The Gallup Poll

Public Opinion 2005

Other Gallup Publications Available from SR Books:

The Gallup Poll Cumulative Index: Public Opinion, 1935–1997
ISBN 0-8420-2587-1 (1999)

The Gallup Poll: Public Opinion Annual Series

2004 (ISBN 0-7425-5138-5)	*1989* (ISBN 0-8420-2344-5)
2003 (ISBN 0-8420-5003-5)	*1988* (ISBN 0-8420-2330-5)
2002 (ISBN 0-8420-5002-7)	*1987* (ISBN 0-8420-2292-9)
2001 (ISBN 0-8420-5001-9)	*1986* (ISBN 0-8420-2275-0)
2000 (ISBN 0-8420-5000-0)	*1985* (ISBN 0-8420-2249-X)
1999 (ISBN 0-8420-2699-1)	*1984* (ISBN 0-8420-2234-1)
1998 (ISBN 0-8420-2698-3)	*1983* (ISBN 0-8420-2220-1)
1997 (ISBN 0-8420-2697-9)	*1982* (ISBN 0-8420-2214-7)
1996 (ISBN 0-8420-2696-0)	*1981* (ISBN 0-8420-2200-7)
1995 (ISBN 0-8420-2695-2)	*1980* (ISBN 0-8420-2181-7)
1994 (ISBN 0-8420-2560-X)	*1979* (ISBN 0-8420-2170-1)
1993 (ISBN 0-8420-2483-2)	*1978* (ISBN 0-8420-2159-0)
1992 (ISBN 0-8420-2463-8)	*1972–77* (ISBN 0-8420-2129-9, 2 vols.)
1991 (ISBN 0-8420-2397-6)	*1935–71* (ISBN 0-394-47270-5, 3 vols.)
1990 (ISBN 0-8420-2368-2)	

International Polls

The International Gallup Polls: Public Opinion, 1979
ISBN 0-8420-2180-9 (1981)

The International Gallup Polls: Public Opinion, 1978
ISBN 0-8420-2162-0-9 (1980)

The Gallup International Opinion Polls: France, 1939, 1944–1975
2 volumes ISBN 0-394-40998-1 (1976)

The Gallup International Opinion Polls: Great Britain, 1937–1975
2 volumes ISBN 0-394-40992-2 (1976)

The Gallup Poll

Public Opinion 2005

EDITED BY
ALEC M. GALLUP AND FRANK NEWPORT

ROWMAN & LITTLEFIELD PUBLISHERS, INC.
Lanham • Boulder • New York • Toronto • Oxford

ACKNOWLEDGEMENTS

The Gallup Poll is a result of the efforts of a number of talented and dedicated individuals. At the Gallup Organization, we wish to express our gratitude to James Clifton, Chairman and CEO; and The Gallup Poll staff, including Jeffrey Jones, Managing Editor; Lydia Saad, Senior Editor; David Moore, Senior Editor; Joseph Carroll, Assistant Editor; and Maura Strausberg, Data Librarian. Special recognition goes to Judith Keneman, Assistant to the Editor in Chief, who was responsible for assembling and editing the manuscript and Julie Ray for her help in reproducing the graphics. Professor Fred Israel, City University of New York and George Gallup, Jr. deserve special credit for their contributions to the first 26 volumes in this series.

ROWMAN & LITTLEFIELD PUBLISHERS, INC.

Published in the United States of America
by Rowman & Littlefield Publishers, Inc.
A wholly owned subsidary of The Rowman & Littlefield Publishing Group, Inc.
4501 Forbes Boulevard, Suite 200, Lanham, Maryland 20706
www.rowmanlittlefield.com

PO Box 317
Oxford
OX2 9RU, UK

ISSN 0195-962X

ISBN-10: 0-7425-5258-6 (cl.)
ISBN-13: 978-0-7425-5258-6 (cl.)

Printed in the United States of America

∞™ The paper used in this publication meets the minimum requirements of American National Standard for Information Sciences—Permanence of Paper for Printed Library Materials, ANSI/NISO Z39.48-1992.

CONTENTS

INTRODUCTION

The Gallup Poll: Public Opinion 2005 contains the findings of the more than 500 daily Gallup Poll reports released to the American public during the year 2005. The latest volume reveals the attitudes and opinions of individuals and key groups within the American population concerning national and international issues and events of the year.

The 2005 volume is the most recent addition to the 32-volume Gallup collection, *Public Opinion, 1935-2054*, the largest compilation of public opinion findings ever published and one of the largest reference works produced on any subject. The Gallup collection documents the attitudes and opinions of Americans (and where appropriate, citizens of other countries) on national and international issues and events from Franklin D. Roosevelt's second term to the present.

Shown in detail are results of the more than 60,000 questions that the Gallup Poll—the world's oldest and most respected public opinion poll—has asked of the public over the last seven decades. Results of the survey questions appear in the nearly 10,000 Gallup Poll reports, reproduced in the 29 volumes. These reports, the first of which was released on October 20, 1935, have been provided to client media on a continuous, two-to-five times per week basis since that time. The contents of the collection are referenced in detail in *The Gallup Poll Cumulative Index* published by Scholarly Resources in 1999.

The 32-volume collection documents public opinion from 1935 to the present in the following five separate and distinct areas:

- *Recording the Public's Response to Major News Events.* Gallup has recorded the public's attitudes and opinions in response to every major news event of the last seven decades. Examples include Adolf Hitler's invasion of the Soviet Union, the bombing of Pearl Harbor, the dropping of the atomic bomb on Hiroshima, the as-

sassination of President John F. Kennedy, the moon landing, the taking of U.S. hostages in Iran, the O. J. Simpson trial verdict, the impeachment of President Bill Clinton, the 9/11/01 terrorist attacks, the Iraq war and Hurricane Katrina and its aftermath.

- *Measuring the Strength of Support for the President, Political Candidates, and Political Parties.* For over seventy years, Gallup has measured, on a continuous basis, the strength of support for the president, for the congressional opposition, and for various political candidates and parties in national elections. This is the role most closely associated with Gallup in the public's mind.

- *Tracking the Public's Attitudes Concerning Enduring Societal Issues.* Since 1935, Gallup has tracked the public's attitudes and opinions concerning a wide range of enduring societal issues, including such narrowly defined issues as abortion and capital punishment as well as broader, multifaceted ones such as crime, the environment, and education. Most of Gallup's long-term subjective social indicators, which are designed to measure social, political, and economic attitudinal trends, are found in this category.

- *Revealing American Lifestyle Trends.* Another ongoing Gallup polling activity has been to document American lifestyles, including periodic measurements of participation in a wide range of leisure activities and other pursuits. Additional examples include frequent series describing the public's tastes and favorites in various areas, and their knowledge level as revealed by national "quizzes" in geography, history, science, politics and the like.

- *Gauging and Charting the Public's Mood.* From its earliest days the Gallup Poll has sought to determine, on an ongoing basis, Americans' satisfaction or dissatisfaction with the direction in which the nation appeared to be headed and with the way they thought that their personal lives were progressing. This process also has involved regular assessments of the people's mood regarding the state of the nation's economy as well as the status of their personal finances, their jobs, and other aspects of their lives.

Two of the most frequently asked questions concerning the Gallup Poll are: Who pays for or provides financial support to the Poll? And who determines which topics are covered by the Poll or, more specifically, who decides which questions are asked on Gallup surveys? Since its founding in 1935 the Gallup Poll has been underwritten by the nation's media. In recent years, funding has come from the national daily newspaper *USA Today*. The Gallup Poll also receives financial support from subscriptions to its premium website service, sales of the monthly magazine, and this annual volume.

Suggestions for poll questions come from Gallup's media subscribers, from other print and broadcast media, and from institutions as well as from individuals, including members of Congress and other public officials, university professors, and foundation executives. In addition, the public themselves are regularly questioned about the problems and issues facing the nation as they perceive them. Their answers establish priorities and provide an up-to-the-minute list of topic areas to explore through the Poll.

The Gallup Poll, as it is known today, began life on October 20, 1935, as a nationally syndicated newspaper feature titled "America Speaks—The National Weekly Column of Public Opinion." For brevity's sake, the media quickly came to refer to the column as The Gallup Poll, after its founder and editor-in-chief, Dr. George H. Gallup. Although Dr. Gallup had experimented during the 1934 congressional and 1932 presidential election campaigns to develop more accurate techniques for measuring public opinion, including scientific sampling, the first Gallup survey results to appear in print were those reported in the initial October 20, 1935, column. (The Roper Poll also began operations in 1935, coinciding closely with the founding of the Gallup Poll, when Elmo Roper began conducting a quarterly public opinion column for *Fortune* magazine).

Although the new scientific opinion polls enjoyed almost immediate popular success, their initial efforts were met with skepticism from many quarters. Critics questioned, for example, how it was possible to determine the opinions of the entire American populace based on only 1,000 interviews or less, or how one know whether people were telling the truth. The credibility of the polls as well as their commercial viability was enhanced significantly, however, when Gallup correctly predicted that Roosevelt would win the 1936 presidential election in a landslide, directly contradicting the forecast of the Literary Digest Poll, the poll of record at that time. The Digest Poll, which was not based on scientific sampling procedures, claimed that FDR's Republican challenger, Alfred M. Landon, would easily win the election.

Over the subsequent six decades scientifically based opinion polls have gained a level of acceptance to where they are used today to investigate virtually every aspect of human experience in most nations of the world. To a large extent, this acceptance is due to the record of accuracy achieved by the polls in pre-election surveys. For example, in the eighteen presidential elections since 1936, the average deviation between Gallup's final pre-election survey figures and the actual election results is 2.1 percentage points and, since 1960, only 1.6 points. Correspondingly, in the thirteen midterm congressional elections measured since 1950, the deviation between Gallup's final election survey figures and the actual election results is 1.1 percentage points. These tests of candidate strength or "trial heats," which were introduced by Gallup in the 1930s (along with the presidential "approval" ratings), demonstrate that scientific survey techniques can accurately quantify public sentiment.

A. M. G.

THE SAMPLE

Most Gallup Poll findings are based on telephone surveys. The majority of the findings reported in Gallup Poll surveys is based on samples consisting of a minimum of 1,000 interviews. The total number, however, may exceed 1,000, or even 1,500, interviews, where the survey specifications call for reporting the responses of low-incidence population groups such as young public-school parents or Hispanics.

Design of the Sample for Telephone Surveys

The findings from the telephone surveys are based on Gallup's standard national telephone samples, consisting of unclustered directory-assisted, random-digit telephone samples utilizing a proportionate, stratified sampling design. The random-digit aspect of the sample is used to avoid "listing" bias. Numerous studies have shown that households with unlisted telephone numbers are different from listed households. "Unlistedness" is due to household mobility or to customer requests to prevent publication of the telephone number. To avoid this source of bias, a random-digit procedure designed to provide representation of both listed and unlisted (including not-yet-listed) numbers is used.

Telephone numbers for the continental United States are stratified into four regions of the country. The sample of telephone numbers produced by the described method is representative of all telephone households within the continental United States.

Only working banks of telephone numbers are selected. Eliminating nonworking banks from the sample increases the likelihood that any sampled telephone number will be associated with a residence.

Within each contacted household, an interview is sought with the adult 18 years of age or older living in the household who has had the most recent birthday (this is a method commonly employed to make a random selection within households without having to ask the respondent to provide a complete roster of adults living in the household). In the event that the sample becomes disproportionately female (due to higher cooperation rates typically observed for female respondents), the household selection criteria are adjusted to select only the male in the household who has had the most recent birthday (except in households where the adults are exclusively female).

A minimum of three calls (and up to six calls) is attempted to each selected telephone number to complete an interview. Time of day and the day of the week for callbacks are varied to maximize the chances of finding a respondent at home. All interviews are conducted on weekends or weekday evenings in order to contact potential respondents among the working population.

The final sample is weighted so that the distribution of the sample matches current estimates derived from the U.S. Census Bureau's Current Population Survey (CPS) for the adult population living in telephone households in the continental United States.

Weighting Procedures

After the survey data have been collected and processed, each respondent is assigned a weight so that the demographic characteristics of the total weighted sample of respondents match the latest estimates of the demographic characteristics of the adult population available from the U.S. Census Bureau. Gallup weights data to census estimates for gender, race, age, educational attainment, and region. Telephone surveys are weighted to match the characteristics of the adult population living in households with access to a telephone.

The procedures described above are designed to produce samples approximating the adult civilian population (18 and older) living in private households (that is, excluding those in prisons, hospitals, hotels, religious and educational institutions, and those living on reservations or military bases)—and in the case of telephone surveys, households with access to a telephone. Survey percentages may be applied to census estimates of the size of these populations to project percentages into numbers of people. The manner in which the sample is drawn also produces a sample that approximates the distribution of private households in the United States. Therefore, survey results also can be projected to numbers of households.

Sampling Tolerances

In interpreting survey results, it should be borne in mind that all sample surveys are subject to sampling error— that is, the extent to which the results may differ from what would be obtained if the whole population surveyed had been interviewed. The size of such sampling errors depends largely on the number of interviews.

The following tables may be used in estimating the sampling error of any percentage. The computed allowances have taken into account the effect of the sample design upon sampling error. They may be interpreted as indicating the range (plus or minus the figure shown) within which the results of repeated samplings in the same time period could be expected to vary, 95 percent of the time, assuming the same sampling procedure, the same interviewers, and the same questionnaire.

Table A shows how much allowance should be made for the sampling error of a percentage. Let us say a reported percentage is 33 for a group that includes 1,000 respondents. First, we go to the row headed "Percentages near 30" and then go across to the column headed "1,000." The number here is 3, which means that the 33 percent obtained in the sample is subject to a sampling error of plus or minus 3 points. Another way of saying it is that very probably (98 chances out of 100) the average of repeated samplings would be somewhere between 29 and 37, with the most likely figure being the 33 obtained.

In comparing survey results in two samples, such as for men and women, the question arises as to how large must a difference between them be before one can be reasonably sure that it reflects a real difference. In Tables B and C, the number of points that must be allowed for in such comparisons is indicated. Table B is for percentages near 20 or 80, and Table C is for percentages near 50. For percentages in between, the error to be allowed for is between those shown in the two tables.

Here is an example of how the tables would be used: Let us say that 50 percent of men respond a certain way and 40 percent of women also respond that way, for a difference of 10 percentage points between them. Can we say with any assurance that the 10-point difference reflects a real difference between men and women on the question? The sample contains approximately 500 men and 500 women.

Since the percentages are near 50, we consult Table C, and since the two samples are about 600 persons each, we look for the number in the column headed "500" that is also in the row designated "500". We find the number 7 here. This means that the allowance for error should be 7 points, and that in concluding that the percentage among men is somewhere between 3 and 17 points higher than the percentage among women, we should be wrong only about 5 percent of the time. In other words, we can conclude with considerable confidence that a difference exists in the direction observed and that it amounts to at least 3 percentage points.

If, in another case, men's responses amount to 22 percent and women's 24 percent, we consult Table B because these percentages are near 20. We look for the number in the column headed "500" that is also in the row designated "500" and see that the number is 5. Obviously, then, the 2-point difference is inconclusive.

TABLE A
Recommended Allowance for Sampling Error of a Percentage

In Percentage Points
(at 95 in 100 confidence level)*
Sample Size

	1,000	750	500	250	100
Percentages near 10	2	2	3	4	6
Percentages near 20	3	3	4	5	9
Percentages near 30	3	4	4	6	10
Percentages near 40	3	4	5	7	10
Percentages near 50	3	4	5	7	11
Percentages near 60	3	4	5	7	10
Percentages near 70	3	4	4	6	10
Percentages near 80	3	3	4	5	9
Percentages near 90	2	2	3	4	6

*The chances are 95 in 100 that the sampling error is not larger than the figures shown.

TABLE B
Recommended Allowance for Sampling Error of the Difference

In Percentage Points
(at 95 in 100 confidence level)*
Percentages near 20 or percentages Near 80

	750	500	250
Size of sample			
750	4		
500	5	5	
250	6	7	8

*The chances are 95 in 100 that the sampling is not larger than the figures shown.

TABLE C
Recommended Allowance for Sampling Error of the Difference

In Percentage Points
(at 95 in 100 confidence level)*

	750	500	250
Size of sample			
750	6		
500	6	7	
250	8	8	10

*The chances are 95 in 100 that the sampling is not larger than the figures shown.

Gallup Poll Accuracy Record
Presidential Elections

	Candidates	Final Gallup Survey	Election Result	Gallup Deviation
2004	Bush	49	51	-2
	Kerry	49	48	1
	Other	2	1	1
2000	Gore	46	48.4	-2.4
	Bush	48	47.9	0.1
	Nader	4	2.7	1.3
	Buchanan	1	0.4	0.6
	Other	1	0.6	0.4
1996	Clinton	52	49.2	2.8
	Dole	41	40.9	0.1
	Perot	7	8.5	-1.5
1992	Clinton	49	43	6
	Bush	37	37.5	-0.5
	Perot	14	18.9	-4.9
1988	Bush	56	53.4	2.6
	Dukakis	44	45.7	-1.7
1984	Reagan	59	58.8	0.2
	Mondale	41	40.6	0.4
1980	Reagan	47	50.8	-3.8
	Carter	44	41	3
	Anderson	8	6.6	1.4
	Other	1	1.6	-0.6
1976	Carter	48	50.1	-2.1
	Ford	49	48	1
	McCarthy	2	0.9	1.1
	Other	1	0.9	0.1
1972	Nixon	62	60.7	1.3
	McGovern	38	37.6	0.4
1968	Nixon	43	43.4	-0.4
	Humphrey	42	42.7	-0.7
	Wallace	15	13.5	1.5

Chronology

2004

December 1 Jailed Palestinian militant and Fatah leader, Marwan Barghouti, announces his candidacy for president of the Palestinian Authority challenging Mahmoud Abbas, the former prime minister.

December 2 Bush nominates former New York City police commissioner Bernard Kerik to replace Tom Ridge as Homeland Security Secretary.

December 6 U.S. Consulate in Jidda, Saudi Arabia attacked by five gunman, killing five employees, none American. Al Qaeda believed to be responsible.

December 7 Hamid Karzai inaugurated as Afganistan's first popularly elected president. Ceremony attended by Vice President Dick Cheney and Defense Secretary Donald Rumsfeld.

The house votes on and passes, 336-75, an expansive overhaul of the country's intelligence community.
IBM sells PC business to Beijing company Lenovo for $1.75 billion.

December 11 Bernard Kerik withdraws nomination for Homeland Security Secretary saying he hired an illegal nanny and failed to pay employer taxes on her behalf.

December 13 Eleven Iraqis killed and more than a dozen wounded by a suicide bomber attack in the fortified Green Zone housing the U.S. Embassy and Iraqi government buildings.

President Bush nominates Michael Leavitt, former governor of Utah and current administrator of the EPS to succeed Tommy Thompson as Secretary of Health and Human Services.

December 17 President Bush signs the Intelligence Reform and Terrorism Act of 2004.

December 26 Earthquake devastates Asia. Eruption strikes Indonesian island of Sumatra with magnitude of 9.0 causing tidal waves across the Indian Ocean. Hundreds of thousands of people die and millions are left homeless in dozens of nations in Asia and East Africa.

2005

January 3 President Bush appoints George H. W. Bush and Bill Clinton as leaders of nationwide campaign to raise funds for victims of December's catastrophic tsunami.

House of Representatives changes ethics rules sothat indicted members may not retain their positions of leadership

January 4 Ali al-Haidari, governor of Baghdad Province, assassinated in pre-election violence in Iraq.

January 6 Hearings for Attorney General nominee Alberto Gonzales dominated by questions about the Abu Ghraib prison abuse.

January 9 Mahmoud Abbas, chairman of the Palestine Liberation Organization, wins Presidency of the Palestinian Authority, succeeding Yasir Arafat, who died in Nov. 2004.

January 12 The White House announces the end of the search for weapons of mass destruction in Iraq is over and no weapons were found.

January 13 U.S. Army reservist Charles Graner found guilty of abusing prisoners at Abu Ghraib prison in Iraq and sentenced to 10 years in a military prison.

January 20 George W. Bush is officially sworn for his second term as President by Supreme Court chief justice William Rehnquist.

January 23 Viktor Yushchenko, after defeating Viktor Yanukovich in a very controversial election, takes oath of office as President of Ukraine

January 26 Senate confirms Condoleezza Rice as Secretary of State.

January 30 About 57% of the Iraqi population, vote in first democratic elections in more than 50 years, selecting a 275-seat National Assembly and 18 provincial assemblies.

January 31 UN Commission investigating violence in Darfur finds war crimes and crimes against humanity have occurred in western Sudan, but not genocide.

February 2 President Bush delivers State of the Union address highlighting his proposed reform of the Social Security system, the fight against terrorism, and his commitment to remaining in Iraq until the establishment of a stable Iraqi democracy.

February 3 Senate confirms Alberto Gonzales in a vote of 60-36 as new Attorney General. Gonzales is the country's first Hispanic attorney general.

February 14 Bush requests an additional $81.9 billion from Congress to cover current-year expenses which include tsunami aid, benefits for families of troops killed in combat and operations in Iraq and Afghanistan.

Kyoto Protocol, the international environmental treaty, goes into effect requiring 35 industrialized nations to reduce heat-trapping emissions. The U.S., which emits the largest amount of gasses in the world, refused to sign the treaty.

February 15 Senate confirms Michael Chertoff as Homeland Security Secretary. He succeeds Tom Ridge.

February 16 National Hockey League season cancelled due to failure on the part of the leagues owners and players to reach a deal on salary cap for players.

February 28 Suicide bombers blows up a car in Hilla, killing 115 people seeking employment with the Iraqi police.

March 7 Bush nominates John Bolton to UN Ambassador. Bolton is a state department official and harsh critic of the United Nations.

March 11 Rape suspect, Brian Nichols, shoots and kills presiding judge, a court stenographer and a sheriff's deputy in Atlanta's Fulton County Courthouse.

March 16 Iraqi assembly meets for the first time in a largely ceremonial meeting. Shiites and Kurds have not yet appointed leaders.

New England Journal of Medicine indicates that obesity may shorten life expectancy of current generation of children by two to five years vs. adults today.

March 17   Ten baseball players, including Mark McGuire and Sammy Sosa, testify at hearings before the House Government Reform Committee to answer questions regarding steroid use in major league baseball.

March 20   Congress intervenes in case of Terri Schiavo, a woman who has been in a persistent vegetative state for 15 years.

March 22   Federal judge, James Whittemore, refused to order Terri Schiavo's feeding tube be reinserted.

March 23   Federal judge, James Whittemore's decision to allow Terri Schiavo's feeding tube be reinserted is upheld by federal appeals court.

March 24   The US Supreme Court refuses the Terri Schiavo case.

March 31   Commission set up by President Bush criticizes Intelligence agencies and calls assessments on Iraq's weapons capabilities "deal wrong" and finds that agencies exaggerated evidence and relied on shaky sources in making their case for the war in Iraq.

Terri Schiavo dies, 13 days after her feeding tube was removed.

April 2   Pope John Paul II dies after a long struggle with Parkinson's disease.

April 8   Pope John Paul II is buried at the Vatican. World leaders gather for the largest funeral for a pope in history.

Prince Charles marries Camilla Parker Bowles.

April 19   New pope selected. Conclave of cardinals selects Cardinal Joseph Ratzinger of Germany.

April 22   Sept. 11 suspect, Zacarias Moussaoui, pleads guilty but denies involvement in Sept 11 terrorist attacks. He claims he was part of a separate plan to fly a plane into the White House.

President Bush selects General Peter Pace to succeed General Richard Myers as Chairman of Joint Chiefs of Staff.

April 24   Benedict XVI is installed as pope at outdoor mass at St. Peter's Square.

May 2   Pfc. Lynndie England pleads guilty to seven criminal counts in Abu Ghraib abuse scandal.

Iraqi cabinet sworn in with six positions yet unfilled as Shiite and Sunni leaders continue to negotiate.

May 4   Judge declares mistral in Pfc. Lynndie England case. Former army specialist Charles Graner, who was convicted in the scandal and is the father of England's child, testifies that the maltreatment of prisoners was permissible which implies that England did not realize she was committing a crime.

May 5   British Prime Minister, Tony Blair, reelected. He becomes first Labour Party prime minister to win three successive terms.

60th Anniversary of Germany's surrender to the allied forces. President Bush, Russian president Vladimir Putin and dozens of heads of state attend military parade in Moscow's Red Square.

May 10   Iraq National Assembly selects a 55-person committee to write a permanent constitution.

May 13	Pentagon recommends the closing of about 800 military bases, offices and installations in a vast restructuring. Job losses estimated at 26,000.
May 16	Women in Kuwait win right to vote in and run for office in local and parliamentary elections by a vote of 35-23.
May 23	President Bush and Afghanistan's Hamid Karzai meet to sign a new strategic partnership to fight against Islamic extremism, foster democratic, and end the illegal opium trade in Afghanistan.
May 24	House passes bill in a 238-194 vote to allow federal financing of stem cell research. President Bush said he will veto the legislation.
May 31	Watergate scandal's "Deep Throat" reveals himself as W. Mark Felt, a former top FBI official.
June 1	SEC Chief William Donaldson announces his resignation amid criticism that he was too tough in enforcing regulations.
June 2	President Bush nominates California congressman Christopher Cox to replace SEC Chief William Donaldson.
June 13	Michael Jackson acquitted by a California jury of 10 charges including molesting a child, conspiracy, and providing alcohol to minors.
June 15	Terri Schiavo autopsy results released indicating that Schaivo's brain had deteriorated to half normal size and no treatment could have helped her. Autopsy also revealed no evidence of abuse.
June 17	Tyco CEO, L. Dennis Kozlowski, and CFO, Mark Swartz, found guilty of fraud, conspiracy and grand larceny.
June 28	President Bush defends war in Iraq in a nationally televised speech on the first

	anniversary of the transfer of sovereignty to Iraqis.
June 28	Gay marriage approved in Canada.
July 1	Sandra Day O'Connor, the nations first woman on the US Supreme Court announces her retirement after 24 years of service.
July 6	London chosen over Paris to host the 2012 summer Olympics
July 7	Bombs explode in London in four coordinated terrorist attacks on the city's subway and bus systems during rush hour killing 52 people, including the attackers.
July 8	Group of Eight industrial nations end summit meeting with pledge to double aid to Africa to $50 billion a year by 2010. Federal appeals court upholds lower court decision that Partial-Birth Abortion Ban Act is unconstitutional.
July 9	North Korea agrees to resume disarmament talks with US, South Korea, China, Japan and Russia in late July.
July 19	President Bush nominates John G. Roberts to succeed Sandra Day O'Connor as an associate justice.
July 21	Terrorists attempt another attack on London's transit system. Bombs on three subway trains and a bus fail to explode.
July 25	U.S. and North Korea officials meet to discuss the eventual dismantling of North Korea's nuclear weapons in exchange for energy and financial assistance.
July 26	The space shuttle *Discovery* launches from Cape Canaveral, FL for a 12 ? day million to the International Space Station. A piece of foam insulation

breaks off from the shuttle's external fuel tank.

July 27 NASA announces it will ground the shuttle fleet.

August 1 President Bush installs John Bolton as US ambassador to the UN during a congressional recess. Democratic senators had refused to put his confirmation to a vote.

August 9 Shuttle Discovery safely returns to Earth after a 14-day mission. This mission included a first-ever spacewalk to remove a piece of material sticking out of the shuttle's skin.

August 19 US Navy ships, the *Kearsarge* and the *Ashland,* docked in Aqaba attacked in Jordan.

Merck, maker of pain medication Vioxx, is found liable by a Texas jury in death of Robert Ernst and awards his widow $253.5 million.

August 29 Hurricane Katrina, a category 4 storm, hits Gulf Coast with vengeance.

August 30 New Orleans, although spared the full force of Katrina, suffers calamitous damage as levees break, submerging about 80% of the city.

August 31 Death toll in New Orleans from Katrina is feared to be in the thousands. Officials call devastation the worst in US history.

September 1 New Orleans descends into chaos as millions are left homeless and displaced by Hurricane Katrina and broken levees.

September 2 President Bush visits New Orleans in an attempt to quell criticism of his administration's response to the Katrina crisis.

September 3 President Bush signs $10.5 billion emergency aid package for the Gulf coast region in response to Hurricane Katrina crisis

Chief Justice William H. Rehnquist dies after battle with thyroid cancer. Rehnquist served on the U.S. Supreme Court for 33 years, 19 of them as chief justice.

September 5 President Bush announces nomination of Supreme Court nominee John Roberts to be chief justice.

September 6 California legalizes same-sex marriage by defining marriage as a union of "two persons."

September 7 Egyptian President Hosni Mubarak faces multi-candidate elections in his bid for a fifth term. Election monitors contend the election is marred by fraud but Mubarak wins overwhelmingly taking 88.5% of vote though voter turnout is low at 23%.

More than 1,000 mourners attend Chief Justice William H. Rehnquist's funeral.

September 9 President Bush removes FEMA director Michael Brown from relief effort in New Orleans. Brown is replaced by David Paulson.

September 12 Confirmation hearings for John Roberts begin. Roberts is nominated to replace William Rehnquist as chief justice of the U.S. Supreme Court and says he will "confront every case with an open mind."

September 14 President Bush, along with other world leaders, endorses millennium development goals at meeting marking the 60th anniversary of the UN.

September 15 President Bush promises, via national TV, to rebuild New Orleans and to help victims with rebuilding, housing and job training.

September 19 Tyco executives, L. Dennis Kozlowski, and Mark Swartz, both sentenced to

8½ years in prison for bilking the company out of $600 million in a stock-fraud scheme and used the money for personal purposes.

September 22 Senate judiciary committee votes 13-5 in favor of nomination of John Roberts to become 17th chief justice of the U.S. Supreme Court

September 24 Hurricane Rita hits the Gulf Coast, causing widespread flooding. Damage estimated at $6 billion.

September 26 Private Lynndie England found guilty of conspiracy to maltreat prisoners, four counts of maltreatment and one count of committing an indecent act in Abu Ghraib scandal.

September 27 Private Lynndie England is sentenced to three years in prison for Abu Ghraib abuse scandal.

Former FEMA chief, Michael Brown, testifies to Congressional committee that he warned the White House and his boss, Michael Chertoff, that Hurricane Katrina would cause catastrophic damage and blames inept response on Louisiana governor Kathleen Babineaux Blanco.

September 28 House Majority Leader Tom DeLay indicted by Texas grand jury of conspiring to violate state's election laws.

September 29 John Roberts confirmed in senate vote of 78-22 as 17th chief justice of the U.S. Supreme Court. Roberts is sworn in after the vote.

October 1 Suicide bombers are suspected in attack in Bali. At least 22 people die following several bomb explosions at tourist sites on the Indonesian island which was also attached in 2002.

October 3 President Bush nominates Harriet Miers, White House counsel, to replace retiring Justice Sandra Day O'Connor. Nomination coincides with opening of Supreme Court, with new Chief Justice John Roberts.

October 5 Defying veto threat by President Bush, Senate votes 90-9 to approve measure that bans the use of "cruel, inhuman or degrading treatment or punishment" of anyone under the custody of the American military.

October 7 The International Atomic Energy Agency and its leader, Mohamed El Baradei share the Nobel Peace Prize.

October 8 An earthquake with a magnitude of 7.6 rocks Pakistani-controlled part of Kashmir. Approximately 54,000 people die in the region and another 800 are said to die in India. The UN estimates that more than 2.5 million are homeless.

October 10 Angela Merkel, leader of the Christian Democratic Union, to become country's first female chancellor. She narrowly prevailed over Chancellor Gerhard Schroeder's Social Democratic Party in September elections.

October 12 Judge lifts contempt order against New York Times reporter Judith Miller. Miller testified about notes from an interview with I. Lewis Libby, Vice President Cheney's chief of staff.

October 15 Millions of Iraqi voters vote on constitution. Participation of Sunnis is mixed.

October 19 Harriet Miers, Supreme Court nominee, is asked by Republican and Democratic leaders of the Senate Judiciary Committee to revise parts of her judicial questionnaire.

Saddam Hussein trial begins. He pleaded not guilty to charges related to the killing of 143 people in the down of Dujail, Iraq, in 1982.

October 24 President Bush chooses Ben Bernanke, his chief economic adviser, to replace Alan Greenspan as chairman of the Federal Reserve Board.

October 25 Number of deaths of U.S. soldiers fighting in Iraq reaches 2,000 representing the number of fatalities since the war began in March 2003.

October 27 Following weeks of blistering criticism from both Democrats and Republicans about her qualifications, Harriet Miers withdraws her nomination to replace Supreme Court Justice Sandra Day O'Connor.

Paris suburbs experience explosive violence after rioters begin setting cars on fire and looting after two boys are accidentally killed while hiding from police.

October 28 Vice President Cheney's chief of staff, I. Lewis Libby, is indicted with one count of obstruction of justice, two of perjury, and two of making false statements in connection with an investigation into who disclosed the identity of a covert CIA officer. He resigns.

October 31 David Addington, VP Cheney's counsel, is named as I. Lewis Libby's replacement as Cheney's Chief of Staff.

President Bush nominates Samuel Alito to the Supreme Court to replace retiring justice Sandra Day O'Connor. Announcement comes days after Harriet Miers withdrew her nomination.

November 2 Venezuelan president Hugo Chavez leads protest of 25,000 anti-Bush demonstrators at a stadium during a summit meeting with Latin American leaders.

November 3 I. Lewis Libby, former chief staff for VP Cheney, pleads not guilty to one count of obstruction of justice, two of perjury and two of making false statements in connection with an investigation into who disclosed the identity of a covert CIA officer.

November 8 Democrats prevail in gubernatorial elections. Many interpret election results to be a reaction to dissatisfaction with President Bush's recent performance.

November 9 New York Times reporter, Judith Miller, agrees to resign. Miller served 85 days in jail over the summer rather than reveal a source to a grand jury investigating the lead of a CIA operative.

November 10 Fifty-seven people are killed and hundreds wounded after bombs explode simultaneously in three hotels in Amman, Jordan. Al-Qaeda in Mesopotamia claims responsibility saying that Jordan had been targeted because it was friendly with the U.S.

November 21 Israeli prime minister Ariel Sharon quits as head of the Likud Party to start a more centrist organization called Kadima.

November 22 German Parliament elects Angela Merkel of the Christian Democratic Party as Germany's chancellor. Merkel is the first woman and the first person from East Germany to lead the country.

December 14 House votes 251-174 to renew Patriot Act, the controversial legislation that extends the government's surveillance powers.

December 15 It is revealed that President Bush signed a presidential order to allow the National Security Agency to conduct surveillance on Americans suspected of being connected to terrorist activity without warrants. This was reported by the New York Times in 2002.

December 19 New Yorkers stranded by transit strike. Talks between Metropolitan Transportation Agency and the Transport Workers Union break down causing the union to declare a general strike

December 21 The Iraqi electoral commission reports that 10.9 million people or 70% of the country's registered voters participated in the first parliamentary elections since the overthrow of Saddam Hussein.

December 22 New York transportation strike ends. The Metropolitan Transportation Authority and the Transport Workers Union have not finalized a contract, however.

"1967"	1966 Dec 8-13	43	45	13
"1966"	1965 Dec 11-16	56	33	11
"1965"	1965 Jan 7-12	65	22	13

Republicans and Democrats have very different expectations for the 2005 economy. Seventy-six percent of Republicans say it will be a year of prosperity, while 80% of Democrats say it will be a year of economic difficulty.

Which is more likely to be true of 2005?

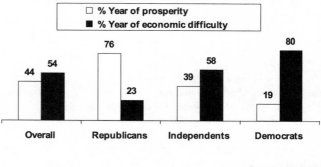

Dec. 17-19, 2004

2005 Predictions: International Affairs

Looking beyond the United States' borders, 69% of Americans expect 2005 to be "a troubled year with much international discord," while 29% say it will be "a peaceful year, more or less free of international disputes."

Americans have also typically taken a pessimistic view in this regard—only in 1959 did a majority of Americans predict that the coming year would be a peaceful year. However, the degree of pessimism is slightly higher in 2005 than in the past—the 69% who feel 2005 will be a troubled year has only been surpassed twice, in Americans' predictions for the years 1966 and 1980. At this time, such a finding is not surprising given the ongoing war in Iraq.

Please tell me which you think is more likely to be true of 2005: A peaceful year, more or less free of international disputes, or a troubled year with much international discord.

		Peaceful year	Troubled year	No opinion
		%	%	%
"2005"	2004 Dec 17-19	29	69	2
"1999"	1998 Dec 28-29	27	69	4
"1998"	1998 Jan 16-18	31	65	4
"1980"	1979 Nov 30-Dec 3	14	80	7
"1979"	1978 Dec 1-4	38	53	9
"1975"	1974 Dec 6-9	29	61	10
"1974"	1973 Nov 30-Dec 3	23	65	11
"1966"	1965 Dec 11-16	11	82	7
"1965"	1965 Jan 7-12	31	57	12
"1963"	1962 Dec 13-18	38	53	9
"1960"	1959 Dec 3-8	54	31	15

A majority of Republicans, Democrats, and independents all expect a troubled 2005, but Republicans are less likely to think so than are independents and Democrats.

January 3, 2005
LESS THAN HALF OF AMERICANS EXPECT PROSPEROUS 2005

by Jeffrey M. Jones, Gallup Poll Managing Editor

More Americans predict 2005 will be a year of economic difficulty for the United States than think it will be a year of prosperity. While nearly 7 in 10 Americans expect 2005 will be a troubled year internationally, a slight majority still believes the United States will increase its power in the world during that time. These predictions come from Gallup's final 2004 poll, conducted Dec. 17-19. Since 1959, Gallup has periodically asked Americans to make predictions about what will happen in the coming year.

Additionally, a recent Gallup poll finds the vast majority of Americans are satisfied with their personal lives as the new year begins. Slightly more than half of Americans also say they are "very happy."

2005 Predictions: The Economy

When asked which of two statements is more likely to be true of 2005, 44% of Americans say it will be a year of economic prosperity, while 54% say it will be a year of economic difficulty.

It is not uncommon for Americans to give pessimistic economic predictions, which are apparently strongly influenced by the state of the current economy. For example, when Gallup asked the question in the 1970s during sluggish economic times, most Americans predicted years of economic difficulty. On the other hand, at times when the economy was strong, such as in the mid-1960s and late-1990s, Americans thought the coming years would be prosperous.

Please tell me which you think is more likely to be true of 2005: A year of economic prosperity, or a year of economic difficulty.

		Prosperity	Difficulty	No opinion
		%	%	%
"2005"	2004 Dec 17-19	44	54	2
"1999"	1998 Dec 28-29	62	34	4
"1998"	1998 Jan 16-18	59	37	4
"1979"	1978 Dec 1-4	21	69	10
"1977"	1976 Dec 10-13	34	54	12
"1976"	1975 Dec 12-15	23	70	7
"1974"	1973 Nov 30-Dec 3	7	85	8
"1973"	1972 Nov 10-13	40	47	13
"1971"	1970 Dec 3-8	18	73	8
"1970"	1969 Oct 17-22	30	61	10
"1969"	1968 Dec 5-10	38	48	15
"1968"	1967 Dec 7-12	42	47	12

Which is more likely to be true of 2005?

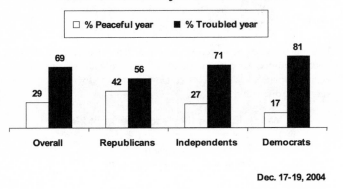

☐ % Peaceful year   ■ % Troubled year

	Overall	Republicans	Independents	Democrats
Peaceful	29	42	27	17
Troubled	69	56	71	81

Dec. 17-19, 2004

Americans give their most optimistic predictions in regards to the United States' position in the world. Just over half of Americans, 51%, say 2005 will be a year in which "America will increase its power in the world," while 44% say it will be "a year when American power will decline."

Despite the slight majority positive view, that still rates as one of the least optimistic assessments in the 15 times Gallup has asked this question. Less than a majority of Americans thought U.S. power would increase in the years 1974 and 1976; all other times, at least 53% expected a more powerful position for the United States.

Please tell me which you think is more likely to be true of 2005: A year when America will increase its power in the world, or a year when American power will decline.

		Increase its power %	*Power will decline* %	*No opinion* %
"2005"	2004 Dec 17-19	51	44	5
"1999"	1998 Dec 28-29	60	33	7
"1998"	1998 Jan 16-18	55	37	8
"1980"	1979 Nov 30-Dec 3	58	30	13
"1979"	1978 Dec 1-4	53	33	15
"1977"	1976 Dec 10-13	58	24	18
"1976"	1975 Dec 12-15	43	44	14
"1974"	1973 Nov 30-Dec 3	29	50	21
"1969"	1968 Dec 5-10	62	21	17
"1968"	1967 Dec 7-12	62	22	15
"1967"	1966 Dec 8-13	66	20	14
"1966"	1965 Dec 11-16	74	14	12
"1965"	1965 Jan 7-12	64	19	17
"1963"	1962 Dec 13-18	84	6	10
"1960"	1959 Dec 3-8	73	10	17

Sixty-seven percent of Republicans say the United States will increase its power in the world in 2005, compared with 48% of independents and 37% of Democrats.

Americans' Personal Lives

As the new year begins, Americans remain positive in their assessment of their personal lives. According to Gallup's Dec. 5-8 poll, 84% of Americans are satisfied with the way things are going in their personal lives, including 58% who say they are very satisfied. Only 14% are dissatisfied.

At least 8 in 10 Americans have expressed satisfaction with their personal lives since 1993. In comparatively few instances since Gallup began asking this question in 1979 has the percentage satisfied dipped below the 80% mark. This has usually occurred at times in which there was a troubled national economy, such as in 1979 and 1992.

In general, are you satisfied or dissatisfied with the way things are going in your personal life?
(Numbers shown in percentages based on yearly averages)

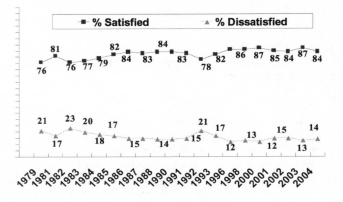
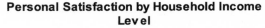

■ % Satisfied   ▲ % Dissatisfied

Satisfied: 76, 81, 76, 77, 79, 82, 84, 83, 84, 83, 78, 82, 86, 87, 85, 84, 87, 84

Dissatisfied: 21, 23, 20, 17, 17, 18, 15, 14, 15, 21, 17, 12, 13, 12, 15, 13, 14

1979 1981 1982 1983 1984 1985 1986 1987 1988 1990 1991 1992 1993 1996 1998 2000 2001 2002 2003 2004

There is a definite relationship between personal satisfaction and income—those living in households with higher income levels are much more likely to say they are satisfied with their personal lives than those living in lower income households. Still, at least 7 in 10 Americans at all income levels say they are satisfied.

Personal Satisfaction by Household Income Level

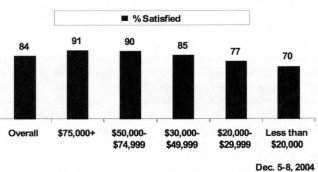

■ % Satisfied

Overall	$75,000+	$50,000-$74,999	$30,000-$49,999	$20,000-$29,999	Less than $20,000
84	91	90	85	77	70

Dec. 5-8, 2004

Additionally, 51% of Americans say that, generally speaking, they are "very happy." Forty-two percent say they are "fairly happy" and only 6% say they are "not too happy." That represents a slight decrease from 55% who said they were very happy in December 2003, the highest percentage Gallup had recorded to date for this measure. The current percentage remains above average by historical standards.

Just as is the case for personal satisfaction, there is also a relationship between household income and expressed happiness, with lower income respondents less likely than higher income respondents to say they are happy.

Survey Methods

These results are based on telephone interviews with randomly selected national samples of 1,002 adults, aged 18 and older, conducted

How happy would you say you are?

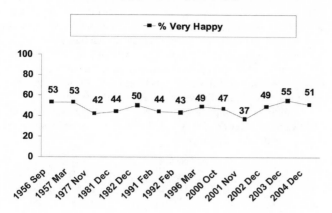

-■- % Very Happy

| | 53 | 53 | 42 | 44 | 50 | 44 | 43 | 49 | 47 | 37 | 49 | 55 | 51 |

1956 Sep, 1957 Mar, 1977 Nov, 1981 Dec, 1982 Dec, 1991 Feb, 1992 Feb, 1996 Mar, 2000 Oct, 2001 Nov, 2002 Dec, 2003 Dec, 2004 Dec

Dec. 17-19, 2004 and 1,003 adults, aged 18 and older, conducted Dec. 5-8, 2004. For results based on these samples, one can say with 95% confidence that the maximum error attributable to sampling and other random effects is ±3 percentage points. In addition to sampling error, question wording and practical difficulties in conducting surveys can introduce error or bias into the findings of public opinion polls.

January 4, 2005
IRAQ, TERRORISM TOP PUBLIC'S AGENDA FOR CONGRESS AND PRESIDENT IN 2005
Top domestic issues: healthcare costs, education, the economy, and Social Security

by David W. Moore, Gallup Poll Senior Editor

A CNN/USA Today/Gallup survey conducted in mid-December finds the war in Iraq and terrorism as the top two issues (among 18 mentioned in the survey) that the American public wants Congress and President George W. Bush to address in 2005. Education, healthcare costs, the economy, and Social Security are the top-ranked domestic issues, just slightly less important to the public than terrorism and Iraq.

How important is it to you that the president and Congress deal with each of the following issues in the next year —is it—extremely important, very important, moderately important, or not that important?

2004 Dec 17-19	(sorted by "extremely/ very important") %	Extremely important Extremely/ Very important %	Not that important %
The situation in Iraq	51	90	1
Terrorism	49	87	3
Healthcare costs	42	87	1
Education	44	86	1
The economy	40	86	1
Social Security	40	82	4
Unemployment	35	77	5
The federal budget deficit	35	77	3
Foreign affairs	31	74	5
Energy policies	27	72	5
Poverty and homelessness	29	71	4
Taxes	26	66	5
Immigration	27	65	8
The environment	24	62	7
Limits on lawsuits	22	52	19
Laws to help blacks and other racial minorities	16	47	18
Abortion	19	41	32
Same-sex marriages or civil unions	16	35	46

The major findings:
- About half of Americans rate the top two issues (Iraq, terrorism) as "extremely" important, while 40% to 44% rate the next four domestic issues (healthcare costs, education, economy, Social Security) that way.
- Slightly more than one in three Americans say unemployment and the federal budget deficit are extremely important.
- Foreign affairs, poverty and homelessness, energy policies, immigration, taxes, the environment, and limits on lawsuits all are rated as extremely important by at least 20% of Americans, with at least a majority saying those issues are either "extremely" or "very" important.
- Laws to help blacks and other racial minorities rank third from the bottom according to "extremely/very important" responses, although slightly fewer people say it is an extremely important issue than say that about abortion. But 32% of Americans give abortion the lowest rating ("not that important"), compared with 18% who give that rating to the racial issue.
- Almost half of all Americans, 46%, give the issue of civil unions or same-sex marriages the lowest rating—saying it is not that important. Just 35% say the issue is either extremely or very important.

Changes in Ratings

There are few changes in the ratings compared with two years ago, in a Jan. 3-5, 2003, poll. Six of the issues measured in mid-December's poll were not rated in the 2003 poll, including poverty and homelessness, energy policies, immigration, limits on lawsuits, laws to help racial minorities, and civil unions or same-sex marriages.

Among the 12 issues included in both polls, only 3 show clearly significant changes: the situation in Iraq, the federal budget deficit, and healthcare costs. More people say these issues are either extremely or very important now than said so two years ago.

(sorted by difference between now and two years ago)	Jan 3-5, 2003 Extremely/ Very important %	Dec 17-19, 2004 Extremely/ Very important %	Difference now vs. two years ago Pct. Pts.
The situation in Iraq	81	90	+ 9
The federal budget deficit	68	77	+ 9
Healthcare costs	81	87	+ 6

Republicans and Democrats Polarized on Agenda

The poll reveals a significant divide between Republicans and Democrats on several issues.
- On only seven issues is there a relative consensus, where the "partisan gap"—the difference between the percentage of each

party rating the issue as "extremely" or "very" important—is less than 10 points. These include foreign affairs, education, the economy, Social Security, Iraq, taxes, and terrorism.

- Five of the top six issues rated by the public are included in this consensus group. Only the issue of healthcare costs shows a major partisan divide among the top six issues.
- The largest differences come on issues that have long divided the two parties—poverty and homelessness, the environment, and racial policies. The partisan gap on these issues exceeds 20 points, with Democrats giving each issue a higher importance rating than do Republicans.
- Limiting lawsuits is the only issue favored by Republicans that shows a partisan gap of greater than 20 points.

2004 Dec 17-19

(% saying "extremely important" or "very important" for president and Congress to deal with)	Republicans (including "leaners") %	Democrats (including "leaners") %	Difference Pct. Pts.
Poverty and homelessness	53	87	+34
The environment	46	76	+30
Laws to help blacks and other racial minorities	35	59	+24
Unemployment	67	85	+18
The federal budget deficit	68	85	+17
Healthcare costs	81	95	+14
Energy policies	66	76	+10
Foreign affairs	70	78	+ 8
Education	83	88	+ 5
The economy	83	88	+ 5
Social Security	81	82	+ 1
The situation in Iraq	91	88	- 3
Taxes	67	62	- 5
Terrorism	92	83	- 9
Abortion	49	36	- 13
Same-sex marriages or civil unions	42	29	- 13
Immigration	72	57	- 15
Limits on lawsuits	64	42	- 22

Note: Bolded issues indicate relative public consensus.

- Democrats give higher importance than Republicans to four additional issues: unemployment, the federal budget deficit, healthcare costs, and energy policies.
- Among Democrats, healthcare costs rank first of all issues, while it ties for fifth among Republicans.
- Besides limiting lawsuits, Republicans give higher importance than Democrats to abortion, civil unions or same-sex marriages, and immigration.
- The three lowest ranking issues for Democrats are civil unions or same-sex marriages, abortion, and limiting lawsuits.
- For Republicans, the three lowest ranking issues are laws to help blacks and other racial minorities, civil unions or same-sex marriages, and the environment.

The results suggest little congruence between Bush's domestic agenda and that of the American public. Tort reform, immigration, and taxes, along with Social Security, have been the domestic issues Bush has pushed the most—but only Social Security ranks among the public's top domestic issues. For the public, healthcare costs and education rank higher than any of Bush's other domestic priorities.

Survey Methods

Results are based on telephone interviews with 1,002 national adults, aged 18 and older, conducted Dec. 17-19, 2004. For results based on the total sample of national adults, one can say with 95% confidence that the maximum margin of sampling error is ±3 percentage points.

For results based on the 478 national adults in the Form A half-sample and 524 national adults in the Form B half-sample, the maximum margins of sampling error are ±5 percentage points.

In addition to sampling error, question wording and practical difficulties in conducting surveys can introduce error or bias into the findings of public opinion polls.

January 5, 2005

PUBLIC DIVIDED ON SOCIAL SECURITY PRIVATIZATION

Americans rate Social Security as high-priority item

by Jeffrey M. Jones, Gallup Poll Managing Editor

George W. Bush has made Social Security reform a top priority for his second term in office. Americans agree that it should be high on the legislative agenda, but don't necessarily agree with a proposal to allow workers to invest a portion of their Social Security taxes in the stock market—something Bush supports. In part, support depends on how the program is described to survey respondents, with support levels in recent polls ranging from 48% to 60%. If Social Security is indeed partially privatized, slightly more than 4 in 10 Americans expect it will not affect them personally, but those who feel they would be affected are about evenly divided as to whether it would help or hurt them.

A Dec. 17-19 CNN/*USA Today*/Gallup poll finds 82% of Americans saying it is at least very important for Congress and the president to deal with Social Security in the next year, including 40% who say it is extremely important. These figures are in line with what Gallup found in 2002 and 2003.

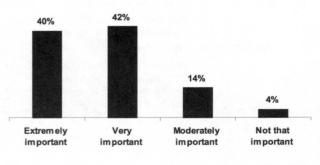

How important is it for Congress/the president to deal with Social Security in the next year?

Extremely important 40% | Very important 42% | Moderately important 14% | Not that important 4%

Dec. 17-19, 2004

Among the 18 policy issues whose importance Americans rated, Social Security ranks among the top 6, behind Iraq (90%), terrorism (87%), healthcare costs (87%), the economy (86%), and education (86%).

Private Investment of Social Security Taxes

One prominent Social Security proposal attracting a lot of attention is the idea of allowing workers to invest part of their Social Security taxes in the stock market. This would provide the possibility of greater returns on a person's investment, but also carries more risk than the safe investments in which the government currently invests Social Security revenues. According to the CNN/*USA Today*/Gallup poll, the public is divided over such a proposal, with 48% in favor and 48% opposed.

The measured level of support for partial Social Security privatization depends somewhat on how the program is described to respondents. Various recent polls have shown support levels for the privatization plan ranging from almost half to 60%.

- A recent Fox News/Opinion Dynamics poll finds 60% saying "people should have the choice to invest privately up to 5% of their Social Security contributions." Only 27% say they should not. This question talks about giving workers the choice and puts a specific number (5%) on how much of the taxes could be invested.
- An ABC News/*Washington Post* poll finds majority support (53%) for "a plan in which people who chose to could invest some of their Social Security contributions in the stock market." Again, this question touches on the "choice" aspect of the program. But only 46% of those who initially said they supported the program continued to do so when they were told that instituting the system may necessitate the government's borrowing up to $2 trillion to set it up.
- A CBS News/*New York Times* poll finds 49% saying it is a "good idea" to allow "individuals to invest portions of their Social Security taxes on their own." Forty-five percent say it is a "bad idea."
- Previous Gallup questions specifying that a portion of Social Security contributions could be invested in "personal retirement accounts" found higher support for privatization than does the current wording that simply talks about investments in stocks and bonds.

The most recent Gallup data show that support for private investment of Social Security taxes varies by subgroup. As is typically the case, younger Americans are much more likely to favor the proposal than are older Americans. Fifty-seven percent of those under age 50 favor the proposal, compared with 37% of those aged 50 and older.

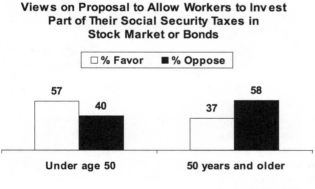

Views on Proposal to Allow Workers to Invest Part of Their Social Security Taxes in Stock Market or Bonds

□ % Favor   ■ % Oppose

Under age 50: 57, 40
50 years and older: 37, 58

Dec. 17-19, 2004

Also, those residing in higher-income households are much more likely to favor the proposal. Sixty percent of Americans living in households whose incomes are $75,000 or more say they favor it. That drops to 51% in households having incomes between $30,000 and $74,999, and 34% in those with incomes less than $30,000.

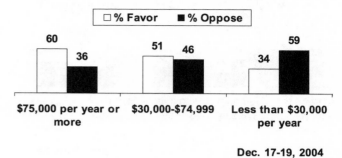

Views on Proposal to Allow Workers to Invest Part of Their Social Security Taxes in Stock Market or Bonds

□ % Favor   ■ % Oppose

$75,000 per year or more: 60, 36
$30,000-$74,999: 51, 46
Less than $30,000 per year: 34, 59

Dec. 17-19, 2004

Perhaps because President Bush has strongly endorsed this reform proposal, Republicans (69%) are nearly three times as likely as Democrats (26%) to favor it.

Expected Personal Impact of Social Security Privatization

The plurality of Americans, 43%, say the proposal to allow private investment of Social Security taxes would have no effect on them personally if it becomes law. Another 29% say it would help them and 26% say it would hurt.

These perceptions also vary by age—those under age 50 are nearly twice as likely to think passage of the proposal would help (42%) rather than hurt (23%) them. The vast majority of Americans currently at retirement age (65 and older), 70%, believe passage of the proposal would not affect them. Those in the pre-retirement years (50 to 64 years old) are most pessimistic: nearly twice as many people in this age group think the proposal would hurt (33%)—rather than help (19%)—them.

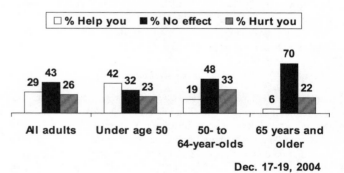

Would Partial Social Security Privatization Help You, Hurt You, or Have No Effect?

□ % Help you   ■ % No effect   ▨ % Hurt you

All adults: 29, 43, 26
Under age 50: 42, 32, 23
50- to 64-year-olds: 19, 48, 33
65 years and older: 6, 70, 22

Dec. 17-19, 2004

Household income levels are also related to the way Americans expect passage of the proposal to affect them. The greater the household income, the more likely people are to think the proposal will help them personally; the less the household income, the more likely people are to think the proposal will hurt them.

Expected Impact of Social Security Privatization on the System

Americans are generally divided in their views on how partially privatizing Social Security would affect the Social Security system and the federal budget.

Would Partial Social Security Privatization Help You, Hurt You, or Have No Effect?

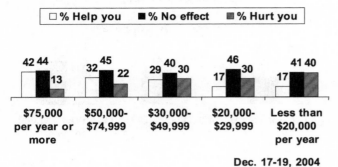

☐ % Help you   ■ % No effect   ▨ % Hurt you

	$75,000 per year or more	$50,000-$74,999	$30,000-$49,999	$20,000-$29,999	Less than $20,000 per year
Help you	42	32	29	17	17
No effect	44	45	40	46	41
Hurt you	13	22	30	30	40

Dec. 17-19, 2004

- Forty-nine percent believe the federal budget deficit would increase significantly if the proposal were passed, while 43% believe the deficit would not increase.
- Forty-seven percent say passing the proposal will strengthen Social Security in the long run, while an equal number believe it will not have this benefit.
- Forty-six percent believe it would reduce benefits to current Social Security recipients, while 48% disagree.
- Americans are less divided in their views of the effect of privatization on future benefits. Fifty-eight percent think the guaranteed Social Security benefits to future recipients would be reduced if the proposal passed, while 36% believe this would not happen.
- Perceptions of the impact of partial Social Security privatization on the system and the federal budget vary significantly by partisanship. Republicans are much more likely than independents or Democrats to expect positive results, and much less likely to anticipate negative results, from the proposal.

	Overall	Democrat	Independent	Republican
Deficit would increase	49%	60%	51%	36%
Future benefits reduced	58%	71%	57%	45%
System stronger in long run	47%	28%	51%	64%
Current benefits reduced	46%	59%	48%	32%

Survey Methods

These results are based on telephone interviews with a randomly selected national sample of 1,002 adults, aged 18 and older, conducted Dec. 17-19, 2004. For results based on this sample, one can say with 95% confidence that the maximum error attributable to sampling and other random effects is ±3 percentage points. In addition to sampling error, question wording and practical difficulties in conducting surveys can introduce error or bias into the findings of public opinion polls.

January 6, 2005

SLIGHT MAJORITY OF AMERICANS SUPPORT MAKING TAX CUTS PERMANENT

Majority support "major changes" or "complete overhaul" to the federal income tax system

by Joseph Carroll, Gallup Poll Assistant Editor

The issue of taxes promises to be at the forefront of debate as President George W. Bush prepares for his second term in office. The president is expected to ask Congress to pass legislation making permanent the tax cuts passed into law during his first term in office that are set to expire over the next several years. Bush is also expected to seek legislation that would simplify the federal income tax system.

A recent CNN/*USA Today*/Gallup poll, conducted Dec. 17-19, finds that a slim majority of Americans support making the Bush tax cuts permanent. A majority of Americans also say that the federal income tax system needs either a complete overhaul or major changes. At the same time, the American public does not think taxes are the most important issue facing Congress and the president this year. Republicans and Democrats differ in their views of the issue of taxes, with Republicans more likely both to support legislation making the tax cuts permanent and to believe major changes to the overall income tax system are necessary.

Public Support for Making Tax Cuts Permanent

A slight majority of Americans, 52%, support making the recent federal income tax cuts permanent, while 40% oppose such a plan. Many fewer Americans endorse the idea of making the cuts permanent now than did so in November 2002.

As you may know, the federal income tax cuts passed into law since George W. Bush became president are set to expire within the next several years. Would you favor or oppose making those tax cuts permanent?

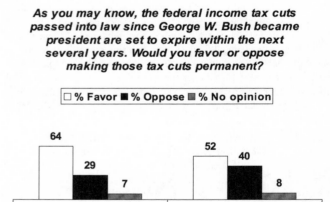

☐ % Favor   ■ % Oppose   ▨ % No opinion

	Nov. 8-10, 2002	Dec. 17-19, 2004
Favor	64	52
Oppose	29	40
No opinion	7	8

Not surprisingly, Republicans are much more likely than Democrats to support making the Bush tax cuts permanent. Seventy-two percent of Republicans (and those who lean toward the Republican Party) support the proposal, compared with only 34% of Democrats (and Democratic leaders).

Americans who live in higher income households are slightly more likely than those living in lower income households to support making the Bush tax cuts permanent.

Tax Code Reform

The poll also finds public support for reforming the federal income tax system. Fifty-nine percent of Americans say the federal income

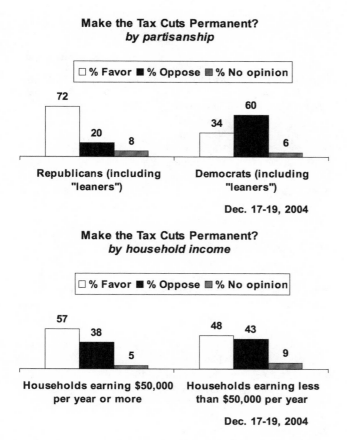

Make the Tax Cuts Permanent?
by partisanship

□ % Favor ■ % Oppose ▨ % No opinion

Republicans (including "leaners"): 72, 20, 8
Democrats (including "leaners"): 34, 60, 6

Dec. 17-19, 2004

Make the Tax Cuts Permanent?
by household income

□ % Favor ■ % Oppose ▨ % No opinion

Households earning $50,000 per year or more: 57, 38, 5
Households earning less than $50,000 per year: 48, 43, 9

Dec. 17-19, 2004

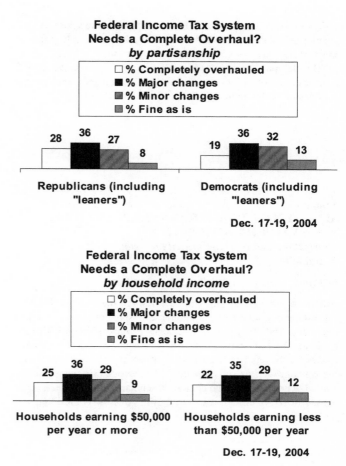

Federal Income Tax System Needs a Complete Overhaul?
by partisanship

□ % Completely overhauled
■ % Major changes
▨ % Minor changes
▨ % Fine as is

Republicans (including "leaners"): 28, 36, 27, 8
Democrats (including "leaners"): 19, 36, 32, 13

Dec. 17-19, 2004

Federal Income Tax System Needs a Complete Overhaul?
by household income

□ % Completely overhauled
■ % Major changes
▨ % Minor changes
▨ % Fine as is

Households earning $50,000 per year or more: 25, 36, 29, 9
Households earning less than $50,000 per year: 22, 35, 29, 12

Dec. 17-19, 2004

tax system either needs to be completely overhauled (24%) or needs major changes (35%). Nearly 3 in 10 Americans say the system needs minor changes, and 11% say the tax system is fine in its current form. These results show little change since 2000.

Republicans are slightly more likely than Democrats to say the federal income tax system should be reformed. More than 6 in 10 Republicans say the tax system needs to be completely overhauled (28%) or needs major changes (36%). This compares with 55% of Democrats who say the system needs a complete overhaul (19%) or major changes (36%).

The poll shows little difference between higher income and lower income households when asked if the federal income tax system should be reformed.

Which of the following statements best represents what you feel about the federal income tax system: it needs to be completely overhauled, it needs major changes, it needs minor changes, (or) it is basically fine the way it is?

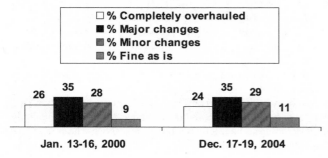

□ % Completely overhauled
■ % Major changes
▨ % Minor changes
▨ % Fine as is

Jan. 13-16, 2000: 26, 35, 28, 9
Dec. 17-19, 2004: 24, 35, 29, 11

Importance of Dealing with Taxes

Although Bush is expected to make tax reform a prominent issue in his second term, Americans are not convinced that taxes are the most important issue facing Congress and the president over the next year. Only about one in four Americans (26%) say taxes are an "extremely" important issue that the president and Congress should address over the next year. An additional 40% say the tax issue is "very" important.

Taxes also rank toward the bottom of the list of 18 issues tested for importance in the poll, only faring better than same-sex marriages or civil unions (with 16% saying that issue is extremely important), laws to help blacks and minorities (16%), abortion (19%), limits on lawsuits (22%), and the environment (24%). The situation in Iraq and terrorism are the top issues in the minds of the public, with about half of Americans rating these as extremely important.

Since Bush took office in 2001, the percentage of Americans rating taxes as an extremely important issue has ranged from a low of 26% to a high of 31%.

Survey Methods

Results are based on telephone interviews with 1,002 national adults, aged 18 and older, conducted Dec. 17-19, 2004. For results based on the total sample of national adults, one can say with 95% confidence that the maximum margin of sampling error is ±3 percentage points.

For results based on the 478 national adults in the Form A half-sample and 524 national adults in the Form B half-sample, the maximum margins of sampling error are ±5 percentage points.

In addition to sampling error, question wording and practical difficulties in conducting surveys can introduce error or bias into the findings of public opinion polls.

January 7, 2005

ALMOST HALF OF AMERICANS REPORT GIVING MONEY FOR TSUNAMI RELIEF

Nearly three-quarters have prayed for victims and their families

by Frank Newport, Gallup Poll Editor in Chief

Americans are closely following the news of the tsunami that devastated the coastal areas of a number of Asian countries and killed more than 150,000 people. Americans have responded with their pocketbooks and hearts. Almost half of Americans report sending money for the relief effort, and nearly three-quarters have prayed for the tsunami victims and their families. Despite criticisms that the United States has not done enough to send aid to the affected countries, 7 in 10 Americans disagree and say that the United States is doing enough.

Americans Highly Focused on Tsunami

The Asian tsunami and the aftermath has become one of the most widely followed news stories of recent decades. The new Gallup Poll shows that 46% of Americans have been following the story very closely and another 43% have been following it somewhat closely. That leaves just about 1 in 10 Americans who have not been following it closely:

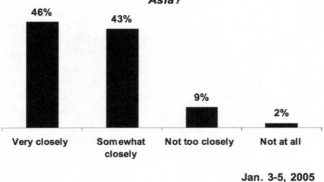

How closely have you been following the news about the recent earthquake and tsunami that struck parts of Asia?

46% Very closely
43% Somewhat closely
9% Not too closely
2% Not at all

Jan. 3-5, 2005

The Gallup Poll has asked this same question about a wide variety of news stories over the last two decades. The attention being paid to this story places it sixth on the list. Only five stories that Gallup has measured have generated more intense levels of interest.

ATTENTION RATINGS IN DETAIL

YEAR	DATE	NEWS EVENT	Very closely %	Some-what closely %	Not too closely %	Not at all %
2001	Sep 14-15	Terrorist attacks on New York City and Washington, D.C.	77	20	2	1
2003	Mar 22-23	War between U.S. and Iraq	63	32	4	1
1997	Sep 6-7	Death of Princess Diana	55	30	11	3
1991	Feb 24	Beginning of ground war in Iraq	53	31	13	3
2002	Oct 21-22	The sniper shootings	50	41	8	1
2005	**Jan 3-5**	**The tsunami that struck parts of Asia**	**46**	**43**	**9**	**2**
2000	Nov 11-12	Situation surrounding Tuesday's presidential election	46	41	10	3

Americans Opening Pocketbooks and Hearts to Tsunami Victims

The American public has responded to the tsunami tragedy both in terms of material gifts and in terms of prayer.

The poll shows that 45% of Americans say they have already given money to relief efforts aimed at benefiting the victims of the tsunami, 74% have prayed for victims of the tsunami and their families, and 26% have contributed material goods or supplies to the relief efforts. (As is always the case when respondents are asked about socially desirable activities, there is the possibility of some over-reporting in these numbers. Additionally, some Americans may believe that their normal donations to a church or synagogue will be spent in part on victim relief. It should be noted that Gallup's question included an option that allowed respondents to indicate that they had "thought about" engaging in each of these three activities, in part designed to lower the social pressure within the interview context to report actually having given aid or prayed for the victims and their families.)

Giving money for tsunami victim relief varies by gender, age, and religion. Women are more likely than men to report having given money, older Americans are more likely than those who are younger to have given aid, and those who attend church frequently are more likely to have given money than those who attend less frequently.

Thinking about ways in which people might support those affected by the tsunami, please tell me if you, by chance, have already done each of the following, if you have thought about doing it, but have not yet done so, or if you have not given much thought to doing it.

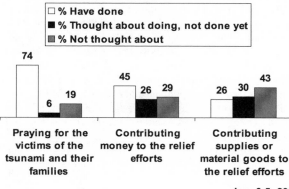

- □ % Have done
- ■ % Thought about doing, not done yet
- ▨ % Not thought about

Praying for the victims of the tsunami and their families: 74, 6, 19

Contributing money to the relief efforts: 45, 26, 29

Contributing supplies or material goods to the relief efforts: 26, 30, 43

Jan. 3-5, 2005

CONTRIBUTION OF MONEY TO AID TSUNAMI VICTIMS AND FAMILIES

	Have contributed %	Thought about contributing/ haven't yet %	Not thought much about contributing %
Overall	45	26	29
Male	40	23	37
Female	49	28	22
18 to 29 yrs.	37	33	30
30 to 49 yrs.	41	26	33
50 to 64 yrs.	51	19	30
65+ yrs.	53	23	21
Attend church weekly	54	22	22
Attend nearly weekly/monthly	42	26	32
Attend less often	40	28	32

The tendency to pray for the tsunami victims and their families is, not surprisingly, related to measures of personal religiosity. Nine in 10 Americans who attend church regularly say they have prayed for those affected by the tsunami, compared with a little more than half of those who attend church less often.

INCIDENCE OF PRAYING FOR VICTIMS AND THEIR FAMILIES

	Have prayed for victims and families %	Thought about praying/ haven't yet %	Not thought much about praying %
Overall	74	6	19
Attend church weekly	92	3	5
Attend nearly weekly/monthly	86	6	8
Attend less often	55	8	35

That a significantly smaller percentage of Americans have contributed supplies or material goods to the relief efforts may stem from the fact that there are fewer ways to directly contribute goods than there is to contribute money.

Majority Thinks the U.S. Is Doing Enough

The efforts of the United States in aiding the victims of the tsunami were initially criticized for being "too little, too late." As recently as this week, for example, ABC's *Good Morning America* anchor Diane Sawyer was questioning Secretary of State Colin Powell about the level of U.S. relief efforts, saying: "With the U.S. now giving $350 million in aid, questions persist about the U.S. initial offer, which was small ..." and "... as you know, there's all kinds of second guessing going on, that America missed a great opportunity, particularly in an intensely Muslim area, to show good faith in the beginning ..."

Powell strongly disagreed with the premise of Sawyer's question. While the new poll did not ask explicitly about the public's reaction to the United States' initial reaction to the tragedy, the results show that Americans believe that at this point, the United States is doing enough to aid the tsunami victims. Seven in 10 say that the United States has been doing enough to help the victims of the tsunami, while about a quarter think the United States should be doing more.

Do you think the United States is doing enough to help the victims of the tsunami, or do you think the United States should be doing more?

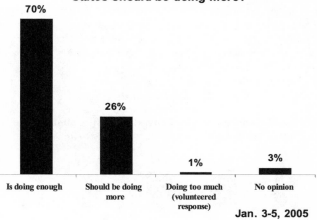

- Is doing enough: 70%
- Should be doing more: 26%
- Doing too much (volunteered response): 1%
- No opinion: 3%

Jan. 3-5, 2005

Do you think the United States is doing enough to help the victims of the tsunami, or do you think the United States should be doing more?

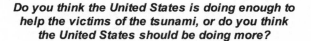

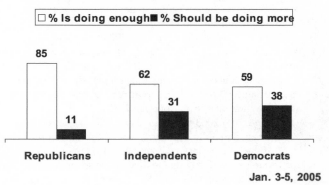

- □ % Is doing enough ■ % Should be doing more

Republicans: 85, 11
Independents: 62, 31
Democrats: 59, 38

Jan. 3-5, 2005

Politics intrudes itself even into a tragedy like this one. With a Republican president and a Republican-controlled Congress, it is perhaps no surprise to find that Republicans are somewhat more likely than Democrats to believe that the United States is doing enough to help the tsunami victims.

Survey Methods

Results are based on telephone interviews with 1,005 national adults, aged 18 and older, conducted Jan. 3-5, 2004. For results based on the total sample, one can say with 95% confidence that the maximum margin of sampling error is ±3 percentage points.

January 10, 2005
PUBLIC GIVES LACKLUSTER REVIEW TO STATE OF THE UNION
Increase seen in pessimism about the future

by Lydia Saad, Gallup Poll Senior Editor

Gallup's annual Mood of the Nation survey, conducted Jan. 3-5, finds the public less than enthusiastic about general conditions in the country.

According to the new poll, only 46% of Americans are satisfied with the way things are going in the nation; 53% are dissatisfied. When asked where the country presently stands on a scale from 0 to 10, 49% rate the country positively, between 6 and 10; about a quarter give it the midpoint rating of 5; and another quarter give expressly negative ratings, between 0 and 4.

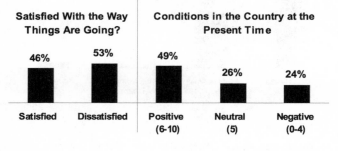

Mood of the Nation

Satisfied With the Way Things Are Going?

46% Satisfied   53% Dissatisfied

Conditions in the Country at the Present Time

49% Positive (6-10)   26% Neutral (5)   24% Negative (0-4)

Jan. 3-5, 2005

These ratings continue a rut in public temperament that seemed to take hold sometime in 2003.

- In 20 of the 25 months since January 2003, more Americans said they were "dissatisfied" than "satisfied" with the way things are going in the United States.
- In polling conducted in January of each year since 2003, barely half the public has given the country a positive review when asked to rate it on a scale from 0 to 10.

The period from 2003 through today stands in contrast to 2001 and 2002, when the public was much more upbeat about the country. In 17 of the 24 months spanning that period, more Americans said they were satisfied than dissatisfied. More specifically, in January 2001—on the eve of George W. Bush's first inauguration—

56% of Americans were satisfied with the state of the country and 73% gave a positive score when they were asked to rate current national conditions. In January 2002—with the country still reeling from the 9/11 terrorist attacks—65% were satisfied with the country and 64% gave national conditions a positive score.

So it's not the best of times, but it's also not the worst of times. According to Gallup trends dating back several decades, the percentage of Americans satisfied with the country or giving it positive ratings on the 0 to 10 scale was much lower in the 1970s and early to mid-1990s. For instance, the low point of satisfaction since Gallup has been using the "satisfied/dissatisfied" measure came in 1979, when only 12% of Americans were satisfied with the state of the country. As recently as 1996, only 24% were satisfied.

High points for satisfaction—when the percentage satisfied reached two-thirds or more—came in the mid-1980s and late 1990s (corresponding with booming economies); in 1991, immediately following the end of the Gulf War; and in the post-9/11 period in 2001 (when Americans were rallying in support of the country).

Recent Ratings Are Steady

Today's results show little recent change.
- The satisfaction measure—initiated by Gallup in 1979 and tracked monthly since October 2000—has found public satisfaction hovering in the mid-40s for the past few months. In fact, except for the initial reading in January 2004, when 55% said they were satisfied, every reading for the past year has found the public more dissatisfied than satisfied with the state of the nation.

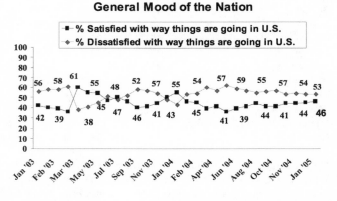

General Mood of the Nation

- % Satisfied with way things are going in U.S.
- % Dissatisfied with way things are going in U.S.

- The 11-point scale on which respondents rate present conditions—first asked in 1959 and updated annually since 2001—produces a slightly more negative assessment today than it did a year ago, when 53% had a positive view of the country. The current rating is similar to that of January 2003, but substantially lower than what was found in 2001 and 2002.

Looking Ahead and Looking Back

This 11-point rating assessment is part of a question sequence known as Gallup's "striving scale." Respondents use the same 0 to 10 scale to indicate where they think the nation stands at the present time, where it will stand five years from now, and where it stood five years ago.

While just 49% think that present conditions rate a positive score on this scale (between 6 and 10), the public is more positive when assessing the past and the future. Three-quarters give positive ratings to conditions five years ago, and 59% believe that conditions five years from now will be positive.

Conditions in the U.S. Today

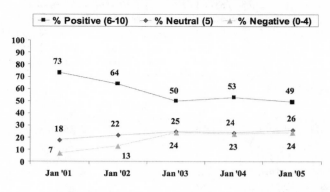

Rating Conditions in the U.S. -- January 2005

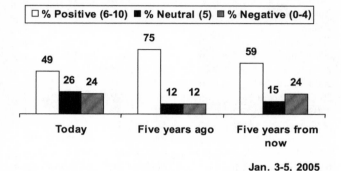

Jan. 3-5, 2005

Still, as with optimism about current conditions, optimism about the future has also declined. Whereas 59% today believe the United States will enjoy positive conditions five years from now, 65% held this view in January 2004.

Rating Conditions in the U.S.—January 2005
percentage of Americans giving a positive rating on a 0-10 scale

	Today	Five Years Ago	Five Years From Now
January 2005	49%	75%	59%
January 2004	53%	72%	65%
Change (pct. pts.)	-4	+3	-6

The cause for this decline in Americans' outlook for the country is not immediately clear. The public's evaluation of the economy—typically an important component of overall public mood—is no worse today than it was a year ago: 41% currently describe the economy as excellent or good, compared with 37% in mid-January 2004.

Satisfaction in Greater Detail

The annual survey also tracks public satisfaction with 28 specific areas of national concern. Between January 2004 and today, public satisfaction declined significantly in 8 of these. They include the nation's military strength and preparedness, the nation's security from terrorism, energy policies, acceptance of homosexuality, the nation's campaign finance laws, the influence of organized religion, the opportunity for a person to get ahead by working hard, and the quality of medical care.

At the same time, satisfaction increased in four areas, including satisfaction with the moral and ethical climate of the country, the nation's crime policies, the amount Americans pay in federal taxes, and the role America plays in world affairs.

More analysis of this specific national satisfaction data will be forthcoming on gallup.com.

Things Look Better at Close Range

While attitudes toward the country are tepid, Americans' satisfaction with the way things are going closer to home remains positive.

- Three-quarters are satisfied with the way things are going in their local communities; only 24% are dissatisfied. This is unchanged from last year.
- About 6 in 10 (59%) say they are satisfied with the way things are going in their states, while 39% are dissatisfied. This is up slightly from 53% satisfied last year.

Most of the increase in satisfaction at the state level comes from residents in the Western region of the United States. This could be the result of changes in attitudes of California residents, who comprise a large share of the survey's Western region. Previous Gallup analysis has found that trust in state government was "atypically low" in the West in the fall of 2003, a fact attributed to very low trust by California residents due to dissatisfaction that led to the ultimate recall of Gov. Gray Davis in October 2003.

% Satisfied With State, by Region

	East	Midwest	South	West
January 2005	47%	63%	61%	61%
January 2004	45%	58%	59%	46%
Change (pct. pts.)	+2	+5	+2	+15

Survey Methods

These results are based on telephone interviews with a randomly selected national sample of 1,005 adults, aged 18 and older, conducted Jan. 3-5, 2005. For results based on this sample, one can say with 95% confidence that the maximum error attributable to sampling and other random effects is ±3 percentage points. In addition to sampling error, question wording and practical difficulties in conducting surveys can introduce error or bias into the findings of public opinion polls.

January 11, 2005
AMERICANS PESSIMISTIC ABOUT FUTURE IN IRAQ
Disapproval of Bush's handling of war in Iraq at 56%

by David W. Moore, Gallup Poll Senior Editor

A new CNN/*USA Today*/Gallup survey shows that Americans continue to be pessimistic about the future in Iraq. Most people are skeptical that peace will be established there within a year, with a clear majority saying that things are going badly in Iraq and expressing disapproval of the way President George W. Bush is handling the situation there. Americans are about evenly divided both as to whether the coming year will see the establishment of a democratic form of government, and whether the decision to go to war in the first place was a mistake or not.

The poll, conducted Jan. 7-9, finds 56% of Americans say they disapprove of the way Bush is handling the situation in Iraq, up from 51% in November 2004. Just 42% approve, down from 47% in November 2004.

Do you approve or disapprove of the way George W. Bush is handling the situation in Iraq?

	Approve %	Disapprove %	No opinion %
2005 Jan 7-9	42	56	2
2004 Nov 7-10	47	51	2
2004 Oct 14-16	46	52	2
2004 Sep 24-26	48	49	3
2004 Aug 9-11	45	52	3
2004 Jun 21-23 ^	42	56	2
2004 Jun 3-6	41	57	2
2004 May 7-9 ^	41	58	1
2004 May 2-4	42	55	3
2004 Apr 16-18	48	49	3
2004 Mar 26-28	51	47	2
2004 Jan 29-Feb 1	46	53	1
2004 Jan 2-5	61	36	3
2003 Dec 5-7	50	47	3
2003 Nov 3-5	45	54	1
2003 Oct 6-8	47	50	3
2003 Sep 8-10	51	47	2
2003 Aug 25-26	57	41	2
2003 Jul 25-27	60	38	2
2003 Jul 18-20	57	39	4
2003 Jul 7-9	58	39	3
2003 Jun 12-15	63	34	3
2003 Apr 14-16	76	21	3
2003 Mar 29-30	71	27	2
2003 Mar 24-25	71	26	3
2003 Mar 14-15	56	41	3
2003 Jan 31-Feb 2	54	42	4
2003 Jan 3-5	55	40	5
2002 Dec 9-10	55	39	6
2002 Oct 21-22	52	40	8

^ Asked of a half sample.

The current level of disapproval is comparable to the public's views last May and June. During the presidential campaign, from August through November last year, disapproval dropped somewhat, averaging just 51%. But with intensified fighting in recent weeks, disapproval has increased.

Disapproval is related to the public's negative assessment of how things are going in Iraq. A clear majority of Americans (59%) believe the war there is going badly, while only 40% believe it is going well. These views are little changed from last month, but they are somewhat more pessimistic than the public's views last August and September.

The poll also finds that 50% of Americans believe the United States made a mistake in sending troops to Iraq, while 48% disagree. These views are roughly comparable to a Gallup survey Jan. 3-5 that found 52% of Americans saying it was not worth going to war in Iraq, and 46% saying it was.

In general, how would you say things are going for the U.S. in Iraq—[ROTATED: very well, moderately well, moderately badly, (or) very badly]?

	Very well %	Moderately well %	Moderately badly %	Very badly %	No opinion %
2005 Jan 7-9	5	35	29	30	1
2004 Dec 5-8	6	34	26	33	1
2004 Sep 24-26	4	42	27	25	2
2004 Aug 9-11 †	5	40	28	25	2
2004 Jul 8-11	5	35	30	29	1
2004 Jun 3-6	6	34	35	25	*
2004 May 21-23	7	35	26	31	1
2004 May 2-4	4	33	32	30	1
2004 Apr 5-8	5	30	31	33	1
2004 Mar 5-7	9	46	28	15	2
2003 Nov 3-5 ^	4	34	34	27	1
2003 Oct 6-8 ^†	6	36	34	24	*
2003 Sep 8-10 ^	6	41	31	21	1
2003 Aug 25-26 ^	6	44	30	19	1
2003 Jul 25-27 ^	10	46	28	15	1
2003 Jul 18-20 ^	6	48	30	15	1
2003 Jun 27-29 ^	5	51	29	13	2
2003 May 30-Jun 1 ^	11	59	22	7	1
2003 May 5-7 ^†	30	56	10	3	1
2003 Apr 22-23 ^†	21	64	12	2	1

^ WORDING: How would you say things are going for the U.S. in Iraq now that the major fighting has ended—[ROTATED: very well, moderately well, moderately badly, (or) very badly]?
† Asked of a half sample.
*Less than 0.5%.

In view of the developments since we first sent our troops to Iraq, do you think the United States made a mistake in sending troops to Iraq, or not?

	Yes %	No %	No opinion %
Iraq			
2005 Jan 7-9	50	48	2
2004 Nov 19-21	47	51	2
2004 Oct 29-31 ^	44	52	4
2004 Oct 22-24	47	51	2
2004 Oct 14-16	47	52	1
2004 Oct 9-10 ^	46	53	1
2004 Oct 1-3	48	51	1
2004 Sep 24-26	42	55	3
2004 Sep 3-5 ^	38	57	5
2004 Aug 23-25 ^	48	50	2
2004 Jul 30-Aug 1	47	51	2
2004 Jul 19-21	50	47	3
2004 Jul 8-11 ^	54	45	1
2004 Jun 21-23 ^	54	44	2
2004 Jun 3-6 ^	41	58	1
2004 May 7-9 ^	44	54	2
2004 Apr 16-18 ^	42	57	1
2004 Jan 12-15 ^	42	56	2
2003 Nov 3-5 ^	39	60	1
2003 Oct 6-8 ^	40	59	1

2003 Jul 7-9 ^	27	72	1
2003 Mar 24-25 ^	23	75	2

^ Asked of a half sample.

When looking to the immediate future in Iraq, most Americans believe it is unlikely that peace and internal security will be established within a year, including 48% of Americans who say it is "very unlikely," and 23% saying "somewhat unlikely." There has been very little change in these views over the last seven months.

Likelihood that peace and internal security will be established

	Very likely %	Some-what likely %	Some-what unlikely %	Very unlikely %	No opinion %
2005 Jan 7-9	6	22	23	48	1
2004 May 21-23 ^	7	22	25	44	2

^ Asked of a half sample.

Americans are somewhat more divided, however, over whether a democratic form of government will be established in Iraq. Despite the upcoming elections scheduled there for the end of this month, 52% of Americans say it is unlikely that a democratic government will be established in Iraq within a year, while 47% say it is likely. These perceptions too have changed little since Gallup's May 2004 survey.

Likelihood that a democratic form of government will be established

	Very likely %	Some-what likely %	Some-what unlikely %	Very unlikely %	No opinion %
2005 Jan 7-9	15	32	23	29	1
2004 May 21-23 ^	12	30	23	32	3

^ Asked of a half sample.

Survey Methods

Results are based on telephone interviews with 1,008 national adults, aged 18 and older, conducted Jan. 7-9, 2005. For results based on the total sample of national adults, one can say with 95% confidence that the maximum margin of sampling error is ±3 percentage points.

For results based on the 480 national adults in the Form A half-sample and 528 national adults in the Form B half-sample, the maximum margins of sampling error are ±5 percentage points.

In addition to sampling error, question wording and practical difficulties in conducting surveys can introduce error or bias into the findings of public opinion polls.

January 11, 2005
GOT HEALTH INSURANCE?

by Joseph Carroll, Gallup Poll Assistant Editor

How many Americans have private health insurance? How many are covered by Medicare or Medicaid? And, how many have no coverage at all?

Each year, Gallup asks the public several different questions designed to measure the type of personal health insurance coverage Americans have. The overall results, compiled from an aggregate of Gallup's November 2003 and November 2004 health and healthcare surveys*, show that roughly 6 in 10 Americans (61%) have private health insurance coverage. Twenty-eight percent of adults nationwide are covered by Medicare or Medicaid, and 11% do not have any health insurance at all.

Health Insurance Coverage

November 2003 and November 2004

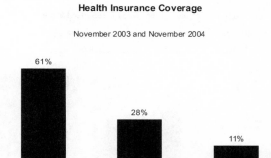

The data show interesting differences in coverage among different demographic subgroups.

Age

- Younger Americans are slightly more likely than those in other age groups to have no health insurance coverage at all (17% of those aged 18 to 29 vs. 12% of those aged 30 to 64 and less than 1% of those aged 65 and older). Sixty-two percent of 18- to 29-year-olds say they have private health insurance, and 21% are covered by Medicare or Medicaid.
- Nearly 8 in 10 adults aged 30 to 64 are covered by private health insurance. Roughly 1 in 10 adults in this age group are covered by Medicare or Medicaid.
- Almost all adults aged 65 and older—98%—are covered by Medicare or Medicaid.

Health Insurance Coverage by Age

■ Private insurance　□ Medicare/Medicaid　▨ No insurance

November 2003 and November 2004

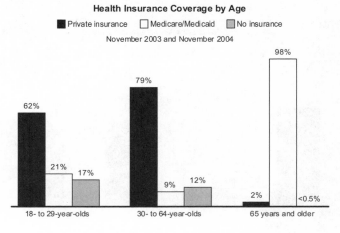

Income

Lower-income households are considerably more likely to be covered by Medicaid or Medicare, while higher-income households are more likely to have private health insurance.

- Half of adults living in households with an annual income of less than $30,000 say they are covered by Medicaid or Medicare. One in three adults (33%) in this income group have private insurance, and 17% have no insurance at all.
- Two in three adults earning between $30,000 and $75,000 per year are covered by private health insurance, while 24% are covered by Medicaid or Medicare and 10% have no coverage.
- Among those living in households earning $75,000 per year or more, 87% have private health insurance. Nine percent are covered by Medicaid or Medicare, and 4% have no insurance coverage.

Health Insurance Coverage by Household Income

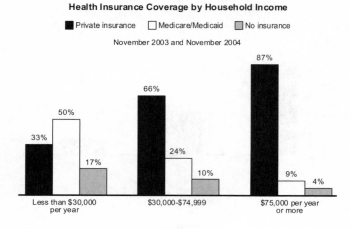

November 2003 and November 2004

Race

More than 6 in 10 non-Hispanic whites (64%) are covered by private health insurance, while 26% are covered by Medicaid or Medicare and 10% have no insurance at all. Blacks, meanwhile, are just as likely to be covered by Medicaid or Medicare (44%) as they are to have private health insurance coverage (45%). Eleven percent of blacks have no healthcare coverage.

Gender

Men are somewhat more likely than women to have private healthcare coverage (64% vs. 59%), while women are slightly more likely

Health Insurance Coverage by Race

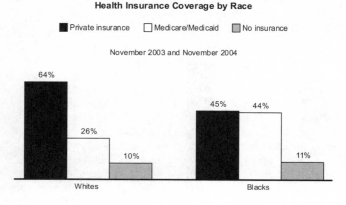

November 2003 and November 2004

Health Insurance Coverage by Gender

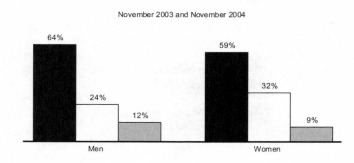

November 2003 and November 2004

to be covered by Medicaid or Medicare (32% to 24%). Women are more represented in the 65 and older population, which may partly explain this difference. Roughly the same proportions of men and women say they have no health insurance, but men are slightly more likely than women to say they have no health insurance.

Physical Disabilities and Long-Term Medical Conditions

Gallup's 2004 health and healthcare survey** asked Americans if they have a "physical disability that limits their activity" or if they have "a long-term medical condition, illness or disease."

Overall, the current data show that 21% of Americans have a physical disability, while 79% do not. Women are slightly more likely than men to say they have a physical disability, by a margin of 25% to 18%. Older Americans also are more likely to report physical disabilities than are younger Americans. Thirty percent of those aged 50 and older have a physical disability, compared with 16% of those aged 30 to 49 and 13% of those aged 18 to 29.

Roughly 3 in 10 Americans (31%) report having a long-term medical condition, while 69% do not. Roughly the same proportion of men and women report having a long-term medical condition. Older Americans are considerably more likely to report having a long-term medical illness than younger people (43% of those aged 50 and older have a long-term condition vs. 24% of those aged 30 to 49 vs. 17% of those aged 18 to 29).

Americans with physical disabilities and long-term medical conditions are more likely than those who do not have these conditions to be covered by Medicaid or Medicare. The data show that 57% of Americans with a physical disability have Medicaid or Medicare coverage, while 33% have private insurance, and 10% have no insur-

Health Insurance Coverage by Physical Disabilities

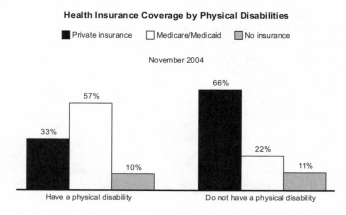

November 2004

ance. It is important to note that those under age 65 with a physical disability may qualify for Medicare and Medicaid. Among those without a physical disability, two in three are covered by private health insurance.

Americans with long-term medical conditions are almost equally likely to be covered by Medicaid or Medicare (46%) as they are to be covered by private insurance (43%). Eleven percent of Americans with a long-term medical condition have no insurance. Two in three Americans who do not suffer from a long-term illness or disease are covered by private health insurance.

Health Insurance Coverage by Long-Term Medical Conditions

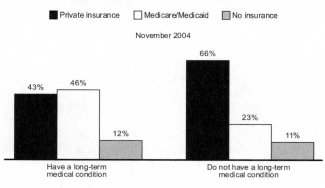

Results are based on telephone interviews with 2,025 national adults, aged 18 and older, conducted Nov. 3-5, 2003, and Nov. 7-10, 2004. For results based on the total sample of national adults, one can say with 95% confidence that the maximum margin of sampling error is ±2 percentage points.

**Results are based on telephone interviews with 1,016 national adults, aged 18 and older, conducted Nov. 7-10, 2004. For results based on the total sample of national adults, one can say with 95% confidence that the margin of sampling error is ±3 percentage points. In addition to sampling error, question wording and practical difficulties in conducting surveys can introduce error or bias into the findings of public opinion polls.*

January 12, 2005
BUSH APPROVAL ON IRAQ DIPS; ECONOMY APPROVAL UP SLIGHTLY
Little change in overall job approval

by Lydia Saad, Gallup Poll Senior Editor

A new CNN/*USA Today*/Gallup poll, conducted Jan. 7-9, updates President George W. Bush's perceived job performance on a number of issues in the news. With his overall job approval rating standing at 52%—about par for the president over the past year—the poll shows Bush also receiving majority public support for his handling of the tsunami disaster, for terrorism, and for education.

Opinion of Bush's handling of the economy is closely divided in the new survey, but his 50% approval score represents the recent

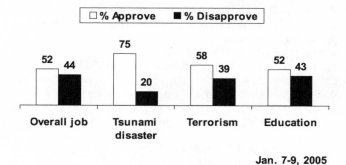

Jan. 7-9, 2005

high-water mark for Bush on this indicator. Approval of Bush on the economy averaged only 45% for all of 2004, and has not reached roughly the 50% level since September (when 49% approved).

In addition to the economy, Bush's ratings are also closely divided for the environment, taxes, and foreign affairs: 47% to 49% approve of his job performance in these areas, and 45% to 49% disapprove.

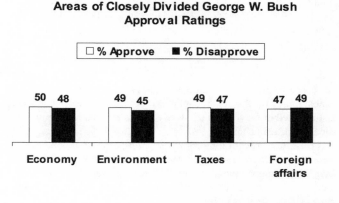

Jan. 7-9, 2005

The public's assessment of Bush skews negative for the situation in Iraq, Social Security, healthcare policy, immigration, and, most of all, the federal budget deficit.

Areas of Majority Disapproval for George W. Bush

☐ % Approve   ■ % Disapprove

	Iraq	Social Security	Healthcare	Immigration	Budget deficit
% Approve	42	41	40	34	32
% Disapprove	56	52	54	54	63

Jan. 7-9, 2005

Job Approval Is Steady

Bush's overall job approval rating is exactly the same today as in the previous poll, conducted Jan. 3-5. It is also consistent with his approval ratings for the past year, which have fluctuated in a fairly narrow range around the 2004 midpoint.

Across 35 individual job approval ratings in 2004, Bush's average score was 51% and his average disapproval score was 46%. Bush's highest overall job ratings in 2004 (60% and 59% approval) were both recorded in January. His lowest approval rating (46%) was recorded in mid-May (a time of significant difficulties in Iraq).

George W. Bush's Job Approval Ratings July 2004 – January 2005

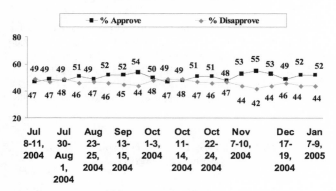

Iraq Job Approval Rating Retreats

Bush's performance on specific issues has also received fairly steady evaluation by the American public. Still, of the five issues that were last updated in November 2004, two—Iraq and the economy—do show significant change.

Bush's approval rating for his handling of the Iraq situation is now 42%, down from 47% in early November. Approval of Bush on Iraq is now comparable to the record low levels seen last spring, coincident with the Abu Ghraib prisoner abuse scandal and a period of heavy U.S. casualties in Iraq.

George W. Bush's Approval Ratings on the Situation in Iraq January 2004 – January 2005

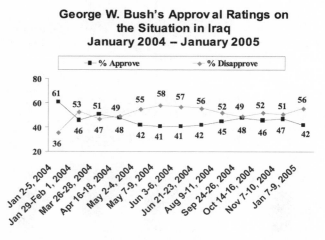

Also, the 50% approval of Bush on the economy appears to be a significant, albeit small, increase, given that the three previous readings (from September through November) averaged 47%.

At the same time, there has been virtually no change in Bush's ratings on terrorism, foreign affairs, or healthcare policy.

Longer-Term Changes

The last time the vast majority of these issues were updated simultaneously was March 2002. It is difficult to compare the 2002 ratings directly with today's ratings, because Bush's overall job approval rating at that time was extraordinarily high—registering 79%—as a result of public reaction to the 9/11 attacks. Presidential approval ratings on specific issues tend to benefit from the halo effect of high overall job approval.

Still, there are some interesting distinctions in the changes among issues between March 2002 and today.

- Public approval of Bush's handling of terrorism (down 28 points since March 2002) and foreign affairs (down 24 points) has fallen to roughly the same degree as the 27-point drop seen in his overall approval rating.
- His approval ratings on several other issues—the federal budget deficit, the economy, taxes, healthcare policy, and education—have fallen by a smaller but still substantial amount (ranging from 11 to 19 points).
- Bush's approval ratings on Social Security and the environment have fallen by fewer than 10 points. However, these were among his least positive issues in March 2002, and ones that experienced little to no inflation from the 9/11 effect; thus, they had less room to fall in the past three years.

Trend in Bush Job/Issue Approval Ratings

	March 2002 %	January 2005 %	Change pct. pts.
Overall job approval	79	52	-27
Terrorism	86	58	-28
Foreign affairs	71	47	-24
The federal budget deficit	51	32	-19
The economy	65	50	-15
Taxes	64	49	-15
Healthcare policy	52	40	-12
Education	63	52	-11
Social Security	47	41	-6
The environment	53	49	-4
The situation in Iraq	*Not asked*	42	—
Immigration	*Not asked*	34	—

Survey Methods

These results are based on telephone interviews with a randomly selected national sample of 1,008 adults, aged 18 and older, conducted Jan. 7-9, 2005. For results based on this sample, one can say with 95% confidence that the maximum error attributable to sampling and other random effects is ±3 percentage points. In addition to sampling error, question wording and practical difficulties in conducting surveys can introduce error or bias into the findings of public opinion polls.

AMERICANS' ECONOMIC ASSESSMENTS MIXED
Four in 10 rate conditions as excellent or good

by Jeffrey M. Jones, Gallup Poll Managing Editor

The beginning of the New Year finds Americans maintaining mixed views on the economy. Four in 10 rate the economic conditions in positive terms, up slightly from the fall but not significantly better than in August and September. More Americans say the economy is getting better than say it is getting worse, but less than half have an optimistic view. Just one in three Americans rate the job market positively—believing now is a good time to find a quality job. However, fewer Americans now view the economy as the most important problem facing the nation than did so in the fall.

Rating of Current Economic Conditions

In Gallup's Jan. 3-5 poll, 41% of Americans rate the economy as either "excellent" (3%) or "good" (38%), while 42% say it is "only fair" and 17% "poor." These are up slightly from the previous three months' data, but not appreciably better than the 39% excellent/good ratings in August and September.

However, the latest poll does mark the first time in a year that the percentage rating the economy as excellent or good has exceeded 40%. Before this month, those ratings had only exceeded 40% a total of four times (out of 61 distinct measurements) since July 2001.

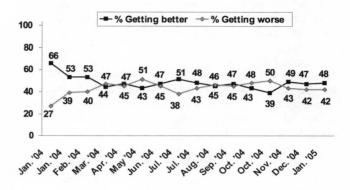

Future Economic Expectations
January 2004 – January 2005

good, time "to find a quality job." Despite the overall negative characterization of the job market, it has been much worse in the recent past. In fact, the 33% saying it is a good time is one of the highest measurements Gallup has measured since it regularly began tracking this question in October 2001. However, the current percentage is down slightly from 36% and 37% readings in December and November, respectively.

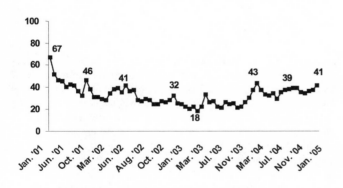

Current Economic Conditions
January 2001 – January 2005
percentage saying "excellent" or "good"

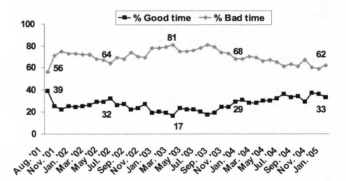

Good Time or Bad Time to Find a Quality Job?
August 2001 – January 2005

General Direction of the Economy

The January poll finds the public continuing, by a small margin, to be more optimistic than pessimistic about the direction in which the economy is headed. Forty-eight percent say the economy is getting better, while 42% say it is getting worse. Those percentages are essentially unchanged from November and December 2004.

While ratings of the current state of the national economy have stayed fairly steady during the last year, Americans' assessments of the economic outlook varied considerably in the past year, from a low of 39% saying the economy is getting better in mid-October to a high of 66% in early January 2004.

The Job Market

Americans continue to believe that job prospects are somewhat grim. By a 62% to 33% margin, the public says it is a bad, rather than

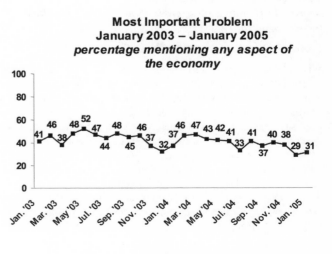

Most Important Problem
January 2003 – January 2005
percentage mentioning any aspect of the economy

Most Important Problem

The poll finds a noticeable decline in the percentage of Americans mentioning some aspect of the economy when they are asked to name the most important problem facing the country—an average of 30% in the last two polls compared with 38% in November and 40% in October.

Looking only at mentions of specific problems, 25% of Americans say the situation in Iraq is the top problem, ranking it ahead of all other issues. Twelve percent mention the economy in general, 11% unemployment, 9% healthcare, and 8% terrorism. The latter figure ties for the lowest percentage mentioning terrorism since the Sept. 11 terrorist attacks.

Most Important Problem Facing the Country Today

Issue	Percent Mentioning
Situation in Iraq	25
Economy (general mentions)	12
Unemployment/Jobs	11
Healthcare	9
Terrorism	8
Dissatisfaction with government leaders	7
Ethical/Moral/Religious decline	6
Poverty/Hunger/Homelessness	5
Social Security/Medicare	5
Education	4

Survey Methods

These results are based on telephone interviews with a randomly selected national sample of 1,005 adults, aged 18 years and older, conducted Jan. 3-5, 2005. For results based on this sample, one can say with 95% confidence that the maximum error attributable to sampling and other random effects is ±3 percentage points. In addition to sampling error, question wording and practical difficulties in conducting surveys can introduce error or bias into the findings of public opinion polls.

January 14, 2005
TERRORISM CONCERNS FADE
Nearly 6 in 10 Americans approve of the way President Bush is handling terrorism

by Joseph Carroll, Gallup Poll Assistant Editor

When Gallup recently asked Americans about the likelihood of a terrorist attack in the United States over the next few weeks, fewer than 4 in 10 said it was very or somewhat likely. This is the lowest percentage that Gallup has found over the past year. Not only do Americans say a terrorist attack is unlikely to occur in the near future, but they are also less likely than they have been in recent months to express concern about becoming victims of terrorism. While fewer than 4 in 10 Americans say the United States is winning the war on terrorism, a slightly larger percentage say neither the United States nor the terrorists are winning. And, Americans continue to rate President George W. Bush's handling of the terrorism issue positively, with roughly 6 in 10 approving.

Expectations of Terrorist Attack Down

The poll, conducted Jan. 7-9, finds that 39% of Americans say it is either very (8%) or somewhat (31%) likely that there will be further acts of terrorism in the United States over the next several weeks. Nearly 6 in 10 Americans (59%) say it is not too or not at all likely to happen.

The perception that a terrorist attack is likely to happen has been higher over the past year than it is now. Last January, 46% of respondents said a terrorist attack was very or somewhat likely to occur. This sentiment increased slightly to 51% in July, and then decreased slightly, to 48% in December.

The current results represent the lowest percentage saying an attack is likely to occur since Gallup first asked the question in 2001. In July 2003, however, the very/somewhat likely percentage was just one point higher, at 40%.

How likely is it that there will be further acts of terrorism in the United States over the next several weeks?

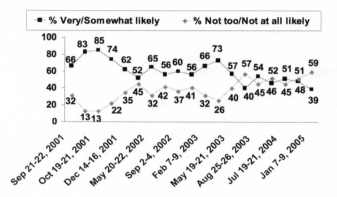

Most Americans also are not likely to believe that a terrorist attack will happen where they live. The poll finds that only 10% of Americans say it is very (2%) or somewhat (8%) likely that there will be a terrorist attack in their communities over the next several weeks. Ninety percent of Americans say an attack in their communities is not that likely, including a slight majority of Americans, 52%, who say it is not at all likely. These results show essentially no change since last year at this time.

How likely is it that there will be further acts of terrorism in YOUR COMMUNITY over the next several weeks?

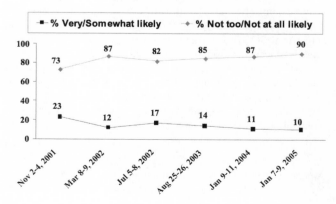

Since this question was first asked, the percentage saying an attack in their communities is likely has been quite low, ranging from a high of 23% in November 2001 to a low of 10% in the current poll.

Terrorism Concerns Down Slightly

Fewer than 4 in 10 Americans say they are very (10%) or somewhat (28%) worried that they or their family members will become victims of terrorism. Sixty-one percent of Americans are not too (37%) or not at all worried (24%).

Americans' concern about becoming terrorism victims fluctuated over the past year, ranging from a low of 28% to a high of 47%. The latest results show a slight decline in concerns about terrorism from what Gallup has found in recent months. In September, 43% of Americans said they were at least somewhat worried about becoming victims of terrorism. This edged up to 47% in October before decreasing to 41% in December.

How worried are you that you or someone in your family will become a victim of terrorism?

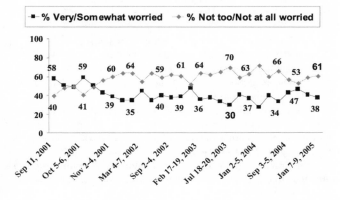

Who's Winning the War Against Terrorism?

Thirty-seven percent of Americans say the United States and its allies are winning the war against terrorism, while 20% say the terrorists are winning. A plurality of Americans, 42%, however, say neither side is winning.

These results show essentially no change since October, but the perceptions that the United States is winning the war on terror were somewhat higher earlier last year. In January, a slim majority (51%) said the United States and its allies were winning, while 14% said the terrorists and 35% said neither side. By mid-July, 40% said the United States was winning, 16% said the terrorists were winning, and 41% said neither side was winning.

Who Do You Think Is Currently Winning the War Against Terrorism?
January 2004—January 2005

	U.S. and its allies %	Neither side %	The terrorists %
2005 Jan 7-9	37	42	20
2004 Oct 9-10	38	41	19
2004 Jul 19-21	40	41	16
2004 Jan 12-15	51	35	14

The perception that the United States is winning the war against terrorism was considerably higher at various points in the past several years.

President Bush Scores Well on Handling Terrorism

The poll also finds that 58% of Americans say they approve of the way Bush is handling the issue of terrorism, while 39% say they disapprove.

The public's approval of how Bush has handled terrorism has shown little change since August 2004, ranging from 57% to 62%. Bush's approval on terrorism was slightly lower in May and June, with monthly averages of 53% in May and 55% in June last year. In March and April, these ratings were at roughly the same level as they are now.

Do you approve or disapprove of the way George W. Bush is handling terrorism?

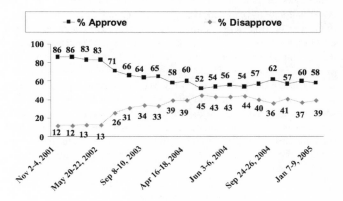

The Jan. 7-9 poll asked Americans to rate Bush's performance on 11 issues facing the nation today. The results show that Bush scores the highest on terrorism out of any of the issues tested.

George W. Bush's Approval Ratings on the Issues
Jan. 7-9, 2005

	Approve %	Disapprove %
Terrorism	58	39
Education	52	43
The economy	50	48
The environment	49	45
Taxes	49	47
Foreign affairs	47	49
The situation in Iraq	42	56
Social Security	41	52
Healthcare policy	40	54
Immigration	34	54
The federal budget deficit	32	63

Survey Methods

Results are based on telephone interviews with 1,008 national adults, aged 18 and older, conducted Jan. 7-9, 2005. For results based on the total sample of national adults, one can say with 95% confidence that the maximum margin of sampling error is ±3 percentage points.

For results based on the 480 national adults in the Form A half-sample and 528 national adults in the Form B half-sample, the maximum margins of sampling error are ±5 percentage points.

In addition to sampling error, question wording and practical difficulties in conducting surveys can introduce error or bias into the findings of public opinion polls.

January 17, 2005

UPDATE: AMERICANS' SATISFACTION WITH ASPECTS OF LIFE IN U.S.

Americans significantly less satisfied with economic issues than four years ago

by Frank Newport, Gallup Poll Editor in Chief

Americans' satisfaction levels with a number of aspects of life in America today have undergone significant changes in the four years of George W. Bush's first term. But there is no clear-cut pattern. Satisfaction with certain elements of life—such as crime-related issues, the amount paid in federal income taxes, and race relations—has improved. But a number of broad measures have deteriorated—particularly those relating to the economy. All in all, Americans are most satisfied with their overall quality of life, the position of women in society, the nation's military strength, and the opportunity for a person who works hard to get ahead. Americans are least satisfied with the availability of affordable healthcare, U.S. efforts to deal with poverty and homelessness, Social Security and Medicare, and immigration levels.

Basic Satisfaction Levels

Gallup has asked Americans every January since 2001 to rate their satisfaction levels with a large list of issues relating to life in the United States.

The table below presents the rank-ordered list of net satisfaction levels based on the January 2005 measures (obtained in Gallup's Jan. 3-5 survey; the complete data are presented at the end of this article). The "net satisfaction" levels are calculated by subtracting the total percentage who say they are dissatisfied with that element of life from the total percentage who say they are satisfied. For example, the +67 for "overall quality of life" is derived from the 83% who are satisfied minus the 16% who are dissatisfied.

State of the Nation/Quality of Life: Net Satisfaction

RANK	2005 Jan 3-5 Based on % satisfied minus % dissatisfied	% NET SATISFACTION (in pct. pts.)
1	The overall quality of life	67
2	The position of women in the nation	41
3	The nation's military strength and preparedness	35
4	The opportunity for a person to get ahead by working hard	33
5	The position of blacks and other racial minorities in the nation	22
6	Our system of government and how well it works	21
7	The nation's security from terrorism	19
8	The nation's policies to reduce or control crime	18
9	The state of race relations	16
10	The influence of organized religion	13
11	The quality of the environment in the nation	12
12 (tie)	The nation's laws or policies on guns	8
12 (tie)	The role America plays in world affairs	8
14	The size and power of the federal government	-2
15	The state of the nation's economy	-4
16	The nation's policies regarding the abortion issue	-5
17	The nation's energy policies	-6
18	The quality of medical care in the nation	-9
19	The quality of public education in the nation	-18
20	The moral and ethical climate	-19
21	The size and influence of major corporations	-21
22	The amount Americans pay in federal taxes	-22
23	The acceptance of homosexuality in the nation	-28
24	The nation's campaign finance laws	-29
25	The level of immigration into the country today	-32
26	The Social Security and Medicare systems	-34
27	The nation's efforts to deal with poverty and homelessness	-41
28	The availability of affordable healthcare	-48

There is obviously a huge variance in the public's satisfaction levels across these 28 items—ranging from the +67 net satisfaction with the overall quality of life to the –48 net satisfaction with the availability of affordable healthcare.

It's difficult to draw broad, overall conclusions from these data, other than to emphasize how widely dispersed the satisfaction levels are.

There are, however, several isolated points that are worth highlighting:

- Americans appear to have a great deal of satisfaction with their overall quality of life. (In a similar fashion, a high percentage of Americans tell us they are satisfied with the way things are going in their personal lives.)
- There are generally high net satisfaction levels with the position of both women and racial/ethnic minorities in America.
- Despite lukewarm satisfaction with the nation's overall economy, there is a much higher level of satisfaction with "the opportunity for a person in this nation to get ahead by working hard."
- Two of the items with the lowest overall net satisfaction levels are ones on President Bush's highly promoted legislative agenda for his new term: Social Security and immigration.

What Does It Mean to Be Dissatisfied?

Interpreting levels of dissatisfaction with several of these issues is not straightforward. For example, it is not immediately apparent whether the low level of satisfaction with immigration is a result of feelings that there should be more immigration, or less immigration. Similarly, the high level of dissatisfaction with the acceptance of homosexuality in the nation could be a result of Americans feeling that there should be *more* tolerance for gays and lesbians, or feelings that there should be *less* tolerance.

For that reason, the January Gallup poll asked follow-up questions to gauge Americans' attitudes about several of these issues; that is, in which direction Americans would like to see the issues changed. For example, Americans were asked if they wanted immigration levels increased or decreased, if they wanted more tolerance or less tolerance for homosexuals, and so forth.

The combination of satisfaction/dissatisfaction data and attitudinal direction data allows for a more complete picture of where Americans stand on these issues. (Again, the complete data are presented at the end of this article.)

Here are some key findings:

SUMMARY TABLES: SATISFACTION ON ISSUES

Corporate Influence (Q.18F/20)

	Total satisfied	Dissat- isfied, want more	Dissat- isfied, want less	Dissat- isfied, keep as now	No opinion
2005 Jan 3-5	38%	2	48	9	3

Americans have an overall net negative level of satisfaction with the size and influence of large corporations, but do those who are dissatisfied want more or less corporate influence? The answer to that question is straightforward. The large majority of Americans who are dissatisfied with the influence of corporations want less influence; very few want corporations to have more influence.

Influence of Organized Religion (Q.18G/21)

	Total satisfied	Dissat- isfied, want more	Dissat- isfied, want less	Dissat- isfied, keep as now	No opinion
2005 Jan 3-5	55%	9	25	8	3

This is an interesting dimension. As is well known, religion was a major factor in the presidential election this year (highly religious Americans were much more likely to vote for Bush than were those who were less religious). In fact, Bush's (and the Republican Party's) connection to evangelical Protestants and the religious right has been a factor in the political landscape throughout Bush's first term.

There is an overall net positive satisfaction level with the influence of organized religion in the country. For those who are dissatisfied, however, the reason is clear from analyzing the direction of desired religious change. Well more than half of those who are dissatisfied say they want religion to have less influence in the country, rather than to have more influence or have its influence stay the same.

Abortion Laws (Q.19A/22)

	Total satisfied	Dissat- isfied, want more strict	Dissat- isfied, want less strict	Dissat- isfied, remain same	No opinion
2005 Jan 3-5	42%	25	11	11	11

There is a slightly higher level of dissatisfaction than satisfaction with national abortion policies. Among the 47% of those who are dissatisfied with abortion, there is a rough split between those who want abortion laws to be made more strict and those who say laws should be made less strict or remain the same.

Gun Laws (Q.19I/23)

	Total satisfied	Dissat- isfied, want more strict	Dissat- isfied, want less strict	Dissat- isfied, remain same	No opinion
2005 Jan 3-5	51%	32	6	5	6

There is a slightly higher level of dissatisfaction than satisfaction. There is little question that dissatisfaction with gun laws in the country is based on a feeling that gun laws should be made more strict.

Acceptance of Homosexuality (Q.19J/24)

	Total satisfied	Dissat- isfied, want more accept- ance	Dissat- isfied, want less accept- ance	Dissat- isfied, accept- ance about right	No opinion
2005 Jan 3-5	32%	19	28	13	8

Considerably more Americans are dissatisfied with the acceptance of homosexuality in the country today than are satisfied (hence the net –28% satisfaction level). But is this dissatisfaction caused by feelings that there should be more tolerance for gays and lesbians, or by feelings that there is already too much acceptance? The data show a somewhat mixed picture. Twenty-eight percent of Americans are both dissatisfied and want less acceptance of homosexuality—a conservative position on the issue. Nineteen percent are dissatisfied and want more acceptance of homosexuality—a more liberal position. But another 13% are dissatisfied and say that acceptance of homosexuality should stay at its current levels. This is a group whose underlying feelings are difficult to interpret. These could be conservatives who want no more change toward liberalization of gay and lesbian rights (for example, legalized gay marriage), or they could be liberals who do not want gay rights further eroded, or possibly a combination of the two.

Level of Immigration (Q.19M/25)

	Total satis- fied	Dissat- isfied, want more	Dissat- isfied, want less	Dissat- isfied, remain same	No opinion
2005 Jan 3-5	30%	4	45	13	8

There is a slightly higher level of dissatisfaction than satisfaction. Dissatisfaction with immigration in the United States today clearly comes from those who want curbs on immigration. Indeed, almost half of all Americans are dissatisfied with the level of immigration and want it restricted further than it is today.

Amount Americans Pay in Federal Income Taxes (Q.19R/26)

	Total satis- fied	Dissat- isfied, want Ameri- cans to pay more	Dissat- isfied, want Ameri- cans to pay less	Dissat- isfied, want taxes to remain same	No opinion
2005 Jan 3-5	38%	5	43	12	2

This is a no-brainer. Those who are dissatisfied with the amount Americans pay in income taxes are strongly likely to say there should be further reductions in taxes. Of interest to us at Gallup is the 5% who say they are dissatisfied with the amount Americans pay in federal income taxes and want them to pay more. Twelve percent are dissatisfied and want Americans to pay approximately the same amount.

Change Over the Four Years
of Bush's First Term

It is not surprising to find that Americans' satisfaction with a number of these issues and dimensions of life have changed over the last four years, that is, between January 2001—when Bush was inaugurated for his first term—and now, when he is about to be inaugurated for his second.

We have presented the changes in the table below, based on the differences between the net satisfaction levels with these issues calculated in January 2001 and the net satisfaction levels calculated in January 2005.

Change in Net Satisfaction Between
January 2001 and January 2005

	Change (pct. pts.)
The nation's laws or policies on guns	+27
The nation's policies to reduce or control crime	+25
The amount Americans pay in federal taxes	+23
The state of race relations	+20
The nation's energy policies	+11
The position of blacks and other racial minorities in the nation	+9
The moral and ethical climate	+7
The nation's military strength and preparedness	+6
The position of women in the nation	+5
The nation's campaign finance laws	+4
The nation's policies regarding the abortion issue	-1
The quality of public education in the nation	-1
The quality of the environment in the nation	-4
The size and power of the federal government	-5
The nation's efforts to deal with poverty and homelessness	-5
The acceptance of homosexuality in the nation	-6
The quality of medical care in the nation	-8
The level of immigration into the country today	-9
The availability of affordable healthcare	-9
The overall quality of life	-12
The Social Security and Medicare systems	-15
Our system of government and how well it works	-17
The role America plays in world affairs	-19
The influence of organized religion	-19
The opportunity for a person in this nation to get ahead by working hard	-21
The size and influence of major corporations	-21
The state of the nation's economy	-45

There is a slightly higher level of dissatisfaction than satisfaction. Net satisfaction levels with five of these dimensions have increased by more than 10 points over the last four years. Interestingly, the highest levels of increased net satisfaction are in terms of perceptions about gun laws and the nation's crime reduction policies. These increased satisfaction levels may reflect the continuation of lower crime rates in most parts of the country. There is no readily apparent explanation for increased satisfaction levels with the state of race relations or the nation's energy policies.

It is less surprising to find that net satisfaction with the amount Americans pay in federal taxes has gone up—given the tax cuts passed in the first Bush term.

The following lost 10 or more points in the net difference between satisfied and dissatisfied:

	Change (pct. pts.)
The overall quality of life	-12
The Social Security and Medicare systems	-15
Our system of government and how well it works	-17
The role America plays in world affairs	-19
The influence of organized religion	-19
The opportunity for a person in this nation to get ahead by working hard	-21
The size and influence of major corporations	-21
The state of the nation's economy	-45

Three aspects of life on which net satisfaction has dropped more than 10 percentage points over the last four years are at least peripherally related to economic issues. The greatest drop of all is in terms of "the state of the nation's economy," which has fallen by 45 net percentage points between January 2001 and January 2005. The other two issues related to the economy are the opportunity for a person to get ahead by working hard, and the size and influence of major corporations. The drop in satisfaction with the overall quality of life may also reflect perceptions of a depressed economy.

The significantly decreased satisfaction with the influence of organized religion may reflect the more prominent role that religion played in analysis of last year's presidential election. The drop in satisfaction with the role America plays in world affairs most probably reflects the worldwide criticism the nation has taken as a result of the war in Iraq.

The decrease in satisfaction with Social Security/Medicare may reflect in part the recent drumbeat of rhetoric from the administration that the systems need fixing, including the president's insistence that Social Security is in a "crisis."

Survey Methods

These results are based on telephone interviews with a randomly selected national sample of 1,005 adults, aged 18 and older, conducted Jan. 3-5, 2005. For results based on this sample, one can say with 95% confidence that the maximum error attributable to sampling and other random effects is ±3 percentage points. In addition to sampling error, question wording and practical difficulties in conducting surveys can introduce error or bias into the findings of public opinion polls.

January 18, 2005

PUBLIC: EARLY TROOP WITHDRAWALS UNLIKELY

Slight majority of Americans say war was a mistake

by David W. Moore, Gallup Poll Senior Editor

With elections in Iraq less than two weeks away, a new CNN/*USA Today*/Gallup survey shows that most Americans expect the elections to take place as planned, but they are not optimistic that the results will lead to early U.S. troop withdrawals from that war-torn country. The poll also shows that Americans are divided over the broader issue of whether U.S. troops should remain in Iraq and whether it was a mistake to send them there in the first place.

The poll, conducted Jan. 14-16, finds that 62% of Americans expect the elections in Iraq will occur as scheduled, up from 51% who felt that way two months ago.

Will Elections Be Held in Iraq at End of January?

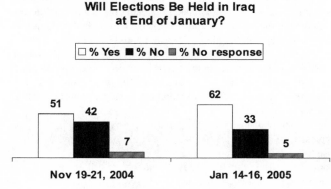

□ % Yes ■ % No ■ % No response

Recently, Secretary of State Colin Powell suggested some U.S. troops might begin withdrawing from Iraq this year, though President George W. Bush declined to confirm Powell's assertion. Instead, Bush said troops would be withdrawn as soon as possible, but that "They won't be leaving until we have completed our mission." The poll shows that only 15% of Americans believe the elections will lead to the withdrawal of U.S. troops within the next few months, while another 43% say it can happen within the next few years. Thirty-eight percent don't see a withdrawal within the foreseeable future.

These views are highly related to party affiliation.

- Eighty percent of Republicans expect troops to be withdrawn within either a few months (18%) or a few years (62%).
- By contrast, only 51% of independents and 44% of Democrats expect troop withdrawals within that time frame.

When Will Elections in Iraq Allow U.S. to Significantly Reduce Troop Strength?

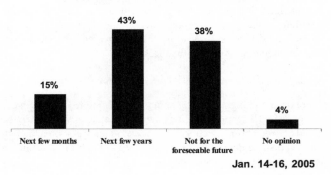

Jan. 14-16, 2005

Elections and Troop Withdrawal
by partisanship

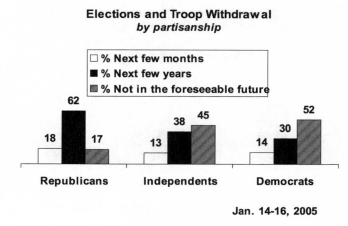

Jan. 14-16, 2005

- Also, just 17% of Republicans say the United States will be forced to leave its troops in Iraq for the foreseeable future, compared with 45% of independents and 52% of Democrats who feel that way.

Public Divided on U.S. Troops in Iraq

Currently, 52% of Americans say the original decision to go to war in Iraq was a mistake, while 47% disagree. Last year in late June through July, there was also a majority who felt the war was a mistake, but during the final months of the election campaign, support for the war improved. From August through the election, a slight majority said the war was not a mistake. Since the election, opinion has gradually become more negative.

Mistake to Send Troops to Iraq?

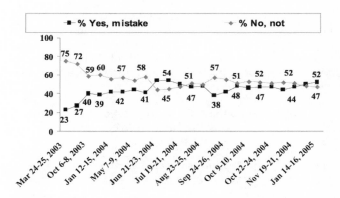

Again, opinions are highly related to party affiliation. Republicans overwhelmingly reject the notion that the war was a mistake, 83% to 16%. Large majorities of independents and Democrats, by contrast, say the war was a mistake—62% to 36% among independents, and 78% to 22% among Democrats.

Apart from whether the original decision was a mistake, half of Americans say the United States should either send more troops (24%) or keep the same number of troops as are there now (26%), while 46% want to withdraw either some or all troops.

For the past year, opinion on this issue has tended toward keeping troops in Iraq or sending more. Last May and June, opinion was almost evenly divided, but the poll in September, in the midst of the presidential campaign, showed a 17-point margin in favor of keeping troops in Iraq or sending more.

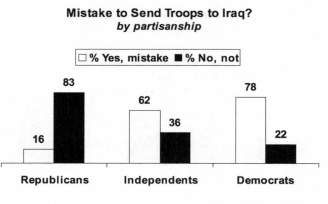

Mistake to Send Troops to Iraq?
by partisanship

□ % Yes, mistake ■ % No, not

Jan. 14-16, 2005

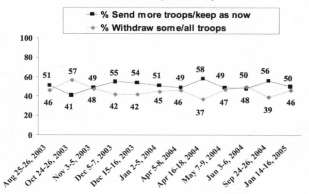

What Should the U.S. Do About the Number of U.S. Troops in Iraq?

- ■ % Send more troops/keep as now
- ◆ % Withdraw some/all troops

As with the other issues related to Iraq, Republicans are much more likely than either independents or Democrats to support keeping the troops in Iraq. By a 3-to-1 margin Republicans want to keep U.S. military forces there or send more, while Democrats want to withdraw some or all troops, by a 2-to-1 margin. Independents are about evenly divided.

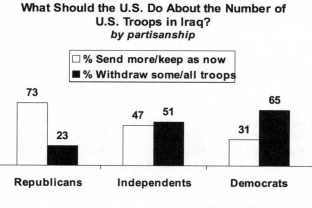

What Should the U.S. Do About the Number of U.S. Troops in Iraq?
by partisanship

□ % Send more/keep as now
■ % Withdraw some/all troops

Jan. 14-16, 2005

Survey Methods

Results are based on telephone interviews with 1,007 national adults, aged 18 and older, conducted Jan. 14-16, 2005. For results based on the total sample of national adults, one can say with 95% confidence that the maximum margin of sampling error is ±3 percentage points. In addition to sampling error, question wording and practical difficulties in conducting surveys can introduce error or bias into the findings of public opinion polls.

January 18, 2005
WILL THE INAUGURATION BOOST BUSH?

by Jeffrey M. Jones, Gallup Poll Managing Editor

Presidential inaugurations are grand scenes in American political life: A popularly elected president takes the oath of office in a public ceremony with the majestic Capitol as the backdrop. Such a prominent event could heal political divisions that could have emerged during the election, and generate a rally in support for the president. Indeed, most new presidents begin their first terms in office with a honeymoon period of high job approval ratings. But what about presidents who were re-elected? Do their second-term inaugurations bring about a boost in support?

A review of historical Gallup job approval data suggests that typically, re-elected presidents do not see their job approval ratings rise following their inaugurations. The one apparent exception to this pattern was Richard Nixon in 1973, though his spike in public support probably resulted from the end of U.S. military action in Vietnam rather than the beginning of his second term as president. Of the five most recent two-term presidents, Nixon is the only one who saw his approval rating significantly increase after taking the oath of office a second time.

President	Pre-inauguration approval rating	Dates of pre-inauguration poll	Post-inauguration approval rating	Dates of post-inauguration poll
Eisenhower	79%	Dec 14-19, 1956	73%	Jan 17-22, 1957
Johnson	71%	Jan 7-12, 1965	70%	Jan 28-Feb 2, 1965
Nixon	51%	Jan 12-15, 1973	67%	Jan 26-29, 1973
Reagan	62%	Jan 11-14, 1985	64%	Jan 25-28, 1985
Clinton	62%	Jan 10-13, 1997	60%	Jan 30-Feb 2, 1997
Bush	52%	Jan 7-9, 2005	—	—

The impact of the inauguration on approval ratings can be better understood by looking at the historical approval ratings for presidents between Election Day and Inauguration Day. The lack of a post-inauguration bounce may be attributed to the fact that some presidents already received a bounce in approval after being re-elected, and the data still show most two-term presidents started out their second terms at or near their term highs.

Dwight Eisenhower

Eisenhower had high approval ratings upon being re-elected, in excess of 70%. His approval ratings remained in the 70% range in the period between his re-election and his second inauguration, although it showed some decay after reaching 79%—the high point in his presidency—in December 1956.

Dwight Eisenhower Job Approval Ratings

November 1956-February 1957

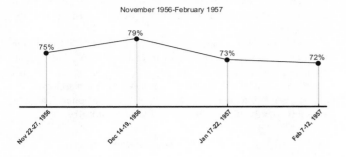

Lyndon Johnson

Like Eisenhower, Johnson had high approval ratings upon re-election, with roughly 7 in 10 Americans giving him a positive review. His approval ratings were quite stable from November 1964 until early February 1965, ranging from 69% to 71%.

Lyndon Johnson Job Approval Ratings

November 1964-February 1965

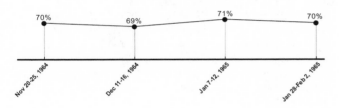

Richard Nixon

As noted, Nixon received a large boost in his approval rating coinciding with his second inauguration. However, in between the two January 1973 Gallup measurements, the United States suspended military action in North Vietnam (on Jan. 15) and signed the Paris Peace Accords that ended U.S. involvement in the Vietnam War (on Jan. 27). Nixon's approval rating had begun to slide following his re-election, from 62% in a Nov. 11-14 poll to 59% in a Dec. 8-11 poll and finally 51% in the Jan. 12-15 poll after the 1972 Christmas bombings.

Richard Nixon Job Approval Ratings

November 1972-January1973

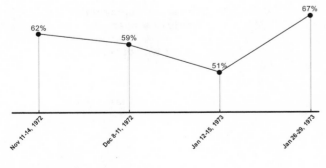

Ronald Reagan

Of the recent two-term presidents, Reagan clearly showed a rise in support following his re-election, though it was a gradual change that

began well before the inauguration. Just before winning a second term in office, 58% of Americans approved of his job as president. That climbed into the 60s in November (before dipping to 59% in December). After inauguration, his approval rating inched up to 64%, one of the highest individual measurements of the Reagan presidency (the high was 68% in May 1981 and again in May 1986).

Ronald Reagan Job Approval Ratings

October 1984-January 1985

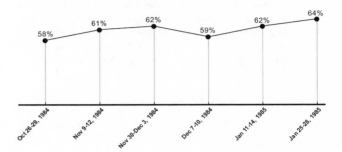

Bill Clinton

Clinton's pattern mirrors that of Reagan. Immediately after being re-elected, Clinton's approval rating jumped from 54% to 58%, where it remained until early January 1997. In a Jan. 10-13 poll, Clinton's job score rose to 62%, which at that time was the highest of his presidency, before falling back slightly to 60% after Inauguration Day.

Bill Clinton Job Approval Ratings

October 1996-February 1997

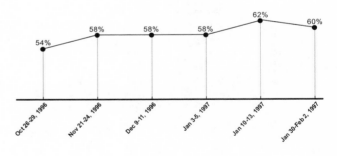

Bottom Line

Despite the pomp and circumstance of Inauguration Day, the event itself seems to have little measurable impact on a president's public support. Likely because presidents (at least recent ones) have tended to get a post-election bounce, with the ceremonies of Inauguration Day providing little additional boost, especially considering that most recent two-term presidents were enjoying some of their highest approval ratings when they began their second terms in office.

George W. Bush is starting out with a lower approval rating (52%) than some of his predecessors, and has already gotten a post-election bounce. Unlike other recent two-term presidents, Bush is actually starting his second term with an approval rating that rates among the lowest of his presidency. Based on history, one would not expect the coming inauguration ceremonies to change that.

January 19, 2005

BUSH AVERAGES 62% APPROVAL IN FIRST TERM

Starts second term at 51%

by Jeffrey M. Jones, Gallup Poll Managing Editor

Today marks the last day of George W. Bush's first term as president. He ends the term with one of the best average job approval ratings of any recent president, due in large part to several rally events in his first term. Bush's 50.1% average for his fourth year in office is the lowest of his presidency to date, and his current rating of 51% ties for the lowest that any recent president has had at the outset of his second term. Terrorism has been a major issue during Bush's presidency, and that is the issue on which he has been rated most highly. Looking back on his first term in office, most Americans believe he did not accomplish a lot of goals that a president could, but most do give him credit for improving the country's military security.

Bush Job Approval Trend

It is hard to describe the first term for Bush without talking about "rally events." These are incidents, usually involving international matters, that trigger a sudden increase in public support for government officials, particularly the president. The Sept. 11, 2001, terror attacks produced the largest rally in presidential job approval that Gallup has measured. Bush's immediate pre-9/11 approval rating of 51% increased to 86% following the attacks, eventually reaching 90%—the highest presidential job score Gallup has measured.

Bush's approval ratings gradually declined after that, remaining above 80% until March 2002, above 70% until July 2002, and above 60% until January 2003.

George W. Bush's Job Approval Ratings: First Term of Presidency

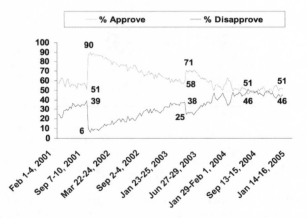

In March 2003, Bush experienced another approval rally, following the onset of U.S. military action in Iraq. His 58% mid-March job approval rating increased to 71% a week later.

The rally after the beginning of the Iraq war did not have the staying power of the post-Sept. 11 rally, though, and the former's effects had fully dissipated by July 2003. Bush's approval rating dropped to a low of 50% in September 2003, shortly after his nationally televised address in which he reported on the difficulty of the situation in Iraq, and asked Congress to support an additional $87 billion in funding for the U.S. efforts there and in Afghanistan.

On Dec. 13, 2003, the U.S. military captured former Iraqi dictator Saddam Hussein, who had fled Baghdad at the start of the mil-

itary action. That caused another bump in support for Bush, to 63%. However, by the end of January, when the Democratic presidential nomination contests dominated the news, Bush's approval hit a new low of 49%.

Bush's approval rating more or less hugged the 50% line during the political season last year, ranging from a low of 46% in May, following reports of Iraqi prisoner abuse, to 54% in September, just prior to the presidential debates. Bush had a 48% job approval rating as he was re-elected, and got a slight "victory bounce" to 53% (and subsequently to 55%) after he defeated John Kerry.

Bush Approval Averages

Overall, Bush averaged a 62.1% job approval rating during his first term—the fourth best among recent presidents, and the second best for a full term behind Eisenhower's 69.6% for 1953 to 1957.

President	Term (dates)	Term average job approval rating (%)
Lyndon Johnson	First (1963-1965)^	74.2
John Kennedy	First (1961-1963)^	70.1
Dwight Eisenhower	First (1953-1957)	69.6
George W. Bush	First (2001-2005)	62.1
George H.W. Bush	First (1989-1993)	60.9
Bill Clinton	Second (1997-2001)	60.7
Dwight Eisenhower	Second (1957-1961)	60.5
Harry Truman	First (1945-1949)^	56.9
Richard Nixon	First (1969-1973)	55.8
Ronald Reagan	Second (1985-1989)	55.3
Lyndon Johnson	Second (1965-1969)	50.3
Ronald Reagan	First (1981-1985)	50.3
Bill Clinton	First (1993-1997)	49.5
Gerald Ford	First (1974-1977)^	47.2
Jimmy Carter	First (1977-1981)	45.5
Harry Truman	Second (1949-1953)	35.4
Richard Nixon	Second (1973-1974)^	34.4

^Partial term

However, as the above review makes clear, Bush's recent numbers have been mediocre. His most recent yearly average was 50.1%, easily the worst of his presidency. While nowhere near the lofty status of his earlier yearly averages, it should be noted that presidents' job approval ratings in re-election years have rarely exceeded 60%.

George W. Bush's Job Approval Ratings: Yearly Averages

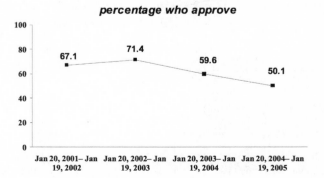

Among the 62 presidential "years" for which Gallup has data, Bush's 50.1% average for 2004-2005 ranks only 39th. His first-year average of 67.1% rates as the 11th best yearly average, his second-year average of 71.4% is the 8th best, and his third-year score of 59.6% is the 27th best.

A look at Bush's quarterly averages shows some slight upward movement in his recent support, probably due to the November "victory bounce." For the 16th quarter of the Bush presidency (from Oct. 20, 2004 to Jan. 19, 2005), an average of 52% of Americans approved of the job he was doing. That is slightly better than averages of 50% in the 15th quarter and 48% in the 14th quarter.

George W. Bush's Job Approval Ratings: Quarterly Averages

percentage who approve

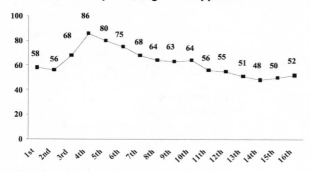

Bush starts his second term with a 51% job approval rating. That is low compared with other presidents at the beginning of their second terms. Harry Truman, Ronald Reagan, and Bill Clinton had approval ratings in excess of 60%, and Dwight Eisenhower and Lyndon Johnson were above 70%. Only Richard Nixon had a comparably low approval rating heading into his second term, and this quickly increased following the end of U.S. military action in Vietnam.

Approval Rating for Presidents Just Prior to Beginning Their Second Terms

President	Pre-inauguration approval rating	Dates of pre-inauguration poll
Truman	69%	Jan 7-12, 1949
Eisenhower	79%	Dec 14-19, 1956
Johnson	71%	Jan 7-12, 1965
Nixon	51%	Jan 12-15, 1973
Reagan	62%	Jan 11-14, 1985
Clinton	62%	Jan 10-13, 1997
Bush	51%	Jan 14-16, 2005

Bush Approval on the Issues

Bush's response to the Sept. 11 terrorist attacks won him high marks from the public. Throughout his first term, he was rated quite positively for his handling of terrorism. An average of 65% approved of Bush's handling of terrorism during his first term, and a healthy 58% still do as he begins his second term.

Bush also averaged above 50% job approval on foreign affairs, education, taxes, Iraq, and the economy in his first term, though education is the only issue other than terrorism on which his latest rat-

ing tops 50%. Bush's weaker points were healthcare and the federal budget. In fact, in the Jan. 7-9 CNN/USA Today/Gallup poll, only 32% approve of Bush's handling of the federal budget deficit.

Issue	Average approval rating	Number of measurements	Most recent	Date of most recent
Terrorism	65%	20	58%	2005 Jan 7-9
Foreign affairs	58%	46	47%	2005 Jan 7-9
Education	58%	8	52%	2005 Jan 7-9
Taxes	55%	10	49%	2005 Jan 7-9
Situation in Iraq	53%	29	42%	2005 Jan 7-9
Economy	51%	52	50%	2005 Jan 7-9
The environment	49%	5	49%	2005 Jan 7-9
Social Security	47%	4	41%	2005 Jan 7-9
Energy	46%	7	33%	2004 Jun 3-6
Healthcare policy	43%	9	40%	2005 Jan 7-9
Federal budget (deficit)	42%	7	32%	2005 Jan 7-9

Bush Accomplishments

A new CNN/USA Today/Gallup poll, conducted Jan. 14-16, asked Americans for a more in-depth assessment of Bush's first term—whether or not he accomplished each of 12 different objectives a president may have.

Next I have some questions about the Bush administration. Whether or not you support Bush, in your view, do you think the Bush administration did or did not do each of the following in its first term in office? How about—[random order]?

2005 Jan 14-16	Yes, did %	No, did not %
Improved military security for the country	62	36
Improved moral values in the United States	50	49
Cut your taxes	46	48
Kept America prosperous	46	50
Increased respect for the presidency	45	52
Improved education	42	52
Improved respect for the United States abroad	32	65
Improved the quality of the environment	31	63
Ensured the long-term strength of the Medicare system	28	63
Healed political divisions in this country	27	68
Improved the healthcare system	26	69
Ensured the long-term strength of the Social Security system	18	74

Apparently, Americans would say Bush has much to do in his second term. Improving military security for the country is the only one of 12 objectives that most Americans credit Bush with achieving in his first term. Half of Americans also say he improved moral values in the country. Less than half of the public says Bush achieved any of the other goals in his first term, with fewer than one in three Americans saying Bush "improved respect for the United States abroad," "improved the quality of the environment," "ensured the long-term strength of the Medicare system," "healed political divisions in this country," "improved the healthcare system," and "ensured the long-term strength of the Social Security system."

These results are based on telephone interviews with randomly selected national samples of approximately 1,000 adults each, aged 18 and older, conducted February 2001 to January 2005. For results based on these samples, one can say with 95% confidence that the maximum error attributable to sampling and other random effects is ±3 percentage points. In addition to sampling error, question wording and practical difficulties in conducting surveys can introduce error or bias into the findings of public opinion polls.

January 20, 2005

PRE-INAUGURATION ATTITUDES REVEAL UNMET EXPECTATIONS, HOPES FOR SECOND TERM

Most say event is a political celebration

*by Frank Newport, Gallup Poll Editor in Chief
and Joseph Carroll, Assistant Editor*

On this Inauguration Day, Americans are much less likely to say that George W. Bush accomplished a series of objectives in his first term than they were to expect he would do so in January 2001. Despite this gap, Americans' views that Bush will accomplish similar objectives in his second term, such as keeping the country prosperous and improving education, are still relatively optimistic.

Several questions included in the latest CNN/*USA Today*/Gallup poll suggest that Americans do not think Bush has a mandate to pursue an exclusively Republican agenda in the coming years; a majority wants him to work with Democrats.

In terms of the inauguration itself, the public feels that it would have been best to have toned down the celebrations because the nation is at war. Americans also perceive that the event is more of a partisan political celebration than a celebration by all Americans of democracy in action. Although few Americans believe that the inauguration ceremonies will do much to help heal the political divisions in this country, the majority also does not believe it is appropriate to protest at the ceremonies.

Expectations for Bush's Second Term

A slight majority of Americans, 51%, say Bush's experience in his first four years as president will make him a better president over the next four years, while 43% say it will not make much difference. Only 6% say his experience will make him a worse president.

When asked what kind of president Bush will be in his second term, a slight majority of respondents say he will be either outstanding (17%) or above average (35%). More than 4 in 10 say he will be below average (23%) or poor (19%). These results show an increase in extreme views of the president—at both ends of the spectrum—compared with what Gallup found in a Jan. 15-16, 2001, poll, suggesting some polarization of attitudes. At that time, only 10% said he would be outstanding, while only 12% said he would be a poor president. Now, as noted, 17% say he will be outstanding while 19% say he will be poor.

The data confirm the hypothesis that Republicans are much more likely than Democrats to say Bush's second term will be outstanding or above average.

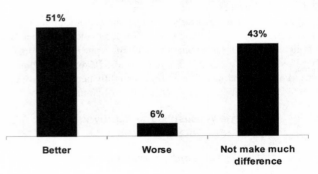

Do you think George W. Bush's experience in his first four years as president will make him a better president in his second term, a worse president, or will it not make much difference either way?

51% — Better
6% — Worse
43% — Not make much difference

Jan. 14-16, 2005

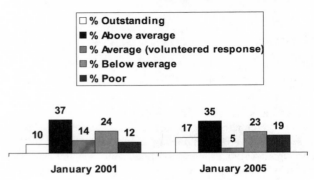

What Kind of President Will George W. Bush Be?

- □ % Outstanding
- ■ % Above average
- ■ % Average (volunteered response)
- ■ % Below average
- ■ % Poor

January 2001: 10, 37, 14, 24, 12
January 2005: 17, 35, 5, 23, 19

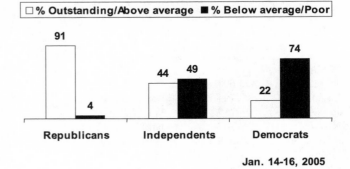

What Kind of President Will George W. Bush Be?
by partisanship

□ % Outstanding/Above average ■ % Below average/Poor

Republicans: 91, 4
Independents: 44, 49
Democrats: 22, 74

Jan. 14-16, 2005

More Specifics on Expectations for Bush's Second Term

Out of a list of 12 objectives, there is only 1 that a majority of Americans say Bush accomplished in his first term: improving military security for the country. Exactly half say he improved moral values; less than half say he accomplished any of the others.

This negative report card on the president's first term in office stands in contrast to the high expectations the public had when Bush started out on his presidential journey four years ago. At that time—in January 2001—Americans were more positive across the board about his chances of accomplishing the objectives than they are today about how well he did, in retrospect.

Expectations Versus Reality: January 2001 and January 2005

	January 2005: Did Bush accomplish these objectives during his first term? %	January 2001: Will Bush accomplish these objectives during his first term? %	Difference pct. pts.
Improve military security for the country	62	81	-19
Improve moral values in the United States	50	55	-5
Cut your taxes	46	49	-3
Keep America prosperous	46	63	-17
Increase respect for the presidency	45	61	-16
Improve education	42	66	-24
Improve respect for the United States abroad	32	58	-26
Improve the quality of the environment	31	42	-11
Ensure the long-term strength of the Medicare system	28	49	-21
Heal political divisions in this country	27	41	-14
Improve the healthcare system	26	46	-20
Ensure the long-term strength of the Social Security system	18	50	-32

The average difference between what people expected of Bush as his first term began and what they say he actually accomplished during that term is –17 percentage points.

The highest discrepancy between the public's expectations of Bush and its views of his accomplishments is in reference to Social Security, followed by improving respect for the United States abroad and improving education. In other words, these three issues appear to be the ones on which Bush most failed to meet expectations, as far as the public is concerned.

The lowest discrepancies are in terms of cutting taxes and improving moral values in this country. Almost as many Americans say Bush accomplished these objectives as thought he would prospectively in January 2001.

Still, Americans continue to be quite optimistic about Bush's prospects in his second term. More Americans believe Bush will succeed, rather than fail, in accomplishing 6 out of the 11 policy and political goals tracked. In fact, Americans are only slightly less positive today than they were four years ago about Bush's chances for success.

Across the board, there is a 13-point difference between the percentage of Americans who say Bush will be able to accomplish the list of objectives in his second term, and those who say he did accomplish them in his first term.

This "optimism gap" is highest in terms of Social Security, improving the healthcare system, improving respect for the United States abroad, improving education, and keeping America prosper-

Retrospective Views and Expectations in January 2005

	January 2005: Did Bush accomplish these objectives during his first term? %	January 2005: Will Bush accomplish these objectives during his second term? %	Difference pct. pts.
Improve military security for the country	62	73	-11
Improve moral values in the United States	50	57	-7
Keep America prosperous	46	62	-16
Increase respect for the presidency	45	54	-9
Improve education	42	58	-16
Improve respect for the United States abroad	32	50	-18
Improve the quality of the environment	31	39	-8
Ensure the long-term strength of the Medicare system	28	42	-14
Heal political divisions in this country	27	33	-6
Improve the healthcare system	26	44	-18
Ensure the long-term strength of the Social Security system	18	40	-22

ous. In other words, the public is apparently most willing to overcome its perceptions of failure on the part of the Bush administration on these issues, and to believe that, whatever the obstacles that stood in the way of accomplishing these objectives, they will be surmounted in Bush's second term.

To be sure, the perceptions that Bush will be able to accomplish these objectives have decreased, but only slightly, as noted, compared to the same perceptions measured in January 2001. More specifically, the average optimism rating is about 5.5 percentage points lower now than it was then.

A Mandate to Advance the Republican Agenda?

Americans are not inclined to believe that Bush's victory over Democratic challenger John Kerry provides him with a mandate to advance the Republican agenda. A majority of Americans, 58%, say that despite his popular and electoral vote victory, Bush should emphasize programs that both parties support. Only about one in three Americans, 36%, say Bush has a mandate.

Gallup asked Americans this question twice in November after the election. At that time, a slightly higher percentage of Americans (63% in both polls) said the president should emphasize programs supported by both parties.

As would be expected, Republicans are more likely than Democrats to say Bush has a mandate, although half of Republicans still say Bush should emphasize bipartisan programs.

Bush's current job approval ratings also underscore the argument that Bush does not have a mandate to advance the Republican agenda in his second term. Only a slight majority of Americans, 51%, approve of the way Bush is handling his job as president, while

Which comes closer to your view — because the election was so close, George W. Bush should emphasize programs that both parties support (or) because he won a majority of the votes, George W. Bush has a mandate to advance the Republican Party's agenda?

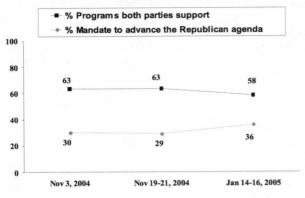

- ▪— % Programs both parties support
- ♦— % Mandate to advance the Republican agenda

Should Bush Emphasize Programs That Both Parties Support, or Does He Have a Mandate to Advance the Republican Agenda?
by partisanship

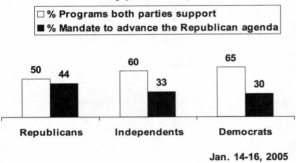

- ☐ % Programs both parties support
- ■ % Mandate to advance the Republican agenda

Jan. 14-16, 2005

Which comes closer to your view -- celebrations at this year's inauguration should be toned down because the country is at war, (or) this year's inauguration should be celebrated in the same way as other inaugurations?

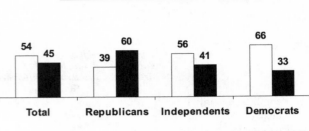

☐ % Toned down ■ % Same as others

Jan. 14-16, 2005

Do you think this year's presidential inauguration ceremonies will help to heal the political divisions in the country, or will they not do much to heal those divisions?

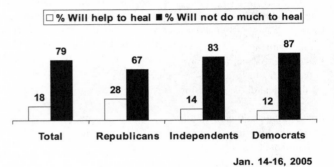

☐ % Will help to heal ■ % Will not do much to heal

Jan. 14-16, 2005

almost as many—46%—disapprove. (Those who disapprove feel more strongly about their attitudes toward Bush than do those who approve, yielding a situation in which 34% of the public now strongly disapproves of the way the president is handling his job, while only 30% strongly approve.)

Key Points About This Year's Inaugural Ceremonies

The CNN/*USA Today*/Gallup poll asked for the public's perspective on this year's inaugural ceremonies:

- A majority of Americans, 54%, say this year's inaugural celebrations should be "toned down" because the country is at war, while 45% say the inauguration should be celebrated in the same way as other inaugurations. Most Republicans say the inauguration should be celebrated in the same way as other inaugurations, while most Democrats feel this year's festivities should be toned down.
- Nearly 8 in 10 Americans (79%) say this year's ceremonies will not do much to heal the political divisions in the country. Eighteen percent say the ceremonies will help to heal them. Republicans are more inclined to say the ceremonies will help to heal the nation's political divisions than are Democrats, but a majority of both groups do not think the ceremonies will help.
- By a 69% to 29% margin, Americans say this week's inauguration is more of "a political celebration by the supporters of the

candidate who won the presidential election" than it is "a celebration by all Americans of democracy in action." Republicans are essentially divided in their views about this week's inauguration, while most Democrats say it is a celebration by the winning candidate's supporters.

- Fifty-five percent of Americans expect Bush's inauguration speech to be excellent (17%) or good (38%), while 28% say it

Do you see this week's inauguration more as — a celebration by all Americans of democracy in action, (or) a political celebration by the supporters of the candidate who won the presidential election?

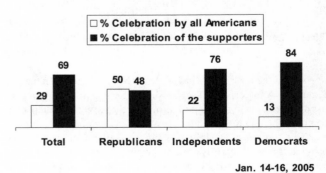

☐ % Celebration by all Americans
■ % Celebration of the supporters

Jan. 14-16, 2005

will be just OK, and 15% say it will be either poor or terrible. Republicans are much more optimistic about Bush's speech than are Democrats. Current expectations for Bush's inaugural speech are slightly lower than were expectations in January 2001, before his first inauguration.

What are your expectations for George W. Bush's inauguration speech? Do you think his speech will be — excellent, good, just OK, poor, or terrible?

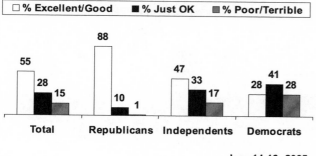

Jan. 14-16, 2005

- Six in 10 Americans (61%) say it is inappropriate for people to protest during the presidential inaugural ceremonies, while 38% say it is appropriate. Democrats are more likely than Republicans to say it is appropriate to protest. In 2001, Gallup found 71% of Americans saying it was inappropriate to protest, while 28% said it was appropriate.

Regardless of whether you think people have a right to protest during the presidential inaugural ceremonies, do you think it is appropriate or inappropriate for them to do so?

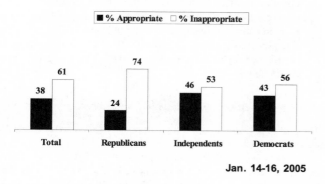

Jan. 14-16, 2005

Survey Methods

These results are based on telephone interviews with randomly selected national samples of approximately 1,000 adults each, aged 18 and older, conducted Jan. 15-16, 2001, and Jan. 14-16, 2005. For results based on these samples, one can say with 95% confidence that the maximum error attributable to sampling and other random effects is ±3 percentage points. In addition to sampling error, question wording and practical difficulties in conducting surveys can introduce error or bias into the findings of public opinion polls.

January 25, 2005
PUBLIC: BUSH HAS A CLEAR PLAN FOR TERRORISM, EDUCATION, ECONOMY
Americans rate confidence in Bush, the president's personal qualities and traits

by Joseph Carroll, Gallup Poll Assistant Editor

Most Americans believe President George W. Bush has a clear plan for preventing terrorism in the United States, for education, and for the economy, but they are not convinced the president has a clear plan for dealing with Iraq, Social Security, healthcare, or the budget deficit. Most Americans express at least some confidence in Bush's ability to handle a number of different objectives over the next four years, including working effectively with Congress to get things done and preventing scandals in his administration. When asked about Bush's personal qualities, at least half of all Americans continue to describe Bush as a strong and decisive leader, as honest and trustworthy, and as someone who inspires confidence, although at somewhat lower levels than at other points in the past several years.

Does Bush Have a Clear Plan for Handling the Issues?

The poll, conducted Jan. 14-16, asked Americans if the president has a clear plan for handling seven issues facing the nation today. A majority of Americans say Bush has a clear plan for preventing terrorism in the country (70%), for education (61%), and for the economy (54%).

Does George W. Bush Have a Clear Plan for Handling the Issues?

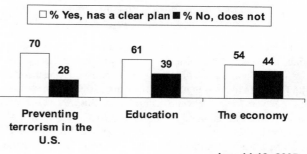

Jan. 14-16, 2005

Just about half of all Americans say Bush has a clear plan for handling the situation in Iraq (49%) and for dealing with Social Security (48%). The public is least likely to say the president has a clear plan for healthcare (43%) and the federal budget deficit (38%).

The ordering of these issues roughly follows Bush's approval ratings—Americans give Bush higher approval ratings on terrorism, education, and the economy, and lower ratings on Iraq, Social Security, and the deficit. The data indicate that more Americans believe Bush has clear plans on these issues than approve of the way he is handling them.

Republicans and Democrats differ substantially in their views of Bush's policy plans. A majority of Republicans say the president has a clear plan for all seven issues, while at least half of all Democrats believe he does not have a clear plan for these issues. Bush fares best among Democrats on the terrorism issue, with 48% saying he has a clear plan.

Use military force wisely	34	56
Secure the nation's long-term economic future	22	56

As the table below illustrates, the public's confidence in Bush to handle some of these tasks has decreased substantially when compared to what it was just before Bush took office in 2001.

Confidence in Bush's Ability to Handle Different Things in the Next Four Years
2001–2005 comparisons, percentage saying "very" or "somewhat" confident

	2001 %	2005 %	Change (pct. pts.)
Use military force wisely	78	56	-22
Prevent major scandals in his administration	77	67	-10
Fulfill the proper role of the United States in world affairs	72	62	-10
Handle an international crisis	71	64	-7
Work effectively with Congress to get things done	74	70	-4

- The poll finds a 22-point drop in Americans' confidence in Bush to use military force wisely. In mid-January 2001, 78% said they were very or somewhat confident in Bush to use force wisely. Now, only 56% are confident.
- Americans express less confidence in Bush to fulfill the proper role of the United States in world affairs, down from 72% in January 2001 to 62% in the current poll.
- There is a decline in the public's confidence in Bush to prevent major scandals in his administration, down from 77% in 2001 to 67% most recently.
- Confidence in Bush's ability to handle an international crisis declined from 71% in 2001 to 64% now. Roughly 7 in 10 Americans expressed this level of confidence in former President Bill Clinton before his inaugurations in 1993 and 1997.
- The poll finds a slight dip, from 74% in 2001 to 70% now, in confidence for Bush to work effectively with Congress to get things done.

Bush's Qualities and Characteristics

The poll asked Americans to indicate whether six different personal characteristics applied to Bush.

At least half of all Americans believe the following characteristics apply to Bush: strong and decisive leader (61%), honest and trustworthy (56%), and inspires confidence (50%). Bush has consistently received high ratings on these three characteristics, although his current ratings are below his first-term averages of 68% for being a strong and decisive leader, 66% for honest and trustworthy, and 63% for inspires confidence.

Fewer than half of all Americans say Bush "cares about the needs of people like you" (45%), is a "person you admire" (45%), and "is in touch with the problems ordinary Americans face in their daily lives" (44%).

Over the course of his first term in office, Bush scored much better, on average, than he currently does for caring about the needs of people (a 58% average across his first term) and for being an admirable person (a 52% average). Gallup asked Americans whether

---

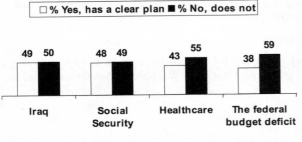

Does George W. Bush Have a Clear Plan for Handling the Issues?

□ % Yes, has a clear plan ■ % No, does not

Iraq	Social Security	Healthcare	The federal budget deficit
49 50	48 49	43 55	38 59

Jan. 14-16, 2005

Does President Bush Have a Clear Plan on the Following Issues?
by partisanship, percentage saying "yes, does have a clear plan"

Jan. 14-16, 2005	Republicans (including "leaners") %	Democrats (including "leaners") %
Preventing terrorism in the United States	89	48
Education	81	37
The economy	81	22
The situation in Iraq	75	19
Social Security	65	28
Healthcare	63	19
The federal budget deficit	54	16

Confidence in Bush to Handle Different Things Over the Next Four Years?

Most Americans express at least some confidence in the president to handle a number of different objectives over the next four years.

At the top of the list of issues in the poll is working effectively with Congress to get things done, for which 70% of Americans say they are "very" or "somewhat" confident in Bush. Next is preventing major scandals in his administration, at 67%, and handling an international crisis, at 64%. (It is important to note that Bush receives the highest "very" confident percentage on handling an international crisis, at 36%.) Fulfilling the proper role of the United States in world affairs has a slightly lower rating, at 62%. Using military force wisely and securing the nation's long-term economic future rank at the bottom of the list, with 56% of Americans saying they are confident in his ability to handle each.

Confidence in Bush's Ability to Handle Different Things in the Next Four Years

Jan. 14-16, 2005	Very confident %	Very/ somewhat confident %
Work effectively with Congress to get things done	26	70
Prevent major scandals in his administration	30	67
Handle an international crisis	36	64
Fulfill the proper role of the United States in world affairs	31	62

George W. Bush Qualities and Characteristics

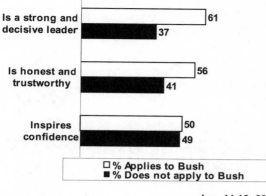

Is a strong and decisive leader: 61 / 37

Is honest and trustworthy: 56 / 41

Inspires confidence: 50 / 49

☐ % Applies to Bush
■ % Does not apply to Bush

Jan. 14-16, 2005

George W. Bush Qualities and Characteristics

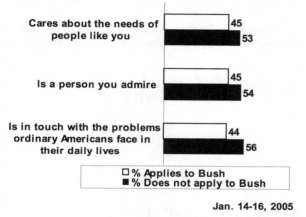

Cares about the needs of people like you: 45 / 53

Is a person you admire: 45 / 54

Is in touch with the problems ordinary Americans face in their daily lives: 44 / 56

☐ % Applies to Bush
■ % Does not apply to Bush

Jan. 14-16, 2005

Bush was in touch with the problems of ordinary Americans only once before, and the results show little change.

Survey Methods

Results are based on telephone interviews with 1,007 national adults, aged 18 and older, conducted Jan. 14-16, 2005. For results based on the total sample of national adults, one can say with 95% confidence that the maximum margin of sampling error is ±3 percentage points.

For results based on the 492 national adults in the Form A half-sample and 515 national adults in the Form B half-sample, the maximum margins of sampling error are ±5 percentage points.

In addition to sampling error, question wording and practical difficulties in conducting surveys can introduce error or bias into the findings of public opinion polls.

January 25, 2005
BUSH REPORT CARD: THE ECONOMY AND FOREIGN AFFAIRS
First-term averages compare favorably with other presidents' averages

by Jeffrey M. Jones, Gallup Poll Managing Editor

In a broad sense, the president's main policy focuses are on the economy and foreign affairs. As such, Gallup has regularly asked Americans whether they approve of the way the president is handling these areas. In George W. Bush's first term in office, an average of 51% of Americans approved of his handling of the economy and 58% approved of the way he handled foreign affairs. Both compare favorably with what other recent presidents have averaged in their terms.

Gallup began asking regularly about economic and foreign affairs approval during the Reagan presidency, so it is possible to compare Bush's averages with the last four presidents', encompassing a total of six four-year terms*.

The Economy

Generally speaking, presidents have not received rave reviews for their performance on the economy. In the last six presidential terms, only two presidents have averaged approval ratings above 50%. Even in Ronald Reagan's second term, when the economic growth was strong, only 48% of Americans on average approved of the way he was handling the economy. That followed a 45% approval rating on the economy in Reagan's first term, which was perhaps more understandable given the recession of 1982.

The elder George Bush suffered a dismal 29% economic approval rating average in his one term as president, largely resulting from a recession in 1991 and the perception throughout the 1992 presidential campaign that the economy was in bad shape. Bill Clinton averaged a 44% economic approval rating in his first term, but a robust 70% in his second term when the economy boomed.

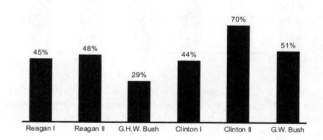

Economic Approval Ratings for Presidents, by Term

Reagan I: 45% | Reagan II: 48% | G.H.W. Bush: 29% | Clinton I: 44% | Clinton II: 70% | G.W. Bush: 51%

George W. Bush also dealt with a recession in his first term, in 2001. Though it was mild and did not last long, his first-term economic approval ratings were helped by a "halo effect" from his high overall job ratings after the Sept. 11 terrorist attacks. From October 2001 through June 2002, at least 6 in 10 Americans approved of Bush's handling of the economy, even though this coincided with the recession and with the spate of corporate scandals. During that time, Bush's overall job rating consistently stayed above 75%.

The trend on Bush's economic approval rating shows it running about 10 points to 15 points below his overall approval rating until about early 2004, when the gap narrowed slightly. The last time both were asked in the same poll (Jan. 7-9, 2005), his overall approval

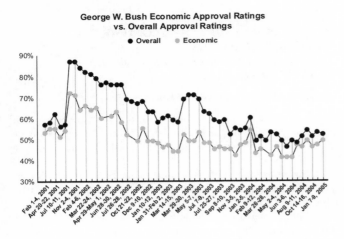

George W. Bush Economic Approval Ratings vs. Overall Approval Ratings

● Overall   ○ Economic

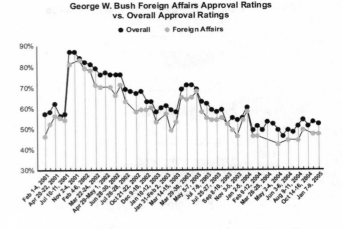

George W. Bush Foreign Affairs Approval Ratings vs. Overall Approval Ratings

● Overall   ○ Foreign Affairs

rating (52%) was three points higher than his economic approval rating (49%).

Foreign Affairs

Americans rated Bush more highly on foreign affairs than on the economy in his first term. His average foreign affairs approval rating was 58%. That is a higher average rating than Reagan or Clinton received in either of their terms—Reagan averaged a 42% foreign affairs approval rating in his first term and 46% in his second; Clinton averaged 45% in his first term and improved to 56% in his second. Of the most recent presidents, the elder George Bush owns the highest average foreign affairs approval rating, 65%, helped greatly by the U.S. victory in the 1991 Persian Gulf War.

Foreign Affairs Job Approval Ratings for Presidents, by Term

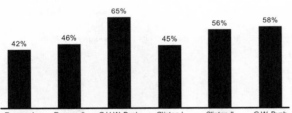

Reagan I	Reagan II	G.H.W. Bush	Clinton I	Clinton II	G.W. Bush
42%	46%	65%	45%	56%	58%

The current president Bush's foreign affairs approval ratings more closely tracked his overall job rating than did his economic rating, although his overall job score was still consistently higher than his foreign affairs rating.

It is notable that both of Bush's two primary issue ratings are lower than his overall rating. Reagan exhibited a similar pattern while in office, while Clinton and the elder George Bush's overall ratings fell between their ratings on the economy and foreign affairs.

While that could suggest that George W. Bush's overall job ratings may be higher than warranted, it is also possible that the public was primarily evaluating Bush on other issues. Obviously, the terrorism issue has been at the forefront of Bush's term in office, and is the reason for his sky-high approval ratings from late 2001-2002. Bush still maintains a positive score on his handling of the terror issue, with 58% approving in the most recent Gallup Poll that measured this.

In his second term, the situation in Iraq could play a similar role. Bush has a much lower approval rating on Iraq (42%), and the war is likely one major reason Bush's job approval ratings were mediocre last year.

If the economy continues to grow in Bush's second term, his economic approval ratings should improve. However, his foreign affairs rating will be influenced by how things evolve in Iraq—a weaker point for Bush—and how well he handles the terror threat, to date, one of his strengths.

Results are based on averages of polls conducted during a president's term, with typical sample sizes of 1,000-1,500.

January 26, 2005
PUBLIC OPINION ON PRIVATIZING SOCIAL SECURITY STILL FLUID
Most see Social Security as important issue for Congress to tackle

by Frank Newport, Gallup Poll Editor in Chief

Reforming Social Security is fast becoming one of the key focus points of both the Bush administration and the Republican Congress. In fact, Senate GOP leaders on Monday said the "Social Security Solvency and Protection Act" would be their top priority for the coming session.

Here are some major questions often asked about public opinion and Social Security, with corresponding answers:

1. Do Americans agree that Social Security is in a "crisis" that must be addressed at once?

No. In the minds of most Americans, it is not in a state of crisis, but clearly has major problems that need to be addressed in the near term.

Here's a basic Gallup question that gives respondents four choices in reference to the Social Security system:

Which of these statements do you think best describes the Social Security system—it is in a state of crisis, it has major problems, it has minor problems, or it does not have any problems?

	Crisis	Major problems	Minor problems	Does not have any problems	No opinion
2005 Jan 7-9	18%	53	24	3	2

From one perspective, more than 7 out of 10 Americans think Social Security has at least major problems. But from another perspective, only a distinct minority are willing to use the "c word" (crisis) to describe the Social Security system as it stands today.

The degree of urgency Americans feel about fixing Social Security is clarified in a separate question that asks when the federal government should make major changes to the system. The results show a divided public: about half of Americans believe that the government should act quickly to do something about Social Security, while the other half would be satisfied with longer-term (or even no) changes.

Do you think the federal government should make major changes in the Social Security system to ensure its long-term future—in the next year or two, within the next 10 years, or do you think major changes are not needed within the next 10 years?

	In the next year or two	Within the next 10 years	Changes not needed within next 10 years	No opinion
2005 Jan 7-9	49%	39	9	3

A December Gallup Poll gave Americans a list of issues and asked for their assessments of the priorities that should be assigned to each in the next year. The results showed that Social Security was tied for fifth on the list, with 40% of Americans saying it was an extremely important issue for Congress and the president to deal with, and a total of 82% saying it was either extremely or very important. Iraq, terrorism, and education were among the issues to which the public gave higher priorities.

Social Security is not a top-of-mind priority when Americans are asked to name the most important problem facing the country today. Only 5% spontaneously mention either Social Security or Medicare in response to this question, putting it far down the list that is dominated by economic issues and Iraq, healthcare quality and costs, and terrorism.

2. Just how much are Americans depending on Social Security income when they retire?

Americans who are not yet retired seemingly hold out few hopes that Social Security will be a substantial source of their retirement income, perhaps due to all of the media attention being given to the system's flaws:

When you retire, how much do you expect to rely on Social Security —[ROTATED: as your main source of income, as a minor source of income, or not at all]?

BASED ON 743 NON-RETIRED ADULTS

	Main source of income %	Minor source of income %	Not at all %	No opinion %
2005 Jan 7-9	18	57	24	1
2000 Aug 11-12	17	55	26	2
1998 Jul 13-14	17	58	23	2

Note that there have been very few changes in these views over the last seven years. Less than a fifth of non-retired Americans say they will depend on Social Security as the main source of their income, while the rest say it will be either a minor source or not a source of income at all.

Contrast this with the reality of the situation for those who are currently retired:

How much do you currently rely on Social Security—[ROTATED: as your main source of income, as a minor source of income, or not at all]?

BASED ON 265 RETIRED ADULTS

	Main source of income	Minor source of income	Not at all	No opinion
2005 Jan 7-9	44%	40	14	2

Forty-four percent of retired Americans say they depend on Social Security as their main source of income, and another 40% say it is a minor income source.

The lack of faith in Social Security as a major future income source (among non-retired workers) is partly reflected by the fact that half of non-retired Americans believe the Social Security system will not be able to pay them a benefit when they retire. Forty-five percent say it will.

Do you think the Social Security system will be able to pay you a benefit when you retire?

BASED ON 743 NON-RETIRED ADULTS

	Yes %	No %	DOESN'T APPLY (vol.) %	No opinion %
2005 Jan 7-9	45	50	1	4
2001 Mar 26-28	52	41	2	5
2000 Aug 11-12	49	42	2	7
1994 Jan	47	52	—	1
1992 Mar	49	49	—	2
1991 Mar	49	48	—	3
1991 Mar	51	42	—	7
1990 Mar	48	47	—	5
1989 Dec	49	47	—	4

There have been some fluctuations in responses to this question over the last 15 years. In the Jan. 7-9 poll, Americans aged 18 to 49 are much less likely to believe Social Security will be able to pay them a benefit when they retire than are those who are older.

3. Do Americans support the concept of privatizing a portion of Social Security?

There is no clear-cut answer to that question. Support for privatizing Social Security varies widely, depending on how the proposed plan is explained to survey respondents.

This is largely because there is not yet a specific, widely understood plan for privatizing Social Security. Americans vaguely comprehend the idea that in privatization, some portion of their potential benefits would be put in private investment accounts, but apparently, they do not understand much more than that. Hence, the devil is in the details. And it is those details (as spelled out in the wording of the various poll questions) that seem to dictate whether respondents respond positively or negatively to a particular description of privatization.

So we find support levels for Social Security privatization that soar as high as 60% in one poll and dip as low as 29% in another. Respondents are most likely to approve of the concept when the question stresses positive things like "choice" and that only 5% of one's Social Security taxes would be involved. They are much more negative when the question stresses that the money would go into the stock market, that such a plan could reduce guaranteed benefits, or that there would be a need to borrow trillions of dollars in the short term (even if the money would be paid back in the future).

The bottom line: Public opinion about the privatization concept is still pretty much up for grabs—depending on how the idea is defined.

Here's the way Gallup asked about privatizing Social Security in its early January poll:

As you may know, one idea to address concerns with the Social Security system would allow people who retire in future decades to invest some of their Social Security taxes in the stock market and bonds, but would reduce the guaranteed benefits they get when they retire. Do you think this is a good idea or a bad idea?

	Good idea	Bad idea	No opinion
2005 Jan 7-9	40%	55	5

A similar question asked by an NBC News/*Wall Street Journal* poll also found 40% support for the concept:

In general, do you think that it is a good idea or a bad idea to change the Social Security system to allow workers to invest their Social Security contributions in the stock market?

	Good idea	Bad idea	Unsure
2005 Jan 13-17	40%	50	10
Source: NBC News/*WSJ* poll			

Both of these questions specifically mention the stock market, which may scare some respondents into being less supportive of privatization.

A Pew Research Center poll found lower support levels in response to a question about privatization that heavily emphasized the idea of a guarantee under the current system:

People have different opinions about how the Social Security system might be changed for the future. When decisions about Social Security's future are being made, which do you think is MORE important: keeping Social Security as a program with a GUARANTEED monthly benefit based on a person's earnings during their working life, OR, letting younger workers DECIDE for THEMSELVES how some of their own contributions to Social Security are invested, which would cause their future benefits to be higher or lower depending on how well their investments perform?

	Guaranteed benefit	Younger workers decide, making benefit variable
2005 Jan 5-9	65%	29
Source: Pew Research Center poll		

But another question wording used in recent months has found significantly higher support levels for the concept of Social Security privatization.

The question, from a December Fox News/Opinion Dynamics poll, asks:

Do you think people should have the choice to invest privately up to 5% of their Social Security contributions, or not?

	Should have choice	Should not have choice
2004 Dec 14-15	60%	27
Source: Fox News/Opinion Dynamics poll		

4. Social Security is clearly an issue of direct relevance to older Americans, and less so in the short term to younger Americans. How do views about Social Security vary by age?

Support for privatizing Social Security varies substantially with age. The older the American, the less he or she supports the idea. In one recent Gallup Poll (using the previously mentioned question wording involving "the stock market and bonds"), support for privatization was 55% among 18- to 29-year-olds, but only 29% among those 65 and older.

Interestingly, it's not the oldest Americans (aged 65+) who ascribe the greatest urgency to doing something about Social Security, but rather those 50-64.

This is presumably because the 50- to 64-year-olds are those for whom retirement is looming large, and who see the possibility of not having Social Security as a real threat. Those 65 and older may realize that their Social Security benefits will probably be protected, regardless of what changes are made (although, as noted, this group is least likely to support the idea of allowing workers to privatize part of their Social Security investments).

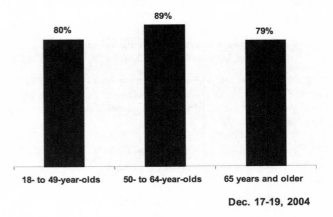

How Important Is It That the President and Congress Deal With Social Security in the Next Year?
percentage saying "extremely" or "very" important

18- to 49-year-olds	50- to 64-year-olds	65 years and older
80%	89%	79%

Dec. 17-19, 2004

5. Are Americans optimistic that something substantive will be done about Social Security in the short term?

No, they are not. Only 40% of Americans say the Bush administration will be able to "ensure the long-term strength of the Social Security system" over the next four years. That's down from the 50% who felt that way in January 2001.

Whether or not you support Bush, do you think the Bush administration will or will not be able to do each of the following in its second term in office? How about—[random order]?

Ensure the long-term strength of the Social Security system

	Yes, will	No, will not	No opinion
2005 Jan 14-16 ^	40%	57	3
2001 Jan 15-16	50%	44	6

^ Asked of a half sample

And despite Bush's discussion of and emphasis on his ideas about privatizing Social Security, just 48% of Americans believe he has a clear plan for handling Social Security, while 49% do not believe this.

It comes as little surprise, then, that when Americans are asked whether Bush did or did not accomplish a long list of objectives in his first term, Social Security is at the absolute bottom of the list. Only 18% think he ensured the long-term strength of the Social Security system.

Next I have some questions about the Bush administration. Whether or not you support Bush, in your view, do you think the Bush administration did or did not do each of the following in its first term in office? How about—?

SUMMARY TABLE: DID THE BUSH ADMINISTRATION DO THE FOLLOWING?

2005 Jan 14-16
(sorted by "yes, did")

	Yes, did %	No, did not %
Improved military security for the country	62	36
Improved moral values in the United States	50	49
Cut your taxes	46	48
Kept America prosperous	46	50
Increased respect for the presidency	45	52
Improved education	42	52
Improved respect for the United States abroad	32	65
Improved the quality of the environment	31	63
Ensured the long-term strength of the Medicare system	28	63
Healed political divisions in this country	27	68
Improved the healthcare system	26	69
Ensured the long-term strength of the Social Security system	18	74

Survey Methods

These results are based on telephone interviews with randomly selected national samples of approximately 1,000 adults each, aged 18 and older, conducted between February 2001 and January 2005. For results based on these samples, one can say with 95% confidence that the maximum error attributable to sampling and other random effects is ±3 percentage points. In addition to sampling error, question wording and practical difficulties in conducting surveys can introduce error or bias into the findings of public opinion polls.

January 27, 2005
AMERICANS FAVOR TAX CUTS, REFORM
But tax issue not a pressing concern for public

by Lydia Saad, Gallup Poll Senior Editor

With President George W. Bush sworn in for a second term and a Republican majority returning to Congress, some ambitious goals are being set for dealing with the federal tax system. One aim is making permanent the various tax cuts passed during the Bush administration's first four years in the White House, which are otherwise set to expire. The other is restructuring the federal tax code to make it fit better with the president's political and economic objectives.

Tuesday, Gallup Poll Editor in Chief Frank Newport addressed the major questions surrounding public support for the Bush administration and Republican Congress' focus on modifying Social Security. Here are answers to some questions often asked about public opinion on tax reform:

1. Do Americans agree that the U.S. tax code needs revamping?

The White House Web site puts the president's tax reform position in these terms: "President Bush believes that America's taxpayers deserve, and our future economic prosperity demands, a simpler, fairer, pro-growth system." The White House acknowledges the first step toward this goal will be the creation of a bipartisan panel to "advise the Secretary of the Treasury on options for reforming the tax code."

Americans generally agree that changes need to be made to the tax system. Fifty-nine percent believe the tax system needs to be "completely overhauled" (24%) or needs "major changes" (35%). Only 40% think the tax system needs "minor changes" or "is fine the way it is."

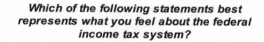

Which of the following statements best represents what you feel about the federal income tax system?

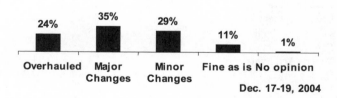

Dec. 17-19, 2004

2. Do Americans agree that tax reform should be a congressional priority?

Earlier this week, Senate Majority Leader Bill Frist (R-Tenn.) promised that tax reform will be among the first pieces of legislation introduced by Republicans in the new session. However, a recent CNN/*USA Today*/Gallup poll suggests that the public does not share that sense of urgency on taxes. When respondents were asked to rate the importance of 18 issues confronting the president and Congress in the next year, taxes ranked 13th, well behind terrorism, education, healthcare costs, and Social Security, among other issues.

Despite favoring an overhaul or major changes to the tax system, only a quarter of Americans think taxes are an "extremely important" issue for the president and Congress to deal with in the coming year.

Because another 40% describe the tax issue as "very important," the overall balance of opinion on this question is in favor of legislative

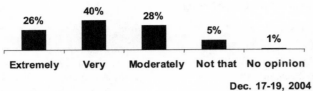

**Importance of President and Congress Dealing
with Taxes in Next Year**

26% — Extremely
40% — Very
28% — Moderately
5% — Not that
1% — No opinion

Dec. 17-19, 2004

action on taxes. Overall, 66% describe the issue as either extremely or very important while only one-third consider it moderately important or not important at all.

However, whether focusing only on those who rate the issue extremely important or including those who call it very important, the tax issue is relatively low on the list of Americans' issue priorities.

- The top-rated issue of importance to Americans is the situation in Iraq: 51% call this extremely important.
- Terrorism, education, healthcare costs, the economy, and Social Security are all cited as extremely important by at least 40% of Americans.
- Taxes ranks on par with immigration, energy policies, and the environment in perceived importance.
- Only tort reform, abortion, minority rights legislation, and gay civil unions rank lower than taxes.

9. How important is it to you that the president and Congress deal with each of the following issues in the next year?

2004 Dec 17-19 (sorted by "extremely important")	Extremely important %	Extremely/ Very important %
The situation in Iraq	51	90
Terrorism	49	87
Education	44	86
Healthcare costs	42	87
The economy	40	86
Social Security	40	82
Unemployment	35	77
The federal budget deficit	35	77
Foreign affairs	31	74
Poverty and homelessness	29	71
Energy policies	27	72
Immigration	27	65
Taxes	26	66
The environment	24	62
Limits on lawsuits	22	52
Abortion	19	41
Laws to help blacks and other racial minorities	16	47
Same-sex marriages or civil unions	16	35

3. Do Americans agree with the president's approach on taxes?

A hallmark of President Bush's first term is the tax cuts he championed in 2001. Last fall, the U.S. House and Senate voted to extend four of these for the third time: three middle-class tax cuts and one business tax cut.

It is Bush's intent to make these tax cuts permanent—a goal favored by a slim majority of Americans. A December CNN/*USA Today*/Gallup poll found 52% of Americans favoring making Bush's federal income tax cuts permanent; 40% are opposed.

However, as the trend shows, this support has waned some compared with November 2002, when 64% were in favor of extending those tax cuts.

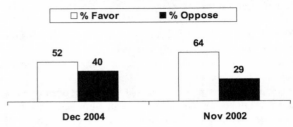

As you may know, the federal income tax cuts passed into law since George W. Bush became president are set to expire within the next several years. Would you favor or oppose making those tax cuts permanent?

□ % Favor   ■ % Oppose

Dec 2004: 52 / 40
Nov 2002: 64 / 29

One reason the latest extension received such strong bipartisan support is that it only involved tax cuts affecting the middle class (such as the $1,000-per-child income tax credit), and not the politically charged capital gains tax cut, which will not expire until 2009. Still, some Democrats in Congress attempted unsuccessfully to offset these tax cuts with increases in taxes on wealthy Americans.

Gallup trend data on tax fairness indicates that Americans are sympathetic to the "tax the rich" argument. Americans tend to believe lower-income people pay too much, and they are divided over whether middle-income people pay too much or pay their fair share. However, they widely believe that wealthy Americans and corporations pay too little.

Amount Groups Pay in Federal Taxes

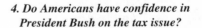

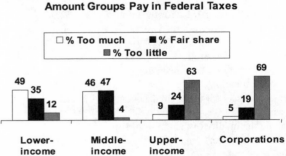

□ % Too much   ■ % Fair share   ▨ % Too little

Lower-income: 49 / 35 / 12
Middle-income: 46 / 47 / 4
Upper-income: 9 / 24 / 63
Corporations: 5 / 19 / 69

April 5-8, 2004

4. Do Americans have confidence in President Bush on the tax issue?

Americans are sharply divided in their assessments of Bush on taxes. According to Gallup's broadest measure, 49% of Americans approve of the way Bush is handling taxes, while 47% disapprove.

The public's current net approval (approval minus disapproval) on Bush's handling of taxes is the lowest tax rating he's received as president. However, Bush's approval rating on taxes tends to be linked with his overall approval rating, and thus the current level could be attributed to the fact that his overall rating is also relatively low.

When asked specifically about tax reform, 49% predict Bush will be able to improve the federal tax system in his second term; 47% say he will not. "Improving the federal tax system" ranks about halfway down a list of actions that the public feels Bush will accomplish in his second term. The list ranges from a high of 73% for improving the country's military security, to a low of 26% for reducing the federal budget deficit.

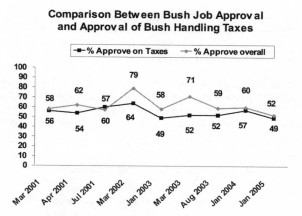

Comparison Between Bush Job Approval and Approval of Bush Handling Taxes

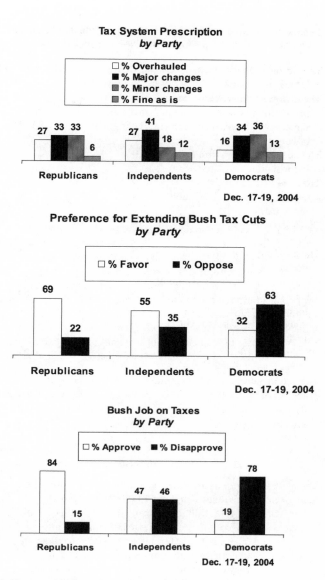

Tax System Prescription
by Party

Dec. 17-19, 2004

Preference for Extending Bush Tax Cuts
by Party

Dec. 17-19, 2004

Bush Job on Taxes
by Party

Dec. 17-19, 2004

11. Next I have some questions about the Bush administration. Whether or not you support Bush, do you think the Bush administration will or will not be able to do each of the following in its second term in office?

2005 Jan 14-16 (sorted by "yes, will")	Yes, will %	No, will not %
Improve military security for the country	73	26
Keep the country safe from terrorism	68	30
Keep America prosperous	62	35
Improve education	58	40
Improve moral values in the United States	57	41
Increase respect for the presidency	54	45
Improve respect for the United States abroad	50	48
Improve the federal tax system	49	47
Improve the healthcare system	44	53
Ensure the long-term strength of the Medicare system	42	53
Ensure the long-term strength of the Social Security system	40	57
Improve the quality of the environment	39	57
Heal political divisions in this country	33	64
Reduce the federal budget deficit	26	70

5. How politicized is the tax issue with the general public?

Republicans and independents see more need for major changes and overhaul of the federal tax system than do Democrats, however these differences are not large. Half of Democrats and 60% of Republicans believe the system needs either major changes or overhaul.

More disagreement is found over the issue of making Bush's first-term tax cuts permanent. Two-thirds of Republicans favor the proposal, whereas nearly two-thirds of Democrats oppose it. Independents side more with Republicans on this issue, as 55% favor the permanent extension of the tax cuts.

The most partisan disagreement is found in reactions to the job Bush is doing on taxes.

6. How do Americans feel about the taxes they pay?

Gallup trends indicate that a majority of Americans (62%) consider the amount they pay in taxes to be "fair." However, only 38% of Americans say they are "very" or "somewhat" satisfied with the amount Americans pay in federal taxes; 60% are "very" or "somewhat" dissatisfied. This positions taxes near the bottom of the list of policy areas Americans are satisfied with, and suggests Bush is on the right track, politically, by pushing for reform.

19. Next, we'd like to know how you feel about the state of the nation in each of the following areas. For each one, please say whether you are—very satisfied, somewhat satisfied, somewhat dissatisfied, or very dissatisfied. If you don't have enough information about a particular subject to rate it, just say so. How about—[ITEMS A-T ROTATED, THEN ITEM U READ]?

2005 Jan 3-5 (sorted by "very satisfied")	Very satisfied %	Total satisfied %	Total dissatisfied %
The nation's military strength and preparedness	28	66	31
The position of women in the nation	21	69	28
The role America plays in world affairs	17	52	44
The position of blacks and other racial minorities in the nation	15	57	35
The nation's laws or policies on guns	15	51	43
The quality of medical care in the nation	15	45	54

2005 Jan 3-5 (sorted by "very satisfied")	Very satisfied %	Total satisfied %	Total dissatisfied %
The nation's security from terrorism	14	58	39
The nation's policies regarding the abortion issue	13	42	47
The nation's policies to reduce or control crime	11	57	39
The quality of the environment in the nation	10	54	42
The state of race relations	9	53	37
The quality of public education in the nation	9	40	58
The Social Security and Medicare systems	8	31	65
The availability of affordable healthcare	7	25	73
The state of the nation's economy	6	47	51
The amount Americans pay in federal taxes	6	38	60
The acceptance of homosexuality in the nation	6	32	60
The nation's efforts to deal with poverty and homelessness	6	28	69
The nation's energy policies	5	39	45
The level of immigration into the country today	4	30	62
The nation's campaign finance laws	4	24	53

Survey Methods

The most recent results are based on telephone interviews with a randomly selected national sample of 1,007 adults, aged 18 and older, conducted Jan. 14-16, 2005. For results based on this sample, one can say with 95% confidence that the maximum error attributable to sampling and other random effects is ±3 percentage points. In addition to sampling error, question wording and practical difficulties in conducting surveys can introduce error or bias into the findings of public opinion polls.

January 28, 2005
PUBLIC: NO IMMEDIATE TROOP WITHDRAWAL AFTER IRAQI ELECTIONS
Americans skeptical about Iraq's future

by David W. Moore, Gallup Poll Senior Editor

With elections in Iraq still on course for Sunday, more Americans have come to believe the elections will actually take place. Few expect that the results will allow the United States to significantly reduce its troops immediately, but a majority of Americans say the elections will allow troop withdrawal at least within the next few years. Expectations about troop withdrawal are highly related to people's partisan orientations, with Democrats much more pessimistic than Republicans.

Earlier Gallup surveys show an American public that is highly skeptical about the future of Iraq—with most people saying peace and

internal security will not be established in the next year, and a majority saying a democratic form of government will not be established.

Election Predictions

The latest CNN/*USA Today*/Gallup survey of Americans' attitudes about the Iraqi elections, conducted Jan. 14-16, shows that 62% of Americans predict the elections in Iraq will take place, while 33% say they will not. These results are more positive than what Gallup found in November, when only 51% expected the elections would occur.

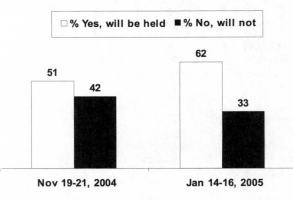

Will the Elections in Iraq Be Held?

□ % Yes, will be held ■ % No, will not

The poll also shows that most Americans are skeptical about any short-term impact the elections might have on the need for U.S. troops in Iraq. Just 15% think the elections will allow the United States to significantly reduce its troop level in that country within "the next few months," while 38% don't expect it to facilitate reductions "for the foreseeable future." Another 43% take a middle position, that the elections will allow troops to be withdrawn in "the next few years."

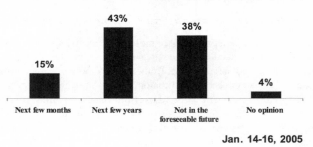

When Do You Think the United States Will Be Able to Significantly Reduce the Number of Troops in Iraq?

Jan. 14-16, 2005

Partisanship and Opinions About Iraq

The current poll shows that people's partisan orientations are highly correlated with their views about the Iraqi elections. Overall, Republicans are more likely to say the elections will occur (69%) than are independents (62%) and Democrats (54%).

Democrats and independents are also much more pessimistic than Republicans about the elections' impact on possible U.S. troop reductions. Fifty-two percent of Democrats and 45% of independents say the elections will *not* allow the United States to significantly reduce its troop strength "for the foreseeable future," while only 17% of Republicans feel that way.

Will the Elections in Iraq Be Held?
based on partisanship

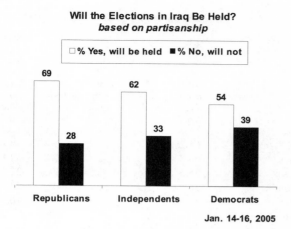

Jan. 14-16, 2005

When Do You Think the United States Will Be Able to Significantly Reduce the Number of Troops in Iraq?
based on partisanship

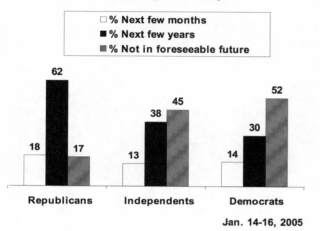

Jan. 14-16, 2005

There are few differences among the three partisan groups as to whether U.S. troops can be withdrawn in the next few months, with only 18% of Republicans, 13% of independents, and 14% of Democrats expressing that view.

The major differences are found in the percentage of each group who say troop reduction is possible within the next several years—62% of Republicans, compared with 38% of independents and 30% of Democrats.

Americans Dubious About Iraq's Future

In a poll conducted last November, Americans were skeptical about whether most Iraqis would treat the elections as legitimate. Only 42% of Americans thought the Iraqis would, while 52% thought they would not.

If the elections in Iraq are held next January, do you think most Iraqis will—or will not—accept the outcome as legitimate?

	Yes, will	No, will not	No opinion
2004 Nov 19-21	42%	52	6

In a survey earlier this month, 71% of Americans said it would be unlikely that peace and security would be established in Iraq in the next year, essentially no different from the opinion expressed last May.

23. Please tell me whether you think each of the following is very likely, somewhat likely, somewhat unlikely, or very unlikely to happen in Iraq in the next YEAR. [ITEMS ROTATED]

A. Peace and internal security will be established

	Very likely	Somewhat likely	Somewhat unlikely	Very unlikely	No opinion
2005 Jan 7-9	6%	22	23	48	1
2004 May 21-23 ^	7%	22	25	44	2

^ Asked of a half sample

B. A democratic form of government will be established

	Very likely	Somewhat likely	Somewhat unlikely	Very unlikely	No opinion
2005 Jan 7-9	15%	32	23	29	1
2004 May 21-23^	12%	30	23	32	3

^ Asked of a half sample

In the same Jan. 7-9 poll, 52% of Americans said it was unlikely that a democratic form of government would be established in Iraq in the next year, while 47% thought it was likely—but only 15% said very likely. These views are slightly more positive than those expressed last May, but they continue to indicate that most Americans are not especially confident the Iraqis will have a democratic form of government by the end of the year.

War Attitudes on the Eve of Elections

Other indications of the public's mood on the eve of the Iraqi elections show a slight majority (52%) of Americans believing it was a mistake to go to war with Iraq in the first place (Jan. 14-16 poll). The same poll found an almost evenly divided public on whether President George W. Bush has a clear plan for handling the situation in Iraq: 49% of Americans say he does; 50% say he does not. A Jan. 7-9 poll found only 42% of Americans approving of the way Bush is handling the Iraqi situation, and 56% disapproving—the highest disapproval rating on this issue since June of last year.

Survey Methods

Results are based on telephone interviews with 1,007 national adults, aged 18 and older, conducted Jan. 14-16, 2005. For results based on the total sample of national adults, one can say with 95% confidence that the maximum margin of sampling error is ±3 percentage points. In addition to sampling error, question wording and practical difficulties in conducting surveys can introduce error or bias into the findings of public opinion polls.

January 31, 2005

GALLUP REVIEW: PARTY SUPPORT IN 2004
Utah, Idaho are most Republican states;
Massachusetts most Democratic

by Jeffrey M. Jones, Gallup Poll Managing Editor

While 2004 rates as a disappointment for Democrats because of their national election losses, the party did make some gains in partisanship among Americans, compared with the prior two years. An analysis of Gallup's 2004 data shows that Massachusetts rates as the most Democratic U.S. state, while Utah and Idaho are the most Republican. A comparison of state partisanship with the 2004 election outcome shows George W. Bush tended to do better in most states than what would be expected based on the states' overall political leanings.

A review of all Gallup national polling from 2004, a total of more than 37,000 individual interviews, finds 34% of Americans identifying themselves as Republicans, 34% as Democrats, and 31% as independents. When independents are asked if they "lean" toward either party, the Democrats pick up an additional 14 percentage points of support (to a total of 48% identifiers and "leaners") while Republican support increases to 45%. The remaining 7% identify themselves as independents and profess no leaning toward either party.

Party Support
2004 Yearly Average

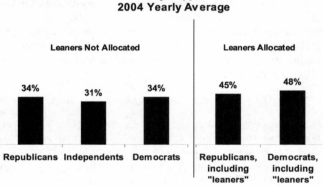

In 2003, equal percentages of Americans (45%) identified with or leaned toward each of the two major parties, the same result as in 2002. So the latest data suggest an increase in Democratic support over the past couple of years, with no change in Republican support. (The basic party identification numbers—which do not take into account independents' leanings—also show about a three-point increase in Democratic identification compared with 2003, from 31% to 34%. Republican identification increased from 32% to 34%, while independent identification dropped from 36% to 31%.)

However, despite the Democratic gains, Republicans were more likely to turn out in the 2004 elections, wiping out the three-point Democratic advantage in party support among all adults. According to Gallup's estimates, 48% of likely voters were Republicans or leaned toward the Republican Party, and 48% were Democrats or leaned toward the Democratic Party.

Party Support in the States

The large number of interviews Gallup conducted last year allows for an in-depth look at partisanship—specifically, how party support varies by state.

Party Identification by State, 2004 Gallup Polls

State	% Republican/ Lean Republican	% Independent (non-leaning)	% Democrat/ Lean Democratic	Number of interviews	Advantage (% Republican minus % Democrat)^ (pct. pts.)
Utah	65.2	5.7	29.1	374	36.1
Idaho	64.8	2.5	32.7	248	32.1
Kansas	58.5	5.6	36.0	396	22.5
Wyoming	58.5	5.2	36.2	103	22.3
Texas	55.5	5.8	38.8	2,236	16.7
South Dakota	55.4	5.7	38.9	98	16.4
Montana	53.4	8.7	37.9	221	15.5
Maine	53.2	6.3	40.5	227	12.8
Nebraska	54.0	4.8	41.2	278	12.8
Indiana	53.2	5.2	41.6	871	11.5
Virginia	52.0	7.3	40.7	964	11.2
Arizona	51.7	6.8	41.5	694	10.3
Mississippi	51.9	4.3	43.8	334	8.1
Georgia	50.4	6.6	43.0	1,026	7.4
South Carolina	51.1	4.9	44.0	535	7.2
Nevada	51.1	4.6	44.3	277	6.8
Alabama	49.9	6.9	43.2	618	6.7
North Dakota	50.3	5.4	44.3	90	6.0
Delaware	48.8	6.7	44.5	106	4.3
Oklahoma	48.9	5.0	46.1	549	2.8
North Carolina	48.3	5.1	46.6	1,108	1.6
Colorado	47.6	6.4	46.0	683	1.5
New Hampshire	46.7	6.9	46.4	200	0.2
Tennessee	46.8	6.5	46.7	816	0.1
West Virginia	48.5	2.8	48.6	283	-0.1
Florida	46.2	6.2	47.6	1,888	-1.4
Missouri	45.0	7.7	47.3	832	-2.3
Ohio	45.2	6.4	48.4	1,601	-3.1
New Mexico	46.0	4.6	49.4	262	-3.4
Pennsylvania	45.2	4.7	50.1	2,141	-4.9
Oregon	44.0	6.6	49.5	611	-5.5
Arkansas	43.7	6.0	50.2	442	-6.5
New Jersey	43.7	5.9	50.5	978	-6.8
Kentucky	43.0	5.9	51.1	676	-8.1
Louisiana	42.6	6.6	50.8	590	-8.2
Michigan	40.9	9.9	49.2	1,229	-8.3
California	42.2	6.0	51.8	3,606	-9.6
Wisconsin	40.5	8.6	50.9	719	-10.4
Minnesota	41.5	6.3	52.3	712	-10.8
Connecticut	41.4	6.1	52.5	478	-11.0
Washington	40.7	6.4	52.9	997	-12.2
Iowa	40.3	6.3	53.4	472	-13.2
Illinois	39.4	5.8	54.9	1,262	-15.5
New York	38.4	6.3	55.3	2,091	-16.9
Maryland	37.5	5.4	57.1	705	-19.5
Rhode Island	35.8	8.6	55.6	156	-19.8
Vermont	33.2	7.2	59.7	129	-26.5
Massachusetts	32.3	6.3	61.4	879	-29.1
District of Columbia	11.4	5.1	83.5	75	-72.1

^ *Positive scores indicate states with a Republican advantage; negative scores indicate those with a Democratic advantage.*

The data show that Utah and Idaho rate as the most Republican states, with roughly 65% of residents in both states identifying themselves as Republicans or saying they lean toward the Republican Party. Four other states have 55% or more of their residents on the Republican side of the ledger: Kansas (59%), Wyoming (59%), Texas (56%), and South Dakota (55%). Eleven additional states have majority Republican identification: Montana, Maine, Nebraska, Indiana, Virginia, Arizona, Mississippi, Georgia, South Carolina, Nevada, and North Dakota.

The most Democratic states are Massachusetts (61%) and Vermont (60%). The District of Columbia is also strongly Democratic, apparently more so than those states, but that is based on a limited sample of capital residents.

Seventeen states have majority Democratic identification. In addition to Massachusetts and Vermont, the states having more than 50% Democratic supporters are Rhode Island, Maryland, New York, Illinois, Iowa, Washington, Connecticut, Minnesota, Wisconsin, California, Louisiana, Kentucky, New Jersey, Arkansas, and Pennsylvania.

The most competitive states—those with nearly equal percentages of Democratic and Republican supporters—include Missouri, Florida, West Virginia, Tennessee, New Hampshire, Colorado, and North Carolina. In all those states, neither party has more than a two percentage-point advantage over the other.

State Partisanship and the 2004 Election

While for the most part, the strongly Democratic states went for Democratic presidential nominee John Kerry and the strongly Republican states went for Bush, the election outcomes in the states did not show a perfect relationship to the states' partisanship. For example, Tennessee was one of the two most evenly balanced states in terms of party support, but Bush won comfortably there. Thus, the state partisanship data displayed above can give an indication of where the candidates did better or worse than could be expected on the basis of the prevailing party leanings of the state.

The graph plots the larger states (those in which Gallup conducted 280 or more interviews in 2004, that is, states with a margin of sampling error of ±6 percentage points or less) on two dimensions: the relative advantage of one party over the other on state partisanship, and the difference between the parties' relative strengths and the outcome of the 2004 election.

2004 Election Outcome Compared With State Partisanship

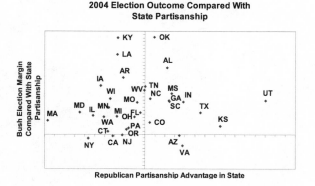

The horizontal axis shows the advantage for one party over the other in terms of each state's partisanship. States farther to the right on this axis (such as Utah) have a greater Republican advantage in party identification, while states to the left (such as Massachusetts) have a greater Democratic Party advantage.

The vertical axis shows the difference between Bush's 2004 election margin in each state and the party advantage in that state. States plotted well above the horizontal line are those where Bush did much better than might be expected, given the partisanship of those states. States plotted below the horizontal line are states in which Kerry did better (or Bush did worse) than would be expected.

For example, Oklahoma is the state farthest above the horizontal line. In 2004, Oklahomans' party affiliations showed a narrow Republican advantage of 3 points (49% to 46%), but the state voted for Bush by a 32-point margin. States close to the horizontal line had 2004 vote outcomes similar to their partisanship—for example, New York had a 17-point Democratic advantage in partisanship, and Kerry won the state's presidential election by virtually the same margin, 18 percentage points.

The graph shows that Bush did better than might be expected, given the state partisanship, in most states. In fact, only a few fall below the horizontal line, suggesting Kerry did better than would be expected (although that does not include several smaller states in which Kerry did better, including Maine, Delaware, and Nevada). The states in which Bush did considerably better were Oklahoma, Kentucky, Louisiana, Alabama, Arkansas, Iowa, Tennessee, Mississippi, and North Carolina.

The fact that Bush tended to do better in the election than what would be expected on the basis of state partisanship alone is likely attributable to several factors.

- As mentioned, Republicans typically are more likely than Democrats to turn out to vote. So everything else being equal, one would expect a Republican candidate to do better than the state's party leanings among all adults because of differences in turnout between Republican and Democratic supporters.
- Bush probably was helped by his status as an incumbent, especially given that the country was at war.
- Despite their long history of Democratic control of local offices, in recent decades Southern states have reliably supported Republican presidential candidates. Gradually, Republicans are replacing the conservative Democratic officeholders in those states, which is evident by the Republicans gaining five Southern Senate seats this past election that were previously held by Democrats. Indeed, the list of states in which Bush did far better than would be expected on partisanship alone is dominated by Southern states.

Survey Methods

These results are based on combined data from 37,330 telephone interviews in Gallup Polls conducted in 2004. For individual states, the maximum margins of sampling error vary from ±2 percentage points for California to ±11 points for North Dakota. The margin of error for Washington, D.C., is ±13 percentage points. The typical state, which would have about 750 interviews, has a margin of sampling error of ±4 percentage points. In addition to sampling error, question wording and practical difficulties in conducting surveys can introduce error or bias into the findings of public opinion polls.

February 1, 2005

HEALTHCARE, NEED FOR MORE MONEY TOP PERSONAL FINANCIAL PROBLEMS

Top economic problem for the country: unemployment/jobs

by David W. Moore, Gallup Poll Senior Editor

A recent Gallup economic poll finds healthcare costs cited as one of the most important financial problems facing American families today. But lack of money in general is the dominant concern of respondents. Overall, 14% of Americans mention healthcare costs, while 13% mention not having enough money to pay their debts, 12% say lack of money or wages in general, and 8% say the high cost of living.

Not counting healthcare costs, a combined total of 31% of Americans mention something about the high cost of living compared with the amount of money they have or earn as the most important problem for their families.

Unemployment/loss of jobs and college expenses are each mentioned by 8%.

What is the most important financial problem facing your family today? [OPEN-ENDED]

	2005 Jan 17-19 %
NET (not enough money, low wages, high cost of living)	**31**
INDIVIDUAL ITEMS	
Healthcare costs	14
Not enough money to pay debts/Too much debt	13
Lack of money/Low wages	12
Unemployment/Loss of job	8
College expenses	8
High cost of living/inflation	8
Retirement savings	6
Taxes	4
Energy costs	3
Social Security	3
Interest rates	1

There are some variations in these problems by age and income.

- Older people are much more likely to mention healthcare costs than are younger people (8% of people under 30 cite healthcare costs, compared with 18% of people 50 and older).
- Younger people are much more likely to mention a lack of money to pay debts (18% of people under 30) than are older people (5% of people 65 and older).

- The more income people have, the more likely they are to mention college expenses as the most serious problem — 2% of people earning under $20,000 a year compared with 17% who earn $100,000 a year or more. It is likely that for many lower-income people, college expenses are not a problem because they don't expect to send their children to college. Their more pressing concerns are daily expenses or because they are older (many senior citizens have relatively low incomes).
- This interpretation is partly supported by the fact that just 3% of people with a high school degree or less say college expenses are the most important problem, compared with 11% among people who have graduated from college.
- With the combined categories of not enough money to pay debts/high cost of living, the disparity between lower- and higher-income people is more evident: 28% of people earning less than $20,000 mention at least one of these two items, compared with 14% of people earning $100,000 a year or more.

When asked to look beyond their personal problems and describe what they feel is the nation's most important economic problem, more Americans (20%) identify unemployment/jobs than any other item, while the war in Iraq comes in second, mentioned by 12%, followed by Social Security at 11%, healthcare at 10%, and the budget deficit at 8%. (These results should not be confused with Gallup's monthly question on "the most important problem" in the country, as this question specifically focuses on the most important *economic* problem.)

What is the most important economic problem facing the country today? [OPEN-ENDED]

	2005 Jan 17-19 %
Unemployment/Jobs	20
Cost of the war in Iraq	12
Social Security	11
Healthcare/Health insurance costs	10
Federal budget deficit	8
Outsourcing of jobs	5
Inflation/Rising prices	3
Taxes	3
Fuel/oil prices	3
George W. Bush/His policies	3
Education reform	3
Welfare	2
Credit cards/overspending	2
Poverty/Hunger/Homelessness	2
Trade deficit	2
Foreign aid/Focus on other countries	2
Wages	2
Illegal immigrants	1
Economy (non-specific)	1
Senior care/Medicare	1
Poorly run government/politics	1
College tuition expenses	1
International relations	1
Lack of money	1
Gap between rich and poor	1
Stock market	*
Interest rates	*
Retirement	*

*Less than 0.5%

Again, there are some differences among demographic subgroups.

- Nonwhites are more likely than whites to cite unemployment/jobs as the most important problem (28% and 17%, respectively).
- The cost of the war in Iraq is cited by 7% of Republicans, but 16% of Democrats.
- Social Security is much more likely to be mentioned by whites (13%) than nonwhites (5%).
- Women are almost twice as likely to mention healthcare (13%) as are men (7%).

Survey Methods

Results are based on telephone interviews with 1,005 national adults, aged 18 and older, conducted Jan. 17-19, 2005. For results based on the total sample of national adults, one can say with 95% confidence that the maximum margin of sampling error is ±3 percentage points. In addition to sampling error, question wording and practical difficulties in conducting surveys can introduce error or bias into the findings of public opinion polls.

February 1, 2005
RELIGION REMAINS FRONT AND CENTER — BUT SHOULD IT?
More Americans preferring that religion have less influence on society

by Albert L. Winseman, Religion and Social Trends Editor

Gallup polling in the first few years of the new millennium suggests a few shifts in Americans' perceptions of the influence religion *has* and *should have* in American life.

A Bumpy Ride

After the turn of the millennium, the Sept. 11 terrorist attacks in 2001 and the high-profile Catholic Church sexual abuse scandal in 2002 seemed to move religion and values to the forefront of American thought. Prominent discussion about the role of values in society throughout the 2004 elections also kept religious topics in the headlines.

The public's perception of religion's influence reflects those headlines, making it a rather bumpy trend from 2001 to the present. In 2000 and the early part of 2001, the percentage of Americans thinking that religion's influence was increasing averaged 37%, and the percentage thinking it was decreasing averaged 57%. Just after the Sept. 11 attacks, 71% of Americans thought the influence of religion was increasing, while 24% thought it was decreasing. By the next year, however, the percentage seeing religion's influence increasing dropped to 53% in March 2002 and dropped even more later in the year, to 43%.

In 2003, the percentage of Americans who said religion's influence was on the rise averaged 39%, and the percentage who thought it was decreasing averaged 56%. However, the 2003 average for those saying influence was on the rise was brought lower because of a low (perhaps anomalous) reading of 32% in November 2003. In 2004, the proportions had evened out: An average of 48% of Americans each thought the influence of religion in American life was increasing and decreasing.

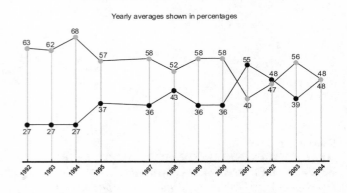

At the present time, do you think religion as a whole is increasing its influence on American life or losing its influence?

● Increasing its influence   ◉ Losing its influence

Yearly averages shown in percentages

Public Warier of Religion's Influence Now

In the last several years, there has been a gradual decline in the percentage of Americans satisfied with the degree of influence organized religion has on society — though this trend was temporarily interrupted by the Sept. 11 terror attacks. In January 2001, 64% of Americans said they were "very" or "somewhat" satisfied with the influence of organized religion on society. In January 2002, the first post-9/11 reading saw the percentage satisfied slightly higher, at 69%. A year later, the percentage who said they were satisfied dropped to 59% in 2003, about where it was in 2004. In the most recent poll, conducted Jan. 3-5, 2005, 55% of Americans now say they are satisfied with religion's influence, and 41% are dissatisfied.

How satisfied are you with the influence of organized religion?

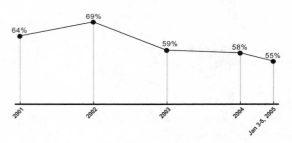

Percentage saying "very" or "somewhat" satisfied

Regardless of whether they think it is waxing or waning, Americans are more divided now as to whether they *approve* of the influence organized religion wields. Since 2001, Gallup has asked the public each January if it would like to see organized religion have more influence on society, less influence, or if its influence should remain about the same. The percentage who say religion should have less influence has slowly increased in the past five years.

In January 2001, 30% of Americans wanted to see religion have more influence, 45% were happy with its level of influence, and 22% wanted religion to have less influence on American life. The percentage desiring less influence increased to 25% in 2003 and 27% in 2004. The latest poll shows 33% of Americans saying that they would prefer that religion have less influence on U.S. society. Meanwhile, the percentage of Americans who say religion should have more influence has fallen back to 26% and the percentage who say its influence should be the same has dropped to 39%.

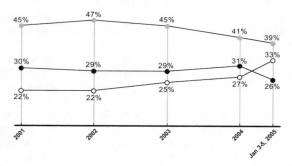

Would you like to see organized religion have more influence, or keep its influence as it is now?

● More influence   ○ Less influence   ○ Keep influence as it is now

Issue Not Going Away

The debate about how much influence religion should have in society is not going to go away anytime soon — particularly since political candidates (Republicans in particular) now recognize the role of values as a potentially effective wedge issue. Furthermore, members of the baby boomer generation are now assuming the primary positions of power in the United States, and as authors William Strauss and Neil Howe argue in their book, *The Fourth Turning,* boomer leaders tend to be passionate about issues of morality. So values, and thereby religion, may remain front and center in policy debates — even though the public may be wary of the ways they are used.

February 1, 2005
AMERICANS' EDUCATION PRIORITIES START WITH THE BASICS
Computer skills important, too

by Steve Crabtree, Contributing Editor

What do today's public school students need to learn to become successful adults in the 21st century? The hottest debates in American education today, such as standardized testing and funding for charter schools, question the fundamental goals of the nation's school system. It's a sign of the times — social and technological progress continually alters what American society needs from its education system (the current focus on ensuring each and every American child receives a rigorous academic education would have seemed strange prior to Horace Mann's novel ideas about universal education in the mid-19th century), and the current revolution in information technology is no exception.

These debates will continue to rage among education pundits. But what attributes and abilities does the *public* think American children should attain in school?

What Are We Aiming For?

In a November 2004 poll*, Gallup asked Americans in an open-ended format what they think the major goal or goals of public education should be. Responses vary, but by far the most common theme — touched on by 37% of Americans — is mastery of essential academic skills such as reading, writing, and basic math. Seventeen per-

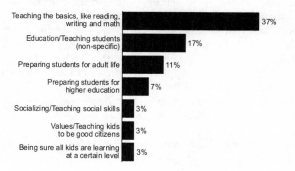

Major Goals of Public Education

We have some questions regarding public education -- that is, kindergarten through 12th grade. First, what do you believe should be the major goal or goals of public education in the U.S.? (open-ended)

Teaching the basics, like reading, writing and math	37%
Education/Teaching students (non-specific)	17%
Preparing students for adult life	11%
Preparing students for higher education	7%
Socializing/Teaching social skills	3%
Values/Teaching kids to be good citizens	3%
Being sure all kids are learning at a certain level	3%

cent said education and teaching students more generally is the major goal, 11% gave a response involving preparation for life after school, and 7% cited preparation for higher education.

Next, Gallup read respondents a list of 12 proposed goals for public education and asked them to rate the importance of each on a 1-to-5 scale. Though most of the 12 goals receive high ratings, the highest-rated items are: Students should be prepared to participate as responsible citizens, students should know how to use computers, students should be able to communicate effectively, and students should have learned how to learn. Less highly valued goals are: Students should have opportunities to discover themselves, students should accumulate facts from the social sciences, literature, and sciences, and students should develop an appreciation of the arts.

Importance of Various Education Goals

On a 1-to-5 scale, where "5" is having great importance, "4" is having much importance, "3" is of some importance, "2" is of little importance, and "1" is not at all important, please rate the importance of some proposed goals for public education (i.e., kindergarten through 12th grade). How about . . .

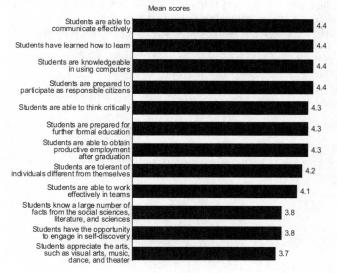

Mean scores

Students are able to communicate effectively	4.4
Students have learned how to learn	4.4
Students are knowledgeable in using computers	4.4
Students are prepared to participate as responsible citizens	4.4
Students are able to think critically	4.3
Students are prepared for further formal education	4.3
Students are able to obtain productive employment after graduation	4.3
Students are tolerant of individuals different from themselves	4.2
Students are able to work effectively in teams	4.1
Students know a large number of facts from the social sciences, literature, and sciences	3.8
Students have the opportunity to engage in self-discovery	3.8
Students appreciate the arts, such as visual arts, music, dance, and theater	3.7

Bottom Line

Mastering basic academic skills and being prepared to participate as responsible citizens are goals that address the fundamental, unchanging role of schools in society, and it's no surprise that Americans gravitate toward these goals. In contrast, that computer skills are ranked second on the list is a testament to a relatively new development: the impact of technology in all circles of American life.

More generally, the data seem to reflect the "back to basics" sentiment that holds sway in education policy today. The Bush administration's current call to increase math and reading testing in high schools has some educators concerned that other opportunities — such as those in the arts or sciences — will be closed off to students. But the general public may well support the idea that whatever the cost, the current overriding priority is seeing that all students have basic reading and math skills.

Results are based on telephone interviews with 1,019 national adults, aged 18 and older, conducted Nov. 3-29, 2004. For results based on the total sample of national adults, one can say with 95% confidence that the maximum margin of sampling error is ±3 percentage points.

February 1, 2005
WHICH HAT BEST FITS THE PRESIDENT?
Public's view of most important role has changed since 2001

by Darren K. Carlson, Government and Politics Editor

During his inauguration speech two weeks ago, President George W. Bush outlined an ambitious agenda for his second term in office. Much of it focused on foreign policy. Suffice it to say, Bush's agenda has changed significantly with the social and political landscape of the country since his first inauguration in January 2001. Accordingly, public opinion about the most important role the president plays has shifted somewhat since then, too.

A CNN/*USA Today*/Gallup Poll* conducted shortly before Bush's inauguration asked Americans what they think is the most important role the president plays. Of the five options respondents were given, "managing the federal government" tops the list, with roughly a third (34%) of Americans saying that role is most important. A quarter (24%) of Americans say "providing moral leadership" is the president's most important role, while another 20% choose "acting as the commander in chief of the military." Rounding out the list are "acting as the chief diplomat in international affairs" (12%) and "proposing legislation" (5%).

The Role of the President

Thinking about the presidency, what do you think is the most important role of the president – acting as the Commander in Chief of the military, proposing legislation, providing moral leadership, managing the federal government, or acting as the chief diplomat in international affairs?

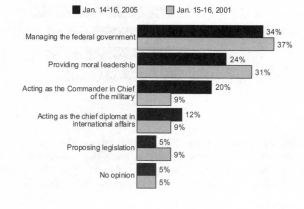

■ Jan. 14-16, 2005   ▨ Jan. 15-16, 2001

	Jan. 14-16, 2005	Jan. 15-16, 2001
Managing the federal government	34%	37%
Providing moral leadership	24%	31%
Acting as the Commander in Chief of the military	20%	9%
Acting as the chief diplomat in international affairs	12%	9%
Proposing legislation	5%	9%
No opinion	5%	5%

Changes Since 2001

Gallup asked this same question just before Bush's 2001 inauguration. Although managing the federal government was the most common response in both years, there have been some important shifts from four years ago. This year, most likely because of the country's embroilment with the war on terror and the war in Iraq, twice as many respondents choose the president's status as military commander as his most important role (20% compared with 9% in 2001).

Fewer Americans say providing moral leadership is the president's most important role — down to 24% from 31% in 2001. Bush's use of a moral platform in his first campaign may have strengthened perceptions of the importance of that role. And as memories of the Bill Clinton-Monica Lewinsky affair become more distant, the public's priorities for the president have shifted to more immediate concerns such as national security.

Politics and Priorities

Republicans and Democrats differ substantially in their views about the president's role. Republicans are much more likely to think the Commander in Chief role is most important; 30% of Republicans say so compared with 17% of independents and 14% of Democrats. Republicans are also more likely to emphasize the president's moral leadership — 28% of Republicans choose this option, compared with 22% of independents and 20% of Democrats.

On the other hand, Republicans are *less* likely than independents or Democrats to emphasize the president's role of managing the federal government. Twenty-seven percent say managing the government is Bush's most important role, compared with 37% of independents and Democrats. Republicans also discount the president's role as a diplomat. Just 4% think acting as the chief diplomat in international affairs is the president's top role, compared with 14% of independents and 18% of Democrats.

These results are based on telephone interviews with a randomly selected national sample of 1,012 adults, aged 18 and older, conducted Jan. 14-16, 2005. For results based on this sample, one can say with 95% confidence that the maximum error attributable to sampling and other random effects is ±3 percentage points. In addition to sampling error, question wording and practical difficulties in conducting surveys can introduce error or bias into the findings of public opinion polls.

February 1, 2005
PRESIDENTIAL APPROVAL VS. FAVORABILITY RATINGS
Presidents usually rated more highly on a personal level than on job performance

by Joseph Carroll, Gallup Poll Assistant Editor

How do presidents' job approval ratings match up with their favorability ratings? A review of Gallup polling* suggests that presidents are usually rated more highly on a personal level than for their job performance.

Gallup finds that the percentage of Americans who rated former President George H.W. Bush and current President George W. Bush favorably was just slightly higher than the percentage who approved of the way they handled their jobs. The same pattern holds true for Bill Clinton's first term in office, but not for his second term. Because of the Monica Lewinsky scandal that rocked Clinton's second term, his favorability ratings plummeted in his last years in office, while his job approval ratings improved and held steady.

It is important to note that while Gallup has tracked presidential approval ratings since the 1930s, it has only more recently asked Americans whether they have a favorable or unfavorable opinion of presidents and other people in the news (prior to asking the current form of the question, respondents were asked to rate basic opinions of presidents and other prominent people on a 10-point scale). This analysis is based on quarterly and yearly averages of these ratings over the past three administrations.

George H.W. Bush

In the elder Bush's final year in office (when Gallup first asked the current version of the favorability question), his favorable ratings were slightly higher than his approval ratings, by 46% to 41%, respectively.

George H.W. Bush: Approval Ratings vs. Favorable Ratings

Based on yearly average for 1992

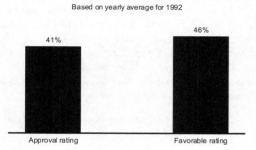

A more detailed look at the 1992 data shows that Bush's favorable ratings were higher than his approval ratings in the first three quarters of the year, differing by seven percentage points in the first quarter and by eight points in the second and third quarters. In the last quarter, Bush's approval rating (49%) and favorable rating (48%) were essentially the same.

George H.W. Bush: Approval Ratings vs. Favorable Ratings
Based on quarterly averages

	Approval ratings %	Favorable rating %	Difference (approval minus favorable)
Jan 20-Apr 19, 1992	42	49	-7
Apr 20-Jul 19, 1992	39	47	-8
Jul 20-Oct 19, 1992	35	43	-8
Oct 20, 1992-Jan 19, 1993	49	48	+1

An interesting pattern developed throughout 1992 for Bush's approval ratings and favorable ratings. Both ratings showed little change from the first to second quarter, then both dropped slightly in the third quarter, before improving in the fourth quarter. The ratings worsened in the summer and early fall during the 1992 presidential election campaign and improved in Bush's final months in office following his defeat against Clinton. Bush's approval ratings were higher in the fourth quarter than at any other time that year,

while his fourth-quarter favorable ratings rebounded to levels found in the first half of the year.

Bill Clinton

The pattern of differences between Clinton's favorability ratings and his job approval ratings changed significantly between his first term and his second term.

In his first term, Clinton's favorable ratings exceeded his job approval ratings each year. During his first year, his favorable ratings averaged 10 percentage points higher than his approval ratings. By his fourth year in office, the two measures differed only by four percentage points, thanks to a higher average job approval rating that year.

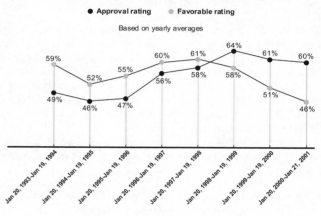

During the first full year of Clinton's second term, his favorable ratings were again higher than his approval ratings, but only by a slim three-point margin.

Then, things began to change. Over the course of his final three years in office, undoubtedly resulting from the impeachment proceedings and the revelations of his relationship with Lewinsky, Clinton's favorable ratings began a steady, gradual decline, shifting from a high of 61% in the first year of his second term to a low of 46% in his last year. His approval ratings, however, edged up slightly in 1998 and held steady in 1999 and 2000, as the economy boomed and the public rallied around the beleaguered president.

A review of Clinton's quarterly averages on these measures show that Clinton's highest favorable rating (65%) occurred during the first quarter of his entire administration, while his highest approval rating came during the height of the impeachment process, with 66% approving of Clinton's job performance during the last quarter of the second year of his second term.

Clinton's lowest quarterly favorable rating was at the end of his second term, with 45% measures both in late 1999/early 2000 and in July to October 2000. His lowest quarterly approval rating was measured relatively early in his first term, with a 41% approval in July to October 1994.

George W. Bush

The current President Bush's approval and favorability ratings were similar during his first two years in office, with his favorable rating just slightly higher than his approval rating. In his first year in office, 69% of Americans viewed the president favorably, while 67% approved of his job performance. The next year, 73% rated Bush fa-

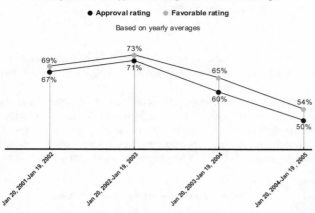

George W. Bush: Approval Ratings vs. Favorable Ratings

● Approval rating ● Favorable rating

Based on yearly averages

vorably, and 71% approved of him. Over the past two years, as both ratings have dropped significantly, the gap between his favorable and approval ratings has increased, with a five-point difference in favorable over approval in 2003 and a four-point difference last year.

Bush's highest quarterly approval rating and quarterly favorable rating occurred in last quarter of 2001, in the immediate months following the 9/11 attacks. At that time, Bush's approval rating was 86%, and his favorable rating was 85%.

Bush's lowest quarterly ratings occurred this past spring, when 48% of Americans approved of Bush and 52% had a favorable opinion of him.

George W. Bush: Approval Ratings vs. Favorable Ratings
Based on quarterly averages

	Approval ratings %	Favorable rating %	Difference (approval minus favorable)
Jan 20-Apr 19, 2001	58	66	-8
Apr 20-Jul 19, 2001	56	64	-8
Jul 20-Oct 19, 2001	68	60	8
Oct 20, 2001-Jan 19, 2002	86	85	+1
Jan 20-Apr 19, 2002	80	N/A	N/A
Apr 20-Jul 19, 2002	75	80	-5
Jul 20-Oct 19, 2002	68	71	-3
Oct 20, 2002-Jan 19, 2003	64	68	-4
Jan 20-Apr 19, 2003	63	68	-5
Apr 20-Jul 19, 2003	64	66	-2
Jul 20-Oct 19, 2003	56	60	-4
Oct 20, 2003-Jan 19, 2004	55	65	-10
Jan 20-Apr 19, 2004	51	55	-4
Apr 20-Jul 19, 2004	48	52	-4
Jul 20-Oct 19, 2004	50	54	-4
Oct 20, 2004-Jan 19, 2005	52	55	-3

These results are based on telephone interviews with randomly selected national samples of approximately 1,000 adults each, aged 18 and older, conducted January 1992 to January 2005. For results based on these samples, one can say with 95% confidence that the maximum error attributable to sampling and other random effects is ±3 percentage points. In addition to sampling error, question wording and practical difficulties in conducting surveys can introduce error or bias into the findings of public opinion polls.

February 2, 2005

STATE OF THE UNION SPEECHES RARELY AFFECT PRESIDENTIAL SUPPORT
Bush ratings not improved by prior speeches

by Jeffrey M. Jones, Gallup Poll Managing Editor

The U.S. Constitution requires that the president update the Congress periodically on the state of the union. This has evolved into an annual televised address and is one of the most anticipated and widely covered news events each year. Observers have long viewed the State of the Union address as an important opportunity for the president to speak directly to the public, and to help increase popular support for his legislative agenda. At times, the State of the Union has taken on added significance, such as George H. W. Bush's attempts to address Americans' concerns about the economy in 1992, and Bill Clinton's address just days after allegations of an affair with a White House intern became public.

A special Gallup analysis of polling data going back to the Carter administration shows that, amid all the pageantry and fanfare associated with the occasion, State of the Union addresses generally do little to help boost a president's ratings. That may be because of the fact that a president's partisan supporters are much more likely to watch the event than are supporters of the opposition party.

The following table shows the pre-State of the Union approval ratings for each president in the Gallup Poll prior to the address, and his approval ratings in the first poll conducted after the address (this does not include addresses given by presidents in their first year in office; though many typically give such speeches, it is usually not under the rubric of a State of the Union address).

Change in President's Job Approval Ratings, Pre- and Post-State of the Union

		Pre-speech approval rating %	Poll dates	Date of speech	Post-speech approval rating %	Poll dates	Change pct. pts.
2004	Bush	53	Jan 12-14	Jan 20	49	Jan 29-Feb 1	-4
2003	Bush	60	Jan 23-25	Jan 28	61	Jan 31-Feb 2	1
2002	Bush	84	Jan 25-27	Jan 29	82	Feb 4-6	-2
2000	Clinton	64	Jan 25-26	Jan 27	63	Feb 4-6	-1
1999	Clinton	69	Jan 15-17	Jan 19	69	Jan 22-24	0
1998	Clinton	59	Jan 25-26	Jan 27	69	Jan 30-Feb 1	10
1997	Clinton	60	Jan 30-Feb 2	Feb 4	57	Feb 24-26	-3
1996	Clinton	46	Jan 12-15	Jan 25	52	Jan 26-29	6
1995	Clinton	47	Jan 16-18	Jan 24	49	Feb 3-5	2
1994	Clinton	54	Jan 15-17	Jan 25	58	Jan 28-30	4
1992	Bush	46	Jan 16-19	Jan 28	47	Feb 6-9	1
1991	Bush	83	Jan 23-26	Jan 29	82	Jan 30-Feb 2	-1
1990	Bush	80	Jan 4-7	Jan 31	73	Feb 8-11	-7
1988	Reagan	49	Jan 22-25	Jan 25	50	Mar 4-6	1
1987	Reagan	48	Jan 16-19	Jan 27	43	Mar 6-9	-5
1986	Reagan	64	Jan 10-13	Feb 4	63	Mar 4-10	-1
1985	Reagan	64	Jan 25-28	Feb 6	60	Feb 15-18	-4
1984	Reagan	52	Jan 13-16	Jan 25	55	Jan 27-30	3
1983	Reagan	37	Jan 21-24	Jan 25	35	Jan 28-31	-2
1982	Reagan	47	Jan 22-25	Jan 26	47	Feb 5-8	0
1980	Carter	56	Jan 5-8	Jan 21	58	Jan 25-28	2
1979	Carter	43	Jan 19-22	Jan 25	42	Feb 2-5	-1
1978	Carter	55	Jan 6-9	Jan 19	52	Jan 20-23	-3

In the 23 cases analyzed here, there are 12 instances in which a president's post-State of the Union approval rating was lower than his rating before the speech, 9 when it was higher, and 2 in which there was no change. Only about a third of these cases (7 out of 23) show differences large enough to suggest real changes in a president's job approval rating, rather than just random variation due to poll sampling.

George W. Bush's approval ratings barely budged following his first two State of the Union addresses. In both instances, his approval ratings were rather high to begin with, but even some dramatic pronouncements, such as terming Iraq, Iran, and North Korea as an "axis of evil," did not cause much change in Bush's job ratings.

It is hard to get a good measurement on the impact of Bush's most recent State of the Union address. Bush gave his 2004 State of the Union speech on Jan. 20, the day after the Iowa caucuses and a week before the New Hampshire primary, both of which helped determine his Democratic Party challenger in the presidential election. Additionally, Gallup's post-State of the Union reading of Jan. 29-Feb. 1 was completed nearly two weeks after the address. That poll also reflected the public's high amount of interest in the Democratic nomination contest, and consequently represented one of the lower points in Bush's support for the year (at 49%). So while Bush's post-State of the Union reading last year was significantly lower than his pre-State of the Union reading, the drop was probably not due to the speech as much as to other events occurring at the same time.

Of the most recent presidents, Clinton seemed most adept at using a State of the Union to help boost his public standing. His approval rating showed significant improvement after three of his seven speeches, including a dramatic increase of 10 percentage points in 1998. That speech was delivered just days after allegations about an affair with White House intern Monica Lewinsky became publicized. Clinton made no mention of that controversy in the 1998 speech, but rather touted the first balanced federal budget in nearly three decades and proposed a variety of new and popular programs in the areas of education, welfare, and Social Security. The 69% approval rating Clinton received following that speech was the second highest of his term, bettered only by a 73% rating immediately after the House of Representatives voted to impeach him (as a result of the Lewinsky scandal) in December 1998.

Clinton also used his 1996 speech, in which he announced an end to the "era of big government," as a springboard to a successful re-election bid. Following that speech, his job approval rating edged past the 50% mark, where it stayed for the remainder of his presidency. Clinton also showed a slight improvement in his approval ratings following his 1994 State of the Union.

The elder Bush was far less successful than Clinton in getting a boost from his State of the Union speeches. However, that probably resulted from the fact that Bush's pre-State of the Union approval ratings in 1990 (80%) and 1991 (83%) were already very high to begin with; both were among the highest Gallup has ever recorded for a president. The 1990 address was given shortly after the United States invaded Panama and successfully captured Manuel Noriega. Also, several Eastern European countries withdrew from the Soviet bloc around that time. The 1991 address was given during early stages of the Persian Gulf War with Iraq.

Bush's 1992 address, though, was seen as an important opportunity for him to address Americans' concerns about a poor economy, and thus to improve his sagging popularity as he began his re-election bid. Prior to the speech, Bush's job approval rating was 46%, and presidents typically need an approval rating above 50% to ensure re-election. However, Bush's State of the Union speech did not do much to change the public's view of him, as his post-State of the Union approval rating was 47%. Bush's approval rating subsequently continued the downward trend that had begun after the Persian Gulf War — falling below 40% by June 1992 — and staying in the 30s until after Clinton defeated him.

Like the elder Bush, Jimmy Carter and Ronald Reagan also saw little improvement in their approval ratings following their State of the Union speeches in the years in which they ran for second terms. Carter's 1980 pre-speech rating of 56% was already somewhat high following rallies in support because of the Iranian hostage crisis and the Soviet invasion of Afghanistan. Reagan's 52% approval rating showed a slight increase to 55% following his 1984 State of the Union address. Surprisingly, his 1984 approval ratings reached only into the high 50s despite his winning 98% of the electoral votes in the election, the most since the awarding of electoral votes was tied to the popular vote in 1828.

Reagan's five-point drop in 1987 probably does not reflect much upon his State of the Union address that year, as the first poll following his address came more than a month after his speech. However, a four-point drop in 1985 may suggest a slight loss of public support following that State of the Union speech.

Partisan audiences

Gallup has conducted reaction polls immediately following several recent State of the Union addresses with those who say they watched the speech. Most of these show a viewing audience heavily tilted toward the president's natural supporters. For example, the audience for last year's speech consisted of 46% Republicans, 28% independents, and only 26% Democrats, compared with a nearly even division in party support among the general public.

The following table shows the partisan composition of Gallup's State of the Union-night poll samples, which give a good indication of the political makeup of the viewing audience. The 1995 address, given shortly after Republicans took control of Congress, is the only recent speech in which the viewing audience roughly approximated national party support. In most other speeches, those from the president's party comprised a much greater percentage of the viewing audience.

Partisan Composition of State of the Union Viewing Audiences, Gallup Polls

Poll date	President (party)	% Speech watchers who were Republican	% Speech watchers who were Democratic	% Speech watchers who were independent
Jan 20, 2004	Bush (R)	46	26	28
Jan 28, 2003	Bush (R)	40	28	31
Jan 29, 2002	Bush (R)	50	25	25
Jan 19, 1999	Clinton (D)	28	40	32
Jan 27, 1998	Clinton (D)	30	37	31
Jan 24, 1995	Clinton (D)	33	33	34
Jan 25, 1994	Clinton (D)	26	41	32

Conclusion

George W. Bush's most recent job approval rating is 51%. It is quite possible this will increase when Gallup next measures it, but that might be due as much or more to a rally in presidential support following the elections in Iraq, as opposed to the State of the Union address. In any case, it will be difficult to measure whether this year's State of the Union address increases Bush's support, just as it has been in other years when significant world events coincided with the yearly address.

Bush has an ambitious second-term agenda, and public support will be a key in getting his proposals passed. However, because those who tune in to hear the speech will skew Republican, it is likely that a disproportionate amount of the viewing audience will already support the Bush agenda.

Survey Methods

Results for pre- and post-State of the Union approval ratings are based on telephone interviews with randomly selected national samples of approximately 1,000 adults, aged 18 and older, conducted between 1990 and 2004, and in-person interviews with approximately 1,500 adults, aged 18 and older, conducted between 1978 and 1988. For results based on these samples, one can say with 95% confidence that the maximum error attributable to sampling and other random effects is ±3 percentage points. In addition to sampling error, question wording and practical difficulties in conducting surveys can introduce error or bias into the findings of public opinion polls.

Results for the party breakdown of the State of the Union audiences are based on telephone interviews with pre-recruited respondents who indicated they planned to watch the State of the Union, and confirmed that they had done so when Gallup called immediately following the speech. The polls represent between 380 and 500 speech watchers, and have a maximum margin of sampling error of ±5 percentage points.

February 3, 2005
SPEECH WATCHERS GIVE BUSH HIGH MARKS
Viewers more positive than last year

by David W. Moore, Gallup Poll Senior Editor

An instant reaction poll of speech watchers last night, a majority of whom were Republicans, found President George W. Bush receiving high marks for his State of the Union address — higher than last year and the year before, though not as high as the ratings he received in his first two years. As a group, speech watchers' positive views of the president increased even more after the address, both generally and about specific policies he proposed.

The major findings of the CNN/*USA Today*/Gallup instant reaction poll are as follows:

- Overall, 86% of speech watchers said their reaction to Bush's address was positive, including 60% who said "very" positive.
  - Last year, 76% said positive, with 45% very positive.
  - Three years ago, shortly after 9/11, 94% were positive and 74% very positive.
- Seventy-seven percent of speech watchers said Bush's proposed policies in general will move the country in the right direction, while 20% said the wrong direction. Last year, the percentage saying the right direction was 70%, while 26% said the wrong direction.
  - In Bush's first two State of the Union addresses, one before and the other after 9/11, speech watchers were more positive

— 91% saying the right direction in 2002, and 84% in 2001.
  - After former President Bill Clinton's two speeches when this sentiment was measured (1994 and 1995), 84% and 83% of speech watchers, respectively, said the president's policies would move the country in the right direction.
- In the pre-speech interview, 67% of people who intended to watch the speech said Bush's policies would move the country in the right direction, compared with 77% who said that after the speech. That 10-point increase is the same as last year's increase, though last year both the figures before and after the speech were lower — 60% and 70%, respectively.
- When asked to evaluate whether Bush's policies in four specific areas would move the country in the right or wrong direction, speech watchers responded positively:
  - On the economy — 71% said the right direction, while 26% said the wrong direction, showing a modest improvement over the 64% to 32% margin measured before the speech.
  - On healthcare — a 70% to 23% ratio of right direction to wrong direction after the speech, which was a large increase from the 55% to 35% ratio before the speech.
  - On Social Security — also a big change, from 51% saying right direction and 38% saying wrong direction before the speech, to a 66% to 29% margin afterward.
  - On the situation in Iraq — a two-to-one margin (66% to 31%) saying right over wrong direction before the speech, to a four-to-one margin afterward (78% to 20%).
- Bush spent a sizeable amount of time during the address outlining the need for changing the Social Security system, and speech watchers as a group reacted positively.
  - Before the speech, 11% cited Social Security as the most important issue for the government to deal with in the next year, but after the speech, 19% expressed that view.
  - After the speech, 74% of speech watchers said Bush made a convincing case for the government to take action on Social Security in the next year or two, while only 24% disagreed.
- Bush's address also appeared to make speech watchers more positive about the economy and Iraq.
  - Prior to the speech, 71% of speech watchers rated the nation's economy today as very good or good, compared with 76% afterward.
  - Similarly, before the speech, 60% said the situation in Iraq was very good or good, while 70% expressed that view afterward.

Republicans Outnumbered Democrats by Two-to-One Margin Among Speech Watchers

Typically, presidential speech watchers disproportionately identify with the party of the president. Last night, the imbalance in favor of the president's party was by more than a two-to-one ratio, with 52% of viewers Republicans and 25% Democrats. Another 22% identified as independents.

That difference of 27 percentage points between Republicans and Democrats compares with 20 points last year, 12 points in 2003, and 25 points in 2002, shortly after 9/11. Among those who watched Clinton's speeches, Democrats outnumbered Republicans by margins that ranged from 7 to 15 percentage points. When former President George H.W. Bush gave his last State of the Union address in 1992, Republicans outnumbered Democrats in the post-speech poll by just six percentage points, 37% to 31%.

Survey Methods

Results are based on telephone interviews with 485 speech watchers, aged 18 and older, conducted Feb. 2, 2005. For results based on the total sample of speech watchers, one can say with 95% confidence that the margin of sampling error is ±5 percentage points.

Survey respondents were first interviewed as part of random national adult samples by Gallup Jan. 31-Feb. 1, 2005, at which time they indicated they planned to watch the President's 2005 State of the Union address and were willing to be re-interviewed by Gallup after the speech. Respondents' pre- and post-speech answers are shown for those questions that were asked on both surveys.

The sample consists of 52% of respondents who identify themselves as Republicans, 25% who identify themselves as Democrats, and 22% who identify themselves as independents.

Polls conducted entirely in one day, such as this one, are subject to additional error or bias not found in polls conducted over several days.

February 4, 2005
SIX IN 10 AMERICANS ARE PRO FOOTBALL FANS
Rates as sport with greatest number of fans

by Jeffrey M. Jones, Gallup Poll Managing Editor

This Sunday, the New England Patriots and Philadelphia Eagles will meet in Super Bowl XXXIX to determine the champion of the National Football League.

More Americans say they are fans of professional football than of any other sport, according to recent Gallup polling. Additionally, pro football rates as the sport with the greatest number of fans among most major demographic groups. One notable exception is women — while a majority of women claim to be professional football fans, more women are fans of figure skating than are fans of any other sport.

Gallup's annual Lifestyle Poll, conducted Dec. 5-8, 2004, asked Americans if they considered themselves fans of 11 different sports. Sixty-four percent say they are fans of professional football (including those who say they are "somewhat of a fan"), giving it a comfortable margin over all other sports in the list. A majority of Americans also identify themselves as fans of college football (54%) and professional baseball (52%). Roughly 4 in 10 Americans are fans of figure skating, college basketball, and professional basketball. Of the 11 sports tested, professional wrestling claims the fewest fans, just 1 in 10 Americans.

Fans of Major Sports, All Americans

Sport	Percentage of Americans Who Are Fans %
Professional football	64
College football	54
Professional baseball	52
Figure skating	41
College basketball	41
Professional basketball	38
Auto racing	30
Professional golf	30
Professional tennis	24
Professional ice hockey	23
Professional wrestling	10

Interestingly, most sports have shown a decline in fan base since the entire list of sports was last asked in 2001. The two exceptions are professional and college football, which have seen their fan bases hold steady. Auto racing and figure skating have each had a nine-point drop in the percentage of Americans calling themselves fans, while hockey has seen an eight-point drop.

Change in Sports Fans, 2004 to 2001

Sport	2001 %	2004 %	Change, pct. pts.
Professional football	63	64	+1
College football	53	54	+1
Professional baseball	56	52	-4
Figure skating	50	41	-9
College basketball	47	41	-6
Professional basketball	44	38	-6
Auto racing	39	30	-9
Professional golf	36	30	-6
Professional tennis	28	24	-4
Professional ice hockey	31	23	-8
Professional wrestling	15	10	-5

DEMOGRAPHIC DIFFERENCES

Gender

Not surprisingly, men are much more likely to say they are fans of individual sports than are women. In fact, there are only two sports for which men are not significantly more likely than women to say they are fans — figure skating and tennis.

Sports Fans, by Gender

Men	Fans %	Women	Fans %
Professional football	77	Figure skating	60
College football	70	Professional football	51
Professional baseball	58	Professional baseball	46
College basketball	49	College football	39
Professional basketball	42	Professional basketball	36
Professional golf	40	College basketball	32
Auto racing	39	Professional tennis	25
Professional ice hockey	28	Auto racing	22
Professional tennis	24	Professional golf	20
Figure skating	21	Professional ice hockey	18
Professional wrestling	14	Professional wrestling	7

The myth of the "football widow" — the wife who is deserted by her husband on Sunday afternoons as he heeds the siren call of NFL games — may have some merit. Nearly 8 in 10 men identify themselves as pro football fans and 7 in 10 men are college football fans — clearly showing the appeal of football to men. A majority of men also identify themselves as baseball fans.

However, professional football also appeals to women, as a slim majority of women are fans of that sport. But figure skating ranks as the top sport for women, with 60% claiming they are fans. That is in stark contrast to just 21% of men who are figure skating fans, rank-

Sports Fans, by Age Group

18- to 29-year-olds		30- to 49-year-olds		50- to 64-year-olds		65 years and older	
Sport	*%*	*Sport*	*%*	*Sport*	*%*	*Sport*	*%*
Pro football	65	Pro football	65	Pro football	63	Pro football	60
Coll. football	56	Coll. football	55	Pro baseball	58	Figure skating	59
Pro basketball	53	Pro baseball	51	Coll. football	52	Pro baseball	56
Coll. basketball	45	Coll. basketball	39	Figure skating	43	Coll. football	54
Pro baseball	41	Auto racing	37	Coll. basketball	39	Coll. basketball	40
Figure skating	29	Figure skating	37	Pro basketball	36	Pro golf	40
Pro ice hockey	27	Pro basketball	34	Auto racing	29	Pro basketball	38
Auto racing	24	Pro golf	28	Pro golf	29	Pro tennis	28
Pro golf	23	Pro ice hockey	27	Pro tennis	24	Auto racing	22
Pro wrestling	23	Pro tennis	26	Pro ice hockey	21	Pro ice hockey	13
Pro tennis	16	Pro wrestling	10	Pro wrestling	7	Pro wrestling	5

ing it behind all sports for men except professional wrestling. That gender gap of 39 points for figure skating fans is the largest for any sport Gallup measured.

Age

Sunday's Super Bowl game should be widely viewed by Americans of all ages. Pro football is no worse than tied for the top sport among all age groups, and at least 6 in 10 Americans in each age group say they are pro football fans. A majority of people in all age groups are college football fans as well.

Several interesting age differences are apparent in the data that show rather distinct sport preferences between the youngest age group (18 to 29) and the oldest age group (65 and older).

- A majority of 18- to 29-year-olds, 53%, identify themselves as pro basketball fans, compared with no more than 38% of those in any other age group.
- Younger Americans are much less likely to be baseball fans, as at least a majority of those in the 30 to 49, 50 to 64, and 65 and older age groups are baseball fans. This is compared to just 41% of those 18 to 29 years old.
- While relatively few Americans are professional wrestling fans, the sport has its greatest appeal among younger Americans. Those in the 18- to 29-year-old age demographic are more than twice as likely as those in any other age category to say they are professional wrestling fans.
- Figure skating is much more popular among older Americans. Fifty-nine percent of those 65 and older are fans of that sport — that is twice the percentage of figure skating fans in the 18- to 29-year-old age group. Only about 4 in 10 Americans between the ages of 30 and 64 are figure skating fans.

- Older Americans are much more likely to say they are professional golf fans — 40% do so, compared with no more than 29% in any other age group.
- Just 13% of Americans aged 65 and older are hockey fans, less than half the proportion of 18- to 29-year-olds and 30- to 49-year-olds (27%) who are fans of that sport.

Race

Professional football rates as the top sport among both whites (62%) and nonwhites (71%). Nonwhites are almost twice as likely to say they are professional basketball fans (63%) as are whites (32%). There is a smaller racial gap of 16 percentage points on college basketball. More than twice as many nonwhites as whites identify themselves as professional wrestling fans. Whites are nearly twice as likely to say they are hockey fans.

Sports Fans, by Race

Whites		Nonwhites	
	%		*%*
Professional football	62	Professional football	71
College football	53	Professional basketball	63
Professional baseball	52	College football	60
Figure skating	41	College basketball	53
College basketball	37	Professional baseball	52
Professional basketball	32	Figure skating	42
Auto racing	32	Professional tennis	35
Professional golf	30	Professional golf	27
Professional ice hockey	25	Auto racing	23
Professional tennis	21	Professional wrestling	20
Professional wrestling	8	Professional ice hockey	13

Sports Fans, by Region

East		Midwest		South		West	
Sport	*%*	*Sport*	*%*	*Sport*	*%*	*Sport*	*%*
Pro football	68	Pro football	68	Coll. football	62	Pro football	60
Pro baseball	58	Coll. football	55	Pro football	60	Pro baseball	57
Coll. football	47	Figure skating	44	Pro baseball	52	Pro basketball	50
Figure skating	40	Pro baseball	43	Coll. basketball	45	Coll. football	49
Coll. basketball	34	Coll. basketball	40	Pro basketball	38	Figure skating	46
Pro basketball	32	Pro basketball	35	Figure skating	37	Coll. basketball	40
Auto racing	32	Auto racing	31	Auto racing	32	Pro golf	31
Pro golf	30	Pro ice hockey	29	Pro golf	30	Pro tennis	26
Pro ice hockey	25	Pro golf	27	Pro tennis	25	Auto racing	25
Pro tennis	24	Pro tennis	22	Pro ice hockey	17	Pro ice hockey	22
Pro wrestling	10	Pro wrestling	11	Pro wrestling	11	Pro wrestling	9

Region

Pro football is either the top sport or essentially tied for the top sport in each region of the country. In the South, college football is as popular as pro football, and in the West, pro baseball is about as popular as pro football.

Survey Methods

Results are based on telephone interviews with 1,003 national adults, aged 18 and older, conducted Dec. 5-8, 2004. For results based on the total sample of national adults, one can say with 95% confidence that the maximum margin of sampling error is ±3 percentage points. Margins of error will be slightly higher for demographic subgroups. In addition to sampling error, question wording and practical difficulties in conducting surveys can introduce error or bias into the findings of public opinion polls.

February 7, 2005
AMERICANS APPEAR OPEN TO ARGUMENTS ON PRIVATIZING SOCIAL SECURITY
Basic support drops after hearing details

by Frank Newport, Gallup Poll Editor in Chief
and Lydia Saad, Senior Editor

To privatize or not to privatize? The answer may depend in part on the looming battle for public opinion on the Social Security issue. For more than a decade, Gallup has been testing the privatization waters with the public, and across that period, the response has been fairly positive. But with unprecedented scrutiny being brought to the concept now that President George W. Bush has elevated it to a national priority, it is unclear whether Americans' historical support for privatization will hold or crumble in the months ahead.

At a fundamental level, Americans still favor the concept of privatization. Findings from a variety of recent questions asked by numerous national public opinion organizations confirm this. When asked about privatization plans in general terms — with little in the way of specifics, or pros and cons, in the question wording — the public is slightly in favor of, or at least divided over, allowing a portion of Social Security contributions to be invested in the stock market.

A good example is an ABC News/*Washington Post* survey conducted in mid-December that asked, "Would you support or oppose a plan in which people who chose to could invest some of their Social Security contributions in the stock market?" Fifty-three percent said they would support the plan, while 44% were opposed.

The Historical Record

In fact, public reaction to Social Security privatization — without qualifications or elaborate explanations — has typically been positive for over a decade. These historical trends make it clear that Americans' support for privatization was not spawned by Bush's recent promotion of the idea.

A review of prior Gallup polling shows majority support for the concept as far back as 1991. In that year, Gallup found that,

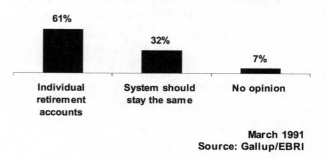

Do you think Social Security taxes, or a portion of those taxes, should go to individual retirement accounts in your name, or do you think the system should stay as it is now?

61% Individual retirement accounts
32% System should stay the same
7% No opinion

March 1991
Source: Gallup/EBRI

when given the choice, 61% of Americans preferred shifting at least a portion of Social Security taxes into individual retirement accounts, while 32% believed the system should be maintained in its current form.

A few years later, in December 1998, Gallup found a similar percentage — 64% — saying they approved of allowing individuals to invest a portion of their Social Security savings in the stock market. (Interestingly, at the same time, only 33% favored allowing the federal government to invest a portion of the Social Security Trust Fund in the stock market.)

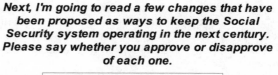

Next, I'm going to read a few changes that have been proposed as ways to keep the Social Security system operating in the next century. Please say whether you approve or disapprove of each one.

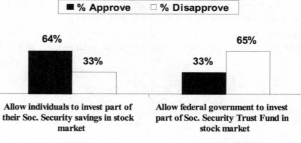

■ % Approve   □ % Disapprove

64% / 33% Allow individuals to invest part of their Soc. Security savings in stock market

33% / 65% Allow federal government to invest part of Soc. Security Trust Fund in stock market

Dec. 4-6, 1998

Four and a half years ago, in the middle of Bush's first presidential election campaign against former Sen. Al Gore, Gallup consistently found two-thirds of Americans amenable to the basic concept of Social Security privatization. Sixty-six percent in an October 2000 poll said they were "for" a law that "would allow people to put a portion of their Social Security payroll taxes into personal retirement accounts that would be invested in private stocks or bonds." Just 30% were against this. These findings were virtually identical to those from a similar question in a June 2000 poll.

From 2000 (including the previously mentioned June poll) to 2003, Gallup tracked public support for privatizing a portion of Social Security with the following question wording:

Though support fluctuated, the percentage in favor was always greater than 50%, including the most recent reading of 62% in October 2003.

A proposal has been made that would allow people to put a portion of their Social Security payroll taxes into personal retirement accounts that would be invested in private stocks and bonds. Do you favor or oppose this proposal?

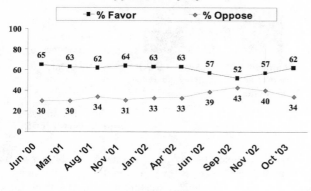

Current Polling

Since the 2004 elections, Gallup and other polling firms have asked about privatization with increasing frequency, using very different approaches to framing the question. The results provide significant insights into public opinion on this important issue.

It appears that Americans are amenable to privatization in principle. The fact that it is being presented as an *option* — one that taxpayers can choose or reject for themselves — is a strong plus with the public. At the same time, charges that the plan puts future retirees' benefits in jeopardy and could cost the Social Security trust fund billions or trillions up front are apparently potent criticisms that could undermine the initial support for privatization that Bush enjoys.

The accompanying table displays 17 different poll questions that have been asked over the last several months about privatizing Social Security, shown in rank order based on the level of support for privatization. The table shows support as high as 60% and as low as 29%:

Poll Questions on Social Security Privatization,
November 2004 – January 2005

Poll dates	Poll sponsor	Attitudes toward privatization		Question wording
		Positive/ Favor %	Negative/ Oppose %	
12/14-15/04	Fox News/ Opinion Dynamics	60	27	Do you think people should have the choice to invest privately up to 5% of their Social Security contributions, or not?
1/12-16/05	ABC News/ *Washington Post*	55	41	Another idea would let workers put some of their Social Security savings into stocks or bonds if they wanted to. That could produce higher or lower benefits depending how the investments perform.
12/1-16/04	Pew Research	54	30	Would you support or oppose this stock market option for Social Security?
1/12-16/05	ABC News/ *Washington Post*	54	41	Generally, do you favor or oppose this proposal (which would allow younger workers to invest a portion of their Social Security taxes in private retirement accounts, which might include stocks or mutual funds)?
12/16-19/04	ABC News/ *Washington Post*	53	44	What would you think of a plan that included both these ideas — a reduction in the rate of growth in Social Security benefits for future retirees, and a stock market option for Social Security contributions? Would you support or oppose that?
1/25-31/05	Quinnipiac Poll	51	43	Would you support or oppose a plan in which people who chose to could invest some of their Social Security contributions in the stock market?
11/18-21/04	CBS News/ *New York Times*	49	45	Do you support or oppose allowing individuals to invest a portion of their Social Security taxes in the stock market?
12/17-19/04	CNN/*USA Today*/ Gallup	48	48	Some people have suggested allowing individuals to invest portions of their Social Security taxes on their own, which might allow them to make more money for their retirement, but would involve greater risk. Do you think allowing individuals to invest a portion of their Social Security taxes on their own is a good idea or a bad idea? As you may know, a proposal has been made that would allow workers to invest part of their Social Security taxes in the stock market or in bonds, while the rest of those taxes would remain in the Social Security system. Do you favor or oppose this proposal?

Date	Source			Question
1/13-17/05	NBC News/ *Wall Street Journal*	46	44	Please tell me which of the following approaches to dealing with Social Security you would prefer — (A) Making some adjustments but leaving the Social Security system basically as is and running the risk that the system will fall short of money as more people retire and become eligible for benefits, OR, (B) changing the Social Security system by allowing people to invest some of their Social Security taxes in private accounts — like IRA's or 401(k)'s — and running the risk that some people will lose money in their private accounts due to drops in the stock market?
1/12-13/05	*Time*	44	47	President Bush favors changing the Social Security system to allow people to invest part of their Social Security payroll tax in stocks and bonds. Do you favor or oppose this proposed change to Social Security?
1/25-26/05	Fox News	44	49	Some people think individuals should be allowed to put a small portion of their Social Security contributions into a personal account, which could be invested in mutual funds. While the personal accounts would be subject to the fluctuations of the stock market, individuals would own the funds when they retire. Others think it is better to leave that money in the Social Security system so it could be used to help pay benefits when you retire. Which comes closer to your view?
1/15-17/05	*L.A. Times*	42	52	As you may have heard, there has been some talk about allowing younger workers to divert payroll tax money from Social Security into private investment accounts which they can then manage themselves. Some people say this is a good thing because it is possible to earn a higher rate of return in the stock market. Others say the stock market is too unpredictable to trust it with Social Security funds. What do you think? Do you approve or disapprove of allowing younger workers to divert their payroll tax money from Social Security into private accounts? (If approve/disapprove, ask: Do you approve/disapprove strongly or do you approve/disapprove somewhat?)
12/9-13/04	NBC News/ *Wall Street Journal*	41	46	As I just mentioned, there is a proposal to allow people to invest some of their Social Security taxes in private retirement accounts that invest in stocks and bonds. Supporters of this idea say that these accounts give people more control over their own money and provide the opportunity to receive more money in retirement. And, because these funds are yours, they can be passed onto your family as part of your estate. Opponents of this idea say that it is expensive because it could cost between one and two trillion dollars over the next 10 years to add these accounts to the system, and it would be dangerous because a major downturn in the stock market could make it impossible to pay Social Security benefits to millions of people. Who do you agree with more on this issue — those who support this idea or those who oppose it?
1/7-9/05	CNN/*USA Today*/ Gallup	40	55	As you may know, one idea to address concerns with the Social Security system would allow people who retire in future

Date	Source			Question
				decades to invest some of their Social Security taxes in the stock market and bonds, but would reduce the guaranteed benefits they get when they retire. Do you think this is a good idea or a bad idea?
1/13-17/05	NBC News/ *Wall Street Journal*	40	50	In general, do you think that it is a good idea or a bad idea to change the Social Security system to allow workers to invest their Social Security contributions in the stock market?
1/13-17/05	NBC News/ *Wall Street Journal*	33	56	Would you favor or oppose a plan to change the Social Security system that includes gradually reducing the amount of money that people receive as their guaranteed Social Security benefit in exchange for allowing workers to invest some of their Social Security taxes in the stock market?
1/5-9/05	Pew Research	29	65	People have different opinions about how the Social Security system might be changed for the future. When decisions about Social Security's future are being made, which do you think is MORE important: keeping Social Security as a program with a GUARANTEED monthly benefit based on a person's earnings during their working life, OR, letting younger workers DECIDE for THEMSELVES how some of their own contributions to Social Security are invested, which would cause their future benefits to be higher or lower depending on how well their investments perform?

What can we learn from an examination of these data?

One obvious conclusion is that Americans' support for Bush's Social Security "reform" plan as measured in these surveys depends on how the question is worded. In turn, this indicates that many Americans do not have firm opinions of the plan in their own minds.

Both proponents and opponents of privatizing Social Security can presumably seek solace in these findings. Proponents can note that a number of basic questions about privatizing find majority or plurality support for the concept. Opponents can note how support drops significantly in many instances when consequences or implications of privatizing Social Security are explained to respondents.

In the broadest terms, it appears there are three ways of asking about Social Security privatization, which result in three levels of support:

1. Questions that ask simply about creating a private investment component to the Social Security system at the option of the worker tend to receive plurality to majority support.
2. Questions that provide relatively balanced pros and cons of the privatization proposal — mentioning both the benefit of saving the system from bankruptcy as well as the financial risks to individual investors — tend to find a plurality or slim majority opposed to the plan.
3. Questions that focus on the financial risks to individual investors — those stating that the plan would reduce guaranteed benefits to retirees without mentioning that this would be compensated for by private investment-account earnings — find larger majorities opposed.

In general, lower support levels are found when questions include phrases such as these:

- "gradually reducing the amount of money that people receive as their guaranteed Social Security benefit"
- "reduce the guaranteed benefits they get when they retire"
- "it is expensive because it could cost between one and two trillion dollars over the next 10 years to add these accounts to the system, and it would be dangerous because a major downturn in the stock market could make it impossible to pay Social Security benefits to millions of people"
- "the stock market is too unpredictable to trust it with Social Security funds"

The questions included in the table above were asked by a variety of polling organizations at different times over the past three months. They were not designed to systematically measure the precise impact of various components or consequences of proposals for privatizing Social Security. The disparate circumstances in which the questions were asked (including in particular the placement of the questions in the various survey contexts and differences in timing of the surveys) could have made a difference in the responses obtained. Some surveys containing these questions had elaborate sequences of questions about Social Security that preceded the questions presented here. Others did not. All of this could have caused variation in the question results.

Thus, at this time, we cannot calibrate with precision exactly how the public will react to the inevitable twists and turns in the debate over Social Security privatization in the months ahead. The fact that the debate is being played out in an extremely partisan context also means that public reaction will be mingled with pre-existing attitudes toward President Bush.

But several conclusions based on available data do appear reasonable:

1. Basic support for the idea of privatizing Social Security has been at the majority level for well over a decade.
2. In the much more politicized environment of the last several months, survey questions asking about Social Security privatization show widely varying support levels.
3. Survey questions that simply ask about the concept of privatizing Social Security (with no qualifications or downsides) tend

to get plurality if not majority support, suggesting that the basic concept still seems like a positive one to many Americans.

4. Questions that remind respondents of problems with privatizing Social Security tend to get significantly lower levels of support, suggesting that opinion is far from well-formed or entrenched at this point.

5. Thus, it appears that the campaign to win the hearts and minds of Americans on this issue is still very much wide open.
   - The Bush administration has an advantage in that public opinion about the concept of privatizing Social Security has generally been positive over the years.
   - The Democrats have an advantage in that majority support for the idea appears to evaporate quite quickly when the public is reminded of downsides associated with changing the Social Security system in its current form.

6. Finally, it is important to note that the privatization issue is rapidly becoming more partisan. The concept is now being actively promoted by a Republican president, and widely criticized by his Democratic congressional opposition. This suggests that public opinion on Social Security could devolve into nothing more than a referendum on the president.

February 8, 2005

BUSH APPROVAL INCREASES TO 57%, HIGHEST RATING IN A YEAR

Iraqi elections likely cause of higher approval rating

by David W. Moore, Gallup Poll Senior Editor

A new CNN/*USA Today*/Gallup survey shows that President George W. Bush's approval rating has increased to 57%, up from 51% three weeks ago. The approval increase appears to be related to the recent Iraqi elections, which the poll shows went better than most Americans expected. In general, the public is more positive now than it was before the elections about the way Bush has handled the situation in Iraq, as well as how the war is faring for the United States. At the same time, the poll shows little change in Bush's job approval rating on the economy or on Social Security.

The poll, conducted Feb. 4-6, shows that Bush's overall approval rating is the highest it has been in over a year. In fact, his approval rating has not exceeded 55% since a Jan. 9-11, 2004, poll, when 59% of Americans indicated their approval of the way Bush was handling the presidency. In the wake of the Democratic primaries and caucuses that followed, along with troubles in Iraq (such as the Abu Ghraib prison scandal), Bush's rating dropped as low as 46% (in May) and then fluctuated around 50% during the rest of the year.

By almost a two-to-one majority (61% to 31%), Americans said the elections in Iraq went better than expected. This perception appears to have led Americans to a generally more positive view about Iraq and about Bush.

The poll shows that 55% of Americans now say the war in Iraq was *not* a mistake, while just last month 52% of Americans felt it *was* a mistake.

Also, there is a 13-point increase in the percentage of Americans who say things are going well for the United States in Iraq — 53% say either "very" or "moderately" well now, compared with 40% prior to the Iraqi elections.

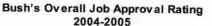
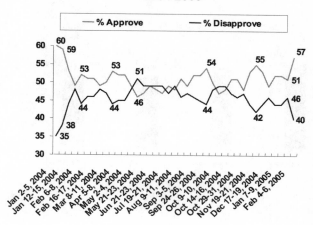

Bush's Overall Job Approval Rating 2004-2005

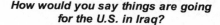
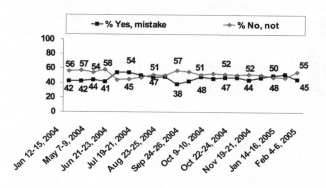

Mistake to Send Troops to Iraq?

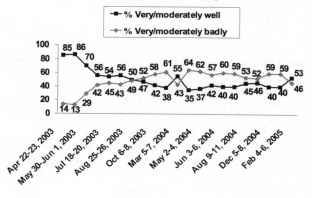

How would you say things are going for the U.S. in Iraq?

These improved perceptions appear to have increased the public's approval of Bush's handling of the situation in Iraq specifically. At the same time, there has not been a significant change in Bush's job approval ratings on either the economy or Social Security, reinforcing the conclusion that the current increase in his overall rating is a result of the Iraqi elections.

The poll shows that Bush's economic approval held steady at 50%, while his Social Security approval rating is now only two percentage points higher than in January (43% to 41%, respectively). That difference is well within the poll's margin of error. Bush's

Little Change in Bush Approval Ratings on Issues Except for Iraq

■ Jan 7-9, 2005 □ Feb 4-6, 2005

Economy	Foreign Affairs	Iraq	Social Security
50% 50%	47% 51%	42% 50%	41% 43%

U.S. Movie Attendance: 1988-2004

How many movies, if any, have you attended in a movie theater in the past 12 months?

● None   ○ 1 to 4 movies in past year   ● 5 or more movies in past year

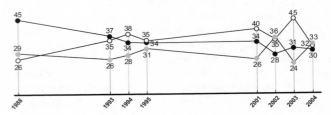

Numbers shown in percentages

foreign affairs approval rating also shows only a slight increase, from 47% to 51%.

Survey Methods

Results are based on telephone interviews with 1,010 national adults, aged 18 and older, conducted Feb. 4-6, 2005. For results based on the total sample of national adults, one can say with 95% confidence that the maximum margin of sampling error is ±3 percentage points. In addition to sampling error, question wording and practical difficulties in conducting surveys can introduce error or bias into the findings of public opinion polls.

February 8, 2005

AMERICANS STILL DRAWN TO THE BIG SCREEN

Sixty-five percent saw at least one movie in the theater in the past year

by Linda Lyons, Education and Youth Editor

Roll out the red carpet. It's the time of year when America pays homage to movie magic. The annual array of star-studded award shows began in January with the Golden Globes and the People's Choice Awards, and last weekend the Screen Actors Guild handed out its statuettes. Movie fans nationwide are already planning Oscar-night parties for Feb. 27 to root for their picks.

But in the age of Netflix and home theater systems, are Americans still actually going out to the movies? A December 2004 Gallup Poll* indicates most still are. Sixty-five percent of Americans reported seeing at least one movie in the theater in the last 12 months, which is consistent with the average percentage since Gallup started asking the question in 1988. Thirty percent of Americans said they had not seen any movies in the theater in the last year.

Young Adults Most Active Moviegoers

Overall, Americans attended an average of 4.7 movies in the theater in the last year. But among those between the ages of 18 and 29, that average is much higher, at 7.9 movies.

Attendance averages drop sharply to 4.4 times in the last year among those aged 30 to 49 — the prime childrearing years. For parents who need to round up a babysitter before leaving the house, the

days of going out to a flick may be gone with the wind, especially when they can just as easily, and more cheaply, pop in a DVD at home.

But movie attendance doesn't appear to rebound among adults whose children are likely to have grown and gone. Adults between the ages of 50 and 64 saw an average of 4.9 movies in the last year, only a slight increase from the 30 to 49 group. Even Americans over 65, most of whom finally have the time to see all the movies they please — and at senior citizen rates — don't appear to be doing so. Those in the oldest group saw an average of only 2.2 movies in the theater in the last year. Sixty-one percent of people 65 and older tell Gallup they did not see any movies in a theater in the last year.

U.S. Moviegoing by Age Group

How many movies, if any, have you attended in a movie theater in the past 12 months?

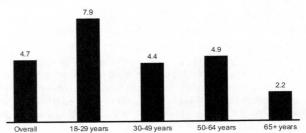

Overall	18-29 years	30-49 years	50-64 years	65+ years
4.7	7.9	4.4	4.9	2.2

And as might be expected given rising ticket prices, Americans who earn $75,000 or more annually saw an average of 5.5 movies in the theater in the last year, while those earning less than $20,000 saw just 3.1 movies.

Other Movie Fans

Are Americans unique in their ongoing love affair with the movies? Not really. Canadians went to the theater slightly less often than Americans did in the last year, averaging 4.0 movies in the last 12 months. And just about the same number of Canadians (33%) and Americans (30%) said they didn't go to any movies. Britons, however, lag behind. British adults averaged seeing 2.9 movies in the theater in the last year. Forty-seven percent of Britons said they did not go to the cinema.

Results in the United States are based on telephone interviews with 1,003 national adults, aged 18 and older, conducted Dec. 5-8, 2004; and 1,011 national adults, aged 18 and older, conducted Dec. 11-14, 2003. For results based on the total sample of national adults,

Movie Attendance in the United States, Canada, and Great Britain

How many movies, if any, have you attended in a movie theater (Great Britain: in a cinema) in the past 12 months?

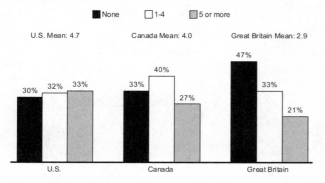

How proud are you to be an American — extremely proud, very proud, moderately proud, only a little proud, or not at all proud?

	Extremely	Very	Moder-ately	Only a little	Not at all	No opinion
	%	%	%	%	%	%
2005 Jan 14-16	61	22	12	3	1	1
2004 Jan 2-5 ^	69	22	5	3	1	*
2003 Jun 27-29	70	20	6	2	1	1
2002 Sep 2-4	69	23	5	1	1	1
2002 Jun 17-19	65	25	6	1	2	1
2001 Jan 10-14	55	32	9	1	1	2

^Asked of a half sample
*Less than 0.5%

one can say with 95% confidence that the maximum margin of sampling error is ±3 percentage points. The survey was conducted by Gallup USA.

Results in Canada are based on telephone interviews with 1,004 national adults, aged 18 and older, conducted Dec. 6-12, 2004. For results based on the total sample of national adults, one can say with 95% confidence that the maximum margin of sampling error is ±3 percentage points. The survey was conducted by Gallup Canada.

Results in Great Britain are based on telephone interviews with 1,009 national adults, aged 18 and older, conducted Dec. 1-21, 2004. For results based on the total sample of national adults, one can say with 95% confidence that the maximum margin of sampling error is ±3 percentage points. The survey was conducted by Gallup UK.

Pride and Politics

Party Affiliation

Republicans have been more inclined to express pride than Democrats when Gallup has asked this question. This may be because Gallup has only asked this question since George W. Bush, a Republican, has been president. Other Gallup measures show substantial partisan fluctuation depending on which party controls the White House. For instance, satisfaction with the state of the nation was higher among Democrats during the Clinton years, while it has been higher among Republicans since Bush took over in 2001.

In 2001, just days before Bush was sworn in as president, Gallup found a 10-point difference between Republicans (including Republican leaners) and Democrats (including Democratic leaners) who said they were extremely proud to be American. Since that time, the gap between the two groups has widened, with the largest difference in 2004, when 82% of Republicans and 57% of Democrats expressed this high level of pride. The latest results show the gap narrowing slightly, with 71% of Republicans and 54% of Democrats saying they are extremely proud.

February 8, 2005
WHO'S PROUD TO BE AN AMERICAN?
Republicans more likely than Democrats to say they are "extremely proud"

by Joseph Carroll, Gallup Poll Assistant Editor

Americans are extremely proud of their country. Since 2001, Gallup has been asking Americans a simple question: "How proud are you to be an American?" The results consistently show that the majority of adults nationwide are proud, and a review of the Gallup data* over the past several years finds some interesting political and racial differences.

Overall Results

In 2001, when Gallup first asked this question, 55% of Americans said they were "extremely" proud to be Americans. This sentiment increased substantially after the Sept. 11 terrorist attacks, to 65% in June 2002 and 69% in September 2002. The percentage of Americans who say they are extremely proud to be American showed little change in 2003 and 2004, but at the beginning of this year, it dropped to 61% — still slightly higher than before the 9/11 attacks but below the level of recent years.

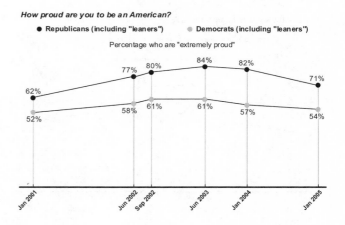

How proud are you to be an American?

● Republicans (including "leaners") ● Democrats (including "leaners")

Percentage who are "extremely proud"

In January 2001, roughly 6 in 10 Republicans said they were extremely proud to be American. This increased dramatically in 2002 and 2003 — reaching a high of 84% in June 2003. By the beginning of 2005, though, the percentage dropped to 71%, which is still higher than what Gallup found among Republicans in 2001.

Among Democrats, the "extremely proud" percentage increased from a low of 52% in 2001 to a high of 61% in 2002 and 2003. It has now declined to 54% — roughly the same as it was in 2001.

Political Ideology

Conservatives are much more likely than moderates or liberals to say they are extremely proud to be American. The percentages of conservatives and moderates expressing this view increased in the period from 2001 to 2002. Among conservatives, this sentiment remained unchanged in 2003 and then declined this year, while views among moderates have shown essentially no change at all since June 2002. The level of pride among liberals shows only modest variation from 2001 through 2003, but Gallup's latest poll finds a significant drop in pride among this group.

How proud are you to be an American?

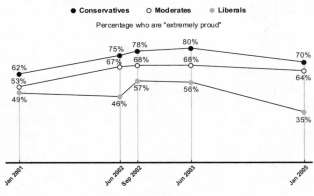

Pride and Race

Since 2001, non-Hispanic whites have been much more likely than nonwhites to say they are extremely proud to be American. The percentage of both non-Hispanic whites and nonwhites who said they are extremely proud increased from 2001 to 2002 and held steady until this year, at which time pride levels decreased.

It might be assumed nonwhites are less likely to be proud since they overwhelmingly identify as Democrats. But even within party groups, the same racial differences are found.

How proud are you to be an American?

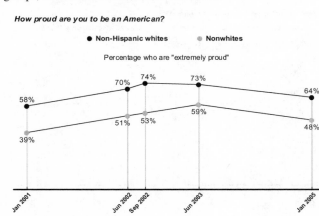

The percentage of non-Hispanic whites who said they are extremely proud to be Americans ranged from a low of 58% in 2001 to a high of 74% in September 2002, about a week before the first anniversary of the 9/11 terrorist attacks. Now, 64% of whites are extremely proud.

Only 39% of nonwhites were extremely proud in 2001. This sentiment increased over the next two years, to a high of 59% in June 2003, before decreasing slightly to 48% most recently.

Pride Among Men and Women

Gallup has consistently found men and women to express roughly the same level of pride since 2001.

How proud are you to be an American?

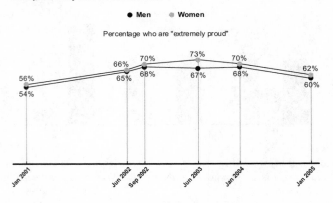

These results are based on telephone interviews with randomly selected national samples of approximately 1,000 adults each, aged 18 and older, conducted January 2001 to January 2005. For results based on these samples, one can say with 95% confidence that the maximum error attributable to sampling and other random effects is ±3 percentage points. In addition to sampling error, question wording and practical difficulties in conducting surveys can introduce error or bias into the findings of public opinion polls.

February 9, 2005

DESPITE BUSH PUSH, LITTLE CHANGE IN VIEWS ON SOCIAL SECURITY
Less than half approve of president's approach to Social Security

by Frank Newport, Editor in Chief

Despite an increase in President Bush's overall job approval rating over the past several weeks, there has been little change in the way Americans view Social Security — the domestic issue Bush has made the centerpiece of his agenda for the coming year.

Americans are no more likely now than they were in January to say Social Security is in crisis or has major problems; Bush's approval rating on handling Social Security has not changed significantly; and support for privatizing Social Security has not changed at all. And while the American public agrees that Social Security has major problems and that the system is likely to go bankrupt by 2042 if no changes are made, less than half of Americans say they favor the president's approach to curing the system.

No Change in Perceived Importance of Social Security

President Bush made Social Security a major focus of his State of the Union address last week and continued that emphasis in his late-week barnstorming trip to five states. Still, a new CNN/*USA Today*/Gallup poll, conducted Feb. 4-6, shows that 17% of Americans say the Social Security system is in crisis and 55% say it has major problems, virtually unchanged from early January.

Which of these statements do you think best describes the Social Security system — it is in a state of crisis, it has major problems, it has minor problems, or it does not have any problems?

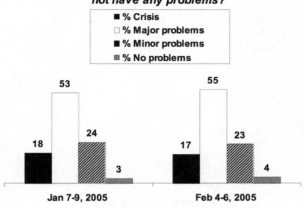

Do you think the Social Security system will — or will not — be bankrupt by the year 2042 if major changes are not made to the system?

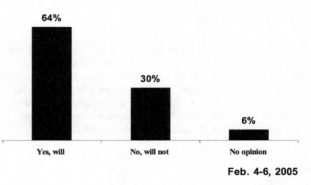

It's also remarkable that despite the Bush administration's increased rhetoric and focus on Social Security in the last couple of months, there has been no significant change between December of last year and now in the percentage of Americans who say Social Security is an extremely important issue for Congress and the president to deal with in the next year. More broadly, views on the importance of dealing with Social Security are no different today from what they were two and a half years ago — in May 2002.

How important is it to you that the president and Congress deal with Social Security in the next year — is it — extremely important, very important, moderately important, or not that important?

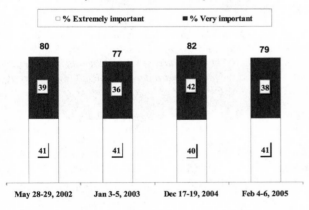

Still, it is important to note that the lack of change in the perceived salience of Social Security should not mask the fact that the public still considers it an issue of importance. Almost three in four Americans say Social Security has major problems or is in a crisis. The poll also shows that almost two-thirds of Americans believe Social Security will be bankrupt by the year 2042 if major changes are not made to the system.

Bush's Approach

In addition to his repeated emphasis on the need to do something to "fix" Social Security, the president is calling on Americans to support his idea of allowing younger workers to invest a portion of their Social Security taxes in private investment accounts.

But all of this recent emphasis on the privatization solution to Social Security's ills has had little impact on public opinion. The new CNN/*USA Today*/Gallup poll shows no change in attitudes toward the concept of privatization compared with views measured in January.

As you may know, one idea to address concerns with the Social Security system would allow people who retire in future decades to invest some of their Social Security taxes in the stock market and bonds, but would reduce the guaranteed benefits they get when they retire. Do you think this is a good idea or a bad idea?

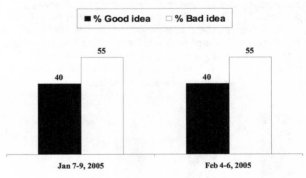

Additionally, less than half of Americans (44%) say they approve of Bush's approach to addressing the Social Security system, while 50% say they disapprove.

Based on what you have heard or read, in general, do you approve or disapprove of George W. Bush's approach to addressing the Social Security system?

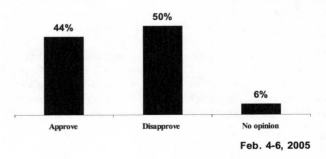

One reason for the relatively tepid reaction to Bush's privatization approach is the fact that Americans are not convinced that individuals would receive higher Social Security benefits if they invested in private investment accounts than they would if the government maintained control of their Social Security taxes.

Suppose Americans were allowed to invest a portion of all the Social Security taxes that they paid in their lifetime in stocks and bonds. When they retired, do you think most Americans would receive - higher Social Security benefits than the government would provide, about the same benefits, or lower Social Security benefits than the government would provide?

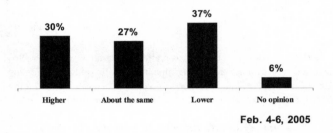

Feb. 4-6, 2005

The poll results indicate that Americans are slightly more optimistic that they personally, compared with the public in general, would benefit from putting their Social Security money into stocks and bonds.

What about you? Do you think that if you had invested a portion of all the Social Security taxes that you have paid in your lifetime in stocks and bonds that you would receive — higher Social Security benefits than the government would provide, about the same benefits, or lower Social Security benefits than the government would provide?

Feb. 4-6, 2005

There is no systematic variation in these views by age. While people aged 30 to 49 are somewhat more likely to believe that private investment would generate higher returns for themselves, that feeling is not shared as widely by those in the 18 to 29 age category; the latter are only slightly more likely than people aged 65 and older to believe that privatization would yield higher returns.

What about you? Do you think that if you had invested a portion of all the Social Security taxes that you have paid in your lifetime in stocks and bonds that you would receive — [ROTATED: higher Social Security benefits than the government would provide, about the same benefits, or lower Social Security benefits than the government would provide]?

	Total %	18- to 29-year-olds %	30- to 49-year-olds %	50- to 64-year-olds %	65 years and older %
Higher Social Security benefits than the government would provide	40	35	48	38	31
About the same benefits	29	36	24	30	29
Lower Social Security benefits than the government would provide	27	27	26	27	30
No opinion	4	2	2	5	10

Politicizing Social Security

It almost goes without saying that privatizing Social Security has now become a very political issue. Much as he did with the war in Iraq, Bush has adopted the privatization issue as a personal crusade, engendering predictable and vociferous objections from his Democratic critics. Thus, it is highly possible that many Americans will simply react to the plan based on their overall evaluations of Bush himself, with Republicans approving of it and Democrats opposing it.

Here is the breakdown of attitudes toward privatizing Social Security by the political orientation of the respondent. The partisan differences are already starkly apparent; almost two-thirds of Republicans are in favor of the concept, while over three-quarters of Democrats are opposed. Independents are also opposed, by more than a two-to-one margin.

As you may know, one idea to address concerns with the Social Security system would allow people who retire in future decades to invest some of their Social Security taxes in the stock market and bonds, but would reduce the guaranteed benefits they get when they retire. Do you think this is a good idea or a bad idea?

	Total %	Republicans %	Independents %	Democrats %
Good idea	40	64	31	18
Bad idea	55	30	64	78
Don't know/Refused	5	6	5	4

Other Ways of Fixing the System

In his State of the Union address, Bush said that all ideas to fix the Social Security system were on the table, including some that were championed by prominent Democrats in the past. The new poll gave the public a list of six possible ways of addressing concerns with the Social Security system apart from privatization, and asked respondents to indicate if each is a good or bad idea.

Assuming there would be no change in Social Security benefits for those who are now age 55 or older, do you think each of the following would be a good idea or a bad idea to address concerns with the Social Security system?

	Good idea %	Bad idea %	No opinion %
Limiting benefits for wealthy retirees	68	29	3
Requiring higher income workers to pay Social Security taxes on ALL of their wages	67	30	3
Further reducing the total amount of benefits a person would receive if they retired early	40	57	3
Increasing Social Security taxes for all workers	37	60	3
Increasing the age at which people are eligible to receive full benefits	35	63	2
Reducing retirement benefits for people who are currently under age 55	29	67	4

One thing is clear from a review of these data. The public is quite willing to sanction changes in the system that would involve increased costs to higher-income Americans, but is decidedly not in favor of more widespread changes such as reductions in benefits or increases in Social Security taxes.

Survey Methods

Results are based on telephone interviews with 1,010 national adults, aged 18 and older, conducted Feb. 4-6, 2005. For results based on the total sample of national adults, one can say with 95% confidence that the maximum margin of sampling error is ±3 percentage points.

In addition to sampling error, question wording and practical difficulties in conducting surveys can introduce error or bias into the findings of public opinion polls.

February 10, 2005
TERRORISM, IRAQ STILL TOP PRIORITIES FOR AMERICANS
Terrorism and Iraq top priorities for Republicans, healthcare costs for Democrats

by Joseph Carroll, Gallup Poll Assistant Editor

Americans say terrorism and the situation in Iraq are top priorities for Congress and President George W. Bush to address over the next year, according to the latest CNN/*USA Today*/Gallup poll. There have only been modest variations in the perceived importance of issues since mid-December. Republicans are more likely than Democrats to say terrorism, same-sex marriages or civil unions, and limits on lawsuits are the top priorities, while Democrats are more inclined to say healthcare costs, education, and the economy. Younger Americans are more likely than any other group to say education is important.

Overall Results

The Feb. 4-6 poll finds that terrorism and the situation in Iraq rank as the most important issues that Congress and the president must deal with over the next year, with 54% of Americans saying terrorism and 53% saying Iraq is extremely important. Following behind terrorism and Iraq are healthcare costs (49%), education (45%), the economy (44%), and Social Security (41%). At the bottom of the list are taxes (31%), same-sex marriages or civil unions (23%), and limits on lawsuits (21%).

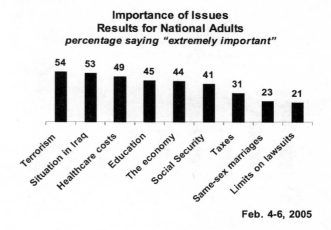

Importance of Issues
Results for National Adults
percentage saying "extremely important"

Terrorism	Situation in Iraq	Healthcare costs	Education	The economy	Social Security	Taxes	Same-sex marriages	Limits on lawsuits
54	53	49	45	44	41	31	23	21

Feb. 4-6, 2005

Since Gallup last asked this question on issue importance in December, there has been a noticeable increase in the perceived importance of five issues: healthcare costs (from 42% to 49%); same-sex marriages or civil unions (16% to 23%); terrorism (49% to 54%); taxes (26% to 31%); and the economy (40% to 44%).

Importance of Issues
Based on national adults, percentage who say "extremely important"

	Dec. 2004 %	Feb. 2005 %	Change, pct. pts.
Healthcare costs	42	49	+7
Same-sex marriages or civil unions	16	23	+7
Terrorism	49	54	+5
Taxes	26	31	+5
The economy	40	44	+4
The situation in Iraq	51	53	+2
Education	44	45	+1
Social Security	40	41	+1
Limits on lawsuits	22	21	-1

Most of these increases may reflect partisan changes. Democrats (including independents who say they "lean" to the Democratic Party) are now more inclined to say that healthcare costs (43% to 55%), education (from 44% to 52%), taxes (23% to 29%), and the economy (42% to 48%) are extremely important. Republicans (including Republican leaners) are more inclined to view terrorism (from 51% to 63%), same-sex marriages (20% to 30%), and taxes (24% to 32%) as extremely important.

Notable is the fact that there has been virtually no change in the perceived importance of Social Security — despite the extraordinary attention it has received in the last several weeks.

Partisanship

Views on the most important issues facing Congress and the president show some variation between Republicans and Democrats.

Terrorism and the situation in Iraq are by far the top issues for Republicans. Sixty-three percent of Republicans (including Republican leaners) say terrorism is extremely important, while 56% say the situation in Iraq. Social Security, healthcare costs, the economy, and education score much lower than terrorism and Iraq, with roughly 4 in 10 Republicans saying these four issues are extremely important.

Importance of Issues
Results for Republicans (including "leaners")
percentage saying "extremely important"

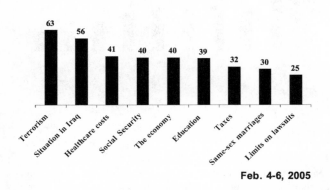

Feb. 4-6, 2005

By comparison, 55% of Democrats (including Democratic leaners) say the issue of healthcare costs is extremely important, making it the top priority for Democrats. Education (52%), the situation in Iraq (51%), and the economy (48%) score only slightly lower.

Importance of Issues
Results for Democrats (including "leaners")
percentage saying "extremely important"

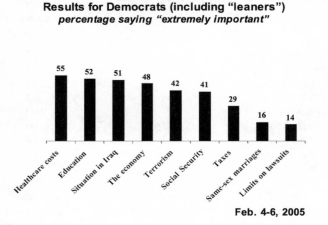

Feb. 4-6, 2005

Overall, Republicans are much more likely than Democrats to say three issues are extremely important: terrorism, by a 63% to 42% margin; same-sex marriages or civil unions, by a 30% to 16% margin; and limits on lawsuits, by a 25% to 14% margin. All three of these are issues that Bush has discussed throughout his re-election campaign last year and in this year's State of the Union address.

Democrats are more likely than Republicans to say healthcare costs (55% to 41%), education (52% to 39%), and the economy (48% to 40%) are extremely important.

Importance of Issues
by party affiliation, percentage who say
"extremely important"

	Republicans (including "leaners")	*Democrats (including "leaners")*	*Difference, pct. pts.*
	%	%	%
Terrorism	63	42	+21
Same-sex marriage or civil unions	30	16	+14
Limits on lawsuits	25	14	+11
The situation in Iraq	56	51	+5
Taxes	32	29	+3
Social Security	40	41	-1
The economy	40	48	-8
Education	39	52	-13
Healthcare costs	41	55	-14

Age

The issue that scores the highest among 18- to 29-year-olds is education, while issues such as terrorism, Iraq, and healthcare costs are more salient among older Americans.

- A majority of adults aged 18 to 29 say education (57%) is extremely important. Moreover, younger Americans are much more likely than people in any other group to say that education is important. Terrorism (49%), healthcare costs (also 49%), the situation in Iraq (47%), and the economy (46%) follow closely behind.
- Among 30- to 49-year-olds, terrorism and Iraq are viewed as the most important issues, with 58% saying terrorism and 57% saying Iraq are extremely important. Next are the economy (47%), education (46%), healthcare costs (44%), and Social Security (also 44%).
- Terrorism (58%), Iraq (57%), and healthcare costs (56%) are the highest-ranking issues among adults aged 50 to 64.
- Among adults aged 65 and older, healthcare costs (49%), the situation in Iraq (48%), and terrorism (47%) are at the top of the priority list. Americans aged 65 and older are much less likely than people in any other age group to say the economy is an extremely important issue.

Importance of Issues
by age, percentage who say
"extremely important"

	18- to 29-year-olds	*30- to 49-year-olds*	*50- to 64-year-olds*	*65 years and older*
	%	%	%	%
Education	57	46	45	33
Healthcare costs	49	44	56	49
Terrorism	49	58	58	47
The situation in Iraq	47	57	57	48
The economy	46	47	48	35
Social Security	38	44	41	40
Taxes	31	34	31	28
Same-sex marriage or civil unions	25	24	21	23
Limits on lawsuits	15	20	22	28

Gender

Women are more likely than men to rate five of the nine issues as extremely important, including terrorism, education, Iraq, the economy, and healthcare costs.

Overall, terrorism and the situation in Iraq are the two most important issues for both men and women. Healthcare costs, the economy, and education are also near the top of the list for both groups.

Importance of Issues
by gender, percentage who say "extremely important"

	Men %	Women %	Difference, pct. pts.
Same-sex marriage or civil unions	24	22	+2
Limits on lawsuits	22	20	+2
Social Security	40	42	-2
Taxes	30	33	-3
Healthcare costs	46	51	-5
The economy	42	47	-5
The situation in Iraq	50	57	-7
Education	41	49	-8
Terrorism	49	60	-11

Survey Methods

These results are based on telephone interviews with 1,010 national adults, aged 18 years and older, conducted Feb. 4-6, 2005. For results based on the total sample of national adults, one can say with 95% confidence that the maximum margin of error attributable to sampling and other random effects is ±3 percentage points. In addition to sampling error, question wording and practical difficulties in conducting surveys can introduce error or bias into the findings of public opinion polls.

February 11, 2005

DNC MEMBERS OPTIMISTIC ABOUT PARTY'S FUTURE, BUT WANT CHANGE
Believe Howard Dean would do an excellent job as party chair

By Jeffrey M. Jones, Gallup Poll Managing Editor

The Democratic National Committee will elect a new chairman Saturday to lead the party for the next four years, with former Vermont Gov. Howard Dean the likely choice. A new poll, conducted by Gallup in conjunction with CNN and *USA Today*, shows Democratic National Committee members are optimistic about the party's future, and most think Dean would do an excellent job as party chair.

The poll of 223 Democratic National Committee members was conducted between Jan. 27 and Feb. 8. While the poll finds that the Democratic Party leadership believes that major changes are needed in the way the Democrats approach elections, three-quarters believe it is very likely the party will win the 2008 presidential election. DNC members favor an electoral strategy that focuses on persuading undecided and swing voters to vote for Democratic candidates, rather than mobilizing existing supporters to vote. They also favor a legislative strategy that attempts to defeat the Republican agenda in

hopes of drawing clear distinctions between the two parties, rather than finding areas of compromise with President George W. Bush and the Republicans in Congress.

Following are the detailed findings of the poll:

The DNC membership has high hopes for Dean as chair — the highest-ranking party position — if he is elected. Sixty-three percent say Dean would do an excellent job as chair and 27% say a good job.

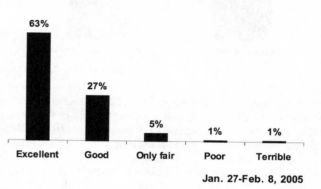

If Howard Dean were elected chair of the Democratic National Committee, what kind of job do you think he would do - excellent, good, only fair, poor, or terrible?

Jan. 27-Feb. 8, 2005

Dean's election is a virtual certainty because all of his major opponents have dropped out of the race. The poll's early results had shown widespread support for Dean among DNC members before the issue of whom they preferred as chair became moot.

Dean would face many challenges if he assumes the role. The poll did not find a single Democratic National Committee member who said the party's approach to winning major elections is "basically fine the way it is." Most say it needs major changes (56%) if not a complete overhaul (8%). Thirty-four percent believe the approach needs only minor changes.

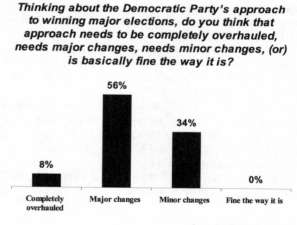

Thinking about the Democratic Party's approach to winning major elections, do you think that approach needs to be completely overhauled, needs major changes, needs minor changes, (or) is basically fine the way it is?

Jan. 27-Feb. 8, 2005

When asked which approach the party should emphasize in order to win future elections, 61% of DNC members say "persuading undecided and swing voters to vote Democratic," while 30% say "mobilizing the Democratic Party's base to turn out to vote." This would mark a shift in the widely reported Democratic Party strategy that focused on turnout in 2004 (though the Republicans are credited with using that approach effectively this past election).

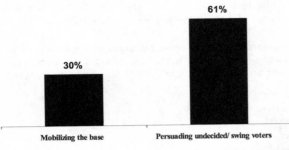

If you had to choose, which of the following do you think is the key to victory for the Democratic Party in future elections—mobilizing the Democratic Party's base to turn out to vote, (or) persuading undecided and swing voters to vote Democratic?

Jan. 27-Feb. 8, 2005

DNC members are hopeful about the 2008 presidential election — three in four DNC members say it is either extremely (30%) or very (47%) likely that the Democratic Party will win that election. Nineteen percent say it is just somewhat likely, and 2% say it is not likely.

Despite their view that the party's election approach needs to change, DNC members do not necessarily blame the party's efforts for the loss in the 2004 presidential election. Nearly half, 49%, say the Democrats lost the election because the "Republicans ran an incumbent president during wartime."

About 4 in 10 believe some aspect of the party's strategy is most to blame for the loss:

- Twenty percent attribute the loss to the Democrats' inability to match the Republicans' grass roots efforts.
- Sixteen percent blame the loss on "the weaknesses of John Kerry as a presidential candidate."
- Seven percent say the Democrats' position on major issues is most to blame for the defeat.

Looking more broadly at the future direction of the party, a slight majority of party leaders, 52%, say the party should become "more moderate," while 23% say "more liberal." One in four had no view on the matter.

Those views are generally in line with what most rank-and-file Democrats believe — a Jan. 14-16 Gallup Poll of Democrats nationwide found 59% saying the party should become more moderate and 35% more liberal.

By a nearly 3-to-1 margin, however, DNC members believe the party should take a more confrontational, rather than cooperative, approach to the second Bush administration. Sixty-eight percent agree that the Democratic Party should "mainly try to defeat the Republican agenda to draw clear distinctions between the two parties," while 24% say it should "mainly try to find areas of compromise with Bush and the Republicans to get things done."

Survey Methods

These results are based on telephone interviews with 223 current members of the Democratic National Committee, aged 18 and older, living in the United States or in U.S. territories, conducted Jan. 27-Feb. 8, 2005. Gallup attempted interviews with the entire group of 434 DNC members who met those conditions.

Question wording and practical difficulties in conducting surveys can introduce error or bias into the findings of public opinion polls.

February 11, 2005
FROM PUBLIC'S PERSPECTIVE, PAST WEEK NOT GOOD ONE FOR BUSH
Approval ratings drop

by Frank Newport, Gallup Poll Editor in Chief and Jeff Jones, Managing Editor

A new Gallup Poll, conducted Feb. 7-10, finds President George W. Bush's job approval rating has dropped to slightly below the levels measured in three January polls, and well below the 57% measured in Gallup's Feb. 4-6 poll that followed the State of the Union address. Furthermore, the president's approval rating on handling the economy has dropped below where it was in January, suggesting that the focus on the new budget and his Social Security plan may have negatively affected the president's public support.

Here's a graph of the president's job approval ratings over the last six months.

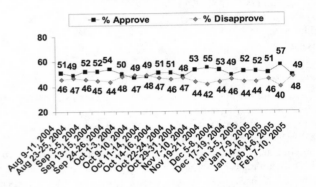

George W. Bush's Job Approval Ratings August 2004 — February 2005

The poll suggests that Bush's public opinion gains following the Iraqi elections and the positive focus on his Feb. 2 State of the Union address have dissipated.

Bush's job approval rating averaged 50% last year, but ranged from 60% in January to 46% in May. His approval ratings hovered around the 50% mark from June until October, but increased after he was re-elected, moving up to 55% in November. That post-election bounce had faded by the end of the year, with Bush ending 2004 at 49% job approval.

The new year brought a slightly higher level of support — Bush averaged 52% in January, which increased to 57% in Gallup's Feb. 4-6 poll, conducted shortly after the Iraqi election and his State of the Union address. The new poll, conducted Feb. 7-10, shows his approval rating is back down to 49% as the news focus has shifted to his proposed federal budget and his plans for changing the Social Security system. Most polling shows a lack of enthusiastic support for his highly publicized focus on privatizing Social Security (and even in Gallup's Feb. 4-6 poll, there were no gains for the president on this dimension, reinforcing the hypothesis that the increasing emphasis on the potential pitfalls of his proposal are now hurting his standing, in the public's eyes).

Changes in presidential job approval (and other public opinion measures) are not unexpected in a highly charged political environment such as appears to be operating in the United States at the moment. In addition to the changes in public opinion monitored by Gallup so far in February, two other nationwide polls released at the end of last week show Bush's approval ratings spread across a six-point range from 45% (Associated Press/Ipsos poll) to 51% (Fox News/Opinion Dynamics poll). Additionally, volatility in the public's mood is suggested in that the AP/Ipsos poll shows the public's confidence in the economy to have dropped to the lowest level in well over a year, while Gallup's tracking measures on perceptions of the economy are essentially unchanged from January, as discussed below.

A Gallup analysis shows that Bush's increase in support in the Feb. 4-6 Gallup Poll came mostly among political independents, whose views are more likely to be influenced by the prevailing political winds than are the views of those with a firm partisan anchor. The president's ratings among independents have now dropped significantly.

The current environment in which the budget and costs of Social Security are the main focus may explain why Bush's job approval rating on handling the economy is now as low as it has been since June of last year, at 45%. It had been 50% in Gallup's Jan. 7-9 poll and stayed at this level in Gallup's Feb. 4-6 poll, even when Bush's overall job rating and foreign affairs approval rating increased.

George W. Bush's Handling of the Economy August 2004 -- February 2005

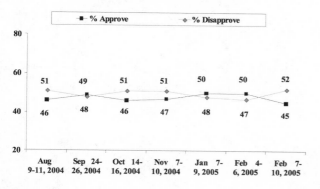

The drop in economic approval rating occurs even though Americans' perceptions of the state of the national economy are unchanged from early January:

- Forty percent of Americans now rate economic conditions in the country as either "excellent" or "good," compared with 41% in a Jan. 3-5 Gallup Poll.
- By a 47% to 44% margin, the public says the economy is getting better rather than worse. In January, 48% said the economy was getting better and 42% worse.
- Similarly, Americans are as satisfied now as they were in January with the way things are going in the United States — 46% of Americans expressed satisfaction in both the Jan. 3-5 and Feb. 7-10 polls.
- One economic measure does show slight improvement. Thirty-eight percent of Americans say now is a "good time to find a quality job," up from 33% in January and reaching a level not seen since August 2001 (although this number has been as high as 37% last November and 36% last July and December).

Bush's foreign affairs approval rating had shown a slight improvement, from 47% in early January to 51% following the Iraqi elections. The current poll measures this rating at 45%, the lowest since August.

Fifty-five percent of Americans approve of the way Bush is handling terrorism — his signature issue. That compares with a slightly higher 58% terrorism approval rating in January, and is Bush's lowest score on the issue since June, when 54% approved.

George W. Bush's Handling of Foreign Affairs August 2004 -- February 2005

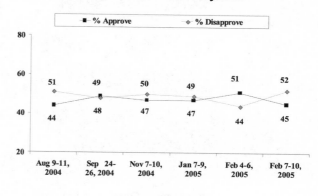

Survey Methods

These results are based on telephone interviews with a randomly selected national sample of 1,008 adults, aged 18 and older, conducted Feb. 7-10, 2005. For results based on this sample, one can say with 95% confidence that the maximum error attributable to sampling and other random effects is ±3 percentage points. In addition to sampling error, question wording and practical difficulties in conducting surveys can introduce error or bias into the findings of public opinion polls.

February 15, 2005
AMERICANS MORE POSITIVE TOWARD ISRAELIS, PALESTINIANS
Still decidedly more sympathetic to Israel

by Jeffrey M. Jones, Gallup Poll Managing Editor

The informal truce between the Israelis and Palestinians announced last week may have encouraged Americans to be more optimistic about the situation in the Middle East. A new Gallup Poll finds Americans rating both sides in the dispute more positively — including the most positive rating ever for the Palestinian Authority. However, by an overwhelming margin, Americans continue to say their sympathies lie with the Israelis. And while Americans are divided as to whether Israel and Arab nations will ever be able to settle their differences, Americans are about as positive as they have ever been on this issue.

The poll was conducted Feb. 7-10, during a Mideast summit at which Israeli Prime Minister Ariel Sharon and recently elected Palestinian Authority President Mahmoud Abbas announced a cease-fire.

Sixty-nine percent of Americans say they have a favorable opinion of Israel, the highest since May 1999 when it was at 68%. Twenty-five percent of Americans view Israel unfavorably. The only time the public's opinion of Israel was more positive was in late January and early February 1991, during the Persian Gulf War, when 79% of Americans expressed positive views of Israel.

Conversely, 27% of Americans have a favorable opinion of the Palestinian Authority — the highest Gallup has recorded since it began measuring this item in 2000. The overall opinion is still decidedly negative, however, with 62% saying they view the Palestinian Authority

Americans' Opinion of Israel

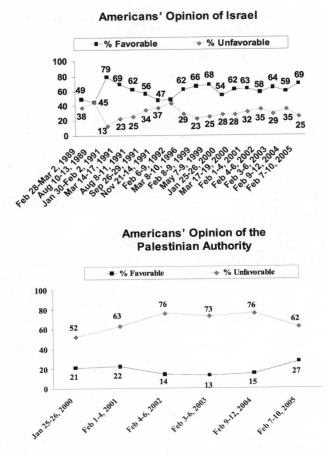

Americans' Opinion of the Palestinian Authority

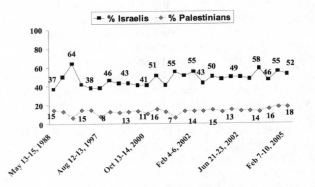

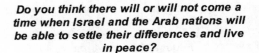

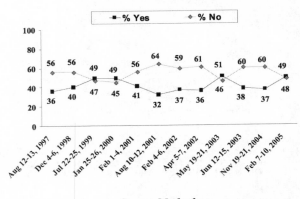

Survey Methods

unfavorably. This is the first rating of the Palestinian Authority since its long-time leader Yasser Arafat died in November 2004.

Despite the more positive views of both sides, Americans' sympathies in the conflict are basically unchanged since last year. Fifty-two percent of Americans say their sympathies lie with the Israelis in the dispute, while 18% say their sympathies lie with the Palestinians, with the remaining 30% not taking sides or offering no opinion. Last year, 55% sympathized with the Israelis and 18% with the Palestinians.

Currently, the level of sympathy for the Palestinians is at its high-water mark. Sympathy toward Israel was at its highest in February 1991, during the height of the Persian Gulf War, when 64% said they sympathized with Israel. However, Americans have always shown very strong support for Israel since this question was first asked in 1988, with margins in favor of the Israelis no less than 2 to 1, and typically higher.

The poll picked up some increasing optimism among Americans that a resolution to the Israeli-Palestinian conflict could be found, as 49% now say there will come a time when the Israelis and Arab nations will "be able to settle their differences and live in peace." That is more positive than a reading from as recently as November 2004 — shortly after Arafat's death — when 37% of Americans were optimistic and 60% were pessimistic about peace prospects between the two sides.

Still, the level of optimism about peace in the Middle East has a history of change. In May 2003 (shortly after President Bush declared an end to major combat operations in the war in Iraq) 51% of Americans said there would come a time of peace in the Middle East. Gallup also measured 49% optimism in July 1999 and January 2000, although that level of optimism had fallen to 32% by August 2001.

These results are based on telephone interviews with a randomly selected national sample of 1,008 adults, aged 18 and older, conducted Feb. 7-10, 2005. For results based on this sample, one can say with 95% confidence that the maximum error attributable to sampling and other random effects is ±3 percentage points. In addition to sampling error, question wording and practical difficulties in conducting surveys can introduce error or bias into the findings of public opinion polls.

February 16, 2005
BYE-BYE, FREEDOM FRIES
Majority of Americans now have "favorable" view of France

by David W. Moore, Gallup Poll Senior Editor

In the wake of France's opposition to the U.S. invasion of Iraq two years ago, a wave of anti-French feelings washed over America. So upset were some Americans that not only did they suggest boycotting all French products, they suggested changing the name of French fries to "freedom fries."

But a lot has happened since then. American enthusiasm for the war in Iraq has abated since the heady days of apparent victory, and in the meantime the French have come to accept the war as a fait accompli. Severe tensions between France and the United States could not remain forever, given the countries' mutual interests on many issues. The recent visit to "old Europe" by the newly sworn-in Secretary of State Condoleezza Rice confirms that both countries are looking for closer relations.

A new Gallup survey suggests that American feelings for the French are decidedly more positive today than they were shortly before the Iraq war began, although not as positive as they were before that. Currently, a majority of Americans, 51%, say they have a favorable view of France, while 43% say their opinion is unfavorable.

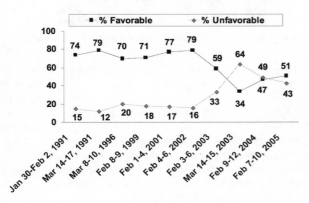

Opinion of France

That eight-point positive margin contrasts with the negative two-point margin last year, when slightly more Americans were unfavorable (49%) than favorable (47%). In 2003, shortly before the United States launched the Iraq war, with strong opposition from the French government, Americans were almost twice as likely to say their opinion of France was unfavorable (64%) rather than favorable (34%).

The recent change in sentiment is not completely unexpected. Most Americans did not view France's opposition to the Iraq war as that of an "enemy." A Gallup survey at the time found 56% of Americans saying France was either an ally or a country friendly to the United States, another 32% saying France was unfriendly, and just 8% characterizing that country as an enemy.

For each of the following countries, please say whether you consider it an ally of the United States, friendly, but not an ally, unfriendly, or an enemy of the United States. How about — [RANDOM ORDER]?

France	Ally	Friendly, not an ally	Unfriendly	Enemy	No opinion
2003 Mar 14-15^	20%	36	32	8	4
2000 May 18-21	50%	40	4	1	5

^ Asked of a half sample

These views were clearly more negative than those expressed in 2000, when 90% of Americans saw France as an ally or friend, just 4% as unfriendly, and 1% as an enemy. But even at the nadir of inter-country relations, the American public remained mostly positive.

It's also true that relatively few Americans at the time took seriously the suggestion to change the name of one of America's most unhealthy foods from French fries to freedom fries. Two-thirds of Americans thought that was a "silly idea," while one-third granted that it was "a sincere expression of patriotism."

As you may know, because France has opposed the U.S. position on Iraq in the United Nations, some restaurants have changed their menus so that foods such as French fries and French toast are now called "freedom fries" or "freedom toast." Do you think this is — [ROTATED: a silly idea (or) a sincere expression of patriotism]?

BASED ON 488 NATIONAL ADULTS IN FORM A

	Silly idea	Sincere expression of patriotism	No opinion
2003 Mar 14-15	66%	33	1

However sincere that expression might have been, just 15% of Americans at the time actually contemplated using the new term, "freedom fries," while 80% said they would stick with the old term.

One possibly cautionary note in this rejuvenation of Franco-American relations is that the current poll shows that 2% of Americans identify France as the "one country anywhere in the world [they] consider to be America's greatest enemy today." No other Western European country is even mentioned. However, mitigating that blight on France's image is the fact that 2% of respondents also say the United States is its own worst enemy.

What one country anywhere in the world do you consider to be America's greatest enemy today? [Open-ended]

	2005 Feb 7-10 %	2001 Feb 1-4 %
Iraq	22	38
North Korea/Korea (non-specific)	22	2
Iran	14	8
China	10	14
Afghanistan	3	*
United States itself	2	1
France	2	—
Saudi Arabia	2	4
Syria	2	—
Russia	2	6
Middle East	1	2
Cuba	*	2
Libya	*	4
Japan	*	1
Palestine	*	1
Israel	*	*
None	2	2
Other	7	4
No opinion	9	11

*Less than 0.5%

Also, despite the increase in favorable ratings, Americans are less positive now than they were before the issue of the war became a point of contention between the United States and France.

The other major Western European country to oppose the United States in the Iraq war was Germany, but that country never took the hit in American public opinion that France did — though positive views of Germany did decline somewhat. While opinion about France was 2-to-1 negative, a plurality of Americans still felt favorable about Germany (49% favorable to 44% unfavorable).

Opinion of Germany

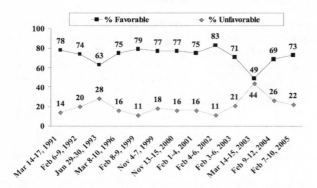

By 2004, Americans were favorably disposed toward Germany by more than a 2-to-1 margin, increasing to more than 3-to-1 in the current poll. The latter rating is comparable to the ratings Americans gave Germany before March 2003.

Despite Germany's agreement with France on the Iraq war issue, Americans never felt that Germany was as unfriendly to the United States as was France. In March 2003, 70% of Americans saw Germany as an ally or friend, compared with 56% who saw France that way.

For each of the following countries, please say whether you consider it an ally of the United States, friendly, but not an ally, unfriendly, or an enemy of the United States. How about — [RANDOM ORDER]?

2003 Mar 14-15^	Ally	Friendly, not an ally	Unfriendly	Enemy	No opinion
France	20%	36	32	8	4
Germany	27%	43	23	3	4

^ Asked of a half sample

Survey Methods

Results in the current survey are based on telephone interviews with 1,008 national adults, aged 18 and older, conducted Feb. 7-10, 2005. For results based on the total sample of national adults, one can say with 95% confidence that the maximum margin of sampling error is ±3 percentage points.

In addition to sampling error, question wording and practical difficulties in conducting surveys can introduce error or bias into the findings of public opinion polls.

February 17, 2005

SOCIAL SECURITY INCHES UP AS A PUBLIC CONCERN

No impact of State of the Union speech seen on public's views on Iraq or the economy

by Lydia Saad, Gallup Poll Senior Editor

President George W. Bush may have hoped to use his latest State of the Union address to jump start public support for making Social Security reform a legislative priority. Indeed, Bush spent nearly one-quarter of his speech addressing Social Security reform. But Gallup measures what Americans consider to be the most important problems facing the nation, and the latest Gallup poll, conducted Feb. 7-10, 2005, suggests Bush had only moderate success sparking support for Social Security change. Over the past month, the percentage mentioning Social Security as the nation's most important problem rose eight percentage points, from 5% in early January to 13% currently.

Social Security as the Most Important Problem

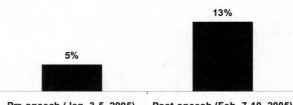

One might have expected Bush's speech to have a bit more impact on public opinion about Social Security, seeing as he positioned it as the primary domestic issue in need of remedy. In fact, more than 1,100 words of Bush's Feb. 2 address to Congress spoke to Social Security issues. The only other domestic issue to come close was the economy, with approximately 700 words in the speech dedicated to economic concerns. But unlike his ideas for Social Security reform, Bush couched his economic proposals — ranging from tax cuts to tort reform — within an upbeat assessment of economic conditions.

Bush's 2005 State of the Union Address

	Number of Words in Speech	Percentage of Speech
Social Security	1,115	22
Iraq	978	19
Building democracy/freedom	881	17
Economy	717	14
Anti-terrorism	415	8
Stem cell research	154	3
Troubled youth	144	3
DNA evidence	104	2
Defense of Marriage Act	100	2
Immigration	93	2
Judicial appointments	73	2
HIV/AIDS	60	1
Introduction/Conclusion	250	5
Total	5,084	100%

No Change in Iraq Assessments

Bush's focus on Iraq in the State of the Union address dealt more with the successes than the challenges still facing the United States in that country. Perhaps as a result, Gallup measured no increase in the public mentioning the situation in Iraq as our country's most important problem. The latest poll finds 24% mentioning Iraq, virtually the same as it has been for several months.

Furthermore, despite Bush's heralding of successful democratic elections in Iraq, there has been no change in Americans' divided assessments of the war in Iraq. About half (48%) say it was worth

Worth Going to War in Iraq?

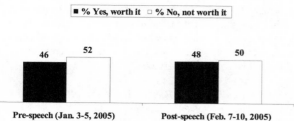

Economic Conditions

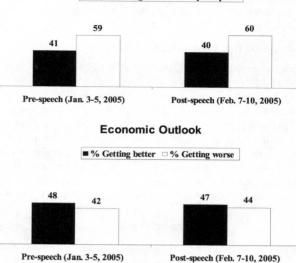

Economic Outlook

going to war in Iraq, up slightly from 46% in January. The other half of the public says it was not worth going to war.

Although Bush dedicated more than 800 words of spirited rhetoric to the virtues of spreading democracy around the globe, Americans are no more convinced today than they were two years ago that this ought to be one of the most important goals of U.S. foreign policy. While a total of 70% consider this goal to be either "very" or "somewhat" important, just 3 in 10 say it is very important. Building democracy in other countries ranks last on a list of nine different foreign policy goals for which Gallup has tracked public support in recent years.

27. Next, I'm going to read a list of possible foreign policy goals that the United States might have. For each one please say whether you think it should be a very important policy goal of the United States, a somewhat important goal, not too important a goal, or not an important goal at all. How about…

2005 Feb 7-10	*Very important* %
Preventing future acts of international terrorism	82
Preventing the spread of nuclear weapons/other weapons of mass destruction	82
Securing adequate supplies of energy	70
Defending our allies' security	57
Maintaining superior military power worldwide	56
Promoting and defending human rights in other countries	52
Protecting weaker nations against foreign aggression	40
Helping to improve the standard of living of less-developed nations	38
Building democracy in other countries	31

No Increase in Consumer Confidence

Bush addressed his first term economic achievements saying, "In the past four years, we provided tax relief to every person who pays income taxes, overcame a recession, opened up new markets abroad, prosecuted corporate criminals, raised homeownership to its highest level in history, and in the last year alone, the United States has added 2.3 million new jobs."

But, according to Gallup's consumer confidence trends, the president did not completely persuade the public. By a 60% to 40% margin, Americans remain more negative than positive in their evaluation of current economic conditions. The 40% now describing the economy as "excellent" or "good" is nearly identical to the 41% recorded in January.

There was also no change in Americans' outlook on the economy. Slightly more still say the economy is getting better rather than

getting worse, by a 47% to 44% margin. That is virtually unchanged from the 48% to 42% margin recorded in January.

In 1994, former president Bill Clinton used his State of the Union address to launch major reform initiatives on healthcare and crime. Gallup's 1994 pre- and post-speech surveys showed double-digit increases in the percentage mentioning both of these problems. There was a 12-point increase in the percentage of Americans naming crime as the most important problem, rising from 37% to 49%. Similarly, the number claiming healthcare problems to be most important rose from 20% to 31%.

Even though the percentage increase was not much different from the 8% seen today for Social Security, the initial level of public concern for healthcare and crime was higher, giving Clinton what appeared to be a mandate for curing those problems in the coming years. Whether Bush has such a mandate on Social Security today remains in question, but it would appear that Bush has more work to do to convince Americans that restructuring Social Security is as imperative as he says it is.

Survey Methods

These results are based on telephone interviews with a randomly selected national sample of 1,008 adults, aged 18 and older, conducted Feb. 7-10, 2005. For results based on this sample, one can say with 95% confidence that the maximum error attributable to sampling and other random effects is ±3 percentage points. In addition to sampling error, question wording and practical difficulties in conducting surveys can introduce error or bias into the findings of public opinion polls.

February 18, 2005

GREATEST U.S. PRESIDENT? PUBLIC NAMES REAGAN, CLINTON, LINCOLN

Most Americans would not want their child to grow up to be president

by Joseph Carroll, Gallup Poll Assistant Editor

Depending on where Americans live, on Monday they'll be celebrating the birthday of the nation's first president, George Washington, or Washington's birthday *and* President Abraham Lincoln's birthday. A recent Gallup Poll asking Americans to name, without prompting, the "greatest United States president," finds Americans most often mentioning Ronald Reagan. Republicans and Democrats differ sharply in their views of the greatest president, with Republicans most often mentioning Reagan and Democrats most often mentioning Bill Clinton. When asked to choose the greater president between Lincoln and Washington, Americans pick Lincoln by a wide margin.

Reagan Tops List

The poll, conducted Feb. 7-10, finds that Reagan is mentioned more often than any other president in history as the greatest, at 20%. Four other presidents trail closely behind: Clinton (with 15% of the mentions), Lincoln (14%), Franklin D. Roosevelt (12%), and John F. Kennedy (also 12%). The current president, George W. Bush, and the first president, Washington, are each mentioned by 5% of Americans.

Whom do you regard as the greatest United States president?

	Feb 7-10, 2005 %	Nov 10-12, 2003 %	Apr 5-6, 2003 %	Feb 9-11, 2001 %	Feb 14-15, 2000 %	Feb 1999 %
Ronald Reagan	20	13	10	18	11	12
Bill Clinton	15	9	11	9	5	12
Abraham Lincoln	14	17	15	14	18	18
Franklin D. Roosevelt	12	11	9	6	12	9
John F. Kennedy	12	17	13	16	22	12
George W. Bush	5	3	11	—	—	—
George Washington	5	7	7	5	5	12
Jimmy Carter	3	3	3	4	3	3
Harry S. Truman	2	3	4	6	3	4
Theodore Roosevelt	2	3	2	2	3	3
Thomas Jefferson	2	3	2	1	3	2
George H.W. Bush	1	2	2	3	3	5
Dwight Eisenhower	1	2	1	1	3	2
Richard Nixon	1	1	1	1	2	2
Other	1	2	2	5	3	1
None	1	*	1	2	*	1
No opinion	3	4	6	7	4	2

2000-2001 questions asked of a half sample
*Less than 0.5%

Since 1999, Gallup has asked this question six times, and over that period, three key points have emerged:
- Lincoln and Kennedy have typically rated at or near the top of the list. In 1999, Lincoln topped the list with a six-percentage point lead over Washington, Kennedy, Reagan, and Clinton. Kennedy led the pack the next year, with a small four-percentage point lead over Lincoln.

- Polling in 2001 and 2003 found no clear-cut victor among the presidents mentioned.
- Reagan has the highest percentage of people mentioning him as the greatest president for the second time. The previous time was in 2001, around celebrations of his 90th birthday. After his death last year, more Americans regard him as the greatest president than did so in November 2003.

Republicans Say Reagan Is Greatest President, Democrats Say Clinton

There are substantial, albeit not necessarily surprising, differences between Republicans' and Democrats' choices for the greatest president in history.

Republicans overwhelmingly say that Reagan is the greatest president in history, with 42% mentioning him. Two other Republican presidents — Lincoln and the current president Bush — follow far behind Reagan, at 14% and 13%, respectively. All told, 76% of Republicans mention a Republican president as the greatest.

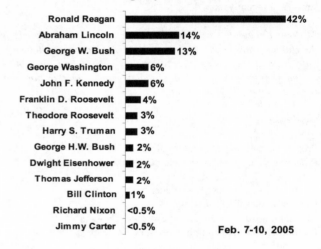

Greatest U.S. President among Republicans

Ronald Reagan	42%
Abraham Lincoln	14%
George W. Bush	13%
George Washington	6%
John F. Kennedy	6%
Franklin D. Roosevelt	4%
Theodore Roosevelt	3%
Harry S. Truman	3%
George H.W. Bush	2%
Dwight Eisenhower	2%
Thomas Jefferson	2%
Bill Clinton	1%
Richard Nixon	<0.5%
Jimmy Carter	<0.5%

Feb. 7-10, 2005

Democrats are most likely to say Clinton is the greatest president, with 31% of Democrats mentioning him. Two other Democratic presidents, Franklin D. Roosevelt (18%) and Kennedy (15%), trail Clinton. Lincoln is the only Republican president identified by a large percentage of Democrats, with 10% saying he is the greatest president. Seventy-two percent of Democrats mention a Democratic president as the greatest.

Among independents, there is no clear consensus as to which president is the greatest. Lincoln, Franklin D. Roosevelt, Kennedy, Clinton, and Reagan are mentioned most frequently.

Age Affects Vote for Greatest U.S. President

There are interesting and significant differences in choice of greatest U.S. president by age, with Americans tending to select a leader from the formative years of their generation.

Clinton is the top choice among 18- to 29-year-olds, while Reagan scores highest for those aged 30 to 49, Kennedy for those aged 50 to 64, and Franklin D. Roosevelt for those aged 65 and older.

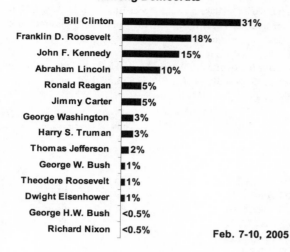

Greatest U.S. President
among Democrats

President	%
Bill Clinton	31%
Franklin D. Roosevelt	18%
John F. Kennedy	15%
Abraham Lincoln	10%
Ronald Reagan	5%
Jimmy Carter	5%
George Washington	3%
Harry S. Truman	3%
Thomas Jefferson	2%
George W. Bush	1%
Theodore Roosevelt	1%
Dwight Eisenhower	1%
George H.W. Bush	<0.5%
Richard Nixon	<0.5%

Feb. 7-10, 2005

Greatest U.S. President
among independents

President	%
Abraham Lincoln	18%
Franklin D. Roosevelt	15%
John F. Kennedy	14%
Bill Clinton	13%
Ronald Reagan	11%
George Washington	5%
Jimmy Carter	3%
Thomas Jefferson	3%
Theodore Roosevelt	3%
Richard Nixon	2%
Harry S. Truman	2%
George W. Bush	2%
George H.W. Bush	1%
Dwight Eisenhower	<0.5%

Feb. 7-10, 2005

Greatest U.S. President by Age Group

	18- to 29-year-olds %	30- to 49-year-olds %	50- to 64-year-olds %	65 years and older %
Bill Clinton	24	16	13	9
Abraham Lincoln	18	15	13	9
Ronald Reagan	15	24	16	19
George W. Bush	10	5	4	3
Franklin D. Roosevelt	8	7	10	31
John F. Kennedy	6	9	23	7
George Washington	5	6	2	7
Theodore Roosevelt	3	3	1	3
Jimmy Carter	1	4	4	1
Thomas Jefferson	1	3	1	1
Harry S. Truman	1	*	4	5
George H.W. Bush	—	2	1	*
Dwight Eisenhower	—	1	2	2
Richard Nixon	—	1	1	1

*Less than 0.5%

Lincoln Beats Washington as the Greater President

When asked to decide the greater president between Washington and Lincoln, Americans choose Lincoln, by 69% to 26%. The same was true six years ago, when Gallup last asked the question.

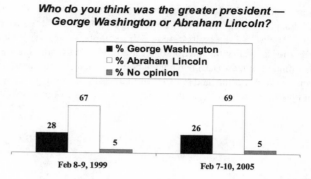

Who do you think was the greater president — George Washington or Abraham Lincoln?

- ■ % George Washington
- □ % Abraham Lincoln
- ■ % No opinion

	Feb 8-9, 1999	Feb 7-10, 2005
George Washington	28	26
Abraham Lincoln	67	69
No opinion	5	5

Although a majority of Americans in all demographic subgroups say Lincoln is the greater president, the data show some modest variations by party affiliation and gender. Republicans (35%) are slightly more likely than Democrats (25%) to say Washington is the greater president. Men are also slightly more inclined than women to say Washington is the greater president, by 32% to 21%.

Majority Wouldn't Want Their Child to Be President

A majority of Americans, 57%, say that if they had a young son or daughter, they would *not* want that child to grow up to be president someday, while 40% would.

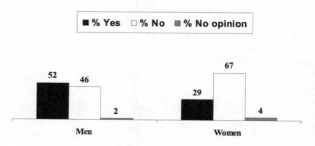

If you had a young son or daughter, would you want that child to grow up to be president someday, or not?

Yes, would want	No, would not	No opinion
40%	57%	3%

Feb. 7-10, 2005

If you had a young son or daughter, would you want that child to grow up to be president someday, or not?
by gender

- ■ % Yes
- □ % No
- ■ % No opinion

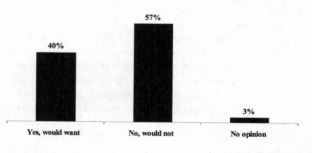

	Men	Women
Yes	52	29
No	46	67
No opinion	2	4

Men and women vary significantly on this measure. Fifty-two percent of men, compared with 29% of women, would want their child to grow up to be president.

Survey Methods

These results are based on telephone interviews with a randomly selected national sample of 1,008 adults, aged 18 and older, conducted Feb. 7-10, 2005. For results based on this sample, one can say with 95% confidence that the maximum error attributable to sampling and other random effects is ±3 percentage points. In addition to sampling error, question wording and practical difficulties in conducting surveys can introduce error or bias into the findings of public opinion polls.

February 22, 2005
AMERICANS DIVIDED ON HOW WORLD VIEWS UNITED STATES
But most Americans still want U.S. to play major role in international politics

by David W. Moore, Gallup Poll Senior Editor

As President George W. Bush continues his European visit, meeting today with European leaders in Brussels at the NATO Summit, a recent Gallup survey shows Americans about evenly divided over the position of the United States in the world today. About half are satisfied, and half are not. A clear majority of the public believes world leaders do not respect Bush, though Americans are divided as to whether the United States is viewed favorably or unfavorably around the world. Most Americans also believe the United States should continue to play at least "a major" role in international politics, but the number saying this country should take "the leading" role has declined somewhat since 9/11.

The poll, conducted Feb. 7-10, finds 48% of Americans satisfied "with the position of the United States in the world today," while 51% are dissatisfied. Polls since May 2000 show Americans mostly satisfied until mid-February 2003, when the United Nations and the United States were in disagreement on whether to go to war in Iraq. At that time, 48% of the public was satisfied and 50% dissatisfied.

After the war began, Americans rallied in support, with satisfaction expressed by a margin of 2 to 1 or better. By February 2004, as the war bogged down, satisfaction dropped to its current level.

On the whole, would you say that you are satisfied or dissatisfied with the position of the United States in the world today?

	Satisfied	Dissatisfied	No opinion
	%	%	%
2005 Feb 7-10	48	51	1
2004 Oct 9-10	42	56	2
2004 Feb 9-12	47	51	2
2003 Apr 14-16	67	30	3
2003 Mar 22-23	69	29	2
2003 Feb 17-19	48	50	2
2003 Feb 3-6	55	43	2
2002 Feb 4-6	71	27	2
2001 Feb 1-4	67	30	3
2000 May 18-21	65	33	2

Apart from satisfaction about the position of the United States in the world, the poll shows that a clear majority of Americans, 60%, believe world leaders do not respect Bush, while only 35% believe he is respected. These results are the worst Gallup has measured during Bush's presidency.

Do you think leaders of other countries around the world have respect for George W. Bush, or do you think they don't have much respect for him?

	Respect him	Don't have much respect	No opinion
	%	%	%
2005 Feb 7-10	35	60	5
2004 Jul 19-21 ^	43	52	5
2004 Feb 9-12	39	57	4
2003 Apr 14-16	46	48	6
2003 Mar 22-23	44	48	8
2003 Feb 17-19	40	55	5
2003 Feb 3-6	46	48	6
2002 Apr 29-May 1	63	31	6
2002 Feb 4-6	75	21	4
2001 Jul 19-22 ^	45	47	8
2001 Jun 8-10	40	46	14
2001 Feb 1-4	49	38	13

^ Asked of a half sample

The only time that a majority of people felt that world leaders respected Bush came in the aftermath of the 9/11 terrorist attacks, in polls conducted in February and late April 2002.

Former President Bill Clinton hardly fared better. In the two Gallup measures taken during his presidency, September 1994 and May 2000, just over half of all Americans thought world leaders did not respect Clinton, while just over 4 in 10 thought world leaders did.

Americans are a little more optimistic about the way the rest of the world views the United States. Forty-eight percent believe the country is rated favorably, and 51% say it is rated unfavorably.

In general, how do you think the United States rates in the eyes of the world — very favorably, somewhat favorably, somewhat unfavorably, or very unfavorably?

	Very favorably	Somewhat favorably	Somewhat unfavorably	Very unfavorably	No opinion
	%	%	%	%	%
2005 Feb 7-10	7	41	39	12	1
2004 Feb 9-12	10	44	34	11	1
2003 Apr 14-16	12	49	28	9	2
2003 Feb 17-19	7	47	34	11	1
2003 Feb 3-6	11	46	34	7	2
2002 Mar 8-9 ^	20	46	26	5	3
2002 Feb 4-6	20	59	17	3	1
2001 Feb 1-4	18	57	20	4	1
2000 May 18-21	20	53	22	4	1

^ Asked of a half sample

Again, this is the most negative perception Gallup has recorded during the Bush presidency — the first time a majority has indicated its belief that the United States is viewed unfavorably.

However the country and its leader might be viewed, Americans want the United States to continue to play either "the leading" or "a major" role in international politics. The percentage saying "leading" role has declined from 26% who said that in February 2002 and February 2003, to 19% today.

Next we would like you to think about the role the U.S. should play in trying to solve international problems. Do you think the U.S. should — [ROTATED: take the leading role in world affairs, take a major role, but not the leading role, take a minor role, (or) take no role at all in world affairs]?

	Leading role %	Major role %	Minor role %	No role %	No opinion %
2005 Feb 7-10	19	53	21	5	2
2004 Feb 9-12	21	53	21	4	1
2003 Feb 3-6	26	53	16	3	2
2002 Feb 4-6	26	52	16	4	2
2001 Feb 1-4	16	57	21	4	2

Survey Methods

Results in the current survey are based on telephone interviews with 1,008 national adults, aged 18 and older, conducted Feb. 7-10, 2005. For results based on the total sample of national adults, one can say with 95% confidence that the maximum margin of sampling error is ±3 percentage points. In addition to sampling error, question wording and practical difficulties in conducting surveys can introduce error or bias into the findings of public opinion polls.

February 22, 2005

HOW YOUNG IS YOUNG ENOUGH TO SUPPORT BUSH'S SOCIAL SECURITY PLAN?
Time may be on younger generation's side

by Steve Hanway, Senior Staff Writer

It's been well documented that younger Americans are more likely than older Americans to support President Bush's proposed changes to Social Security, which would allow people to put a portion of their Social Security benefits into private investment accounts. When Gallup asked Americans in a recent poll* whether they approve or disapprove of Bush's approach to Social Security, Americans under 50 are divided, while those aged 50 and older are far more negative about it. The 18- to 29-year-old age group is the only one with a higher percentage in approval than in dissent.

Will Investment Accounts Yield Higher Returns?

To some extent, the difference may reflect the younger generation's greater opportunity to compound stock market returns over a longer period, and thus withstand extended periods of potential negative returns. But could the difference also reflect greater optimism about the power of the stock market?

It doesn't look that way. Eighteen- to 29-year-olds are not the most optimistic age group when asked whether investing Social Security taxes in private accounts would yield higher benefits for Amer-

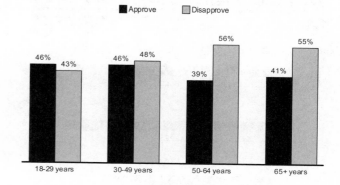

Do you approve or disapprove of the way George W. Bush is handling Social Security?

icans than what the current government system provides. A plurality (36%) of 18- to 29-year-olds think most Americans would receive *lower* benefits from private investments than the current system provides (33% of young adults think people would receive the same benefits either way, and 28% think private accounts would yield higher benefits for most Americans).

On the other hand, a plurality (38%) of adults between the ages of 30 and 49 think most Americans would get *higher* benefits through investing in personal accounts (only 24% think benefits would be the same and 34% think benefits would be lower). Americans 50 and older are at least as negative if not more so than 18- to 29-year-olds regarding the benefits that the proposed private system would yield.

Impact of Investment Accounts on Most Americans

Suppose Americans were allowed to invest a portion of all the Social Security taxes that they paid in their lifetime in stocks and bonds. When they retired, do you think most Americans would receive: higher Social Security benefits than the government would provide, about the same benefits, or lower Social Security benefits than the government would provide?

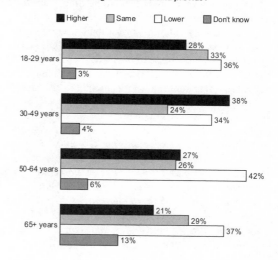

Gallup also asked how people think they might fare *personally* if they could invest their Social Security taxes rather than remaining in the current system. Americans are much more optimistic about their ability to get better returns investing their Social Security taxes than what they feel most Americans could get. But again, adults aged 30 to 49 are most optimistic — nearly twice as many in this age group think they would receive higher returns (48%) as think they would receive lower returns (26%).

Personal Impact of Investment Accounts

What about you? Do you think that if you had invested a portion of all the Social Security taxes that you have paid in your lifetime in stocks and bonds that you would receive: higher Social Security benefits than the government would provide, about the same benefits, or lower Social Security benefits than the government would provide?

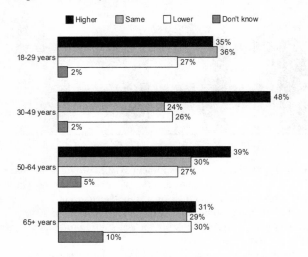

■ Higher ▨ Same ☐ Lower ▨ Don't know

18-29 years: 35% / 36% / 27% / 2%

30-49 years: 48% / 24% / 26% / 2%

50-64 years: 39% / 30% / 27% / 5%

65+ years: 31% / 29% / 30% / 10%

Why are Americans between 30 and 49, who are the most optimistic that they personally (as well as most Americans) could get higher Social Security payments by privately investing their taxes still as likely to oppose Bush's plan as to favor it? The sense of security among 30- to 49-year-olds may have waned; Gallup's 2004 Personal Finances survey found they are considerably less likely than 18- to 29-year-olds to feel their monthly savings — or their income — will increase over the next six months.

Bottom Line

In a way, "thirtysomethings" and "fortysomethings" are the first "401(k) generation," more accustomed to making their own personal investment decisions for retirement, rather than relying on guaranteed pensions. Living and working through a great bull run of the 1990s, they may have a great sense of the market's power to produce superior returns over the long haul. However, the inclination against investment in place of guaranteed benefits highlights the appeal of a nationwide safety net immune to the vagaries of the stock market — a system that remains true to the name "Social *Security*."

Results are based on telephone interviews with 1,010 national adults, aged 18 and older, conducted Feb, 4-6, 2005. For results based on interviews with 112 18- to 29-year-olds, one can say with 95% confidence that the margin of error is ±9 percentage points. For results based on interviews with 367 30- to 49-year-olds, one can say with 95% confidence that the margin of error is ±5 percentage points. For results based on interviews with 279 50- to 64-year-olds or 240 adults 65 and older, one can say with 95% confidence that the margin of error is ±6 percentage points.

February 23, 2005
"AXIS OF EVIL" COUNTRIES SEEN AS AMERICA'S GREATEST ENEMIES
Most favorably rated countries are Great Britain and Canada, with Japan a close third

by David W. Moore, Gallup Poll Senior Editor

A recent Gallup survey, conducted Feb. 7-10, finds the American public citing North Korea, Iran, and Iraq as the United States' greatest enemies. Three years ago, in his 2002 State of the Union address, President George W. Bush specifically charged these three countries with fomenting terrorism and declared that "states like these, and their terrorist allies, constitute an axis of evil, arming to threaten the peace of the world."

The year before that, in a Feb. 1-4, 2001, poll, Americans had a very different view of the world. Thirty-eight percent considered Iraq as "America's greatest enemy," the highest number identifying any country that way. Another 14% mentioned China, with Iran mentioned by 8%, Russia by 6%, and Saudi Arabia and Libya each by 4%. Only 2% mentioned North Korea.

But the current poll finds that today, 22% of Americans each identify Iraq and North Korea as America's top enemies, while another 14% mention Iran. China was a distant second four years ago, but now it is ranked fourth, mentioned by 10% of respondents.

What one country anywhere in the world do you consider to be America's greatest enemy today? [Open-ended]

	2005 Feb 7-10 %	2001 Feb 1-4 %
Iraq	22	38
North Korea/ Korea (non-specific)	22	2
Iran	14	8
China	10	14
Afghanistan	3	*
United States itself	2	1
France	2	—
Saudi Arabia	2	4
Syria	2	—
Russia	2	6
Middle East	1	2
Cuba	*	2
Libya	*	4
Japan	*	1
Palestine	*	1
Israel	*	*
None	2	2
Other	7	4
No opinion	9	11

*Less than 0.5%

Much of the change in opinion over the past four years, of course, is influenced by America's war on terrorism as well as the war in Iraq, in the aftermath of the 9/11 terrorist attacks. Iran and North Korea have both taken more aggressive international postures about their possessing nuclear weapons, in part, they argue, as a defensive response to possible U.S. military action — an argument that U.S. officials dismiss as an excuse for their warlike intentions.

Still, the ongoing conflict between the United States and these two countries is reflected in the American public's ratings of countries around the world. Eighty-two percent of Americans rate Iran unfavorably, and 80% rate North Korea the same way — the highest unfavorable ratings for any of the 24 countries mentioned in the poll. Iraq comes in third, with an unfavorable rating of 66% — far lower than the other two countries in the "axis of evil." The lower unfavorable rating is no doubt a reflection of the fact that with Saddam Hussein out of power and U.S. forces in Iraq, the country is less of a danger to the United States than is either North Korea or Iran.

Next, I'd like your overall opinion of some foreign countries. First, is your overall opinion of [RANDOM ORDER] very favorable, mostly favorable, mostly unfavorable, or very unfavorable? How about — [INSERT NEXT ITEM]?

2005 Feb 7-10 (sorted by "total favorable")	Total favorable %	Total unfavorable %
Great Britain	91	4
Canada	86	10
Japan	81	14
Poland	78	9
India	75	18
Mexico	74	21
Germany	73	22
Israel	69	25
Ukraine	67	18
Egypt	64	26
Russia	61	33
Indonesia	57	28
Jordan	54	32
France	51	43
China	47	47
Pakistan	41	49
Afghanistan	40	54
Saudi Arabia	36	58
Iraq	29	66
Cuba	28	65
The Palestinian Authority	27	62
Syria	25	60
North Korea	13	80
Iran	12	82

Iraq's unfavorable rating is only a point different from the negative rating given to Cuba, which Americans have long viewed in unfavorable terms. Almost a decade ago, Cuba's rating was even more negative — with 81% expressing an unfavorable opinion, and only 10% a favorable one.

The most positive ratings these days go to Great Britain (91% favorable rating) and Canada (86%), mostly English-speaking countries with a great deal of shared culture with the United States. Close behind is Japan (81% favorable), which has shown a significant rise in American popularity in the past decade. In the mid-1990s, when the United States and Japan clashed over trade policy, Americans were about evenly divided in their ratings.

The greatest changes over the past year are found in Americans' ratings of Pakistan, the Palestinian Authority, India, Afghanistan, and Israel — whose net favorable to unfavorable ratings have all improved by at least 20 percentage points.

Changes in Country Ratings From 2004 to 2005 of at Least 20 Percentage Points

Country	Favorable 2005 %	Unfavorable 2005 %	Net rating 2005 Pct. pts.	Favorable 2004 %	Unfavorable 2004 %	Net rating 2004 Pct. pts.	Change: net 2005 minus net 2004 Pct. pts.
Pakistan	41	49	-8	28	64	-36	+28
Palestinian Authority	27	62	-35	15	76	-61	+26
India	75	18	+57	61	29	+32	+25
Afghanistan	40	54	-14	28	65	-37	+23
Israel	69	25	+44	59	35	+24	+20

The more positive views of the Palestinian Authority and Israel are no doubt tied to both Israeli Prime Minister Ariel Sharon's policy of withdrawal from Gaza, as well as the emergence of new leadership in the Palestinian Authority following Yasser Arafat's death. The prospects for peace in that area of the world are clearly more positive now than they were a year ago.

Media coverage of elections in Afghanistan last October probably accounts for much of the increase in favorable feelings about that country. It could be that there were carry-over effects for Pakistan's rating, which also increased significantly since last year. Given that the two countries are neighbors and that their names sound alike, it could be that many Americans had improved favorable impressions of both countries.

India's increased rating may be part of a sympathy reaction to the tsunami disaster that resulted from an earthquake in the Indian Ocean on Dec. 26, 2004. Also, the conflict between Pakistan and India this past year may not have been as salient in the news as it was the year before.

Survey Methods

Results in the current survey are based on telephone interviews with 1,008 national adults, aged 18 and older, conducted Feb. 7-10, 2005. For results based on the total sample of national adults, one can say with 95% confidence that the maximum margin of sampling error is ±3 percentage points. In addition to sampling error, question wording and practical difficulties in conducting surveys can introduce error or bias into the findings of public opinion polls.

February 24, 2005
HILLARY CLINTON'S GENDER ADVANTAGE
Senator has more positive image among women, even those who are Republican and independent

by Frank Newport, Gallup Poll Editor in Chief

New York Sen. Hillary Clinton has a substantially more favorable image among women than among men — a gender advantage that persists even among Republicans and independents. This suggests that Clinton has the potential to draw the votes of women who might ordinarily not consider voting for a Democratic candidate in the 2008 presidential election. Clinton also has a more positive image among younger voters, but has a less positive image among both men and women who are married.

Background

Clinton, at this early stage, is the front-runner for the Democratic nomination for president in 2008. That status has been confirmed by a number of polls of Democrats, including two CNN/*USA Today*/Gallup polls conducted since the November 2004 presidential election. In the first such poll, Clinton was included along with Massachusetts Sen. John Kerry and former North Carolina Sen. John Edwards, and was the top voter getter among Democrats. The second such poll, conducted Feb. 4-6, 2005, yielded similar results:

Next, I'm going to read a list of people who may be running in the Democratic primary for president in the next election. After I read all the names, please tell me which of those candidates you would be most likely to support for the Democratic nomination for President in the year 2008 — [ROTATED: New York Sen. Hillary Rodham Clinton, former North Carolina Sen. John Edwards, Massachusetts Sen. John Kerry] —or would you support someone else?

BASED ON 423 DEMOCRATS OR DEMOCRATIC LEANERS

BASED ON 383 DEMOCRATS OR DEMOCRATIC LEANERS WHO ARE REGISTERED TO VOTE

2005 Feb 4-6	All Democrats/ Democrat leaners %	Democrats/ Democratic leaners who are registered to vote %
Hillary Rodham Clinton	40	40
John Kerry	25	25
John Edwards	17	18
Other	6	6
All/any	2	1
None	4	4
No opinion	6	6

It is of course very early to use current poll results as an accurate predictive gauge of what will happen as the presidential primaries get underway in January 2008, less than three years from now. A review of Gallup Polls conducted in the two or three years before past presidential elections shows that the early indications often bear little relationship to what actually happened in those elections. In some years the early front-runner for the Democratic candidate was out of the running by the time the primaries began, while in other years the eventual nominee wasn't well known enough to be included in early polls — if the person was included, they registered hardly any support (Jimmy Carter prior to 1976, Michael Dukakis prior to 1988, and Bill Clinton prior to 1992).

Furthermore, as Sen. Clinton herself points out frequently, she has the difficult challenge of facing the voters of New York in the 2006 Senate race, putting her in the awkward position of having to explain her future presidential plans while running to represent New York State in the Senate.

Still, Sen. Clinton is a universally known politician, and a person who has generated extraordinary attention since she first entered the national spotlight 13 years ago. These facts make a focus on her presidential potential both relevant and interesting, even at this early stage in the process.

Sen. Clinton's possible presidential candidacy generates even more interest because she would become the first woman to be a major party's presidential candidate, and of course, if elected president, she would become the first female president in the nation's history.

This raises a few questions: Would Sen. Clinton have an advantage in a general election in 2008 because she is a woman? Would female voters ordinarily inclined to vote for the Republican candidate have a greater tendency to vote for Sen. Clinton because of the opportunity to be a part of electing the first female president? Additionally, is there an age or marital factor in Sen. Clinton's appeal?

We gain some insights into the answers to these questions by analyzing Sen. Clinton's image among various demographic groups using a combined dataset of 4,001 interviews based on five separate surveys from 2003-2004 in which the public was asked if they had a favorable or unfavorable opinion of her. Although having a favorable opinion of a politician is not necessarily the same thing as voting for him or her, at this juncture these favorability ratings can reasonably stand as surrogates for potential voting behavior.

The basic results show a significant gender gap in the public's opinions of Sen. Clinton:

Opinion of Hillary Clinton
Based on interviews conducted 2003-2004

	Favorable %	Unfavorable %	Number of interviews
TOTAL	**53**	**42**	**4,001**
Men	48	48	1,915
Women	58	37	2,086

Women are more likely than men to have a favorable opinion of Sen. Clinton, by a 10-point margin. But could this gender gap in favorable opinions of Sen. Clinton be caused, at least in part, by the fact that women tend to be more Democratic in their politics in general than are men?

To answer this question, the table below looks at the difference in the public's opinions of Sen. Clinton by gender within groups of Americans who identify themselves as Republicans, independents, and Democrats.

Opinion of Hillary Clinton
Based on interviews conducted 2003-2004

	Favorable %	Unfavorable %	Number of interviews
TOTAL	**53**	**42**	**4,001**
Republicans	*24*	*73*	*1,260*
Men	20	78	620
Women	29	67	640
Independents	*55*	*39*	*1,492*
Men	49	45	773
Women	61	33	719
Democrats	*82*	*15*	*1,222*
Men	80	15	514
Women	83	14	708

It is clear that the gender gap in the public's opinions of Sen. Clinton operates to some degree even within political categories:

- Republican women are 9 points higher in their favorable rating and 11 points lower in their unfavorable rating of Sen. Clinton than are Republican men.

- Women who are Independents are 12 points higher in their favorable rating and 12 points lower in their unfavorable rating of Sen. Clinton than are Independents who are men.
- There is fairly little gender distinction in favorable ratings of Sen. Clinton among Democrats, among whom both men and women are very positive.

While these are not huge differences, they do support the basic hypothesis that Sen. Clinton could bring to the table an advantage among Republican and independent women, an advantage that could make a difference in a close election. Of particular importance is the big difference between her image among independent men, which essentially breaks even, and her image among independent women, where her favorable ratings outweigh her unfavorable ratings by almost a 30-point margin.

The Age Factor

Sen. Clinton has a decidedly more positive image among Americans under age 30 than she does among those who are older:

Opinion of Hillary Clinton
Based on interviews conducted 2003-2004

	Favorable %	Unfavorable %	Number of interviews
TOTAL	53	42	4,001
Age 18 to 29	61	33	725
Age 30 to 49	53	44	1,671
Age 50 to 64	51	46	880
Age 65 and older	51	43	689

The origins of this younger skew in appeal for Sen. Clinton are not immediately apparent (She is now 57 years old, and will be 61 at the time of the 2008 election). The ultimate value in a presidential election of having strong appeal to younger voters is also unclear. As was seen in this past year's election, having a strong appeal to the youngest group of voters does not automatically transfer into real votes, given the historic fact that the younger the voter, the less likely he or she is to actually turn out and vote.

There is an interesting gender and age interaction in the public's opinions of Sen. Clinton:

Opinion of Hillary Clinton
Based on interviews conducted 2003-2004

	Favorable %	Unfavorable %	Number of interviews
TOTAL	53	42	4,001
Age 18 to 29	61	33	725
Men	51	44	367
Women	71	23	358
Age 30 to 49	53	44	1,671
Men	46	50	828
Women	59	38	843
Age 50 to 64	51	46	880
Men	47	49	407
Women	54	43	471
Age 65 and older	51	43	689
Men	51	44	305
Women	51	41	384

There is a significant gender gap in the public's opinions of Sen. Clinton among those aged 18 to 29 and among those aged 30 to 49, much less of a gap among 50- to 64-year-olds, and no gap among those 65 and older. In short, Sen. Clinton's strongest constituency would appear to be among women under age 50.

Does this age gap persist even when the partisan orientation of the respondent is controlled? To answer this question, we can look at the public's opinions of Sen. Clinton within age groups and within party orientation. In order to keep sample sizes as large as possible, in this chart those who are politically independent but who lean toward the Republican Party have been included with Republicans, and those who are independent and lean Democratic have been included with Democrats.

Opinion of Hillary Clinton
Based on interviews conducted 2003-2004

	Favorable %	Unfavorable %	Number of interviews
TOTAL	53	42	4,001
Age 18 to 29	61	33	725
Republican, including leaners	40	53	279
Democrat, including leaners	81	15	360
Age 30 to 49	53	44	1,671
Republican, including leaners	30	68	757
Democrat, including leaners	76	19	737
Age 50 to 64	51	46	880
Republican, including leaners	22	75	409
Democrat, including leaners	80	17	399
Age 65 and older	51	43	689
Republican, including leaners	20	74	283
Democrat, including leaners	78	17	337

Here we see the persistence of the age gap in the public's favorable opinions of Sen. Clinton even within party groups. Clinton has a 40% favorable rating among 18- to 29-year-old Republicans, declining to 30% among Republicans aged 30 to 49, and then down to 22% and 20% among those aged 50 to 64 and 65 and older, respectively.

On the other hand, there is little difference in the public's opinions of Sen. Clinton among Democrats by age. About 8 in 10 Democrats have a favorable opinion of her regardless of age.

A Marriage Gap?

The data show a basic and substantial marriage gap in Sen. Clinton's appeal:

Opinion of Hillary Clinton
Based on interviews conducted 2003-2004

	Favorable %	Unfavorable %	Number of interviews
TOTAL	53	42	1,476
Married	45	52	779
Not married*	62	31	697

* 'Not married' includes those who are living together with a partner, widowed, divorced, separated, and never married.

Americans who are not married have a significantly more favorable view of Sen. Clinton than those who are married.

Again, the basic nature of politics in America today holds possible explanations for these patterns. Married voters in general are more likely to be Republicans, while those who are not married are more likely to be Democrats.

The table examines the relationship between marital status and the public's opinions of Sen. Clinton within political groups:

Opinion of Hillary Clinton
Based on interviews conducted 2003-2004

	Favorable %	Unfavorable %	Number of interviews
TOTAL	**53**	**42**	**1,476**
Republican	*24*	*73*	
Married	20	80	318
Not married*	29	66	184
Independent	*55*	*39*	
Married	50	44	278
Not married*	64	27	263
Democrat	*82*	*14*	
Married	82	15	178
Not married*	85	10	246

* 'Not married' includes those who are living together with a partner, widowed, divorced, separated, and never married.

The gap by marriage in the public's opinions of Sen. Clinton is evident among Republicans and independents, but much less so among Democrats. In other words, Sen. Clinton's image suffers among Republicans and independents who are married.

The marriage gap is evident among both genders, and is slightly larger among women.

Opinion of Hillary Clinton
Based on interviews conducted 2003-2004

	Favorable %	Unfavorable %	Number of interviews
TOTAL	**53**	**42**	**1,476**
Men	*48*	*48*	*701*
Married	41	55	435
Not married*	53	41	266
Women	*58*	*37*	*773*
Married	50	49	343
Not married*	68	25	430

* 'Not married' includes those who are living together with a partner, widowed, divorced, separated, and never married.

Although the sample sizes involved here are small, the data suggest that the marriage gap persists among Republican women (with those who are married having a less favorable opinion of Sen. Clinton than those who are not married), and among Democratic men (with those married having a less favorable opinion).

Opinion of Hillary Clinton
Based on interviews conducted 2003-2004

	Favorable %	Unfavorable %	Number of interviews
TOTAL	**53**	**42**	**1,476**

	Favorable %	Unfavorable %	Number of interviews
Republicans, including leaners			
Men			
Married	23	75	257
Not married*	25	71	109
Women			
Married	26	74	175
Not married*	43	49	150
Democrats, including leaners			
Men			
Married	69	23	143
Not married*	81	11	133
Women			
Married	81	18	137
Not married*	83	12	246

* 'Not married' includes those who are living together with a partner, widowed, divorced, separated, and never married.

Summary

Sen. Clinton appears to bring to the table a specific advantage among women and younger voters, and has more difficulty among married Americans, regardless of gender.

Survey Methods

Results are based on telephone interviews conducted in five separate surveys in 2003 and 2004, with national adults, aged 18 and older. The maximum margin of error for the data varies based on the sample sizes noted in the tables above. In addition to sampling error, question wording and practical difficulties in conducting surveys can introduce error or bias into the findings of public opinion polls.

February 25, 2005
PUBLIC: U.N. NOT DOING A GOOD JOB, BUT STILL NECESSARY
Six in 10 Americans say U.N. plays a necessary role in world affairs

by Jeffrey M. Jones, Gallup Poll Managing Editor and Joseph Carroll, Assistant Editor

A recent Gallup Poll shows the American public continuing to give the United Nations low marks for the way it has handled issues it has had to face, but still believing the United Nations has a role to play in world affairs. Americans' basic opinions of the United Nations are still as negative now as they were immediately before the Iraq war, even though ratings of individual countries opposed to the war have recovered since then. Still, 6 in 10 Americans say the United Nations plays a necessary role in the world today and two in three Americans believe it should play at least a major role in world affairs. Only 13% of Americans believe the United States should give up its U.N. membership.

These results are based on Gallup's annual World Affairs poll, conducted Feb. 7-10.

Thirty-six percent of Americans say the United Nations is doing a good job of trying to solve the problems it has had to face, while

United Nations Doing a Good Job or a Poor Job?

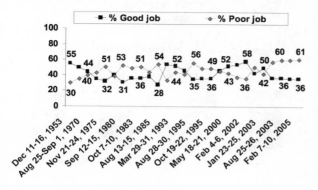

61% say it is doing a poor job. These views have remained about the same since just before the Iraq war.

Meanwhile, the poll shows that views of foreign nations such as France and Germany — which opposed military action in Iraq — have improved since then.

Over the years, opinion of the way in which the United Nations has handled its job has fluctuated in response to international events. At its most positive, though, only slightly more than half of Americans have given the United Nations positive evaluations. Gallup's first poll in which this question was asked, in 1953, showed that 55% said it was doing a good job; the highest was 58% a few months after the Sept. 11 terror attacks.

At a more basic level, 43% of Americans say they have an overall favorable view toward the United Nations, while 48% have an unfavorable view. That puts it on par with the way Americans rate the countries of Pakistan and China, for example.

Despite these generally negative evaluations, Americans believe the United Nations has its place in international matters. Sixty-four percent say the "United Nations plays a necessary role in the world today," while 34% say it does not. The percentage of Americans seeing the United Nations as necessary is down considerably from the last (and only other) time Gallup asked Americans this question. In 1997, 85% of Americans thought the United Nations played a necessary role.

When asked to assess the role the United Nations *should* play in world affairs, two in three Americans say it should play either a major role (47%) or a leading role (21%). Only 27% say it should play a minor role. These views have been fairly stable over the last several years.

The United States and United Nations have had their share of disagreements over the years — in addition to the Iraq war, the United States did not pay its U.N. member dues for several years in

the 1990s. However, relatively few Americans are willing to say that the United States should give up its membership — something some politicians have argued. Only 13% of Americans agree with that idea, while 85% disagree.

U.S. Give Up Its Membership in the U.N.?

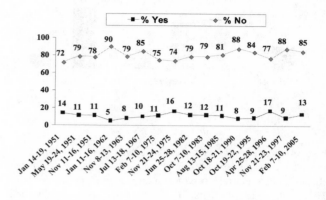

Party Affiliation Shapes Views of United Nations

Gallup consistently finds Republicans rating the United Nations less positively than do Democrats.

Democrats are twice as likely as Republicans are to say the United Nations is doing a good job in dealing with the issues it has had to face. The partisan gap has grown since war with Iraq became a possibility. From 2000 to early 2002, the gap between Democrats and Republicans averaged 15 percentage points. From late 2002 until the present, the gap has averaged 24 points.

United Nations Doing a Good Job or Poor Job?
by partisanship percentage saying "good job"
Selected Trend: 2000-2005

	Republicans %	Independents %	Democrats %
2005 Feb 7-10	22	37	48
2004 Feb 9-12	24	37	47
2003 Aug 25-26	23	39	47
2003 Mar 14-15	24	41	44
2003 Jan 23-25	36	50	65
2002 Oct 21-22	33	39	54
2002 Feb 4-6	53	56	65
2001 Feb 1-4	47	52	63
2000 May 18-21	41	54	59

Gallup also finds similar differences when asking Americans whether they have a favorable or unfavorable view of the United Nations. Only one in four Republicans say they have a favorable opinion, while 60% of Democrats rate the United Nations favorably.

Only a slight majority of Republicans (52%) say the United Nations plays a necessary role in world affairs, compared with 74% of Democrats. In 1997, when this question was last asked, Gallup found only slight partisan differences, with 81% of Republicans and 87% of Democrats saying the United Nations plays a necessary role.

Republicans and Democrats also differ in their views of the role the United Nations should play. Fifty-eight percent of Republicans say it should play a leading (16%) or major role (42%). That compares with 77% of Democrats (23% say it should play a leading role, 54% a major role).

Role the United Nations Should Play in World Affairs

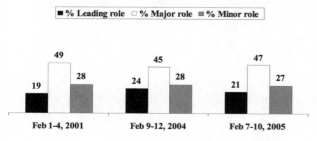

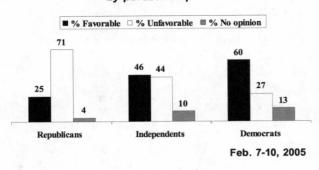

Favorable or Unfavorable Opinion of the United Nations?
by partisanship

Feb. 7-10, 2005

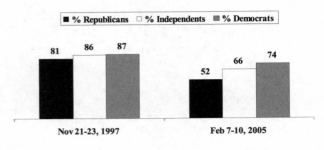

Does the U.N. Play a Necessary Role in World Affairs?
by partisanship
percentage saying "yes"

Survey Methods

These results are based on telephone interviews with a randomly selected national sample of 1,008 adults, aged 18 and older, conducted Feb. 7-10, 2005. For results based on this sample, one can say with 95% confidence that the maximum error attributable to sampling and other random effects is ±3 percentage points.

For results based on the 504 national adults in the Form A half-sample and 504 national adults in the Form B half-sample, the maximum margins of sampling error are ±5 percentage points.

In addition to sampling error, question wording and practical difficulties in conducting surveys can introduce error or bias into the findings of public opinion polls.

	Favorable %	Unfavorable %	Never heard of %	No opinion %
Catholics				
2005 Feb 25-27	93	4	*	3
2003 Oct 6-8	88	9	1	2
2002 Apr 29-May 1	78	17	1	4
Non-Catholics				
2005 Feb 25-27	73	14	2	11
2003 Oct 6-8	68	20	2	10
2002 Apr 29-May 1	57	28	2	12

*Less than 0.5%

Most Catholics, 64%, also think the pope rates as either a "great" world leader or "one of the greatest" world leaders in their lifetimes. Another 22% say he is "good," while just 13% think of him as either average (10%) or below average (3%).

Non-Catholics are not as positive, but still 35% say he is at least a "great" world leader, and another 33% say good. Just 20% say he is average and 5% say below average.

Thinking about some of the prominent world leaders during your lifetime, how do you think Pope John Paul II rates—as—one of the greatest, great, but not one of the greatest, good, average, or below average?

	One of the greatest %	Great, not one of the greatest %	Good %	Average %	Below average %	No opinion %
Catholics						
2005 Feb 25-27	38	26	22	10	3	1
Non-Catholics						
2005 Feb 25-27	17	18	33	20	5	7

Catholics have become more positive about the pope's positions on issues than they were in 1987 and again in 2003. Currently, a clear majority believes his positions are "about right," while 33% say his positions are too conservative. In October 2003, only 49% of Catholics said his positions were about right, and 38% said too conservative.

March 1, 2005

CATHOLICS DIVIDED ON POSSIBLE RESIGNATION OF POPE

62% of Catholics say pope's positions on issues are "about right"

by David W. Moore, Gallup Poll Senior Editor

In the wake of Pope John Paul II's continued sickness, a new CNN/*USA Today*/Gallup survey finds a slight majority of Catholics, 51%, saying the pope should remain in office until he dies, while 43% think he should resign now because of health reasons.

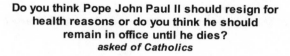

Do you think Pope John Paul II should resign for health reasons or do you think he should remain in office until he dies?
asked of Catholics

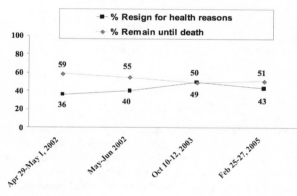

The pope is currently recovering from a throat operation, his second stay in the hospital this year. On Feb. 1 he was rushed to the hospital with breathing problems, but was let out 10 days later. He returned to the same hospital on Feb. 24. The pope has referred to this hospital as Vatican Three, because he has spent the most time there other than at the Vatican Palace and his summer retreat south of Rome.

Because of recurrent health problems, the question about the pope's possibly resigning has been asked of Catholics three times previous to this survey—twice in 2002 and once in 2003. In 2002, a clear majority said he should stay in office until death, while in 2003 Catholics were evenly divided.

Opinion of Pope John Paul II

Catholics have a highly positive view of the pope. Overall, 93% of Catholics say they have a favorable opinion, while just 4% say unfavorable. Even non-Catholics are mostly positive, by a 73% to 14% margin.

In your opinion, is Pope John Paul II too conservative in his position on issues, too liberal, or about right?
asked of Catholics

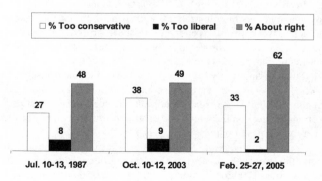

Not surprisingly, most Catholics say the selection of a new pope would matter to them—44% say a "great deal," and another 30% say a "moderate amount." Only a quarter of Catholics say it wouldn't matter much or at all to them who the next pope will be.

How much will it matter to you who the Catholic Church chooses as the next pope when the time comes to do so—a great deal, a moderate amount, not much, or not at all?

	Great deal %	Moderate amount %	Not much %	Not at all %	No opinion %
Catholics					
2005 Feb 25-27	44	30	17	8	1
Non-Catholics					
2005 Feb 25-27	7	16	34	41	2

Whom the Catholic Church chooses as its next pope matters a great deal or moderate amount to 23% of non-Catholics as well.

Survey Methods

Results in the current survey are based on telephone interviews with 1,008 national adults, aged 18 and older, conducted Feb. 25-27, 2005. For results based on the total sample of national adults, one can say with 95% confidence that the maximum margin of sampling error is ±3 percentage points. For results based on the sample of 241 Catholics, the maximum margin of sampling error is ±7 percentage points. For results based on the sample of 767 non-Catholics, the maximum margin of sampling error is ±4 percentage points. In addition to sampling error, question wording and practical difficulties in conducting surveys can introduce error or bias into the findings of public opinion polls.

March 1, 2005
MORE INCOME MEANS MORE TOYS
Upper-income Americans spend 213% more on recreation, entertainment

by Lydia Saad, Gallup Poll Senior Editor

What would you spend your money on if you suddenly had extra discretionary income at your disposal? According to a new Gallup economic measure, the answer is probably toys—or at least the adult equivalent of toys in the form of entertainment and recreation.

In a Feb. 21-24 survey*, Gallup asked Americans to estimate how much money their households will spend in the current month on each of four types of expenditures. Of these, groceries account for the most spending, followed by clothes purchases, then recreation and entertainment, and then dining out.

This ranking holds for upper- and lower-income households alike. However, upper-income Americans—those earning above the roughly $40,000 U.S. median household income level—spend proportionally more on recreation and entertainment than on any of the other three types of purchases.

Overall, the *median* dollar amount Americans say they will spend this month (February) for each type of expenditure is $300 for groceries, $100 for clothing, $100 for recreation and entertainment, and $75 for eating dinner out at restaurants. *Mean* spending values—the numeric average of all responses in each category—are substantially higher because of some big spenders at the upper margin. Gallup finds that Americans will spend an average of $361 per household this month on groceries, $222 will be spent on clothing, $176 on entertainment and recreation, and $116 on dining out.

	Mean (including zero)	Median
Groceries	$361	$300
Clothing	$222	$100
Entertainment	$176	$100
Eating dinner out	$116	$75

Discretionary Dollars Steered Toward Clothing and Entertainment

It is obvious that the higher one's income, the more money one has to spend. The sum of all four expenditures for households earning $40,000 or more (about half of all U.S. households) is about twice what those earning under $40,000 will spend: $1,158 vs. $554.

However, the data reveal that those in higher-income households plan to spend proportionally more money on some items than on others. Americans in upper-income households say they will spend less than double what those in lower-income households will spend on groceries ($433 vs. $277—or about 56% more). They will also spend about double (109% more) dining out. And they will spend much more than double on clothing (158% more) and on recreation/entertainment (213% more).

Mean Spending Estimate for February by Household Income Level

	Less than $40,000	$40,000+	Difference
Groceries	$277	$433	+56%
Dining out	$74	$155	+109%
Clothing	$120	$310	+158%
Recreation	$83	$260	+213%
Total	$554	$1,158	+109%

A Possible Forecasting Tool

Just how accurately can Americans predict their monthly spending in these categories? That's an important question in helping determine how well monthly changes in spending estimates might correspond with actual retail spending patterns. To get a gauge on accuracy, the survey included questions that asked respondents to indicate how accurate they felt their estimates were — "reasonably accurate" or "mainly a guess."

The responses vary, with respondents indicating that their estimate of dining out is the most accurate, followed by groceries and then entertainment/recreation. About half believe their estimate of clothing spending is accurate.

Is that estimate for what you will actually spend—[ROTATED: reasonably accurate (or is it) mainly a guess]?

	Reasonably accurate %	Mainly a guess %	No opinion %
Eating dinner out	71	27	2
Groceries	64	31	5
Entertainment/recreation	59	37	4
Clothing	51	44	5

Men and women have roughly equal confidence in the accuracy of their estimates in each category.

	Men %	Women %
Eating dinner out	75	66
Groceries	64	63
Entertainment/recreation	58	60
Clothing	49	53

Bottom Line

Consumer confidence data typically include questions tracking public perceptions of the national or local economy plus questions measuring Americans' confidence in their personal finances. However valuable these measures may be as indicators of overall economic mood, recent research has questioned the utility of these measures in predicting future economic activity. Gallup has an annual measure of Americans' Christmas holiday spending that has proven to be a remarkably reliable indicator of whether the retail holiday season is going to be a boom or a bust. The question, typically asked in mid-November, simply asks respondents to estimate how much money they will spend on Christmas presents that year.

Along the same lines, it is possible that the best way to know how much consumers will spend each month is to simply ask them. The four questions included in the mid-February survey ask about four expenditure categories that account for the bulk of Americans' discretionary spending—what they buy after their housing costs and other bills are paid. Time will tell, but questions that tap whether Americans feel flush enough to spring for filet mignon at the grocery store or are willing to pay for an extra night out at the movies could provide important information to supplement the prevailing measures of consumer confidence.

*Results are based on telephone interviews with 1,003 national adults, aged 18 and older, conducted Feb. 21-24, 2005. For results based on the total sample of national adults, one can say with 95% confidence that the margin of sampling error is ±3 percentage points.

For results based on the 519 national adults in the Form A half-sample and 484 national adults in the Form B half-sample, the maximum margins of sampling error are ±5 percentage points.

For results based on the sample of 626 adults employed full or part time or unemployed adults looking for work, the maximum margin of sampling error is ±4 percentage points.

In addition to sampling error, question wording and practical difficulties in conducting surveys can introduce error or bias into the findings of public opinion polls.

March 2, 2005
MAJORITY DISAPPROVAL FOR BUSH ON SOCIAL SECURITY
Overall approval rating steady at 52%

by Jeffrey M. Jones, Gallup Poll Managing Editor

George W. Bush's ratings for handling Social Security have dropped in recent weeks, and now a majority of Americans disapprove of the way he is handling that issue. Additionally, as debate on the Social Security system has intensified, Americans now perceive less urgency for reform: fewer say major changes are needed to the sys-

tem within the next two years than did so in January. The public is divided over whether the greater risk is to take a private investment approach to Social Security reform or rely on the current system to pay full benefits when workers retire. Bush's overall job approval rating is holding steady at 52%.

According to the Feb. 25-27 CNN/*USA Today*/Gallup poll, 35% of Americans approve and 56% disapprove of the way Bush is handling the issue of Social Security. That compares with a 43% approval rating immediately following the State of the Union address, in which Bush made the case for significant reforms to the system. So far this year, Bush has failed to gain majority public support for his approach to the Social Security issue.

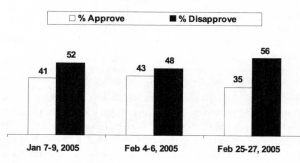

George W. Bush's Approval Ratings on Social Security

At this point, the poll finds Americans more inclined to say they trust the Democratic Party (47%) than the Republican Party (37%) when it comes to handling the issue of Social Security retirement benefits.

Americans now show a diminished sense of urgency to reform the Social Security system when compared to earlier this year. A Jan. 7-9 poll found just under half of Americans, 49%, saying that "the federal government should make major changes in the Social Security system" in the next year or two "to ensure its long-term future." Thirty-nine percent said the federal government should make major changes within the next 10 years, and only 9% said major changes were not needed within the next 10 years. Now, 38% say action needs to be taken in the short term, 37% in the longer term, and 22% say not at all.

This change may be due to the fact that the Social Security issue has come into sharper focus nationally. As a result, it has become

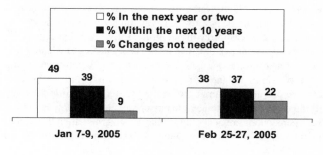

Do you think the federal government should make major changes in the Social Security system to ensure its long-term future — in the next year or two, within the next 10 years, or do you think major changes are not needed within the next 10 years?

more partisan in nature, with Bush and the Republicans tending to favor a more aggressive approach to reform while the Democrats favor a more measured approach. Americans today tend to see the issue in Republican and Democratic terms, and adopt a position more in line with that of their preferred party. In fact, the data show most of the change regarding the urgency for more immediate reform coming among Democrats.

Perceived Need for Major Changes to Social Security System, by Party Identification

	Jan 7-9			Feb 25-27		
	Dem %	Ind %	Rep %	Dem %	Ind %	Rep %
Changes needed in 1-2 years	53	48	45	33	41	40
Changes needed within 10 years	35	39	45	31	32	47
Changes not needed within next 10 years	11	8	8	34	23	9

In January, a majority of Democrats, 53%, said major changes were needed in the next two years and only 11% said they were not needed within the next 10 years. Now, Democrats are three times more likely to say major changes are not needed in the next 10 years (34%) and significantly less likely to believe major changes are needed during this session of Congress (33%). Independents are also now more likely to believe no major changes are needed (23%) than they were in January (8%). Republicans' views have changed relatively little in the last two months.

Shifting opinions on the perceived need for changes to the Social Security system are also apparent by age. Americans aged 50 and older are much less likely now than in January to favor major changes in the next two years. In January, the plurality of members of this age group said such changes were needed in the next two years and only 13% said major changes were not needed in the next 10 years. Now, 29% say major changes are not needed and only 27% believe changes are needed in the next two years.

Perceived Need for Major Changes to Social Security System, by Age

	Jan 7-9		Feb 25-27	
	18-49 %	50+ %	18-49 %	50+ %
Changes needed in 1-2 years	53	45	45	27
Changes needed within 10 years	40	38	36	40
Changes not needed within next 10 years	7	13	16	29

Clearly, the private investment approach to reforming Social Security—long championed by Bush—entails risks. While that approach holds out the promise of paying higher benefits when workers retire, it also could result in significantly lower benefits if the investments do not pan out. The public is divided as to whether that risk is greater for the average worker than the risk involved in relying on the system to pay the current level of benefits. Forty-six percent perceive private investment to be the greater risk, while 50% say relying on the system to pay the current level of benefits is riskier. These perceptions are generally similar by subgroup, though Democrats tend to see private investment as riskier and Republicans are

more likely to believe that relying on the current system to pay benefits is the more risky approach.

Bush's Ratings

Social Security is the issue on which Bush receives the lowest ratings of the five tested in the poll. Sixty percent approve of the way he is handling terrorism, and half give him passing marks on foreign affairs. This last figure is unchanged following Bush's European trip last week.

The public is divided on Bush's handling of the economy, with 48% approving and 49% disapproving. And Americans disapprove rather than approve of Bush's handling of Iraq by a 53% to 45% margin.

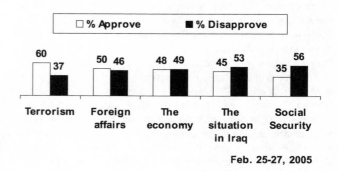

George W. Bush's Approval Ratings on Issues

Feb. 25-27, 2005

Bush's overall job approval rating of 52% is right in line with the most recent measurements (49% in a Feb. 7-10 poll and 51% in a Feb. 21-24 poll), after showing a temporary increase to 57% immediately following the State of the Union address and the Iraqi elections.

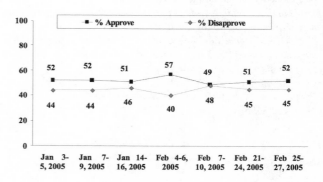

George W. Bush's Job Approval Ratings

In fact, aside from that recent 57% rating and a slightly higher rating in November following his re-election victory, Bush's approval rating has hovered around the 50% mark since January 2004.

Survey Methods

These results are based on telephone interviews with a randomly selected national sample of 1,008 adults, aged 18 and older, conducted Feb. 25-27, 2005. For results based on this sample, one can say with 95% confidence that the maximum error attributable to sampling and other random effects is ±3 percentage points. For results based on the 526 national adults in the Form A half-sample and 482 national adults in the Form B half-sample, the maximum margins of sampling error are ±5 percentage points. In addition to sampling error, question wording and practical difficulties in conducting surveys can introduce error or bias into the findings of public opinion polls.

March 3, 2005
AMERICANS REMAIN DIVIDED OVER IRAQ WAR
Slightly less than half say it was a mistake to send U.S. troops

by Frank Newport, Gallup Poll Editor in Chief

The war in Iraq continues to dominate domestic and international news coverage, and remains at the forefront of public concern in the United States. Gallup's February update on Americans' perceptions of the most important problem facing the country found that 24% of Americans mentioned the situation in Iraq—the largest specific problem response given in the survey.

There are two major questions that can be asked about public opinion on Iraq. First, what is the level of support for the decision to invade Iraq and depose Saddam Hussein? Second, what do Americans think about the situation in Iraq looking ahead?

Mistake to Send Troops to Iraq?

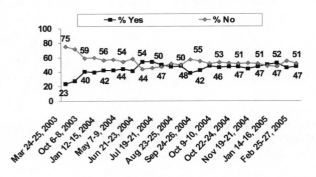

Mistake to Get Involved in War?

The most recent CNN/*USA Today*/Gallup poll, conducted Feb. 25-27, shows that 47% of Americans think that it was a mistake for the United States to send troops to Iraq, while 51% say that it was not.

Gallup first asked this "mistake" question in August 1950—shortly after America became immersed in the Korean War. Gallup asked Americans if they believed the United States "made a mistake in deciding to defend Korea, or not?" Gallup tracked responses to that question through January 1953, and then picked up the sequence in regards to the Vietnam War beginning in August 1965. More recently, Gallup asked the mistake question 26 separate times in relation to U.S. military involvement in the first Persian Gulf War in 1990 and 1991, and again asked the question about U.S. military involvement in Yugoslavia in 1999 and in Afghanistan following the Sept. 11 terrorist attacks.

Gallup began using the mistake question in regards to U.S. military involvement in Iraq in March 2003, and Gallup has tracked responses to that question 24 times in the two years since.

The pattern of responses to the mistake question has not been consistent or linear in direction. Only three times (mid-summer 2004 and twice in January 2005) has a majority of Americans agreed that sending U.S. troops to Iraq was a mistake. But most recent surveys show that opinion on the war remains quite divided, with the percent of Americans saying military action was a mistake hovering just under 50% in several recent surveys. It is perhaps most reasonable to conclude that the Iraq war still divides the country, with no strong consensus having developed that sending troops to Iraq either was or was not a mistake.

The public's perception of the situation in Iraq started out quite positively, reflecting the initial news coverage of the successful completion of the war effort's primary objective: the deposition of Hussein. Only a quarter of Americans in late March 2003—just a few weeks after the war began—thought that the effort was a mistake. Similar perceptions persisted through the summer of 2003 (for example, only 27% of Americans said sending troops to Iraq was a mistake in July 2003). By the fall of 2003, however, the mistake percentage was up to 40%, and it crept above 50% by June and July 2004. This increase was fueled in part by the criticism about the war from Democrats during the presidential race, and in part by developments in Iraq itself, including the publicity surrounding the Abu Ghraib prison scandal.

These more negative assessments were short-lived, however. In late August and early September, the Republican National Convention provided a more positive interpretation of the war on terrorism and the war in Iraq, and in the first Gallup poll that asked about Iraq following that convention, the mistake percentage decreased to 38%.

Since that time there has been some fluctuation in the public's views of the war, with an uptick (to 52%) in the mistake percentage at the beginning of this year, a drop (to 45%) in early February (following the Iraqi elections at the end of January), and now a slight rise (to 47%) in Gallup's most recent survey.

The war in Iraq has been highly associated with George W. Bush and his personal convictions that the war be fought. It is therefore no surprise to find that vast differences continue in the way Americans look at the war based on their political orientations.

Mistake to Send Troops to Iraq?
by party affiliations

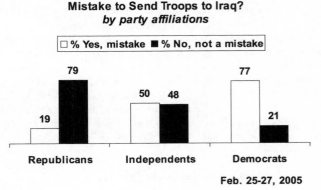

Feb. 25-27, 2005

Very few Republicans say that sending U.S. troops to Iraq was a mistake, while relatively few Democrats say that it was *not* a mistake.

One of the reasons why more Americans do not agree that sending troops to Iraq was the right thing to do is almost certainly because they don't think that U.S. efforts in Iraq have been successful.

Only 43% of Americans say that the United States and its allies are winning the war in Iraq. And although very few say that the

Who Is Winning the War in Iraq?

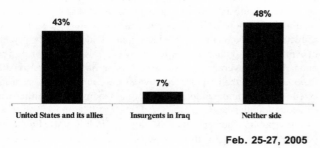

Feb. 25-27, 2005

**George W. Bush's Approval on Iraq
January 2004 – February 2005**

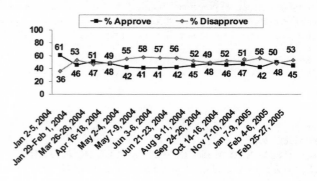

insurgents in Iraq are winning, about half say that neither side is winning the war.

Looking Ahead

What is the future of U.S. military involvement in Iraq? Most Americans are quite pessimistic when asked to estimate how long they think it will be necessary to keep a significant number of U.S. troops in Iraq.

Just your best guess, how much longer do you think the U.S. will have a significant number of troops in Iraq—less than a year, one to two years, three to five years, six to 10 years, or longer than 10 years?

	Less than a year %	One to two years %	Three to five years %	Six to 10 years %	Longer than that %	No opinion %
2005 Feb 25-27	4	29	42	13	9	3
2004 Jun 21-23	8	28	40	14	9	1

Only one-third of Americans believe that it will be necessary to keep a significant number of U.S. troops in Iraq for only another year or two (or less). A majority of Americans say that troops will be in Iraq for three years or more, including one out of five Americans who say that troops will be in Iraq for six years or longer.

Despite the relatively successful Iraqi elections in late January, these sentiments have not changed significantly from when Gallup last asked this question in June 2004.

Americans who believe that the war in Iraq was a mistake are more likely than those who believe it wasn't a mistake to perceive that it will be necessary to keep troops in Iraq for a long time. But even a majority of those who say that the war was not a mistake believe that a significant number of troops will be in Iraq for three years or more.

Bush's Handling of the Situation in Iraq

Not surprisingly, given the public's mixed sentiments on Iraq, public opinion of President Bush's handling of the situation in Iraq also varies.

Forty-five percent of Americans currently approve of the president's handling of Iraq, while a slight majority, 53%, disapprove. This is not the low point for Bush on this measure, but it is at the lower end of the range of his Iraq approval ratings over the last two years.

Bush received his lowest Iraq approval rating, 41%, in June 2004, roughly coinciding with an increase in the percentage of Americans

who thought that sending troops to Iraq was a mistake. Bush's highest marks on Iraq came in the months after the war began in the spring of 2003, reaching a 76% approval rating in April of that year. Bush also scored relatively well on his handling of the situation in Iraq in early January of last year—shortly after the capture of Hussein.

Survey Methods

These results are based on telephone interviews with a randomly selected national sample of 1,008 national adults, aged 18 and older, conducted Feb. 25-27, 2005. For results based on this sample, one can say with 95% confidence that the maximum error attributable to sampling and other random effects is ±3 percentage points. In addition to sampling error, question wording and practical difficulties in conducting surveys can introduce error or bias into the findings of public opinion polls.

March 7, 2005
MAJORITY OF AMERICANS SAY CHARGES AGAINST MICHAEL JACKSON ARE TRUE
Blacks divided on Jackson's guilt

by Joseph Carroll, Gallup Poll Assistant Editor

As the second week of Michael Jackson's child molestation trial begins today, a recent CNN/*USA Today*/Gallup poll shows that a majority of Americans say the charges against him are true. A majority of Americans also say that Jackson will receive a fair trial. Blacks and whites differ in their views of Jackson's guilt or innocence, with most whites saying the charges against Jackson are true, while blacks are divided on the issue.

The poll was conducted Feb. 25-27, on the eve of the trial, and shows 75% of Americans saying the charges that Jackson sexually abused a boy are definitely (22%) or probably (53%) true. Only 16% believe the charges are untrue, and 9% have no opinion. An early February poll found 69% of Americans believing the charges to be true and 19% taking the opposite view.

Gallup asked two similar versions of this question in late 2003 and early 2004. In early December 2003, after Jackson's initial arrest in this matter, 62% said the allegations were true. This sentiment dipped to 54% in mid-December, probably due to the fact that the authorities had not yet formally charged Jackson when the poll was

Do you personally believe the charges that Michael Jackson sexually abused a boy are definitely true, probably true, probably not true, or definitely not true?

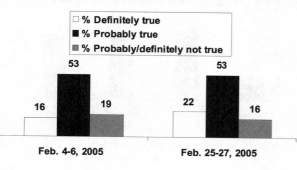

□ % Definitely true
■ % Probably true
▨ % Probably/definitely not true

Feb. 4-6, 2005
Feb. 25-27, 2005

Do you think Michael Jackson will — or will not — receive a fair trial?

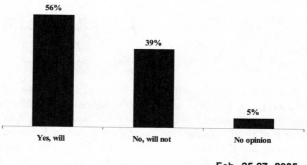

Feb. 25-27, 2005

conducted. By late January/early February 2004, two in three respondents, 67%, said the allegations were true.

Whites, Blacks Differ in Their Views of Jackson's Guilt

In order to better examine the views of whites and blacks in this matter, Gallup combined the results of its Feb. 4-6, 2005, and Feb. 25-27, 2005, polls. The results show that the vast majority of non-Hispanic whites, 75%, say the charges against Jackson are definitely (19%) or probably (56%) true. Only 14% say they are not true. Blacks are more divided in their views of Jackson's guilt, with 51% saying the charges are true, and 42% saying they are not true.

Charges Against Michael Jackson True or Not True?
by racial groups

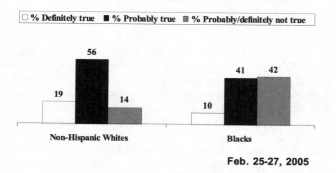

□ % Definitely true   ■ % Probably true   ▨ % Probably/definitely not true

Non-Hispanic Whites
Blacks

Feb. 25-27, 2005

The opinions of blacks were quite different immediately following Jackson's arrest in 2003. At that time, nearly two in three blacks said the allegations against Jackson were untrue. Roughly two in three whites at the time said they were true.

Fair Trial for Jackson?

Whenever a case attracts a lot of media attention, questions are raised as to whether the defendant will get a fair trial—since prospective jurors may have been exposed to speculation about the person's guilt or innocence before hearing the full range of evidence in court. Americans, however, are not overly concerned about this—56% say Jackson will get a fair trial; 39% say he will not.

Nonwhites are more skeptical that Jackson will receive a fair trial. The poll shows that 59% of non-Hispanic whites say Jackson will get a fair trial, compared with only 45% of nonwhites. (These results are based on the sample of all nonwhites because the sam-

ple size of blacks is too small to report reliably on the "fair trial" question.)

The data also show some differences by age. Thirty-eight percent of adults aged 18 to 29 say Jackson will get a fair trial, compared with 54% of 30- to 49-year-olds and 64% of adults aged 50 and older.

The O.J. Simpson Case

This is not the first highly publicized court case that Gallup has tracked in recent years. In 1994 and 1995, Gallup repeatedly asked Americans whether the charges that O.J. Simpson murdered his ex-wife, Nicole Brown Simpson, and her friend, Ronald Goldman, were true.

In early February 1995, just after the Simpson trial had begun, Gallup found that roughly two in three Americans said the charges against Simpson were true—a slightly lower percentage than Gallup currently finds for Jackson.

Throughout the 36 weeks of the trial, the percentage of Americans saying the charges against Simpson were true ranged from 61% to 75%. In June 2004, on the 10th anniversary of the deaths of Nicole Brown Simpson and Goldman, Gallup found that 78% of Americans still believed that O.J. Simpson committed the murders.

Do you personally believe the charges that O.J. Simpson murdered Nicole Brown Simpson and Ronald Goldman are definitely true, probably true, probably not true, or definitely not true?

	Definitely true %	Probably true %	Definitely/ Probably true %	Definitely/ Probably not true %
2004 Jun 3-6	35	43	78	16
1999 Feb 26-28	35	38	73	21
1996 Dec 9-11	36	38	74	18
1996 Apr/May	35	40	75	20
1995 Oct 19-22	30	40	70	22
1995 Oct 5-7	30	37	67	25
1995 Sep 29-30	30	33	63	23
1995 Aug 28-30	30	37	67	23
1995 Jul 20-23	29	40	69	21
1995 Jul 7-9	34	39	73	19
1995 Jun 5-6	33	42	75	17
1995 Apr 17-19	24	41	65	22
1995 Mar 17-19	17	44	61	24
1995 Feb 3-5	20	45	65	22
1995 Jan 16-18	24	46	70	19
1994 Oct 7-9	14	48	62	21

	Definitely true %	Probably true %	Definitely/ Probably true %	Definitely/ Probably not true %
1994 Sep 18, 20	14	47	61	20
1994 Jul 15-17	16	51	67	20
1994 Jul 1-3	12	50	62	21
1994 Jun 22	10	56	66	16

There is an interesting difference between the Jackson case and the Simpson case: blacks are more likely to say Jackson is guilty at this early stage of the trial than they were to say Simpson was guilty at the start of his trial. As the Simpson trial got underway, the majority of blacks said the charges against Simpson were *not* true, while roughly a quarter of blacks said the charges were true. About one in five blacks were unsure of Simpson's guilt at the time.

Survey Methods

Results in the current survey are based on telephone interviews with 1,008 national adults, aged 18 and older, conducted Feb. 25-27, 2005. For results based on the total sample of national adults, one can say with 95% confidence that the maximum margin of sampling error is ±3 percentage points.

For results based on the sample of 1,674 non-Hispanic whites, in polls conducted Feb. 4-6, 2005, and Feb. 25-27, 2005, the maximum margin of sampling error is ±3 percentage points.

For results based on the sample of 144 blacks, in polls conducted Feb. 4-6, 2005, and Feb. 25-27, 2005, the maximum margin of sampling error is ±9 percentage points.

In addition to sampling error, question wording and practical difficulties in conducting surveys can introduce error or bias into the findings of public opinion polls.

March 8, 2005
MORALITY METER: AMERICANS DISSATISFIED WITH ETHICAL CLIMATE
Satisfaction with moral conditions declines with age

by Linda Lyons, Education and Youth Editor

The moral and ethical climate in the United States is uncomfortable for many Americans. Fifty-nine percent of Americans are somewhat (29%) or very (30%) dissatisfied with the United States' moral and ethical climate, according to Gallup's annual Mood of the Nation poll*. Four in 10 Americans are very (7%) or somewhat (33%) satisfied.

What springs to mind when Gallup asks Americans to assess the nation's "moral and ethical climate"? In follow-up interviews with some of the poll's respondents, the answers are diverse. Sexual and violent content in television and movies, prejudice, the economy, environmental waste, plagiarism in schools, corporate scandals, gay rights, and divorce are just a few of the topics that people associate with the moral and ethical climate in America.

Younger Americans Most Satisfied With Moral and Ethical Climate

The poll finds a gap in the way Americans of different ages assess moral conditions in the United States. Nearly half (47%) of the

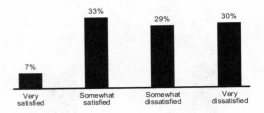

Current Satisfaction With Moral and Ethical Climate

Next, I'm going to read some aspects of life in America today. For each one, please say whether you are very satisfied, somewhat satisfied, somewhat dissatisfied, or very dissatisfied... the moral and ethical climate.

youngest adults, those aged 18 to 29, are satisfied with the moral and ethical climate in America, but satisfaction diminishes progressively with age, as it has since Gallup began asking the question in 2001. Only a third (32%) of adults aged 65 and older are satisfied.

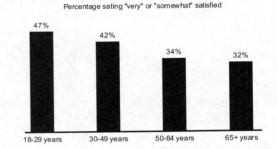

Satisfaction With Moral and Ethical Climate by Age

Next, I'm going to read some aspects of life in America today. For each one, please say whether you are very satisfied, somewhat satisfied, somewhat dissatisfied, or very dissatisfied... the moral and ethical climate.

Percentage sating "very" or "somewhat" satisfied

When explaining why he is "somewhat satisfied" with the moral and ethical climate in America today, an 18-year-old from Texas says, "Although I still think there is a lot more work to be done, I'm encouraged that the government has started to crack down on unethical business practices. And I am also glad Americans are beginning to accept gays as equals."

Contrast that relatively optimistic attitude with that of a 58-year-old man from Florida who is "very dissatisfied" with America's moral and ethical climate. "Corporations are not accountable for their actions; the bankruptcy laws are too lenient; too many credit cards are offered to people who can't afford to get into debt. It seems the more money you have, the more you can get away with in this country," he says. "No one's trying to help the average American anymore."

No Partisan Gap?

The November 2004 presidential election exit polls showed that among Americans who selected "moral values" as the top reason for their vote (22% of all voters), 80% voted Republican and just 18% voted Democratic (see "Moral Values Important in the 2004 Exit Polls" in Related Items). So it may surprise some that Republicans and Democrats are equally satisfied with the moral and ethical climate in America.

That wasn't always the case. In 2001, the gap between the two political parties was significant, with Democrats more satisfied than Republicans with morals and ethics in America. In 2001, 42% of Democrats were satisfied with the moral and ethical climate, compared with 31% of Republicans. That gap has narrowed each year

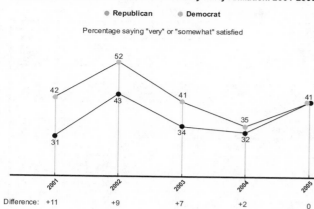

Satisfaction With Moral and Ethical Climate by Party Affiliation: 2001-2005

Republican   Democrat

Percentage saying "very" or "somewhat" satisfied

	2001	2002	2003	2004	2005
Republican	42	52	41	35	41
Democrat	31	43	34	32	41

Difference: +11   +9   +7   +2   0

and the latest survey shows 41% of both Republicans and Democrats are satisfied.

It is unclear why the gap between Republicans and Democrats has narrowed, and whether the current leadership in the White House has anything to do with it. Among the 7% of Americans who say they are "very satisfied" is a 63-year-old Republican from New Jersey. "I am so grateful to have a president who stands morally and ethically tall, and who shows the kind of leadership that we didn't always have in the past administration," she says. "Of course not everything is perfect in this country, but having moral leadership we can believe in sets the tone for the rest of us." A "very dissatisfied" 58-year-old Florida Democrat says his distress over the current Republican administration is probably driving his views.

Bottom Line

Opinion polls measure a complex set of attitudes based on individual experience. For instance, a 37-year-old black respondent from Florida who is "somewhat dissatisfied" with the moral and ethical climate is most concerned with the negative images of blacks on television, in the movies, and videos. "To me, that's immoral and unethical," the respondent says.

It's difficult to generalize about the diverse and often-personal reasons for Americans' assessments of something like moral climate—but that doesn't make the aggregation of those views any less important. Americans have plenty of different reasons underpinning their views of the state of morality in the United States. Regardless of those underpinnings, Americans continue to be more dissatisfied than satisfied.

Results are based on telephone interviews with 1,005 national adults, aged 18 and older, conducted Jan. 3-5, 2005. For results based on the total sample of national adults, one can say with 95% confidence that the maximum margin of sampling error is ±3 percentage points.

**Results are based on telephone interviews with 1,016 national adults, aged 18 and older, conducted Nov. 7-10, 2004. For results based on the total sample of national adults, one can say with 95% confidence that the maximum margin of sampling error is ±3 percentage points.

March 8, 2005
AMERICANS' FINANCIAL WOES
Healthcare costs become a greater concern as Americans age

by Joseph Carroll, Gallup Poll Assistant Editor

Over the past two months, Gallup has been asking Americans to name "the most important financial problem facing your family today." Overall, the top financial problems facing American families today include healthcare costs and lack of money or low wages. Americans also mention the level of debt, unemployment, college expenses, retirement savings, and the high cost of living or inflation.

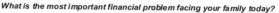

What is the most important financial problem facing your family today?

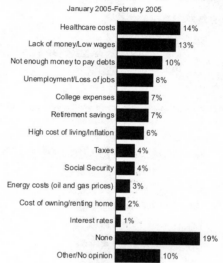

January 2005-February 2005

Healthcare costs	14%
Lack of money/Low wages	13%
Not enough money to pay debts	10%
Unemployment/Loss of jobs	8%
College expenses	7%
Retirement savings	7%
High cost of living/Inflation	6%
Taxes	4%
Social Security	4%
Energy costs (oil and gas prices)	3%
Cost of owning/renting home	2%
Interest rates	1%
None	19%
Other/No opinion	10%

However, aggregated results from surveys in January and February reveal that not all American families have the same financial problems—there are some interesting differences among different groups of people.

Money, Wages Top Problem for Blacks, Health Costs for Whites

Money, wages, paying off debt, and healthcare costs are the important financial problems for both whites and blacks, but blacks are much more likely than whites to mention lack of money or low wages as the top problem.

One in four blacks (26%) say lack of money or low wages is the most important financial problem facing their families today. Not having enough money to pay debts, at 18%, and healthcare costs, at 10%, follow.

Among whites, healthcare costs top the list (at 15%), followed by lack of money or wages (11%), debt (9%), unemployment (8%), and college expenses (8%).

College, Debt Top Problem for Younger Americans, Health Costs for Older Americans

Healthcare costs become a greater concern to Americans as they age. Younger adults mention paying for college and paying off debts most frequently.

- **18- to 29-year-olds**. The top financial problems for younger Americans include not having enough money to pay debts

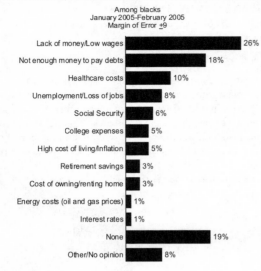

Among blacks
January 2005-February 2005
Margin of Error ±9

Lack of money/Low wages	26%
Not enough money to pay debts	18%
Healthcare costs	10%
Unemployment/Loss of jobs	8%
Social Security	6%
College expenses	5%
High cost of living/Inflation	5%
Retirement savings	3%
Cost of owning/renting home	3%
Energy costs (oil and gas prices)	1%
Interest rates	1%
None	19%
Other/No opinion	8%

What is the most important financial problem facing your family today?

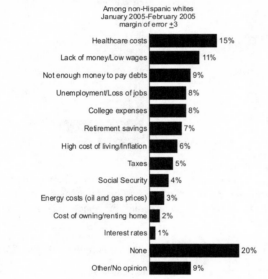

Among non-Hispanic whites
January 2005-February 2005
margin of error ±3

Healthcare costs	15%
Lack of money/Low wages	11%
Not enough money to pay debts	9%
Unemployment/Loss of jobs	8%
College expenses	8%
Retirement savings	7%
High cost of living/Inflation	6%
Taxes	5%
Social Security	4%
Energy costs (oil and gas prices)	3%
Cost of owning/renting home	2%
Interest rates	1%
None	20%
Other/No opinion	9%

Most Important Financial Problem by Age
January-February 2005

	18- to 29-year-olds	30- to 49-year-olds	50- to 64-year-olds	65 years and older
Not enough money to pay debts	14%	13%	7%	4%
Lack of money/Low wages	13%	14%	14%	9%
Unemployment/Loss of jobs	10%	8%	8%	5%
College expenses	10%	10%	6%	1%
Healthcare costs	8%	13%	19%	18%
High cost of living/Inflation	6%	7%	5%	6%
Taxes	4%	5%	5%	3%
Cost of owning/renting a home	4%	2%	2%	2%
Social Security	3%	2%	4%	9%
Energy costs (oil and gas prices)	3%	4%	3%	2%
Retirement savings	1%	7%	12%	5%
Interest rates	1%	1%	2%	2%
None	19%	14%	18%	32%
Other/No opinion	14%	10%	6%	8%

Day-to-Day Expenses Problem for Lower-Income Households

Household income affects views on the top financial problem facing Americans today. Higher-income households are slightly more likely than lower-income households to mention college expenses and retirement savings, while lower-income households more frequently mention lack of money or low wages and healthcare costs.

- Those earning less than $30,000 per year are most likely to say lack of money and low wages is the top financial problem, mentioned by 21% of respondents, followed by healthcare costs (16%), unemployment (13%), and paying off debts (11%).
- For households earning between $30,000 and $50,000 per year, healthcare costs (14%), lack of money (14%), and paying off debts (13%) are the salient issues.
- The most important financial problems for those earning between $50,000 and $75,000 per year are essentially the same as those earning between $75,000 and $100,000 per year: healthcare costs, college expenses, lack of money or low wages, paying off debts, and retirement savings.
- Among those earning between $75,000 and $100,000 per year, the top problems are healthcare costs (19%), college expenses (12%), retirement savings (9%), money or wages (9%), and not having enough money to pay off debts (9%).
- College expenses (15%), retirement savings (12%), and healthcare costs (9%) are the most important financial problems for those earning $100,000 per year or more.

Democrats More Likely Than Republicans to Say Money, Wages, Unemployment

The data show some slight variations by partisanship, with Democrats more likely than Republicans to say lack of money and unemployment are the top financial problems and Republicans more likely to not name any financial problems. These differences may result from Republicans being generally more likely to live in higher-income households than Democrats.

(14%), lacking money or having low wages (13%), being unemployed (10%), and paying for college (10%).
- **30- to 49-year-olds**. Among Americans in this age group, money and wages (14%), paying off debts (13%), healthcare costs (13%), and college expenses (10%) are top problems.
- **50- to 64-year-olds**. Healthcare costs, at 19%, are the top financial problem for Americans aged 50 to 64, followed by money and wages (14%) and retirement savings (12%). More Americans in this age group mention retirement savings as the top financial problem than in any other age group.
- **65 years and older**. The most important financial problem for older Americans is healthcare costs, mentioned by 18% of respondents aged 65 and older. Lack of money and Social Security follow, each mentioned by 9% of Americans in this age group. Those aged 65 and older more often cite Social Security as the top problem than do younger Americans. They also are the most likely age group to not mention any problem.

Most Important Financial Problem by Household Income

January-February 2005

	Less than $30,000	$30,000-$49,999	$50,000-$74,999	$75,000-$99,999	$100,000 per year or more
Lack of money/Low wages	21%	14%	11%	9%	3%
Healthcare costs	16%	14%	17%	19%	9%
Unemployment/Loss of jobs	13%	7%	4%	5%	7%
Not enough money to pay debts	11%	13%	9%	9%	5%
High cost of living/Inflation	8%	5%	7%	6%	4%
Social Security	6%	3%	1%	3%	3%
College expenses	4%	5%	11%	12%	15%
Energy costs (oil and gas prices)	4%	3%	3%	2%	3%
Cost of owning/renting a home	3%	3%	3%	2%	2%
Retirement savings	2%	8%	8%	9%	12%
Taxes	2%	2%	4%	5%	7%
Interest rates	*	2%	1%	2%	1%
None	13%	20%	22%	16%	24%
Other/No opinion	8%	11%	8%	8%	9%

*Less than 0.5%

Among Republicans, the most important financial problems are healthcare costs (13%), college expenses (10%), money and wages (9%), and paying off debts (9%). Twenty-three percent of Republicans do not name any top financial problem in their families, compared with 20% of independents and 15% of Democrats.

Healthcare costs, lack of money and low wages, paying off debts, and unemployment are the top financial problems facing Democrats' families. Fourteen percent of Democrats say the top problem is lack of money and wages, while only 9% of Republicans mention this. Democrats are just slightly more likely than Republicans to say unemployment is the top problem, by a four-point margin.

Independents most frequently mention healthcare costs, lack of money or low wages, and paying down debts as their families' top financial problems.

Most Important Financial Problem by Party Affiliation

January-February 2005

	Republicans	Independents	Democrats
Healthcare costs	13%	16%	15%
Lack of money/Low wages	9%	15%	14%
Not enough money to pay debts	9%	10%	11%
Unemployment/Loss of jobs	6%	8%	10%
Retirement savings	7%	7%	7%
High cost of living/Inflation	5%	6%	7%
College expenses	10%	5%	7%
Social Security	2%	4%	4%
Energy costs (oil and gas prices)	2%	3%	4%
Taxes	6%	3%	3%
Cost of owning/renting a home	2%	3%	2%
Interest rates	1%	1%	2%
None	23%	20%	15%
Other/No opinion	10%	8%	9%

Few Differences Between Men and Women

The results show few differences by gender; the most important financial problems for both groups are healthcare costs, lack of money, and paying off debts.

Most Important Financial Problem by Gender

January-February 2005

	Men	Women
Healthcare costs	14%	15%
Lack of money/low wages	12%	13%
Not enough money to pay debts	10%	10%
Unemployment/loss of jobs	7%	8%
College expenses	6%	9%
Retirement savings	7%	7%
High cost of living/inflation	7%	5%
Taxes	6%	3%
Social Security	4%	3%
Energy costs (oil and gas prices)	3%	3%
Cost of owning/renting a home	2%	3%
Interest rates	1%	1%
None	21%	18%
Other/no opinion	10%	9%

These results are based on telephone interviews with a randomly selected national sample of 2,008 adults, aged 18 and older, conducted Jan. 17-19, 2005, and Feb. 25-27, 2005. For results based on this sample, one can say with 95% confidence that the maximum error attributable to sampling and other random effects is ±3 percentage points.

In addition to sampling error, question wording and practical difficulties in conducting surveys can introduce error or bias into the findings of public opinion polls.

March 10, 2005

PUBLIC BELIEVES MEN, WOMEN HAVE EQUAL ABILITIES IN MATH, SCIENCE
Nearly 7 in 10 say genders are equal in this respect

by Jeffrey M. Jones, Gallup Poll Managing Editor

Harvard University President Lawrence Summers sparked a controversy with his widely reported comments in January on why there are fewer women than men in math and science professions. He raised the possibility that biological differences or differences in personal choices between men and women could be more important than either early socialization or some form of gender discrimination. Debate soon ensued as to whether men really are better than women at math and science, and if so, the reasons why.

A recent CNN/*USA Today/*Gallup poll found that a significant majority of Americans disagree with the assumption that men are better than women at math and science, saying the two genders are about the same in this regard. However, about one in five Americans are willing to say that men are superior to women in math and science, although this group is divided as to whether that is due more to innate differences or more to societal influences.

Gender Differences in Math and Science

The Feb. 25-27 poll finds 68% of Americans saying men and women are about the same when it comes to their math and science abilities. Slightly more than one-fifth of Americans, 21%, believe men are superior in these areas, while 8% think women are superior.

Which comes closest to your view — men are better at math and science than women, men and women are about the same, or women are better at math and science than men?

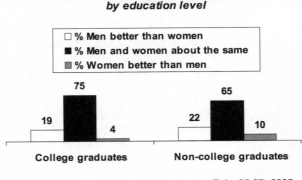

Feb. 25-27, 2005

Majorities in all key demographic subgroups of the population believe that parity exists between the genders in terms of their math and science abilities. Perhaps most importantly, the data show that men and women have nearly identical views—most members of both groups say the genders are equal, and similar proportions of men and women who perceive differences say men are better. Sixty-eight percent of men believe the genders are equal, 19% say men are better, and 9% say women are better, while 68% of women believe abilities are equal, 23% say men are better, and 8% believe women are better.

Some opinion differences are apparent by education and political views.

College graduates (75%) are more likely than non-college graduates (65%) to believe the genders are equal in their math and science abilities. Non-college graduates believe men are better than women by a 22% to 10% margin, while among college graduates the margin is slightly larger—19% say men are better and 4% women.

Men vs. Women at Math and Science by education level

☐ % Men better than women
■ % Men and women about the same
■ % Women better than men

College graduates: 19, 75, 4
Non-college graduates: 22, 65, 10

Feb. 25-27, 2005

Democrats (71%) and independents (72%) are more likely than Republicans (61%) to believe the genders have comparable abilities in math and science. Republicans are nearly five times more likely to say men are better (29%) than to say women are better (6%), while Democrats are about as likely to say men are better (16%) as to say women are better (12%). Independents fall in between, with 18% saying men are better and 8% women.

Men vs. Women at Math and Science by party affiliation

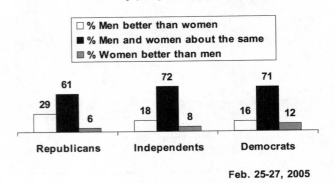

☐ % Men better than women
■ % Men and women about the same
■ % Women better than men

Republicans: 29, 61, 6
Independents: 18, 72, 8
Democrats: 16, 71, 12

Feb. 25-27, 2005

Why the Difference?

If either gender is in fact better than the other at math and science, the reasons are probably numerous and difficult to pinpoint. The poll asked those respondents who believe men are better at math and science to choose among two possible explanations—one focusing on biological differences (or "nature") and the other on societal and cultural differences (or "nurture"). Equal percentages of those who believe men have an advantage say it is due to "differences between boys and girls that are present at birth" as say the perceived advantage is due to "differences in the way society and the educational system treat boys and girls."

Just your best guess, is that due more to—[ROTATED: differences between boys and girls that are present at birth, (or more to) differences in the way society and the educational system treat boys and girls]?

	Differences present at birth	Way society/ educational system treats boys and girls	No opinion
2005 Feb 25-27	48%	48	4

Survey Methods

These results are based on telephone interviews with a randomly selected national sample of 1,008 adults, aged 18 and older, conducted Feb. 25-27, 2005. For results based on this sample, one can say with 95% confidence that the maximum error attributable to sampling and other random effects is ±3 percentage points. In addition to sampling error, question wording and practical difficulties in conducting surveys can introduce error or bias into the findings of public opinion polls.

March 11, 2005

BLOGS NOT YET IN THE MEDIA BIG LEAGUES
Very few Americans read them with any frequency

by Lydia Saad, Gallup Poll Senior Editor

> *If you would not be forgotten, as soon as you are dead and rotten, either write things worth reading, or do things worth the writing.*
>
> — Benjamin Franklin

Whether they are seeking immortality or just letting off steam, Web bloggers are multiplying in number and are seemingly affecting American media and political insiders, at the very least. But whether bloggers are directly influencing the broader public is questionable. According to a new CNN/*USA Today*/Gallup poll, relatively few Americans are generally familiar with the phenomenon of blogging, in which individuals, ranging from famous to anonymous, post running narratives of their thoughts and observations on whatever interests them.

Three-quarters of the U.S. public uses the Internet at work, school, or home, but only one in four Americans are either very familiar or somewhat familiar with blogs (the shortened form of the original "Web logs"). More than half, 56%, have no knowledge of them. Even among Internet users, only 32% are very or somewhat familiar with blogs.

As you may know, there are Web sites known as "blogs" or "Web logs," where people sometimes post their thoughts. How familiar are you with "blogs" — very familiar, somewhat familiar, not too familiar, or not at all familiar?

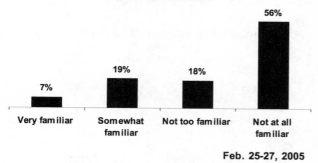

Feb. 25-27, 2005

More to the point, fewer than one in six Americans (15%) read blogs regularly (at least a few times a month). Just 12% of Americans read blogs dealing specifically with politics this often. Among Internet users, the numbers are similarly low: 19% and 15%, respectively.

Web Logs Dish Up Low "Ratings"

Political commentator and prolific blogger Andrew Sullivan calls blogging "opinion journalism" and "democratic journalism." In May 2002, he wrote a "Must Read" article for *Wired* magazine titled, "The Blogging Revolution," in which he touted blogs as the next big thing:

This, at least, is the idea: a publishing revolution more profound than anything since the printing press. Blogger could be to words what Napster was to music—except this time, it'll really work. Check back in a couple of years to see whether this is yet another concept that online reality has had the temerity to destroy.

Well, it has been almost three years, and, while blogging is certainly wielding some influence in media and political circles, tradi-

Frequency of Reading "Blogs" on the Internet

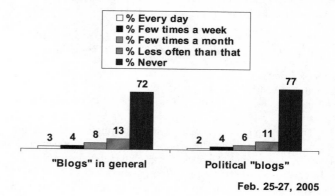

Feb. 25-27, 2005

tional news outlets are still the dominant sources of information for the American public. (Blogging is also so new that the 2003 edition of Microsoft Word thinks it's a typo at this writing.)

According to a December 2004 Gallup Poll, the percentage of Americans getting their news on a daily basis from the mainstream media is 51% for local television news, 44% for local newspapers, 39% for cable news networks, 36% for the nightly broadcast network news, and 21% for radio talk shows. By contrast, only 3% of Americans say they read Internet blogs every day, and just 2% read politics-focused blogs daily.

Blogs Reading Defines Generations

Blog readers are younger than the population at large. Although 17% of the public is aged 18 to 29, a quarter of all blog readers (those who read even occasionally) are in this age bracket. At the older extreme, 17% of Americans are 65 and older, but only 6% of blog readers are this old.

Age Distribution of Americans According to Blog Readership

	Read blogs*	National Adults
	%	%
Age 18 to 29	25	17
Age 30 to 49	47	41
Age 50 to 64	22	25
Age 65+	6	17
	100%	100%

*Blog readership is defined as reading blogs every day, a few times a week, a few times a month, or less often than that. Only those who say they never read blogs are excluded.

This age skew reflects both the younger demographic of the Internet-connected universe as well as a greater likelihood of young people on the Internet, compared with older Internet users, to gravitate toward blogs.

	Percentage of Americans who use the Internet	Percentage of Internet users who read blogs
	%	%
Age 18 to 29	91	44
Age 30 to 49	88	37
Age 50 to 64	75	34
Age 65+	33	28

Said differently, monthly-plus readership of blogs is 21% among 18- to 29-year olds, 16% among those 30 to 49, 14% among those 50 to 64 and just 7% among those 65 and older.

	Age 18 to 29 %	Age 30 to 49 %	Age 50 to 64 %	Age 65+ %
At least monthly	21	16	14	7
Less than monthly	19	17	11	3
Never	59	68	75	90

The age gap in blog reading is particularly noteworthy because it is a complete reversal of the typical age pattern gap for news consumption. Gallup finds Americans' use of all traditional news media to be positively correlated with age. (For instance, only 32% of 18- to 29-year-olds read a local paper every day, versus 61% of those 65 and older.)

Gallup finds no gender differences in blog readership, or according to party affiliation. There are slight differences by political outlook, as about a quarter of liberals (24%) say they read blogs at least monthly, compared with 15% of conservatives and 12% of moderates.

Survey Methods

These results are based on telephone interviews with a randomly selected national sample of 1,008 adults, aged 18 and older, conducted Feb. 25-27, 2005. For results based on this sample, one can say with 95% confidence that the maximum error attributable to sampling and other random effects is ±3 percentage points.

For results based on the sample of 788 Internet users, the maximum margin of sampling error is ±4 percentage points. For results based on the sample of 297 adults who read "blogs" on the Internet, the maximum margin of sampling error is ±6 percentage points.

In addition to sampling error, question wording and practical difficulties in conducting surveys can introduce error or bias into the findings of public opinion polls.

March 14, 2005
PUBLIC APPROVAL OF CONGRESS DECLINES; BUSH APPROVAL STEADY
Lowest rating for Congress in a Gallup Poll since fall 1999

by David W. Moore, Gallup Poll Senior Editor

A new Gallup survey, conducted March 7-10, shows a drop in public approval of the way Congress is handling its job, but no change in President George W. Bush's approval rating. A majority of Americans are dissatisfied with the way things are going in the country, little changed from last month, and about the same level it has been for over a year. The situation in Iraq heads the list of the most important problems facing the country, while Social Security, terrorism, the economy in general, and healthcare essentially tie for second.

According to the poll, 37% of Americans approve, but 53% disapprove, of the way Congress is handling its job. Last month, the comparable figures were 45% approve to 48% disapprove. The current figures are the lowest that Gallup has measured since September 1999, though approval was as low as 40% just last October.

Do you approve or disapprove of the way Congress is handling its job?

	Approve %	Disapprove %	No opinion %
2005			
2005 Mar 7-10	37	53	10
2005 Feb 7-10	45	48	7
2005 Jan 3-5	43	48	9
2004			
2004 Dec 5-8	41	50	9
2004 Nov 7-10	41	52	7
2004 Oct 11-14	40	51	9
2004 Sep 13-15	41	52	7
2004 Aug 9-11	40	52	8
2004 Jul 8-11	40	53	7
2004 Jun 3-6	41	52	7
2004 May 2-4	41	52	7
2004 Apr 5-8	43	51	6
2004 Mar 8-11	42	51	7
2004 Feb 9-12	41	51	8
2004 Jan 12-15	48	45	7

The decline in approval comes across the political spectrum. Compared with last month, Republicans show a decline of 10 points, independents 6 points, and Democrats 9 points. The lower approval rating would thus appear to be less related to any specific bill that Congress has passed, which would cause a more partisan response, and more to the fact that members are facing some controversial issues. Typically, news coverage does not portray Congress in a favorable light when members spend a great deal of time debating legislative issues and arguing with each other.

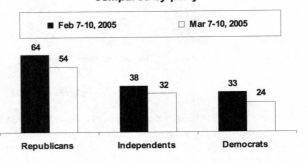

Percentage Who Approve of Job Congress Is Doing
compared by party

	■ Feb 7-10, 2005	□ Mar 7-10, 2005
Republicans	64	54
Independents	38	32
Democrats	33	24

At the same time, Bush's approval rating remains at 52%, the same as it was two weeks ago, and three points higher than what Gallup measured a month ago. Bush's approval has averaged 52% since the beginning of the year.

Do you approve or disapprove of the way George W. Bush is handling his job as president?

	Approve %	Disapprove %	No opinion %
2005			
2005 Mar 7-10	52	44	4
2005 Feb 25-27	52	45	3
2005 Feb 21-24	51	45	4
2005 Feb 7-10	49	48	3

2005	Approve %	Disapprove %	No opinion %
2005 Feb 4-6	57	40	3
2005 Jan 14-16	51	46	3
2005 Jan 7-9	52	44	4
2005 Jan 3-5	52	44	4

The poll also shows that 56% of Americans are dissatisfied with the way things are going in the country today, while only 42% are satisfied. Americans were dissatisfied last month as well, by 52% to 45%.

In general, are you satisfied or dissatisfied with the way things are going in the United States at this time?

2005	Satisfied %	Dissatisfied %	No opinion %
2005 Mar 7-10	42	56	2
2005 Feb 21-24	45	52	3
2005 Feb 7-10	46	52	2
2005 Jan 3-5	46	53	1
2004			
2004 Dec 5-8	45	53	2
2004 Nov 7-10	44	54	2
2004 Oct 29-31 ^	44	53	3
2004 Oct 11-14	41	57	2
2004 Sep 13-15	41	56	3
2004 Aug 9-11	44	55	1
2004 Jul 8-11	41	57	2
2004 Jun 3-6	39	59	2
2004 May 2-4	36	62	2
2004 Apr 5-8	41	57	2
2004 Mar 8-11	39	60	1
2004 Feb 9-12	45	54	1
2004 Jan 12-15	46	53	1
2004 Jan 2-5	55	43	2

^ Asked of a half sample

This measure has been remarkably consistent for over a year, since mid-January 2004.

As is typically the case, Americans who identify with the party of the president are more satisfied than other partisans. In the current survey, 69% of Republicans are satisfied, compared with just 36% of independents, and only 18% of Democrats.

When asked what they think is the most important problem facing the United States today, 25% of Americans say the situation in Iraq, 12% say Social Security, 10% say the economy in general, and 9% each say terrorism and healthcare.

What do you think is the most important problem facing this country today? [Open-ended]

	Mar 7-10, 2005 %	Feb 7-10, 2005 %	Jan 3-5, 2005 %	Dec 5-8, 2004 %
ECONOMIC PROBLEMS (NET)	**28**	**29**	**31**	**29**
1 Economy in general	10	12	12	12
2 Unemployment/Jobs	8	7	11	10
3 Federal budget deficit/ Federal debt	3	5	3	3
4 Fuel/Oil prices	2	1	1	2
5 Taxes	2	2	2	2
6 Wage issues	2	*	1	*
7 High cost of living/Inflation	1	2	1	1
8 Lack of money	1	1	2	1
9 Gap between rich and poor	*	1	1	1
10 Corporate corruption	*	*	*	1
11 Foreign trade/Trade deficit	*	*	1	*
12 Recession	*	—	*	—
NON-ECONOMIC PROBLEMS (NET)	**80**	**83**	**76**	**76**
1 Situation in Iraq/War	25	24	25	23
2 Social Security	12	12	4	2
3 Terrorism	9	9	8	12
4 Poor healthcare/hospitals; high cost of healthcare	9	10	9	7
5 Education/poor education/ access to education	6	5	4	3
6 Dissatisfaction with government/Congress/ politicians/candidates; Poor leadership; corruption	6	7	7	6
7 National security	5	4	3	4
8 Ethics/Moral/Religious/ Family decline; dishonesty; lack of integrity	4	6	6	10
9 Poverty/Hunger/ Homelessness	3	4	5	2
10 Foreign aid/Focus overseas	3	4	3	1
11 Immigration/Illegal aliens	3	3	2	2
12 International issues /problems	2	3	2	3
13 Crime/Violence	2	1	2	1
14 Lack of respect for each other	2	1	2	2
15 Children's behavior/ way they are raised	2	*	*	1
16 Drugs	1	1	2	2
17 Judicial system/Courts/Laws	1	1	2	2
18 Environment/Pollution	1	1	1	1
19 Unifying the country	1	1	1	2
20 Welfare	1	1	1	*
21 Care for the elderly	1	1	*	*
22 Medicare	1	1	1	*
23 Lack of energy sources; the energy crisis	*	*	*	*
24 Homosexuality/Gay issues	*	1	*	*
25 Abortion	*	1	1	1
26 Cancer/Diseases	*	—	*	*
27 Abuse of power	*	*	*	*
28 Overpopulation	*	—	*	*
29 Race relations/Racism	*	*	1	*
30 Election year/Presidential choices/Election reform	*	*	*	*
31 Guns/Gun control	*	*	*	—

	Mar 7-10, 2005 %	Feb 7-10, 2005 %	Jan 3-5, 2005 %	Dec 5-8, 2004 %
The media	—	1	*	1
Child abuse	—	—	—	*
Other non-economic	1	2	3	3
No opinion	3	2	4	2
Total	**133%**	**138%**	**134%**	**145%**

Totals add to more than 100% due to multiple responses.
*Less than 0.5%

The pattern of responses is little changed over the past several months, except for the emergence of Social Security as one of the top concerns—following the major emphasis given this issue by the president and Congress in recent weeks.

Survey Methods

Results in the current survey are based on telephone interviews with 1,004 national adults, aged 18 and older, conducted March 7-10, 2005. For results based on the total sample of national adults, one can say with 95% confidence that the maximum margin of sampling error is ±3 percentage points.

In addition to sampling error, question wording and practical difficulties in conducting surveys can introduce error or bias into the findings of public opinion polls.

March 15, 2005
WILL AMERICANS BUY THE NEW MARTHA?
Her public image has partially recovered

by Lydia Saad, Gallup Poll Senior Editor

Fresh from prison, a visibly relieved Martha Stewart spoke to her staff at Martha Stewart Living Omnimedia, Inc., last week about the future of the company. Without ever mentioning the "p" word, Stewart expressed that her legal ordeal has changed her; that she has a new appreciation for the comforts of home, a new understanding of the needs of everyday people, and a new willingness to credit her employees.

While Stewart might be a better person for her recent experiences, is she better off with the American public? She is far better off today than two years ago, when she was in the midst of a legal battle over her December 2001 sale of ImClone Systems stock*. But she is still worse off than before these troubles began. Stewart's favorable rating has rebounded to about where it stood when Gallup first measured it in 1999, but her unfavorable rating has since doubled.

The impact of Stewart's bad publicity—as well as the good publicity she apparently earned from behind the gates of Alderson Federal Prison Camp—is well-chronicled in Gallup's favorable ratings trend on Stewart.

- In that earliest rating, from an October 1999 survey, about half of Americans (49%) had a favorable impression of Stewart and 16% had an unfavorable impression, with the remainder either neutral or not familiar with her.

- In the first few days after the federal investigation into her sale of ImClone Systems stock became public, Stewart's image was 46% favorable and 27% unfavorable.
- By the following month, Stewart's image had plunged: only 30% viewed her favorably and 39% unfavorably.
- In June 2003, immediately following her indictment, Stewart's image hit the lowest point recorded by Gallup: 33% favorable and 52% unfavorable.
- In February of this year, just one month before Stewart was released from prison, her ratings were once again more positive than negative: 53% favorable vs. 32% unfavorable.

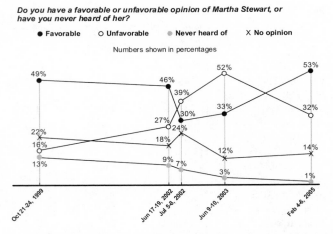

Do you have a favorable or unfavorable opinion of Martha Stewart, or have you never heard of her?

When Stewart stepped down as CEO of the company in June 2003, it was unclear whether she would ever again be the face of Martha Stewart Living Omnimedia (MSO). From the homecoming she received from corporate executives and staff, it now seems clear she will. As far back as last fall, the new CEO, Susan Lyne, spoke to *Newsweek* about Stewart's importance to the future of the brand.

Holding May Be Easier Than Growing

While Stewart will likely be as visible as ever, Lyne does plan some changes. In the same interview, she indicated that while holding on to its traditional market, the company is aiming to expand by targeting new publications at a somewhat younger demographic (25-year-olds to 40-year-olds).

Of course the fundamental demographic for MSO has been, and probably always will be, women. Six years ago, a majority of women (55%) had a favorable view of Stewart, and just 19% had an unfavorable view of her. After falling into the 30s during the stock scandal, Stewart's favorable rating among women has reverted to 55%, while her unfavorable rating remains somewhat elevated, at 32%.

The trend in Stewart's favorability ratings by age may spell trouble, however, if the company is going after a younger demographic. Although Stewart's overall favorable rating has recovered to 53%, this has occurred almost exclusively among people 50 and older.

Between 1999 and today (leaving out the interim period when her favorability sank), the percentage viewing Stewart favorably rose by double digits among those aged 50 to 64 (+12) and 65+ years of age (+19). It rose by only 5 points among those aged 18 to 29 and fell by 6 points among those aged 30 to 49.

When taking into account changes in both the percentage favorable and the percentage unfavorable, as is done with the shift in "net favorable" statistic, it is clear that Stewart's image has been hardest hit among the 30- to 49-year-old demographic.

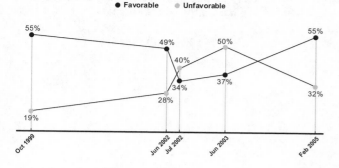

Trend in Views of Martha Stewart Among Women

● Favorable ○ Unfavorable

55% ... 49% ... 50% ... 55%
40%
34% ... 37%
28%
19% ... 32%

Oct 1999 | Jun 2002 | Jul 2002 | Jun 2003 | Feb 2005

Trend in Stewart's Image Rating by Age

	18-29	30-49	50-64	65+
October 1999				
Favorable	44%	53%	47%	42%
Unfavorable	21%	16%	19%	11%
No opinion	35%	31%	34%	47%
February 2005				
Favorable	49%	47%	59%	61%
Unfavorable	39%	37%	29%	22%
No opinion	12%	16%	12%	17%
Shift in % favorable	+5	-6	+12	+19
Shift in Net Favorable*	-13	-27	-2	+8

*Net Favorable defined as percent favorable minus percent unfavorable

When looking at age and gender together, we see no shift in the percentage of men 18 to 49 holding a favorable opinion of Stewart (44% today vs. 44% in 1999), a slight decrease among women 18 to 49 (-6 points), a modest increase among women 50+ (+9) and a substantial increase among men 50+ (+23).

Trend in Stewart's Image Rating by Gender/Age

	Men 18-49	Women 18-49	Men 50+	Women 50+
October 1999				
Favorable	44%	57%	38%	51%
Unfavorable	16%	20%	8%	19%
No opinion	40%	23%	54%	30%
February 2005				
Favorable	44%	51%	61%	60%
Unfavorable	40%	36%	24%	28%
No opinion	16%	13%	15%	12%
Shift in % favorable	0	-6	+23	+9
Shift in Net Favorable*	-24	-22	+7	0

*Net Favorable defined as percent favorable minus percent unfavorable

These shifts may not be the type of movement her stockholders are hoping for. But as has been seen in the past, opinions of Stewart can turn on a dime. It may take nothing more than a successful debut of her version of the *Apprentice* to ignite support from the younger demographic.

Stewart's Appeal Strengthened With Lower-Income Households

The findings by household income could be good news for the Martha Stewart Everyday line of household products sold through Kmart, but could run counter to the interests of her magazine and the higher-end furniture line.

Her favorable rating among people living in lower-income households (those earning less than $30,000 annually) has increased 12 points (from 42% in 1999 to 54% today). That figure has increased only 3 points among middle-income earners and declined by 5 points among those earning $75,000 or more.

Trend in Stewart's Image Rating by Income

	$75,000+	$30,000-$74,999	Less than $30,000
October 1999			
Favorable	56%	52%	42%
Unfavorable	20%	18%	13%
No opinion	24%	30%	45%
February 2005			
Favorable	51%	55%	54%
Unfavorable	34%	32%	32%
No opinion	15%	13%	14%
Shift in % favorable	-5	+3	+12
Shift in Net Favorable*	-19	-11	-7

*Net Favorable defined as percent favorable minus percent unfavorable

Bottom Line

Stewart's public image has partially recovered from the battering it took during the ImClone scandal. Having a favorable image above the 50% line today is a good thing. Having an elevated unfavorable rating, however, means less opportunity for converting neutral Americans into fans, and more work at managing or reducing those unfavorables.

This problem is seen across all demographics. Even among groups with whom her favorable rating has increased since 1999, her net favorable rating (percentage favorable minus percentage unfavorable) is still lower than six years ago.

The good news for Stewart in the demographic trends is that a majority of women again view her favorably. She should also welcome the fact that a component of the traditional market segment—older women—is back in her fold. The decline in favorability among younger women (particularly pronounced when looking at her net favorable rating) could be a problem, however, as the new management team at MSO tries to expand the company.

*Results are based on telephone interviews with 1,010 national adults, aged 18 and older, conducted Feb. 4-6, 2005. For results based on the total sample of national adults, one can say with 95% confidence that the margin of sampling error is ±3 percentage points.

March 16, 2005
AMERICANS' VIEWS OF U.S. ENERGY SITUATION UNCHANGED
Slightly more likely to express personal worry about energy costs, availability

by Jeffrey M. Jones, Gallup Poll Managing Editor

Rising oil prices have yet to affect Americans' assessment of the country's energy situation, because the public currently rates the energy situation as no more serious than in the past two years. However, Americans do show higher concern about the availability and affordability of energy than in the previous two years. The public still tilts toward conservation and environmental protection over increased energy production as ways to address the energy situation. George W. Bush's ratings for improving the nation's energy policy are now the worst of his presidency.

These results are based on Gallup's annual Environment poll, conducted March 7-10.

Thirty-one percent of Americans rate the "energy situation in the United States" as "very serious," little changed from the last two years, when 29% and 28%, respectively, said it was very serious. The only departure from that level of concern in recent years came in 2001. Rolling blackouts and rising gas prices caused 58% to assess the energy situation as very serious in May of that year.

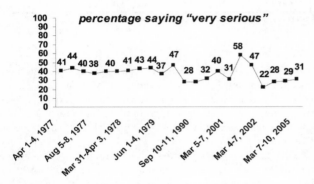

How serious would you say the energy situation is in the United States — very serious, fairly serious, or not at all serious?

percentage saying "very serious"

Overall, 39% of Americans say they worry "a great deal" about the "availability and affordability of energy." Twenty-six percent say they worry "a fair amount," 26% "only a little," and 8% "not at all."

That represents a slightly higher level of worry compared with last year's polling, and much higher than in 2003. Last year, 35% expressed a great deal of worry; in 2003, just 27% did so. Still, concern has not reached the same level it did in 2001, when 46% said they worried a great deal.

A slight majority of Americans, 52%, think the United States is "likely to face a critical energy shortage during the next five years."

Next I'm going to read a list of problems facing the country. For each one, please tell me if you personally worry about this problem a great deal, a fair amount, only a little, or not at all? First, how much do you personally worry about the availability and affordability of energy?

percentage saying "great deal"

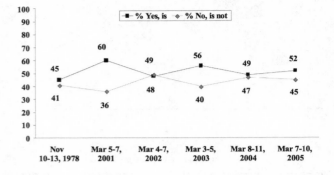

Do you think that the United States is or is not likely to face a critical energy shortage during the next five years?

Forty-five percent disagree. Those numbers have fluctuated in recent years, reaching as high as 60% predicting a shortage (in 2001).

These assessments of the energy situation vary according to one's household income—with those at lower income levels showing greater concern.

Views of Energy Situation by Household Income

	Less than $30,000 %	$30,000-$74,999 %	$75,000 and above %
Percentage who say energy situation is "very serious"	39	32	26
Percentage who worry "a great deal" about energy availability/ affordability	48	40	29
Percentage who expect critical energy shortage in next five years	62	53	44

Dealing With the Energy Situation

When asked to choose the proper approach to solving the nation's energy problems, the public is more likely to come down on the side of conservation and environmental protection than production and increasing energy supplies.

Consistent with past results, Americans by a 2-to-1 margin say the United States should emphasize greater consumer conservation of existing energy supplies (61%) rather than "production of more oil, gas, and coal supplies" (28%). The only deviation from that general pattern occurred in May 2001, when Americans favored conservation, but by a slimmer 47% to 35% margin.

Americans do not show nearly the same level of consensus when asked to choose the higher priority between protecting the environment and development of energy supplies, but still side against increased development. In the latest poll, 52% say priority should be given to environmental protection, while 39% say development of energy supplies should get the higher priority. The latest results are marginally more pro-environment than in the past two years, and are about the same as the results in earlier years.

These attitudes are influenced by one's political orientation. Republicans come down much more on the side of production, while Democrats (as well as independents) fall more on the side of environmental protection. While all partisan groups show a preference for conservation over production to address the nation's energy problems, Democrats show the strongest margin in favor of it.

Which of the following approaches to solving the nation's energy problems do you think the U.S. should follow right now — emphasize production of more oil, gas, and coal supplies (or) emphasize more conservation by consumers of existing energy supplies?

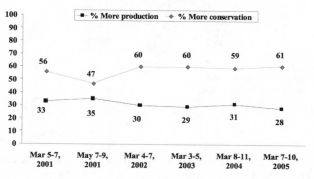

With which one of these statements about the environment and energy production do you most agree — protection of the environment should be given priority, even at the risk of limiting the amount of energy supplies — such as oil, gas, and coal — which the United States produces (or) development of U.S. energy supplies — such as oil, gas, and coal – should be given priority, even if the environment suffers to some extent?

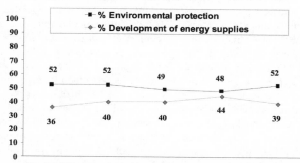

Energy Attitudes by Party Affiliation

	Repub-lican	Inde-pendent	Democrat
Approach U.S. should follow to solve nation's energy problems			
Conservation of existing supplies	50%	65%	71%
More production of oil, gas, coal	37%	25%	22%
Which should be given a higher priority			
Environmental protection	33%	60%	65%
Development of U.S. energy supplies	58%	30%	27%

Low Marks for Bush

Public support for Bush's energy policy shows continued decline; his current ratings are the worst of his administration. Each time

Gallup has asked whether Bush is doing a good job or a poor job of "improving the nation's energy policy," the percentage saying "a good job" has been lower than the previous time. Currently, just 32% say he is doing a good job, while 54% say he is doing a poor job.

Do you think George W. Bush is doing a good job or a poor job in handling each of the following issues as president? How about — improving the nation's energy policy?

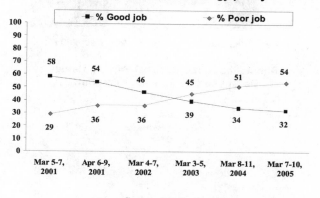

Survey Methods

These results are based on telephone interviews with a randomly selected national sample of 1,004 adults, aged 18 and older, conducted March 7-10, 2005. For results based on this sample, one can say with 95% confidence that the maximum error attributable to sampling and other random effects is ±3 percentage points. In addition to sampling error, question wording and practical difficulties in conducting surveys can introduce error or bias into the findings of public opinion polls.

March 18, 2005

PUBLIC LEANS AGAINST OIL EXPLORATION IN ARCTIC RESERVE

About a third of Americans would not be upset if oil exploration occurs or not

by David W. Moore, Gallup Poll Senior Editor

The U.S. Senate voted Wednesday on a budget resolution that could pave the way for Congress to authorize oil drilling in the Arctic National Wildlife Refuge (ANWR) in Alaska. With the issue now treated as a budget matter, the likelihood for passage appears greater than in recent years, when the issue was brought up separately and opponents were able to filibuster the Senate to block passage.

A new Gallup survey reveals a public that leans against oil exploration in ANWR, though a sizable number of people don't appear to care strongly about the issue either way. According to the poll, conducted March 7-10, 53% say ANWR should not be opened up to oil exploration, while 42% say it should. These views represent a slight shift in opinion from three years ago, when Americans opposed oil exploration by 56% to 35%.

Despite the apparent closeness of opinion on this matter, a follow-up question reveals greater intensity among opponents than supporters. Less than half of the supporters of oil exploration say they

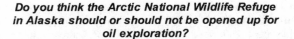

Do you think the Arctic National Wildlife Refuge in Alaska should or should not be opened up for oil exploration?

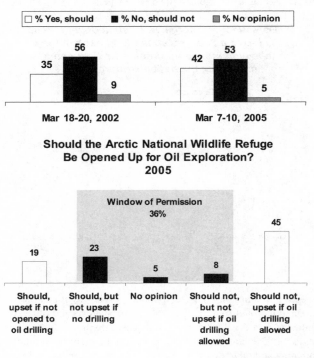

Should the Arctic National Wildlife Refuge Be Opened Up for Oil Exploration? 2002

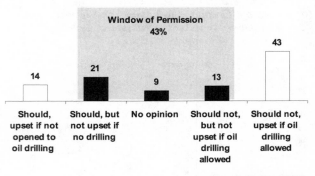

March 18-20, 2002

would be "very" or "somewhat" upset if exploration did not happen, but the majority of opponents say they would be very or somewhat upset if exploration did occur.

These results suggest that more than a third of all respondents, 36%, don't care enough about the issue to be upset one way or the other. When first asked about the issue, 23% say they feel ANWR should be open to oil exploration, but later admit that they would not be upset if it didn't happen. Another 8% initially oppose oil exploration, but subsequently say they would not be upset if it did happen. Five percent have no opinion at all on the matter.

This group of Americans can be classified as having a "permissive" opinion, either not having an opinion, or not caring if their own opinion prevails. Instead, they appear willing to permit political leaders to do whatever they think is preferable.

The percentage of Americans with permissive opinions is somewhat smaller now than it was three years ago, though the basic pattern of responses is quite similar. At that time, 43% of respondents expressed a permissive opinion on oil exploration, including 21% who were in favor but said they would not be upset if it didn't happen, 13% who opposed the idea but said they would not be upset if it did happen, and 9% who had no opinion.

Among those who feel strongly enough about the issue to be either very or somewhat upset if their opinion does not prevail, the ratio of opposition to support is about 2-to-1, with 45% intensely opposed and just 19% intensely in favor.

Gallup's overall results can be compared with other polls, which have shown conflicting opinions on ANWR. These polls show that opinion on this issue is highly influenced by whether the question on oil exploration is asked in an energy framework or an environmental framework. Harris Interactive, for example, found a slight major-

ity of Americans in favor of oil drilling, but it was framed in the context of "reform" in order to "decrease our reliance on foreign oil." The Gallup question that found majority opposition was included amid other questions on a survey on the environment.

The results of Gallup's current poll, as well as the other polls, suggest that overall public opinion on the issue of ANWR is "fuzzy"—its measurement highly susceptible to the context in which the issue is discussed. The debate that will likely unfold in the weeks ahead, as Congress considers whether to authorize oil drilling in the Arctic reserve, may help bring that opinion into greater focus. Currently, the permissive opinion analysis suggests that more than a third of Americans are susceptible to being persuaded in either direction.

The analysis also shows major differences by party. Republicans are much more likely to intensely favor allowing oil exploration in ANWR (31%) than are independents (14%) or Democrats (11%). Similarly, 59% of Democrats are intensely opposed, compared with 48% of independents and 30% of Republicans.

Republicans are evenly divided in terms of their intense opinions on the matter, 31% intensely in favor to 30% intensely opposed. However, when Republicans with permissive opinions are included, the figures show Republicans with net support by 59% to 37%.

A similar pattern appears between the other two groups of partisans. When permissive opinions are included, the margins against opening up ANWR are reduced.

• For independents, intense opinions show a 48% to 14% margin of opposition. When permissive opinions are included, the margin is 58% to 37% opposed.

Should the Arctic National Wildlife Refuge Be Opened Up for Oil Exploration? by Party

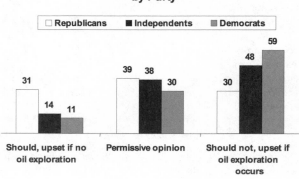

- For Democrats, 59% are intensely opposed, 11% intensely in favor. With permissive opinions included, opposition is 68% to 27%.

Survey Methods

Results in the current survey are based on telephone interviews with 1,004 national adults, aged 18 and older, conducted March 7-10, 2005. For results based on the total sample of national adults, one can say with 95% confidence that the maximum margin of sampling error is ±3 percentage points.

In addition to sampling error, question wording and practical difficulties in conducting surveys can introduce error or bias into the findings of public opinion polls.

March 22, 2005
PUBLIC SUPPORTS REMOVAL OF FEEDING TUBE FOR TERRI SCHIAVO
Majority of Americans would do the same if they had child or spouse in similar condition

by David W. Moore, Gallup Poll Senior Editor

A new CNN/*USA Today*/Gallup survey finds a majority of Americans supporting the decision by a state judge to remove the feeding tube that was keeping Florida woman Terri Schiavo alive. The poll also finds that a clear majority of Americans, if faced with a similar situation in the case of a spouse or child, would also remove life support. The public's attention to the Schiavo case, despite massive media coverage, is well below the degree that the public has followed other major news stories of the last several years.

The Florida woman has been in a persistent vegetative state since 1990, and doctors have told her family that she has no chance of recovering. But her husband and parents disagree over whether to keep her alive with the aid of a life support system. A Florida state judge ordered the feeding tube removed last Friday, in accordance with the wishes of Michael Schiavo, the woman's husband. But Congress passed a highly unusual bill on Monday morning, immediately signed by President George W. Bush, authorizing the federal courts to intervene.

The poll, conducted March 18-20, shows that 66% of Americans have been following the case either "very" closely (27%) or "somewhat" closely (39%), while another 33% say they have not been following the issue closely—either "not too closely" (21%) or "not at all" (12%). This level of attention to the story is not high in the context of other major news events of the last few years. However, given the intervention by Congress and the president, one might expect attention to increase.

When told that the feeding tube had been removed, 56% of Americans agreed that it was the right thing to do, while 31% disagreed.

As you may know, on Friday the feeding tube keeping Terri Schiavo alive was removed. Based on what you have heard or read about the case, do you think that the feeding tube should or should not have been removed?

2005 Mar 18-20	Should have %	Should not have %	No opinion %
OVERALL	**56**	**31**	**13**
HOW CLOSELY FOLLOW			
Very closely	56	40	4
Somewhat closely	62	29	9
Not closely	48	26	26
CHURCH ATTENDANCE			
Weekly	51	37	12
Nearly weekly/monthly	55	31	14
Seldom/never	60	27	13
PARTY AFFILIATION			
Republicans	54	35	11
Independents	54	31	15
Democrats	62	26	12
POLITICAL IDEOLOGY			
Conservatives	50	38	12
Moderates	57	29	14
Liberals	69	22	9

A comparison of responses by various subgroups of people shows majority support in most of the groups. People who are following the issue very closely show the lowest percent of no opinion, with 56% in favor of removing the tube and 40% against. Just 4% are undecided.

Some observers have characterized the issue as a political one, with conservatives and Republicans lining up on one side and liberals and Democrats on the other. The poll shows majority support among conservatives, Republicans, and people who attend church on a weekly basis. There is proportionally greater support among liberals, Democrats, and people who seldom or never attend church, but the differences among these subgroups are not nearly as pronounced as they often are on high salience issues.

When asked what they would do if they had a child or spouse in the same condition as Terri Schiavo, a clear majority of Americans said they would remove the feeding tube.

Suppose you had a (child/spouse) who was in the same condition as Terry Schiavo, and it were up to you to decide whether to keep that child alive through the use of a feeding tube. What would you, personally, decide to do in that situation [ROTATED—remove the feeding tube (or) keep the feeding tube in place]?

	Remove	Keep in place	No opinion
Child	56%	34	10
Spouse	61%	30	9

There is a slight difference in the percentage of the public who would remove a feeding tube from a child compared with the percentage who would remove a feeding tube from a spouse. But those differences are within the poll's margins of error for the sub samples of respondents asked one question or the other.

Survey Methods

Results in the current survey are based on telephone interviews with 909 national adults, aged 18 and older, conducted March 18-20,

2005. For results based on the total sample of national adults, one can say with 95% confidence that the margin of sampling error is ±4 percentage points.

In addition to sampling error, question wording and practical difficulties in conducting surveys can introduce error or bias into the findings of public opinion polls.

March 22, 2005
PUBLIC: SIXTEEN TOO YOUNG TO DRIVE
Parents cautiously optimistic

by Linda Lyons, Education and Youth Editor

"Young novice drivers are at significant risk on the road because they lack both the judgment that comes with maturity and the skill that comes with experience." Few would argue with this statement from the Insurance Institute for Highway Safety. But at what age are young people mature enough to exercise good judgment on the road?

A CNN/*USA Today*/Gallup poll of U.S. adults, conducted in December 2004*, shows the majority of Americans (61%) say people should be 17 years old or older before they are permitted to get a driver's license; just 37% say 16 or younger. The plurality of Americans, 42%, think 18 is the right age. These findings represent a significant shift in public opinion from a decade ago.

At what age do you think people should be permitted to have a driver's license?

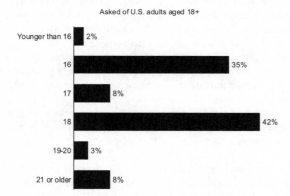

Opinion Shifts in Favor of Older Drivers

Not long ago, many more Americans than do so today thought 16 was the appropriate age at which teens should be able to get a driver's license. In 1995, 46% said 16 was the right age, 30% said 18, and 23% mentioned other ages.

What took place over the last 10 years that might have influenced that shift? During the 1990s, faced with rising accident rates among teens, most states implemented some variation of a Graduated Driver Licensing (GDL) law. The laws vary in strength from state to state, but all encompass a basic principle—delaying a full-fledged, unrestricted driver's license, while prolonging the learning process under less risky conditions until drivers turn 18 (see "Phasing in Teen Drivers" in Related Items). The publicity the GDL laws generated may have made more Americans aware of the dangers of driving too young.

At what age do you think people should be permitted to have a driver's license?

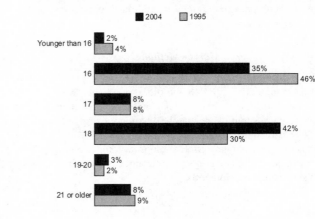

Women Cautious About Young Drivers

While 42% of men think 16 is the right age to begin driving, just 29% of women agree. Women are somewhat more cautious about young drivers than men are; nearly half of women (47%) say 18 is the right age for a driver's license, as do 37% of men.

At what age do you think people should be permitted to have a driver's license?

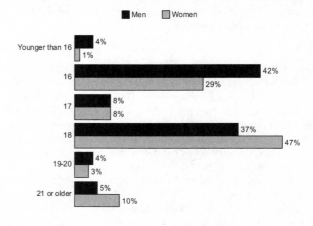

Younger Drivers on Young Drivers

Young adults—those between age 18 and 29, who were likely most recently licensed as drivers—are more inclined to say licenses should be given at age 18 (43%) than age 16 (36%).

Parents Weigh In

Most parents with children between the ages of 12 and 18 seem to view the prospect of their children driving with cautious optimism. When asked to name the appropriate age for teens to begin driving, one might expect many parents to say, "40 sounds about perfect." But just 11% of parents with children between the ages of 12 and 18 say the right age to get a driver's license is "21 or older." An equal percentage of parents with children in this age range say 16 (37%) and 18 (37%) is the appropriate age to become a licensed driver.

*Results are based on telephone interviews with 1,002 national adults, aged 18 and older, conducted Dec. 17-19, 2004. For results based on the total sample of national adults, one can say with 95% confidence that the maximum margin of sampling error is ±3 percentage points.

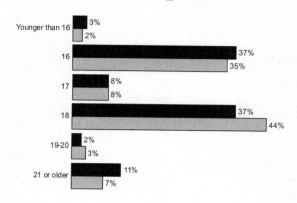

At what age do you think people should be permitted to have a driver's license?

■ Parents of children 12-18　▢ No children 12-18

Younger than 16: 3% / 2%
16: 37% / 35%
17: 8% / 8%
18: 37% / 44%
19-20: 2% / 3%
21 or older: 11% / 7%

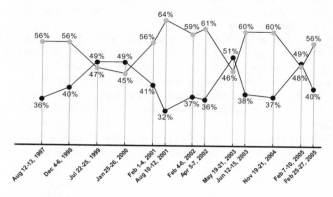

Do you think there will or will not come a time when Israel and the Arab nations will be able to settle their differences and live in peace?

● Yes, there will come a time　● No, there will not

Aug 12-13, 1997: 36% / 56%
Dec 4-6, 1998: 40% / 56%
Jul 22-25, 1999: 49% / 47%
Jan 25-26, 2000: 49% / 45%
Feb 1-4, 2001: 41% / 56%
Aug 10-12, 2001: 32% / 64%
Feb 4-6, 2002: 37% / 59%
Apr 5-7, 2002: 36% / 61%
May 19-21, 2003: 51% / 46%
Jun 12-15, 2003: 38% / 60%
Nov 19-21, 2004: 37% / 60%
Feb 7-10, 2005: 49% / 48%
Feb 25-27, 2005: 40% / 56%

When Will Arabs and Israelis Settle Differences and Live in Peace?

Based on those who say peace will come about

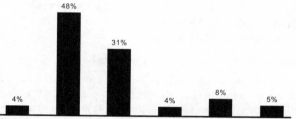

Next year: 4%
Next 5 years: 48%
Next 25 years: 31%
Next 50 years: 4%
After that: 8%
No opinion: 5%

March 22, 2005
AMERICANS' HOPES FOR MIDEAST PEACE WANE—AGAIN
Only one in five expect peace in next five years

by Lydia Saad, Gallup Poll Senior Editor

The news from the Holy Land was mostly good as the New Year began. On Jan. 9, Mahmoud Abbas was chosen in open elections to succeed Yasser Arafat as president of the Palestinian people. On Feb. 2, Abbas and Israeli Prime Minister Ariel Sharon announced they would participate in a peace summit. The two met in Sharm el-Sheik, Egypt, on Feb. 8 and verbally agreed to suspend the hostilities that have gripped the region since the Palestinians launched a second *intifada* in September 2000.

It appears one or another (or both) of these events, widely reported as reasons for new hope in the Arab-Israeli conflict, inspired optimism about the region among some Americans. In a Feb. 7-10 Gallup Poll*, 49% of Americans said they believed there will come a time when Israel and the Arab nations will settle their differences and live in peace, up from 37% two months earlier.

But, as is so often the case, that optimism faded quickly; this time, most likely because a Palestinian suicide bomber bombed a Tel Aviv nightclub on Feb. 25, killing four Israelis and injuring about 50 others. A Feb. 25-27 CNN/*USA Today*/Gallup poll* conducted on the heels of the attack found a nine-point drop in optimism from earlier in the month. According to that poll, just 40% of Americans agree the conflict will be resolved, while 56% disagree.

The latest 40% figure is not the lowest level of optimism Gallup has recorded on this measure. That low came in the summer of 2001—a time of severe hostilities between the two sides—when only 32% of Americans felt the Arabs and Israelis would eventually settle their differences.

The Feb. 7-10 measure of 49% is not technically the highest level of optimism recorded (that was 51% in May 2003), but it is consistent with the upper end of the range for this trend.

Peace Not Around the Corner

Even optimism about Middle East peace is tempered with a good dose of realism about the timetable. Only a small fraction (4%) of Americans who predict peace believe it will come about in the next year. Altogether, about half of Middle East optimists (52%) believe peace will be achieved within the next five years, while 43% say it will take longer than that.

When factoring in the majority of Americans who are pessimistic about the outlook for peace, only one in five Americans (21%) expect peace to occur within the next five years, while another 17% say it will take longer.

Bottom Line

They say hope springs eternal, but not when it comes to Americans' outlook for peace between Arabs and Israelis. The cycle of U.S. optimism about the chances for peace in the Middle East closely follows the cycle of peace accords and violence that define recent Arab-Israeli relations. At their most encouraged, 51% of Americans have said they believe peace is within reach. At their worst, just 32% have been hopeful.

Late last week, Palestinian militant groups brought together by Abbas agreed to halt violence against Israel for the duration of

When Will Arabs and Israelis Settle Differences and Live in Peace?

Based on national adults

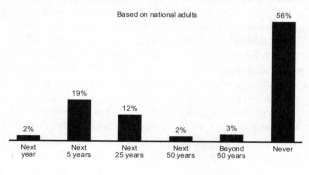

Next year: 2%
Next 5 years: 19%
Next 25 years: 12%
Next 50 years: 2%
Beyond 50 years: 3%
Never: 56%

2005, if Israel will release 8,000 Palestinian prisoners and agree to a similar cease-fire. Israel reportedly welcomed the offer and agreed to aspects of it, with some counter terms of its own. Presuming this holds until the next polling opportunity, it will be interesting to see how Americans react to the news.

Perhaps as long as U.S. optimism shifts within the fairly narrow (32% to 51%) historical range, those attitudes should be considered "normal." But when, and if, the level of optimism reaches well above the 50% line, then it may be a sign that real changes are at hand.

Results are based on telephone interviews with 1,008 national adults, aged 18 and older, conducted Feb. 7-10, 2005, and 1,008 national adults, aged 18 and older, Feb. 25-27, 2005. For results based on the total sample of national adults, one can say with 95% confidence that the maximum margin of sampling error is ±3 percentage points.

March 22, 2005
ARE AMERICANS UNITED IN MORE NEGATIVE ECONOMIC ASSESSMENTS?
Perceptions and politics related

by Jeffrey M. Jones, Gallup Poll Managing Editor

Americans have become more pessimistic about the direction of the nation's economy. In Gallup's initial 2005 poll, 48% of Americans said the economy was getting better and 42% said worse. A more recent poll, conducted March 7-10, finds 41% say it is getting better and 50% say it is getting worse.

Economy Getting Better or Worse?

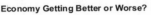

● Getting better ● Getting worse

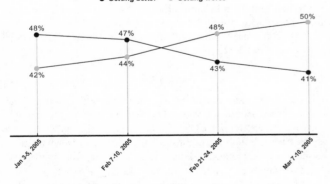

That represents a net shift of 15 points, from a 6-point net positive assessment (48% better, 42% worse) to a 9-point net negative assessment (41% better, 50% worse). Have all Americans become more pessimistic about the national economy, or are certain groups mainly responsible for the shift in opinion? An analysis of Gallup's Jan. 3-5 and March 7-10 polls* provides some answers.

Compared with their opinions in January, Americans in most demographic groups have become more negative in their assessments of the economy's course. Of the 30 groups analyzed, 27 now see the economy in less positive terms than they did in the early January poll.

The table summarizes the changes. The figures represent the net assessment of the economy (% getting better - % getting worse) for January and March, as well as the net change between the two periods.

Change in Ratings of Economy's Direction by Subgroup

	January	March	Change
Male	+13	+2	-11
Female	+1	-19	-20
White	+16	-4	-20
Nonwhite	-27	-26	+1
	January	*March*	*Change*
18 to 29 yrs old	+3	+4	+1
30 to 49 yrs old	+15	-8	-23
50 to 64 yrs old	-1	-17	-16
65+ yrs old	0	-14	-14
East	-8	-19	-11
Midwest	+1	-12	-13
South	+18	-12	-30
West	+10	+8	-2
Urban	+6	-18	-24
Suburban	+6	+7	+1
Rural	+9	-28	-37
High school or less	-1	-18	-17
Some college	+8	-17	-25
College grad only	+27	+17	-10
Post-grad	+5	+2	-3
Income $75,000+	+14	+8	-6
Income $30,000-<$75,000	+13	-7	-20
Income <$30,000	-13	-31	-18
Conservative	+27	+21	-6
Moderate	+3	-21	-24
Liberal	-21	-31	-10
Republican	+58	+38	-20
Independent	-19	-26	-7
Democrat	-25	-44	-19
Employed	+15	-3	-18
Not employed	-4	-19	-15

The most change has primarily occurred among groups that had much more positive assessments of the economy's momentum in January. The largest shifts occurred among: rural residents (-37), Southerners (-30), 30- to 49-year-olds (-23), urban residents (-24), those with some college education (-25) and political moderates (-24). All those groups have moved from a net positive to a net negative assessment from January until now.

Relatively small changes occurred among suburban residents and Westerners. While that could indicate that economic conditions in those areas are good and staying that way, it could also be attributed to sampling variation given the smallish sample sizes of these groups. Other groups showing little change in their economic evaluations include nonwhites and younger Americans (18 to 29). Nonwhites were decidedly negative about the economy's course and remain so. Younger Americans were just slightly more optimistic than pessimistic in both January and March.

After the shifts in opinion, the following groups now are most optimistic about the economy's direction—Republicans (+38), conservatives (+21), and those with a college degree but no postgraduate education (+17). Democrats (-44), liberals (-31), those in lower-income households (-31), rural residents (-28), independents

(-26), and nonwhites (-26) are now most pessimistic about the nation's economy. Clearly, one's politics is related to his or her perceptions of the economy.

Bottom Line

Americans' views on the economy's momentum can be quite fluid, and the recent results reflect that. After relatively optimistic evaluations at the outset of the year, Americans by and large have grown more pessimistic in the past few months.

Results are based on interviews with 1,005 adults, 18 and older, conducted Jan. 3-5, 2005, and 1,004 adults, 18 and older, conducted March 7-10, 2005. For results based on these samples, one can say with 95% confidence that the maximum error attributable to sampling is ±3 percentage points.

Margins of sampling error for subgroups will be higher.

March 23, 2005
MAJORITY AGREES WITH JUDGE'S DECISION IN SCHIAVO CASE
Few see hope for improvement in her condition if kept alive

by Jeffrey M. Jones, Gallup Poll Managing Editor

A one-night CNN/*USA Today*/Gallup poll finds a slim majority of Americans agreeing with a federal judge's decision in the Terri Schiavo case. The decision effectively denied a request by Schiavo's parents to re-insert the feeding tube helping to keep her alive, pending further legal action in the matter. Relatively few Americans see much hope for improvement in Schiavo's condition, even if the feeding tube were re-inserted permanently.

A majority of Americans express sympathy for both sides in the dispute—Schiavo's husband, who wants the feeding tube removed to end her life, and Schiavo's parents—though more are sympathetic with the parents than with the husband. Still, most Americans believe husband Michael Schiavo is being truthful when he says his wife told him she did not want to be kept alive by artificial means.

By wide margins, Americans disapprove of the actions of President George W. Bush and the Republicans in Congress in the Schiavo case. Americans also disapprove of the actions of the Democrats in Congress, but to a smaller degree. The public is divided in its view of the media's handling of the case.

Detailed findings of the March 22 poll follow.

By a 52% to 39% margin, Americans agree with the federal judge's decision that resulted in the feeding tube—removed on Friday—not being re-inserted. Two in three Americans hold their views with some conviction: 37% strongly agree with the judge's decision; 30% strongly disagree.

As you may know, Terri Schiavo is a Florida woman in a persistent vegetative state who was being kept alive through the use of a feeding tube. The feeding tube was removed on Friday, an action that will result in her death within about two weeks. A federal judge made a ruling in the case today.

First, do you agree with the federal judge's decision that resulted in the feeding tube being left unattached, or do you disagree and think the federal judge should have ordered the feeding tube to be re-attached?

	Agree with decision that left feeding tube unattached	Disagree, should have ordered feeding tube re-attached	No opinion
2005 Mar 22	52%	39	9

Do you agree/disagree strongly, or only moderately?

COMBINED RESPONSES (Q.1-2)

	Agree strongly	Agree only moderately	Disagree only moderately	Disagree strongly	No opinion
2005 Mar 22	37%	15	9	30	9

Relatively few Americans believe there is much chance for significant improvement in Terri Schiavo's condition if the feeding tube were put back in place permanently. In fact, a majority, 54%, says there is "no chance whatsoever" that Schiavo's brain activity would show significant improvement under those circumstances, agreeing with several court-appointed physicians in the many legal proceedings surrounding the matter. Only 29% say there is a slight chance of improvement. Thirteen percent say there is a good chance, including 4% who believe the chances are "very good."

Just your best guess, if the feeding tube that was helping to keep Terri Schiavo alive were reinserted on a permanent basis, how much of a chance do you think there is that she would eventually show significant improvement in her brain activity—a very good chance, a good chance, a slight chance, or no chance whatsoever?

	Very good chance	Good chance	Slight chance	No chance whatsoever	No opinion
2005 Mar 22	4%	9	29	54	4

The poll finds that Americans are sympathetic to both sides in the dispute—husband Michael Schiavo and parents Bob and Mary Schindler. However, despite the fact that a majority of Americans agree with the husband's side of the case, Americans express much greater sympathy toward the parents than toward the husband. Fifty-five percent of Americans say they feel "very sympathetic" toward the Schindlers, and an additional 31% say they are somewhat sympathetic. By comparison, 37% are very sympathetic and 32% are somewhat sympathetic toward Michael Schiavo.

Based on what you have heard or read about this case, how do you feel toward—[RANDOM ORDER]—very sympathetic, somewhat sympathetic, somewhat unsympathetic, or very unsympathetic?

	Very sympathetic	Somewhat sympathetic	Somewhat unsympathetic	Very unsympathetic	No opinion
Bob and Mary Schindler, parents of Terri Schiavo	55%	31	5	5	4
Michael Schiavo, husband of Terri Schiavo	37%	32	9	18	4

Many Americans appear to be taking sides in the issue. Those who say they are very sympathetic toward the Schindlers are much more likely to disagree (55%) than agree (38%) with the federal judge's ruling. Conversely, those who are very sympathetic toward Michael Schiavo support the judge's decision by a substantial margin (76% to 19%).

Still, most Americans believe Michael Schiavo is being forthright in saying that Terri expressed a wish not to be kept alive by artificial means—21% say he is definitely telling the truth and 43% say he probably is. One in four do not believe his statements are truthful.

As you may know, Michael Schiavo said his wife, Terri, told him that she would not want to be kept alive by artificial means. Do you think he is—[ROTATED: definitely telling the truth, probably telling the truth, probably not telling the truth, (or) definitely not telling the truth]?

	Definitely telling the truth	Probably telling the truth	Probably not telling the truth	Definitely not telling the truth	No opinion
2005 Mar 22	21%	43	17	8	11

The public is giving a collective thumbs-down to politicians' involvement in the Schiavo case. A majority, 52%, disapproves of the way Bush has handled the case, and a near-majority (47%) disapproves of the way Republicans in Congress have handled it. Even Americans who are very sympathetic with the Schindlers are more likely to disapprove than approve of the actions of the Republican congressional delegation, and are evenly divided in their views of Bush's involvement.

More Americans disapprove (42%) than approve (28%) of the actions of the Democrats in Congress in this matter, though a substantial 30% have no opinion.

In contrast, the media comes out looking relatively good: 43% approve and 46% disapprove of the way the media has handled the case.

Do you approve or disapprove of the way each of the following has handled the case involving Terri Schiavo? How about—[RANDOM ORDER]?

2005 Mar 22 (sorted by "approve")	Approve %	Disapprove %	No opinion %
The media	43	46	11
George W. Bush	31	52	17
The Democrats in Congress	28	42	30
The Republicans in Congress	26	47	27

Survey Methods

These results are based on telephone interviews with a randomly selected national sample of 620 adults, aged 18 and older, conducted March 22, 2005. For results based on this sample, one can say with 95% confidence that the maximum error attributable to sampling and other random effects is ±4 percentage points. In addition to sampling error, question wording and practical difficulties in conducting surveys can introduce error or bias into the findings of public opinion polls.

Polls conducted entirely in one day, such as this one, are subject to additional error or bias not found in polls conducted over several days.

March 24, 2005
SUPPORT FOR IRAQ WAR REMAINS DIVIDED
Three key measures find support for the war split

by Joseph Carroll, Gallup Poll Assistant Editor

This past Saturday, March 19, marked the second anniversary of the start of the war in Iraq. Americans are now divided in their overall support for the war, in their ratings of President George W. Bush's handling of it, and in their views of how things are going in Iraq. This is a much different picture from what Gallup found at the start of the war, when the vast majority of Americans supported the United States' efforts in Iraq. Americans have become much more positive, however, in their overall view of Iraq as a country, although the majority still has an unfavorable opinion of Iraq.

Americans Split in Support for War

Over the past two years, Gallup has tracked three key measures to gauge public support for the war in Iraq. At the start of the war, the vast majority of Americans supported the war efforts. By the summer of 2003, after the president had declared victory in Iraq and the fighting continued in cities throughout the country, support for the war began to diminish. Last year, on most measures, Americans were closely divided in their views of the war, but were generally more negative than positive in their assessment of the conflict. For the past few months, Americans have been divided on all three of these measures.

1. In view of the developments since we first sent our troops to Iraq, do you think the United States made a mistake in sending troops to Iraq, or not?

The latest CNN/*USA Today*/Gallup poll, conducted March 18-20, finds that a slim majority of Americans, 51%, say it was *not* a mistake to send troops to Iraq; 46% say it was a mistake.

When the war started, only 23% of adults nationwide said it was a mistake to send troops to Iraq, while three-quarters of respondents said it was not a mistake. The percentage of Americans saying it was a mistake gradually increased, and by the end of 2003, reached the 40% range. It was not until the summer of 2004 when a majority of Americans first said it was a mistake to send troops to Iraq.

The more recent trend, since the start of 2005, shows greater fluctuation in the public's responses to this question. In January, more Americans said it was a mistake to send troops than said it was *not* a mistake. That changed when Americans became much more positive about the situation in Iraq following the elections in that country at the end of January, with the majority (55%) saying it was not a mistake and 45% saying it was. Since then, positive assess-

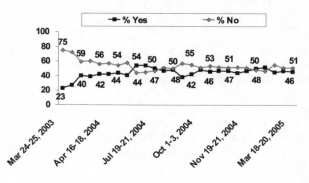

Mistake to Send Troops to Iraq?

ments have receded somewhat, but remain more positive than at the beginning of the year.

2. Do you favor or oppose the U.S. war with Iraq?

Forty-seven percent of Americans support the U.S. war with Iraq; the exact same percentage opposes it.

Gallup asked this question seven times in March and April 2003. The vast majority of Americans supported the war at that time, with support ranging from 68% to 72%. When Gallup asked this question again in October 2003, support had declined, but a majority of Americans, 54%, still supported it. Last November, following Bush's victory in the presidential election against Massachusetts Sen. John Kerry, Americans were divided in their reaction to the war. This same divide remains today.

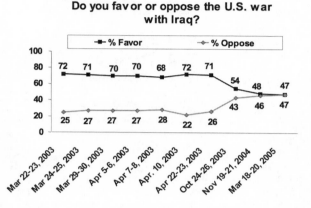

Do you favor or oppose the U.S. war with Iraq?

3. All in all, do you think it was worth going to war in Iraq, or not?

Another question Gallup has used to measure the public's feelings about going to war asks whether the war was "worth it," or not.

At the start of the war, two in three Americans said it was worth going to war in Iraq. At least half of all Americans expressed this sentiment until the end of January 2004. Since that time, the results of this question have fluctuated significantly, ranging from a low of 44% to a high of 56% saying it was worth it. Most recently, Americans have been divided on this measure. According to a Feb. 7-10 poll, 48% say it was worth going to war, while 50% say it was not.

Public Also Divided on How Things are Going in Iraq

A slight majority of Americans, 52%, say things are currently going well for the United States in Iraq, while 45% say things are going

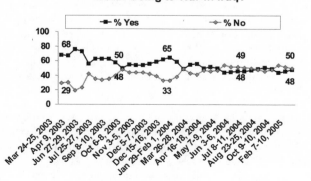

Worth Going to War in Iraq?

badly. These results show little change from early February, when they became more positive right after the elections in Iraq took place. Throughout 2004, the public tended to say things were not going well in Iraq.

Gallup first asked this question a month after the war in Iraq started. At that time, 85% said things were going well in Iraq. Views on the war stayed at this level until the end of May 2003, at which point Americans became less likely to say things were going well.

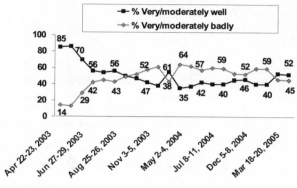

How Would You Say Things Are Going For The U.S. in Iraq?

When asked who is winning the war in Iraq, 43% of Americans say the United States is winning, while 7% say the insurgents in Iraq are winning. Slightly fewer than half of Americans, 48%, say neither side is winning.

Who do you think is currently winning the war in Iraq?

	U.S. and its allies	Insurgents in Iraq	Neither side	No opinion
2005 Feb 25-27	43%	7	48	2
2004 Nov 19-21	44%	7	46	3
2004 Oct 22-24 ^	35%	10	53	2

^ Asked of a half sample

At the start of the war, the overwhelming majority of Americans said the United States was winning. Only about one in five said neither side was winning, and few said Iraq was winning. (The response options on this question were changed as it became clear that the Iraqi insurgents were the United States' primary enemy in the conflict).

Who do you think is currently winning the war in Iraq?

	U.S. and its allies	Iraq	Neither side	No opinion
2003 Mar 29-30	74%	1	23	2
2003 Mar 24-25	74%	1	21	4
2003 Mar 22-23	84%	*	14	2

*Less than 0.5%

Slight Majority Disapproves of Bush's Handling of Iraq

Gallup's Feb. 25-27 poll shows that a slight majority of Americans, 53%, disapprove of the way Bush is handling the situation in Iraq, while 45% approve. Earlier in February, Americans were essentially split, with 50% approving and 48% disapproving. The current results are roughly similar to ratings Gallup measured during the past few months.

The Public's Approval of George W. Bush's Handling of Situation in Iraq

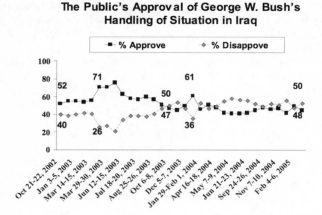

Prior to the start of the Iraq war, Bush's approval rating on Iraq was in the mid-50% range. Approval of Bush then surged once the war started, to 71% in late March 2003 and 76% in April 2003. Bush's approval on Iraq began to wane after that point, dipping as low as 41% in May 2004.

Americans More Favorable Toward Iraq This Year

Gallup periodically asks Americans if they have a favorable or unfavorable opinion of various countries around the world. Americans' opinions of Iraq have improved substantially since the war in Iraq began. From 1991 through 2003, less than 1 in 10 Americans said they had a favorable opinion of Iraq. In 2004, Iraq's favorable ratings increased to 21%. This year, the ratings increased again, this time to 29%. Still, two in three Americans in this year's survey view Iraq negatively.

The Public's Opinion Of Iraq

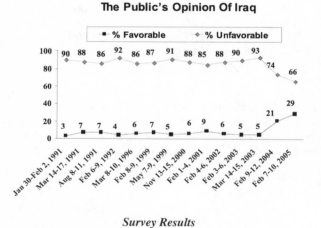

Survey Results

Results in the current survey are based on telephone interviews with 909 national adults, aged 18 and older, conducted March 18-20, 2005. For results based on the total sample of national adults, one can say with 95% confidence that the maximum margin of sampling error is ±4 percentage points. In addition to sampling error, question wording and practical difficulties in conducting surveys can introduce error or bias into the findings of public opinion polls.

March 25, 2005

BUSH APPROVAL DROPS AMID SOURING ECONOMIC VIEWS

Two-year low in economic rating of the future

by David W. Moore, Gallup Poll Senior Editor

President George W. Bush's approval rating is now at 45%, according to the latest CNN/*USA Today*/Gallup poll, conducted March 21-23. This is the lowest such rating Bush has received since taking office, although it is not significantly different from the 46% approval rating he received in May 2004.

George W. Bush's Job Approval Ratings November 2004 – March 2005

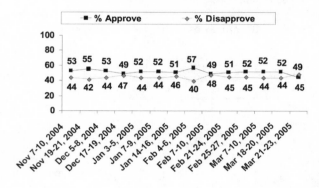

In the last three Gallup surveys, conducted in late February and early March, Bush's job approval rating was 52%. The timing of the seven-point drop suggests that the controversy over the Terri Schiavo case may be a major cause. New polls by ABC and CBS News show large majorities of Americans opposed to the intervention by Congress and the president in the Schiavo case, and Gallup's Tuesday-night poll shows a majority of Americans disapprove of the way Bush has handled the Schiavo situation. Almost all recent polling has shown that Americans approve of the decision to remove Schiavo's feeding tube.

But the CNN/*USA Today*/Gallup survey suggests that the public's increasingly dismal views about the economy, and about the way things are going in general, could also be factors in Bush's lower approval rating.

A month ago, the public was more dissatisfied than satisfied with the country's direction by a margin of seven points; 52% of Americans said they were dissatisfied with the way things were going in the United States at that time, compared with 45% who were satisfied. But the current poll shows that the margin of dissatisfaction has increased to 21 points, 59% dissatisfied to 38% satisfied.

Gallup's economic measures also show a continual decline since the beginning of the year. Thirty-two percent of Americans rate current economic conditions as excellent or good, while 24% say poor. That eight-point positive margin is the smallest since Gallup found a two-point margin last May. At the beginning of this year, 41% rated the economy as excellent or good, while just 17% said poor— a 24-point positive margin. Earlier this month, the positive margin was 19 points, 35% to 16%.

Even more dramatic is the greater pessimism about the future of the nation's economy. Fifty-nine percent of Americans say the economy is getting worse, just 33% say better—a 26-point negative margin. Earlier this month, the net negative rating was just nine points, with 50% saying the economy was getting worse, and 41% saying better. This is the worst rating on this measure in two years.

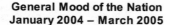

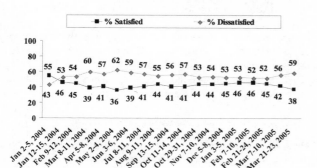

Current Economic Conditions
March 2004 – March 2005

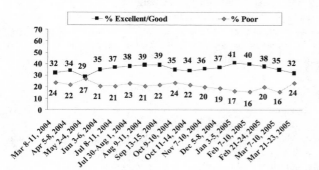

Economic Outlook
March 2004 – March 2005

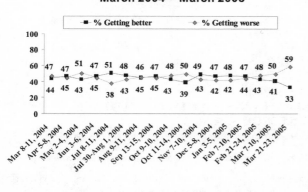

The Importance of Rising Gas Prices

One factor contributing to the economic malaise is almost certainly the rising price of gas and oil. In an open-ended question, 17% of Americans cited fuel prices as the most important economic problem facing the country, up from just 5% who said that a month ago, and 3% who mentioned it in mid-January.

What is the most important economic problem facing the country today? [OPEN-ENDED]

	Mar 21-23, 2005 %	Feb 21-24, 2005 %	Jan 17-19, 2005 %
Fuel/Oil prices	17	5	3
Unemployment/Jobs/Wages	17	22	22
War in Iraq	11	9	14

	Mar 21-23, 2005 %	Feb 21-24, 2005 %	Jan 17-19, 2005 %
Social Security	10	10	12
Healthcare/Health insurance costs	7	10	11
Federal budget deficit	7	9	9
Outsourcing of jobs	7	6	5
Lack of money	3	4	1
Inflation/Rising prices	3	2	3
Illegal immigrants	2	1	1
Education reform	2	2	3
Credit cards/Overspending	2	1	2
Taxes	2	2	3
George W. Bush/His policies	1	1	3
Poverty/Hunger/Homelessness	1	2	2
Gap between rich and poor	1	1	1
Welfare	1	1	2
Economy (non-specific)	1	1	1
Senior care/Medicare	1	1	1
Trade deficit	1	2	2
Poorly run government/politics	1	1	1
Foreign aid/Focus on other countries	1	1	2
Retirement	1	1	*
Stock market	*	*	*
Interest rates	*	1	*
International relations	*	*	1
College tuition expenses	—	—	1
Other	4	5	8
None	1	1	1
No opinion	9	10	8

Percentages add to more than 100% because of multiple responses.
*Less than 0.5%

When asked to identify the most important financial problem facing their families, 10% said energy costs—up from just 3% who mentioned that in February and January.

What is the most important financial problem facing your family today? [OPEN-ENDED]

	Mar 21-23, 2005 %	Feb 21-24, 2005 %	Jan 17-19, 2005 %
Healthcare costs	14	14	15
Energy costs	10	3	3
Lack of money/Low wages	10	13	12
Not enough money to pay debts/ Too much debt	8	7	14
Retirement savings	7	7	7
Unemployment/Loss of job	7	8	8
Cost of owning/renting a home	6	5	*
College expenses	6	7	8
High cost of living/inflation	5	4	8
Taxes	4	4	4
Social Security	2	4	3
Interest rates	1	1	1
Other	2	4	7
None	18	21	18
No opinion	6	4	4

Percentages add to more than 100% because of multiple responses.
*Less than 0.5%

The factors contributing to increasing dissatisfaction with the way Bush is handling his job also appear to be causing some Americans to drift toward identification with the Democratic Party, at least temporarily. The poll shows that the percentages of Americans who say they identify "as of today" as either a Republican or an independent are down slightly, from 35% Republican in Gallup's last poll to 32% in this poll, and from 31% independent to 29% independent. Identification with the Democratic Party is up from 32% to 37%. These relatively slight changes do not suggest a fundamental shift in the partisan structure in America today so much as they reflect a more negative mood at the moment toward both the president and his party.

Survey Methods

Results in the current survey are based on telephone interviews with 1,001 national adults, aged 18 and older, conducted March 21-23, 2005. For results based on the total sample of national adults, one can say with 95% confidence that the margin of sampling error is ±3 percentage points.

In addition to sampling error, question wording and practical difficulties in conducting surveys can introduce error or bias into the findings of public opinion polls.

March 25, 2005
SIX IN 10 AMERICANS TO ATTEND CHURCH THIS EASTER
Eighty-four percent of Americans identify with a Christian religion

by Frank Newport, Gallup Poll Editor in Chief

It is safe to predict that America's churches will be more crowded than usual this Sunday as Christians celebrate the Easter holiday. A recent Gallup Poll found that slightly more than 6 in 10 Americans plan on attending church on Easter.

Do you plan on attending church services this coming Easter Sunday, or not?

	Yes %	No %	No opinion %
2005 Mar 21-23	62	37	1
2002 Mar 18-20	64	31	5
1991 Mar 21	68	29	3

Although this self-reported Easter church attendance figure is down from similar measures obtained in the weeks before Easter in 2002 and 1991, it is still significantly higher than normal attendance. Gallup data collected in 2004 indicate that 44% of Americans reported having attended church in the last seven days, and that the same percentage said, on average, they attend church at least once a week or almost every week.

Who is most likely to be in the pews on Easter Sunday? Women, older Americans, and those who don't live in the West.

- Women are significantly more likely to be attending services than are men, by a 69% to 55% margin.

- Sixty-nine percent of Americans aged 65 and older say they will be attending services, compared with 59% of those aged 18 to 29.
- Almost three-quarters of women aged 50 and older will be attending church on Easter.
- Attendance will be lowest in the West, where only 52% will be attending Easter services, while at least 6 in 10 Americans in the Midwest, East, and South will be in the pews.
- There is little difference in projected Easter service attendance between Protestants and Catholics.

Americans' Religious Preferences

Although the United States is a diverse nation in terms of its citizens' specific religious affiliations, it is predominantly a Christian nation. Gallup's 2004 compilation of religion data shows that more than 8 in 10 Americans identify with a type of Christian religion: 24% Catholic, 50% Protestant, and 10% who can be classified as identifying with some other form of Christianity.

Gallup's 2004 data also indicate that 9% of Americans say they have no religious preference, and another 2% do not answer the question. That leaves just about 5% of all adult Americans who have a religious preference that is not Christian-related.

Survey Methods

These results are based on telephone interviews with a randomly selected national sample of 1,001 adults, aged 18 and older, conducted March 21-23, 2005. For results based on this sample, one can say with 95% confidence that the maximum error attributable to sampling and other random effects is ±3 percentage points. In addition to sampling error, question wording and practical difficulties in conducting surveys can introduce error or bias into the findings of public opinion polls.

March 28, 2005
BASEBALL FANS HAVE LITTLE PATIENCE FOR STEROID ABUSE
Fans have little trust in Congress to help fix the problem

by Mark Gillespie, Gallup Poll Senior Broadcast Producer

As baseball's spring training winds down and doctors review the first round of drug tests for the new season, a new CNN/*USA Today*/ Gallup poll finds fans are very concerned about the impact of performance-enhancing drugs on the national pastime, and that one in four are willing to say the drugs are "ruining" the game. The poll, conducted March 18-20, also shows that fans believe an average of 4 in 10 Major League Baseball players have used steroids or other performance-enhancing drugs within the past five years.

The poll was conducted after a hearing by the House Government Reform Committee into the sport's steroid problem and testing program on March 17. During that hearing, baseball players and executives defended the sport's new testing program against an onslaught of criticism from members of Congress. Mark McGwire, who acknowledged using the steroid precursor androstenedione during his record-setting 70-homer season in 1998, refused to directly answer questions during the hearing about whether he used other performance-enhancing drugs during his career.

McGwire told the committee he wanted to focus on the positive and look to the future, and pledged to help efforts aimed at persuading young athletes to stay away from steroids. However, the Gallup survey found most fans believe McGwire would likely have tested positive for steroids had a testing program been in place during his career (McGwire retired after the 2001 season; baseball did not ban steroid use until 2002 and started a testing program in 2003). More than three out of four baseball fans (77%) now believe McGwire used steroids despite his repeated denials during his career. In addition, only 53% of American adults have a favorable opinion of McGwire now, compared with 87% in a December 1998 Gallup Poll following his record-setting season.

Sammy Sosa and Rafael Palmeiro, two other players implicated in a controversial new book by admitted steroid user and former player Jose Canseco, both flatly denied any steroid use during their testimony before the committee. However, baseball fans are more likely to believe Palmeiro than Sosa, who remains the only player to hit 60 or more home runs in each of three seasons. Sixty-two percent of fans believe Sosa has used steroids, compared with 30 percent for Palmeiro. As with McGwire, the public's opinion of Sosa has also been damaged—falling from 83% favorable in December 1998 to 55% in the new CNN/*USA Today*/Gallup poll.

The one player not in the hearing room who might have been able to add to the discussion was Barry Bonds of the San Francisco Giants—accused by many of being the poster boy for steroid abuse. Bonds testified in 2003 before a federal grand jury investigating the BALCO Laboratories steroid case, and according to records leaked to a San Francisco newspaper, denied that he knowingly used steroids allegedly supplied by his personal trainer, who is one of four people facing criminal charges in the case.

Bonds, who expects to miss a great deal of the upcoming season because of injuries, has hit 703 home runs during his career so far, and is on track to surpass Babe Ruth's total of 714 homers when he returns to the lineup. However, 75% of baseball fans believe at least some of those homers were hit with the aid of steroids or other performance-enhancing drugs.

What Happens Next?

The hearing has already resulted in changes to the sport's drug testing plan. Baseball Commissioner Bud Selig has announced that fines alone will no longer be an option for disciplining players who test positive for steroid use. The possibility of fines was part of the plan agreed to by team owners and the players' union, sparking outrage from members of the House committee. As a result of a new agreement between the owners and the union, Selig says any player caught using steroids will face suspension.

Half of fans trust Major League baseball to handle the steroid issue on its own, according to the new poll, while 48% say they have little or no trust in the sport to police itself. The threat of congressional action to require a stronger drug testing policy inspires little confidence as well, with only 38% of fans placing their trust in Congress to handle the steroid issue.

Will Baseball Suffer Permanent Damage?

The new poll found that 39% of Americans consider themselves to be baseball fans, down from 43% last December. However, it must be noted that this figure is subject to seasonal variations, and routinely peaks after the end of a season, with a slight drop during the winter. As an example, 43% of Americans declared themselves to be baseball fans in November 2003 (after the Chicago Cubs and Boston Red Sox nearly made the World Series), and support slipped to 36% at the start of the 2004 season, in a March 2004 Gallup Poll. The current level of 39% is in line with polls conducted since the end of the 1994-1995 baseball players' strike.

However, failure to address the steroid issue conclusively could have a long-term impact on the game's popularity. The new poll found 23% of fans who believe steroid use is ruining the game of baseball, and another 63% who say it is a serious problem. Just 8% say it is not serious, and 5% believe the game has actually improved because of steroid use.

Survey Methods

These results are based on telephone interviews with a randomly selected national sample of 909 adults, aged 18 and older, conducted March 18-20, 2005. For results based on this sample, one can say with 95% confidence that the maximum error attributable to sampling and other random effects is ±4 percentage points. For results based on the sample of 443 baseball fans, the maximum margin of sampling error is ±5 percentage points. In addition to sampling error, question wording and practical difficulties in conducting surveys can introduce error or bias into the findings of public opinion polls.

March 29, 2005
PUBLIC: RICE HANDLING NEW JOB WELL
Opinion varies dramatically by party

by Darren K. Carlson, Government and Politics Editor

Condoleezza Rice is a busy lady. In February, she was mending rifts and strengthening ties in Europe and the Middle East. In March, she was championing democracy and stressing global partnership in South and East Asia. So far *this year*, the newest secretary of state has visited 19 countries, from Pakistan to Poland, racking up more than 54,000 travel miles as she promotes U.S. foreign policy.

What is the public's take on how the Bush administration's chief diplomat is handling her job? By and large, it's positive. A March 18-20 CNN/*USA Today*/Gallup poll*, conducted as Rice was finishing her tour of six Asian nations, found a majority of Americans (61%) approve of the way Rice is handling her job. Roughly a quarter (24%) disapprove, and 15% have no opinion.

Do you approve or disapprove of the way Condoleezza Rice is handling her job as secretary of state?

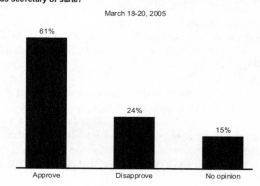

March 18-20, 2005

Not surprisingly, opinion of how Rice is handling her job varies dramatically by political party affiliation, with more than twice as many Republicans approving as Democrats. More than 8 in 10 Republicans (85%) express approval, compared with 57% of political independents and just 40% of Democrats.

Job Approval for Secretary of State Condoleezza Rice

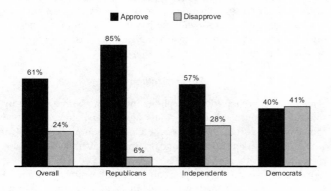

Favorable Rating Comparisons

In February, Gallup also asked Americans for their more basic opinions on Rice. The results are somewhat similar to her job approval rating, with roughly 6 in 10 Americans (59%) saying they have a favorable opinion of her, and slightly more than a quarter (27%) expressing an unfavorable opinion. Gallup's trend on this question dates back to October 2003, when Rice was national security adviser. After a 55% reading in October 2003, Rice's favorable rating dipped slightly (to 50%) in March 2004. Her favorable rating has since hovered in the 60% range.

Please say if you have a favorable or unfavorable opinion of this person -- or if you have never heard of him or her. . .Secretary of State Condoleezza Rice.

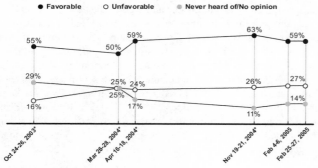

*Wording: National Security Adviser, Condoleezza Rice

How does Rice's favorable rating compare with those of her two most recent predecessors at the State Department? Her current rating is similar to those of the first female secretary of state, Madeleine Albright, who served during President Bill Clinton's second term (1997-2001). Albright's favorable rating was in the 60% range while serving as secretary of state.

Rice's favorable rating is significantly lower than that of Colin Powell, who served from 2001 to 2005. During his tenure as secretary of state, Powell's favorable rating averaged 85%—among the highest ratings of any figure Gallup has tested. Powell's ratings have been high since he became a national figure while serving as the Chairman of the Joint Chiefs of Staff during the Persian Gulf War in the early 1990s.

Race and Gender

Rice is a black woman, so it is possible that she may be thought more highly of by women and nonwhite Americans than by men and white Americans. This doesn't appear to be the case—Rice's job approval rating is nearly identical among women and men, and her favorable rating is actually *lower* among women than among men (56% compared with 62%). Among nonwhite respondents, her favorability sags substantially, which is likely because nonwhites tend to identify as Democrats. Rice's job approval rating among nonwhites is 42%, compared with 66% among whites; her favorability among nonwhite respondents is 44%, compared with 64% among whites. So despite her unique background compared with prior secretaries of state, Rice is still largely evaluated in partisan terms.

*These results are based on telephone interviews with randomly selected national samples of 1,008 adults and 909 adults, aged 18 and older, conducted Feb. 25-27, and March 18-20, 2005, respectively. For results based on these samples, one can say with 95% confidence that the maximum error attributable to sampling and other random effects is ±3 percentage points. In addition to sampling error, question wording and practical difficulties in conducting surveys can introduce error or bias into the findings of public opinion polls.

March 29, 2005
AMERICANS CHOOSE DEATH OVER VEGETATIVE STATE
Most would have feeding tube removed for their child, spouse, or themselves

by Lydia Saad, Gallup Poll Senior Editor

The court of public opinion has been no more favorable to Terri Schiavo's parents, Robert and Mary Schindler, than have been the state and federal courts that rebuffed their various requests to reinsert the feeding tube that keeps their daughter alive. Yes, Americans feel sympathetic toward the Schindlers, but on the legal question that is their real concern, every national media poll conducted to date about the Schiavo situation has found a majority of Americans agreeing with the court rulings that prevented reinserting the tube that was removed on March 18.

- A CNN/*USA Today*/Gallup poll conducted March 18-20* found 56% of Americans in agreement with the original removal of the feeding tube, with a question that was preceded by a description of Schiavo as "a Florida woman who has been in a persistent vegetative state since 1990."
- A CBS News poll on March 21-22 described Schiavo as being in a persistent vegetative state, and found 61% agreeing with the decision to remove her feeding tube.
- A Fox News/Opinion Dynamics poll conducted March 1-2 found 59% in favor of removing Schiavo's feeding tube, when told that she has been in "a so-called persistent vegetative state since 1990."
- An ABC News poll on March 20 found 63% of Americans in agreement with the removal, with a question that characterized Schiavo as suffering from irreversible brain damage, having no consciousness, and being on life support.

The Schindlers have argued that polling—and media coverage of the case more generally—has erred in telling the public that Schiavo is in a persistent vegetative state (PSV). They assert that their daughter is responsive, and at least two neurologists who observed Schiavo or reviewed her medical records say that she may have been misdiagnosed with PSV, and is, rather, in a "minimally conscious state."

Being in a vegetative state clearly has strong connotations for Americans. Whether Americans perceive much of a difference between being "a vegetable" and in a "minimally conscious state" is an open question.

A Gallup Poll from 1997 on death and dying found that being in a vegetative state was the most troubling end-of-life possibility to Americans among 24 different medical, emotional, practical, and spiritual problems that can confront people at death.

More than half of Americans said that "the possibility of being vegetable-like for some period of time" worries them "a great deal" when they think about their deaths. This exceeded concern for how family or loved ones will be cared for (44%), not having the chance to say good-bye to someone (39%) and even the possibility of great physical pain (32%).

Some people, when they think about their death, worry about practical matters, or emotional matters, or medical or spiritual matters … When you do think about your own death, how much, if at all, does each of these (practical/ emotional/ medical/ spiritual) matters worry you—a great deal, somewhat, not too much, or not at all?

The Gallup Organization*
May 1997

	% a great deal
The possibility of being vegetable-like for some period of time	53
How your family or loved ones will be cared for	44
Not being forgiven by God	42
Not having the chance to say good-bye to someone	39
Dying when you are removed or cut off from God or a higher power	38
The possibility of great physical pain before you die	32
Thinking that your death will be the cause of inconvenience and stress for those who love you	29
Not reconciling with others	25
The possibility of not having access to your own doctor or hospital	23
The possibility of not having access to life-saving medical technology	23
Not being forgiven by someone for something you did	23
The possibility of continued emotional suffering	21
The possibility of being alone when you are dying	21
Having other people make medical decisions about you	20
Not having a blessing from a family member or clergy person	19
What it will be like for you after you die	18
Not having made or updated a will	18
Not having completed your life work	16
The idea of being in a hospital if you are dying	14
Not being alive and part of this world	13
Not having made burial arrangements	11
Wondering whether anyone will miss you or remember you over time	10

	% a great deal
Having somebody go through your possessions after you have died	6
What they will say about you at your funeral	4

(*) Survey conducted for the Nathan Cummings Foundation and Fetzer Institute

Mercy, Not Malice

A combined 73% of Americans say they worry "a great deal" or "somewhat" about the possibility of being vegetable-like. Given this, it is not surprising that if Americans believe someone is in a vegetative state, they may consider removal of the feeding tube to be an act of mercy.

This earlier finding is reinforced by recent polling showing that most Americans would choose to remove the feeding tube for themselves, their spouse, or even a child if one of these were in the same condition as Schiavo.

- According to a recent ABC News poll, only 16% of Americans would want to be kept alive, themselves, while 78% would not.
- According to a 2003 Fox News poll, 74% would want their guardian to remove the feeding tube.
- According to a recent CNN/*USA Today*/Gallup survey, 56% and 61% would remove the feeding tube on behalf of a child or spouse, respectively.

Majority Support Doctor-Assisted Suicide

But it is not just for cases as extreme as PSV patients that Americans believe doctors should be allowed to hasten death. A clear majority of Americans believe doctor-assisted suicide should be legal for terminally ill patients. This is true regardless of whether the question specifies the illness is causing the patient severe pain. In May 2004, Gallup found approximately two-thirds of Americans in support of doctor-assisted suicide for people with incurable diseases:

- 69% said that in cases "when a person has a disease that cannot be cured" doctors should be allowed to "end the patient's life by some painless means if the patient and his family request it."
- 65% said that in cases "when a person has a disease that cannot be cured and is living in severe pain" doctors should be allowed to "assist the patient to commit suicide if the patient requests it."

Of course in these hypotheticals, the doctor has the patient's consent. Terri Schiavo had no living will (neither do most Americans according to a recent ABC News poll) so there is no way to know for certain if she would have wanted to continue living in her condition. But, perhaps because they would have their own feeding tubes removed under Schiavo's conditions, Americans are inclined to believe Michael Schiavo's claim that this would have been his wife's wish.

In a March 22 CNN/*USA Today*/Gallup poll, 64% of Americans said they thought Michael Schiavo was definitely or probably telling the truth when he said that Terri told him she would not want to be kept alive by artificial means.

Bottom Line

U.S. District Judge James Whittemore expressed the apparent sentiment of most Americans, when, in his latest ruling in the case, he wrote: "The court would be remiss if it did not once again convey its appreciation for the difficulties and heartbreak the parties have endured throughout this lengthy process." More than four in five Americans told Gallup they feel sympathetic toward the Schindlers, and three in five feel sympathetic for Michael Schiavo.

From the sidelines, Americans perceived that Terri Schiavo's mental condition was unlikely to ever improve. They believed her husband when he said that it would not have been her wish to be indefinitely sustained through a feeding tube. Most Americans know that they, themselves, would not want to persist in that state. All of this helps to explain why Americans would so roundly and consistently agree with the courts on the removal of Schiavo's feeding tube, even if that sentiment is profoundly disappointing to her parents.

Results are based on telephone interviews with 620 national adults, aged 18 and older, conducted March 22, 2005. For results based on the total sample of national adults, one can say with 95% confidence that the maximum margin of sampling error is ±4 percentage points.

Results are based on telephone interviews with 909 national adults, aged 18 and older, conducted March 18-20, 2005. For results based on the total sample of national adults, one can say with 95% confidence that the margin of sampling error is ±4 percentage points.

Survey done by Nathan Cummings Foundation and Fetzer Institute. Methodology: Conducted by Gallup Organization during May, 1997 and based on telephone interviews with a national adult sample of 1,200.

March 30, 2005
BUSH'S APPROVAL RATING IN PERSPECTIVE
Most other presidents had worse low points

by Jeffrey M. Jones, Gallup Poll Managing Editor

Last week's CNN/*USA Today*/Gallup poll measured the lowest job approval rating of George W. Bush's presidency to date—45%, one point lower than his previous low. While not good news for Bush, there are some silver linings for him in that other presidents' lowest approval ratings were much lower and that Bush's average rating while in office remains among the most positive for recent presidents. Nevertheless, Bush's public support is significantly lower than support for all other two-term presidents at similar points in their second terms.

Gallup's March 21-23 poll, conducted during the controversy over government involvement in the Terri Schiavo case and in the midst of rising gas prices, found 45% of Americans approving and 49% disapproving of the way Bush is handling his job as president. Bush received a similar 46% approval rating and slightly higher 51% disapproval rating last May, following reports of abuse of Iraqi prisoners by U.S. soldiers.

Even though Bush's approval rating has hit a personal low, it is still relatively high by historical standards when compared to other presidents at their low points. In fact, Bush's low rating is higher than the lows of all other recent presidents except John Kennedy and Dwight Eisenhower. Four presidents hit bottom below the 30% approval level—Harry Truman (23%), Richard Nixon (24%), Jimmy Carter (28%), and the elder George Bush (29%). Four others bottomed out below 40%—Lyndon Johnson (35%), Gerald Ford (37%), Ronald Reagan (35%), and Bill Clinton (37%). Kennedy's low point was 56%; Eisenhower's, 49%.

Low Approval Ratings for Presidents, Gallup Polls

President	Low approval rating	Disapproval at time of low approval rating	Date of low approval rating
Truman	23%	61%	1951 Nov 11-16
	23%	67%	1952 Jan 6-11
Eisenhower	49%	33%	1960 Jul 16-21
Kennedy	56%	29%	1963 Sep 12-17
Johnson	35%	52%	1968 Aug 7-12
Nixon	24%	63%	1974 Jul 12-15
	24%	66%	1974 Aug 2-5
Ford	37%	39%	1975 Jan 10-13
	37%	43%	1975 Mar 28-31
Carter	28%	59%	1979 Jun 29-Jul 2
Reagan	35%	56%	1983 Jan 28-31
G.H.W. Bush	29%	60%	1992 Jul 31-Aug 2
Clinton	37%	49%	1993 Jun 5-6
G.W. Bush	45%	49%	2005 Mar 21-23

Most presidents' low approval ratings can be attributed to events that were demonstrably not going well for the United States—specifically, the Korean War for Truman, the Vietnam War and racial tensions for Johnson, imminent impeachment for Nixon over the Watergate scandal, the energy crisis for Carter, and flagging economies for Ford, Reagan, and Bush the elder.

Also of note is that Johnson's and the elder Bush's low points came in polls completed just after the opposition parties held their presidential nominating conventions, which likely served to focus the nation's attention on its problems and to lay the blame for those squarely on the president's shoulders.

Bush's Presidency in Historical Perspective

In large part because of his response to the Sept. 11 terror attacks, George W. Bush remains one of the most highly rated presidents in Gallup annals. His term-to-date average approval rating of 61% is surpassed by only Kennedy and Eisenhower, and is the same as his father's.

Average Job Approval Ratings for Presidents, Gallup Polls
sorted by rating

President	Average approval rating for full presidency
Kennedy	70%
Eisenhower	65%
G.H.W. Bush	61%
G.W. Bush	61%
Johnson	55%
Clinton	55%
Reagan	53%
Nixon	49%
Ford	47%
Truman	45%
Carter	45%

Earlier in his term, the younger Bush's average approval rating rivaled that of Kennedy—after two full years in office, Bush's average job rating was 69%. But that cumulative average has been increasingly weighed down by ratings consistently around 50% for the better part of a year. In fact, nearly all of Bush's approval ratings since early 2004 have been below average by historical standards, given that the average Gallup presidential approval rating since the 1930s is 56%.

Thus, Bush's full-term average of 61% is more a reflection of where Bush has been than where he is going. All other presidents who were re-elected to a second term had approval ratings well above 50% in the March following their re-election.

Presidential Approval Ratings in March After Re-Election Year

President	Approval Rating	Date
Truman	57%	1949 Mar 6-11
Eisenhower	65%	1957 Mar 15-20
Johnson	69%	1965 Mar 18-23
Nixon	57%	1973 Mar 30-Apr 2
Reagan	56%	1985 Mar 8-11
Clinton	59%	1997 Mar 24-26
Bush	45%	2005 Mar 21-23

Bush still has more than three full years left in his second term, and he faces considerable challenges, including the war in Iraq, the war on terrorism, record budget deficits, and Social Security reform. His ability to successfully negotiate these issues will help determine if 45% is the absolute low point of his presidency or if his approval ratings will achieve new lows.

March 31, 2005
MAJORITY AGAINST "BUSH'S APPROACH" TO SOCIAL SECURITY
Support for private accounts depends on how reform is described

by Lydia Saad, Gallup Poll Senior Editor

President George W. Bush's proposal to restructure Social Security with private investment accounts remains less than popular with the American people. A March 18-20 CNN/*USA Today*/Gallup poll measured support for the proposal with three different questions, and found the public evenly divided, at best, on the issue.

Republicans are the only partisan group showing majority support for Bush's approach to addressing the long-term fiscal problems with the Social Security system. Democrats are solidly against it, while independents lean toward the Democrats' sentiments.

Most Americans feel fairly well informed about the debate over the future of Social Security. However, self-reported level of knowledge on the issue has little bearing on attitudes about Bush's plan. Those who say they understand the debate "very well" are generally no more supportive or opposed to Bush's plan than those who understand it only "somewhat" well, or not well at all.

"Bush's Approach" to Social Security Sparks Negative Reaction

One measure of support for Bush's plan simply asks respondents whether they "approve or disapprove of George W. Bush's approach to addressing the Social Security system," without providing any specific details of what that approach entails. By a 53% to 40% margin, the current results show net opposition.

These results are similar to the 50% disapproval and 44% approval ratings recorded in early February. The 4-percentage point drop in approval between February and March is within the margin of sampling error for this survey.

Support for Private Investment Limited, but Varies

A second question asks about the concept of private investment accounts, without associating the concept with President Bush, and without mentioning any specific pros and cons. The question simply describes the proposal as one "that would allow workers to invest part of their Social Security taxes in the stock market or in bonds, while the rest of those taxes would remain in the Social Security system."

Americans are divided in their reaction to this question, with 45% favoring the proposal and 47% opposing it. This question was previously asked in December 2004, with similar results.

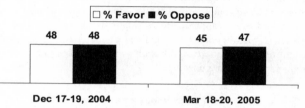

As you may know, a proposal has been made that would allow workers to invest part of their Social Security taxes in the stock market or in bonds, while the rest of those taxes would remain in the Social Security system. Do you favor or oppose this proposal?

A third question—asking Americans whether they think private investment accounts are a good idea or a bad idea—provides more information about the plan. Most notably, it specifies that the plan is intended to "address concerns with the Social Security system," that it "would allow people who retire in future decades to invest some of their Social Security taxes in the stock market and bonds," and that it "would reduce the guaranteed benefits" of those future retirees.

This wording generates the least support for Bush's plan of the three questions. Only 33% of Americans consider the plan as described a good idea, while 59% call it a bad idea. Support for the idea dropped 7 percentage points since the first week of February.

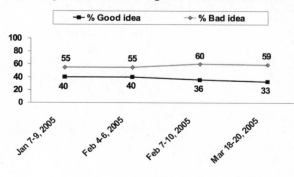

As you may know, one idea to address concerns with the Social Security system would allow people who retire in future decades to invest some of their Social Security taxes in the stock market and bonds, but would reduce the guaranteed benefits they get when they retire. Do you think this is a good idea or a bad idea?

This is the only question of the three that detects any significant change in attitudes about the proposal in recent months.

How fixed Americans' attitudes are on the issue—and how influenced they will be by future debate over Bush's plan—may partially depend on how knowledgeable they are about Social Security reform, and whether that knowledge base changes over time. Already, the public describes itself as fairly well informed. Nearly one-third of Americans (31%) say they understand the current debate over the future of the Social Security system "very well," while another 50% understand it "somewhat well." Only 18% of Americans say they understand it "not too well," or not at all.

Would you say you understand the current debate over the future of the Social Security system very well, somewhat well, not too well, or not at all?

	Very well	Some-what well	Not too well	Not at all	No opinion
2005 Mar 18-20	31%	50	13	5	1

For now, there is no correlation between self-described knowledge of the debate and attitudes toward Bush's plan. Those who say they understand the debate very well are similar in their views to those who understand it somewhat well. In both cases, a majority disapproves of Bush's approach to dealing with Social Security.

Those who do not have a good understanding of the debate also disapprove of his approach, though a substantial minority of this group admits they are unsure.

Based on what you have heard or read, in general, do you approve or disapprove of George W. Bush's approach to addressing the Social Security system?

by understanding of the Social Security debate

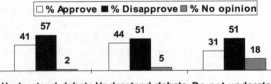

March 18-20, 2005

Republican Support Less Than Democratic Opposition

One problem for Bush is that Democrats are more unified in their views of Social Security reform than are Republicans. Just two-thirds of Republicans (65%) approve of Bush's approach, while 81% of Democrats disapprove of it. More than half of independents, 55%, disapprove of Bush's approach, which is almost exactly the average of Republican (25%) and Democrat (81%) disapproval.

Based on what you have heard or read, in general, do you approve or disapprove of George W. Bush's approach to addressing the Social Security system?

by party affiliation

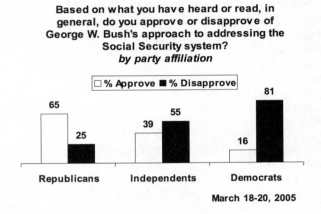

March 18-20, 2005

Survey Methods

These results are based on telephone interviews with a randomly selected national sample of 909 adults, aged 18 and older, conducted March 18-20, 2005. For results based on this sample, one can say with 95% confidence that the maximum error attributable to sampling and other random effects is ±4 percentage points. For results based on the 443 national adults in the Form A half-sample and 466 national adults in the Form B half-sample, the maximum margins of sampling error are ±5 percentage points.

heard or read about the case, do you think that the feeding tube should or should not have been removed?

	Should have	Should not have	No opinion
2005 Mar 18-20	56%	31	13

TIME/SRBI

Terri Schiavo has been in what doctors call a persistent vegetative or coma-like state for 15 years, with no higher brain activity. Her husband says that Terri would not want to be kept alive artificially in this state. He has asked that the feeding tube that keeps her alive be removed. Her parents disagree, saying that Terri would not want to die this way, and contend that her condition could be improved. A Florida judge upheld her husband's request to remove the feeding tube. Do you agree or disagree with the decision to remove her feeding tube?

	Agree	Disagree	Unsure
2005 Mar 22-24	59%	35	7

CBS News

(Terri Schiavo has been in a persistent vegetative state since 1990. Terri's husband says his wife would not want to be kept alive under these circumstances and he wants her feeding tube removed. Terri's parents believe her condition could improve and they want the feeding tube to remain.) What do you think should have happened in this case? Should the feeding tube have been removed or should it have remained? Partial sample (N=321)

	Removed	Remained	Unsure
2005 Mar 21-22	61%	28	11

It is important to note that the questions all provide the respondent with basic information about the situation, including the words "persistent vegetative."

Some critics have argued that these descriptions are inaccurate and that the resulting responses are biased. Recent questions that ask for opinions about the Schiavo case give an explanation or preamble, so it is impossible to determine with precision what the impact of the specific question wording is on the responses.

However, there are several reasons to believe that Americans most likely support the idea of Schiavo being allowed to die, regardless of the question wording involved.

First, recent poll results indicate that there has been a great deal of attention paid to the case. If a situation is well known to respondents, in general, they are less likely to be affected by the particular way in which the situation is described.

Second, responses to a recent Gallup Poll question show that most Americans believe that Schiavo would not have recovered significantly even if the tube had been replaced, suggesting that the public has a basic belief that she was beyond improvement:

Just your best guess—If the feeding tube that was helping to keep Terri Schiavo alive were reinserted on a permanent basis, how much of a chance do you think there is that she would eventually show significant improvement in her brain activity: a very good chance, a good chance, a slight chance, or no chance whatsoever?

	Very good	Good	Slight	None	Unsure
2005 Mar 22	4%	9	29	54	4

April 1, 2005
THE TERRI SCHIAVO CASE IN REVIEW
Support for her being allowed to die consistent

by Frank Newport, Gallup Poll Editor in Chief

Terri Schiavo lived in relative obscurity for much of her 41 years, but in the last two years, she was at the center of what eventually became a national obsession and firestorm of controversy. Naturally, in today's hothouse media environment, controversy nets intense media coverage. As a result, a large majority of Americans ultimately reached the point at which they said they were following the Schiavo situation at least somewhat closely.

There wasn't a great deal of public opinion polling on this case until recently, but we have seen enough survey research accumulate just in the last several weeks to allow us to reach several conclusions.

1. A majority of Americans believe that it was appropriate that Terri Schiavo's feeding tube be removed and that she be allowed to die.

Gallup first asked a question relating to the Schiavo case (although not mentioning her by name) in October 2003:

When a patient is in a persistent vegetative state caused by irreversible brain damage, do you think his or her spouse should or should not be allowed by law to make a final decision to end the patient's life by some painless means?

	Yes, should be allowed	No, should not be allowed	No opinion
2003 Oct 24-26	80%	17	3

At that point, well before the case became a major media focus, 8 in 10 Americans said that a spouse should be allowed to make a final decision to end his or her spouse's life.

Most other questions asked since then have dealt specifically with the Schiavo case, usually by giving respondents a description of the situation, and then asking their opinions. All have shown majority support for allowing Schiavo to die.

Here are some recent examples:

Gallup

(How closely have you been following the news about Terri Schiavo, a Florida woman who has been in a persistent vegetative state since 1990, and whose parents and husband disagree over whether she should be kept alive) As you may know, on Friday the feeding tube keeping Terri Schiavo alive was removed. Based on what you have

A majority of Americans also appear to believe that Schiavo's husband, Michael, was telling the truth when he argued that she would not want to be kept alive—again suggesting that the public's agreement that she be allowed to die is rooted in more than a temporary response to the way in which specific questions were worded:

As you may know, Michael Schiavo said his wife, Terri, told him that she would not want to be kept alive by artificial means. Do you think he is definitely telling the truth, probably telling the truth, probably not telling the truth, or definitely not telling the truth? Options rotated

	Definitely truth	Probably truth	Probably not truth	Definitely not truth	Unsure
2005 Mar 22	21%	43	17	8	11

2. Americans did not approve of government intervention into this case.

This is one of the most consistent public opinion findings relating to the Schiavo case. Results from a number of poll questions, asked after Congress passed legislation and President George W. Bush signed it into law early in the morning of March 21, have shown strong opposition to government involvement in the situation.

Here are several examples of these questions:

TIME/SRBI

Congress met in a special session this past weekend to pass legislation moving the Schiavo case from the Florida state courts, which have repeatedly ruled to remove the feeding tube, to the federal court system. Regardless of your opinion on the Schiavo case, do you think it was right for Congress to intervene in this matter, or not?

	Right	Not right	Unsure
2005 Mar 22-24	20%	75	5

How about President Bush, who signed the legislation this weekend moving jurisdiction to the federal courts? Was it right for him to intervene, or not?

	Right	Not right	Unsure
2005 Mar 22-24	24%	70	6

Do you think that Congress and the President's intervention had more to do with their values and principles, or more to do with politics?

	Value and principles	Politics	BOTH (vol.)	NEITHER (vol.)	Unsure
2005 Mar 22-24	25%	65	4	1	5

If your congressman voted to move the Schiavo case to the federal courts, would this make you more likely to vote for him or less likely?

	More likely	Less likely	DOESN'T MATTER (vol.)	Unsure
2005 Mar 22-24	21%	54	18	7

CBS News

Do you think Congress and the President should be involved in deciding what happens to Terri Schiavo, or is this a matter Congress and the President should stay out of?

	Should be involved	Should stay out	Unsure
2005 Mar 21-22	13%	82	5

Regardless of your opinion about the Terri Schiavo case, in general, do you think the federal government should decide whether it is legal for family members to remove a patient from life support, or should each state government decide, or are these issues something the government should stay out of?

	Federal	State	Government stay out	Unsure
2005 Mar 21-22	9%	13	75	3

Congress has passed a bill that would require Terri Schiavo's case to be heard in U.S. federal court. Do you think Congress passed this bill because they really care about what happens in this case, or do you think they passed the bill to advance a political agenda?

	Really care	Political agenda	BOTH (vol.)	NEITHER (vol.)	Unsure
2005 Mar 21-22	13%	74	3	1	9

Gallup

Do you approve or disapprove of the way each of the following has handled the case involving Terri Schiavo? How about [see below]?

2005 Mar 22 (sorted by "approve")	Approve %	Disapprove %	Unsure %
The media	43	46	11
George W. Bush	31	52	17
The Democrats in Congress	28	42	30
The Republicans in Congress	26	47	27

3. Americans would want their child or spouse to die if they were in a similar situation. More broadly, the American public supports the related concept of doctor-assisted suicide.

Gallup asked Americans what they would do if they had a relative in the same condition as Schiavo. The results show that by about a 2-to-1 ratio, Americans say they would personally have a feeding tube removed if the situation involved a child and if the situation involved a spouse:

Suppose you had a child who was in the same condition as Terri Schiavo, and it were up to you to decide whether to keep that child alive through the use of a feeding tube. What would you, personally, decide to do in that situation [ROTATED — remove the feeding tube (or) keep the feeding tube in place]?

	Remove	Keep in place	No opinion
2005 Mar 18-20	56%	34	10

Suppose you had a spouse who was in the same condition as Terri Schiavo, and it were up to you to decide whether to keep your spouse alive through the use of a feeding tube. What would you, personally, decide to do in that situation [ROTATED — remove the feeding tube (or) keep the feeding tube in place]?

	Remove	Keep in place	No opinion
2005 Mar 18-20	61%	30	9

Gallup has asked questions about "doctor-assisted" suicide since 1947. A majority of Americans were opposed in the 1947 and 1950 surveys, but polls conducted since 1973 have shown consistent majority support. Gallup has asked this question regularly in May of each of the last four years, and in these surveys, between 65% and 72% have supported the concept.

When a person has a disease that cannot be cured, do you think doctors should be allowed by law to end the patient's life by some painless means if the patient and his family request it?

	Yes %	No %	No opinion %
2004 May 2-4	69	29	2
2003 May 19-21	72	25	3
2002 May 6-9	72	26	2
2001 May 10-14	65	31	4
1996 Jul 26-28	69	26	5
1996 Apr 9-10	75	22	3
1990 Nov 15-18	65	31	4
1973 Jul 6-9	53	40	7
1950 Jan 8-13	36	54	10
1947 Jun 6-11	37	54	9

When a person has a disease that cannot be cured and is living in severe pain, do you think doctors should or should not be allowed by law to assist the patient to commit suicide if the patient requests it?

	Should %	Should not %	No opinion %
2004 May 2-4	65	31	4
2003 May 19-21	62	36	2
2002 May 6-9	62	34	4
2001 May 10-14	68	27	5
1999 Mar 12-14^	61	35	4
1998 Jun 5-7^	59	39	2
1997 Jun 23-24^	57	35	8
1997 Jan 3-5^	58	37	5
1996 Jul 26-28^	52	42	6

^1996-1999 WORDING: *When a person has a disease that cannot be cured and is living in severe pain, do you think doctors should be allowed by law to assist the patient to commit suicide if the patient requests it, or not?*

4. The long-term impact of the Schiavo situation is difficult to determine, but it is clear that the case has generated a strong interest in living wills. Americans are also concerned that the Schiavo case may lead to a situation in which Congress intervenes in the lives of Americans in the years to come.

Polls conducted by various organizations over the last several weeks have shown that about a third of Americans have living wills. But a poll conducted by *TIME* magazine shows that almost 7 in 10 Americans who do not have living wills say the Schiavo case made them "think about drafting a living will or discussing with your family your wishes for medical treatment should you be unable to communicate them yourself."

TIME/SRBI

(Terri Schiavo has been in what doctors call a 'persistent vegetative' or coma-like state for 15 years, with no higher brain activity. Her husband says that Terri would not want to be kept alive artificially in this state. He has asked that the feeding tube that keeps her alive be removed. Her parents disagree, saying that Terri would not want to die this way and contend that her condition could be improved. A Florida judge upheld her husband's request to remove the feeding tube.) …Has the Schiavo case made you think about drafting a living will or discussing with your family your wishes for medical treatment should you be unable to communicate them yourself?

Subpopulation/Note: Those who do not currently have a living will (62%)

	Yes	No	Don't know
2005 Mar 22-24	69%	30	1

There will no doubt continue to be speculation about the long-term implications of the Schiavo case on the nation's political and judicial systems. Conservatives have argued that the case will be a rallying cry for those who want to do more to ensure that the country embraces a "culture of life," while liberals have argued that there may be a backlash against those who attempt to legislate personal decisions. Given that the majority of Americans are clearly against government intervention in the case, the results of a recent CBS poll on the topic may not be surprising. The poll shows that two-thirds of Americans are apparently worried that this case will allow Congress to intervene in Americans' lives in the future:

Do you think that Congress' actions in this case would make it easier for Congress to intervene in the lives of individual Americans in the future? If Yes: Are you concerned about that, or not?

	Easier/ Concerned	Easier/ Not Concerned	Not easier	Unsure
2005 Mar 21-22	68%	9	17	6

Survey Methods

Results in the current survey are based on telephone interviews with 909 national adults, aged 18 and older, conducted March 18-20, 2005. For results based on the total sample of national adults, one can say with 95% confidence that the maximum margin of sampling error is ±4 percentage points.

In addition to sampling error, question wording and practical difficulties in conducting surveys can introduce error or bias into the findings of public opinion polls.

April 4, 2005
AMERICAN CATHOLICS REVERE POPE, DISAGREE WITH SOME MAJOR TEACHINGS
Seven in 10 expect church to make Pope John Paul II a saint

by David W. Moore, Gallup Poll Senior Editor

With the death of Pope John Paul II, most American Catholics believe that history will judge him favorably—either as a great pope, or even one of the greatest ever. Seven in 10 predict the Catholic Church will make him a saint. Most American Catholics also say the choice of the next pope will matter to them personally, and also to the world. But American Catholics seem not to care where the next pope comes from—they are equally willing to have him come from Africa, Asia, or Latin America.

As for the future, many Catholics appear to disagree with church teachings in several areas—use of birth control, allowing priests to marry, making church doctrine less strict on stem cell research, and allowing women to become priests. The poll shows that a majority of Catholics support each of those policies, while Pope John Paul II was adamantly against all of them. About half of American Catholics also would allow Catholics to remarry after a divorce, without getting an annulment. And more than a third would like to make church doctrine less strict on abortion.

The poll, conducted April 1-2, shows that almost 9 in 10 American Catholics believe Pope John Paul II will go down in history as either a "great" pope (21%) or one of the greatest popes ever (67%).

How do you think Pope John Paul II will go down in history—as— one of the greatest popes, great, but not one of the greatest, good, average, or below average?

	One of the greatest	Great, not one of the greatest	Good	Average	Below average	No opinion
Catholics						
2005 Apr 1-2	67%	21	7	2	1	2

Seventy-one percent believe the church will make him a saint, up from 51% who felt that way in October 2003.

Do you think Pope John Paul II will—or will not—be made a saint by the Catholic Church?

	Yes, will	No, will not	No opinion
Catholics			
2005 Apr 1-2	71%	18	11
2003 Oct 10-12	51%	39	10

About 9 in 10 Catholics also believe that it will matter to the world either a great deal (55%) or a moderate amount (34%) whom the church chooses as its next pope. Even three-quarters of non-Catholics believe the choice will matter to the world.

Just your best guess, how much will it matter to the world whom the Catholic Church chooses as the next pope—a great deal, a moderate amount, not much, or not at all?

	Great deal	Moderate amount	Not much	Not at all	No opinion
Catholics					
2005 Apr 1-2	55%	34	7	4	—
Non-Catholics					
2005 Apr 1-2	41%	35	14	8	2

Americans are less likely to say the choice of the new pope will matter to them personally than to say it will matter to the world, though it will matter personally to a clear majority (65%) of Catholics. Not surprisingly, among non-Catholics, only 23% say the choice will matter to them, while 76% say it will not.

How much will it matter to you who the Catholic Church chooses as the next pope—a great deal, a moderate amount, not much, or not at all?

	Great deal	Moderate amount	Not much	Not at all	No opinion
	%	%	%	%	%
Catholics					
2005 Apr 1-2	36	29	16	19	*
2005 Feb 25-27 ^	44	30	17	8	1
Non-Catholics					
2005 Apr 1-2	8	15	19	57	1
2005 Feb 25-27 ^	7	16	34	41	2

*Less than 0.5%

^ WORDING: How much will it matter to you who the Catholic Church chooses as the next pope when the time comes to do so—a great deal, a moderate amount, not much, or not at all?

One of the themes many Catholic observers articulated on television during the final days of Pope John Paul II's life was the inspiration Catholics received from the pope's suffering. The poll shows that about half of all Catholics, but 68% of Catholics who attend church weekly, found inspiration in the way Pope John Paul II handled his health problems.

Would you say you have found inspiration in the way Pope John Paul II has handled his health problems, or has it not affected you, personally, that strongly?

	Found inspiration	Not affected that strongly	No opinion
Catholics			
All	51%	48	1
Weekly churchgoers	68%	32	0

As for the future pope, about 8 in 10 Catholics say it is acceptable for him to come from Latin America, Africa, or Asia.

Would you find it acceptable or unacceptable if the College of Cardinals chose the next pope from one of the following areas? How about [RANDOM ORDER]?

2005 Apr 1-2
(sorted by "acceptable")

Catholics	Acceptable	Unacceptable	No opinion
Latin America	85%	12	3
Africa	80%	17	3
Asia	78%	19	3

About a third of all Catholics (including a third among weekly churchgoers) would also like the new pope to be more liberal than Pope John Paul II, while about 6 in 10 think the new pope should be about the same.

If you had to choose, do you think the College of Cardinals should select as the next pope someone who is—[ROTATED: more conservative than John Paul II, about the same, or more liberal than John Paul II]?

	More conservative	About the same	More liberal	No opinion
Catholics				
All	4%	59	34	3
Weekly churchgoers	1%	64	33	2

Although only a third of Catholics say they want the new pope to be more liberal than Pope John Paul II, clear majorities say they want the new pope to adopt policies that were clearly unacceptable to Pope John Paul II. Among all Catholics, 78% support allowing Catholics to use birth control, 63% allowing priests to marry, 59% making church doctrine on stem cell research less strict, and 55% allowing women to become priests.

Do you think the next pope should—or should not—[RANDOM ORDER]?

BASED ON 254 CATHOLICS

2005 Apr 1-2 (sorted by "yes, should")	Yes, should %	No, should not %	No opinion %
Allow Catholics to use birth control	78	21	1
Allow priests to marry	63	36	1
Make church doctrine on stem cell research less strict	59	36	5
Allow women to become priests	55	44	1
Allow Catholics to divorce and remarry without getting an annulment	49	48	3
Make church doctrine on abortion less strict	37	59	4

In addition, Catholics are evenly divided on allowing members of their faith to remarry after a divorce without getting an annulment, and 37% support making church doctrine on abortion less strict.

Only about half of all people who identify as Catholics say they attend church on a weekly basis, who—for purposes of comparison—are classified here as "practicing Catholics." Even among this group, large numbers support changes in church doctrine that Pope John Paul II opposed and that are likely to be opposed by any new pope.

Do you think the next pope should—or should not—[RANDOM ORDER]?

BASED ON 101 CATHOLICS WHO ATTEND CHURCH WEEKLY

2005 Apr 1-2 (sorted by "yes, should")	Yes, should %	No, should not %	No opinion %
Allow Catholics to use birth control	68	29	3
Allow priests to marry	48	52	0
Make church doctrine on stem cell research less strict	46	48	6
Allow women to become priests	44	56	0
Allow Catholics to divorce and remarry without getting an annulment	37	63	0
Make church doctrine on abortion less strict	29	69	2

Survey Methods

Results in the current survey are based on telephone interviews with 1,040 national adults, aged 18 and older, conducted April 1-2, 2005. For results based on the total sample of national adults, one can say with 95% confidence that the maximum margin of sampling error is ±3 percentage points.

For results based on the sample of 786 non-Catholics, the maximum margin of sampling error is ±4 percentage points.

For results based on the sample of 254 Catholics, the maximum margin of sampling error is ±7 percentage points.

For results based on the sample of 101 Catholics who attend church weekly, the maximum margin of sampling error is ±11 percentage points.

In addition to sampling error, question wording and practical difficulties in conducting surveys can introduce error or bias into the findings of public opinion polls.

April 5, 2005
AMERICANS FEELING PINCH OF HIGHER GAS PRICES
About 6 in 10 Americans experiencing hardship, including 15% who say "serious" hardship

by David W. Moore, Gallup Poll Senior Editor

The average price of gas is now at $2.15, up 10 cents from two weeks ago, and up 40 cents from last year. A new CNN/*USA Today*/Gallup survey finds that these higher gas prices are taking their toll on American consumers. Almost 6 in 10 say the higher prices are causing a hardship, including 15% who say the hardship is "serious." More than a third of Americans have cut back on spending because of the higher prices, and about half have cut back significantly on the amount of driving they do. Lower-income Americans feel especially hard hit.

The poll, conducted April 1-2, finds that 58% of Americans have experienced hardship, the first time in the past six years that a majority has expressed this view. Though no survey was taken on this issue in 2002, that was because there was no spike in prices. The current finding represents a significant increase in the number of Americans feeling a negative effect from higher gas prices.

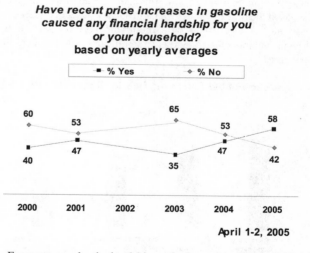

Have recent price increases in gasoline caused any financial hardship for you or your household?
based on yearly averages

— ■ % Yes   ◆ % No

April 1-2, 2005

For most people, the hardship so far is modest, but for 15% of all Americans, the hardship is a serious one.

Have recent price increases in gasoline caused any financial hardship for you or your household?

Is that a severe hardship that affects your ability to maintain your current standard of living, or is it a moderate hardship that affects you somewhat but does not jeopardize your current standard of living?

	Serious hardship	Moderate hardship	No hardship	No opinion
2005 Apr 1-2	15%	43	42	*

*Less than 0.5%

If prices continue to rise, the number of Americans who say they will feel the pinch is also likely to rise. When those who say the prices have not caused them financial problems were asked at what price level they would feel financially squeezed, the results suggest that 60% of all Americans feel the pinch when gas prices are at $2.00 per gallon, 70% would feel the pinch at $2.50 per gallon, 84% at $3.00 per gallon, and 94% if the price goes higher than that. (Another 2% say they would feel no hardship at any price level, and 4% express no opinion.)

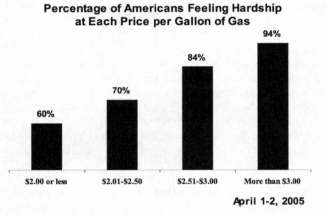

Percentage of Americans Feeling Hardship at Each Price per Gallon of Gas

April 1-2, 2005

Actions Taken Because of Higher Gas Prices

More than 7 in 10 consumers say that because of higher prices, they have made more of an effort to find the gas station with the cheapest gas in their areas. More than half have seriously considered buying a more fuel-efficient car. About half have cut back on their driving, and more than a third have significantly cut their household spending.

Done Each of the Following Due to Higher Gas Prices?

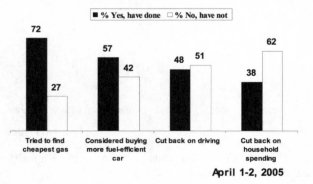

April 1-2, 2005

A comparison of actions taken by household income levels finds that lower-income consumers are especially hard hit by the higher prices. About 7 in 10 of the lowest income consumers (with household incomes of less than $20,000 a year) report cutting back on driving,

and separately, cutting back on spending. The percentages decline with increasing income, so that only 3 in 10 of the highest income households ($75,000 a year or more) report cutting back on driving, and 2 in 10 report cutting back on spending.

Done the Following Due to Higher Gas Prices?
by household income

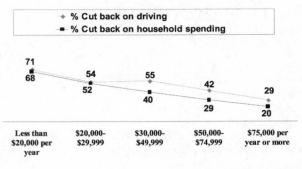

April 1-2, 2005

The other two actions taken by consumers are not strongly related to income. In general, high- and low-income consumers are about equally likely to consider a more fuel-efficient car. And from low-income to high-income consumers, there is only a slight decline in the percentage trying to find the cheapest gas in their neighborhoods— 77% among people with incomes under $20,000 a year down to 67% among people with incomes of $75,000 a year or more.

Done the Following Due to Higher Gas Prices?
by household income

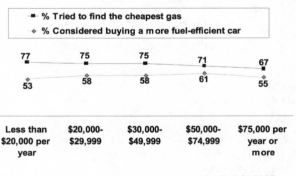

April 1-2, 2005

Survey Methods

Results in the current survey are based on telephone interviews with 1,040 national adults, aged 18 and older, conducted April 1-2, 2005. For results based on the total sample of national adults, one can say with 95% confidence that the maximum margin of sampling error is ±3 percentage points. In addition to sampling error, question wording and practical difficulties in conducting surveys can introduce error or bias into the findings of public opinion polls.

April 5, 2005

AMERICANS INSECURE ABOUT SOCIAL SECURITY

Only affordability and availability of healthcare is larger concern

by Darren K. Carlson, Government and Politics Editor

Since March 2001, Gallup has annually asked Americans to rate their personal level of worry with a number of social, economic, and political issues in the United States. The "Social Security system," which was included on the list of issues for the first time this year,* debuted among the top concerns. Of the 12 items Gallup tested, only "the availability and affordability of healthcare" is a larger concern for the public than Social Security. Roughly half (48%) of Americans worry a "great deal" about Social Security and another 24% worry a "fair amount." Slightly more than a quarter (27%) worry about the issue "only a little" or "not at all."

Worry About Social Security

Next I'm going to read a list of problems facing the country. For each one, please tell me if you personally worry about this problem a great deal, a fair amount, only a little, or not at all? First, how much do you personally worry about -- the Social Security system?

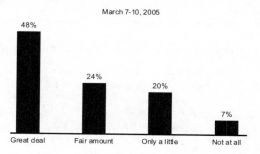

March 7-10, 2005

Because this is the first year Social Security was included in the survey, it is unclear whether the Bush administration's current initiative to reform Social Security through private investment accounts has elevated Americans' level of concern with that issue. However, Americans are much more likely now than in the past to cite Social Security as the most important problem facing the country.

Demographically, Americans nearing retirement are most likely to say they worry a great deal about Social Security. Forty-four percent of 18- to 29- year-olds say they worry about Social Security a great deal, as do 49% of 30- to 49-year-olds. More than half (54%) of 50- to 64-year-olds worry a great deal, compared with 43% of those aged 65 and older—many of whom are probably already collecting Social Security.

Worry about Social Security is also directly related to household income. Americans with higher incomes—who are less likely to depend on Social Security for retirement income—are also less likely than other Americans to say they worry about it a great deal. Thirty-seven percent of those with annual household incomes of $75,000 or more worry a great deal about the Social Security system, compared with 62% of Americans earning $30,000 a year or less.

Energy Anxiety

How does concern about Social Security compare with concerns about other political "hot button" issues of the day?

With gas prices topping $2 per gallon across the country, Americans are feeling the pinch. Although fewer Americans are worried about "the availability and affordability of energy" than they are about Social Security, concern about energy is up. Nearly 4 in 10 Ameri-

cans (39%) worry a great deal about energy supplies, up 4 percentage points from March 2004, and up 12 points from March 2003. However, the level of worry about energy today is still *lower* than it was in March 2001, when 46% of Americans worried a great deal about energy availability.

Worry About Energy

Next I'm going to read a list of problems facing the country. For each one, please tell me if you personally worry about this problem a great deal, a fair amount, only a little, or not at all? First, how much do you personally worry about -- the availability and affordability of energy?

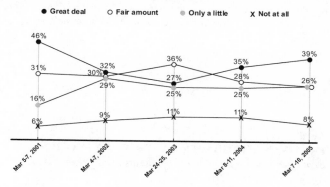

It is possible that energy concerns have risen since the poll was conducted in early March, especially since the price of oil has reached record highs.

Terrorism Less Troubling?

The possibility of a terrorist attack still troubles many Americans, but not to the degree it did in 2002 and 2003. Forty-one percent of Americans say they worry a great deal about the possibility of a terrorist attack in the United States—about the same percentage that worry a great deal about the availability and affordability of energy. The percentage worried about terrorism is in line with the percentage from last year (42%), but significantly lower than the 49% who worried a great deal about a terrorist attack in 2002 and 2003.

Worry About Terrorism

Next I'm going to read a list of problems facing the country. For each one, please tell me if you personally worry about this problem a great deal, a fair amount, only a little, or not at all? First, how much do you personally worry about -- the possibility of future terrorist attacks in the U.S.?

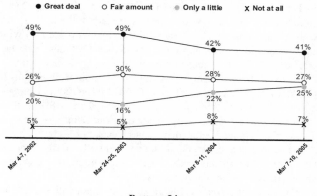

Bottom Line

Public awareness and worry about different issues will ebb and flow along with current events. Today's oil prices are causing worry about energy to trend upward. When it comes to terrorism, the fact that no attacks have occurred since 2001 has allowed the public's level of concern to remain fairly static. Whether the current battle over Social Security reform will lead to increased or decreased worry about that issue may depend on its outcome—namely, whether Bush can muster enough support in Congress for reform.

These results are based on telephone interviews with a randomly selected national sample of 1,008 adults, aged 18 and older, conducted March 7-10, 2005. For results based on this sample, one can say with 95% confidence that the maximum error attributable to sampling and other random effects is ±3 percentage points. In addition to sampling error, question wording and practical difficulties in conducting surveys can introduce error or bias into the findings of public opinion polls.

April 5, 2005
PARTISANSHIP SHAPES VIEWS OF COUNTRIES
Republicans more likely than Democrats to rate Iraq, Afghanistan favorably

by Joseph Carroll, Gallup Poll Assistant Editor

Americans' views of several countries around the world vary significantly depending on their party affiliation. Recent Gallup polling shows that Republicans and Democrats differ most in their ratings of nations in which the United States has taken military action following the Sept. 11, 2001, terrorist attacks, and in ratings of some of the countries that have supported or opposed U.S. military action in Iraq.

Gallup's Feb. 7-10 poll* shows that Republicans are much more likely than Democrats to rate Iraq and Afghanistan favorably, while Democrats are more favorable than Republicans toward France and Germany. Democrats are also more positive than Republicans about Iran and North Korea—two nations, along with Iraq, that President George W. Bush described as part of the "axis of evil" in his 2002 State of the Union address.

Overall Results

Republicans, including independents who lean toward the Republican Party, are most likely to differ from Democrats, including Democratic leaners, in their favorable views of Iraq (41% vs. 19%) and Afghanistan (49% vs. 34%). Republicans also view the following nations more favorably than Democrats do: Israel, Ukraine, Pakistan, Great Britain, Saudi Arabia, and Japan.

Democrats, meanwhile, are more likely than Republicans to favorably rate France (67% vs. 34%), Cuba (35% vs. 20%), Germany (80% vs. 67%), Iran (18% vs. 7%), and North Korea (18% vs. 8%). Views of Canada, Indonesia, Syria, Mexico, and China also are more favorable among Democrats than Republicans.

Republicans and Democrats show essentially no difference in their ratings of six other nations—Poland, Jordan, India, Russia, Egypt, and the Palestinian Authority.

For the most part, these favorability gaps are small enough that the majority of Republicans and Democrats are, nevertheless, in agreement in their views of each country. The major exception to this is France: 67% of Democrats view this country favorably, while 34% of Republicans view it favorably.

Opinion of Countries Around the World

Feb. 7-10, 2005
Percentage saying "very" or "mostly" favorable

	Republicans (including "leaners")	Democrats (including "leaners")	Gap (Republicans minus Democrats)
Iraq	41%	19%	+22
Afghanistan	49%	34%	+15
Israel	76%	65%	+11
Ukraine	73%	63%	+10
Pakistan	46%	38%	+8
Great Britain	96%	89%	+7
Saudi Arabia	41%	34%	+7
Japan	85%	79%	+6
Poland	80%	78%	+2
Jordan	56%	55%	+1
India	75%	75%	0
Russia	62%	64%	-2
Egypt	63%	66%	-3
The Palestinian Authority	24%	28%	-4
China	45%	50%	-5
Mexico	72%	78%	-6
Syria	21%	27%	-6
Indonesia	54%	62%	-8
Canada	82%	91%	-9
North Korea	8%	18%	-10
Iran	7%	18%	-11
Germany	67%	80%	-13
Cuba	20%	35%	-15
France	34%	67%	-33

Partisan Views of Nations Changed With Start of Iraq War

Republicans' and Democrats' opinions of several nations shifted as the United States made its case for going to war in Iraq in early 2003.

France. Republicans and Democrats showed essentially no difference in their views of France in 2001 and 2002. However, favorable views of France dropped substantially among both groups in early 2003, but much more so among Republicans than Democrats. Among Democrats, France's favorable ratings reached a low of 46% in mid-March 2003, while ratings dropped all the way to 20% among Republicans. Since that time, ratings of France have improved among both groups, but Democrats are now twice as likely as Republicans to rate that country positively.

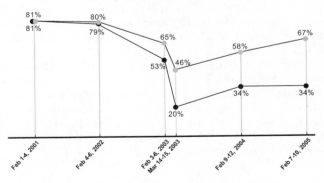

Opinion of France

● Republicans   ● Democrats

Percentage saying "very" or "mostly" favorable

Germany. Republicans rated Germany more favorably than Democrats did in 2001 and 2002. But, Republicans' favorable ratings of Germany plummeted to 37% about a week before the start of the Iraq war. The favorable ratings also dropped among Democrats at that time, but only to 61%. Since 2003, ratings of Germany have rebounded among both Republicans and Democrats, but

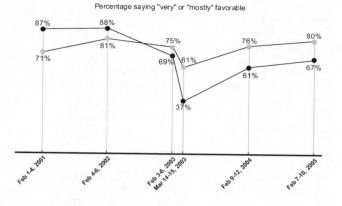

Opinion of Germany
● Republicans   Democrats
Percentage saying "very" or "mostly" favorable

87%   88%   75%   76%   80%
71%   81%   69% 61%   67%
            37%   61%

Feb 1-4, 2001   Feb 4-6, 2002   Feb 3-6, 2003 / Mar 14-15, 2003   Feb 9-12, 2004   Feb 7-10, 2005

Republicans continue to view Germany less favorably than Democrats do.

Iraq. Few Americans rated Iraq favorably prior to the start of the Iraq war. Fewer than 1 in 10 Republicans and Democrats rated Iraq favorably from 2001 to 2003. Last year, the favorable ratings of Iraq surged among both Republicans and Democrats, with a 23-point increase from March 2003 to February 2004 among Republicans and a 9-point increase among Democrats. The latest poll finds another jump in Republicans' favorable ratings of Iraq, from 28% to 41%, but essentially no change in Democrats' views of the country.

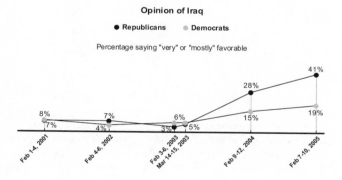

Opinion of Iraq
● Republicans   Democrats
Percentage saying "very" or "mostly" favorable

8%   7%   6%   41%
7%   4%   3% 5%   28%
                  15%   19%

Feb 1-4, 2001   Feb 4-6, 2002   Feb 3-6, 2003 / Mar 14-15, 2003   Feb 9-12, 2004   Feb 7-10, 2005

Afghanistan. In 2002 and 2003, Gallup found only slight variations in ratings of Afghanistan among Republicans and Democrats. Favorable ratings of Afghanistan increased among Republicans in 2004, from 26% to 36%, while they remained unchanged among Demo-

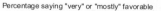

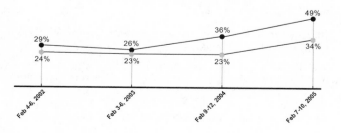

Opinion of Afghanistan
● Republicans   Democrats
Percentage saying "very" or "mostly" favorable

29%   26%   36%   49%
24%   23%   23%   34%

Feb 4-6, 2002   Feb 3-6, 2003   Feb 9-12, 2004   Feb 7-10, 2005

crats last year. In 2005, ratings increased among both groups, with nearly half of Republicans rating the country favorably and only about a third of Democrats doing so.

North Korea. Republicans and Democrats have shown essentially no difference in their views of North Korea until this year, when 18% of Democrats rated the country favorably, compared with only 8% of Republicans.

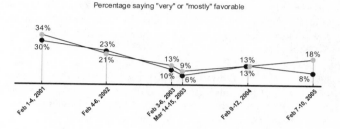

Opinion of North Korea
● Republicans   Democrats
Percentage saying "very" or "mostly" favorable

34%   23%   13%   18%
30%   21%   10% 9% 13%
                 6% 13%   8%

Feb 1-4, 2001   Feb 4-6, 2002   Feb 3-6, 2003 / Mar 14-15, 2003   Feb 9-12, 2004   Feb 7-10, 2005

Iran. As Gallup found with North Korea, there have only been slight partisan variations in ratings of Iran from 2001 through 2004. The current poll, however, finds an 11-point gap between Republicans and Democrats, with Democrats rating Iran more favorably than Republicans do.

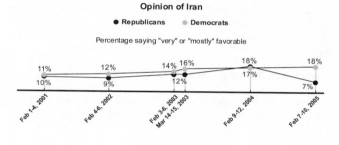

Opinion of Iran
● Republicans   Democrats
Percentage saying "very" or "mostly" favorable

11%   12%   14% 16% 18%   18%
10%   9%   12%   17%   7%

Feb 1-4, 2001   Feb 4-6, 2002   Feb 3-6, 2003 / Mar 14-15, 2003   Feb 9-12, 2004   Feb 7-10, 2005

Bottom Line

Republicans and Democrats differ in their views of many countries around the world. Over the past two years, Democrats have grown relatively more favorable toward nations that opposed the war in Iraq, while Republicans have grown relatively more positive about nations the United States has invaded since the 9/11 terrorist attacks.

This year, Gallup also found partisan differences emerging in views of North Korea and Iran.

*Results are based on telephone interviews with 1,008 national adults, aged 18 and older, conducted Feb. 7-10, 2005. For results based on the total sample of national adults, one can say with 95% confidence that the maximum margin of sampling error is ±3 percentage points. In addition to sampling error, question wording and practical difficulties in conducting surveys can introduce error or bias into the findings of public opinion polls.

April 6, 2005

PUBLIC SENDS MIXED MESSAGES ON SOCIAL SECURITY REFORM

Wants political leaders to act more quickly, but rates other issues as higher priorities

by Jeffrey M. Jones, Gallup Poll Managing Editor

Americans express a desire for political leaders to move more quickly on Social Security legislation, but at the same time assign a higher priority to several other issues, including terrorism, gas prices, and healthcare costs. Those who think political leaders are moving too slowly on Social Security are slightly more likely to blame George W. Bush and the Republicans in Congress than the Democrats in Congress. Bush's approval rating on Social Security remains low, as does support for the idea of allowing private investment of Social Security taxes.

To date, neither President Bush nor the congressional leaders of either party have made a formal legislative proposal on Social Security. The April 1-2 CNN/*USA Today*/Gallup poll gauged public reaction to the lack of legislative progress on the Social Security issue. Sixty-one percent of Americans say political leaders are moving "too slowly" in taking up legislation to change the Social Security system, while 29% say they are moving at an appropriate pace. Seven percent volunteer that leaders are moving too quickly.

This generally negative assessment of the progress is shared about equally by most key demographic groups. Republicans (64%) are about as likely as Democrats (61%) and independents (58%) to feel that political leaders are moving too slowly on the issue.

Those who say leaders are moving too slowly are slightly more likely to assign blame for this to Bush and the Republicans in Congress (40%) rather than the Democrats in Congress (32%). Seventeen percent say both are to blame, and 4% say neither is.

Who Is to Blame for Slow Progress on Social Security?

among those who say political leaders are moving too slowly on Social Security legislation

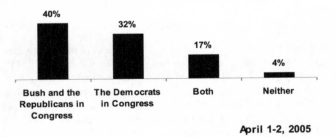

April 1-2, 2005

Overall, nearly 8 in 10 Americans say it is very important for Congress and the president to deal with Social Security in the next year, including 37% who say it is "extremely important." However, Americans assign higher priorities to several other issues, including terrorism, healthcare costs, gas prices, and the economy.

Rated Issue Importance

2005 Apr 1-2 (sorted by "extremely important")	Extremely important %	Extremely/Very important %
Terrorism	47	88
Healthcare costs	46	88
Gas prices	44	79
The economy	41	87
Social Security	**37**	**79**
Changes to how the federal courts handle moral issues	20	47

The percentage (37%) who say Social Security is an extremely important issue represents a slight decline from early February. Immediately after Bush's State of the Union address, 41% of Americans rated the issue as extremely important. Forty percent said it was extremely important in December.

Private Investment

Despite a desire for more action on Social Security, Americans show only limited support for the most talked-about reform proposal—allowing workers to invest a portion of their Social Security taxes in stocks and bonds. Thirty-nine percent favor such a proposal and 56% are opposed, a decline from 48% support in December.

As you may know, a proposal has been made that would allow workers to invest part of their Social Security taxes in the stock market or in bonds, while the rest of those taxes would remain in the Social Security system. Do you favor or oppose this proposal?

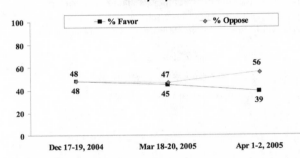

A separate question measured support for private investment of Social Security taxes but told respondents that such a proposal would entail a reduction in future guaranteed Social Security benefits. Just 33% of Americans say this proposal is a "good idea," while 61% say it is a bad one.

Bush's Handling of the Issue

Just 35% of Americans approve of the way George W. Bush is handling the Social Security issue, while 57% disapprove. That ties for the lowest rating of his administration on this issue to date.

Bush is rated more positively on most other issues tested in the poll, except for his handling of the Terri Schiavo case. However, only on terrorism do a majority of Americans approve of Bush. His latest overall job approval rating is 48%, a slight improvement from 45% the previous week.

Do you approve or disapprove of the way George W. Bush is handling—[RANDOM ORDER]?

2005 Apr 1-2 (sorted by "approve")	Approve %	Disapprove %
Terrorism	57	40
His job as president (overall job approval)	*48*	*48*

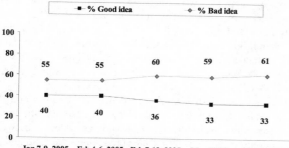

As you may know, one idea to address concerns with the Social Security system would allow people who retire in future decades to invest some of their Social Security taxes in the stock market and bonds, but would reduce the guaranteed benefits they get when they retire. Do you think this is a good idea or a bad idea?

	■ % Good idea	◆ % Bad idea

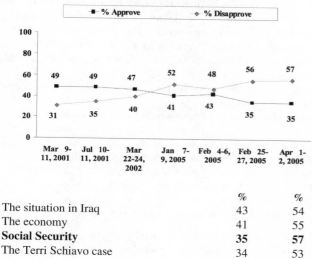

	Jan 7-9, 2005	Feb 4-6, 2005	Feb 7-10, 2005	Mar 18-20, 2005	Apr 1-2, 2005
% Bad idea	55	55	60	59	61
% Good idea	40	40	36	33	33

George W. Bush's Approval Ratings for Handling Social Security

	■ % Approve	◆ % Disapprove

	Mar 9-11, 2001	Jul 10-11, 2001	Mar 22-24, 2002	Jan 7-9, 2005	Feb 4-6, 2005	Feb 25-27, 2005	Apr 1-2, 2005
% Approve	49	49	47	52	48	56	57
% Disapprove	31	35	40	41	43	35	35

	%	%
The situation in Iraq	43	54
The economy	41	55
Social Security	**35**	**57**
The Terri Schiavo case	34	53

Bush's low marks on Social Security are understandable given the lack of progress on the issue as well as his public support for the relatively unpopular idea of private investment accounts. Some critics have charged that those accounts will seriously harm the Social Security system, because funds needed to pay for them would have to be borrowed from the existing Social Security trust fund. While the accounts hold out the promise of paying higher benefits to retirees than what may be possible under the current system, they also entail the risk of lower benefits if the investments do not pan out.

The poll asked Americans for their sense of what Bush's intentions are for Social Security. Generally speaking, the public is divided, with 50% saying Bush is trying to ensure the long-term stability of the system, while 46% say he is trying to dismantle it. These opinions are strongly partisan in nature—84% of Republicans believe Bush is trying to ensure the stability of Social Security, while 77% of Democrats believe he is trying to dismantle it. Independents are more likely to say Bush is trying to dismantle Social Security (51%) than to say he is trying to ensure its long-term stability (43%).

Survey Methods

These results are based on telephone interviews with a randomly selected national sample of 1,040 adults, aged 18 and older, conducted April 1-2, 2005. For results based on this sample, one can say with 95% confidence that the maximum error attributable to sampling and other random effects is ±3 percentage points.

For results based on the 519 national adults in the Form A half-sample and 521 national adults in the Form B half-sample, the maximum margins of sampling error are ±5 percentage points. For results based on the sample of 612 adults who say the political leaders in this country are moving too slowly in taking up legislation to change the Social Security system, the maximum margin of sampling error is ±4 percentage points.

In addition to sampling error, question wording and practical difficulties in conducting surveys can introduce error or bias into the findings of public opinion polls.

April 8, 2005
U.S. CATHOLICS VARY WIDELY ON MORAL ISSUES
Active Catholics much more conservative

by Frank Newport, Gallup Poll Editor in Chief

The death of Pope John Paul II has focused attention on the future of the Catholic Church and the importance of the next pope and his positions on key doctrinal and moral issues. Pope John Paul II's conservative stances were positively received in some quarters, but most observers agree that many Catholics consider themselves out of sync with church positions and that this disjuncture has possible long-term negative implications.

Although most of the world's Catholics live outside the United States, an analysis of American Catholics' characteristics, attitudes, and opinions provides useful insights into the challenges the church faces in the years ahead.

A special Gallup Poll review of data on American Catholics—about a quarter of the adult U.S. population—shows that Catholics as a whole tend to express views similar to those of non-Catholics on many moral issues. The two groups also share similar demographic characteristics (although Catholics are more likely to live in the East and to be Hispanic). A detailed examination of the Catholic population's views on moral issues, however, reveals significant differences within the broad Catholic population. The third of American Catholics who are active churchgoers tend to be older and much more conservative on moral issues than are those who attend church less frequently or do not attend church at all. This latter group of lapsed Catholics, who are younger and constitute about a third of all Catholics, are much more likely to say that such things as abortion, the death penalty, and stem cell research are morally acceptable.

Catholics on Six Moral Issues

Each May, Gallup asks Americans to rate the acceptability of a series of moral and ethical issues ranging from abortion to wearing animal fur.

For the purposes of this analysis, we looked at six moral issues on which the Catholic Church has taken a position: abortion, the death penalty, doctor-assisted suicide, homosexual behavior, divorce, and research using stem cells derived from human embryos. In order to provide larger sample sizes and more stable estimates, we combined data from 2002, 2003, and 2004 in this analysis.

Moral Acceptability of Six Issues
Based on Gallup Polls Conducted in May 2002, May 2003, and May 2004
% Morally acceptable

	Catholics %	Non-Catholics %
Abortion	37	39
Death penalty	63	65
Doctor-assisted suicide	48	50
Homosexual behavior	48	39
Divorce	68	64
Stem cells/Human embryos	55	53
Sample size	734	2,284

There are no significant differences between Catholics and non-Catholics in their views of the moral acceptability of five of these issues, although homosexual behavior is more likely to be perceived as morally acceptable among Catholics than it is among non-Catholics.

Differences Within the Catholic Population in the U.S.

These data suggest that Americans who identify as Catholic are not substantially different from everybody else in terms of their positions on these key moral issues.

But as noted, the Catholic population in the United States today is not monolithic. In particular, data show that the rate of church attendance among Catholics has drifted downward over the years, resulting in a situation in which about a third of Catholics report attending church weekly, about a third say they attend less than weekly or monthly, and about a third say they seldom or never attend.

These are vastly different groups of Catholics. Demographically, the active Catholics who attend weekly are much older than less active Catholics. More importantly, an analysis of self-reported moral acceptability of the six issues shows extraordinary differences among the three groups of Catholics as determined by their church attendance.

Moral Acceptability of Six Issues
Based on Gallup Polls Conducted in May 2002, May 2003, and May 2004
Based on Catholics Only
% Morally acceptable

	Catholics who attend church weekly %	Catholics who attend church nearly every week or monthly %	Catholics who seldom or never attend church %
Abortion	20	34	54
Death penalty	45	64	77
Doctor-assisted suicide	32	48	62
Homosexual behavior	35	45	63
Divorce	55	66	82
Stem cells/Human embryos	37	58	68

The pattern is consistent on all six issues. The moral acceptability of each issue is lowest among Catholics who attend church weekly, somewhat higher among those who attend less frequently, and much higher among those who seldom or never attend.

The differences are striking. Only 20% of active Catholics who attend church weekly say that abortion is morally acceptable. That percentage rises to 34% among those who attend nearly every week or monthly, and jumps to 54% among lapsed Catholics who rarely attend church. There are similar differences on each of the other issues.

Overall, significant majorities of Catholics who seldom or rarely attend church find each of these six issues to be morally acceptable, while less than a majority of the active Catholic group finds five of the six morally acceptable (the exception is divorce, morally acceptable to 55% of active Catholics).

These data are a striking representation of the problems the Catholic Church faces today, in some ways suggestive of the strategic issues facing a political candidate who has to decide between appealing only to the party faithful or broadening the campaign to appeal to a larger group of voters. In the United States, there is a hard-core group of older Catholics who attend church frequently, and who have quite conservative positions on moral issues that are in line with the official Vatican doctrine. But this group constitutes way less than a majority of all Americans who identify themselves as Catholics. Another group attends church, but less frequently, and is also less conservative on moral issues. Finally, there is the group of younger Catholics who seldom or never attend church, and who have positions on moral issues that tend to be quite at odds with official church dogma.

Any organization tends to pay most attention to its loyal and most active members of course, and it would be logical if the Catholic Church were to continue to adopt positions that active churchgoers approved of. But Gallup data suggest that church attendance has been declining among Catholics over the last quarter-century, and if those younger Catholics who are not attending remain at odds with church doctrine on key issues, it is less likely that they can be persuaded to become more active in the years to come.

A Portrait of Catholics in U.S. Today

An analysis of more than 24,000 interviews conducted in 2004, in which Americans were asked their religious identification, indicates that Catholics—as a group—are not substantially different from non-Catholics on most demographic dimensions.

Catholic Representation Within Demographic, Geographic, and Political Subgroups
Based on Gallup Polls Conducted in 2004

	Catholic %	Non-Catholic %
Men	24	76
Women	24	76
East	37	63
Midwest	26	74
South	16	84
West	22	78
HS or less	23	77
Some college	24	76
College grad	27	73
Post-grad	25	75

	Catholic %	Non-Catholic %
Less than $20,000	20	80
$20,000 - <$30,000	20	80
$30,000 - < $50,000	24	76
$50,000 - < $75,000	25	75
$75,000 +	28	72
Non-Hispanic white	24	76
Non-Hispanic black	7	93
White Hispanic	58	42
Black Hispanic	40	60
Asian	23	77
Other race/DK	30	70
Refused race	8	92
18-29 years	25	75
30-49 years	25	75
50-64 years	23	77
65+ years	24	77
Republican	23	77
Independent	24	76
Democrat	26	74
Conservative	23	77
Moderate	27	74
Liberal	22	78

In particular, there are no significant differences by age or gender in identification with the Catholic Church, and very small differences by most other dimensions.

The exceptions are as follows:

- Americans living in the East are significantly more likely to be Catholics than in the other three major regions of the country. Americans living in the South are significantly less likely to be Catholics.
- Catholics are slightly more highly represented in higher-income categories than they are in lower-income categories.
- Hispanics are much more likely to be Catholics than non-Hispanic whites and blacks, although more than 4 in 10 Hispanics are not Catholics.

Survey Methods

These results are based on telephone interviews with randomly selected national samples of adults, aged 18 and older, conducted in 2002, 2003 and 2004, as noted in the tables. The margin of errors associated with these data varies depending on the size of the samples involved.

In addition to sampling error, question wording and practical difficulties in conducting surveys can introduce error or bias into the findings of public opinion polls.

April 12, 2005
NATION'S HUNGER, HOMELESSNESS TROUBLE AMERICANS
Nonwhites worry more than whites

by Linda Lyons, Education and Youth Editor

Anyone who's been in a big city has seen them. Some people avert their eyes and hurry by; others drop coins, or even bills, in their hands. But lone panhandlers aren't the only faces of poverty in the United States. Many families with children also find themselves in soup kitchens and shelters.

That's one reason, perhaps, why nearly two-thirds of Americans are concerned about hunger and homelessness in the nation, according to a March 2005 Gallup Poll*. "I was recently without a job for 18 months," says a 54-year-old respondent from Arizona in a follow-up interview, "and it made me realize that most of us take our good fortune for granted. But bad luck can happen to anyone." More than a third of respondents (37%) say they worry "a great deal" and another 27% worry "a fair amount" about hunger and homelessness. Thirty-five percent of Americans worry only a little or not at all.

Worry About Hunger and Homelessness

Next I'm going to read a list of problems facing the country. For each one, please tell me if you personally worry about this problem a great deal, a fair amount, only a little, or not at all . . . Hunger and homelessness.

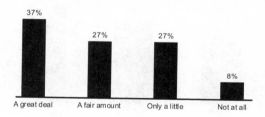

The poverty rate and number of families in poverty increased from 9.6% and 7.2 million in 2002 to 10% and 7.6 million in 2003, according to 2003 U.S. Census Bureau data. For all children under 18, the poverty rate increased from 16.7% in 2002 to 17.6% in 2003. The number in poverty rose, from 12.1 million to 12.9 million.

Poverty and Race

It's no surprise that nonwhites worry more than whites do about hunger and homelessness, 52% compared with 33%. According to the U.S. Census Bureau, in 2003, 8.2% of non-Hispanic whites lived below the poverty threshold, 24.4% of non-Hispanic blacks lived below the poverty threshold, and 22.5% of Hispanics lived below that threshold.

Worry About Hunger and Homelessness by Race

Percentage worrying "a great deal"

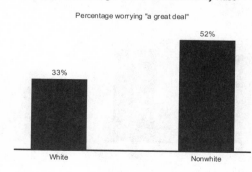

Ideological Differences

Forty-six percent of self-identified liberals worry "a great deal" about hunger and homelessness, compared with 29% of conservatives. But some conservatives may be sympathetic to the plight of the poor even if they don't express worry, as evidenced by the remarks of one poll respondent. An 82-year-old ideologically conservative woman from Missouri says she does not worry at all about hunger and homelessness in the United States. But she quickly qualifies her response: "It's not that I'm not concerned about others. I know poverty and homelessness are huge problems in the big cities. But I live in a small town where I'm not faced with it on a daily basis so I don't think much about it. However, I'm a member of the local Methodist church and we do give money to groups all over the country and the world to help alleviate suffering."

A 68-year-old man from Maryland, a self-described "100%, military-loving, flag-waving conservative," says he worries "a fair amount" about hunger and homelessness in this country. "I'm a conservative, but only on certain issues … The U.S. is the land of milk and honey and charity should begin at home. We send too much aid overseas to countries that despise us," he concludes.

Worry About Hunger and Homelessness by Ideology

Percentage worrying "a great deal"

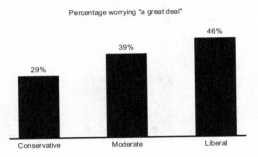

Poverty and Religion

People who attend church or synagogue on a regular basis are slightly more likely to worry a great deal about hunger and homelessness than those who seldom or never attend. Forty-one percent of weekly attendees say they worry "a great deal," compared with 32% of those who rarely or never go to religious services. Religious organizations have historically spearheaded programs to help the needy—operating soup kitchens and rummage sales and providing daycare for children, among other efforts.

Some churches have begun housing the homeless. Interfaith Hospitality Network (IHN), a national nonprofit organization, sets up a network of local churches to house and feed homeless families until they can secure permanent housing. When Trinity Church in Princeton, N.J., wanted to help the growing number of homeless families in the area, outreach minister Margaret Prescott contacted IHN and worked with church members to transform a house on church property into transitional housing for homeless families, most of whom she notes are mothers with small children.

Can they possibly do more? "Absolutely yes," says Prescott, "The next step for Trinity is to buy property to place at least two to three more families in transitional housing in the next five years." Prescott feels that with recent cuts in federal funds for housing assistance, the need for assistance from religious and nonprofit groups is greater than ever: "We will only have more homeless families in the years ahead, not fewer."

Results are based on telephone interviews with 1,004 national adults, aged 18 and older, conducted March 7-10, 2005. For results based on the total sample of national adults, one can say with 95% confidence that the maximum margin of sampling error is ±3 percentage points.

April 12, 2005
MAJORITY OF AMERICANS WANT TO START OWN BUSINESS
The lure of entrepreneurship is especially felt among young men

by David W. Moore, Gallup Poll Senior Editor

Be your own boss—it sounds great in principle. Illusions of power and setting your own schedule, perhaps also of wealth far beyond what you could earn working for someone else.

That lure of entrepreneurship has snared a majority of Americans, according to a recent CNN/*USA Today*/Gallup survey*. The poll finds that this aspiration is neither political nor religious, nor related to education or current income. It's primarily a youthful dream, held more by men than women.

About two-thirds of all Americans are employed either full or part time these days (including some who are technically "retired"). Ten percent of all adults are self-employed, including just 4% who own their own business and have employees working for them. But the poll, conducted March 18-20, finds that if given a choice of starting their own business or working for someone else, 57% of Americans would opt for the former, while 40% would choose to work for someone else. Among people who are actually employed, the margin in favor of being their own boss is even greater—61% to 38%.

Start your own business, or work for someone else?

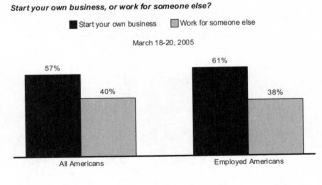

This preference is especially characteristic of young people. By a margin of 72% to 27%, they would prefer to start their own business rather than work for someone else. The proportions shift with increasing age, so that among people 65 and older, more would rather work for someone else (49%) than be their own boss (40%).

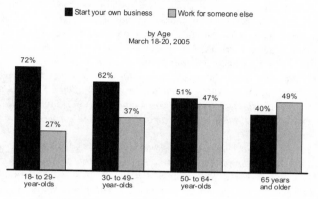

Start your own business, or work for someone else?

■ Start your own business ☐ Work for someone else

by Age
March 18-20, 2005

Men prefer the option of starting their own business by almost a 2-to-1 margin, 63% to 34%. Women barely lean in that direction, 50% to 46%.

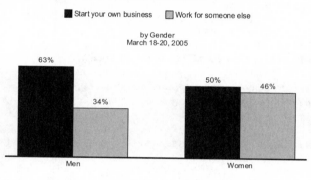

Start your own business, or work for someone else?

■ Start your own business ☐ Work for someone else

by Gender
March 18-20, 2005

The gender gap persists across age categories. Among adults under age 50, men are 14 percentage points more likely than women to choose being their own boss, 72% vs. 58%. Among people 50 and older, there is an 11-point gender gap in that choice—52% of men compared with 41% of women.

While views on this issue are not significantly related to income or education, nor to partisan views such as party or ideology, there

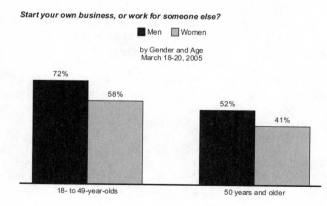

Start your own business, or work for someone else?

■ Men ☐ Women

by Gender and Age
March 18-20, 2005

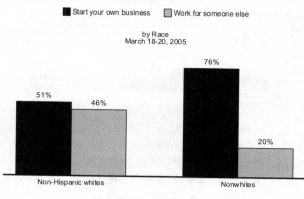

Start your own business, or work for someone else?

■ Start your own business ☐ Work for someone else

by Race
March 18-20, 2005

is a large racial gap. Whites are about evenly divided on the matter, 51% to 46% in favor of starting their own business; nonwhites want that opportunity by an almost 4-to-1 ratio, 76% to 20%.

Results in the current survey are based on telephone interviews with 1,001 national adults, aged 18 and older, conducted March 18-20, 2005. For results based on the total sample of national adults, one can say with 95% confidence that the margin of sampling error is ±3 percentage points.

In addition to sampling error, question wording and practical difficulties in conducting surveys can introduce error or bias into the findings of public opinion polls.

April 12, 2005
HEALTHCARE CONCERNS WHITES, LIFE-AND-DEATH MATTER FOR BLACKS
Six in 10 Americans worry "a great deal" about affordability and availability

by Rick Blizzard, Health and Healthcare Editor

It's that time of year again in Washington. The cherry trees blossom, tourists flock to the National Mall—and Congress begins negotiations over the federal budget.

Near the top of this year's agenda are cuts needed to address the deficit, and various healthcare programs are undoubtedly under discussion. But if Gallup's March 7-10 poll* is any indication, healthcare probably isn't the best place for major cuts. When presented with a list of 12 social, economic, and political problems facing the country, Americans are most likely to choose "the availability and affordability of healthcare" as the issue they worry about most. Six in 10 Americans (60%) worry about this issue "a great deal." Social Security is a distant second with 48% worrying a great deal.

That sentiment is reflective of a speech Franklin Delano Roosevelt once gave. "The success or failure of any government in the final analysis must be measured by the well-being of its citizens," Roosevelt argued. "Nothing can be more important to a state than its public health; the state's paramount concern should be the health of its people." Roosevelt would be pleased that overall health status and life expectancy in the United States have improved dramatically since the 1930s—but he'd also recognize that these improvements haven't lessened public concern about the nation's healthcare system.

Concern About Healthcare in the United States

Next I'm going to read a list of problems facing the country. For each one, please tell me if you personally worry about this problem a great deal, a fair amount, only a little, or not at all? First, how much do you personally worry about. . . ?

Percentage saying "great deal"

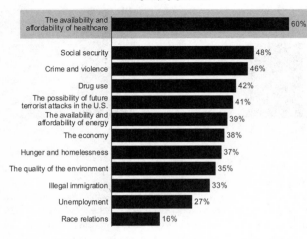

The availability and affordability of healthcare	60%
Social security	48%
Crime and violence	46%
Drug use	42%
The possibility of future terrorist attacks in the U.S.	41%
The availability and affordability of energy	39%
The economy	38%
Hunger and homelessness	37%
The quality of the environment	35%
Illegal immigration	33%
Unemployment	27%
Race relations	16%

Who Is Concerned About Healthcare?

A majority of Americans in almost every group worry a great deal about healthcare availability and cost. But an aggregate of the last four years' data on this question**, which allows for a more in-depth look at subgroups, shows black Americans are more concerned than whites.

Worry "A Great Deal" About Availability and Affordability of Healthcare

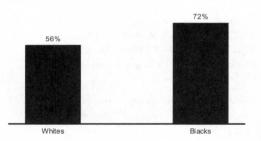

Whites	Blacks
56%	72%

Blacks have good reason to be more concerned than whites about healthcare in the United States. The Office of Minority Health at the U.S. Centers for Disease Control and Prevention reports:

- The infant death rate for black Americans is more than double that of whites.
- The death rate for heart disease is 40% higher for black Americans than it is for whites.
- The death rate for cancer is 30% higher for black Americans than it is for whites.
- Black American women, despite having almost as high a mammography screening rate as white women, have a higher death rate from breast cancer.

The medical journal *Health Affairs* recently published an article titled, "What If We Were Equal? A Comparison of the Black-White Mortality Gap in 1960 and 2000." The authors have found that the gap between black and white mortality rates changed little between 1960 and 2000, and the gap actually grew worse for black infants and black men over the age of 35.

Bottom Line

When it comes to the United States' black population, it appears the U.S. government is not living up to FDR's ideal. Blacks are extremely likely to say they worry about access to healthcare—and their worries are justified. Even as the push to reform Social Security grabs headlines, the Medicare system is approaching crisis, as is Medicaid in many states. How will legislators respond? Will they aggravate the problem for short-term budgetary gain, or lead the charge toward reforming healthcare and protecting public health? Where black Americans are concerned, the issue is one of social justice—and for many a matter of life or death.

*Results are based on telephone interviews with 1,004 national adults, aged 18 and older, conducted March 7-10, 2005. For results based on the total sample of national adults, one can say with 95% confidence that the maximum margin of sampling error is ±3 percentage points.

**Results are based on telephone interviews with 4,023 national adults, aged 18 and older, conducted March 2002 to March 2005. For results based in the sample of 3,406 whites, the margin of sampling error is ±2 percentage points. For results based in the sample of 253 blacks, the margin of sampling error is ±7 percentage points.

April 13, 2005
PUBLIC: MIXED REACTION TO FEDERAL INCOME TAXES
Most say upper-income people and corporations pay too little, though most also say their own tax bill is fair

by David W. Moore, Gallup Poll Senior Editor

As the deadline nears for taxpayers to file their annual income tax returns, a new Gallup survey finds Americans expressing mixed feelings about the fairness of the tax. Most say upper-income people and corporations pay too little taxes and lower-income people pay too much, but most Americans say their own tax bill is fair. A slight majority also says federal income taxes are too high. The "worst," or "least fair," tax: the local property tax, followed by the federal income tax, with the Social Security tax, state income tax, and state sales tax tying for third.

The poll, conducted April 4-7, shows that 61% of Americans say the income tax they will have to pay this year is fair, while 34% say it is not.

During World War II, from 1943 to 1945, Gallup found that more than 8 in 10 Americans said income taxes were fair, but in the immediate postwar period (1946), that number fell to about 6 in 10 Americans. When Gallup began asking the question again in 1997, the public was more evenly divided. After the 9/11 terrorist attacks, the percentage saying "fair" jumped to 58%, up from 51% the previous April. In April 2003, shortly after the Iraq war was launched, the percentage jumped even higher to 64%, about the level of the post-World War II sentiment.

The Iraq war and the war on terrorism followed major tax cuts passed by the Congress and signed by the president. Whether these tax cuts or U.S. involvement in war are more responsible for the change in opinion is impossible to determine. The fact that the per-

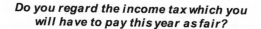

Do you regard the income tax which you will have to pay this year as fair?

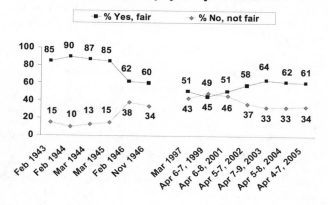

centage saying "fair" jumped in April 2003, however, suggests that wartime patriotism is a major, if not sole, influence.

While 61% of Americans say the federal income tax they have to pay is fair, 51% also say the amount they have to pay is too high. One might think that if people say their tax bill is fair, they wouldn't also say it is too high. But the poll shows that 29% of people who say their taxes are fair also say they have to pay too much.

Do you consider the amount of federal income tax you have to pay as too high, about right, or too low?

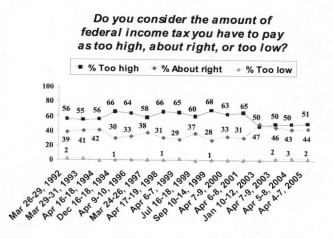

From the 1992 presidential campaign until the Republicans won majority control of the U.S. House of Representatives in 1994, just over a majority of Americans said they had to pay too much in taxes. Over the next seven years, as the Republicans pushed tax-cut legislation, an average of 64% of Americans expressed that view. In the first poll following the 9/11 terrorist attacks, the percentage complaining of excess taxation dropped dramatically—just 47% said income taxes were too high, not much different from the 51% who express that sentiment in the current poll.

Again, one could attribute some of the change in opinion to the actual tax cuts that have passed during the Bush administration, though history suggests it is national security rather than tax cuts themselves that more significantly influence people's opinion on this issue. In March 1949, during the Berlin blockade that had been imposed by the Soviet Union in June of the previous year, the percentage saying taxes were too high dropped to 43% from 57% the previous March. The only other time in the post-World War II period that less than a majority of Americans complained of taxes that were too high occurred during the Berlin Crisis of 1958-1962. In three

polls during that time, Gallup found an average of 48% saying taxes were too high. After the crisis appeared to be over, an early summer 1962 poll found 63% with that view, though there had been no significant increase in the tax rate.

Majority of Upper-Income People Say They Pay Too Little Taxes; Lower- and Middle-Income People Agree

While most Americans say the amount of taxes they pay is fair, large majorities also say the amount corporations and upper-income people pay is too little, and a slight majority says the amount lower-income people pay is too much.

Does [each group noted below] pay its FAIR share in federal taxes, pay too MUCH or pay too LITTLE?

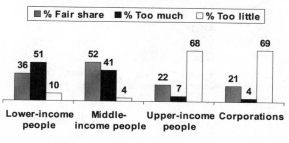

April 4-7, 2005

About 16% of all Americans identify themselves as either "upper class" or "upper middle class." A majority of this group, 52%, says upper-income people pay too little taxes. Among people who identify themselves as "working/lower class" or "middle class," large majorities agree—77% and 67%, respectively.

Do upper-income people pay their fair share in federal taxes, pay too much, or pay too little?
compared by self-identified socioeconomic class

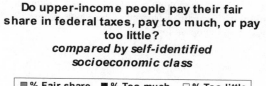
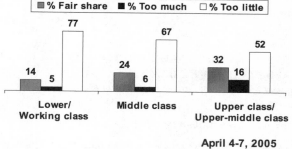

April 4-7, 2005

Recent news reports suggest that the federal government fails to collect up to $350 billion in taxes every year because people cheat on their returns. But this year, the Internal Revenue Service says it is making a special effort to go after corporations, upper-income people, and small businesses, to make sure the taxes are paid. The poll shows that Americans are divided over how difficult it is to cheat on income taxes. Thirty percent say it is becoming harder to do so, 21% say it is easier, and 35% say there has been no change.

Do you believe it is becoming—[ROTATED: easier for someone to cheat on their income taxes, has there been no change, or is it becoming harder for someone to cheat on their income taxes]?

	Easier	No change	Harder	No opinion
2005 Apr 4-7	21%	35	30	14

Which is the worst tax people have to pay? The winner, as it was two years ago, is the property tax, followed by the federal income tax. Three other taxes essentially tie for third place—state income tax, state sales tax, and the Social Security tax.

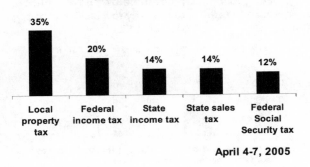

Which do you think is the worst tax — that is the least fair?

April 4-7, 2005

Survey Methods

Results in the current survey are based on telephone interviews with 1,010 national adults, aged 18 and older, conducted April 4-7, 2005. For results based on the total sample of national adults, one can say with 95% confidence that the maximum margin of sampling error is ±3 percentage points. For results based on the 503 national adults in the Form A half-sample and 507 national adults in the Form B half-sample, the maximum margins of sampling error are ±5 percentage points. In addition to sampling error, question wording and practical difficulties in conducting surveys can introduce error or bias into the findings of public opinion polls.

April 14, 2005

SURGE IN AMERICANS' PLANS TO FILE TAXES ELECTRONICALLY THIS YEAR

Majority of Americans under age 50 plan to file returns electronically

by Joseph Carroll, Gallup Poll Assistant Editor

As many Americans scramble to finish their federal income tax returns by April 15, a new Gallup economic poll finds that Americans are now just as likely to say they will file their tax returns by mail as they are to file them electronically, with younger Americans much more likely to do so than older Americans. This is the highest proportion of Americans saying they plan to file their returns electronically since Gallup first asked the question eight years ago.

A recent Experian/Gallup Personal Credit Index survey also shows that most Americans expect to receive a tax refund this year, and that they will use their refunds mostly to pay off bills and debt.

Over half of Americans who owe money to the government say they will pay the Internal Revenue Service (IRS) the entire amount without borrowing money, while about one in four plan to borrow money to pay their taxes in full, or plan to participate in an IRS installment payment plan.

Americans Split About Filing Tax Returns by Mail or Electronically

The Gallup poll on economy and finance, conducted Apr. 4-7, finds that Americans are equally likely to say they will file their tax return by mail (43%) as they are to file electronically (44%). In all previous years when this question was asked, more people indicated they would file by regular mail than electronically.

In 1997, when this question was first asked, more than three in four Americans said they planned to file their tax returns by mail, and only one in six said electronically. Since that time, there has been a gradual increase in electronic filing. By 2003, only a slim majority of Americans, 52%, said they planned to file by mail, while one-third (34%) said they would file their returns electronically.

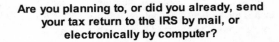

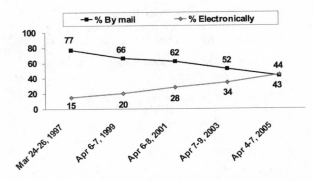

Are you planning to, or did you already, send your tax return to the IRS by mail, or electronically by computer?

Over the years, electronic filing has gained popularity among people in all age groups, but this is the first year when Americans under age 50 are more likely to file their taxes electronically than to file them by mail.

Are you planning to, or did you already, send your tax return to the IRS by mail, or electronically by computer?

	Ages 18 to 29		Ages 30 to 49		50 years and older	
	Mail %	Electronically %	Mail %	Electronically %	Mail %	Electronically %
2005 Apr 4-7	35	57	38	55	50	30
2003 Apr 7-9	42	43	51	40	59	23
2001 Apr 6-8	53	43	59	34	69	13
1999 Apr 6-7	64	26	66	25	69	11
1997 Mar 24-26	73	26	78	17	76	8

As the table illustrates, the rate of increased electronic submissions is highest among 30- to 49-year-olds, with the rate increasing from 17% in 1997 to 55% now — an increase of 38 percentage points. By comparison, 18- to 29-year-olds show an increase in electronic filing of 31 percentage points (from 26% in 1997 to 57% earlier this month), and the oldest group shows an increase of 22 percentage points (from 8% to 30%).

More than 6 in 10 Americans Expect to Receive a Tax Refund

More than 8 in 10 Americans (85%) say they will file their taxes by the April 15 deadline, while only 7% say they expect to take an extension. This is according to the latest Experian/Gallup Personal Credit Index survey, conducted Mar. 14-20, which asked Americans several questions about this year's federal income taxes.

More than 6 in 10 Americans say they have received or expect to receive a tax refund, while 21% say they owe or expect to owe this year. When asked about last year's income taxes, two in three Americans said they received a refund, while 19% said they owed money.

What Taxpayers Expect in 2004 and Experienced in 2003 From Their Federal Income Tax Returns

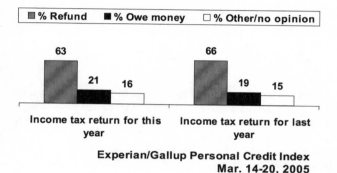

Experian/Gallup Personal Credit Index
Mar. 14-20, 2005

Americans who owe the federal government money on this year's tax return say they owe an average of $2,205. This includes 30% of Americans who owe less than $1,000, 22% who owe between $1,000 and $5,000, and 10% who owe $5,000 or more. About one-third say they do not know how much they owe.

Nearly 7 in 10 respondents who owe the government money this year say they will pay the entire amount without borrowing money to do so, while 8% say they will pay the whole amount but will need to borrow money. Roughly one in five Americans say they are paying the money on an IRS installment plan.

The average expected refund this year is $2,065. This includes refunds from 25% who expect to receive less than $1,000, 14% who

How People Plan to Pay What They Owe the IRS
among those who owe money on this year's returns

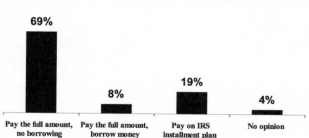

Experian/Gallup Personal Credit Index
Mar. 14-20, 2005

expect between $1,000 and $2,000, 22% who expect between $2,000 and $5,000, and 8% who say they will get back $5,000 or more. One in five Americans say they do not know how much of a refund they will receive this year.

Among those receiving a refund this year, nearly half (49%) say they will use the money to pay off bills or debt, while 31% will invest or save it, 9% will make a large purchase, and 6% will spend it on a vacation.

How will you spend your refund?
among those who will receive a tax refund this year

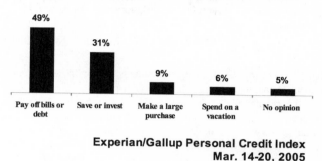

Experian/Gallup Personal Credit Index
Mar. 14-20, 2005

Survey Methods for the Gallup Poll on Economy and Finance

These results are based on telephone interviews with a randomly selected national sample of 1,010 adults, aged 18 and older, conducted April 4-7, 2005. For results based on this sample, one can say with 95% confidence that the maximum error attributable to sampling and other random effects is ±3 percentage points. In addition to sampling error, question wording and practical difficulties in conducting surveys can introduce error or bias into the findings of public opinion polls.

April 15, 2005
NRA VIEWED FAVORABLY BY MOST AMERICANS
Majority of Americans favor arming pilots, but not school officials

by Lydia Saad, Gallup Poll Senior Editor

With National Rifle Association members now gathered in Houston for the NRA's 134th annual meeting, a recent Gallup Poll finds that public opinion of the nation's leading pro-gun lobby is fairly positive. Six in 10 Americans say they view the organization favorably, while about a third of Americans view it unfavorably.

Despite this positive tilt, favorable opinions of the NRA are relatively soft. Only 18% view the NRA "very" favorably, while an almost equal number, 15%, view it "very" unfavorably. People with a less intense feeling split 42% favorably to 19% unfavorably.

Positive ratings of the NRA are a bit more prevalent today than when previously measured, but that could be attributed to the fact that the NRA image question in the latest survey was preceded by a new series of questions about gun use. These questions may have enhanced

Overall Opinion of the NRA

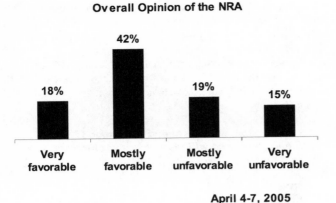

April 4-7, 2005

the NRA's ratings by focusing respondents first on the self-defense aspect of guns.

In particular, Gallup found that 62% of Americans believe arming pilots with guns would make airplanes safer; only a third believe armed pilots would make planes more dangerous. Americans are more divided on the effect of arming judges in courtrooms, with 50% saying the measure would make courtrooms more dangerous versus 43% who say it would make the courts safer. Americans mostly agree, however, that arming school officials would make schools more dangerous (73%).

Impact of Arming Occupations/ Locations With Guns

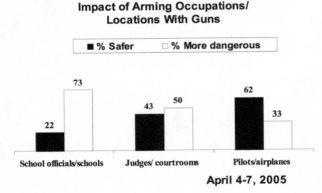

April 4-7, 2005

Recent high-profile crimes have propelled each of these proposals into the national spotlight. But as the data show, a majority of Americans believe the risks involved with arming judges and school officials outweigh the potential of those same officials being defenseless against the rare violent attacker. This is somewhat in line with Americans' attitudes about personal gun ownership. According to Gallup's 2004 Crime survey, 42% say having a gun in the house makes it a safer place to be, while 46% say it makes the home more dangerous.

Attitudes are different about pilots, possibly because pilots are already entrusted with their passengers' lives, and because the memory of the horrifying 9/11 terrorist hijackings is still vivid.

Incoming NRA President Sandra S. Froman recently proposed arming school officials as a way of lowering school violence. "I'm not saying that that means every teacher should have a gun or not, but what I am saying is we need to look at all the options at what will truly protect the students," she said. However, NRA Executive Vice President Wayne LaPierre told the *Houston Chronicle* the NRA is "...not backing national legislation to arm teachers."

NRA Viewed Positively in the Past

Although the latest NRA favorable rating could be somewhat inflated because of the question order, previous Gallup Polls on the NRA have generally showed a majority of Americans viewing it favorably. When last asked in May 2000, 52% had a favorable view of the NRA, while 39% had an unfavorable view. Similar results were found in April 1999. Only in June 1995 did Gallup find a slim majority of Americans (51%) feeling unfavorably toward the NRA.

Trend in NRA Favorable Ratings

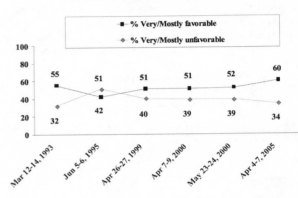

Favorable impressions of the NRA go beyond gun owners. The current 60% favorable rating is much higher than the 40% of Americans who told Gallup they have a gun in their home or on their property in an October 2004 survey.

Still, the demographic pattern of favorable views of the NRA is broadly similar to the pattern of gun ownership. Men, Southerners, rural residents, Republicans, and self-described conservatives are among the groups most likely to say they own guns, and are also among the most favorably disposed to the NRA.

The only obvious exception to this rule is older Americans. Although those aged 65 and older are among the most likely of any age group to own guns (45%), they show the least favorable attitudes toward the NRA of all age groups (49% favorable).

Democrats and liberals have a distinctly negative view of the NRA. A majority of Americans falling into these groups (53% and 60%, respectively) view the organization unfavorably.

Gun Ownership vs. Favorable Views of NRA by Demographic Subgroups

	Own a Gun (Oct 11-14, 2004)	Favorable to NRA (Apr 4-7, 2005)
	%	%
National adults	40	60
Men	49	70
Women	33	51
Aged 18 to 29	30	64
Aged 30 to 49	41	65
Aged 50 to 64	45	60
Aged 65 and older	45	49
East	27	57
Midwest	40	62
South	50	67
West	40	51

	Own a Gun (Oct 11-14, 2004)	Favorable to NRA (Apr 4-7, 2005)
	%	%
Urban	29	56
Suburban	40	57
Rural	56	73
Republican	53	78
Independent	36	62
Democrat	31	41
Conservative	49	77
Moderate	38	57
Liberal	29	38

Survey Methods

These results are based on telephone interviews with a randomly selected national sample of 1,010 adults, aged 18 and older, conducted April 4-7, 2005. For results based on this sample, one can say with 95% confidence that the maximum error attributable to sampling and other random effects is ±3 percentage points. In addition to sampling error, question wording and practical difficulties in conducting surveys can introduce error or bias into the findings of public opinion polls.

April 18, 2005

VOLATILE QUARTER FOR BUSH LOOKS AVERAGE IN FINAL ANALYSIS

Latest average similar to previous four

by Jeffrey M. Jones, Gallup Poll Managing Editor

George W. Bush's 17th quarter in office, the first of his second term, was somewhat of a wild ride. Beginning his second term with relatively weak approval ratings (51% just prior to his inauguration), Bush's numbers got a shot of adrenaline following the Iraqi elections and the State of the Union address in early February. That boost quickly faded, however, and Bush's ratings took a dive to 45%—the lowest of his presidency—after he signed a bill allowing federal courts to hear lawsuits in the Terri Schiavo case. His two most recent ratings show Bush gaining back some of that public support.

George W. Bush's Job Approval Ratings During the 17th Quarter of His Administration

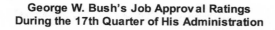

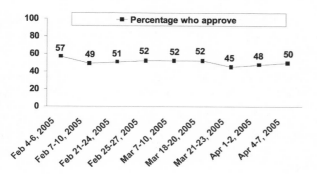

Amid all the ups and downs, Bush's approval rating for the quarter averaged 50.7%. That is right in line with his averages for the previous four quarters, suggesting little change in public support for Bush over the past year.

George W. Bush's Job Approval Ratings — Quarterly Averages for His Administration

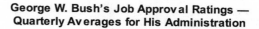

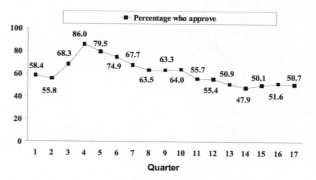

From a historical perspective, the current quarterly average of 50.7% ranks 149th out of 236 presidential quarters for which Gallup has data, going back to the Truman administration. That puts the current quarter in just the 37th percentile of all presidential quarters—a far cry from Bush's quarterly averages in the 4th through 6th quarters of his presidency, which rank among the highest Gallup has ever measured.

Historical Comparison

Most other presidents were well above the 50% job approval mark at similar points in their presidencies: Dwight Eisenhower at 69.0%, Richard Nixon at 60.8%, Ronald Reagan at 58.0%, and Bill Clinton at 57.5%. The lone exception was Lyndon Johnson, who—unlike the other presidents—was not beginning his second term during the 17th quarter of his presidency, but rather, nearing the end of it. An average of 44.3% of Americans approved of Johnson at that time. In Johnson's first full quarter after being re-elected (January to April 1965)—similar to where Bush and the other presidents were in their 17th quarters—he averaged 68.4% job approval.

Presidents' 17th Quarter Average Approval Ratings

President	Dates	Average Approval Rating	Number of Measurements
Eisenhower	Jan 20-Apr 19, 1957	69.0%	4
Johnson	Oct 20, 1967-Jan 19, 1968	44.3%	4
Nixon	Jan 20-Apr 19, 1973	60.8%	4
Reagan	Jan 20-Apr 19, 1985	58.0%	4
Clinton	Jan 20-Apr 19, 1997	57.5%	4
G.W. Bush	Jan 20-Apr 19, 2005	50.7%	9

Apart from Nixon, most other presidents' 18th quarter averages were similar to their 17th quarter averages. Add to this that Bush has had five consecutive quarters of similar job approval ratings, and his prospects for an improvement during the next three months do not appear good.

That is due in large part to the public's highly polarized views of Bush. In the past year, an average of only 15% of Democrats have approved of Bush, compared with 43% of independents and 90% of

Republicans. That Democratic average could be depressed somewhat, given that 2004 was an election year and partisan feelings were running high, but just 17% of Democrats have approved of Bush, on average, since last November. By comparison, Clinton got passing marks from 27% of Republicans throughout his presidency.

Absent some dramatic international or domestic event that could produce a rally in support, Bush's approval ratings are unlikely to improve substantially in the near term. In the long term, the state of the economy and Bush's ability to handle pressing issues such as Social Security, Iraq, and energy costs will help determine whether Bush can break out of the low 50% approval range, or whether he will slip below that level.

Survey Methods

These results are based on an average of nine Gallup Polls conducted by telephone during the 17th quarter of Bush's presidency—January 20-April 19, 2005—each with approximately 1,000 adults aged 18 and older.

April 19, 2005

AMERICANS TURN MORE NEGATIVE TOWARD SAME-SEX MARRIAGE

Fifty-seven percent favor a constitutional amendment defining marriage as between a man and woman

by Frank Newport, Gallup Poll Editor in Chief

The issue of same-sex marriage continues to absorb the attention of voters and lawmakers in various venues across the country. Last week, Republican Sen. Sam Brownback of Kansas began a series of hearings in the U.S. Senate focusing on an amendment to the U.S. Constitution that would ban gay marriage and which would also overturn state laws that legalized same-sex marriage. Voters in Brownback's home state recently passed a constitutional amendment banning same-sex marriage by a 70% to 30% margin, making Kansas the 18th state to have passed such an amendment. Jim Backlin, legislative affairs vice president for the Christian Coalition of America, said in an interview with the Salem *Statesman Journal* that up to 34 states could have laws or constitutional amendments defining marriage as between a man and a woman by late next year.

At the same time, gay and lesbian rights groups are fighting the efforts to pass such amendments. Matt Foreman, executive director for the National Gay and Lesbian Task Force, said in a press release that "Our nation is continuing to witness something that has not happened since our constitution was first ratified in 1791—essentially a national referendum inviting the public to vote to deprive a small minority of Americans of rights that the majority takes for granted and sees as fundamental."

An Amendment to the U.S. Constitution?

The process of amending the U.S. Constitution does not directly involve a public vote, but rather the vote of two-thirds of the members of both the U.S. Senate and House of Representatives, and then ratification by the legislatures of three-quarters of the states (although in some instances ratification can be done by state convention in each

state). The opinion of the general public, however, no doubt has and will continue to play an important part in the debate in the national Congress, and would certainly be a part of discussions at the state level if a marriage amendment is ever passed and sent to the states for ratification.

Thus, it is of importance to note that public support for an amendment to the U.S. Constitution that would define marriage as "being between a man and a woman, thus barring marriages between gay or lesbian couples" has now risen to 57% in a recent Gallup Poll, the highest measured across the seven times the question has been asked using this wording since the summer of 2003. The poll, conducted March 18-20, shows that 37% of Americans oppose such a constitutional amendment. Support has ranged from a previous high point of 53% in mid-February 2004 to a low point of 47% in early February of 2004 to the current 57%:

Would you favor or oppose a constitutional amendment that would define marriage as being between a man and a woman, thus barring marriages between gay or lesbian couples?

	Favor %	Oppose %	No opinion %
2005 Mar 18-20	57	37	6
2004 Jul 19-21 ^	48	46	6
2004 May 2-4	51	45	4
2004 Mar 5-7	50	45	5
2004 Feb 9-12	53	44	3
2004 Feb 6-8 ^	47	47	6
2003 Jul 18-20	50	45	5

^ Asked of a half sample

The proposal for a constitutional amendment banning same-sex marriages originated from Republican members of the U.S. House and Senate, and for the most part has been pushed by Republicans at the state level (and endorsed by President George W. Bush last year). It is no surprise, therefore, to find that Republicans are much more likely to support the idea than either independents or Democrats.

Would you favor or oppose a constitutional amendment that would define marriage as being between a man and a woman, thus barring marriages between gay or lesbian couples?

	Favor %	Oppose %
Republicans	71	24
Independents	51	45
Democrats	45	47

Still, as can be seen, even among Democrats nationally in the March 18-20 poll, support for a constitutional amendment essentially breaks even.

The table displays the level of support for the marriage amendment among other subgroups of Americans in the March 18-20 Gallup survey:

Would you favor or oppose a constitutional amendment that would define marriage as being between a man and a woman, thus barring marriages between gay or lesbian couples?

	Favor %	Oppose %
Men	59	37
Women	55	38

	Favor	Oppose
	%	%
18-29	56	39
30-49	61	34
50-64	51	45
65+	56	33
East	53	43
South	65	29
Midwest	56	36
West	49	45
Weekly churchgoers	67	27
Monthly churchgoers	62	33
Seldom/Never go to church	46	48
Postgraduate degree	42	55
College degree	54	44
Some college	64	32
High school or less	56	34

There are not major differences in support by gender or age, although in this poll Americans aged 50 to 64 are slightly less likely to favor the amendment than those in other age groups. Support is highest in the South and lowest in the West, and significantly higher among those who attend church regularly than among those who seldom or never attend. The highest levels of opposition to the amendment come among Americans with postgraduate degrees.

Basic Support for Legalized Same-sex Marriage

The March 18-20 poll also shows that 68% of Americans say that marriages between homosexuals should not be recognized by law as valid. As was the case for the concept of a constitutional amendment, the responses to this question reflect the highest opposition to same-sex marriage measured since Gallup started asking the question in this format in January 2000.

Do you think marriages between homosexuals should or should not be recognized by the law as valid, with the same rights as traditional marriages?

	Should be valid	Should not be valid	No opinion
	%	%	%
2005 Mar 18-20 ^	28	68	4
2004 Jul 19-21 ^	32	62	6
2004 Mar 5-7	33	61	6
2004 Feb 16-17	32	64	4
2004 Feb 6-8 ^	36	59	5
2003 Dec 15-16	31	65	4
2003 Oct 24-26	35	61	4
2003 Jun 27-29	39	55	6
2000 Jan 13-16	34	62	4

^ Asked of a half sample

Support for the concept of a civil union between same-sex couples has historically been higher than support for a fully legal marriage. In May 2004, for example, a Gallup survey found 49% of Americans favored and 48% opposed a law that "would allow homosexual couples to legally form civil unions, giving them some of the legal rights of married couples."

Would you favor or oppose a law that would allow homosexual couples to legally form civil unions, giving them some of the legal rights of married couples?

	Favor	Oppose	No opinion
	%	%	%
2004 May 2-4	49	48	3
2003 Jul 25-27	40	57	3
2003 May 5-7	49	49	2
2002 May 6-9	46	51	3
2002 Apr 8-11	45	46	9
2002 Feb 8-10	41	53	6
2001 May 10-14	44	52	4
2000 Oct 25-28 ^	42	54	4

^ WORDING: Suppose that on election day this year you could vote on key issues as well as candidates. Please tell me whether you would vote for or against each one of the following propositions. Would you vote—[RANDOM ORDER]? (For or against a law that would allow homosexual couples to legally form civil unions, giving them some of the legal rights of married couples)

The March 18-20 poll included a question that gave respondents three possible arrangements between gay and lesbian couples — same-sex marriages, civil unions, or neither same-sex marriages nor civil unions—and asked them to choose which they thought should be recognized as legally valid.

Which of the following arrangements between gay or lesbian couples do you think should be recognized as legally valid—same-sex marriages, civil unions, but not same-sex marriages, or neither same-sex marriages nor civil unions?

	Same-sex marriages	Civil unions	Neither	No opinion
	%	%	%	%
2005 Mar 18-20 ^	20	27	45	8
2004 Nov 19-21	21	32	43	4

^ Asked of a half sample

These data suggest that close to half of all Americans are willing to accept some type of legally valid arrangement among same-sex couples, although the plurality of these Americans tilt toward favoring a civil union concept rather than official marriage.

Survey Methods

These results are based on telephone interviews with a randomly selected national sample of 909 adults, aged 18 and older, conducted March 18-20, 2005.

For results based on the 443 national adults in the Form A half-sample and 466 national adults in the Form B half-sample, the maximum margins of sampling error are ±5 percentage points. For results based on this sample, one can say with 95% confidence that the maximum error attributable to sampling and other random effects is ±3 percentage points. In addition to sampling error, question wording and practical difficulties in conducting surveys can introduce error or bias into the findings of public opinion polls.

April 19, 2005

CONGRESSIONAL APPROVAL LOWEST IN FIVE YEARS

Decline most dramatic in lower-income households

by Joseph Carroll, Gallup Poll Assistant Editor

Americans' ratings of Congress have dropped an average of eight percentage points in the past two months and are lower now than at any other point since spring 2000. Congressional ratings have declined among almost every demographic subgroup, with the most notable changes occurring among lower-income Americans and highly educated people. These changes come at a time when Congress has been busy debating Social Security reform, finalizing next year's budget, and passing controversial legislation regarding the Terri Schiavo case.

At the beginning of 2005, congressional approval ratings were in the low- to mid-40% range. Ratings have declined in the past two months, and now fewer than 4 in 10 Americans (38%) say they approve of Congress.

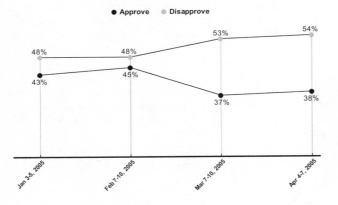

Congressional Job Approval Ratings: 2005

Aggregated Gallup Poll data* collected over these past four months allow for an analysis of where the drop from January-February to March-April has occurred. The analysis shows that the decline in support is rather general, as most demographic subgroups tend to show a drop and these are all about the same magnitude. However, departures from this general pattern are evident in household income and education groups.

Household Income

Congressional approval ratings declined most dramatically among Americans living in lower-income households. Congressional ratings among Americans with household incomes of less than $30,000 a year dropped 12 percentage points between the first two months of the year and the subsequent two months. Meanwhile, ratings decreased only six points among Americans in households with incomes between $30,000 to $74,999, and showed no change at all among those living in households with total earnings of $75,000 or more.

Early in the year, ratings of Congress were similar among people at all income levels; now they are much lower among those in households earning less than $30,000 per year.

Education

Congressional approval ratings actually improved in recent months among Americans with postgraduate educations, while ratings fell

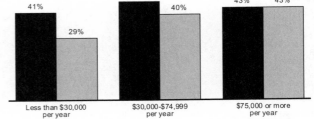

Congressional Job Approval Ratings by Annual Household Income

by roughly equal proportions among college graduates, those with some college education, and those with a high school education or less. Earlier in the year, postgraduates rated Congress much more negatively than people with lower levels of education; now, approval ratings of Congress are roughly the same among respondents of all educational backgrounds.

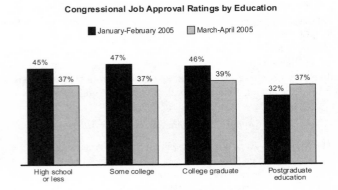

Congressional Job Approval Ratings by Education

Political Viewpoints

Approval of Congress declined about equally among Republicans (eight points) and Democrats (seven points), while independents showed essentially no change. Republicans continue to rate the GOP-controlled Congress much more positively than Democrats do.

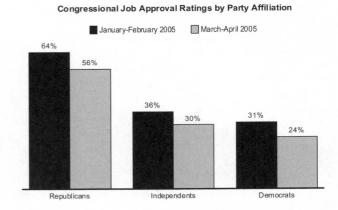

Congressional Job Approval Ratings by Party Affiliation

Likewise, self-described ideological conservatives continue to view Congress more positively than moderates or liberals do. Approval of Congress among moderates has dropped eight points, from 41% to 33%, in the past few months. Ratings fell by slightly smaller amounts among conservatives (from 56% to 52%) and liberals (from 28% to 22%).

Gender, Age, and Race

Ratings of Congress have dropped more or less uniformly among gender, age, and racial groups.

Bottom Line

Congress definitely took a public relations hit with its unpopular action in the Schiavo case—more than 7 in 10 Americans said they disapproved of its involvement. Negative economic perceptions, as currently exist, also tend to take a toll on Americans' evaluations of the national legislature. Congress' ratings in recent years have broken some uncharted positive territory, but in recent years, and recent months, the arrow is pointing downward.

Results are based on telephone interviews with 2,013 national adults, aged 18 and older, conducted Jan. 3-5, 2005, and Feb. 7-10, 2005. For results based on this sample, one can say with 95% confidence that the margin of sampling error is ±2 percentage points. Results are based on telephone interviews with 2,014 national adults, aged 18 and older, conducted March 7-10, 2005 and April 4-7, 2005. For results based on this sample, one can say with 95% confidence that the margin of sampling error is ±2 percentage points.

April 19, 2005

FEWER AMERICANS SAY IRAQ WAR "WORTH IT"

Support varies by political party, race, and age

by Darren K. Carlson, Government and Politics Editor

Reminders that the war is far from over temper signs of progress in Iraq. A new Iraqi government is elected amid great fanfare, yet insurgents continue nearly daily attacks on civilians, police officers, and U.S. soldiers. Water and power are reportedly being restored in many areas; meanwhile militants kidnap an American contractor.

American opinion about Iraq is still mixed, but at this point it appears the negatives outweigh the positives. According to the most recent Gallup Poll* on the subject, fewer Americans say the situation in Iraq was worth going to war over than say that it was not.

Public Opinion Shift on Iraq

Shortly after the war began two years ago, most Americans thought the situation in Iraq was worth going to war over. In a March 24-25, 2003, poll, 68% said the war was worth it, and this sentiment climbed as high as 76% immediately following the fall of Baghdad. Support gradually declined over the summer and dropped to a low of 50% in September, after President Bush asked Congress for an additional $87 billion to fund the war, which he admitted was not going well in a nationally televised address. War support got a boost with the capture of Saddam Hussein in December 2003, but that proved to be short-lived.

By the end of January 2004, Gallup found for the first time less than a majority saying the war was worth it. Support rebounded somewhat in the spring, but tumbled again in May after news of U.S.

soldiers abusing Iraqi prisoners made headlines. Since that time, support has been below the 50% mark with one exception (in late August 2004). The April 1-2 Gallup Poll shows 45% of Americans saying the war was worth it, while 53% say it was not.

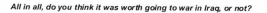

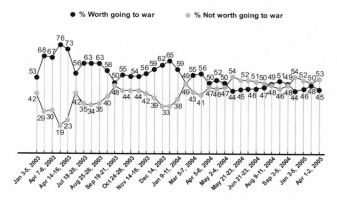

All in all, do you think it was worth going to war in Iraq, or not?

● % Worth going to war   ● % Not worth going to war

Party Matters Most

While the public overall is fairly evenly split about the value of the war in Iraq, levels of support vary by political party, race, and age. Democrats are much less likely than Republicans to say it was worth going to war in Iraq. Nearly 8 in 10 Republicans (79%) say it was worth going to war, while just 19% say it was not worth it. Among Democrats, only 17% say it was worth it and 82% say it was not. The divide among political independents is not as wide: a third (36%) say it was worth going to war, while 61% say it was not.

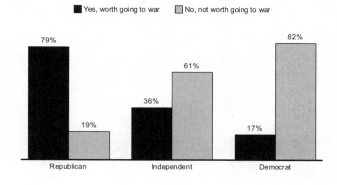

All in all, do you think it was worth going to war in Iraq?

■ Yes, worth going to war   ▢ No, not worth going to war

Race and Age

The political split is related to the persistent racial divide in opinions of the war. White respondents are ambivalent—50% say the war was worth it and 48% say it was not. In contrast, 7 in 10 nonwhite respondents (72%) say the war was not worth it, compared with 26% who say it was.

The oldest and the youngest Americans are the least likely to think it was worth going to war in Iraq. A majority of 18- to 29-year-olds and a majority of Americans aged 65 and older think it was *not* worth going to war. Americans between the ages of 30 and 64 are more evenly split.

These results are based on telephone interviews with a randomly selected national sample of 1,040 adults, aged 18 and older, conducted April 1-2, 2005. For results based on this sample, one can say with 95% confidence that the maximum error attributable to sampling and other random effects is ±3 percentage points. In addition to sampling error, question wording and practical difficulties in conducting surveys can introduce error or bias into the findings of public opinion polls.

April 19, 2005
WHICH IS THE UNFAIREST TAX OF THEM ALL?
Disgruntlement likely to grow

by Dennis Jacobe, Chief Economist, The Gallup Organization

Six in 10 Americans say the income tax they paid this year is fair, according to an April 4-7 Gallup Poll*. But when asked which tax is the *worst,* or least fair, tax they pay, 1 in 3 Americans point to local property tax over federal income tax, Social Security tax, state income tax, and state sales tax. This is bad news for local governments and public education systems, which remain highly dependent on local property taxes as their major source of revenue.

More importantly, recent economic trends suggest the public's disgruntlement will only grow as local property taxes are likely to increase in the months and years ahead. Could this mean another property tax revolt?

The Worst Tax

One in five Americans (20%) say the federal income tax is the most unfair form of taxation, while 14% each identify the state sales tax and state income tax, and 12% name Social Security taxes. In sharp contrast to these percentages, 35% of Americans—nearly twice as many as for any other tax—say local property taxes are the most unfair.

Which do you think is the worst tax -- that is the least fair – federal income tax, federal Social Security tax, state income tax, state sales tax, or local property tax?

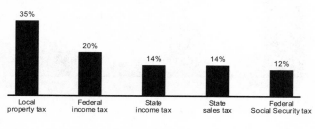

Necessary Evil

In economic theory, property taxes have little to recommend them on equity grounds; they vary widely across the country, raise significant questions about assessed values versus real values, and can impact the optimal allocation of investment dollars to real estate in the United States.

On the other hand, many fiscal theorists tend to view local property taxes as a necessary evil in terms of the entire U.S. tax structure. They argue that property taxes: 1) have the advantage of being direct taxes that are hard to shift to other taxpayers; 2) are largely predictable in advance; 3) are usually identified by the specific local needs they are used to address; and 4) are determined at the local government level. Probably most importantly, local property taxes are the only real source of revenue that federal and state authorities leave to local governments as a major funding source.

A Growing Problem

The reason property taxes tend to be most difficult for the average taxpayer to handle is the fact that it's a wealth-based tax, rather than an income-based or expenditure-based tax. So when housing values soar, as they have during recent years, the value of homeowners' properties increases, as do their property taxes. However, this appreciation in asset values doesn't provide homeowners with added realizable income, and the appreciation of home values is not treated as current income for other federal or state tax purposes.

As a result, homeowners are being required to add to their monthly housing payments to pay increased property taxes, even if their incomes remain stagnant or decline. At the same time, increased real estate taxes are causing monthly payments required to buy a home to increase for first-time homebuyers. Given this context, it is not surprising many Americans feel property taxes are unfair.

In addition, property taxes help pay for local services, including public education. During recent years, many local areas have experienced a flood of new residents because of illegal immigration. Increasing the property taxes to pay for these externalities, which are not controllable at the local level, also generates a perception of unfairness.

Finally, as the population ages, the number of older "empty nesters" and retired couples is increasing. These older Americans may feel it is unfair for them to have to pay for many services they do not use. Even more importantly, many retired people living on fixed incomes may feel they are being pushed out of their homes as property taxes eat up an ever-growing share of their income.

A Property Tax Revolt

Unfortunately, many of the underlying trends creating pressure for higher property taxes are unlikely to dissipate. There is no real national immigration policy, so local communities seem destined to face the challenges of increased service needs on their own. The baby boomers are approaching retirement, so the issue of paying increased real estate taxes on a fixed income is likely to grow. And while housing values seem to be increasing at an excessive rate, many people will continue to live in homes they could not afford to buy at today's prices even if the current housing boom takes a breather.

Many years ago, surging real estate taxes led to a property tax revolt in California. With one in three Americans currently viewing property tax as the most unfair form of taxation, and their property tax burden likely to increase in the coming years, another revolt may become a reality in the not too distant future.

*Results are based on telephone interviews with 507 national adults, aged 18 and older, conducted April 4-7, 2005. For results based on this total sample, one can say with 95% confidence that the maximum margin of sampling error is ±5 percentage points.

April 21, 2005

PUBLIC'S ENVIRONMENTAL OUTLOOK GROWS MORE NEGATIVE

But no increase in public worry about environment quality

by Lydia Saad, Gallup Poll Senior Editor

This year's Earth Day, which will be observed Friday, is marked by a slight increase in pessimism about the environment among Americans. According to Gallup's annual environment survey, conducted March 7-10, half the public is negative about environmental conditions and only a quarter is positive; another quarter offers a mixed assessment. This is according to Gallup's environmental index, which takes into account ratings of current environmental conditions as well as perceptions of whether the environment is improving or worsening.

Gallup Environmental Rating Index

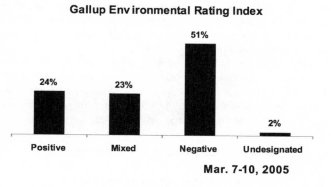

Mar. 7-10, 2005

As the trend in this index shows, the current distribution is five points more negative than was recorded last year, and is the most negative Gallup has recorded since the index was established in 2001.

Gallup Environmental Rating Index

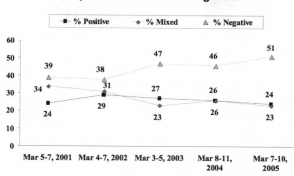

Gallup combines Americans' answers to two basic ratings of the environment to create the index of environmental attitudes.

- Respondents who perceive current environmental conditions as "excellent" or "good" *and* believe the environment is staying the same or getting better are considered "positive" about the environment.
- Those who rate the environment as "only fair" *and* getting worse—or who rate the environment as "poor" *and* say it is staying the same or worsening—are considered "negative" about the environment.
- Most others are categorized as "mixed."

In this year's environment poll, 41% of Americans characterize the overall quality of the environment in the United States today as "excellent" or "good." About half (48%) rate it "only fair," while 10% call it "poor." There has been no significant change in this measure over the past year.

At the same time, perceptions about the direction in which the environment is headed have worsened. Sixty-three percent of Americans, up from 58% in March 2004, say the quality of the environment in the country is getting worse. Only 29% (down from 34% last year) now say it is getting better.

Still No Surge of Concern

Despite a dimming view of the environment's future, there has been little change in Americans' level of worry about the quality of the environment. Only 35% of Americans—identical to last year—say they worry a great deal about the quality of the environment. Another 30% worry a fair amount, while 34% express little to no worry.

Public anxiety about the environment has held relatively steady since 2002—the percentage who worry a great deal or fair amount has fluctuated between 62% and 68%. However, concern about the environment was higher in March 2001, when 77% were this worried.

Worried About the Quality of the Environment?

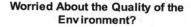

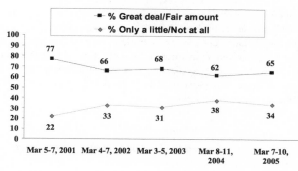

The reason for the decline in concern between March 2001 and March 2002 could very well be the intervening 9/11 terrorist attacks. Heightened concern about terrorism caused Americans to show less concern about several issues, such as the environment, crime, and drugs.

Gallup also sees no change in the percentage of Americans naming the environment as the most important problem facing the United States today. The environment has rarely been mentioned by more than 5% of the public in recent years (significantly higher percentages mentioned the environment as the nation's top problem in the years immediately after the first Earth Day celebration in 1970). More recently, the figure has been in the 1% to 2% range. This is the case today, as just 1% name the environment as the top problem. Rather than the environment, the economy, Social Security, and issues related to terrorism and the Iraq situation lead the list of issues Americans see as most pressing.

Social Security Eclipses Environment as Long-Term Problem

A different test of how important the environment is to Americans comes from another open-ended question that asks them to project what the most important problem will be 25 years from now.

The environment was once the leading long-term problem perceived by Americans, but now Social Security and the economy overshadow it. Since 2000, the percentage of Americans naming the environment as the most important problem that will face the United

States in 25 years has dwindled from 14% to 6%. Initially, the economy replaced the environment as the No. 1 long-term concern but, with its increasing prominence in public debate, Social Security has gained momentum on this measure and now swamps all other issues.

Looking ahead, what do you think will be the most important problem facing our nation 25 years from now?

		Mar 2005	Mar 2004	Mar 2003	Mar 2002	Mar 2001	Apr 2000
2005 Rank							
1	Social Security	23	10	5	6	8	4
2	Economy in general	9	12	14	12	5	3
3-tie	**Environment**	**6**	**8**	**9**	**10**	**11**	**14**
3-tie	Healthcare	6	6	6	5	3	3
4-tie	Lack of energy sources/energy crisis	5	2	8	5	7	1
4-tie	Federal budget deficit/federal debt	5	4	2	2	3	1
4-tie	Fear of war	5	4	6	7	4	2

Partisan Attitudes

Attitudes on the environment are predictably partisan. A majority of Republicans describe current environmental conditions in positive terms, while Democrats are more critical. Half of Republicans perceive the environment as improving, while four in five Democrats say it is getting worse. As a result, about four times as many Republicans as Democrats (42% vs. 10%) are identified as "positive" on Gallup's environmental index.

Environmental Index by Party ID

	Republican	Independent	Democrat
Positive	42	19	10
Mixed	24	26	19
Negative	31	52	71
Undesignated	3	3	*
	100%	100%	100%

*Less than 0.5%

A Women's Issue

More interesting is that women are more critical of environmental conditions than are men. Fifty-seven percent of women, overall, are negative about the environment, compared with 44% of men.

Environmental Index by Gender

	Men	Women
Positive	31	18
Mixed	23	22
Negative	44	57
Undesignated	2	3
	100%	100%

This gender gap can be almost entirely attributed to the differences among Republicans. Republican women are nearly twice as likely as Republican men (41% vs. 24%) to be negative in their environmental assessments. There is virtually no difference in the environmental outlook of Democratic men and Democratic women. Similar results by gender within party were observed last year.

Environmental Index by Gender With Party ID**

	Republican men	Republican women	Democratic men	Democratic women
Positive	50	33	9	8
Mixed	23	23	18	21
Negative	24	41	73	70
Undesignated	3	3	*	1
	100%	100%	100%	100%

*Less than 0.5%
**Republicans includes independents who lean toward the Republican Party. Democrats includes independents who lean toward the Democratic Party.

Global Warming

Hollywood gave us a global warming disaster movie—*The Day After Tomorrow*—in 2004. Though it was the No. 6 top-grossing movie of the year, it doesn't appear to have stirred up a great deal of alarm among Americans about global warming.

By its own admission, the public is not well positioned to make much sense of the issue. Only 16% of Americans say they understand the issue of global warming "very well." Another 54% say they understand it "fairly well," while 3 in 10 say "not very well" or "not at all." This is virtually unchanged from last year.

How Well Understand Global Warming Issue?

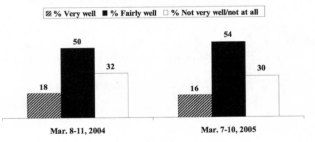

Even prior to the debut of *The Day After Tomorrow* in May 2004, Americans appeared to have accepted that global warming is a real phenomenon. In March 2004, about half of Americans said that the effects of global warming were already happening, while two-thirds expected the effects would be apparent in their lifetimes.

Those figures are essentially the same today.

- About 7 in 10 Americans (69%) believe the effects of global warming have already occurred or will occur in their own lifetimes.
- Roughly one in five (19%) think the effects will only affect future generations.
- Just 9% are completely skeptical, saying that deleterious effects from global warming will never happen.

There has been a slight change since 2004 in Americans' perceptions about the seriousness of global warming. But this change simply marks a return to where attitudes stood in 2003. Just under a third of Americans (31%) say that news reports about global warming generally exaggerate the problem. Just over a third (35%) believe the news generally underestimates the problem. Another 29% think that news coverage of the issue is generally on the mark.

Longer term, however, Gallup has recorded a slight increase in perceptions that the problem is generally underestimated, from 27% in 1997 to 35% today.

Trend in Perceptions About News Coverage of Global Warming

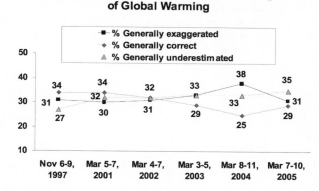

- ■ % Generally exaggerated
- ◆ % Generally correct
- ▲ % Generally underestimated

| | Nov 6-9, 1997 | Mar 5-7, 2001 | Mar 4-7, 2002 | Mar 3-5, 2003 | Mar 8-11, 2004 | Mar 7-10, 2005 |

Survey Methods

The latest results are based on telephone interviews with a randomly selected national sample of 1,004 adults, aged 18 and older, conducted March 7-10, 2005. For results based on this sample, one can say with 95% confidence that the maximum error attributable to sampling and other random effects is ±3 percentage points. In addition to sampling error, question wording and practical difficulties in conducting surveys can introduce error or bias into the findings of public opinion polls.

April 26, 2005

PUBLIC DOUBTS "SMARTS" OF U.S. INTELLIGENCE COMMUNITY

Half of Americans say Bush administration deliberately misled country

by Joseph Carroll, Gallup Poll Assistant Editor

The U.S. intelligence community was "dead wrong" in its accounts that Iraq had weapons of mass destruction prior to the start of the war two years ago, according to a recent presidential commission report. The commission also stated that the intelligence community knows little about possible nuclear threats to the United States from nations across the globe.

The criticism comes at a time when the American public is skeptical about the United States' intelligence efforts. Less than half of Americans are confident in the U.S. intelligence community. Additionally, half now believe that the Bush administration deliberately misled the public about whether Iraq possessed weapons of mass destruction.

Slim Majority of Americans Not Confident in Intelligence Community

An April 1-2 CNN/*USA Today*/Gallup poll* finds that 52% of Americans are not confident that "the U.S. intelligence community is giving the administration accurate information about possible threats to the U.S. from places such as Iran and North Korea." Forty-seven percent express confidence, but only 10% say they are "very confident."

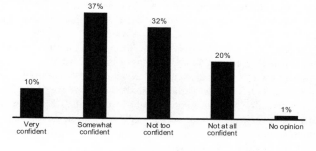

How confident are you that the U.S. intelligence community is giving the administration accurate information about possible threats to the U.S. from places such as Iran and North Korea?

Half Say Bush Administration Deliberately Misled the Public

Americans are split as to whether the Bush administration deliberately misled the public about possible weapons of mass destruction in Iraq, with 50% saying the administration misled the public and 48% saying it did not.

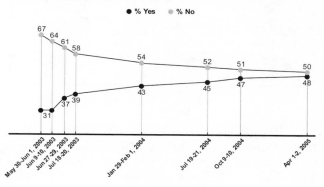

Do you think the Bush administration deliberately misled the American public about whether Iraq has weapons of mass destruction, or not?

● % Yes　● % No

That represents the highest proportion of Americans saying the country was misled since Gallup first asked this question about two years ago. Over time, there has been a slow, gradual increase in the percentage saying the administration deliberately misled Americans, from 31% in May and June of 2003 to the current 50%.

Partisan Politics?

Republicans and Democrats differ substantially in their views of the intelligence community and the Bush administration, with Republicans much more positive than Democrats.

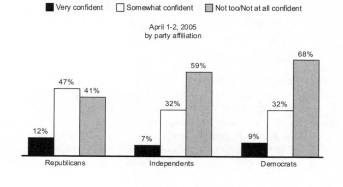

Confidence in the U.S. Intelligence Community

■ Very confident　☐ Somewhat confident　▦ Not too/Not at all confident

April 1-2, 2005
by party affiliation

Nearly 6 in 10 Republicans say they are very (12%) or somewhat (47%) confident that the intelligence community is giving the administration accurate information about possible threats to U.S. security. Only about 4 in 10 Democrats and independents say the same.

Only 14% of Republicans say the Bush administration deliberately misled Americans about weapons of mass destruction in Iraq, compared with more than 8 in 10 Democrats (82%). Republicans have shown only modest variations in their responses to this question historically, ranging from a low of 8% to a high of 15%. Democrats, however, have become substantially more suspicious about the administration, as only about half initially thought the Bush administration had misled the public.

Do you think the Bush administration deliberately misled the American public about whether Iraq has weapons of mass destruction, or not?

Percentage saying "yes, did mislead" by party affiliation

	Republicans	Independents	Democrats
Apr 1-2, 2005	14%	58%	82%
Oct 9-10, 2004	10%	51%	80%
Jul 19-21, 2004	11%	62%	76%
Jan 29-Feb 1, 2004	10%	43%	75%
Jul 18-20, 2003	14%	41%	59%
Jun 27-29, 2003	15%	38%	59%
Jun 9-10, 2003	8%	37%	48%
May 30-Jun 1, 2003	9%	31%	51%

Bottom Line

The federal government has been examining the intelligence failures of federal agencies like the FBI and CIA ever since the Sept. 11, 2001, terrorist attacks against New York City and Washington, D.C. High-profile reports of these investigations such as that by the Sept. 11 commission are shedding light on the weaknesses of the U.S. intelligence gathering system, thus it is understandable that many Americans have doubt about its effectiveness.

Results are based on telephone interviews with 1,040 national adults, aged 18 and older, conducted April 1-2, 2005. For results based on the total sample of national adults, one can say with 95% confidence that the margin of sampling error is ±3 percentage points.

April 26, 2005
PREACHING TO ANOTHER CHURCH'S CHOIR?
Practicing Protestants' moral views more consistent with Catholic Church

by Jeffrey M. Jones, Gallup Poll Managing Editor

The Catholic Church has been in the spotlight in recent weeks following the passing of its former leader, Pope John Paul II, and the election of a new one, Pope Benedict XVI. The Catholic Church's teachings on moral issues such as abortion, homosexuality, divorce, sex before marriage, and the death penalty are sometimes controversial given that many of the church's positions are deemed out of touch with modern societal norms. Even those who identify as

Catholics in the United States hold views on moral issues that differ from church teachings.

As might be expected, though, Gallup Poll data confirm that committed Catholics are much more likely to share the church's views on moral issues than are non-committed Catholics. Gallup surveys also reveal that on many moral issues, practicing *Protestants,* as a group, are more likely than even practicing Catholics to hold traditional moral positions like those taught by the Catholic Church.

Each May, as part of the annual Values and Beliefs poll, Gallup asks Americans to rate the moral acceptability of a series of issues, such as abortion, divorce, and the death penalty. Combined data from the 2002-2004 polls* allows for a more in-depth look at the views by religious affiliation and level of commitment.

Life and Death Issues

The Catholic Church views human life as sacred and as such is officially opposed to any practices that are thought to prematurely end it, such as abortion, the death penalty, euthanasia, and medical research using stem cells derived from human embryos.

U.S. Catholics tend to be in step with the church's teaching on abortion—54% say abortion is morally wrong. But most Catholics depart from church teachings on the death penalty (only 32% say it is morally wrong) and stem cell research (39%), and nearly half stray on the area of doctor-assisted suicide (46%).

Percentage of U.S. Catholics Who Find Practices Morally Wrong by Frequency of Church Attendance

Issue	All Catholics (N=760) %	Attend weekly (N=265) %	Attend nearly weekly/ monthly (N=224) %	Seldom/ Never attend (N=269) %
Abortion	54	74	53	37
Death penalty	32	49	30	18
Doctor-assisted suicide	46	63	43	32
Medical research involving stem cells obtained from human embryos	39	56	36	28

However, in all cases, Catholics who attend church weekly are more likely to express views consistent with church teachings than Catholics who attend less frequently. That is the case even on the death penalty, something favored by roughly two in three Americans overall.

Marriage and Sex

The Catholic Church views marriage as a holy sacrament that is divinely ratified, and thus the union of man and woman cannot be dissolved. In fact, as a general rule, the Catholic Church does not allow divorced Catholics to remarry in the church unless they get their first marriages annulled. Similarly, the church preaches that sexual relations should only occur within marriages. These beliefs obviously allow no room for homosexual relations, something the church regards as a sin.

Gallup's data show most U.S. Catholics do not hold views consistent with church teachings on sex and marriage. Only one in four say divorce is morally wrong, one in three say sex between an unmarried man and woman is wrong, and less than half say the same of having a baby outside marriage and homosexual relations. One notable exception is that Catholics—like all Americans—condemn extramarital affairs.

Percentage of U.S. Catholics Who Find Practices Morally Wrong by Frequency of Church Attendance

Issue	All Catholics (N=760) %	Attend weekly (N=265) %	Attend nearly weekly/ monthly (N=224) %	Seldom/ Never attend (N=269) %
Divorce	25	34	29	14
Sex between unmarried man and woman	32	52	34	13
Having a baby outside of marriage	42	54	44	31
Married men and women having an affair	91	92	91	91
Homosexual behavior	46	58	50	32

Just as on life and death issues, Catholics who attend church weekly are much more likely to express views consistent with the church's positions on sex and marriage, with the exception of divorce. A majority views premarital sex, conceiving a baby out of wedlock, and homosexual behavior as morally wrong. On these issues, Catholics who attend nearly weekly or monthly generally disagree with the church, but their opinions are closer to those of Catholics who attend every week than those who rarely or never go to mass.

Practicing Catholics vs. Practicing Protestants

Centuries ago, Protestant denominations developed out of disagreements with the practices of the Catholic Church. Mainline Protestant denominations have produced scores of offshoot denominations over the years, most of which are much less hierarchical and much more democratic than the Catholic Church. As such, there is no single Protestant voice or set of teachings as exists in the Catholic Church.

But because both are Christian faiths, there is some overlap in beliefs. The Gallup data show that the most committed Protestants' generally traditional views on moral issues dovetail with Catholic Church teachings on morality, even if those views are not necessarily based on the same doctrine. In fact, on most of the issues tested, practicing Protestants' moral views are more consistent with Catholic Church teachings than even the most committed Catholics' views.

Percentage of Weekly Church-Attending Catholics and Protestants Who Find Practices Morally Wrong

Issue	Catholics who attend church weekly (N=265) %	Protestants who attend church weekly (N=515) %
Abortion	74	78
Death penalty	49	29
Doctor-assisted suicide	63	73
Homosexual behavior	58	80
Sex between unmarried man and woman	52	75
Married men and women having an affair	92	96
Divorce	34	48
Medical research involving stem cells obtained from human embryos	56	55
Having a baby outside of marriage	54	75

For example, 80% of Protestants who attend church weekly say homosexual behavior is morally wrong, compared with 58% of Catholics who go to church each week. Protestants who attend church weekly are also much more likely to view extramarital sex as wrong (75% compared with 52% of practicing Catholics), having a baby outside marriage (75% to 54%), divorce (48% to 34%) and doctor-assisted suicide (73% to 63%).

The two groups express similar views on abortion and stem cell research, with majorities of practicing Catholics and Protestants opposed to both.

Practicing Protestants (29%) are much less likely to view the death penalty as morally wrong than are practicing Catholics (49%), the one issue on which practicing Catholics convey views more similar to the Catholic teachings than practicing Protestants do.

Of course, religion is not the sole influence on one's views on moral issues. In the United States, especially, moral issues have become politicized. Thus, one reason that practicing Protestants' views more closely adhere to generally conservative Catholic Church teachings is that the former group is more homogeneous (that is, conservative) politically. Sixty-two percent of Protestants who attend services weekly identify themselves as ideological conservatives, while 28% say they are moderate and 10% liberal. In contrast, a plurality of weekly attending Catholics, 45%, say they are ideologically moderate. Forty-one percent say they are conservative and 13% liberal.

Practicing Catholics are as likely to say they are Democrats (40%) as Republicans (38%), while practicing Protestants are much more likely to be Republicans (46%) than Democrats (30%).

Bottom Line

The Catholic Church's traditional views on moral issues are sometimes criticized for being too out of step with U.S. society's increasingly liberal moral outlook. However, Protestants with a strong commitment to their faith would find Catholic teachings right in line with their own moral outlooks. While U.S. Catholics as a group do not necessarily adhere to the church's positions, practicing American Catholics and Protestants tend to agree with the substance of the moral messages coming from the church.

*Results are based on aggregated data from telephone interviews drawn from nationally representative samples of approximately 1,000 respondents in polls conducted in early May 2002, 2003, and 2004.

For results based on the total sample of 760 Catholics, one can say with 95% confidence that the maximum error attributable to sampling and other random effects is ±4 percentage points.

For results based on the sample of 265 Catholics who attend church weekly, the maximum margin of sampling error is ±7 percentage points.

For results based on the sample of 224 Catholics who attend church nearly every week or monthly, the maximum margin of sampling error is ±7 percentage points.

For results based on the sample of 269 Catholics who seldom or never attend church, the maximum margin of sampling error is ±7 percentage points.

For results based on the sample of 515 Protestants who attend church weekly, the maximum margin of sampling error is ±5 percentage points.

April 26, 2005
ECONOMIC INDICATORS CONTINUE DOWNWARD SLIDE
Rising gas/oil prices appear major factor in recent decline

by David W. Moore, Gallup Poll Senior Editor

The latest Gallup survey finds Americans to be the most pessimistic they have been in two years about where the economy is headed. Today, 61% say the economy is getting worse, while just 31% say better—a net negative 30 percentage points. That is the worst rating since early March 2003—just prior to the beginning of the war in Iraq—when Americans gave the economy a net negative rating of 44 points, with 67% saying the economy was getting worse and only 23% saying better.

Economic Outlook
April 2004 -- April 2005

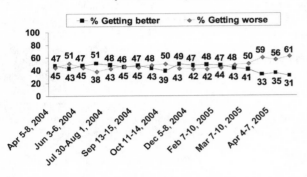

On another economic measure, Americans are not quite so pessimistic, with 31% rating the current economy as excellent or good and 24% as poor—a net positive of seven percentage points, a point less than last month's rating. Earlier this month, public sentiment appeared to improve slightly, as the net positive moved up to 14 points in the April 4-7 survey, only to fall back in the latest survey.

Current Economic Conditions
April 2004 -- April 2005

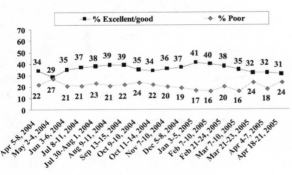

The current rating is the least optimistic since May of last year, when 29% of Americans said the economy was either excellent or good, and 27% said poor.

The lower ratings these past two months appear to be fueled principally by public concerns about higher gas prices. Again this month, the public identifies the top two economic problems facing the country as oil/gas prices and unemployment/jobs. The latter has been at the top of the list for the past several months, but the problem of higher fuel and oil prices jumped to the top last month and remains there now.

What is the most important economic problem facing the country today? [OPEN-ENDED]

	Apr 18-21, 2005 %	Mar 21-23, 2005 %	Feb 21-24, 2005 %	Jan 17-19, 2005 %
Fuel/oil prices	19	17	5	3
Unemployment/Jobs/Wages	18	17	22	22
War in Iraq	8	11	9	14
Social Security	7	10	10	12
Healthcare/Health insurance costs	7	7	10	11
Lack of money	6	3	4	1
Outsourcing of jobs	5	7	6	5
Federal budget deficit	5	7	9	9
Inflation/Rising prices	4	3	2	3
Education reform	2	2	2	3
Illegal immigrants	2	2	1	1
Taxes	2	2	2	3
Credit cards/Overspending	1	2	1	2
Poverty/Hunger/Homelessness	1	1	2	2
Trade deficit	1	1	2	2
Retirement	1	1	1	*
Economy (non-specific)	1	1	1	1
Poorly run government/Politics	1	1	1	1
Gap between rich and poor	1	1	1	1
George W. Bush/His policies	1	1	1	3
Foreign aid/Focus on other countries	1	1	1	2
Welfare	1	1	1	2
Senior care/Medicare	1	1	1	1
Stock market	*	*	*	*
Interest rates	*	*	1	*
International relations	*	*	*	1
College tuition expenses	*	—	—	1
Other	4	4	5	8
None	1	1	1	1
No opinion	8	9	10	8

*Less than 0.5%
Percentages add to more than 100% due to multiple responses.

The war in Iraq, Social Security, and healthcare costs round out the top five most frequently mentioned national problems for the economy. When asked to name the most important economic problems facing their families (rather than the country as a whole), the public identifies lack of money/low wages, healthcare costs, and energy costs among the top three. Energy costs emerged among the top three items last month, paralleling responses about the most important problem facing the national economy.

What is the most important financial problem facing your family today? [OPEN-ENDED]

	Apr 18-21, 2005 %	Mar 21-23, 2005 %	Feb 21-24, 2005 %	Jan 17-19, 2005 %
Lack of money/Low wages	15	10	13	12
Healthcare costs	14	14	14	15

	Apr 18-21, 2005 %	Mar 21-23, 2005 %	Feb 21-24, 2005 %	Jan 17-19, 2005 %
Energy costs	11	10	3	3
Retirement savings	8	7	7	7
Too much debt/Not enough money to pay debts	8	8	7	14
Unemployment/Loss of job	7	7	8	8
College expenses	7	6	7	8
High cost of living/inflation	5	5	4	8
Cost of owning/renting a home	4	6	5	*
Taxes	3	4	4	4
Social Security	1	2	4	3
Interest rates	1	1	1	1
Other	5	2	4	7
None	15	18	21	18
No opinion	5	6	4	4

*Less than 0.5%

Percentages add to more than 100% due to multiple responses.

Partisan Economy

The public rates the economy as though it were primarily a politically partisan activity. Both on the current rating of economic conditions and the economic outlook, Republicans and Democrats appear to see very different worlds.

Among Republicans, the ratio of excellent/good to poor ratings of current economic conditions is 59% to 7%—a 52-point net positive margin. Among independents, the margin is a net -4 points, with 26% saying poor and only 22% saying excellent/good. Among Democrats, the margin is a net -25 points, 38% poor to 13% excellent/good.

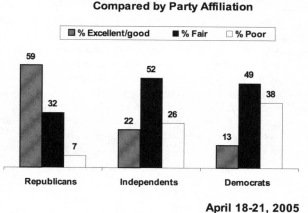

Ratings of Current Economic Conditions Compared by Party Affiliation

■ % Excellent/good ■ % Fair □ % Poor

April 18-21, 2005

When rating the economic outlook, Republicans are mostly positive, with 56% saying the economy is getting better and 35% saying worse. Both independents and Democrats, on the other hand, express mostly pessimistic views—69% getting worse to 22% getting better among independents, and 81% worse to 13% better among Democrats.

Survey Methods

Results in the current survey are based on telephone interviews with 1,003 national adults, aged 18 and older, conducted April 18-21, 2005. For results based on the total sample of national adults, one

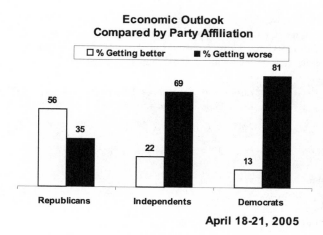

Economic Outlook Compared by Party Affiliation

□ % Getting better ■ % Getting worse

April 18-21, 2005

can say with 95% confidence that the maximum margin of sampling error is ±3 percentage points.

In addition to sampling error, question wording and practical difficulties in conducting surveys can introduce error or bias into the findings of public opinion polls.

April 27, 2005
"BE A DOCTOR" IS THE MOST COMMON CAREER ADVICE
Nursing still perceived as a woman's job

by Lydia Saad, Gallup Poll Senior Editor

The fact that "Take Your Daughter to Work" day—launched by the Ms. Foundation for Women in 1993 as a way to boost girls' self-esteem and expand their horizons—has now become "Take Our Daughters and Sons to Work" day speaks to modern society's insistence on gender equality in the workplace. It's the same demand that got Harvard University's president in trouble earlier this year when he implied that men and women might not have identical aptitudes for the hard sciences.

A recent Gallup Poll finds that, compared with 1950—when Americans differentiated between men and women in assigning career options—there is great similarity today in the occupations people believe would be good for young men and for young women to pursue. Americans think both young men and young women would be well advised to enter a medical field, with "be a doctor" the single most frequently occurring advice for both genders.

The April 18-21 Gallup Poll includes two open-ended questions asking respondents to name the kind of work or career they would recommend if a young man or young woman came to them for advice.

M.D. Stands for Most Desirable Career

As youngsters join their parents at work on Thursday for this year's "Take Our Daughters and Sons to Work" day, the most common career advice Americans have for young men and women is that they become doctors. One in five Americans say this would be their choice for young women, and 17% choose it for young men.

Medicine was also the leading choice when Gallup first asked this question—focused only on young men—in 1949. At that time,

28% said it would be the best career, and that level held through 1973. When the question about careers for young women was first asked in 1950, only 2% recommended that they become doctors, but that figure has gradually climbed to where it is today.

Trend in the Percentage Advising Young People to Become Doctors

	2005 %	2001 %	1998 %	1985 %	1973 %	1967 %	1953 %	1950 %	1949 %
Recommended for young men	17	12	8	8	28	30	29	29	28
Recommended for young women	20	15	11	7	—	—	—	2	—

Women are nearly twice as likely as men to recommend that young people pursue an M.D. About one-quarter of women recommend medicine for young men as well as for young women. In contrast, only 11%-14% of men say they would tell a young man or young woman to become a doctor.

Percentage Advising Young People to Become Doctors, by Gender
April 2005

	Men %	Women %
Recommended for young men	11	22
Recommended for young women	14	25

In addition to medicine, the top five careers chosen for young men include computers (11%), a trade or industrial job (8%), business or sales (8%), and technology/electronics (8%).

Top Five Careers Recommended for Young Men
April 2005

	%
Doctor/Medical field	17
Computers	11
Trades/Industrial/Blue collar	8
Business/Self-employed/Sales	8
Technology/Electronics	8

The "top five" list for young women is slightly different. As with young men, medicine, computers, and business are in the top five recommendations, but the list for women includes nursing and teaching, rather than trade and technology careers.

Top Five Careers Recommended for Young Women
April 2005

	%
Doctor/Medical field	20
Nursing	13
Teaching	9
Computers	8
Business/Self-employed/Sales	6

Only four years ago, the computer field edged out medicine as the most widely recommended occupation. In fact, computers reigned on this list from 1985 through 2001—a period spanning both the introduction of computer technology as a field and the dot-com boom in the late 1990s. But since the dot-com boom went bust and there has been a substantial move to outsource computer jobs abroad, the percentage of Americans mentioning computers has dropped by about half.

Trend in the Percentage Advising Young People to Go Into Computers

	2005 %	2001 %	1998 %	1985 %	1950 %
Recommended for young men	11	18	19	27	—
Recommended for young women	8	16	16	22	—

Another profession that has lost much favor is engineering. At its peak in 1953, one in five Americans recommended engineering as a profession for young men. Today that figure is only 5%. It has never been a very popular choice for young women.

Trend in Percentage Advising Young People to Go Into Engineering

	2005 %	2001 %	1998 %	1985 %	1973 %	1967 %	1953 %	1950 %
Recommended for young men	5	2	2	6	13	14	20	16
Recommended for young women	3	1	1	2	—	—	—	0

Occupations Where Gender Bias Persists

Despite some slight differences in the rank order of occupations, the only substantial difference in the recommended professions for young men and young women is the percentage mentioning nursing. Whereas 13% say they would advise young women to enter nursing, less than one-half of one percent mention this for young men.

Much smaller, though statistically significant, differences are seen for teaching as a profession (more likely to be chosen for women), as well as computers, technology/electronics, and trades/industrial jobs (all more likely to be chosen for men).

Occupations With Gender Differences
April 2005

	Recommended for young men %	Recommended for young women %	Difference (men minus women) %
Nursing	*	13	-13
Teaching	5	9	-4
Technology/Electronics	8	5	+3
Computers	11	8	+3
Trades/Industrial/Blue collar	8	2	+6

*Less than 0.5%

Combining the mentions of all technical jobs (including computers, technology/electronics, and engineering) provides even stronger evidence that young men are more likely to be associated with these sorts of jobs than are young women (24% vs. 16%).

The slight tendency for teaching to be seen as a female profession is almost entirely due to women being more likely to recommend this line of work to young women. Whereas about equal percentages of women and men recommend teaching as a profession to young men (5% and 4%, respectively), women are much more likely than men to recommend teaching as a profession to young women (12% vs. 5%).

Generational Change

Gallup's career advice trend indicates that a few professions historically associated with women have gone the way of poodle skirts. In 1950, 8% of Americans recommended home economics to young women, 8% recommended secretarial/clerical jobs, 4% mentioned dressmaking or fashion, and 4% mentioned being an airline stewardess. Today, only 2% of Americans mention secretarial work, and less than one half of one percent recommend any of the others as professions for young women.

Survey Methods

These results are based on telephone interviews with a randomly selected national sample of 1,003 adults, aged 18 and older, conducted April 18-21, 2005. For results based on this sample, one can say with 95% confidence that the maximum error attributable to sampling and other random effects is ±3 percentage points. In addition to sampling error, question wording and practical difficulties in conducting surveys can introduce error or bias into the findings of public opinion polls.

April 28, 2005
IF YOU HAD 15 MINUTES WITH PRESIDENT BUSH...
Most common advice: Get out of Iraq

by Frank Newport, Gallup Poll Editor in Chief

It wasn't uncommon in the old days for presidents of the United States to personally entertain the public—holding receptions, meeting average citizens in greeting lines, and taking occasions to hear what the people of the country were thinking and feeling.

But no more. In today's high security environment, of course, that's much less possible. The president of the United States is highly protected, and rarely, if ever, comes into enough contact with the average citizens of the country to get any kind of unfiltered feedback or advice.

Polling helps in that regard. Well-done scientific polls provide an assessment of what the people of the country are thinking and feeling at any given point in time. These polls provide an invaluable connection between elected representatives and the people they represent.

Although President George W. Bush has publicly proclaimed that he doesn't pay attention to polls, it is clear that his White House staff and advisors—particularly White House Deputy Chief of Staff Karl Rove—monitor public opinion as measured in polls quite carefully.

Most polls measure public opinion on issues as framed by the pollster: assessments of certain policy initiatives or overall reaction to plans, legislation, and events. From time to time, Gallup thinks it is useful to simply let Americans share what's on their minds, without prompting or pre-ordained question categories.

So Gallup's April 18-21, 2005, national poll of 1,003 randomly selected Americans included this simple question: *"If you could talk with President Bush for 15 minutes and give him advice about anything that's on your mind, what would you tell him?"*

The answers are fascinating and informative, ranging the gamut from simple praise or criticism for Bush's job performance, to a focus on very specific issues like abortion, immigration, and reforming welfare, to those who implore Bush to fix major problems such as the economy, healthcare, education, and, above all, the war in Iraq.

Reading through these comments is a fascinating exercise, and provides a unique and direct insight into the directions the American people would give to their commander in chief if given a chance.

In order to facilitate that process, Gallup listed responses from the more than 1,000 respondents to the survey question, along with the respondents' ages and genders.

But, not surprisingly, the answers Americans give in response to this question tend to fall into certain patterns and broad types of answers. Gallup coders read through each answer and placed it where possible into broader categories. These categories provide a more systematic view of exactly what the individual citizens want their president to do:

If you could talk with President Bush for 15 minutes and give him advice about anything that's on your mind, what would you tell him? [OPEN-ENDED]

	2005 Apr 18-21 % of Americans Giving Response
IRAQ WAR	**28**
End the war in Iraq/get out	22
Stay the course in Iraq/finish the job	3
War (non-specific)	3
SOCIAL SECURITY	**14**
Leave Social Security alone	6
Social Security (non-specific)	4
Fix Social Security/make solvent for future	4
GENERAL PRAISE, CRITIQUE	**11**
Doing a good job	6
Disapprove of job he is doing/resign office	5
ECONOMY	**10**
Economy needs to be improved	3
Reduce the federal budget deficit	2
Unemployment/jobs	2
Taxes	2
Cost of living/inflation	1
Reduce foreign trade deficit	*
ENERGY/GAS PRICES	**8**
Control prices of fuel/oil/Improve energy policies/ Need more alternatives	8
INEQUALITY	**7**
Improve domestic care for Americans/help those in need in the U.S.	3

Close the gap between rich and poor/stop catering to the rich	2
Stop corporate greed	1
Reform welfare	1

HEALTHCARE — 6
Improve overall healthcare system/Make it available/affordable to all	4
Increase Medicare coverage	2

MORALITY/MORAL ISSUES — 6
Keep the faith/good moral standards	2
Tell the truth/honest with the public	2
Separate church and state	1
Abortion issues	1

IMMIGRATION — 4
Close borders/restrict immigration	4

EDUCATION — 3
Improve/reform education	3

FOREIGN AID — 3
Foreign aid/focus overseas	3

INTERNATIONAL ADVICE — 2
International problems/stay out of others' business	2

GOVERNMENT/CONGRESS — 2
Government/Congress/politicians	2

ENVIRONMENT — 2
Improve/revamp environmental policies	2

COURTS/JUDICIAL SYSTEM — 1
Improve judicial system/courts	1

None	2
Other	7
No opinion	8

Percentages add to more than 100% due to multiple responses.
*Less than 0.5%

Several patterns emerge from a review of these categorized responses:

1. Iraq—The single bit of advice for the president that occurs more than any other is to end the war in Iraq and get U.S. troops home. This advice is offered by about 280 of the 1,003 Americans interviewed, or more than one in five. In short, despite Bush's focus on domestic issues in recent months, it is clear that a substantial sector of the public is still very worried about the nation's occupancy in Iraq.

2. Social Security—Americans, particularly those in the 50- to 64-year-old age group, are clearly worried about Social Security, and more than 1 in 10 would use their visit with the president to talk about what's going to happen to the Social Security system. Unfortunately for the president, Americans seem to be as likely to be concerned about the possible harm that could be done to the system as much as they are about reforms. It appears that many Americans, in short, are concerned about the cure being worse than the disease.

3. The economy—There is clear concern about the economy, although perhaps not at as high a level as recent consumer confidence numbers might suggest.

4. Energy prices—A little less than 10% of Americans would implore the president to do something about energy prices.

5. Financial inequality—It appears that a significant number of Americans, particularly Democrats, would ask the president to do something about the poor, welfare, and the current differences between the haves and the have-nots in the country.

6. Healthcare—Not a dominant concern, but some Americans would focus the president's attention on making healthcare more available, reigning in healthcare costs, and improving Medicare coverage.

7. Morality—About 6% of Americans in one way or the other would talk to the president about moral standards in the country today.

Age Differences

Here are the top five categories of advice for President Bush within four major age groups of Americans:

Age 18 to 29		Age 30 to 49	
Get out of Iraq	29%	Get out of Iraq	17%
Lower energy costs	10	Lower energy costs alone	9
Stay the course in Iraq alone	6	Fix healthcare	7
Good job	5	Good job	6
Disapprove	5	Disapprove	5
Improve education	5		

Age 50 to 64		Age 65 and older	
Get out of Iraq	25%	Get out of Iraq	21%
Lower energy costs	9	Leave Social Security alone	14
Leave Social Security	7	Good job	7
Disapprove	7	Lower energy costs	6
Social Security (non-specific)	6	Fix immigration	5
Fix Social Security	6		

One thing that is very clear is the high level of concern about Social Security among those Americans who are now 50- to 64-years-old — the group that includes many people who are most likely to be focused on retirement, although not yet in the Social Security system.

It is also clear that younger Americans, ages 18 to 29, are more likely to mention Iraq than those who are older.

Regional Differences

East		South	
Get out of Iraq	26%	Get out of Iraq	17%
Disapprove	9	Lower energy costs	10
Lower energy costs	8	Good job	8
Good job	6	Social Security (non-specific)	7
Social Security (non-specific)	5	Lower immigration	6
Provide more equal care	5		
Improve economy	5		

Midwest		West	
Get out of Iraq	22%	Get out of Iraq	25%
Lower energy costs	10	Disapprove	8
Leave Social Security alone	9	Leave Social Security alone	7
Fix healthcare	7	Good job	5
Good job	5	Fix immigration	5
Improve economy	5		
Improve education	5		
Get less involved overseas	5		

Regional differences to some degree reflect the differences in the regions' political orientations. Bush's highest level of support comes in the South, so it is not surprising that negative comments about getting out of Iraq are lower in the South, where favorable comments about Bush are higher.

Also, those living in the West and South are more likely to mention immigration concerns.

Party Differences

The differences in advice by party are fairly predictable. Republicans would be much more likely to say to the president that he's doing a good job, and much less likely to give him critical advice regarding Iraq. Independents and Democrats are more likely to offer critical advice regarding Iraq, and Democrats—not surprisingly—are more likely than average to offer a general negative comment.

Republicans		Independents		Democrats	
Doing a good job	13%	End the war in Iraq/get out	26%	End the war in Iraq/get out	31%
End the war in Iraq/get out	10	Leave Social Security alone	6	Disapprove	9
Control fuel oil prices/ energy policies	10	Control fuel oil prices/ energy policies	6	Control fuel oil prices/ energy policies	9
Social Security (non-specific)	6	Disapprove	5	Leave Social Security alone	8
Improve healthcare	6	Good job	4	Improve healthcare	5

There are two other interesting differences by party:
- Democrats are more likely than average to implore the president to do something about inequality and the problem of haves and have-nots in society.
- Republicans are more likely than average to want the president to do something about immigration.

Survey Methods

These results are based on telephone interviews with a randomly selected national sample of 1,003 adults, aged 18 and older, conducted April 18-21, 2005. For results based on this sample, one can say with 95% confidence that the maximum error attributable to sample and other random effects is ±3 percentage points. In addition to sampling error, question wording and practical difficulties in conducting surveys can introduce error and bias into the findings of public opinion polls.

April 29, 2005

MOST AMERICANS BELIEVE CHARGES AGAINST MICHAEL JACKSON PROBABLY TRUE
Muted racial divide in Jackson case compared with O.J. Simpson case

by David W. Moore, Gallup Poll Senior Editor

The racial division that characterized public opinion about O.J. Simpson's murder trial in 1995 is largely muted in Michael Jackson's child molestation trial. The latest Gallup survey shows that a large majority of whites believe the charges against Jackson are either definitely or probably true, similar to whites' opinions about the murder charges against Simpson in 1994 and 1995. Large majorities of blacks, however, said the charges against Simpson were either definitely or probably not true, leading to a large racial gap in attitudes on the matter. About Jackson, blacks are much more divided, leaning—by a modest margin—toward the probability that he is guilty.

The most recent Gallup survey about Jackson was conducted April 18-21. Only a third of Americans say they are following the trial very or somewhat closely. By comparison, in a July 1-3, 1994, Gallup survey, 72% of Americans said they had been following news about the Simpson murder charges either very or somewhat closely. Public attention remained high throughout the following year, as reflected a year later in a July 6, 1995, Gallup survey. At that time, just after the prosecution in the case rested, 66% of Americans said they had seen or heard a "great deal" or "moderate amount" about the trial.

How Much Paying Attention to News About Michael Jackson/O.J. Simpson

HOW CLOSELY FOLLOW:	Very closely	Somewhat closely	Not too closely	Not at all	No opinion
Michael Jackson 2005 Apr 18-21	6%	27	43	24	*
O.J. Simpson 1994 Jul 1-3	25%	47	21	6	1

HOW MUCH HEARD:	Great deal	Moderate amount	Only a little	Nothing at all	No opinion
O.J. Simpson 1995 Jul 6	38%	28	29	4	1

*Less than 0.5%

The current poll shows that 70% of Americans believe the charges against Jackson are true—including 12% who say "definitely" and 58% who say "probably" true. In two previous surveys taken in February this year, 69% and 75% indicated the charges were true, little different from current opinion.

Do you personally believe the charges that Michael Jackson sexually abused a boy are—[ROTATED: definitely true, probably true, probably not true, (or) definitely not true]?

	Definitely true %	Probably true %	Probably not true %	Definitely not true %	No opinion %
2005 Apr 18-21	12	58	13	2	15
2005 Feb 25-27	22	53	13	3	9
2005 Feb 4-6	16	53	17	2	12

A comparison of these views by race shows that even among blacks, more adults are likely to believe that the charges are at least probably true than to believe they are at least probably not true. (To provide a more substantial number of black respondents, the results of the three surveys this year were combined.) An average of the responses among whites over the three surveys shows that whites believe the charges against Jackson are true, by 75% to 13%. Among blacks, the margin is much lower, with 49% saying the charges are at least probably true, and 41% saying they are at least probably not true.

Charges Against Jackson Are:

	Definitely/ Probably true	Definitely/ Probably not true	No opinion
Whites (3 polls)	75%	13	12
Blacks (3 polls)	49%	41	10

The margin among whites saying the charges are true is 62 percentage points, compared with 8 points among blacks—for a net racial gap of 54 points.

While this gap is not insignificant, the overall results show that even among blacks, a plurality agrees with the majority of whites. Also, in comparison with differences between blacks' and whites' attitudes about the Simpson case, the current racial gap is relatively modest.

For example, in a July 20-23, 1995, survey, Gallup found that a large majority of whites believed the charges against Simpson were true, by 75% to 15%—similar to the percentages in the Jackson case. Among blacks, however, a large majority believed the charges were not true, by 60% to 25%.

Charges Against Simpson Are:

	Definitely/ Probably true	Definitely/ Probably not true	No opinion
1995 Jul 20-23			
Whites	75%	15	10
Blacks	25%	60	15

The margin among whites for Simpson was 60 points, while the margin among blacks was a minus 35 points—for a net racial gap of 95 points.

The racial gap remained substantial, even after Simpson's acquittal. When asked whether the jury made the right or the wrong decision, a majority of whites said it was wrong, while an overwhelming majority of blacks said it was right.

Jury Decision in the Simpson Case Is:

	Right decision	Wrong decision	No opinion
1995 Oct 19-22			
Whites	36%	53	11
Blacks	89%	6	5

Among whites, the margin saying the decision was wrong was 17 points, with 53% saying it was the wrong decision and 36% saying it was right. Blacks said the decision was right by an 83-point margin, 89% to 6%. The net racial gap is 100 points, almost twice as large as the racial gap in the Jackson case.

Survey Methods

Results in the current survey are based on telephone interviews with 1,003 national adults, aged 18 and older, conducted April 18-21, 2005. For results based on the total sample of national adults, one can say with 95% confidence that the maximum margin of sampling error is ±3 percentage points. The combination of three surveys included 206 black respondents, for a maximum margin of error of ±8 percentage points.

In addition to sampling error, question wording and practical difficulties in conducting surveys can introduce error or bias into the findings of public opinion polls.

Fifty-two percent of Americans say they are worried about "not being able to pay medical costs in the event of a serious illness or accident," the only other issue for which a majority expresses worry. Four in 10 are worried about paying the costs of normal healthcare and being able to maintain their current standard of living. Americans are far less worried about paying normal monthly bills, their mortgages or housing payments, and the minimum payments on their credit cards.

Retirement

The poll asked an extensive battery of questions about non-retirees' plans for retirement, as well as current retirees' experience.

In general, non-retirees have fairly positive overall attitudes toward retirement, despite the rather high level of concern about retirement and the substantial proportion of Americans who do not expect to live comfortably during retirement. When given a choice, 69% of non-retirees say they are "looking forward to retirement," while 25% say they are "dreading" it.

But those attitudes are not an indication that Americans are counting the days until their working days end. Sixty-four percent of non-retirees say they would like to work part-time when they retire, while 33% would like to stop working altogether.

Also, Gallup asked non-retirees at what age they would retire if money were no object. The data suggest they would not necessarily jump at the chance; the average age was 51. Fourteen percent would retire at age 65 or older.

If you were rich enough so that money were no object, at what age would you like to retire, or would you have retired?

Based on non-retirees

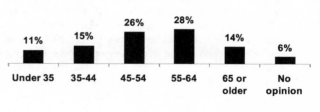

April 4-7, 2005

May 2, 2005
RETIREMENT EXPECTATIONS, REALITY NOT ENTIRELY CONSISTENT
Retirement continues to be public's greatest financial concern

by Jeffrey M. Jones, Gallup Poll Managing Editor

Gallup's annual Personal Finance poll finds that retirement is the financial issue Americans are most worried about. While most non-retirees say they are looking forward to retirement, just over half think they will be able to live comfortably when they retire. Non-retirees' expectations for retirement differ from the actual experience of current retirees in a few respects: on average, non-retirees expect to retire four years later than the average age when current retirees stopped working; and retirees rely to a much greater extent on Social Security income than non-retirees expect to.

Financial Concerns

The April 4-7 poll shows that retirement savings is once again Americans' top financial concern, based on reactions to a list of seven items included in the survey. Six in 10 Americans are either very (30%) or moderately (30%) worried about "not having enough money for retirement." Retirement has been the chief financial worry of Americans for each of the last five years.

2005 Apr 4-7 (sorted by "very worried")	Very worried %	Moderately worried %	Total "Worried" %	Total "Not worried" %
Not having enough money for retirement	30	30	60	37
Not being able to pay medical costs of a serious illness/accident	30	22	52	47
Not being able to pay medical costs for normal healthcare	23	19	42	56
Not being able to maintain the standard of living you enjoy	14	27	41	59
Not having enough to pay your normal monthly bills	13	17	30	69
Not being able to pay your rent, mortgage, or other housing costs	10	13	23	73
Not being able to make the minimum payments on your credit cards	7	9	16	67

Despite these relatively positive views on retirement, just slightly more than half of non-retired Americans, 53%, say they think they will have enough money to live comfortably when they retire; 40% do not think so. That represents a slight drop from each of the prior three years, when 59% said they thought they would have enough money in retirement. It compares with 72% of all Americans who say they have enough to live comfortably now—and 73% of retired Americans who say they are now living comfortably.

Nearly half of non-retirees expect a 401(k) plan or Individual Retirement Account to be a major source of income when they retire, significantly more than any of the other sources tested in the poll. Given the uncertainty regarding the future of the Social Security system in its current form, it is perhaps not surprising that only 28% of non-retirees say Social Security will be a major source of retirement funding. About one in four expect a pension plan or their home equity to be a major source of income during retirement.

Enough Money to Live Comfortably?

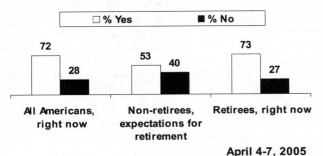

April 4-7, 2005

Expected Retirement Income Sources, Non-Retirees

	Major source %	Major or Minor source %
401(k), IRA, etc.	49	82
Social Security	28	81
Pension plan	28	59
Home equity	26	67
Stocks/mutual funds	21	62
Savings account/CDs	18	73
Part-time work	18	69
Annuities/insurance	9	43
Inheritance	7	35
Rent/royalties	6	30

Gallup has annually updated these trends and found consistent results from year to year.

Non-retirees' expectations differ significantly from retirees' reality. Social Security is clearly the dominant source of income among those who are now retired—88% say it is a source of income, including 58% who say it is a major source. Only half of retirees rely on a 401(k) or IRA plan, including just one in five who rely on it a great deal. That could be due to the fact that these savings vehicles are relatively new creations, and may not have been options for (especially older) retirees.

Pension plans are the number-two source of income for current retirees, with over a third saying they are a major income source.

Retirement Income Sources, Retirees

	Major source %	Major or Minor source %
Social Security	58	88
Pension plan	36	58
Home equity	25	44
401(k), IRA, etc.	21	50
Stocks/mutual funds	12	44
Savings account/CDs	11	52
Annuities/insurance	6	32
Part-time work	6	23
Inheritance	3	16
Rent/royalties	2	15

In general, non-retirees are more likely to expect to rely on all of the sources of income to some degree than current retirees do, except for Social Security (the difference on pension plans is negligible). Thus, although many non-retirees expect to rely on a wide range of sources to fund retirement, relatively few current retirees actually do.

Retirement Funds: Major + Minor Sources

	Non-retirees %	Retirees %	Difference Pct. pts.
401(k), IRA, etc.	82	50	+32
Social Security	81	88	-7
Savings account/CDs	73	52	+19
Part-time work	69	23	+46
Home equity	67	44	+23
Stocks/mutual funds	62	44	+18
Pension plan	59	58	+1
Annuities/insurance	43	32	+11
Inheritance	35	16	+19
Rent/royalties	30	15	+15

Another disconnect between expectation and reality concerns retirement age. The average age of expected retirement for non-retirees is 64, and 56% expect to retire at age 65 or older. Those who are currently retired report an average age of 60 at the time of retirement, and only 29% retired at age 65 or older.

Retirement Age

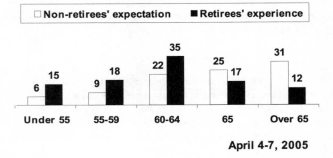

April 4-7, 2005

It is unclear whether the differences on retirement age or funding are due to somewhat unrealistic expectations for retirement on the part of non-retirees, or whether they are a reflection of the growing realities concerning retirement. In the past few decades, the age at which Americans are eligible to receive Social Security benefits has increased. Additionally, Social Security gives higher payouts if recipients begin receiving benefits at a later age. Both factors may have encouraged Americans to retire (or want to retire) at later ages. Indeed, the reported average age of retirement for retirees, according to Gallup's data, has increased from 57 in 1991 to the current 60, and the expected average age of retirement has climbed from 60 in 1995 to the current 64.

The differences between non-retirees' expectations and retirees' reality concerning the funding sources of retirement may also be influenced by societal or policy changes. For example, many companies no longer offer pension plans to their workers, and 401(k) plans are growing in popularity as an alternative. Also, the looming concerns about the long-term financial prospects of the Social Security system may be conditioning younger Americans to seek other sources of income to support them during their retirement years.

Survey Methods

These results are based on telephone interviews with a randomly selected national sample of 1,010 adults, aged 18 and older, conducted April 4-7, 2005. For results based on this sample, one can say with 95% confidence that the maximum error attributable to sampling and other random effects is ±3 percentage points. In addition to sampling error, question wording and practical difficulties in conducting surveys can introduce error or bias into the findings of public opinion polls.

For the results based on the sample of 767 non-retirees, the maximum margin of sampling error is ±4 percentage points.

For results based on the sample of 243 retirees, the maximum margin of sampling error is ±7 percentage points.

In addition to sampling error, question wording and practical difficulties in conducting surveys can introduce error or bias into the findings of public opinion polls.

May 3, 2005

PUBLIC WARM TO NUCLEAR POWER, COOL TO NEARBY PLANTS
Gender, politics affect responses

by Darren K. Carlson, Government and Politics Editor

Against the backdrop of soaring gas prices, President George W. Bush spoke twice last week—including a prime-time news conference—about developing more oil refineries and nuclear plants as a way to lessen American dependence on foreign oil. A secure energy future for America, Bush said, must include more nuclear power.

On one aspect of the energy plan, increased reliance on nuclear power, Americans are currently more positively than negatively oriented. Gallup's recent Environment poll* found a slight majority of Americans favor using nuclear energy to provide electricity. But a majority opposes the idea of a nuclear energy plant being built in their areas.

Currently, 54% of Americans favor using nuclear energy as a way to provide electricity for the United States—17% "strongly favor" the idea, and 37% "somewhat favor" it. On the other side, 43% say they either "strongly" (22%) or "somewhat oppose" (21%) the idea of using nuclear energy for electricity.

These most recent results are right in line with public opinion from last year and also in 1994. In 2001, support for nuclear energy use was slightly lower.

Overall, do you strongly favor, somewhat favor, somewhat oppose, or strongly oppose the use of nuclear energy as one of the ways to provide electricity for the U.S.?

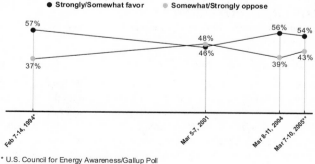

● Strongly/Somewhat favor   ● Somewhat/Strongly oppose

* U.S. Council for Energy Awareness/Gallup Poll
** Based on 494 national adults in Form A

Public Says 'No Thanks' to Nuclear Neighborhoods

Though more Americans than not favor the use of nuclear energy in a broad sense, most don't like the idea of a plant in their areas, which is understandable given the risks of nuclear power production. A majority of Americans (63%) say they oppose the construction of a nuclear energy plant in their areas—4 in 10 oppose the idea strongly, while another 1 in 5 say they're somewhat opposed. Slightly more than a third of Americans (35%) favor the construction of a plant near them—11% favoring the idea strongly; 24% somewhat favoring it.

Overall, do you strongly favor, somewhat favor, somewhat oppose, or strongly oppose the construction of a nuclear energy plant in your area as one of the ways to provide electricity for the U.S.?

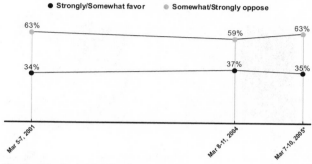

● Strongly/Somewhat favor   ● Somewhat/Strongly oppose

*Based on 510 national adults in Form B

Gender, Politics Affect Responses

Some groups are significantly more likely to favor nuclear power as an energy source, on both a national and local level. On the question of plants as an energy source for the United States, a majority of men (69%) favor the idea, while 29% oppose. Among women, just 40% favor the use of nuclear power, and 56% oppose. When asked about construction of a plant in their areas, 44% of men favor the notion, compared with just 28% of women.

Republicans are more likely than Democrats and political independents to favor nuclear power. On the question of using nuclear energy to provide electricity in the United States, 66% of Republicans approve, compared with 56% of independents, and 40% of Democrats. Nearly half of Republicans (46%) also say they favor the construction of a nuclear power plant in their areas. Among independents, just 31% favor this idea, and the percentage dwindles to just 27% among Democrats.

*These results are based on telephone interviews with randomly selected national samples of 494 and 510 adults, aged 18 and older, conducted March 7-10, 2005. For results based on these samples, one can say with 95% confidence that the maximum error attributable to sampling and other random effects is ±5 percentage points. In addition to sampling error, question wording and practical difficulties in conducting surveys can introduce error or bias into the findings of public opinion polls.

	Men 18-49	Men 50+	Women 18-49	Women 50+
Enjoy spending	48	44	54	38
Enjoy saving	51	52	42	55
No opinion	1	4	4	7
	100%	100%	100%	100%

May 3, 2005
WHO SAVES IN AMERICA—AND WHO SPENDS?
Most Americans claim to live within their means

by Lydia Saad, Gallup Poll Senior Editor

Politics is not the only force that divides the country—a recent Gallup survey* revealed that Americans also split nearly equally between spenders and savers. Half of Americans say they are the type of person who more enjoys saving money, while 46% more enjoy spending it.

Do you enjoy spending money or saving money?

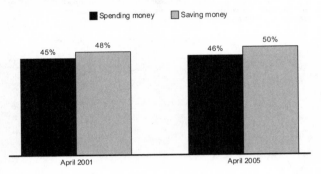

Americans are often berated for not saving enough, but consumer spending is so important to the nation's economic well-being that one has to wonder which team—the spenders or the savers—President George W. Bush and his economic advisers are rooting for. Democratic Americans may be doing more than their share to keep recession at bay. The majority of Democrats, compared with just 39% of Republicans, say they more enjoy spending money.

	Republican	Independent	Democrat
Enjoy spending	39	46	54
Enjoy saving	58	49	43
No opinion	3	5	3
	100%	100%	100%

Women are often typecast as "shopaholics," but men appear to be no different in their orientation toward money. Men and women are virtually identical in their answers to this question: 46% of both groups say they more enjoy spending money, while 51% of men and 48% of women say they prefer saving it.

Greater differences in attitudes about money are observed by age, with the penchant for spending highest among younger Americans. A slim majority of those aged 18 to 29 and 30 to 49 say they more enjoy spending money. Those aged 50 and older prefer saving it.

	18-29	30-49	50-64	65+
Enjoy spending	51	51	45	34
Enjoy saving	48	46	50	59
No opinion	1	3	5	7
	100%	100%	100%	100%

Putting gender and age together, we see that younger women are the most likely to get a thrill from shopping, while older women are the least likely. In fact, the 13-point gap in the percentage of older versus younger women who enjoy spending is one of the largest demographic distinctions seen in this data (second only to the 15-point difference between Republicans and Democrats).

Only slight differences are seen according to household earnings, with those living in higher-income households slightly more likely to say they enjoy spending money than those in lower-income households.

What Does It Mean?

While interesting, one's orientation toward money appears to bear little relation to one's financial well-being. Those who describe their personal financial situation as "excellent" or "good" are essentially no more likely to enjoy saving money than those whose situation is "only fair" or "poor."

Most Americans claim to be living within their means: 85% of savers and 76% of spenders attest to this in the recent survey. The percentage admitting they are living beyond their means is only marginally higher among spenders than savers: 24% vs. 14%.

Perhaps most relevant for the economy, savers are no more likely than spenders to project an increase in their level of spending in the near future. Just 24% of spenders and 25% of savers say that their spending level is likely to increase over the next six months.

Bottom Line

People may have feelings about spending money—whether they like it or don't. The data suggest that spenders may be slightly worse off financially than savers, but for the most part, one's self-identification as a spender or saver doesn't appear to be a major indicator of financial well-being.

*Results are based on telephone interviews with 1,003 national adults, aged 18 and older, conducted April 18-21, 2005. For results based on the total sample of national adults, one can say with 95% confidence that the margin of sampling error is ±3 percentage points.

May 3, 2005
CRYSTAL METH, CHILD MOLESTATION TOP CRIME CONCERNS
Seventy-five percent of rural Americans very concerned about meth

by Joseph Carroll, Gallup Poll Assistant Editor

When presented with a list of six crimes that could happen in their local communities, a recent CNN/*USA Today*/Gallup poll finds that Americans express the greatest concern about child molestation and the sale and use of methamphetamines or "crystal meth." The public also expressed considerable worry about the sale and use of cocaine as well as identity theft, but is less worried about violent crime or terrorism.

Two in Three Americans "Very Concerned" About Child Molestation, Crystal Meth

The poll, conducted Feb. 25-27*, asked Americans to rate their level of concern on five different aspects of crime in their local communities. In a separate question, Gallup also asked Americans to describe their level of concern about identity theft, the crime in which someone steals personal information, such as a Social Security number, and uses that information to commit fraud.

Sexual molestation of children and the use or sale of methamphetamines top the list of these local crime worries, with roughly two in three Americans saying they are "very concerned" about these two issues. The use or sale of cocaine, with 61% saying they are very concerned, and identity theft, with 59%, follow closely behind. Americans are less concerned about violent crime, although a slim majority (52%) still says it is very concerned about it. Just about a third of all Americans, 36%, say they are very concerned about acts of terrorism occurring in their local communities.

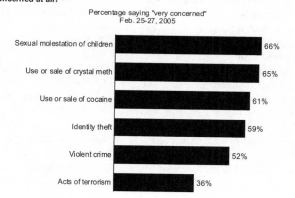

Americans' Crime Concerns

How concerned are you about each of the following happening in your local community – very concerned, somewhat concerned, not too concerned, or not concerned at all?

Percentage saying "very concerned"
Feb. 25-27, 2005

- Sexual molestation of children — 66%
- Use or sale of crystal meth — 65%
- Use or sale of cocaine — 61%
- Identity theft — 59%
- Violent crime — 52%
- Acts of terrorism — 36%

Crystal Meth a Concern in Rural Communities, the Midwest, South, and West

News reports depict how the sale and use of crystal meth has been surging in rural and suburban communities across the country in recent years, particularly in the Midwest and the West.

The current poll finds that a slight majority of Americans (53%) living in the eastern part of the country say they are very concerned about crystal meth. However, this sentiment is much higher among those living in the Midwest (68%), the South (68%), and the West (70%).

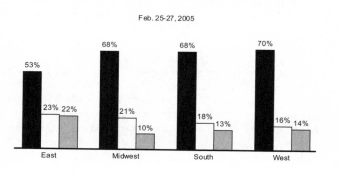

Concern About Crystal Meth, by Region

■ Very concerned   □ Somewhat concerned   ■ Not too/Not at all concerned

Feb. 25-27, 2005

	East	Midwest	South	West
Very concerned	53%	68%	68%	70%
Somewhat concerned	23%	21%	18%	16%
Not too/Not at all	22%	10%	13%	14%

People residing in suburban areas are less likely than people in urban or rural areas to say they are very concerned about crystal meth. Seventy-five percent of adults living in rural areas and 67% of adults in urban areas say they are very concerned about the drug, compared with 60% of those living in suburban communities.

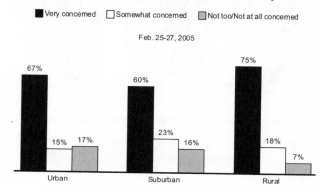

Concern About Crystal Meth, by Type of Community

■ Very concerned   □ Somewhat concerned   ■ Not too/Not at all concerned

Feb. 25-27, 2005

	Urban	Suburban	Rural
Very concerned	67%	60%	75%
Somewhat concerned	15%	23%	18%
Not too/Not at all	17%	16%	7%

When comparing Americans' concerns about crystal meth with their concerns about cocaine, the data also show some differences by region and type of community. Roughly two in three adults living in the Midwest say they are very concerned about the use or sale of crystal meth, while 55% of those living in that region are concerned about cocaine. Among residents living in the West, 70% are very concerned about crystal meth, compared with 61% who are concerned about cocaine. The data show only slight variations among residents in the eastern and southern parts of the country on these two measures.

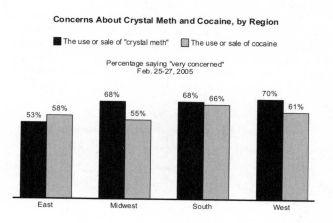

Concerns About Crystal Meth and Cocaine, by Region

■ The use or sale of "crystal meth"   ■ The use or sale of cocaine

Percentage saying "very concerned"
Feb. 25-27, 2005

	East	Midwest	South	West
Crystal meth	53%	68%	68%	70%
Cocaine	58%	55%	66%	61%

There are only modest differences in the levels of concern about crystal meth compared with cocaine in urban and suburban communities. Americans living in rural communities, however, are more likely to express concern about crystal meth than about cocaine.

Women, People in Lower-Income Households More Concerned About Child Molestation

The ongoing and highly publicized Michael Jackson child molestation case has propelled the issue to the forefront of the news over the past several months.

Gallup's data show that women are much more likely than men to be concerned about child molestation, although majorities of both

Concerns About Crystal Meth and Cocaine, by Type of Community

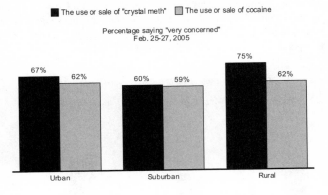

■ The use or sale of "crystal meth" ☐ The use or sale of cocaine

Percentage saying "very concerned"
Feb. 25-27, 2005

Concerns About Sexual Molestation of Children, by Gender

■ Very concerned ☐ Somewhat concerned ☐ Not too/Not at all concerned

Feb. 25-27, 2005

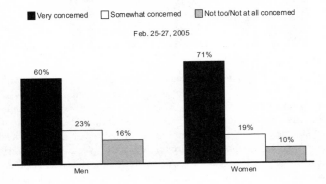

groups are worried about it. Slightly more than 7 in 10 women say they are very concerned, compared with 60% of men.

Americans living in lower-income households are also more likely to express concern about sexual abuse of children than are those in higher-income households. More than three in four adults earning less than $30,000 per year say they are very concerned about child molestation, while 64% of those earning between $30,000 and $75,000 per year, and just 54% of those earning $75,000 per year or more express this level of concern.

Concerns About Sexual Molestation of Children, by Household Income

■ Very concerned ☐ Somewhat concerned ☐ Not too/Not at all concerned

Feb. 25-27, 2005

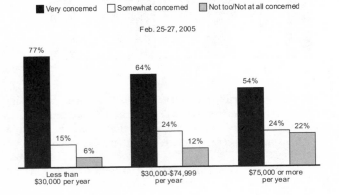

Interestingly, the poll finds no difference in the levels of concern about child molestation between parents of children aged 18 and younger and those who do not have young children.

These results are based on telephone interviews with a randomly selected national sample of 1,008 adults, aged 18 and older,

conducted Feb. 25-27, 2005. For results based on this sample, one can say with 95% confidence that the maximum error attributable to sampling and other random effects is ±3 percentage points. In addition to sampling error, question wording and practical difficulties in conducting surveys can introduce error or bias into the findings of public opinion polls.

May 4, 2005
BUSH FAILS TO IGNITE PUBLIC SUPPORT FOR REFORM
Social Security debate is stagnating

by Lydia Saad, Gallup Poll Senior Editor

Using a live, nationally televised address and a cross-country barnstorming tour, President George W. Bush has been putting his all into building public support for his Social Security plan in recent weeks, but to little avail so far. The latest CNN/*USA Today*/Gallup poll finds little change in Americans' opinions about Bush's substantive positions on Social Security. There has also been no change in the percentage of Americans approving of the job Bush is doing on the issue compared with a month ago.

The overall picture for Bush remains lackluster. In particular, only 27% of Americans would like to see Congress pass a Republican-backed plan for Social Security this year. Nearly as many would prefer to see a Democratic-backed plan passed (22%), but the plurality of Americans (46%) say it would be better for them if no plan were passed this year. Also, just 35% of Americans today approve of the job Bush is doing on Social Security, while 58% disapprove. Those approval figures are nearly identical to the previous measures, taken in early April and late February.

George W. Bush's Handling of Social Security

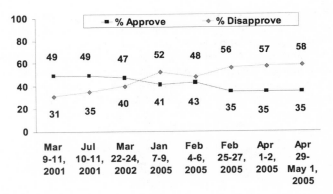

Public reaction to the centerpiece of Bush's reform plan—private accounts—remains more negative than positive. About half of Americans (52%) say they oppose allowing workers to invest part of their Social Security taxes in stocks or bonds; just 44% favor this. There has been no statistically significant change in support for private investment accounts since Gallup first tested this in December.

Americans are even more resistant to the idea of indexing Social Security benefits for future retirees—an idea conceived by a Demo-

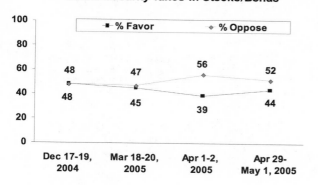

Allowing Workers to Invest Part of Their Social Security Taxes in Stocks/Bonds

- % Favor ■   - % Oppose ◆

	Dec 17-19, 2004	Mar 18-20, 2005	Apr 1-2, 2005	Apr 29-May 1, 2005
Oppose	48	47	56	52
Favor	48	45	39	44

cratic financier and promoted by Bush at his press conference last week—whereby benefits would be curbed along a sliding scale for middle- and upper-income Americans. Only 38% favor this proposal, while 54% oppose it.

Americans are so opposed to this means-testing proposal that, when given a choice, the majority, 53%, say they would rather see taxes raised than have benefits cut (38%).

Americans Would Postpone Changes

Underlying all of these attitudes is a basic belief among Americans that the Social Security system needs to be fixed, and that it will require some hard choices. Bush has failed to capitalize on this sentiment in part because a majority of Americans don't believe the need for action is that urgent.

- While 81% say major changes in Social Security are needed in the foreseeable future, only 45% think such changes are needed in the next year or two. Thirty-six percent say changes should be made within the next 10 years and 16% believe they are not necessary.

- There has been a slight increase since late February—from 38% to 45%—in the percentage of Americans saying that reform should occur in the next year or two. This change might be due to Bush's recent efforts to promote his plan. However, the current level is still slightly lower than the 49% who favored quick action in January.

- Only 35% of Americans believe it is possible to ensure the long-term future of Social Security without either raising their taxes or cutting their Social Security benefits. Most (62%) think such a painless solution is not possible.

- A slim majority of Americans (53%) believe that the system of changes Bush is proposing will result in a reduction in their own Social Security benefits.

Democrats Fail to Persuade

It is clear that President Bush's proposal to restructure Social Security has been met with a resounding thud. But Democrats may be overreaching with their contention that Bush wants to "dismantle" the system. Only 41% of Americans believe Bush wants to dismantle Social Security, as some Democrats have charged; the majority (55%) says he is trying to ensure its long-term stability. There has even been a slight increase this month (from 50% to 55%) in the percentage of Americans crediting Bush with pure motives.

By contrast, Americans are about evenly divided over whether the Democrats are mainly trying to preserve Social Security (49%)

or are trying to use the issue to hurt Republicans (46%) in the next elections.

While Washington politicos are playing a game of charge and countercharge over who has Americans' best interests at heart, the public has a fairly balanced reaction to the two parties' approaches to Social Security reform. The percentage of Americans who say they are worried that the Republicans will go too far in changing the Social Security system and the percentage who are worried that the Democrats will not go far enough are about equal (62% and 61%, respectively).

Naturally, Democrats tend to be the ones worried that the Republicans will go too far. What's interesting is that Democratic respondents are nearly as likely as Republican respondents to say they are worried that the Democrats won't go far enough.

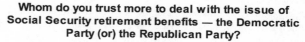

% Very/Somewhat Worried About Each Party's Approach to Social Security
by Party ID

	Republicans	Independents	Democrats
Worried Republicans will go too far	35%	66%	86%
Worried Democrats won't go far enough	66%	58%	58%

More generally, however, by a 46% to 36% margin, Americans have more faith in Democrats than in Republicans to handle Social Security.

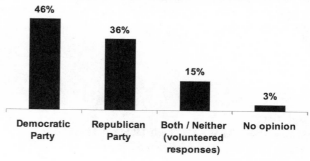

Whom do you trust more to deal with the issue of Social Security retirement benefits — the Democratic Party (or) the Republican Party?

Democratic Party	Republican Party	Both / Neither (volunteered responses)	No opinion
46%	36%	15%	3%

April 29-May 1, 2005

This is not new, however. Not only are these figures nearly identical to where they stood two months ago, but Gallup polling for the past decade or so has shown that Democrats have consistently had about a 10- to 15-point advantage over Republicans on this issue. So, rather than expanding their advantage, Democrats are at the low end of their historical advantage on Social Security.

Cynical Seniors

Of the various age groups, America's seniors are the most critical of Bush on the Social Security issue, and the least likely to support his various reform proposals.

- Only 29% of those 65 and older, compared with 36% of those under 65, say they approve of Bush's handling of Social Security.

- Though there are no significant differences by age with respect to Bush's means-testing proposal, the percentage favoring

Bush's privatization plan falls from 51% among those 18 to 49, to 39% among those 50 to 64, to 30% among those 65 and older.

- The majority of Americans under 65 believe that Bush's plan would result in a cut in their Social Security benefits. While only 36% of seniors hold that view, this figure could be viewed as significant, given the extent to which Bush has emphasized that his plan would not affect current retirees in any way.

Perceived Effect of Bush's Plan on Your Social Security Benefits

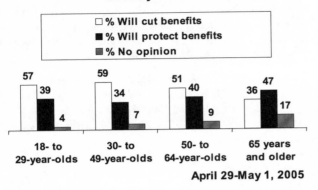

□ % Will cut benefits
■ % Will protect benefits
■ % No opinion

18- to 29-year-olds	30- to 49-year-olds	50- to 64-year-olds	65 years and older
57 39 4	59 34 7	51 40 9	36 47 17

April 29-May 1, 2005

Survey Methods

These results are based on telephone interviews with a randomly selected national sample of 1,006 adults, aged 18 and older, conducted April 29-May 1, 2005. For results based on this sample, one can say with 95% confidence that the maximum error attributable to sampling and other random effects is ±3 percentage points. In addition to sampling error, question wording and practical difficulties in conducting surveys can introduce error or bias into the findings of public opinion polls.

May 5, 2005
AMERICANS' VIEWS OF THE IRAQ WAR SOUR
President Bush's approval ratings on Iraq hold steady at 42%

by Joseph Carroll, Gallup Poll Assistant Editor

Americans' views of the war in Iraq have turned more negative in recent weeks, continuing a trend that began shortly after the Iraqi elections. Fifty-seven percent of Americans now say it was *not* worth going to war in Iraq—the most negative results Gallup has recorded on this measure. A majority of Americans now say things are going badly for the United States in Iraq, a switch from the post-election period in Iraq, when a majority gave a positive assessment of the situation there. Americans are more divided as to whether or not it was a mistake to send troops to Iraq, and President George W. Bush's job approval rating on Iraq has settled back down to the low 40% range after reaching 50% immediately following the Iraqi elections.

Majority of Americans Say Iraq War Was not "Worth It"

The latest CNN/*USA Today*/Gallup poll, conducted April 29 - May 1, shows that only 41% of Americans say it was worth going to war in Iraq, while a majority of Americans, 57%, say it was not worth it.

Worth Going to War in Iraq?
Selected Trend: January 2004 — May 2005

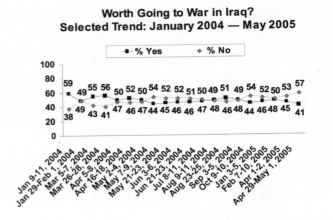

This is the lowest level of support that Gallup has found on this question since the war started in March 2003.

Over the course of this year, the results to this question have shown modest fluctuations. In early January, a slim majority of Americans, 52%, said the war was *not* worth it. Then, Americans were more divided in their views in early February, with 48% saying it was worth it and 50% saying it was not. At the beginning of April, Americans became more negative, with 45% saying it was worth it and 53% saying it was not worth it, and the most recent poll finds views growing still more negative.

Public Divided as to Whether It Was a "Mistake to Send Troops to Iraq"

While a clear majority of Americans believe the war effort was not worth it, the public is more reluctant to term the decision to send troops a "mistake." Gallup's other basic measure of support for the war is now evenly divided, with 49% saying it was a mistake to send troops and 48% saying it was not.

Mistake to Send Troops to Iraq?
Selected Trend: January 2004 — May 2005

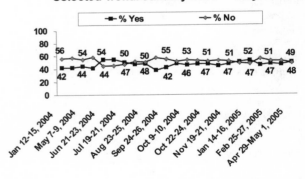

Since the start of the year, this question's trend shows greater fluctuation. In mid-January, more Americans said it was a mistake (52%) to send troops than said it was *not* a mistake (47%). That changed when Americans became much more positive about the situation in Iraq following the elections in that country at the end of January, with the majority (55%) then saying it was *not* a mistake and 45% saying it was. Since then, positive assessments have receded, and now the percent who believe the war was not a mistake has fallen back below 50%.

Majority of Americans Say
War in Iraq Going "Badly"

A majority of Americans, 56%, say things are currently going badly for the United States in Iraq, while just 42% say things are going well. These results show a shift in opinion during the past several months, although views were more negative at the start of the year.

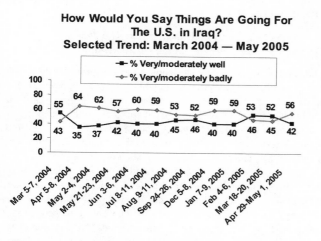

How Would You Say Things Are Going For The U.S. in Iraq?
Selected Trend: March 2004 — May 2005

In February and March polls, following the elections in Iraq, a slight majority of Americans—53% in early February and 52% in mid-March—said things were going well in Iraq. Fewer than half said things were going badly in those two polls. At the beginning of the year, however, views on this measure were much more negative, with 40% saying things were going well and 59% saying things were going badly for the United States in Iraq.

Americans are now four times as likely to say things are going "very badly" (25%) than to say they are going "very well" (6%).

Bush Approval on Iraq Holds
Steady at 42%

A majority of Americans, 55%, disapprove of the way President Bush is handling the situation in Iraq, while 42% approve. Bush began the year with the same 42% approval rating, which is in line with the lowest approval ratings of his presidency, but saw it spike to 50% following the Iraq elections. Since that time it has declined, falling five percentage points by late February and three additional percentage points since then.

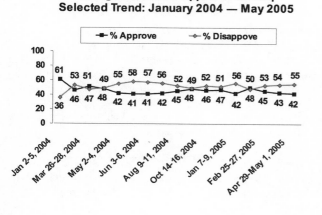

George W. Bush's Approval on Iraq
Selected Trend: January 2004 — May 2005

Nearly Half of Americans Say U.S. Soldiers
Have Stopped Abusing Iraqi Prisoners

A year ago, Americans also gave quite negative assessments of the war. That is in part due to the Abu Ghraib prisoner abuse scandal involving American soldiers, many of whom are now facing trial. More than 6 in 10 Americans say the abuse of Iraqi prisoners by U.S. soldiers bothers them a "great deal" or a "fair amount"—down significantly since Gallup asked this question last year when the media first reported the cases of prisoner abuse. At that time, nearly 8 in 10 Americans were bothered a great deal (54%) or fair amount (25%) by the abuse.

Would you say the abuse of Iraqi prisoners by U.S. soldiers bothers you — a great deal, a fair amount, not much, or not at all?

Although most Americans are still bothered by these incidents, nearly half of Americans, 49%, say U.S. soldiers have stopped abusing Iraqi prisoners. Thirty-seven percent say soldiers are still abusing Iraqi prisoners in a similar way today.

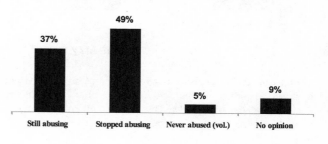

Do you think U.S. soldiers are still abusing Iraqi prisoners in a similar way today, or do you think they have stopped abusing Iraqi prisoners?

April 29 - May 1, 2005

Survey Methods

Results in the current survey are based on telephone interviews with 1,006 national adults, aged 18 and older, conducted April 29 - May 1, 2005. For results based on the total sample of national adults, one can say with 95% confidence that the maximum margin of sampling error is ±3 percentage points. For results based on the 492 national adults in the Form A half-sample and 514 national adults in the Form B half-sample, the maximum margins of sampling error are ±5 percentage points.

In addition to sampling error, question wording and practical difficulties in conducting surveys can introduce error or bias into the findings of public opinion polls.

May 6, 2005

NEARLY 8 IN 10 AMERICANS CALL GAS PRICES "UNFAIR"

Majority expects prices will continue to rise

by Jeffrey M. Jones, Gallup Poll Managing Editor and Joseph Carroll, Gallup Poll Assistant Editor

A recent CNN/*USA Today*/Gallup poll finds much discontent with current gas prices, as the vast majority of Americans believe the gas prices they are currently paying are "unfair." Most think gas prices will continue to rise, rather than stabilize or even return to lower levels.

Americans are also clearly unhappy with the way President George W. Bush is handling gas prices. Just more than one in four approve of his handling of the issue, and two-thirds believe there are reasonable things he can do to lower gas prices, despite his assertions that there is little he can do. A majority of Americans find Bush to blame for the gas prices, but foreign countries that produce oil and U.S. oil companies are more likely to be blamed.

The April 29-May 1 poll finds 78% of Americans terming the gas prices they are currently paying as "unfair," and just 20% saying they are "fair."

Prices You Are Paying for Gasoline Fair or Unfair?

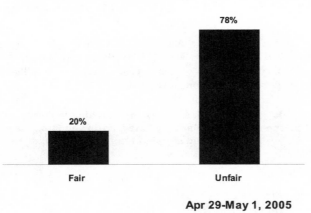

Apr 29-May 1, 2005

Americans do not expect relief from the high prices anytime soon. In fact, a majority of Americans expect gas prices will continue to rise over the next six months. Thirty-three percent believe gas prices will stabilize, and just 9% predict they will go back down.

Will the Price of Gasoline Continue to Rise, Stabilize, or Go Back Down Over the Next Six Months?

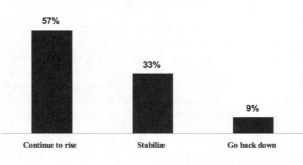

Apr 29-May 1, 2005

The data show that people residing in the West, who have consistently suffered much higher gas prices than the rest of the country, are more likely than those living elsewhere to say prices will continue to rise. Sixty-six percent of people in the West say prices will continue to rise, compared with 55% of those in the East, 56% of those in the Midwest, and 53% of those in the South.

Democrats express similar pessimism. Two in three Democrats, 66%, say gas prices will continue to rise, compared with only 44% of Republicans.

Bush Scores Low on Handling Gas Prices, Most Say He Should Do Something

A substantial majority of Americans, 67%, disapprove of the way Bush is handling the gas price issue, while just 27% approve. Bush's approval rating on gas prices shows sharp partisan differences, with a slight majority of Republicans (53%) approving of his handling of the issue and nearly 9 in 10 Democrats (88%) disapproving. Of the six issues tested in the poll, including the economy, Iraq, foreign affairs, and Social Security, Bush scores lowest on gas prices.

That low score likely results from what the public perceives as inaction on the issue. The poll finds 67% of Americans saying there are "reasonable steps that Bush should take right now that would significantly lower gas prices in the country." Twenty-nine percent say there are not any steps that Bush should take. Bush has said that there is little he could do as president to lower gas prices in the short term.

Reasonable Steps That President Bush Should Take That Would Significantly Lower Gas Prices?

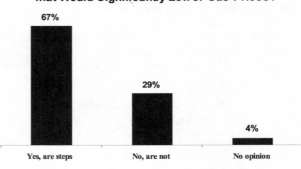

Apr 29-May 1, 2005

Democrats are much more likely than Republicans to want Bush to do something about gas prices. Seventy-nine percent of Democrats say there are steps Bush should take to combat high gas prices, a view shared by 68% of independents and even 54% of Republicans.

Blame for High Gas Prices

Most Americans (65%) assign either "a great deal" (38%) or a "moderate amount" (27%) of blame to Bush for the recent increase in gas prices. However, Americans are more inclined to blame foreign countries that produce oil (77% blame them, including 50% who blame them a great deal) and oil companies in the United States (79% blame them, including 47% who do so a great deal). Just slightly more than half of Americans also blame people who drive "vehicles that use a lot of gasoline."

Survey Methods

Results in the current survey are based on telephone interviews with 1,006 national adults, aged 18 and older, conducted April 29-May 1,

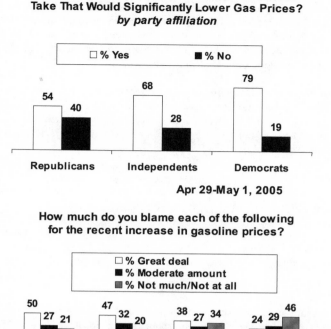

Reasonable Steps That President Bush Should Take That Would Significantly Lower Gas Prices?
by party affiliation

☐ % Yes   ■ % No

	Republicans	Independents	Democrats
% Yes	54	68	79
% No	40	28	19

Apr 29-May 1, 2005

How much do you blame each of the following for the recent increase in gasoline prices?

☐ % Great deal
■ % Moderate amount
▨ % Not much/Not at all

	Foreign countries that produce oil	Oil companies in the U.S.	Bush administration	Those who drive gas guzzlers
% Great deal	50	47	38	24
% Moderate amount	27	32	27	29
% Not much/Not at all	21	20	34	46

Apr 29-May 1, 2005

2005. For results based on the total sample of national adults, one can say with 95% confidence that the maximum margin of sampling error is ±3 percentage points.

In addition to sampling error, question wording and practical difficulties in conducting surveys can introduce error or bias into the findings of public opinion polls.

May 10, 2005

CONGRESS JOB APPROVAL AT 35%, LOWEST IN EIGHT YEARS

About 4 in 10 Americans say most congressional reps unethical

by David W. Moore, Gallup Poll Senior Editor

These are not good days for Congress. The latest Gallup survey shows that only 35% of Americans approve of the way Congress is handling its job, and almost 4 in 10 say *most* Republicans and, separately, *most* Democrats in Congress are unethical. When asked about members of Congress going on a trip funded by a lobbyist, an action that has caused House Majority Leader Tom DeLay to come under severe criticism and possible investigation by the House ethics committee, more than 8 in 10 say it is at least a "moderately serious" ethical problem. Overall, the public's low esteem of congressional members holds about equally for both Republicans and Democrats.

The latest survey on Congress' approval rating was conducted May 2-5, 2005 showing that 35% of Americans approve and 57% disapprove of the way Congress is handling its job. That is the lowest approval rating and highest disapproval rating for Congress since July 1997.

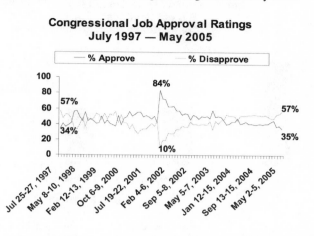

Congressional Job Approval Ratings July 1997 — May 2005

Ratings of Congress are highly related to people's party affiliation. But even Republicans—whose party controls both the House and the Senate—approve of Congress by only a slim 49% to 45% margin. Independents and Democrats strongly disapprove—by margins of 62% to 28%, and 66% to 26%, respectively.

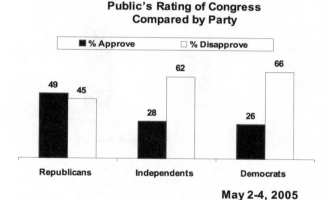

Public's Rating of Congress Compared by Party

■ % Approve   ☐ % Disapprove

	Republicans	Independents	Democrats
% Approve	49	28	26
% Disapprove	45	62	66

May 2-4, 2005

It is impossible to determine the exact causes for this continuing slide in the public's approval rating of Congress, but the recent wrangling over the filibuster rule, intervention in the Terri Schiavo case, and charges of unethical conduct lodged against DeLay almost certainly have all contributed.

In a survey conducted at the end of April, 56% of Americans said that most Republicans in Congress are ethical, and 38% said they are unethical. Regarding Democrats, the pattern was almost identical—55% said most Democrats in Congress are ethical and 39% said most are unethical.

Generally speaking, do you think—[ROTATED: Most Republicans in Congress/Most Democrats in Congress]—are ethical or unethical?

2005 Apr 29-May 1	Ethical %	Unethical %	No opinion %
Most Republicans in Congress	56	38	6
Most Democrats in Congress	55	39	6

Most Republicans think that Republicans in Congress are ethical, but independents are about evenly divided on the issue and Democrats are inclined to think of congressional Republicans as unethical.

Most Republicans in Congress Are Ethical/Unethical, Compared by Party

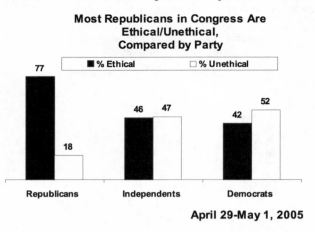

April 29-May 1, 2005

On the other hand, most Democrats think congressional Democrats are ethical, and a slight majority of Republicans agree. Independents are about evenly divided.

Most Democrats in Congress Are Ethical/Unethical, Compared by Party

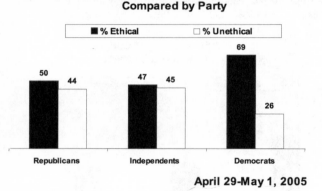

April 29-May 1, 2005

Recently, DeLay has come under fire for a variety of actions his critics call unethical, including taking trips funded by a lobbyist and the presence of his wife and daughter on the payrolls of various lobbying organizations. The charges may well have hurt DeLay's standing among the American public (as well as the overall image of Congress), as 38% of Americans say they have an unfavorable opinion of him, while 27% say favorable. In July 2003, more people were favorable (33%) than unfavorable (19%).

Next, we'd like to get your overall opinion of some people in the news. As I read each name, please say if you have a favorable or unfavorable opinion of these people—or if you have never heard of them. First, ... How about ... [ITEMS A-C ROTATED, ITEM D READ LAST]

A. House Republican Leader, Tom DeLay

	Favorable %	Unfavorable %	Never heard of %	No opinion %
2005 Apr 29-May 1	27	38	22	13
2005 Apr 1-2	27	31	26	16
2005 Feb 4-6	29	24	24	23
2003 Jul 25-27	33	19	34	14

In the wake of charges against DeLay, his unfavorable rating has climbed 14 points in the past three months, although his favorable rating has dropped only two points in the same period of time.

Most Americans believe that lobbyist-funded trips, like the kind DeLay is accused of taking, constitute either a "very serious" (46%) or "moderately serious" (36%) ethical matter.

If the member of Congress who represents your district in the U.S. House of Representatives went on a trip that was paid for by a lobbyist, would you consider that to be—a very serious ethical matter, moderately serious, not too serious, or not a serious ethical matter at all?

	Very serious	Moderately serious	Not too serious	Not serious at all	No opinion
2005 Apr 29-May 1	46%	36	12	4	2

Opinion on this issue is only slightly related to party affiliation, with 78% of Republicans, 80% of independents, and 90% of Democrats saying it is at least a moderately serious matter.

Survey Methods

Results in the two surveys mentioned in this release are based on telephone interviews, each with about 1,000 national adults, aged 18 and older, one conducted April 29-May 1, 2005 and the other May 2-4, 2005. For results based on the samples of national adults in each survey, one can say with 95% confidence that the maximum margin of sampling error is ±3 percentage points.

In addition to sampling error, question wording and practical difficulties in conducting surveys can introduce error or bias into the findings of public opinion polls.

May 10, 2005
ARE WOMEN HARDWIRED FOR WORRY?
Cultural roles, income may offer explanation

by Lydia Saad, Gallup Poll Senior Editor and Linda Lyons, Education and Youth Editor

Are women born worriers?

Each year in March, Gallup measures the degree to which Americans are concerned about various U.S. domestic policy issues. While levels of concern can change from year to year, one finding remains constant: women tend to express higher degrees of worry than men do. This inevitably leads to the question: Are women more troubled by societal problems, more prone to anxiety in general, or simply more comfortable admitting they worry?

In this year's survey*, women were significantly more likely than men to say they worry "a great deal" about 7 of the 12 issues tested. The gender gaps are particularly large for hunger/homelessness and crime—17 points and 16 points, respectively. Significant gaps are also evident for drug use, the environment, the economy, Social Security, and terrorism. On no issue are men significantly more worried than women.

Percentage Worried "a Great Deal" About Each Problem

Next I'm going to read a list of problems facing the country. For each one, please tell me if you personally worry about this problem a great deal, a fair amount, only a little, or not at all. First, how much do you personally worry about . . .

■ Women ☐ Men ▨ Difference (women minus men)

Problem	Women	Men	Difference
Hunger/Homelessness	45%	28%	17 points
Crime/Violence	53%	37%	16 points
Drugs	48%	35%	13 points
Environment	42%	29%	13 points
Economy	42%	33%	9 points
Social Security	52%	44%	8 points
Terrorism	45%	37%	8 points
Availability and affordability of healthcare	63%	58%	5 points
Unemployment	29%	26%	3 points
Availability and affordability of energy	39%	39%	0 points
Illegal immigration	33%	33%	0 points
Race relations	16%	16%	0 points

Women and Anxiety

To determine whether these gaps really do indicate a higher level of anxiety among women about the problems, as opposed to a gender-role difference in men's versus women's willingness to *confess* anxiety, we must look at some other data.

A study reported two years ago in the journal *Psychiatric Genetics* found a significantly higher propensity toward anxiety among women than men. The study involved clinical research measuring brainwaves and DNA blood samples in men and women—thereby sidestepping the problem of differential propensities to admit anxiety.

Does this finding also explain why Gallup polling from 2003 and 2004 shows women are slightly more likely than men to say they experience stress? Thirty-nine percent of women say they are frequently stressed, compared with 32% of men. So, it's possible that women are just wound a bit more tightly, and therefore are more likely to feel anxious about some social problems.

In fact, according to the Mayo Clinic, not only are women about twice as likely as men to experience clinical depression in their lives, they're also significantly more likely to experience generalized anxiety disorder. "Women are very anxious," observes someone who spends a lot of time with women—a 42-year-old hairdresser from New Jersey. "A lot of the women I know take medication for anxiety. I do, too. Before I started taking Zoloft," she says, referring to a drug used to treat both depression and anxiety, "I worried about everything."

Cultural Role

Cultural roles offer a possible explanation; specifically, motherhood may cause women to be more sensitive to societal problems. "I think women look at things from a very maternal perspective—they want to know how things like crime, drugs, the environment, and the economy will affect their own children," says a 40-year-old mother of

two from Florida. "Also, I'm concerned a great deal about social issues like hunger and homelessness and I want my children to be aware that others aren't as lucky as we are."

If maternity was the predominant explanation, one might expect to see women with children under 18 at home showing more concern than other women. That's not the case; there are only slight differences between women with and without children under 18. Where there is a significant difference—as seen with worry about hunger/homelessness and Social Security—it is women without young children who are more worried.

Percentage of Women Worried "a Great Deal" About Each Problem

Next I'm going to read a list of problems facing the country. For each one, please tell me if you personally worry about this problem a great deal, a fair amount, only a little, or not at all. First, how much do you personally worry about . . .

■ Have children under 18 ☐ Have no children under 18 ▨ Difference

Problem	Have children under 18	Have no children under 18	Difference
Economy	43%	41%	+2
Terrorism	46%	44%	+2
Drugs	48%	47%	+1
Environment	40%	42%	-2
Crime/Violence	51%	54%	-3
Hunger/Homelessness	39%	49%	-10
Social Security	44%	57%	-13

It could certainly be the case that all mothers—those with grown children as well as those with young children—share the psychological traits that would affect their tendency to worry. Thus a further line of research (not possible with the current data) would compare the attitudes of all mothers to women with no children.

Income

The fact that women, on average, have lower incomes compared with men, may also help explain why women are more sensitive to some social problems. This hypothesis is supported to some degree by Gallup's data. Overall, respondents in lower-income households are more likely to say they worry about drug use, the environment, the economy, and Social Security. Because more women than men fall into the lower-income category of $30,000 or less a year (32% of women versus 21% of men), it therefore holds that income is a significant explanatory variable in the worry gap between men and women.

Furthermore, income seems to make a bigger difference among women than men when it comes to worrying. Lower-income women are significantly more worried than women in higher-income households about several problems—hunger, crime, the economy, the environment, drugs, and Social Security. This income pattern is seen to a lesser degree with men.

Bottom Line

Still, lower-income women are more worried than lower-income men about the problems Gallup examined—so income is not an overriding explanatory factor. There is something about women (especially lower-income women) that makes them prone to worry.

Next I'm going to read a list of problems facing the country. For each one, please tell me if you personally worry about this problem a great deal, a fair amount, only a little, or not at all. First, how much do you personally worry about . . .

	Men		Women	
	Less than $30,000	$30,000+	Less than $30,000	$30,000+
Hunger/Homelessness	44%	25%	65%	35%
Crime/Violence	52%	35%	70%	44%
Environment	36%	28%	49%	38%
Economy	38%	33%	53%	37%
Terrorism	36%	38%	58%	38%
Drugs	53%	31%	63%	41%
Social Security	56%	42%	66%	47%

Several respondents indicated they feel that "something" is a combination of nature and nurture—psychological differences formed to address different social roles. "I think men are programmed not to worry about things they can't control," says a 55-year-old male respondent. "They're more focused on the immediate things they have to do to take care of their families."

The Florida mom quoted earlier has a similar idea. "I think women are hardwired differently—they are more compassionate and they see a broader perspective than men," she says. "They have to, because they juggle so many activities and issues every day."

*These results are based on telephone interviews with a randomly selected national sample of 1,004 adults, aged 18 and older, conducted March 7-10, 2005. For results based on this sample, one can say with 95% confidence that the maximum error attributable to sampling and other random effects is ±3 percentage points. In addition to sampling error, question wording and practical difficulties in conducting surveys can introduce error or bias into the findings of public opinion polls.

May 10, 2005

IN GREENSPAN WE TRUST? PUBLIC CONFIDENCE IN ECONOMIC LEADERS SHAKEN
Faith in Bush lowest in years

by Darren K. Carlson, Government and Politics Editor

High oil prices, stock market fluctuations, and sluggish growth are giving consumers plenty of reasons to worry about the economy, and those worries are taking a toll on their opinions of various economic policy setters. A recent Gallup Poll* finds Americans expressing the least amount of confidence since 2001 in the economic leadership of President George W. Bush and Federal Reserve Chairman Alan Greenspan. Confidence in the economic leadership of Republicans and Democrats in Congress is diminished as well.

The April 4-7 poll shows that slightly more than half of Americans have a "great deal" or "fair amount" of confidence in Bush and Greenspan to do or recommend the right thing for the economy. As has typically been the case, Americans express less confidence in the partisan leaders in Congress—with 47% confident in the Republican leadership on the economy and 42% confident in the Democrats.

As I read some names and groups, please tell me how much confidence you have in each to do or to recommend the right thing for the economy -- a great deal, a fair amount, only a little, or almost none. How about . . .

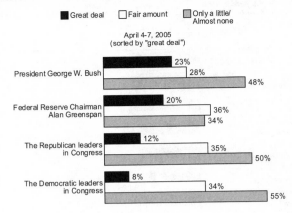

Downward Trends for Bush and Greenspan

The percentage of Americans expressing at least a fair amount of confidence in Bush's economic leadership is the lowest in several years. The high point for public confidence in Bush's economic leadership came in 2002, when nearly three-fourths (73%) of Americans had a great deal or fair amount of confidence in his economic ability, Since then, confidence dropped to 65% in 2003, 55% in 2004, and again to the current 51%.

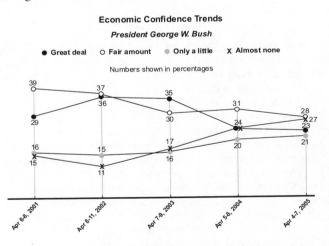

Economic Confidence Trends
President George W. Bush

While Greenspan's ratings are not as negative as Bush's, the pattern in confidence is similar. The percentage of Americans with a great deal or fair amount of confidence in Greenspan has never been lower. There has been a significant negative shift since 2001, with confidence falling from 74% then to 56% now.

Congressional Economic Leadership Not Viewed With Confidence

A downward trend is evident among Republicans and Democrats as well. Compared with their high marks in 2001, confidence has dropped 19 points for Republicans (from 66% to 47%) and 24 points for Democrats (from 66% to 42%).

Politics Plays a Role

The vast majority of Republicans (84%) say they have at least a fair amount of confidence in Bush's ability to recommend the right thing

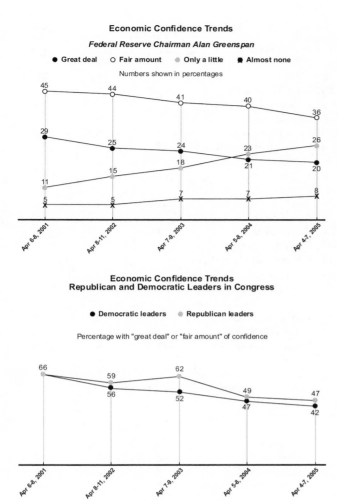

Economic Confidence Trends
Federal Reserve Chairman Alan Greenspan

● Great deal   ○ Fair amount   ● Only a little   ■ Almost none

Numbers shown in percentages

Economic Confidence Trends
Republican and Democratic Leaders in Congress

● Democratic leaders   ● Republican leaders

Percentage with "great deal" or "fair amount" of confidence

for the economy, compared with just 44% of political independents and 22% of Democrats. Along those same lines, Republicans (76%) are much more likely than Democrats (21%) to express confidence in the Republican congressional leaders. And, though not as strongly, Democrats (60%) are more likely than Republicans (31%) to have confidence in the Democratic congressional leadership's ability to handle the economy.

Though Greenspan has served under Republican and Democratic presidents, confidence in him is more robust among Republicans. Sixty-nine percent of Republicans say they have a great deal or fair amount of confidence in Greenspan, compared with 53% of independents and just 46% of Democrats.

These results are based on telephone interviews with a randomly selected national sample of 1,010 adults, aged 18 and older, conducted April 4-7, 2005. For results based on this sample, one can say with 95% confidence that the maximum error attributable to sampling and other random effects is ±3 percentage points. In addition to sampling error, question wording and practical difficulties in conducting surveys can introduce error or bias into the findings of public opinion polls.

May 11, 2005
PUBLIC'S MOOD REMAINS DOUR
Bush approval at 50%; general satisfaction at 39%

by David W. Moore, Gallup Poll Senior Editor

The latest Gallup survey finds the public's mood little changed over the past several weeks. President George W. Bush's approval rating is at 50%, up two points from the last two measures. Satisfaction with the way things are going remains in the doldrums—39% of Americans are satisfied, 58% are dissatisfied. And Gallup's two basic economic questions show a still-gloomy public.

The survey, conducted May 2-5, finds Americans still about evenly divided as to whether they approve or disapprove of the way Bush is handling his job as president. Bush appeared to get a slight boost from his successful re-election, averaging a 52% approval rating from January through mid-March. But in the past six measures, including his current 50% rating, Bush has averaged a 48% approval rating. Since his re-election, his rating has averaged 51%.

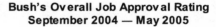

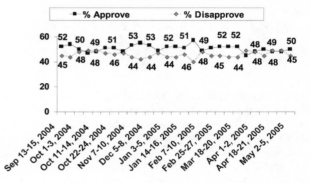

Bush's Overall Job Approval Rating
September 2004 — May 2005

Satisfaction with the way things are going in the country has remained essentially unchanged over the past seven weeks, with 38% of Americans expressing satisfaction in mid-March and again in early April, and 39% saying they are satisfied in the latest poll. Just before, and just after, the presidential election, 44% of Americans were satisfied, only a little better than the current reading.

This satisfaction rating is substantially below the higher ratings Gallup measured in the months after Sept. 11, 2001, and also the high ratings in the late 1990s during the robust economic years of the dot-com boom. Still, the satisfaction level is not as bad as it has been at

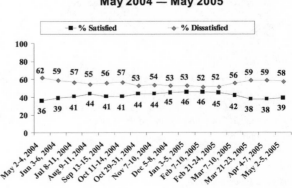

General Mood of the Country
May 2004 — May 2005

other points in the past. In the summer of 1992, for example, only 14% of Americans were satisfied with the way things were going in the United States, and only 12% were satisfied in July 1979.

Recently there has been little change in the public's ratings of the economy, although they are currently much worse than the ratings earlier this year.

Overall, 31% of Americans rate economic conditions as either excellent or good, and 25% rate them as poor. That 6-point positive gap is essentially unchanged from the 7-point gap in late April, but is much smaller than the 19-point gap in early March and the 24-point gap at the beginning of the year.

Current Economic Conditions
May 2004 — May 2005

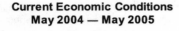
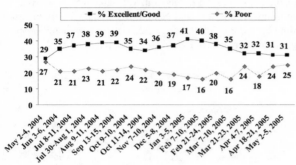

Similarly, the public economic outlook is more negative now than it was at the beginning of the year. Currently, 61% of Americans say the economy is getting worse, and 32% say better—similar to the 61% worse and 31% better ratings in late April. But in early March, only 50% said the economy was getting worse, and 41% said better. And at the beginning of the year, more people expressed a positive than a negative rating—with 48% expecting the economy to improve and just 42% expecting it to get worse.

Economic Outlook
May 2004 — May 2005

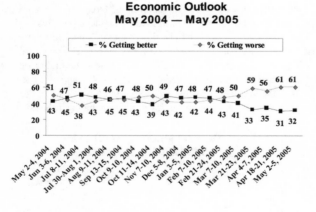

The poll also shows that the public's view of the most important problem facing the country today is about the same as it was a month ago. The war in Iraq continues to head the list, followed by the economy in general. Social Security, fuel/oil prices, jobs, and healthcare are close behind.

What do you think is the most important problem facing this country today? [Open-ended]

		May 2-5, 2005 %	Apr 4-7, 2005 %	Mar 7-10, 2005 %
ECONOMIC PROBLEMS (NET)		**33**	**34**	**28**
1	Economy in general	12	12	10
2	Fuel/Oil prices	8	9	2
3	Unemployment/Jobs	8	8	8
4	Federal budget deficit/ Federal debt	3	3	3
5	High cost of living/ inflation	1	3	1
6	Taxes	1	1	2
7	Lack of money	1	1	1
8	Wage issues	1	1	2
9	Corporate corruption	*	*	*
10	Foreign trade/Trade deficit	*	*	*
11	Gap between rich and poor	*	1	*
	Recession	—	—	*
NON-ECONOMIC PROBLEMS (NET)		**74**	**73**	**80**
1	Situation in Iraq/War	21	18	25
2	Social Security	9	8	12
3	Poor healthcare/ hospitals; high cost of healthcare	7	7	9
4	Dissatisfaction with government/Congress/ politicians/candidates; Poor leadership; corruption	5	5	6
5	Terrorism	5	8	9
6	Immigration/Illegal aliens	5	4	3
7	Education/Poor education/ Access to education	5	6	6
8	Poverty/Hunger/ Homelessness	4	2	3
9	Crime/Violence	4	1	2
10	Ethics/Moral/Religious/ Family decline; dishonesty; lack of integrity	4	6	4
11	National security	3	3	5
12	Foreign aid/Focus overseas	2	2	3
13	International issues/ problems	2	2	2
14	Judicial system/ Courts/Laws	2	2	1
15	Lack of energy sources; the energy crisis	1	1	*
16	Lack of respect for each other	1	1	2
17	Medicare	1	2	1
18	Children's behavior/ way they are raised	1	1	2
19	Unifying the country	1	1	1
20	Environment/Pollution	1	1	1
21	Care for the elderly	1	1	1
22	Race relations/Racism	1	1	*
23	Drugs	1	1	1
24	Welfare	1	1	1
25	Homosexuality/Gay issues	*	1	*

	May 2-5, 2005 %	Apr 4-7, 2005 %	Mar 7-10, 2005 %
26 Abortion	*	1	*
27 The media	*	*	—
28 Abuse of power	*	*	*
29 Overpopulation	*	*	*
30 Election year/Presidential choices/Election reform	*	—	*
31 Guns/Gun control	*	—	*
Cancer/Diseases	—	*	*
Child abuse	—	*	—
Other non-economic	4	3	1
No opinion	3	2	3
Total	130%	131%	133%

*Less than 0.5%

Survey Methods

Results in the current survey are based on telephone interviews with 1,005 national adults, aged 18 and older, conducted May 2-5, 2005. For results based on the total sample of national adults, one can say with 95% confidence that the maximum margin of sampling error is ±3 percentage points.

In addition to sampling error, question wording and practical difficulties in conducting surveys can introduce error or bias into the findings of public opinion polls.

May 12, 2005

AMERICANS CLOSELY DIVIDED INTO PRO-CHOICE AND PRO-LIFE CAMPS
Pro-life side more attentive to Supreme Court appointments

by Lydia Saad, Gallup Poll Senior Editor

No fewer than four U.S. Supreme Court justices are on the retirement watch list by virtue of their age, their health, or both—with conservative Chief Justice William Rehnquist's exit being the most widely anticipated. Although his replacement would not likely alter the political balance of the high court with respect to abortion cases, any vacancy is likely to spark a colossal political battle in Washington—and if history is any guide, that battle is likely to include a debate on abortion.

Gallup recently asked Americans how important it is to them, personally, that future U.S. Supreme Court nominees share their views on abortion. Just under half of Americans, 45%, say this is very important, 31% say it is somewhat important, and a combined 23% say it is not too important or not important at all.

This is a case where the percentage saying "very important" is particularly relevant, because it is the best indication of who will take an active role in lobbying for or against Supreme Court nominees on the basis of their abortion stance.

So who comprises this potentially active group (the 45% of Americans who say it is very important that future nominees share their views on abortion)?

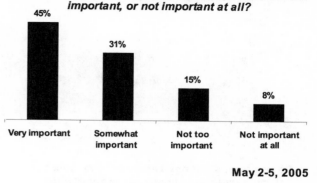

Now thinking about future nominees to the United States Supreme Court, how important is it to you, personally, that they share your views on the abortion issue — very important, somewhat important, not too important, or not important at all?

May 2-5, 2005

More than half (53%) are people who describe themselves as pro-life on the abortion issue; about 4 in 10 (39%) say they are pro-choice. This contrasts with Americans as a whole, who are more evenly divided on abortion. Nationally, 48% of Americans call themselves pro-choice and 44% call themselves pro-life. Clearly, pro-life supporters have the edge in terms of their interest in the abortion position of future Supreme Court nominees.

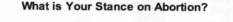

What is Your Stance on Abortion?

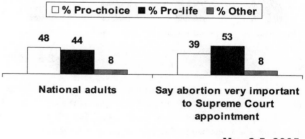

May 2-5, 2005

Women comprise the majority of the "very important" group (61%), while just 39% are men. By a 55% to 39% margin, these women tend to identify themselves as pro-life rather than pro-choice. Similarly, by a 50% to 39% margin, these men tend to be pro-life. Politically, 37% are Republican, 36% are Democratic, and 27% are independent.

National Trends

As noted, Americans are about evenly divided into the pro-choice and pro-life camps (48% and 44%). This close division, with a slight edge for the pro-choice side, has been the case for the past seven years. Prior to that, Gallup recorded somewhat higher identification with the pro-choice side. For instance, in September 1995, 56% were pro-choice and 33% pro-life.

According to Gallup's longest-running trend on abortion, asked since 1975, the majority of Americans (53%) take a moderate position on the issue, saying abortion should be legal only under certain circumstances. This leaves 45% who take one of two absolutist positions on either end of the spectrum: 23% say abortion should be legal under any circumstances, and 22% say it should be illegal in all circumstances.

What is Your Stance on Abortion?
Trend Data

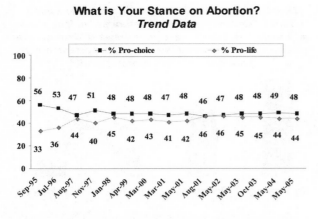

Do you think abortions should be legal under any circumstances, legal only under certain circumstances, or illegal in all circumstances?

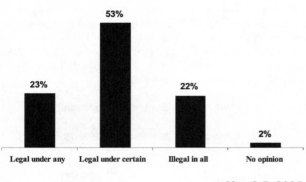

May 2-5, 2005

The percentage saying abortion should be illegal in all circumstances has been inching up in the last few years—from 15% in 2000 to 22% today—but this is the first time since 1985 that this extreme anti-abortion view has been essentially at parity with the extreme pro-abortion rights position.

Do you think abortions should be legal under any circumstances, legal only under certain circumstances, or illegal in all circumstances?
Trend Data

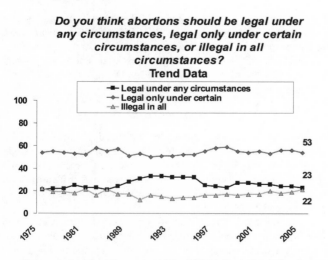

It is not clear how important this shift in the political landscape will be if a Supreme Court vacancy needs to be filled during President George W. Bush's last term in office. But there is no doubt that the landscape has changed since the last two times a Republican pres-

ident filled a Supreme Court vacancy—in 1990 and 1991, when President George H. W. Bush nominated David Souter and Clarence Thomas, respectively. Compared to the early 1990s, however, Americans today are much less likely to say abortion should be legal under any circumstances, and more likely to say that it should be illegal in all circumstances.

Do you think abortions should be legal under any circumstances, legal only under certain circumstances, or illegal in all circumstances?
Then and Now

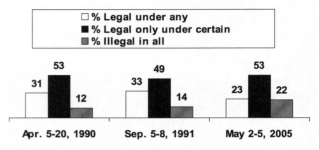

Both Souter and Thomas refrained from articulating clear positions on abortion during their confirmation hearings, and both were ultimately confirmed. Thomas has been one of three reliably pro-life justices on the court, while Souter has sided with the pro-choice majority on such cases as Stenberg v. Carhart, which struck down a Nebraska ban on partial birth abortion.

Whether George W. Bush appoints someone with a more visible track record on abortion, or who is more forthcoming with his or her views in the confirmation hearings, may partly depend on what the expected public reaction would be to an admittedly pro-life justice.

As the Gallup data suggest, pro-life Americans have the edge over the pro-choice public in intensity when it comes to Supreme Court appointments. Theoretically, this should translate into more pro-life communication to members of the U.S. Senate, larger pro-life rallies supporting or opposing a nominee, and more pro-life support at election time. However, the pro-choice contingent that cares about these appointments is not insignificant, and it will undoubtedly wage a pitched battle of its own.

Survey Methods

These results are based on telephone interviews with a randomly selected national sample of 1,005 adults, aged 18 and older, conducted May 2-5, 2005. For results based on this sample, one can say with 95% confidence that the maximum error attributable to sampling and other random effects is ±3 percentage points. In addition to sampling error, question wording and practical difficulties in conducting surveys can introduce error or bias into the findings of public opinion polls.

May 16, 2005

SOCIETY'S MORAL BOUNDARIES EXPAND SOMEWHAT THIS YEAR

More say death penalty, embryonic stem cell research, and out-of-wedlock births are OK

by Joseph Carroll, Gallup Poll Assistant Editor

The boundaries of moral propriety have expanded a bit in the last year, according to Gallup's annual Values and Beliefs survey, which tracks public perceptions of the morality of many issues and personal behaviors. Specifically, more Americans today than a year ago say that the death penalty, embryonic stem cell research, and having a baby out of wedlock are morally acceptable. At the same time, the survey shows no significant changes in the perceived morality of 13 other items.

Americans are most likely to say the death penalty, divorce, medical testing on animals, gambling, wearing fur clothing, and embryonic stem cell research are morally acceptable, while adultery, polygamy, cloning humans, and suicide are viewed as the least acceptable.

More generally, the survey shows that few Americans describe the current state of moral values in this country positively, and most say moral values are getting worse. The public's ratings of moral values in this country have shown only modest variations over the past several years.

Death Penalty Is Acceptable, but Adultery, Polygamy, Human Cloning Are Not

Over the past several years, Gallup has asked Americans to evaluate the moral acceptability of a number of issues facing the country.

Six issues in the current poll, conducted May 2-5, are viewed as morally acceptable by at least 6 in 10 Americans—including the death penalty, which tops the list this year: 70% say it is morally acceptable. Other issues widely held to be morally acceptable are divorce (66%), medical testing on animals (66%), gambling (64%), buying and wearing fur clothing (64%), and medical research using stem cells obtained from human embryos (60%).

Next on the list is sex between an unmarried man and woman, and having a baby outside of marriage, both of which are viewed as morally acceptable by a majority of Americans (58% and 54%, respectively). Between half and one-third of Americans say doctor-assisted suicide (49%), homosexual relations (44%), abortion (40%), and cloning animals (35%) are morally acceptable.

The four issues that are the least acceptable are suicide (13%), cloning humans (9%), polygamy (6%), and married men and women having an affair (5%).

Moral Acceptability of Issues

May 2-5, 2005
(sorted by percentage saying "morally acceptable")

	Morally acceptable %	Morally wrong %
The death penalty	70	25
Divorce	66	27
Medical testing on animals	66	30
Gambling	64	32
Buying and wearing clothing made of animal fur	64	32
Medical research using stem cells obtained from human embryos	60	33

	Morally acceptable %	Morally wrong %
Sex between an unmarried man and woman	58	39
Having a baby outside of marriage	54	43
Doctor-assisted suicide	49	46
Homosexual relations	44	52
Abortion	40	51
Cloning animals	35	61
Suicide	13	82
Cloning humans	9	87
Polygamy, when one husband has more than one wife at the same time	6	92
Married men and women having an affair	5	93

Since 2001, when Gallup first asked this question, there have only been modest variations in the results for most of the items on the list. The results this year show interesting changes in views about the death penalty, stem cell research, and having a baby outside of marriage.

The death penalty. Gallup's 2001 survey found that 63% of Americans said the death penalty was morally acceptable. This sentiment showed only minor variations from 2002 through 2004. Now, the perceived moral acceptability of the death penalty has reached its highest point to date, with 70% saying it is acceptable.

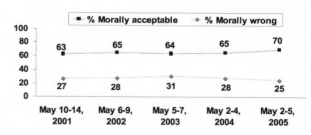

Morally Acceptable or Morally Wrong?
The Death Penalty

Medical research using stem cells obtained from human embryos. The moral acceptability of embryonic stem cell research also reached a new high this year, with 60% saying it is acceptable. In the three previous polls in which Gallup asked this question, only a slight majority of Americans said embryonic stem cell research was morally acceptable.

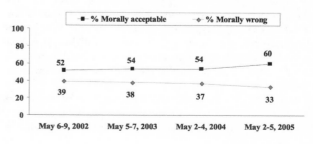

Morally Acceptable or Morally Wrong?
Embryonic Stem Cell Research

Having a baby outside of marriage. Fifty-four percent of Americans currently say it is morally acceptable to have a baby outside of marriage—the highest percentage Gallup has found on this measure. In recent years, the percentage saying this was morally acceptable hovered around the 50% mark, with ratings at 45% in 2002, 51% in 2003, and 49% in 2004.

Morally Acceptable or Morally Wrong?
Having a Baby Outside of Marriage

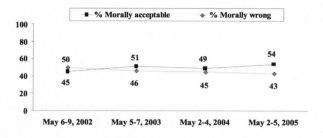

Three other issues—medical testing on animals, buying or wearing clothing made from animal fur, and cloning animals—also reached the highest percentages to date, in terms of their perceived moral acceptability among Americans. However, these high points are not significantly higher than what Gallup has found in recent years.

One in Five Americans Give Positive
Ratings to Country's Moral Values

The poll also finds that only about one in five Americans rate the overall state of moral values in the country today as excellent (2%) or good (17%). Nearly 4 in 10 adults nationwide rate moral values as poor. Over the past four years that Gallup has asked this question, the results have essentially been the same each year, with one minor exception. In 2003, the percentage rating morality in the country as poor was slightly lower, at 35%.

Current State of Moral Values in the Country

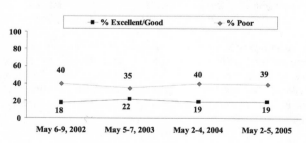

Americans remain quite pessimistic that the state of moral values in the country is going to improve in the future. More than three in four Americans, 77%, say moral values in the country are getting worse; only 16% say they are getting better. These results show no change since last year, but Americans were just slightly more optimistic about the outlook for morality in 2002 and 2003. In those two polls, one in four Americans said the state of moral values was getting better, while two-thirds said it was getting worse.

The responses to these two questions can be combined to produce an overall "moral values outlook" measure. All told, the data show that 70% of Americans categorize the state of moral values as

Outlook for the State of Moral Values in the Country

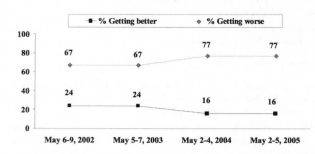

negative. Nine percent have a positive outlook on moral values, and 18% have mixed views. These results also show no change since last year. However, Americans were marginally less negative about the state of moral values in 2002 and 2003, when roughly two in three categorized the state of moral values as negative.

Moral Values Outlook Groups

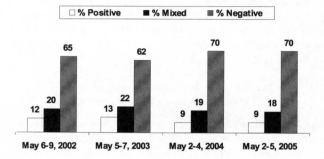

Interestingly, ratings of moral values do not show huge variations between Republicans and Democrats. Nearly three in four Republicans (74%) categorize the state of moral values as negative, compared with two in three Democrats (68%).

Survey Methods

Results in the current survey are based on telephone interviews with 1,005 national adults, aged 18 and older, conducted May 2-5, 2005. For results based on the total sample of national adults, one can say with 95% confidence that the maximum margin of sampling error is ±3 percentage points. In addition to sampling error, question wording and practical difficulties in conducting surveys can introduce error or bias into the findings of public opinion polls.

May 17, 2005
THREE IN FOUR AMERICANS SUPPORT EUTHANASIA
Significantly less support for doctor-assisted suicide

by David W. Moore, Gallup Poll Senior Editor

Gallup's latest annual survey on values and beliefs suggests that 75% of Americans support euthanasia—allowing a doctor to take the life of a patient who is suffering from an incurable disease and wants to die. But the survey also finds that a much smaller proportion of Americans, 58%, support doctor-assisted suicide for patients in the same condition.

The apparent conflict in values appears to be a consequence of mentioning, or not mentioning, the word "suicide." When asked if doctors should be allowed to end the life of a patient who is suffering from an incurable disease and wants to die, 75% of Americans say "yes." But when asked if doctors should be allowed to help a patient commit suicide under the same circumstances, only 58% of Americans say "yes."

The exact wording for each of the questions is as follows:

When a person has a disease that cannot be cured, do you think doctors should be allowed by law to end the patient's life by some painless means if the patient and his family request it?

BASED ON 516 NATIONAL ADULTS IN FORM A

	Yes	No	No opinion
2005 May 2-5	75%	24	1

When a person has a disease that cannot be cured and is living in severe pain, do you think doctors should or should not be allowed by law to assist the patient to commit suicide if the patient requests it?

BASED ON 489 NATIONAL ADULTS IN FORM B

	Should	Should not	No opinion
2005 May 2-5	58%	39	3

The poll shows that support for euthanasia has increased significantly over the past half-century, going from 37% support in 1947 to 75% now. The trend also shows that usually there is a significant gap in views between euthanasia and doctor-assisted suicide. In 1996, when Gallup first asked about doctor-assisted suicide, support was about 20 points lower than for euthanasia. In 2002, 2003, and this year, there have also been major differences. In 2001 and 2004, however, differences between the two actions were minor.

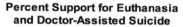

Percent Support for Euthanasia and Doctor-Assisted Suicide

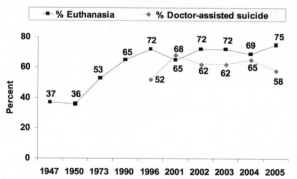

Comparison by Subgroups

An examination of the responses by various demographic characteristics shows that the people who are most likely to be affected by the difference in question wording are evangelical Christians, and to a lesser extent young males and rural residents.

- Among evangelical Christians, 61% support euthanasia, while only 32% approve of doctor-assisted suicide—a net difference of 29 points. Among all Americans, the difference is 17 points.

- Eighty-seven percent of men under the age of 50 support euthanasia, but only 63% support doctor-assisted suicide—a difference of 24 points.
- Seventy-one percent of rural residents support euthanasia, while only 47% support doctor-assisted suicide—a net difference also of 24 points.

May 2-5, 2005	Support Euthanasia %	Support Doctor-Assisted Suicide %	Lower Support for Doctor-Assisted Suicide vs. Euthanasia Difference in Pct. Pts.
All	75	58	-17
Gender			
Male	84	64	-20
Female	66	53	-13
Age by Gender			
Under 50/Male	87	63	**-24**
50+/Male	82	65	-17
Under 50/Female	63	50	-13
50+/Female	69	56	-13
Religion			
Protestants	70	52	-18
Catholics	75	60	-15
Evangelical Christians	61	32	**-29**
Frequency of Attending Church			
Weekly	51	30	-21
Almost weekly	87	66	-21
Seldom/never	85	76	-9
Region			
East	82	61	-21
Midwest	73	53	-20
South	71	52	-19
West	76	69	-7
Type of Community			
Urban	78	59	-19
Suburban	75	62	-13
Rural	71	47	**-24**
Ideology			
Conservative	63	44	-19
Moderate	83	66	-17
Liberal	82	71	-11
Party			
Republicans	65	52	-13
Independents	79	68	-11
Democrats	79	57	-22

Other major findings include the following:
- There is a major gender gap in support for euthanasia, with 84% of men indicating support, compared with 66% of women. On doctor-assisted suicide, the gap narrows—64% of men support it, compared with 53% of women.
- Weekly churchgoers are far less likely to support either method of ending a patient's life than are people who attend church less frequently or never attend.
- Conservatives are 19 percentage points less likely than liberals to support euthanasia, and 27 percentage points less likely than liberals to support doctor-assisted suicide.

- Republicans are somewhat less likely (65%) to support euthanasia than are Democrats (79%). But Democrats are more likely to be affected by question wording, so that there is little difference in support between Democrats (57%) and Republicans (52%) for doctor-assisted suicide.

Although Americans support doctor-assisted suicide by a 58% to 39% margin, they are less likely to say that the action is moral—49% say it is morally acceptable, and 46% say it is morally wrong.

Personal Behavior

The poll shows that 38% of Americans believe they would *not* consider "ending [their] life by some painless means," even if they were suffering from an incurable disease and were living in "severe pain." Fifty-nine percent say they would consider such an option.

- Women are more likely than men to say they would not consider ending their lives—44% vs. 29%, respectively.
- Half of all conservatives (51%) say they would not consider that option, compared with only 26% of moderates and 33% of liberals.
- Weekly churchgoers show the most opposition, 69%, while people who attend church almost weekly or less often are far less opposed—25% and 22%, respectively.
- Evangelical Christians also have a high level of opposition (62%) to ending their lives in that situation.

When it comes to being "in a persistent vegetative state with no hope of for significant recovery," 85% of Americans say they would want to have their life support removed. That is the state that Terri Schiavo's doctors described for Schiavo before her feeding tube was removed and she died. Much of the controversy was over her exact state and whether she had any hope of significant recovery.

There are some differences in views on this matter when compared by various subgroups, but the differences are relatively small. Very large majorities of all subgroups would not want to persist indefinitely in a vegetative state. The following groups of people, who are most opposed to euthanasia or doctor-assisted suicide, nevertheless would want their life support removed:

- Rural residents—84%
- Conservatives—83%
- Women—83%
- Republicans—82%
- Southerners—81%
- Weekly churchgoers—75%
- Evangelical Christians—70%
  Percentages are higher for other subgroups.

Survey Methods

Results in the current survey are based on telephone interviews with 1,005 national adults, aged 18 and older, conducted May 2-5, 2005. For results based on the total sample of national adults, one can say with 95% confidence that the maximum margin of sampling error is ±3 percentage points.

For results based on the 516 national adults in the Form A half-sample and 489 national adults in the Form B half-sample, the maximum margins of sampling error are ±5 percentage points.

In addition to sampling error, question wording and practical difficulties in conducting surveys can introduce error or bias into the findings of public opinion polls.

May 17, 2005
AMERICANS REMAIN POSITIVE ABOUT PERSONAL FINANCES
Most believe they are living within their means

by Raksha Arora, Business and Economy Editor

Personal saving rates are at historic lows and rock-bottom interest rates have fueled debt burdens, causing some economic experts to worry about the state of personal finances for the average American household. Federal Reserve Board Governor Susan Schmidt Bies acknowledged in a recent speech that some "pockets of financial stress exist among households," but "the sector as a whole appears to be in good shape."

Americans don't necessarily disagree with that assessment, given their generally upbeat responses to questions about their personal finances from two April Gallup Polls.

Personal Finances

In an April 4-7 poll*, 52% of Americans reported their personal finances were excellent or good, and 48% said they were only fair or poor. Americans' opinions of their personal financial situations have remained relatively stable over the last five years. There have been few drastic changes in the proportion who describe their personal finances as excellent, good, fair, or poor. If climbing debt burdens have worsened finances in the last few years—this is not reflected in the overall trend.

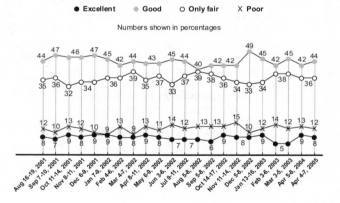

The majority of Americans are comfortable with their personal finances, according to an April 18-21 poll**. Fifty-seven percent claim they aren't worried about their family finances; that number has remained stable since the beginning of the year.

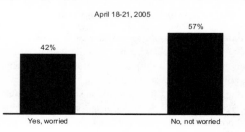

Gallup asked Americans in the April 4-7 poll whether they feel their financial situations are getting better or worse. About half of Americans express an optimistic view about their financial situations and a third believe things are getting worse, while 15% volunteered that things would remain the same. Americans have always been more positive than negative in their answers to this question.

Right now, do you think your financial situation as a whole is getting better or getting worse?

● Getting better   ○ Getting worse

Numbers shown in percentages

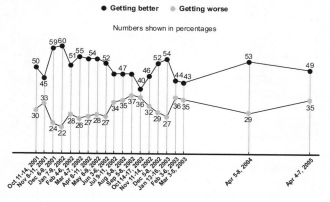

Are American Families Stretched Too Thin?

Much of the world may see American consumers as hedonistic big spenders, but Gallup data reveal the majority of Americans believe they are living within their means. About 8 in 10 American consumers (81%) feel they aren't overextending themselves financially, despite the low average personal savings rate of 1%.

Would you say that you and your family are presently living within your means, somewhat beyond your means, or far beyond your means?

April 4-7, 2005

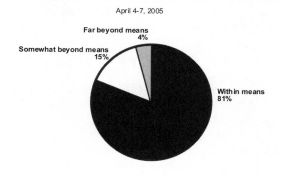

Far beyond means 4%
Somewhat beyond means 15%
Within means 81%

That number has held steady even as debt burdens have increased and the overall savings rate has decreased. Gallup received basically the same response when the question was asked in 1974, 1975, and 1984.

Income, Spending, Saving Expected to Hold Steady

Comfortable with their *current* financial status, most Americans do not see much change in store over the next six months. About half of consumers believe their incomes, their monthly savings, and their spending levels will remain the same, in line with what Gallup typically finds. No more than a quarter of Americans expect these things to decrease. A larger percentage of Americans, 39%, predict their personal debt burdens will come down, compared with 41% who expect no change in their debt levels and just 17% who expect to take on more debt.

*Results are based on telephone interviews with 1,010 national adults, aged 18 and older, conducted April 4-7, 2005. For results based on the total sample of national adults, one can say with 95% confidence that the margin of sampling error is ±3 percentage points.

**Results are based on telephone interviews with 1,003 national adults, aged 18 and older, conducted April 18-21, 2005. For results based on the total sample of national adults, one can say with 95% confidence that the margin of sampling error is ±3 percentage points.*

May 17, 2005

RETIREMENT AGE EXPECTATIONS AND REALITIES

Average retirement age increasing

by Joseph Carroll, Gallup Poll Assistant Editor

Many factors enter into Americans' retirement age decisions, not the least of which is probably whether they enjoy their jobs, but also whether they can afford to stop working. Each year Gallup chronicles retirement age trends by asking non-retired Americans the age they expect to retire at and asking retired Americans the age at which they retired. For the first time this year, Gallup also asked non-retired adults the age at which they would retire if they were rich enough to do so.

The results show some fascinating differences, with non-retired adults expecting to retire several years later than the actual retirement age of current retirees. Non-retired adults also say they would retire at a much earlier age if they could afford to financially.

Retirement Expectations

Gallup's annual survey on the economy and personal finance*, conducted April 4-7, shows that the average age at which non-retired adults plan to retire is 64. According to the full distribution of responses, 15% of non-retired Americans plan to retire before their 60th birthday, 22% plan to retire between the ages of 60 and 64, 25% plan to retire at age 65, and 31% plan to retire when they are older than that.

At what age do you expect to retire?
Among non-retired adults

	Under 55	55-59	60-64	65	Over 65	Never retire	No answer	Mean
Apr 4-7, 2005	6%	9%	22%	25%	31%	--	7%	64
Apr 5-8, 2004	9%	11%	21%	26%	26%	--	7%	64
Apr 7-9, 2003	8%	11%	23%	28%	22%	--	8%	63
Apr 8-11, 2002	7%	15%	21%	26%	21%	--	10%	63
Dec 15-18, 1995	15%	12%	23%	29%	15%	5%	4%	60
Nov 6-8, 1995	16%	11%	20%	34%	12%	3%	4%	60

In the 10 years since Gallup first asked this question, the mean age at which people plan to retire has increased slightly. In 1995, the average planned retirement age was 60. This increased to age 63 in polls conducted in 2002 and 2003, and then to age 64 in 2004 and 2005.

While the mean age at which people plan to retire has edged up slightly, the percentage of non-retired adults who say they plan to retire after age 65 is now the highest it has ever been. This figure has increased from 12% in 1995 to 31% in the latest survey.

There are some slight, but real, differences in retirement age predictions according to the current age of respondents, with younger adults expecting to retire earlier than those 50 and older. On average, those aged 18 to 29 say they plan to retire by age 62, while those aged 30 to 49 plan to retire at age 65 and those aged 50 and older at age 66.

Retirement expectations also vary by household income levels, with the highest-income households planning to retire a few years earlier than those in lowest-income households. Adults living in households earning less than $30,000 per year say they expect to retire at age 66, on average. Those earning between $30,000 and $75,000 per year plan to retire at age 64, and those earning more than $75,000 per year plan to retire at age 63.

But ... What If You Were Rich?

We've all heard the stories of jackpot lottery winners who claim they will keep their day jobs pumping gas, but would most Americans really continue to work if money were no object?

As opposed to the average age of 64 for retirement predictions under normal circumstances, non-retired adults say they would retire, on average, at age 51 if they were "rich enough so that money were no object." Eleven percent would retire before age 35, 15% between the ages of 35 and 44, and 26% between the ages of 45 to 54. But 28% would hold on until somewhere between 55 to 64, and 14% until they are 65 or older.

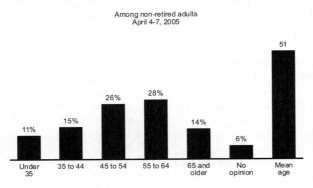

If you were rich enough so that money were no object, at what age would you like to retire, or would you have retired?

Among non-retired adults
April 4-7, 2005

Younger respondents are much more likely than older respondents to say they would retire at a younger age if they were wealthy. On average, 18- to 29-year-olds would retire at age 42, while 30- to 49-year-olds would retire at age 50, and those aged 50 and older would retire at age 59.

However, the poll finds no significant differences in the answers of people of different income levels when asked, hypothetically, at what age they would retire if income were not a factor. Those earning less than $30,000 per year would retire, on average, at age 51; those earning between $30,000 and $75,000 would retire at age 50; and those earning $75,000 per year or more would also retire at age 50.

And ... When Do Retirees Leave the Workforce?

Current retirees tell Gallup that they left the workforce, on average, at age 60—four years earlier than non-retired adults expect to retire.

This includes a third who retired before age 60, 35% who retired between the ages of 60 and 64, 17% who retired at age 65, and 12% who retired after that.

At what age did you retire?

Among retirees

	Under 55	55-59	60-64	65	Over 65	No opinion	Mean
Apr 4-7, 2005	15%	18%	35%	17%	12%	3%	60
Apr 5-8, 2004	17%	18%	37%	14%	12%	2%	60
Apr 7-9, 2003	21%	14%	34%	12%	15%	4%	59
Apr 8-11, 2002	19%	19%	34%	13%	11%	4%	59
Apr 1993	27%	18%	25%	14%	11%	5%	57
Apr 1992	21%	16%	36%	13%	8%	6%	58
May 1991	28%	12%	36%	11%	7%	6%	57

This question has been asked by Gallup since 1991, and since that time, the mean age at which people retired has shown only modest changes. In 1991, the average age that people retired was 57. Now, that age is 60.

Results are based on telephone interviews with 1,010 national adults, aged 18 and older, conducted April 4-7, 2005. For results based on the total sample of national adults, one can say with 95% confidence that the maximum margin of sampling error is ±3 percentage points. For results based on the sample of 767 non-retired adults, the maximum margin of sampling error is ±4 percentage points. For results based on the sample of 243 retired adults, the maximum margin of sampling error is ±7 percentage points. In addition to sampling error, question wording and practical difficulties in conducting surveys can introduce error or bias into the findings of public opinion polls.

May 18, 2005
CHURCH ATTENDANCE AND PARTY IDENTIFICATION
Frequency of church attendance strongly related to partisanship

by Frank Newport, Gallup Poll Editor in Chief

There is a strong correlation in America today between one's religiosity and one's political status. This *political status* includes both the political party with which one identifies as well as the candidate for whom one votes.

Gallup's final survey conducted before the 2004 election estimated that 63% of voters who attended church weekly or almost every week voted for Bush; 37% voted for Kerry. Sixty percent of those who seldom or never attended church indicated a vote choice for Kerry; 40% voted for Bush. The same directional patterns have been observed between self-reported importance of religion and vote choice.

There was a good deal of interest in this connection between religion and politics last year. But it is not a totally new phenomenon. In 2000, 54% of those who attended church weekly or almost weekly voted for Bush, while 37% voted for Gore. Gallup surveys indicated that in both 1992 and 1996, Bill Clinton did better than his opponent among those who seldom or never attended church.

In short, religious Americans skew strongly toward voting for the Republican candidate for president. Highly religious white Protestant or non-Catholic Americans in particular skew strongly toward the Republican candidate. Black Americans are very much the exception; they skew heavily toward the Democratic candidate, regardless of their religiosity.

This review focuses not on the vote in a particular election, but rather, on partisan identification. The analysis is based on a very large aggregated sample of almost 30,000 Gallup Poll interviews conducted in 2004, in which questions about church attendance were included.

Church Attendance and Partisan Identification

The table displays the percentage of those in each church attendance category who identify with the two major parties or are independents. It also displays a difference score based on the percentage of Democrats minus the percentage of Republicans, and a calculated value of "macropartisanship." This last variable is based on the percentage of those who identify as Democrats divided by the percentage who identify as either Democrats or Republicans. The macropartisanship variable, in short, is a convenient way of expressing how Democratic in orientation a given group is.

Partisanship by Church Attendance
Aggregated Sample of Gallup Poll Interviews
Conducted in 2004

	Republican %	Independent %	Democrat %	% Dem − % Rep pct. pts.	Macropartisanship [% Dem ÷ (% Dem + % Rep)]
Once a week	45%	25%	30%	-15	40
Almost every week	40	27	33	-8	45
Once a month	32	31	37	5	54
Seldom	29	34	37	8	56
Never	22	43	35	13	61

Here's this same relationship presented graphically.

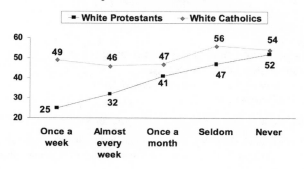

Macropartisanship
% Democratic
by church attendance

The basic pattern is clear. Americans who attend church frequently are significantly more likely to be Republicans and less likely to be Democrats than those who attend church less frequently. Note also that Americans who never attend church are significantly more likely to say they have no partisan choice (i.e., are independent) than are those who attend church, even infrequently.

These data are for all Americans, regardless of race, creed, or color. Numerous studies have shown, however, that being black is one of the strongest available predictors of identifying with the Democratic Party. Gallup data also show that blacks are very religious. Therefore, the strong positive relationship between church attendance and identification with the Republican Party as presented above is actually attenuated somewhat because the black respondents included in the dataset have the opposite relationship.

The table on church attendance and race corrects for this problem by separating whites and blacks into two samples.

Partisanship by Church Attendance and Race
Aggregated Sample of Gallup Poll
Interviews Conducted in 2004

Race	Church attendance	Rep %	Ind %	Dem %	% Dem − % Rep pct. pts.	Macropartisanship [% Dem ÷ (% Dem + % Rep)]
White	Once a week	51	25	24	-27	32
	Almost every week	46	28	26	-20	36
	Once a month	37	31	31	-6	46
	Seldom	32	34	33	1	51
	Never	24	43	33	9	58
Black	Once a week	9	25	65	56	88
	Almost every week	6	22	71	65	92
	Once a month	5	23	72	67	94
	Seldom	4	26	70	66	95
	Never	4	38	58	55	94

The basic relationship between church attendance and partisanship for whites follows the same pattern as is observed for the total sample—not surprising, given that whites constitute the significant majority of the total population.

Among blacks, the relationship isn't strong, principally because blacks are overwhelmingly Democratic regardless of church attendance. Still, there is a slight tendency for blacks who attend once a week to be less Democratic than those who attend less often. Also, blacks who never attend church are more likely to be independents than are those who attend at least occasionally.

Church Attendance and Partisanship:
White Protestants and White Catholics

A major focus of the analysis of religion's impact on politics is evangelical Protestants, who are widely assumed to be significantly different from Catholics and other Protestants in the way in which their religion is manifested in their daily lives and actions. For the purpose

Macropartisanship
%Democratic
by church attendance

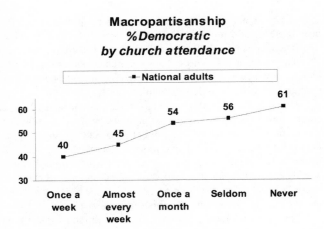

of analysis, this table shows the relationship between church attendance and partisanship only among white Protestants.

Partisanship by Church Attendance
White Protestants Only
Aggregated Sample of Gallup Poll Interviews Conducted in 2004

Church attendance	Rep %	Ind %	Dem %	% Dem – % Rep pct. pts.	Macro-partisanship [% Dem ÷ (% Dem + % Rep)]
Once a week	60	21	20	-40	25
Almost every week	50	26	24	-26	32
Once a month	43	27	30	-13	41
Seldom	37	30	33	-4	47
Never	31	37	33	2	52

The relationship pattern here is the same as the one observed for the total sample, but one that reflects white Protestants' tendency across the board to be even more Republican in orientation. Four of the five church attendance groups are less than 50% Democratic (based on the macropartisanship measure). Only the group who "never" attends services is slightly more Democratic than Republican. The proportion of white Protestants who attend church weekly is remarkably Republican, as can be seen.

What about white Catholics?

Partisanship by Church Attendance
White Catholics Only
Aggregated Sample of Gallup Poll Interviews Conducted in 2004

Church attendance	Rep %	Ind %	Dem %	% Dem – % Rep pct. pts.	Macro-partisanship [% Dem ÷ (% Dem + % Rep)]
Once a week	38	27	36	-2	49
Almost every week	39	27	34	-5	47
Once a month	37	31	32	-5	46
Seldom	29	33	38	9	57
Never	31	33	36	5	54

The relationship between church attendance and partisanship is flatter among white Catholics than is the same relationship among white Protestants. There is little difference in the macropartisanship variable among Catholics who attend church weekly, almost every week, or once a month. But those who attend less frequently—seldom or never—do move somewhat above the 50% mark.

Macropartisanship
%Democratic
by church attendance

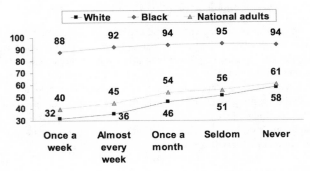

Overall, the spread in the macropartisanship score between the group of Catholics who are most likely to be Republicans and the group who are most likely to be Democrats is just 11 points. Among white Protestants, macropartisanship ranges between 25% and 52%, a spread of 27 points.

In other words, there is a very strong relationship between frequency of church attendance and identifying with the Republican Party among white Protestants, and a much more muted such relationship among Catholics, who tend to be significantly more Democratic in orientation across the board.

Survey Methods

Results are based on telephone interviews with 29,575 national adults, aged 18 and older, aggregated from various surveys conducted from January to December 2004. The margin of sampling error varies, depending on the sample size. In addition to sampling error, question wording and practical difficulties in conducting surveys can introduce error or bias into the findings of public opinion polls.

May 19, 2005
AMERICANS' VIEWS OF DEATH PENALTY MORE POSITIVE THIS YEAR
Nearly three in four favor it as a penalty for convicted murderers

by Jeffrey M. Jones, Gallup Poll Managing Editor

Gallup's annual Moral Values and Beliefs poll finds that Americans are more positive in their orientation toward the death penalty than they have been in the past several years. Across a wide range of questions on the topic, Americans show a slight but noticeable increase in death penalty support. Compared with a year ago, more Americans say they support the death penalty as punishment for murder, more choose it over life imprisonment as the preferred punishment for murder, and more Americans believe the death penalty is applied fairly in this country.

Additionally, a majority of Americans now say the death penalty is not imposed often enough. There has also been a significant decline since 2003 in the percentage who believe that innocent people have been executed under the death penalty in the past five years. The increase in support for the death penalty is apparent across most societal subgroups.

Basic Support for the Death Penalty

The May 2-5, 2005, Gallup Poll finds 74% of Americans saying they favor the death penalty for a person convicted of murder, while 23% are not in favor. That represents a recent high in support, tied with a 74% reading in May 2003. Gallup has asked this version of the death penalty question since 1936, with a high water mark in support of 80% in 1994, and a low of 42% in 1966.

Are you in favor of the death penalty for a person convicted of murder?

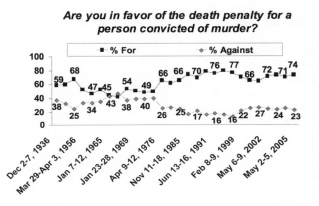

A second question on death penalty support—asking respondents whether the death penalty or life imprisonment with no possibility of parole is the better penalty for murder—also shows an increase in pro-death penalty sentiment. Fifty-six percent of Americans say the death penalty is the better punishment, while 39% choose life imprisonment. The last time support for the death penalty was this high was in 1999, when 56% also said they preferred that option. The highest support for the death penalty that Gallup has measured on this question (dating back to 1985) was 61% in August 1997.

By a nearly two-to-one margin, men say they prefer the death penalty (65%) to life imprisonment (33%). Women, however, are about equally divided in their views, with 47% preferring the death penalty and 46% life imprisonment. This gender gap has been evident in previous years, but both groups are more likely to favor the death penalty this year than in the past.

Consistent with their basic support for the use of the death penalty, 70% of Americans say it is "morally acceptable," while 25% say it is "morally wrong." From 2001-2004, a lower percentage of Americans—between 63% and 65%—considered the death penalty morally acceptable.

Application of the Death Penalty

For the first time since Gallup began asking about the application of the death penalty in 2001, a majority of Americans say the death

If you could choose between the following two approaches, which do you think is the better penalty for murder: the death penalty (or) life imprisonment, with absolutely no possibility of parole?

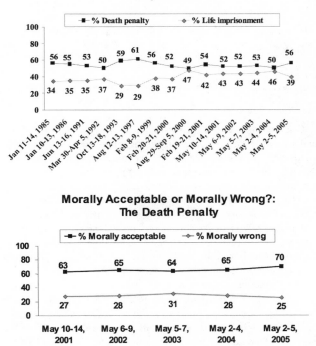

Morally Acceptable or Morally Wrong?: The Death Penalty

penalty is not imposed often enough. Fifty-three percent hold this view, while 24% say it is imposed the right amount of time, and 20% say it is imposed too often. Last year, 48% said the death penalty was not imposed often enough, 25% the right amount of time, and 23% too often. In 2001, public opinion on this matter was very different. At that time, just 38% said the death penalty was not used enough, 34% said the right amount of time, and 21% too often.

In your opinion, is the death penalty imposed: too often, about the right amount, or not often enough?

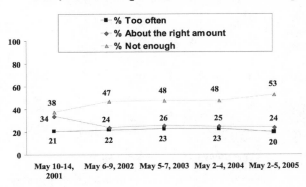

Sixty-one percent say that, generally speaking, the death penalty is applied fairly in the United States today, while 35% say it is applied unfairly. In 2003, 60% also said the death penalty was applied fairly, but in other years the percentage has been in the low-to-mid 50% range.

Generally speaking, do you believe the death penalty is applied fairly or unfairly in this country today?

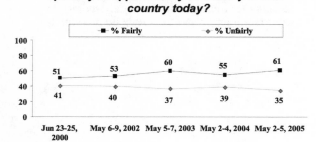

One possible reason for the increase in support for the death penalty is a declining belief that innocent people are being executed. Gallup finds a significant decrease in the percentage of Americans who believe that, in the past five years, innocent people have been executed under the death penalty—from 73% in May 2003 to 59% this year.

At the beginning of the decade, several death row inmates whose cases were reopened were found to be not guilty of the crime for which they received the death penalty. This led the state of Illinois—where many of those cases occurred—to institute a moratorium on executions, which remains in effect today. Maryland also imposed a moratorium in 2002, which has since been lifted.

Most Americans believe that executions of innocent people are rare—two in three believe this has happened in 5% or fewer cases in the last five years, including one-third who say it has not happened at all. Only 6% believe it has happened in more than 20% of the cases—less than half the percentage who said this in 2003 (13%).

How often do you think that a person has been executed under the death penalty who was, in fact, innocent of the crime he or she was charged with—do you think this has happened in the past five years, or not?[IF YES:] Just your best guess, about what percent of people who are executed under the death penalty are really innocent of the crime they were charged with?

	2005 May 2-5 %	2003 May 5-7 %
None/Has not happened	33	22
1-5%	34	40
6-10%	8	9
11-20%	6	6
21-50%	5	11
More than 50%	1	2
No opinion	13	10
Mean	6.6%	8.8%
Median	1%	2%

Variations in Death Penalty Support

In its long history of polling on the death penalty, Gallup has consistently found that different groups are more or less likely to favor the death penalty. Those differences are apparent this year, as well. The following table shows the percentage of each group who finds the death penalty morally acceptable, comparing it to last year and reporting any change. In general, most groups show a slight increase in death penalty support compared with last year.

View of Death Penalty as Morally Acceptable or Morally Wrong, by Subgroup

Group	% Morally acceptable, 2004 %	% Morally acceptable, 2005 %	Change
All Americans	65	70	+5
Men	72	79	+7
Women	59	61	+2
White	70	73	+3
Non-white	45	58	+13
18-29 years old	69	64	-5
30-49 years old	71	74	+3
50-64 years old	61	69	+8
65 years and older	57	67	+10
High school education or less	67	72	+5
Some college education	73	71	-2
Four-year college graduate	61	69	+8
Post-graduate education	53	61	+8
Household income less than $30,000	57	67	+10
Household income $30,000-$74,999	70	70	0
Household income $75,000 or more	69	73	+4
Liberal	47	59	+12
Moderate	66	70	+4
Conservative	74	75	+1
Democrat	53	59	+6
Independent	68	71	+3
Republican	77	79	+2
Attend church weekly	61	63	+2
Attend nearly weekly/monthly	62	69	+7
Seldom/never attend church	72	75	+3
Protestant	66	69	+3
Catholic	69	70	+1

To summarize the major differences in subgroup support:

- Men are much more likely to find the death penalty morally acceptable than women.
- Whites are more supportive of capital punishment than non-whites.
- Those with a post-graduate education are slightly less supportive of the death penalty than people with lower levels of education.
- Conservatives are much more likely to view the death penalty more morally acceptable than are liberals.
- Likewise, Republicans are much more pro-death penalty than Democrats.
- People who attend church or religious services on a regular basis are less likely to support the death penalty than those who seldom or never attend.

These results are based on telephone interviews with a randomly selected national sample of 1,005 adults, aged 18 and older, conducted May 2-5, 2005. For results based on this sample, one can say with 95% confidence that the maximum error attributable to sampling and other random effects is ±3 percentage points. In addition to sampling error, question wording and practical difficulties in conducting surveys can introduce error or bias into the findings of public opinion polls.

May 20, 2005

GAY RIGHTS ATTITUDES A MIXED BAG

Broad support for equal job rights, but not for gay marriage

by Lydia Saad, Gallup Poll Senior Editor

Though Americans have grown increasingly tolerant of homosexuality over the past three decades, U.S. public opinion on the subject is still ambiguous. Most Americans believe homosexuals deserve equal rights in the workplace, but people are closely divided over whether homosexuality is an acceptable way of life. Barely half believe homosexual relations between consenting adults should be legal, and a majority says such relations are immoral. Fewer than half want to see gay marriages legally sanctioned.

According to Gallup trends, by the late 1990s public attitudes toward homosexuals had advanced considerably compared with the 1970s, and even with the early 1990s. The percentage saying homosexuals should have equal job opportunities grew from 56% in 1977 to 74% in 1992 and to 88% by 2003. Similarly, the percentage saying homosexuality should be considered an acceptable alternative lifestyle was only 34% in 1982 and 38% in 1992, but expanded to 50% by 1999.

However, that progression has largely stalled in the last few years. Today, the percentage saying the homosexual lifestyle should be considered acceptable remains at just 51%, while 45% say it should not be acceptable.

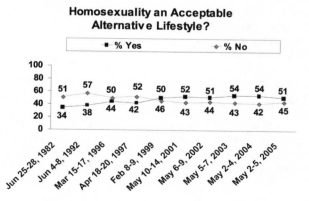

Homosexuality an Acceptable Alternative Lifestyle?

Similarly, there has been little movement since 2001 in the percentage saying they personally believe homosexual relations are morally acceptable. Since 2001, that figure has averaged 42%, and stands at 44% today. A slim majority of Americans—ranging between

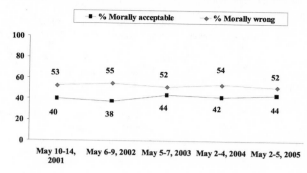

Americans' Views of Homosexual Relations

52% and 55%—have consistently said that homosexual relations are morally wrong.

Much Resistance to Homosexuals in the Clergy, as Teachers

Even though Americans say homosexuals should have equal job rights, generally, they make sharp distinctions among the types of professions homosexuals should be hired for. Three-quarters or more say homosexuals should be hired as salespersons, doctors, in the armed forces, and for the president's cabinet; a majority believes they should be hired as high school teachers. But there is substantial resistance for having homosexuals employed as members of the clergy or as grade school teachers. Though a slim majority believes homosexuals should serve as grade school teachers, more than 4 in 10 Americans think they should not. Americans are evenly divided over homosexuals in the clergy.

Should Homosexuals Be Hired for These Professions?

	Yes	No
	%	%
Salesperson	90	7
Doctors	78	19
The armed forces	76	22
As a member of the president's cabinet	75	23
High school teachers	62	36
Elementary school teachers	54	43
Clergy	49	47

Gallup recorded significant movement in these occupation trends between 1992 and 1999, with public support expanding for homosexuals being employed in most of these professions. But as with other indicators, these figures have changed relatively little over the past six years.

Not helping matters for gay rights advocates is that recent scandals in the Catholic Church over priests sexually abusing young boys may have spilled over into attitudes about homosexuals serving as teachers or clergy. Between 2003 and 2005, Gallup recorded seven-point declines in the percentage saying homosexuals should be hired as clergy (from 56% to 49%), and in the percentage saying homosexuals should be hired as elementary teachers (from 61% to 54%). There has been a five-point decline (from 67% to 62%) in the percentage saying homosexuals should be hired as high school teachers. At the same time, there were smaller (and not statistically significant) declines in support for hiring homosexuals as doctors, members of the president's cabinet, in the armed forces, and as salespersons.

Changes in Support for Homosexuals in Different Professions

	Doctors %	President's cabinet %	Armed forces %	H.S. teachers %	Elem. teachers %	Sales-persons %	Clergy %
Change since 2003	-4	-4	-4	-5	-7	-2	-7
2005 May 2-5	78	75	76	62	54	90	49
2003 May 19-21	82	79	80	67	61	92	56
2001 May 10-14	78	75	72	63	56	91	54
1999 Feb 8-9	75	74	70	61	54	90	54
1996 Nov 21-24	69	71	65	60	55	90	53
1992 Jun 4-8	53	54	57	47	41	82	43

Public Frowns on Gay Marriage

President George W. Bush has called for a constitutional amendment that would define marriage as a union between a man and a woman, thereby superseding state and local laws that permit gay marriage. According to a Gallup Poll taken in late April, Americans tend to agree with Bush on this issue. The majority says that marriages between homosexuals should not be recognized as legally valid; only 39% say they should be valid.

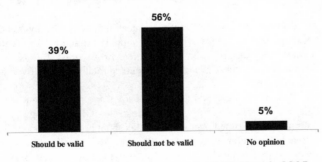

Do you think marriages between homosexuals should or should not be recognized by the law as valid, with the same rights as traditional marriages?

April 29-May 1, 2005

Similarly, a slim majority favors a constitutional amendment that would bar marriages between gay or lesbian couples. Public opinion about this has been relatively stable since Gallup first asked the question in 2003.

While gays battle for the right to marry, it might surprise some to know that, more fundamentally, barely half of Americans believe

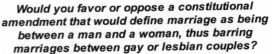

Would you favor or oppose a constitutional amendment that would define marriage as being between a man and a woman, thus barring marriages between gay or lesbian couples?

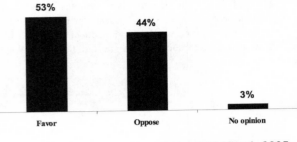

April 29-May 1, 2005

that homosexual relations between consenting adults should be legal. This attitude has changed relatively little since 1977 when 43% supported homosexual relations being legal. While this figure peaked at 60% in 2003, it stands at only 52% today.

"Gay" Label Elicits More Support Than "Homosexual"

As with many issues, public opinion about homosexuality can be influenced by nuances of question wording. In a split-sample experiment, Gallup tested alternative terms for referencing gay Americans and found that the wording used does make some difference. Referencing this population as "gays and lesbians" results in somewhat more favorable, pro-gay responses than does using the term "homosexuals."

Specifically, the percentage of Americans saying that this population should be hired as high school and elementary teachers is 9 to 10 points higher when the question is asked about "gays and lesbians" rather than "homosexuals."

34/35. Do you think [Q.34: homosexuals/Q.35: gays and lesbians] should or should not be hired for each of the following occupations? First, ... Next, ... [RANDOM ORDER]?

2005 May 2-5 (sorted by "should")	Homosexuals %	Gays and Lesbians %	Difference, in Pct. Pts.
Salesperson	90	93	+3
Doctors	78	81	+3
The armed forces	76	79	+3
As a member of the president's cabinet	75	78	+3
High school teachers	62	71	+9
Elementary school teachers	54	64	+10
Clergy	49	53	+4

There is no significant difference between the percentage of Americans favoring equal job opportunities for "gays and lesbians" (90%) than for "homosexuals" (87%), but this is most likely because support is almost universal on this item, and has little room for expansion.

Survey Methods

These results are based on telephone interviews with a randomly selected national sample of 1,005 adults, aged 18 and older, conducted May 2-5, 2005. For results based on this sample, one can say with 95% confidence that the maximum error attributable to sampling and other random effects is ±3 percentage points.

For results based on the 516 national adults in the Form A half-sample and 489 national adults in the Form B half-sample, the maximum margins of sampling error is ±5 percentage points.

In addition to sampling error, question wording and practical difficulties in conducting surveys can introduce error or bias into the findings of public opinion polls.

May 24, 2005
PUBLIC CONFLICTED IN FILIBUSTER DEBATE
A third say both parties acting like "spoiled children"

by David W. Moore, Gallup Poll Senior Editor

A substantial majority of Americans are paying little attention to the debate over the Senate's filibuster rule, according to the latest CNN/*USA Today*/Gallup survey. After being informed about the issue, 48% of respondents say they favor the Democrats' side and 40% favor the Republicans' side. However, when the question is posed differently, 35% of respondents favor the position that Republicans are arguing for, while 19% favor the position that Democrats prefer.

Clear majorities of respondents say the Republicans and, separately, the Democrats are acting like "spoiled children" rather than "responsible adults." But a majority believes that at least one party is acting responsibly, while a third believes members of both parties are acting like "spoiled children."

How Closely Following?

The poll, conducted May 20-22, finds that only 17% of Americans are following the filibuster issue "very closely," and another 26% are following it "somewhat closely." The 43% total is up from 35% measured at the end of April, but still shows that close to 6 in 10 Americans are not giving the issue much consideration.

How closely have you been following the news about the use of the filibuster on judicial nominations in the U.S. Senate—very closely, somewhat closely, not too closely, or not at all?

	Very closely %	Somewhat closely %	Not too closely %	Not at all %	No opinion %
2005 May 20-22	17	26	20	37	*
2005 Apr 29-May 1	12	23	28	37	*

*Less than 0.5%

When told that the Democrats are using the filibuster to prevent President George W. Bush's judicial nominees from being confirmed, and the Republicans are trying to change the rules to allow an up-or-down vote on all nominees, respondents divide as to which course of action they prefer. Thirty-five percent want the rules changed to get the up-or-down vote, another 34% want to retain the filibuster but still have the up-or-down vote, and 19% want to preserve the filibuster to prevent the vote.

As you may know, President Bush has nominated some people as federal judges who have not yet been confirmed by the Senate. The Democrats in the Senate have used a filibuster to prevent those nominees from being confirmed. In response, the Republicans in the Senate are trying to change the rules to prevent the use of filibusters on judicial nominations so that all are subject to an up-or-down vote.

Which comes closest to your view—[ROTATED: you want to see the filibuster rule preserved and you do not want those judicial nominees confirmed, you want to see the filibuster rule preserved, but you would like to see the Senate have an up-or-down vote on those nominees, or you want to see the filibuster rules changed so that those judicial nominees are subject to an up-or-down vote]?

	Option 1 *Preserve filibuster, do not want vote*	Option 2 *Preserve filibuster, would like to see vote*	Option 3 *Want rules changed*	*No opinion*
2005 May 20-22	19%	34	35	12

These are the results of a question asked of half the sample. Note that the compromise option (Option 2) is not a realistic choice from the two parties' perspectives, as the whole point of the Democratic filibuster is to prevent an up-or-down vote on some of Bush's nominees. Democratic senators are aware that with a Republican majority in the Senate, such a general vote would almost surely mean the nominees would be confirmed. The Democratic position in this question is Option 1, supported by 19% of Americans, while the Republican position is Option 3, supported by 35%.

Half of the sample in the poll was asked not what specific position they prefer, but in general which party's position they favor. The results show that more people choose the Democratic Party's position than choose the Republican Party's position.

In the current controversy over the filibuster, whose side do you generally favor—[ROTATED: the Republicans in the Senate (or) the Democrats in the Senate]?

BASED ON 517 NATIONAL ADULTS IN FORM A

	Republicans	Democrats	BOTH (vol.)	NEITHER (vol.)	No opinion
2005 May 20-22	40%	48	1	7	4

(vol.) = Volunteered response

One reason for this apparent contradiction is that many people don't know much about the issue and are basing their responses primarily upon what they hear in the survey. Among people who have followed the issue "very closely," however, there is greater consistency in results.

Which comes closest to your view—

	Option 1 *Preserve filibuster, do not want vote* %	Option 2 *Preserve filibuster, would like to see vote* %	Option 3 *Want rules changed* %	*No opinion* %
Overall	19	34	35	12
How closely following				
Very	38	28	31	3
Somewhat	21	44	31	4
Not	12	30	39	19

Note that the "very" attentive respondents favor the Democratic position (Option 1) over the Republican position (Option 3) by a 38% to 31% margin. Among people with lower levels of attention, the Republican position is favored over the Democratic position.

Support for the Democratic Party is also higher among people who pay close attention to the filibuster issue.

In the current controversy over the filibuster, whose side do you generally favor—[ROTATED: the Republicans in the Senate (or) the Democrats in the Senate]?

BASED ON 517 NATIONAL ADULTS IN FORM A

	Republicans %	Democrats %	BOTH (vol.) %	NEITHER (vol.) %	No opinion %
All	40	48	1	7	4
How closely follow					
Very	40	53	2	5	0
Somewhat	45	45	3	6	1
Not	37	48	*	8	7

(vol.) = Volunteered response
*Less than 0.5%

People who are following the issue "very closely" favor the Democrats by 53% to 40%, but people who are following it only "somewhat closely" divide evenly, 45% for each party. People who say they haven't been following the issue favor the Democrats by 48% to 37%.

These results might suggest that people who pay more attention to the issue are disproportionately Democrats, but that is not the case. Eighteen percent of Republicans and 17% of Democrats say they have been following the issue "very closely."

How closely have you been following the news about the use of the filibuster on judicial nominations in the U.S. Senate—very closely, somewhat closely, not too closely, or not at all?

	Very closely %	Somewhat closely %	Not too closely %	Not at all %	No opinion %
All	17	26	20	37	*
Republicans	18	28	21	33	*
Independents	15	26	19	40	*
Democrats	17	25	19	39	0

*Less than 0.5%

A Plague on Both Houses? Not Quite …

Overall, a substantial majority of Americans, 58%, say the Republicans are acting like spoiled children, and 54% also say that about Democrats.

In the current debate over federal judges and the filibuster, do you think the Republican leaders in the Senate are—[ROTATED: acting like responsible adults (or are they) acting like spoiled children]?

BASED ON 489 NATIONAL ADULTS IN FORM B

	Responsible adults	Spoiled children	NEITHER (vol.)	No opinion
2005 May 20-22	31%	58	3	8

(vol.) = Volunteered response

In the current debate over federal judges and the filibuster, do you think the Democratic leaders in the Senate are—[ROTATED: acting like responsible adults (or are they) acting like spoiled children]?

BASED ON 489 NATIONAL ADULTS IN FORM B

	Responsible adults	Spoiled children	NEITHER (vol.)	No opinion
2005 May 20-22	36%	54	2	8

(vol.) = Volunteered response

But it is not true that a majority of Americans say that about *both* parties. Only about a third of Americans, 36%, say both parties are behaving badly, while 15% say both parties are behaving responsibly. An additional 20% say the Democrats are acting responsibly and the Republicans are acting like spoiled children, while 16% say the reverse—that Democrats are the spoiled children and Republicans are the responsible adults.

How Are Republicans and Democrats Acting

Both parties acting like spoiled children	Both parties acting responsibly	Democrats responsible; Republicans spoiled	Republicans responsible; Democrats spoiled	No opinion on one party or the other
36%	15	20	16	13

These results show that a bare majority of Americans, 51%, believe at least one party is acting responsibly, 36% say neither is, and 13% aren't sure.

Survey Methods

Results in the current survey are based on telephone interviews with 1,006 national adults, aged 18 and older, conducted May 20-22, 2005. For results based on the total sample of national adults, one can say with 95% confidence that the maximum margin of sampling error is ±3 percentage points.

For results based on the 517 national adults in the Form A half-sample and 489 national adults in the Form B half-sample, the maximum margins of sampling error are ±5 percentage points.

In addition to sampling error, question wording and practical difficulties in conducting surveys can introduce error or bias into the findings of public opinion polls.

May 24, 2005
AMERICANS WEIGH IN ON EVOLUTION VS. CREATIONISM IN SCHOOLS
Responses vary by religiosity, education, ideology

by Darren K. Carlson, Government and Politics Editor

Earlier this month, the Kansas Board of Education conducted public hearings about possible revisions to the state's science standard. The debate centered on the proposal to include the theory of "intelligent design"—which claims the natural world is so complex and well-ordered that it must have been created by an intelligent being—in the state's science curriculum for public schools.

Scientists and evolution advocates claim intelligent design is veiled creationism, and have urged the Kansas board to keep the current evolution-friendly curriculum in place. The board plans to consider the proposed changes by August. With conservative Republicans having captured a majority of the board seats in last year's elections, current speculation is the board will approve at least some of the proposed changes.

This controversy isn't confined to Kansas. Similar debates have been raised in Ohio, Michigan, Pennsylvania, and other states. However, a recent CNN/*USA Today*/Gallup poll* reveals that many Americans wouldn't be distressed if either intelligent design or the theory of evolution were taught in their local classrooms.

In March, Gallup asked Americans whether they would be upset if public schools in their communities taught the theory of creationism—"the idea that human beings were created by God in their present form and did not evolve from other species of animals." A majority, 76%, say they would *not* be upset if creationism were taught in their schools, while 22% say they *would* be upset.

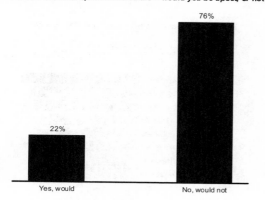

By way of comparison, Gallup also asked respondents whether they would be upset if the theory of evolution—"the idea that human beings evolved from other species of animals"—were taught in their local schools. A smaller majority, 63%, would not be upset if evolution were taught in schools, while roughly a third (34%) say they would be upset.

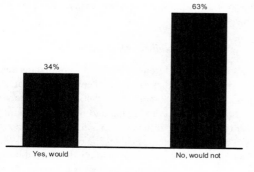

One, but Not the Other?

Combined responses to these two questions show a plurality of Americans (45%) are permissive on the topic—that is, it wouldn't upset them if either creation or evolution were taught in the local schools. But those with a preference for only one theory or the other are more likely to come down on the side of creationism—30% of Americans say they would be upset if only evolution were taught, while 18% would be upset if only creationism were taught.

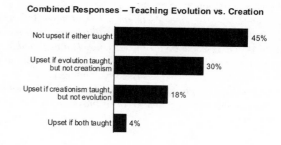

Religion, Education, and Ideology

Certain groups of Americans are more likely to be upset if only evolution were taught in schools. Obviously, religiosity is an important factor. Among those who attend church weekly, half (53%) say they would be upset if only evolution were taught in schools. This compares with 32% of nearly weekly or monthly churchgoers and just 13% of those who seldom attend church.

Responses also vary by education level and political ideology. Thirty-seven percent of Americans with a high school education or less say they would be upset if their schools taught evolution but not creation, compared with only 17% of those with a postgraduate education.

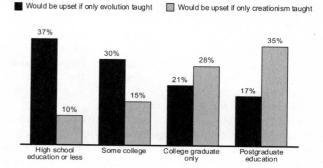

Nearly twice as many self-described conservatives (45%) as moderates (22%) or liberals (20%) would be upset by an evolution-only science curriculum.

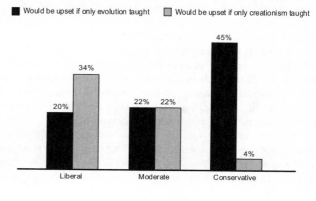

Bottom Line

The percentage of Americans who actively want creation, not evolution, to be taught in schools may seem relatively modest at 30%, but this number is significantly larger than the percentage who actively want evolution to be taught over creation.

These results are based on telephone interviews with a randomly selected national sample of 1,001 adults, aged 18 and older, conducted March 21-23, 2005. For results based on this sample, one can say with 95% confidence that the maximum error attributable to sampling and other random effects is ±3 percentage points. In addition to sampling error, question wording and practical difficulties in conducting surveys can introduce error or bias into the findings of public opinion polls.

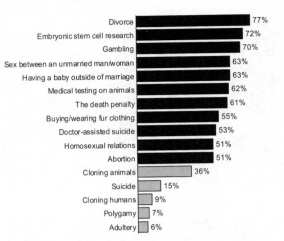

Moral Acceptability of Issues Among Democrats
May 2-5, 2005
Percentage saying each item is "morally acceptable"

May 24, 2005
PARTY LINES SHAPE VIEWS OF WHAT'S MORALLY ACCEPTABLE
Embryonic stem cell research sees surge in support among Democrats

by Joseph Carroll, Gallup Poll Assistant Editor

Gallup's annual survey on values and beliefs asked Americans to rate 16 issues as "morally acceptable" or "morally wrong." A review of the data shows substantial differences between Republicans' and Democrats' views of what is morally acceptable.

Republicans find the death penalty, buying and wearing fur clothes, and animal testing to be the most morally acceptable items on the list, while Democrats rate divorce, embryonic stem cell research, and gambling as the most morally acceptable. The issues with the largest partisan gaps include embryonic stem cell research, abortion, having a baby out of wedlock, divorce, buying and wearing fur clothes, and the death penalty.

Over the past several years, while there have been significant gaps between what Republicans and Democrats find morally acceptable, these gaps have shown only minor variations, with the lone exception of embryonic stem cell research, which has seen a surge in support among Democrats.

What Do Republicans and Democrats Consider Acceptable?

The poll, conducted May 2-5*, finds that Democrats (including independents who lean toward the Democratic Party) view more issues as morally acceptable than Republicans do (including those independents who lean toward the Republican Party).

Of the 16 issues tested in the poll, a majority of Democrats view 11 of them as morally acceptable: divorce, embryonic stem cell research, gambling, sex between an unmarried man and woman, having a baby outside of marriage, medical testing on animals, the death penalty, buying and wearing clothing made of animal fur, doctor-assisted suicide, homosexual relations, and abortion.

At least 7 in 10 Republicans say the death penalty, buying and wearing clothing made of animal fur, and medical testing on animals is morally acceptable. A majority of Republicans also say gambling, divorce, and sex between an unmarried man and woman is acceptable.

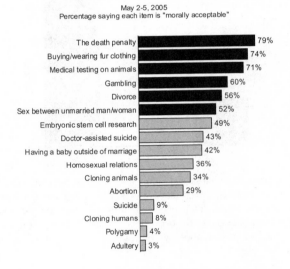

Moral Acceptability of Issues Among Republicans
May 2-5, 2005
Percentage saying each item is "morally acceptable"

The bottom of the list is essentially the same for both Republicans and Democrats. The issues that are least acceptable to both groups are suicide, cloning humans, polygamy, and married men and women having affairs.

The Republican-Democratic Divide

There are substantial differences between Republicans and Democrats in the issues viewed as morally acceptable this year.

Republicans are much more likely than Democrats to view three issues as morally acceptable: buying and wearing clothing made of animal fur (74% for Republicans, 55% for Democrats), the death penalty (79% to 61%), and medical testing on animals (71% to 62%).

Democrats, meanwhile, are more likely than Republicans to rate eight issues as morally acceptable. There is at least a 20-point difference between Democrats' and Republicans' views of embryonic stem cell research (72% to 49%), abortion (51% to 29%), having a baby outside of marriage (63% to 42%), and divorce (77% to 56%). Democrats also are more inclined than Republicans to say homosexual relations (51% to 36%), sex between an unmarried man and woman (63% to 52%), doctor-assisted suicide (53% to 43%), and gambling (70% to 60%) are morally acceptable.

Moral Acceptability of Issues Among Republicans and Democrats
May 2-5, 2005
Percentage saying each item is "morally acceptable"

	Republicans (including "leaners")	Democrats (including "leaners")	Difference (Reps. Minus Dems.)
Buying and wearing clothing made of animal fur	74%	55%	+19
The death penalty	79%	61%	+18
Medical testing on animals	71%	61%	+9
Cloning humans	8%	9%	-1
Cloning animals	34%	36%	-2
Polygamy, when one husband has more than one wife at the same time	4%	7%	-3
Married men and women having an affair	3%	6%	-3
Suicide	9%	15%	-6
Gambling	60%	70%	-10
Doctor-assisted suicide	43%	53%	-10
Sex between an unmarried man and woman	52%	63%	-11
Homosexual relations	36%	51%	-15
Divorce	56%	77%	-21
Having a baby outside of marriage	42%	63%	-21
Abortion	29%	51%	-22
Medical research using stem cells obtained from human embryos	49%	72%	-23

Year-to-Year Changes

Since Gallup first began asking this question, Republicans' and Democrats' views on what is morally acceptable have shown only modest variations on a year-to-year basis. The one issue that changed dramatically this year—possibly because of an increased focus on the issue following the death of actor Christopher Reeve and former President Ronald Reagan last summer, and during the fall campaign—involves views about embryonic stem cell research.

In 2002, there was only a two-point difference between Republicans and Democrats on this measure, with 52% of Republicans and 54% of Democrats saying embryonic stem cell research was morally acceptable. Over the next two years, the gap widened slightly, with Democrats growing more accepting of this type of research and Republicans holding steady in their views. Now, the latest poll finds a 23-point margin between Republicans and Democrats, with just about half of Republicans and more than 7 in 10 Democrats saying stem cell research is acceptable.

Results are based on telephone interviews with 1,010 national adults, aged 18 and older, conducted April 4-7, 2005. For results

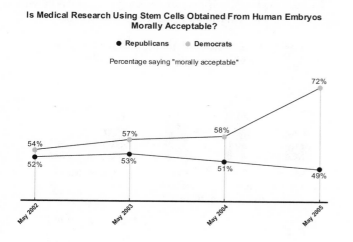

Is Medical Research Using Stem Cells Obtained From Human Embryos Morally Acceptable?

● Republicans   ○ Democrats

Percentage saying "morally acceptable"

based on the total sample of national adults, one can say with 95% confidence that the margin of sampling error is ±3 percentage points. For results based on the sample of 455 Republicans and those independents that lean to the Republican Party, the maximum margin of sampling error is ±5 percentage points. For results based on the sample of 471 Democrats and those independents that lean to the Democratic Party, the maximum margin of sampling error is ±5 percentage points.

In addition to sampling error, question wording and practical difficulties in conducting surveys can introduce error or bias into the findings of public opinion polls.

May 25, 2005
BUSH RATINGS SHOW DECLINE
At low points for his handling of economy, Iraq, Social Security

by Jeffrey M. Jones, Gallup Poll Managing Editor

Opinions of George W. Bush are at or near lows for his presidency, according to the latest CNN/*USA Today*/Gallup poll. Bush's 46% approval rating is just one point higher than the low of his term, and his ratings on the economy, Iraq, and Social Security have never been lower. Only 4 in 10 Americans say they agree with Bush on issues that matter most to them, and just a bare majority says he has the personality and leadership qualities a president should have.

The May 20-22 poll finds 46% of Americans approving and 50% disapproving of the job Bush is doing as president. In late March, 45% approved of Bush, the lowest Gallup has measured during the Bush presidency. There were modest signs of recovery in public support for Bush in April and early May, including a pair of 50% approval ratings during that time. But now, in the midst of concerns about the economy and controversy over some of his judicial nominations, his approval rating has dipped again.

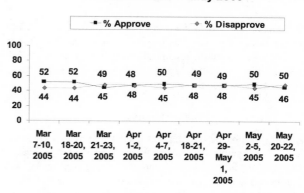

**Bush's Overall Job Approval Rating
March 2005 — May 2005**

Aside from Richard Nixon, who was dealing with the Watergate scandal, all two-term presidents since Truman were comfortably above 50% during the month of May following their re-election. With only a few exceptions, Bush's approval rating has hovered around 50% since February 2004.

Bush on the Issues

Just 40% of Americans say they agree with Bush "on the issues that matter most" to them. Fifty-seven percent say they disagree. While this question is not updated on a regular basis, this is clearly the worst reading of Bush's presidency. The prior low was 46% agreement in September 2003.

Please tell me whether you agree or disagree with George W. Bush on the issues that matter most to you.

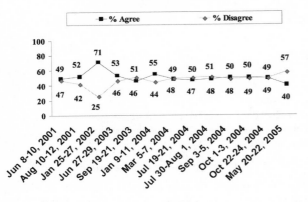

With that backdrop, it is not surprising that Americans' ratings of Bush for handling specific issues are among the lowest (if not the lowest) of his presidency. Specifically,

- Forty percent of Americans approve of Bush's handling of the economy. Forty-one percent was the previous low mark, reached several times.
- Forty-four percent approve of Bush on foreign affairs; his low on this was a 42% reading last May.
- Forty percent approve of the way Bush is dealing with the situation in Iraq, the lowest of his term. He received 41% ratings in May and June 2004.
- Thirty-three percent approve of Bush's handling of Social Security. It had been at 35% in three separate polls since late February.
- Fifty-five percent approve of Bush on terrorism. His low mark on this issue was 52% in May 2004.

On a personal level, Bush is also taking a bit of a hit. A bare majority of Americans, 52%, say they agree that "Bush has the personality and leadership qualities a president should have," while 45% disagree. That is down from 57% just before his re-election, and is the lowest percentage on this measure to date.

Survey Methods

These results are based on telephone interviews with a randomly selected national sample of 1,006 adults, aged 18 and older, conducted May 20-22, 2005. For results based on this sample, one can say with 95% confidence that the maximum error attributable to sampling and other random effects is ±3 percentage points. In addition to sampling error, question wording and practical difficulties in conducting surveys can introduce error or bias into the findings of public opinion polls. For results based on the 517 national adults in the Form A half-sample and 489 national adults in the Form B half-sample, the maximum margins of sampling error are ±5 percentage points.

Please tell me whether you agree or disagree that George W. Bush has the personality and leadership qualities a president should have.

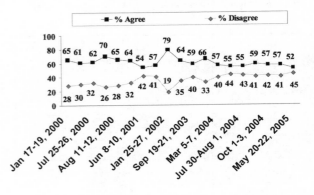

May 26, 2005
AMERICANS OK WITH USING EMBRYOS IN MEDICAL RESEARCH
60% think such research is morally acceptable

by Lydia Saad, Gallup Poll Senior Editor

President George W. Bush has drawn a line in the sand over embryonic stem cell research, saying he will veto proposed legislation to expand funding for such research should it reach his desk. A bill passed Tuesday in the U.S. House of Representatives would permit federal funding for medical studies that utilize stem cells derived from surplus embryos lying fallow in fertility clinics.

"This bill would take us across a critical ethical line by creating new incentives for the ongoing destruction of emerging human life," Bush said. "Crossing this line would be a great mistake."

The ethical line so clear to Bush does not resonate with the majority of Americans. While about 4 in 10 adults agree with Bush's position, more than half the public agrees with the substance of the House bill. This includes 42% who would ease current restrictions on taxpayer funding of research involving human embryos, and 11% who would place no restrictions on such funding.

Unlike abortion, which is morally troubling to a majority of Americans, 60% of the public recently told Gallup that medical research

Preferred Approach to Funding Medical Research Involving Embryonic Stem Cells

May 20-22, 2005

Moral Acceptability of Issues

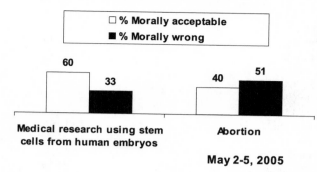

□ % Morally acceptable
■ % Morally wrong

Medical research using stem cells from human embryos		Abortion	
60	33	40	51

May 2-5, 2005

using stem cells obtained from human embryos is morally acceptable; one-third disagrees.

This finding is not particularly surprising, given that, though Americans are generally ambivalent about abortion, they are generally supportive of it being legal in the first trimester of pregnancy. According to a January 2003 Gallup poll, 66% of Americans believe abortion should be legal in the first three months of pregnancy. (Conversely, 68% think it should be illegal in the second three months, and 84% think it should be illegal in the last three months.)

If two-thirds of Americans are comfortable with abortion being legal in the first trimester, then it stands to reason that a majority would be comfortable with using discarded embryos for medical research.

Republicans and Democrats Disagree

According to the May 20-22, 2005, CNN/*USA Today*/Gallup poll, a majority of Republicans hold views consistent with Bush's anti-research position, while a majority of Democrats are in agreement with the pro-research position inherent in the House bill.

Nearly 6 in 10 Republicans (59%) prefer to maintain the current restrictions on stem cell research funding, or prohibit such funding altogether. Just over one-third of Republicans (36%) believe the funding restrictions should be eased or lifted. By contrast, 6 in 10 Democrats would like to see expanded funding opportunities, while about 4 in 10 (38%) would like the current restrictions maintained or strengthened.

Independents are nearly identical to Democrats in their preferences on this issue.

Republicans are a bit further removed from Bush on the moral aspect of embryonic stem cell research. An equal number of Republicans—47%—say such research is morally acceptable as say it is morally wrong. However, Democrats are still much more

Partisan Preferences on Government Funding of Embryonic Stem Cell Research

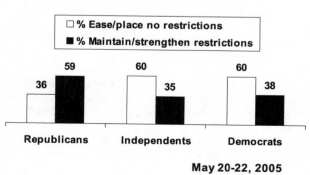

□ % Ease/place no restrictions
■ % Maintain/strengthen restrictions

Republicans		Independents		Democrats	
36	59	60	35	60	38

May 20-22, 2005

supportive of the research; 72% consider it morally acceptable, while just 20% say it is wrong.

Mid-Level Attention Being Paid to the Issue

Americans are paying an average amount of attention to the current stem cell research debate, compared with Gallup's measurement of public attention to a wide variety of issues and stories that have been in the news over the past decade.

Approximately 6 in 10 Americans (58%) say they are following the debate very or somewhat closely. Another 27% are following it "not too closely," while just 15% are not following it at all. This is higher than the 42% paying close attention to the recent filibuster controversy, but lower than the 66% who closely followed the Terri Schiavo case.

Across 150 news attention measures taken by Gallup since 1991, the average percentage paying very or somewhat close attention has been 60%.

The current level of attention to the stem cell research funding debate is slightly higher than the attention paid the last time the issue took center stage in American politics in 2001. A Gallup poll conducted in August 2001—just a few days before Bush announced his decision to authorize government funding on a limited number of existing embryonic stem cell lines—found 55% following the issue closely and 23% not following it at all.

Supporters of expanding federal funding of this research appear to be more energized in the current debate than are the detractors. By a 68% to 31% margin, those closely following the issue tend to be in favor of relaxing federal funding restrictions. By contrast, by a 53% to 39% margin, those not paying close attention tend to agree more with Bush's position.

Survey Methods

These most recent results are based on telephone interviews with a randomly selected national sample of 1,006 adults, aged 18 and older, conducted May 20-22, 2005. For results based on this sample, one can say with 95% confidence that the maximum error attributable to sampling and other random effects is ±3 percentage points. In addition to sampling error, question wording and practical difficulties in conducting surveys can introduce error or bias into the findings of public opinion polls.

May 27, 2005
GAS PRICE HARDSHIPS WON'T ALTER AMERICANS' VACATION PLANS
A slight majority will drive less this summer because of gas prices

by Joseph Carroll, Gallup Poll Assistant Editor

As summer unofficially starts this Memorial Day weekend, a recent CNN/*USA Today*/Gallup poll finds that nearly 6 in 10 Americans say the recent hikes in gas prices have caused financial hardship for their households. This is unchanged from April and continues to represent the highest percentage expressing this sentiment since Gallup first asked the question in 2000. More than half of Americans also say that gas prices will cause them to drive less than expected this summer, while a slightly lower percentage say gas prices will cause them to alter their summer vacation plans.

"Financial Hardship" Remains at High Level

The poll, conducted May 20-22, finds that 59% of Americans say the recent gas price increases have caused financial hardship for their households. Forty-one percent say these increases have not caused any financial hardship. This remains at the high level measured in early April this year, when 58% said the gas price increases had caused financial hardship and 42% said they had not.

Have recent price increases in gasoline caused any financial hardship for you or your household?

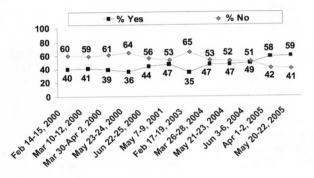

Gallup first asked this question in February 2000 and has periodically re-asked it as gas prices have risen in recent years. At that initial point in 2000, 40% said price increases had caused a financial hardship. Not until this year did a majority of Americans say gas price increases were causing financial hardship. It is worth noting that this financial hardship percentage has stayed high even though gas prices have leveled off or declined in recent weeks in some parts of the country.

Certain groups of Americans are more inclined to say gas prices have caused financial difficulties in their households:

- More than 7 in 10 adults earning less than $30,000 per year say gas price increases are causing a financial hardship for their households. This compares with 62% of those earning between $30,000 and $75,000 and just 41% of those earning $75,000 a year or more.
- Younger Americans are much more likely than older Americans to report financial hardship, with 71% of 18- to 29-year-olds, 59% of 30- to 49-year-olds, and 54% of those aged 50 and older expressing this sentiment.
- Two in three women say the recent gas price increases have caused financial hardship, compared with just about half of men.
- Seventy-two percent of nonwhites say gas prices have caused hardship, while only 55% of whites feel this way.
- There are only modest regional differences, with Southerners just slightly more likely than those living elsewhere to say gas prices have caused hardship.

Gas Price Increases Causing Financial Hardship?
May 20-22, 2005

	Yes, caused hardship %	No, not caused hardship %
Gender		
Men	51	49
Women	67	33

	Yes, caused hardship %	No, not caused hardship %
Race		
Whites	55	45
Nonwhites	72	27
Age		
18- to 29-year-olds	71	29
30- to 49-year-olds	59	41
50 years and older	54	46
Income		
$75,000 or more per year	41	59
$30,000-$74,999	62	38
Less than $30,000 per year	71	29
Region		
East	55	45
Midwest	58	42
South	65	35
West	56	44

Americans Plan to Drive Less This Summer, but Won't Alter Vacation Plans

Fifty-five percent of Americans say gas prices will cause them to drive less than they might have otherwise this summer, while 43% say prices will not cause them to drive less. These results are roughly the same as Gallup found last May. This measure reached its highest point in May 2001, when 58% said they would drive less. Although the level of financial hardship caused by high gas prices is at an all-time high, the effect of that hardship on summer driving plans is actually slightly lower than in 2001.

Will the price of gas cause you to drive less than you might have otherwise this summer, or not?

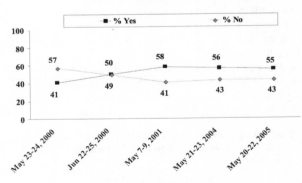

While a majority of Americans say they plan to drive less this summer because of gas prices, a smaller percentage will alter their summer vacation plans. Fifty-three percent of Americans say they will not alter their summer vacation plans, while 46% say they will. (The poll did not ask how many Americans were planning to take a vacation this summer, so some of the respondents may not intend to take a vacation.)

Americans living in lower-income households are much more likely than those in upper-income households to say they will drive less this summer and that they will alter their summer vacation

Will the price of gas cause you to alter your summer vacation plans, or not?

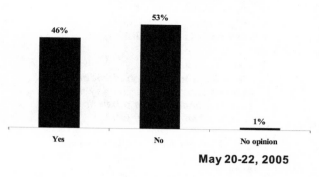

May 20-22, 2005

**Current Economic Conditions
January — May 2005**

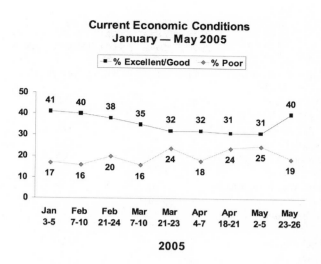

plans. The poll did not find any difference by age on these two measures.

Survey Methods

Results in the current survey are based on telephone interviews with 1,006 national adults, aged 18 and older, conducted May 20-22, 2005. For results based on the total sample of national adults, one can say with 95% confidence that the maximum margin of sampling error is ±3 percentage points.

For results based on the 517 national adults in the Form A half-sample and 489 national adults in the Form B half-sample, the maximum margins of sampling error are ±5 percentage points.

In addition to sampling error, question wording and practical difficulties in conducting surveys can introduce error or bias into the findings of public opinion polls.

May 31, 2005
AMERICANS SOMEWHAT MORE POSITIVE ABOUT ECONOMY
Drop in concern about gas prices may be one reason

by Frank Newport, Gallup Poll Editor in Chief

Americans have become somewhat less negative about the direction of the U.S. economy, and more positive when asked to rate economic conditions in the country at this time. Despite this improvement, economic attitudes remain quite negative in absolute terms, and a slight majority of Americans continue to say economic conditions are getting worse. Fewer Americans than in recent months mention energy costs as the top economic problem facing the nation today, suggesting that lessening concern about the price of gas may be one factor behind the more positive perceptions. But only 4 in 10 Americans say now is a good time to find a quality job, little changed from previous months.

Ratings of the National Economy

Ratings of both the current economy and the direction of the economy have become more positive in the current poll.

Forty percent of Americans now rate economic conditions in this country as excellent or good, 41% say they are only fair, and 19% say they are poor.

That's obviously not a strongly positive reading, but in perspective, it's the most positive since early February of this year. And the current reading marks a clear break from the more consistently negative readings Gallup has recorded over the last several months.

In similar fashion, there has been a significant change in the American public's responses to the question about whether economic conditions in this country as a whole are getting better or getting worse.

**Economic Outlook
January — May 2005**

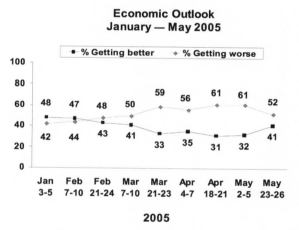

Although still negative, the 52% "getting worse" figure is the lowest since March, and is significantly lower than the 61% recorded in mid-April and early May.

Overall, it's fair to say that while Americans are not exuberant about the economy, they are no longer as negative as they have been in the last two months or so.

Why the Increase in Optimism?

Gallup's late May poll asks Americans to name—without prompting—what they perceive to be the most important economic problem facing the country.

The results for this question show a clear drop in the percentage of Americans who believe that fuel or oil prices are the most important economic problem.

What is the most important economic problem facing the country today? [OPEN-ENDED]

	May 23-26, 2005 %	Apr 18-21, 2005 %	Mar 21-23, 2005 %	Feb 21-24, 2005 %	Jan 17-19, 2005 %
Unemployment/ Jobs/Wages	18	18	17	22	22
War in Iraq	11	8	11	9	14
Healthcare/Health insurance costs	11	7	7	10	11
Fuel/Oil prices	10	19	17	5	3
Outsourcing of jobs	8	5	7	6	5
Social Security	6	7	10	10	12
Inflation/Rising prices	5	4	3	2	3
Lack of money	4	6	3	4	1
Federal budget deficit	4	5	7	9	9
Illegal immigrants	4	2	2	1	1
Trade deficit	3	1	1	2	2
Taxes	3	2	2	2	3
Education reform	2	2	2	2	3
Credit cards/ Overspending	2	1	2	1	2
Poverty/Hunger/ Homelessness	2	1	1	2	2
Poorly run government/ Politics	1	1	1	1	1
Economy (non-specific)	1	1	1	1	1
Gap between rich and poor	1	1	1	1	1
Welfare	1	1	1	1	2
Senior care/Medicare	1	1	1	1	1
George W. Bush/ His policies	1	1	1	1	3
Retirement	1	1	1	1	*
Foreign aid/Focus on other countries	1	1	1	1	2
Stock market	*	*	*	*	*
Interest rates	*	*	*	1	*
International relations	*	*	*	*	1
College tuition expenses	*	*	—	—	1
Other	7	4	4	5	8
None	2	1	1	1	1
No opinion	9	8	9	10	8

Percentages add to more than 100% due to multiple responses.

*Less than 0.5%

While only 3% and 5% of Americans mentioned energy costs as the nation's top economic problem in January and February, respectively, that percentage jumped to 17% in March and then 19% last month. Now, it's down again—to 10%.

Correlation is no proof of causation, of course, and Gallup has no way of ascertaining precisely whether the drop in concern about energy costs is the driving factor behind the more optimistic view of the national economy. It seems reasonable to assume, however, that it is at least one of the causes.

This conclusion is borne out by the fact that mentions of other economic concerns remain roughly the same: 18% mention jobs, 11% the war in Iraq, and 11% healthcare costs. (Somewhat fewer

Americans name Social Security as the top economic concern than did so at the beginning of the year.)

The constancy in concern about jobs is also shown in responses to a closed-ended question that asks: "Thinking about the job situation in America today, would you say that it is now a good time or a bad time to find a quality job?"

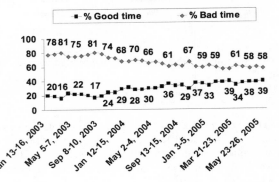

Thinking about the job situation in America today, would you say that it is now a good time or a bad time to find a quality job?

The results show no major increase in positive responses compared to previous months this year, although, from a long-term perspective, Americans are now somewhat more optimistic when answering this question than they were in 2003 and much of 2004.

All in all, overall economic optimism is increasing, but perceptions of an improved job market are apparently not the cause.

Survey Methods

These results are based on telephone interviews with a randomly selected national sample of 1,004 adults, aged 18 and older, conducted May 23-26, 2005. For results based on this sample, one can say with 95% confidence that the maximum error attributable to sampling and other random effects is ±3 percentage points. In addition to sampling error, question wording and practical difficulties in conducting surveys can introduce error or bias into the findings of public opinion polls.

May 31, 2005
JOB MARKET RATED MORE POSITIVELY IN SOUTH, WEST
Trends in East, Midwest relatively flat

by Jeffrey M. Jones, Gallup Poll Managing Editor

Twice each month, Gallup updates Americans' perceptions of the job market by asking the public if it is now a "good or bad time to find a quality job." Americans are generally more pessimistic than optimistic about current job prospects, but their views are more positive now than in recent years. A closer look at the data shows consistent regional variation in assessments of the job market this year, with those in the West and the South more optimistic than those in the East and the Midwest.

According to an aggregate of Gallup data since March*, 31% of those residing in the East and 30% of those residing in the Midwest say it is a good time to find a quality job. By comparison, 42% of those in the South, and 42% of those in the West, say it is a good time.

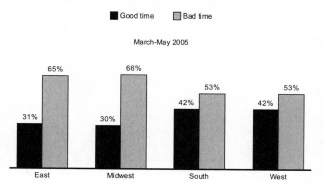

Good/Bad Time to Find a Quality Job, by Region

■ Good time   ▨ Bad time

March-May 2005

East: 31% / 65%
Midwest: 30% / 66%
South: 42% / 53%
West: 42% / 53%

These relationships persist even when controlling for other factors that are related to job market assessments, including partisanship, income, and employment status. And the differences are not necessarily reflections of differential ratings of the economy by region—while perceptions of the national economy vary somewhat by region, these gaps are not as large as the gaps by region in job market assessments.

Ratings of National Economy, by Region, March-May 2005

	East	Midwest	South	West
Rate economy as excellent or good	29%	32	36	34
Say economy is getting better	32%	34	36	36

The trends show that perceptions of the job market weren't all that different in January and especially February. Divergence was first evident in late February and has persisted since. In the West, job market assessments improved in each poll from early January to early March, and have leveled off somewhat since. In the South, a slightly different pattern is evident, with ratings of the job market higher in the three most recent months than at earlier points in the year. The trends in the East and Midwest have been relatively flat, especially in the last two months.

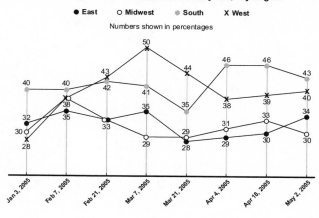

Percentage "Good Time to Find a Quality Job," by Region

● East   ○ Midwest   ◉ South   X West

Numbers shown in percentages

The regional differences in job market perceptions are generally in line with regional estimates of employment provided by the Bureau of Labor Statistics in its May 20 report. For example, the biggest gains this year in non-farm employment have been in Nevada, Arizona, Utah, Oregon, and Florida—four Western states and one Southern state. The Midwest generally had the highest level of unemployment this year (while the Northeast has the lowest unemployment rate, none of the states in the region show significant job growth).

Gallup's new May 23-26 poll suggests stability in ratings of the job market at the national level, with slightly fewer than 4 in 10 Americans saying it is a good time to find a quality job (as has been the case since February, save for a slightly lower 34% reading in mid-March). Those data suggest that Midwest residents may be rating the job market more positively now, but still behind those of the South and West, while Eastern residents continue to give substantially more negative ratings.

Results are based on an aggregate of 5,023 telephone interviews with randomly selected national samples of adults, age 18 and older, conducted March 7-May 5, 2005.

For results based on the 1,150 residents of the East, 1,136 residents of the Midwest, 1,614 residents of the South, and 1,123 residents of the West, the maximum margins of sampling error are ±3 percentage points.

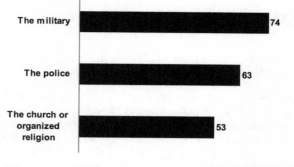

Top-Tier Institutions

percentage saying they have "a great deal" or "quite a lot" of confidence

The military — 74
The police — 63
The church or organized religion — 53

May 23-26, 2005

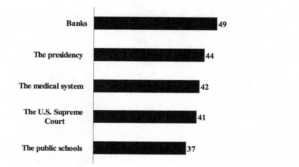

Middle-Tier Institutions

percentage saying they have "a great deal" or "quite a lot" of confidence

Banks — 49
The presidency — 44
The medical system — 42
The U.S. Supreme Court — 41
The public schools — 37

May 23-26, 2005

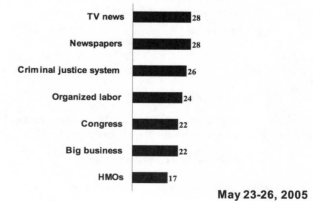

Bottom-Tier Institutions

percentage saying they have "a great deal" or "quite a lot" of confidence

TV news — 28
Newspapers — 28
Criminal justice system — 26
Organized labor — 24
Congress — 22
Big business — 22
HMOs — 17

May 23-26, 2005

June 1, 2005

MILITARY AGAIN TOPS "CONFIDENCE IN INSTITUTIONS" LIST

Ratings of the president, Congress, and the Supreme Court are all down

by Lydia Saad, Gallup Poll Senior Editor

Gallup's 2005 reading of public confidence in major institutions operating in U.S. society finds little change, compared with a year ago, in Americans' ratings at the top of the list. These include the military, ranked No. 1, as well as the police, organized religion, and banks.

However, several institutions that typically appear toward the bottom of this list—organized labor, the criminal justice system, and Congress—have experienced declines in public confidence since last year. Confidence in the presidency, which ranks No. 5 on this year's list, and confidence in the Supreme Court, ranked No. 7, also declined.

Gallup's annual measure of public confidence in institutions is based on the question, "Now I am going to read you a list of institutions in American society. Please tell me how much confidence you, yourself, have in each one—a great deal, quite a lot, some, or very little?" ("None" is allowed as a volunteered response.) The rank order of institutions is based on the combined "a great deal" plus "quite a lot" figures.

The Basic Ranking

Only 3 U.S. institutions out of the 15 included in the May 23-26 poll command a high degree of confidence from at least half of Americans: the military, the police, and the church or organized religion. (In previous years, banks, the presidency, the Supreme Court, newspapers, and public schools have each crossed the 50% threshold.) The 74% rating given to the military continues to make it the institution engendering the most confidence of any of those tested—and by a healthy margin.

Several organizations are rated highly by between 40% and 50% of Americans. These are banks, the presidency, the medical system, and the U.S. Supreme Court.

Close to 4 in 10 Americans (37%) say they have a great deal or quite a lot of confidence in the public schools.

Roughly one in four have high confidence in television news, newspapers, the criminal justice system, organized labor, Congress, and big business.

Health maintenance organizations (HMOs) are rated highly by only 17% of Americans.

Trends Are Down

There are no major shifts in public confidence this year—at least none on par with the 15-point decline in confidence in organized reli-

gion that occurred between 2001 and 2002 over the Catholic church's sexual abuse scandal, or the 13-point increase in confidence in the military that occurred in the same period (following the Sept. 11 terrorist attacks).

The only significant changes recorded this year are all declines in confidence. These occur in relation to five institutions, and range from five to eight percentage points.

	May 2004 %	May 2005 %	Change pct. pts.
The presidency	52	44	–8
The criminal justice system	34	26	–8
Congress	30	22	–8
Organized labor	31	24	–7
The U.S. Supreme Court	46	41	–5

Confidence in the presidency ratings are generally linked with job approval ratings of the sitting president. However, the eight-point decline in confidence in the presidency this year is not reflected in President Bush's approval rating spanning the same period. Bush's approval rating today is 48%, versus 47% in May 2004. Whatever the reason, the decline in confidence in the presidency is most pronounced among Democrats nationally, although Republicans are also slightly less positive on this measure than they were a year ago.

Confidence in the Presidency
by partisanship
(% Great deal/Quite a lot of confidence)

	Republicans %	Independents %	Democrats %
May 2004	85	40	33
May 2005	79	35	18
Change	*–6 pct. pts.*	*–5 pct. pts*	*–15 pct. pts.*

The eight-point overall decline in confidence in Congress is seen to a similar degree among Republicans (–7 points) and Democrats (–12 points). The exact cause for this bipartisan decline is unclear, although Congress has been the source of much controversy this year, including its involvement in the Terri Schiavo feeding tube case, partisan battles over federal court nominees, and ethical clouds over House Majority Leader Tom DeLay.

Whatever the cause, the 22% confidence rating for Congress today is the lowest it has been in eight years.

Confidence in Congress
by partisanship
(% Great deal/Quite a lot of confidence)

	Republicans %	Independents %	Democrats %
May 2004	35	22	31
May 2005	28	20	19
Change	*–7 pct. pts.*	*–2 pct. pts.*	*–12 pct. pts.*

Similarly, the five-point decline seen in confidence in the Supreme Court occurred about equally among Republicans and Democrats.

Confidence in the Supreme Court
by partisanship
(% Great deal/Quite a lot of confidence)

	Republicans %	Independents %	Democrats %
May 2004	53	41	47
May 2005	47	36	42
Change	*–6 pct. pts.*	*–5 pct. pts.*	*–5 pct. pts.*

Gallup also recorded an eight-point decline in confidence in the criminal justice system (now 26%, down from 34%), and a seven-point decline in confidence in organized labor (now 24%, down from 31%). The drop in confidence in the criminal justice system is about even by party.

Confidence in the Criminal Justice System
by partisanship
(% Great deal/Quite a lot of confidence)

	Republicans %	Independents %	Democrats %
May 2004	39	30	34
May 2005	31	19	28
Change	*–8 pct. pts.*	*–11 pct. pts.*	*–6 pct. pts.*

The drop in confidence in organized labor is more pronounced among Democrats than among Republicans.

Confidence in Organized Labor
by partisanship
(% Great deal/Quite a lot of confidence)

	Republicans %	Independents %	Democrats %
May 2004	22	30	43
May 2005	19	22	34
Change	*–3 pct. pts.*	*–8 pct. pts.*	*–9 pct. pts.*

Other Notables

- The last five years have been bad for journalism. Since 2000, trust in television news has declined from 36% to 28%, and trust in newspapers has declined from 37% to 28%. The current ratings represent the lowest trust levels for both of these institutions, although trust in newspapers has been as low as 29% (in 1994).
- Trust in organized religion remains where it was last year, at 53%. This represents a partial recovery from 2002, when the Catholic church's sexual abuse scandal drove this confidence level down to 45%, but it is still below the 56% to 60% level maintained before the scandal.

Survey Methods

These results are based on telephone interviews with a randomly selected national sample of 1,004 adults, aged 18 and older, conducted May 23-26, 2005. For results based on this sample, one can say with 95% confidence that the maximum error attributable to sampling and other random effects is ±3 percentage points. In addition to sampling error, question wording and practical difficulties in conducting surveys can introduce error or bias into the findings of public opinion polls.

June 3, 2005
ABOUT HALF OF AMERICANS READING A BOOK
Most say Internet has not affected their reading habits

by David W. Moore, Gallup Poll Senior Editor

About one in every two Americans is engrossed in some type of book, according to Gallup's latest measure of the public's reading habits. About half of Americans also say they have read more than five books in the past year, not much different from the number reported a decade and a half ago. There is no widespread pattern as to how people select their books—some choose by the author, others based on recommendations from their friends, and still others by browsing in a bookstore or library.

The poll, conducted May 20-22, finds 47% of adults saying they are presently reading a book, up from 37% who reported that in 1990, and 23% in 1957.

Do you happen to be reading any books or novels at present?

	Yes %
2005 May 20-22	47
1990 Dec 13-16	37
1957 Mar 15-20	23
1954 Nov 11-16	22
1952 Oct 5-10	18
1949 Dec 2-7	21
1949 Nov 27-Dec 2	21
1949 Jan 22-27	21

The poll also shows that 83% of Americans say they have started to read at least 1 book sometime in the past year, including 31% who say they have read more than 10 books, and 6% who have read more than 50.

During the past year, about how many books, either hardcover or paperback, did you read either all or part of the way through?

	None %	1-5 %	6-10 %	11-50 %	51 + %	No answer %	Mean (w/ zero)	Median
2005 May 20-22	16	38	14	25	6	1	*14.2*	5
2002 Dec 5-8	18	31	15	27	8	1	*15.8*	6
2001 Dec 6-9 ^	13	38	16	23	8	1	*14.5*	5
1999 Sep 10-14	13	30	16	31	7	2	*17*	7
1999 Jul 13-14	12	24	18	34	10	3	*20*	10
1990 Dec 13-16	16	32	15	27	7	3	*11*	6
1978 Jul 21-Aug 14	8	29	17	29	13	4	—	—

^Asked of a half sample

The median number of books read is five—about half of Americans have read more than that, and half have read fewer than that, including 16% who say they did not even start a book last year.

Who is reading books? Women more than men, people aged 30 and older more than people aged 18 to 29, the higher educated more than the less educated, people who closely follow other news events, and frequent rather than infrequent moviegoers.

Reading a Book?

	Yes %
Overall	47
Gender	
Male	42
Female	53
Age	
18-29	40
30-49	47
50-64	51
65+	47
Education	
High school or less	33
Some college	46
College grad	63
Postgraduate	74
How closely follow filibuster	
Very	64
Somewhat	55
Not close	39
How frequently attend movies	
High frequency	62
Moderate frequency	49
Not at all	33
Movie attendance vs. five years ago	
More often	56
Same	47
Less often	44

- The gender gap is in the double digits—53% of women vs. 42% of men are currently reading a book, an 11-point difference.
- Among people in the three older age groups, the percentages reading a book are similar (47% to 51%), but significantly higher than the percentage among people younger than 30 (40%).
- It's no surprise that education correlates highly with reading a book, going from 33% among Americans with a high school education or less to 74% among Americans with at least some postgraduate experience.
- People following current events are also more likely to read books. The poll included questions on the U.S. Senate filibuster and on stem cell research. The more people were paying attention to either issue, the more likely they were also to be reading a book. For example, among people who were following the

controversy over the U.S. Senate filibuster "very closely," 64% were reading a book, compared with 55% among people following the controversy "somewhat closely" and just 39% among people not following the issue closely. The same pattern was also evident by how closely people were following the issue of stem cell research.

- Movie attendance does not appear to depress book reading. The more movies people attend, the more likely they are to be reading books—from 33% who didn't attend a movie last year, to 49% among people who attended a few movies, to 62% who attended several movies.
- Also, among people who say they are attending movies more often than they did five years ago, 56% are presently reading a book, compared with 47% among people attending the same number of movies as in the past, and 44% among people attending movies less often.

There is no single way that best describes how Americans select the books they read. Thirty percent of adults who read a book in the last year do so based on an author they like, 27% on a recommendation from someone they know, and 22% by browsing at a bookstore or library.

Which of the following is the main way you generally select the books you read—[ROTATED: based on a recommendation from someone you know, by choosing an author whose books you like, based on book reviews you've read, by browsing a bookstore or library, based on an advertisement you've seen, by browsing an Internet site]—or do you select them another way?

BASED ON 855 ADULTS WHO READ AT LEAST ONE BOOK IN THE PAST YEAR

	2005 May 20-22 %	1999 Sep 10-14 %
By choosing an author whose books you like	30	26
Based on a recommendation from someone you know	27	27
By browsing a bookstore or library	22	26
Based on book reviews you've read	7	6
By subject (vol.)	6	2
By browsing an Internet site	3	1
Based on an advertisement you've seen	2	3
Other	2	7
No opinion	1	1

Few people choose a book based on book reviews (7%) or by browsing an Internet site (3%), and only 2% say they were influenced to read a book by an advertisement.

Most people, 73%, say the Internet has not affected their reading habits, but 16% say that because they spend more of their free time on the Internet, they are reading fewer books. Just 6% say that the Internet has influenced them to read more, by making it easier to find out about, and purchase, books.

Which best describes the effect that the Internet has had on the amount of time that you, personally, spend reading books—[ROTATED: you are reading more books now because it is easy to buy books on the Internet and to find out about the books you want to read, the Internet has not affected the amount of time you spend reading books, or you are reading fewer books because you are spending more of your free time on the Internet instead of reading books]?

	Reading more books	Not affected	Reading fewer books	No opinion
2005 May 20-22	6%	73	16	5

Survey Methods

Results in the current survey are based on telephone interviews with 1,006 national adults, aged 18 and older, conducted May 20-22, 2005. For results based on the total sample of national adults, one can say with 95% confidence that the maximum margin of sampling error is ±3 percentage points.

In addition to sampling error, question wording and practical difficulties in conducting surveys can introduce error or bias into the findings of public opinion polls.

June 7, 2005
UPDATE: HILLARY RODHAM CLINTON AND THE 2008 ELECTION
Slight majority says they would consider voting for her

by Frank Newport, Gallup Poll Editor in Chief

New York Sen. Hillary Rodham Clinton has yet to formally declare her candidacy for the 2008 presidential nomination, in part because she faces a re-election bid for her U.S. Senate seat from New York next year. However, Sen. Clinton's husband, former President Bill Clinton, did nothing to dampen speculation about her presidential bid when he was quoted as saying last week that his wife would make a "magnificent" president.

Like her husband, Hillary Clinton has been no stranger to controversy over the last 13 years. Her near-celebrity status—coupled with the chance that she could become the first female president in U.S. history—have served to make her the most talked about potential presidential candidate more than two and a half years before the first 2008 primaries.

History indicates that it is too early to make any realistic assessments of what will happen in a presidential election this far in advance. But it is interesting, nevertheless, to take stock of several interesting aspects of public opinion about Clinton, based on several recent polls.

1. Hillary Clinton has near-universal name recognition, which could be either a blessing or a curse.

It is no great shock to find that well over 9 out of 10 Americans have an opinion about Clinton. In fact, only 6% of Americans interviewed in

Gallup's mid-May poll claimed that they did not know enough about her to have either a favorable or unfavorable opinion. This "no opinion" percentage for Clinton has been in the single digits for over 10 years, suggesting that she is a figure on the American political scene who, in general, certainly needs no introduction to the population.

Whether this level of very high name recognition is good or bad for a presidential candidate is open to discussion. A well-known figure doesn't have to waste time and money gaining name identification in a political contest, but at the same time a very well known figure often has an ingrained image in the minds of the public that is hard to change. It is perhaps interesting to note that the last two Democrats who won the presidency (Bill Clinton and Jimmy Carter) were virtual unknowns on the national political scene three years before their election year. At the same time, as a sitting vice president, Al Gore was very well known to the public three years before his failed bid for the presidency in 2000.

2. Hillary Clinton has a generally favorable image in the eyes of Americans, but there is a core of about 4 in 10 who view her unfavorably.

Clinton's current numbers are 55% favorable and 39% unfavorable, remaining stable over the past year, but slightly improved from January 2001 through 2003—after her husband left office. Clinton's lowest favorable rating of 43% came in January 1996, when Congress had been shut down and at which time her husband also had low public opinion ratings. Sen. Clinton was most favorably evaluated during the Monica Lewinsky/impeachment crisis, reaching an all-time high of 67% favorable in December 1998, presumably as a result of sympathy from the public for her "aggrieved spouse" role at that time.

Hillary Rodham Clinton

2005	Favorable %	Unfavorable %	No opinion %
2005 May 20-22	55	39	6
2005 Feb 25-27	53	41	6
2004			
2004 Jul 19-21 ^	56	38	6
2003			
2003 Oct 24-26	51	44	5
2003 Sep 19-21	54	40	6
2003 Jun 27-29 ^	52	44	4
2003 Jun 9-10	53	43	4
2003 Mar 14-15	45	46	9
2002			
2002 Dec 16-17	48	46	6
2002 Sep 23-26	47	44	9
2001			
2001 Aug 3-5	51	44	5
2001 Mar 5-7	44	53	3
2001 Feb 19-21	49	44	7
2001 Feb 1-4	52	43	5
2000			
2000 Nov 13-15	56	39	5
2000 Oct 25-28	52	43	5
2000 Aug 4-5	45	50	5
2000 Feb 4-6	55	39	6

1999	Favorable %	Unfavorable %	No opinion %
1999 Dec 9-12	48	48	4
1999 Sep 23-26	56	40	4
1999 Aug 3-4	56	41	3
1999 Jul 22-25	62	35	3
1999 Jun 25-27	56	42	2
1999 Mar 5-7	65	31	4
1999 Feb 19-21	65	30	5
1999 Feb 4-8	66	31	3
1998			
1998 Dec 28-29	67	29	4
1998 Oct 9-12 ‡	63	33	4
1998 Sep 14-15	61	33	6
1998 Aug 21-23	61	33	6
1998 Aug 10-12	60	36	4
1998 Aug 7-8	60	35	5
1998 Feb 13-15	60	36	4
1998 Jan 30-Feb 1	64	34	2
1998 Jan 24-25	61	33	6
1998 Jan 23-24	60	35	5
1997			
1997 Dec 18-21	56	38	6
1997 Oct 27-29	61	34	5
1997 Jun 26-29	51	42	7
1997 Feb 24-26	51	42	6
1997 Jan 31-Feb 2	55	39	6
1997 Jan 10-13	56	37	7
1996			
1996 Oct 26-29 ‡	49	43	8
1996 Aug 28-29 †	51	41	8
1996 Aug 16-18 †	47	48	5
1996 Aug 5-7 †	48	45	7
1996 Jun 18-19	46	47	6
1996 Mar 15-17	47	48	5
1996 Jan 12-15	43	51	6
1995			
1995 Jul 7-9	50	44	6
1995 Mar 17-19	49	44	7
1995 Jan 16-18	50	44	6
1994			
1994 Nov 28-29	50	44	6
1994 Sep 6-7	48	47	5
1994 Jul 15-17	48	46	6
1994 Apr 22-24	56	40	4
1994 Mar 25-27	52	42	6
1994 Mar 7-8	55	40	5
1994 Jan 15-17	57	36	7
1993			
1993 Nov 2-4	58	34	8
1993 Sep 24-26	62	27	11
1993 Aug 8-10	57	33	10

^ Asked of a half sample
† Based on likely voters
‡ Based on registered voters

2002-March 2003 WORDING: New York Senator Hillary Rodham Clinton

By way of comparison, the same mid-May poll in which Clinton was most recently evaluated included a measure of the image of the Democratic and Republican Senate leaders. Senate Republican Leader Bill Frist (also a possible candidate in 2008) has a very mixed image (26% favorable, 24% unfavorable). Senate Democratic Leader Harry Reid has a similarly mixed rating (22% favorable, 19% unfavorable). Both men have large "no opinion" percentages. Democratic National Committee chairman (and 2004 presidential candidate) Howard Dean has a 35% favorable, 33% unfavorable rating.

By comparison, the latest Gallup reading on the image of President George W. Bush from early April shows him with a 54% favorable and 45% unfavorable reading, just slightly more negative than Hillary Clinton's. Measured in early February, Bill Clinton had a 56% favorable and 41% unfavorable ratio.

3. Hillary Clinton's image has a significant gender gap, with a more favorable image among women than among men.

In the most recent poll, Clinton has a 61% favorable to 34% unfavorable image among women, compared with a 48% to 45% image ratio among men.

Women in general are more likely to be Democrats than Republicans, so a Democratic politician usually has a more favorable image among women than among men. But previous in-depth Gallup analysis has shown that Clinton's gender advantage among women extends even to those women who consider themselves Republican and independent. This suggests that a Clinton candidacy might have the ability to bring in the votes of women who usually would not consider voting for a Democratic candidate, providing an edge that could be decisive in a close election.

4. Hillary Clinton is the front-runner for her party's nomination.

Gallup's last survey asking Democrats to indicate who they want to be their party's nominee in 2008 was conducted in early February, and showed Clinton to be far and away the front-runner among the Democratic candidates listed.

CNN/USA Today/Gallup Poll. Feb. 4-6, 2005, Nationwide
Next, I'm going to read a list of people who may be running in the Democratic primary for president in the next election. After I read all the names, please tell me which of those candidates you would be most likely to support for the Democratic nomination for president in the year 2008: New York Senator Hillary Rodham Clinton, former North Carolina Senator John Edwards, Massachusetts Senator John Kerry—or would you support someone else? [Names rotated. N=383 Democrats and Democratic leaners who are registered to vote; MoE ± 6.]

	%
Hillary Rodham Clinton	40
John Kerry	25
John Edwards	18
Other	6
ALL/ANY (vol.)	1
NONE (vol.)	4
Unsure	6

(vol.) = Volunteered response

A more recent Marist College Poll, conducted in mid-April, shows essentially the same thing.

Marist College Poll. April 18-21, 2005. Nationwide.
If the 2008 Democratic presidential primary were held today, whom would you support if the candidates are [see below]? [N=376 Democrats and Democratic leaners who are registered to vote; MoE ± 5.]

	4/18-21/05	2/14-16/05
	%	%
Hillary Clinton	40	39
John Kerry	18	21
John Edwards	16	15
Joe Biden	7	5
Wesley Clark	4	4
Russ Feingold	2	2
Bill Richardson	1	2
Mark Warner	-	1
Evan Bayh	-	1
Tom Vilsack	-	-
Unsure	12	10

It should be noted, however, that trial heats this far out from an election are mostly a reflection of name recognition, rather than people's careful assessment of each candidate's position on issues or abilities to be president. For example, Democratic candidate Connecticut Sen. Joe Lieberman consistently led the early trial heats for the 2004 election, but didn't do particularly well in Iowa and New Hampshire and quickly dropped out of the race.

5. Over half of Americans say they would consider voting for Hillary Clinton in the general election, although there is a substantial minority who say they would not.

Gallup's mid-May poll asked Americans to indicate how likely they would be to vote for Clinton if she were to run for president in 2008. The results show that a slight majority of registered voters (52%) say they would be "somewhat likely" or "very likely" to vote for her, while 47% say they would be "not very likely" or "not at all likely" to vote for her.

If Hillary Rodham Clinton were to run for president in 2008, how likely would you be to vote for her—very likely, somewhat likely, not very likely, or not at all likely?

	Very likely	Somewhat likely	Not very likely	Not at all likely	No opinion
National Adults	%	%	%	%	%
2005 May 20-22 ^	29	24	7	39	1
2003 Jun 9-10	21	21	12	44	2
2000 Nov 13-15 †	26	21	12	39	2
Registered Voters	%	%	%	%	%
2005 May 20-22 ^	28	24	7	40	1
2003 Jun 9-10	20	21	12	45	2
2000 Nov 13-15 †	26	21	12	39	2

^ Asked of a half sample.
† WORDING: If Hillary Rodham Clinton were to run for president in 2004 or 2008, how likely would you be to vote for her—very likely, somewhat likely, not very likely, or not at all likely?

The fact that 40% of registered voters are strongly against voting for Clinton ("not at all likely"), while 28% are strongly in favor ("very likely") suggests that she begins a potential quest for the presidency with a built-in core opposition that is larger than her built-in core support.

In recent months, several polls have pitted Clinton against selected Republican nominees in a hypothetical trial heat for the general election—with varying results. It appears that Republican Arizona Sen. John McCain, a presidential candidate in 2000 and a potential candidate in 2008, tests best against Clinton at this time, owing in large part to McCain's significant appeal outside the Republican Party.

6. Hillary Clinton is still tagged with the "liberal" label by a majority of voters.

Here are the results of a question asking Americans to indicate whether they perceive Clinton to be a liberal, moderate, or conservative.

Do you consider Hillary Rodham Clinton to be—[ROTATED: a liberal, a moderate, or a conservative]?

	Liberal	Moderate	Conservative	No opinion
National Adults	%	%	%	%
2005 May 20-22	54	30	9	7
Registered Voters				
2005 May 20-22	56	30	9	5

The fact that few voters perceive Clinton to be a conservative is not surprising in the least. But the gap between the views of Clinton as a "liberal" versus "moderate" may end up being more significant. There has been a good deal of press coverage in recent months about actions taken by Clinton suggesting she is trying to draw closer to the middle in her ideological positioning, including in particular some more moderate statements on abortion. Clinton may be attempting to avoid the "far left" label, which could make it more difficult for any Democratic candidate to win a general election. The current data suggest that she may have continued work to do in this regard.

There are no trend data on this question, so we have no way of knowing whether or not Clinton's image may have changed. But it's a fair presumption that she will be focusing on the challenge of moderating her image between now and 2008 (assuming that she makes the run for the presidency) while at the same time attempting to avoid the "flip-flopping" image that the Bush campaign used to hurt John Kerry's image in last year's election.

Survey Methods

These results are based on telephone interviews with a randomly selected national sample of 1,006 adults, aged 18 and older, conducted May 20-22, 2005. For results based on this sample, one can say with 95% confidence that the maximum error attributable to sampling and other random effects is ±3 percentage points.

For results based on the sample of 383 Democrats or Democratic leaners who are registered to vote, the maximum margin of sampling error is ±6 percentage points.

In addition to sampling error, question wording and practical difficulties in conducting surveys can introduce error or bias into the findings of public opinion polls.

June 7, 2005
LAST WISHES: HALF OF AMERICANS HAVE WRITTEN WILLS
Most don't have living wills

by Linda Lyons, Education and Youth Editor

Death, like taxes, is certain. And like taxes, it's one of the least pleasant topics to contemplate, let alone discuss with others. Even so, a recent Gallup Poll* indicates half of American adults have faced up to the inevitable and written a last will and testament, directing where or to whom their worldly assets should be distributed when they leave this one.

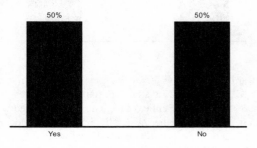

Do you have a will that describes how you would like your money and estate to be handled after your death, or not?

That leaves the other half of Americans at risk of dying intestate—meaning their assets will be distributed not according to their wishes, but those of their state of residence.

Gallup recontacted some of our survey respondents to ask *why* they haven't written a will. "I just haven't gotten around to it," says Dave, a 37-year-old respondent from North Dakota. Other reasons are even simpler. "I don't have a will because I don't have very much," says Nilda, a 52-year-old Florida woman. "We've had some recent deaths in the family so I'm sure my family would be able to settle who gets what amicably. Now if my circumstances should change," she adds, "if I won the lottery, for instance—then I would *definitely* write a will."

Age Is a Factor

It's no surprise that older Americans are far more likely than younger Americans to have a will. Seven in 10 (71%) respondents aged 50 and older have a will, compared with 37% of people under 50.

Providing for one's loved ones is among the most important reasons to make a will. Married people (54%) are somewhat more likely than those who aren't married (44%) to have wills. "My husband and I travel together frequently," says Ann, a 40-year-old respondent from Colorado. "Eight years ago—around the time our third child was born—we decided we had better take care of it just in case of an accident. We wrote a will and appointed a guardian for the children at the same time."

Living Wills

The publicity surrounding the death of Terri Schiavo, the Florida woman whose feeding tube was removed after years of legal wrangling between her husband and parents, spurred a flurry of interest in living wills—directives to family and medical staff about end-of-life wishes. Schiavo was emblematic of the majority of Americans (59%) who do not have a living will dictating in writing exactly how much or how little intervention they would prefer if they were in a similar medical situation. Forty percent of Americans have living wills**.

Do you, personally, have a living will, or not?

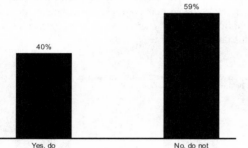

Edward Kahn, a New Jersey attorney whose law firm concentrates in wills and trusts, says he expected to see interest in living wills increase after the Schiavo case, and was surprised when his office didn't have that experience. "It's an important document to have … I find that most of my clients do not want to be kept alive artificially if there's no hope," Kahn says. "Not only do they not want to burden their families, they don't want to live if they can't define their own choices."

As with having wills that deal with the distribution of assets, age is also a factor in whether people have living wills. The tendency to have a living will increases with age. Nineteen percent of 18- to 29-year-olds say they have living wills, as do 32% of 30- to 49-year-olds, 46% of 50- to 64-year-olds, and 67% of those 65 and older.

Dave has no plans to ever write a living will. "The Terri Schiavo case actually lessened my interest in living wills," he says. "It became apparent to me that family members can contest anything if they want to. Here in North Dakota, we can donate organs on our driver's licenses, but if the family doesn't want to do it, they don't have to donate them. So I feel it's a waste of time to write it all down. I've just told everyone what I want and hope they will honor my wishes."

Bottom Line

With so many Web sites devoted to easy, do-it-yourself wills—either free or for a nominal fee—there is really no excuse for not recording your final wishes in writing if you really want to. But many Americans may be deterred by the squeamishness of having to think about their own deaths. Kahn says his clients almost always make excuses

for not taking care of writing a will sooner. "But people just don't want to deal with it," he says. "It's a difficult thing for anyone to have to think about."

Results are based on telephone interviews with 489 national adults, aged 18 and older, conducted May 2-5, 2005. For results based on the sample of national adults, one can say with 95% confidence that the margin of sampling error is ±5 percentage points.

**Results are based on telephone interviews with 1,005 national adults, aged 18 and older, conducted May 2-5, 2005. For results based on the total sample of national adults, one can say with 95% confidence that the margin of sampling error is ±3 percentage points.*

June 7, 2005
YOUNG, OLD HAVE VASTLY DIFFERENT EXPECTATIONS FOR SHORT-RUN FINANCES
Most younger Americans expect change

by Jeffrey M. Jones, Gallup Poll Managing Editor

Gallup's polling on personal finances* shows that Americans generally expect specific aspects of their personal financial situations—including their income, spending, savings and debt—to remain stable in the short term. Among those who expect change, optimists outnumber pessimists by a wide margin. A closer look at the data shows that financial expectations vary widely by age, with most younger Americans expecting their situations to change for the better in the short run, while older Americans expect things to stay the same.

Each month, Gallup asks Americans whether they expect their income, savings, spending, and debt to increase, decrease, or remain the same in the next six months. The data underscore the idea that most Americans' finances remain pretty steady in the short term.

This stability is evident in two ways. First, there is little variation from month to month in Gallup's estimates of Americans' predictions for their short-term income, spending, savings, and debt. For example, Gallup typically finds about a quarter of Americans expecting their spending to increase in the next six months, about a quarter expecting it to decrease, and about half expecting it to stay the same.

Second, the most common response across three of the four categories (income, savings, and spending) is that things will "stay the same" in the next six months. The one exception is that slightly more Americans predict their debt load will decrease (42%) than say it will stay the same (38%).

Americans' Expectations for Their Personal Financial Situations, January-May 2005

	Income	Savings	Spending	Debt
% Increase	40	40	28	18
% Stay the same	51	42	48	38
% Decrease	8	15	24	42

However, not all Americans are alike in expecting little change in their personal financial situations. Younger Americans are more likely than older Americans to expect changes in their spending, saving, income, and debt over the next six months. Most young adults, aged 18 to 29, believe their incomes and savings will increase, and 4 in 10 expect their spending to go up.

In general, expectations for personal financial situations grow more stable by age group—18- to 29-year-olds expect the most change in all four aspects, 30- to 49-year-olds expect less change than 18- to 29-year-olds but more than those in older age groups, and so on. A majority of those age 65 and older expect all four financial aspects to remain the same, with income expectations the most stable—70% expect their incomes to remain the same in the next six months.

Personal Finance Expectations by Age, 2005

	18-29 yrs %	30-49 yrs %	50-64 yrs %	65 yrs and older %
Income				
Increase	55	47	33	16
Stay the same	39	45	55	70
Decrease	6	7	11	11
Spending				
Increase	40	30	21	18
Stay the same	40	45	49	61
Decrease	20	24	29	20
Savings				
Increase	56	44	35	23
Stay the same	30	40	45	55
Decrease	13	14	17	15
Debt				
Increase	24	20	14	10
Stay the same	33	30	39	57
Decrease	42	49	45	25

In all groups, the percentage who expect their savings to increase is about the same as the percentage who expect their incomes to increase. For example, 55% of those in the 18- to 29-year-old age group expect their income to increase, and 56% expect their savings to increase. Older Americans are slightly more likely to expect their savings to increase (23%) than their income to increase (16%), but expectations for increased savings are not far below expectations for increased income in any group.

In all age groups except those 65 and older, a smaller percentage expects spending to increase than expects income to increase. Among the oldest age group, 18% expect their spending to increase while 16% expect their income to increase.

So among most Americans, expectations of higher incomes are associated with expectations of increased savings, but not necessarily increased spending.

Bottom Line

These results likely reflect the general pattern of Americans' financial situations, with younger Americans expecting their incomes to increase as they get established in their jobs, allowing them to increase their savings and spending. Whether that improvement actually occurs in the six-month window or just reflects the optimism of youth is another matter that these data cannot answer. As people age, their financial situations likely stabilize, as do their expectations regarding their finances in the near future. And when Americans reach retirement age—and often live on fixed incomes from Social Security benefits and work pensions—they expect their financial situations to change little in the short term.

These results are based on combined data from 5,032 telephone interviews with randomly selected national samples of U.S. adults, age 18 and older, conducted January-May 2005. For results based on this sample, one can say with 95% confidence that the maximum margin of error associated with sampling is ±1 percentage point.

For results based on the sample of 587 18- to 29-year-olds, the maximum margin of sampling error is ±4 percentage points.

For results based on the sample of 1,876 30- to 49-year-olds, the maximum margin of sampling error is ±3 percentage points.

For results based on the sample of 1,421 50- to 64-year-olds, the maximum margin of sampling error is ±3 percentage points.

For results based on the sample of 1,094 Americans 65 and older, the maximum margin of sampling error is ±3 percentage points.

June 8, 2005
MORE AMERICANS SEEING VULNERABILITY IN U.S. DEFENSE
Still, nearly half say the military is as strong as it should be

by Joseph Carroll, Gallup Poll Assistant Editor

In mid-May, the Pentagon announced a proposal for downsizing military bases, including shutting down 33 large bases within the United States. President George W. Bush supports the measure to close these military bases in an effort to make the military more efficient in fighting the war on terrorism. By September, the Base Realignment and Closure Commission will submit to Bush a list of bases that would be closed, for his approval or disapproval. If the president approves, Congress would have to pass a joint resolution to keep the base closures from happening. Although it is not a cost-cutting measure per se, this reallocation of resources does raise the issue of defense spending, more generally.

Gallup's February World Affairs survey found a plurality of Americans believing the federal government was spending the right amount on the military and defense. The rest of the public was evenly divided as to whether the government is spending too little or too much on national defense. Nearly half of Americans said the country's national defense is as strong as it should be, while 4 in 10 said it is not strong enough and 1 in 10 said it is stronger than it needs to be. Since last year, both the percentage of Americans saying the government is spending too little on the military and the percentage saying the military is not strong enough have increased. (It is important to note that this poll was conducted before the announcement of military base closings.)

Military Spending

The latest update, conducted Feb. 7-10, found Americans evenly split as to whether the government is spending "too little" (30%) or "too much" (30%) on national defense. A plurality, 38%, says the government is spending "about the right amount." While the percentage of Americans saying the government is spending too much shows little change since last year, the percentage saying "too little" increased by eight points and the percentage saying "about the right amount" decreased by seven points.

Since Gallup first asked this question in 1969, the results have fluctuated significantly. Throughout the late 1960s and 1970s, a majority or a plurality of Americans said the government was spending too much on the military, although this percentage showed a

Trend: Military Spending

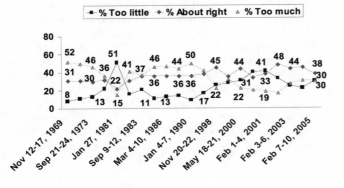

Trend: Strength of the Military

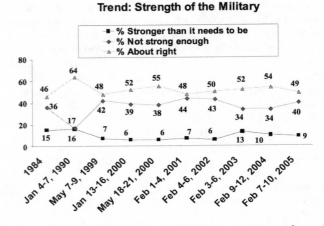

gradual decline over this time period. There was a brief shift in opinion following Ronald Reagan's inauguration in 1980, when about half of Americans said the government was spending too little on defense. In the remaining years of Reagan's administration, though, Americans were most likely to say the government was spending too much on defense. This sentiment reached a high of 47% in 1986.

By 1998, opinions had shifted once again, with a plurality of Americans saying the government was spending the right amount on the military. That poll found the rest of the public divided as to whether the government was spending too much (22%) or too little (26%) on defense.

Then, in 2000, as the presidential race between Democratic candidate Al Gore and Republican candidate George W. Bush headed into the heat of the fall campaign season, 40% of Americans said the government was spending too little on defense, while 34% said the right amount and 20% said too much. This sentiment persisted through the initial days of Bush's presidency in 2001. But since the Sept. 11 attacks, Gallup has found that a plurality of Americans feel the government is spending the right amount on defense.

Over the past several years, Gallup has found substantial partisan differences about government spending on the military. Among Republicans in the most recent poll, just 9% say the government is spending too much, while 39% say too little. A slim majority of Republicans, 51%, say the government is spending the right amount for military and defense purposes. Among Democrats, 41% say the government is spending too much, 25% say too little, and 33% say the right amount.

Military Strength

The Feb. 7-10 poll found that nearly half of Americans, 49%, said that in terms of its strength, the country's national defense is "about right"

at the present time. Forty percent said it is not strong enough, up six points from last year. Nine percent felt it is stronger than necessary.

Since this question was first asked in 1984, few Americans have ever told Gallup that the country's defense is stronger than necessary, but there have been significant variations in the percentages of Americans saying it is not strong enough or about right.

Before the start of the current Bush administration, Americans consistently said the strength of the country's defense was about right, with percentages ranging from 46% to 64%. The percentages of Americans who said the country's defense was not strong enough ranged from 17% to 42% during this same period.

When Bush first took office in 2001, Americans were almost evenly divided as to whether the national defense was about right (48%) or not strong enough (44%). Over the next three years, after the Sept. 11 attacks and then the war in Iraq, increasing numbers of Americans said the country's defense was about right. Last year, a majority of Americans, 54%, said the national defense was about right, while only a third (34%) said it was not strong enough.

Republicans and Democrats differ slightly in their views about the strength of the country's military. Five percent of Republicans say the military is stronger than it needs to be, while 40% say it is not strong enough, and a majority (55%) says it is about right. Among Democrats, 11% say it is stronger than necessary, 41% say it is not strong enough, and 45% say about right.

Another question, from Gallup's January Mood of the Nation poll, asked Americans how satisfied they were with the "nation's military strength and preparedness." The results showed that two in three Americans said they were "very" (28%) or "somewhat" satisfied (38%). This sentiment is down considerably this year—roughly

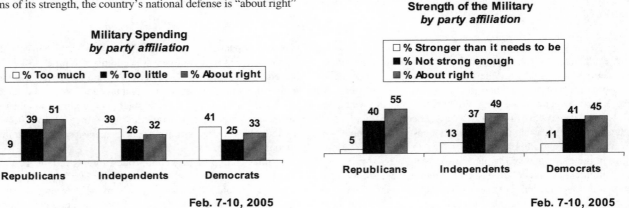

8 in 10 Americans said they were satisfied with the strength and preparedness of the military in polls conducted from 2002 through 2004.

Survey Methods

These results are based on telephone interviews with a randomly selected national sample of 1,008 adults, aged 18 and older, conducted Feb. 7-10, 2005. For results based on this sample, one can say with 95% confidence that the maximum error attributable to sampling and other random effects is ±3 percentage points. In addition to sampling error, question wording and practical difficulties in conducting surveys can introduce error or bias into the findings of public opinion polls.

June 9, 2005

SEX OFFENDER REGISTRIES ARE UNDERUTILIZED BY THE PUBLIC

Two-thirds think it's likely they live by a convicted child molester, but only 23% have checked

by Lydia Saad, Gallup Poll Senior Editor

The February rape and murder of 9-year-old Jessica Lunsford in Florida by a convicted sex offender helped spur U.S. Attorney General Alberto Gonzales to recently announce plans to put a National Sex Offender Registry on the Internet this summer. But as some recent Gallup polling suggests, the key to whether the new registry is effective at reducing child sex crimes could be the amount of effort that goes into publicizing its existence.

Even now, virtually all Americans have access to state records indicating whether convicted sex offenders are living in their local communities, but according to a recent CNN/*USA Today*/Gallup poll, only 38% of Americans think their state maintains such a resource. As a result, only about one-quarter of Americans have checked these lists. The rate is slightly higher among parents of minor children, but only 36% of these people have checked the available registries.

The 1996 federal Megan's Law—so-named after 7-year-old Megan Kanka, who was raped and murdered by a neighboring sex offender—requires all states to maintain an updated registry of sex offenders once they are released into the community. The law also compels states to make this information available to the public, with some latitude concerning how this "notification" component is implemented.

The merits of publicizing this information are virtually undisputed by the public at large. An April 29 - May 1, 2005, Gallup survey finds 94% of Americans in favor, and only 5% opposed, to laws requiring registration of people convicted of child molestation.

Also, there is relatively little sympathy for the argument that such laws will lead to harassment of people named on these registry lists. Only one-third of Americans are very or somewhat concerned about this; 44% are not at all concerned, while another 21% are not too concerned.

Rather, most Americans see the need for public access to information about where sex offenders are living:

- Two-thirds of Americans presume that someone convicted of child molestation probably lives in their neighborhood: 66%

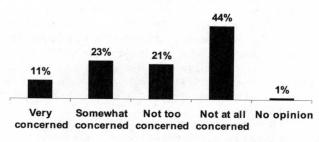

How concerned are you that those laws will lead to harassment of the people whose names are on the lists — very concerned, somewhat concerned, not too concerned, or not at all concerned?

Apr. 29-May 1, 2005

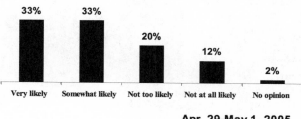

Likelihood That a Convicted Child Molester Lives in Your Neighborhood

Apr. 29-May 1, 2005

think this is very or somewhat likely and only 12% think it is not at all likely.

- Sixty-five percent of Americans believe that child molesters cannot, generally, be rehabilitated.

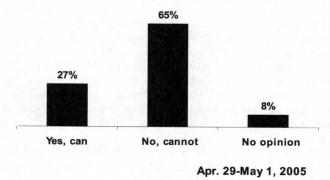

Just your best guess, do you think people who commit the crime of child sexual molestation can be successfully rehabilitated to the point where they are no longer a threat to children, or not?

Apr. 29-May 1, 2005

- Seventy-seven percent say that people who sexually molest children are less likely than other types of serious criminals to be successfully rehabilitated.

What Registry?

Despite all of the national publicity about Megan's Law since its passage in 1996, and despite the fact that, according to a May 2005 speech by Gonzales, 48 states provide Internet-based access to these lists, a majority of Americans are uncertain about whether a publicly available list of sex offenders is maintained in their area. Only 38% say that such a list is maintained, while 4% say it is not maintained and 58% are unsure.

The percentage of Americans who have ever checked a sex offender list is even smaller. Just 23% of U.S. adults have done this, including 36% of adults who are parents of children under the age of 18.

Men and women are about equally likely to have checked such a list, but the rate of checking is slightly higher in urban areas than it is in rural areas (26% to 18%, respectively). Also, residents in the East are less likely to have checked than are those living in other regions of the country.

More limited access to the Internet could be dampening the ability of people from lower income households to review their local registry, but even those in higher income households exhibit a low rate of checking.

Percent Who Have Checked Their Local Sex Offender Registry

	%
Men	25
Women	21
Urban	26
Suburban	23
Rural	18
East	15
Midwest	26
South	24
West	27
$75,000 or more in household income	33
$50,000 - $74,999	31
$30,000 - $49,999	19
Less than $30,000	12
Parents of children under 18 years of age	36
No children under 18 years of age	16

Americans' perceptions about the likelihood that a convicted child molester lives in their neighborhood also has relatively little bearing on whether or not people look up their locale on a sex offender registry. Even those who think it is "very likely" that a child molester lives in their neighborhood are unlikely to have ever checked (only 37% have). The rate is 18% among those who think the chances a child molester lives in the neighborhood are "somewhat likely," 13% among those who say "not too likely" and 23% among those who say "not at all likely."

What does matter is awareness of the existence of state registries. Six in 10 respondents (61%) who believe their state does maintain a registry say they have checked it.

That most Americans are unaware that their state provides this service suggests that a national registry—combined with a national public awareness campaign to raise awareness of the registry and how to access it—could be what is needed to make Megan's Law more effective.

Survey Methods

These results are based on telephone interviews with a randomly selected national sample of 1,006 adults, aged 18 and older, con-

ducted April 29-May 1, 2005. For results based on this sample, one can say with 95% confidence that the maximum error attributable to sampling and other random effects is ±3 percentage points. For results based on the 492 national adults in the Form A half-sample and 514 national adults in the Form B half-sample, the maximum margins of sampling error are ±5 percentage points. For results based on the sample of 381 adults who say they live in an area that maintains a registry of child sex offenders, the maximum margin of sampling error is ±6 percentage points.

In addition to sampling error, question wording and practical difficulties in conducting surveys can introduce error or bias into the findings of public opinion polls.

June 10, 2005
POLITICAL MALAISE CONTINUES
Bush approval at 47%; general satisfaction at 38%

by David W. Moore, Gallup Poll Senior Editor

The latest Gallup survey finds Americans about evenly divided in their assessment of how well President George W. Bush is handling his job, but decidedly negative in their assessment of Congress and of how things are going in the country. Iraq and the economy continue to top the public's list of most important problems facing the country.

The poll, conducted June 6-8, shows that 47% of Americans approve, and 49% disapprove, of Bush's job performance. In the past nine polls, since the third week in March, Bush has averaged a 48% to 48% approval to disapproval rating. In the previous nine Gallup readings, taken between Jan. 3 and March 20, Bush averaged a 52% to 44% approval to disapproval rating.

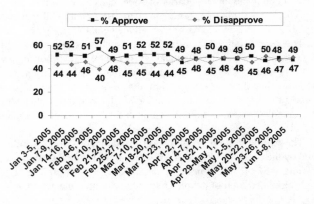

**Bush's Overall Job Approval Ratings
January 2005 – June 2005**

The public's rating of Congress is far more negative than its rating of Bush. Just 34% of Americans approve of the job Congress is doing, while 59% disapprove—the lowest Gallup rating since July 1997. Last month's rating was almost as bad—35% approval to 57% disapproval—but earlier this year, more than 4 in 10 approved. In 2004, approval did not dip below the 40% mark; and in 2003, it hovered just at or below the 50% level for the first seven months, but averaged only 42% for the rest of the year.

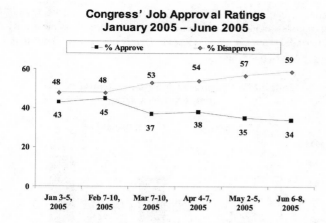

**Congress' Job Approval Ratings
January 2005 – June 2005**

	Jan 3-5, 2005	Feb 7-10, 2005	Mar 7-10, 2005	Apr 4-7, 2005	May 2-5, 2005	Jun 6-8, 2005
% Approve	43	45	37	38	35	34
% Disapprove	48	48	53	54	57	59

Satisfaction with the way things are going in the country has remained essentially unchanged over the past 11 weeks, with 38% of Americans expressing satisfaction in mid-March and again in early April, rising slightly to 41% in late May and then falling back to its current reading of 38%.

This satisfaction rating is substantially below the high ratings Gallup measured both in the months after Sept. 11, 2001, and in the late 1990s during the robust economic years of the dot-com boom. Still, the satisfaction level is not as low as it has been at other points in the past. In the summer of 1992, for example, only 14% of Americans were satisfied with the way things were going in the United States, and only 12% were satisfied in July 1979.

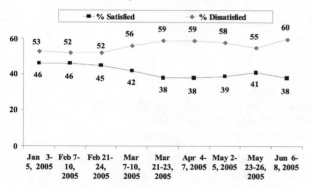

**Satisfaction With Way Things Are Going in U.S.
January 2005 – June 2005**

	Jan 3-5, 2005	Feb 7-10, 2005	Feb 21-24, 2005	Mar 7-10, 2005	Mar 21-23, 2005	Apr 4-7, 2005	May 2-5, 2005	May 23-26, 2005	Jun 6-8, 2005
% Satisfied	46	46	45	42	38	38	39	41	38
% Dissatisfied	53	52	52	56	59	59	58	55	60

Compared with a month ago, the poll also shows little change in the public's view of the most important problem facing the country today. The war in Iraq continues to head the list, mentioned by 22% of Americans, followed by the economy in general (12%), unemployment (9%), healthcare (9%), terrorism (8%), and a general dissatisfaction with government and politicians (8%).

What do you think is the most important problem facing this country today? [Open-ended]

	Jun 6-8, 2005 %	May 2-5, 2005 %	Apr 4-7, 2005 %
ECONOMIC PROBLEMS (NET)	**30**	**33**	**34**
Economy in general	12	12	12
Unemployment/Jobs	9	8	8
Fuel/Oil prices	4	8	9
Federal budget deficit/ Federal debt	3	3	3
Taxes	1	1	1
High cost of living/Inflation	1	1	3
Lack of money	1	1	1
Wage issues	1	1	1
Gap between rich and poor	1	*	1
Foreign trade/Trade deficit	*	*	*
Corporate corruption	*	*	*
Recession	—	—	—
NON-ECONOMIC PROBLEMS (NET)	**74**	**74**	**73**
Situation in Iraq/War	22	21	18
Poor healthcare/hospitals; high cost of healthcare	9	7	7
Terrorism	8	5	8
Dissatisfaction with government/ Congress/ politicians/ candidates; poor leadership; corruption	8	5	5
Social Security	6	9	8
Ethics/Moral/ Religious/ Family decline; dishonesty; lack of integrity	6	4	6
Immigration/Illegal aliens	5	5	4
Foreign aid/Focus overseas	5	2	2
Education/Poor education/ Access to education	5	5	6
Poverty/ Hunger/ Homelessness	4	4	2
Judicial system/Courts/Laws	2	2	2
International issues/ problems	2	2	2
National security	2	3	3
Crime/Violence	2	4	1
Drugs	2	1	1
Children's behavior/ way they are raised	1	1	1
Environment/Pollution	1	1	1
Medicare	1	1	2
Welfare	1	1	1
Lack of respect for each other	1	1	1
Abortion	1	*	1
Homosexuality/Gay issues	*	*	1
Care for the elderly	*	1	1
Lack of energy sources; the energy crisis	*	1	1
Unifying the country	*	1	1
The media	*	*	*
Overpopulation	*	*	*
Race relations/ Racism	*	1	1
Child abuse	*	—	*
Abuse of power	—	*	*
Election year/Presidential choices/Election reform	—	*	—
Guns/Gun control	—	*	—
Cancer/Diseases	—	—	*

	Jun 6-8, 2005 %	May 2-5, 2005 %	Apr 4-7, 2005 %
Other non-economic	5	4	3
No opinion	3	3	2
TOTAL	135%	130%	131%

* Less than 0.5%

Social Security has fallen in importance as the White House has focused its attention on other issues. While 12% of Americans mentioned this issue as the most important in February and March, just 6% mention it in the current survey.

Partisan Polarization

As with previous surveys, this poll shows major differences in perceptions by party affiliation.

While 88% of Republicans approve of Bush's job performance, just 11% of Democrats approve—a difference of 77 points. Only 40% of independents approve, making them closer to the Democrats than to the Republicans.

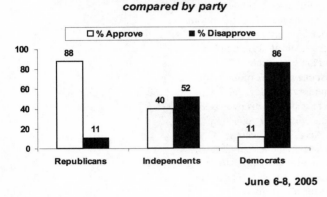

Bush's Overall Job Approval Rating
compared by party

June 6-8, 2005

Polarization is not as great on the public's approval of Congress. Exactly half, 50%, of Republicans approve, compared with only 21% of Democrats—a 29-point difference. Again, independents are closer to Democrats than Republicans, with a 30% approval rating.

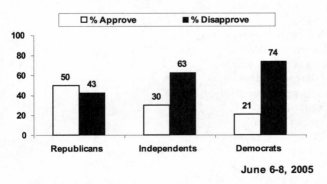

Congress' Job Approval Rating
compared by party

June 6-8, 2005

The general mood question—satisfaction with the way things are going in the country—shows a substantial polarization between Republicans and Democrats, though smaller than on Bush approval.

Among Republicans, 67% are satisfied, compared with 13% among Democrats—a 54-point difference. As with the other two measures, independents are somewhat closer to Democrats in their views than they are to Republicans.

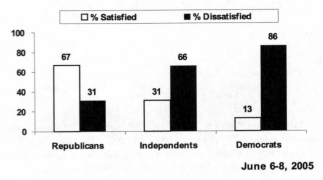

Satisfaction With Way Things Are Going in U.S.
compared by party

June 6-8, 2005

Survey Methods

Results in the current survey are based on telephone interviews with 1,002 national adults, aged 18 and older, conducted June 6-8, 2005. For results based on the total sample of national adults, one can say with 95% confidence that the maximum margin of sampling error is ±3 percentage points.

In addition to sampling error, question wording and practical difficulties in conducting surveys can introduce error or bias into the findings of public opinion polls.

June 13, 2005
NEARLY 6 IN 10 AMERICANS SUPPORT TROOP REDUCTIONS IN IRAQ
Basic support for the war near all-time low

by Jeffrey M. Jones, Gallup Poll Managing Editor

A new Gallup Poll finds most Americans favoring a partial or complete withdrawal of U.S. troops in Iraq, and for the first time, a majority say they would be upset with the president if he decided to send more troops. This comes at a time when basic support for the war is as low as it has been since the war began. The poll probed Americans' reasons for believing the war was or was not worth fighting. Those who favor the war generally cite the Bush administration's various stated motivations for going to war, such as freeing the Iraqi people from an oppressive regime. Those who oppose the war believe there was insufficient justification for going to war, or say the costs have been too high given the lack of progress.

The June 6-8 poll finds 56% of Americans saying it was *not* worth going to war in Iraq, while 42% say it was worth it. These results are essentially the same as in a late April/early May poll (41% worth it, 57% not worth it), which represent the lowest levels of war support since fighting began in March 2003. Since last October, at least half of Americans have consistently said the war was not worth it.

Worth Going to War in Iraq?
Selected Trend: January 2004 —
June 2005

weapons of mass destruction (17%), Iraq not posing a threat to the United States (15%), or that the United States should not police the world (11%). Those who base their opposition on the status of the war cite the number of people killed or wounded (15%), the war being poorly planned (8%), a lack of progress made (3%), or a lack of resolution (3%).

In your own words, why do you think the situation in Iraq was NOT worth going to war over? [OPEN-ENDED; MULTIPLE RESPONSES ALLOWED]

BASED ON ADULTS WHO SAY THE SITUATION IN IRAQ WAS NOT WORTH GOING TO WAR OVER

	Jun 6-8, 2005 %	Jun 27-29, 2003 %
Fraudulent claims/No weapons of mass destruction/Lied to the people about them	17	24
All people killed/wounded	15	24
Iraq was not a threat to the U.S./ Not justified in attacking	15	—
Stop policing the world/Not our business	11	11
Poorly planned	8	—
All about big business/oil/gas	7	7
Needed more evidence/time to investigate/ make a case for war	5	12
Bush's personal vendetta	5	—
Need to take care of own problems first	5	3
They have been fighting for years/ cannot stop them	5	—
Not making any progress	3	—
Nothing has been resolved	3	—
Other countries are more of a threat	3	6
It is going on too long	3	—
U.S. looks like a bully trying to control the world	2	7
The U.S. has made things worse	2	—
The Iraqis do not want us there	2	—
Costing the U.S. too much money	2	—
Opposed to war/Needed to be handled peacefully	1	9
Other	16	8
No opinion	2	3

Gallup asked Americans to explain their positions on the Iraq war. Supporters are most likely to agree with the various motivations for going to war advanced by the Bush administration—to combat terrorism, to free the Iraqi people from oppression, to protect the United States from the Iraq threat, and to remove Saddam Hussein from power. Nine percent say they support the war as a means of promoting peace in the Middle East and 7% say the U.N. resolutions against Iraq needed to be enforced.

In your own words, why do you think the situation in Iraq was worth going to war over? [OPEN-ENDED; MULTIPLE RESPONSES ALLOWED]

BASED ON ADULTS WHO SAY THE SITUATION IN IRAQ WAS WORTH GOING TO WAR OVER

	Jun 6-8, 2005 %	Jun 27-29, 2003 %
Because of Sept. 11/To stop terrorism	20	13
Need to free the Iraqi people/stop the oppression	20	18
Protect the nation/Stop the threat to world security	19	30
Removing Saddam Hussein from power (evil/cruel dictator)	16	27
To promote democracy/peace in the Middle East	9	5
U.N. resolutions needed enforcement/ doing what the U.N. should've done	7	—
To show that you cannot mess with the United States	6	4
Protect freedom	4	—
To stop weapons of mass destruction from being sold or made	3	8
Protect our oil interests	2	—
Create world peace	2	—
Other	12	4
No opinion	1	3

Opponents generally cite two broad classes of responses for their anti-war stance—being opposed to the initial decision to go to war and negative assessments of the war's progress. The former category is represented by responses such as false claims that Iraq had

U.S. Troop Levels in Iraq

Gallup finds Americans much more likely to favor reducing U.S. troops in Iraq than increasing or maintaining the status quo. Given a choice of four options, 59% say the United States should withdraw some (31%) or all (28%) of its troops, while 26% say the number should be kept the same as now and 10% say it should be increased.

That is a significant increase in support for troop reduction since the question was last asked. In February, immediately following the Iraqi elections, 49% favored a reduction in the number of U.S. troops in Iraq. The current percentage favoring troop reductions is the highest Gallup has found to date, just slightly above a 57% reading in October 2003.

A follow-up question asks those who favor troop reduction or maintenance of the status quo whether they would be "upset" if the

What Should the United States Do About Troop Levels in Iraq?

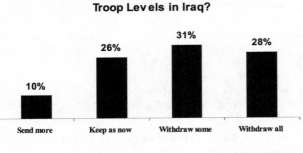

| Send more | Keep as now | Withdraw some | Withdraw all |
| 10% | 26% | 31% | 28% |

June 6-8, 2005

president decides to send more troops to Iraq. This question is designed to gauge how much latitude the president might have in this area, as many Americans who express a preference for the status quo or a reduction might nevertheless support the president if he decided that increased troop levels were necessary. Fifty-six percent of all Americans say they would be upset if Bush sent more troops to Iraq, while 37% would not be. That is the first time a majority of the public said it would be upset with an increase in troops since Gallup first asked the follow-up in April 2004.

Upset if George W. Bush Sends More Troops to Iraq?

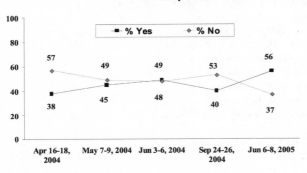

- % Yes   - % No

	Apr 16-18, 2004	May 7-9, 2004	Jun 3-6, 2004	Sep 24-26, 2004	Jun 6-8, 2005
Yes	38	45	48	40	56
No	57	49	49	53	37

Seventy-six percent of Democrats say they would be upset if Bush sent more troops to Iraq, more than double the percentage of Republicans (32%). Independents (61%) are more aligned with Democrats than Republicans on this matter.

More generally, 72% of Democrats say they favor a partial or complete withdrawal from Iraq, along with 65% of independents and

What Should the United States Do About Troop Levels in Iraq?
by party affiliation

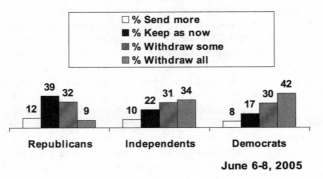

- □ % Send more
- ■ % Keep as now
- ■ % Withdraw some
- ■ % Withdraw all

	Republicans	Independents	Democrats
Send more	12	10	8
Keep as now	39	22	17
Withdraw some	32	31	30
Withdraw all	9	34	42

June 6-8, 2005

41% of Republicans. Forty-two percent of Democrats favor a complete withdrawal of U.S. troops from Iraq.

Survey Methods

These results are based on telephone interviews with a randomly selected national sample of 1,002 adults, aged 18 and older, conducted June 6-8, 2005. For results based on this sample, one can say with 95% confidence that the maximum error attributable to sampling and other random effects is ±3 percentage points. In addition to sampling error, question wording and practical difficulties in conducting surveys can introduce error or bias into the findings of public opinion polls.

June 14, 2005
HIGH SCHOOL: WORST OF TIMES OR BEST OF TIMES?
Most wish they'd hit the books a little harder

by Heather Mason Kiefer, Contributing Editor

As another school year draws to a close, many of the nation's high school seniors are graduating, signing each other's yearbooks, and reflecting upon their experiences of the past four years. When they look back on high school later in life, are their memories more likely to be positive or negative?

A recent Gallup Poll Panel survey* asked 1,000 U.S. adults to describe how much they enjoyed their high school years. The results suggest most enjoyed them. A small percentage of panel respondents, 7%, described their time in high school as "the best time" in their lives. A little more than half (54%) said high school was "a great time" in their lives, while a little more than a third (35%) described that period as "a so-so time." Only 4% said their years in high school were "the worst years" of their lives.

Would you describe high school as:
Asked of U.S. adults

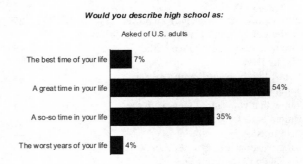

The best time of your life	7%
A great time in your life	54%
A so-so time in your life	35%
The worst years of your life	4%

Importance of High School

Academically and socially, high school is a transition period between childhood and adulthood. Academic responsibilities increase, and students are given more freedom than they had in middle school to navigate their own way through the school day and interact with peers. The importance of a high school education is obvious in today's society, but which high school learning experiences are particularly essential for turning schoolchildren into productive, self-sufficient adults?

Responses to the panel survey reflect the idea that being successful in high school is about more than just getting good grades. When respondents were asked in an open-ended question to name the "single most important thing" they learned in high school, the largest percentage gave answers related to "social skills" or "getting along with others." Academic pursuits weren't disregarded—12% mentioned various academic subjects, 13% study habits, and 8% the importance of getting a good education.

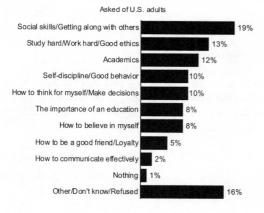

What was the single most important thing you learned in high school? (open-ended)

Asked of U.S. adults

Social skills/Getting along with others	19%
Study hard/Work hard/Good ethics	13%
Academics	12%
Self-discipline/Good behavior	10%
How to think for myself/Make decisions	10%
The importance of an education	8%
How to believe in myself	8%
How to be a good friend/Loyalty	5%
How to communicate effectively	2%
Nothing	1%
Other/Don't know/Refused	16%

If I Could Do It All Over Again ...

Although many people don't feel academic skills were the most important things they learned in high school, a majority do wish they'd hit the books a little harder. Six in 10 respondents (60%) said they wish they'd spent more time on their grades in high school. In contrast, just 16% said they wish they'd spent more time "partying and having a good time." Fifty-one percent wish they'd spent more time on music and art—two subjects that tend to receive a minimal amount of emphasis in high school. Thirty-five percent wish they'd spent more time playing sports.

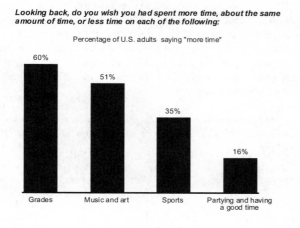

Looking back, do you wish you had spent more time, about the same amount of time, or less time on each of the following:

Percentage of U.S. adults saying "more time"

Grades	Music and art	Sports	Partying and having a good time
60%	51%	35%	16%

Bottom Line

Some popular movies about high school, such as *Mean Girls* and *Heathers*, portray students who experience extreme angst and unhappiness, while others such as *Bring It On* illustrate teenagers enjoying their time in high school. Gallup data suggest most people experience something in between these two extremes—they don't

see high school as the best time in their lives, but very few see it as the worst time either.

*These results are based on telephone interviews with a randomly selected national sample of 1,000 adults in the Gallup Poll Panel of households, aged 18 and older, conducted March 1 to March 22, 2005. For results based on this sample, one can say with 95% confidence that the maximum error attributable to sampling and other random effects is ±3 percentage points. In addition to sampling error, question wording and practical difficulties in conducting surveys can introduce error or bias into the findings of public opinion polls.

June 14, 2005

DO AMERICANS GIVE WOMEN A FIGHTING CHANCE?
Service other than active combat OK with Americans

by Darren K. Carlson, Government and Politics Editor

After two weeks of intense House debate, a measure that sought to limit women's roles in active military combat was withdrawn late last month. Women are currently prohibited from serving in infantry, armor, and some artillery units, but serve in combat support units. The measure essentially would have forced the Army to strictly comply with a 1994 Pentagon policy barring female soldiers from direct ground combat below the brigade level. Senior Army leaders opposed the measure, citing the potential loss of at least 21,000 combat support-related jobs and confusion among troops serving in Iraq.

A recent CNN/*USA Today*/Gallup poll* shows that a majority of Americans support women serving in combat zones as support for ground troops and serving anywhere in Iraq. However, most oppose women serving as "ground troops who are doing most of the fighting."

The survey asked respondents about women serving in three different military roles. A substantial majority (72%) of Americans favor women "serving anywhere in Iraq." Two-thirds (67%) support women serving in combat zones as support for ground troops. But when asked about women "serving as ground troops who are doing most of the fighting," just 44% are in favor.

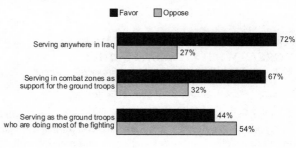

Next, I will read you a list of jobs in the military. Do you favor or oppose having women do each of the following? How about . . . ?

■ Favor ■ Oppose

	Favor	Oppose
Serving anywhere in Iraq	72%	27%
Serving in combat zones as support for the ground troops	67%	32%
Serving as the ground troops who are doing most of the fighting	44%	54%

Who's Most Willing to Let Women Fight?

Women are slightly more likely than men to favor the idea of women serving as ground combat troops, 47% compared with 42%. The

House measure that proposed limits on women's roles in combat was Republican-sponsored, and the poll finds Republican identifiers (37%) less likely to favor women serving as ground troops in combat than are independents (49%) or Democrats (47%).

Age is a particularly significant factor in American's views of whether women should serve as ground combat troops. The youngest American adults (those aged 18 to 29) are most likely to favor the idea of women participating in heavy fighting, and support decreases with age: 60% of 18- to 29-year-olds favor the idea, as do half (50%) of 30- to 49-year-olds, 36% of those aged 50 to 64, and only 33% of people aged 65 and older. The age differences could reflect the changes in women's roles in recent military conflicts—which is what younger Americans have only known—or a tendency among younger Americans to be more liberal.

Next, I will read you a list of jobs in the military. Do you favor or oppose having women do each of the following? . . . How about serving as the ground troops who are doing most of the fighting?

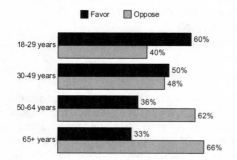

The data also show similar age differences in regard to views of whether women should serve in combat zones in a supporting role or serve in Iraq.

Results are based on telephone interviews with 1,006 national adults, aged 18 and older, conducted May 20-22, 2005. For results based on the total sample of national adults, one can say with 95% confidence that the maximum margin of sampling error is ±3 percentage points. In addition to sampling error, question wording and practical difficulties in conducting surveys can introduce error or bias into the findings of public opinion polls.

June 14, 2005

INSTANT REACTION: PLURALITY OF PUBLIC DISAGREES WITH JACKSON VERDICT

Majority of whites disagree, majority of nonwhites agree

by David W. Moore, Gallup Poll Senior Editor

Forty-eight percent of Americans disagree, and 34% agree, with the not guilty verdict in the Michael Jackson child molestation case, according to a CNN/*USA Today*/Gallup instant reaction poll conducted last night.

As you may know, the jury in the Michael Jackson trial announced their verdict today that Jackson is NOT guilty of sexually molesting a young boy. Do you agree or disagree with the verdict?

	Agree	Disagree	No opinion
2005 Jun 13	34%	48	18

In 1995, after the verdict was announced in the murder trial of O.J. Simpson, an instant reaction poll also found more Americans disagreeing than agreeing with the jury, and by an even larger margin than in the Jackson case—56% to 33%.

As you many know, the jury in the O.J. Simpson trial announced their verdict today that Simpson is not guilty on both charges of murder. Do you agree or disagree with the verdict?

	Agree	Disagree	MIXED (vol.)	No opinion
1995 Oct 3	33%	56	4	7

(vol.) = Volunteered response

The current poll also shows a major racial divide in attitudes. Whites disagree with the decision by about a 2-to-1 margin (54% to 28%), while nonwhites take the opposite point of view, also by about a 2-to-1 margin (56% to 26%).

Reactions to Jury Verdicts

	Agree	Disagree	No opinion
JACKSON CASE			
2005 June 13	%	%	%
All adults	34	48	18
BY RACE			
Whites	28	54	18
Nonwhites	56	26	18
SIMPSON CASE			
1995 Oct 3			
All adults	33	56	11
BY RACE			
Whites	27	62	11
Nonwhites	67	24	9

The Simpson case provided a somewhat more racially divided public than did the Jackson case—but in both situations, clear majorities of whites disagreed with clear majorities of nonwhites.

When asked whether different sentiments characterized their reactions to the verdict, about half of all respondents say they are "surprised," a third are "sad," a little over a quarter are "pleased," while a little under a quarter are "outraged."

Please tell me whether each of the following describes or does not describe your reaction to the jury's verdict. How about [RANDOM ORDER]?

2005 Jun 13 (sorted by "yes, describes")	Yes, describes %	No, does not %	No opinion %
Surprised	47	52	1
Sad	34	62	4
Pleased	27	67	6
Outraged	24	73	3

By comparison, slightly more Americans were surprised about the verdict in the Simpson case than in the Jackson case, many more Americans were sad, but about the same percentages were outraged and pleased.

Trends for comparison: The O.J. Simpson verdict

1995 Oct 3	Yes, describes %	No, does not %	No opinion %
Surprised	52	47	1
Sad	50	48	2
Outraged	28	69	3
Pleased	26	71	3

A clear majority of Americans, 62%, believe that Jackson's celebrity status was a major factor in the jury's verdict, while about half that number say his celebrity status was either a minor factor (17%) or not a factor at all (18%).

Just your best guess, do you think Michael Jackson's celebrity status was a major factor, a minor factor, or not a factor at all in the jury's verdict?

	Major factor	Minor factor	Not a factor at all	No opinion
2005 Jun 13	62%	17	18	3

During and after the trial, some observers suggested that with a not guilty verdict, Jackson might try a comeback, either with a world tour or a new album. The poll indicates that about half of Jackson's fan base has stayed with him, while the other half has not.

Which comes closest to your view—[ROTATED: you were never a fan of Michael Jackson, you were a fan of Michael Jackson before the charges about misconduct with young boys first surfaced, but you are not a fan now, or you are still a fan of Michael Jackson]?

	Never a fan %	Fan before charges, not a fan now %	Still a fan %	No opinion %
All adults	50	22	25	3
BY AGE				
18-49	36	28	33	3
50+	69	14	15	2

Overall, 50% of all Americans say they are not now, nor have they ever been, Jackson fans. Another 22% say they used to be fans, but are not any longer. That leaves 25% of adults who say they are still fans, including 33% of people under 50, and 15% of people 50 and older. If these numbers hold up in the ensuing weeks and months, this would be a very sizable base if Jackson attempts a comeback.

While the Jackson case received a great deal of media attention, the public was more mesmerized by the Simpson trial 10 years ago. The poll shows that half of all Americans say they personally watched or listened to the Jackson verdict, while 80% said they personally watched or listened to the Simpson verdict.

Did you personally watch or listen to the verdict announcement on television or radio today as it was being announced, or did you hear about it later?

	Personally watched/ listened to	Heard about it later	No opinion
2005 Jun 13	49%	50	1

Trends for comparison: The O.J. Simpson verdict

	Personally watched/ listened to	Heard about it later	No opinion
1995 Oct 3	80%	19	1

Survey Methods

Results in the current survey are based on telephone interviews with 635 national adults, aged 18 and older, conducted June 13, 2005. The jury's verdict that found Jackson not guilty on 10 separate counts was announced to the public shortly after 5 p.m. Eastern Daylight Time. The national poll of 635 adults was conducted between 6 p.m. and 8:30 p.m. EDT.

For results based on the total sample of national adults, one can say with 95% confidence that the maximum margin of sampling error is ±4 percentage points.

In addition to sampling error, question wording and practical difficulties in conducting surveys can introduce error or bias into the findings of public opinion polls.

Polls conducted entirely in one day, such as this one, are subject to additional error or bias not found in polls conducted over several days.

June 15, 2005
ECONOMIC RATINGS RETREAT SLIGHTLY OVER PAST TWO WEEKS
Americans also more pessimistic about finding a "quality job"

by Joseph Carroll, Gallup Poll Assistant Editor

Americans' perceptions about the state of the nation's economy are down slightly from a few weeks ago, suggesting that any momentum in consumer confidence that may have built up in May is not being sustained. Still, these ratings are more positive than they were in mid-April and early May. Americans also grew somewhat more pessimistic about the job situation in the country this month. Three in 10 Americans mention the economy as the most important problem facing the country today, which is down slightly over the past two months.

Current Economic Conditions

The poll, conducted June 6-8, finds that 35% of Americans rate the current economy as "excellent" or "good," while 20% rate it as "poor." These results show a slight drop since late May, at which time Gallup (and other polls) found an increase in consumer optimism about the economy. This suggests that last month's uptick in economic ratings was not the beginning of a sustained surge. Still, the current ratings are higher now than they were in mid-April and early May.

Ratings of the nation's economy were much more positive at the beginning of the year. In January and early February, Gallup found a net positive score (the percentage describing the economy as excellent

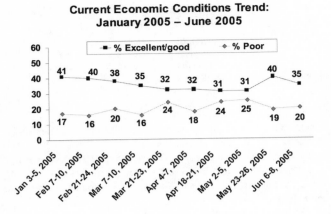

**Current Economic Conditions Trend:
January 2005 – June 2005**

or good minus the percentage describing it as poor) of 24 points. By mid-March, perceptions about the economy began to sour, with the net score dropping to 8 points. These ratings reached their low point for the year, so far, in early May, with a score of 6 points, before rebounding to a score of 21 points a few weeks ago. Now, as noted, the ratings have fallen back.

Economic Outlook

About a third of Americans (35%) in the latest poll say economic conditions in the country are getting better, while the majority of adults nationwide, 55%, say they are getting worse. These results are essentially the same as what Gallup found at the beginning of April, before optimism on this measure declined in mid-April and early May. But these ratings—like the numbers reviewed above—are lower than what Gallup found at the end of May.

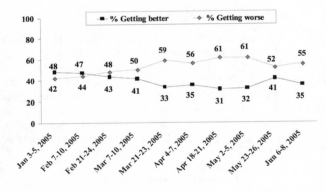

**Economic Outlook Trend:
January 2005 – June 2005**

Americans' assessments of the direction of the nation's economy were much more optimistic earlier in the year. In January, Americans were more positive than negative about the direction of the economy, with 48% saying economic conditions were getting better and 42% saying they were getting worse. By mid-February, the reverse was true, with 48% saying conditions were getting worse and 43% saying conditions were getting better. Perceptions of the economic outlook became more pessimistic over the next several months, before they rebounded somewhat by the end of May, with 41% saying conditions were getting better and 52% saying getting worse in Gallup's May 23-26 survey.

A Good Time to Find a Quality Job?

Americans have also grown somewhat more negative about the job situation in the country. The latest poll finds that 35% of Americans say now is a good time to find a quality job, while more than 6 in 10 Americans (62%) say it is a bad time. Over the past two months, just under 4 in 10 Americans have said it was a good time to find a quality job.

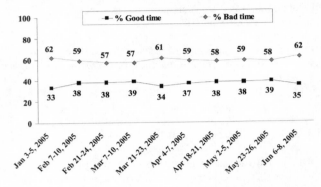

**Good or Bad Time to Find a Quality Job?
Selected Trend: January 2005 – June 2005**

At the beginning of the year, a January Gallup poll found roughly the same results as measured today—33% said it was a good time to find a quality job and 62% said it was a bad time. In February and early March, Americans became more optimistic about jobs in the country, with nearly 4 in 10 saying it was a good time. The public's sentiment about the job situation dipped slightly in late March, but bounced back to the 40% range in April and May.

Rating the Economy as the Most Important Problem

Every month, Gallup asks Americans, without prompting, to name the "most important problem facing this country today." The latest results show that 30% of Americans mention some aspect of the economy, including the general state of the economy (12%), unemployment or jobs (9%), fuel or oil prices (4%), or the federal budget deficit (3%), as the top problem.

The percentage of Americans mentioning some aspect of the economy as the top problem has varied only slightly over the course of the year. In January, 31% of Americans mentioned the economy. This sentiment dipped slightly to 28% by March, before increasing to 34% in April. In May, 33% named the economy. The current results show a modest decline in economic mentions, to 30%.

What else, other than the economy, do Americans mention as the nation's top problem? Twenty-two percent say the situation in Iraq, 9% healthcare, 8% terrorism, 8% issues concerning the government or politicians, 6% Social Security, and 6% ethics and moral issues.

Survey Methods

Results in the current survey are based on telephone interviews with 1,002 national adults, aged 18 and older, conducted June 6-8, 2005. For results based on the total sample of national adults, one can say with 95% confidence that the maximum margin of sampling error is ±3 percentage points.

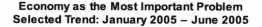

**Economy as the Most Important Problem
Selected Trend: January 2005 – June 2005**

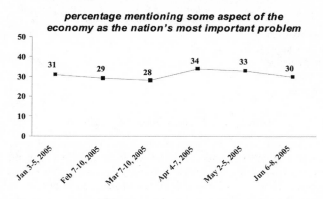

In addition to sampling error, question wording and practical difficulties in conducting surveys can introduce error or bias into the findings of public opinion polls.

June 16, 2005

THREE IN FOUR AMERICANS BELIEVE IN PARANORMAL

Little change from similar results in 2001

by David W. Moore, Gallup Poll Senior Editor

About three in four Americans profess at least one paranormal belief, according to a recent Gallup survey. The most popular is extrasensory perception (ESP), mentioned by 41%, followed closely by belief in haunted houses (37%). The full list of items includes:

	Believe in %
Extrasensory perception, or ESP	41
That houses can be haunted	37
Ghosts/that spirits of dead people can come back in certain places/situations	32
Telepathy/communication between minds without using traditional senses	31
Clairvoyance/the power of the mind to know the past and predict the future	26
Astrology, or that the position of the stars and planets can affect people's lives	25
That people can communicate mentally with someone who has died	21
Witches	21
Reincarnation, that is, the rebirth of the soul in a new body after death	20
Channeling/allowing a 'spirit-being' to temporarily assume control of body	9

A special analysis of the data shows that 73% of Americans believe in at least one of the 10 items listed above, while 27% believe in none of them. A Gallup survey in 2001 provided similar results—76% professed belief in at least one of the 10 items.

Number of paranormal items people believe in	Percent	Cumulative percent
10	1%	1%
9	2	3
8	3	6
7	3	9
6	6	15
5	7	22
4	10	32
3	11	43
2	14	57
1	16	73
None	27	100

The "cumulative percent" column shows that more than one-fifth of all Americans, 22%, believe in five or more items, 32% believe in at least four items, and more than half, 57%, believe in at least two paranormal items. Only 1% believe in all 10 items.

Three other items included in the survey, but which do not necessarily reflect paranormal beliefs, include beliefs in "psychic or spiritual healing or the power of the human mind to heal the body," "that people on earth are sometimes possessed by the devil," and "that extra-terrestrial beings have visited earth at some time in the past."

The healing powers of the mind have been demonstrated empirically, reflected in the power of placebos, among other examples. More than half of Americans, 55%, believe in this connection.

The poll shows that 42% of Americans believe that "people on this earth are sometimes possessed by the devil." However, it is unclear how many people treat that statement literally, and how many interpret it in metaphorical terms. Thus, for purposes of this analysis, that item was excluded.

Strictly speaking, visits from aliens are not part of paranormal beliefs. Although definitive scientific evidence of such visits is lacking, in principle the existence of extra-terrestrial beings and their ability to visit earth are subject to empirical verification.

All of the other 10 items listed above require the belief that humans have more than the "normal" five senses.

Comparison by Demographic Subgroups

The poll shows no statistically significant differences among people by age, gender, education, race, and region of the country. Christians are a little more likely to hold some paranormal beliefs than non-Christians (75% vs. 66%, respectively), but both groups show a sizeable majority with such beliefs.

Several items show modest declines since 2001 in the percentage of people who profess to believe in them, though the overall percentage of people with at least one paranormal belief has declined only slightly—from 76% in 2001 to 73% now.

The largest declines since 2001 are found in the number of people who believe in ESP (41% now compared with 50% in 2001), clairvoyance (26% now, 32% in 2001), ghosts (32% vs. 38%), mentally communicating with the dead (21% vs. 28%), and channeling (9% vs. 15%).

Survey Methods

Results in the current survey are based on telephone interviews with 1,002 national adults, aged 18 and older, conducted June 6-8, 2005.

For results based on the total sample of national adults, one can say with 95% confidence that the maximum margin of sampling error is ±3 percentage points. In addition to sampling error, question wording and practical difficulties in conducting surveys can introduce error or bias into the findings of public opinion polls.

June 17, 2005
AMERICANS' WORRY ABOUT PERSONAL FINANCES HOLDS STEADY
Energy costs have declined as a budget concern

by Lydia Saad, Gallup Poll Senior Editor

The U.S. Labor Department's consumer price index fell by 0.1% in May following months of rising prices, but Americans' level of financial anxiety and their estimated retail spending patterns have been fairly stable since February. This is according to Gallup's monthly economic poll, last updated May 23-26.

The poll also finds that while no single issue dominates the list of most important financial challenges Americans say their families are facing, "healthcare costs" lead, with 18% mentioning this issue. Mentions of "energy costs," which peaked as a concern in April, have since receded.

Financial Worry Has Not Changed

The percentage of Americans who say they are worried about their families' personal financial situations has consistently hovered in the 40% range this year. Approximately 6 in 10 are not worried.

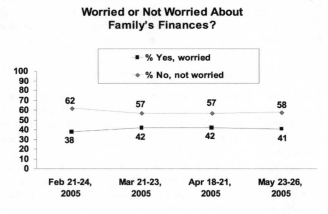

Worried or Not Worried About Family's Finances?

Few Americans, just 15% in May, say they are *very* worried about family finances.

Naturally, concern about one's finances is highly related to household income. Only a small fraction of those in households earning $100,000 or more annually are very or somewhat worried (14%), compared with two-thirds of those earning less than $30,000 a year. The broad middle class—encompassing about 6 in 10 Americans who say their incomes fall between $30,000 and $100,000—tends not to be worried.

Financial Worry by Household Income

	$100,000 or more	$50,000- $99,999	$30,000- $49,999	Less than $30,000
	%	%	%	%
Very worried	3	9	13	36
Somewhat worried	11	23	33	31
Total worried	*14*	*32*	*46*	*67*
Not worried	86	68	54	32

Grocery Bill Exceeds Other Expenditures

The stability in Americans' sense of their personal finances is also evident in a monthly measure tracking Americans' estimates of the amount of money their households will spend that month in four areas: groceries, clothing, dining out, and entertainment and recreation.

In May, the median spending estimates were $300 for groceries and $100 each for clothing, eating out, and entertainment. The *mean* spending estimates—the numeric average of all responses in each category—are higher because big spenders drive up this figure.

According to Americans' May spending projections, the average household grocery bill for the month was $365. That's higher than the $248 Americans expected to spend on entertainment, the $227 anticipated for clothing, and the $123 for dining at a restaurant.

Household Spending Estimates for May

	Mean (including zero)	Median
Groceries	*$365*	*$300*
Clothing	*$227*	*$100*
Eating dinner out	*$123*	*$100*
Entertainment	*$248*	*$100*

The expenditure estimates have been quite steady since Gallup began tracking them in February. One exception is an $81 increase in Americans' expected spending on clothing between March and April, from $170 to $251. That corresponds with national retail sales data showing a significant uptick in sales at clothing and accessories stores in April. (The Census Bureau MARTS data show a 2.7% increase in clothing/accessories spending in April compared with March—representing the largest month-to-month increase observed across all retail sales categories for April.)

Retail Clothing Sales

	Americans' mean spending estimate for May	National retail sales, month-to-month % change*
2005 May 23-26	*$227*	-0.8
2005 Apr 18-21	*$251*	+2.7
2005 Mar 21-23	*$170*	-2.1
2005 Feb 21-24	*$222*	+2.0

*MARTS data

Pump Pressure Eases

The Labor Department reported a 4.4% decline in gasoline prices in May—the biggest one-month decline since last July. That drop is certainly reflected in Gallup's monthly measure of the financial issues confronting average Americans. The percentage of Americans naming energy costs as the most important financial problem facing their families fell from 11% in April to 5% in May. At the same time, the percentage mentioning healthcare costs rose from 14% to 18%.

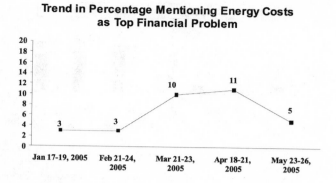

Trend in Percentage Mentioning Energy Costs as Top Financial Problem

Healthcare costs lead the list of financial concerns facing families, followed by lack of money/low wages (mentioned by 12%), and retirement savings (9%); financial debt, unemployment, and college expenses are each mentioned by 8%.

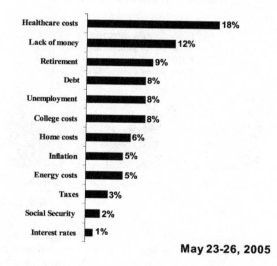

What is the most important financial problem facing your family today?

May 23-26, 2005

Survey Methods

These results are based on telephone interviews with a randomly selected national sample of 1,004 adults, aged 18 and older, conducted May 23-26, 2005. For results based on this sample, one can say with 95% confidence that the maximum error attributable to sampling and other random effects is ±3 percentage points. In addition to sampling error, question wording and practical difficulties in conducting surveys can introduce error or bias into the findings of public opinion polls.

June 20, 2005

MOST POPULAR SEASON COMING TO AN END
Spring rates ahead of summer, fall

by Jeffrey M. Jones, Gallup Poll Managing Editor

If you find you are not in the best mood while reading this article, it may be because you are doing so on Americans' least favorite day of the week, on the last day of the most popular season. A recent Gallup Poll finds that more Americans pick spring as their favorite season and Monday as their least favorite day of the week. Americans clearly prefer Friday and the weekend days to the other days of the week, with Friday a slight overall favorite. There is no consensus in terms of the public's favorite month, with May, June, October, and December most frequently mentioned. A majority of Americans also say they are a "morning person" rather than a "night person."

Seasons

The June 6-8 Gallup Poll finds 36% of Americans naming spring as their favorite season of the year, while 27% prefer fall, 25% summer, and just 11% winter. Each time Gallup has asked the question—in 1947, 1960, and this year—spring is the season the public has been most likely to name as its favorite.

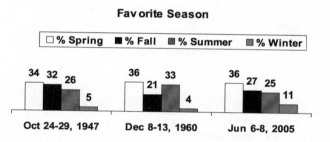

Favorite Season

Favorite seasons differ by age group. For example, Americans aged 18 to 29 are the group least likely to prefer spring (24%), while those 65 and older are most likely to prefer it (53%). Younger Americans are much more likely to prefer summer than are those in older age groups, and, in fact, summer is the top choice among this age group. That could be because many in this age group are students or recently were students, and summer meant a break from classes. Younger Americans are also the age group most likely to say winter is their favorite season.

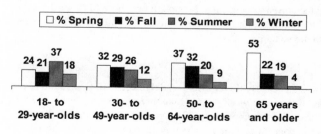

Favorite Season by age group

June 6-8, 2005

Months

The poll shows a lack of consensus when Americans are asked to name their favorite month. Fourteen percent say May, 13% October, 12% June, and 12% December. The months mentioned least often are January, February, and March.

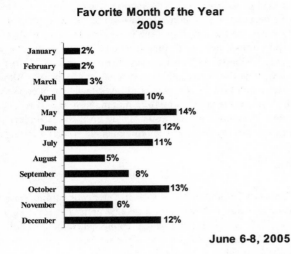

Favorite Month of the Year 2005

January	2%
February	2%
March	3%
April	10%
May	14%
June	12%
July	11%
August	5%
September	8%
October	13%
November	6%
December	12%

June 6-8, 2005

Gallup asked this question previously in 1960, at which time May and June were the favorites, mentioned by 19% and 18%, respectively.

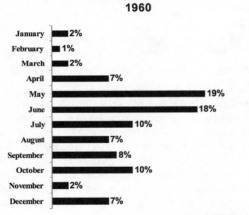

Favorite Month of the Year 1960

January	2%
February	1%
March	2%
April	7%
May	19%
June	18%
July	10%
August	7%
September	8%
October	10%
November	2%
December	7%

Dec. 8-13, 1960

It is unclear whether there might be a seasonal effect in responses to this question, because the 1960 poll was conducted in December and the current poll in June. In 1960, more chose May and June than did so this year, and more now choose November and December than did so then.

Days of the Week

Americans clearly prefer Friday and the weekend days to the beginning of the work week—more than three in four say Friday (29%), Saturday (25%), or Sunday (23%) is their favorite day of the week. That is consistent with data on this question from 1990, though in that poll, Saturday (27%) had a slight edge over Sunday (24%) and Friday (21%).

Favorite Day of the Week

numbers shown in percentages

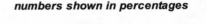

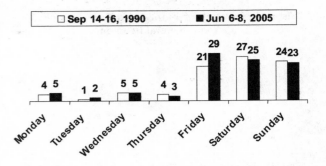

There are differences in favorite day of the week by age. Those in younger age groups are more likely to peg Friday as their favorite day, while those in older age groups are more likely to choose Sunday.

Favorite Day of the Week by age group

numbers shown in percentages

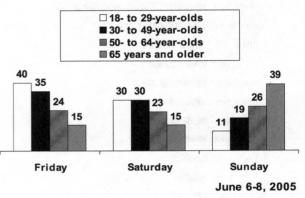

June 6-8, 2005

Older Americans' preference for Sunday is largely driven by the fact that older women favor that day. Among women aged 50 and older, 38% say Sunday is their favorite, 16% Saturday, and 17% Friday. Men aged 50 and older are about equally likely to choose Friday (25%), Saturday (23%), or Sunday (23%) as their favorite. Older women's preference for Sunday could be related to their tendency to be more religious than other age and gender groups, and less likely to be employed.

Gallup also asked Americans to name their least favorite day of the week. Monday is the overwhelming choice, mentioned by 65% of Americans. All other days are in the single digits.

Monday was also the least favorite day when Gallup asked the question in 1990, but now slightly more Americans choose it than did so then (65% compared with 59%).

The data show that Americans' disdain for Monday apparently fades as they grow older and stop working. Seventy-five percent of 18- to 29-year-olds, 72% of 30- to 49-year-olds, 59% of 50- to 64-year-olds, and 49% of those 65 and older say Monday is their least favorite day. Despite the drop among the oldest age group, Monday still is this group's least favorite day; the difference is attributable to the fact that

Least Favorite Day of the Week

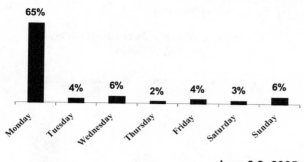

June 6-8, 2005

22% of those 65 and older volunteer that they do not dislike any day in particular. Similarly, 70% of working Americans rate Monday as their least favorite day, compared with 59% of non-working Americans.

Time of Day

To get a sense of the public's preferred time of day, Gallup asked Americans if they considered themselves a "morning person" or a "night person." A majority, 53%, say they are morning people, while 43% say they are at their best at night. Those results are similar to what Gallup found in 1990, when 50% said they were morning people and 40% night people.

Are You a Morning Person or a Night Person?

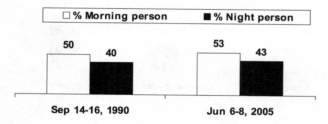

| Sep 14-16, 1990 | Jun 6-8, 2005 |

Americans in most age groups say they are morning people. One dramatic exception occurs among young adults—by a 70% to 29% margin, 18- to 29-year-olds say they are night people. In all other age groups, at least a slim majority say they are morning people.

The results also differ by race: 57% of whites say they are morning people, while 39% say they are night people; among nonwhites, 59% say they are night people and 37% morning people.

Are You a Morning Person or a Night Person?
by age group

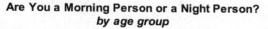
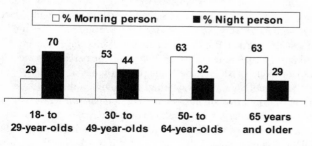

June 6-8, 2005

Survey Methods

These results are based on telephone interviews with a randomly selected national sample of 1,002 adults, aged 18 and older, conducted June 6-8, 2005. For results based on this sample, one can say with 95% confidence that the maximum error attributable to sampling and other random effects is ±3 percentage points. In addition to sampling error, question wording and practical difficulties in conducting surveys can introduce error or bias into the findings of public opinion polls.

June 21, 2005

MAJORITY OF AMERICANS OPPOSE WAR WITH IRAQ
But majority supports continued operation of Guantanamo Bay detention facility

by David W. Moore, Gallup Poll Senior Editor

According to the latest CNN/*USA Today*/Gallup survey, 59% of Americans oppose the war with Iraq, while just 39% favor it—a substantial change from a March poll, when the public was evenly divided, 47% in favor and 47% opposed. This is the first time that a majority has expressed opposition to the war on this question, although these results parallel the findings from a June 6-8 Gallup Poll, which found 56% of Americans saying it was not worth going to war in Iraq, and 59% supporting at least a partial withdrawal of troops from that country.

Support for U.S. War With Iraq

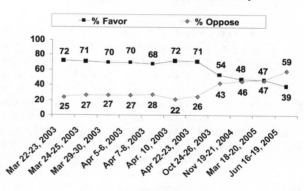

The decline in support for the war is found among Republicans and independents, with little change among Democrats. A substantial majority of Republicans continue to support the war, but the percentage in favor (70%) is 11 percentage points lower than it was in March (81%). Among independents, support has dropped by eight points (from 40% to 32%). Democrats show a 2-point increase in support, along with a 4-point increase in opposition, for a net negative increase of 2 points (from a net 63-point opposition in March to a 65-point opposition in June).

Public Favors Guantanamo Base Detention Facility

In recent weeks, various political leaders and media organizations around the world have called for shutting down the detention facility

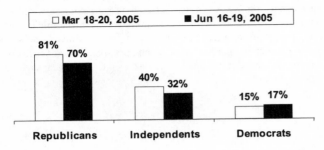

Support for U.S. War With Iraq
by party affiliation
percentage saying "favor"

☐ Mar 18-20, 2005　■ Jun 16-19, 2005

	Republicans	Independents	Democrats
Mar 18-20	81%	40%	15%
Jun 16-19	70%	32%	17%

at the Guantanamo Naval Base, where the United States holds captive more than 500 prisoners, mostly from Afghanistan and Iraq. Opponents include several prominent Republican leaders, such as Florida Sen. Mel Martinez, a former George W. Bush cabinet member, as well as prominent Democrats, such as former presidents Bill Clinton and Jimmy Carter.

But the poll suggests that the public has yet to be persuaded. Overall, 58% say the government should continue to operate the facility, while 36% want to close it.

As you may know, since 2001, the United States has held people from other countries who are suspected of being terrorists at a detention facility in Guantanamo Bay in Cuba. Based on what you have heard or read, do you think the U.S. should—[ROTATED: continue to operate this facility (or do you think the U.S. should) close this facility and transfer the prisoners to other facilities]?

	Continue to operate	Close facility	No opinion
2005 Jun 16-19	58%	36	6

Several news stories recently have reported on alleged abuses of prisoners at Guantanamo. The U.S. military has admitted using coercive interrogation techniques, although it denies such techniques amount to torture. When asked about U.S. treatment of prisoners at the base, 52% of Americans say they approve and 37% disapprove—though intensity of feeling is not widespread. A majority of Americans feel "strongly" about the issue, and they split toward approval rather than disapproval by 33% to 23%. Another 44% do not feel strongly about the issue, including 11% who have no opinion, 19% who approve, and 14% who disapprove.

In general, do you approve or disapprove of the way the U.S. is treating the prisoners being held at Guantanamo Bay in Cuba? Do you [approve/disapprove] strongly, or not strongly?

COMBINED RESPONSES (Q.31-32)

	Approve, strongly	Approve, not strongly	Disapprove, not strongly	Disapprove, strongly	No opinion
2005 Jun 16-19	33%	19	14	23	11

These views are highly related to party affiliation, although the polarization between Republicans and Democrats is somewhat less than what is measured on support for the war in Iraq. Seventy-five percent of Republicans want to keep the detention facility open,

compared with 38% of Democrats—a difference of 37 points. By contrast, there is a 53-point difference between the two parties in their support for the war with Iraq.

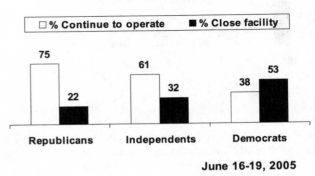

Continue to Operate Guantanamo Bay?
by party affiliation

☐ % Continue to operate　■ % Close facility

	Republicans	Independents	Democrats
% Continue to operate	75	61	38
% Close facility	22	32	53

June 16-19, 2005

Similarly, 73% of Republicans approve of U.S. treatment of prisoners at Guantanamo, compared with 31% of Democrats—a 42-point difference.

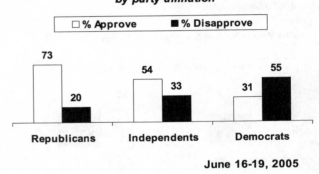

Approve of the Way U.S. Treating Prisoners Held at Guantanamo Bay?
by party affiliation

☐ % Approve　■ % Disapprove

	Republicans	Independents	Democrats
% Approve	73	54	31
% Disapprove	20	33	55

June 16-19, 2005

Public Concern About War on Terror Declines

The poll shows that since the end of the 2004 presidential election, Americans have become less concerned about terrorism. In three measures in 2004, the public was about evenly divided as to how likely there would be more terrorist attacks "over the next several weeks." About half thought such attacks were "very" or "somewhat" likely, while the other half thought they were "not too" or "not at all" likely. But in the two readings in 2005, a clear majority of Americans say the attacks are not likely.

Similarly, in 2004, Americans were most worried about becoming a victim of terrorist attacks shortly before the presidential election, with 47% "very" or "somewhat" worried and 53% "not too" or "not at all" worried. But since that time, the percentage who are worried has dropped nine points (to 38%), and the percentage who are not worried has also increased nine points (to 62%).

Satisfaction with the way things are going for the United States in the war on terrorism has declined in comparison with a similar reading in February, from a poll conducted immediately following the Iraqi elections. But current sentiment (52% satisfied to 47% dissatisfied) is now essentially back to what it was before the election in Iraq.

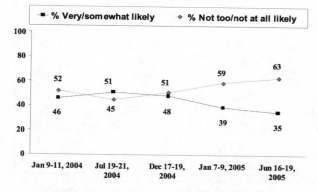

How likely is it that there will be further acts of terrorism in the United States over the next several weeks?

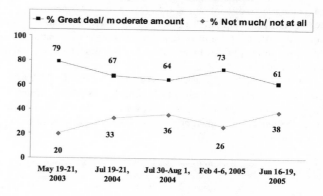

How much confidence do you have in the Bush administration to protect U.S. citizens from future acts of terrorism?

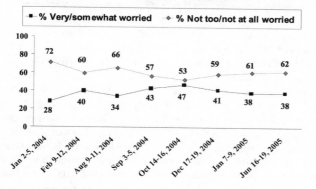

How worried are you that you or someone in your family will become a victim of terrorism?

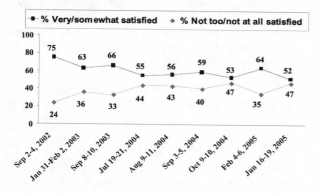

How satisfied are you with the way things are going for the U.S. in the war on terrorism?

that at least half of all Americans have expressed disapproval of Bush's overall job performance, the other time occurring in late May of this year, when 50% disapproved.

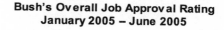

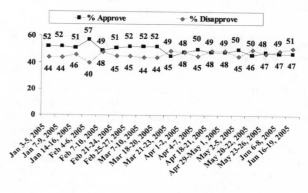

Bush's Overall Job Approval Rating January 2005 – June 2005

Survey Methods

Results in the current survey are based on telephone interviews with 1,006 national adults, aged 18 and older, conducted June 16-19, 2005. For results based on the total sample of national adults, one can say with 95% confidence that the maximum margin of sampling error is ±3 percentage points.

In addition to sampling error, question wording and practical difficulties in conducting surveys can introduce error or bias into the findings of public opinion polls.

Confidence in the Bush administration to protect U.S. citizens has also declined since February, though it remains high—61% have a "great deal" or "moderate amount" of confidence, while just 38% have little or none at all. Current sentiment is similar to what it was last summer, though there was a spike in confidence in February.

Bush's approval rating, 47%, remains unchanged since the previous poll at the beginning of this month, although approval is down 10 points from the Feb. 4-6 poll, when the two previous readings on terrorism were taken.

The current 51% disapproval ties with Bush's highest disapproval rating ever, measured in May 2004. It is only the third time

June 21, 2005

AMERICANS' CONFIDENCE IN HIGH COURT DECLINES
Current rating among lowest ever

by Joseph Carroll, Gallup Poll Assistant Editor

For many Americans, June represents a time to plan summer vacations, to lounge by the pool, or to relax after a long school year. For some, though, especially the political junkies among us, it is most notable as the time when the U.S. Supreme Court hands down a flurry of decisions before taking its annual recess.

A recent Gallup Poll*, conducted May 23-26, asked Americans to rate their level of confidence in 15 institutions in American society, including the Supreme Court. The Supreme Court ranks in the middle of the list, much lower than the military, police, and organized religion, but higher than HMOs, big business, Congress, and organized labor.

Overall, 4 in 10 Americans say they have a great deal (16%) or quite a lot (25%) of confidence in the court. This 41% confidence rating is among the lowest Gallup has ever found for this institution, and it perpetuates a gradual decline in the public's confidence over the past three years.

Confidence in Institutions Trends: The U.S. Supreme Court

Percentage saying "great deal" or "quite a lot"

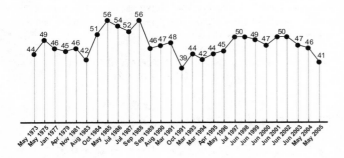

In 1973, about four months after the court ruled on the controversial *Roe v. Wade* case, Gallup found that 44% of Americans expressed confidence in the Supreme Court. Americans' confidence in the court showed only modest fluctuations over the next decade, but by 1984, ratings increased to the point at which a slim majority of Americans, 51%, expressed confidence in the court. Confidence reached its high point over the next several years, with a 56% confidence rating in 1985 and another 56% rating in 1988.

The low point in the public's assessment of the Supreme Court came during the confirmation hearings of Clarence Thomas in 1991. In mid-October of that year, 39% of Americans said they were confident in the Supreme Court. Throughout the rest of the 1990s, confidence in the court gradually increased, reaching 50% in 1997 and 1998.

When President George W. Bush took office in 2001, half of Americans expressed confidence in the court. Views have gradually declined since then, falling to 47% in 2003, 46% in 2004, and 41% this year. This decline in recent years may result from some controversial court decisions on affirmative action and homosexual relations.

Partisan Differences

Generally, Republicans' and Democrats' opinions about the court aren't vastly divergent. When there are differences, there is a tendency for Republicans to express higher levels confidence in the court than Democrats express.

Republicans and Democrats were not radically different in their confidence with the court from 1973 until 1984, at which point 57% of Republicans and only 44% of Democrats said they were confident in the court.

Throughout President George H.W. Bush's term in office, Republicans expressed higher levels of confidence in the court than Democrats did, and during the Thomas confirmation hearings in

**Confidence in Institutions Trends:
The U.S. Supreme Court by Party Affiliation**

Percentage saying "great deal" or "quite a lot"

	Republicans	Independents	Democrats	Republican Minus Democrats
May 23-26, 2005	47%	36%	42%	+5
May 21-23, 2004	53%	41%	47%	+6
Jun 9-10, 2003	56%	44%	42%	+14
Jun 21-23, 2002	53%	50%	46%	+7
Jun 8-10, 2001	61%	42%	46%	+15
Dec 15-17, 2000	67%	45%	40%	+27
Jun 22-25, 2000	48%	48%	44%	+4
Jun 25-27, 1999	47%	45%	58%	-11
Jun 5-7, 1998	52%	51%	48%	+4
Jul 25-27, 1997	51%	48%	52%	-1
May 28-29, 1996	43%	46%	46%	-3
Mar 25-27, 1994	45%	38%	45%	0
Mar 22-24, 1993	44%	41%	47%	-3
Oct 10-13, 1991	46%	37%	36%	+10
Feb 28-Mar 1, 1991	50%	53%	44%	+6
Sep 7-10, 1989	54%	44%	41%	+13
Jul 10-13, 1987	58%	52%	49%	+9
Oct 24-27, 1986	57%	56%	52%	+5
May 17-20, 1985	58%	54%	55%	+3
Oct 6-10, 1984	57%	55%	44%	+13
Nov 20-23, 1981	51%	42%	46%	+5
Apr 6-9, 1979	47%	39%	46%	+1
Jan 7-10, 1977	43%	46%	48%	-5
May 30-Jun 2, 1975	53%	45%	52%	+1
May 4-7, 1973	48%	44%	44%	+4

1991, there was a 10-point partisan difference, with 46% of Republicans and 36% of Democrats expressing confidence.

Over the next several years, there were only slight partisan variations on this measure. But, in 1999, Democrats were significantly more likely than Republicans to express confidence in the court, by a 58% to 47% margin. There were no extremely controversial rulings during this time, but this may have been the result of Democrats rallying during the impeachment of President Bill Clinton earlier that year.

The most dramatic party differences followed the court's decision regarding the Florida vote recount that effectively ended the presidential election in 2000 and allowed Bush to become president.

In June 2000, Gallup found only minor differences between Republicans' and Democrats' level of confidence in the court. But, by December, after the court decision that gave Bush the presidency, there was a 27-point difference, with 67% of Republicans expressing confidence in the Supreme Court while only 40% of Democrats did the same. These differences settled down slightly by June 2001. That poll found 61% of Republicans and 46% of Democrats saying they were confident in the court.

Over the past two years, the partisan gap that emerged after the 2000 election has gradually diminished, and today Republicans are only slightly more likely than Democrats to have confidence in the Supreme Court.

Ideological Differences

The current poll finds that self-described conservatives, moderates, and liberals are roughly even in their overall confidence in the Supreme Court. Since the 2000 presidential election, liberals have shown only modest variations in confidence ratings, while confidence among conservatives has declined steadily. Conservatives' ratings of the court now are at roughly the same levels they were in June 1999 and June 2000.

In 1998, Gallup found that at least half of conservatives (50%) and moderates (54%) expressed confidence in the Supreme Court, while 45% of liberals felt this way. In June 1999 and June 2000, confidence among conservatives dropped to 43%, while moderates and liberals continued to rate the court roughly the same way as they did in 1998.

After the court's ruling in the 2000 presidential election, confidence among conservatives surged to 58%, but decreased slightly

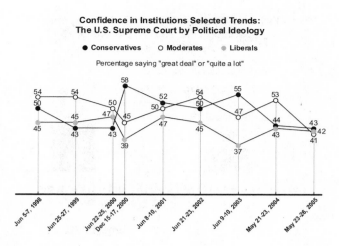

**Confidence in Institutions Selected Trends:
The U.S. Supreme Court by Political Ideology**

● Conservatives   ○ Moderates   ● Liberals

Percentage saying "great deal" or "quite a lot"

among moderates and liberals. Over the next two years, conservatives became less likely to say they were confident, but at least half still expressed confidence.

Gallup's 2004 survey, the first conducted after the court's controversial ruling on homosexual relations in June 2003, found that ratings among conservatives dropped to 44%, and were now at roughly the same level as liberals (43%). A slight majority of moderates, 53%, said they were confident in the court last year. This year, views among conservatives and liberals remained unchanged, but dropped 12 points among moderates.

Bottom Line

The public's current confidence rating in the U.S. Supreme Court is among the lowest that Gallup has found historically. Republicans and Democrats currently show only modest differences in their views of the court—a much different picture from what Gallup found after the 2000 election controversy when Republicans were much more likely than Democrats to express confidence. Conservatives, moderates, and liberals have roughly the same level of confidence in the court, but since 2000, ratings of the court among conservatives have dropped significantly.

*Results are based on telephone interviews with 1,004 national adults, aged 18 and older, conducted May 23-26, 2005. For results based on the total sample of national adults, one can say with 95% confidence that the margin of sampling error is ±3 percentage points. In addition to sampling error, question wording and practical difficulties in conducting surveys can introduce error or bias into the findings of public opinion polls.

June 22, 2005
MANY AMERICANS RELUCTANT TO SUPPORT THEIR CHILD JOINING MILITARY
Nearly half would suggest a different occupation

by Jeffrey M. Jones, Gallup Poll Managing Editor

While the U.S. Army has struggled to meet its monthly recruitment quotas in the midst of the Iraq war, a new Gallup Poll finds only a bare majority of Americans would support their child's decision to enter the military, while a substantial proportion would suggest their child try a different occupation. That is a significant decline when compared with previous data on this question from 1999. The poll also finds most Americans oppose mandatory military training for young men; something the public consistently favored a half-century ago. Additionally, an October 2004 Gallup survey showed only minimal support for re-instituting the military draft.

The June 16-19 poll asked Americans how they would react if they had a son or daughter who was planning to enter the military. Fifty-one percent say they would support that step, while 48% would suggest a different occupation. When The Associated Press asked the same question in 1999, 66% of Americans said they would support their child's decision, while only 29% would suggest their child try something else.

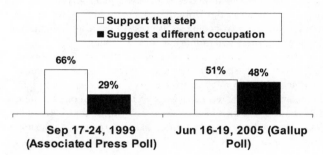

If you had a son or daughter who was planning to enter the military, would you support that step or would you suggest a different occupation?

□ Support that step
■ Suggest a different occupation

66%   29%
Sep 17-24, 1999
(Associated Press Poll)

51%   48%
Jun 16-19, 2005 (Gallup Poll)

This reluctance to support a military career is not a reflection on the military itself. The military remains the most positively rated institution according to Gallup's annual confidence in institutions poll, with more than 7 in 10 expressing confidence. In fact, slightly more Americans express confidence in the military today (74%) than did so in 1999 (68%). A more likely explanation probably lies in the realization that military service is more dangerous today given the ongoing war in Iraq.

Americans' views on the war are strongly related to their willingness to support a military career for their son or daughter. Among those who favor the war with Iraq, 81% say they would support their child if he or she decided to enter the military and 18% would suggest a different occupation. But among those who oppose the war, just 30% would support their child's wishes while 69% would suggest an alternate career path.

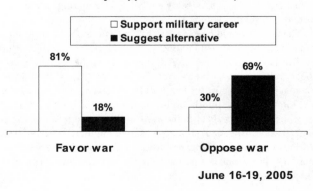

Support Son or Daughter Joining the Military?
by support for war in Iraq

□ Support military career
■ Suggest alternative

81%   18%
Favor war

30%   69%
Oppose war

June 16-19, 2005

That relationship persists even when taking into account one's party affiliation, which is strongly related to both support for the war and for a hypothetical military career for one's child. Overall, Republicans are more likely to favor the war and to say they would support their child's wanting to enter the military. However, the vast majority of Republicans who oppose the war say they would try to talk their child out of a military career. And while Democrats are generally opposed to the war and a military career for their children, Democrats who favor the war overwhelmingly say they would support their children if they opted for military service.

There are only slight differences between those who have personally served in the military and those who have not. Fifty-six percent of veterans would support their son or daughter if they expressed a desire to enter the military, as would 49% of those who did not serve in the military.

Mandatory Service?

To date, few have suggested compulsory military service for young men and women in the United States as a remedy to the lag in recruitment. That may be, in part, because of the realization that public support for required military service is lacking.

The current poll updated a Gallup question on mandatory military service, last asked 50 years ago. Currently, 35% of Americans favor and 62% oppose "requiring every able-bodied young man in this country when he reaches the age of 18, to spend one year in military training and then join the reserves." During the 1950s, at least a majority of Americans favored mandatory training, with support climbing as high as 76% in May 1955.

Would you favor or oppose requiring every able-bodied young man in this country when he reaches the age of 18, to spend one year in military training and then join the reserves?

	Favor %	Oppose %	No opinion %
2005 Jun 16-19	35	62	3
1955 Dec 8-13	69	23	8
1955 May 12-17	76	18	6
1955 Feb 10-15	71	20	9
1955 Jan 20-25	73	22	5
1954 Dec 2-7	75	22	3
1954 Aug 26-31	72	22	6
1952 Feb 28-Mar 5	60	33	7
1951 Dec 9-14	56	28	16

Those with prior military service are much more likely to favor mandatory military training than those who have not served. Veterans favor compulsory service by a 63% to 34% margin, while non-veterans oppose it by a 68% to 29% margin.

The public would be even less likely to favor the re-institution of the military draft. An October 2004 CNN/*USA Today*/Gallup poll found that just 14% of Americans said the United States should "return to the military draft," while 85% said it should not. In recent years, support for the draft has been about as low as it is now, though it was slightly higher in January 2003, a few months before the Iraq war began. In the early 1980s, just a few years after the draft was suspended, support was much higher. In early 1980, then-President Jimmy Carter re-instituted the Selective Service registration requirement as a partial response to the Soviet invasion of Afghanistan.

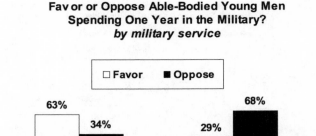

Favor or Oppose Able-Bodied Young Men Spending One Year in the Military?
by military service

☐ Favor   ■ Oppose

| 63% | 34% | 29% | 68% |

Served in the military   **Did not serve in the military**

June 16-19, 2005

Do you think the United States should return to the military draft at this time, or not?

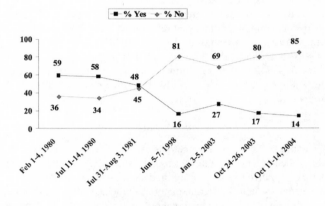

Survey Methods

These results are based on telephone interviews with a randomly selected national sample of 1,006 adults, aged 18 and older, conducted June 16-19, 2005. For results based on this sample, one can say with 95% confidence that the maximum error attributable to sampling and other random effects is ±3 percentage points. In addition to sampling error, question wording and practical difficulties in conducting surveys can introduce error or bias into the findings of public opinion polls.

June 23, 2005
AMERICANS FAMILIAR WITH, FOND OF BILLY GRAHAM
One in six have heard him in person

by Lydia Saad, Gallup Poll Senior Editor

About 200,000 people are expected to attend the Greater New York Billy Graham Crusade in New York City this weekend—likely his last crusade—but that number is dwarfed by the number of Americans who have witnessed Rev. Graham's preaching since he began his ministry more than 50 years ago.

According to a recent Gallup Poll, one in six adult Americans living today—or 35 million people—recall having heard Graham in person at some point in their lives. In addition, more than half of Americans, 52%, say they have heard Graham on the radio, while 85% have seen him on television.

Americans' Lifetime Exposure to Billy Graham

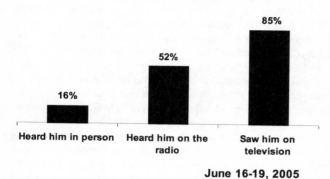

June 16-19, 2005

Graham's longevity has enabled him to build large audiences, and it has also given him an important Gallup Poll distinction. Graham has appeared in the top 10 of Gallup's list of most admired men more times (48) than any other man since the list's inception in 1948. His nearest competition is primarily comprised of U.S. presidents and Pope John Paul II. Ronald Reagan is second to Graham with 31 appearances on the list.

One in Five Are Critical of Graham

The new poll, conducted June 16-19, finds that Graham is widely popular with Americans, but also has his share of detractors. Two-thirds of Americans (66%) view Graham favorably, while 20% view him unfavorably.

- Graham's favorable-to-unfavorable ratio is highest among seniors, low-income Americans, those living in the South, Republicans, Protestants, and churchgoers more generally. Close to 75%, or more, of individuals in these categories view Graham favorably.
- Graham is seen unfavorably most among non-Christians (a category that includes non-religious Americans along with those of non-Christian faiths), as well as with politically liberal Americans and those in households earning $100,000 a year or more. Non-Christians are evenly divided in their opinions about Graham: 39% view him favorably, 40% unfavorably. Although 37% of liberals and 28% of high income Americans view him unfavorably, majorities of these groups still view Graham more favorably than not.

Graham Most Popular With Protestants

As a non-denominational evangelical Christian who attracted millions to his weekly radio address and numerous television specials, Graham was once dubbed "Pope of Protestant America" by *Time* magazine. Indeed, Graham's reach is particularly deep within the American Protestant community. Nineteen percent of all Protestants have heard Graham in person, two-thirds have heard him on the radio, and nearly all have seen him on television.

Most Catholics and non-Christians have also seen Graham on television, but less than half have heard him on the radio. Eleven percent of Catholics and 5% of non-Christians have heard Graham in person.

Exposure to Graham by Religious Affiliation

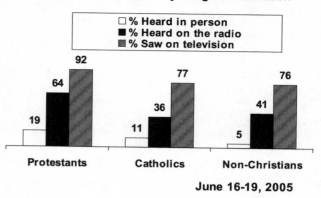

June 16-19, 2005

Graham's popularity among different religious groups also varies. Whereas 81% of Protestants tell Gallup they have a favorable view of Graham, that figure is only 58% among Catholics and 39% among non-Christians.

Graham's popularity among Catholics and non-Christians is partially suppressed by the fact that larger proportions of these groups, compared with Protestants, have no opinion of him. However, his unfavorable ratings among Catholics and non-Christians are also higher than among Protestants.

Personal View of Graham by Religious Affiliation

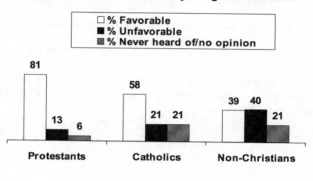

June 16-19, 2005

A Generational Decline in Graham's Influence

Graham is now 86 years old, and his frail health has kept him out of the public eye for the last several years. This change in his visibility is evident in young adults' levels of exposure to him.

Overall, 14% of Americans have no opinion of Graham, but that figure is 45% among young adults.

Similarly, those between the ages of 18 to 29 are about half as likely as those ages 50 and older to have ever seen or heard Graham in a public appearance. Young adults are only slightly less likely than those ages 30 to 49 to have heard Graham in person or on the radio, but they are much less likely to have ever seen him on television.

Survey Methods

These results are based on telephone interviews with a randomly selected national sample of 1,006 adults, aged 18 and older, conducted June 16-19, 2005. For results based on this sample, one can say with 95% confidence that the maximum error attributable to sampling and other random effects is ±3 percentage points. In addition

Personal View of Graham by Age

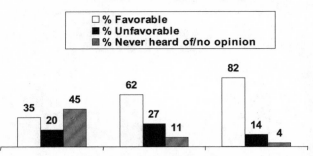

□ % Favorable
■ % Unfavorable
▨ % Never heard of/no opinion

	18- to 29-year-olds	30- to 49-year-olds	50 years and older
Favorable	35	62	82
Unfavorable	20	27	14
Never heard of/no opinion	45	11	4

June 16-19, 2005

Exposure to Graham by Age

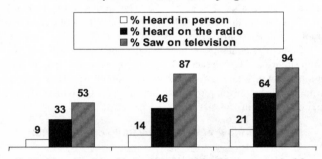

□ % Heard in person
■ % Heard on the radio
▨ % Saw on television

	18- to 29-year-olds	30- to 49-year-olds	50 years and older
Heard in person	9	14	21
Heard on the radio	33	46	64
Saw on television	53	87	94

June 16-19, 2005

to sampling error, question wording and practical difficulties in conducting surveys can introduce error or bias into the findings of public opinion polls.

June 24, 2005
WHO ARE THE EVANGELICALS?
Estimates vary widely

by Frank Newport, Gallup Poll Editor in Chief

What will likely be the Rev. Billy Graham's last U.S. evangelistic crusade starts this weekend, and the event has refocused attention on the group of religious Americans known as evangelicals. The term *evangelical* has been in general use for many years, but a more precise definition of exactly who this group is has been the subject of more intense focus in recent decades as evangelicals have become increasingly visible and active in American society. Evangelicals received a great deal of news coverage during the presidential election last fall, and more recently—from a totally different perspective—were featured in a *Business Week* magazine cover story that investigated their influence on the U.S. economy.

About 8 in 10 Americans adhere to some form of Christianity. Who among this group are the evangelicals? There is no easy answer to that question. There are perhaps as many different ways to define evangelicals as there are those attempting to define them.

Two Approaches to Defining Evangelicals

Broadly speaking, there are two basic ways to approach the objective of defining evangelicals: adherence to some specific belief or religious practice criteria and self-definition (that is, just asking people whether they consider themselves evangelical).

The list of possible belief and religious practice criteria that can be used to qualify individuals as evangelicals can quickly become mind-boggling. Gallup at times in the past has attempted to define evangelicals as those who answer affirmatively to three questions: (1) whether they have been born again or have had a born-again experience, (2) whether they have encouraged other people to believe in Jesus Christ, and (3) whether they believe the Bible is the actual word of God. In 1980, about 19% of the adult population agreed with all three statements. In a recent Gallup Poll update in May of this year, a quite similar 22% of all Americans agreed with all three statements.

Even more elaborate criteria have been used by other researchers. One research firm (The Barna Group) argues that individuals must answer positively to as many as nine different questions in order to qualify. Not surprisingly, only 7% of the U.S. adult population qualifies as evangelical using these restrictive criteria.

The obvious problem with any procedure that qualifies people as evangelical based on agreement with a set of statements is the lack of consensus on what those statements should be. There are so many different possible criteria, one could envision a series of 20 or more statements necessary for individuals to agree with in order to be included under the "evangelical" umbrella.

The second approach outlined is much simpler, focusing primarily on a simple self-definitional question: "Would you describe yourself as a 'born again' or evangelical?" Here is how Americans have responded to this question since 1991:

	Yes %	No %	No opinion %
2005 Apr 18-21	42	53	5
2004 Dec 5-8	39	55	6
2004 Jun 3-6	42	54	4
2003 Nov 10-12	43	53	4
2003 May 30-Jun 1	41	53	6
2003 Feb 17-19	41	54	5
2002 Dec 9-10	46	48	6
2002 Mar 18-20	46	50	4
2001 Dec 14-16	42	49	9
2001 Feb 19-21	45	49	6
2000 Aug 24-27	44	50	6
2000 Mar 17-19	46	47	7
1999 Dec 9-12	46	48	6
1999 Apr 30-May 2	45	47	8
1998 Jun 22-23	44	48	8
1997 Aug 12-13	45	47	8
1997 Mar 24-26^	43	51	6
1996 Nov 21-24^	41	52	7
1996 Sep 3-5^	42	52	6
1996 Jul 26-28^	36	59	5
1996 Jun 27-30^	35	58	7
1995 Dec 15-18^	43	52	5
1995 Aug 28-30^	39	54	7
1995 May 11-14^	39	53	8
1994 Jun 25-28^	39	53	8
1994 Mar 28-30^	45	48	7

	Yes	No	No opinion
	%	%	%
1993 Oct 28-30^	43	51	6
1993 Sep 13-15^	44	51	5
1993 Mar^	46	50	4
1992 Apr 9-12^	42	52	6
1991 Nov 21-24^	41	54	5

^November 1991-March 1997 WORDING: Would you describe yourself as a "born-again" or evangelical Christian?

This question is typically asked of the entire U.S. population. The range of affirmative responses since 1991 has been between a low point of 35% in a June 1996 survey and a high point of 46% in 1993, 1999, 2000, and 2002. The average across the years is 42%, which matches the results of the most recent April survey.

Further Restrictions on Self-Definitional Criteria

Some individuals who identify themselves as evangelicals are members of subgroups that many informed observers would agree don't fit in an evangelical category as conceived. These would include, in particular, people who are not Christian (but who agree with the "born again or evangelical" criterion). Additionally, for practical purposes, it is often reasonable to exclude nonwhites and Catholics from the evangelical category.

Why? Black Americans, as a whole, are highly religious and likely to say that they are evangelical or born again. Any sample of self-defined born agains or evangelicals thus includes a number of black Americans. But for the purposes of analysis involving political variables, the presence of blacks in the sample of evangelicals can be confusing. A large percentage of blacks have historically identified with the Democratic Party. Thus, for most analytical purposes, including blacks as part of the sample of evangelicals confounds the analysis, particularly when one discusses the relationship between being evangelical and certain political stances.

Also, a perhaps surprisingly high percentage of Catholics (19%) say they are born again or evangelical. Catholics in general may think of themselves that way, but again, for analytical purposes, Catholics are historically different enough from members of traditionally non-Catholic, Protestant denominations to warrant their exclusion from an evangelical definition. Hence the usual decision to exclude Catholics from the "evangelical category."

That any non-Christians agree with the born-again or evangelical label is also surprising, but for obvious reasons we want to remove them from the calculations. That goes for those who say they have no religious preference as well.

Thus, one procedure for defining evangelicals (the one to be used in the following analysis) consists of these three criteria:

1. Respondents must agree that the label "born again" or "evangelical" describes them.
2. Respondents must be white.
3. Respondents must be self-identified members of a Christian faith other than Catholic.

Twenty-six percent of Americans meet these criteria (based on an aggregated random sample of 3,000 interviews in which this evangelical question was asked in 2004 and 2005). By way of comparison, about 19% of the population is white and a member of a Christian faith other than Catholic, but do not agree with the born-again/evangelical label; 22% are white Catholics (regardless of their beliefs); 11% are black; and the rest of the population (those that do not identify as either white or black, those with no religious preference, those identifying with Eastern religions and so forth) constitute 22% of the population.

Evangelicals and Religiosity

Are these evangelicals (as defined) indeed more religious than average Americans—as we would expect? The table displays the relationship between this definition of evangelical and self-reported importance of religion:

Importance of Religion by Evangelical Grouping

Religious summary: race, religion, born-again status	Importance of religion in life		
	Very important	Fairly important	Not very important
	%	%	%
White, Protestant/Other Christian, born again	84	13	2
White, Protestant/Other Christian, not born again	41	38	22
White, Catholic	50	36	14
Black	83	10	6
All others	40	24	34
Total	59	25	16

It is clear that describing oneself as a born again or evangelical is tantamount to saying that religion is very important in one's life. Eighty-four percent of evangelicals agree that religion is very important in their lives, compared with just 41% white, non-Catholic Christians who are not born again or evangelical.

Here is the relationship between evangelical status and church attendance:

Church Attendance by Evangelical Grouping

Religious summary: race, religion, born-again status	Often attend church				
	Once a week	Almost every week	Once a month	Seldom	Never
	%	%	%	%	%
White, Protestant/ Other Christian, born again	53	15	11	16	5
White, Protestant/ Other Christian, not born again	15	11	19	41	14
White, Catholic	37	7	17	30	9
Black	51	12	19	14	4
All others	21	5	11	27	34
Total	35	10	13	26	14

Note the significant relationship between being evangelical and church attendance. Two-thirds of those in the white, non-Catholic Christian evangelical group attend church weekly or almost every week. Those white, non-Catholic Christians who don't accept the evangelical label are less than half as likely to attend church that often.

Who Are the Evangelicals?

The table shows the percentage of a variety of demographic subgroups in the population who are in the evangelical group:

Demographic	White, Protestant/ Other Christian, born again %	White, Protestant/ Other Christian, not born again %	White, Catholic %	Black %	All others %
TOTAL SAMPLE	26	19	22	11	22
East	15	19	34	11	21
Midwest	30	21	25	8	16
South	38	17	13	16	17
West	16	20	19	5	40
High school or less	30	17	20	14	20
Some college	27	18	22	11	22
College grad	25	21	25	7	22
Postgrad	15	24	26	6	29
Republican-no lean	42	19	21	2	17
Independent-all	17	21	22	9	31
Democrat-no lean	18	18	23	21	20
18-29	20	15	25	14	26
30-49	27	18	21	12	23
50-64	28	21	20	8	23
65+	30	24	22	8	17
Less than $20,000	24	19	18	18	21
$20,000 to less than $30,000	26	20	18	11	25
$30,000 to less than $50,000	31	17	20	14	19
$50,000 to less than $75,000	27	20	24	6	24
$75,000 and above	22	21	26	7	24
Conservative	40	16	22	9	14
Moderate	20	21	23	12	24
Liberal	12	22	21	11	34
Male	25	20	23	10	23
Female	27	18	22	12	22

It is significant to note that the representation of white, non-Catholic Christian evangelicals is not extremely strongly correlated with any demographic or regional variable. In other words, evangelicals are to a large degree represented throughout the U.S. population. Evangelicals do skew downscale, a little older, and toward the middle of the country (that is, away from either coast). But these differences are not large.

Importantly, it appears that the relationship between political variables and evangelical status (as defined here) is stronger than any other demographic or regional variable included in this analysis. There is a 24-percentage-point difference in the percentage of Republicans who are evangelicals as opposed to Democrats and a similarly large distinction between the representation of evangelicals among conservatives and liberals.

We can look at these data in a slightly different fashion. Fifty-seven percent of white, non-Catholic Christians who are evangelicals are Republicans, compared with just 34% of white non-Catholic Christian non-evangelicals who are Republicans.

Survey Methods

These results are based on telephone interviews with an aggregated group of randomly selected national samples of more than 3,000 adults, aged 18 and older, conducted by Gallup in 2004 and 2005. The sample is comprised of three separate surveys, which included the "evangelical" question as discussed above. For results based on this sample, one can say with 95% confidence that the maximum error attributable to sampling and other random effects is ±2 percentage points. In addition to sampling error, question wording and practical difficulties in conducting surveys can introduce error or bias into the findings of public opinion polls.

June 28, 2005
PUBLIC SKEPTICAL ON ULTIMATE SUCCESS OF U.S. EFFORTS IN IRAQ
Clear majority says Bush has no clear plan for dealing with Iraq

by David W. Moore, Gallup Poll Senior Editor

The latest CNN/*USA Today*/Gallup survey finds Americans about evenly divided on whether the United States can ever establish a stable government in Iraq. Among those who say it can, most expect success within five years. Other poll findings show slight majorities of Americans who want a timetable for removal of troops from Iraq and who think the war was a mistake. A clear majority of people say that President George W. Bush has no clear plan for dealing with the war in Iraq. Just 40% approve of Bush's handling of the situation there. Bush's overall job approval is at 45%, with 53% disapproving—the worst negative to positive ratio in Bush's presidency.

Secretary of Defense Donald Rumsfeld told Chris Wallace of *Fox News Sunday* on June 26 that "Insurgencies tend to go on 5, 6, 8, 10, 12 years," implying that the war in Iraq may not be "in the last throes," as suggested by Vice President Dick Cheney in a June 20 interview with Larry King on CNN. This new projection of how long the Iraq war might last could exacerbate an already widespread skepticism among Americans as to whether or not the United States will ever be able to establish a stable government in Iraq.

According to the latest CNN/*USA Today*/Gallup survey, just 49% say the United States will achieve that goal, while 45% say it will not. But the positive half of the public has more optimistic assumptions about how long it will take to establish a stable government than Rumsfeld. Almost three-quarters of Americans expect success within five years, while Rumsfeld says five years is probably a minimum; the war could last as long as a dozen years.

Do you think the United States will—or will not—ever be able to establish a stable government in Iraq that will allow the U.S. to withdraw its troops from Iraq?

	Yes, will	No, will not	No opinion
2005 Jun 24-26	49%	45	6

Just your best guess, how long do you think it will take for the U.S. to establish a stable government in Iraq—one year or less, two to three years, four to five years, six to ten years, or longer than ten years?

	One year or less	*2-3 years*	*4-5 years*	*6-10 years*	*Longer than 10 years*	*No opinion*
2005 Jun 24-26	5%	39	29	17	8	2

COMBINED RESPONSES

	2005 Jun 24-26 %
Yes, will establish a stable government	**49**
(Establish strong/independent government in one year or less)	*(2)*
(2-3 years)	*(19)*
(4-5 years)	*(15)*
(6-10 years)	*(8)*
(Longer than 10 years)	*(4)*
(Unsure)	*(1)*
No, will not	**45**
No opinion	**6**

The importance of this issue can be seen in the fact that more than half of all Americans (51%) already think it is best for the United States to set a timetable for removing troops from Iraq, "and stick to that timetable regardless of what is going on in Iraq at the time."

Another 44% say it would be better to keep troops in Iraq until the situation improves, "even if that takes many years."

If you had to choose, which do you think is better for the U.S.— [ROTATED: to keep a significant number of troops in Iraq until the situation there gets better, even if that takes many years, (or) to set a time-table for removing troops from Iraq and to stick to that timetable regardless of what is going on in Iraq at the time]?

	Keep troops in Iraq until situation gets better	*Set timetable for removing troops from Iraq*	*No opinion*
2005 Jun 24-26	44%	51	5

The poll also shows that over the past several months, Americans are increasingly pessimistic that the United States and its allies are winning the war. Just 34% say they are, while 14% say the insurgents are winning, and 50% say neither side is.

Who do you think is currently winning the war in Iraq—the U.S. and its allies, the insurgents in Iraq, or neither side?

	U.S. and its allies %	*Insurgents in Iraq %*	*Neither side %*	*No opinion %*
2005 Jun 24-26	34	14	50	2
2005 Feb 25-27	43	7	48	2
2004 Nov 19-21	44	7	46	3
2004 Oct 22-24 ^	35	10	53	2
^ Asked of a half sample				

These views are more pessimistic than what Americans expressed in February (during the time of the Iraqi elections) and even last November.

At the same time, many Americans have had second thoughts about whether the original decision to launch the war against Iraq was justified—today, 53% say it was a mistake, while 46% disagree.

In view of the developments since we first sent our troops to Iraq, do you think the United States made a mistake in sending troops to Iraq, or not?

Iraq	*Yes, a mistake %*	*No, not %*	*No opinion %*
2005 Jun 24-26	53	46	1
2005 Apr 29-May 1 ^	49	48	3
2005 Mar 18-20 ^	46	51	3
2005 Feb 25-27	47	51	2
2005 Feb 4-6	45	55	*
2005 Jan 14-16	52	47	1
2005 Jan 7-9	50	48	2
2004 Nov 19-21	47	51	2
2004 Oct 29-31 ^	44	52	4
2004 Oct 22-24	47	51	2
2004 Oct 14-16	47	52	1
2004 Oct 9-10 ^	46	53	1
2004 Oct 1-3	48	51	1
2004 Sep 24-26	42	55	3
2004 Sep 3-5 ^	38	57	5
2004 Aug 23-25 ^	48	50	2
2004 Jul 30-Aug 1	47	51	2
2004 Jul 19-21	50	47	3
2004 Jul 8-11 ^	54	45	1
2004 Jun 21-23 ^	54	44	2
2004 Jun 3-6 ^	41	58	1
2004 May 7-9 ^	44	54	2
2004 Apr 16-18 ^	42	57	1
2004 Jan 12-15 ^	42	56	2
^ Asked of a half sample			
* Less than 0.5%			

Two related items:

Americans are evenly divided as to whether the war with Iraq has made the United States safer from terrorism. Forty-three percent say it has, but 46% say it has not.

Do you think the war with Iraq has made the U.S. safer—or less safe—from terrorism?

BASED ON 505 NATIONAL ADULTS IN FORM A

	Safer %	*Less safe %*	*NO CHANGE (vol.) %*	*No opinion %*
2005 Jun 24-26 ^	43	46	8	3
2004 Oct 1-3	47	45	5	3
2004 Jun 21-23	37	55	6	2
2004 Mar 5-7	50	37	10	3
2003 Dec 15-16 ^	56	33	9	2
2003 Nov 14-16	48	43	7	2
2003 Oct 24-26	45	43	10	2

	Safer %	Less safe %	NO CHANGE (vol.) %	No opinion %
2003 Apr 22-23	58	33	8	1
2003 Apr 10 †	51	37	9	3

(vol.) Volunteered response
^ Based on a half sample
† Polls conducted entirely in one day, such as this one, are subject to additional error or bias not found in polls conducted over several days.

Despite the Bush administration's claim that the war in Iraq is part of the larger war against terrorism, the public is evenly divided on that matter. Forty-seven percent agree, but 50% believe the war is "an entirely separate military action."

Do you consider the war in Iraq to be part of the war on terrorism which began on September 11, 2001, or do you consider it to be an entirely separate military action?

BASED ON 504 NATIONAL ADULTS IN FORM B

	Part of war on terrorism %	Separate military action %	No opinion %
2005 Jun 24-26 ^	47	50	3
2004 Oct 1-3	50	47	3
2004 Jul 19-21 ^	51	47	2
2004 Mar 26-28	50	48	2
2003 Aug 25-26	57	41	2

^ Asked of a half sample

Public Evaluation of Bush's Handling of the Situation in Iraq

Given these pessimistic assessments, it is not surprising that Bush's current approval rating on the war is among the lowest the president has received—40% approve and 58% disapprove. In early February, amid coverage of the Iraqi elections, public approval of Bush on the issue was evenly divided, but since then the public has become more critical.

	Approve %	Disapprove %	No opinion %
2005 Jun 24-26	40	58	2
2005 May 20-22 ^	40	56	4
2005 Apr 29-May 1	42	55	3
2005 Apr 1-2	43	54	3
2005 Feb 25-27	45	53	2
2005 Feb 4-6	50	48	2
2005 Jan 7-9	42	56	2
2004 Nov 7-10	47	51	2
2004 Oct 14-16	46	52	2
2004 Sep 24-26	48	49	3
2004 Aug 9-11	45	52	3
2004 Jun 21-23 ^	42	56	2
2004 Jun 3-6	41	57	2
2004 May 7-9 ^	41	58	1
2004 May 2-4	42	55	3
2004 Apr 16-18	48	49	3
2004 Mar 26-28	51	47	2

	Approve %	Disapprove %	No opinion %
2004 Jan 29-Feb 1	46	53	1
2004 Jan 2-5	61	36	3

^ Asked of a half sample

Perhaps even more telling is that an increasing number of Americans believe that Bush does not have a clear plan for how to deal with the situation in Iraq. Currently, 61% say he does not, up from 50% who expressed that opinion in January of this year. Only 37% say he does have a clear plan.

Do you think George W. Bush does—or does not—have a clear plan for handling the situation in Iraq?

	Yes, does %	No, does not %	No opinion %
2005 Jun 24-26	37	61	2
2005 Jan 14-16 ^	49	50	1
2004 Oct 1-3	49	49	2
2004 Sep 24-26	52	44	4
2004 Jul 30-Aug 1	42	56	2
2004 Jul 19-21	45	54	1
2003 Dec 15-16 †	51	45	4
2003 Sep 8-10 †	40	59	1
2003 Aug 25-26 †	44	54	2

^ Asked in a rotation with other issues.
† WORDING: Do you think the Bush administration does—or does not—have a clear plan for handling the situation in Iraq?

These negative views on the war cannot help but affect Bush's overall approval rating, which the poll now shows at 45%. Another 53% disapprove. That net eight-point negative margin is the largest measured by Gallup during Bush's presidency.

Do you approve or disapprove of the way George W. Bush is handling his job as president?

2005	Approve %	Disapprove %	No opinion %
2005 Jun 24-26	45	53	2
2005 Jun 16-19	47	51	2
2005 Jun 6-8	47	49	4
2005 May 23-26	48	47	5
2005 May 20-22	46	50	4
2005 May 2-5	50	45	5
2005 Apr 29-May 1	48	49	3
2005 Apr 18-21	48	49	3
2005 Apr 4-7	50	45	5
2005 Apr 1-2	48	48	4
2005 Mar 21-23	45	49	6
2005 Mar 18-20	52	44	4
2005 Mar 7-10	52	44	4
2005 Feb 25-27	52	45	3
2005 Feb 21-24	51	45	4
2005 Feb 7-10	49	48	3
2005 Feb 4-6	57	40	3
2005 Jan 14-16	51	46	3
2005 Jan 7-9	52	44	4
2005 Jan 3-5	52	44	4

Survey Methods

Results in the current survey are based on telephone interviews with 1,009 national adults, aged 18 and older, conducted June 24-26, 2005. For results based on the total sample of national adults, one can say with 95% confidence that the maximum margin of sampling error is ±3 percentage points.

For results based on the 505 national adults in the Form A half-sample and 504 national adults in the Form B half-sample, the maximum margins of sampling error are ±5 percentage points.

In addition to sampling error, question wording and practical difficulties in conducting surveys can introduce error or bias into the findings of public opinion polls.

June 28, 2005

WHAT WILL GET AMERICANS OUT TO THE MOVIES?

Lower ticket prices might change their minds

by Linda Lyons, Education and Youth Editor

Obi-wan Kenobi wasn't Hollywood's only hope in reversing its longest box-office slump in 20 years, but so far, none of the summer blockbusters—not even the Caped Crusader—has been able to save Movie City. Results from a recent Gallup survey* likely won't relieve industry-watchers' concern about sagging box-office figures, either.

Movie Habits

Asked directly if their movie-going habits have changed in the last five years, nearly half of Americans (48%) say they are visiting movie theaters less often, 36% say they go about the same amount, and only 15% say they think they're going out to see *more* movies than they did five years ago.

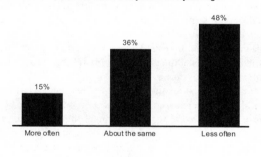

Are you going to see movies in a theater more often, about the same number of times, or less often than you did five years ago?

Settling In

Why do more Americans say they're less likely to go out to the movies these days? When given a choice of four reasons why they might not go to the theaters more often, 33% say they "prefer to watch movies at home." Twenty-four percent say that "it costs too much to go to the movies," and 19% attribute it to the "poor quality" of movies today. One in five (21%) say they just don't have the time.

The poll asked Americans whether five factors would make them *more* likely to see a movie in a theater. Seven in 10 say they would be more likely to attend a movie showing if "the tickets and

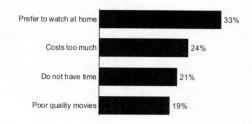

concessions cost less money," including 43% who say this would make them "much more likely." Roughly the same percentage say that better quality films would make them more likely to go to the movies, although somewhat fewer (36%) say it would make them "much more likely" to do so. About half would be at least somewhat more likely to attend if "the theaters were better" or if "there were better controls on audience behavior." Forty-two percent say a delay of two years before movies appeared on DVD or VHS would increase their likelihood of seeing a movie in a theater.

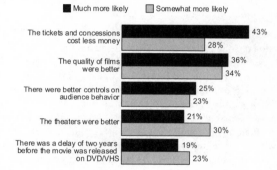

Would you be much more likely, somewhat more likely, or not more likely to see movies in a theater if . . .

The poll also asked the public which of four factors would be most important in getting them to see a movie in the theater. Personal recommendations from friends and relatives was most likely chosen, and by a 2-to-1 margin over the other options. Twenty-one percent said commercials for the movie are important in getting them to see a movie in a theater, 16% say the starring actors in the film, and just 14% say positive reviews from movie critics.

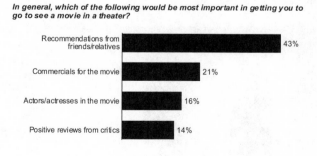

In general, which of the following would be most important in getting you to go to see a movie in a theater?

Bottom Line

Perhaps the new crop of blockbusters, such as *War of the Worlds* or *Fantastic Four*, will help lure Americans back to the cinema. But even if people prefer their living rooms to the multiplex, they needn't worry about seeing studio executives living on the street. Things have changed since Hollywood's golden days, when movie studios were totally dependent on box-office revenues. DVD sales now contribute more to a movie's profits than tickets sales; according to a recent *Variety* article, to date 2005 income from DVD sales is three times higher than box-office ticket earnings.

* Results are based on telephone interviews with 1,006 national adults, aged 18 and older, conducted May 20-22, 2005. For results based on the total sample of national adults, one can say with 95% confidence that the maximum margin of sampling error is ±3 percentage points.

In addition to sampling error, question wording and practical difficulties in conducting surveys can introduce error or bias into the findings of public opinion polls.

June 28, 2005

PUBLIC: FIGHT FAIR TO FILL SUPREME COURT SPOT

Majority says Democrats should work to defeat nominee with whom they disagree

by Lydia Saad, Gallup Poll Senior Editor

The heated rhetoric swirling around President George W. Bush's nomination of John Bolton for U.S. ambassador to the United Nations, as well as the filibuster fracas over the president's federal judicial nominations, have offered a preview of how future battles over Supreme Court nominations might be waged.

It is inevitable that, should U.S. Supreme Court Chief Justice William Rehnquist retire at the end of the current court term (as some have speculated), his departure will set off a political brawl between Bush, who will try to replace him with an equally conservative justice, and the Senate Democrats, who will demand someone more liberal.

How will Americans react to such an encounter? A recent Gallup Poll* tested Americans' tolerance for political disagreement over the next Supreme Court appointment, and found that, ideally, Americans want Bush and the Senate Democrats to reach consensus.

Asked whether Bush should stick with his first choice to fill a vacancy on the Supreme Court or choose someone more palatable to the Democrats if the Democrats object to his first choice, a slim majority of Americans—51%—opt for the latter. Less than half—46%—believe Bush should still nominate his first choice if that person proves to be controversial.

What should Bush do if Senate Democrats object to his preferred Supreme Court nominee?

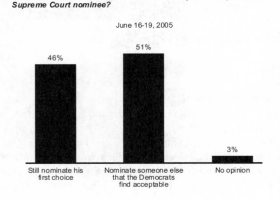

(The fiction here is that Bush could be satisfied with someone whom the Democrats also find acceptable. But reacting to that assumption, Americans think Bush should be willing to yield on his first choice.)

What about the Democrats? Should the Democrats in the Senate confirm any Bush Supreme Court nominee so long as that person is legally and ethically qualified, or should the Democrats work to defeat a nominee whom they disagree with politically in order to compel the president to pick someone more acceptable?

The same CNN/*USA Today*/Gallup poll, conducted June 16-19, 2005, finds Americans siding more with the Democrats than with Bush when given this choice. Fifty-three percent say the Democrats should work to defeat a nominee whom they disagree with on important issues, while just 40% say they should vote to confirm such a nominee.

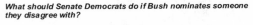

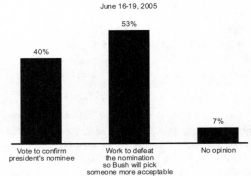

Clearly Americans don't think the Senate Democrats should rubber-stamp just anyone Bush chooses for the job of Supreme Court justice. They would prefer to see the two sides work (perhaps fight) until they arrive at someone both can support.

Rehnquist Vacancy Should be Filled by Another Conservative?

Complicating the matter, neither Bush nor the Senate Democrats has a mandate from the public over the political direction of the Supreme Court. The largest segment of Americans, 41%, says that in the event of a vacancy, they would like Bush to nominate someone who will make the court more conservative than it currently is. Another 30% would like him to make the court more liberal than it is, while 24% want him to keep the court as it is now.

Of course, if Rehnquist were to retire, this suggests that Americans would want Bush to nominate another conservative justice. That is because a total of 65% of Americans either want the court to remain as it is or become more conservative. But by the same token, were Justice John Paul Stevens or some other liberal member of the court to create a vacancy, 54% would prefer a liberal replacement.

Bottom Line

In 1987, Ronald Reagan nominated Judge Robert Bork to fill the vacancy left by Justice Lewis F. Powell Jr. Bork's views, particularly on the right to privacy and judicial restraint, outraged liberals, and he was ultimately rejected on a 58-42 vote by the then Democrat-controlled Senate. Reagan later nominated Judge Anthony Kennedy (who was perceived as a more moderate conservative than Bork), and he was easily confirmed.

Preferred Impact of New Justice on the Supreme Court

June 16-19, 2005

More liberal	30%
More conservative	41%
Keep as it is now	24%
No opinion	5%

The current data suggest that Americans today would applaud how that process unfolded. But, according to the *Washington Post*, some conservative leaders who assembled in Washington, D.C. in April called for Kennedy to be impeached over his perceived liberal (and what they view as unconstitutional) votes. To say Kennedy has been a disappointment to conservatives would be an understatement.

Bush won't want to nominate a Kennedy of his own, and therefore it is doubtful he will yield very easily to the Democrats if a battle ensues over his first choice. A major difference between 1987 and today is that the Republicans are in the majority and will most likely confirm anyone Bush chooses. However, without a 60-vote majority, Bush still has to contend with the Senate Democrats who will threaten to block a confirmation vote with a filibuster.

If the dilemma is resolved by a "nuclear" maneuver, such as changing the filibuster rule for judicial confirmations, and the political atmosphere in Washington is forever poisoned, Americans may be left wondering why the two sides couldn't have compromised their hard-line positions, and simply settled on someone tolerable to both sides.

Results are based on telephone interviews with 1,003 national adults, aged 18 and older, conducted June 16-19, 2005. For results based on the total sample of national adults, one can say with 95% confidence that the margin of sampling error is ±3 percentage points.

In addition to sampling error, question wording and practical difficulties in conducting surveys can introduce error or bias into the findings of public opinion polls.

June 30, 2005
LITTLE FOR BUSH TO SAVOR IN LATEST SOCIAL SECURITY POLLING
Still "no" to private investment accounts

by Lydia Saad, Gallup Poll Senior Editor

The news for President George W. Bush on Social Security is not good. His approval ratings on Social Security are the worst they have been all year, and more Americans have faith in the Democrats than in the Republicans to deal with the issue. A majority of Americans continue to oppose private investment accounts—Bush's core idea for addressing the Social Security system. And while a majority of Americans acknowledge Bush has proposed a Social Security plan, fewer describe it as a clear plan.

Decidedly Weak Approval on Social Security

According to the June 24-26, 2005, CNN/*USA Today*/Gallup poll, only 31% of Americans approve of Bush's handling of Social Security; 64% disapprove. That amounts to a -33 net approval rating on Social Security, which is lower than where he stood even a month ago, and is substantially lower than results from earlier in the year.

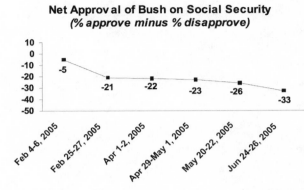

Net Approval of Bush on Social Security
(% approve minus % disapprove)

Bush's declining ratings on Social Security are possibly part of a larger pattern that is not directly related to his specific performance on the issue. His dwindling support on Social Security parallels a decline in his overall job approval rating, and is similar to the trend seen for his handling of the economy and Iraq.

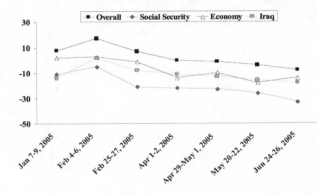

Comparison of Bush Net Approval Ratings
(% approve minus % disapprove)

No to Private Investment Accounts

Still, the important fact remains that a majority of Americans seem resistant to Bush's idea of establishing private investment accounts within the Social Security system—at least as Gallup describes that idea. Fifty-three percent of Americans say they oppose a proposal that would "allow workers to invest part of their Social Security taxes in the stock market or in bonds, while the rest of those taxes would remain in the Social Security system." Just 44% favor this. These results are nearly identical to those measured in late April.

Party affiliation presents the biggest distinctions in support for private accounts. About two-thirds of Republicans (69%) favor the idea, while three-quarters of Democrats (74%) and a majority of independents (59%) oppose it.

But the differences are almost as stark according to the age of respondents. Adults under age 50 generally favor the idea while those 50 and older oppose it.

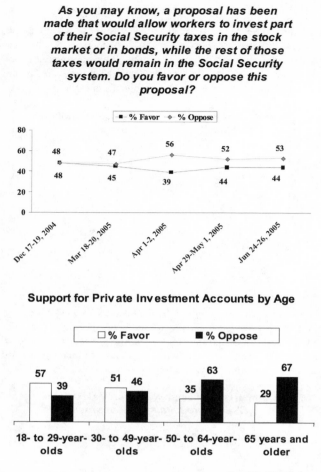

As you may know, a proposal has been made that would allow workers to invest part of their Social Security taxes in the stock market or in bonds, while the rest of those taxes would remain in the Social Security system. Do you favor or oppose this proposal?

Support for Private Investment Accounts by Age

June 24-26, 2005

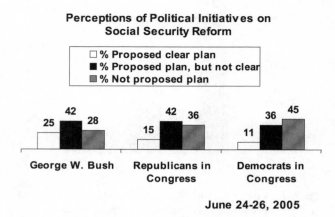

Perceptions of Political Initiatives on Social Security Reform

□ % Proposed clear plan
■ % Proposed plan, but not clear
▨ % Not proposed plan

June 24-26, 2005

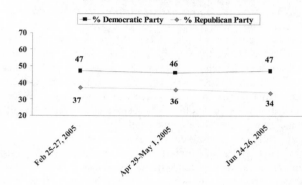

Who do you trust more to deal with the issue of Social Security retirement benefits?

opposing Bush's plan without having one of their own. However, Americans still choose the Democrats over the Republicans as the party they trust more to deal with Social Security retirement benefits.

Not Even an "A" for Effort

Bush gets moderate credit from Americans for having proposed a plan for addressing the Social Security system. Two-thirds (67%) acknowledge he has a plan, compared with less than half (47%) who say the same of the Democrats in Congress. However, only a quarter of Americans believe Bush has proposed a clear plan, leaving a great deal of room for improvement on this front.

Republicans might hope that Bush's Social Security initiative leaves Democrats vulnerable to being seen as obstructing the issue—

Survey Methods

These results are based on telephone interviews with a randomly selected national sample of 1,009 adults, aged 18 and older, conducted June 24-26, 2005. For results based on this sample, one can say with 95% confidence that the maximum error attributable to sampling and other random effects is ±3 percentage points. In addition to sampling error, question wording and practical difficulties in conducting surveys can introduce error or bias into the findings of public opinion polls.

Despite these results, the poll suggests some erosion of support if the war persists for a long time. Half of Americans, 49%, say it is better for the United States to set a timetable for removing troops from Iraq and "to stick to that timetable regardless of what is going on in Iraq at the time." The other half, 48%, would keep troops in Iraq until things get better, "even if that takes many years."

If you had to choose, which do you think is better for the U.S.— [ROTATED: to keep a significant number of troops in Iraq until the situation there gets better, even if that takes many years, (or) to set a timetable for removing troops from Iraq and to stick to that timetable regardless of what is going on in Iraq at the time]?

	Keep troops in Iraq until situation gets better	Set timetable for removing troops from Iraq	No opinion
2005 Jun 29-30	48%	49	3
2005 Jun 24-26	44%	51	5

The current views are slightly more positive toward keeping the troops in Iraq than the views measured in the June 24-26 poll, but the differences are within the polls' margins of error.

One key to continued support is the public's perception about whether the United States and its allies are making progress in the war. The poll shows that a clear majority, 58%, believes that progress is being made, while just 34% believe allied forces are losing ground to the insurgents.

Which comes closer to your view—[ROTATED: the U.S. and its allies are making progress in Iraq, (or) the U.S. and its allies are losing ground to the insurgents in Iraq]?

	Making progress	Losing ground	No opinion
2005 Jun 29-30	58%	34	8

While a majority of Americans continue to support keeping troops in Iraq, they are more critical about whether it was necessary or even worth it in the first place.

A slight majority, 52%, say it was not worth going to war, while 46% say it was. This is slightly more positive than what Gallup measured in a June 6-8 poll, but it is consistent with the pattern of responses on this issue this year.

All in all, do you think it was worth going to war in Iraq, or not?

	Worth it %	Not worth it %	No opinion %
2005 Jun 29-30	46	52	2
2005 Jun 6-8	42	56	2
2005 Apr 29-May 1^	41	57	2
2005 Apr 1-2	45	53	2
2005 Feb 7-10	48	50	2
2005 Jan 3-5	46	52	2
2004 Oct 9-10 ^	44	54	2

July 1, 2005
PUBLIC: PULLOUT FROM IRAQ WOULD BE HARMFUL TO U.S.
No major change in opinion following Bush speech

by David W. Moore, Gallup Poll Senior Editor

A new Gallup Poll finds most Americans saying it would be harmful to the United States if it withdrew its troops from Iraq before the situation stabilizes there.

A majority also says that it is necessary to keep U.S. troops in Iraq to thwart terrorist attacks on the United States, that the United States and its allies are making progress in Iraq, and that the Bush administration is doing a good job in providing the proper number of troops and right equipment to prevent unnecessary casualties.

The poll was conducted June 29-30, in the two days following President George W. Bush's nationally televised speech to troops at Fort Bragg, N.C., Tuesday night.

In his speech, the president presented his arguments for staying the course in Iraq, saying it was essential for U.S. security. But the poll suggests that he changed few people's minds on the issue. Some of the questions showed slightly more positive views of the war, but the differences between the public's views now and what Gallup measured on the weekend before Bush's speech are small and within the polls' margins of error.

The most widespread consensus among Americans is that a precipitous pullout of American troops would be harmful, a point repeatedly stressed by the president. Sixty-four percent of Americans say if troops were withdrawn before the situation stabilized in Iraq, it would do "more harm than good" to the United States. Just 28% say it would do "more good than harm."

If the United States pulled its troops out of Iraq before things stabilize there, do you think that would —[ROTATED: do more harm than good to the U.S., (or) do more good than harm to the U.S.]?

	More harm than good	More good than harm	No opinion
2005 Jun 29-30	64%	28	8

When people were asked more specifically whether it was necessary to keep U.S. troops in Iraq "in order to prevent additional acts of terrorism in the United States," a smaller majority, 55%, said it was necessary, while 41% disagreed.

Thinking about the current situation, do you think it is—or is not— necessary for the United States to keep its troops in Iraq NOW in order to prevent additional acts of terrorism in the U.S.?

	Worth it %	Not worth it %	No opinion %
2004 Sep 3-5 ^	49	48	3
2004 Aug 23-25 ^	51	46	3
2004 Aug 9-11 ^	49	48	3
2004 Jul 8-11 ^	47	50	3
2004 Jun 21-23 ^	46	51	3
2004 Jun 3-6 ^	46	52	2
2004 May 21-23	45	52	3
2004 May 7-9 ^	44	54	2
2004 May 2-4	50	47	3
2004 Apr 16-18 ^	52	46	2
2004 Apr 5-8	50	47	3
2004 Mar 26-28	56	41	3
2004 Mar 5-7	55	43	2

^ Asked of a half sample

Similarly, when asked whether it was necessary to go to war with Iraq in 2003 in order to prevent additional acts of terrorism, Americans say "no" by a slight majority, 51% to 46%.

Do you think it was—or was not—necessary for the United States to invade Iraq in 2003 in order to prevent additional acts of terrorism in the U.S.?

	Yes, was necessary	No, was not	No opinion
2005 Jun 29-30	46%	51	3

Also, Americans remain divided about how the war with Iraq has affected U.S. security. Forty-four percent say the war has made the United States safer, while 39% say less safe.

Do you think the war with Iraq has made the U.S. safer—or less safe—from terrorism?

	Safer %	Less safe %	NO CHANGE (vol.) %	No opinion %
2005 Jun 29-30	44	39	13	4
2005 Jun 24-26 ^	43	46	8	3
2004 Oct 1-3	47	45	5	3
2004 Jun 21-23	37	55	6	2
2004 Mar 5-7	50	37	10	3
2003 Dec 15-16 ^	56	33	9	2
2003 Nov 14-16	48	43	7	2
2003 Oct 24-26	45	43	10	2
2003 Apr 22-23	58	33	8	1
2003 Apr 10 †	51	37	9	3

(vol.) = Volunteered response
^ Based on a half sample
† Polls conducted entirely in one day, such as this one, are subject to additional error or bias not found in polls conducted over several days.

The results in this poll are slightly more positive than those measured in the June 24-26 poll, but not because more people say the war has made the country safer. The difference is that fewer people say the war has made the country "less safe," while more say there has been no change.

Other results from the poll give mixed reviews to the Bush administration.

Some critics have charged the president with not doing enough to protect U.S. troops from becoming casualties in Iraq, by not providing the right equipment and by not sending enough troops to fight the insurgents. But a majority of Americans seem to dismiss these arguments. Fifty-five percent say the Bush administration is doing a good job in that area, while 42% say a poor job.

How would you rate the job the Bush administration is doing in providing the proper number of troops and right equipment needed to prevent unnecessary casualties in Iraq? Would you say they are doing—[ROTATED: a very good job, a good job, a poor job, (or) a very poor job]?

	Very good job	Good job	Poor job	Very poor job	No opinion
2005 Jun 29-30	10%	45	29	13	3

On the other hand, the poll also shows that a solid majority of Americans, 58%, believe Bush does not have a clear plan for handling the situation in Iraq, while just 38% say he does.

Do you think George W. Bush does—or does not—have a clear plan for handling the situation in Iraq?

	Yes, does %	No, does not %	No opinion %
2005 Jun 29-30	38	58	4
2005 Jun 24-26	37	61	2
2005 Jan 14-16 ^	49	50	1
2004 Oct 1-3	49	49	2
2004 Sep 24-26	52	44	4
2004 Jul 30-Aug 1	42	56	2
2004 Jul 19-21	45	54	1
2003 Dec 15-16 †	51	45	4
2003 Sep 8-10 †	40	59	1
2003 Aug 25-26 †	44	54	2

^ Asked in a rotation with other issues
† WORDING: Do you think the Bush administration does—or does not—have a clear plan for handling the situation in Iraq?

These views are little changed from the June 24-26 poll.

Finally, whatever the slight changes in attitudes on Iraq, the public shows virtually no change in its overall evaluation of the president. His job approval is 46% in the current poll, just one point higher than the lowest rating of his presidency.

Do you approve or disapprove of the way George W. Bush is handling his job as president?

2005	Approve %	Disapprove %	No opinion %
2005 Jun 29-30	46	51	3
2005 Jun 24-26	45	53	2
2005 Jun 16-19	47	51	2
2005 Jun 6-8	47	49	4
2005 May 23-26	48	47	5
2005 May 20-22	46	50	4
2005 May 2-5	50	45	5
2005 Apr 29-May 1	48	49	3
2005 Apr 18-21	48	49	3

2005	Approve %	Disapprove %	No opinion %
2005 Apr 4-7	50	45	5
2005 Apr 1-2	48	48	4
2005 Mar 21-23	45	49	6
2005 Mar 18-20	52	44	4
2005 Mar 7-10	52	44	4
2005 Feb 25-27	52	45	3
2005 Feb 21-24	51	45	4
2005 Feb 7-10	49	48	3
2005 Feb 4-6	57	40	3
2005 Jan 14-16	51	46	3
2005 Jan 7-9	52	44	4
2005 Jan 3-5	52	44	4

Survey Methods

Results in the current survey are based on telephone interviews with 883 national adults, aged 18 and older, conducted June 29-30, 2005. For results based on the total sample of national adults, one can say with 95% confidence that the maximum margin of sampling error is ±4 percentage points.

In addition to sampling error, question wording and practical difficulties in conducting surveys can introduce error or bias into the findings of public opinion polls.

The distribution of party affiliation, compared with the last poll, is as follows:

	Republicans	Independents	Democrats
2005 Jun 29-30	29%	31	38
2005 Jun 24-26	33%	32	34

July 5, 2005
SPECIAL ANALYSIS: AMERICANS DIVIDE INTO FOUR GROUPS ON IRAQ WAR
Greatest number think war a mistake, want timetable for withdrawal

by Jeffrey M. Jones, Gallup Poll Managing Editor

George W. Bush has said there are two tracks in the war in Iraq—a military track and a political track. Americans' views on the war likely have two components as well—whether or not Americans support the initial decision to go to war in 2003, and whether or not they think the United States should continue its military efforts in Iraq. Indeed, a recent Gallup Poll asking Americans why they supported or opposed the war found the most common reasons given were agreement or disagreement with going to war in the first place and an assessment of the United States' progress (or lack thereof) in the war effort. An analysis of recent Gallup Poll data shows that most Americans are consistent in their views, holding pro- or anti-war opinions on both counts. But a sizable proportion shows evidence of mixed views on the war.

Two Dimensions of War Support

Support for the decision to go to war is measured by Gallup's historical trend question of whether the United States made a "mistake in

sending troops to Iraq." In the June 24-26 CNN/*USA Today*/Gallup poll, 53% of Americans said it was a mistake while 46% said it was not.

Support for continuing the military efforts is measured by a newer question that asks whether the United States should set a timetable for withdrawing its troops (and stick to it regardless of what is happening in Iraq), or keep a significant number of troops in Iraq until the situation is stable, even if that takes many years. The same poll found 51% of Americans favoring a timetable and 44% wanting to keep troops in Iraq as long as needed. (Gallup conducted a poll in the days following Bush's nationally televised address on Iraq last Tuesday night, and found no fundamental change in Americans' views of the Iraq war.)

However, Americans do not neatly divide into two large pro- and anti-war groups, as the divided views on the two questions might suggest. There are really four camps that Americans fall into when evaluating the ongoing war in Iraq. The largest segment of Americans, 36%, is anti-war on both questions—they believe it was a mistake to send troops to Iraq and believe the United States should set a timetable for withdrawal. A slightly smaller proportion, 30%, is pro-war on both dimensions—they do not believe it was a mistake to send troops and believe the United States should keep troops in Iraq as long as needed.

Twenty-eight percent of Americans have mixed views of the war—14% agree with the decision to go to war but think the United States should now look to withdraw troops. This group can be considered to be "losing patience." Another 14% believe the United States made a mistake in going to war, but think the country should keep troops in Iraq anyway until the situation stabilizes; these can be considered to be "feeling boxed in."

Opinion on Iraq War and Troops in Iraq

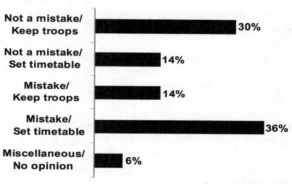

June 24-26, 2005

Iraq Opinion by Subgroup

The following table shows how members of key demographic subgroups fall into the four categories of Iraq opinion.

Group	Pro-war: War not a mistake/ Keep troops %	Losing patience: War not a mistake/ Set timetable %	Feeling boxed in: War a mistake/ Keep troops %	Anti-war: War a mistake/ Set timetable %
Male	35	12	19	30
Female	25	17	10	40
White	34	15	14	31
Nonwhite	14	11	15	53

Group	Pro-war: War not a mistake/ Keep troops	Losing patience: War not a mistake/ Set timetable	Feeling boxed in: War a mistake/ Keep troops	Anti-war: War a mistake/ Set timetable
	%	%	%	%
18-29 yrs old	20	17	13	42
30-49 yrs old	34	19	12	31
50-64 yrs old	31	12	15	37
65 yrs and older	28	8	20	36
HS or less	24	14	14	41
Some college	32	17	14	33
College grad	37	15	14	30
Postgraduate	33	10	19	34
Democrat	10	10	19	56
Independent	23	14	18	39
Republican	57	20	6	11
Liberal	8	11	20	56
Moderate	23	18	16	37
Conservative	51	13	9	21

Between 60% and 70% of every demographic group shown above has either pro- or anti-war attitudes. In other words, the proportions holding consistent views and the proportions holding mixed (or, perhaps, conflicted) views of the war are similar across demographic subgroups.

However, the groups differ in terms of the general thrust of their war views. For example, 35% of men agree with the decision to go to war and want to stay the course, while only 25% of women share this view. Four in 10 women think the war was a mistake and want the United States to set a timetable for withdrawal, as do just 30% of men.

Younger adults (those between the ages of 18 and 29) are twice as likely to hold consistent anti-war views as to hold consistent pro-war views. In other age groups, the distribution of pro- versus anti-war opinions is much closer.

Two of the largest subgroup differences are by race and party. A majority of nonwhites (53%) are anti-war, while 14% are pro-war and 26% have mixed views. Whites are much more divided in their views—34% are pro-war, 31% anti-war, and 29% have mixed opinions.

Republicans' and Democrats' war opinions are nearly mirror images of each other. Fifty-six percent of Democrats are anti-war, 19% are feeling boxed in, 10% are losing patience, and 10% are pro-war. On the other hand, 57% of Republicans are pro-war, 20% are losing patience, 6% are feeling boxed in, and only 11% are anti-war.

Survey Methods

These results are based on telephone interviews with a randomly selected national sample of 1,009 adults, aged 18 and older, conducted June 24-26, 2005. For results based on this sample, one can say with 95% confidence that the maximum error attributable to sampling and other random effects is ±3 percentage points. In addition to sampling error, question wording and practical difficulties in conducting surveys can introduce error or bias into the findings of public opinion polls.

July 6, 2005
CHOOSING A NEW SUPREME COURT JUSTICE
Fifty-seven percent of weekly churchgoers say choice of next justice matters a great deal to them

*by Frank Newport, Gallup Poll Editor in Chief and
Joseph Carroll, Assistant Editor*

Last week's announcement that U.S. Supreme Court Justice Sandra Day O'Connor will retire has made her potential replacement the major domestic news story of the moment. Some estimates are that tens of millions of dollars will be spent in the intense lobbying effort from both sides as President George W. Bush ponders his choice to replace O'Connor on the bench. A number of recent Gallup polls have asked the American public about the issues involved in appointing a new justice to the court. What follows is a review of several key points derived from the results.

How Much Does the Next Supreme Court Justice Matter to Americans?

A recent CNN/*USA Today*/Gallup survey, conducted prior to O'Connor's retirement announcement, finds that nearly half of Americans, 48%, say the choice of a new Supreme Court justice matters a great deal to them. An additional 26% say it matters a moderate amount, and about one in four say it does not matter much (19%) or at all (7%).

Suppose one of the U.S. Supreme Court justices retires this year. How much would the choice of a new Supreme Court justice matter to you — a great deal, a moderate amount, not much, or not at all?

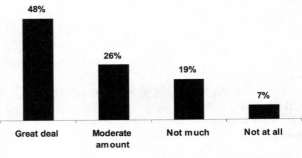

June 24-26, 2005

In general, the choice of the next Supreme Court justice appears to be most important to those who attend church weekly, to those who are politically or ideologically committed to one side of the political spectrum or the other (as opposed to moderates and independents), and to older Americans.

Conversely, the choice appears to be least important to those who are less likely to have strong opinions on politics, younger Americans, and those who seldom or never attend church.

More generally, at least half of the respondents in the following groups say the choice of a new justice matters a great deal to them: weekly churchgoers (57%), liberals (56%), conservatives (55%), weekly churchgoers who are white (55%), men aged 50 and older (54%), women aged 50 and older (52%), women (50%), Republicans (50%), and Democrats (50%).

How much would the choice of a new Supreme Court justice matter to you?

	June 24-26, 2005 Percentage saying "great deal"
	%
Weekly churchgoers	57
Liberals	56
Conservatives	55
White weekly churchgoers	55
Men, aged 50 and older	54
Women, aged 50 and older	52
Women	50
Republicans	50
Democrats	50
Nearly weekly/monthly churchgoers	49
All U.S. adults	48
Women, aged 18 to 49	48
Men	47
Independents	45
Those who seldom/never attend church	43
Men, aged 18 to 49	41
Moderates	40

Groups for which the choice of the next justice does not matter as much include those who attend church on a semi-regular basis (49%), women aged 18 to 49 (48%), men (47%), independents (45%), those who rarely or ever attend church (43%), men aged 18 to 49 (41%), and moderates (40%).

The Impact of Abortion

Much of the attention being paid to the selection of a new Supreme Court justice is based on the potential for O'Connor's replacement to affect future court rulings on the controversial issue of abortion. More specifically, press accounts suggest that conservatives are energized by the prospect of a new justice overturning the Roe v. Wade decision, while liberals would appear to be greatly worried about exactly that same possibility.

Historically, only a minority of Americans have told Gallup that abortion should be totally illegal, while a majority says it should be legal under certain circumstances. Most recently, a June 24-26 Gallup poll found that 55% of Americans said abortion should be legal under certain circumstances, while 24% said it should be legal under any circumstances, and 20% said it should be illegal in all circumstances. The 55% who say abortion should be legal in some circumstances breaks down to 40% who say it should be legal in just a few instances, and 15% who say it should be legal under most circumstances.

When asked specifically if they would want the new justice to vote to overturn Roe v. Wade or to vote to uphold that decision, Americans overwhelmingly would want that justice to uphold the decision (65%) rather than overturn it (29%).

In fact, less than a majority of most traditionally conservative groups favor overturning Roe v. Wade.

Three traditionally conservative groups of Americans—while above average in wanting a new justice who would overturn Roe—are essentially divided in their views about the decision: weekly churchgoers, regardless of race (49% of whom say overturn to 45% who say keep), conservatives (47% to 46%), and Republicans (46% to 47%).

White weekly churchgoers are more likely than any other group included in this analysis to say that they would want the new justice to vote to overturn Roe v. Wade—but even among this group only

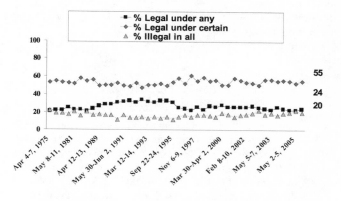

Do you think abortions should be legal under any circumstances, legal only under certain circumstances, or illegal in all circumstances?

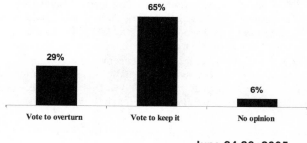

If one of the U.S. Supreme Court justices retired, would you want the new Supreme Court justice to be someone who would vote to overturn Roe v. Wade — the decision that legalized abortion — or vote to uphold it?

June 24-26, 2005

52% offer this response while 41% saying they would want to keep Roe v. Wade.

As the table below shows, at least 6 in 10 Americans in the rest of the demographic subgroups in this analysis would want the new Supreme Court justice to vote to uphold the decision.

If one of the U.S. Supreme Court justices retired, would you want the new Supreme Court justice to be someone who would vote to overturn Roe v. Wade—the decision that legalized abortion—or vote to uphold it?

	June 24-26, 2005 Vote to overturn	Vote to keep
	%	%
White weekly churchgoers	52	41
Weekly churchgoers	49	45
Conservatives	47	46
Republicans	46	47
Women, aged 18 to 49	32	64
Women	31	64
Women, aged 50 and older	30	63
All U.S. adults	29	65
Men, aged 50 and older	29	65
Nearly weekly/monthly churchgoers	29	64
Men	28	66
Men, aged 18 to 49	28	67

	June 24-26, 2005 Vote to overturn %	Vote to keep %
Democrats	22	76
Moderates	21	74
Independents	21	71
Those who seldom/never attend church	18	79
Liberals	16	81

A More Liberal or More Conservative Court?

Do Americans want the U.S. Supreme Court to become more conservative, more liberal, or would they want to maintain its current political balance? Gallup's June 16-19 poll finds that 41% of Americans say they would like the court to become more conservative, while 30% would want it more liberal, and 24% would keep it as it is now.

Those Americans who are most likely to say they want the court to become more conservative include (not surprisingly) those who identify themselves as conservatives (71% more conservative to 8% more liberal), Republicans (64% to 10%), whites who attend church weekly (60% to 17%), and all Americans who go to religious services on a weekly basis (55% to 19%).

Those who are most likely to want the Supreme Court to become more liberal include self-defined liberals (70% more liberal to 10% more conservative) and Democrats (46% to 25%). Slightly more than a third of those who rarely or never go to church (37%), and younger men (36%) say they want the court to become more liberal.

One interesting note about partisan differences—Republicans are more inclined to want the court to become more conservative than Democrats are in wanting the court to become more liberal.

Suppose one of the U.S. Supreme Court Justices retires at the end of this term. Would you like to see President Bush nominate a new justice who would make the Supreme Court—[ROTATED: more liberal than it currently is, more conservative than it currently is]—or who would keep the Court as it is now?

	June 16-19, 2005		
	More liberal %	More conservative %	Keep same as now %
Liberals	70	10	17
Democrats	46	25	24
Those who seldom/ never attend church	37	30	27
Men, aged 18 to 49	36	37	26
Independents	34	35	27
Nearly weekly/monthly churchgoers	32	44	21
Men	32	40	24
Moderates	32	29	35
Women, aged 18 to 49	31	41	23
All U.S. adults	30	41	24
Women	28	42	25
Women, aged 50 and older	26	43	26
Men, aged 50 and older	25	46	22
Weekly churchgoers	19	55	22
White weekly churchgoers	17	60	20
Republicans	10	64	23
Conservatives	8	71	18

Views of Alberto Gonzales

Although Bush has given no official indication of whom he is considering nominating to replace O'Connor, some news reports have focused on long-time Bush friend Alberto Gonzales, the recently confirmed Attorney General of the United States. Some conservatives have expressed reservations about Gonzales (despite the fact that he is a Republican and closely tied to Bush) because decisions he made while serving on the Texas state Supreme Court are viewed as having favored abortion rights and affirmative action programs.

Currently, Gallup finds Americans view Gonzales more favorably than unfavorably—by an almost two-to-one margin—but half of Americans do not know enough about him to rate him.

Those who view Gonzales favorably include Republicans (44% favorable rating), conservatives (42%), and men (41% rating among older men, 39% among all men, and 38% among younger men).

Gonzales is viewed least favorably among Democrats, liberals, and women. There is thus no sign—as of late June—that conservatives and/or Republicans have anything less than the favorable opinion of Gonzales that would be expected, although this question did not ask specifically for opinions of a Gonzales nomination to the Supreme Court. It is important to note that a large percentage of respondents in these groups are unfamiliar with Gonzales.

Opinion of Alberto Gonzales

	June 24-26, 2005		
	Favorable %	Unfavorable %	Never heard of/ no opinion %
Republicans	44	5	51
Conservatives	42	9	49
Men, aged 50 and older	41	20	39
Men	39	18	43
Men, aged 18 to 49	38	17	45
Nearly weekly/ monthly churchgoers	38	11	51
Independents	34	19	47
All U.S. adults	32	17	51
Moderates	31	16	53
Those who seldom/ never attend church	31	20	49
Weekly churchgoers	30	17	53
White weekly churchgoers	30	16	54
Women, aged 18 to 49	27	14	59
Women	26	15	59
Women, aged 50 and older	24	17	59
Liberals	20	34	46
Democrats	20	25	55

What Will Bush and the Democrats in the Senate Do?

Over the past few weeks, Gallup has asked Americans several questions about what the Republicans and Democrats might do in the process to appoint a new Supreme Court justice.

- Roughly two in three Americans say it is at least somewhat likely that the president would appoint someone to the court who would let his or her religious beliefs inappropriately influence his or her legal decisions. About a third say this is not likely.
- More than 8 in 10 Americans say it is very (58%) or somewhat (28%) likely that the Democrats in the Senate would attempt to block Bush's nominee for inappropriate political reasons. Twelve percent say this is not too or not at all likely.

How likely do you think it is that Bush would appoint someone to the U.S. Supreme Court who would let their religious beliefs inappropriately influence their legal decisions?

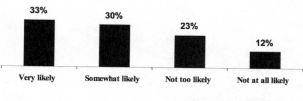

Very likely	Somewhat likely	Not too likely	Not at all likely
33%	30%	23%	12%

June 24-26, 2005

How likely do you think it is that the Democrats in the Senate would attempt to block Bush's nominee for inappropriate political reasons?

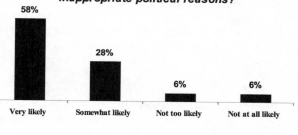

Very likely	Somewhat likely	Not too likely	Not at all likely
58%	28%	6%	6%

June 24-26, 2005

- Earlier in June, Gallup asked a question about what Bush should do if he nominates someone that he thinks is the best person for the job but that almost all the Democrats in the Senate oppose because of that nominee's stance on important issues. A slim majority of Americans in that poll, 51%, say Bush should nominate another person who the Democrats find acceptable in this instance, while 46% say he should still nominate that person.

Suppose President Bush decides to nominate the person who he thinks is the best choice for the U.S. Supreme Court, but almost all the Democrats in the Senate oppose the nominee because they disagree with that person on important issues. Should President Bush: still nominate the person he thinks is best for the job, or should he nominate another well qualified person whom the Democrats find acceptable?

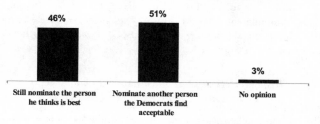

Still nominate the person he thinks is best	Nominate another person the Democrats find acceptable	No opinion
46%	51%	3%

June 16-19, 2005

- Another question in that mid-June poll asked Americans about what the Democrats in the Senate should do if they oppose Bush's nominee because they disagree with that person on important issues. A slight majority of Americans, 53%, say the Democrats in the Senate should work to defeat the nomination, while 40% say they should vote to confirm the nominee.

Suppose almost all the Democrats in the Senate oppose President Bush's nominee for the U.S. Supreme Court because they disagree with that person on important issues. Should the Democrats in the Senate: still vote to confirm the president's nominee _unless_ they believe that the person is not qualified legally or ethically, or should they work to defeat the nomination to try to get the president to pick someone that is more acceptable to them?

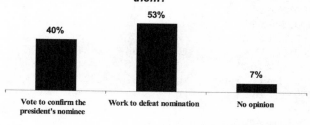

Vote to confirm the president's nominee	Work to defeat nomination	No opinion
40%	53%	7%

June 16-19, 2005

Survey Methods

These results are based on telephone interviews with a randomly selected national sample of 1,009 adults, aged 18 and older, conducted June 24-26, 2005. For results based on this sample, one can say with 95% confidence that the maximum error attributable to sampling and other random effects is ±3 percentage points. In addition to sampling error, question wording and practical difficulties in conducting surveys can introduce error or bias into the findings of public opinion polls.

July 7, 2005
PUBLIC AMBIVALENT ABOUT NEW IMMIGRANTS
About half want to curtail immigration, though clear majority says it is good for the country

by David W. Moore, Gallup Poll Senior Editor

By an almost two-to-one margin, Americans say that immigration is a good, rather than bad, thing for this country today. Yet, the public is about evenly divided as to whether immigration should be curtailed, as opposed to being kept at its current level or increased. Americans are also divided as to whether immigrants in the long run become productive citizens and pay their fair share of taxes or cost the government too much money by using too many public services, and whether immigrants mostly help or hurt the economy. As for illegal immigrants, most Americans oppose making it easier for them to become citizens.

These results come from a Gallup survey conducted June 6-25, 2005, which included large oversamples of both blacks and Hispanics. The poll finds that Hispanics are much more favorable toward immigration and the impact of immigrants than are either blacks or non-Hispanic whites.

The poll shows that 46% of Americans want immigration into the United States to decline, while 16% say it should be increased and another 34% would keep it at the current level.

In your view, should immigration be kept at its present level, increased, or decreased?

	Present level %	Increased %	Decreased %	No opinion %
2005 Jun 6-25	34	16	46	4
2004 Jun 9-30	33	14	49	4
2003 Jun 12-18	37	13	47	3
2002 Sep 2-4	26	17	54	3
2002 Jun 3-9	36	12	49	3
2001 Oct 19-21	30	8	58	4
2001 Jun 11-17	42	14	41	3
2001 Mar 26-28	41	10	43	6
2000 Sep 11-13	41	13	38	8
1999 Feb 26-28 ^	41	10	44	5
1995 Jul 7-9	27	7	62	4
1995 Jun 5-6	24	7	65	4
1993 Jul 9-11	27	6	65	2
1986 Jun 19-23 †	35	7	49	9
1977 Mar 25-28	37	7	42	14
1965 Jun 24-29	39	7	33	20

^ Asked of a half sample
† CBS/*New York Times* poll

These views have varied little during the past four years, with the percentage saying immigration should be decreased varying from a low of 41% in 2001 to a high of 49% in 2002 and 2004.

In the early and mid-1990s, anti-immigration sentiment was considerably more widespread than it is now. Also, the public rated the economy much more negatively then than they do now.

Despite the current caution about the rate of immigration, 61% of Americans say that immigration is a good thing for this country today, while only 34% say it is a bad thing. Gallup's polls during the past four years have consistently shown a substantial margin giving a positive evaluation of immigration.

On the whole, do you think immigration is a good thing or a bad thing for this country today?

	Good thing %	Bad thing %	MIXED (vol.) %	No opinion %
2005 Jun 6-25	61	34	3	2
2003 Jun 12-18	58	36	4	2
2002 Jun 3-9	52	42	4	2
2001 Jun 11-17	62	31	5	2

(Vol.) Volunteered response

Despite the general positive view about immigration, Americans are about evenly divided about the economic impact of more immigrants into this country.

One question shows that 49% believe immigrants in the long run become productive citizens and pay their fair share of taxes, while 44% disagree.

Which comes closer to your point of view—[ROTATED: immigrants in the long-run become productive citizens and pay their fair share of taxes, (or) immigrants cost the taxpayers too much by using government services like public education and medical services?]

	Pay fair share of taxes %	Cost taxpayers too much %	No opinion %
2005 Jun 6-25	49	44	7
2000 Sep 11-13	48	40	12
1999 Feb 26-28	47	45	8
1994 Dec 16-18	36	57	7
1993 Jul 9-11	37	56	7

Views were much more negative in the early 1990s, when substantial majorities of Americans expressed the more negative view—that immigrants cost taxpayers too much money. Those negative results could have reflected the more dire economic conditions that many people were experiencing compared with the economic situation in recent years.

Americans today are also divided on whether immigrants mostly help the economy by providing low cost labor, or hurt the economy by driving wages down. Last year, Americans expressed the more negative assessment by greater than a two-to-one margin (65% said immigrants hurt the economy, while 30% said they helped). This year, the margin is more modest—49% say immigrants hurt, 42% say they help the economy.

Do you think immigrants—[ROTATED: mostly help the economy by providing low cost labor, (or) mostly hurt the economy by driving wages down for many Americans?]

	Mostly help %	Mostly hurt %	NEITHER (vol.) %	BOTH (vol.) %	No opinion %
2005 Jun 6-25	42	49	3	3	3
2004 Jan 9-11 ^	30	65	2	1	2
2000 Sep 11-13	44	40	7	3	6
1999 Feb 26-28	42	48	3	1	6
1993 Jul 9-11	28	64	2	2	4

(Vol.) Volunteered response
^ Asked of a half sample

The low marks in 2004 could partially be the result of the presidential campaign, during which Democrats criticized Republicans and President George W. Bush for the state of the economy. In 1993, Gallup recorded a similarly low evaluation of immigrants, at a time when the public's rating of the economy was much lower than it is today.

While Americans are generally divided over the economic impact of immigrants, they are decidedly against making it easier for illegal immigrants to become citizens. Just 28% want to make it easier, while 70% are opposed.

Hispanics Much More Favorable to Immigration Than Non-Hispanic Whites and Blacks

The poll shows relatively small differences in attitudes about immigration and the impact of immigrants between blacks and non-Hispanic whites. But it shows a major gulf in attitudes between Hispanics and the other two groups.

Only 32% of Hispanics want to curtail immigration, compared with 44% of blacks and 50% of non-Hispanic whites.

While 74% of Hispanics say that immigration is a good thing for the country today, just 60% of non-Hispanic whites and 55% of blacks agree.

In your view, should immigration be kept at its present level, increased, or decreased?

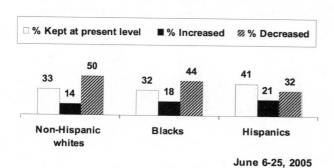

June 6-25, 2005

On the whole, do you think immigration is a good thing or a bad thing for this country today?

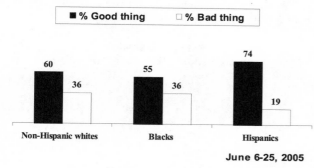

June 6-25, 2005

Blacks and non-Hispanic whites are about evenly divided as to whether immigrants ultimately pay their fair share of taxes. Most Hispanics take a positive view—66% say immigrants do pay their fair share, while only 27% disagree.

Which comes closer to your point of view: immigrants in the long-run become productive citizens and pay their fair share of taxes, or immigrants cost the taxpayers too much by using government services like public education and medical services?

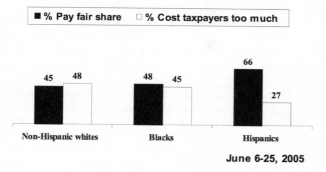

June 6-25, 2005

Blacks are most likely to say that immigrants hurt rather than help the economy, by 66% to 26%. A smaller majority of non-Hispanic whites agree, by 52% to 39%. But most Hispanics take the opposite point of view, saying that immigrants help rather than hurt the economy by 66% to 27%.

Do you think immigrants: mostly _help_ the economy by providing low cost labor, or mostly _hurt_ the economy by driving wages down for many Americans?

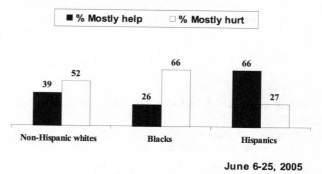

June 6-25, 2005

Finally, large majorities of both blacks (67%) and non-Hispanic whites (79%) are opposed to making it easier for illegal immigrants to become citizens, while a large majority of Hispanics (70%) takes the opposite point of view.

Do you think the United States should or should not make it easier for illegal immigrants to become citizens of the United States?

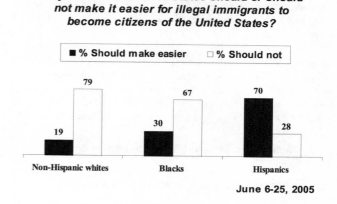

June 6-25, 2005

Survey Methods

Results are based on telephone interviews with 2,264 national adults, aged 18 and older, conducted June 6-25, 2005, including oversamples of blacks and Hispanics that are weighted to reflect their proportions in the general population. For results based on the total sample of national adults, one can say with 95% confidence that the maximum margin of sampling error is ±5 percentage points.

Results for the sample of 807 non-Hispanic whites, aged 18 and older, are based on telephone interviews conducted June 6-25, 2005. For results based on the total sample, one can say with 95% confidence that the maximum margin of sampling error is ±7 percentage points.

Results for the sample of 802 blacks, aged 18 and older, are based on telephone interviews conducted June 6-25, 2005. For results based on the total sample, one can say with 95% confidence that the maximum margin of sampling error is ±5 percentage points.

Results for the sample of 511 Hispanics, aged 18 and older, are based on telephone interviews conducted June 6-25, 2005. For results based on the total sample, one can say with 95% confidence that the maximum margin of sampling error is ±5 percentage points. (181 out of the 511 interviews with Hispanics were conducted in Spanish).

In addition to sampling error, question wording and practical difficulties in conducting surveys can introduce error or bias into the findings of public opinion polls.

July 11, 2005
AMERICANS EXPRESS CONFIDENCE IN NASA
Most say they are fairly confident agency can prevent another space shuttle disaster

by Jeffrey M. Jones, Gallup Poll Managing Editor

NASA is preparing to launch the space shuttle Discovery on Wednesday, which would be the first space shuttle mission since the Columbia disaster in February 2003. A new CNN/*USA Today*/Gallup poll finds most Americans say they have at least a fair amount of confidence in NASA to prevent another such disaster. Nearly three in four Americans favor a continuation of the manned space shuttle program, and a majority believes NASA is moving at an appropriate pace in restarting it. A majority also evaluates NASA positively for the job it is doing overall.

The June 24-26 poll finds 74% of Americans saying the United States should continue the manned space shuttle program, while 21% disagree. Historically, Americans have supported the program, even in the immediate aftermath of the Challenger and Columbia shuttle disasters. Gallup Polls conducted following those disasters showed 8 in 10 Americans favoring a continuation of the program.

Continue the Manned Space Shuttle Program?

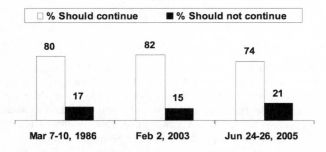

Public support for the continuation of shuttle missions may be related to Americans' confidence that NASA can avoid another such disaster. The poll finds 76% saying they have either a great deal (20%) or fair amount (56%) of confidence in NASA to prevent a similar event. That's about the same level of confidence that Americans expressed after the two shuttle explosions in 1986 and 2003, although more Americans had a great deal of confidence in NASA in those polls than do currently.

An earlier CNN/*USA Today*/Gallup poll, conducted in late April and early May, found two in three Americans saying NASA is moving "at the right pace" in restarting the shuttle program, while 18% say "too quickly" and 10% say "too slowly." NASA had initially scheduled the Discovery launch for May, but postponed it to make some additional repairs.

Confidence in NASA

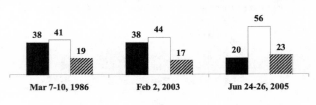

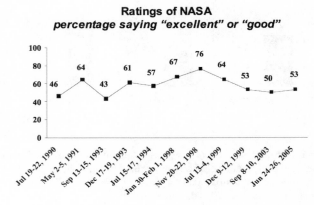

NASA Viewed Positively Overall

At a more basic level, 53% of Americans say NASA is doing an "excellent" or "good" job. Thirty-four percent say "fair" and 6% say "poor." Those views have remained remarkably stable since 1999. NASA was rated significantly more positively in 1998 when it sent former Sen. John Glenn into space, and lower in 1993 when NASA "lost" the Mars Observer probe and was having trouble getting clear pictures from the Hubble telescope.

Ratings of NASA are fairly consistent by subgroup, with the main exception coming in terms of age. Sixty percent of Americans below age 50 say NASA is doing an excellent or good job, compared with just 43% of those aged 50 or older.

Mars Mission

While Americans express support for NASA in general and the space shuttle program in particular, they are apparently less likely to favor a mission to Mars, one of NASA's (and President George W. Bush's) future goals for space exploration. Fifty-eight percent say they oppose setting aside the money for an attempted Mars landing, while 40% are in favor.

Gallup asked the same question in 1999 and 1969 (immediately after the moon landing) and found similar results.

Men and women take very different views of funding a Mars landing. Men favor funding such a mission by 51% to 47%, but women oppose it by 68% to 29%. Additionally, 47% of adults under age 50 support the United States undertaking a mission to Mars, compared with just 31% of those aged 50 and older.

Survey Methods

These results are based on telephone interviews with a randomly selected national sample of 1,009 adults, aged 18 and older, con-

Send an Astronaut to Mars?

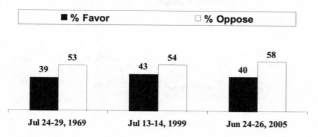

ducted June 24-26, 2005. For results based on this sample, one can say with 95% confidence that the maximum error attributable to sampling and other random effects is ±3 percentage points. In addition to sampling error, question wording and practical difficulties in conducting surveys can introduce error or bias into the findings of public opinion polls.

July 12, 2005
PUBLIC: LIKELIHOOD OF TERRORIST ATTACK IN UNITED STATES NOW HIGHER
Sharp jump in number of Americans who say Iraq has made U.S. less safe from terrorism

by David W. Moore, Gallup Poll Senior Editor

A new CNN/*USA Today*/Gallup survey this past weekend shows that the July 7 terrorist attacks in London have raised the specter of more terrorism in the United States, with a majority of Americans now expecting an imminent attack.

There is also a sharp increase in the percentage who say the war in Iraq has made the country less safe from terrorism, and that terrorism is the most important problem facing the country.

Still, there is virtually no change in public opinion about who is winning the war on terrorism or the Bush administration's ability to protect U.S. citizens from terrorism.

Bush's approval is at 49%, up from 46% at the end of June.

The poll, conducted July 7-10, finds that a majority of Americans, 55%, now believe that terrorists will strike in this country within the next several weeks, up from only 35% who held that view last month.

How likely is it that there will be further acts of terrorism in the United States over the next several weeks?

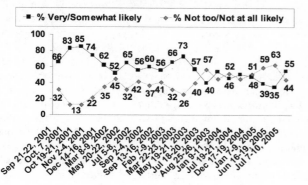

In October 2001, following the 9/11 terrorist attacks, more than 8 in 10 Americans expected further strikes, but over time that expectation declined. It rose again as the United States prepared to invade Iraq in early 2003, reaching 73% just after the launch of the war. Again, expectations of more terrorist acts declined, but fluctuated with events in Iraq.

At the beginning of this year, as Iraq prepared for and eventually held elections, the number of Americans expecting more terrorism in the United States dropped. Last month was the lowest level measured by Gallup since September 2001. The current level is the highest since August 2003, when 54% of Americans said new terrorist strikes were likely.

Another consequence of the attacks in London is that more Americans now believe that the war in Iraq has made the United States less safe from terrorism. Less than two weeks ago, a Gallup survey showed only 39% saying "less safe," but that is up to 54% in the latest poll. The percentage who say the Iraq war has made the United States safer declined by four points, from 44% at the end of June to 40% now. Most of the increase in the "less safe" assessment apparently comes from people who said last month that the war had no effect on U.S. safety.

Do you think the war with Iraq has made the U.S. safer — or less safe — from terrorism?

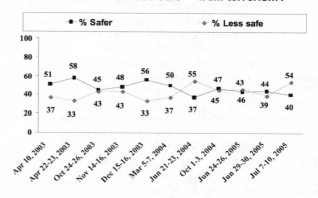

Other evidence for the heightened salience of terrorism is that 17% of Americans now say it is the most important problem facing the country today. Last month, just 8% volunteered terrorism as the most important problem.

While the attacks in London made Americans more likely to think another strike is imminent in the United States, opinion is little changed on the public's evaluation of the war or of the Bush administration's ability to protect the country.

Most Important Problem
percentage mentioning terrorism

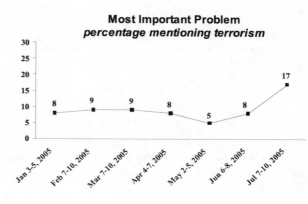

Currently, 34% of Americans believe the United States and its allies are winning the war against terrorism, virtually unchanged from the 36% who expressed that view last month. Still, the current figure represents a 6-point decline from a year ago, and a 17-point decline from January 2004, when 51% of Americans thought the United States and its allies were winning.

Who do you think is currently winning the war against terrorism?

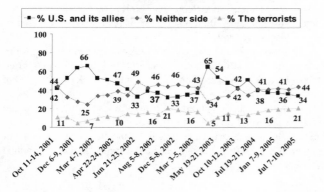

The public's assessment of a U.S. victory was highest when the United States successfully ousted the Taliban from power in Afghanistan. In January 2002, 66% of Americans said the United States was winning. That optimism declined over the next year, though it surged again when the United States invaded Iraq, reaching 65%. The optimism began declining shortly after Bush announced the end of major fighting in Iraq, and reaching a low of 34% in the latest poll. It averaged 35% between June and December 2002.

Despite the relatively negative assessment of how the war on terrorism is going, there has been no recent change in the mostly positive rating of the Bush administration's ability to protect U.S. citizens from terrorism. Sixty-one percent of Americans say they have either a "great deal" or a "moderate amount" of confidence in the Bush administration on this matter, identical to last month's measure.

How much confidence do you have in the Bush administration to protect U.S. citizens from future acts of terrorism?

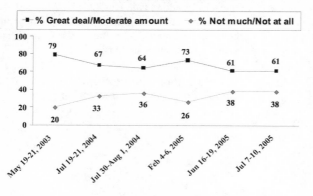

Current views are somewhat less positive than they were in February, when 73% expressed high confidence. After Bush announced the end of major fighting in Iraq in May 2003, confidence was even higher, at 79%.

Bush's Overall Job Approval Rating January 2005 — July 2005

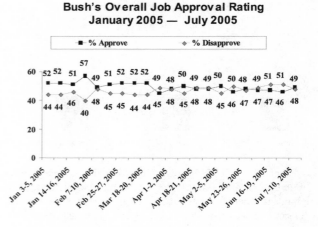

Since the end of March, Bush's approval rating, as measured by Gallup, has fluctuated between 45% and 50%, averaging just over 47%. The three-point increase in Bush's job approval rating from last month is within the poll's margin of error.

Survey Methods

Results are based on telephone interviews with 1,006 national adults, aged 18 and older, conducted July 7-10, 2005. For results based on the total sample of national adults, one can say with 95% confidence that the maximum margin of sampling error is ±3 percentage points. For results based on the 489 national adults in the Form A half-sample and 517 national adults in the Form B half-sample, the maximum margins of sampling error are ±5 percentage points.

In addition to sampling error, question wording and practical difficulties in conducting surveys can introduce error or bias into the findings of public opinion polls.

July 12, 2005
ONE-THIRD OF AMERICANS BELIEVE DEARLY MAY NOT HAVE DEPARTED
Belief declines with age

by Linda Lyons, Education and Youth Editor

Most people love a good ghost story, especially one that takes place in a haunted house. The 1979 horror classic, *Amityville Horror*—in which a family moves into a large house with malevolent ghostly inhabitants—spawned a remake released this spring. Among this year's other supernatural offerings are *Dark Water,* a tale about a haunted New York apartment, and *Boogeyman*, about a man who is forced to face the dark demons in his childhood home.

In a June 6-8 poll*, 37% of Americans told Gallup they believe in haunted houses, while 46% say they don't, and 16% aren't sure.

Belief in haunted houses declines with age. Fifty-six percent of young adults between the ages of 18 and 29 believe in them, but belief drops to 39% among 30- to 49-year-olds, to 30% among those between the ages of 50 and 64, and to just one in four (26%) among Americans 65 and older.

Many people not only believe in haunted houses, they actually seek them out on vacations, according to Danica Shurlan, front desk

Haunted Houses

For each of the following items I am going to read you, please tell me whether it is something you believe in, something you're not sure about, or something you don't believe in. How about . . . that houses can be haunted?

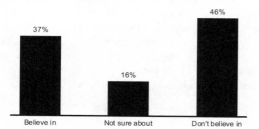

Belief in Ghosts by Age Group

Those saying "believe in"

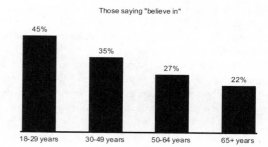

Belief in Haunted Houses, by Age Group

For each of the following items I am going to read you, please tell me whether it is something you believe in, something you're not sure about, or something you don't believe in. How about . . . that houses can be haunted?

Percentage saying "believe in"

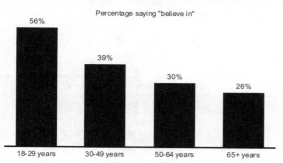

compared with 35% of 30- to 49-year-olds and 27% of 50- to 64-year-olds. Just 22% of respondents aged 65 and older believe.

The tendency to believe in some paranormal occurrences varies by ideology—political conservatives appear significantly more skeptical than either moderates or liberals. Twenty-eight percent of conservatives believe in haunted houses versus 42% of moderates and 42% of liberals. Similar patterns emerge with respect to ghosts—25% of conservatives believe in ghosts, compared with 35% of moderates and 42% of liberals. Age could partly explain the ideological differences—younger adults tend to identify more as liberals than older adults do, and younger adults are more likely to believe.

For each of the following items I am going to read you, please tell me whether it is something you believe in, something you're not sure about, or something you don't believe in. How about . . .

Percentage saying "believe in"

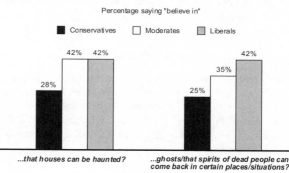

manager at the Concord (Mass.) Colonial Inn. "Room 24 is the big attraction—we call it our "room with a view-ing," she says. It's haunted, according to local lore—and to the many guests who have witnessed strange happenings while sleeping in it. One legend holds that the resident apparition is a Revolutionary War surgeon who cared for wounded soldiers at the inn in 1775. "It's always either/or," says Shurlan, "People either ask *for* the room specifically or ask to be put far, far away from it."

Ghost Stories

Haunted houses and otherworldly inhabitants go hand in hand, so it makes sense that a similar proportion of Americans believe in ghosts as believe in the houses they haunt. About a third (32%) say they believe in ghosts, while nearly half (48%) do not. About a fifth (19%) say they aren't sure about the existence of spirits.

As with haunted houses, belief in ghosts declines with age. Forty-five percent of Americans between the ages of 18 and 29 believe,

Ghosts

For each of the following items I am going to read you, please tell me whether it is something you believe in, something you're not sure about, or something you don't believe in. How about . . . ghosts/that spirits of dead people can come back in certain places/situations?

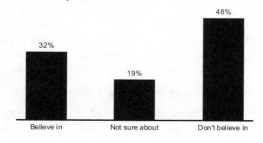

Ghostly Sightings

It is apparent to one woman that younger people are more receptive to encounters with spirits than are older people. Suzanne Scanlan, 60, wasn't even aware that she had a ghost in her 100-year-old house in Canton, Miss., until her daughter, Jessica, moved back home at age 24. "She was sleeping in the middle bedroom at the top of the stairs when she saw a black shadow moving up and down the stairway," she says. "Jessica has *never* slept in that room again—in fact, none of my children have." Although there was no mention of a ghost when the family bought the house in 1991, they have since been told that an old woman died in the kitchen many years ago.

John Ridge, one of Scanlan's neighbors, is among the three-quarters of 50- to 64-year-olds who do not believe in ghosts. Ridge, 59, recently bought a 153-year-old house in Canton that reportedly has its own live-in ghost—one Susan Nelson Priestley, the wife of the original owner. Neighbors say they often see her at night, sitting by the window in the bedroom where she died from Yellow Fever in 1858. "The real estate broker told me it was a haunted house right from the start," Ridge says, "but since I don't really believe in ghosts, it didn't bother me." Ridge reports no sightings yet, but he did have a close call the first night he spent in his new old house. "I got up in the middle of the night and passed through a very cold air patch in the hallway. I thought 'uh-oh,' but when I calmed down enough to look around, discovered I was standing under an air conditioning vent. It was a great relief—at least for now."

Results are based on telephone interviews with 1,002 national adults, aged 18 and older, conducted June 6-8, 2005. For results based on the total sample of national adults, one can say with 95% confidence that the margin of sampling error is ±3 percentage points.

July 12, 2005
WHO ARE THE PEOPLE IN YOUR NEIGHBORHOOD?
South reports highest proportion of blacks; West reports highest number of Hispanics, recent immigrants

by Joseph Carroll, Gallup Poll Assistant Editor

Gallup's annual update on race relations* suggests that Americans generally live in areas populated with people from their own racial or ethnic backgrounds. More than 8 in 10 non-Hispanic whites say they live in areas where there are many whites, while at least 6 in 10 blacks and Hispanics say many people of their respective backgrounds live in their neighborhoods. Few whites, blacks, or Hispanics say they live in areas highly populated by recent immigrants or Asians.

Racial Differences?

The poll, conducted June 6-25, asked Americans how many people of various races and ethnic backgrounds lived in their areas—"many, some, only a few, or none." The results to this question among non-Hispanic whites, blacks, and Hispanics suggest that these different groups tend to live in areas with relatively few of those from different backgrounds.

Composition of Neighborhoods by Racial and Ethnic Groups
June 6-25, 2005

	% of non-Hispanic whites who say there are "many" of each group in area	% of blacks who say there are "many" of each group in area	% of Hispanics who say there are "many" of each group in area
Whites	86%	45%	52%
Blacks	28%	66%	32%
Hispanics	32%	26%	61%
Asians	12%	6%	13%
Recent immigrants	14%	18%	30%

Three main conclusions:

1. Non-Hispanic whites are most likely to live in areas in which there are large numbers of their own race. Eighty-six percent live in areas in which there are "many" whites. By contrast, only 66% of blacks live in areas in which there are many blacks, and only 61% of Hispanics live in areas in which there are many Hispanics. Looked at differently, these data suggest that a third or more of blacks and Hispanics live in areas in which their race or ethnic group is in the decided minority.

2. Whites generally tend to live in areas in which there are less likely to be substantial concentrations of blacks and Hispanics. Only about one in three non-Hispanic whites say that there are many blacks or Hispanics in their neighborhoods. By way of contrast, 45% of blacks and 52% of Hispanics say that there are many whites in their neighborhoods.

3. Only relatively small percentages of members of all three of these groups say that there are many Asians or recent immigrants in their neighborhoods. The highest concentration of recent immigrants exists in Hispanic neighborhoods.

Regional Differences?

When looking at these results among all U.S. adults, the data show some vast differences by regions across the country—in the South, respondents tend to say there are many blacks, while in the West, areas tend to be highly populated by Hispanics and recent immigrants. Residents in the West are also slightly less likely than people elsewhere to say there are many whites living around them.

Composition of Neighborhoods by Regions
June 6-25, 2005
Percentage saying "many" live in area

	East	Midwest	South	West
Whites	80%	78%	78%	68%
Blacks	33%	26%	49%	19%
Hispanics	20%	21%	39%	55%
Asians	15%	11%	7%	17%
Recent immigrants	10%	10%	13%	33%

- Roughly 8 in 10 Americans living in the East, Midwest, and South say there are many whites in their neighborhoods, while slightly more than two in three respondents in the West say this.
- Nearly half of those living in the South (49%) say there are many blacks in their areas. This compares with about a third of those in the East, roughly one in four Midwesterners, and but fewer than one in five respondents in the West.
- A majority of people living in the West (55%) say there are many Hispanics in their areas. This percentage is much lower in the South (39%), and is even lower in the Midwest (21%) and East (20%).
- A third of respondents in the West say there are many recent immigrants in their areas, while only about 1 in 10 respondents living elsewhere offer this response.
- The data show only minor regional differences in the percentage saying there are many Asians in their area, though Southerners are least likely to say this.

These distinctions mirror what the U.S. Census reported in 2000. The Census showed that 24.3% of Western residents are Hispanic, more than twice the proportion in the East (9.8%), Midwest (4.9%), and South (11.6%). According to the Census, 18.9% of Southern residents are black, a significantly higher proportion than in the East (11.4%), Midwest (10.1%), and West (4.9%). The proportion of whites is lowest in the West (58.4%) compared with 73.4% in the East, 81.4% Midwest, and 65.8% South.

Differences by Household Income Levels?

Gallup also finds differences by household income—Americans living in higher-income households are somewhat more likely than are those living in lower-income households to say there are many Asians in their areas. The reported concentration of whites is much greater among those living in middle- and upper-income households than lower-income households. There is also a slight tendency for lower-income households to say there are many Hispanics living around them. The data show essentially no differences by household income levels for the percentage saying there are many blacks or recent immigrants living in their areas.

Composition of Neighborhoods by Household Income

June 6-25, 2005
Percentage saying "many" live in area

	Less than $30,000 per year	$30,000-$74,999	$75,000 or more per year
Whites	61%	81%	85%
Blacks	37%	31%	32%
Hispanics	40%	35%	28%
Asians	9%	9%	19%
Recent immigrants	20%	15%	18%

As the table illustrates, 85% of adults earning $75,000 per year or more say there are many whites living in their areas, while only 61% of those whose income is less than $30,000 per year offer this response. Similarly, 19% of adults in high-income households say there are many Asians in their areas, while 9% of those in lower-income households say this.

Four in 10 adults earning less than $30,000 per year say there are many Hispanics in their areas. This compares with 28% of those living in households with incomes of $75,000 or more per year.

Bottom Line

These data suggest that Americans tend to live in neighborhoods largely populated by people of similar racial or ethnic backgrounds—86% of non-Hispanic whites, 66% of blacks, and 61% of Hispanics report living in areas where there are many people from their own backgrounds. These results also show the South reports the highest proportion of blacks, while the West reports the highest number of Hispanics and recent immigrants. Higher-income households report a higher proportion of whites and Asians in their areas than those in lower-income households, while lower-income households report more Hispanics in their areas than those in higher-income households.

Results are based on telephone interviews with 2,264 national adults, aged 18 and older, conducted June 6-25, 2005, including oversamples of blacks and Hispanics that are weighted to reflect their proportions in the general population. For results based on the total sample of national adults, one can say with 95% confidence that the maximum margin of sampling error is ±5 percentage points.

Results for the sample of 807 non-Hispanic whites, aged 18 and older, are based on telephone interviews conducted June 6-25, 2005. For results based on the total sample, one can say with 95% confidence that the margin of sampling error is ±7 percentage points.

Results for the sample of 802 blacks, aged 18 and older, are based on telephone interviews conducted June 6-25, 2005. For results based on the total sample, one can say with 95% confidence that the margin of sampling error is ±5 percentage points.

Results for the sample of 511 Hispanics, aged 18 and older, are based on telephone interviews, conducted June 6-25, 2005. For

results based on the total sample, one can say with 95% confidence that the margin of sampling error is ±5 percentage points. (181 out of the 511 interviews with Hispanics were conducted in Spanish).

July 13, 2005
AMERICANS' VIEWS OF ECONOMY UNCHANGED AFTER LONDON BOMBINGS
No signs of significant change in recent months

by Frank Newport, Gallup Poll Editor in Chief

The Gallup Poll's first read on consumer confidence after last Thursday's London terror bombings shows little positive or negative change. Americans remain generally pessimistic about the economy, only about a third rate the current economy as excellent or good, and a majority say that now is not a good time to be looking for a quality job.

Competing Pressures

Competing pressures could conceivably pull consumer confidence in two directions. Some so-called "hard" economic news coming from government and other official sources has been positive of late. The gross domestic product grew at 4.4% in 2004, the best in five years; the unemployment rate in June was the lowest since September 2001; and existing home values have continued their almost meteoric rise.

At the same time, rising gas prices certainly signify bad news for most Americans who drive and/or who are not directly employed in the energy business. There was also the possibility that last week's London terror bombings would dampen consumer optimism, reminding Americans of the general fragility of the U.S. economy in an unsettled world environment.

Perhaps these types of concerns balance themselves out in the final analysis—or at least have a minimal independent impact on consumer attitudes. The latest Gallup Poll update on consumer perceptions of the economy, conducted July 7-10 (after the terror bombings in London), shows basically no change in those perceptions.

Current Economic Conditions

Consumer ratings of the current U.S. economy are roughly the same as the previous three measures obtained in late May and early

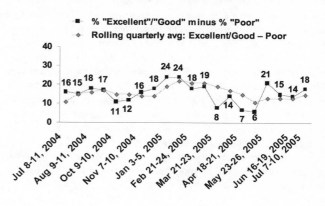

Current Economic Conditions

June, but are slightly more positive than the low points on this measure from mid-March to early May. Thirty-six percent of Americans now rate the economy as excellent or good, 45% rate it as only fair, and 18% rate it as poor. At one point in early May, 31% rated the economy as excellent or good, 44% as only fair, and 25% as poor. By way of contrast, 41% rated the economy as excellent or good in the first poll of the year in early January, and 17% rated it as poor.

None of these represent highly substantial changes at any point this year. Indeed, from a longer-range perspective, Americans' ratings of the current economy are obviously much lower than they were in the late 1990s and in 2000, but are also higher than they were in 2003. While there has been no sign that the public is returning to the more robust attitudes of five or six years ago, attitudes are sustaining themselves above the level of two years ago.

Economic Outlook

The same basic pattern is evident in the trend data on Americans' perceptions of the economy's direction. Fifty-four percent of Americans now say the economy is getting worse, while 35% say it is getting better. In early January and early February, there was a net positive optimism rating, with slightly more Americans saying the economy was getting better than saying it was getting worse.

Net optimism dropped slightly in late February before dropping further, to its lowest levels of the year, in late April and early May. It has rebounded slightly since then. Again, however, these are all relatively small changes.

Economic Outlook

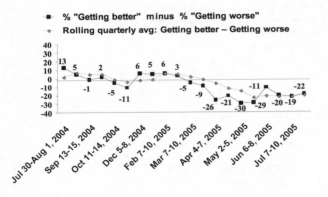

The high point in recent years for economic optimism was in January 2000, when 69% said the economy was getting better, while just 23% said it was getting worse. The low point came just before the Sept. 11, 2001, terrorist attacks, when 19% said the economy was getting better and 70% said it was getting worse.

It is important to note that Americans were generally more optimistic about the economy's direction throughout most of last year than they are now. In July 2004, for example, 51% said the economy was getting better, while 38% said it was getting worse. In fact, in 10 out of 15 surveys in 2004, Americans had a net positive outlook on the economy. In 2005, out of 12 surveys, Americans, on balance, have been optimistic about the economy in only the first 2 of the year—in January and early February. In short, the first half of this year has in general been marked by more economic pessimism than was the case throughout 2004.

Job Outlook

There is no substantive change here either. Fifty-seven percent of those who are employed or unemployed and looking for work say it's a bad time to find a quality job, while 41% say it's a good time.

Good or Bad Time to Find a Quality Job?
based on those who are employed or who are unemployed but looking for work

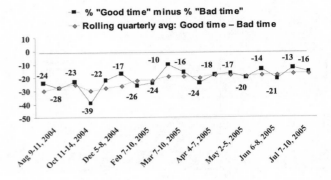

The 41% on the positive side of the ledger in response to this jobs question is not great, but substantially above where it has been within the last several years. In March 2003, for example, only 16% of workers said it was a good time to find a quality job.

Bottom Line

Americans' views of the national economy remain fairly steady—and weak. On balance, more Americans perceive the economy as getting worse than getting better, and only a little more than a third are willing to rate the current economy as excellent or good. Just about 4 out of 10 workers say it's a good time to find a quality job.

These readings of consumer confidence have not changed materially over the last month or two and did not change significantly as a result of the London bombings of last Thursday.

The broad picture shows that the American public's feelings about the economy are more positive now than they were in 2003, but well below the heights to which consumer confidence had risen at the time of the economic boom of the late 1990s.

Additionally, consumer optimism about the economy (the percentage saying the economy is getting better minus the percentage saying it is getting worse) has in general been less positive this year than it was throughout much of 2004.

Survey Methods

These results are based on telephone interviews with a randomly selected national sample of 1,006 adults, aged 18 and older, conducted July 7-10, 2005. For results based on this sample, one can say with 95% confidence that the maximum error attributable to sampling and other random effects is ±3 percentage points. For results based on the sample of 632 adults employed full- or part-time or unemployed adults looking for work, the maximum margin of sampling error is ±4 percentage points. In addition to sampling error, question wording and practical difficulties in conducting surveys can introduce error or bias into the findings of public opinion polls.

July 14, 2005

AMERICANS MOSTLY UPBEAT ABOUT CURRENT RACE RELATIONS

Majority of blacks believe relations with whites will always be problematic

by Lydia Saad, Gallup Poll Senior Editor

As the National Association for the Advancement of Colored People (NAACP) meets in Milwaukee this week for its 96th annual convention, Gallup's annual Minority Rights and Relations poll reports both encouraging and not so encouraging attitudes about relations between whites and blacks in the United States.

The June 6-25, 2005, survey includes large oversamples of blacks and Hispanics that allow for statistically reliable analyses of their views, in addition to the views of non-Hispanic whites.

On the positive side, most Americans are upbeat when asked to rate the quality of overall relations between whites and blacks. Roughly two-thirds of Americans—including majorities of whites and blacks—believe these inter-race relations are "very" or "somewhat" good.

Public perceptions of how well whites and blacks get along are about the same as perceptions of white-Hispanic relations. Seventy percent of Americans describe relations between whites and Hispanics as either very or somewhat good. By comparison, Americans are slightly more likely to think that whites and Asians have good relations (79%). Americans are somewhat less likely to believe that blacks and Hispanics get along (56%).

Percent Saying Each Pair of Races Has Very/Somewhat Good Relations

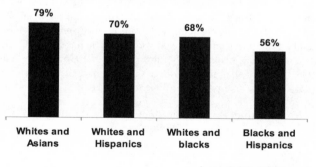

Percent of All Americans Saying Each Pair of Races Has Very/Somewhat Good Relations

June 6-25, 2005

A separate question finds that a majority of Americans believe only a few whites and blacks dislike members of the other race. However, a substantial number disagrees: 43% of blacks say that many or all white people dislike blacks. Similarly, 41% of whites say that many or all black people dislike whites.

A slightly higher level of discouragement is evident in a question asking whether relations between whites and blacks will "always be a problem" or whether "a solution will eventually be worked out." Just half of all Americans believe the country will work out relations between whites and blacks; nearly as many (46%) believe race relations will pose a persistent problem.

A Closer Look at Race Relations Ratings

Roughly two-thirds (68%) of the nation's adults describe black-white relations as very or somewhat good; only 29% consider them very or somewhat bad.

Majorities of blacks and whites perceive relations between the two groups positively. Hispanics are a bit less positive in their assessment.

Would you say relations between whites and blacks are very good, somewhat good, somewhat bad, or very bad?

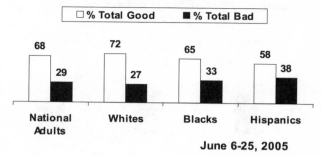

June 6-25, 2005

Ratings of relations between whites and Hispanics and between whites and Asians are also positive:

- Seventy percent of adults say that relations between whites and Hispanic are either very or somewhat good. This includes 73% of whites, 67% of Hispanics, and 61% of blacks saying that relations between whites and Hispanics are good.
- Overall, nearly 8 in 10 Americans say that white-Asian relations are good. This includes 81% of whites, 72% of blacks, and 73% of Hispanics saying white-Asian relations are good.

Black-Hispanic relations are a potential difficulty for the country today. Black-Hispanic relations receive less positive reviews than black-white relations, in part because a significant minority of Hispanics (40%) perceive trouble in this area. By contrast, most blacks (77%) believe black-Hispanic relations are good; only 16% consider them bad. A significant minority of whites (32%) also think black-Hispanic relations are bad.

Would you say relations between blacks and Hispanics are very good, somewhat good, somewhat bad, or very bad?

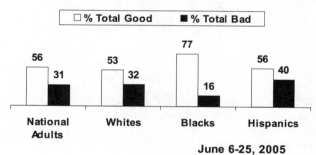

June 6-25, 2005

Close to Half Think Black-White Tensions Will Persist

Despite Americans' generally positive assessment of white-black relations today, when asked specifically "Do you think that relations between blacks and whites will always be a problem for the United States, or that a solution will eventually be worked out?", 46% of Americans take the pessimistic view. Half say "a solution will eventually be worked out."

While white Americans are a little more optimistic than pessimistic about the outlook for race relations (51% believe there will eventually be a solution, 46% disagree), blacks are considerably more negative (57%) than positive (41%).

Do you think that relations between blacks and whites will always be a problem for the United States, or that a solution will eventually be worked out?

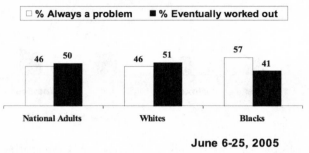

June 6-25, 2005

The long-term trend on this question shows that Americans were most optimistic about resolving black-white tensions when polling began on this question in 1963. Gallup found more negative attitudes during much of the 1990s, a decade marked by the Rodney King incident, the Los Angeles riots, and the O.J. Simpson murder trial. Since 2001, perceptions have been about evenly divided.

Trend in Outlook for Black-White Relations

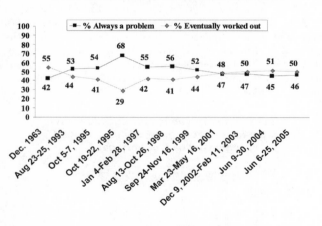

Many Perceive Racial Enmity

The "cup is half empty or half full" conundrum regarding race relations is perhaps most evident in a question asking Americans to estimate the extent of hostility between whites and blacks. On the one hand, a majority of blacks believe that only a few whites dislike blacks. Also, a majority of whites believe that only a few blacks dislike whites.

But depending on one's perspective, the fact that a sizeable minority of people perceive widespread bigotry could be troubling. More than one-third of U.S. adults believe that many or almost all white people dislike blacks; 34% of whites and 43% of blacks hold this view.

Similarly, 4 in 10 Americans believe that many or all blacks dislike whites. Whites and Hispanics are slightly more likely than blacks to hold this view.

Do you think only a few white people dislike blacks, many white people dislike blacks, or almost all white people dislike blacks?

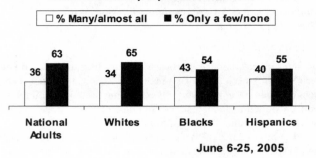

June 6-25, 2005

Do you think only a few black people dislike whites, many black people dislike whites, or almost all black people dislike whites?

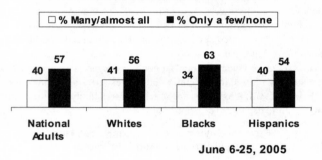

June 6-25, 2005

Gallup first asked these questions in 1992. Since then, there has been little change in perceptions of how whites feel about blacks, but perceptions of blacks' feelings toward whites have increased. In 1992 and 1995—spanning the King and Simpson controversies—more than half of Americans perceived widespread animosity by blacks toward whites. This gradually improved as of 1996, and by June 1998, attitudes were more positive than negative. The balance of opinion today remains more positive than negative.

Trend: How Many Black People Dislike Whites?

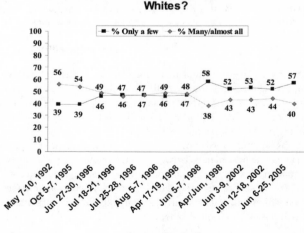

Survey Methods

These results are based on telephone interviews with a randomly selected national sample of 1,375 adults, aged 18 years and older, including a main sample of 1,004 national adults and oversamples of blacks and Hispanics. Telephone interviews were conducted from June 6-25, 2004.

For results based on the total sample of 2,264 national adults, one can say with 95% confidence that the maximum error attributable to sampling and other random effects is ±5 percentage points.

Results based on the subsample of whites include interviews with 807 non-Hispanic white adults and have a maximum margin of sampling error of ±7 percentage points. Results based on the subsample of blacks include interviews with 802 black national adults and have a maximum margin of sampling error of ±5 percentage points. Results based on the subsample of Hispanics include interviews with 511 Hispanic national adults (including 181 conducted in Spanish) and have a maximum margin of sampling error of ±7 percentage points.

In addition to sampling error, question wording and practical difficulties in conducting surveys can introduce error or bias into the findings of public opinion polls.

July 15, 2005

MOST WOULD APPLAUD FEMALE, HISPANIC COURT NOMINEE

But few see either as an essential characteristic of the next justice

by Jeffrey M. Jones, Gallup Poll Senior Editor

As President George W. Bush continues to mull over his choice of nominee for a new Supreme Court justice, a CNN/*USA Today*/Gallup poll finds most Americans would apparently welcome a female or Hispanic nominee, but few see either as an essential characteristic of the next justice. Earlier polling found a slight preference for a justice who would make the court more conservative, but Americans also clearly prefer a justice who would not overturn the *Roe v. Wade* decision on abortion rights.

Americans tend to believe the organized lobbying campaigns by liberal and conservative groups will do more harm than good to getting the best justice, but Democrats are more likely to believe such efforts will help. The public currently has the most negative view of the Supreme Court it has had since 2000.

The Next Justice

A July 7-10 CNN/*USA Today*/Gallup poll finds most Americans saying that a female or Hispanic justice would be a good idea, but few think choosing such a nominee is essential. Some have argued that Sandra Day O'Connor should be replaced by a female justice just as Thurgood Marshall was replaced by another black justice, Clarence Thomas, in 1991. Just 13% say it is essential that the next justice is a woman, but an additional 65% say it would be a good idea. An additional 18% say it doesn't matter to them, and 2% say it would be a bad idea.

Democrats and Republicans differ little in their assessments that choosing a woman would be a good idea, but Democrats are more likely to say it is essential to replace the retiring O'Connor with another woman.

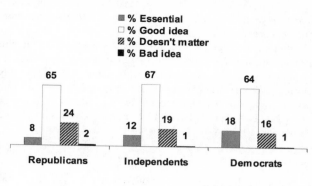

Next Supreme Court Justice a Woman?

- ■ % Essential
- □ % Good idea
- ▨ % Doesn't matter
- ■ % Bad idea

	Republicans	Independents	Democrats
% Essential	8	12	18
% Good idea	65	67	64
% Doesn't matter	24	19	16
% Bad idea	2	1	1

July 7-10, 2005

Bush has hinted that he would like to be the first president to nominate a Hispanic to the Supreme Court, and again most Americans say that would be a good idea (63%), but few believe it is essential (4%). Twenty-seven percent say it doesn't matter to them if the next justice is Hispanic, and 4% say it would be a bad idea.

A June 16-19 CNN/*USA Today*/Gallup poll asked Americans about the ideology of the next Supreme Court justice. The plurality of Americans, 41%, say they would like to see "Bush nominate someone who would make the Supreme Court more conservative than it currently is," while 30% want a justice who would make the court more liberal, and 24% want the composition of the court to be kept as it is now. O'Connor is generally believed to be a moderate conservative who often is the swing vote in determining whether the more liberal or more conservative justices prevail in court rulings. [The poll was conducted prior to the announcement of O'Connor's retirement, so it is unclear if that would have affected public opinion on this matter.]

As one might expect, conservatives overwhelmingly prefer a nominee who would move the court to the right and liberals overwhelmingly prefer a nominee who would move the court to the left. Moderates are more divided in their views. The overall preference for a conservative nominee is likely related to the fact that Americans are roughly twice as likely to identify as conservative as liberal.

Despite the slight preference for a more conservative court, by a wide margin, Americans are not in favor of overturning the court's rulings on abortion rights, something that some see as possible if

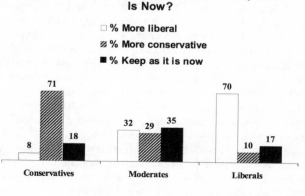

Next Supreme Court Justice Make the Court More Liberal, More Conservative, or Keep as It Is Now?

- □ % More liberal
- ▨ % More conservative
- ■ % Keep as it is now

	Conservatives	Moderates	Liberals
% More liberal	8	32	70
% More conservative	71	29	10
% Keep as it is now	18	35	17

June 16-19, 2005

Bush replaces O'Connor with a strong pro-life justice. The July 7-10 poll shows 63% of Americans against overturning the *Roe v. Wade* decision that established a constitutional right to an abortion, while 28% are in favor.

Americans' views on overturning *Roe* are strongly related to their ideological identification—liberals are overwhelmingly against overturning the decision (84% to 9%), while conservatives are evenly divided in their views, as 45% would like to see the decision reversed and 45% would not. Moderates come down strongly on the side of keeping *Roe* as the law, with only 17% in favor of overturning it and 77% opposed.

Political Context

Earlier polling showed nearly half of Americans, 48%, saying the choice of the next Supreme Court justice mattered a great deal to them. An additional 26% say it mattered a "moderate amount," so clearly most have something invested in the decision of who the next justice is.

Additionally, public approval of the court is the lowest Gallup has measured since it began tracking Supreme Court job approval in 2000. A June 24-26 CNN/*USA Today*/Gallup poll found 42% approving of the court, after approval had been above 50% in all prior measurements. The poll was conducted immediately after the court announced its controversial decision on eminent domain, but before it announced its split decisions on the displays of Ten Commandments monuments on government property (prior Gallup polling showed three in four Americans saying the court should allow state governments to do so).

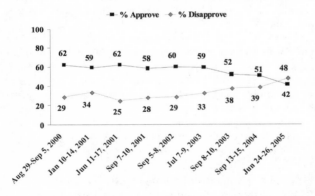

U.S. Supreme Court Approval Ratings

With that background, it may not be surprising that extensive organized lobbying efforts from both sides of the ideological spectrum are beginning over the choice of the next justice. These groups are using, or plan to use, campaign-style techniques such as television ads, direct mail, and traditional lobbying to pressure Bush and senators to put a justice in place that is most acceptable to them.

The public tends to think these efforts will do more harm than good. A majority of Americans, 54%, believe such campaigns will be "harmful to getting the best person on the court," while 39% say they will be helpful.

There are partisan differences on this count. By a 49% to 43% margin, Democrats say such campaigns will be helpful. In contrast, Republicans say they will be harmful by a 63% to 32% margin. Independents are more likely to believe they will be harmful. Democrats' belief that such efforts will aid the process may be based on the

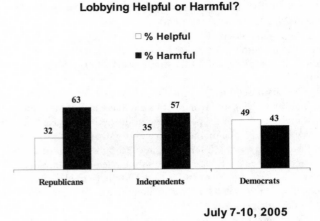

Lobbying Helpful or Harmful?

July 7-10, 2005

notion that heavy political pressure on Bush might force him to choose a moderate, rather than a conservative, justice.

Survey Methods

These results are based on telephone interviews with a randomly selected national sample of 1,006 adults, aged 18 and older, conducted July 7-10, 2005. For results based on this sample, one can say with 95% confidence that the maximum error attributable to sampling and other random effects is ±3 percentage points. In addition to sampling error, question wording and practical difficulties in conducting surveys can introduce error or bias into the findings of public opinion polls.

July 18, 2005

WINE GAINS MOMENTUM AS AMERICANS' FAVORITE ADULT BEVERAGE

Special analysis shows different shifts in drinking preferences by age

by Lydia Saad, Gallup Poll Senior Editor

For the first time in Gallup's measurement of Americans' drinking preferences, there is a statistical tie between wine and beer as the alcoholic beverage adult drinkers say they drink most often. As recently as last year, beer edged out wine as Americans' standard drink. Today, 39% of drinkers in the United States say they drink wine most often, while 36% say they usually drink beer. This is according to Gallup's annual Consumption Habits poll, conducted July 7-10, 2005.

Overall, 63% of Americans say they drink alcohol, which is consistent with the rate of drinking recorded for most of the six decades Gallup has asked this question. The major exception is the period from 1976 through 1981, when 69%-71% said they drank alcohol.

Most of the latest change in Americans' preference for type of drink is seen in the percentage naming wine, up six points from 33% in 2004. This is the first significant shift in wine preferences recorded in the last eight years.

When Gallup asked Americans about their drinking preferences in 1992, beer was the runaway leader, with 47% naming it; just 27%

**Do you most often drink liquor, wine, or beer?
asked of those who drink alcohol**

Wine: 39%
Beer: 36%
Liquor: 21%
All equally (vol.): 3%

July 7-10, 2005

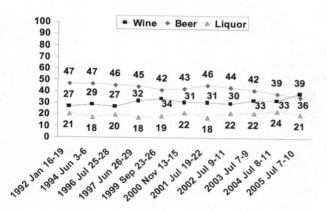

Trend in Preferred Drink

Wine: 27, 29, 27, 32, 34, 31, 31, 30, 33, 33, 36
Beer: 47, 47, 46, 45, 42, 43, 46, 44, 42, 39, 39
Liquor: 21, 18, 20, 18, 19, 22, 18, 22, 22, 24, 21

1992 Jan 16-19, 1994 Jun 3-6, 1996 Jul 25-28, 1997 Jun 26-29, 1999 Sep 23-26, 2000 Nov 13-15, 2001 Jul 19-22, 2002 Jul 9-11, 2003 Jul 7-9, 2004 Jul 8-11, 2005 Jul 7-10

named wine. Liquor has consistently ranked third, with between 18% and 24% naming it as their preferred drink.

Given the overall trends, one might assume that beer drinkers have merely switched over to wine. But a close review of the data suggests a more complicated pattern of changes in alcohol consumption since 1992. With one demographic group, beer drinking is giving way to liquor, while among another, beer is losing ground to wine; with still another, the preference for liquor is declining while wine is gaining.

The net result is a decrease in the percentage of drinkers naming beer as their standard drink (from 47% in 1992 to 36% today) and a commensurate increase in wine drinkers (from 27% to 39%), with no change in those preferring liquor (21%).

In Search of a Keg Party

One of the biggest trends Gallup sees in drinking patterns over the past decade is a crumbling of the once-dominant positioning of beer among young adults.

It appears that young adults are trading in their beer mugs for martini glasses, in droves. Beer is still the preferred drink of nearly half of adults aged 18-29*, but the figure is down compared with 10—and even 5—years ago. In contrast, the percentage saying they usually drink liquor has more than doubled, from 13% to 32%.

Beer is also losing ground among middle-aged Americans. The percentage of those 30-49 who most often drink beer has declined from 48% in the early '90s to 40% in the last two years. Both liquor and wine have made corresponding gains among this age segment as a result.

The percentage of beer drinkers among older Americans—those 50 and older—appears stable at around 30%. Wine has con-

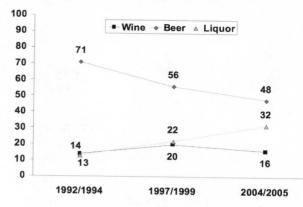

Trend in Preferred Drink: 18- to 29-year-olds

% who drink each type most often

Beer: 71, 56, 48
Liquor: 13, 22, 32
Wine: 14, 20, 16

1992/1994, 1997/1999, 2004/2005

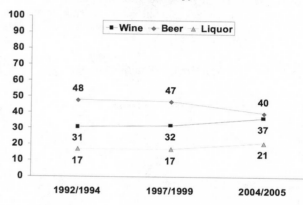

Trend in Preferred Drink: 30- to 49-year-olds

% who drink each type most often

Beer: 48, 47, 40
Wine: 31, 32, 37
Liquor: 17, 17, 21

1992/1994, 1997/1999, 2004/2005

sistently been the top drink preferred by this age category, although since 1994, the percentage choosing wine has increased further (from 37% to 45%), while the percentage for liquor has declined (from 30% to 20%).

Despite the downward trend in the percentage of young adults whose preferred drink is beer, it remains their top choice as of Gallup's July 2005 survey. Wine and beer are closely matched as the

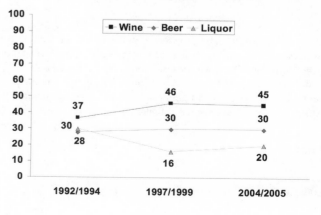

Trend in Preferred Drink: 50+ years

% who drink each type most often

Wine: 37, 46, 45
Beer: 30, 30, 30
Liquor: 28, 16, 20

1992/1994, 1997/1999, 2004/2005

Drinking Preferences, by Age

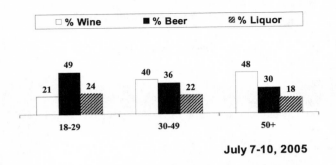

	□ % Wine	■ % Beer	▨ % Liquor

July 7-10, 2005

preferred drink of those 30-49, while wine is the clear leader among those 50 and older.

The Gender Gap in Drinking

Men prefer beer; women prefer wine. That has been the case throughout Gallup's tracking of this measure. Even in 1992, when beer was chosen by nearly 2-to-1 over wine among all drinkers, only 27% of women named beer as their standard drink, while 43% named wine. Since then, wine has gained in popularity among both sexes, but especially among men.

% Who Prefer Wine, by Gender

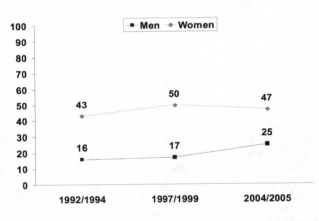

This advance for wine has come at the expense of beer. There has been virtually no change in preference for liquor among men and women, but the percentage naming beer has declined since 1992/1994 by 12 points among men, and by 6 points among women.

Minorities Switching to Wine

The national shift from beer to wine is especially pronounced among the nonwhite population. The long-term increase in preference for wine (since 1992/1994) has been +7 percentage points among white Americans, but +17 points among nonwhites. Similarly, the percentage of those preferring beer has fallen by 10 points among whites, but by 15 points among nonwhites.

Wine	Whites	Nonwhites
1992/1994	29	22
1997/1999	34	28
2004/2005	36	39

% Who Prefer Beer, by Gender

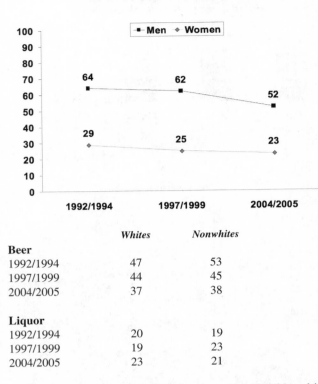

Beer	Whites	Nonwhites
1992/1994	47	53
1997/1999	44	45
2004/2005	37	38
Liquor		
1992/1994	20	19
1997/1999	19	23
2004/2005	23	21

Future Gallup releases will review the extent of problem drinking in America, focusing on the relationship between age, type of alcohol preferred, and the self-reported tendency to sometimes drink too much.

* NOTE: Demographic trends are reported on the basis of two-year averages in order to increase sample size, and therefore, statistical reliability.

Survey Methods

These results are based on telephone interviews with a randomly selected national sample of 1,006 adults, aged 18 and older, conducted July 7-10, 2005. For results based on this sample, one can say with 95% confidence that the maximum error attributable to sampling and other random effects is ±3 percentage points.

July 19, 2005
BUSH'S LATEST QUARTERLY AVERAGE A NEW LOW
Second-term average stands at 49%

by Jeffrey M. Jones, Gallup Poll Managing Editor

The war in Iraq and negative views on the economy are likely dragging down President George W. Bush's recent job approval ratings, which are among the worst of his presidency.

In his 18th quarter in office—spanning the dates from April 20 to July 19—Bush averaged a 47.4% job approval rating. That average includes a term-low-tying individual rating of 45% in a June 24-26 poll. The average was propped up slightly by the 49% rating Bush received just after the London terrorist attacks. Notably, in all but 3 of the 10 Gallup Polls conducted during the quarter, more Americans expressed disapproval than approval of Bush.

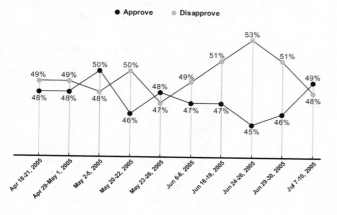

George W. Bush Job Approval During His 18th Quarter in Office

● Approve ● Disapprove

The 47.4% average is the lowest of Bush's presidency to date, just below the 47.9% average in his 14th quarter in office (April-July 2004). Those are the only two times Bush's quarterly average rating has dipped below 50% approval.

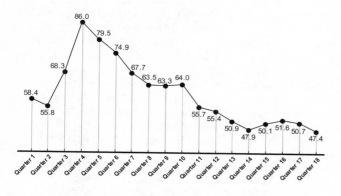

Quarterly Job Approval Averages for George W. Bush

From a historical perspective, the 47.4% current average ranks 171st out of 236 presidential quarters for which Gallup has data, going back to the Harry Truman presidency. That places it just outside the bottom quarter of all averages, ranking in the 27th percentile.

Other second-term presidents had significantly higher 18th-quarter averages than Bush. For example, Dwight Eisenhower averaged 63.6%, Ronald Reagan 58.7%, and Bill Clinton 56.3%. Bush's current average may be most comparable to Truman's 48.7%, registered less than a year after his famous come-from-behind victory in 1948.

Richard Nixon was also below the 50% mark shortly after being re-elected, averaging just 44% approval as the effects of the Watergate scandal were beginning to take hold in April-June 1973. Incidentally, that represented the last time Nixon averaged above 40% approval for a quarter until his resignation from office.

Lyndon Johnson had a 42% average in his 18th quarter, the lowest Gallup has measured. But unlike other presidents whose 18th quarters came in the first year of their second terms in office, John-

son's came in the last year he was in office because his presidency began in the third year of Kennedy's term.

18th-Quarter Approval Averages of Recent U.S. Presidents

President	Average approval rating	Dates of quarter	Number of polls during quarter
Truman	48.7%	Jul 20-Oct 19, 1949	3
Eisenhower	63.6%	Apr 20-July 19, 1957	5
Johnson	42.0%	Jan 20-Apr 19, 1968	4
Nixon	44.0%	Apr 20-Jul 19, 1973	6
Reagan	58.7%	Apr 20-Jul 19, 1985	3
Clinton	56.3%	Apr 20-Jul 19, 1997	3
Bush	47.4%	Apr 20-Jul 19, 2005	10

Broadly speaking, presidents who have had similar quarterly averages to Bush's most recent one did not show much improvement going forward, mostly because they were nearing the ends of their presidencies (as with Nixon and Johnson as shown in the table and Reagan at a later stage of his second term; also with Ford and Carter who spent large spans of their single terms below the 50% mark). There are, of course, exceptions to the general pattern. Clinton and Reagan both had quarterly averages similar to Bush's 47.4% at earlier stages of their presidencies, but eventually saw the needles on their approval ratings moving in a positive direction.

Clearly, Bush is off to an inauspicious start to his second term in office. He had averaged a 62% approval rating during his first term in office, but after two quarters, his second-term average stands at 49%. The White House may be feeling a bit under siege lately—in addition to flagging approval ratings and criticism of the war effort, the media are focused on top adviser Karl Rove's potentially revealing classified information to a reporter and the looming battle over Bush's choice of the next Supreme Court nominee.

Results are based on an average of 10 polls of 800 to 1,000 national adults, age 18 and older, conducted between the dates of April 18-July 10, 2005. Each poll has a maximum margin of sampling error of no more than 4 percentage points.

July 19, 2005
BLACK SUPPORT FOR BUSH, GOP REMAINS LOW
No change in the last year

by Jeffrey M. Jones, Gallup Poll Managing Editor

Republican Party leaders reached out to the black community last week with speeches by President Bush to a black group in Indiana and by party chairman Ken Mehlman to the NAACP convention in Milwaukee. The speeches were designed to convince blacks that minorities have made gains in home and small-business ownership during the Bush administration and to convince blacks that Republican policies on education, Social Security, and aid to religious charities would benefit them.

Results of the recent Gallup Minority Relations poll reveal that blacks continue to show very low levels of support for Bush and few identify politically as Republicans. In contrast, Hispanics are more likely to approve of Bush than are blacks, but on balance, Hispanics are more likely to disapprove than approve of him. Non-Hispanic whites continue to show higher levels of support for Bush and the Republican Party than do blacks or Hispanics, but are currently divided in their views of the job Bush is doing as president.

Bush Approval

In recent Gallup Polls, Bush's job approval ratings have ranked among the lowest of his presidency—in the mid- to high-40% range, including a term-low 45% rating in late June. According to the June 6-25, 2005, Minority Relations poll, none of the major racial or ethnic groups in the United States show solid support for Bush. Most notably, blacks are highly unlikely to support Bush—just 16% of blacks approve of him while 77% disapprove. Hispanics are more than twice as likely as blacks to approve of Bush (41%) and whites are nearly three times as likely (47%) to do so, but those groups are at least as likely to disapprove as to approve of Bush.

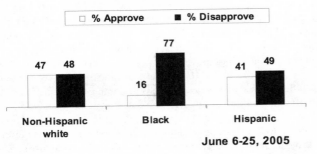

George W. Bush Approval, by Race/Ethnic Group, 2005

The data show essentially no change in blacks' and Hispanics' views of Bush compared with last year's poll. In June 2004, 16% of blacks and 40% of Hispanics approved of Bush. As a group, whites have shown a significant decline, from 61% to 47%. Thus, the slight decline in Bush support from around the 50% mark a year ago to the mid- to high-40s this year has come mostly among non-Hispanic whites.

An analysis of data from prior Minority Relations polls underscores the erosion in Bush's support over the past several years from its post-9/11 highs. The drop was dramatic for blacks and Hispanics between 2003 and 2004, when support for the Iraq war first started to decline, and has since leveled off. While whites showed some decline in their approval rating of Bush between 2003 and 2004, there has been a much larger decay in the last year.

Bush Job Approval by Racial and Ethnic Group, June Minority Relations Polls

	2001 %	2002 %	2003 %	2004 %	2005 %
Non-Hispanic whites	58	74	69	61	47
Blacks	37	41	32	16	16
Hispanics	59	73	67	40	41

Party Support

While Bush's approval ratings have fluctuated over the past several years, support for the Republican and Democratic parties by racial and ethnic groups has stayed fairly steady.

For example, the percentage of blacks identifying as Republicans has stayed in a narrow range of 5% to 9% in the last five years, while blacks' identification as Democrats has consistently exceeded 60%. Blacks have been about twice as likely (if not greater) to identify as Democrats as independents.

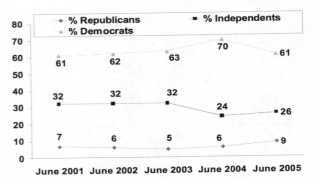

Party Identification Among Blacks, 2001—2005, Minority Relations Polls

The current 9% Republican identification for blacks is slightly higher than what Gallup has measured in the Minority Relations polls to date, but it is not clear if that represents a real increase since the change is well within the margin of sampling error for the black sample.

In Gallup's final 2004 pre-election poll, Bush received 7% of the black vote. While still minuscule, it was an apparent improvement on his 3% support in 2000. However, given the small samples of blacks in those polls, it is not certain that Bush increased his vote share among blacks. The national exit poll, which has larger samples of blacks, suggested a slight increase in Bush's share of the black vote in 2004.

Both the Republicans and Democrats have made great efforts to appeal to Hispanics, who now represent the largest minority group in the United States. On the whole, Hispanics are more likely to identify as Republicans than are blacks, but more Hispanics align themselves with the Democratic Party (32%) than the Republican Party (18%). Notably, nearly half of Hispanics, 47%, do not affiliate with either party.

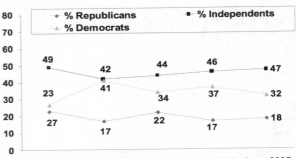

Party Identification Among Hispanics, 2001—2005, Minority Relations Polls

If anything, the data on party identification among whites show the extent to which the Democratic Party has to rely on the minority vote to build winning electoral coalitions. Less than 30% of non-Hispanic whites have identified as Democrats in the Minority Relations polls, while Republican support has been around 36% (save for a perhaps aberrant reading of 47% in the June 2004 poll). Whites, like Hispanics, are also more likely to identify as independents than Democrats, although not quite to the degree that Hispanics do.

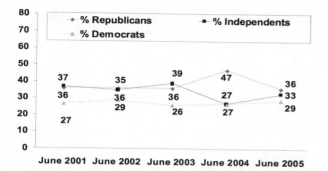

Party Identification Among Non-Hispanic Whites, 2001—2005, Minority Relations Polls

Party Support Varies by Age

A look inside the recent poll data among blacks reveals little difference in party identification due to gender or education level. However, younger blacks are much less likely than older blacks to support the Democratic Party.

Among blacks aged 50 and older, 73% identify as Democrats, 16% as independents, and only 6% as Republicans. But just over half of blacks aged 18 to 49 identify as Democrats (55%), with higher proportions identifying as independents (26%) and Republicans (11%). In prior years' polls, younger blacks were also less likely to identify as Democrats and more likely to identify as independents, but not necessarily more likely to identify as Republicans.

The difference in party support by age could be due to the politics of the civil rights struggles in the 1960s, something likely to be remembered well by older blacks. The Democratic Party strongly supported civil rights legislation but the Republican Party did not. In fact, during his speech to NAACP members, Mehlman apologized for the party's attitude toward blacks in the past.

The data also show that older Hispanics are more likely than younger Hispanics to identify with the Democratic Party, while younger Hispanics are quite likely to be independent. In the latest Minority Relations poll, 49% of Hispanics aged 50 and older identify as Democrats, while 21% are Republicans, and 25% independent. In contrast, a plurality of Hispanics aged 18 to 49 are independent (52%), while 28% are Democrat and 18% Republican.

Generally speaking, younger Americans of all backgrounds are more likely to be independent than are older people, but as people age they generally align themselves with one or the other party. The data suggest young Hispanics are especially likely to be up-for-grabs when it comes to party loyalty, and the parties will surely struggle to gain a foothold on Hispanic political loyalties. While black loyalties are firmly in line with the Democrats, a significant proportion of younger blacks have yet to come into the Democratic fold.

Survey Methods

These results are based on telephone interviews with a randomly selected national sample of 2,264 national adults, including over-samples of blacks and Hispanics, aged 18 and older, conducted June 6-25, 2005. For results based on the total sample, one can say with

95% confidence that the maximum margin of sampling error is ±5 percentage points.

Results for the sample of 807 non-Hispanic whites, aged 18 and older, are based on telephone interviews conducted June 6-25, 2005. For results based on the total sample, one can say with 95% confidence that the maximum margin of sampling error is ±7 percentage points.

Results for the sample of 802 blacks, aged 18 and older, are based on telephone interviews conducted June 6-25, 2005. For results based on the total sample, one can say with 95% confidence that the maximum margin of sampling error is ±5 percentage points.

Results for the sample of 511 Hispanics, aged 18 and older, are based on telephone interviews, conducted June 6-25, 2005. For results based on the total sample, one can say with 95% confidence that the maximum margin of sampling error is ±5 percentage points. (181 out of the 511 interviews with Hispanics were conducted in Spanish).

In addition to sampling error, question wording and practical difficulties in conducting surveys can introduce error or bias into the findings of public opinion polls.

July 19, 2005

LIBERTY VS. SECURITY: PUBLIC MIXED ON PATRIOT ACT
Majority familiar with the law

by Darren K. Carlson, Government and Politics Editor

The recent bombings in London served as a tragic reminder that the war on terrorism is ongoing. It's a war fought with public policy changes as well as machine guns and mortar. In the United States, the Patriot Act is the legal backbone of the country's anti-terrorism measures. Controversy has swirled around the act since its inception in late 2001. Government officials argue the law is vital for obtaining information about U.S. residents who are suspected of having terrorist ties, but civil libertarians argue the act is turning America into a police state.

Recent Gallup polling on the Patriot Act* allows a look beyond the rhetoric of government officials and civil libertarians, to explore the opinions of all Americans. Results show self-reported awareness of the act is high, while public opinion about the act's effect on Americans' civil liberties is mixed.

Majority Familiar With Act

Gallup asked respondents how familiar they are with the Patriot Act. A majority of Americans—64%—say they are either "very" or "somewhat" familiar with the law, although just 12% claim to be very familiar. A quarter of Americans (25%) say they are "not too familiar" with the law, and 11% are "not at all familiar."

Americans with more education are more likely to be familiar with the law. Twenty percent of those with a postgraduate education say they are very familiar with the law, compared with only 6% of those with a high school education or less.

Gallup asked about familiarity with the Patriot Act using slightly different question wording in 2003 and 2004. Those results suggest the public has become slightly more familiar with the Patriot Act in the last two years.

Awareness of the Patriot Act

As you may know, shortly after the terrorist attacks on September 11, 2001, a law called the Patriot Act was passed. That law deals with the ways the federal government can obtain private information on people living in the U.S. who are suspected of having ties with terrorists. How familiar are you with the Patriot Act – very familiar, somewhat familiar, not too familiar, or not at all familiar?

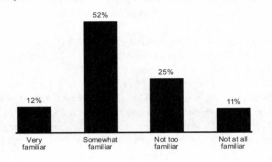

Very familiar	Somewhat familiar	Not too familiar	Not at all familiar
12%	52%	25%	11%

Does the Law Go Too Far?

A follow-up question asked respondents whether they think the Patriot Act goes too far, is about right, or doesn't go far enough in restricting people's civil liberties in order to investigate suspected terrorism. The plurality of Americans, 41%, say the law is about right in terms of protecting civil liberties. More Americans, however, believe it goes too far (30%) than believe it does not go far enough (21%).

Does the Patriot Act Go Too Far?

Based on what you have read or heard, do you think the Patriot Act -- goes too far, is about right, or does not go far enough – in restricting people's civil liberties in order to investigate suspected terrorism?

Goes too far	About right	Not far enough	No opinion
30%	41%	21%	8%

Partisanship is a major factor when it comes to public opinion about the Patriot Act. More than a third (37%) of Democrats think it goes too far in restricting civil liberties, as do 4 in 10 political independents (40%)—but only 12% of Republicans think the Patriot Act goes too far. Most Republicans, 61%, believe the Patriot Act is "about right" in trading off protection from terrorism with protection of civil liberties.

It appears familiarity might breed some contempt when it comes to the Patriot Act. Among Americans who say they are very familiar

Based on what you have read or heard, do you think the Patriot Act . . .

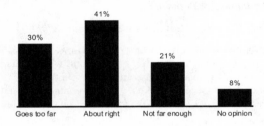

■ Very familiar with Patriot Act □ Somewhat familiar with Patriot Act ▨ Not familiar with Patriot Act

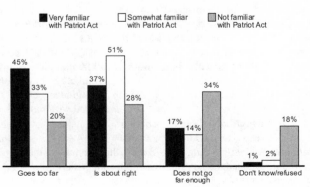

	Goes too far	Is about right	Does not go far enough	Don't know/refused
Very familiar	45%	37%	17%	1%
Somewhat familiar	33%	51%	14%	2%
Not familiar	20%	28%	34%	18%

with the law, 45% believe it goes too far in restricting civil liberties, while a third (33%) of those who are somewhat familiar think so. Just 20% of those who are not familiar with the law think it goes too far.

*These results are based on telephone interviews with a randomly selected national sample of 1,009 adults, aged 18 and older, conducted June 24-26, 2005. For results based on this sample, one can say with 95% confidence that the maximum error attributable to sampling and other random effects is ±3 percentage points. In addition to sampling error, question wording and practical difficulties in conducting surveys can introduce error or bias into the findings of public opinion polls.

July 19, 2005
POST-9/11 PATRIOTISM REMAINS STEADFAST
Nonwhites least likely to feel highly patriotic

by Joseph Carroll, Gallup Poll Assistant Editor

Summer is a season full of patriotic celebrations—baseball games, firework displays, barbecues, and Fourth of July picnics remind Americans every year of their national identity. But just how patriotic are Americans feeling this year?

A recent CNN/*USA Today*/Gallup poll*, conducted a week before the Fourth of July holiday, shows more than 7 in 10 Americans describe themselves as "extremely" (26%) or "very" (46%) patriotic. About one in five U.S. adults say they are somewhat patriotic, and 5% say they are not especially patriotic.

These results are essentially unchanged since the question was last asked in 2002, when 71% of Americans expressed a high level of patriotism, but slightly higher than they were in 1994 and 1999. In both of those surveys, roughly two in three Americans said they were patriotic.

How patriotic are you? Would you say extremely patriotic, very patriotic, somewhat patriotic, or not especially patriotic?

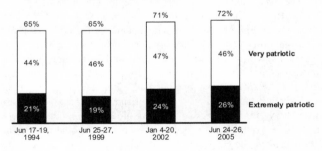

	Jun 17-19, 1994	Jun 25-27, 1999	Jan 4-20, 2002	Jun 24-26, 2005
Total	65%	65%	71%	72%
Very patriotic	44%	46%	47%	46%
Extremely patriotic	21%	19%	24%	26%

This increase in feelings of patriotism between 1999 and 2002 stems from an increase in the percentage of Americans describing themselves as "extremely" patriotic. About one in five Americans in the 1994 and 1999 polls said they were extremely patriotic, compared with roughly one in four in the 2002 and 2005 surveys. The Sept. 11, 2001, terrorist attacks elevated Americans' sense of patriotism—that is clear from a second Gallup trend question, which has shown no less than 61% (and as many as 70%) of Americans saying they are "extremely proud" to be American in five separate polls conducted following 9/11, compared with only 55% in a January 2001 poll.

Race, Gender, Age Affect Patriotism

Some Americans are more likely than others to express high levels of patriotism.

Eighty percent of whites say they are extremely or very patriotic, while only 46% of nonwhites say this. Nonwhites are the least likely demographic subgroup among those analyzed to express high levels of patriotism.

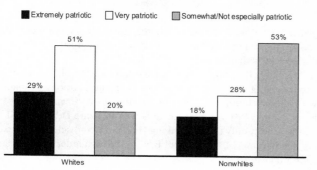

Patriotism by Race

The poll also finds differences in patriotism by age and gender. Overall, men (76%) are somewhat more likely than women (68%) to say they are extremely or very patriotic. Likewise, people aged 50 and older (79%) are more likely than younger Americans (67% of those under age 50) to be patriotic.

The interaction of age and gender produces an interesting result—younger women prove to be significantly less likely to express a high degree of patriotism than other age and gender groups. Sixty percent of women between the ages of 18 and 49 say they are extremely or very patriotic. That compares with 78% among women aged 50 and older. At least three-fourths of men in both age groups say they are highly patriotic.

Patriotism by Gender and Age

	Extremely patriotic	Very patriotic	Extremely/Very patriotic	Somewhat/Not especially patriotic
Gender				
Men	29%	47%	76%	23%
Women	23%	45%	68%	31%
Age				
18 to 49 years	27%	40%	67%	35%
50 years and older	26%	53%	79%	20%
Gender and Age				
Men, aged 18 to 49	35%	40%	75%	25%
Men, aged 50 and older	24%	56%	80%	19%
Women, aged 18 to 49	19%	41%	60%	40%
Women, aged 50 and older	28%	50%	78%	22%

Politics

Perhaps not surprisingly, Americans' levels of patriotism divide sharply along political lines. Eighty-one percent of those who identify themselves as politically conservative say they are extremely or very patriotic. That compares with just 57% of Americans who say they are politically liberal. Seventy-three percent of self-identified political moderates consider themselves highly patriotic.

Similarly, 85% of Republicans describe themselves as extremely or very patriotic, compared with 66% of both independents and Democrats.

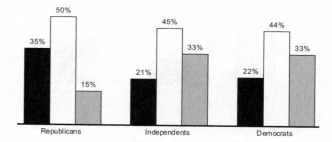

Patriotism by Party Affiliation

This partisan divide has narrowed between Gallup's 1999 and 2005 surveys. In both 1999 and 2005, Republicans were most likely to say they are highly patriotic. But the percentage of Democrats who say they are extremely or very patriotic has increased more significantly over the last six years than the percentage of independents or Republicans who say so. In 1999, 56% of Democrats said they were patriotic, and that percentage is now 10 percentage points higher. The increase among Republicans was slightly smaller, at six points (from 79% in 1999 to 85% today) and there has been essentially no change among independents (63% to 66%).

*Results are based on telephone interviews with 1,009 national adults, aged 18 and older, conducted June 24-26, 2005. For results based on the total sample of national adults, one can say with 95% confidence that the margin of sampling error is ±3 percentage points. In addition to sampling error, question wording and practical difficulties in conducting surveys can introduce error or bias into the findings of public opinion polls.

July 19, 2005
WHERE DO HISPANIC AMERICANS STAND ON RELIGION, POLITICS?
Nearly two-thirds identify as Catholic

by Linda Lyons, Education and Youth Editor

In July 2001, U.S. Census data showed that Hispanics surpassed blacks as the largest minority group in the United States. Hispanics make up about 14% of the U.S. population today and the Census Bureau predicts that, based on continued immigration and birth rates, they will constitute 25% by 2050. An aggregate of 2004 and 2005 data from Gallup's annual Minority Relations poll* allows a close look at the major religious and political affiliations of Hispanic Americans.

Religious Identity

Forty-nine percent of Hispanics say they attend services once a week or almost every week and another 17% attend at least once a month. One-third of Hispanics (32%) say they seldom or never attend church. Looking at an aggregate from surveys conducted in 2004, 44% of Americans say they attend once a week or almost every week and 10% attend at least once a month; 41% say they seldom or never attend. Hispanics are slightly less likely than the overall population to say they seldom or never attend.

Hispanic Political Affiliation

As of today, do you consider yourself a Republican, a Democrat, or an independent?

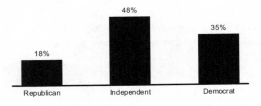

Nearly two-thirds of Hispanics (63%) self-identify as Catholic, while 16% say they are Protestant. Another 10% align with other Christian faiths; just 6% say they have no religious affiliation at all. About 9 in 10 Hispanics identify with a Christian religion, which is slightly higher than the 84% of Americans in general.

Hispanic Religious Preference

What, if any, is your religious preference -- are you Protestant, Roman Catholic, Jewish, Mormon, Muslim, or an Orthodox religion such as the Greek or Russian Orthodox Church?

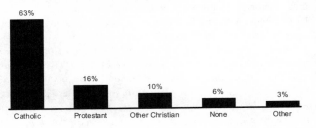

"Although nearly all Hispanics arrive in this country as Catholics, so many more options are available to them when they get to the United States," says the Rev. Javier Diaz-Munoz, a priest who works closely with the Hispanic community in New Jersey. "Protestant churches, especially, are very active here. They offer a lot of social services to Hispanics."

Diaz-Munoz sees attendance increasing in his diocese, especially at the Spanish-language services. "Several years ago, we conducted mass in Spanish in 14 parishes; today there are 19. In Trenton alone, where the majority of Hispanics are from Mexico and Guatemala, we get 500 to 600 people at Spanish language services every Saturday and Sunday."

Political Identity

The effect of the booming Hispanic population on American politics has been fully recognized in recent presidential elections. As with religion, Hispanic Americans are becoming less homogeneous politically—raising concerns among leading Democrats that the Hispanic population's political leanings can no longer be taken for granted. At this point, however, Hispanics still aren't identifying as Republicans in large numbers. The plurality of Hispanics (48%) remain independent of either major political party. Thirty-five percent say they are Democrats, and 18% say they are Republicans. (For an extended analysis on Hispanics and party affiliation, see "Black Support for Bush, GOP Remains Low" in Related Items.)

Newsweek's recent cover story on Hispanic Americans reports that the connection between religion and politics is particularly troubling to Democratic leaders, who fear religious Hispanics are more likely to identify with conservative values. But are religious His-

panics (as defined by frequent church attendance) more likely than less religious Hispanics (who attend church infrequently) to associate themselves with the GOP?

Gallup's data don't show much difference in political attitudes between religious and non-religious Hispanics. Among Hispanics who attend church once a week or almost every week, 21% are Republicans, 48% are independents, and 31% are Democrats. The numbers shift only slightly among Hispanics who seldom or never attend church—14% are Republicans, 49% are independents, and 37% are Democrats.

Hispanic Political Affiliation by Church Attendance

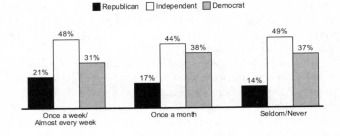

Bottom Line

The exploding Hispanic population is poised to influence every aspect of American life—particularly religion and politics. Tracking its varied attitudes and preferences will be a full-time job for demographers, marketers, sociologists, educators, politicians, religious leaders, and virtually everyone else with a long-term stake in American economic and cultural life.

These results are based on an aggregated sample of 1,007 Hispanic adults, aged 18 and older, from telephone interviews conducted June 9-30, 2004 and June 6-25, 2005. For results based on this sample, one can say with 95% confidence that the maximum error attributable to sampling and other random effects is ±4 percentage points. In addition to sampling error, question wording and practical difficulties in conducting surveys can introduce error or bias into the findings of public opinion polls.

July 20, 2005

INCREASED SUPPORT FOR SMOKING BANS IN PUBLIC PLACES
But still widespread opposition to complete ban

by David W. Moore, Gallup Poll Senior Editor

Gallup's latest annual poll on the public's consumption habits finds a significant increase in support over the past two years for banning smoking in selected public places.

This change is not because Americans have suddenly become more concerned about second-hand smoke, which has been recognized by the vast majority of Americans as harmful at least since the mid-1990s. Instead, it is likely that as various state and local governments have acted to restrict smoking, the public culture has moved in the same direction.

The groups showing the greatest movement toward banning smoking are Republicans, frequent churchgoers, and nonsmokers—though even smokers show some movement in that direction as well.

The poll, conducted July 7-10, shows that 34% of Americans want to completely ban smoking in hotels and motels, up from 25% who expressed that view two years ago.

What Is Your Opinion About Smoking in the Following Places?
percentage saying "totally ban smoking"

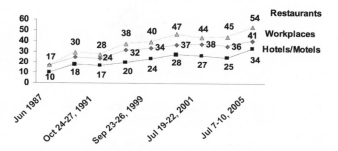

Support for banning smoking in the workplace and in restaurants has also increased since 2003—by five points for the workplace (from 36% to 41%), and by nine points for restaurants (45% to 54%). For the first time, a majority favors a total ban on smoking in restaurants.

Eighteen years ago, when Gallup first measured Americans' views on public smoking restrictions, only 10% to 17% supported banning smoking in these locations. The vast majority opted instead for setting aside certain areas for smoking and other areas where smoking would not be permitted. In the workplace, and in hotels and motels, majorities of Americans still prefer that smoking areas be set aside rather than that smoking be banned altogether, although the trend is clearly in favor of banning smoking in these public places.

Smoking Restrictions in Public Places

	Set aside areas %	Totally ban %	No restrictions %	No opinion %
Hotels and motels	60	34	5	1
Workplaces	56	41	2	1
Restaurants	42	54	3	1
Bars	40	29	28	3

Bars remain an area where about two-thirds of Americans oppose a ban. Forty percent would favor setting aside areas within a

What Is Your Opinion About Smoking in Bars?

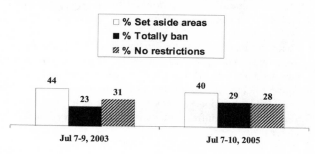

bar for smoking, while 28% say smoking should be allowed anywhere within a bar.

Current views show a modest movement toward banning smoking in bars, from 23% two years ago to 29% now.

Despite the increased acceptance of smoking bans in public places, more than 8 in 10 Americans oppose a complete ban on smoking in this country, while only 16% are in favor of making it illegal to smoke at all. These numbers have varied only slightly over the years.

Should smoking in this country be made totally illegal, or not?

BASED ON 489 NATIONAL ADULTS IN FORM A

	Yes, made illegal %	No, not made illegal %	No opinion %
2005 Jul 7-10	16	83	1
2003 Jul 7-9	16	84	*
2001 Jul 19-22	14	84	2
1994 Mar 11-13	11	86	3
1990 Nov Jul 6-8	14	84	2

* Less than 0.5%

Increased Support Compared by Selected Groups

Republicans are more likely than Democrats or independents to show increased support for smoking bans in restaurants, hotels and motels, and the workplace.

Currently, 62% of Republicans want to ban smoking in restaurants, up from 47% in 2003—a 15-point increase. By contrast, independents are eight points more likely to support a ban in restaurants (from 40% to 48%), while Democrats are only five points more likely (from 48% to 53%).

A similar pattern is found among partisans about smoking in hotels and motels. Forty-one percent of Republicans support a smoking ban in these establishments, compared with 28% of independents and 33% of Democrats. For Republicans, the current figures represent an increase of 15 percentage points over a similar reading in 2003, but only a 6-point increase for independents, and a 5-point increase for Democrats.

In the workplace, Republicans show an increase in support by 11 points (from 36% in 2003 to 47% in 2005) and independents by 5 points (32% to 37%). Democrats show an insignificant one-point decline, from 41% to 40%.

The poll also finds that frequent churchgoers are more likely to support bans on smoking than are infrequent churchgoers, and also more likely to reflect an increase in support from 2003.

- In the workplace, weekly churchgoers show an increase of 12 percentage points in support (41% to 53%), compared with essentially no change among the least frequent churchgoers (33% to 34%).
- That same pattern is found for restaurants—a 13-point increase for frequent churchgoers (51% to 64%), compared with a 5-point increase for people who rarely attend (42% to 47%).
- And for hotels and motels, frequent churchgoers are 14 points more likely to support a smoking ban now than they were two years ago, while infrequent churchgoers show only a 5-point increase.

It is expected that much of the increased support for banning smoking would come from nonsmokers. Indeed, compared with two years ago, nonsmokers' support for total bans on smoking in hotels and motels (up 11 percentage points), workplaces (8 points), and restaurants (9 points) has grown significantly. But the poll shows that even smokers are now more willing to ban smoking rather than just setting aside smoking and nonsmoking areas.

The largest increase in smokers' support is found for restaurants, with 31% supporting a ban on smoking, up from 21% two years ago. In hotels and motels, the increase is slight—up five points, from just 6% to 11%. In the workplace, however, smokers show essentially no change in their views from two years ago—only 15% prefer a ban now, compared with 17% in 2003.

Survey Methods

Results are based on telephone interviews with 1,006 national adults, aged 18 and older, conducted July 7-10, 2005. For results based on the total sample of national adults, one can say with 95% confidence that the maximum margin of sampling error is ±3 percentage points.

For results based on the 489 national adults in the Form A half-sample, the maximum margin of sampling error is ±5 percentage points.

For results based on the sample of 216 smokers, the maximum margin of sampling error is ±7 percentage points.

For results based on the sample of 790 nonsmokers, the maximum margin of sampling error is ±4 percentage points.

In addition to sampling error, question wording and practical difficulties in conducting surveys can introduce error or bias into the findings of public opinion polls.

July 22, 2005
FEWER YOUNG ADULTS DRINKING TO EXCESS
No change in reported overindulgence among older Americans

by Lydia Saad, Gallup Poll Senior Editor

Alcohol is a double-edged sword for society. Although the moderate enjoyment of alcohol may have health and lifestyle benefits for drinkers, the effects of alcoholism and drunken driving can be devastating. Gallup asks two questions that provide rough gauges of the negative effects of alcohol on Americans. Both were recently updated in Gallup's annual Consumption Habits survey, conducted July 7-10, 2005.

Gallup finds that 21% of drinkers—equivalent to 13% of all adult Americans—admit that they sometimes drink too much. This is down from the early 1990s, particularly among young adults.

From 1992 to 1994, nearly half of young adults (aged 18 to 29) said they occasionally drank too much, making them the most binge-prone age group. However, in the last two years, that figure has averaged just 30%, comparable to the percentage of middle-aged Americans who say they sometimes drink too much.

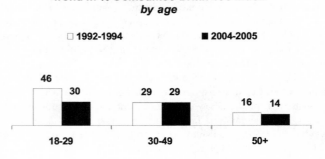

Three in 10 Americans report that alcohol has been the source of trouble within their own families. This figure is higher than it was a decade ago, and significantly higher than in the 1970s.

One in Five Occasionally Overdoes It

The percentage saying they sometimes drink too much averaged 30% between 1985 and 1994, but has averaged 23% since.

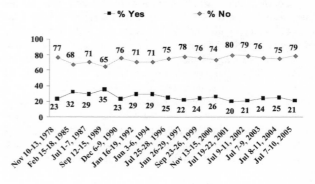

Although this long-term decrease in reported occasional overindulgence is encouraging, the fact that it has not decreased further since 1996 could explain why the rate of drunken-driving fatalities has also been at a stalemate for the past decade. Government statistics show a steep decline in alcohol-related highway deaths between 1982 and 1994. This corresponds with the emergence of anti-drunken-driving campaigns such as Mothers Against Drunk Driving (MADD), which spawned stiff new drunken-driving penalties nationwide. But since 1994, the number of alcohol-related highway deaths has changed little.

Three in 10 Perceive Drinking as a Cause of Trouble in Family

A different picture emerges from Gallup's trend on drinking-related family problems. The percentage having this experience inched up from the 12% to 15% range recorded in 1947 and for much of the 1970s. By 1981, this figure was typically over 20%, and by 1997, it was typically over 30%.

Has drinking ever been a cause of trouble in your family?

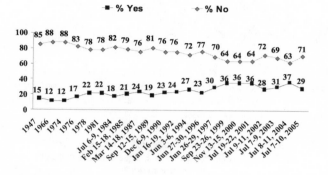

Does this represent a true increase in the effect of problem drinking on families, or merely an increased willingness to admit that such problems exist? With relatively small demographic differences in reported experience with problem drinking, the answer is not clear.

Fewer Young Adults Drinking to Excess (or So They Say)

Drinking too much on occasion is moderately correlated with age. Gallup's data from 2004-2005* show that those under age 50 are about twice as likely as those aged 50 and older to say they sometimes drink too much. The current rate is 30% among those aged 18 to 29 and 29% of those 30 to 49, but only 14% among those 50 and older.

This pattern was quite different a decade ago. From 1992 to 1994, nearly half of young adults said they occasionally drank too much. By contrast, a comparison of 1992-1994 and 2004-2005 data finds little or no change in the percentage of middle-aged and older Americans who say they sometimes drink too much.

Shrinking Gender Gap

Gallup's aggregated trend data show that, over the past two years, men have been slightly more likely than women to say they sometimes drink too much, 27% vs. 20%. But this gender gap is narrower than it was in the early 1990s when 35% of men, compared with 22% of women, sometimes drank more than they should.

Apart from age, another major predictor of overindulgence is the type of alcohol one tends to drink. Those who say they most often drink beer are somewhat more likely than those who prefer liquor to occasionally drink too much. Wine drinkers are the least likely to report occasionally exceeding their limits.

The percentage of beer drinkers who sometimes drink too much has declined from 40% in 1992-1994 to 29% in 2004-2005. This mostly results from the reported decrease in drinking too much among young adults, currently the only age group that names beer as its most preferred alcoholic drink.

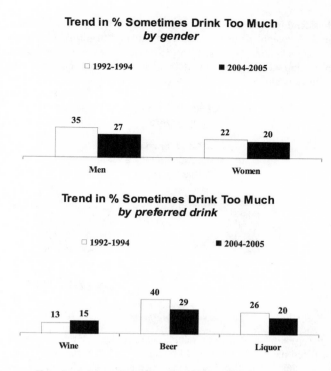

Few Americans Consider Alcohol Beneficial to Health

Some medical studies in recent years have suggested potential health benefits associated with moderate drinking. However, the Gallup measures on this indicate that most Americans don't embrace this finding. Americans are nearly as likely to believe that moderate drinking is bad for one's health (22%) as believe it is good for one's health (25%), while the largest segment believes it makes no difference (51%).

Since this question was first asked in 2001, there has only been a slight change in public perceptions, with a minor shift toward the view that alcohol is beneficial.

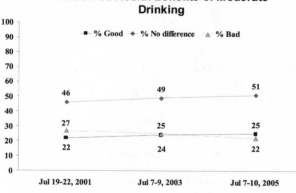

Perceived Health Benefits of Moderate Drinking

A common clinical definition for moderate drinking is one drink per day for non-pregnant women and two drinks per day for men. Because Gallup's question defines drinking in moderation as "one or two drinks a day," some women could perceive this as being over the suggested daily allowance. The net perception among women is that drinking is bad for one's health (27% say bad vs. 19% say good), while the net perception among men is that drinking is good for one's health (31% vs. 17%). However, even among men, the prevailing view is that drinking in moderation makes no difference to one's health.

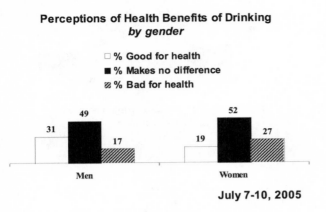

Perceptions of Health Benefits of Drinking by gender

□ % Good for health
■ % Makes no difference
▨ % Bad for health

July 7-10, 2005

Survey Methods

These results are based on telephone interviews with a randomly selected national sample of 1,006 adults, aged 18 and older, conducted July 7-10, 2005. For results based on this sample, one can say with 95% confidence that the maximum error attributable to sampling and other random effects is ±3 percentage points. For results based on the sample of 658 adults who drink alcoholic beverages, the maximum margin of sampling error is ±4 percentage points.

In addition to sampling error, question wording and practical difficulties in conducting surveys can introduce error or bias into the findings of public opinion polls.

Note: Demographic trends are reported on the basis of two-year averages in order to increase sample size, and therefore, statistical reliability.

July 26, 2005
PUBLIC: NOT ENOUGH SAFEGUARDS FOR MASS TRANSIT
But generally satisfied with steps to protect airlines

by David W. Moore, Gallup Poll Senior Editor

Following the initial terrorist bombings in London on July 7, Americans have become more worried about terrorism here in the United States. The most recent CNN/*USA Today*/Gallup survey finds a nine-point increase since June in the number of Americans who are worried about personally becoming a victim of terrorism.

In the current poll, 47% of Americans express some worry about becoming a terrorist victim, up from 38% who expressed that view in the June 16-19 poll.

However, the current poll also shows that the additional terrorist acts in London since the initial bombings have not caused Americans to become more worried about further attacks in the United States in the next several weeks. Today, more than half of all Americans, 57%, say it is likely there will be further acts of terrorism in

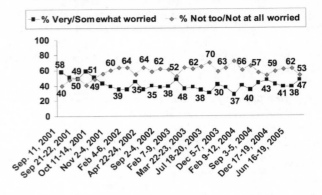

How worried are you that you or someone in your family will become a victim of terrorism?

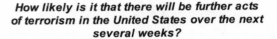

the United States in the next several weeks, very similar to the 55% measure Gallup obtained two weeks ago after the London bombings, but up substantially from mid-June. At that time, just 35% said further terrorist attacks were likely.

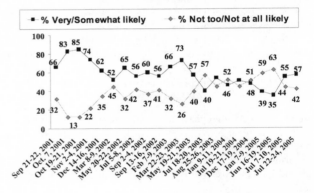

How likely is it that there will be further acts of terrorism in the United States over the next several weeks?

Given how easily it appeared that terrorists were able to attack the subway and bus system in London, Americans are not confident that the U.S. government has done enough to prevent terrorist acts on the mass transit systems in this country. Fifty-three percent say the federal government has not done enough, while 39% say it has, and another 2% say it has already done too much.

These views contrast with the public's perception of how much the government has done to protect the airlines. Fifty-seven percent say it has done "the right amount," while 35% say not enough, and 5% say too much.

Significant Partisan Differences

A comparison of responses to these terrorism questions by party affiliation shows some major differences in perceptions. Relatively few Republicans, 38%, are worried about becoming a terrorist victim, with 62% not worried. By contrast, independents and Democrats are about evenly divided—with independents leaning slightly in the worried direction, 51% to 49%, and Democrats showing about the same results, 52% to 48%.

The differences among the partisan groups are more modest in the prediction of further terrorism in the United States. Majorities of all three groups say such attacks are likely, though the mar-

Worried About Terrorism?
by party affiliation

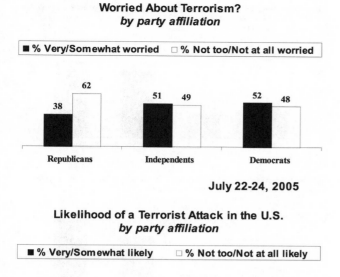

■ % Very/Somewhat worried   □ % Not too/Not at all worried

July 22-24, 2005

Likelihood of a Terrorist Attack in the U.S.
by party affiliation

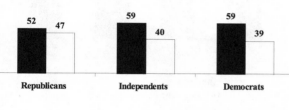

■ % Very/Somewhat likely   □ % Not too/Not at all likely

July 22-24, 2005

gins are larger among independents and Democrats than among Republicans.

By 52% to 47%, Republicans say terrorist attacks are likely within the next several weeks, while the comparable figures among independents and Democrats are 59% to 40%, and 59% to 39%, respectively.

Partisan differences are also modest in the public's assessment of government efforts to protect the mass transit systems in the United States. While 52% of Republicans say the government has done enough and only 39% say not enough, majorities of the other two partisan groups, 59% each, say the government has not done enough, while only about a third in each case say it has.

Similarly, the three partisan groups show major differences in their responses about government efforts to protect the airlines. By close to a 3-to-1 margin, Republicans say the government has

Preventing Acts of Terrorism on Mass Transit Systems in the U.S.
by party affiliation

■ % Too much   ▨ % Right amount   □ % Not enough

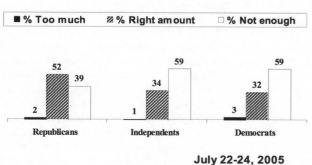

July 22-24, 2005

done enough rather than not enough, while Democrats are evenly divided. In this case, independents are more like Republicans than Democrats.

Preventing Acts of Terrorism on Airplanes
by party affiliation

■ % Too much   ▨ % Right amount   □ % Not enough

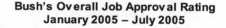

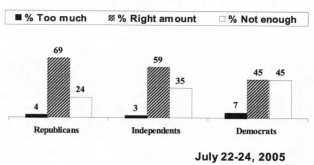

July 22-24, 2005

The poll also showed no difference in President George W. Bush's approval rating from two weeks ago. It is currently at 49%, identical to the July 7-10 measure, and little different from what it has been for the past several months.

Bush's Overall Job Approval Rating
January 2005 – July 2005

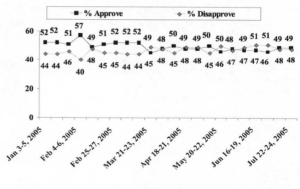

Survey Methods

Results are based on telephone interviews with 1,006 national adults, aged 18 and older, conducted July 22-24, 2005. For results based on the total sample of national adults, one can say with 95% confidence that the maximum margin of sampling error is ±3 percentage points.

In addition to sampling error, question wording and practical difficulties in conducting surveys can introduce error or bias into the findings of public opinion polls.

July 26, 2005

MINORITIES STILL STRUGGLE TO MEET BASIC NEEDS

Roughly a third of blacks, Hispanics didn't have enough money to buy food

by Raksha Arora, Business and Economy Editor

The cover story of the February 2005 issue of *Black Enterprise* magazine, which honored the 75 most influential blacks in corporate America, featured 18 black CEOs of powerful companies such as American Express, Time Warner, and Merrill Lynch. In 1993, there were only two black CEOs on the list. U.S. Census figures also suggest progress among minority communities: In 2003, 22% of black families lived below the poverty line, down from 31% a decade before. Among Hispanic families, the number dropped similarly, from 27% in 1993 to 21% in 2003. During the same time, the percentage of white families was steadier—9% lived below the poverty line in 1993, compared with 8% in 2003.

Despite that progress among blacks and Hispanics, data from Gallup's June 2005 Minority Relations poll* reveal that minorities still have singularly different life experiences from their white counterparts. Blacks and Hispanics are much more likely than whites to express concern about their personal finances, and to say they struggle to meet the most basic needs.

Gallup asked respondents how often they have to worry that their family incomes will not be enough to cover their expenses and bills. Forty-three percent of blacks say this is a concern they must face "all" or "most of the time"; only 26% of whites express the same degree of concern.

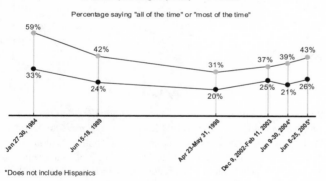

How often do you worry that your total family income will not be enough to meet your family's expenses and bills -- all of the time, most of the time, some of the time, or almost never?

● Whites (including Hispanics)   ● Blacks

Percentage saying "all of the time" or "most of the time"

*Does not include Hispanics

Forty-one percent of Hispanics say they worry about meeting their bills and expenses "most" or "all of the time."

Worry Over Basic Necessities

Beyond their concern about their finances, blacks and Hispanics also differ significantly from whites in their reports of being unable to meet some basic needs. For example, 36% of Hispanics and 31% of blacks say there have been times in the last year when they did not have enough money to buy food their families needed. That compares with just 11% of whites.

The same holds true for the question about whether respondents have had enough money to buy clothing for their families. Forty-five percent of Hispanics and 37% of blacks say there have been times in

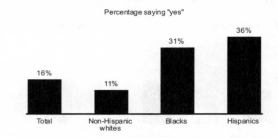

Have there been times during the last year when you did not have enough money to buy food your family needed?

Percentage saying "yes"

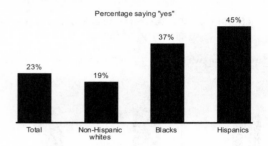

Have there been times during the last year when you did not have enough money to buy clothing your family needed?

Percentage saying "yes"

the last year when they did not have enough money to buy clothing; just 19% of non-Hispanic whites say the same.

Bottom Line

Despite decades of reform, activism, and economic progress, many minorities still struggle for basic necessities. These data illustrate the fact that the American dream continues to elude a significant proportion of the U.S. population.

Results are based on telephone interviews with 2,264 national adults, aged 18 and older, conducted June 6-25, 2005, including oversamples of blacks and Hispanics that are weighted to reflect their proportions in the general population. For results based on the total sample of national adults, one can say with 95% confidence that the maximum margin of sampling error is ±5 percentage points.

July 26, 2005

DO SPARKS FLY WHEN BLACKS AND WHITES ARE NEIGHBORS?

Those in racially integrated areas have more negative views on how blacks and whites really feel

by Lydia Saad, Gallup Poll Senior Editor

Does familiarity breed harmony or conflict when it comes to racial and ethnic relations in the United States? More to the point, does living in a well-integrated area—a place where at least one other race or ethnic group besides one's own is represented in large numbers—lead to more positive or more negative perceptions of race and ethnic relations?

Results from Gallup's 2005 Minority Relations poll* suggest that the racial and ethnic makeup of one's community has little bearing on Americans' overall perceptions of relations between whites and blacks, between whites and Hispanics, or between Hispanics and blacks. For instance, blacks living in heavily Hispanic areas are no different from blacks living among few Hispanics in their perceptions of how well blacks and Hispanics get along. The same can be said of whites' and blacks' perceptions of white-black relations.

On the other hand, the influence of integration is evident in whites' and blacks' perceptions of how members of the two races view each other on a more personal level. With a pair of questions asking respondents to estimate how many whites and blacks dislike people of the other race, Gallup finds that those living in more racially integrated environments appear to have more negative views about how blacks and whites really feel toward each other.

Ratings of Race Relations Not Affected by Community Makeup

Gallup asked respondents: *Would you say relations between whites and blacks [in the United States] are very good, somewhat good, somewhat bad, or very bad?*

The encouraging result is that a majority of blacks and whites—regardless of the degree to which they live in integrated communities—positively view overall relations between whites and blacks.

Sixty-two percent of blacks living in areas populated by "many whites" say that relations between whites and blacks are good in the United States these days; only 35% consider them bad. Roughly three-fourths of blacks living among "some whites" and 61% of those living among only a few or no whites say relations are good.

Blacks' Views of White-Black Relations

Number of Whites in Area

	Many whites	Some whites	Only a few/no whites
Overall Rating			
Good	62%	74	61
Bad	35%	26	38

Similarly, whites' perceptions of white-black relations do not vary according to whether whites are living in an area where there are many blacks, some blacks, or only a few or no blacks. Roughly 7 in 10 whites across all these categories positively perceive white-black relations.

Whites' Views of White-Black Relations

Number of Blacks in Area

	Many blacks	Some blacks	Only a few/no blacks
Overall Rating			
Good	73%	70	72
Bad	27%	27	26

Community makeup also does not affect whites' views of white-Hispanic relations and blacks' views of black-Hispanic relations.

Whites' Views of White-Hispanic Relations

Number of Hispanics in Area

	Many Hispanics	Some Hispanics	Only a few/no Hispanics
Overall Rating			
Good	78%	68	71
Bad	21%	28	26

Blacks' Views of Black-Hispanic Relations

Number of Hispanics in Area

	Many Hispanics	Some Hispanics	Only a few/no Hispanics
Overall Rating			
Good	74%	79	80
Bad	17%	19	15

Although the June 6-25 survey includes large oversamples of blacks and Hispanics that allow for statistically reliable analyses of their views, the sample sizes of Hispanics living in areas with less than "many" whites and blacks are too small to be used for this analysis.

Integrated Blacks and Whites Perceive the Most Racial Enmity

The same survey probed Americans' perceptions of racial hostility with this pair of questions:

Do you think only a few white people dislike blacks, many white people dislike blacks, or almost all white people dislike blacks?

Do you think only a few black people dislike whites, many black people dislike whites, or almost all black people dislike whites?

Whites who live in areas where there are many blacks are more likely to say that "many white people dislike blacks" (44%) than those who live in areas where there are just some (30%) or only a few (31%) blacks. At the same time, the prevalence of blacks in their communities does not affect whites' perceptions of how many blacks dislike whites.

The question for future study is whether whites living in highly integrated areas are simply more aware of white hostility toward blacks (perhaps integrated whites are more vocal about it), or whether there is, in fact, more white hostility toward blacks in these environments.

Whites' Views of White-Black Relations

Number of Blacks in Area

	Many blacks	Some blacks	Only a few/no blacks
How many blacks dislike whites?			
Only a few/none	58%	52	58
Many/all	40%	44	39
How many whites dislike blacks?			
Only a few/none	55%	69	69
Many/all	44%	30	31

Blacks are also more likely to perceive acrimony between the races when they live in predominantly white areas. However, these blacks perceive a higher rate of black dislike for whites as well as white dislike for blacks.

Among blacks who live in areas populated by many whites, 41% believe that many blacks dislike whites. This is significantly higher than the 26% who live among only some whites. Half of blacks living in well-integrated areas believe that many whites dislike blacks. This is significantly higher than the 39% of blacks who live where there are only a few or no whites.

Blacks' Views of White-Black Relations

	Number of Whites in Area		
	Many whites	*Some whites*	*Only a few/no whites*
How many blacks dislike whites?			
Only a few/none	58%	70	63
Many/all	41%	26	35
How many whites dislike blacks?			
Only a few/none	48%	52	57
Many/all	50%	43	39

Bottom Line

Americans' overall view of white-black relations is generally rosy, and evidently not informed by personal experiences with integration. That could be because respondents are answering the question in broader terms.

But ask something more specific, like "how many white people dislike blacks?" and respondents can be witnesses to the world around them. This report from the trenches—from those on the front lines, as it were, of race relations—is disquieting.

*These results are based on telephone interviews with a randomly selected national sample of 1,375 adults, aged 18 years and older, including a main sample of 1,004 national adults and oversamples of blacks and Hispanics. Telephone interviews were conducted from June 6-25, 2004.

For results based on the total sample of 2,264 national adults, one can say with 95% confidence that the maximum error attributable to sampling and other random effects is ±5 percentage points.

Results based on the subsample of whites include interviews with 807 non-Hispanic white adults and have a maximum margin of sampling error of ±7 percentage points. Results based on the subsample of blacks include interviews with 802 black national adults and have a maximum margin of sampling error of ±5 percentage points. Results based on the subsample of Hispanics include interviews with 511 Hispanic national adults (including 181 conducted in Spanish) and have a maximum margin of sampling error of ±7 percentage points.

In addition to sampling error, question wording and practical difficulties in conducting surveys can introduce error or bias into the findings of public opinion polls.

July 27, 2005
WHITE HOUSE LEAK HAS LITTLE EFFECT ON BUSH HONESTY RATINGS
Ratings stable compared with most recent readings, but near lows for his presidency

by Jeffrey M. Jones, Gallup Poll Managing Editor

A new CNN/*USA Today*/Gallup poll finds that George W. Bush's personal honesty rating is the lowest of his term, but his ratings apparently have not suffered much, if at all, as a result of the probe into White House leaks of classified information. Only about half of Americans are following the controversy closely, but the prevailing

sentiment is that Bush adviser Karl Rove did something unethical, if not illegal, when he revealed the identity of a CIA operative to reporters. Bush's ratings on other characteristics—including his values and his ability to manage the government—are also at lows for his presidency. His current approval rating is 49%, which is a slight improvement from where he stood in late June.

The July 22-24 poll finds 54% of Americans saying Bush is honest and trustworthy and 44% saying he is not. That is essentially unchanged from a 56% honesty rating found in April, long before the White House leak controversy erupted. In fact, Bush's image on this dimension has been quite stable since the beginning of 2004.

George W. Bush: Is Honest and Trustworthy

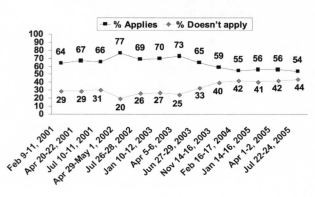

However, the percentage who believe Bush to be honest has unmistakably declined since its post-9/11 highs. At the same time, Bush's overall approval rating was generally falling (after mid-2003, arguably due to the difficulties in Iraq). As such, it is more likely that the decline in the honesty rating is part of that larger pattern.

Contrary to what the Gallup data indicate, some news reports have suggested that Bush's honesty ratings may have declined in part due to the leak controversy—citing a Pew Research Center for the People and the Press survey. That July 13-17 Pew poll showed just 49% saying that Bush "impress[es]" them as "trustworthy," compared with 62% who said that in a September 2003 Pew survey. The interpretation of a decline in trustworthiness is correct, but the implication that the decline is a recent development is not correct, as the Gallup data indicate.

Gallup has shown an 11 percentage-point decline in Bush's honesty ratings since June 2003, compared with Pew's 13-point decline since September 2003, so it is clear that Bush's honesty ratings have gone south in the last two years. But Gallup's frequent intervening measures indicate that the decline had mostly occurred by early 2004, and since then, perceptions of Bush's honesty and trustworthiness have generally stabilized.

Ethics of the Bush Administration

The new CNN/*USA Today*/Gallup poll also asked Americans for more general ratings of the ethics of the Bush administration as a whole. Overall, 55% of Americans rate the ethical standards of the Bush administration as "excellent" (8%) or "good" (47%). Twenty-four percent say they are "not good" and 18% say they are "poor." Gallup last measured the Bush administration's ethics before the Iraq war began, in July 2002, and they were much more positive then (74% rated them as excellent or good).

A majority of Americans, 58%, also say the ethical practices of the Bush administration are *not* worse than previous administrations, while 39% believe they are. Gallup asked the same question in the July 2002 poll, at which time just 16% said Bush administration ethics were worse than previous administrations and 80% said they were not.

So while ratings of Bush administration ethics are much less positive now than at earlier stages in his presidency, they are still in positive territory.

The Leak Controversy

One reason the leak controversy may not be affecting Bush's honesty ratings much is that just over half of Americans say they are following the news about the White House leak very (17%) or somewhat (34%) closely. When asked about Rove's actions in the matter, 25% say he did something illegal, and an additional 37% say he did something unethical but not illegal. Just 15% believe Rove did not do anything seriously wrong, and the remaining 23% have no opinion.

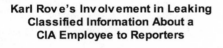

Karl Rove's Involvement in Leaking Classified Information About a CIA Employee to Reporters

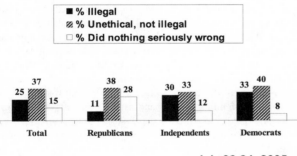

- ■ % Illegal
- ▨ % Unethical, not illegal
- ▢ % Did nothing seriously wrong

July 22-24, 2005

Evaluations of Rove's actions are closely tied to partisanship—Democrats (73%) are much more likely than Republicans (49%) to say Rove acted illegally or unethically.

The public is divided over whether Bush should fire Rove—40% say he should, 39% say he should not, and 21% have no opinion. Bush indicated earlier that he would fire anyone in his administration who leaked classified information. However, he since has said he would fire someone who committed a crime in leaking such information (Rove apparently did not reveal the identity of CIA operative Valerie Plame by name, which would not be a crime). Democrats (53%) are more than twice as likely as Republicans (21%) to believe Bush should fire Rove.

Americans are more inclined to believe that Rove should resign from the administration—49% say he should, 31% say he should not, and 20% have no opinion. Again, there are wide gaps in opinion by party—65% of Democrats believe Rove should resign, compared with just 26% of Republicans.

An analysis of the data shows that those following the story closely are much more likely than those not following the story to believe that Rove did something wrong. Thirty-six percent of the attentive group says Rove did something illegal and 40% say he did something unethical. A majority of this group also says Bush should fire Rove, and two-thirds say Rove should resign.

	Following closely	Not following closely
Did something illegal	36%	13%
Did something unethical	40%	34%
Did not do anything wrong	19%	12%
No opinion	4%	41%
Should be fired	54%	25%
Should not be fired	41%	38%
No opinion	5%	37%
Should resign	66%	32%
Should not resign	31%	31%
No opinion	4%	37%

One might assume from these results that Democrats are simply following the story more closely than Republicans. While that is true, the margin is relatively small—54% of Democrats say they are following the story closely, compared with 48% of Republicans. Regardless of party affiliation, those following the controversy are more likely to take a negative view of Rove in this matter. Attentive Democrats and independents are especially likely to hold negative views, however.

The data suggest that while the leak controversy may not have affected Bush's honesty ratings to date, it still could if it becomes a bigger issue. There is a significant gap in Bush's honesty ratings between those following the controversy closely (48%) and those who are not (61%).

Other Bush Ratings

Even though the leak controversy has yet to cause Bush's honesty ratings to decline, the current 54% rating is the lowest Gallup has measured to date. Bush's ratings on two other personal characteristics are also at or near lows for his presidency.

Half of Americans say Bush "shares your values" and 48% say he does not. In April of this year, 55% said Bush shared their values. The previous low reading was 52% in February 2004.

George W. Bush: Shares Your Values

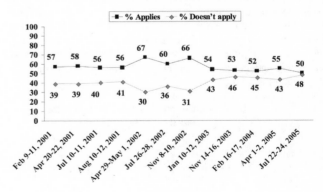

Fifty-three percent say Bush "can manage the government effectively," while 45% disagree. This also is the lowest reading for Bush to date, but this item was last asked in early 2003.

Bush does comparatively better on the "strong and decisive leader" dimension than the others, something that has been typical throughout his presidency. The current 62% rating on this characteristic is little

George W. Bush:
Can Manage the Government Effectively

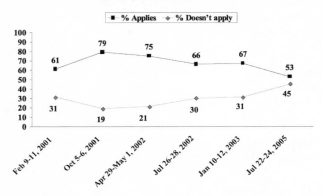

changed from January. Unlike the other characteristics in this poll, Bush has received worse ratings on his leadership at other points in his presidency. In August 2001, only 55% thought Bush was a strong leader.

George W. Bush:
Is a Strong and Decisive Leader

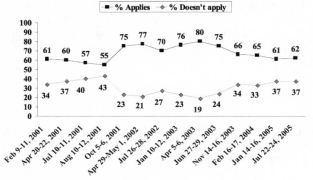

Generally speaking, Bush receives ratings for his personal characteristics that are more positive than those he receives for his job performance. His ratings on these four personal characteristics are at least slightly better than his current 49% job approval rating. That approval rating is unchanged from a Gallup Poll conducted two weeks earlier, and is a slight improvement from a 45% term-low reading in late June. The fact that Bush's approval rating has remained steady (or even increased) during the height of the leak controversy underscores the notion that Bush is not taking much of a personal hit from it.

Bush's Overall Job Approval Rating
April — July 2005

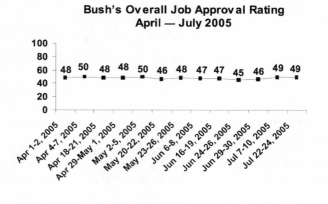

Survey Methods

These results are based on telephone interviews with a randomly selected national sample of 1,006 adults, aged 18 and older, conducted July 22-24, 2005. For results based on this sample, one can say with 95% confidence that the maximum error attributable to sampling and other random effects is ±3 percentage points. In addition to sampling error, question wording and practical difficulties in conducting surveys can introduce error or bias into the findings of public opinion polls.

July 28, 2005
NO EVIDENCE OF DECLINING SUPPORT FOR IRAQ WAR
But Americans doubtful U.S. will ultimately "win"

by Lydia Saad, Gallup Poll Senior Editor

A new CNN/*USA Today*/Gallup poll, conducted July 22-24, shows that Americans are about as supportive of U.S. involvement in Iraq currently as they have been for the past year, with little change in the public's optimism regarding successful completion of the mission.

This finding may seem contrary to the continued violence from insurgency forces in Iraq and the release of grim statistics about the ill-preparedness of Iraq's internal security forces. But the maintenance of public opinion at previous levels perhaps reflects some tempering of the negative news from Iraq by news of the forthcoming Iraqi elections. It is even more likely that these public opinion levels are evidence that there is a partisan structure to views about Iraq—with most Republicans defending the war and most Democrats opposing it—that is quite fixed, and not particularly susceptible to volatile events.

A slim majority of Americans are supportive of President George W. Bush's administration's decision to enter the Iraq war, even though more than half are doubtful the United States will win the conflict, and nearly 6 in 10 are doubtful that the United States will establish a stable democracy in Iraq.

Iraq War "Not a Mistake"

Fifty-three percent of Americans say that it was not a mistake to send troops to Iraq, while 46% say it was. This represents a slight improvement compared with a June Gallup poll, when the majority (53%) said sending troops was a mistake.

However, the current result is consistent with the general range of support for the war that has been evident since last fall. Throughout this period, Americans have been closely divided in their assessments of the United States' involvement in Iraq, with the slight majority usually saying that sending troops was not a mistake.

Doubt Democracy Will be Achieved

Americans are no more—or less—confident today than they were last April about the United States' chances for creating a stable democratic government in Iraq. Only 37% think this will happen, while 58% say it will not.

Optimism on this question was slightly higher last November in polling conducted after a major U.S. military offensive in Fallujah, Iraq; but even then, less than half of the public felt the U.S. would achieve its goal of helping Iraq develop a stable democracy.

Mistake to Send Troops to Iraq?
March 2003 — July 2005

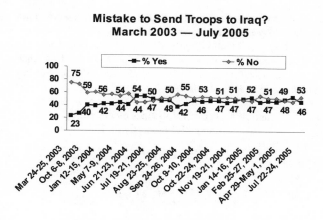

Will U.S. Establish a Stable Government in Iraq?

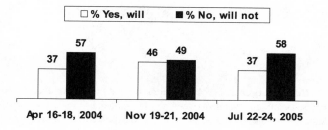

Americans are slightly more confident about the chances that the United States will win the war in Iraq than they are about democracy succeeding, but the majority (53%) predicts the U.S. will not win. Specifically, 43% think America will win the war, 21% say the U.S. can win but won't, and 32% think victory is not possible.

Which comes closest to your view about the war in Iraq — you think the U.S. will win the war in Iraq, you think the U.S. can win the war in Iraq, but you don't think it will win, or you do not think the U.S. can win the war in Iraq?

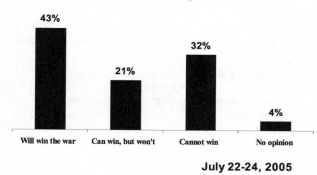

July 22-24, 2005

Americans are closely divided on the question of whether the Bush administration deliberately misled Americans about the threat of an armed Iraq. Fifty-one percent say the administration misled the public about whether Iraq has weapons of mass destruction; 47% say it did not.

This is not the first time that public opinion has tilted against the Bush administration on this measure. Public doubts about the administration's candor in leading America to war have been building gradually since the beginning of June 2003, and finally reached the 50% mark this past April. Prior to this spring, the majority believed the administration did not mislead the public.

Do you think the Bush administration deliberately misled the American public about whether Iraq has weapons of mass destruction, or not?

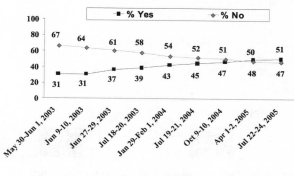

Partisan Divide

Partisan attitudes continue to be the public's most notable distinctions about the Iraq war. Republicans tend to see the war in a positive light, while Democrats are mostly critical of the conflict. Independents also tend to be more negative than positive about the venture.

The strongest partisan differences in the four questions from the latest poll which measure opinions about the Iraq war are the perceptions of whether the Bush administration misled the public about the security threat posed by Iraq. More than four in five Republicans (85%) defend the administration on this charge, compared with only 15% of Democrats—a 70 percentage-point difference.

Did Bush Administration Deliberately Mislead Americans?

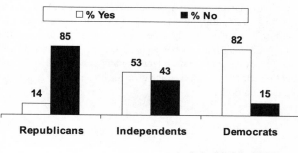

July 22-24, 2005

Republicans and Democrats are slightly closer in their views on whether sending U.S. troops to Iraq was a mistake (a 52 percentage-point gap). They are much closer in their outlooks for winning the war and establishing democracy, mostly because Republicans tend to be less positive on these dimensions of the Iraq war than they are on the other two.

Summary of Pro-Bush Iraq Views

	Republican %	Democratic %	Percentage-point difference
Did not deliberately mislead	85	15	70
No, Iraq war not a mistake	82	30	52
U.S. will win Iraq war	63	26	37
Will establish democracy in Iraq	61	22	39

Bush's Image

Although a majority of Americans now say the Bush administration misled the public about the existence of weapons of mass destruction in Iraq, a slim majority of Americans still believe that President Bush is generally honest and trustworthy.

The Credibility Factor

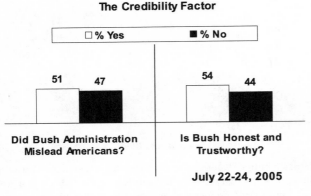

July 22-24, 2005

A comparison of the two questions shows most of those who think the administration misled the public (77%) also believe Bush is not honest and trustworthy, while a sizable minority of this group (21%) believes he is. Naturally, there is closer to a one-to-one correlation in the views of those who defend the administration's position on the justification for attacking Iraq. Nearly 9 in 10 (89%) of those that think the Bush administration didn't mislead the public think Bush is honest and trustworthy, while just 9% say he is not.

Survey Methods

These results are based on telephone interviews with a randomly selected national sample of 1,006 adults, aged 18 and older, conducted July 22-24, 2005. For results based on this sample, one can say with 95% confidence that the maximum error attributable to sampling and other random effects is ±3 percentage points. In addition to sampling error, question wording and practical difficulties in conducting surveys can introduce error or bias into the findings of public opinion polls.

July 29, 2005
BUSH APPROVAL AT 44%
Lowest measurement of his presidency

by Jeffrey M. Jones, Gallup Poll Managing Editor

A new Gallup Poll finds a decline in George W. Bush's job approval rating. After standing at 49% approval in the prior two CNN/*USA Today*/Gallup polls conducted this month, now just 44% of Americans say they approve of Bush, a new low mark for the president. The poll also shows a drop in Bush's favorable rating to 48%, which is the first time it has dropped below 50% since Gallup began tracking this opinion in 1999. Four in 10 Americans are satisfied with the way things are going in the country, which is essentially unchanged from early July. The poll shows continued positive momentum for the Democratic Party in terms of national party identification and rat-

ings of the two major political parties, both of which were evident before the drop in Bush approval occurred.

The July 25-28 Gallup Poll finds 44% of Americans approving and 51% disapproving of the job Bush is doing as president. Bush's prior low approval rating was 45%, which occurred once in March and once again in June of this year.

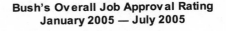
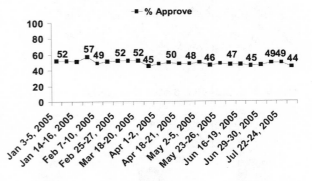

Bush had been at 49% approval in the first two July polls, which represented an improvement over where he stood in late June. To a large degree, then, the decline observed in the new poll could simply represent a fading of a short-term boost to Bush's public standing. His higher July numbers may have been a product of the increased focus on terrorism following the London terror attack on July 7 and an attempted attack on July 21, as well as the attack in Egypt on July 23. Both July polls were conducted in the immediate aftermath of those attacks (July 7-10 and July 22-24). Also, Bush's selection of John Roberts as Supreme Court nominee on July 19 has been well received by the public, but any boost in support from that would likely be short-lived.

A closer look at the data reveals that Bush's recent approval ratings were higher because of independents' more positive evaluations, which have now returned to their late June levels. Republicans' and Democrats' evaluations of Bush have been more stable in recent weeks.

The more negative evaluation of Bush is not confined to his approval rating. Just 48% of Americans now say they have a favor-

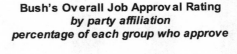
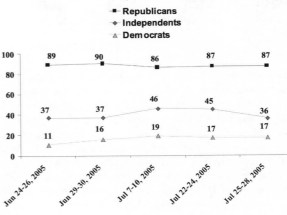

able opinion of him, while 50% have an unfavorable view. Bush's previous low favorable rating was 51%, measured twice last October (Bush also had a 51% favorable rating in a September 2000 poll of registered voters).

Opinion of George W. Bush
February 2001 — July 2005

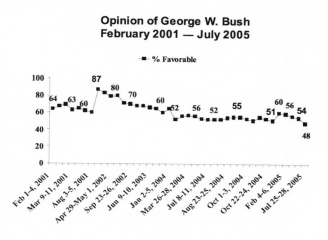

Bush's prior favorable rating—from April—was 54%. At that time, he had a 48% job approval rating.

Even while Bush's ratings are falling, other core Gallup ratings show more stability.

- For example, 40% of Americans are satisfied with the way things are going in the country, and 58% are dissatisfied. In early July, 42% were satisfied and 57% dissatisfied.
- Ratings of the national economy also show little change. In early July, 36% said economic conditions were excellent or good and 18% said poor. Thirty-five percent said the economy was getting better and 54% said worse. Now, 32% rate the economy as excellent or good (23% as poor) and 35% say it is getting better and 53% say getting worse.
- While the Iraq war could be responsible the general descent into the mid-to-high 40% approval range for Bush over the last two years, there has been little change in the public's views on Iraq in recent polls to suggest it is behind Bush's current rating. The

July 22-24 poll showed fewer Americans (46%) calling the war in Iraq "a mistake" than did so in June (53%).

Democrats Faring Better

Recent Gallup Polls have shown growing positive momentum for the Democratic Party, even while Bush's ratings were somewhat higher. For example, the July 22-24 CNN/*USA Today*/Gallup poll found 52% of Americans rating the Democratic Party favorably, while just 46% give a favorable rating to the Republican Party. When the question was last asked in April, each party was rated favorably by 50% of Americans.

Additionally, Gallup has observed a consistent edge for the Democrats in terms of national party identification in its recent polls. In the current poll, 33% say they are Democrats, 28% Republicans, and 37% independents. This is the fourth consecutive poll in which Democrats have outnumbered Republicans in Gallup Polls.

Party Identification, Recent Gallup Polls

	% Democrat	*% Republican*	*% Independent*
July 25-28	33	28	37
July 22-24	36	32	31
July 7-10	35	30	33
June 29-30	38	29	31

For comparison's sake, the party identification averages were evenly divided in Gallup Polls conducted in the first half of 2005 (34% Republican and 33% Democratic) and in all of 2004 (34% Republican and 34% Democratic).

Survey Methods

These results are based on telephone interviews with a randomly selected national sample of 1,010 adults, aged 18 and older, conducted July 25-28, 2005. For results based on this sample, one can say with 95% confidence that the maximum error attributable to sampling and other random effects is ±3 percentage points. In addition to sampling error, question wording and practical difficulties in conducting surveys can introduce error or bias into the findings of public opinion polls.

should confirm Roberts. Among those who are not Christian, only 28% support this. (Forty-four percent of non-Christians oppose his confirmation, and 28% have no opinion.)

Initial support for Roberts' confirmation is similar to what Gallup has found for two other Supreme Court nominees over the past 14 years. A few weeks after President George H.W. Bush nominated Clarence Thomas in July 1991 but before the Anita Hill allegations came to light, a slight majority of Americans, 52% supported Thomas serving on the court. And, in mid-June 1993, days after her nomination, Gallup also found a slim majority of Americans, 53%, supporting confirmation for President Bill Clinton's nominee, Ruth Bader Ginsburg.

Trend: Support for U.S. Supreme Court Nominees

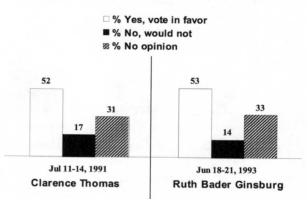

□ % Yes, vote in favor
■ % No, would not
▨ % No opinion

Jul 11-14, 1991
Clarence Thomas

Jun 18-21, 1993
Ruth Bader Ginsburg

Gallup also asked about another, much more controversial Supreme Court nominee in 1987. After Ronald Reagan nominated Robert Bork to serve on the court, an August/September 1987 poll found fewer than 4 in 10 Americans supporting his confirmation.

Big Political Fight on the Horizon?

While Americans support Roberts serving on the court, they are more divided about how the Senate confirmation hearings will go. A slim majority of respondents, 51%, predict there will be a major fight between Republicans and Democrats that will drag on for a long time, while 42% say it will be a relatively easy process in which both parties come to an agreement.

Forty-Six Percent of Americans View Roberts Favorably

Slightly less than half of Americans, 46%, say they have a favorable opinion of Roberts, while only 13% have an unfavorable opinion. A

Which do you think is more likely to occur during the Senate confirmation hearings for Roberts: a relatively easy process in which Republicans and Democrats come to an agreement, (or) a major fight between Republicans and Democrats that would drag on for a long time?

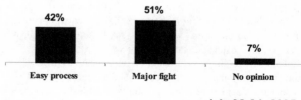

July 22-24, 2005

August 1, 2005

PUBLIC SUPPORTS ROBERTS SERVING ON U.S. SUPREME COURT

A slim majority says Senate confirmation hearings will be a major political fight

by Joseph Carroll, Gallup Poll Assistant Editor

A recent CNN/*USA Today*/Gallup poll finds that nearly 6 in 10 Americans say they would like the Senate to confirm U.S. Circuit Judge John Roberts Jr. to the U.S. Supreme Court. However, Americans are not convinced that the confirmation hearings will go smoothly. A slim majority expects a major fight between Republicans and Democrats. When it comes to the abortion issue, a majority of Americans say the Senate should insist that Roberts explain his views, but the public also feels that a nominee's position about whether to keep or overturn the *Roe v. Wade* decision should not be the lone factor that would disqualify the person from serving on the court.

Support for Roberts' Confirmation

Americans would like the Senate to confirm Roberts, according to the July 22-24 poll conducted just days after President George W. Bush nominated him to the U.S. Supreme Court. The poll finds that 59% of Americans say they would like to see the Senate vote in favor of Roberts serving on the Supreme Court, while 22% would not. Nearly one in five do not have an opinion.

As you may know, John Roberts is the person nominated to serve on the Supreme Court. Would you like to see the Senate vote in favor of Roberts serving on the Supreme Court, or not?

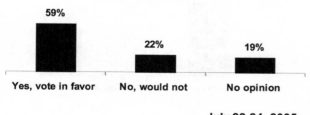

July 22-24, 2005

Perhaps not surprisingly, support for Roberts is related to party affiliation. More than 8 in 10 Republicans say the Senate should vote in favor of Roberts, while 5% do not support his confirmation and 13% have no opinion. Among Democrats, just 42% support Roberts' confirmation, while 35% do not and 23% have no opinion.

Also, the poll finds essentially no difference in support between Catholics and Protestants, even though Roberts is Catholic. More than 6 in 10 Protestants (65%) and Catholics (62%) say the Senate substantial number of Americans, 41%, do not know enough about the nominee at this point to rate him.

Again, the poll finds Republicans much more likely than Democrats to view Bush's nominee favorably; Democrats are much more likely to withhold judgment at this point. Seventy percent of Republicans view Roberts favorably, while nearly half of Democrats (49%) say they do not know enough about Roberts to have an opinion. Democrats who give an opinion of Roberts are equally divided between positive and negative evaluations.

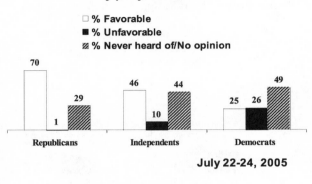

Opinion of U.S. Supreme Court Nominee John Roberts by party affiliation

☐ % Favorable
■ % Unfavorable
▨ % Never heard of/No opinion

July 22-24, 2005

The Abortion Issue

How important will Roberts' stance on abortion be in the confirmation process? That answer is unknown at this point, but the poll provides some clues.

Americans' positions on abortion seem to have relatively little influence on shaping support for Roberts. A majority of those who say they are pro-life (69%) as well as pro-choice (52%) on the abortion issue support Roberts' confirmation, although those who are pro-life are more likely to do so.

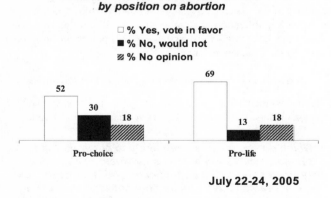

Support for John Roberts' Confirmation by position on abortion

☐ % Yes, vote in favor
■ % No, would not
▨ % No opinion

July 22-24, 2005

The American public says the Senate should insist that Roberts explain his views on abortion. Six in 10 Americans (61%) say the senators should insist that Roberts explain his views prior to confirming him to the court, while 37% say he should be allowed to refuse to answer questions on the subject.

This sentiment is somewhat stronger now than it was when Thomas was nominated in July 1991. At that time, 54% said Thomas should have to explain his views on abortion, while 39% said he should be allowed to refuse to answer.

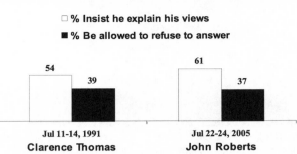

When the U.S. Senate holds hearings on the Clarence Thomas/John Roberts nomination, do you think senators should insist that he explain his views on abortion before confirming him, or should he be allowed to refuse to answer questions about abortion?

☐ % Insist he explain his views
■ % Be allowed to refuse to answer

| Jul 11-14, 1991 Clarence Thomas | Jul 22-24, 2005 John Roberts |

The survey also asked Americans if a nominee's position on the *Roe v. Wade* decision should disqualify the nominee from serving.

Half of the respondents in the survey were asked:

*If a nominee for the U.S. Supreme Court favors **keeping** the Roe v. Wade decision on abortion, in your view, should that alone disqualify that person from serving on the Supreme Court, or not?*

And the other half of the respondents were asked this question:

*If a nominee for the U.S. Supreme Court favors **overturning** the Roe v. Wade decision on abortion, in your view, should that alone disqualify that person from serving on the Supreme Court, or not?*

The results to both questions suggest that the vast majority of Americans do not think a nominee's views about the *Roe v. Wade* decision should be the sole factor to disqualify that candidate. Only 13% say a nominee should be disqualified if that person favors keeping the *Roe v. Wade* decision. A higher percentage, but still far from a majority (25%), says a nominee should be disqualified if the person wants to overturn the decision.

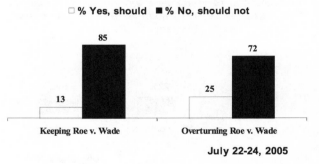

If a nominee for the U.S. Supreme Court favors keeping/overturning the Roe v. Wade decision on abortion, in your view, should that alone disqualify that person from serving on the Supreme Court, or not?

☐ % Yes, should   ■ % No, should not

| Keeping Roe v. Wade | Overturning Roe v. Wade |

July 22-24, 2005

Survey Methods

Results are based on telephone interviews with 1,006 national adults, aged 18 and older, conducted July 22-24, 2005. For results based on the total sample of national adults, one can say with 95% confidence that the maximum margin of sampling error is ±3 percentage points.

For results based on the 497 national adults in the Form A half-sample and 509 national adults in the Form B half-sample, the maximum margins of sampling error are ±5 percentage points.

In addition to sampling error, question wording and practical difficulties in conducting surveys can introduce error or bias into the findings of public opinion polls.

August 2, 2005

BACK-TO-SCHOOL WILL TEST THE ECONOMY'S STRENGTH

Consumer confidence declines even as economists tout second quarter results

by Dennis Jacobe, Chief Economist, The Gallup Organization

On July 29, the Commerce Department reported that the U.S. economy grew at a 3.4% annual rate during the second quarter as consumer spending increased at a 3.3% annual rate. While these numbers are down from the first quarter, they represent a strong economic performance, particularly in light of the fact that retail gasoline prices averaged $2.23 a gallon during the second quarter, compared to $1.97 during the first three months of the year.

While the economy's performance from April to June produced euphoria on Wall Street, Gallup's consumer confidence measures declined at the end of July. The Conference Board's Consumer Confidence Index also showed a decline for the month, while the University of Michigan's Consumer Sentiment Index remained essentially unchanged.

So, why aren't consumers more optimistic about the future of the U.S. economy? Will consumers continue to spend even if their confidence level continues to decline? What is the outlook for back-to-school sales?

Perceptions of Current Economic Conditions

According to a July 25-28 Gallup Poll, the percentage of consumers rating the economy "good" or "excellent" declined from 36% in early July to 32% at the end of the month. At the same time, the percentage rating the economy "poor" increased to 23% from 18% earlier in the month. The current difference of 9 percentage points (percentage good/excellent minus percentage poor) is at its lowest point since early May. It is also far below the 24 percentage-point difference registered in January and early February.

Current Economic Conditions
Selected Trend: January — July 2005

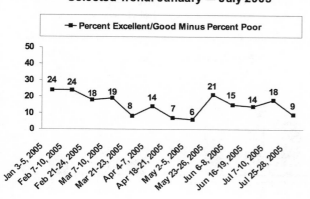

Consumer Expectations

Fifty-three percent of consumers say current economic conditions in the country as a whole are "getting worse" in late July, compared to only 35% who say they are "getting better." This difference of -18 percentage points (percentage getting better minus percentage getting worse) is about where it was in early July, but far below the positive differences recorded in January and early February.

Economic Outlook
Selected Trend: January — July 2005

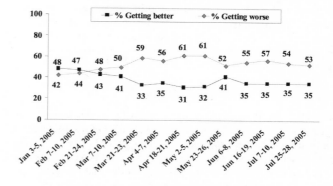

Why Aren't Consumers More Optimistic?

Four in 10 Americans say they are worried about their families' finances right now, with 15% saying they are very worried and 25% saying they are somewhat worried. In spite of two good quarters of economic growth, this percentage is up slightly from the 38% measured in February.

One reason so many consumers continue to worry about their family finances involves gas prices. Although the economy's second quarter performance led some on Wall Street to declare that the U.S. economy can do very well even with oil prices at $60 a barrel, a closer look at gasoline prices suggests differently. Gasoline prices hit $2.28 on April 11, according to the U.S. Energy Information Administration. Shortly thereafter, gas prices fell steadily from their April peak, declining to $2.10 a gallon by the end of May. Since then, gasoline prices have increased once more and averaged $2.29 a gallon at the end of July—up $0.40 from one year ago.

The drop in gas prices led to an improvement in consumer confidence and consumer spending as the second quarter progressed. Recent increases in gas prices, however, are doing just the opposite. Given increasing prices at the pump, it is easy to see why consumer confidence is declining.

Will Wealth Effects Spur Back-to-School Spending?

Of course, the question for back-to-school shopping is whether the current weakening in consumer confidence will translate into a decline in retail sales. Normally, barring a surge in employment in the near term or a rash of significant discounting like that taking place in the automobile industry, one would assume that falling consumer confidence would mean declining retail sales.

The current economic situation could be different, however, because of today's wealth effects. Many consumers feel richer because of the gains they have made as the value of their homes and their equity investments have surged. Since these equity gains are easily liquefied in today's economy by way of home equity loans and lines of credit, they could provide an added stimulus to consumer spending. However, increasing interest rates and growing debt levels may combine with higher prices at the pump to discourage spending even among these better-off consumers.

On the other hand, the numerous consumers who are not enjoying the wealth gains being created in the current economy are probably the best explanation of how consumer confidence can remain weak even as the overall economy performs well. These consumers are unlikely to increase their spending in the face of increasing pump prices.

In sum, the strong performance of the U.S. economy during the first two quarters of this year does not necessarily guarantee more of the same, or something even better, during the remainder of 2005. Instead, increasing gas prices, higher interest rates, and declining consumer confidence suggest just the opposite. In this context, the real test of the economy's underlying strength is likely to be consumer back-to-school spending.

Survey Methods

Results are based on telephone interviews with 1,010 national adults, aged 18 and older, conducted July 25-28, 2005. For results based on the total sample of national adults, one can say with 95% confidence that the maximum margin of sampling error is ±3 percentage points. In addition to sampling error, question wording and practical difficulties in conducting surveys can introduce error or bias into the findings of public opinion polls.

August 2, 2005
BLACKS REMAIN BEARISH ON ECONOMY
Economic ratings improve among whites and Hispanics

by Raksha Arora, Business and Economy Editor

Americans as a whole are gloomy about economic conditions, but minorities appear to be particularly dejected. Gallup's annual Minority Relations poll* reveals a continuing gulf in views of current economic conditions, as well as the specific economic problems facing the nation.

Economic Conditions

In four Gallup Minority Relations polls since 2001, white Americans have been consistently more optimistic than blacks about the state of the economy, with Hispanics' perceptions ranging somewhere in between and aligning closer to whites'. Hispanics' and whites' ratings of economic conditions improved from 2003 to 2005, with whites' perceptions improving more than Hispanics'. But black Americans remain as pessimistic about economic conditions as they were in 2003. According to the June 6-25 poll, 40% of whites rate economic conditions as excellent or good, as do 32% of Hispanics. Only 14% of blacks say the same.

Blacks are also far more bearish than whites and Hispanics about future economic conditions in the United States. In 2005, 37% of whites and 33% of Hispanics say economic conditions are getting better. About half that percentage of blacks—18%—say conditions are improving. In 2003, twice as many whites as blacks said they believe that economic conditions in the country as a whole are getting better.

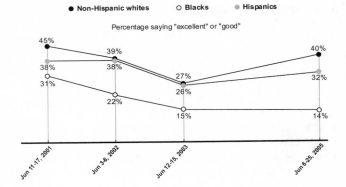

How would you rate economic conditions in this country today – as excellent, good, only fair, or poor?

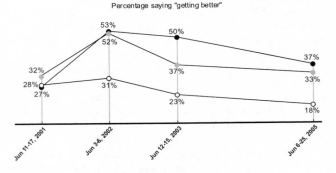

Right now, do you think that economic conditions in this country as a whole are getting better or getting worse?

Most Important Problem

When asked to name the most important problem facing the country, the three racial and ethnic groups attach similar importance to the economy in general and rising fuel prices. But they diverge on the subject of unemployment. Nineteen percent of blacks name unemployment/jobs as the most important problem facing the country, significantly more than the percentage of whites (11%) or Hispanics who do the same (7%). That has also been the case in other past Gallup Minority Relations polls (with the exception of 2003 when economic ratings were worse among whites and Hispanics than they are now).

The finding of differences in the perceived importance of unemployment is consistent with the higher unemployment rate among blacks—in June, the unemployment rate among blacks was 10.3%, 4.3% among whites, and 5.8% among Hispanics. These disparities have been evident for at least the last decade.

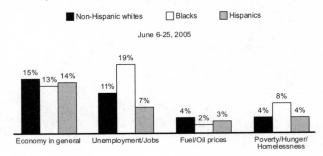

What do you think is the most important problem facing this country today?

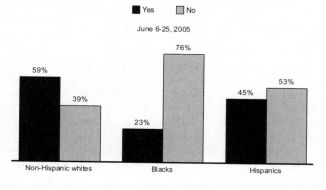

Do you feel that racial minorities in this country have equal job opportunities as whites, or not?

■ Yes   ☐ No

June 6-25, 2005

Echoing the concern about unemployment among black Americans, the majority of blacks believe racial minorities in the United States do not have the same access to job opportunities that whites enjoy. More than two-thirds (76%) of blacks say minorities do not have equal job opportunities as whites; 53% of Hispanics and 39% of whites agree.

Results are based on telephone interviews with 2,264 national adults, aged 18 and older, conducted June 6-25, 2005, including oversamples of blacks and Hispanics that are weighted to reflect their proportions in the general population. For results based on the total sample of national adults, one can say with 95% confidence that the maximum margin of sampling error is ±5 percentage points.

August 2, 2005

GENDER DIFFERENCES IN VIEWS OF JOB OPPORTUNITY

Fifty-three percent of Americans believe opportunities are equal

by Jeffrey M. Jones, Gallup Poll Managing Editor

Although women represent a majority of the population, they are still a minority in the U.S. workforce, and achieving equality there is an ongoing struggle. Gallup's annual Minority Rights and Relations poll assessed the public's views on job opportunities for women and finds a growing perception that women are achieving parity with men. Men continue to be more likely than women to have that view, but the views of both men and women on this issue are sometimes moderated or enhanced when their other characteristics are taken into account.

For the first time since the question has been tracked, the June 6-25 Gallup Poll* finds a majority of Americans saying that women have equal job opportunities with men. Fifty-three percent of Americans believe job opportunities are equal for the sexes and 46% do not. In 2003, 49% thought women had equal opportunities and 50% did not.

Men are more likely to believe that women have achieved equality of opportunity in the workforce. Sixty-one percent of men say so, and a majority of men have held that view since 2001. This year, 45% of women say women have equal job opportunities, which is the highest percentage with that view since Gallup first asked this question.

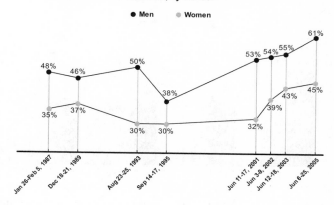

Percentage Believing Women Have Equal Job Opportunities With Men, by Gender

● Men   ● Women

Additionally, women are also much more likely than men to favor affirmative action programs for women—65% do compared with 53% of men. The poll finds 59% of Americans overall favoring such programs, while 34% are opposed.

Moving Beyond Gender

The relationships between gender and perceptions of gender issues in the workplace are straightforward, but many of these become more complex when taking into account respondents' other characteristics in addition to gender.

For example, there are significant age gaps on views of job equality, but only among men. Sixty-five percent of men under age 50 believe women have equal job opportunities, compared with 54% of men age 50 and older. Younger and older women are about equally likely to believe women have equal job opportunities (47% of women aged 18 to 49, 45% of women aged 50 and older).

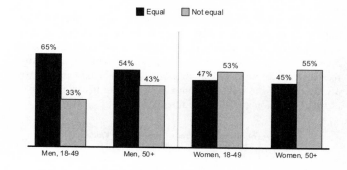

Perceptions of Equal Job Opportunities for Women, by Gender and Age

■ Equal   ☐ Not equal

Employment status is also related to views on women's job opportunities, but again, only among men. Both working and non-working women answer the question on job opportunity similarly—45% of women who are currently employed say women have equal job opportunities, as do 46% of nonworking women. In contrast, 67% of working men believe women have equal job opportunities, compared with 49% of nonworking men.

Ideological differences are pronounced—62% of all conservatives say women have equal opportunities, compared with 52% of moderates and 39% of liberals. What is interesting is that conservatives answer the question similarly regardless of gender—61%

Perceptions of Equal Job Opportunities for Women, by Gender and Employment Status

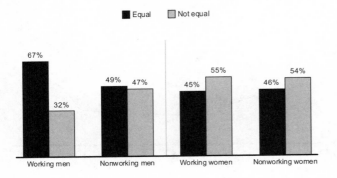

of conservative men and 63% of conservative women believe women have equal job opportunities. There are large gender gaps among moderates and liberals, however. Sixty-eight percent of moderate men believe women have equal opportunities, compared with 38% of moderate women. Forty-nine percent of liberal men and 30% of liberal women think women have equal opportunities in the workplace.

Perceptions of Equal Job Opportunities for Women, by Gender and Political Ideology

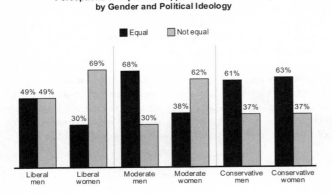

Oddly enough, despite their belief that women have equal job opportunities, 61% of conservative women still favor affirmative action programs for women; a far cry from the 38% of conservative men who do. Sixty-seven percent of moderate women favor affirmative action, compared with 56% of moderate men. Among liberals, the gender gap is almost nonexistent, 76% of liberal men favor affirmative action as do 69% of liberal women.

Views of Affirmative Action Programs for Women, by Gender and Political Ideology

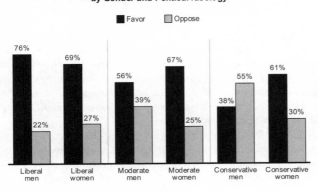

Bottom Line

As the poll shows, Americans are becoming more optimistic that women are getting the same chances as men in the job market. While men are more optimistic than women are, age, employment status, and political philosophy can also influence the way people evaluate the situation beyond any effects attributable to gender. Given that people's views about equality of job opportunity are affected by a number of different variables (in some fairly complex ways), it may take more than just objective data that women are achieving equality to see the public reach a consensus on the issue and for the gender gap in perceptions to erode.

Results are based on telephone interviews with 2,264 national adults, aged 18 and older, conducted June 6-25, 2005, including oversamples of blacks and Hispanics that are weighted to reflect their proportions in the general population. For results based on the total sample of national adults, one can say with 95% confidence that the maximum margin of sampling error is ±5 percentage points.

For results based on the sample of 904 men, one can say with 95% confidence that the margin of sampling error is ±8 percentage points.

For results based on the sample of 1,201 women, one can say with 95% confidence that the margin of sampling error is ±7 percentage points.

August 3, 2005

ELECTION 2008: REPUBLICAN CANDIDATES FARE BETTER IN EARLY TRIAL HEATS
Public's view of John Kerry growing more negative

by Jeffrey M. Jones, Gallup Poll Managing Editor

Even though the next presidential election is more than three years away, those who might pursue the office are already testing the waters in New Hampshire, in Iowa, and at other gatherings where party power brokers are present. The latest Gallup Poll assessed the public's overall views of four possible contenders for the office and tested how they would fare today in a hypothetical election.

A majority of Americans say they have favorable views of Republican and former New York City mayor Rudy Giuliani, Sen. Hillary Rodham Clinton, D-N.Y., and Sen. John McCain, R-Ariz. On the other hand, more Americans view Sen. John Kerry, D-Mass., unfavorably than favorably, and his ratings have grown more negative since his loss to George W. Bush in last fall's presidential election. The trial heat match-ups show the two possible Republican candidates holding an edge over the two Democratic candidates among registered voters.

Favorable Ratings of Contenders

The July 25-28 Gallup Poll asked Americans to rate four politicians whom many currently consider the early front-runners in the next presidential election. This is based in part on their relatively high public profiles, on the belief that they are thought to be seriously considering presidential runs in 2008, and also on early polling by Gallup and other organizations on Republicans' and Democrats' preferences for their respective parties' nominees in the next election.

Of the four, Giuliani is rated most positively, with 64% of Americans saying they have a favorable opinion of him and only 19% with an unfavorable opinion. Clinton (53%) and McCain (51%) have similar favorable ratings, although Clinton is the much better-known figure (only 4% do not have an opinion of her, compared with 27% for McCain). Clinton's unfavorable ratings (43%) are nearly twice as high as McCain's (22%).

Favorable Ratings

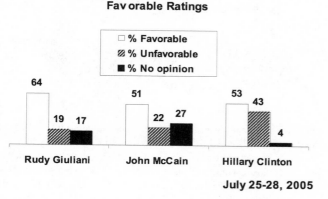

- ☐ % Favorable
- ▨ % Unfavorable
- ■ % No opinion

Rudy Giuliani 64, 19, 17
John McCain 51, 22, 27
Hillary Clinton 53, 43, 4

July 25-28, 2005

Kerry is the only candidate of the four with higher unfavorables (48%) than favorables (42%). That is a significant shift from last fall, when Kerry averaged a 52% favorable rating and a 44% unfavorable rating in five October Gallup Polls leading up to the presidential election. At least a majority of Americans had viewed Kerry favorably following his surprise victory in the Iowa caucuses and continuing through Gallup's final pre-election poll.

Opinion of John Kerry

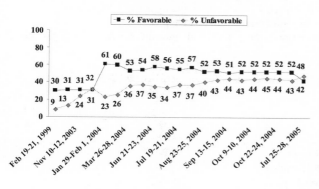

- ■ % Favorable
- ◆ % Unfavorable

Trial Heat Match-ups

The poll suggests the Republican candidates have an edge at this point, with at least a slight lead in all four trial heats. Clinton appears to be the stronger of the two Democratic candidates, while the two Republican candidates fare similarly against both Democrats.

By a 50% to 45% margin, registered voters say they would vote for McCain over Clinton. Giuliani enjoys the same edge over Clinton.

The Republicans do even better when matched up against Kerry; both lead the Massachusetts senator by 54% to 41% margins among registered voters.

In any election, there are at least four ways one can achieve victory.

- by winning a greater share of the independent vote
- by maintaining higher party loyalty than one's opponent does

2008 Trial Heats

among registered voters

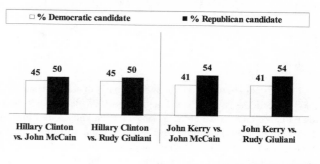

- ☐ % Democratic candidate
- ■ % Republican candidate

Hillary Clinton vs. John McCain 45, 50
Hillary Clinton vs. Rudy Giuliani 45, 50
John Kerry vs. John McCain 41, 54
John Kerry vs. Rudy Giuliani 41, 54

July 25-28, 2005

- by winning a greater proportion of votes from those who normally support the other party
- by getting more of one's supporters to turn out to vote

These are certainly not mutually exclusive possibilities—for example, it is possible that a candidate could get a higher share of the independent vote but lose because the other candidate's supporters had higher turnout. In most elections, most or all of the factors would probably work in the same candidate's favor. The late July poll allows for a test of the first three possibilities, and the analysis shows that the Republican candidates currently have an edge on all three.

First, at least half of independent registered voters prefer the Republican candidates regardless of the match-up, while support for the Democratic candidates among this group ranges between 35% and 41% in the four trial heats.

Second, party loyalty is higher among Republican registered voters than among Democratic registered voters. Specifically, 87% of Republican registered voters say they would vote for Giuliani and for McCain if each were running against Clinton, while Democratic registered voters' support for Clinton in both match-ups is slightly lower, at 80%. At least 9 in 10 Republican registered voters say they would support McCain or Giuliani when matched up with Kerry, while only about three in four Democrats indicate they would support Kerry.

Finally, related to the above, the Republican candidates are gaining a greater share of the Democratic vote than the Democratic candidates are gaining of the Republican vote. Close to one in five Democrats say they would support McCain or Giuliani versus Clinton, while only 11%-12% of Republicans are supporting Clinton in either match-up. An even higher proportion of Democrats would support McCain or Giuliani versus Kerry.

Support for 2008 Presidential Candidates by Party, Among Registered Voters

	Democrat	Independent	Republican
Trial Heat 1			
Clinton	80%	40%	11%
McCain	19%	51%	87%
Trial Heat 2			
Clinton	80%	41%	12%
Giuliani	18%	50%	87%

	Democrat	Independent	Republican
Trial Heat 3			
Kerry	74%	35%	10%
McCain	25%	53%	90%
Trial Heat 4			
Kerry	76%	38%	7%
Giuliani	22%	53%	91%

These data are not likely to predict what will actually happen in 2008. Indeed, the issues that will define the 2008 election—let alone the party's choice of candidates—are not even known. But the data do give a sense of the candidates' basic appeal at this time, and the contenders likely will be relying on poll data such as these as one factor in helping to determine whether or not they will formally seek the presidency.

Survey Methods

These results are based on telephone interviews with a randomly selected national sample of 1,010 adults, aged 18 and older, conducted July 25-28, 2005. For results based on this sample, one can say with 95% confidence that the maximum error attributable to sampling and other random effects is ±3 percentage points. In addition to sampling error, question wording and practical difficulties in conducting surveys can introduce error or bias into the findings of public opinion polls.

For results for the sample of 922 registered voters, one can say with 95% confidence that the maximum error attributable to sampling and other random effects is ±4 percentage points.

August 4, 2005
INCREASED OPTIMISM ABOUT JOBS MAINLY AMONG REPUBLICANS, HIGH-INCOME HOUSEHOLDS
Republicans becoming more optimistic, but not Democrats

by Frank Newport, Gallup Poll Editor in Chief

Although Americans are not highly positive about the condition of the current job market, they have become more so than they were in late 2002 and early 2003. This increase in optimism about jobs has occurred selectively, with the largest increases occurring among Republicans and those with high household incomes. Democrats and Americans living in lower-income households are only marginally more positive now than they were in late 2002 and early 2003.

Gallup began asking Americans a basic job market question—"Thinking about the job situation in America today, would you say that it is now a good time or a bad time to find a quality job?"—on a monthly basis beginning in August 2001.

Thirty-nine percent of Americans said that it was a good time to find a quality job in that August 2001 poll, the exact same percentage as recorded in Gallup's July 7-10, 2005 poll. This question's similar starting and ending points mask the fact, however, that there has been a good deal of change during the intervening four years.

Americans became steadily more negative about finding quality jobs in 2001 and 2002, reaching a low point in March 2003 when

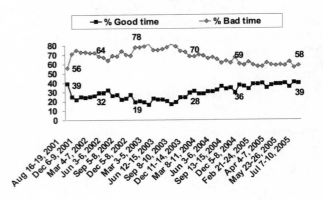

Good Time to Find a Quality Job?
Selected Trend: Aug. 2001 — July 2005

only 16% said that it was a good time to find a quality job. In August 2003, only 17% agreed it was a good time to find a quality job.

Positive perceptions of the job market began to climb modestly after that point, reaching 31% in January 2004, 37% in November 2004, and 40% in June 2005 (and 39%, as noted, in Gallup's early July poll).

Thus, the public's view of the job market reached a 4-year low in late 2002 and early 2003, while positive perceptions have increased in recent months and now equal the 4-year high in August 2001.

(Polling done by the University of Connecticut suggests that responses to this same "quality job" question were much more positive in the late 1990s and in 2000—at the tail end of the dot-com boom.)

Who Has Become More Positive?

A special Gallup analysis of 4,006 interviews conducted from December 2002 through March 2003, when the percent agreeing that it was a good time to find a quality job was 18%, shows that almost all key subgroups were relatively negative about the job market. In other words, there is relatively little difference among key subgroups.

Perceptions of the Job Market
Interviews Conducted Dec. 2002-March 2003
n=4,006

	Good time	Bad time	Don't know
	%	%	%
Total	18	79	3
Republican	25	71	4
Independent	16	82	2
Democrat	14	84	2
18- to 29-years-old	24	75	1
30- to 39-years-old	21	77	2
40- to 49-years-old	19	80	1
50- to 59-years-old	16	82	2
60- to 69-years-old	14	83	3
70 years old or older	12	82	6
East	16	82	2
Midwest	16	81	3
South	21	77	2
West	20	76	3
Less than $20,000	19	79	2
$20,000-$29,999	15	82	3
$30,000-$49,999	18	79	2
$50,000-$74,999	19	79	2
$75,000+	19	79	2

Republicans and 18- to 29-year-olds are slightly more likely than others to respond affirmatively to the "good job" question during this time period, but generally there is remarkably little variation across subgroups.

The results from December 2002 through March 2003 can be compared to a combined sample of 8,037 interviews conducted from March 2005 through July 2005. The overall percentage agreeing that it is a good time to find a quality job in this aggregated sample is 37%. The percentage of those who agreed that it was a good time to find a quality job essentially doubled from an average of 18% from late 2002-early 2003 to 37% during the last several months.

But there is now significant variation across subgroups in agreement with this question.

Perceptions of the Job Market
Interviews Conducted March 2005-July 2005
n=8,037

	Good time %	Bad time %	Don't know %
Total	37	59	4
Republican	59	37	4
Independent	33	63	4
Democrat	21	77	2
18- to 29-years-old	42	56	2
30- to 39-years-old	44	54	2
40- to 49-years-old	38	59	3
50- to 59-years-old	34	63	2
60- to 69-years-old	33	62	5
70 years old or older	31	60	8
East	32	64	3
Midwest	33	64	3
South	43	53	4
West	40	56	4
Less than $20,000	27	69	4
$20,000-$29,999	32	65	3
$30,000-$49,999	36	61	3
$50,000-$74,999	38	59	3
$75,000+	48	49	3

The change in perceptions of the job situation from late 2002-early 2003 to this year did not occur proportionately across the key demographic groups outlined above. Instead, the data show disproportionate increases among Republicans, those with higher household incomes, and to some degree those living in the South and West.

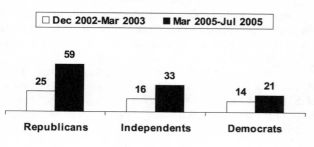

Good Time to Find a Quality Job?
percentage saying yes
by party affiliation

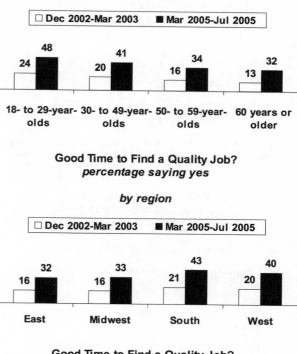

Good Time to Find a Quality Job?
percentage saying yes
by age groups

Good Time to Find a Quality Job?
percentage saying yes
by region

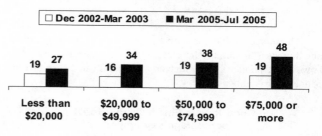

Good Time to Find a Quality Job?
percentage saying yes
by household income

The Power of Party

The data show that Americans' partisan identification has become an increasingly important predictor of their views of the labor market—much more so than just 1 or 2 years ago.

Regardless of income category, Republicans are more positive about the job market than are independents, who in turn are more positive than are Democrats. At the same time, there is a very strong effect of household income level among Republicans, such that positive views of the job market jump from 38% among the lowest income group to 70% among the highest.

The effect of income is much more muted among the other two political groups. Independents whose households make $75,000 a year or more are somewhat more positive than other independents. But among Democrats, household income makes very little difference at all. Democrats are quite negative about the job market regardless of their personal household income. In short, for Democrats, political party affiliation trumps income.

Good Time to Find a Quality Job?
percentage saying yes
Mar. 2005 — July 2005

by age groups and party affiliation

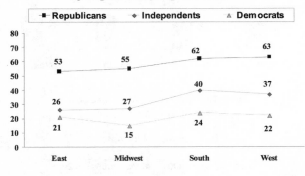

There is a decline in positive perceptions of the job market as age increases among all three political groups. Regardless of age, however, Republicans remain much more optimistic than either independents or Democrats.

Good Time to Find a Quality Job?
percentage saying yes
Mar. 2005 — July 2005

by household income and party affiliation

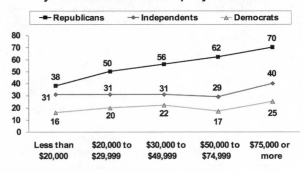

There is a slight tendency for those living in the South and West to be more positive about the job market than those living in the East and Midwest across the three political groups, but, again, Republi-

cans are substantially more optimistic than are independents or Democrats regardless of region.

Survey Methods

These results are based on telephone interviews with randomly selected national samples of adults, aged 18 and older, conducted during the time periods noted above. The combined sample sizes are noted above as well. For results based on these samples, one can say with 95% confidence that the maximum error attributable to sampling and other random effects is ±2 percentage points or less. In addition to sampling error, question wording and practical difficulties in conducting surveys can introduce error or bias into the findings of public opinion polls.

August 5, 2005

MAJORITY SUPPORTS USE OF ATOMIC BOMB ON JAPAN IN WWII

Say bombing saved American lives by shortening the war, but divided on whether it saved Japanese lives

by David W. Moore, Gallup Poll Senior Editor

Six decades after the United States dropped atomic bombs on Hiroshima and Nagasaki, which effectively ended World War II, a majority of Americans, 57%, say they approve of using the bombs, while 38% disapprove.

As you may know, the United States dropped atomic bombs on Hiroshima and Nagasaki in August 1945 near the end of World War II. Looking back, would you say you approve or disapprove of using the atomic bomb on Japanese cities in 1945?

	Approve	Disapprove	No opinion
	%	%	%
2005 Jul 25-28	57	38	5
1995 Jul 20-23	59	35	6
1994 Dec 2-5	55	39	6
1991 Nov 21-24	53	41	6
1990 Jul 19-21	53	41	6
1945 Aug 10-15 ^	85	10	5

^WORDING: *Do you approve or disapprove of using the new atomic bomb on Japanese cities?*

The views expressed around the 60th anniversary of that historic event, the only time atomic weapons have ever been used in war, are not much different from the views expressed 10 years ago around the 50th anniversary. But approval differs substantially from the overwhelming support Americans gave just a few days after the bombs were dropped in August 1945. At that time, 85% said they approved and just 10% disapproved.

A major factor in President Harry S. Truman's decision to bomb Hiroshima and Nagasaki was that the bombs would hasten the end of the war and thus save American lives. Today, 80% of Americans believe the bombs did in fact save American lives by shortening the war. Ten years ago, the percentage was slightly higher, at 86%.

Do you think dropping the atomic bombs saved American lives by shortening the war, or not?

	Yes, saved American lives	No, did not	No opinion
2005 Jul 25-28	80%	16	4
1995 Jul 20-23	86%	7	7

The public is more ambivalent, however, about the long-term consequences to the Japanese people. While 41% of Americans say they think that dropping the atomic bombs saved more Japanese lives than would have been lost if the war had continued, 47% believe that dropping the bombs ultimately cost more Japanese lives. These views are not much different from those measured 10 years ago.

Do you think that dropping the atomic bombs saved more Japanese lives than would have been lost if the war had continued, or did dropping the bomb COST more Japanese lives?

	Saved more Japanese lives	Cost more Japanese lives	No opinion
2005 Jul 25-28	41%	47	12
1995 Jul 20-23	40%	45	15

Gender, Party, and Age Differences

The poll shows that men are much more likely than women, and Republicans are more likely than Democrats, to express positive views about the bombing in Japan. To a lesser extent, older people are more positive than younger people.

Overall, 73% of men, but only 42% of women, approve of the bombing. Similarly, 73% of Republicans, 53% of independents, and just 47% of Democrats approve. An irony here is that it was a Democratic president who made the decision to drop the bombs, though now Democrats give the least support among the three partisan groups.

The large gender gap is not due solely to the fact that men disproportionately identify as Republicans and women as Democrats. Even within the party faithful, there are large differences in views between men and women.

Among Republican men, 87% approve of the bombing, compared with 60% of Republican women—a gender gap of 27 percentage points. Among independents, the gap is even larger, at 40 percentage points (71% of men approve vs. just 31% of women). And among Democrats, the gender gap is 26 percentage points (63% of men approve, as do 37% of women).

PERCENTAGE OF EACH GROUP WHO APPROVE OF DROPPING ATOMIC BOMBS ON JAPAN

	Republicans	Independents	Democrats	Difference Republicans vs. Democrats
Male	87%	71%	63%	+24
Female	60%	31%	37%	+23
Difference males vs. females	+27	+40	+26	

Note that among each gender group, the differences between Republicans and Democrats are similar. Eighty-seven percent of male Republicans approve, compared with 63% of male Democrats,

a difference of 24 percentage points. Similarly, 60% of female Republicans, while only 37% of female Democrats, approve—a difference of 23 percentage points.

Younger people are somewhat less likely to approve of the bombing than are older people—an average of 53% approval among people under age 50, compared with 63% among people 50 and older.

Similar patterns of differences by gender and party are also found on the other two questions about the bombing. Men and Republicans are more likely than their counterparts to say the bombing helped save American and Japanese lives.

Survey Methods

Results are based on telephone interviews with 1,010 national adults, aged 18 and older, conducted July 25-28, 2005. For results based on the total sample of national adults, one can say with 95% confidence that the maximum margin of sampling error is ±3 percentage points.

In addition to sampling error, question wording and practical difficulties in conducting surveys can introduce error or bias into the findings of public opinion polls.

August 8, 2005
AMERICANS REJECT EXTREME ANTI-PRIVACY SECURITY MEASURES
National ID cards OK, but not random searches or electronic snooping

by Lydia Saad, Gallup Poll Senior Editor

The recent London suicide bombings seem to have elevated Americans' own anxiety about terrorism, although not to as great an extent as did the 9/11 terrorist attacks against the United States. Since the London bombings, there has been a sustained increase in Americans' expectations that a terrorist attack is likely to happen in the United States in the next few weeks. There has been a less pronounced increase in Americans' personal fear that they or a family member will be a terrorism victim.

Still, Gallup finds that Americans are not so fearful that they are willing to surrender their personal privacy. In the name of domestic security, most Americans are willing to endure metal detectors and security checks at buildings, and are in favor of a national ID card. They also think it's OK for the police to profile Arab Americans at airports. But most reject more extreme measures, such as allowing the police to search people and homes at random or without a warrant, expanding government surveillance of e-mail and telephone calls, and suspending the right to a speedy trial of terrorist suspects who are U.S. citizens.

More Americans Expect a Terrorist Event Than Fear It

In Gallup polling conducted right after the July 7 backpack bombings that killed 52 passengers on London's transit system, there was a sharp increase in the percentage of Americans saying that an act of terrorism was likely to happen in the United States within the next several weeks. This figure was only 35% in June, but shot up to 55% in a CNN/*USA Today*/Gallup poll conducted July 7-10, and it remains at about the same level today.

According to a July 22-24 CNN/*USA Today*/Gallup poll, only 12% of Americans think another terrorist incident is "very likely" to happen in the coming weeks, but a combined 57% say it is "very" or "somewhat" likely.

Likelihood of Terrorist Attack in U.S. Happening Soon

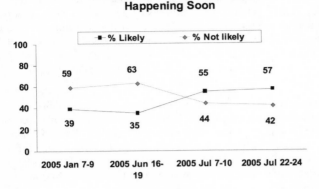

By comparison, Gallup finds a smaller increase between June and today in the percentage of Americans who are personally worried that they or a family member will be a victim of terrorism. Forty-seven percent of Americans now say they are worried this will happen, up from 38% in June.

Comparison of Change in Terrorism Concerns

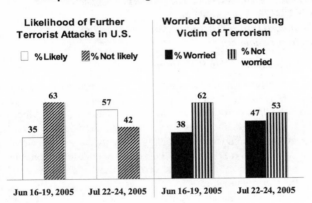

Terrorism fears today are somewhat lower than they were in the first few weeks after Sept. 11, 2001, when terrorist hijackers brought down the World Trade Center towers, crashed into the Pentagon, and would have directed a fourth airplane at a target in Washington, D.C., if not for the plane's heroic passengers.

Ten days after those attacks, Gallup found a similar level of fear to today's about being a victim of terrorism (47% today vs. 49% in September 2001), but a much higher expectation that further acts of terrorism were imminent (57% today vs. 66% then).

Privacy Concerns Trump Security

Finding the right balance between liberty and security has been an ongoing challenge for policymakers since 9/11. Controversy over the Patriot Act is a case in point, and now a similar battle is being waged in the United Kingdom, where Prime Minister Tony Blair has just proposed tight new restrictions on Muslims.

As much as Americans want to be safe from terrorism, they are reluctant to expand government surveillance of private communica-

Concern About Terrorism: Post-9/11, Pre-London, Post-London

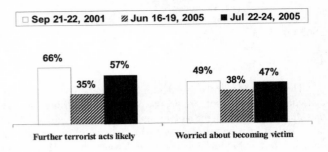

tion or suspend basic privacy rights such as freedom from unreasonable searches.

A supermajority (two-thirds or more) of Americans do support making metal detectors and identity verification a routine part of entering buildings and other public places; a similar number support the establishment of a national ID card. More than half also are in favor of subjecting all Arabs, including Arab Americans, to special security checks at airports.

Next, please tell me if you would favor or oppose each of the following as a means of preventing terrorist attacks in the United States. How about—[random order]?

	Favor %	Oppose %
Requiring every person going into an office building or public place to go through a metal detector	81	18
Requiring mass transit systems like subways, buses, and trains to institute security systems similar to what is found in airports	78	20
Requiring every person going into an office building or public place to show ID	70	30
Requiring all Americans to carry a national ID card	66	33
Requiring Arabs, including those who are U.S. citizens, to undergo special, more intensive security checks before boarding airplanes in the U.S.	53	46

Americans are closely split on whether police should be able to do random checks of pedestrians or whether Arabs in the United States should be required to carry a special ID.

	Favor %	Oppose %
Allowing police to stop people on the street at random and ask them to show their ID	48	51
Requiring Arabs, including those who are U.S. citizens, to carry a special ID	46	53

A majority of Americans oppose giving the government the authority to search through people's library loan records.

	Favor %	Oppose %
Allowing the government to search a list of books people have checked out of the library	37	60

A supermajority of the public opposes random police checks of people's possessions; increased government surveillance of Americans through their mail, e-mail, and telephones; suspension of certain legal rights for terrorism suspects; and allowing police to enter people's homes without a search warrant.

	Favor %	Oppose %
Allowing police to stop people on the street at random to search their possessions	29	70
Making it easier for legal authorities to read mail, e-mail, or tap phones without the person's knowledge	25	73
Allowing the government to imprison U.S. citizens who are suspected of terrorism without putting them on trial for years	21	75
Allowing police to enter a person's home at any time without a search warrant	6	93

A subset of these items was first tested in September 2001, shortly after the 9/11 attacks, and the results were not much different then. Americans were only slightly more likely at that time than they are now to favor some of these proposals.

Republicans More Security Minded

Public reaction to these proposals is quite similar across different demographic groups. The largest differences tend to be according to politics, with Republicans being the most likely to favor certain proposals.

This is especially evident with respect to some of the least popular strategies, such as making it easier for legal authorities to conduct surveillance on private communication, and allowing the police to stop people on the street at random to search their possessions. Still, the majority of Republicans oppose these measures.

Percentage Favoring Measures to Fight Terrorism: Areas of Greatest Partisan Disagreement

	Republicans %	Independents %	Democrats %
Allowing police to conduct random searches on people	41	21	23
Making it easier for legal authorities to conduct surveillance on private communication	35	22	16
Allowing the government to search individuals' library loan records	46	30	34
Allowing the government to imprison U.S. terrorist suspects without putting them on trial for years	30	19	14

Survey Methods

These results are based on telephone interviews with a randomly selected national sample of 1,006 adults, aged 18 and older, conducted July 22-24, 2005. For results based on this sample, one can say with 95% confidence that the maximum error attributable to sampling and other random effects is ±3 percentage points. In addi-

tion to sampling error, question wording and practical difficulties in conducting surveys can introduce error or bias into the findings of public opinion polls.

August 9, 2005
WHO'S WORRIED ABOUT THEIR WEIGHT?

by Joseph Carroll, Gallup Poll Assistant Editor

Whether they're cutting carbs or trimming fat, Americans constantly take steps to control their weight, and companies are making millions of dollars each year on diet programs.

But just how worried are Americans about their weight today? A recent Gallup Poll* asked that very question and found that nearly half of Americans say they worry about their weight at least some of the time. The other half say they rarely or never worry about their weight.

How often do you worry about your weight? Would you say you worry all of the time, some of the time, not too often, or never?

Date	All of the time	Some of the time	Not too often	Never
Jul 7-10, 2005	15%	34%	29%	22%
Jul 22-25, 1999	15%	27%	34%	24%
Oct 11-14, 1990	7%	27%	33%	33%

The current results represent the highest percentage of Americans saying they worry about their weight all or some of the time since Gallup first asked this question 15 years ago. In 1990, only about a third of Americans (34%) said they worried about their weight at least some of the time. This sentiment increased to 42% in 1999, and then edged up again this year, to 49%.

Who's Worried?

Which groups of Americans spend time worrying about their weight? The answer: People who already see themselves as overweight, women (especially younger women), people who otherwise think they have an unhealthy diet, and to a lesser extent, people who drink alcohol.

Weight

Americans who describe their weight situations as overweight are substantially more likely than those who describe their weight as about right or underweight to say they worry about their weight all or some of the time. Nearly 7 in 10 self-described overweight adults, 69%, say they spend time worrying about their weight, compared with a third (33%) of those who say they are about right or underweight.

The results are similar for those who have tried to lose weight in the past and those who have not. Sixty-three percent of Americans who report that they have tried to lose weight in the past say they worry about their weight at least some of the time, while only 17% of those who have never tried to lose weight worry this often.

How Often Do You Worry About Your Weight?

■ All or some of the time　□ Not too often/Never

July 7-10, 2005

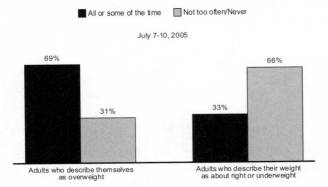

How Often Do You Worry About Your Weight?
By Description of Diet

■ All or some of the time　□ Not too often/Never

July 7-10, 2005

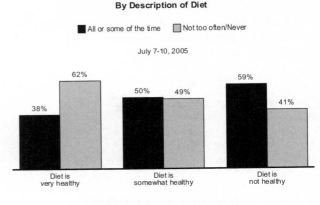

Gender and Age

A majority of women, 57%, say they worry about their weight, while fewer than 4 in 10 men (39%) do so. This pattern has been consistent since Gallup first asked this question in 1990. At that time, 46% of women and only 21% of men said they worried about their weight. And, in 1999, 52% of women said they worried, compared with 31% of men.

Interestingly, younger women (those aged 18 to 49) are much more likely to worry about their weight than are older women (those aged 50 and older) or men of any age. The latest poll finds that 62% of younger women worry about their weight all or some of the time, while 51% of older women do so. Among men, 40% of younger men and 38% of older men say they worry this often.

How Often Do You Worry About Your Weight?
By Gender and Age

■ All or some of the time　□ Not too often/Never

July 7-10, 2005

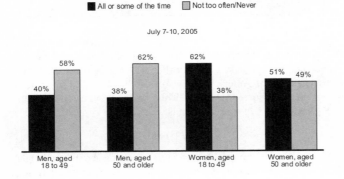

Diet and Personal Health

Americans who describe their diet as "very healthy" and those who say their personal health is "excellent" are substantially less likely to say they spend time worrying about their weight.

Thirty-eight percent of those who say their diet is very healthy say they worry all or some of the time about their weight. Among those who say their diet is somewhat healthy, this sentiment increases to 50%, and among those with a poor diet, 59% say they worry.

Similarly, 39% of those who describe their health as excellent say they worry about their weight, compared with 53% of those who report "only" good health, as well as 53% of those in fair or poor health.

Results are based on telephone interviews with 1,006 national adults, aged 18 and older, conducted July 7-10, 2005. For results based on the total sample of national adults, one can say with 95%

How Often Do You Worry About Your Weight?
By Description of Current Health

■ All or some of the time　□ Not too often/never

July 7-10, 2005

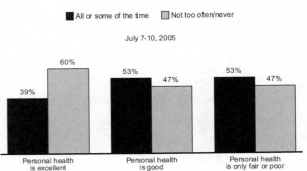

confidence that the maximum margin of sampling error is ±3 percentage points. In addition to sampling error, question wording and practical difficulties in conducting surveys can introduce error or bias into the findings of public opinion polls.

August 9, 2005
MAJORITY OF AMERICANS MAINTAIN NEGATIVE VIEWS ON IRAQ
Believe war has made the United States "less safe" from terrorism

by David W. Moore, Gallup Poll Senior Editor

In the wake of the intensive news coverage of American casualties in Iraq in the past couple of weeks, Americans have become somewhat more critical of the war than they were two weeks ago. Nevertheless, President Bush's approval rating remains steady at 45%, compared with 44% two weeks ago, and an average of 46.5% since June.

Today, 54% say the United States made a mistake in sending troops to Iraq, up from 46% who expressed that view in a July 22-24 poll, but not much different from a poll in late June.

The view that it was a mistake to go to war in Iraq is reinforced by a separate question that asks if it was "worth going to war in Iraq or not." This question was asked of half the sample, while the other half of the sample was asked if "sending troops to Iraq" was a mistake. The same percentage, 54%, say that it was not worth going to war as say sending troops to Iraq was a mistake.

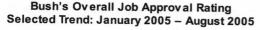

Bush's Overall Job Approval Rating
Selected Trend: January 2005 – August 2005

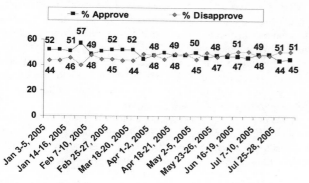

Mistake to Send Troops to Iraq?
Selected Trend: October 2004 – August 2005

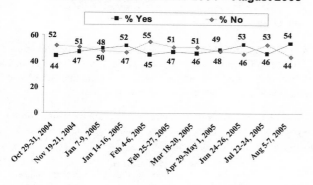

Worth Going to War in Iraq?
Selected Trend: October 2004 – August 2005

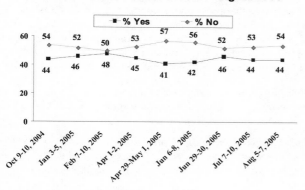

A majority of Americans have consistently said the war was not worth it since last October, although at the same time, Americans have not been as consistently willing to say sending troops was a mistake. Just before the presidential election last year, only 44% of Americans said it was a mistake, while 54% said it was not. Yet, at about the same time, a majority of Americans were also saying the war was not worth it.

One possible explanation for these findings is that the word "mistake" is a harsher judgment than "not worth it," and Americans were reluctant to make the harsher judgment. But the current poll suggests that in today's news environment, Americans are not as likely to hold back their criticisms.

On other questions, however, there is little change in the mostly negative perceptions about the war. A majority of Americans today say the war is going badly rather than well, by a 56% to 43% margin, not much different from what Gallup measured last May. Opinion was more positive after the elections in Iraq, but it has deteriorated to levels measured this past December and January.

How would you say things are going for the U.S.
in Iraq?
Selected Trend: September 2004 – August 2005

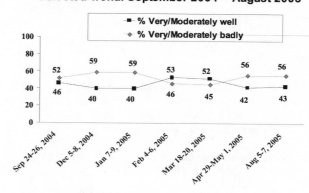

The most significant change in longer-term tracking of trends on Iraq was measured in a June 6-8 poll, when a solid majority of Americans, 59%, said the United States should withdraw some or all of its troops from Iraq. That was the first time Gallup had shown a substantial majority in favor of troop withdrawal.

Troop Levels in Iraq
Selected Trend: September 2004 –
August 2005

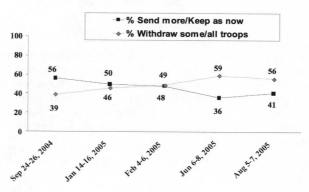

This month, the margin has tightened slightly, with 56% opting for troop withdrawal—though the change is well within the poll's margin of error. Still, by a four-point margin, the 33% who say that the United States should withdraw all of its troops is the largest measured across the 15 times this question has been asked.

One of Bush's justifications for the war is that it would be less dangerous for the United States to fight terrorists in Iraq than to fight terrorists who come here. Generally, the polls have shown the public's agreement with that premise. However, in June 2004 and again in July and August of this year, clear majorities disagree. The current poll, and another a month ago, now show a clear majority saying the war in Iraq has made the United States "less safe" from terrorism.

War in Iraq Made U.S. Safer From Terrorism?

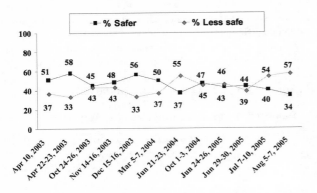

One argument is that while the Iraq war may make the world and the United States more susceptible to terrorist attacks in the short run, in the long run the Iraq war will make the country safer. The poll shows a divided public on this issue—48% disagree, but 42% agree.

War in Iraq Made U.S. Safer From Terrorism? Now vs. in the Long Run

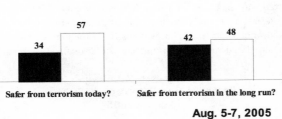

Aug. 5-7, 2005

Survey Methods

Results are based on telephone interviews with 1,005 national adults, aged 18 and older, conducted Aug. 5-7, 2005. For results based on the total sample of national adults, one can say with 95% confidence that the maximum margin of sampling error is ±3 percentage points.

In addition to sampling error, question wording and practical difficulties in conducting surveys can introduce error or bias into the findings of public opinion polls.

August 10, 2005
SPACE SHUTTLE PROGRAM A "GO" FOR AMERICANS
Majority believes NASA is doing an excellent or good job

by Frank Newport, Gallup Poll Editor in Chief

The successful landing of the Space Shuttle Discovery on Tuesday has allowed NASA to begin to focus on next steps. The space shuttle program has been officially suspended until NASA figures out how to solve problems relating to the foam insulation that covers the shuttle, but NASA administrator Michael Griffin has said he would like to get the next space shuttle launched and back into space by the end of the year.

Although safety and technical aspects of the shuttle program are obviously the most important determinants of future launch plans, public opinion can also be an important part of the thinking about the program's future. Presidents since John F. Kennedy have used space travel as a way to rally Americans around a common cause and to give them a vision for something beyond themselves. If that vision is no longer part of the public's psyche, congressional willingness to appropriate money could dwindle away.

At this point, it appears that a large majority of Americans support the idea that the space shuttles should continue to fly. A Gallup Poll conducted in late June found that three-quarters of Americans felt the United States should continue the manned space shuttle program.

Do you feel the U.S. should—or should not—continue the manned space shuttle program?

	Should continue	Should not continue	No opinion
2005 Jun 24-26	74%	21	5

A poll completed this past weekend (before the successful return of the shuttle to Edwards Air Force base in California early Tuesday morning) found that 83% of Americans are confident that NASA can make the space shuttle safe to fly on future missions.

How confident are you that NASA can make the space shuttle safe to fly on future missions—very confident, somewhat confident, not too confident, or not at all confident?

	Very confident	Somewhat confident	Not too confident	Not at all confident	No opinion
2005 Aug 5-7	41%	42	13	3	1

A CBS News poll conducted July 29-Aug. 2 found 59% support for continuing the space shuttle program, "given the costs and risks involved in space exploration."

Interestingly, support for the continuation of the space shuttle program was highest in the immediate aftermath of the Challenger and Columbia disasters that occurred, respectively, in 1986 and 2003.

2003: In light of the space shuttle disaster yesterday in which the seven astronauts were killed do you feel the U.S. should or should not continue the manned space shuttle program?

1986: In light of the space shuttle disaster in January (1986) in which the seven astronauts were killed, do you feel the U.S. should or should not continue the manned space shuttle program?

	Should continue	Should not continue	No opinion
2003 Feb 2 ^	82%	15	3
1986 Mar 7-10	80%	17	3

^ Polls conducted entirely in one day, such as this one, are subject to additional error or bias not found in polls conducted over several days.

CBS News also found high support for the aforementioned question (75%) in a poll conducted in February 2003, after the Columbia disaster.

NASA's Image

Ratings for the job NASA is doing rose slightly in the weekend poll. Sixty percent of Americans now give NASA an excellent or good rating, slightly higher than the 53% positive rating the space agency received in late June.

How would you rate the job being done by NASA—the U.S. space agency? Would you say it is doing an excellent, good, only fair, or poor job?

	Excellent %	Good %	Only fair %	Poor %	No opinion %
2005 Aug 5-7	16	44	29	8	3
2005 Jun 24-26	11	42	34	6	7
2003 Sep 8-10	12	38	36	10	4
1999 Dec 9-12	13	40	31	12	4
1999 Jul 13-4	20	44	20	5	11
1998 Nov 20-22	26	50	17	4	3
1998 Jan 30-Feb 1	21	46	21	4	8
1994 Jul 15-17	14	43	29	6	8
1993 Dec 17-19	18	43	30	7	2
1993 Sept 13-15	7	36	35	11	11
1991 May 2-5	16	48	24	6	6
1990 July 19-22	10	36	34	15	5

The lowest ratings NASA has received in recent years came in September 1993, when just 43% gave it an excellent or good rating. The highest rating came in November 1998 (76% excellent or good), after the successful space shuttle mission involving former astronaut John Glenn, then in his 70s.

What About the Costs?

Gallup Polls have also shown the perhaps not surprising finding that support for space exploration drops when Americans are reminded of its costs.

In May 1961, the month in which President John Kennedy made his dramatic announcement that the United States should focus on sending a man to the moon before the decade was finished, almost 6 out of 10 Americans said they opposed spending $40 billion to send a man to the moon.

It has been estimated that it would cost the United States $40 billion—or an average of about $225 per person—to send a man to the moon. Would you like to see this amount spent for this purpose, or not?

	Yes %	No %	No opinion %
1961 May	33	58	9

Similarly, three separate Gallup Polls conducted in 1969, 1999, and June of this year have found majority opposition to the idea of setting aside money to land an astronaut on Mars.

There has been much discussion about attempting to land an astronaut on the planet Mars. How would you feel about such an attempt—would you favor or oppose the United States setting aside money for such a project?

	Favor %	Oppose %	No opinion %
2005 Jun 24-26	40	58	2
1999 Jul 13-14	43	54	3
1969 Jul 24-29	39	53	8

It is interesting to note that this question about manned space flight to Mars raised the hackles of NASA administrator Griffin when moderator Tim Russert asked him about it on NBC's "Meet the Press" on July 31. Griffin had this to say:

Well, when you poll and ask the question that way, you can get almost any answer you like. It's very close to those, "Have you stopped beating your wife?" questions. If I ask the question in a different way, I might get a very different answer. The way I would ask it is, "NASA will spend about 5% or less of the money which is spent on national defense each year for the next 20 years. What would you like to see done with that money. Given that we're going to spend that money on the American space program, what would you like to see done with it?" and then list various options. "Returning to the moon, eventually going to Mars, exploring the asteroids and other planets, or would you rather that the United States space program be confined to lower-Earth orbit as we have been for the last 30 years?" And I strongly suspect that if confronted with choices, if confronted with the knowledge that we're going to be spending money on space and confronted with choices about where we should spend that money, that those poll results would change dramatically.

Of course, Griffin is correct in stipulating that an alternatively worded question about sending humans to Mars would have elicited different responses. There is little doubt that the type of wording suggested by Griffin would have resulted in an increased level of support for the idea of going to Mars.

But the conclusion derivable from the basic question of funding for a manned trip to Mars still holds: When reminded that it will cost money, Americans' initial reaction to the idea of sending astronauts to Mars is fairly tepid. Griffin and others (including, perhaps, President Bush, if he picks up on his previously announced support for a Mars mission) have their work cut out for them as they seek to expand Americans' support for the idea in the months and years ahead.

Survey Methods

Results are based on telephone interviews with 1,004 national adults, aged 18 and older, conducted Aug. 5-7, 2005. For results based on the total sample of national adults, one can say with 95% confidence that the maximum margin of sampling error is ±3 percentage points.

In addition to sampling error, question wording and practical difficulties in conducting surveys can introduce error or bias into the findings of public opinion polls.

August 11, 2005
HILLARY CLINTON EASILY PACES DEMOCRATIC FIELD
Two-thirds of Americans rate her as a strong leader

by Jeffrey M. Jones, Gallup Poll Managing Editor

A new CNN/*USA Today*/Gallup poll finds New York Sen. Hillary Rodham Clinton as the clear early favorite of the Democratic Party's rank-and-file for the 2008 presidential nomination. On the Republican side, former New York City Mayor Rudy Giuliani and Arizona Sen. John McCain are closely matched, with Secretary of State Condoleezza Rice coming in third. Majorities of Americans view Clinton as a strong and decisive leader, as likeable, and as caring and honest. However, Americans are more inclined to believe she would divide rather than unite the country, and less than half believe she shares their values.

Presidential Preference

The August 5-7 poll asked Democrats and Republicans who they are most likely to support in the 2008 presidential primaries. Clinton has a sizeable lead over the rest of the Democratic field, as 40% of Democratic registered voters prefer her to other possible nominees. Massachusetts Sen. John Kerry and former North Carolina Sen. John Edwards are the closet pursuers, at just 16% and 15%, respectively. Nine percent favor Delaware Sen. Joe Biden, while 5% or less currently support retired general Wesley Clark (5%), New Mexico Governor Bill Richardson (3%), Indiana Sen. Evan Bayh (3%), and Virginia Governor Mark Warner (2%).

2008 Democratic Primary Trial Heats
among registered Democrats/Democratic leaners

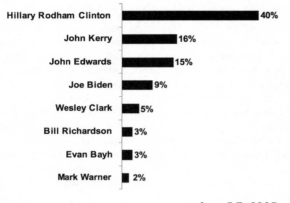

Aug. 5-7, 2005

On the Republican side, 27% of registered voters support Giuliani and 24% back McCain. Rice is the choice of 19% of Republican registered voters. The remaining Republicans tested in the poll are all in single digits, including Senate Majority Leader Bill Frist of Tennessee (9%), Massachusetts Governor Mitt Romney (4%), New York Governor George Pataki (3%), Virginia Sen. George Allen (3%), and Kansas Sen. Sam Brownback (2%). Less than 1% chose Nebraska Sen. Chuck Hagel.

Last month, a Gallup poll tested how some of those candidates might fare in a general election match-up. Both Giuliani and McCain had slight 50%-45% leads over Clinton in trial heats among registered voters, and larger 54%-41% leads over Kerry.

These results give an indication of early candidate support, but are not necessarily predictive of what will happen during the 2008 primaries or general election. Results of a poll question that asked Americans about their current orientations to the 2008 election underscore that caution. Just 16% say they have a good idea of whom they will support, 52% say they are following the news about the election but have not seriously considered whom they will support, and 31% say they are not following the news about it closely.

Views of Clinton

Much of the early focus on the 2008 election has been on Clinton, the former first lady who could become the first woman to win a

2008 Republican Primary Trial Heats
among registered Republicans/Republican leaners

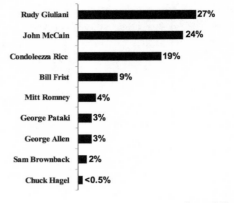

Aug. 5-7, 2005

party's presidential nomination. A July 25-28 Gallup poll found 53% of Americans rating her favorably and 43% unfavorably.

The current poll delves more deeply into public perceptions of the New York senator by asking Americans to rate Clinton on a series of personal characteristics.

Thinking about the following characteristics and qualities, please say whether you think each applies or doesn't apply to Hillary Clinton. How about—[RANDOM ORDER]?

2005 Aug 5-7 (sorted by "applies")	Applies %	Doesn't apply %
Is a strong and decisive leader	68	30
Is likable	60	39
Cares about the needs of people like you	54	43
Is honest and trustworthy	53	43
Shares your values	44	51
Would unite the country and not divide it	41	53

Nearly 7 in 10 describe Clinton as a "strong and decisive leader," and at least a majority believes she is "likable," "cares about the needs of people like you," and is "honest and trustworthy."

At 53%, she compares favorably to her husband, former President Bill Clinton, on the honesty dimension. Gallup's most recent reading on him, from July 2000, found only 21% of Americans describing him as honest and trustworthy. That was a dramatic drop from the 61% who described him that way shortly after he took office in 1993, long before the Monica Lewinsky scandal.

Hillary Clinton's honesty ratings are comparable to the current president's. A late July CNN/*USA Today*/Gallup poll finds 54% saying George W. Bush is honest and trustworthy.

Her apparent weaknesses at this point are on values and uniting the country. Currently, 50% of Americans say the Republican president Bush shares their values, compared with 44% for Clinton. Recently, Clinton has received a lot of attention for apparently urging the Democratic Party to take a more moderate approach on the abortion issue.

Likewise, only 41% say Clinton would unite the country, while 53% disagree. It is unclear to what degree that is a reflection on her versus a commentary on the highly partisan nature of politics in the United States today, since the question has not been asked recently about other politicians. When Gallup asked a slightly different question about Bush earlier this year, the public was evenly divided in its view of whether Bush was a "uniter" or a "divider."

The results for Clinton vary dramatically by party affiliation—65% of Democrats believe Clinton would unite the country, compared with just 39% of independents and 21% of Republicans.

As was the case in the 2004 election, the public will evaluate the next group of presidential candidates to a large degree on their ability to handle the terrorism issue. A majority of Americans, 57%, believes Clinton would be at least somewhat effective in dealing with terrorism, but only 17% say she will be very effective. Roughly 4 in 10 believe she would not be very effective on the terror issue.

How Effective Would Hillary Clinton be in Dealing With Threat of Terrorism?

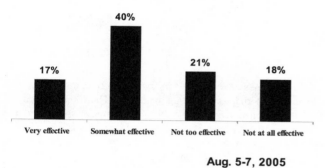

Aug. 5-7, 2005

Aside from being the first woman nominee of a major party, Clinton would also be the first spouse of a former president to seek the office. The poll finds that the public views Hillary Clinton's marriage to Bill Clinton as more of a liability than an asset. Forty-three percent of Americans say her marriage to Bill Clinton makes them less likely to vote for her, 30% say more likely, and 26% say it makes no difference. These views are strongly partisan—with Democrats saying it makes them more likely to support Hillary Clinton and Republicans less likely, with independents fairly evenly divided.

Does the fact that Hillary Clinton is married to Bill Clinton make you more likely to vote for her or less likely to vote for her if she ran for president in 2008?

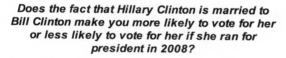

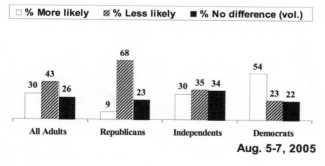

Aug. 5-7, 2005

Survey Methods

These results are based on telephone interviews with a randomly selected national sample of 1,004 adults, aged 18 years and older, conducted August 5-7, 2005. For results based on this sample, one can say with 95% confidence that the maximum error attributable to sampling and other random effects is ±3 percentage points. In addi-

tion to sampling error, question wording and practical difficulties in conducting surveys can introduce error or bias into the findings of public opinion polls.

For results based on the sample of 406 Republicans and Republican leaners who are registered to vote, the maximum margin of sampling error is ±5 percentage points.

For results based on the sample of 424 Democrats and Democratic leaners who are registered to vote, the maximum margin of sampling error is ±5 percentage points.

August 15, 2005
MOST SMOKERS WANT TO QUIT, BUT FEEL THEY ARE ADDICTED
More than 8 in 10 Americans believe smoking very harmful to smokers

by Jeffrey M. Jones, Gallup Poll Managing Editor

Former smoker and ABC News anchor Peter Jennings' recent death from lung cancer has done a lot to remind people about the health dangers associated with smoking. Gallup polling shows that Americans overwhelmingly acknowledge the dangers of smoking, though smokers are somewhat less likely to do so. Over time, the number of smokers in the U.S. adult population has dropped, as has the reported daily number of cigarettes that smokers smoke. Most of the roughly one-quarter of Americans who smoke would like to quit, but most also feel they are addicted to cigarettes. Heavy smokers are much more likely than light smokers to feel they are addicted, but not more likely to express a desire to quit.

Smoking Incidence

Gallup's annual Consumption Habits poll, conducted July 7-10 this year, tracks Americans' smoking habits and their attitudes toward smoking. About one in four Americans say they smoke cigarettes; this proportion has changed little since the mid-1990s. However, it has decreased substantially from when Gallup began asking about it in the 1940s. A 1944 Gallup Poll found 41% of Americans saying they smoked cigarettes in the past week. The highest percentage of reported smoking that Gallup recorded was 45% in 1954.

Have You Smoked in the Past Week?

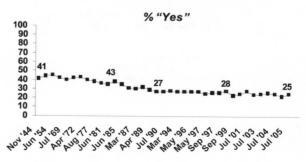

Thirty percent of nonsmokers say they have smoked cigarettes on a regular basis at some point in their lives, meaning nearly half of the adult population has regularly smoked cigarettes.

Americans' Smoking Habits

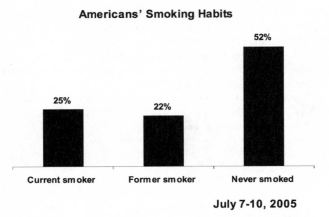

July 7-10, 2005

One silver lining in the smoking data is that those who smoke today report smoking fewer cigarettes each day on average than did smokers of the past. The July 2005 poll finds a majority of smokers saying they smoke less than one pack per day, which has been the case since 1999. The current data show 4 in 10 smokers indicating they smoke a pack or more per day, while polling in the late 1970s and early 1980s found about 6 in 10 smokers saying they smoked a pack or more a day.

Percentage of Smokers Who Smoke One Pack or More Per Day

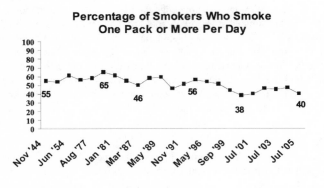

Risks With Smoking

Even before Jennings' death, Americans were well aware of the harm smoking could do to their health. Eight in 10 Americans believe smoking is very harmful to smokers. Fifty-three percent say second-hand smoke is very harmful to adults. Both results have been quite consistent over the past four years.

Perceptions of Harm From Smoking and Secondhand Smoke

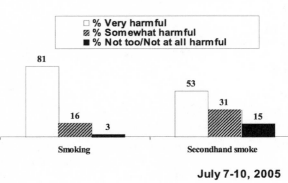

July 7-10, 2005

Americans, too, are well aware of the link between smoking and lung cancer. In 2001, 71% of Americans said smoking was "a major cause of lung cancer," 11% said it was a minor cause, and just 16% said science hadn't been able to establish a link between the two.

Perceptions of the Link Between Cigarette Smoking and Lung Cancer

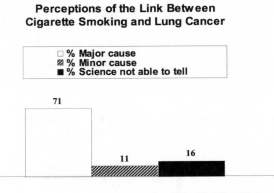

July 19-22, 2001

As a group, smokers clearly recognize the risks inherent in their habit, but are perhaps less willing to admit it. The 2001 poll showed that 77% of nonsmokers—but only 57% of smokers—believed that smoking is a major cause of lung cancer. In the July 2005 poll, 86% of nonsmokers say smoking is very harmful to those who smoke, compared with just 65% of smokers.

Still, the vast majority of smokers would like to quit. The recent Consumption Habits poll finds 76% of smokers saying they would like to give up smoking. This percentage has ranged between 76% and 82% since 1999. Gallup has always found at least a majority of smokers expressing a desire to quit, dating back to the initial asking in 1977.

Smokers: Like to Give Up Smoking?

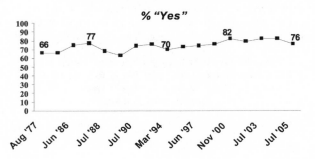

In 1990, Gallup found 61% of smokers saying they considered themselves addicted to cigarettes. That percentage has increased over time—currently, 74% say they are addicted, and at least 7 in 10 have said so since 1997.

A Closer Look at Smokers

Because Gallup has asked the smoking questions consistently over the years, the poll results can be combined to look at a larger sample of smokers. The following analyses are based on smokers' answers to poll questions from 2000 to 2005.

Smokers can be classified into one of four groups, according to whether or not they consider themselves addicted to cigarettes and whether or not they want to give up smoking. A majority of smokers consider themselves addicted to cigarettes and would also like to

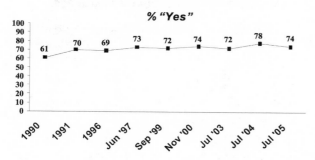

Smokers: Addicted to Cigarettes?

% "Yes"

give up smoking. Another 17% do not consider themselves addicted but still would like to quit. Eleven percent consider themselves addicted but do not want to give up smoking.

Smoker Typology, 2000-2005 Gallup Poll Data

Addicted and want to give up smoking	63%
Addicted, do not want to give up smoking	11
Not addicted, want to give up smoking	17
Not addicted, do not want to give up smoking	7

The desire to quit is more prevalent among smokers who believe they have an addiction. Eighty-five percent of smokers who consider themselves addicted would like to give up smoking, compared with 69% of those who do not consider themselves addicted.

Heavy smokers—those who smoke more than one pack per day—are more likely to believe they are addicted to cigarettes, but not more likely to want to quit. Ninety-three percent of smokers who smoke more than a pack per day believe they are addicted to cigarettes (as do 90% of those who smoke between a half pack and a full pack daily). In contrast, only 60% of those who smoke half a pack or less per day believe they are addicted.

However, heavy smokers are only slightly less likely than light smokers to say they want to quit smoking, though that difference is within the poll's margin of error.

Smokers' Attitudes Toward Smoking,
by Amount Smoked Per Day

	Half pack or less	More than half a pack to a full pack	More than one pack
Addicted	60%	90%	93%
Would like to quit	82%	80%	74%

An analysis shows that smokers aged 60 and older are more likely to say they are addicted to cigarettes but less likely to say they want to quit smoking than are smokers aged 18 to 34.

Two in three smokers between the ages of 18 and 34 say they are addicted to smoking, while 80% of smokers in the 35 to 59 age group and 76% of smokers aged 60 and older agree.

A majority of all three smoker age groups express a desire to quit smoking, but a higher proportion of 18- to 34-year-old smokers (80%) and 35- to 59-year-old smokers (80%) do so than do smokers aged 60 and older (69%).

Survey Methods

These results are based on telephone interviews with a randomly selected national sample of 1,006 adults, aged 18 and older, con-

ducted July 7-10, 2005. For results based on this sample, one can say with 95% confidence that the maximum error attributable to sampling and other random effects is ±3 percentage points. In addition to sampling error, question wording and practical difficulties in conducting surveys can introduce error or bias into the findings of public opinion polls.

August 16, 2005
AUGUST GALLUP POLL SHOWS NO UPTICK IN CONSUMER OPTIMISM
Majority continues to say economy getting worse

by Frank Newport, Gallup Poll Editor in Chief

How is the U.S. economy doing? To a significant degree, the answer to that question depends on whom you ask. Many official economic statistics look relatively promising. The government reported over 200,000 new jobs were created in July, retail sales are up, manufacturing is up, leading economic indicators are up, and the economy is robust enough in general to prompt the Federal Reserve Board to continue to raise short-term interest rates.

Last week President Bush expressed his confidence in the economy. He is quoted on the Web site www.whitehouse.gov as saying, "The economy of the United States is strong, and the foundation for sustained growth is in place."

But it's not at all clear that the average American agrees that the economy is strong, and it's equally unclear if Americans share the bullish outlook on the economy that the official statistics might suggest.

Gallup's August economic update shows that Americans, on average, continue to believe that economic conditions in the United States are getting worse, not better. Only a little more than a third are willing to rate the economy as "excellent" or "good." A majority says it is a bad time to find a quality job. And about a third of Americans tell us that some aspect of the economy is the most important problem facing the country today.

In none of these instances are there signs of a sustained recovery in consumer confidence. In most cases, the public's views on the economy remain more depressed than they were at the beginning of this year or on average last year.

The following chart presents the trends on two key measures of the economy since the beginning of the Bush administration.

Rating the Nation's Economy

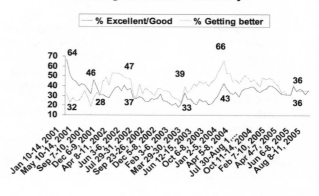

The relative optimism of the American public—measured as the percentage who say the U.S. economy has been getting better (as opposed to getting worse)—has been the more volatile of these two measures, swinging from a Bush administration low point of 19% in Sep. 7-10, 2001 (just before the 9/11 terrorist attacks) to a high point of 66% in Jan. 2-5, 2004.

The average "getting better" percentage across the Bush administration has been 39.4%. The current 36% "getting better" figure is thus slightly below average for the time period since January 2001.

We can describe the pattern of economic optimism across the four and a half years of the Bush administration as follows:

1. Two periods of relative optimism—the first coming late in 2001 and into 2002, and the second coming in late 2003 and extending into early 2004.
2. A decidedly downbeat period from the summer of 2002 to the summer of 2003.
3. The current period of mid-range doldrums.

The public's views of the current economy—measured as the percentage of Americans rating the economy as excellent or good—is less volatile, and can be described as follows:

1. Low relative ratings in 2002 and 2003, with a Bush administration low point of 18% rating the economy as excellent or good in Feb. 17-19, 2003.
2. A Bush administration high point of 51% in February 2001, just as Bush took office (and 67% in an early January 2001 poll before he was inaugurated).
3. Relative high points in these ratings came in spring 2002 and late 2003/early 2004.

Currently, 36% of Americans rate the economy as excellent or good, slightly above the average of 33% for the four and a half years of the Bush administration so far.

Here's a more detailed look at the data for the past 12 months.

Current Economic Conditions
Selected Trend: August 2004 – August 2005

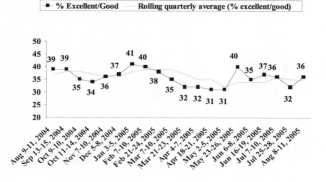

Both economic optimism ("getting better") and the rating of current economic conditions (percentage excellent or good) reached their low points for the year in mid-March through early May, and have recovered slightly since that point. The current readings, however, are still lower than they were as the year began. Additionally, as can be seen, economic confidence has been very steady across the summer months, showing no signs of significant upward movement.

Jobs?

Forty-two percent of Americans who are working or looking for work say that now is a good time to find a quality job, basically unchanged

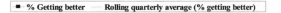

Economic Outlook
Selected Trend: August 2004 – August 2005

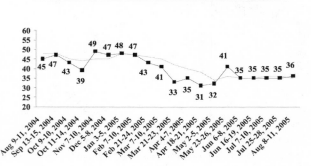

for the year. This perception of the job market is, however, somewhat higher than it was in 2003, when at one point (Mar. 3-5, 2003) only 16% of workers or those looking for work said that it was a good time to look for a quality job.

The Economy as Most Important Problem

Thirty-two percent of Americans mention some aspect of the economy as the most important problem facing the country today, which is little changed from previous months' polls, conducted this year. The specific economic problems mentioned by Americans are:

Most Important Problem Facing Country, Economic Problems

	%
The economy in general	13
Unemployment/jobs	8
Fuel/oil prices	8
High cost of living/inflation	3
Federal budget deficit	2
Lack of money; Taxes; Wage issues	1% each

Survey Methods

These results are based in part on telephone interviews with a randomly selected national sample of 1,001 adults, aged 18 and older, conducted Aug. 8-11, 2005. For results based on this sample, one can say with 95% confidence that the maximum error attributable to sampling and other random effects is ±3 percentage points. In addition to sampling error, question wording and practical difficulties in conducting surveys can introduce error or bias into the findings of public opinion polls.

August 16, 2005
SIX IN 10 AMERICANS HAVE ATTEMPTED TO LOSE WEIGHT
Women more likely than men to diet

by Joseph Carroll, Gallup Poll Assistant Editor

Some people increase their cardio regimen, while others hire personal trainers and nutritionists and still others merely reduce the number of carbs, fat, or calories in their diet. No matter what people are doing, many are trying to lose weight. A recent Gallup Poll finds that attempts to lose weight are common among the U.S. population, and a substantial proportion of Americans have attempted to lose weight several times in their lives.

Gallup's annual survey on Consumption Habits*, conducted July 7-10, finds that Americans report that they have tried to lose weight an average of seven times in their lives. This includes 24% of Americans who have tried to lose weight once or twice, 28% who have tried between 3 and 10 times, and 11% who have tried more than 10 times. A third of Americans, 34%, say they have never tried to lose weight.

How many different times, if any, have you seriously tried to lose weight in your life?

Date	Once or twice	Three to 10 times	More than 10 times	Never	No opinion	Mean
Jul 7-10, 2005	24%	28%	11%	34%	3%	7.3
Jul 22-25, 1999	25%	25%	8%	40%	2%	4.6
Oct 18-21, 1990	30%	18%	5%	44%	3%	4.0

The current poll shows a significant increase in reported weight loss attempts over the past 15 years. In 1990, a Gallup Poll found that Americans tried to lose weight four times in their lives, on average. In 1999, the average was five times. These two surveys found a higher percentage of Americans reporting that they have never tried to lose weight, and fewer reporting that they have dieted three or more times.

Who's Trying to Lose Weight?

Certain groups of Americans are more likely to attempt weight loss than others: overweight Americans rather than average or under-weight Americans, women rather than men, those who do not eat a very healthy diet rather than those who do, and those who do not describe their health as excellent rather than those who do.

Weight Description

Americans who describe their current weight situation as overweight are much more likely than those who are about right or underweight to say they have tried to lose weight. Overweight Americans report that they have attempted diets an average of 13 times, compared with 3 times among those who are about right or underweight.

How many different times, if any, have you seriously tried to lose weight in your life?

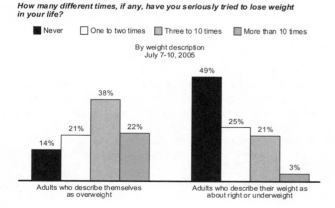

Nearly half of those who are about right or underweight say they have never attempted to lose weight, while only 14% of overweight respondents have never tried. Six in 10 overweight Americans have tried to lose weight three or more times.

Gender and Age

Women are much more likely than men to say they have tried to lose weight before. On average, men report that they have tried to lose weight five times in their lives, while women say they have made an average of 10 attempts.

Slightly less than half of men (45%) say they have never attempted to lose weight, compared with only 23% of women. Among women, 25% have tried to lose weight once or twice, while 46% have tried three or more times. Among men, 23% have tried once or twice to lose weight, while only 31% have made three or more attempts.

How many different times, if any, have you seriously tried to lose weight in your life?

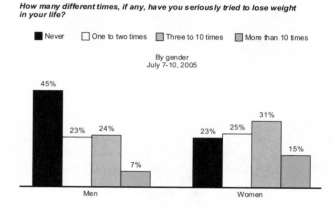

There are also some slight variations by age, with the youngest adults (aged 18 to 29) and seniors (aged 65 and older) reporting fewer attempts at weight loss than those in the 30 to 64 age range. Adults aged 18 to 29 and adults aged 65 and older have tried to lose weight an average of 4 times each, while 30- to 49-year-olds have attempted weight loss an average of 8 times and 50- to 64-year-olds an average of 10 times.

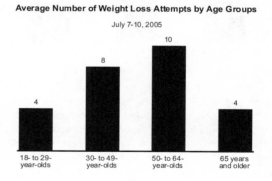

Last week, in an analysis about weight concerns, Gallup reported that younger women were much more likely than older women or men of any age to worry about their weight all or some of the time. Despite the difference in expressed worry, younger and older women have made about the same number of attempts at weight loss, on average. On average, younger women (aged 18 to 49) have tried to lose weight 9 times, while older women (aged 50 and older) have tried 11 times. Younger and older men both report an average of five weight loss attempts.

Diet

On average, Americans who describe their diet as "very healthy" say they have attempted to lose weight five times in their lives. This is slightly lower than those who describe their diet as somewhat healthy or not healthy, with an average of eight weight loss attempts and nine attempts, respectively.

Average Number of Weight Loss Attempts by Description of Diet

July 7-10, 2005

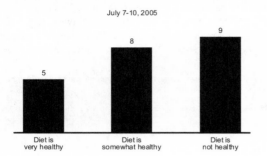

Personal Health Description

Those who describe their health as "excellent" say they have tried to lose weight about four times, on average. This compares with eight times among those who describe their personal health as "good" and 13 times among those describing it as "only fair" or "poor."

Average Number of Weight Loss Attempts by Description of Personal Health

July 7-10, 2005

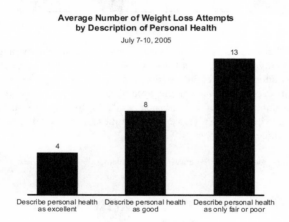

Results are based on telephone interviews with 1,006 national adults, aged 18 and older, conducted July 7-10, 2005.

For results based on the total sample of national adults, one can say with 95% confidence that the margin of sampling error is ±3 percentage points. In addition to sampling error, question wording and practical difficulties in conducting surveys can introduce error or bias into the findings of public opinion polls.

August 16, 2005

PUBLIC BACKS FEDERAL FUNDING FOR NEW STEM CELL RESEARCH
Weekly churchgoers, conservatives less supportive

by Linda Lyons, Education and Youth Editor

Senate Majority Leader Bill Frist, an honored speaker at the first evangelical Christian Justice Sunday rally last April, wasn't invited to Justice Sunday II in Tennessee last weekend. Frist may have been snubbed because he recently changed his position on government spending to support research on newly created stem cells obtained from human embryos, angering many conservative Christians who feel stem cells attained that way destroy human life.

According to a new CNN/*USA Today*/Gallup poll*, the majority of Americans (56%) agree with Frist that the federal government should "fund research that would use newly created stem cells obtained from human embryos." Forty percent say the government should not fund such research.

Do you think the federal government should -- or should not – fund research that would use newly created stem cells obtained from human embryos?

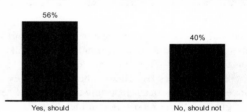

Those results are generally in line with what Gallup has found in its polling on the stem cell research issue. For example, in a May Gallup Poll, 60% of Americans described "medical research using stem cells obtained from human embryos" as morally acceptable, while 33% said it was morally wrong. Also in May, a CNN/*USA Today*/Gallup poll showed 53% favoring no restrictions or an easing of current restrictions of government funding of stem cell research, while 24% favored keeping the current restrictions in place and 19% opposed any kind of government funding of stem cell research.

Frequent Churchgoers, Conservatives Less Supportive of Federal Funding

Weekly churchgoers and ideological conservatives, in particular, are less supportive of federal funding for stem cell research. In the current poll, just 37% of weekly churchgoers support the funding of newly created stem cells obtained from human embryos, compared with 55% of Americans who attend church nearly weekly or monthly, and 69% of those who seldom or never attend church. Forty-two percent of conservatives agree that the government should fund research involving stem cells created from human embryos, versus 64% of moderates and 73% of liberals.

The House of Representatives passed a bill allowing an expansion of government financing of stem cell research in May, and the Senate may take it up as early as this fall. President George W. Bush, who believes using human embryos for research disregards the sanctity of life, has vowed to veto the bill if the Senate passes it. At that point, Congress will need a two-thirds majority of both houses to override the veto.

These results are based on telephone interviews with a randomly selected national sample of 1,004 adults, aged 18 and older,

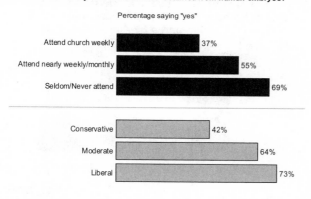
conducted Aug, 5-7, 2005. For results based on this sample, one can say with 95% confidence that the maximum error attributable to sampling and other random effects is ±3 percentage points. In addition to sampling error, question wording and practical difficulties in conducting surveys can introduce error or bias into the findings of public opinion polls.

August 17, 2005
GENDER STEREOTYPES PREVAIL ON WORKING OUTSIDE THE HOME
Modest backlash among women against working; men warming up to staying home

by David W. Moore, Gallup Poll Senior Editor

The second wave of the women's movement, which surged onto the public agenda in the early 1970s, was stimulated in part by controversy over the proper role of women and men at home and at work. Should women be allowed to work outside the home as the principal breadwinners? Should men be allowed to stay at home as the principal caretakers?

The latest Gallup Poll shows that if they were free to choose, a majority of women would opt for the traditional female role of staying at home, while a larger majority of men would prefer the traditional male role of working outside the home. But over the years, there has been a sea change in attitudes on this subject.

In 1938, a Gallup Poll asked Americans if they approved or disapproved of a married woman earning money in business or industry if her husband was capable of supporting her. More than three in four—78%—said they disapproved; just 22% approved. Men and women expressed about the same level of disapproval. For most Americans of that time, it was the husband's responsibility to be the provider, the wife's responsibility to be the nurturer.

But these views changed, as more and more women took paying jobs, and many women who did not work outside the home became frustrated with the roles they were expected to play. By 1970, about a third of women were already working outside the home, and another quarter wished they could. Four years later, a Roper poll showed that 36% of women said they "would prefer to have a job outside of the home," while 60% would rather "stay home to take care of the house and family."

That decisive majority view in favor of the traditional role of women disappeared in Roper's 1978 poll, when slightly more women opted for working outside the home, by 49% to 45%.

Work Outside the Home or Stay at Home?
among women

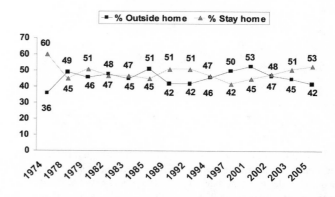

Since then, no clear consensus in either direction has emerged, with small majorities of women sometimes opting for working outside the home and, as measured in the latest Gallup survey, small majorities sometimes favoring the traditional role of family caretaker. These variations are mostly within the respective polls' margins of error, suggesting a mostly divided opinion among women.

Still, the recent figures from 2001 to the present show women moving in the direction of preferring the more traditional role. Four years ago, a majority of women favored working outside the home by 53% to 45%, while today a majority favors staying at home by 53% to 42%.

The first measurement of men's attitudes on this question came in 1983, with 72% of men preferring to work outside the home and just 21% preferring to stay at home. Two years later, the margin in favor of working was even larger, 86% to 12%. Since then, there has been a slow movement toward men staying at home, with the strongest support for that position recorded in the current poll—but still more than 2-to-1 favor work, 68% to 27%.

Work Outside the Home or Stay at Home?
among men

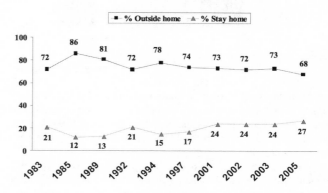

A comparison of men's and women's attitudes on working outside the home shows a persistently large gender gap over the years, at 27 points in 1983, and at 26 points today. During this period, the gap expanded to its largest size of 39 points in 1989, and shrank to its smallest size of 20 points in 2001.

Work Outside the Home or Stay at Home?
Percentage Saying "Work Outside the Home"

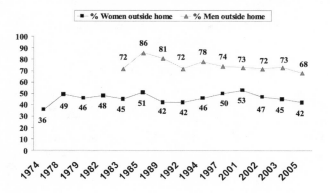

Percentage of Men and Women Who *Prefer to Work Outside the Home* Rather Than Stay at Home to Take Care of House and Family *Compared by Age*

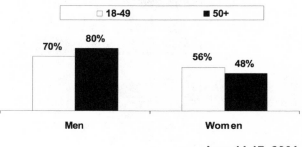

June 11-17, 2001

A suggestion of what the future might hold can be seen in a comparison of attitudes by age. Fewer men under age 50 want to work outside the home than men 50 and older, with 65% and 72%, respectively, expressing that view. These results suggest that in the long run, more men may be opting for the nontraditional role of being family caretaker. The difference is small, however, and needs to be treated cautiously.

Among women, there is little difference in attitudes by age. If anything, younger women are slightly less likely to choose working outside the home (40%) than are older women (43%). The difference is well within the poll's margin of error, but the results indicate at least that younger women are not moving in a nontraditional direction more than older women.

Percentage of Men and Women Who *Prefer to Work Outside the Home* Rather Than Stay at Home to Take Care of House and Family *Compared by Age*

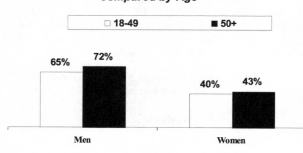

Aug. 8-11, 2005

A similar comparison of attitudes measured in 2001 shows startling differences. In that survey, younger women were more likely than older women to prefer working outside the home, 56% vs. 48%. Overall, 53% of women preferred that option, compared with 42% in the current poll.

These results show that over the past four years, younger women—much more than older women—have turned away from working outside the home. Today, only 40% of younger women choose that option, compared with 56% of younger women in 2001—a 16-point decline. Among older women, the decline is more modest—from 48% four years ago to 43% today.

Among men, the changes in each age group tend to reinforce the overall and gradual movement toward staying at home. Today, 65%

of younger men want to work outside the home, compared with 70% four years ago. Among older men, 72% want to work, down from 80% in 2001.

Survey Methods

Current results are based on telephone interviews with 1,001 national adults, aged 18 and older, conducted Aug. 8-11, 2005. For results based on the total sample of national adults, one can say with 95% confidence that the maximum margin of sampling error is ±3 percentage points.

August 18, 2005
MCCAIN HAS BROAD, BUT NOT DEEP, APPEAL
Senator viewed similarly by partisan groups

by Jeffrey M. Jones, Gallup Poll Managing Editor

Arizona Senator John McCain is likely to be one of the major contenders for the 2008 Republican presidential nomination. McCain, a Vietnam War hero, has a generally conservative voting record in the United States Senate, but may be best known for some notable breaks from the Republican caucus on issues such as campaign finance reform and judicial nominations.

Gallup polling during the last several years shows McCain's favorable ratings running in the low 50s. While other politicians have similar favorable ratings, what sets McCain apart is that he is viewed similarly across party and ideological lines. A closer analysis of the data hints that McCain's support is not particularly strong among conservative Republicans, the constituency whose support will be key to winning the party's presidential nomination.

McCain's most recent favorable rating, from a July 25-28 Gallup Poll, is 51%. Twenty-two percent view him unfavorably, and 27% have no opinion. These figures are in line with what Gallup has found for McCain since 2002.

Combining the data from the four separate 2002-2005 surveys allows for a more detailed look at the public's opinions of McCain. Remarkably, the numbers show little variation due to political ideology—53% of self-identified conservatives, 53% of self-identified moderates, and 52% of self-identified liberals view

Opinion of John McCain

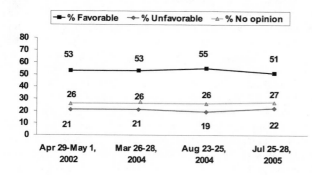

McCain favorably. Conservatives (25%) and liberals (23%) are about equally likely to view him negatively.

The same pattern is evident by party affiliation—54% of Republicans, 51% of independents, and 53% of Democrats view him favorably. McCain's negatives are slightly higher among *Republicans* (25%) than independents and Democrats (19% each).

The aggregated data allow a detailed look at ideological groups within specific parties. Again, McCain's ratings are similar even across these more precisely defined groups. The notable exception are pure independents—that is, those who do not identify with, nor "lean" to, either political party—who have only 37% favorable ratings due to a high proportion of those without an opinion of McCain. But the ratio of positive-to-negative views among this group is still better than 2-to-1, as is the case with the other groups.

Views of John McCain, by Party and Ideology
(2002-2005 aggregate)

	Favor- able %	Unfavor- able %	No opinion %	Net favor- able
Liberal Democrat	57	23	19	+34
Moderate Democrat	55	14	30	+41
Conservative Democrat	51	20	30	+31
Pure independent	37	17	46	+20
Moderate/Liberal Republican	51	20	28	+31
Conservative Republican	56	27	17	+29

Interestingly, moderate Democrats give McCain the highest net favorable rating at +41 (55% favorable minus 14% unfavorable). In fact, McCain's net ratings are no worse, and in some instances better, among the three Democratic groups than among the two Republican groups. McCain's net favorable rating among conservative Republicans is only +29, given this group's higher proportion of unfavorable views of McCain.

McCain in Context

On the surface, McCain's favorable ratings look similar to many other politicians. Take for example New York Senator Hillary Rodham Clinton, who could be McCain's rival in the 2008 presidential election. Clinton has a nearly identical 54% favorable rating average across the last four measurements (taken in 2004 and 2005) to McCain's 53%. However, Clinton's unfavorable ratings are much higher than McCain's, while substantially more Americans have no opinion of McCain.

Despite their similar favorable ratings, Clinton's and McCain's ratings look dramatically different beneath the surface. Views of Clinton are highly positive among those on the left of the American political spectrum, and highly negative among those on the right. Specifically, 80% of liberals have a favorable opinion of Clinton, compared with 59% of moderates and only 34% of conservatives. There is a similar divide by party, with 84% of Democrats, 53% of independents, and 24% of Republicans viewing the New York senator favorably.

The divergence of the public's views of Clinton are even greater when taking respondents' party affiliations and ideologies into account, showing a steep decline when moving from left to right on the political spectrum. For example, 85% of liberal Democrats have a favorable view of Clinton compared with just 17% of conservative Republicans. The net score for Clinton among liberal Democrats is +74, compared with -63 among conservative Republicans—a gap of 137 points.

Views of Hillary Rodham Clinton, by Party and Ideology
(2004-2005 aggregate)

	Favor- able %	Unfavor- able %	No opinion %	Net favor- able
Liberal Democrat	85	11	4	+74
Moderate Democrat	80	15	5	+65
Conservative Democrat	76	17	6	+59
Pure independent	46	40	14	+6
Moderate/Liberal Republican	37	58	6	-21
Conservative Republican	17	80	3	-63

A side-by-side graph of McCain's and Clinton's net ratings by partisan and ideological group underscore the differences. McCain's appeal is consistent across groups, but shallow in the sense that no group views him extremely positively. On the other hand, Clinton's appeal varies by group, but the three Democratic factions have overwhelmingly positive views of her.

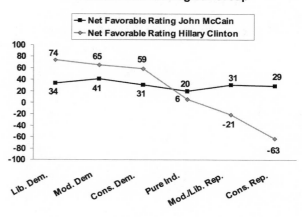

Partisan and ideological divergence in public opinion of politicians is not confined to Clinton or even Democrats more generally. When Gallup last asked for overall opinions of President George W. Bush in a July 25-28 poll, 72% of conservatives, 42% of moderates, and 18% of liberals viewed him favorably. The results by party were even more polarized—89% of Republicans, 41% of independents, and 19% of Democrats viewed Bush favorably.

Even former New York City Mayor Rudy Giuliani, whose 64% favorable rating makes him one of the most popular Republican politicians, has much higher ratings among Republicans (80%) than independents (60%) or Democrats (56%).

McCain and the 2008 Nomination

Gallup has twice asked Republicans for their preference for their party's 2008 nominee from among a list of possible candidates. While McCain placed no worse than second in either poll, in both cases his support is lower among conservative Republicans than among moderate or liberal Republicans.

Last November, Gallup asked Republicans to choose their preferred 2008 nominee from among Giuliani, McCain, and Florida Governor Jeb Bush. McCain's support was 10 percentage points higher among liberal and moderate Republicans than among conservative Republicans. Jeb Bush appealed more to conservatives than liberals and moderates, while Giuliani's support was roughly equal between the two groups.

Preference for the Republican Nomination
November 2004 Gallup Poll

	All Republicans %	Liberal/ Moderate Republicans %	Conservative Republicans %
Rudy Giuliani	47	49	47
John McCain	26	33	23
Jeb Bush	17	7	22

A CNN/*USA Today*/Gallup poll conducted earlier this month asked Republicans to choose from a longer list of contenders (which excluded Bush, who has indicated he does not plan to run for the 2008 nomination). While McCain and Giuliani are closely matched among all Republicans, the data suggest McCain's support is lower among conservative Republicans, though the difference is within the margin of error for this subgroup. Again, there is little difference in Giuliani's support by ideological affiliation.

Preference for the Republican Nomination
August 2005 CNN/USA Today/Gallup Poll

	All Republicans %	Liberal/ Moderate Republicans %	Conservative Republicans %
Rudy Giuliani	27	29	27
John McCain	24	27	22
Condoleezza Rice	18	19	16
Bill Frist	8	4	11
Mitt Romney	4	6	3
George Allen	3	3	4
Sam Brownback	2	3	1
George Pataki	1	4	3
Chuck Hagel	<1	1	<1

Implications

In a political environment characterized by widespread party polarization, it is hard to predict whether McCain's broad—yet shallow—

appeal will be an asset or a weakness. It could be a weakness as most Republican presidential primaries are limited to registered members of that party, but it could be an asset in states with open primaries, those that allow independent (and in some cases Democratic) voters to participate in the Republican primary. Michigan and New Hampshire are two such states, and are two states in which McCain defeated George W. Bush in 2000. But McCain's victories in 2000 were limited and, aside from Michigan and his home state of Arizona, were confined to the more liberal and moderate Northeastern states. McCain's 2000 showing is consistent with his current appeal.

However, if McCain does well in the primaries and secures the Republican nomination, he could be a formidable candidate, especially against someone like Clinton who has more limited appeal outside her party. But McCain's fairly modest appeal to Republicans could also hurt his ability to mobilize supporters to work for and contribute to his campaign, as well as turn out to vote for him on Election Day.

Survey Methods

These results are based on telephone interviews with a randomly selected national sample of 3,538 adults, aged 18 and older, conducted April 29-May 1, 2002, March 26-28, 2004, Aug. 23-25, 2004, and July 25-28, 2005. For results based on this sample, one can say with 95% confidence that the maximum error attributable to sampling and other random effects is ±2 percentage points. In addition to sampling error, question wording and practical difficulties in conducting surveys can introduce error or bias into the findings of public opinion polls.

August 22, 2005
RESTAURANTS HIGHEST-RATED INDUSTRY; OIL AND GAS LOWEST
Views of education, accounting, and farming and agriculture up this year

by Joseph Carroll, Gallup Poll Assistant Editor

Gallup's annual update on the images of various business and industry sectors in the country finds the restaurant industry, the computer industry, agriculture, and the grocery industry viewed most favorably by Americans. The oil and gas industry, typically the most negatively rated, saw its ratings decline even further this year as the prices of oil and gasoline reached new heights. Views of education, accounting, and agriculture are all up this year compared with 2004, while ratings of the oil and gas industry, the federal government, and the sports industry have declined and are now the lowest Gallup has measured for them. The image of the movie industry also took a hit this year.

Overall Rankings

Each year since 2001, Gallup has asked Americans to rate more than 20 business and industry sectors in the country on a five-point scale ranging from very positive to very negative. A net image score is calculated by subtracting the percentage saying "very negative" or "somewhat negative" from the percentage saying "very positive" or "somewhat positive." The middle rating of "neutral" is not factored into these scores.

The latest poll, conducted Aug. 8-11, finds that Americans have a net positive view (more people rating them positively than negatively) of 15 industries and a net negative view (more rating them negatively than positively) of 10.

Business and Industry Sector Ratings
Aug. 8-11, 2005

	Total positive %	Neutral %	Total negative %	Net image pct. pts.
Restaurant industry	58	31	8	+50
Computer industry	57	30	10	+47
Farming and agriculture	58	27	13	+45
Grocery industry	58	27	15	+43
Retail industry	52	31	15	+37
Travel industry	48	35	13	+35
Accounting	42	40	14	+28
Internet industry	46	27	22	+24
Banking	46	31	22	+24
Real estate industry	46	29	23	+23
Education	52	18	29	+23
Publishing industry	42	35	20	+22
Automobile industry	42	29	26	+16
Telephone industry	40	31	27	+13
Airline industry	38	32	27	+11
Electric and gas utilities	36	24	38	-2
Television and radio industry	35	25	38	-3
Sports industry	33	26	38	-5
Advertising and public relations industry	30	32	35	-5
Movie industry	33	25	39	-6
The federal government	33	20	45	-12
Pharmaceutical industry	29	22	47	-18
Healthcare industry	32	16	50	-18
The legal field	27	24	47	-20
Oil and gas industry	20	17	62	-42

At the top of the list is the restaurant industry, with a net positive rating of +50, followed by the computer industry (+47), farming and agriculture (+45), and the grocery industry (+43). Next on the list are the retail industry (+37), the travel industry (+35), accounting (+28), the Internet industry (+24), banking (+24), the real estate industry (+23), education (+23), and the publishing industry (+22). The automobile industry, the telephone industry, and the airline industry also receive net positive ratings from the public.

The oil and gas industry is by far the most negatively rated business sector, with a -42 net rating. Also near the bottom of the list are the legal field (-20), the healthcare industry (-18), the pharmaceutical industry (-18), and the federal government (-12). In addition, Americans rate the movie industry, advertising and public relations, the sports industry, television and radio, and the electric and gas utilities more negatively than positively.

Since 2001, the computer industry has consistently scored at the top of the list, with the exception of Gallup's 2002 poll, in which computers were tied with the restaurant industry in the top spot. The food industries (restaurants, grocery, and agriculture) usually fare well each year, as does the retail industry. The oil and gas industry has ranked at the bottom in each of the past five surveys, while the medical fields (healthcare and pharmaceuticals) and the legal field are also consistently among the most poorly rated.

Images of Education, Accounting, and Agriculture Improve This Year

The public's views of three business sectors improved considerably this year.

Education. Americans' image of education in this country improved dramatically since last year, but is at roughly the same level as it was in 2003. In 2001, education had a +18 rating. This dipped slightly to +11 in 2002, but then jumped to +21 in 2003. Last year, it had a +13 rating, which increased this year to +23.

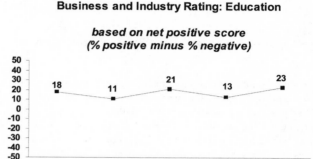

Business and Industry Rating: Education
based on net positive score (% positive minus % negative)

Accounting. Even though the accounting sector fares better this year, these ratings are still lower than they were before the accounting scandals in late 2001 and 2002 at major corporations like Enron and WorldCom. The current score for the accounting sector is +28, up from +20 last year. In 2001, Americans rated this sector with a net +39 score, but after the accounting scandals came to light in 2002, its net score dropped to 0.

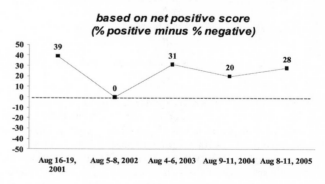

Business and Industry Rating: Accounting
based on net positive score (% positive minus % negative)

Farming and agriculture. The public's view of this sector is higher now than it has been over the past three years, but is essentially the same as it was in 2001. Farming and agriculture received a +35 rating in 2002 and showed little change in 2003 and 2004, before edging up to a +45 score this year.

Views of Oil and Gas, Sports, Movies, and Federal Government Down

Americans' assessment of four business sectors declined this year.

The oil and gas industry. Since Gallup started asking this question, Americans' views of the oil and gas industry have always been at or

**Business and Industry Rating:
Farming and Agriculture**

*based on net positive score
(% positive minus % negative)*

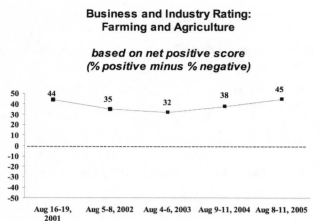

| Aug 16-19, 2001 | Aug 5-8, 2002 | Aug 4-6, 2003 | Aug 9-11, 2004 | Aug 8-11, 2005 |

**Business and Industry Rating:
The Sports Industry**

*based on net positive score
(% positive minus % negative)*

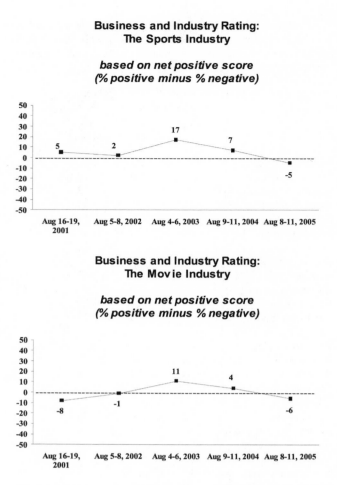

| Aug 16-19, 2001 | Aug 5-8, 2002 | Aug 4-6, 2003 | Aug 9-11, 2004 | Aug 8-11, 2005 |

near the bottom of the list of business sectors. However, with this year's soaring oil prices, the current poll finds that the ratings of the oil and gas industry are the worst that Gallup has ever measured. In 2001, the oil and gas industry received a net negative score of -30. These ratings improved in 2002 and again in 2003, with respective scores of -19 and -8, before growing more negative in 2004 (-37) and 2005 (-42).

**Business and Industry Rating:
The Movie Industry**

*based on net positive score
(% positive minus % negative)*

**Business and Industry Rating:
The Oil and Gas Industry**

*based on net positive score
(% positive minus % negative)*

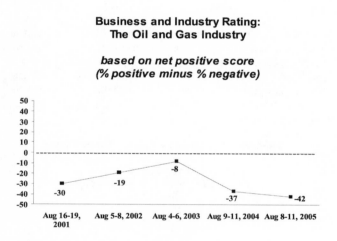

| Aug 16-19, 2001 | Aug 5-8, 2002 | Aug 4-6, 2003 | Aug 9-11, 2004 | Aug 8-11, 2005 |

eral government scored a +6 rating; this decreased to -5 last year and again to -12 this year. Gallup polling this year has shown significant declines in public ratings of Congress and President George W. Bush.

The sports industry. Views of the sports industry dropped more than those for any other business sector this year. In 2001 and 2002, these ratings were essentially neutral, at +5 and +2, respectively. Then, ratings increased to +17 in 2003, before decreasing to +7 last year and then dropping significantly this year, to -5. The decline this year could be a result of revelations about steroid use in Major League Baseball or the National Hockey League strike that canceled the 2004-2005 season.

The movie industry. Ratings of the movie industry in 2005 declined to levels that Gallup first measured in 2001. At that time, the industry received a -8 rating. This improved in 2002 (-1) and 2003 (+11), but dropped slightly in 2004 (+4). Views declined once again this year, to a -6 rating. The movie industry has received a lot of negative press due to a slump in box office revenue for much of the year and complaints about the quality of this year's crop of movies.

The federal government. Gallup's image ratings of the federal government have declined each of the past three years. In 2003, the fed-

**Business and Industry Rating:
The Federal Government**

*based on net positive score
(% positive minus % negative)*

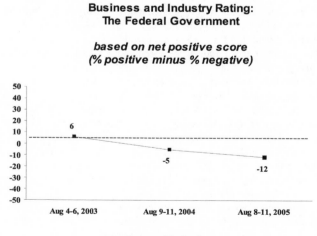

| Aug 4-6, 2003 | Aug 9-11, 2004 | Aug 8-11, 2005 |

Survey Methods

Results are based on telephone interviews with 1,001 national adults, aged 18 and older, conducted Aug. 8-11, 2005. For results based on the total sample of national adults, one can say with 95% confidence that the maximum margin of sampling error is ±3 percentage points.

For results based on the 497 national adults in the Form A half-sample and 504 national adults in the Form B half-sample, the maximum margins of sampling error are ±5 percentage points.

In addition to sampling error, question wording and practical difficulties in conducting surveys can introduce error or bias into the findings of public opinion polls.

August 23, 2005

SHIFT IN PUBLIC PERCEPTIONS ABOUT UNION STRENGTH, INFLUENCE

Majority of Americans continue to approve of labor unions

by Jeffrey M. Jones, Gallup Poll Managing Editor

A recent Gallup poll shows Americans are apparently aware of the difficulties labor unions in the United States are facing. Conducted shortly after several large unions left the AFL-CIO over disagreements about the organization's strategy, the poll finds a majority of Americans predicting that labor unions will be weaker in the future. And in a shift from previous years, a plurality of Americans now say they would like to see unions have more influence in the United States than they have today. Basic support for unions has always been fairly high—with at least a majority approving of unions—and this year's results show little change from the recent past.

The Aug. 8-11 poll, conducted after the AFL-CIO split but before the recent Northwest Airlines mechanics' strike, shows a majority of Americans, 53%, now expect that unions in this country will become weaker in the future. That represents a 12-point increase in the percentage predicting a weakening of union power from last year, and it is the first time a majority has held this view. Nineteen percent of Americans currently believe unions will be stronger in the future and 25% believe there will be no change.

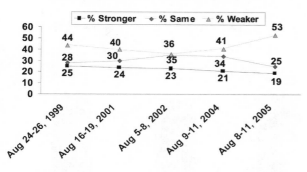

Thinking about the future, do you think labor unions in this country will become — stronger than they are today, the same as today, (or) weaker than they are today?

The current increase in expectations of weaker union power is broadly based, with most subgroups showing an increase compared with last year.

Perhaps as a result of the recognition of the new challenges facing organized labor, there has been a change in the public's expressed preference about union influence. Now, a plurality of 38% say they would like to see unions have more influence than they have today,

while 30% say less influence, and 29% say the same amount. Prior to this year, the plurality response had always been the "same amount" of influence.

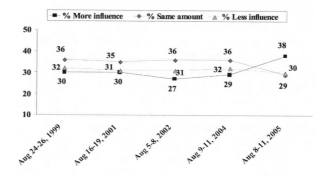

Would you, personally, like to see labor unions in the United States have — more influence than they have today, the same amount as today, (or) less influence than they have today?

Democrats have typically expressed a desire for greater union influence, and the prevalence of Democrats holding that view has increased substantially this year, from 46% to 60%. The percentage of independents saying unions should have more influence this year has also increased since last year, but there has been little change among Republicans.

Preference for Union Influence in the United States

	Democrats		Independents		Republicans	
	2004	2005	2004	2005	2004	2005
	%	%	%	%	%	%
More influence	46	60	30	38	14	17
Same	37	26	36	35	33	26
Less influence	15	12	30	22	50	53

Basic Support for Labor Unions

Despite the changes in perceptions about union influence, Americans' basic attitudes about unions are stable. Fifty-eight percent of Americans approve of labor unions, while 33% disapprove. A year ago, 59% approved, and approval has ranged in a fairly narrow band from 58% to 66% since 1967.

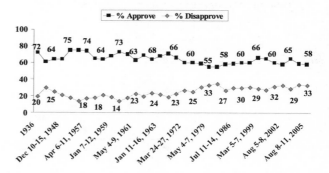

Labor Union Approval Ratings

Union approval was generally higher prior to the 1970s, according to historical Gallup Polls. Save for a few exceptions, from 1936 to 1967 roughly two-thirds or more of Americans said they approved of labor unions. The height of support was 75%, reached in 1953 and 1957, while the low points were readings of 55% in 1979 and 1981.

Support for unions today is strongly related to one's political leaning—Democrats (77%) are twice as likely as Republicans (38%) to approve. Sixty percent of independents approve.

The poll finds 19% of U.S. households claiming union membership. Eleven percent of Americans overall say they are personally members of unions.

Survey Methods

These results are based on telephone interviews with a randomly selected national sample of 1,001 adults, aged 18 and older, conducted Aug. 8-11, 2005. For results based on this sample, one can say with 95% confidence that the maximum error attributable to sampling and other random effects is ±3 percentage points. In addition to sampling error, question wording and practical difficulties in conducting surveys can introduce error or bias into the findings of public opinion polls.

August 23, 2005
RACE, IDEOLOGY, AND SUPPORT FOR AFFIRMATIVE ACTION
Personal politics has little to do with blacks' support

by Jeffrey M. Jones, Gallup Poll Managing Editor

Affirmative action programs remain one of the more controversial social policies in the United States. The Supreme Court ruled in 2003 that race can be a factor in college admissions, as long as it is not the overriding factor. As a whole, the American public is quite divided about affirmative action programs designed to help racial minorities gain admission to colleges and to secure jobs. As one might expect, whites' and blacks' views on the policy differ.

Overall Support for Affirmative Action

Gallup's annual Minority Rights and Relations poll* finds 50% of Americans favor "affirmative action programs for racial minorities," while 42% oppose such programs. Previous surveys in this series have shown similar results, with slightly more Americans expressing support than opposition.

Opinion of Affirmative Action Programs for Racial Minorities

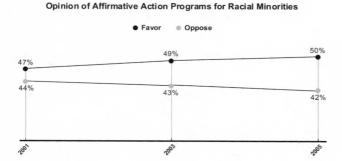

Support for affirmative action has been known to vary depending on how the question is worded, particularly when the question describes the programs in more detail. Surveys conducted in the past five years

by the major polling firms show a range of support from as low as 38% (when the term "racial preferences" is used) to as high as 64%.

Regardless of the wording, all polling on affirmative action shows blacks overwhelmingly support it. In the latest Gallup Poll, 72% of blacks say they favor affirmative action programs, while only 21% are opposed. Among whites, the story is different. Whites are much more divided, with opponents outnumbering supporters by a 49% to 44% margin. The results for both whites and blacks have been consistent over time.

Support for Affirmative Action Programs by race, 2005

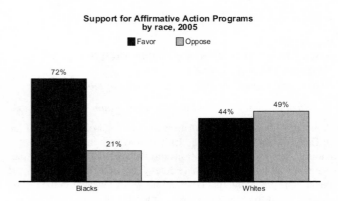

Those views likely stem from the belief among a majority of whites (59%) that blacks in this country have equal job opportunities with whites, while only 23% of blacks agree. Roughly three in four blacks believe that they do not have equal job opportunities in this country.

Black Versus White Support for Affirmative Action

What might explain the differences in support for affirmative action by race? An analysis of the Minority Rights and Relations poll data shows that blacks' support for affirmative action is consistent even for those whose political belief systems differ, suggesting personal politics has little to do with their views on the issue. However, for whites, support for affirmative action programs is highly related to political ideology.

Among blacks, 76% of self-described conservatives, 71% of moderates, and 76% of liberals favor affirmative action programs for minorities.

Support for Affirmative Action Programs by ideology, among blacks

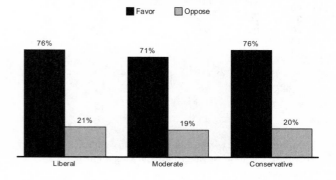

Among whites, on the other hand, most conservatives oppose affirmative action, while more moderates and liberals support than oppose it. Fifty-nine percent of liberal whites, compared with 50%

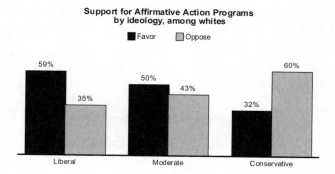

Support for Affirmative Action Programs by ideology, among whites

■ Favor ▢ Oppose

	Liberal	Moderate	Conservative
Favor	59%	50%	32%
Oppose	35%	43%	60%

of moderate whites and 32% of conservative whites say they favor affirmative action programs for minorities.

While there appear to be slight differences for blacks by party, the differences are not statistically significant.

A special statistical analysis (the results of which are not shown here) that allows one to predict Americans' support for affirmative action based on their demographic and political characteristics shows that race is by far the strongest predictor. Ideology is the next strongest, but its effect is only half as large as that found for race.

When the same analysis is run just among blacks, thus controlling for their race, none of the other demographic characteristics (such as gender, age, or education) or political characteristics (ideology and partisanship) is predictive of their support. Only household income comes close to being a significant predictor. Thus, affirmative action views among blacks appear to be almost entirely influenced by their race (or more precisely, the experiences and characteristics that blacks as a group tend to share).

Bottom Line

One of the reasons for the controversy over affirmative action is that it divides the American public. Obviously, blacks and whites differ in their views, and Hispanics also tend to be much more supportive than whites, though not as supportive as blacks. Even among whites, views of affirmative action are polarized, but along political lines.

Results are based on telephone interviews with 2,264 national adults, aged 18 and older, conducted June 6-25, 2005, including oversamples of blacks and Hispanics that are weighted to reflect their proportions in the general population. For results based on the total sample of national adults, one can say with 95% confidence that the maximum margin of sampling error is ±5 percentage points.

Results for the sample of 807 non-Hispanic whites, aged 18 and older, are based on telephone interviews conducted June 6-25, 2005. For results based on the total sample, one can say with 95% confidence that the margin of sampling error is ±7 percentage points.

Results for the sample of 802 blacks, aged 18 and older, are based on telephone interviews conducted June 6-25, 2005. For results based on the total sample, one can say with 95% confidence that the margin of sampling error is ±5 percentage points.

August 24, 2005
IRAQ VERSUS VIETNAM: A COMPARISON OF PUBLIC OPINION
Gallup reviews public opinion during the Vietnam War and the current war in Iraq

by Frank Newport, Gallup Poll Editor in Chief and Joseph Carroll, Assistant Editor

Will the war with Iraq turn into "another Vietnam" for the United States? Sunday, on ABC's "This Week," Republican Sen. Chuck Hagel stated that the situation in Iraq is not "dissimilar to where we were in Vietnam," and that "the longer we stay there, the more similarities [to Vietnam] are going to come together." White House counselor Dan Bartlett responded: "We respect Sen. Hagel. He's a decorated Vietnam War veteran. But we couldn't disagree more."

It is obviously too early to predict the verdict of future historians who will compare the two wars. There are significant differences between them, and the Iraq conflict has not yet approached the depth of U.S. involvement in Vietnam, which saw more than 500,000 U.S. troops deployed in that country by 1968 and which ultimately resulted in more than 58,000 U.S. military deaths.

Still, the Iraq war was a major theme in last year's presidential election, as was Vietnam in the elections of 1968 and 1972—and the Iraq war is now a dominant subject in news coverage, just as Vietnam was in the 1960s and early 1970s.

An important focus today is the battle for public opinion on Iraq—as eventually it was in Vietnam. Recent polls showing declining support for the Iraq war in the United States have received much media attention. This has not only prompted President Bush to make speeches explicitly asking for continuing public support for the war (two speeches on Iraq this week alone), but has, in addition, provoked commentators to begin invoking the Vietnam comparison. The highly publicized protest vigil of Cindy Sheehan outside Bush's ranch in Crawford, Texas, has also provoked memories of the protests that ultimately played such a large part in the Vietnam saga.

Just how comparable are the two wars as far as public opinion is concerned? That's a difficult question to answer in many ways. Many of the questions asked then about Vietnam and now about Iraq are quite specific to the circumstances involved and do not allow for perfect comparisons. Plus, the environment in which the Vietnam War played out was significantly different from the environment now. Vietnam began in the middle of the Cold War, just 20 years after the conclusion of World War II. Iraq began in the middle of a "war on terrorism" declared by the Bush administration in the wake of the terrorist attacks of Sept. 11, 2001.

But, there are several Gallup Poll questions asked during both wars that provide some public opinion comparability. An analysis of the trend patterns for each provides important insights into the nature of public opinion in both situations.

Gallup asked the public to assess whether the United States made a "mistake" in sending troops into Vietnam, and has asked the same question since March 2003 about Iraq. Gallup consistently asked Americans to name the "most important problem" facing the country during the years of both conflicts, and to evaluate how the presidents involved were handling both war situations.

The bottom line: Americans were much quicker to consider the Vietnam War to be a major problem facing the country than has been the case for the Iraq war. But at the same time, a majority of Americans began to call Iraq a "mistake" within about a year and three months of its beginning, while it took over three years for a majority to call Vietnam a mistake. Lyndon Johnson's job approval ratings for handling Vietnam dropped to lower levels than has been the case—so far—for George W. Bush.

Mistake?

One of Gallup's key measures used to assess public support for both the Vietnam War and the current war in Iraq asks Americans whether or not it was a "mistake" to send troops to those countries. The data trends for both wars (that is, every time the question was asked about Vietnam and every time it has been asked about Iraq to date) are presented in the accompanying graphs.

In order to provide a comparative basis between the two wars, the results have been aggregated into quarterly averages and the trend lines have been plotted, based on the first quarter of the year in which each war began in earnest—1965 for Vietnam and 2003 for Iraq. Gallup first asked the "mistake" question about the Vietnam War in August 1965 (the third quarter of the first year of the war) and about the Iraq war in March 2003 (the first quarter of the first year of the war).

As the graph illustrates, Americans have become negative about the war in Iraq more quickly than they did for the Vietnam War.

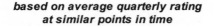

Mistake to Send Troops to Vietnam/Iraq?
percentage saying "yes"

*based on average quarterly rating
at similar points in time*

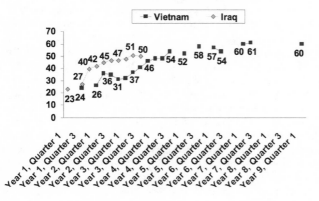

The latest quarterly average for Iraq shows that 50% say it was a mistake to send troops (the most recent single measure on this indicator, from an Aug. 5-7 Gallup Poll, shows 54% saying the war was a mistake).

In the comparable quarter for the Vietnam War (the third quarter of the war's third year—that is, the third quarter of 1967), Gallup found 41% saying the conflict was a mistake. It was not until the third quarter of the fourth year of the Vietnam War (August-September 1968) that a majority of Americans said the war was a mistake. In short, it took longer for a majority of Americans to view the Vietnam War as a mistake than has been the case for Iraq.

(There is one caveat in these comparisons: A larger percentage of Americans in the Vietnam years said they did not have an opinion about Vietnam than has been the case for Iraq.)

When the war in Iraq started in March 2003, only 23% of adults nationwide said it was a mistake to send troops to Iraq, while three-quarters said it was not a mistake. The percentage of Americans saying it was a mistake gradually increased, and by the end of 2003, it

reached the 40% range. By June 2004, just one year and three months after the war began, a majority of Americans reached the conclusion that the war was a mistake.

Since that time, there have been significant fluctuations in the public's responses to this question—usually in reaction to events relating to Iraq.

Mistake to Send Troops to Iraq?

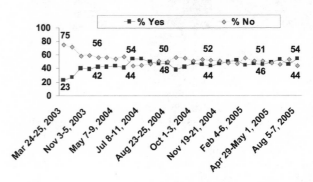

About six months after Johnson began large-scale U.S. involvement in Vietnam in 1965, Gallup found just 24% of Americans saying it was a mistake to send troops, while 60% said it was not. At least a plurality of all Americans continued to say it was not a mistake until July 1967, almost two and a half years after the United States had increased its military presence in Vietnam. In that July poll, a plurality still supported the notion that it was not a mistake to send troops to Vietnam, by a 48% to 41% margin.

Mistake to Send Troops to Vietnam?

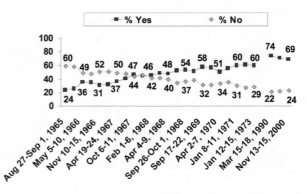

The tide began to turn by October 1967, when more Americans said it was a mistake to send troops to Vietnam (47%) than said it was not (44%). For nearly a year, this pattern persisted.

Finally, in an August 1968 poll, Gallup found for the first time that a majority of Americans, 53%, said it was a mistake to send troops to Vietnam. This was three and a half years into the war.

(Opposition to the Vietnam War, as measured by this "mistake" question, continued to grow, as the percentage of Americans who said it was a mistake averaged 55% in 1969 and 1970, then increased to 60% in 1971 and 1973. When asked this question in retrospect, Americans have continued to say they feel it was a mistake to send troops to Vietnam. Most recently, three polls conducted from 1990 to 2000 found about 7 in 10 Americans saying it was a mistake.)

Most Important Problem

Another measure of public opinion about the nation's involvement in war is provided by responses to Gallup's long-term, open-ended trend asking Americans to name "the most important problem facing the country today."

The number of Americans who identified the Vietnam War as the most important problem facing the country fluctuated significantly over the course of the war. But only a year and a half into the war, in August 1966, an overwhelming 69% identified Vietnam or the war as the nation's top problem. These responses don't necessarily indicate that 69% of Americans thought involvement in Vietnam was a bad decision. But the fact that about 7 out of 10 Americans said Vietnam was the nation's top problem by 1966 shows how quickly it began to dominate the nation's consciousness.

The open-ended mentions of Iraq in response to this question have been much less dominant so far, ranging from 5% in August 2003 to 27% in the latest poll and in a June 2004 poll. (Gallup had found higher percentages mentioning Iraq as the top problem leading up to the start of the war.) Today—about two years and five months after the war began—27% of Americans mention Iraq as the top problem, essentially as high as this measure has gone since the war began in 2003.

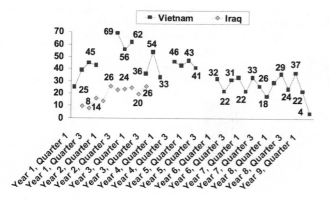

Most Important Problem Facing the Country based on average quarterly rating at similar points in time

War Approval

Lyndon Johnson

After some 184,000 troops were deployed to South Vietnam by the end of 1965, Gallup found majority approval for Johnson's handling of Vietnam in four separate polls.

But this was the only time that a majority would support Johnson's handling of Vietnam.

By mid-April of 1966, fewer than half of all Americans, 47%, approved of Johnson's handling of Vietnam. From May to December 1966, Johnson's Vietnam approval showed a slight dip, averaging 42% during that period. In May and June 1966, for the first time, more Americans disapproved than approved of Johnson's handling of the war.

A decline that was more obvious occurred in 1967, with approval averaging 37% for the year and falling as low as 27% in August, which would be the low point in Johnson's administration.

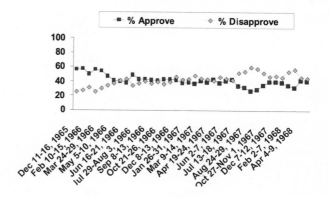

Lyndon Johnson's Approval on Vietnam

George W. Bush

Bush's Iraq approval ratings were quite steady, with an average of 54%, prior to the start of the war in March 2003. Immediately following the initiation of military action in Iraq, Bush's approval on Iraq spiked to 71%. It increased to 76% after the fall of Baghdad in mid-April. A month and a half after Bush announced the end of major combat in Iraq on May 1, 2003, his approval rating on Iraq decreased to 63%.

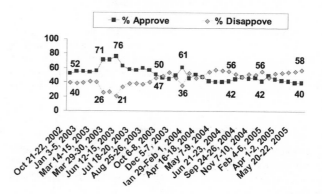

George W. Bush's Approval on Iraq

Bush's Iraq approval remained quite steady in July and August 2003, ranging between 57% and 60%. Moving into the fall of 2003, the ratings started to decrease, from 51% in September to 47% in October to 45% in November. In early December, Bush's Iraq rating was 50%. This increased to 61% in an early January 2004 poll, the first Gallup Poll conducted after the capture of Saddam Hussein.

After the post-capture 61% rating, Bush's Iraq approval dropped to 46% in late January and early February 2004. These ratings increased slightly to 51% in March, before dropping back to 48% in April amid reports describing numerous attacks against U.S. soldiers in Iraq. After media reports in early May detailed incidents of U.S. soldiers abusing Iraqi prisoners at Abu Ghraib, Bush's Iraq approval dropped to 41%. In the last half of 2004, Bush's ratings on Iraq improved, ranging from 42% to 48%.

Bush's approval ratings on Iraq have been in the low 40% range throughout this year, with the exception of a 50% rating following the elections in Iraq in late January. His most recent Gallup Poll rating, from a June 24-26 poll, is the lowest of his administration, at 40%.

In summary, Bush's ratings on Iraq—so far—have been higher than Johnson's ratings on Vietnam. Bush now averages a 51% approval rating on Iraq across 36 polls conducted from October 2002 through June 2005. Johnson averaged only 41% over 38 polls from December 1965 to May 1968.

Summary

Although public support for both the Vietnam and the Iraq wars was strong as each conflict began, at least as measured by Gallup's "mistake" question, opposition to the latter has escalated much more quickly. Within a year and three months of the Iraq war's inception, a majority of Americans said it was a mistake. It wasn't until over three years after the inception of the Vietnam War that a majority called it a mistake.

At the same, Americans much more quickly perceived that the Vietnam War was a major problem facing the United States, with over two-thirds naming it as the nation's most important problem within the war's second year. By contrast, even today, some two years and five months after the Iraq war began, only a little more than a fourth of Americans say it is the nation's top problem.

In short, Americans have been quicker to oppose the Iraq war, but less likely to consider it the top problem facing the nation.

With all of this, it is worth remembering that a good deal of the significant societal impact of the Vietnam War did not take place until long after the war's two-and-a-half-year mark (essentially where the Iraq war is today). Vietnam continued to be a major factor in American life as late as the presidential election of 1972—some seven years after it began. And—as noted above—the cost of the Vietnam War in terms of human lives was ultimately many degrees higher than the cost of the Iraq war so far. But the fact that a majority of Americans already say Iraq was a mistake, and that it has become perhaps the most significant issue facing the Bush administration today suggests that comparisons between the two situations are not totally unreasonable.

Survey Methods

These results are based on telephone interviews with randomly selected national samples of at least 1,000 adults, aged 18 and older. For results based on these samples, one can say with 95% confidence that the maximum error attributable to sampling and other random effects is ±3 percentage points. In addition to sampling error, question wording and practical difficulties in conducting surveys can introduce error or bias into the findings of public opinion polls.

August 26, 2005
PUBLIC FAVORS VOLUNTARY PRAYER FOR PUBLIC SCHOOLS
But strongly supports moment of silence rather than spoken prayer

by David W. Moore, Gallup Poll Senior Editor

A new Gallup survey confirms that whatever arguments political leaders make about separation of church and state in the public schools, most Americans don't seem to be persuaded. Large majorities continue to favor allowing voluntary prayer in public schools, and believe

that religion has too little presence in them. Still, if given a choice, most people prefer a moment of silence, rather than a spoken prayer.

The poll, conducted Aug. 8-11, finds 76% of Americans favor "a constitutional amendment to allow voluntary prayer in public schools," while just 23% oppose such an amendment. This is not new. In 1983, a similar poll showed 81% in favor, and polls in the past decade show about three-quarters of Americans consistently supportive.

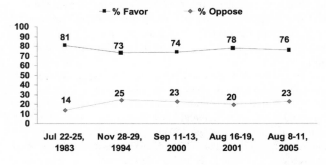

Amendment to Allow Voluntary Prayer in Public Schools

A major stumbling block for any such amendment would be the type of voluntary prayer allowed. The poll shows that only 23% of Americans prefer some type of spoken prayer, while 69% favor a moment of silence for contemplation or silent prayer. These views are essentially the same as those expressed a decade ago in a similar poll.

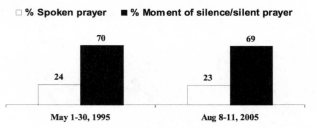

If you had a choice, which would you prefer in the local public schools: spoken prayer, (or) a moment of silence for contemplation or silent prayer?

Related to their support of school prayer, most Americans also believe that religion should have a greater "presence" in public schools. Just 11% say religion already has "too much" presence, and 27% say it has the right amount. A clear majority of Americans, 60%, believe religion has "too little" presence. These views are similar to those expressed in a 2001 Gallup survey.

Not surprisingly, views on this matter are highly related to religious orientation, and to a lesser extent, party affiliation.

- The more frequently people attend church, the more likely they are to favor a constitutional amendment permitting voluntary prayer—from 88% among people who attend weekly to 63% among those who seldom or never attend.
- Protestants are most likely to favor school prayer (82%), followed closely by Catholics (75%). A majority of non-Christians oppose a constitutional amendment, by 55% to 44%.
- Among party groups, Republicans are most likely to support an amendment (88%), but both independents (72%) and Democrats (67%) also give majority support.

Thinking about the presence that religion currently has in public schools in this country, do you think religion has too much of a presence in public schools, about the right amount, (or) too little of a presence in public schools?

☐ % Too much   ▨ % Right amount   ■ % Too little

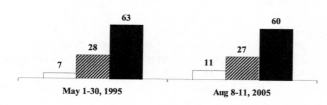

May 1-30, 1995	Aug 8-11, 2005
7 28 63	11 27 60

Please tell me whether you favor or oppose a constitutional amendment to allow voluntary prayer in public schools.

	Favor %	Oppose %
Overall	76	23
Church attendance		
Weekly	88	11
Nearly weekly/Monthly	82	17
Seldom/Never	63	35
Religious affiliation		
Protestants	83	17
Catholics	75	21
Non-Christians	44	55
Party		
Republicans	88	12
Independents	72	25
Democrats	67	32

A majority of all major demographic subgroups of Americans surveyed prefer a moment of silent prayer to spoken prayer. The greatest support for spoken prayer is found among weekly churchgoers (39%), while only 10% of infrequent churchgoers favor that type of prayer.

Protestants (30%) are twice as likely as Catholics (15%) to want a spoken prayer, and three times as likely as non-Christians (10%).

Differences are slight among party groups, from 26% support for spoken prayer among Republicans to 21% among Democrats.

If you had a choice, which would you prefer in the local public schools—[ROTATED: spoken prayer, (or) a moment of silence for contemplation or silent prayer]?

	Spoken prayer %	Moment of silence/ silent prayer %	NEITHER (vol.) %	BOTH (vol.) %
Overall	23	69	5	3
Religious attendance				
Weekly	39	57	2	2
Nearly weekly/Monthly	24	70	2	4
Seldom/Never	10	80	8	2
Religious affiliation				
Protestants	30	63	3	4
Catholics	15	80	4	*
Non-Christians	10	75	15	0

	Spoken prayer %	Moment of silence/ silent prayer %	NEITHER (vol.) %	BOTH (vol.) %
Party				
Republicans	26	67	2	5
Independents	22	70	6	2
Democrats	21	71	6	2

(vol.) = volunteered response

While 60% of all Americans believe that religion has too little of a presence in public schools, 79% of frequent churchgoers believe that. Only 42% of infrequent churchgoers say there is too little religious presence.

Protestants (71%) are much more likely than Catholics (51%) to express that view, while non-Christians are more likely to say there is too much presence (38%) than too little (22%).

Republicans as a whole give responses similar to those of Protestants, with 73% saying there is too little religious presence. Fifty-six percent of independents and 51% of Democrats agree with that perception.

Thinking about the presence that religion currently has in public schools in this country, do you think religion has—[ROTATED: too much of a presence in public schools, about the right amount, (or) too little of a presence in public schools]?

	Too much of a presence %	About the right amount %	Too little of a presence %	No opinion %
Overall	11	27	60	2
Religious attendance				
Weekly	3	18	79	0
Nearly weekly/Monthly	5	28	65	2
Seldom/Never	20	35	42	3
Religious affiliation				
Protestants	6	22	71	1
Catholics	8	38	51	3
Non-Christians	38	37	22	3
Party				
Republicans	5	20	73	2
Independents	11	31	56	2
Democrats	16	31	51	2

Survey Methods

Results are based on telephone interviews with 1,001 national adults, aged 18 and older, conducted Aug. 8-11, 2005. For results based on the total sample of national adults, one can say with 95% confidence that the maximum margin of sampling error is ±3 percentage points.

In addition to sampling error, question wording and practical difficulties in conducting surveys can introduce error or bias into the findings of public opinion polls.

August 26, 2005

BUSH APPROVAL RATING CONTINUES TO DROP

Current 40% approval is lowest of administration to date

by Frank Newport, Gallup Poll Editor in Chief
and Jeff Jones, Managing Editor

A new Gallup Poll reflects further erosion in President George W. Bush's job approval rating, continuing the slow but steady decline evident throughout the year so far. The poll—conducted Aug. 22-25—puts Bush's job approval rating at 40% and his disapproval rating at 56%. Both are the most negative ratings of the Bush administration. Bush's previous low point in approval was 44% (July 25-28, 2005) and his previous high point in disapproval was 53% (June 24-26, 2005).

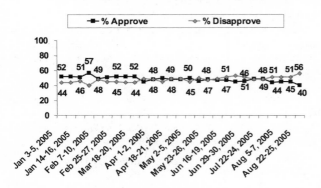

Bush's average approval rating for the last three Gallup Polls—all conducted in August—is 43%. The rolling average has been steadily declining throughout the year. Bush's average approval ratings for January, February, and March of this year were in the 50% to 52% range, but they then began declining slowly in subsequent months. Bush's average approval rating in May was 48%, declining to 46% in June, rising slightly in July, and then declining again to the current three-poll average of 43%.

The following chart shows the rolling average for Bush's job approval rating this year, with each average consisting of three poll measurements.

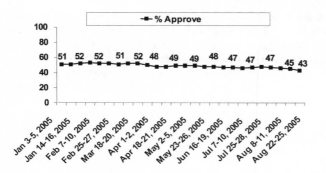

The current poll finds a drop in support for Bush among independents, and a small drop in support among Republicans to the lowest level of his administration.

In two July polls in which Bush averaged an overall 49% approval rating, an average of 46% of independents approved. In the subsequent three polls (July 25-28, Aug. 5-7, and Aug. 8-11), Bush's overall approval average dropped to 45%, and his average support among independents fell to 37%. Now, in the current poll, 32% of independents approve. (An average of 41% of independents have approved across all 2005 polls to date, excluding the most recent poll.)

Bush's support among Republicans—although still very high—is now at the lowest level of his administration. His current 82% approval rating among Republicans is down from the 85%, 86%, 87%, 87%, and 86% recorded in the last five polls prior to this one, and is below the 89% Republican approval rating he has received across all 2005 polls before the most recent poll. He has averaged a 92% approval rating among Republicans for his entire presidency.

Bush's approval rating among Democrats remains very low. His current 13% is down slightly from his 2005 average (excluding the current poll) of 17% and down from his administration average among Democrats of 35%.

Bush Approval by Party Identification

	Current poll	2005 average (not including current poll)	Presidency average (2001-2005)
	%	%	%
Overall	40	49	61
Republicans	82	89	92
Independents	32	41	56
Democrats	13	17	35

Historical Comparisons

There have been seven U.S. presidents re-elected to a second term since World War II (although two of them—Harry Truman and Lyndon Johnson—had initially ascended to the presidency without being elected). Here's where they stood in August of the year after their re-election (or, in the case of Truman, in June):

President	Time	Approval rating
Harry Truman	June 1949 (No July or August 1949 measure)	58%
Dwight Eisenhower	August 1957	63
Lyndon B. Johnson	August 1965	65
Richard Nixon	August 1973	34
Ronald Reagan	August 1985	61
Bill Clinton	August 1997	61
George W. Bush	August 2005	43

Bush's current 43% job approval rating is the lowest of all of these presidents with the exception of Richard Nixon, who was beset by the woes of Watergate by the summer of 1973. (Of course, Bush's most recent 40% is lower still by comparison.)

Satisfaction

The drop in President Bush's job approval rating has been accompanied by a continuing drop in the American public's overall satisfaction with the way things are going in the United States today.

Just 34% of Americans are satisfied with the way things are going in this country in the Aug. 22-25 Gallup Poll, while 62% are dissatisfied. This is the lowest satisfaction level of the entire Bush administration to date and is the lowest recorded by Gallup since January 1996.

The average satisfaction rating for 2005 before this poll has been 41%. The average for the five June, July, and August polls before this one in which satisfaction has been rated is 40%.

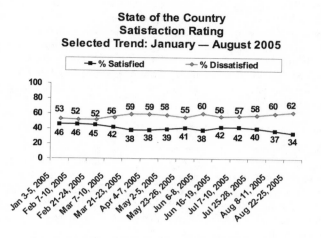

State of the Country Satisfaction Rating
Selected Trend: January — August 2005

Thirty-five percent of poll respondents identified themselves as Democrats, 29% as Republicans, and 34% as independents.

Survey Methods

These results are based on telephone interviews with a randomly selected national sample of 1,007 adults, aged 18 and older, conducted Aug. 22-25, 2005. For results based on this sample, one can say with 95% confidence that the maximum error attributable to sampling and other random effects is ±3 percentage points. In addition to sampling error, question wording and practical difficulties in conducting surveys can introduce error or bias into the findings of public opinion polls.

August 30, 2005

NEARLY TWO IN THREE CONSUMERS SAY THE ECONOMY IS GETTING WORSE
Surging oil and gas prices lead Americans' economic concerns

by Dennis Jacobe, Chief Economist, The Gallup Organization

As oil prices soar past $70 a barrel in response to the potential damage created by Hurricane Katrina, there are widespread predictions of another surge in gas prices at the pump, and a slowdown in the U.S. economy. While the coming "soft-patch" in the economy will most likely be attributed to Katrina, the reality is that consumers' expectations for the economy were already tumbling in response to increasing gas prices prior to the storm hitting southern Louisiana on Monday (Aug. 30).

In a new Gallup Poll (Aug. 22-25), taken about a week before Katrina hit the Gulf Coast, two in three consumers say the economy is getting worse while only 28% say it is getting better. This suggests that the modest declines reported by both the University of Michigan on Friday (Aug. 26) and the Conference Board on Monday

(Aug. 30) were significantly out-of-date even as they were announced. Of course, Katrina, and the storm's aftermath, are likely to significantly exacerbate consumers' already plummeting expectations.

Consumer Expectations for the Economy

In this latest poll, 63% of consumers say current economic conditions in the country as a whole are "getting worse." This is the highest level of negative economic expectations recorded by Gallup since just before the beginning of the war in Iraq (March 3-5, 2003) when the percentage of consumers saying economic conditions were getting worse reached 67%.

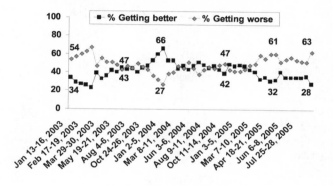

Economic Outlook
Selected Trend: January 2003 – July 2005

Most Important Economic Problem

The worsening of consumer expectations appears to be closely associated with consumer concerns about surging fuel and oil prices. When asked to name the most important economic problem facing the country today, 34% of consumers point to increasing fuel and oil prices as August comes to a close. This is up 20 percentage points from July 25-28 and 15 percentage points from April 18-21. It is also more than twice the percentage of consumers who mention unemployment/jobs/wages and three times the number who point to the war with Iraq as the most important problem.

Most Important Economic Problem
(numbers shown in percentages)

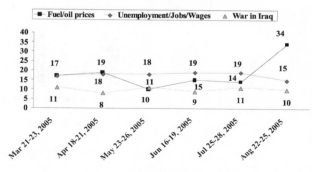

Gas Prices and Consumer Expectations

In fact, the relationship between higher gas prices at the pump and consumers' negative expectations for the economy is stunning. Gasoline prices averaged $1.78 as of Jan. 3, 2005 according to the Energy Information Administration. Gas prices peaked for the first half of the year at $2.28 on April 11, 2005, and were at $2.24 on May 2, 2005. The percentage of consumers saying economic conditions were getting worse increased from 42% in early January to 61% in late April and early May.

Gas prices fell steadily from their April peak, declining to $2.12 a gallon by early June. Over the same period, the percentage of consumers saying economic conditions were getting worse dropped to 55% in June from the 61% of late April and early May.

Since June, gasoline prices have significantly increased once more and averaged $2.61 a gallon as of Aug. 27, 2005—up $0.83 from January. Although there was a lag in the consumer response to these price increases, the percentage of consumers saying the economy is getting worse surged to 63% in Gallup's Aug. 22-25 poll—up 11 percentage points from early August and 21 percentage points from January.

	Price of gasoline $	Those saying "getting worse" %
Early January	1.78	42
Early February	1.91	44
Early March	2.00	50
Early April	2.22	56
Early May	2.24	61
Early June	2.12	55
Early July	2.33	54
Early August	2.37	52
Late August	2.61	63

Family Finances

More than 4 in 10 Americans say they are worried about their family's finances right now with 17% saying they are "very worried" and 27% saying they are "somewhat worried." However, the amount of worry differs significantly by income. One in four consumers having annual incomes of $100,000 or more say they are worried about their family's finances. Nearly twice as many (45%) of those with annual incomes of between $30,000 and $50,000 say they are worried. And, two in three of those with incomes under $30,000 a year say they are worried about their family's finances.

Concern About Family Finances

□ % Yes, worried   ■ % No, not worried

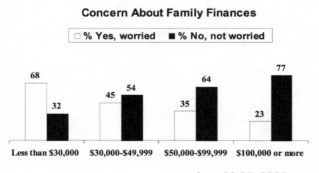

Aug. 22-25, 2005

In a letter released July 18, 2005, Federal Reserve Board Chairman Alan Greenspan told Congress that higher energy prices may restrain economic growth by three-quarters of a percentage point this year. While this doesn't sound too bad, this prediction preceded the August surge in pump prices and the arrival of Hurricane Katrina.

Past Gallup polling suggests that there is a severe psychological effect on consumers when gas prices at the pump hit $3.00 a gallon. Whether gas prices reach that level on average across the nation and

whether it has a more severe impact on consumers or not, clearly today's gas prices and the plunging consumer expectations they create threaten another economic soft-patch.

How likely are consumers to continue buying SUVs, even at "employee prices" given the surge in fuel costs? Can the housing boom continue as the cost of heating and cooling those homes soars? More importantly, what will happen to consumer spending as higher gas prices disproportionately impact lower- and middle-income families and those who have to drive long distances to reach their jobs?

Right now, it looks like the "Oil Grinch" may succeed in stealing Christmas, particularly from many lower- and middle-income consumers as well as the retailers and other companies that serve them.

Survey Methods

Results are based on telephone interviews with 1,007 national adults, aged 18 and older, conducted Aug. 22-25, 2005. For results based on the total sample of national adults, one can say with 95% confidence that the maximum margin of sampling error is ±3 percentage points. In addition to sampling error, question wording and practical difficulties in conducting surveys can introduce error or bias into the findings of public opinion polls.

August 30, 2005
AMERICANS IN LABOR UNIONS
Who wears the union label?

by Joseph Carroll, Gallup Poll Assistant Editor

Last month, the AFL-CIO split, with more than 4 million members of the Teamsters union, the Service Employees International Union, and the United Food and Commercial Workers union disaffiliating themselves from the labor federation.

About 1 in 10 Americans currently say they belong to a labor union. A review of historical Gallup Poll data shows that represents a decrease from the 1940s and 1950s, when roughly one in six belonged to a union. Current polling shows that union membership is higher among government workers than among private-sector or nonprofit employees, among middle-aged Americans than among younger adults or senior citizens, among men than among women, and in middle-income households than among higher-income or lower-income households. Union membership is lower in the South than in other regions across the country.

Membership Trends

Since the 1940s, Gallup has asked Americans whether they belong to a labor union. An analysis of the results to this question at selected points in time since the mid-1940s shows that reported membership in unions has held steady for the past 20 years, but it is slightly lower now than it was from the mid-1940s through the mid-1970s. The following analysis is based on yearly averages of self-reported union membership on a decade-by-decade basis over the past 60 years.

It is important to note that Gallup's reported estimates of union membership are slightly lower than the Bureau of Labor Statistics reports, mostly attributable to the fact that Gallup has historically asked this question of all Americans and the Bureau of Labor Statistics measures wage and salary workers.

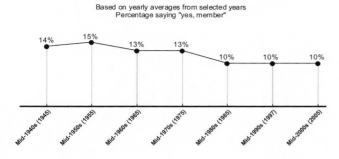

Selected Trend: Labor Union Membership

Based on yearly averages from selected years
Percentage saying "yes, member"

14% — 15% — 13% — 13% — 10% — 10% — 10%

Mid-1940s (1945) — Mid-1950s (1955) — Mid-1960s (1965) — Mid-1970s (1975) — Mid-1980s (1985) — Mid-1990s (1997) — Mid-2000s (2005)

The trend in union membership shows a slight, gradual decline over the past 60 years. In 1945, an average of 14% of Americans surveyed that year said they belonged to a labor union. Union membership was essentially the same in 1955, with an average of 15% of Americans reporting membership that year.

But then, self-reported membership began to decline gradually. In 1965 and 1975, 13% of Americans said they belonged to a union. In 1985, the average fell to 10%. These results have shown no change in Gallup Polls conducted in 1997 and 2005. (Gallup did not include its labor union question polls conducted in 1995 and 1996, so the results from 1997 were used in this analysis.)

Who's a Member?

To examine union members more closely, Gallup aggregated the results of its past five August surveys* that asked this question. The results show some interesting differences among segments of the population.

Among all adults who say they are employed full time or part time, 12% report that they belong to a labor union. Government employees are substantially more likely to be union members than are employees of private companies or nonprofit organizations. Roughly a third of government employees (31%) belong to a labor union. This compares with 12% of employees of nonprofit organizations and 8% of employees working for private businesses.

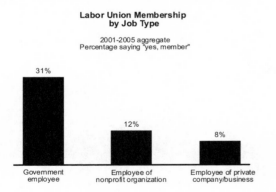

Labor Union Membership by Job Type

2001-2005 aggregate
Percentage saying "yes, member"

31% — Government employee
12% — Employee of nonprofit organization
8% — Employee of private company/business

Americans who live in the South are less likely than those living elsewhere in the country to belong to a labor union. Only 4% of Southerners say they are members, while 10% of Westerners, 11% of Easterners, and 11% of Midwesterners report membership.

About one in eight adults between the ages of 30 and 64 say they are union members. This is significantly higher than it is among 18-

Labor Union Membership by Region

2001-2005 aggregate
Percentage saying "yes, member"

11% — East
11% — Midwest
4% — South
10% — West

Labor Union Membership by Age

2001-2005 aggregate
Percentage saying "yes, member"

4% — 18- to 29-year-olds
11% — 30- to 49-year-olds
12% — 50- to 64-year-olds
5% — 65 years and older

to 29-year-olds, of whom only 4% report membership, and among those aged 65 and older, 5% of whom are members.

Americans in middle-income households are slightly more likely than those in higher-income households and lower-income households to belong to a union. Only 5% of those living in households earning less than $30,000 per year belong to a labor union. This compares with 12% among those living in households earning between $30,000 and $75,000 per year and 9% among those earning $75,000 or more per year.

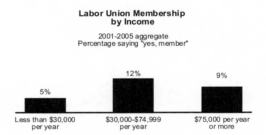

Labor Union Membership by Income

2001-2005 aggregate
Percentage saying "yes, member"

5% — Less than $30,000 per year
12% — $30,000-$74,999 per year
9% — $75,000 per year or more

Men are twice as likely as women to report being in a union, by a 12% to 6% margin. The results among employed men and women show little difference, with 13% of men and 10% of women saying they belong to a union.

Republicans, at 6%, are slightly less likely than Democrats (10%) or independents (10%) to say they belong to labor unions.

The data also show some slight variations by education level. Thirteen percent of those with postgraduate educations belong to a labor union, most likely teachers or college professors. This compares with 7% of college graduates, 10% of those with some college education, and 7% of those with a high school diploma or less.

Results are based on in-person telephone interviews with at least 1,000 national adults, aged 18 and older. For results based on the total sample of national adults, one can say with 95% confidence that the margin of sampling error is ±3 percentage points.

In addition to sampling error, question wording and practical difficulties in conducting surveys can introduce error or bias into the findings of public opinion polls.

September 1, 2005
SEVEN IN TEN AMERICANS HURT BY GAS PRICES

Public approval for President Bush's handling of the issue: 20%

by David W. Moore, Gallup Poll Senior Editor

As the price of oil temporarily surged above $70 a barrel in the wake of Hurricane Katrina, a new CNN/*USA Today*/Gallup survey, conducted Aug. 28-30, finds that rising gas prices are already negatively affecting most Americans. About 7 in 10 report suffering hardship from higher gas prices, with widespread expectations that prices will rise even higher during the next year.

More people blame the oil companies than the politicians in Washington for the higher prices, although a substantial number of people also blame the Bush administration and to a lesser extent the Republican and Democratic members of Congress. Only 20% of Americans approve of the way President George W. Bush has handled the issue.

The poll was conducted before Bush said that he would consider releasing oil from the nation's Strategic Petroleum Reserve, a policy officially announced Aug. 31 by the U.S. Department of Energy. While the action caused a drop in crude oil prices that same day, wholesale fuel prices continued to rise in afternoon trading.

According to the poll, 69% of Americans say they have experienced a hardship because of rising gas prices, including 18% who say it is a "severe" hardship that affects their "ability to maintain [their] current standard of living."

Have recent price increases in gasoline caused any financial hardship for you or your household?

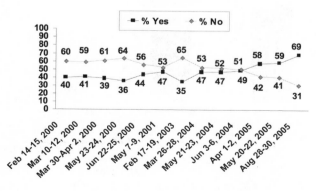

Expectations are for a continuing increase in prices. The average price people report paying for a gallon of gas these days is $2.65, while the average expectation for the price of gas one year from now is $3.16—a 51 cent per gallon increase.

Political Fallout

The poll shows that more people blame the U.S. oil companies than blame politicians, with 54% of Americans saying the oil companies are to blame a "great deal," and another 30% saying a "moderate amount."

Still, 63% of Americans blame the Bush administration either a great deal or moderate amount, while 57% blame congressional Republicans. Fewer Americans assign blame to congressional Democrats (46%).

How much do you blame each of the following for the recent increase in gasoline prices—a great deal, a moderate amount, not much, or not at all? How about—[RANDOM ORDER]?

2005 Aug 28-30 (sorted by "great deal")	Great deal %	Great deal/ moderate amount %	Not much/ not at all %
Oil companies in the U.S.	54	84	15
The Bush administration	38	63	36
The Republicans in Congress	27	57	40
The Democrats in Congress	12	46	50

Bush's approval rating on handling the issue is down seven percentage points from May 2005, when it was at 27%. Bush's rating on gas prices is by far the lowest approval rating on the issues measured in the poll. Bush scores best on his handling of terrorism, with a 53% approval rating. On all other issues, a majority of Americans disapprove of Bush's performance.

Do you approve or disapprove of the way George W. Bush is handling—[RANDOM ORDER]?

2005 Aug 28-30 (sorted by "approve")	Approve %	Disapprove %
Terrorism	53	44
Foreign affairs	43	52
The situation in Iraq	40	59
The economy	38	60
Healthcare policy	32	60
Gas prices	20	76

Bush's overall job approval rating is 45%, up from 40% a week ago, which was the lowest rating of his presidency. An analysis of the ratings over the three-day interviewing period shows a slight increase in support for the president after Hurricane Katrina struck some of the Gulf Coast states. It is not unusual for presidents to experience an increase in public support following national tragedies.

Gas Prices and New Cars

Most Americans (75%) say that when they buy or lease their next vehicle, gas mileage will be a more important consideration for them than it was in the past.

When you buy or lease your next vehicle, will the car's gas mileage be a more important consideration for you than it has been in the past, or will it not be any more important to you?

2005 Aug 28-30	More impor- tant	Not more impor- tant	LESS IMPOR- TANT (vol.)	DON'T DRIVE (vol.)	No opinion
	75%	22	*	1	2

*Less than 0.5%

Only a bare majority, 55%, would consider purchasing a gas-electric hybrid vehicle. Still, interest is strong among this group of people. Most of those who would consider a hybrid also say they would make the purchase even if it cost $3,000 more than the "standard model of the same vehicle." The devoted hybrid respondents represent 45% of all Americans.

Suppose you were going to buy a new vehicle. Would you seriously consider buying a car or SUV that is a gas-electric hybrid, or not? If the hybrid vehicle cost $3,000 more than the standard model of the same vehicle, would you still seriously consider buying it, or not?

	2005 Aug 28-30 %
Yes, seriously consider	55
(Even if $3,000 more)	(45)
(Not if $3,000 more)	(9)
(unsure)	(1)
No, would not	43
No opinion	2

Survey Methods

Results are based on telephone interviews with 1,007 national adults, aged 18 and older, conducted Aug. 28-30, 2005. For results based on the total sample of national adults, one can say with 95% confidence that the maximum margin of sampling error is ±3 percentage points. For results based on the 507 national adults in the Form A half-sample and 500 national adults in the Form B half-sample, the maximum margins of sampling error are ±5 percentage points.

In addition to sampling error, question wording and practical difficulties in conducting surveys can introduce error or bias into the findings of public opinion polls.

September 2, 2005
AMERICANS SYMPATHIZE WITH PROTESTING MOM
No evidence her campaign has changed public attitudes on Iraq

by Lydia Saad, Gallup Poll Senior Editor

Most Americans sympathize with Cindy Sheehan, the grieving mother who led an anti-war protest outside President George W. Bush's Texas ranch for most of August. A majority of Americans also say Bush should meet with her. Still, less than half of Americans agree with the actions Sheehan has taken in her opposition to the Iraq war. And, despite her efforts to draw public attention to anti-war arguments, Sheehan's tactics have not appeared to increase public opposition to the Iraq war.

Americans supported the Iraq war as it began in March 2003, but attitudes began to sour significantly about a year ago, and have remained characteristically negative through most of this summer. Today, more than half of Americans disapprove of the way Bush is handling Iraq, think the original decision to go to war was a mistake, and favor at least partial troop withdrawal from Iraq.

- Only 40% of Americans approve, while 59% disapprove of the way Bush is handling Iraq—nearly identical to results in late June, when 40% approved and 58% disapproved.
- Fifty-three percent of Americans think going to war in Iraq was a mistake, similar to the 54% who said this in early August.
- Fifty-three percent of Americans favor a reduction of U.S. troops in Iraq, similar to the 56% in August. Today's percentage includes 26% who prefer withdrawing all troops, and 27% who favor withdrawing some troops.
- Although Sheehan and her supporters have called for an immediate withdrawal of all U.S. troops, the percentage of Americans with this view has actually fallen since early August, from 33% to 26%, while the percentage in favor of sending more troops has increased slightly.

Which comes closest to your view about what the U.S. should now do about the number of U.S. troops in Iraq?

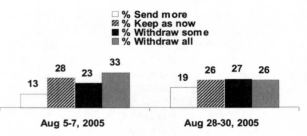

Sheehan's Plea for Meeting Gets Mixed Reaction

Sheehan's 24-year-old son was killed in Iraq in April, and Sheehan demanded that Bush defend his administration's rationale for going to war in Iraq in a face-to-face meeting with her in which she can also air her grievances.

Although Bush staff members have met with Sheehan, the president's refusal to meet with her during this episode (he already met with her once) risks looking callous, as the majority of Americans—58%—say Bush should meet with her; only 41% say he should not.

Should George W. Bush Meet With Cindy Sheehan?

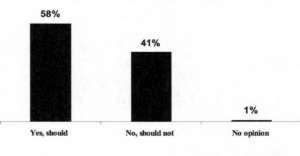

Aug. 28-30, 2005

Naturally, most Americans (74%) who think the war was a mistake think Bush should meet with Sheehan, while most war supporters (59%) do not think he should.

Attitudes on this question follow a similar pattern by political affiliation—although relative to some other issues, these attitudes are not strongly partisan. Nearly three-quarters of Democrats (72%) and

63% of independents think Bush should meet with Sheehan, while the majority of Republicans (58%) think he should not.

Sheehan clearly has Americans' sympathy for the loss of her son. Overall, 91% of Americans say they sympathize with her over this. But this sympathy does not guarantee support for her political activism. Only 42% of Americans both sympathize with her and agree with her actions against the war. About half of Americans sympathize with her but disagree with her actions (49%). Another 6% do not have much sympathy for her because of her actions.

Which comes closest to your view of Cindy Sheehan?

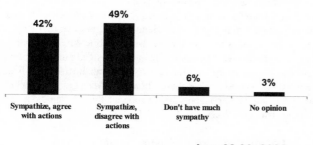

Aug. 28-30, 2005

Protest Having Limited Impact on Bush, Americans

Bush's refusal to meet with Sheehan has not appeared to hurt him politically. Not only has his approval rating for his handling of Iraq remained stable, but a new measure finds that Americans, by a 2-to-1 margin, believe Bush sincerely cares about the families of U.S. soldiers killed in Iraq.

Just your best guess, do you think George W. Bush does or does not sincerely care about the families of U.S. soldiers killed in Iraq?

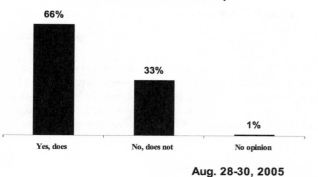

Aug. 28-30, 2005

Meanwhile, Sheehan's protest is doing little to inspire fellow resisters to become active against the Iraq war. Only 13% of Americans (including 21% of those saying the Iraq war was a mistake) say that the events surrounding the Sheehan news story have made them more likely to get involved in anti-war activities. A nearly equal percentage—12% of Americans—say it has made them more likely to get involved in pro-war activities.

Americans Doubt Iraq Will Be Stabilized

Although Bush has thus far declined to meet with Sheehan for a second time (they met once this spring at an event for the parents of

Have the events surrounding Cindy Sheehan made you: more likely to get involved in anti-war activities, have they made no difference to you, or have they made you more likely to get involved in pro-war activities?

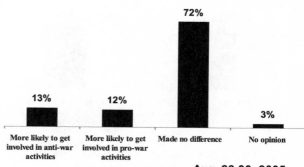

Aug. 28-30, 2005

fallen soldiers), he articulated his rationale for staying the course in Iraq in a V-J Day commemoration speech on Tuesday.

In that speech, Bush argued that America's continued military involvement in Iraq is needed to prevent terrorists and insurgents from taking control of that country—which would include Iraq's oil fields as well as the government. Bush also expressed confidence that the war will result in a free and democratic Iraq.

Americans marginally agree with Bush that a democratic government will be established in Iraq and that the Iraqi government will be friendly to the United States. Slightly more than half the public says it is likely these things will happen in the long run, and close to half, if not the majority, says these will happen within the next year.

Signs of Optimism in Americans' Outlook for Iraq

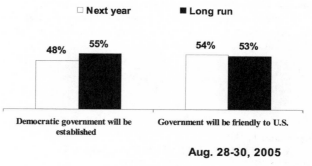

Aug. 28-30, 2005

At the same time, Americans remain pessimistic about the military challenges that Iraq presents. Less than half think peace and security will be established in Iraq, either next year (30%) or even in the long run (43%). The majority says this is unlikely.

Additionally, most Americans predict that, over the next year, U.S. military casualties will continue to mount at the same rate or even a higher rate than now. Forty-two percent of Americans consider this very likely and another 40% say somewhat likely. Only 16% of Americans think it is unlikely.

Survey Methods

These results are based on telephone interviews with a randomly selected national sample of 1,007 adults, aged 18 and older, conducted Aug. 28-30, 2005. For results based on this sample, one can

Outlook for Peace and Security in Iraq

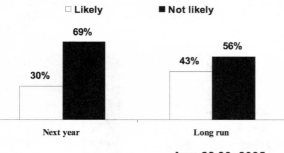

☐ Likely　　■ Not likely

Next year: 30% Likely, 69% Not likely
Long run: 43% Likely, 56% Not likely

Aug. 28-30, 2005

How Likely U.S. Casualties in Iraq Will Continue at Same or Higher Rate Than Now?

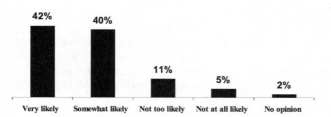

Very likely 42% | Somewhat likely 40% | Not too likely 11% | Not at all likely 5% | No opinion 2%

Aug. 28-30, 2005

say with 95% confidence that the maximum error attributable to sampling and other random effects is ±3 percentage points.

For results based on the 507 national adults in the Form A half-sample and 500 national adults in the Form B half-sample, the maximum margins of sampling error are ±5 percentage points.

In addition to sampling error, question wording and practical difficulties in conducting surveys can introduce error or bias into the findings of public opinion polls.

September 6, 2005

PUBLIC MOST INTERESTED IN HEARING ROBERTS' VIEWS ON ABORTION

Slim majority continues to favor his confirmation

by Jeffrey M. Jones, Gallup Poll Managing Editor

Senate confirmation hearings for Supreme Court nominee John Roberts, scheduled to begin Tuesday, have been delayed because of the passing of Chief Justice William Rehnquist. A recent CNN/*USA Today*/Gallup poll finds that most Americans say they plan to follow the hearings at least somewhat closely, which may take on added meaning given President George W. Bush's decision to nominate Roberts for chief justice. The public is more inclined to believe that Roberts should answer questions regarding his views on specific issues rather than limiting his responses to questions on his general judicial philosophy. When Americans are asked what they most want to learn about Roberts, the most frequent response concerns his views on abortion. Americans currently favor Roberts'

confirmation by a 2-to-1 margin, but many still do not have an opinion on the matter.

The impending hearings are the first on a Supreme Court justice since Stephen Breyer was confirmed in 1994. Roughly 6 in 10 Americans say they plan to follow the hearings very (18%) or somewhat (41%) closely, according to the Aug. 28-30 poll (conducted before Rehnquist's death on Saturday). Slightly less than half of Americans say Roberts' confirmation matters to them—including 20% who say it matters a great deal and 27% who say a moderate amount.

Recent nominees have done their best to avoid answering most questions on controversial issues such as abortion, especially after Robert Bork's answers to such questions contributed to his being denied a seat on the court after he was nominated by Ronald Reagan. Nevertheless, a majority of Americans, 55%, believe that Roberts *should* answer questions on specific issues, while 42% disagree and say he should answer only questions about his general judicial philosophy. Views on this matter vary by partisanship—Republicans are more inclined to think Roberts should answer only philosophical questions, while independents and Democrats think he should answer specific issue questions.

Do you think John Roberts should — answer questions from the senators about his views on specific issues such as abortion or affirmative action, (or should he) only answer questions from the senators about his general judicial philosophy?

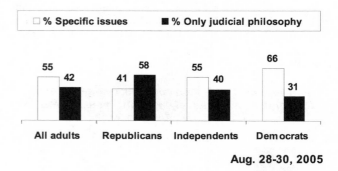

☐ % Specific issues　　■ % Only judicial philosophy

All adults: 55 / 42
Republicans: 41 / 58
Independents: 55 / 40
Democrats: 66 / 31

Aug. 28-30, 2005

The poll asked Americans to name, without prompting, what they are most interested in learning about Roberts during the hearings. Twenty-eight percent mention something about his views on abortion, by far the most common response. Other issues mentioned include minority rights and civil rights, economics, and gay marriage and homosexual rights.

As you may know, senators will be asking John Roberts about his views on a variety of subjects. On what subjects would you most like to hear John Roberts' views during his confirmation hearings? [OPEN-ENDED]

	2005 Aug 28-30 %
Abortion/*Roe v. Wade*/Women's right to choose	28
Minority rights/Civil rights	6
Economics	6
Gas/Oil prices	5
Judicial system reform/Supreme Court issues	5
Constitutional views	4
Gay marriage/Homosexual rights	4
Healthcare	4

	2005 Aug 28-30
	%
Religious issues	3
War	3
Death penalty/Capital punishment	3
Morals/Family values	3
Crime	2
Education reform	2
Stem cell research	2
Terrorism	2
Foreign affairs	2
Affirmative action	2
His background (qualifications/integrity)	1
Immigration	1
Gun control	1
Privacy laws	1
Eminent domain	1
Other	14
Nothing	11
Everything	1
No opinion	19

Note: Percentages add to more than 100% due to multiple responses.

Democrats (37%) are more likely than independents (22%) or Republicans (26%) to want to learn about Roberts' views on abortion.

Whether senators ultimately vote to confirm Roberts will depend to at least some degree on how he answers their questions. Should they disagree with his positions on specific issues but otherwise think he is qualified to serve, most Americans believe senators should still vote to confirm Roberts. Fifty-four percent say senators would *not* be justified in voting against Roberts purely because of issue disagreements, while 40% say they would be justified in doing so.

These views show a dramatic partisan divide. By a 69% to 28% margin, Republicans say senators would not be justified in voting against Roberts based only on policy disagreements, while Democrats believe senators *would* be justified in doing so, by a 55% to 40% margin.

Suppose the upcoming confirmation hearings indicate that John Roberts is qualified and has no ethical problems. Do you think U.S. senators would be justified — or unjustified — in voting against him if they disagree with his stance on current issues such as abortion or affirmative action?

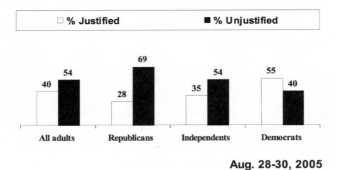

Aug. 28-30, 2005

Current Support for Roberts

The poll finds 52% of Americans currently in favor of Roberts' confirmation, while 26% are opposed and another 22% have no opinion.

These results are in line with two earlier polls on Roberts, conducted after Bush nominated him to replace retiring Justice Sandra Day O'Connor, though his support was slightly higher immediately after Bush's announcement.

As you may know, John Roberts is a federal judge who has been nominated to serve on the Supreme Court. Would you like to see the Senate vote in favor of Roberts serving on the Supreme Court, or not?

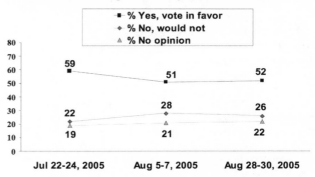

When asked to predict what the ideological slant of Roberts' decisions might be as a justice, 48% of Americans say "about right." Twenty-four percent think he would be "too conservative" and 8% "too liberal." One in five have no opinion.

The same question was asked about two other recent Supreme Court nominees. In June 1993, 47% of Americans said Ruth Bader Ginsburg would be about right, 14% said she would be too liberal, 4% too conservative, and 35% had no opinion. In a July 1991 poll, 46% said Clarence Thomas would be about right, with 20% saying too conservative, 7% too liberal and 27% having no opinion.

Views of Rehnquist

Supreme Court justices—even the chief justice—are typically not widely known by the general public (with Clarence Thomas an exception). In the most recent survey asking about Rehnquist—a May 20-22 CNN/*USA Today*/Gallup poll—38% of Americans did not have an opinion about the chief justice. However, opinion toward Rehnquist was decidedly more positive (46%) than negative (16%). The 46% favorable rating was actually the lowest for Rehnquist in four measurements, as 50% to 53% rated him favorably in polls conducted in 1999, 2000, and 2004.

Opinions of William Rehnquist, Gallup Polls

	Favor-able	Unfavor-able	Never heard of	No opinion
	%	%	%	%
2005 May 20-22	46	16	21	17
2004 Nov 19-21	53	20	13	14
2000 Dec 15-17	50	15	19	16
1999 Jan 8-10	51	8	18	23

Survey Methods

These results are based on telephone interviews with a randomly selected national sample of 1,007 adults, aged 18 and older, conducted Aug. 28-30, 2005. For results based on this sample, one can say with 95% confidence that the maximum error attributable to sampling and other random effects is ±3 percentage points. In addition to sampling error, question wording and practical difficulties in conducting surveys can introduce error or bias into the findings of public opinion polls.

September 6, 2005
CONGRESS RECONVENES AMID LOW PUBLIC APPROVAL
Opinion varies by party, age

by Darren K. Carlson, Government and Politics Editor

As Congress returns to session this week, lawmakers have their work cut out for them. They must address the aftermath of Hurricane Katrina, rising oil prices, and a number of other foreign and domestic policy issues. A recent Gallup Poll* shows congressional leaders also have work to do in terms of public perceptions, as Americans' approval of how Congress is handling its job remains low.

According to the Aug. 8-11 poll, slightly more than a third (36%) of Americans approve of the way Congress is handling its job. A majority—58%—disapprove. These most recent results are consistent with findings from July, continuing the recent trend of ratings in the mid-30% range.

Do you approve or disapprove of the way Congress is handling its job?

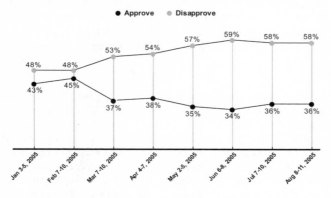

Congress' approval ratings have not been below 40% for as many months since the spring and summer of 1997. However, the current ratings are still significantly higher than Congress' low points. In March 1992 only 18% approved, and in June 1979 only 19% approved.

Opinion Varies by Political Party, Age Group

Political party affiliation affects Americans' opinions of Congress. More than half of Republicans (57%) approve of the way the current GOP-controlled Congress is doing its job, compared with less than a third of independents (29%) and only 22% of Democrats.

Congressional approval also varies by age, although less than a majority of every age group gives Congress a positive appraisal. Forty-three percent of 18- to 29-year-olds approve of the way Congress is handling things, as do 41% of those between the ages of 30 and 49. But, job approval is lower among Americans aged 50 to 64, just 29% approve, and among those aged 65 and older, 26% approve.

Do you approve or disapprove of the way Congress is handling its job?

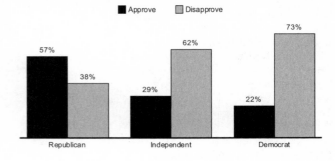

Gallup research has shown consistent age differences such as these in congressional job approval all the way back to the first measurement in 1974.

*These results are based on telephone interviews with a randomly selected national sample of 1,001 adults, aged 18 and older, conducted Aug. 8-11, 2005. For results based on this sample, one can say with 95% confidence that the maximum error attributable to sampling and other random effects is ±3 percentage points. In addition to sampling error, question wording and practical difficulties in conducting surveys can introduce error or bias into the findings of public opinion polls.

September 7, 2005
PUBLIC SKEPTICAL NEW ORLEANS WILL RECOVER
Criticism, but little outrage, for Bush's and federal agencies' response to hurricane

by David W. Moore, Gallup Poll Senior Editor

A new CNN/*USA Today*/Gallup survey finds the public skeptical that New Orleans will ever completely recover from Hurricane Katrina, but also supportive of making the effort to rebuild the city. Even those who predict full recovery expect the process to take many years.

The poll also finds the public largely divided in its evaluation of the response by President George W. Bush and the federal government, though more people are critical than supportive of their efforts. The public is also highly critical of gas companies for the rise in prices, saying the industry is taking advantage of the situation to charge unfair prices.

The poll, conducted Sept. 5-6, finds almost all Americans, 93%, agreeing that Hurricane Katrina is the worst natural disaster in their lifetimes.

Thinking about natural disasters such as hurricanes, floods, earthquakes, or fires, do you consider Hurricane Katrina to be the worst natural disaster in the U.S. in your lifetime, or not?

	Yes, is	No, is not	No opinion
2005 Sep 5-6	93%	7	*

*Less than 0.5%

A majority, 56%, is even skeptical that New Orleans will ever completely recover from the hurricane. Among those who think recovery is possible, they predict on average that it will take more than nine years, with a majority saying a minimum of six years.

Do you think the city of New Orleans will ever completely recover from the effects of Hurricane Katrina, or not?

	Yes, will completely recover	No, will not	No opinion
2005 Sep 5-6	42%	56	2

Just your best guess, how many years will it take for New Orleans to completely recover? [OPEN-ENDED]

BASED ON 268 ADULTS WHO SAY THE CITY OF NEW ORLEANS WILL COMPLETELY RECOVER FROM THE EFFECTS OF HURRICANE KATRINA

	2 years or less %	3-5 years %	6-10 years %	11-20 years %	More than 20 years %	No opinion %	Mean	Median
2005 Sep 5-6	10	33	41	8	5	3	9.3 years	7 years

Still, a substantial majority, 63%, believes that New Orleans should be rebuilt as a major city.

Do you think New Orleans should—or should not—be rebuilt as a major city?

	Yes, should	No, should not	No opinion
2005 Sep 5-6	63%	34	3

No Apparent Outrage With Government's Response to Hurricane

Despite widespread criticism of the response by Bush and, separately, the federal government, to the problems caused by the hurricane, the public seems on balance only mildly critical. Forty-two percent say Bush did a "bad" (18%) or "terrible" (24%) job, but 35% rate his response as either "great" (10%) or "good" (25%).

Do you think—[RANDOM ORDER]—has/have done a—great, good, neither good nor bad, bad, or terrible job—in responding to the hurricane and subsequent flooding?

	Great %	Good %	Neither good nor bad %	Bad %	Terrible %	No opinion %
George W. Bush	10	25	21	18	24	2
Federal government agencies responsible for handling emergencies	8	27	20	20	22	3
State and local officials in Louisiana	7	30	23	20	15	5

Federal agencies received a similar rating, with 42% of Americans giving a low rating and 35% a high one. The public was about evenly divided on state and local officials in Louisiana—37% giving a high rating and 35% a low one.

The ratings for Bush are highly related to party affiliation.
- By a margin of 69% to 10%, Republicans give Bush a positive rather than negative rating for his response.
- Democrats give almost a mirror opposite—66% negative to 10% positive.
- Independents side with the Democrats, giving a more modest margin—47% negative to 29% positive.

When asked to identify who was *most* responsible for the problems in New Orleans after the hurricane, 38% of Americans said no one was really to blame, while 13% cited Bush, 18% the federal agencies, and 25% state and local officials.

Who do you think is MOST responsible for the problems in New Orleans after the hurricane—[ROTATED: George W. Bush, federal agencies, (or) state and local officials], or is no one really to blame?

	George W. Bush	Federal agencies	State/ local officials	No one to blame	No opinion
2005 Sep 5-6	13%	18	25	38	6

Few Americans feel that any top official in the agencies responsible for handling emergencies should be dismissed from office—just 29% say someone should be fired, while 63% disagree.

Do you think that any of the top officials in the federal agencies responsible for handling emergencies should be fired, or don't you think so?

	Yes, should be fired	No, don't think so	No opinion
2005 Sep 5-6	29%	63	8

Police are trying to get the remaining residents in New Orleans to evacuate, because of health and safety problems. Americans agree with this effort by better than a 2-to-1 margin, 66% to 30%.

Which comes closer to your view—[ROTATED: all residents of New Orleans should evacuate the city (or) the residents of New Orleans who are still in the city should be allowed to stay]?

	All residents should evacuate city	Residents still in the city should be allowed to stay	No opinion
2005 Sep 5-6	66%	30	4

The public tends to be upbeat about the efforts being made to deal with the disaster. Sixty-two percent feel the progress being made in the region is satisfactory, while 35% say it is not.

Based on what you have seen or read in the past day or two, do you think the progress made in dealing with the situation is satisfactory, or not?

	Yes, is	No, is not	No opinion
2005 Sep 5-6	62%	35	3

As for the effect of the hurricane on gas prices, Americans express a cynical view—by 79% to 18%, they believe that gas companies are taking advantage of the situation to charge unfair prices.

Which comes closer to your view—[ROTATED: the gas companies are charging a fair price given the conditions caused by the hurricane, (or) the gas companies are taking advantage of the situation and charging unfair prices]?

	Charging fair price given conditions	Taking advantage, charging unfair prices	No opinion
2005 Sep 5-6	18%	79	3

Survey Methods

Results are based on telephone interviews with 609 national adults, aged 18 and older, conducted Sept. 5-6, 2005. For results based on the total sample of national adults, one can say with 95% confidence that the maximum margin of sampling error is ±4 percentage points.

For results based on the sample of 268 adults who say the city of New Orleans will completely recover from the effects of Hurricane Katrina, the maximum margin of sampling error is ±6 percentage points.

In addition to sampling error, question wording and practical difficulties in conducting surveys can introduce error or bias into the findings of public opinion polls.

September 8, 2005
SLIM MAJORITY DISSATISFIED WITH EDUCATION IN THE U.S.
Most parents think children's school properly emphasizing key subjects

by Jeffrey M. Jones, Gallup Poll Managing Editor

As children across the United States begin another school year, a recent Gallup Poll shows that a slim majority of Americans are dissatisfied with the quality of education in the country, a change after a slightly more positive rating last year. As usual, though, parents of children in kindergarten through grade 12 are overwhelmingly satisfied with the education their own children are receiving. Two in three parents say their child's school is placing the right amount of emphasis on reading and English and math. In fact, a majority of parents believe their child's school is appropriately emphasizing all but one of 11 subject areas or activities tested in the poll (foreign language being the one exception).

Gallup's Aug. 8-11 Work and Education Poll finds 46% of Americans are satisfied and 51% dissatisfied with "the quality of education students receive in kindergarten through grade 12 in the U.S. today." Those numbers are more negative than last year, when 53% were satisfied, but generally in line with what Gallup has measured in recent years. The recent low point was a 61% dissatisfaction rating in 2000, but typically just half or more of Americans have expressed dissatisfaction.

As the level of dissatisfaction with education has declined since 2000, so has its salience as an area of concern for Americans. This is understandable given the emergence of terrorism, the economy, and the war in Iraq as major issues for the country in recent years.

In October 2000, shortly before the presidential election, 17% of Americans mentioned education when asked to name the most

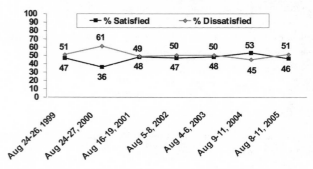

Satisfaction With K-12 Education in U.S. Today

important problem facing the country, placing it at the top of the list. Ten percent or more of Americans cited education as the country's top concern in all but two polls conducted between Jan. 1997 and Sept. 10, 2001.

That changed after 9/11. No more than 8% of Americans have mentioned education as the nation's top problem since Oct. 2001, with an average of just 5% of mentions to the question. In the recent Work and Education Poll, just 5% say education is the most important problem, placing it well behind the Iraq war (mentioned by 27%) as well as the economy in general (13%) and terrorism (10%).

Difference in Education Satisfaction by Subgroup

There are consistent regional differences in the way Americans rate the nation's education system. Namely, residents living in the West are slightly less likely to express satisfaction. Only 37% of Western residents say they are satisfied with the quality of education for school-age children, compared with 45% of those living in the South, 50% in the East, and 50% in the Midwest. Gallup has found similar regional variation in its previous data on this question.

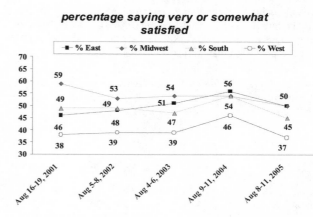

Satisfaction With K-12 Education in U.S. Today by region

percentage saying very or somewhat satisfied

Parents of school-age children are only slightly more positive in their evaluation of the national education system (50%) than Americans without children in school (43%).

Ratings of Own Child's Education Much More Positive

Satisfaction levels with the U.S. education system, as usual, stand in stark contrast to the level of satisfaction K-12 parents give to their own children's education. Seventy-eight percent of K-12 parents say they are satisfied "with the quality of education [their] oldest child is receiving," while only 20% are dissatisfied. Thirty-three percent say they are "completely satisfied."

These ratings have remained quite stable in the last three years, after being slightly lower in 2001 and 2002.

Satisfaction With Education Oldest Child Receives

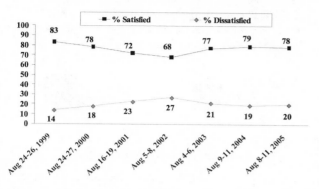

The poll finds parents' satisfaction with their child's education is fairly broad-based and extends to specific evaluations of different subject areas and activities. When asked if their child's school places too much, too little, or the right amount of emphasis on a variety of subjects and activities, a majority of parents say the right amount in almost every case. That includes 66% who say their child's school is placing the proper emphasis on reading and English and 65% who say the same about math. The lone exception to this general contentment comes in the area of foreign languages—46% say their oldest child's school places too little emphasis on these, while 42% say the right amount.

Now thinking about the school your oldest child attends, do you think there is too much emphasis, the right amount, or too little emphasis on [RANDOM ORDER]?

BASED ON 311 K-12 PARENTS

2005 Aug 8-11 (sorted by "right amount")	Too much emphasis	Right amount	Too little emphasis	NOT APPLIC- ABLE (vol.)	No opinion
	%	%	%	%	%
Reading and English	5	66	28	*	1
Math	2	65	31	1	1
Art and music	5	61	32	1	1
Sciences	5	60	31	2	2
Health	3	60	33	2	2
Composition or writing	3	60	35	*	2
History	2	60	34	2	2
Physical education	4	58	35	1	2
Sports	18	57	20	4	1
Preparing for standardized tests	18	52	24	3	3
Foreign languages	4	42	46	6	2

*Less than 0.5%

K-12 parents are more inclined to think schools are doing too little in the various areas than too much. On only two items—preparing for standardized tests and sports—do more than 10% say their oldest child's school is doing too much. Even in the controver-

sial area of standardized tests, a key component for measuring school performance in President George W. Bush's No Child Left Behind Act, more parents say that their child's school spends too little rather than too much time preparing for standardized tests.

Survey Methods

These results are based on telephone interviews with a randomly selected national sample of 1,001 adults, aged 18 and older, conducted Aug. 8-11, 2005. For results based on this sample, one can say with 95% confidence that the maximum error attributable to sampling and other random effects is ±3 percentage points. In addition to sampling error, question wording and practical difficulties in conducting surveys can introduce error or bias into the findings of public opinion polls.

For results based on the sample of 311 parents with children in grades K-12, the maximum margin of sampling error is ±6 percentage points.

September 9, 2005
AMERICANS SENSE A "NEW NORMAL" AFTER 9/11
Most say U.S., their lives, still not back to normal

by Lydia Saad, Gallup Poll Senior Editor

Americans' current perceptions of the effect the 9/11 attacks have had on the United States and on themselves, personally, are similar to what these perceptions were on the first anniversary of the attacks. Even four years after the attacks, an Aug. 28-30 CNN/*USA Today*/ Gallup poll finds most Americans feeling that neither the country nor their own lives have fully returned to normal since terrorists killed nearly 3,000 people on Sept. 11, 2001.

While these evaluations haven't changed since 2002, Americans appear a bit more pessimistic now than they were then about the likelihood that normalcy will ever be fully restored to the country or to their own lives. Nearly two-thirds now say the country will never completely return to normal, while close to half say the same for themselves.

Evaluations of Current Conditions Since 9/11

When asked to evaluate how the country is faring since 9/11, a slim majority of Americans (54%) say the United States is not back to normal, while 42% believe it is "somewhat" back to normal. Thus, 96% of Americans perceive that the country remains changed by the event. Only a scant few (4%) say things are "completely back to normal." These attitudes—collected before the full scale of the Hurricane Katrina disaster was known—are virtually identical to previous measures in 2002 and 2003.

The apparent effect of 9/11 on Americans' personal lives is less severe, but still widespread. A total of 62% of Americans indicate that their lives remain changed by 9/11, including 24% who say their lives are not back to normal, and 38% who say they are only somewhat back to normal.

About one-quarter of Americans say the event did not change their lives, while an additional 14% say it did affect them, but their lives have since completely rebounded.

Evaluating the United States After 9/11

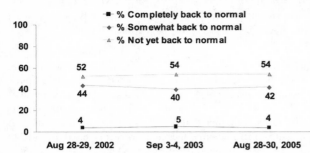

- ■ % Completely back to normal
- ◆ % Somewhat back to normal
- △ % Not yet back to normal

	Aug 28-29, 2002	Sep 3-4, 2003	Aug 28-30, 2005
Not yet back to normal	52	54	54
Somewhat back to normal	44	40	42
Completely back to normal	4	5	4

Evaluating One's Personal Life After 9/11

- □ % Life did not change/Completely back to normal
- ▨ % Changed, somewhat back to normal
- ■ % Changed, not yet back to normal

	Aug 28-29, 2002	Aug 28-30, 2005
Life did not change	42	38
Changed, somewhat	37	38
Changed, not yet	20	24

Americans' recovery from 9/11 is quite consistent across demographic groups. Perhaps somewhat remarkably, urban residents are no more likely than those living in the suburbs or rural areas to say that their lives remain changed. There are also no substantial differences on this indicator by region, gender, or age. There are, however, some slight differences by party ID. Seventeen percent of Republicans say their lives are still not back to normal, compared with 30% of Democrats and 25% of independents.

Expectations for Getting Back to "Normal"

When asked to think about the outlook for restoring normalcy in the United States, only a third of Americans (33%) believe the country will eventually return to normal, if it hasn't already. But 63% think it will never return to the way it was before 9/11.

Americans are notably more pessimistic on this measure than they were in 2002 or 2003. At those times, Gallup found more than 4 in 10 Americans expressing optimism that the country would fully recover, and only half the public saying things would never return to normal.

Similarly, Americans are more pessimistic than they were in 2002 about their own lives returning to normal. Today, 42% believe

Outlook for the United States After 9/11

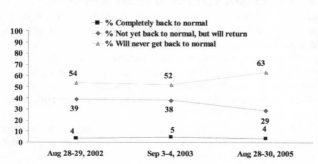

- ■ % Completely back to normal
- ◆ % Not yet back to normal, but will return
- △ % Will never get back to normal

	Aug 28-29, 2002	Sep 3-4, 2003	Aug 28-30, 2005
Will never get back to normal	54	52	63
Not yet back to normal, but will return	39	38	29
Completely back to normal	4	5	4

their lives will never completely return to normal, up from 32% in 2002. At the same time, the percentages saying their lives are already mended or predicting they will eventually recover are each down slightly compared with 2002.

Americans' Outlook for Their Lives After 9/11

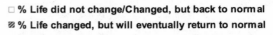

- □ % Life did not change/Changed, but back to normal
- ▨ % Life changed, but will eventually return to normal
- ■ % Life changed, will not return to normal

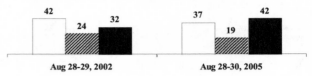

	Aug 28-29, 2002	Aug 28-30, 2005
Life did not change	42	37
Changed, but will eventually return	24	19
Changed, will not return	32	42

Government Earns Modest Praise

According to the recent poll, Americans generally believe the government's anti-terrorist efforts since the 9/11 attacks have made the country safer from terrorism. But relatively few say the government has made the country a lot safer. Rated separately, the government agencies responsible for preventing terrorist attacks and the U.S. Congress are viewed similarly on this measure.

Only 17% say government anti-terror agencies have made the country a lot safer since Sept. 11, 2001. Another 55% say they have made the country a little safer. Fifteen percent say they have made no difference and 12% say they have made the country less safe.

Similarly, only 17% say Congress has made the country a lot safer through the role it has played in preventing terrorist attacks in the United States. Another 49% say it has made the country a little safer, 21% say it has made no difference, and 12% say it has reduced safety.

Government's Effect on Safety From Terrorism

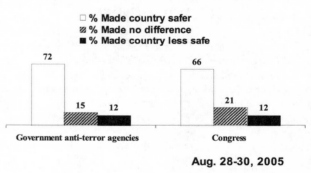

- □ % Made country safer
- ▨ % Made no difference
- ■ % Made country less safe

	Government anti-terror agencies	Congress
Made country safer	72	66
Made no difference	15	21
Made country less safe	12	12

Aug. 28-30, 2005

Long-Term Decline in Positive Reviews of War on Terror

Despite these generally positive reviews of the government's anti-terror efforts, public satisfaction with the war on terrorism is down sharply compared with previous measures. Shortly before the first anniversary of 9/11, in September 2002, 75% of Americans were either very or somewhat satisfied with the way things are going for the United States in the war on terrorism. By September 2004, that figure had fallen to 59%, and today it is 51%.

Americans' views of who is winning the war on terrorism have changed a great deal over the past few years. While few Americans have ever said the terrorists are winning, the perception of whether

Public Satisfaction With U.S. War on Terrorism

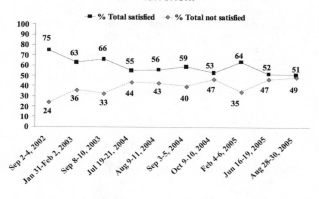

the United States and its allies are winning or neither side is winning goes back and forth. Today—as has been the case for the past year—the slight plurality of Americans say neither side is winning.

Who Is Winning the War on Terrorism?

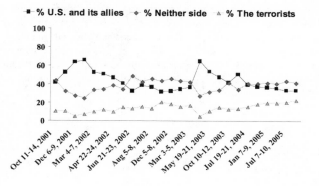

Survey Methods

These results are based on telephone interviews with a randomly selected national sample of 1,007 adults, aged 18 and older, conducted Aug. 28-30, 2005. For results based on this sample, one can say with 95% confidence that the maximum error attributable to sampling and other random effects is ±3 percentage points. In addition to sampling error, question wording and practical difficulties in conducting surveys can introduce error or bias into the findings of public opinion polls.

September 12, 2005
PERCEPTION OR REALITY? THE EFFECT OF STATURE ON LIFE OUTCOMES
Americans believe that height confers advantages in the workplace

by Jack Ludwig

Does it really matter if someone is noticeably shorter or taller than someone else? Shorter people may be more likely to need help in

reaching the highest shelves, and to feel submerged in a crowd, while taller folks may be more prone to bumping their heads and may feel decidedly more cramped in standard-sized airline seats. But what about things that *really* matter? What about feelings of self-confidence in social situations, or being respected—or promoted—at work?

The recently completed Gallup/Pfizer Survey of Opinions on the Social Impact of Stature measured perceptions of a random sample of Americans regarding the relative fortunes of adults who are noticeably shorter or taller than their peers. Although the survey did not directly assess whether taller or shorter people actually experience different outcomes, Gallup found ample evidence that Americans believe that one's stature has a decided effect on a variety of important dimensions.

Height Preferences

Before asking about the importance of height, Gallup asked the random sample of Americans whether they would prefer to be taller, shorter, or to remain at their present height. The majority of respondents (61%) say they would choose to stay as they are. Only a negligible number would like to be shorter (2%). But more than one in three American adults would like to be taller—and the number is remarkably similar for men (35%) and women (38%).

Americans' Height Preferences

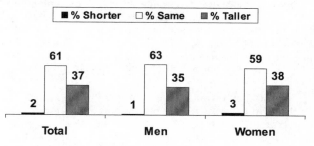

How does this preference for being taller vary by the actual height of the respondent? To find out, Gallup divided the sample into thirds. For men, the bottom third of reported height was 5 feet 8 inches and under; the middle third, 5 feet 9 inches to 5 feet 11 inches; and the top third was 6 feet and taller. For women, the bottom third in reported height was 5 feet 3 inches and under; the middle third, 5 feet 4 inches to 5 feet 5 inches; and the tallest third was 5 feet 6 inches and taller.

Among the shortest third of men in the sample (those 5 feet 8 inches and under), 45% wish to be taller, while 54% say they would prefer to remain at their current height. But even among men who are 6 feet and taller (the tallest third of the male sample) 19% would like to be taller still, while 78% say they would prefer to stay at their current height if they had the opportunity to change it. Only 3% of this group would like to be shorter.

The parallel results for women are generally quite similar. Among the tallest third of women in the sample (those 5 feet 6 inches and taller), 20% say they would prefer to be still taller, while 74% would like to remain at their current height and only 7% wish to be shorter. At the other end of the spectrum, among the shortest third of women interviewed (those 5 feet 3 inches and under), 56% wish to be taller—a higher number than the comparable percentage among men—while 44% would prefer to remain at their current height.

Stature in the Workplace

Various reports over the years have argued that taller men have an advantage in the workplace, and some studies have argued that the taller candidate for U.S. president is almost always more likely to win (the most recent exception being John Kerry, who was taller than George W. Bush, yet lost the 2004 election).

Americans certainly tend to presume that height confers advantages in the workplace. Asked whether noticeably taller or noticeably shorter men have an easier time being respected at work, an overwhelming majority of Americans (86%) give the edge to taller men, while only 7% think shorter men have an easier time being respected, and another 7% volunteer that taller and shorter men have equal chances.

When the same question was asked about women, the results were similar, although not quite as lopsided: 71% think noticeably taller women have an easier time being respected at work, while 17% believe shorter women have the easier time, and 11% volunteer that neither group has an advantage. This view that taller women have an easier time being respected on the job than do shorter women was expressed by both men and women, but the perception was more prevalent among women (74% versus 15%) than among men (68% versus 20%).

Who has the easier time being respected at work — adult men/women who are noticeably shorter than other men/women their age, or adult men/women who are noticeably taller than other men/women their age?

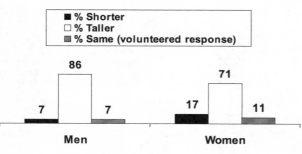

Americans' belief that tall people have an advantage over short people is not limited to vague outcomes such as "respect" among coworkers. Gallup asked a parallel set of questions about the effect of height on one's chances of being promoted at work. The perceived advantages of height when it comes to one's chances for promotion are slightly less pronounced than they are in relation to respect, but the patterns are markedly similar. As with the respect question, the perception that increased height favorably affects promotion chances is less widespread for women than it is for men.

The Bottom Line

The data reviewed above are, after all, only opinions about whether shorter or taller people reap advantages or disadvantages from their stature, not proof that these dynamics exist in the workplace. But they do suggest that stature might belong among characteristics such as gender, age, and race that—irrespective of their relevance—can have a bearing on outcomes in the workplace and beyond. They reveal a remarkable degree of consensus among Americans that a pattern of thinking and behavior that could be given the name "heightism" exists. Beliefs cannot be taken as proof, but beliefs as

Who has the easier time being promoted at work — adult men/women who are noticeably shorter than other men/women their age, or adult men/women who are noticeably taller than other men/women their age?

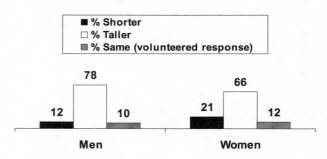

broadly shared as the ones that are the focus of this survey beg to be taken seriously.

Survey Methods

These results are based on telephone interviews with a randomly selected national sample of 1,509 adults, aged 18 and older, conducted May 18-July 7, 2005. For results based on this sample, one can say with 95% confidence that the maximum error attributable to sampling and other random effects is ±3 percentage points. In addition to sampling error, question wording and practical difficulties in conducting surveys can introduce error or bias into the findings of public opinion polls.

September 13, 2005
PUBLIC: RESPONSE TO KATRINA BETTER NOW THAN JUST AFTER HURRICANE HIT
Katrina third most closely followed news event after 9/11, Iraq War

by David W. Moore, Gallup Poll Senior Editor

Most Americans were not impressed with the initial response to Hurricane Katrina, but according to the latest CNN/*USA Today*/Gallup survey, majorities of Americans now say that the people and officials involved in the rescue effort are doing a good job. The weekend poll shows Americans were inclined to fire Federal Emergency Management Agency Director Michael Brown (who resigned from FEMA on Monday). Most Americans believe that government agencies in New Orleans should have been better prepared, and they support the proposal for an independent investigation into the problems with the government's response. But they reject the notion that race or poverty were reasons why the government was slow to respond.

The poll, conducted Sept. 8-11, finds that 58% of Americans say they have been following the news about the hurricane "very closely" and another 38% "somewhat closely." Only the terrorist attacks on 9/11 and the war with Iraq found more Americans paying "very" close attention to those events—out of a list of over 150 events tracked by Gallup since the early 1990s.

The vast majority of Americans have also reacted emotionally to the events in the Gulf Coast—98% say they have felt sadness, 78% shock, and 62% anger.

When asked about the initial response to Hurricane Katrina, majorities of Americans are critical of President George W. Bush, FEMA and federal government agencies responsible for handling emergencies, state and local officials in Louisiana, and the residents of New Orleans. However, when asked how these same groups were responding to the hurricane in the past few days, majorities of Americans say each person or group has been doing a good job.

[INITIAL RESPONSE:] *Now thinking about what happened* immediately after Hurricane Katrina hit and NOT what has happened in the past few days, *how would you rate the way—[RANDOM ORDER]—initially responded to the hurricane—as very good, good, poor, or very poor?*

[SUBSEQUENT RESPONSE:] *Now thinking about what has happened* in the past few days *in the areas affected by Hurricane Katrina and NOT what happened immediately after it hit, how would you rate the way—[RANDOM ORDER]—has responded to the hurricane in the past few days—as very good, good, poor, or very poor?*

2005 Sep 8-11 (sorted by "initial response")	*Initial* (total good) %	*Recent* (total good) %
George W. Bush	44	58
The residents of New Orleans	39	59
State and local officials in Louisiana	38	57
FEMA/federal government agencies responsible for handling emergencies	36	56

The results show little differentiation among the four groups, suggesting the public believes blame for the problems should be shared by many. In that regard, 70% believe there should be an independent investigation into the problems with the government's response; only 29% disagree.

By a 47% to 37% margin, with the rest expressing no opinion, Americans were of the opinion (in the weekend poll) that at least one person, FEMA Director Michael Brown, should be fired. (Brown resigned on Monday, Sept. 12. Last Friday, Coast Guard Vice Admiral Thad Allen replaced Brown as commander of Hurricane Katrina relief operations. Bush supported Homeland Security Secretary Michael Chertoff's decision to reassign Brown.)

The public does not accept the argument "that there was no way for [government agencies] to adequately prepare for a hurricane that strong." Instead, by a 71% to 28% margin, the public believes that the agencies should have been better prepared. Americans are also more likely to believe that the slow response was a result of bureaucratic inefficiency (49%) than a lack of adequate preparation (40%).

Effects of Hurricane Katrina

Most Americans say the effects of Katrina will hurt them financially in the next year. Forty-three percent expect to be hurt "a lot" by Katrina, and another 37% expect to be hurt "a little." Such expectations are highly related to household income, with 58% of people earning less than $30,000 a year saying they will be hurt a lot, compared with only 29% who earn $75,000 a year or more.

Despite criticisms of the government about its response to Katrina, clear majorities of Americans have confidence in the federal government's ability to respond both to future natural disasters, and to terrorist attacks.

- Sixty percent of Americans express a "great deal" or "moderate amount" of confidence in the federal government to respond to natural disasters, compared with 40% who have "not much" confidence or "none at all."
- Similarly, 63% have confidence in the federal government to respond to terrorist attacks, while 37% do not.

Q.28 How much confidence do you have in the federal government's ability to respond to future natural disasters—a great deal, a moderate amount, not much, or none at all?

Q.29 How much confidence do you have in the federal government's ability to respond to future terrorist attacks—a great deal, a moderate amount, not much, or none at all?

	Great deal %	*Moderate amount* %	*Not much* %	*None at all* %	*No opinion* %
Natural disasters	22	38	28	12	—
Terrorist attacks	21	42	25	12	*

*Less than 0.5%

President Bush

Despite initial criticisms of the federal government's slow response to Katrina, Bush's overall job approval rating remains essentially where it was at the end of August. Currently, 46% approve of his overall performance, compared with 45% in an Aug. 28-30 poll, both up slightly from a 40% reading earlier in mid-August. Fifty-one percent disapprove of the way Bush has been handling his job as president.

Americans are slightly less positive about Bush's handling of the response to Hurricane Katrina, with 43% approving and 54% disapproving.

News Media

The public approves of the way the news media have covered the disaster—77% of Americans say the media have acted "responsibly" in their coverage; only 20% say "irresponsibly."

Nevertheless, 49% of Americans say the media are spending too much time trying to figure out who is responsible for the problems in the areas affected by the hurricane, compared with 48% who say that about Democratic leaders in Congress, and 31% about congressional Republican leaders.

Survey Methods

Results are based on telephone interviews with 1,005 national adults, aged 18 and older, conducted Sept. 8-11, 2005. For results based on the total sample of national adults, one can say with 95% confidence that the maximum margin of sampling error is ±3 percentage points.

For results based on the 533 national adults in the Form A half-sample and 472 national adults in the Form B half-sample, the maximum margins of sampling error are ±5 percentage points.

In addition to sampling error, question wording and practical difficulties in conducting surveys can introduce error or bias into the findings of public opinion polls.

The poll did not dial into some of the areas of Louisiana and Mississippi that were declared federal disaster areas following Hurricane Katrina. This amounts to about 0.75% of the U.S. population.

September 13, 2005

BLACKS: WHITES HAVE ADVANTAGE IN COLLEGE ADMISSIONS

Whites more likely to say chances are the same

by Linda Lyons, Education and Youth Editor

Financial considerations aside, access to a college education depends on an intricate combination of factors including grades, college entrance test scores, class rank, course of study, quality of the high school attended, and extracurricular activities. Race can also be a factor—though not an overriding factor—in deciding who is in and who is out, according to a landmark 2003 Supreme Court decision involving the University of Michigan law school.

This year, Americans were asked: "If two equally qualified students, one black and one white, applied to a major U.S. college or university, who would have the better chance of being accepted?" Nearly half of Americans (47%) say each has the same chance; 29% say the white student has a better chance and 20% say the black student*.

Who Has the Better Chance to Gain Admission?

If two equally qualified students, one white and one black, applied to a major U.S. college or university, who do you think would have the better chance of being accepted to the college – the white student, the black student, or would they have the same chance?

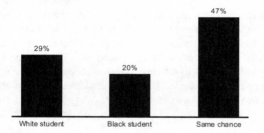

As on many issues involving race, whites and blacks have different opinions regarding which race currently fares better in the college admissions process. Half of non-Hispanic whites (50%) say each student has an equal chance of being accepted; 24% say the black student would have the edge, while 21% think the white student would have the advantage. In contrast, a solid majority of blacks (64%) say the white student would have a better chance of being accepted, while only 4% say the black student would have the better chance. Twenty-nine percent of blacks say chances are equal for both.

Whites' perceptions have changed since the last time Gallup asked this question, just prior to the 2003 Supreme Court decision.

Better Chance to Gain Admission by Race

If two equally qualified students, one white and one black, applied to a major U.S. college or university, who do you think would have the better chance of being accepted to the college – the white student, the black student, or would they have the same chance?

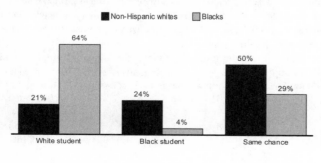

Overall, Americans are now more likely to say that blacks and whites have the same chance of being accepted into college, compared with sentiment in 2003. In 2003, 34% of whites said the black student had the better chance, compared with 24% who say that today. Although the Supreme Court upheld the concept of affirmative action for minority students in principle, it struck down the practice of admissions offices assigning additional points to students based *solely* on race—a fine distinction that may have created a more positive attitude toward affirmative action on the part of whites.

Many black Americans are starkly aware of the educational disparity between the poor, urban schools that many black children attend and schools in more affluent, largely white suburbs. This disparity may be one reason for the difference of opinion between blacks and whites on this question. With access to often superior secondary education, white students may benefit from more rigorous academic tracks that prepare them more fully for college-level work. The College Board reports that in 2005, combined average SAT verbal and math scores were 1068 for whites and 864 for blacks.

Affirmative Action Plays a Role

Why do one in four whites say the equally qualified black student would have a better chance of getting into college? That figure may reflect knowledge of past and present affirmative action programs used on college campuses. Designed in the 1960s to remedy the effects of discrimination by helping minorities gain entrance into college, black Americans clearly support affirmative action programs, while whites are more divided (see "Race, Ideology, and Support for Affirmative Action" in Related Items).

Additionally, respondents were asked in the same survey whether they think affirmative action programs "ensure that well-qualified minorities get access to the schools and jobs that they deserve, or these programs give preferential treatment to minorities in school admissions and jobs—even when those minorities are less qualified than other applicants." The majority of whites (54%) tend to view affirmative action programs as giving preferential treatment to minorities in work and education, while the majority of blacks (65%) generally think that they mainly ensure access for minorities that they otherwise might not get.

Majority of Young Adults Discern a Fair Process

Younger Americans, aged 18 to 29, who are nearest to the traditional college age, are particularly likely to view the system as evenhanded. Young adults are significantly more likely than older adults to say equally qualified students of both races have an equal chance of getting into college—59% of 18- to 29-year-olds compared with 44% of adults aged 30 and older. As encouraging as this may be, race is still, by far, the overriding factor in gauging attitudes about college access. A majority of both younger and older blacks say the white student has a better chance to get in.

Bottom Line

College and university access increased for all Americans during the latter part of the 20th century. The number of white Americans earning a bachelor's degree or higher has tripled, from 8% in 1960 to 26% in 2000. During the same time period, blacks have nearly *quintupled* their college graduation rate—in 1960, just 3% of blacks earned a college degree, compared with more than 14% today.

*Results are based on telephone interviews with 2,264 national adults, aged 18 and older, conducted June 6-25, 2005, including

Better Chance to Gain Admission by Age Group

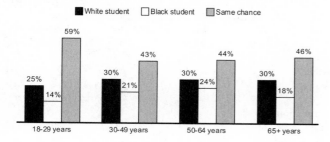

If two equally qualified students, one white and one black, applied to a major U.S. college or university, who do you think would have the better chance of being accepted to the college – the white student, the black student, or would they have the same chance?

■ White student ☐ Black student ▨ Same chance

oversamples of blacks and Hispanics that are weighted to reflect their proportions in the general population. For results based on the total sample of national adults, one can say with 95% confidence that the maximum margin of sampling error is ±5 percentage points.

Results for the sample of 807 non-Hispanic whites, aged 18 and older, are based on telephone interviews conducted June 6-25, 2005. For results based on the total sample, one can say with 95% confidence that the margin of sampling error is ±7 percentage points.

Results for the sample of 802 blacks, aged 18 and older, are based on telephone interviews conducted June 6-25, 2005. For results based on the total sample, one can say with 95% confidence that the margin of sampling error is ±5 percentage points.

September 13, 2005

WORKERS DESCRIBE JOBS, PAY, AND HOURS

Half of American workers paid hourly

by Joseph Carroll, Gallup Poll Assistant Editor

Gallup periodically queries Americans about their job status to better understand what work is like for the typical American worker. The latest update, taken from Gallup's Aug. 8-11 poll*, finds that most American workers currently hold just one job and spend an average of 42 hours a week at work. About one in five employed adults in the country work in blue-collar professions, while the rest work as executives or in some other white-collar profession. Half of workers are paid an hourly wage, while roughly 4 in 10 receive a salary and only 6% are paid mostly on commission.

Jobs Trends

Overall, about 6 in 10 Americans are employed, with roughly half employed full time and about 1 in 10 part time. American employees work 42 hours per week on average (this sample includes respondents who are both full- and part-time workers). This includes 16% of Americans who work fewer than 35 hours per week, 45% who work between 35 and 44 hours, and 39% who work more than 45 hours per week.

The average number of hours people work in a given week has shown only modest fluctuations since 1989, ranging from 42 hours a week to 44 hours a week. However, the trends on this measure show a slight decline in the percentage of Americans working more than 45 hours a week. In 1999, Gallup found that 45% of U.S. workers said they worked 45 hours or more per week. This percentage has slowly and gradually declined since then. The current results are now at levels Gallup recorded from 1989 through 1993. Since 1999, the percentage of workers saying they work between 35 and 44 hours has increased slightly.

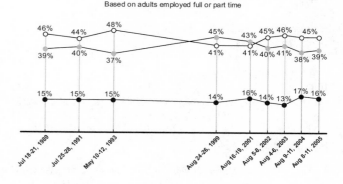

Trend in Number of Hours Worked

● <35 hours ○ 35-44 hours ● 45 hours

Based on adults employed full or part time

The vast majority of employed adults, 83%, say they currently hold only one job. Thirteen percent have two jobs at the present time, and 4% work three or more jobs. Results on this question have shown essentially no change since it was first asked in 1999.

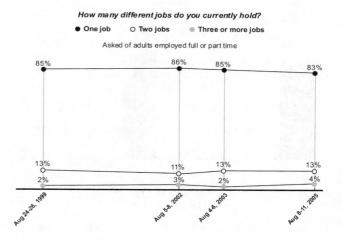

How many different jobs do you currently hold?

● One job ○ Two jobs ● Three or more jobs

Asked of adults employed full or part time

When workers are asked about the specific type of work they do, about one in four (24%) say they are employed in some professional specialty, in fields such as law, medicine, computer science, engineering, or social work. Twenty percent say they are administrative or managerial executives, with jobs such as chief executive, financial officer, or auditor.

About 1 in 10 workers each categorized their jobs as administrative personnel (12%), operators and laborers (11%), or service (10%). Other general categories of professions mentioned include sales (8%), precision production, craft, and repair (8%), technical (3%), farming, fishing, or forestry (1%), and the military (1%).

Being as specific as possible and using any job titles you may have, please tell me the kind of work you do based on adults employed full or part time

	2005 Aug 8-11 %	2003 Aug 4-6 %	2002 Aug 5-8 %
Professional Specialty	24	22	19
Executive: Administrative and Managerial	20	15	18
Administrative	12	17	13
Operators, Fabricators and Laborers	11	12	11
Service	10	14	12
Sales	8	8	8
Precision Production, Craft, and Repair	8	6	11
Technical	3	1	4
Farming/Forestry/Fishing	1	1	1
Military	1	2	1
Other	2	1	1
No Opinion	*	1	1

*Less than 0.5%

Half of American employees say they are paid hourly, while 39% receive salaries, and 6% are paid on commission. These results are essentially the same as they were in August 2002.

How are you paid at work: do you have a salary, are you paid by the hour, (or) are you mostly paid on commission?

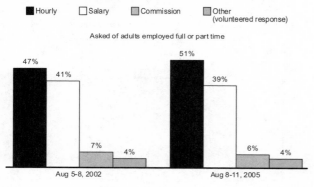

■ Hourly　□ Salary　■ Commission　□ Other (volunteered response)

Asked of adults employed full or part time

Variations by Type of Americans' Jobs

In order to better understand the way different groups of American workers describe their current employment situations, Gallup combined the results of its past three surveys on this question from August 2002, August 2003, and August 2005.

Gallup also categorized workers' responses to the type of work they do into three broad categories: professional or executive jobs, which include executives, managers, and specialists; other white-collar jobs, which include technical professions in health, science, and engineering, sales, and administrative personnel; and blue-collar professions, which include service jobs, farming or fishing, repair persons, laborers, and military personnel.

As the table shows, there are some interesting differences by gender, education level, and household income on this measure.

Job Description by gender, education level, and household income 2002-2005 Aggregate based on adults employed full or part time

	Professional/ Executive %	Other white collar %	Blue collar %
Gender			
Men	36	29	35
Women	46	48	7
Education			
High school or less	20	43	37
Some college	34	44	23
College graduates	55	37	8
Postgraduate	79	17	4

More than 9 in 10 women work in white-collar professions (46% in professional or executive and 48% in other white-collar professions), and just 7% work in blue-collar professions. Among men, 36% work in professional or executive professions, while 29% work in some other white-collar profession, and 35% work in blue-collar jobs.

Workers with a higher level of education are more likely to describe their jobs as professional or executive. Nearly 8 in 10 workers (79%) with postgraduate education work in a professional or executive job, compared with 55% of those with a college degree, 34% of those with some college education, and 20% of those with a high school education or less.

Differences in Type of Compensation for Workers

The combined results of Gallup's 2002 and 2005 surveys also show interesting differences in the way in which various groups are paid.

A majority of women (56%) say they are paid hourly wages, while 37% say they are on salary. Among men, compensation is almost equally divided between an hourly wage (43%) and a salary (42%). This difference may reflect the fact that women are more likely than men to be employed part time (11% to 5%), while men are more likely than women to be employed full time (61% to 39%).

Compensation by Gender 2002-2005 Aggregate

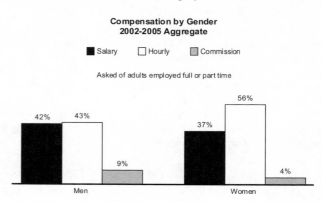

■ Salary　□ Hourly　■ Commission

Asked of adults employed full or part time

Workers with higher levels of education are more likely to receive salaries than are less educated workers. More than three in four workers with postgraduate education (77%) are on salary, compared with 55% of college graduates, 29% of those with some college education, and 24% of those with a high school education or less.

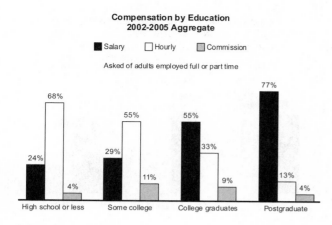

**Compensation by Education
2002-2005 Aggregate**

■ Salary   □ Hourly   ▨ Commission

Asked of adults employed full or part time

More than 6 in 10 workers in households earning $75,000 per year or more say they are paid salaries. By comparison, nearly three in four workers in households earning less than $30,000 per year are paid hourly.

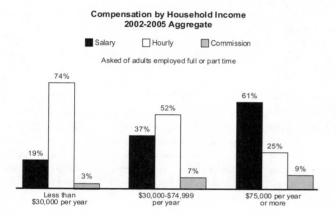

**Compensation by Household Income
2002-2005 Aggregate**

■ Salary   □ Hourly   ▨ Commission

Asked of adults employed full or part time

Sixty-one percent of those who are employed as a professional or executive are paid salaries, while 30% are paid hourly. Among other white-collar professionals, 60% are paid by the hour and 29% are paid a salary, and among blue-collar workers, 66% are paid hourly and only 18% are on salary.

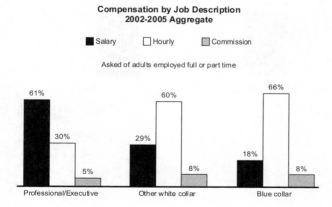

**Compensation by Job Description
2002-2005 Aggregate**

■ Salary   □ Hourly   ▨ Commission

Asked of adults employed full or part time

*Results are based on telephone interviews with 564 adults employed full or part time, aged 18 and older, conducted Aug. 8-11, 2005. For results based on the total sample of national adults, one

can say with 95% confidence that the margin of sampling error is ±4 percentage points.

Results are based on telephone interviews with 1,702 employed adults, aged 18 and older, conducted across four surveys from August 2002 through August 2005, the maximum margin of sampling error is ±3 percentage points.

Results are based on telephone interviews with 1,132 employed adults, aged 18 and older, taken from two surveys conducted August 2002 and August 2005, the maximum margin of sampling error is ±3 percentage points.

In addition to sampling error, question wording and practical difficulties in conducting surveys can introduce error or bias into the findings of public opinion polls.

September 14, 2005
BLACKS BLAST BUSH FOR KATRINA RESPONSE
Most believe racism was responsible for delays in providing relief

by Lydia Saad, Gallup Poll Senior Editor

Whites and blacks have sharply differing reactions to the federal government's response to Hurricane Katrina, with blacks more likely than whites to believe that racial bias was a factor in slowing the government's response, and blacks especially critical of President Bush's performance.

Aside from Bush, whites and blacks have similar perspectives on how various entities handled themselves in the Hurricane Katrina disaster. Most whites and blacks agree that FEMA, state and local Louisiana authorities, and New Orleans residents did a poor job initially, but that in recent days each has been doing a good job.

There is much more of a racial divide in assessments of Bush. Only 15% of blacks versus 49% of whites say Bush did a good job initially. Only 36% of blacks versus 63% of whites say Bush has been doing a good job in recent days.

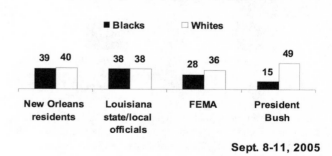

Initial Response to Hurricane Katrina
percentage "very good" or "good"

■ Blacks   □ Whites

Sept. 8-11, 2005

Blacks See Racial Bias at Work

There is a wide racial gap in perceptions of the role that the hurricane victims' socioeconomic status played in the federal government's willingness to get involved. The vast majority of blacks believe the government was slow in rescuing people specifically because the people affected are primarily black, and also because they are poor. Whites overwhelmingly reject these explanations.

Response to Hurricane Katrina in Recent Days
percentage "very good" or "good"

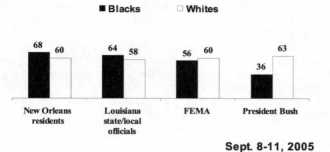

Sept. 8-11, 2005

Do you think one reason the federal government was slow in rescuing these people was because many of them were poor, or was that not a reason?

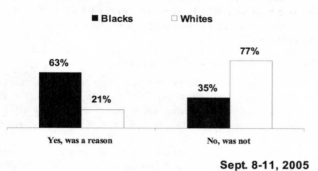

Sept. 8-11, 2005

Do you think one reason the federal government was slow in rescuing these people was because many of them were black, or was that not a reason?

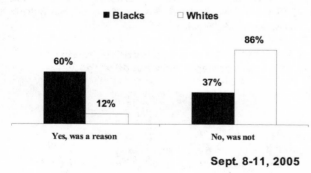

Sept. 8-11, 2005

These perceptions likely explain why blacks tend to be more likely than whites to report feeling anger in response to Hurricane Katrina and its aftermath (76% of blacks vs. 60% of whites).

At the same time, nearly all whites and blacks say they have felt sadness, and close to 8 in 10 have felt shock.

Blacks' Basic Ratings of Bush Haven't Changed

Whether the New Orleans crisis has harmed Bush's reputation in the black community or merely reinforced pre-existing criticism of him is not entirely clear. On the surface, it appears as if the federal

Personal Reaction to Hurricane Katrina and Aftermath

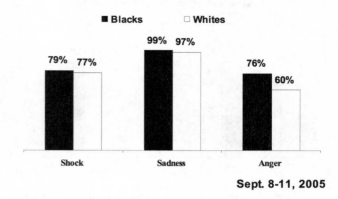

Sept. 8-11, 2005

response to Hurricane Katrina has not changed blacks' fundamental perceptions of Bush or the Republican Party—perceptions that were already quite negative.

The percentage of blacks approving of the job Bush is doing as president is 14% today, little different from the 15% recorded in August. Similarly, the percentage of blacks holding a favorable view of the Republican Party is now 16%, versus 18% earlier this year.

Finding Fault

While Bush appears to be the focal point for blacks' anger about the less-than-optimal government response to Hurricane Katrina, blacks as well as whites find plenty of blame to go around.

About 7 in 10 whites, and a similar proportion of blacks, believe that the government agencies in New Orleans responsible for dealing with natural disasters could have been better prepared to respond to Hurricane Katrina.

Views of New Orleans' Government Agencies That Deal With Natural Disasters

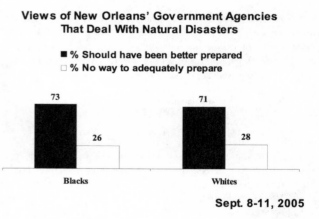

Sept. 8-11, 2005

When asked whether the mayor of New Orleans, the residents of New Orleans, Bush, or no one is most to blame for the fact that so many residents were trapped in New Orleans after the hurricane, the plurality of blacks (37%) cite President Bush. However, the combined percentage who blame either the mayor of New Orleans (20%) or the residents themselves (11%) is nearly as large.

Whites spread out their blame more evenly. About one-quarter each blame the mayor, the residents, and no one, while the fewest number of whites (15%) blame Bush.

Who Is the Most to Blame for New Orleans' Residents Being Trapped After Hurricane?

■ Blacks ☐ Whites

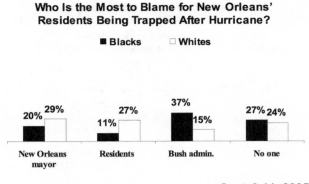

Sept. 8-11, 2005

Whites and blacks are in much closer agreement in their evaluations of FEMA Director Michael Brown (who has subsequently resigned his position). Only about one in five whites and blacks view Brown favorably, while about half view him unfavorably.

Opinion of FEMA Director Michael Brown

■ % Favorable   ▨ % Unfavorable   ☐ % No opinion

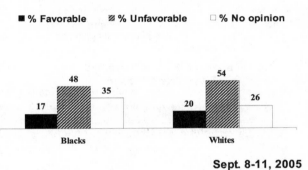

Sept. 8-11, 2005

Much greater disparity is seen in blacks' and whites' reactions to New Orleans Mayor Ray Nagin. Most blacks have favorable impressions of Nagin, who is black, while whites are about evenly divided in their assessments of him.

Opinion of New Orleans Mayor Ray Nagin

■ % Favorable   ▨ % Unfavorable   ☐ % No opinion

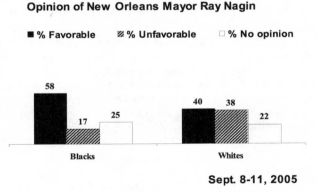

Sept. 8-11, 2005

Not only do blacks perceive racial bias in the federal government's handling of the post-Katrina situation, but when asked to choose between two explanations for why the government had difficulty responding, most blacks opt for the more critical reason. Fifty-six percent of blacks say it was due to "neglecting domestic needs like emergency preparedness and infrastructure." The slim majority of whites, 51%, choose the more benign explanation of "bureaucratic inefficiency."

Which was the greater obstacle to the federal government's response to the hurricane?

■ % Neglecting domestic needs
☐ % Bureaucratic inefficiency

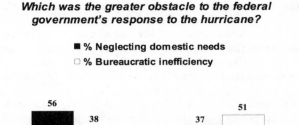
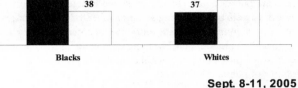

Sept. 8-11, 2005

Highlighting the degree to which politics play a role in perceptions of blame, blacks tend to say that the Republicans in Congress are spending too little time in figuring out who is to blame for the problems in the areas affected by Katrina (60% of blacks say this), while whites tend to say Democrats are spending too much time on this (49%). The majority of whites think the media are also spending too much time (51%), while most blacks (58%) think the media are spending the right amount of time on this issue.

Additional Findings

Three-quarters of blacks (77%), compared with only 44% of whites, consider the post-hurricane looters in New Orleans to have been mostly desperate people trying to keep themselves alive. Half of whites and only 16% of blacks view them as mostly criminals taking advantage of the situation.

Blacks are bothered, while whites are not, by the use of the term "refugees" to describe the residents of areas hit by Hurricane Katrina who have had to evacuate. The Rev. Jesse Jackson, among other civil rights figures, has stated that the use of the term is racist in this context, saying U.S. citizens should never be called "refugees."

A majority of whites (67%) and an especially large percentage of blacks (88%) would like to see an independent investigation conducted to review the problems with the government's response to the hurricane.

Blacks are a bit more optimistic than whites that when New Orleans is rebuilt, government planners will succeed in making the city less segregated than it was before the hurricane. Close to half of blacks (46%), but only 32% of whites, think planners will be at least somewhat successful at achieving this goal.

Whites and blacks have slightly different responses to how they would react if they were confronted with a New Orleans-like situation. Most whites (67%) say that if their homes and communities were destroyed in a natural disaster, they would want to go back and rebuild their lives there; only 29% would move to another community. Blacks are more evenly divided, as only 54% say they would go back and rebuild while 41% say they would relocate.

Survey Methods

These results are based on telephone interviews with 262 blacks, aged 18 and older, conducted Sept. 8-11, 2005, some of which were drawn from Gallup's Sept. 8-11 national sample and some of which were drawn from a special black oversample. The combined sample of blacks is weighted to be representative of U.S. blacks. For results based on the total sample, one can say with 95% confidence that the maximum margin of sampling error is ±7 percentage points.

Results for the sample of 848 whites, aged 18 and older, are based on telephone interviews with non-Hispanic whites conducted Sept. 8-11, 2005, and drawn from the national sample poll. For results based on the total sample, one can say with 95% confidence that the maximum margin of sampling error is ±4 percentage points.

For results based on the samples of 223 and 230 blacks, the maximum margin of sampling error is ±7 percentage points.

For results based on the samples of 388 and 460 whites, the maximum margin of sampling error is ±5 percentage points.

In addition to sampling error, question wording and practical difficulties in conducting surveys can introduce error or bias into the findings of public opinion polls.

The sample for this survey did not include the areas of Louisiana and Mississippi that were declared federal disaster areas following Hurricane Katrina. This accounts for about 0.75% of the U.S. population.

September 15, 2005
AMERICANS SUPPORT ROBERTS' CONFIRMATION
Half of Americans have a favorable opinion of nominee

by Joseph Carroll, Gallup Poll Assistant Editor

The United States Senate Judiciary Committee continues confirmation hearings today regarding the nomination of U.S. Circuit Judge John Roberts Jr. to serve as the Chief Justice of the U.S. Supreme Court. The latest CNN/*USA Today*/Gallup poll finds that nearly 6 in 10 Americans say they would like the Senate to confirm Roberts to the high court. Support for Roberts' confirmation is higher now than it was in August, and is at the same level Gallup recorded when President George W. Bush first nominated Roberts in late July. Half of Americans say they have a favorable view of Roberts, while only about one in six view him unfavorably and one-third have no opinion. Blacks and Democrats are much less likely than whites and Republicans to support Roberts' confirmation and to view him favorably.

Support for Roberts' Confirmation

The poll, conducted Sept. 8-11, finds that 58% of Americans support the Senate confirming Roberts to serve as Chief Justice of the Supreme Court. Twenty-seven percent oppose his confirmation and 15% have no opinion.

Gallup has asked this question four times since President Bush nominated Roberts in late July, initially to replace retiring Justice Sandra Day O'Connor. At that time, 59% of Americans said the Senate should confirm Roberts. Then, in August, support for Roberts' confirmation decreased slightly, but still a slim majority of Americans (51% in early August and 52% in late August) supported his confirmation. Gallup polling conducted after Bush nominated Roberts to serve as chief justice upon the recent death of Chief Justice William Rehnquist—but before the Senate confirmation hearings began this week—finds support for his confirmation at 58%.

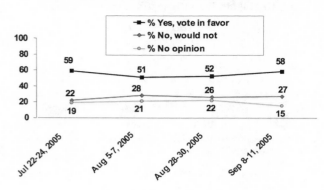

Support for Roberts' Confirmation

Republicans continue to show substantially higher levels of support for Roberts' confirmation than Democrats. Nearly 8 in 10 Republicans (79%) say the Senate should confirm Roberts to the Supreme Court, while 7% say the Senate should not confirm him and 14% have no opinion. These results compare with just 41% of Democrats who support the confirmation, 46% who oppose it, and 13% who have no opinion. Republican support has remained essentially unchanged since late July, while support among Democrats dipped in August but is now back to the level Gallup first measured.

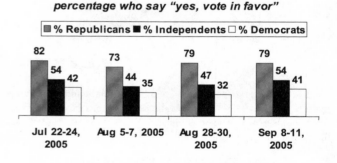

Support for Roberts' Confirmation
by party affiliation

percentage who say "yes, vote in favor"

Opinion of Roberts

The poll also asked Americans for their overall opinion of the Supreme Court nominee. Fifty percent of Americans say they have a favorable opinion of Roberts, while 17% have an unfavorable opinion and 33% do not have an opinion about him. The percentage of Americans with no opinion of Roberts has decreased since late July, while the favorable and unfavorable percentages have increased proportionately.

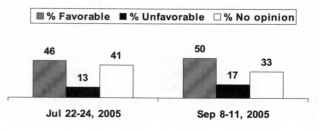

Opinion of John Roberts

Americans' opinions of Roberts also show sharp partisan differences. Two in three Republicans (67%) have a favorable opinion of Roberts, while 4% have an unfavorable opinion and 29% have no opinion. Democrats are more divided in their view of Roberts, with 35% rating him favorably and 31% unfavorably. Thirty-four percent of Democrats do not have an opinion about Roberts.

Since late July, Republicans have shown essentially no change in their ratings of Roberts. However, Democrats have become more willing to rate Roberts since that time. In July, half of Democrats did not know enough about Roberts to rate him, while the rest were equally divided in their view of him.

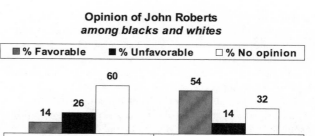

Opinion of John Roberts
among blacks and whites

Opinion of John Roberts
by party affiliation

	Favorable %	Unfavorable %	NEVER HEARD OF/ NO OPINION (vol.) %
2005 Sep 8-11			
Republicans	67	4	29
Independents	47	17	36
Democrats	35	31	34
2005 Jul 22-24			
Republicans	70	1	29
Independents	46	10	44
Democrats	25	26	49

Blacks More Negative Than Whites
About Roberts' Confirmation

The Sept. 8-11 poll, which included an oversample of blacks, finds substantial differences between whites' and blacks' assessments of Roberts.

Blacks are much less likely than whites to say the Senate should vote to confirm Roberts as Chief Justice of the Supreme Court. Among blacks, only 27% support his confirmation to the Court, while 44% oppose it and 29% do not have an opinion either way. Among whites, 61% support the confirmation, 23% oppose it, and 16% offer no opinion.

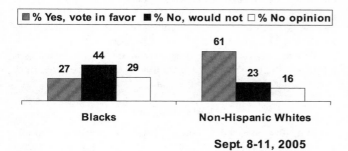

Support for Roberts' Confirmation
among blacks and whites

Blacks also are more negative than positive in their ratings of Roberts, with 14% rating him favorably and 26% unfavorably. The majority of blacks (60%) do not know enough about the nominee to rate him. In contrast, a majority of whites (54%) rate Roberts favorably, 14% rate him unfavorably, and 32% do not have an opinion.

Survey Methods

Results are based on telephone interviews with 1,005 national adults, aged 18 and older, conducted Sept. 8-11, 2005. For results based on the total sample of national adults, one can say with 95% confidence that the maximum margin of sampling error is ±3 percentage points. Results for the sample of 262 blacks, aged 18 and older, are based on telephone interviews conducted Sept. 8-11, 2005, some of which were drawn from Gallup's Sept. 8-11 national sample and some of which were drawn from a special black oversample. The combined sample of blacks is weighted to be representative of U.S. blacks. For results based on the total sample, one can say with 95% confidence that the maximum margin of sampling error is ±7 percentage points.

Results for the sample of 848 non-Hispanic whites, aged 18 and older, are based on telephone interviews conducted Sept. 8-11, 2005 drawn from the national sample poll. For results based on the total sample, one can say with 95% confidence that the maximum margin of sampling error is ±4 percentage points.

In addition to sampling error, question wording and practical difficulties in conducting surveys can introduce error or bias into the findings of public opinion polls.

The poll did not dial into some of the areas of Louisiana and Mississippi that were declared federal disaster areas following Hurricane Katrina. This amounts to about 0.75% of the U.S. population.

September 16, 2005
BUSH GETS NEGATIVE VIEWS FOR HANDLING THE HURRICANE
Fewer rate him as a strong and decisive leader

by Jeffrey M. Jones, Gallup Poll Managing Editor

Despite a generally negative evaluation of George W. Bush's response to Hurricane Katrina, Americans' more basic views of the president have changed little in recent weeks. Compared with the results of an Aug. 28-30 CNN/*USA Today*/Gallup poll—conducted as the hurricane hit parts of Louisiana, Mississippi, and Alabama—Bush's overall approval rating and his rating for handling specific issues have remained essentially the same. Views of Bush as a strong and decisive leader, typically one of his strengths, have slipped in the past few weeks.

Bush Approval Ratings

A majority of Americans, 54%, disapprove of the way Bush is handling the response to Hurricane Katrina, while 43% approve. As on most measures of the president, views divide along partisan lines—76% of Republicans approve, compared with just 15% of Democrats. Slightly more than one in three independents (36%) give Bush positive marks for his response to the crisis.

While that measure gives an overall assessment of Bush's response to the hurricane, the poll also asked the public to rate the job he did immediately after the hurricane hit, and in more recent days. Forty-four percent of Americans say the way he initially responded to the hurricane was good and 55% say it was poor. Reviews of his recent handling of the situation are more positive—58% say his response has been good and 40% say it has been poor. That general pattern of more negative initial ratings and more positive recent ratings is also found in the public's evaluations of how FEMA, Louisiana state and local officials, and the residents of New Orleans reacted.

Ratings of Initial and More Recent Response to Hurricane Katrina

2005 Sep 8-11	Initial (% good)	Recent (% good)
George W. Bush	44	58
The residents of New Orleans	39	59
State and local officials in Louisiana	38	57
FEMA/Federal government agencies responsible for handling emergencies	36	56

The fact that partisanship so heavily influences the ratings of Bush's overall response to the hurricane may explain the lack of change in other views of him. Forty-six percent of Americans approve and 51% disapprove of the job Bush is doing as president, according to the Sept. 8-11 poll. In the Aug. 28-30 poll, 45% of Americans approved. These approval ratings are among the lowest of Bush's presidency, and at least a majority of Americans have disapproved since late July. Bush's low point—a 40% approval rating in an Aug. 22-25 poll—was measured before the hurricane.

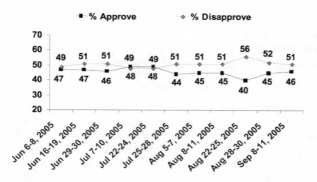

Bush's Overall Job Approval Rating
Selected Trend: June 2005 — September 2005

Bush's overall rating tends to be somewhat higher than most of his ratings for handling specific issues. Bush is rated more negatively on Iraq (40%), the economy (39%), and gas prices (22%). Bush earns his highest mark on how he has handled terrorism, as he has since Sept. 11, 2001. However, the current 52% approval rating on that issue is tied for the lowest of his presidency.

Ratings of George W. Bush on Issues

2005 Sep 8-11 (sorted by "approve")	% Approve	% Disapprove
Terrorism	52	45
Overall job approval	*46*	*51*
The response to Hurricane Katrina	43	54
The situation in Iraq	40	58
The economy	39	58
Gas prices	22	71

Aside from his response to Katrina, which was measured for the first time in this poll, Bush's issue ratings have basically not changed since the late August poll.

George W. Bush Issue Approval Ratings, late August and early September

	Aug 28-30 %	Sep 8-11 %
Terrorism	53	52
The situation in Iraq	40	40
The economy	38	39
Gas prices	20	22

There has, however, been some evidence of post-hurricane change in the public's ratings of Bush's personal characteristics. Most notably, fewer Americans (52%) now say he is a strong and decisive leader than did so in the late August poll (60%). On the other hand, there has been a slight increase in Bush's ratings on the "cares about the needs of people like you" dimension, from 44% to 48%. Ratings of Bush as inspiring confidence have held steady.

	Aug 28-30 %	Sep 8-11 %
Is a strong and decisive leader	60	52
Cares about the needs of people like you	44	48
Inspires confidence	47	46

The poll also asked about whether Bush displays good judgment in a crisis—47% say he does, 52% say he does not. There is no pre-hurricane reading on this measure for the president.

Most Americans disagree with the controversial assertion—made by rapper Kanye West during a telethon for hurricane victims—that Bush doesn't care about black people. In the poll, 62% of Americans say he does care, and 31% say he does not. However, black Americans see things differently—just 21% of blacks believe Bush cares about them, while 72% say he does not.

Overall, just 14% of blacks approve of the job Bush is doing as president, roughly the same as the ratings blacks have given Bush over the first eight months of the year.

Survey Methods

These results are based on telephone interviews with a randomly selected national sample of 1,005 adults, aged 18 and older, conducted Sept. 8-11, 2005. For results based on this sample, one can say with 95% confidence that the maximum error attributable to sampling and other random effects is ±3 percentage points. In addition to sampling error, question wording and practical difficulties in conducting surveys can introduce error or bias into the findings of public opinion polls.

Results for the sample of 262 blacks, aged 18 and older, are based on interviews conducted Sept. 8-11, 2005, some of which were drawn from Gallup's Sept. 8-11 national sample and some of which were drawn from a special black oversample. The combined sample of blacks is weighted to be representative of U.S. blacks. For results based on the total sample, one can say with 95% confidence that the margin of sampling error is ±7 percentage points.

September 19, 2005

AMERICANS' DOUR ECONOMIC ATTITUDES LITTLE AFFECTED BY KATRINA

Americans very negative on economy both before and after hurricane

by Frank Newport, Gallup Poll Editor in Chief

What has been the impact of Hurricane Katrina on consumer confidence in the United States economy? Gallup's first September update on Americans' views of the economy suggests that the hurricane may be having little effect at all. Confidence in the economy, which was low and dropping in August just before Katrina's landfall, continues to be low in September, showing little change in either direction after the events of the last few weeks. Economic concerns remain the most important problem facing the country—again, little changed from August.

Gallup's new economic update does show, however, a slight uptick in Americans' perceptions that inflation and unemployment will increase in the months ahead.

These results are based on Gallup's sample of 921 Americans interviewed Sept. 12-15, and are compared against more than 2,000 interviews conducted at two points in August.

The Economy

Americans were very much down on the economy before Katrina. Sixty-three percent of Americans in Gallup's Aug. 22-25 economic update said economic conditions were getting worse in the country as a whole, while only 28% said they were getting better. That was as low as had been measured since March 2003.

Now, after Katrina, there has been little change. Americans remain deeply pessimistic, with only a slight and statistically insignificant increase in the negative perceptions of the economy's direction.

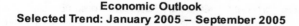

Economic Outlook
Selected Trend: January 2005 – September 2005

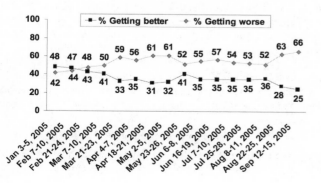

Ratings of current economic conditions in the country were relatively negative in August, and remain so now. Thirty-one percent of Americans now rate the economy as excellent or good, while 44% say it is "only fair" and 25% say it is poor. Those numbers are little changed from August.

Current Economic Conditions
Selected Trend: January 2005 – September 2005

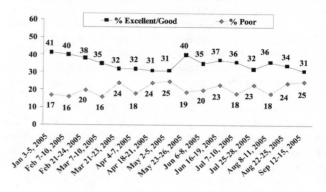

In both instances, then, the data suggest little support for the hypothesis that the hurricane itself has made a material difference in Americans' confidence in the U.S. economy. The August Gallup surveys showed that Americans were particularly troubled by the increase in gas prices, but despite the fact that prices have spiked even higher as a result of Katrina, there does not appear—at least at this point—to have been further erosion in the public's views of the economy.

Most Important Problem

Katrina neither amplified Americans' perceptions that the economy is the nation's top problem, nor did it diminish them.

Asked to name the most important problem facing the country, 32% of Americans in the Sept. 12-15 survey mention some aspect of the economy, a figure that is roughly comparable to what Gallup measured in August and the months that preceded.

What do you think is the most important problem facing this country today? [Open-ended]

		Sep 12-15, 2005	Aug 8-11, 2005	Jul 7-10, 2005
		%	%	%
	ECONOMIC PROBLEMS (NET)	**32**	**32**	**27**
1	Economy in general	11	13	10
2	Fuel/Oil prices	8	8	6
3	Unemployment/Jobs	4	8	8
4	Federal budget deficit/ Federal debt	3	2	1
5	High cost of living /Inflation	2	3	2
6	Lack of money	2	1	1
7	Wage issues	2	1	1
8	Gap between rich and poor	1	*	*
9	Taxes	1	1	1
10	Corporate corruption	1	*	*
11	Foreign trade/Trade deficit	1	*	1
12	Recession	*	—	—

		Sep 12-15, 2005	Aug 8-11, 2005	Jul 7-10, 2005
		%	%	%
NON-ECONOMIC PROBLEMS (NET)		**71**	**78**	**82**
1	Situation in Iraq/War	16	27	25
2	Natural disaster relief effort and funding	13	—	—
3	Dissatisfaction with government/ Congress/ politicians/ candidates; poor leadership; corruption	9	7	6
4	Ethics/Moral/Religious/ Family decline; dishonesty; lack of integrity	7	6	6
5	Terrorism	6	10	17
6	Poverty/Hunger/ Homelessness	4	5	5
7	National security	4	3	4
8	Education/Poor education/ Access to education	3	5	3
9	Foreign aid/Focus overseas	3	2	2
10	Poor healthcare/hospitals; high cost of healthcare	3	8	7
11	Immigration/Illegal aliens	2	5	4
12	Lack of energy sources; the energy crisis	2	2	1
13	Lack of respect for each other	2	1	*
14	International issues/problems	1	2	2
15	Judicial system/Courts/Laws	1	2	3
16	Social Security	1	3	4
17	Unifying the country	1	1	1
18	Race relations/Racism	1	*	*
19	Lack of military defense	1	—	*
20	Welfare	1	1	1
21	Environment/Pollution	1	1	1
22	The media	*	*	*
23	Abuse of power	*	*	*
24	Drugs	*	2	2
25	Overpopulation	*	—	*
26	Election year/Presidential choices/Election reform	*	*	*
27	Care for the elderly	*	*	*
28	Children's behavior/ way they are raised	*	2	*
29	Abortion	*	1	1
30	Medicare	*	1	1
31	Child abuse	*	*	*
32	Homosexuality/Gay issues	*	*	*
	Crime/Violence	—	2	1
	Guns/Gun control	—	—	*
	Cancer/Diseases	—	—	—
	Other non-economic	2	5	2
	No opinion	3	3	3
	Total	123%	144%	133%

*Less than 0.5%

Thirteen percent of Americans mention some aspect of Katrina or disaster relief and disaster funding as the nation's top problem.

That is, of course, up from 0% in August. The big change in response to this "most important problem" question between August and September involves the salience of Iraq. While 27% of Americans said Iraq was the nation's top problem in August, only 16% mention it now in the aftermath of Katrina.

In short, the hurricane has—at least temporarily—lowered the top-of-mind salience of the Iraq war for Americans, but it has done little to change the perceived importance of the economy as a problem facing the nation.

Inflation and Unemployment

One of the concerns about the economic impact of Katrina has been inflation. Not only have gas prices spiked, but there has been speculation that the price of many other goods and services may increase as well. Americans seem mindful of this possibility. The new poll finds that 76% believe inflation will go up over the next six months, including 33% who say it will go up a lot. That's the highest expectation of an increase in inflation that Gallup has measured since this tracking trend began in October 2001 (although in May of this year, 74% said inflation would go up).

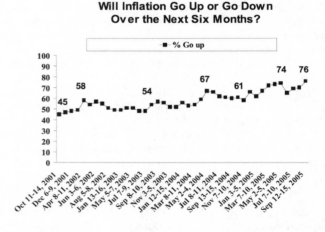

Will Inflation Go Up or Go Down Over the Next Six Months?

There has also been an increase in views that unemployment will increase in the next six months, from 44% who said it would go up a little or a lot in August to 52% this month. This change may well be a direct result of Americans' views that the hurricane put people living in the Gulf Coast out of work, at least temporarily.

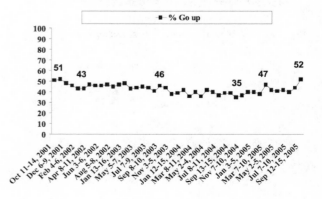

Will Unemployment Go Up or Go Down Over the Next Six Months?

Spending

It's rare to find major changes in Americans' spending plans. Survey after survey shows that the plurality or even the majority of Americans say their spending plans will remain the same rather than increasing or decreasing over the coming six months.

In the latest survey, 29% of Americans say their spending will increase over the next six months, 29% say it will decrease, and 42% say it will remain the same. That's not materially changed from Gallup's August poll or from polls conducted in previous months this year.

It appears obvious that Americans' actual retail spending is not always directly correlated with attitudes expressed in surveys. Too many factors like discounts, sales, introductions of highly desired products, and even the weather can affect spending regardless of the consumer's mood. Still, it would not be out of the question to assume that Katrina and its aftermath might affect the public's stated intentions about spending. That has not happened. There is no sign from these data that Katrina or the run-up in gas prices has significantly affected Americans' self-reported spending plans.

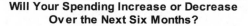

Will Your Spending Increase or Decrease Over the Next Six Months?

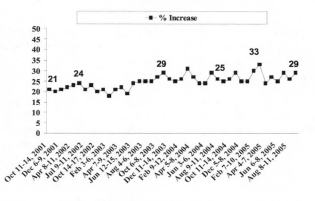

Survey Methods

Results are based on telephone interviews with 921 national adults, aged 18 and older, conducted Sept. 12-15, 2005. For results based on the total sample of national adults, one can say with 95% confidence that the maximum margin of sampling error is ±4 percentage points.

In addition to sampling error, question wording and practical difficulties in conducting surveys can introduce error or bias into the findings of public opinion polls.

The poll did not dial into some of the areas of Louisiana and Mississippi that were declared federal disaster areas following Hurricane Katrina. This amounts to about 0.75% of the U.S. population.

September 20, 2005
IS CONFIDENCE IN U.S. FOOD SUPPLY WILTING?
Americans positive about grocery store, restaurant food safety

by Chris McComb, Senior Staff Writer

Accusations that the government responded slowly to the devastation that Hurricane Katrina caused have prompted renewed focus on the United States' vulnerabilities, both to natural disasters and potential terrorist attacks. One pivotal safety concern is the nation's food supply.

Gallup's July 2005 Consumption Habits poll* (conducted before Hurricane Katrina) shows few Americans express a great deal of confidence in the federal government's ability to protect the food supply. Only 19% of Americans have "a great deal" of confidence in the federal government's ability "to ensure the safety of the food supply in the U.S," but an additional 61% have a fair amount. Only 20% have little or no confidence.

The percentage who are highly confident in the U.S. government in this regard has declined compared with last year's data. At that time, 31% expressed a great deal of confidence. This year's data are more similar to what Gallup found in earlier polls on this topic.

Gallup has asked this question several times over the last six years. The only time fewer Americans expressed a great deal of confidence in the government's ability to protect the food supply was September 1999, in a poll conducted just weeks after two large E. coli outbreaks in New York and Illinois.

How much confidence do you have in the federal government to ensure the safety of the food supply in the U.S., would you say you have -- a great deal, a fair amount, not much, or none at all?

Percentage saying "a great deal" of confidence

Americans Confident in Safety of Food in Grocery Stores, Restaurants

Despite persistent recalls from food suppliers and distributors, and scares such as the human fingertip "discovered" in a serving of chili at a Wendy's in San Jose, Calif., earlier this year (later determined to be a fraud), majorities of U.S. adults express confidence in the safety of food available at grocery stores and restaurants. Eighty-eight percent of Americans feel confident that grocery store food is safe, and 76% are confident that restaurant food is safe. Confidence in these food sources has increased since these questions were first asked in 1999, though large majorities were confident at that time as well.

Bottom Line

The post-Sept. 11 spotlight on safety issues, including food safety, may have faded somewhat over the past four years, but that does not mean anxieties have been completely assuaged. In a January 2003

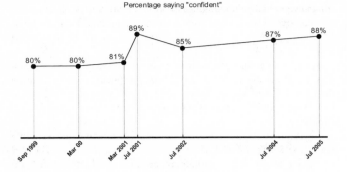

Do you feel confident or not confident that the food available at most grocery stores is safe to eat?

Percentage saying "confident"

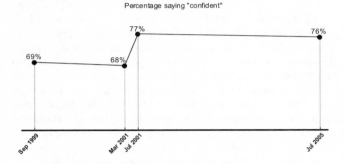

Do you feel confident or not confident that the food served at most restaurants is safe to eat?

Percentage saying "confident"

report, the Food Safety and Inspection Services, a public health regulatory agency of the U.S. Department of Agriculture, stated: "biological and chemical threats to the nation's food supply are a growing source of public concern." Americans seem to be in tune to this anxiety, with most of them expressing at least some level of wariness about the government's ability to protect the nation's food.

Results are based on telephone interviews with 1,006 national adults, aged 18 and older, conducted July 7-10, 2005. For results based on the total sample of national adults, one can say with 95% confidence that the margin of sampling error is ±3 percentage points.

September 20, 2005
FEAR OF CHILDREN'S SAFETY AT SCHOOL REMAINS LOW
Environment a big fear factor

by Jeffrey M. Jones, Gallup Poll Managing Editor

Armed security guards and metal detectors greeted Red Lake (Minn.) High School students at the start of this school year. The safety measures were put in place after a student shot and killed five classmates, a security guard, a teacher, and himself last spring. That is one extreme example of the dangers children face while at school, but dangers also exist in the forms of guns and knives in student lockers and the normal bullying that is common in most school settings.

Gallup regularly asks parents of school-aged children how much they fear for their oldest child's safety when they are at school*. In the last three years, the percentage of parents with children in kindergarten through grade 12 who say they fear for that child's

safety at school has ranged between 21% and 28%, with the vast majority of parents not expressing fear. That is a significant decline from the 55% of parents who expressed fear in April 1999, immediately after the Columbine High School shootings took place. In fact, the current year's 21% figure is the lowest Gallup has measured. Fear has typically increased in the immediate wake of highly publicized school shootings, and dissipated when none have been widely reported.

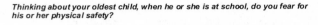

Thinking about your oldest child, when he or she is at school, do you fear for his or her physical safety?

● Yes, fear   ○ No, do not

Based on K-12 parents
Numbers shown in percentages

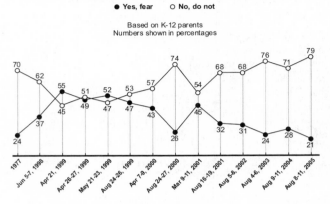

An analysis of Gallup data from the last three years on this question shows that some parents are more likely to express concern than others. In general, it appears that the environment of the child's school greatly affects parents' level of fear.

Income is the strongest predictor of worry—parents with lower levels of annual household income are much more likely to be worried than are middle- and upper-income parents. That probably reflects the areas in which the child attends school—as higher-income parents are more likely to live in the lower-crime suburbs, while lower-income parents are probably more likely to live in higher-crime areas. Additionally, higher-income parents are much more likely than lower-income parents to send their children to private or parochial schools (according to the Gallup data, 17% of parents whose annual household income is $75,000 or more send their children to private or parochial school, compared with 8% of those whose annual household income is less than $30,000).

Forty percent of parents living in households with annual incomes that are less than $30,000 say they fear for their oldest child's safety at school, compared with 21% of parents in $30,000 to $74,999 households and just 16% of parents in households in which the income is $75,000 or greater.

Fear for Child's Safety at School by Household Income

■ Fear   ▢ Do not fear

Numbers shown in percentages

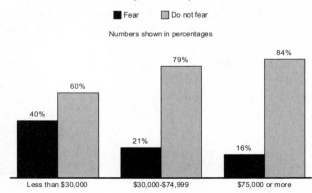

Race also is related to safety fears, even when taking into account household income. Black parents are nearly twice as likely as non-Hispanic white parents to say they fear for their oldest child's safety at school. Thirty-nine percent of black parents express fear, compared with 19% of white parents.

Parents whose oldest child attends public school (26%) are nearly twice as likely to express concern about that child's safety as parents who send the child to private or parochial schools (15%). Again, this difference is apparent even when controlling for household income.

Fear for Child's Safety at School by Type of School

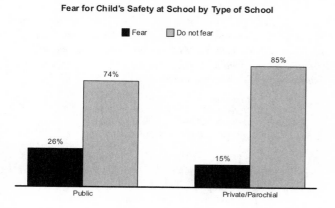

■ Fear   ▨ Do not fear

Whether true or not, private and parochial schools are generally thought to impose stricter discipline on students. These schools also have an advantage over public schools in that they are smaller, which allows for easier classroom control, and they often have the time to deal with any concerns *before* they become problems. Additionally, it is also possible that because these schools choose their students, they can keep the environment safer.

On the surface, it does not appear that a child's school level is related to parents' expressed fear. Twenty-four percent of parents whose oldest child is in elementary school (kindergarten through grade 5) say they fear for their child's safety, compared with 26% whose oldest child attends middle school (grades 6 to 8) and 23% of parents whose eldest child is in high school (grades 9 to 12).

However, a closer look at the data suggests that within those gross grade divisions, there is some evidence of a difference. Parents whose children are younger relative to the other students in their school are more likely to express worry. For example, 29% of parents whose oldest child is attending high school in grade 9 or 10 say they are fearful for their oldest child's safety, compared with 17% of parents whose child attends high school and is in grade 11 or 12—a statistically significant difference. Also, the data suggest that parents whose oldest child is in kindergarten or grade 1 are more likely to fear for their child's safety than parents whose children also attend elementary school but are in grades 2 or 3 or in grades 4 or 5.

Bottom Line

In general, it appears a child's school environment heavily influences fear for a child's safety while at school. The location of the school, whether it is a public or private institution, and the child's age relative to other students in the same school all influence the level of fear.

Results are based on 886 interviews with parents of K-12 children, taken from larger polls of the adult population conducted Aug.

4-6, 2003, Aug. 9-11, 2004, and Aug. 8-11, 2005. For results based on this sample, the maximum margin of sampling error is ±4 percentage points.

Margins of error for subgroups of parents will be higher.

September 20, 2005
BUSH RATINGS REACH LOW POINTS OF PRESIDENCY
Public skeptical about spending for reconstruction in New Orleans

by David W. Moore, Gallup Poll Senior Editor

Despite President George W. Bush's major address to the country last week, his popularity has sunk to the lowest level of his presidency. According to the latest CNN/*USA Today*/Gallup survey, only 40% of Americans approve of his overall job performance, which tied with one previous reading in August as the lowest score he has received since taking office in 2001. His disapproval reading of 58% is two points higher than the previous record measured last month.

2005	Approve %	Disapprove %	No opinion %
2005 Sep 16-18	40	58	2
2005 Sep 12-15	45	52	3
2005 Sep 8-11	46	51	3
2005 Aug 28-30	45	52	3
2005 Aug 22-25	40	56	4
2005 Aug 8-11	45	51	4
2005 Aug 5-7	45	51	4

On several other measures, Bush also fares worse than at any time in his presidency. His approval for handling the economy is at 35%, for foreign affairs 38%, and for Iraq 32%. His Iraq rating is eight points lower than his previous low of 40%, which he maintained from May through early September.

Do you approve or disapprove of the way George W. Bush is handling—[RANDOM ORDER]?

2005 Sep 16-18
(sorted by "approve")

	Approve %	Disapprove %
The response to Hurricane Katrina	41	57
Overall job approval	40	58
Foreign affairs	38	58
The economy	35	63
The situation in Iraq	32	67

Forty-one percent of Americans approve of the president's handling of the response to Hurricane Katrina, while 57% disapprove—down slightly from the 43% to 54% rating Bush received for Katrina in early September.

Bush's image among Americans has suffered not only in the way he has handled his job, but in his personal characteristics as well. Perhaps the most positive image of the president has been that of a strong and decisive leader, a trait that was used to contrast Bush with

Democratic Sen. John Kerry during the recent presidential election. Even as late as the end of August, a week after Hurricane Katrina hit, Americans viewed the president as a strong leader by a 60% to 40% margin. The latest results show a divided public—with a slight majority, 51%, saying that trait does not apply to Bush, and 49% saying it does.

Thinking about the following characteristics and qualities, please say whether you think it applies or doesn't apply to George W. Bush. How about—[ROTATED]?

2005 Sep 16-18 (sorted by "applies")	Applies %	Doesn't apply %
Is a strong and decisive leader	49	51
Is honest and trustworthy	47	50
Cares about the needs of people like you	42	56

Similarly, Americans are now considerably less likely to think of Bush as being honest and trustworthy than they did during most of his presidency and even earlier this year. As late as July, a clear majority, 54%, thought of Bush that way, with 44% expressing disagreement. Today, Americans lean in the opposite direction—50% say he is not honest and trustworthy; 47% say he is.

On whether he "cares about the needs of people like you," a decisive majority says Bush does not—by 56% to 42%. This view is reinforced by a separate question, asked later in the survey, about whether Bush had taken steps to help victims of Hurricane Katrina because of his sincere concern about the victims or because of political reasons. Americans choose political reasons by 56% to 42%.

Just your best guess, do you think George W. Bush has taken steps to help victims of Hurricane Katrina—[ROTATED: mostly because he sincerely cares about the victims, (or) mostly for political reasons]?

	Sincerely cares about the victims	Political reasons	No opinion
2005 Sep 16-18	42%	56	2

Aftermath of Hurricane Katrina

Overwhelmingly, the public believes that Hurricane Katrina will require the average American to make sacrifices in the form of higher taxes or cuts in government benefits.

In order for the federal government to handle the problems caused by Hurricane Katrina, do you think the average American will have to make major sacrifices in the form of higher taxes or cuts in government programs that benefit them, minor sacrifices, or no sacrifices at all?

	Major sacrifices	Minor sacrifices	No sacrifices	No opinion
2005 Sep 16-18	45%	48	6	1

And the vast majority of Americans, 84%, say they are willing to do that—although only 20% of Americans are willing to make "major" sacrifices while 64% say they would be willing to make "minor" sacrifices.

Would you, personally, be willing to make major sacrifices, minor sacrifices or no sacrifices at all in your taxes or government benefits to allow the government to spend money to address the problems caused by Hurricane Katrina?

	Major sacrifices	Minor sacrifices	No sacrifices	No opinion
2005 Sep 16-18	20%	64	14	2

Still, a clear majority of Americans, 54%, want the federal government to pay for the costs of Hurricane Katrina by cutting spending for the war in Iraq, while only 17% want taxes raised, 15% prefer an increase in the federal budget deficit, and 6% opt for cuts in domestic programs.

If you had to choose, which of the following would you say would be the best way for the government to pay for the problems caused by Hurricane Katrina—[ROTATED: increase the federal budget deficit, raise taxes, cut spending for the war in Iraq, (or) cut spending for domestic programs such as education and health care]?

	Increase federal budget deficit	Raise taxes	Cut spending for war in Iraq	Cut spending for domestic programs	OTHER (vol.)	No opinion
2005 Sep 16-18	15%	17	54	6	5	3

(vol.) = Volunteered response

Also, Americans are more worried that the government will spend too much on the problems caused by Katrina and ignore other problems facing the country, than they are worried that the government will spend too little to help the victims of Katrina.

Thinking about the money the federal government plans to spend on the problems caused by Hurricane Katrina, which worries you more—[ROTATED: that the federal government will spend TOO MUCH on these problems and ignore other problems the country faces, (or) that the federal government will spend TOO LITTLE on these problems and not adequately fix the problems caused by the hurricane]?

	Will spend too much	Will spend too little	NOT WORRIED (vol.)	No opinion
2005 Sep 16-18	50%	40	5	5

(vol.) = Volunteered response

As for government efforts to address the problems, most Americans express limited optimism. By 45% to 27%, Americans approve of the proposals Bush outlined in his address to the nation last week, though 28% volunteered no opinion.

Based on what you have heard or read, do you approve or disapprove of the proposals George W. Bush outlined in his speech on Thursday night to handle the problems caused by Hurricane Katrina in New Orleans and other areas of the Gulf Coast?

	Approve	Disapprove	No opinion
2005 Sep 16-18	45%	27	28

And when asked how much confidence they had in the Bush administration to respond to the current problems caused by Katrina, as well as future natural disasters and terrorist attacks, most Americans are guardedly optimistic. From 24% to 29% express a "great deal" of confidence, while from 30% to 40% have little or no confidence. Another 30% to 40% have a "moderate" amount of confidence.

How much confidence do you have in the Bush administration's ability to do each of the following—a great deal, a moderate amount, not much, or none at all? How about—[RANDOM ORDER]?

2005 Sep 16-18 (sorted by "great deal")	Great deal %	Moderate amount %	Not much %	None at all %	No opinion %
Assist the victims of Hurricane Katrina	29	41	20	10	*
Improve the government's ability to respond to future acts of terrorism	29	30	27	13	1
Rebuild New Orleans and other areas of the Gulf Coast region	25	43	21	10	1
Improve the government's ability to respond to future natural disasters	24	36	27	13	*

*Less than 0.5%

Despite their relatively sanguine view on these issues, the vast majority of Americans want an independent panel, not Congress, to investigate the government's slow response to Hurricane Katrina.

As you may know, some people have called for an investigation into the problems the government had in responding to Hurricane Katrina. Who would you rather see conduct this investigation—[ROTATED: an independent panel (or) Congress]?

	Independent panel	Congress	No opinion
2005 Sep 16-18	81%	18	1

Survey Methods

Results are based on telephone interviews with 818 national adults, aged 18 and older, conducted Sep. 16-18, 2005. For results based on the total sample of national adults, one can say with 95% confidence that the maximum margin of sampling error is ±4 percentage points.

In addition to sampling error, question wording and practical difficulties in conducting surveys can introduce error or bias into the findings of public opinion polls.

September 21, 2005
SUPPORT FOR U.S. POLICY IN IRAQ IS DWINDLING
Clear majority now says sending troops was a mistake

by Lydia Saad, Gallup Poll Senior Editor

While the Bush administration is trying to emphasize positive developments on the political front in Iraq, the recent escalation of rebel violence there—in addition to public concerns about the costs of recovering from Hurricane Katrina—may be costing President Bush some public support for his Iraq policy.

Public approval of Bush's overall handling of the situation in Iraq has tumbled eight points in just the past week, from 40% in a Sept. 8-11 poll to 32% in the most recent CNN/*USA Today*/Gallup poll, conducted Sept. 16-18. In fact, exactly 40% of Americans had approved of Bush's handling of Iraq in each of the previous four measures, dating back to May. Now, for the first time since the start of the Iraq war in 2003, two-thirds of Americans disapprove of the job he is doing on Iraq.

Bush's Handling of Situation in Iraq

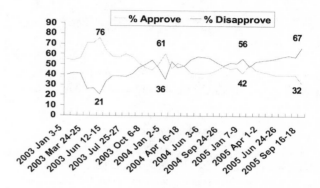

The percentage saying the United States made a mistake in sending troops to Iraq has also reached a new high of 59%, up six points from earlier this month.

Did the U.S. Make a Mistake in Sending Troops to Iraq?

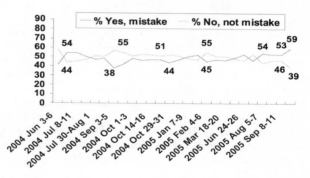

Also at a record high is the percentage of Americans favoring a reduction of U.S. troops in Iraq. More than 6 in 10 (63%) say the United States should now withdraw all or some of its troops from Iraq—compared with an average of 55% who said this in August. Only about one-third would prefer to see the number of U.S. forces in that country maintained or strengthened.

The shift toward troop withdrawal is seen about evenly among Republicans, independents, and Democrats, just as the decline in Bush's approval rating on Iraq is similar by party.

While increased support for troop withdrawal is consistent with the general decline in support for U.S. involvement in Iraq recorded elsewhere in the poll, it could also reflect Americans' view that the costs of rebuilding New Orleans and helping the victims of Hurricane Katrina should be paid with money currently earmarked for Iraq.

When given four budgetary options, 54% of Americans choose cutting spending for the war in Iraq as the best way for the government to pay for the problems caused by Hurricane Katrina. Only

U.S. Forces in Iraq

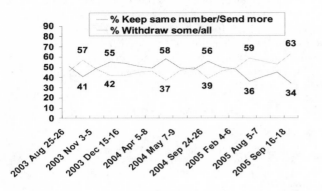

Survey Methods

These results are based on telephone interviews with a randomly selected national sample of 818 adults, aged 18 and older, conducted Sept. 16-18, 2005. For results based on this sample, one can say with 95% confidence that the maximum error attributable to sampling and other random effects is ±4 percentage points. In addition to sampling error, question wording and practical difficulties in conducting surveys can introduce error or bias into the findings of public opinion polls.

small fractions of Americans opt for raising taxes (17%), increasing the federal budget deficit (15%), or cutting back on domestic programs (6%).

Insurgent Violence Shaking Americans' Resolve?

Rebels continue to attack U.S. military targets in Iraq, taking the lives of roughly two American soldiers per day; the total number of U.S. troops killed since the beginning of the Iraq war is expected to surpass 2,000 in November.

But this is not likely the cause for the sudden and sharp decline in public support for the Bush administration's Iraq policy seen in the latest poll. Rather, the perception that a civil war may be erupting between Sunni rebels and the Shiite Arab majority could be deepening Americans' sense that Iraq is descending into a quagmire.

The Sept. 16-18 poll comes on the heels of what one report described as "the deadliest day of attacks in Baghdad since the invasion of March 2003." Last Wednesday (Sept. 14), a dozen or so suicide bombings and other attacks claimed the lives of more than 150 Iraqi civilians and security personnel, only to be followed by more bombings and more than 30 killed on Thursday.

Contrary to this hypothesis, however, a Gallup Poll conducted Sept. 12-15—spanning the period of the Baghdad attacks—found no drop in the percentage of Americans saying it was worth going to war in Iraq. The latest poll found 45% saying it was worth it and 53% not worth it—nearly identical to an early August poll.

Is Katrina a Factor?

Another possible explanation for Americans' declining support for the Iraq war could be the financial connection between Iraq and the recovery from Hurricane Katrina. Gallup's Sept. 12-15 survey found the percentage of Americans naming Iraq as the nation's most important problem down sharply compared with August (dropping from 27% to 16%) at the same time that 13% mentioned Katrina as the nation's top problem. It is possible that Americans' concerns about the costs involved in hurricane recovery could be draining public support for continued U.S. military involvement in Iraq.

An Iraq backlash from Katrina was not evident in Gallup's Sept. 8-11 survey. At that time, attitudes about Bush's handling of Iraq were identical to those measured before Katrina made landfall south of New Orleans on Aug. 29. But as media coverage of Katrina has shifted from rescuing residents and dealing with refugees to the price of recovery, it's quite possible that the link Americans make between Katrina and Iraq has strengthened.

September 23, 2005
MOST AMERICANS TENTATIVE ABOUT ORIGIN-OF-LIFE EXPLANATIONS
Public says evolution, creationism probably true; divided on intelligent design

by David W. Moore, Gallup Poll Senior Editor

Last month, President George W. Bush fueled renewed debate about teaching evolution in schools, when he opined that "intelligent design" should be taught along with evolution as competing theories explaining the origins of life. Gary Bauer, a Christian conservative leader who ran against Bush in the 2000 Republican primaries, asserted that intelligent design "is not some backwater view. It's a view held by the majority of Americans."

Gallup polling suggests that indeed most Americans believe God played some part in the development or creation of the human species, though relatively few people are very familiar with the term "intelligent design." While close to half of all Americans (45%) say they are "very familiar" with evolution, and an equal percentage say that about creationism, only 17% say they are this familiar with intelligent design.

How familiar would you say you are with each of the following explanations about the origin and development of life on Earth—very familiar, somewhat familiar, not too familiar, or not at all familiar? How about—[RANDOM ORDER]?

2005 Aug 5-7 (sorted by "very familiar")	Very familiar	Somewhat familiar	Not too familiar	Not at all familiar	No opinion
	%	%	%	%	%
Evolution	45	37	10	7	1
Creationism	45	29	15	9	2
Intelligent design	17	28	27	25	3

The percentages who say they are either "very" or "somewhat" familiar with each explanation are 82% for evolution, 74% for creationism, and 45% for intelligent design.

When it comes to expressing a firm belief in one explanation or another, most Americans are unwilling to say that any of the items are either "definitely" true or false.

Forty percent of people have a "definite" view of evolution, with 20% saying evolution is definitely true and 20% saying definitely false. By comparison, 37% have a clear-cut view about creationism (29% definitely true, 8% definitely false), and just 18% express unambiguous feelings about intelligent design (8% definitely true, 10% definitely false).

For each of the following, please say whether you believe it is—[ROTATED: definitely true, probably true, probably false, (or) definitely false] as an explanation for the origin and development of life on Earth? How about—[RANDOM ORDER]?

2005 Aug 5-7 (sorted by "definitely true")	Definitely true %	Probably true %	Probably false %	Definitely false %	Not familiar with %	No opinion %
Creationism	29	29	18	8	11	5
Evolution	20	35	14	20	8	3
Intelligent design	8	23	22	10	28	9

While many people are not completely sure about the validity of each of the explanations for the origins of life, majorities believe that creationism and evolution are at least probably true, while people are evenly divided about intelligent design. By 58% to 26%, a majority of Americans express their belief in creationism; by 55% to 34%, a majority also accept evolution. But 32% of Americans tend to reject intelligent design, while 31% say it is probably true.

In principle, the possibility exists that one could believe in both evolution and intelligent design. While many evolutionists suggest that random mutations are at the heart of evolutionary change, many other people who accept evolution nevertheless believe that at some removed point in time, God set the evolutionary process in motion.

However, the conflicts between creationism and evolution appear irreconcilable. Evolution posits millions of years of change, and the emergence of the human species from apes. Creationism accepts the literal creation story in the Bible, which essentially says that about 6,000 years ago God created all living things, including humans, as they currently exist.

The poll shows, however, that many Americans apparently do not recognize the irreconcilability of creationism and evolution. Twenty-nine percent say that both explanations are either definitely or probably true, while 47% accept only one or the other of the explanations—26% say creationism is probably true, but evolution is not; and 21% say that evolution is probably true, and creationism is not. Another 4% say both explanations are probably false, and 20% have no opinion.

Comparison of Beliefs About Evolution and Creationism

	"Probably" true/false %
Both probably true	29
Evolution probably true, creationism not	21
Creationism probably true, evolution not	26
Both probably false	4
No opinion about one or both	20

If we look only at the people who have "definitely" decided whether each explanation is true or false, we find only 25% of Americans with a firm view about the two explanations. Five percent believe both are definitely true, while 2% believe both are definitely false. Another 13% believe creationism is definitely true and evolution is definitely false; while 5% believe evolution is definitely true and creationism is definitely false.

Comparison of Beliefs About Evolution and Creationism

	"Definitely" true/false %
Both definitely true	5
Evolution definitely true, creationism not	5
Creationism definitely true, evolution not	13
Both definitely false	2
No opinion about one or both	75

Views About Origins of Life Related to Church Attendance

There are some differences in views among Protestants and Catholics on the explanation for the origin of life, but the major differences appear to be among people classified by how frequently they attend church.

People who seldom or rarely attend are much more likely to believe in evolution (71%) than are people who attend weekly (33%). Also, there are differences by education—the higher the level of education, the more likely people are to believe in evolution.

Evolution	Definitely/ Probably true %	Definitely/ Probably false %	Not familiar/ no opinion %
Overall	55	34	11
Church attendance			
Weekly	33	56	11
Near weekly/Monthly	52	36	12
Seldom/Never	71	18	11
Education			
High school or less	46	32	22
Some college	56	39	5
College grad	60	36	4
Postgrad	74	24	2

Not surprisingly, those correlations are reversed for creationism. Seventy-three percent of weekly churchgoers believe creationism is probably true, compared with 63% of occasional churchgoers, and just 48% of people who rarely or never attend.

Education also appears to be correlated with belief in creationism, but the differences in views are primarily between postgraduates and the rest of the group. Postgraduates are about evenly divided as to whether creationism is true or false, while the other educational groups all show significant majorities who believe creationism is true.

Creationism	Definitely/ Probably true %	Definitely/ Probably false %	Not familiar/ No opinion %
Overall	58	26	16
Church attendance			
Weekly	73	13	14
Near weekly/Monthly	63	20	17
Seldom/Never	48	37	15
Education			
High school or less	57	20	23
Some college	64	23	13
College grad	63	27	10
Postgrad	48	45	7

Results are based on telephone interviews with 1,004 national adults, aged 18 and older, conducted Aug. 5-7, 2005. For results based on the total sample of national adults, one can say with 95% confidence that the margin of sampling error is ±3 percentage points.

In addition to sampling error, question wording and practical difficulties in conducting surveys can introduce error or bias into the findings of public opinion polls.

September 22, 2005

PUBLIC MOST SATISFIED WITH GOVERNMENT'S HANDLING OF PARKS, OPEN SPACE

Decline in satisfaction with handling of military, national defense

by Jeffrey M. Jones, Gallup Poll Managing Editor

Of all the major functions the federal government performs, the American public is most satisfied with the work the government is doing in the area of national parks and open space. The public is least satisfied with the government's handling of the nation's finances, poverty, and healthcare. There are only 5 of 17 areas for which more Americans are satisfied than dissatisfied. Republicans are more likely to express satisfaction than Democrats in all areas.

Gallup's annual Governance poll, conducted Sept. 12-15, asked the public to rate its satisfaction with the various functions the federal government performs—loosely based on the various cabinet agencies. Seventy-one percent of Americans say they are satisfied with the government's work in the area of national parks and open space, placing it far ahead of the second ranked area on the list—the nation's military and national defense.

In all, there are only five areas in which at least half the public is satisfied—national parks, the nation's military and defense, agriculture and farming, transportation, and homeland security.

Americans are least satisfied with the government's handling of the nation's finances, poverty, healthcare, and energy policy, all with only about one in four Americans satisfied. In the wake of Hurricane Katrina, one in three are satisfied with the government's handling of natural disasters.

Next, we are going to name some major areas the federal government handles. For each one, please say whether you are satisfied or dissatisfied with the work the government is doing

Area	Satisfied %	Dissatisfied %
National parks and open space	71	27
The nation's military and national defense	59	40
Agriculture and farming	56	38
Transportation	56	42
Homeland security	50	49
Environmental issues	48	51
Public housing and urban development	47	49
Criminal justice	47	52
Labor and employment issues	44	54
Foreign affairs	41	58
Education	41	59

Area	Satisfied %	Dissatisfied %
Job creation and economic growth	39	60
Responding to natural disasters	33	66
Energy policy	27	71
Healthcare	24	75
Poverty	24	75
The nation's finances	23	76

Gallup asked this question in 2001, immediately before the Sept. 11 terror attacks. Many agencies have seen their ratings change since then—with roughly half showing improved ratings and half showing worse ratings.

Change in Americans' Ratings of Federal Government Functions, 2001-2005

	2001	2005	Percentage Point Change
National parks and open space	64	71	+7
Agriculture and farming	49	56	+7
Criminal justice	40	47	+7
Education	38	41	+3
Labor and employment issues	42	44	+2
Environmental issues	46	48	+2
Job creation and economic growth	39	39	0
Public housing and urban development	49	47	-2
Poverty	26	24	-2
Healthcare	27	24	-3
The nation's military and national defense	65	59	-6
Transportation	65	56	-9
Energy policy	38	27	-11
The nation's finances	34	23	-11
Foreign affairs	57	41	-16
Homeland security	—	50	—
Responding to natural disasters	—	33	—

The biggest positive changes—all showing 7 percentage point increases in satisfaction compared with 2001—are national parks, agriculture, and criminal justice. Americans rate education, labor, and the environment more positively than in 2001, but not significantly so.

Some of the greatest changes during the past four years have come on the negative side of the ledger—the biggest drop has come in the government's handling of foreign affairs, down 16 points from 2001. Military and defense, which was among the three highest rated government areas in 2001, has seen its satisfaction rating fall. The war in Iraq is a likely explanation for both declines.

High gas prices are a likely reason that satisfaction with the government's handling of energy policy is down 11 points, even though the 2001 ratings were already quite negative. There has been a similar drop in terms of the government's handling of the nation's finances, likely due to the exploding deficits brought about by increased efforts to prevent terrorism, the Iraq war, the series of income tax cuts passed in 2001-2002, and now efforts to rebuild after Hurricane Katrina. Ratings of transportation have also fallen significantly, from 65% in 2001 to 56% today.

Party differences are evident in all areas, with Republicans significantly more satisfied than Democrats for all functions. That is not surprising since a Republican administration is running the government. The largest gaps between Republicans and Democrats are in the areas of national defense and foreign affairs, both showing differences of greater than 50 percentage points in rated satisfaction. The smallest partisan gap—still 9 percentage points—is in the area of criminal justice.

Party Differences in Ratings of Government Functions

	Republican %	Independent %	Democrat %	Rep-Dem Difference
The nation's military and national defense	88	57	34	+54
Foreign affairs	70	35	19	+51
Responding to natural disasters	63	24	14	+49
Labor and employment issues	69	43	20	+49
Job creation and economic growth	67	33	20	+47
Homeland security	75	45	30	+45
The nation's finances	49	17	5	+44
Public housing and urban development	68	42	32	+36
Poverty	43	18	10	+33
Environmental issues	68	43	35	+33
Education	61	34	29	+32
Healthcare	36	20	16	+20
Agriculture and farming	70	49	53	+17
Transportation	66	54	49	+17
National parks and open space	81	68	65	+16
Energy policy	37	22	24	+13
Criminal justice	52	44	43	+9

Survey Methods

These results are based on telephone interviews with a randomly selected national sample of 921 adults, aged 18 and older, conducted Sept. 9-12, 2005. For results based on this sample, one can say with 95% confidence that the maximum error attributable to sampling and other random effects is ±3 percentage points. In addition to sampling error, question wording and practical difficulties in conducting surveys can introduce error or bias into the findings of public opinion polls.

September 27, 2005

TRUST IN NEWS MEDIA REBOUNDS SOMEWHAT THIS YEAR

Plurality of Americans still describe news media as too liberal

by Joseph Carroll, Gallup Poll Assistant Editor

Half of Americans say they trust the mass media when it comes to reporting the news fully, accurately, and fairly, according to Gallup's annual Governance survey. Trust and confidence in the news media is up significantly since last year, but it is still slightly lower than

what Gallup has found in recent years. The most common view of the political leanings of the news media is that they are too liberal—close to half of Americans say this—followed by more than a third who say they are about right. The smallest number describes the news media as too conservative. Republicans are much less likely than Democrats to express confidence in the media, but are much more likely to perceive bias in the news media, with most Republicans saying they are too liberal.

Trust in Media Up This Year, Still Lower Than in Recent Years

The poll, conducted Sep. 12-15, finds that half of Americans say they have a great deal (13%) or fair amount (37%) of trust and confidence in the mass media, while the other half say they do not have very much trust (37%) or none at all (12%). The current results show an increase in the public's trust and confidence in the media since last year, but the results are still slightly lower than what Gallup has recorded in recent years.

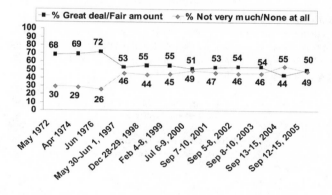

Trust and Confidence in the Mass Media Trend

When Gallup first asked this question in 1972, trust and confidence in the mass media was much higher than it is today, with 68% Americans expressing confidence in 1972; the high point on this measure came in 1976, when 72% of respondents said they had a great deal or fair amount of trust and confidence in the media.

By 1997, when Gallup resurrected the question, this sentiment had declined substantially. Still, a majority of Americans, 53%, expressed confidence in the media. These results showed only modest variations between 1997 and 2003 before dropping substantially to 44% last year, matching the low point of the trend. Confidence in the media has rebounded somewhat this year, but still remains below recent levels.

A Plurality of Americans Say News Media Are Too Liberal

When asked about the news media's political slant, Americans are much more likely to say they are too liberal (46%) than they are to say they are about right (37%) or too conservative (16%).

Those views are consistent with what Gallup has measured since 2001. The percentage of Americans saying the news media are too liberal has ranged between 45% and 48%, and has always been the plurality response. There has been a slight increase in the public's sentiment that the media are too conservative, from 11% in 2001 to 16% today.

Is the News Media Too Liberal, Too Conservative, or Just About Right?

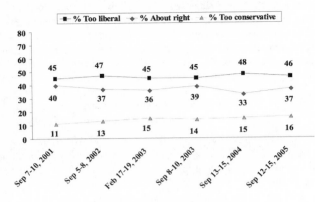

Is the News Media Too Liberal, Too Conservative, or Just About Right?
by party affiliation

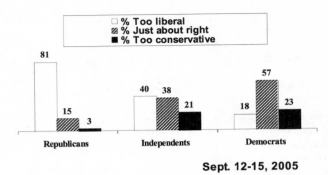

Sept. 12-15, 2005

Republicans and Democrats Differ in Views of News Media

These two measures show substantial differences between Republicans and Democrats.

About 3 in 10 Republicans (31%) say they have a great deal or fair amount of trust and confidence in the media, while the vast majority of Republicans (69%) say they have very little or no trust in the media. The results are essentially opposite among Democrats, with 70% expressing a great deal or fair amount of confidence in the media and 30% very little or no confidence.

Trust in Mass Media
by party affiliation

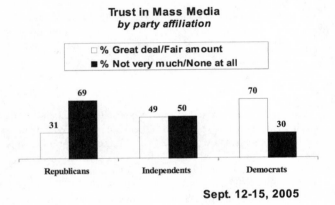

Sept. 12-15, 2005

Eight in 10 Republicans (81%) say the news media are too liberal, while 15% say they are about right, and just 3% say they are too conservative. Among Democrats, a majority (57%) says the news media are just about right, while the rest are almost equally divided in their description of the news media as too liberal (18%) and too conservative (23%).

Survey Methods

These results are based on telephone interviews with a randomly selected national sample of 921 adults, aged 18 and older, conducted Sep. 12-15, 2005. For results based on this sample, one can say with 95% confidence that the maximum error attributable to sampling and other random effects is ±3 percentage points. In addition to sampling error, question wording and practical difficulties in conducting surveys can introduce error or bias into the findings of public opinion polls.

September 28, 2005
TRUST IN FEDERAL GOVERNMENT NOT SHAKEN BY KATRINA
Little recent change in confidence in government to handle domestic problems

by Lydia Saad, Gallup Poll Senior Editor

Gallup's annual Governance survey, conducted Sept. 12-15, suggests that the events surrounding Hurricane Katrina have thus far had little effect on Americans' fundamental levels of confidence in the federal government, just as Katrina had little immediate impact on Gallup's ratings of President George W. Bush. In contrast, the 9/11 terrorist attacks immediately boosted Bush's approval ratings and ultimately strengthened public confidence in the federal government for a sustained period.

The percentage of Americans who now trust the federal government in Washington to handle domestic problems stands about where it did when last measured seven months ago: 53% have either a great deal or a fair amount of confidence. In February the figure was 56%.

Americans' overall trust and confidence in the executive branch of the federal government has declined slightly compared with the

Confidence in Government on Domestic Problems

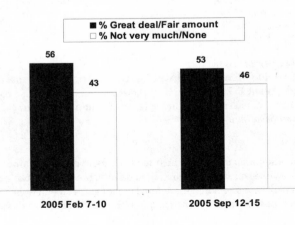

previous reading—it was 58% in September 2004 vs. 52% today—but this conforms with a slight dip in Bush's overall job approval rating over the same period.

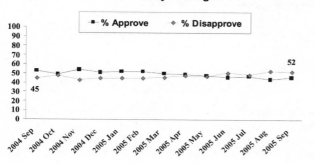

There has also been no significant year-to-year change in public trust in state and local governments. About two-thirds of Americans today say they have trust and confidence in these, nearly identical to last September's readings.

Media and Executive Branch Have Low Ranking

The Governance survey audits Americans' confidence levels in a variety of entities that contribute to public affairs in the United States: the three branches of the federal government, state and local governments, public officials themselves, the media, and the American public. Of these, Americans express the greatest amount of trust in the American public and the least in the mass media and the executive branch of government.

Nearly four in five Americans say they have a great deal or fair amount of trust in the American people "when it comes to making judgments under our democratic system about the issues facing our country."

The next-most-highly rated civic players are local governments, the judicial branch of the federal government, and state governments. About two-thirds of Americans rate each of these highly.

Roughly 6 in 10 give high marks to the legislative branch of the federal government and to the men and women who serve in public office.

Just half give high marks to the mass media for "reporting the news fully, accurately, and fairly"; 49% say they have not very much or no confidence at all in the mass media. Similarly, just 52% express confidence in the executive branch of government, while 48% express little or no confidence.

Trust in Federal Government's Abilities

Gallup's frequent measurement of two questions included in the Governance survey shows that 9/11 corresponded with a sharp increase in Americans' trust in the federal government to handle domestic as well as international problems. Between September 2001 and October 2001, the percentage expressing confidence in the government's handling of these areas increased from 68% to 83% for international problems, and from 60% to 77% for domestic problems. Confidence levels remained elevated in subsequent polls conducted in February and June 2002, but by September 2002 these had returned to pre-9/11 levels.

Since 2002, there has been a continued slide in public confidence on these two dimensions—a slide that corresponds with increasing

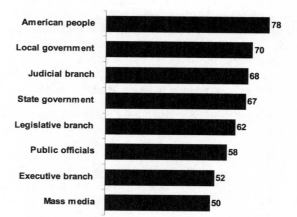

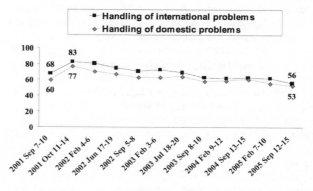

public concerns about the Iraq war and the U.S. economy, and with decreasing ratings of President Bush more generally.

Decreasing public support for the Iraq war is the most likely explanation for the six-point decline since February of this year in the government's ratings on its handling of international problems. Since that time, the percentage saying they approve of the job Bush is doing on Iraq has fallen from 50% to 40% and the percentage saying that sending troops to Iraq was a mistake has risen from 45% to 53%. (Subsequent Gallup measures of Bush approval on Iraq are even lower than they were at the time of the Governance poll.)

Similarly, since early February, the percentage of Americans expressing positive sentiments about the U.S. economy has declined from 34% to 21%.

Other Recent Trends

Besides reduced public confidence in the federal government's handling of international problems and in the executive branch of government more specifically, the other significant changes recorded this year are a slight increase in public trust in media and a slight decline in trust in public officials.

Americans' trust in the media has partially rebounded after declining from 54% in 2003 to 44% last year. (The cause of last year's drop is not clear, but the most visible news controversy at the time involved CBS News anchor Dan Rather's reliance on faulty documents in his report that was critical of President Bush's service in the National Guard.) Today, 50% say they have at least a fair amount of trust and confidence in the news media.

Confidence in News Media

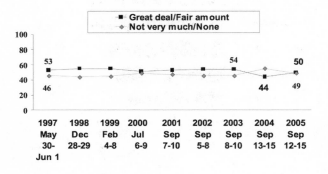

The percentage of Americans saying they have a great deal or fair amount of trust in the men and women serving in public office fell five points over the past year, from 63% in 2004 to 58% today. But last year's level was unusually high, so that the current figure is consistent with where this stood in 2002 and 2003.

Confidence in Public Officials

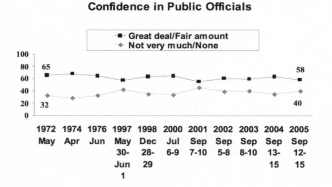

At the same time, there has been no significant change in Americans' expressed confidence in the judicial or legislative branches, or in state or local governments, or in the American people.

Ratings Disparities Among the Parties

Republicans and Democrats differ sharply in the levels of confidence expressed toward the executive branch, as well as toward the news media. Republicans are much more positive about the executive branch than are Democrats—naturally so, given that the head of the executive branch (President Bush) is a Republican. Democrats, who are much more likely than Republicans to be satisfied with the political leanings of the news media, give much higher confidence ratings to the media.

All other partisan differences—even with respect to the legislative branch of government, currently controlled by the Republican Party—are relatively minor.

% Trust a Great Deal/ Fair Amount by Party ID	Republicans	Independents	Democrats
	%	%	%
Executive branch	90	43	25
American public	82	74	78
Judicial branch	75	64	65
Local government	75	63	72
Public officials	67	51	58
Legislative branch	67	56	65
State government	66	66	67
News/Mass media	31	49	70

Survey Methods

These results are based on telephone interviews with a randomly selected national sample of 921 adults, aged 18 and older, conducted Sept. 12-15, 2005. For results based on this sample, one can say with 95% confidence that the maximum error attributable to sampling and other random effects is ±4 percentage points. In addition to sampling error, question wording and practical difficulties in conducting surveys can introduce error or bias into the findings of public opinion polls.

September 29, 2005
PUBLIC'S RATINGS OF PARTIES LOW IN HISTORICAL PERSPECTIVE
Democrats gain edge on party identification

by Jeffrey M. Jones, Gallup Poll Managing Editor

Recent Gallup polling finds the public with at best middling views of the Democratic and Republican parties. Fewer than half rate each party favorably, and as many give a negative evaluation of the Republican Party as give a positive one. The parties maintain their recent positioning on the issues—Americans view Republicans as better able to handle international matters, while they consider Democrats better in dealing with the economy. General impressions of each party largely center on their ideological orientation, the public's basic favorable or unfavorable views of the parties, and on the parties' perceived biases toward the rich or poor. Finally, an analysis of trends in partisanship nationwide during recent months shows a slight shift toward the Democratic Party.

Ratings of the Parties

A Sept. 8-11 CNN/*USA Today*/Gallup poll finds less than half of the public with a favorable view of either party. Overall, Americans have a net positive view of the Democratic Party—47% rate it favorably and 41% unfavorably. The public views the GOP evenly—45% have a favorable opinion and 45% an unfavorable opinion. Both current ratings are worse than the historical averages. Since Gallup first asked this question in 1992, the average favorable ratings of the Democratic and Republican parties have been 53% and 50%, respectively.

Both parties' ratings are down significantly from earlier points this year. In fact, the 45% rating of the Republican Party is the lowest since 1999, when the unpopular attempt to impeach President Bill Clinton hurt the party's rating.

Opinion of the Republican Party

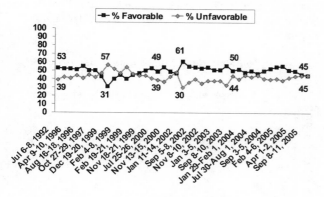

The 47% rating of the Democratic Party is among the lowest Gallup has measured since 1992, with only a 46% rating earlier this year being lower.

Opinion of the Democratic Party

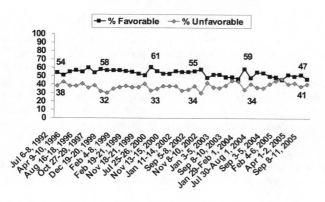

General Impressions of the Parties

Gallup's Sept. 12-15 Governance poll asked Americans—on an open-ended basis—to say what came to mind when they think of each party. The most common responses reflect the parties' ideological orientations, their perceived biases toward particular economic groups, and the public's basic favorable or unfavorable opinions of the parties.

Specifically, the most common responses about the Republican Party are an overall favorable view of it (14% mention this), the party being "conservative" (12%), and the perception that the party "caters to the rich" (11%). Eleven percent simply said they had an unfavorable view of the party (11%). In general, the basic impressions of the GOP are similar to what they were in 2001, when Gallup last asked the question.

*Now, we'd like to ask you about your impressions of the two major political parties. What comes to mind when you think of **the Republican Party**?*

	2005 Sep 12-15 %	2001 Sep 7-10 %
Favorable	14	12
Conservative	12	16
Cater to the rich	11	11
Unfavorable	11	13

	2005 Sep 12-15 %	2001 Sep 7-10 %
Cater to big business	6	7
Self-centered/out for themselves	6	1
Untrustworthy	5	2
High morals	4	2
Money	3	5
George W. Bush	3	3
Greedy	3	2
Close-minded/not open to new ideas	2	1
For the people	2	2
For smaller/less government	1	1
Trustworthy	1	2
Arrogant	1	1
Poor economic conditions	1	2
Lower taxes	1	1
Fiscally conservative	1	1
An elephant	*	1
Poor environmental record	*	*
Other	7	13
None	8	7
No opinion	7	7

*Less than 0.5%
Percentages add to more than 100% due to multiple responses.

Republican and Democratic identifiers give very different responses to this question. The most common impression Republicans have of the Republican Party (i.e., the party with which they personally identify) is their overall "favorable opinion" of the party. On the other hand, Democrats are most likely to mention the Republican Party's "catering to the rich" when asked for their impressions of the GOP.

Most Common Impressions of the Republican Party, by Party Identification

Republicans		Independents		Democrats	
1. Favorable	33%	1. Unfavorable	13%	1. Cater to the rich	24%
2. Conservative	18%	2. Conservative	11%	2. Unfavorable	12%
3. High morals	6%	3. Favorable	9%	3. Self-centered	10%
4. Unfavorable	6%	4. Cater to the rich	9%	4. Conservative	9%
5. For the people	4%	5. Cater to big business	7%	5. Cater to big business	8%
6. Self-centered	4%	6. Untrustworthy	6%	6. Untrustworthy	8%

About one in five Americans describes the Democratic Party as "liberal," a perception that has become more common since 2001, when 13% mentioned this. Seventeen percent say the Democrats are "for the people; the working, middle, and lower classes." Twelve percent mention a basic unfavorable view of the party, while 7% mention a basic favorable view.

Now, we'd like to ask you about your impressions of the two major political parties. What comes to mind when you think of the Democratic Party?

	2005 Sep 12-15 %	2001 Sep 7-10 %
Liberal	22	13
For the people/For the working, middle, lower class	17	15

	2005 Sep 12-15 %	2001 Sep 7-10 %
Unfavorable	12	11
Favorable	7	11
Socially conscious/progressive	5	4
Fair	5	4
Big spending/spend a lot of money	4	3
Self-centered/out for themselves	3	1
Bill Clinton	2	3
Untrustworthy	2	3
High taxes	2	1
Big government	2	3
Corrupt/crooks/scandals	2	4
Good economic conditions	1	2
Labor unions	1	1
Conservative	1	1
Give money away	1	2
Lack of morals	1	2
Welfare	1	1
Pro-choice	*	1
Good environmental record	*	1
Al Gore	*	1
Other	8	11
None	9	7
No opinion	5	6

*Less than 0.5%

Percentages add to more than 100% due to multiple responses.

Democrats' dominant impression of their own party is that it is "for the people; for the middle, lower, and working classes"—one in three Democrats mentions this. Among both Republicans and independents the Democratic Party's "liberal" ideology is the most commonly held impression.

Most Common Impressions of the Democratic Party, by Party Identification

Republicans		Independents		Democrats	
1. Liberal	31%	1. Liberal	22%	1. For the people	33%
2. Unfavorable	14%	2. Unfavorable	15%	2. Favorable	15%
3. For the people	7%	3. For the people	12%	3. Liberal	12%
4. Big spenders	6%	4. Socially conscious	6%	4. Fair	8%
5. Self-centered	5%	5. Big spenders	4%	5. Unfavorable	7%
6. Socially conscious	5%	6. Favorable	4%	6. Socially conscious	5%

A separate question asked Americans to judge the parties on a relative basis on two main policy spheres—international affairs and the economy. Americans continue to give the Republicans an edge on international affairs, while the Democrats maintain their perceptual advantage on the economy. The Sept. 12-15 Gallup Poll finds 48% saying the Republican Party does a better job of protecting the country from "international terrorism and military threats," compared with 37% who say this of the Democrats. That advantage is similar, though slightly smaller, than what Gallup has measured during the past few years.

By a 46% to 41% margin, Americans say the Democratic Party will do a better job than the Republican Party of keeping the coun-

try prosperous during the next few years. Democrats hold a slight advantage in this regard in the last two polls. In 2002, the parties were even, but in the prior two years Democrats held the advantage as they do now.

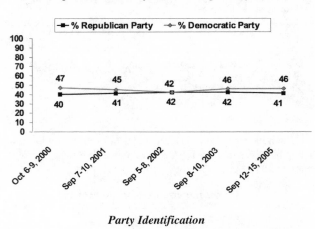

Party to Better Keep the Country Prosperous

Party Identification

In terms of the general public's party identification, the momentum is clearly on the side of the Democrats. In Gallup polling from July to September, the Democrats have an average three-point advantage in party identification among the general public, 34% to 31%, with another 34% of Americans identifying as independents. In the first quarter of this year, Republicans had an average 35% to 33% advantage. In the second quarter, the parties shared the same average, with both at 33%.

The precise breakdown of identification with the parties in a particular survey varies from poll to poll, in part because of short term changes in the political environment and also to the topics and content of that particular survey.

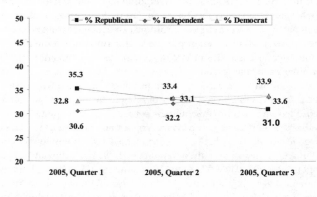

Party Affiliation

Survey Methods

These results are based on telephone interviews with a randomly selected national sample of 921 adults, aged 18 and older, conducted Sept. 12-15, 2005. For results based on this sample, one can say with 95% confidence that the maximum error attributable to sampling and other random effects is ±3 percentage points. In addition to sampling error, question wording and practical difficulties in conducting surveys can introduce error or bias into the findings of public opinion polls.

September 30, 2005
PUBLIC DIVIDED OVER FUTURE IDEOLOGY OF SUPREME COURT
Few believe it is essential next nominee is a woman or minority

by Jeffrey M. Jones, Gallup Poll Managing Editor

With John Roberts now confirmed as chief justice, George W. Bush prepares to announce a second nominee to the Supreme Court. A new CNN/*USA Today*/Gallup poll finds Americans closely divided as to whether that nominee should make the Supreme Court more conservative, more liberal, or not change the court's ideological makeup. While many have speculated that Bush may choose a woman or racial or ethnic minority to replace retiring Justice Sandra Day O'Connor, few Americans see this as an essential quality of the next nominee. The Supreme Court's recent job approval rating has recovered after taking a hit near the end of the court's last term.

Court Ideology

The Sept. 26-28 CNN/*USA Today*/Gallup poll finds 33% of Americans saying Bush should nominate a Supreme Court justice who would make the court more conservative, 30% who think it should be made more liberal, and 29% who say it should be kept the same as now.

There has been a shift since this summer. A June 16-19 poll, conducted shortly before O'Connor announced her retirement, found 41% of Americans favoring a more conservative court, with 30% preferring a more liberal court and 24% wanting no change.

Would you like to see President Bush nominate a new justice who would make the Supreme Court — more liberal than it currently is, more conservative than it currently is — or who would keep the court as it is now?

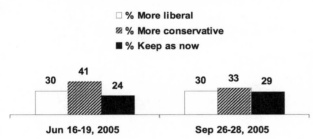

As one would expect, most self-described conservatives (57%) want to see the court go in a more conservative direction, but an even higher percentage of liberals (73%) want to see it become more liberal. A plurality of moderates prefer to maintain the status quo, but more moderates prefer a more liberal (30%) to a more conservative (20%) court.

Court Diversity

Bush has hinted that the court's racial, ethnic, and gender diversity will be a consideration when he chooses the next nominee. That the new nominee would take O'Connor's seat may add pressure to choose a woman. Bush reportedly has long favored naming a Hispanic to the court. However, the poll finds that most Americans, 51%, say the next justice's race, ethnicity, or gender does not matter to them. Only 12% say it is "essential that the next justice is Hispanic, black, or a woman," while an additional 28% say it is "a good idea, but not essential."

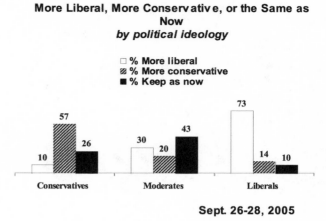

More Liberal, More Conservative, or the Same as Now
by political ideology

Sept. 26-28, 2005

A recent *Newsweek* poll shows that the public thinks diversity should be a consideration in the choice. The Sept. 8-9 *Newsweek* poll finds 66% saying Bush should strongly consider naming another woman to serve on the court, and 60% say he should strongly consider naming another black or a Hispanic to the court. But the Gallup data suggest that people do not view a female or minority nomination as a requirement.

In the new CNN/*USA Today*/Gallup poll, a randomly selected half of respondents were asked the general question about whether the next court nominee should be either black, Hispanic, or a woman. The other half was asked about each characteristic in isolation. In each case, a majority of Americans say the nominee's gender, race, or ethnicity does not matter to them.

- Fifty-five percent say it does not matter if the next justice is a woman, while 14% say it is essential the next justice is female, and 29% say it is a good idea, but not essential.
- Sixty-nine percent say it does not matter if the next justice is Hispanic; only 3% say it is essential and 23% say it is a good idea.
- Seventy-one percent say it does not matter if the next justice is black, 5% say it is essential, and 22% say it is a good idea.

In all cases, Democrats are more likely than Republicans to see these characteristics as either essential or desirable qualities in the next justice, while the vast majority of Republicans say none of these characteristics matters to them.

Supreme Court Approval

The vacancies that O'Connor's impending retirement and the death of former Chief Justice William Rehnquist created have attracted attention to the court. In general, most Americans give the Supreme Court a positive review overall—according to a Sept. 12-15 Gallup Poll, 56% approve of the way it is handling its job, while 36% disapprove.

That is a dramatic improvement from as recently as this past summer. A June 24-26 CNN/*USA Today*/Gallup poll conducted near the end of the last term found just 42% of Americans approving and 48% disapproving of the court—the most negative reading Gallup has measured since it began tracking approval in 2000. That June poll was conducted on the heels of the court's controversial decision permitting broader government power to seize privately held land.

Republicans (65%) are much more likely than independents (54%) or Democrats (47%) to approve of the Supreme Court's performance. In June, there were essentially no party differences—44% of Republicans, 42% of independents, and 40% of Democrats approved. The court's eminent domain decision was largely criticized by those who

Supreme Court Approval Ratings

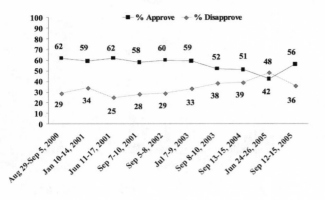

fear it gave too much power to government, a view typically held by Republicans. But apparently the possible effect of that decision on Republicans' (and to a lesser extent, independents') views of the court has faded.

Survey Methods

These results are based on telephone interviews with a randomly selected national sample of 1,007 adults, aged 18 and older, conducted Sept. 26-28, 2005. For results based on this sample, one can say with 95% confidence that the maximum error attributable to sampling and other random effects is ±3 percentage points. In addition to sampling error, question wording and practical difficulties in conducting surveys can introduce error or bias into the findings of public opinion polls.

The two Gallup updates on this getting better/getting worse measure taken in September show only a slight deterioration in attitudes compared to late August, and no change whatsoever between the Sept. 12-15 and Sept. 26-28 measures. In short, consumer optimism about the direction of the economy has been quite stable over the last month—albeit quite negative.

There has been less of a negative tilt in Americans' assessments of the "economic conditions in this country today" over the last several months—either before or after Katrina.

Economic Conditions
Selected Trend: January 2005 — September 2005

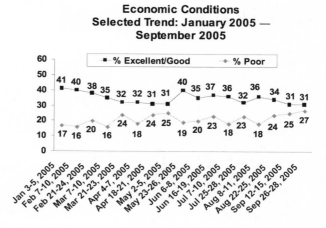

Thirty-one percent of Americans now rate economic conditions as excellent or good, little changed from measures in late July, August, and early September. In fact, similarly negative reads on the economy were measured in March, April, and May of this year, and even more negative reads on the economy were prevalent at many points in 2003. In other words, Americans' assessments of the current economy at the moment are downbeat, but not remarkably so in the context of readings taken over the last two or three years.

What's Behind the Numbers?

Americans believe high energy costs continue to be the top economic problem facing the nation, according to Gallup's Sept. 26-28 poll. Concern about energy is followed by worries about unemployment, dealing with natural disasters, the war in Iraq, the federal budget deficit, and healthcare costs.

What is the most important economic problem facing the country today? [OPEN-ENDED]

	Sep 26-28, 2005 %	Aug 22-25, 2005 %	Jul 25-28, 2005 %	Jun 16-19, 2005 %	May 23-26, 2005 %	Apr 18-21, 2005 %
Fuel/Oil prices	25	34	14	15	10	19
Unemployment/ Jobs/Wages	14	15	19	19	18	18
Dealing with natural disasters	11	—	—	—	—	—
War in Iraq	11	10	11	9	11	8
Federal budget deficit	6	5	5	6	4	5
Healthcare/Health insurance costs	6	6	7	12	11	7
Outsourcing of jobs	4	5	7	5	8	5
Lack of money	3	2	4	5	4	6

October 3, 2005

CONSUMER VIEWS ON ECONOMY SHOW LITTLE CHANGE AS SEPTEMBER ENDS
Outlook on future still grim

by Frank Newport, Gallup Poll Editor in Chief

Americans remain negative about the direction of the U.S. economy and the majority say current economic conditions are only fair or poor. There is little evidence to suggest that these attitudes have become significantly more negative as a result of Hurricanes Katrina and Rita. Gallup's biweekly data show that the big drop in positive sentiment came in late August, before Katrina struck the Gulf Coast. In fact, Americans' concerns over rising fuel prices appear to have abated to some degree by late September. The public is less likely now than a month ago to mention energy costs as the top economic problem facing the nation, and fewer Americans say energy prices are causing them personal financial hardship than did so two weeks ago. There is no clear-cut indication in the data that Americans plan on spending less in several key categories now compared to what they reported a month ago, an important factor as the nation's retailers attempt to recover from a sluggish August.

Rating the U.S. Economy

Gallup measures the public's view of the economy on a biweekly basis, using pinpoint surveys of no more than four days' duration. This pattern of frequent, intense measurement makes it possible to more precisely assess the effects of high-profile events on consumer sentiment than do monthly consumer surveys conducted over a period of weeks.

The trend in consumer views of the U.S. economy's direction (e.g., is the economy getting worse or better?) shows that a more negative pattern of responses was established in late August, *before* Hurricane Katrina made landfall in Louisiana, Mississippi, and Alabama.

Economic Outlook
Selected Trend: January 2005 — September 2005

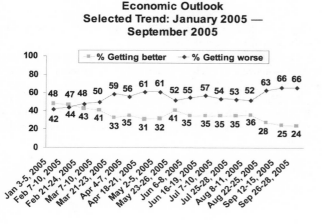

	Sep 26-28, 2005	Aug 22-25, 2005	Jul 25-28, 2005	Jun 16-19, 2005	May 23-26, 2005	Apr 18-21, 2005
Inflation/Rising prices	4	4	4	5	5	4
Taxes	3	2	2	4	3	2
Illegal immigrants	2	2	2	3	4	2
Poverty/Hunger/ Homelessness	2	3	2	2	2	1
Poorly run government/Politics	2	1	1	2	1	1
Education reform	2	2	1	4	2	2
George W. Bush/ His policies	1	1	1	1	1	1
Gap between rich and poor	1	1	1	1	1	1
Credit cards/ Overspending	1	1	2	2	2	1
Welfare	1	1	1	1	1	1
Trade deficit	1	1	3	2	3	1
Foreign aid/Focus on other countries	1	*	1	1	1	1
Senior care/Medicare	1	1	1	1	1	1
Interest rates	1	*	1	*	*	*
Economy (non-specific)	1	2	1	2	1	1
Social Security	1	3	4	6	6	7
Security/Threat of terrorism	*	2	3	1	—	—
Companies closing/ No growth	*	1	2	1	—	—
International relations	*	1	*	*	*	*
College tuition expenses	*	*	1	*	*	*
Retirement	—	*	1	1	1	1
Stock market	—	—	*	*	*	*
Other	5	5	6	9	7	4
None	*	1	1	1	2	1
No opinion	7	6	8	9	9	8

*Less than 0.5%
Percentages add to more than 100% due to multiple responses.

There have been some changes in these perceptions over the last several months:

- Energy costs zoomed up in importance as the top economic problem facing the nation in August, but have come back down slightly. In other words, despite the increasing cost of gasoline in the immediate aftermath of Katrina in early September, the public is less likely now than a month ago to say high fuel costs are the most important economic problem facing the nation.
- Eleven percent say dealing with natural disasters is the top economic problem, the first time this issue has appeared as a category in response to this question.
- Mentions of the cost of the Iraq war have stayed relatively stable and prevalent over the past year.

Gallup asks Americans in a slightly different fashion to talk about the most important financial problem facing their families today.

What is the most important financial problem facing your family today? [OPEN-ENDED]

	Sep 26-28, 2005 %	Aug 22-25, 2005 %	Jul 25-28, 2005 %	Jun 16-19, 2005 %	May 23-26, 2005 %	Apr 18-21, 2005 %
Energy costs/Oil and gas prices	17	20	8	7	5	11
Healthcare costs	11	10	13	17	18	14
Lack of money/ Low wages	10	11	11	12	12	15
Too much debt/Not enough money to pay debts	8	6	7	6	8	8
High cost of living/ Inflation	7	6	6	8	5	5
College expenses	7	6	7	7	8	7
Unemployment/ Loss of job	6	7	8	7	8	7
Cost of owning/ renting a home	5	3	4	6	6	4
Taxes	4	3	4	3	3	3
Retirement savings	3	5	6	6	9	8
Interest rates	1	1	1	1	1	1
Lack of savings	1	1	1	2	—	—
Social Security	1	2	1	2	2	1
Transportation/ Commuting costs	1	1	1	2	—	—
State of the economy	1	*	1	1	—	—
Stock market/ Investments	*	1	1	1	—	—
Controlling spending	*	1	1	1	—	—
Other	4	4	4	6	4	5
None	18	16	17	16	16	15
No opinion	4	5	5	3	4	5

*Less than 0.5%
Percentages add to more than 100% due to multiple responses.

The cost of energy tops the list, as it did in late August, followed by concerns over healthcare costs, lack of money, too much debt, the high cost of living, college expenses, and unemployment. As was the case in terms of discussion of economic problems facing the nation as a whole, concerns about energy costs are less likely to be mentioned now than they were in August.

Family Worries

Gallup doesn't find much change in Americans' self-reported worries about their families' finances.

Four out of 10 Americans worry about their finances, but this number is statistically unchanged across the eight times this question has been asked since February of this year.

In other words, despite the downturn in consumer views of the U.S. economy, there has been little change in consumers' views of their own family financial situations—at least as measured by this "worry" question.

Spending?

Gallup has asked Americans for a number of months to estimate how much they are planning on spending "this month" across four cate-

Worried About Family's Finances?

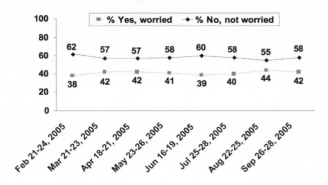

gories: groceries, clothing, eating dinner at a restaurant, and entertainment, vacation travel, or recreational activities.

The trend lines for the average estimates across these categories are represented in the accompanying graph.

Monthly Spending Estimates for Household Expenses

based on average dollar amount

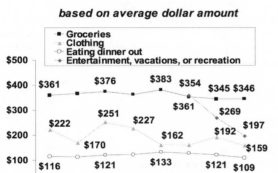

The last two months have shown a slight downtick in estimated average spending on groceries compared to previous months this year.

Average self-reported spending on clothing has varied since February, reaching its highest points in April and May, and its lowest points in June, July, and the current September reading.

The current reading on intended amount to be spent on eating out over the next month—$109—is technically the lowest recorded since February, but statistically, it is not significantly different from other readings earlier this year.

There has been a significant drop-off in self-reported spending on entertainment/vacation travel/recreational activities this month compared to July and August. This is reasonably likely to be a result of the end of the summer vacation season and therefore not necessarily an indication of an abnormal reduction in retail spending in this category.

Survey Methods

These results are based on telephone interviews with a randomly selected national sample of 1,007 adults, aged 18 and older, conducted Sept. 26-28, 2005. For results based on this sample, one can say with 95% confidence that the maximum error attributable to sam-

pling and other random effects is ±3 percentage points. In addition to sampling error, question wording and practical difficulties in conducting surveys can introduce error or bias into the findings of public opinion polls.

October 4, 2005
NEARLY HALF OF AMERICANS THINK U.S. WILL SOON HAVE A WOMAN PRESIDENT
Most say they would vote for a qualified woman

by Jeffrey M. Jones, Gallup Poll Managing Editor

The success of the recent television show "Commander in Chief," with actress Geena Davis playing the role of the president, has intensified discussion about the likelihood of having a woman as the nation's chief executive. Speculation about a female president is already high, given the expectation that New York Sen. Hillary Rodham Clinton will likely seek the Democratic presidential nomination in 2008. A recent CNN/*USA Today*/Gallup poll finds that the vast majority of Americans say they would personally vote for a qualified woman for president. Slightly less than half the public thinks that the United States will have a female president within the next 10 years, but most think there will be a female president within 25 years.

The Sept. 8-11 poll finds nearly half of Americans, 46%, think the United States will have a female president within the next 10 years, and an additional 41% say within the next 10 to 25 years. In 2001, 40% of Americans said there would be a female president within the next 10 years.

Overall, how long do you think it will be before a woman is elected president — within the next 10 years, within the next 25 years, within the next 100 years, sometime longer than that, or never?

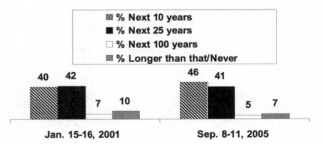

Women (51%) are more likely than men (40%) to believe that there will be a female president within the next 10 years. A majority of Democrats, 52%, think the United States will have a female president within the next 10 years, compared with 40% of Republicans.

Eighty-six percent of Americans say that they, personally, would vote for a qualified woman for president. Democrats (94%) are more likely than Republicans (76%) to say they would vote for a woman, though the vast majority of each political group is supportive.

One issue with asking people whether they would vote for a female president is that some respondents may tell the interviewer they would do so even if in reality they would not, to avoid expressing a view about women that could be considered prejudicial. At times, survey researchers will ask respondents to assess their *neighbors'* intentions. This allows respondents to express a seemingly gender-biased view without appearing to be biased themselves. Using this approach, support for a female president is significantly lower, but still registers as a majority—61% of Americans say their neighbors would vote for a qualified woman, while 34% say their neighbors would not.

The direct and indirect results taken together suggest that most Americans would vote for a female president, though the actual percentage of who would do so is unclear. Interestingly, less than half of Republicans, 47%, believe their neighbors would vote for a qualified woman for president, compared with 72% of Democrats who share this view. For both parties, the percentage who believe their neighbors would vote for a woman is more than 20 percentage points lower than the percentage who say that they, personally, would vote for a woman.

Would you, personally, vote for a qualified woman for president, or not?
Do you think most of your neighbors would vote for a qualified woman for president, or not?

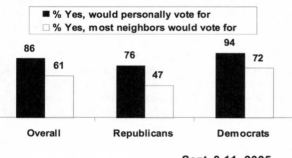

Sept. 8-11, 2005

The poll also attempted to assess if Americans saw a difference in a male or female president in the dominant policy spheres—national security and domestic policy. Americans are more inclined to say that a male president is better able to handle national security, and a female domestic policy. But a substantial proportion volunteers that the gender of the president makes no difference in either arena.

Do you think a man (or a) woman president would better handle national security/domestic policy?

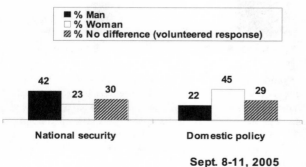

Sept. 8-11, 2005

Democrats' and Republicans' views diverge in their assessment of both policy areas, with Democrats saying a female president would better handle both, while Republicans say a male president would do a better job in both.

By a 57% to 8% margin, Republicans say that a man would better handle national security than a woman. Democrats show a slight preference for a female (37%) than a male (31%) president in this arena.

The reverse is true in regards to domestic policy—Democrats overwhelmingly believe a female (62%) president is preferable to a male (13%), while Republicans show a slight preference for a man (34%) over a woman (30%) to handle domestic policy.

	Man	Woman	No difference
	%	%	%
National security			
Democrats	31	37	27
Independents	37	27	32
Republicans	57	8	31
Domestic policy			
Democrats	13	62	22
Independents	19	45	32
Republicans	34	30	32

Survey Methods

These results are based on telephone interviews with a randomly selected national sample of 1,005 adults, aged 18 years and older, conducted Sept. 8-11, 2005. For results based on this sample, one can say with 95% confidence that the maximum error attributable to sampling and other random effects is ±3 percentage points. In addition to sampling error, question wording and practical difficulties in conducting surveys can introduce error or bias into the findings of public opinion polls.

October 4, 2005
THE GROUP BETTER KNOWN AS "NEWS JUNKIES"
Attentive elite skews older, more partisan

by Lydia Saad, Gallup Poll Senior Editor

When events such as the indictment of Republican leader Tom DeLay occur, it's tempting to look for evidence of a ripple effect in the broader political environment—in this case, a possible decline of public trust in the Republican Party or even President George W. Bush. While trust may or may not erode in time, it is helpful to remember that most Americans are less than riveted to U.S. politics, and thus a seismic event inside the Washington, D.C., Beltway may barely be noticed outside of it.

Gallup has yet to do any polling on DeLay's situation, specifically. But we regularly track public attention to American politics with a question that asks: "Overall, how closely do you follow news about national politics—very closely, somewhat closely, not too closely, or not at all?"

The most recent results come from the annual Governance poll, conducted Sept. 12-15, 2005. According to that survey, only about one in four of all national adults, 28%, follow the news about national politics very closely. Another 48% follow it somewhat closely, 18% say they follow it "not too closely," while 5% say they don't follow national politics at all. The 28% paying very close attention is similar to what Gallup found in 2002 and 2003.

Last year, the percentage bumped up to 36%, but this was most likely because the poll was conducted during the height of the 2004 election season. An average of the last five Governance polls*, spanning 2001 to 2005, also puts the percentage paying very close attention to political news at 28%.

That 28% presumably represents a majority of the audience for the talking heads and chattering pundits who provide the daily news and then thrash it out 24/7. They are the attentive elite—perhaps better known as "news junkies"—whose early reactions to the news could be pivotal in how a political event plays out.

Attentive Elite Skews Older, More Partisan

So who are the attentive elite? According to Gallup's 2001-2005 data, attention to national politics is strongly correlated with age, and, at every age level, men are more likely than women to be highly attentive.

The percentage saying they follow the news of national politics very closely rises from 13% among 18- to 24-year-olds to 38% among those aged 55 to 64. Attention increases gradually among the intervening age groups, but then holds at the 38% level among those 55 and older.

Attention to News by Age

Overall, how closely do you follow news about national politics?

Percentage saying "very closely"

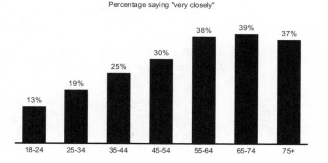

Gallup finds that by a 33% to 23% margin, men are more likely than women to follow political news very closely. In other words, women are about a third less likely than men to be attentive. This ratio holds at almost every age group looked at. However, the gap between men and women narrows some among seniors.

Solid identifiers with either major political party are more likely to be attentive than are political independents. About 3 in 10 Republicans (31%) and Democrats (28%) say they pay very close attention to political news, compared with only 20% of pure independents (that is, independents who don't lean toward either the Republican or Democratic parties).

Attentiveness is clearly linked with political participation. Gallup's data from 2004 show that those who closely follow political news were three times as likely (44% vs. 15%) to say they had voted in the 2000 election. More generally, registered voters are more than twice as likely as non-registered voters (31% vs. 13%) to say they follow the news closely. In fact, nearly half of non-registered voters admit they do not pay close attention to the news.

Bottom Line

When Washington insiders are looking for Americans' reactions to political news events, the first responders are presumably those paying closest attention to the news. They are the ones whose views are most likely to be affected by information or an event—particularly when it is not a major event that gets saturation news coverage. Not only do relatively few Americans pay very close attention to polit-

Attention to News by Age and Gender

Overall, how closely do you follow news about national politics?

■ Male ▨ Female

Percentage saying "very closely"

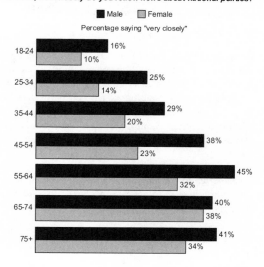

Attention to News by Party ID

Overall, how closely do you follow news about national politics?

Percentage saying "very closely"

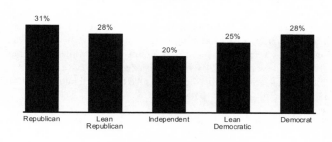

Attention to News by Voter Status

Overall, how closely do you follow news about national politics?

■ Very closely ☐ Somewhat closely ▨ Not too/Not at all closely

Percentage saying "very closely"

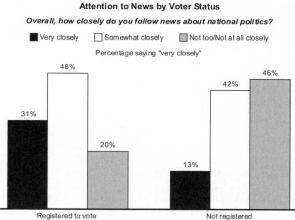

ical news, but those who do tend to be older and more strongly partisan, and therefore could be less susceptible to shifting their political attitudes.

*The aggregate database on which these results are based includes telephone interviews with 4,976 randomly selected national adults aged 18 and older, drawn from five separate surveys conducted each September from 2001 through 2005. Results based on the total sample have a margin of error of ±2 percentage points.

October 5, 2005
PUBLIC REACTION TO MIERS LUKEWARM
Nomination triggers mostly partisan responses

by David W. Moore, Gallup Poll Senior Editor

If Harriet Miers is an unknown to most members of Congress, then she must be even more obscure to the general public. Yet, most people are willing, even at this early stage, to express an opinion—although an opinion highly conditioned by their partisan orientation.

Overall, 44% of Americans rate President George W. Bush's choice of Miers to replace Sandra Day O'Connor on the Supreme Court as "excellent" or "good," while 41% rate the choice as "only fair" or "poor."

Generally speaking, how would you rate Bush's choice of [name of nominee] as a nominee to the U.S. Supreme Court—as excellent, good, only fair, or poor?

	Excellent	Good	Only fair	Poor	No opinion
Harriet Miers (2005 Oct 3-4)	11%	33	25	16	15
John Roberts (2005 Jul 20)	25%	26	20	14	15

This is a somewhat lower rating than what Chief Justice John Roberts received when he was nominated to the Supreme Court in July. Fifty-one percent gave him a high rating, 34% a low rating.

Not unexpectedly, Miers' rating is highly related to people's partisan orientation. Overwhelmingly, Republicans give her a high rating (72% excellent or good, just 16% fair or poor), while Democrats give her a low rating (24% excellent or good, 62% fair or poor). Independents are evenly divided: 41% give her a high rating and 41% a low rating.

Generally speaking, how would you rate Bush's choice of Harriet Miers as a nominee to the U.S. Supreme Court—as excellent, good, only fair, or poor?

Harriet Miers	Excellent/ Good %	Only fair/ Poor %	No opinion %
Overall	44	41	15
Republicans	72	16	12
Independents	41	41	18
Democrats	24	62	14

Similarly, more people had positive first impressions of Roberts than of Miers. Forty-two percent say their "first impressions" of Miers are positive, compared with 54% who felt positively about Roberts.

How would you describe your first impressions of [name of candidate]? Would you say they are—[ROTATED: very positive, somewhat positive, neither positive nor negative, somewhat negative, (or) very negative]?

	Very positive	Somewhat positive	Neither	Somewhat negative	Very negative	No opinion
Miers (2005 Oct 3-4)	14%	28	34	10	4	10
Roberts (2005 Jul 20)	26%	28	21	8	7	10

Again, these views are highly related to partisan orientation. Sixty-seven percent of Republicans have positive first impressions of Miers, compared with 40% of independents and just 26% of Democrats.

How would you describe your first impressions of Harriet Miers? Would you say they are—[ROTATED: very positive, somewhat positive, neither positive nor negative, somewhat negative, (or) very negative]?

Harriet Miers	Positive %	Neither %	Negative %	No opinion %
Overall	42	34	14	10
Republicans	67	21	7	5
Independents	40	36	13	11
Democrats	26	42	22	10

Conservatives Less Supportive of Miers Than of Roberts

The poll shows that the lower ratings received by Miers than Roberts are due principally to the opinions of conservatives. While moderates and liberals are about as likely to rate Miers as an "excellent" or "good" choice as they are to rate Roberts that way, conservatives are considerably less likely to give Miers the high rating.

Percentage Rating Each Candidate as an "Excellent" or "Good" Choice

	Roberts %	Miers %	Difference Pct. pts.
Conservatives	77	58	-19
Moderates	46	43	- 3
Liberals	17	23	+ 6

Similarly, when asked their first impressions of the two candidates, conservatives are much less likely to say their first impressions of Miers are positive (57%) than they were to say they had positive impressions of Roberts (77%). Moderates are also less positive about Miers, but the difference between their views of Roberts and Miers is just 14 points, compared with the 20-point difference among conservatives. Liberals are about as positive about Miers (26%) as they were about Roberts (23%).

Percentage Saying They Have "Positive" First Impressions of Each Candidate

	Roberts %	Miers %	Difference Pct. pts.
Conservatives	77	57	-20
Moderates	53	39	-14
Liberals	23	26	+ 3

Miers' Gender of Little Impact on Public Support

One of the defining characteristics of Miers' nomination is that so few people know much about her legal views. Having never served as a judge, and having been Bush's legal confidante for most of the past decade, Miers has left virtually no "paper trail" of opinions for observers to study. The public views this lack of a legal record as much more negative than positive.

Thinking about Harriet Miers' background, does each of the following make you—[ROTATED: more likely to support her nomination, does it make no difference to you, or does it make you less likely to support her nomination]? How about—[RANDOM ORDER]?

2005 Oct 3-4 (sorted by "more likely")	More likely %	No difference %	Less likely %	No opinion %
She is a woman	29	66	5	*
She has close personal ties to George W. Bush	16	38	44	2
Her views on most major issues are not known	12	33	49	6
She has never served as a judge	10	42	46	2

*Less than 0.5%

Most people, 66%, are neither positive nor negative about the fact that Miers is a woman. But 29% say her gender makes them more likely to support her candidacy, while just 5% say it makes them less likely to support her.

A separate question finds that only 18% of Americans would have been upset if Bush had *not* nominated a woman.

The other three characteristics—her close personal ties to Bush, the fact that her views on most issues are not known, and the lack of service as a judge—are all perceived by the public as net negative marks on her candidacy.

Women are more likely than men to be impressed with Miers because she is a woman. Nineteen percent of men say her gender makes them more likely to support her, compared with 37% of women who feel that way. Partisan differences are relatively minor.

Miers' close personal ties to Bush are much more objectionable to Democrats than to Republicans, with 68% of Democrats saying these ties make them less likely to support her, compared with 47% of independents who feel that way, and just 11% of Republicans.

Miers' lack of a public record also bothers Democrats more than it does Republicans—63% of Democrats say this factor makes them less likely to support her, while 46% of independents and 36% of Republicans agree.

Some of Miers' supporters are touting her lack of experience as a judge in positive terms, saying it would give the court more breadth of experience. Most Americans, however, do not accept that point of view. Her lack of judicial experience causes 58% of Democrats to be less supportive of her candidacy, compared with 45% of independents and 32% of Republicans.

Similar to what people expressed about the Roberts candidacy this year, and the Clarence Thomas candidacy in 1991, a majority of Americans, 55%, believe that senators should insist that Miers explain her views on abortion during the hearings on her nomination, while 42% disagree.

When the U.S. Senate holds hearings on the [name of nominee] nomination, do you think senators should insist that he/she explain his/her views on abortion before confirming him/her, or should he/she be allowed to refuse to answer questions about abortion?

	Insist he/she explain his/her views %	Allowed to refuse to answer %	No opinion %
Harriet Miers (2005 Oct 3-4)	55	42	3
John Roberts (2005 Jul 22-24)	61	37	2
Clarence Thomas (1991 Jul 11-14)	54	39	7

Again, these views are highly related to partisan orientation: 68% of Democrats believe Miers should be required to state her views on abortion, compared with 57% of independents, and just 39% of Republicans.

Survey Methods

Results are based on telephone interviews with 803 national adults, aged 18 and older, conducted Oct. 3-4, 2005. For results based on the total sample of national adults, one can say with 95% confidence that the maximum margin of sampling error is ±4 percentage points.

In addition to sampling error, question wording and practical difficulties in conducting surveys can introduce error or bias into the findings of public opinion polls.

October 6, 2005
MOST SENIORS EXPECT TO SKIP MEDICARE PRESCRIPTION DRUG PROGRAM
Only 22% say they will join; federal government projects 68%

by David W. Moore, Gallup Poll Senior Editor

A new CNN/*USA Today*/Gallup survey suggests that enrollment for the federal government's new Medicare prescription drug benefit program, scheduled to go into effect on Jan. 1, 2006, may fall well short of government projections.

Health and Human Services projects that some 29.3 million out of 43.1 million Medicare beneficiaries will join the program. But the poll suggests that only about one-third of the people who are expected to enroll will actually do so. The poll also suggests that few seniors (people 65 and older) understand the program, and in the past three months there has been little progress in educating them about it.

The survey of 760 seniors occurred in three stages—July 22-24, Aug. 5-7, and Sept. 26-28, with about 250 interviewed in each group. Overall, only 12% of seniors say they understand the program "very" well, and another 24% say "somewhat" well. Sixty-one percent understand little or nothing at all about the program.

As you may know, the government is instituting an optional prescription drug benefit program for Medicare recipients. How well do you, personally, understand the prescription drug benefit program that will be offered to Medicare recipients—very well, somewhat well, not too well, or not at all?

	Very well %	Somewhat well %	Not too well %	Not at all %	No opinion %
Composite	12	24	35	26	3
2005 Sep 26-28	12	25	32	29	2
2005 Aug 5-7	12	25	33	26	4
2005 Jul 22-24	11	23	40	24	2

During the past few months the percentages have remained stable, suggesting that there has been no increase in understanding, despite the fact that the deadline for joining the program has moved much closer.

Intentions to join the program have also remained stable, with just about one in five seniors (22%) saying they will join, and the rest either saying they will not join (61%) or that they do not know if they will (17%).

Do you plan to join the new prescription drug benefit program for Medicare recipients, or not?

	Yes %	No %	No opinion %
Composite	22	61	17
2005 Sep 26-28	24	54	22
2005 Aug 5-7	24	63	13
2005 Jul 22-24	20	65	15

That 22% enrollment expectation contrasts with the much more optimistic projection by Health and Human Services of 68% of eligible Medicare recipients. It is possible that the 17% of poll respondents claiming no opinion will eventually enroll, but that would still make the total far short of the government's projection. Clearly, the government has a major challenge of persuasion if it is to meet its enrollment expectations.

As an incentive to join the program, there are severe penalties for most eligible recipients who do not enroll within the enrollment period. But so far this fact either is not well known, or it is not affecting intentions. The poll shows that seniors who say they understand the program "very" or "somewhat" well are about as likely to join as people who understand the program less well.

Do you plan to join the new prescription drug benefit program for Medicare recipients, or not?

	Yes %	No %	No opinion %
How well understand program			
Very well	21	71	8
Somewhat well	21	71	8
Not too well	27	53	20
Not at all	21	56	23

Among seniors who do not understand the program well, there is more uncertainty than among those who say they understand the program very or somewhat well, with about one in five of the less informed groups expressing no opinion. But the percentage saying they will join varies little among the four groups.

There are few differences in the intentions between men and women, but the poll shows that higher income respondents are somewhat less likely to say they will join the program than lower income respondents.

Thirty-one percent of seniors in households with less than $20,000 in annual income expect to enroll, compared with just 18% of seniors in households with annual incomes of $50,000 or more. About one in five of the middle income groups expect to enroll.

Do you plan to join the new prescription drug benefit program for Medicare recipients, or not?

	Yes %	No %	No opinion %
By annual household income			
Less than $20K	31	49	20
$20K to <$30K	21	64	15
$30K to <$50K	22	62	16
$50K +	18	70	12

It is worthwhile noting that half of even the lowest income seniors say they will not join, suggesting that Americans do not necessarily see the program as the economic benefit it was intended to be. Perhaps with additional information, more seniors will become persuaded of the program's benefits. But at this stage, enrollment in the Medicare program is likely to be far short of what the government expects.

Survey Methods

Results are based on telephone interviews with 760 adults, aged 65 and older, conducted July 22-24, 2005, Aug. 5-7, 2005, and Sept. 26-28, 2005. For results based on this sample, one can say with 95% confidence that the maximum margin of sampling error is ±4 percentage points. In addition to sampling error, question wording and practical difficulties in conducting surveys can introduce error or bias into the findings of public opinion polls.

October 7, 2005
MOST AMERICANS APPROVE OF INTERRACIAL DATING
Practice not uncommon in U.S.

by Jeffrey M. Jones, Gallup Poll Managing Editor

Most Americans say they approve of interracial dating. Even though a majority of whites approve, they are somewhat less likely to approve of interracial dating than are blacks or Hispanics. Interracial and interethnic dating is not uncommon in the United States, according to self-reports in the survey. Slightly less than half of Americans say they have dated someone from a different racial or ethnic background, with Hispanics more likely than whites or blacks to say this. Younger Americans are much more likely to approve of interracial dating and to have dated someone from a different racial or ethnic background.

Gallup's annual Minority Rights and Relations poll delved into the topic of interracial dating to see whether Americans approve or disapprove of whites and blacks dating. One half of the sample, which included larger numbers of blacks and Hispanics than in a typical poll, was asked about a *black man* dating a *white woman*. The other half was asked about a *white man* dating a *black woman*. The poll finds 75% of Americans approving of a white man dating a black woman, and 71% approving of a black man dating a white woman. The difference is not statistically significant.

The distinction between the race of the man and woman makes little difference for blacks and Hispanics, but appears to affect whites' approval of interracial dating to a small degree. Seventy-two percent of whites approve of a white man dating a black woman, while 65% of whites approve of a black man dating a white woman.

There are substantial differences by age in approval of interracial dating. Those in the 18- to 29-year-old age category are nearly unanimous in their approval, but approval declines significantly with each succeeding age category, to the point at which less than half of senior citizens approve.

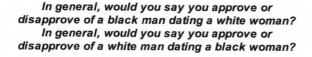

In general, would you say you approve or disapprove of a black man dating a white woman?
In general, would you say you approve or disapprove of a white man dating a black woman?

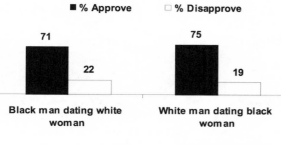

■ % Approve   □ % Disapprove

	Black man dating white woman	White man dating black woman
Approve	71	75
Disapprove	22	19

June 6-25, 2005

In general, would you say you approve or disapprove of a black man dating a white woman?
In general, would you say you approve or disapprove of a white man dating a black woman?

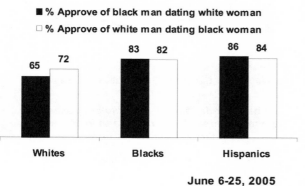

■ % Approve of black man dating white woman
□ % Approve of white man dating black woman

	Whites	Blacks	Hispanics
Black man dating white woman	65	83	86
White man dating black woman	72	82	84

June 6-25, 2005

Percentage Approving of Interracial Dating, by Age

	18 to 29 yrs	30 to 49 yrs	50 to 64 yrs	65 yrs+
Black man dating white woman	95%	77	61	45
White man dating black woman	95%	85	64	46

Interracial and Interethnic Dating in Practice

In addition to measuring the public's attitudes toward interracial dating, the poll also measured the extent to which people have dated someone with similar or different racial and ethnic backgrounds from their own.

As one would expect, most Americans, 92%, say they have dated someone of their own racial or ethnic background in their lifetimes—97% of whites have dated a white person, 95% of blacks have dated a black person, and 83% of Hispanics have dated another Hispanic. But it is not uncommon for people to report dating someone from a different racial or ethnic background—48% of Americans overall say they have done so, including 69% of Hispanics, 52% of blacks, and 45% of whites.

Younger Americans—who are more approving of interracial dating—are also more likely to have dated a person from a different racial or ethnic background. Sixty percent of 18- to 29-year-olds have

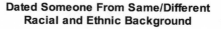

Dated Someone From Same/Different Racial and Ethnic Background

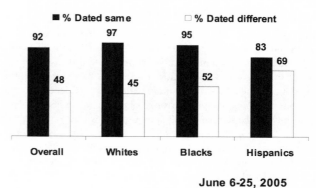

■ % Dated same   □ % Dated different

	Overall	Whites	Blacks	Hispanics
Dated same	92	97	95	83
Dated different	48	45	52	69

June 6-25, 2005

done so, compared with 53% of 30- to 49-year-olds, 46% of 50- to 64-year-olds, and only 28% of those 65 and older.

There are no appreciable gender differences in the incidence of dating someone from one's own race or ethnic background. However, there are differences by gender when it comes to dating someone from a different racial or ethnic background.

Black men (64%) are significantly more likely to say they have dated a non-black than are black women (42%). Hispanic men (74%) are also more likely than Hispanic women (65%) to say they have dated a non-Hispanic. White men (48%) are about as likely as white women (43%) to have dated a nonwhite.

That general pattern holds when looking at the data in more detail—black men are much more likely than black women to say they have dated whites, Hispanics, and Asians. Men of all racial and ethnic backgrounds are significantly more likely than women of all backgrounds to say they have dated an Asian.

Dating People of Various Racial and Ethnic Backgrounds, by Race and Gender

	Dated a Non-Hispanic white %	Dated a black %	Dated a Hispanic %	Dated an Asian %
All Americans	85	34	36	18
Men	88	34	38	28
Women	83	34	34	9
All non-Hispanic whites	97	24	29	18
White men	99	25	30	27
White women	96	24	28	9
All blacks	44	95	28	12
Black men	56	97	40	24
Black women	35	94	18	3
All Hispanics	64	34	83	19
Hispanic men	69	39	86	31
Hispanic women	60	29	81	8

Overall, blacks are much more likely to say they have dated a white (44%) than a Hispanic (28%) or an Asian (12%). Hispanics are twice as likely to say they have dated a white (64%) than a black (34%), and only 19% of Hispanics have dated an Asian. Whites are slightly more likely to say they have dated a Hispanic (29%) than a black (24%) or an Asian (18%).

Survey Methods

Results are based on telephone interviews with 2,264 national adults, aged 18 and older, conducted June 6-25, 2005, including oversamples of blacks and Hispanics that are weighted to reflect their proportions in the general population. For results based on the total sample of national adults, one can say with 95% confidence that the maximum margin of sampling error is ±5 percentage points.

Results for the sample of 807 non-Hispanic whites, aged 18 and older, are based on telephone interviews conducted June 6-25, 2005. For results based on the total sample, one can say with 95% confidence that the margin of sampling error is ±7 percentage points.

Results for the sample of 802 blacks, aged 18 and older, are based on telephone interviews conducted June 6-25, 2005. For results based on the total sample, one can say with 95% confidence that the margin of sampling error is ±5 percentage points.

Results for the sample of 511 Hispanics, aged 18 and older, are based on telephone interviews, conducted June 6-25, 2005. For results based on the total sample, one can say with 95% confidence that the margin of sampling error is ±5 percentage points. (181 out of the 511 interviews with Hispanics were conducted in Spanish.)

October 10, 2005

DEMOCRATS GROWING WARY OF FEDERAL GOVERNMENT'S POWER

Republicans generally satisfied with federal power

by Lydia Saad, Gallup Poll Senior Editor

The American public is evenly divided over whether the federal government these days has too much power. Exactly half of Americans interviewed in Gallup's 2005 Governance Survey, conducted Sept. 12-15, say the federal government has too much power. The same number believes the government is doing too many things that should be left to individuals and businesses. Somewhat fewer, 37%, believe the government "poses an immediate threat to the rights and freedoms of ordinary citizens."

The perception that the federal government has too much power is more widespread today than it has been in recent years. Between 2002 and 2003, Gallup recorded only a slight increase in the percentage of all national adults saying the government has too much power (from 39% to 43%). The bigger change came in just the past year, with the figure jumping eight points—from 42% in 2004 to 50% today.

Democrats, in particular, have grown more critical of government power. Between 2002 and today, the percentage of Democrats saying the government has too much power increased by 20 points, with more than half of that increase occurring in the past year. There have been much smaller increases (five points) in the percentages of Republicans and independents taking this position.

The percentage of national adults saying the federal government poses a threat to the rights and freedoms of ordinary citizens has also increased, rising from 30% when first asked in 2003, to 35% in 2004, to 37% today.

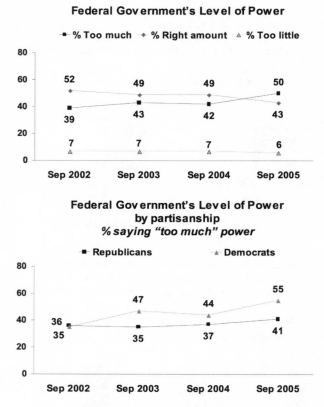

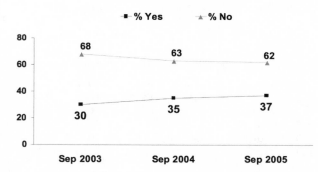

At the same time, there has been virtually no variability in Americans' broader assessments of the *role* of government. This conclusion is based on the trend for a Gallup Governance Poll question asking whether people agree more that "the government is trying to do too many things that should be left to individuals and businesses" or that "government should do more to solve our country's problems." The results from September for each of the last four years (the same surveys on which the government power questions were asked) show between 49% and 51% saying the government is doing too much, and 41% to 44% saying the government should do more.

What Sparked Power Concerns?

Whether the heightened sense that the federal government is too powerful reflects concerns about government power specifically, or disagreement with the Bush administration more generally, is not clear.

Role of Government in Solving Nation's Problems

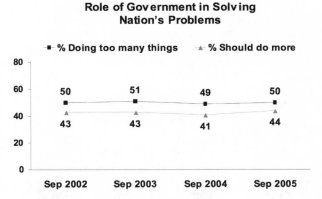

Gallup's measure of government power was instituted in September 2002, nearly a year after the anti-terrorism law known as the USA Patriot Act was enacted in response to the 9/11 attacks. Thus, the trend does not document the initial impact the Patriot Act may have had on attitudes toward government compared with previous points in time. However, the percentage in 2002 saying the government was too powerful (39%) was relatively small, suggesting that the Patriot Act did not immediately ignite a firestorm of concern about infringements on personal freedoms.

Another potential factor explaining increased criticism of government power is the rather sharp decline of President Bush's general popularity since 2002. Across Gallup's annual Governance polls, Bush's approval fell from 66% in September 2002, to 52% in September 2003 and 2004, to 45% in September 2005. With much of this decline occurring among Democrats, it is not unexpected that Democrats would become concomitantly more critical of other aspects of the federal government, such as its level of power.

Power vs. Role of Government

This is not to say that Democrats have abandoned their traditional philosophy in favor of an active government. In answer to Gallup's *role of government* question, 57% of Democrats say they want the government to do more to solve the country's problems; only 37% think the government is doing too much.

Republicans tend to take the opposing view on this question. Nearly two-thirds say the government is doing too many things that should be left to individuals and businesses.

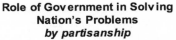
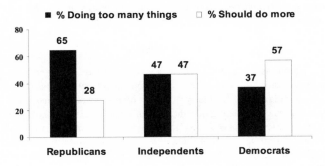

The result is that Republicans and Democrats hold what some might consider incongruous sets of attitudes.

Republicans are generally satisfied with the government's level of power: 56% say the federal government has about the right amount of power. But most Republicans (65%) also hold the conventional GOP view that the federal government is doing too many things that should be left to the private sector.

Democrats, on the other hand, are generally critical of the amount of power the federal government uses: 55% say it has too much power; but the majority (57%) also believe the government should do more to solve the nation's problems.

Survey Methods

These results are based on telephone interviews with a randomly selected national sample of 921 adults, aged 18 and older, conducted Sept. 12-15, 2005. For results based on this sample, one can say with 95% confidence that the maximum error attributable to sampling and other random effects is ±4 percentage points. In addition to sampling error, question wording and practical difficulties in conducting surveys can introduce error or bias into the findings of public opinion polls.

The sample for this survey did not include the areas of Louisiana and Mississippi that were declared federal disaster areas following Hurricane Katrina. This accounts for about less than 1% (0.75%) of the U.S. adult population.

October 11, 2005
HEIGHT MATTERS: MORE FOR BOYS THAN GIRLS
What Americans believe about the importance of height for preteens and teenagers

by Jack Ludwig, Contributing Editor

For young people whose bodies are still growing, height can be a volatile characteristic. Uncertainty about the timing and intensity of growth spurts can leave teens and preteens shorter than their peers at one point in time and taller at another. This volatility makes it interesting to wonder about how much a young person's height really matters. How much real importance does youthful stature have for success and social development during these formative years? Does it affect their ability to make friends, to be involved in sports, or to approach social situations with self-confidence?

In a recently completed Gallup/Pfizer Survey of Opinions on the Social Impact of Stature, we asked a random sample of U.S. adults to give us their opinions about the relative fortunes of young people who are noticeably shorter or taller than their peers. Although the survey did not directly assess whether taller or shorter young people actually experience different outcomes, we found compelling evidence that American adults believe that stature has important consequences for preteens and teenagers.

We asked separate questions about preteens and teenagers and about boys and girls in each age grouping, a feature that lends interesting nuance to our findings. While opinions are largely the same whether the questions focus on preteens or teenagers, height is believed to have a very different significance for boys than for girls.

When asked whether noticeably taller or noticeably shorter young people have an easier time getting involved in sports, the results are similar whether the questions are asked about preteens or teenagers. Adults overwhelmingly believe that noticeably taller young people have an easier time getting involved in sports than noticeably shorter young people, regardless of age grouping or gender of the child. However, in both age groupings, height is believed to be a more important asset for boys than for girls. Eighty-seven percent of adults believe that noticeably taller preteen boys will have an easier time, while 10% say that noticeably shorter preteen boys will have an easier time.

For preteen girls, 81% of adults believe that taller girls have an advantage in getting involved in sports, while 13% say that shorter girls have the advantage. Essentially, the same pattern exists when the questions focus on teenagers—Americans believe that height has a decided effect on involvement in sports for young people, and that the benefits of height are somewhat greater for boys than for girls.

Perceived Effect of Height on Involvement in Sports for Boys and Girls

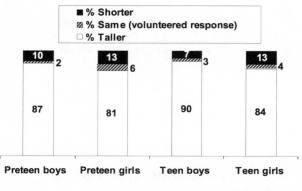

May 18-July 7, 2005

Question wording: *If you had to guess, who do you think has the easier time getting involved in sports—(preteen/teen) (boys/girls) who are noticeably shorter than other (boys/girls) their age, or (preteen/teen) (boys/girls) who are noticeably taller than other (boys/girls) their age?*

We also ask about the impact of height on young people's ease in making friends and their ease in feeling self-confident in social situations—dimensions extremely important in a young person's social development. On these dimensions, opinions differ dramatically depending on the gender of the child—much more dramatically than when the questions focus on athletic involvement.

When we asked whether noticeably shorter or noticeably taller young people had an easier time making friends, adults give a slight (but statistically significant) edge to shorter girls. Fifty-eight percent believe that noticeably shorter teenage girls have an easier time making friends, while 33% say that noticeably taller teenage girls have an easier time. But when teenage boys are the subject of the question, opinions are much more lopsided and in the opposite direction. Seventy-three percent of adults say that noticeably taller boys had an advantage in making friends, while only 21% give shorter boys the edge. Once again, the patterns for preteens and teenagers show no meaningful differences: shorter girls are believed to have an advantage over taller girls in making friends, but taller boys are perceived to have a decisive advantage over shorter boys.

This enormous gulf between the perceived consequences of height for boys and girls in making friends is larger than any measured in the Gallup/Pfizer survey for any other dimension either for young people or adults. That it shows up on a dimension that is so fundamental to social adjustment and integration is both striking and sobering.

Perceived Effect of Height on Ease of Making Friends for Boys and Girls

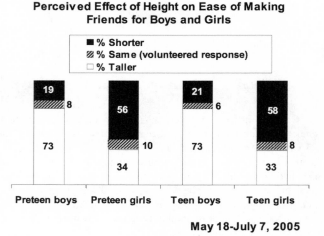

May 18-July 7, 2005

Question wording: *If you had to guess, who do you think has the easier time making friends—(preteen/teen) (boys/girls) who are noticeably shorter than other (boys/girls) their age, or (preteen/teen) (boys/girls) who are noticeably taller than other (boys/girls) their age?*

The final question we asked about young people probed opinions on the impact of height on general feelings of self-confidence in social situations. Forty-nine percent of adults say that noticeably shorter preteen girls have an easier time making friends, while 45% say that noticeably taller preteen girls have an easier time. However, opinions were strikingly divergent when we asked about preteen boys: an overwhelming 81% said that taller boys have an easier time feeling self-confident, while only 15% said that noticeably shorter boys have an advantage.

The results of the parallel set of questions (asking about teenagers instead of preteens) are once again remarkably similar. To be sure, teenage girls are believed to have a slightly greater edge than their preteen male counterparts if they're noticeably shorter, but the differences by age group dwarf the differences across the gender line.

Question wording: *If you had to guess, who do you think has the easier time feeling self-confident in social situations—(preteen/teen) (boys/girls) who are noticeably shorter than other (boys/girls) their age, or (preteen/teen) (boys/girls) who are noticeably taller than other (boys/girls) their age?*

Final Thoughts

The opinions reflected in our survey are disquieting, although they certainly help to make sense of anxious questions that parents of young children—particularly of young boys—frequently ask pediatricians. The fascinating question, unanswered by our survey results, is why these perceptions exist. It is relatively easy to understand how people might believe that the height of young people might affect their involvement in sports, since size—in certain sports at least—confers distinct advantages. But what is the relevance of height to feeling self-confident in social situations? Why should height affect

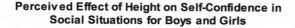

Perceived Effect of Height on Self-Confidence in Social Situations for Boys and Girls

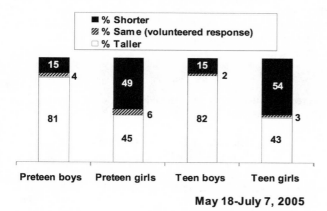

- ■ % Shorter
- ▨ % Same (volunteered response)
- □ % Taller

May 18-July 7, 2005

how easily a young person makes friends? Why do these perceptions exist? And why is height seen as so much more of a social asset for boys than it is for girls?

Granted, these are, after all, only opinions about whether shorter or taller young people reap advantages or disadvantages from their statures, not proof that these dynamics exist. But our results do suggest that stature might belong among characteristics such as gender, age, and race that—irrespective of their relevance—can have a bearing on important outcomes for young people. Whether you consider these results to be proof of "heightism" or not, the fact that these opinions are so broadly shared makes them deserving of careful consideration, and begs for an explanation of why they are so widely believed.

Survey Methods

These results are based on telephone interviews with a randomly selected national sample of 1,509 adults, aged 18 and older, conducted May 18-July 7, 2005. Randomly selected subsamples of this overall sample were asked questions about preteens (733 adults) and teenagers (777 adults). For results based on samples of this size, one can say with 95% confidence that the maximum error attributable to sampling and other random effects is ±4 percentage points. In addition to sampling error, question wording and practical difficulties in conducting surveys can introduce error or bias into the findings of public opinion polls.

October 12, 2005

AMERICANS WANT LEADERS TO PAY ATTENTION TO PUBLIC OPINION

But still skeptical of standard sample sizes used by pollsters

by Frank Newport, Gallup Poll Editor in Chief

The American public believes the nation would be better off if its leaders paid more attention to the views of the public and to public opinion polls. Americans also have more trust and confidence in the views of the people than in any of the three branches of the federal

government, state or local government, or the mass media. At the same time, the majority of Americans paradoxically don't believe that a random sample of 1,000 adults—the sample size of a typical public policy poll—can accurately reflect the views of the nation's population. Republicans are less likely to want leaders to pay attention to polls than are independents and Democrats.

Should Leaders Follow Public Opinion More Closely?

More than 7 in 10 Americans say the nation would be better off "if the leaders of our nation followed the views of the public more closely," and more than 6 in 10 agree that the nation would be better off if leaders "followed the views of public opinion polls more closely."

If the leaders of our nation followed the views of the public more closely, do you think the nation would be better off, or worse off than it is today?

	Better off %	Worse off %	NO DIFFER- ENCE (vol.) %	No opinion %
2005 Sep 12-15	73	22	3	2
2001 Sep 7-10	75	18	4	3
1996 Apr 25-28 ^	80	11	—	9
1975 Oct 3-6	67	16	9	8

(vol.) = Volunteered response
^ Asked of a half sample

If the leaders of our nation followed the views of public opinion polls more closely, do you think the nation would be better off, or worse off than it is today?

	Better off %	Worse off %	NO DIFFER- ENCE (vol.) %	No opinion %
2005 Sep 12-15	61	33	3	3
2001 Sep 7-10	63	27	6	4
1996 Apr 25-28 ^	73	14	—	13

(vol.) = Volunteered response
^ Asked of a half sample

The difference of 12 percentage points in the "better off" responses between the "views of the public" and "public opinion polls" wording may suggest that "poll" has a mildly pejorative connotation. Still, the majority support for the idea of leaders paying more attention to polls per se reinforces the conclusion that the public is talking about more than just public opinion as expressed in elections.

In general, regardless of how the question is phrased, it is clear that Americans fairly strongly believe the nation would be well served if its leaders paid closer attention to the views of the average American—and presumably less attention to special interests, lobbyists, party bosses, and so forth.

President George W. Bush has frequently stated that he does not govern by paying attention to polls, and has argued that his view of leadership is based on a president doing what he thinks is right rather than what polls show the public wants.

With this in mind, it is perhaps not surprising to find that Republicans are less likely than independents or Democrats to believe the nation would be better off if its leaders paid more attention to public opinion.

SHOULD LEADERS FOLLOW THE VIEWS OF THE PUBLIC AND PUBLIC OPINION POLLS MORE CLOSELY?

If the leaders of our nation followed the views of the public more closely, do you think the nation would be better off, or worse off than it is today?

	Republicans	Independents	Democrats
Better off	63%	70%	85%
Worse off	31	24	11
No difference/ No opinion	6	6	4

If the leaders of our nation followed the views of public opinion polls more closely, do you think the nation would be better off, or worse off than it is today?

	Republicans	Independents	Democrats
Better off	49%	58%	76%
Worse off	44	37	17
No difference/ No opinion	7	5	7

It may also be possible that Republicans—currently enjoying control of the White House, the House of Representatives, and the Senate—feel it is less necessary to pay attention to the public's views. Additionally, with polls showing that a majority of Americans disapprove of the job President Bush is doing, and that a majority disapprove of administration policies on issues such as Iraq, Democrats may feel more comfortable at the moment saying the people's voice should be listened to.

There are significant differences in responses to these questions by educational level. Americans with the highest levels of educational attainment—those with postgraduate degrees—are less likely to say the nation would be better off if its leaders followed either the views of the public or public opinion polls. This is particularly true when it comes to public opinion polls. On the other hand, Americans with high school educations or less are more likely to believe the nation *would* be better off if leaders paid attention to either the views of the public or public opinion polls.

SHOULD LEADERS FOLLOW THE VIEWS OF THE PUBLIC AND PUBLIC OPINION POLLS MORE CLOSELY?

If the leaders of our nation followed the views of the public more closely, do you think the nation would be better off, or worse off than it is today?

	Post-graduate	College grad	Some college	High school or less
Better off	62%	69%	73%	78%
Worse off	35	24	21	17
No difference/ No opinion	3	7	6	5

If the leaders of our nation followed the views of public opinion polls more closely, do you think the nation would be better off, or worse off than it is today?

	Post-graduate	College grad	Some college	High school or less
Better off	44%	57%	57%	72%
Worse off	47	36	35	25
No difference/ No opinion	9	7	8	3

Trust and Confidence

The recent Gallup Poll asked respondents how much trust and confidence they had in each of eight different entities.

How Much Trust and Confidence Do You Have in the Following?

(sorted by "Great deal/Fair amount")	Great deal/ Fair amount %	Not very much/ None at all %
American people as a whole when it comes to making judgments about issues facing the country	78	22
Your local government	70	30
Judicial branch	68	31
Your state government	67	33
Legislative branch	62	37
Men and women in political life in this country	58	40
Executive branch	52	48
Mass media	50	49

Consistent with the finding that Americans would like leaders to pay more attention to the views of the public, these data show that Americans have the highest level of trust in themselves—followed by local government, the judicial branch, and state government.

One Thousand People?

Despite the fact that a majority of Americans believe the nation would be better off if leaders paid more attention to public opinion polls, relatively few believe in the random-sample methodology that is at the heart of today's polls.

As you may know, most national polls are typically based on a random sample of 1,000 U.S. adults. Do you think a sample of this size accurately reflects the views of the nation's population, or not?

	Yes, reflects	No, does not	No opinion
2005 Sep 12-15	30%	68	2

TREND FOR COMPARISON:

2001 Sep 7-10^	21%	75%	4%
1996 Jul 25-28^	28	68	4
1996 Apr 25-28^	28	68	4
1985^	28	56	15

^ QUESTION WORDING: Do you think a sample of 1,500 or 2,000 people can accurately reflect the views of the nation's population, or that it is not possible with so few people?

As can be seen, this distrust of the power of random sampling—using what appear to be very small numbers of respondents—is not new. Previous polling has reinforced the conclusion that while Americans approve of the concept and philosophy of polling as a way of measuring the will of the people, they don't understand how the small number of people involved in a typical sample can possibly represent millions in the general population.

There is no difference in response to this question by party or by education. This latter finding is particularly interesting. Better-educated Americans are no more likely than those with less education to believe that a random sample of 1,000 can represent the total population.

Summary

Americans—perhaps not surprisingly—have great faith in themselves as a guiding force in a democracy. As a result, they think the nation would be better off if their elected representatives paid more, rather than less, attention to the views of the people, including those views as measured in public opinion polls.

There is a significant paradox in these data, however. Americans still don't understand how a random sample of only 1,000 people can accurately represent the views of millions of Americans. The public, in short, accepts the philosophic underpinnings of polling and its use by elected leaders, but has yet to be convinced that polling works.

Survey Methods

These results are based on telephone interviews with a randomly selected national sample of 921 adults, aged 18 and older, conducted Sept. 12-15, 2005. For results based on this sample, one can say with 95% confidence that the maximum error attributable to sampling and other random effects is ±4 percentage points. In addition to sampling error, question wording and practical difficulties in conducting surveys can introduce error or bias into the findings of public opinion polls.

The sample for this survey did not include the areas of Louisiana and Mississippi that were declared federal disaster areas following Hurricane Katrina. This accounts for about less than 1% (0.75%) of the U.S. adult population.

October 13, 2005

MOST AMERICANS ENGAGED IN DEBATE ABOUT EVOLUTION, CREATION

Majorities have thought about it and care which explanation is correct

by Jeffrey M. Jones, Gallup Poll Managing Editor

The debate about how human beings came to exist on Earth has simmered in American public discourse for a long time. Most Americans are engaged in the debate to some degree, according to a recent CNN/*USA Today*/Gallup poll—three-quarters say they have thought at least a moderate amount about the origin of human beings, and two-thirds say it matters to them which theory about how human beings came to exist is correct. Americans are more likely to endorse a purely creationist view of the origin of humans than a purely evolutionary view or a view involving elements of both. Majorities of the public say evolution and creationism should be taught in public school science classes, while fewer believe intelligent design should be taught.

Basic Views About Origin of Human Beings

The Sept. 8-11 CNN/*USA Today*/Gallup poll asked Americans to choose from three explanations for the origin of man:

Which of the following statements comes closest to your views on the origin and development of human beings—[ROTATED: human beings have evolved over millions of years from other forms of life and God guided this process, human beings have evolved over millions of years from other forms of life, but God had no part in this process, or God created human beings in their present form exactly the way the Bible describes it]?

Fifty-three percent say God created humans in their present form the way the Bible describes it, essentially endorsing a strict creationist explanation. Twelve percent endorse the strict evolutionary perspective—that humans evolved from other species, but without any divine intervention. Thirty-one percent choose the modified perspective, believing human beings evolved from other species but with God guiding the process. That closely matches the perspective commonly known as "intelligent design."

Earlier Gallup polling shows similar results, with between 44% and 47% favoring the strict creationist viewpoint. Those questions, however, used slightly different question wordings that did not mention the Bible specifically as does the current wording. That may explain the higher support for creationism in the Sept. 8-11 poll. Nevertheless, in Gallup polling, the public has always been most likely to endorse creationist explanations for the origin of human beings.

That does not mean that Americans reject evolutionary theories. An Aug. 5-7 CNN/*USA Today*/Gallup poll asked Americans to rate whether each of the three theories were definitely true, probably true, probably false, or definitely false. Fifty-eight percent said creationism was definitely or probably true, but a majority, 55%, also said evolution was definitely or probably true. One in three Americans believe the evolution explanation is false. Fewer believe intelligent design is true, likely because a significant proportion of the public is unfamiliar with the term (28%, while an additional 9% did not have an opinion).

Views of Different Explanations for the Origin and Development of Life on Earth

	Defi-nitely true %	Prob-ably true %	Prob-ably false %	Defi-nitely false %	Not familiar with %	No opinion %
Creationism	29	29	18	8	11	5
Evolution	20	35	14	20	8	3
Intelligent design	8	23	22	10	28	9

Majorities of Americans also believe that evolution and creationism should be taught in public school science classes—in fact, more say evolution should be taught (61%) than say creationism should be taught (54%). Fewer than half say the same about intelligent design, again because many Americans are unfamiliar with that theory.

Should Different Explanations for Origin of Man be Taught in Public School Science Classes?

	Yes, should %	No, should not %	Unsure %	No answer %
Evolution	61	20	19	*
Creationism	54	22	23	1
Intelligent design	43	21	35	1

*Less than 0.5%

Public Involvement in the Debate

It is unclear exactly how well Americans understand the different theories. The Sept. 8-11 poll attempted to gauge a sense of the public's involvement in the debate by asking how much they have thought about the different explanations, and how much it matters to them which is correct.

Forty-one percent of Americans say they have thought a great deal about these issues, with an additional 35% saying they have given a moderate amount of thought to them. Less than one in four say they have not thought about it much (17%) or at all (6%).

Interestingly, people differ in the amount they have thought about human origin according to the view they most closely subscribe to. Among those who believe in evolution and say God had no part in the process, a majority (54%) say they have thought a great deal about how human beings came to exist. That compares with 43% of those who prefer the strict creationist view and 35% of those who believe man evolved with divine guidance.

Amount of Thought Given to Origin of Human Beings
by preferred explanation

	Evolved, God not involved %	Evolved, God guiding %	Created as Bible says %
Great deal	54	35	43
Moderate amount	31	49	29
Not much/Not at all	11	15	19

Because the proportion of people who subscribe to the purely evolutionary view is small, the views of the group who have thought about the issue a great deal are not that different from the general public in their views about how humans came to exist on Earth—55% believe God created humans in their present form, 27% believe God guided the evolutionary process, and 16% believe God had no part in the evolutionary process.

View of Origin of Human Beings
by Amount of Thought Given to Issue

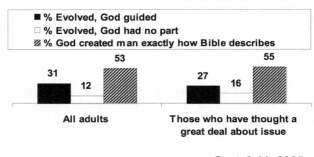

■ % Evolved, God guided
□ % Evolved, God had no part
▨ % God created man exactly how Bible describes

All adults: 31, 12, 53
Those who have thought a great deal about issue: 27, 16, 55

Sept. 8-11, 2005

Overall, 40% of Americans say it matters a great deal to them which theory is correct, and an additional 26% say a moderate amount. One in three Americans say it doesn't matter to them much (19%) or at all (14%).

While those who believe in the strict evolutionary view are more likely to say they have thought about the issues, they are *least* likely to say it matters to them a great deal. A majority of people who subscribe to the creationist view are much more likely to say it matters a great deal to them which is correct.

How Much Does it Matter to You Which Theory is Correct?
by view of human origin

	Evolved, God not involved %	Evolved, God guiding %	Created as Bible says %
Great deal	21	29	54
Moderate amount	38	26	20
Not much/Not at all	41	44	25

In general, then, people who adhere to the evolutionary view of the origin of humans are more likely to have thought a lot about the issue, but less likely to say it matters to them that their theory is right. People who adopt an orthodox creationist view are less likely to have thought a lot about the issue, but more likely to say it matters to them which is correct.

Past Gallup analyses have shown that people who believe in creationism are much more religious, and the fact that their religion and views of human origin are closely linked likely explains why they are so invested in which theory of the origin of human beings is correct.

Survey Methods

These results are based on telephone interviews with a randomly selected national sample of 1,005 adults, aged 18 and older, conducted Sept. 8-11, 2005. For results based on this sample, one can say with 95% confidence that the maximum error attributable to sampling and other random effects is ±3 percentage points. In addition to sampling error, question wording and practical difficulties in conducting surveys can introduce error or bias into the findings of public opinion polls.

October 14, 2005
AT LEAST 100,000 KATRINA VICTIMS STILL SEPARATED FROM FAMILIES
Half of victims who requested Red Cross aid still living in temporary housing or shelter

by David W. Moore, Gallup Poll Senior Editor

Six weeks after Hurricane Katrina hit New Orleans and surrounding areas, a special CNN/*USA Today*/Gallup survey of hurricane victims finds many still separated from their families, including a large number of parents still not reunited with their children. Tens of thousands of people have lost their jobs and their homes, and many are concerned about the possibility of another Katrina-like disaster. Though New Orleans Mayor Ray Nagin is now urging residents of the city to return to their homes, many apparently will not do so.

The survey was conducted Sept. 30-Oct. 9, using a random sample of hurricane victims who have applied to the Red Cross for assistance. The Red Cross database includes more than 463,000 names, and the poll interviewed a random sample of 1,510 of these people by telephone, some by landline and others by cell phone.

Some of the major findings:

Half of this group reported that they were separated from other family members for at least a day as a result of Katrina, and 22%—which projects to more than 100,000—say their families are still not reunited. The actual number among all hurricane victims could be higher, because the survey included Red Cross applicants only.

Six percent of parents with children under age 18 who have applied for Red Cross aid are still not reunited with their children. That translates into almost 15,000 parents, which could even be higher once parents who have not applied for Red Cross aid are taken into account.

In addition to being separated from family members, the poll also assessed the extent to which these hurricane survivors experienced other hardships:

	%
Worried about elderly family members living in the path of the hurricane	73
Feared for your life	53
Were separated for at least a day from family members you had been living with	51
Had a vehicle damaged	41
Went without food for at least a day	40
Went without drinking water for at least a day	34
Spent at least one night in an emergency shelter	25
Lost a pet or had to abandon one	20
Were a victim of a crime	7
Were physically injured or hurt	6

Thirty-two percent of the sample of Red Cross applicants—projectable to about 150,000 people—say that the home or apartment they were living in either was destroyed or damaged so badly they cannot live in it.

While half of the Red Cross applicants are now living in the same place they were before the hurricane hit, 25% (116,000 people) are living in someone else's home, 13% (60,000) are living in an apartment or house they rented after the disaster, 8% (37,000) are still living in a hotel or motel, 2% (9,000) in an emergency shelter, and 1% (4,600) in a camper or trailer.

Most of the people living in someone else's home are living with other family members (66%), while 25% are living with friends, and 9% with people they didn't know before the hurricane.

Nearly 7 in 10 respondents say they were employed before Katrina hit, but only 62% of that group is currently employed. Thirty-seven percent of the previously employed (116,000) do not have a job at the present time.

The vast majority of these victims, 81%, think it is likely that another natural disaster like Hurricane Katrina will hit their communities again at some point in their lives. Forty-nine percent say that is very likely to occur; another 32% say somewhat likely.

Given the fears, it is perhaps surprising how many people expect to return to their communities. About half, 51%, are already back there, while another 14% say they will definitely return and 13% say they will probably return. Nineteen percent are skeptical that they will go back—8% say they definitely will not, and 11% say probably not.

While the New Orleans mayor is urging all residents to return, 16% of New Orleans residents who applied for Red Cross assistance (more than 21,000) say they will definitely not return, and another 23% (31,000) say they probably will not return.

There was much controversy as to why many people did not evacuate their homes before the hurricane and floods hit. Among the people surveyed, 67% say they evacuated before the storm hit, 3% did so during the storm, 15% did so after it had passed, while 15% did not evacuate at all.

Among those who did not evacuate before the storm hit, the most frequently cited reasons given fall into two categories: 1) misjudgment, and 2) difficulty in leaving.

The misjudgment category includes: the misperception that the hurricane was not going to be as bad as it turned out to be, that the respondents' homes could withstand the force of the storm, that they were safely far enough away from the coast, and that they waited until the last minute and it was too late.

The difficulty in leaving category includes: trying to keep the family together, having no transportation, not having enough money to leave, having no place to go, needing to work, not being informed, not having enough gasoline, and being in poor health.

What are some of the reasons why you did NOT evacuate BEFORE Hurricane Katrina hit? [OPEN-ENDED]

BASED ON 492 RESPONDENTS WHO DID NOT EVACUATE BEFORE HURRICANE KATRINA HIT (± 5 PCT PTS)

	2005 Sep 30-Oct 9
	%
Misjudgment	57
Didn't think it would be that bad/prior hurricanes not as bad as predicted	40
Thought my house structure was sound/ could withstand it	7
Thought our distances from the coast was safe	7
Waited until the last minute and it was too late	5
Difficulty in leaving	39
Was keeping family together	7
Had no transportation/not reliable	6
Couldn't afford to leave/No money	6
No place to go	5
Had to work	5
Wasn't fully advised on what to do/Not a mandatory evacuation	5
Availability of gas/Afraid would be stuck in traffic without gas	3
Poor health/Couldn't due to medical issues	2
Had to stay and protect my property/ possessions/animals	5
Faith in God/Put destiny in God's hands	2
Stubborn/Hard-headed/Didn't want to leave	2
Other	5
None	1
No opinion	1

Percentages add to more than 100% due to multiple responses.

Survey Methods

This poll was conducted in cooperation with the American Red Cross. Results are based on telephone interviews with a sample of 1,510 adults, aged 18 and older, drawn randomly from the American Red Cross database of applicants seeking assistance due to the effects of Hurricane Katrina. Interviews were conducted Sept. 30-Oct. 9, 2005.

The vast majority of applicants provided a working contact telephone number to the Red Cross. Gallup did reverse phone lookups to obtain telephone numbers for the portion of the selected sample that did not provide a contact number. Where necessary, Gallup interviewers tracked down updated telephone numbers when respondents had moved from their previous location. Interviews were conducted on both landline and cellular telephones. Full details on the poll methodology can be found at poll.gallup.com.

In addition to sampling error, question wording and practical difficulties in conducting surveys can introduce error or bias into the findings of public opinion polls.

October 17, 2005
KATRINA VICTIMS: FEAR REPLACED BY RELIEF, BUT MAJORITY STILL SCARRED
Two-thirds continue to experience anxiety

by Lydia Saad, Gallup Poll Senior Editor

While the rest of the country looked on with sadness, shock, and anger, the residents of the Gulf Coast who suffered Hurricane Katrina's fury experienced intense feelings of anxiety, including fear, devastation, depression, helplessness, and stress. In more recent days, these acute feelings have subsided, and many more victims are expressing relief along with a restored sense of normalcy in their lives. Still, a majority of survivors are experiencing negative reactions, including nearly a third who have strongly negative feelings—even six weeks after the storm hit.

Survivors' Emotional Responses Post-Katrina: Then and Now

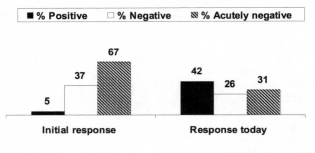

Sept. 30-Oct. 9, 2005

These are the findings of a special CNN/*USA Today*/Gallup survey of people who have applied to the American Red Cross for assistance as a result of Hurricane Katrina. The poll was conducted by telephone (landline and cell phone) Sept. 30-Oct. 9, and includes a random sample of 1,510 adult Katrina victims (from a Red Cross database of more than 463,000 people who applied to the Red Cross for aid).

Respondents were asked to describe, in their own words, the feelings they had in the initial days of the storm and its aftermath. Fear was the most common feeling, expressed by 22%. Many simply said they were "scared," while others said they were "scared to death." Still others gave specific reasons for being fearful.

"I got emphysema and asthma. When the power went out, I thought I was going to die. My neighbors brought a generator. I did not think I was going to live through it."

"Well, the kinds of emotions I felt were scary, because for me to have my first child in the hurricane that was to hit Louisiana the way it did, it was scary. Because I didn't know which items I would need … didn't know which items that a newborn baby would need."

"Very bad. My roof was flying away, the water was coming on the floor in my house, and we didn't have any lights, and I had 18 people in my house, and we were all very scared."

Some of the comments reinforce the finding (discussed in the related item by David Moore) that many residents did not evacuate before the storm because, for various reasons, they did not appreciate its potential severity.

"It didn't really hit me until the after effect of the canals, the levees busting. Once that happened, that's when we really had to deal with it; that's what scared us and let us know we really had to leave."

Other comments reveal the profound level of anxiety brought on by the separation of family members.

"Very anxious and not knowing what was going on in the parish and if the family members got out in time."

"Anxiety; being away from my children. My kids were in Houston and I was in Atlanta."

An analysis of the verbatim responses finds that two-thirds of Katrina survivors felt one or more deeply negative emotions in the initial days after the storm made landfall. In addition to being scared, this includes those who were "devastated," "shocked," "stressed," and "upset." Altogether, 67% of respondents named one or more emotions that Gallup classifies as "acutely negative."

Emotions in First Few Days: Acutely Negative Responses (net 67%)

Scared/Afraid (net)	22%
Stressed/Overwhelmed/Distraught (net)	9
Devastated	7
Shock/Shocked	7
Upset	6
Depressed	5
Bad	4
Lost/Don't know where to turn	4
Anxious/Anxiety	3
Disbelief	3
Angry/Anger	2
Horrible	2
Feelings of loss (loved one/home)	2
Unbelievable	2
Crying	1
Helplessness	1
Terrible	1

(Table adds to more than 67% due to multiple responses.)

Thirty-seven percent reported having seemingly less severe negative emotions, including feeling nervous, uncertain, sad, and "emotional."

"I was very sad and depressed—one day I had a roof over my head and the next day it was gone."

Emotions in First Few Days: Negative Responses (net 37%)

Sad	9%
Worried	7
Uncertainty	6
Emotional/All kinds of emotions	4
Confused	3
Frustrated	3
Nervous	3
Hurt	2

Concerned	2
Surprised	1
Apprehension	1

(Table adds to more than 37% due to multiple responses.)

A relatively small number—5%—report feeling one or more positive emotions in the first few days of Katrina and her aftermath.

"To be honest, relieved that my trailer was still here."

"We were feeling relief that we could get away from the coast. It took quite awhile, but we did get away. Then, we were doubly concerned for those who could not get away from the coast. Then, we got to Georgia, and we found a place to stay."

Emotions in First Few Days:
Positive Responses (net 5%)

Blessed (God was with me)	1%
Happy	1
Hopeful/Hope	1
Relieved/Relief	1
Thankful	1
Calm/Stable	1
Feeling better/back to normal	1

(Table adds to more than 5% due to multiple responses.)

Many Still Sad and Anxious, but Also Relieved

Responses are markedly different to a question asking survivors to describe their current emotions. Gallup asked, "Now thinking about your emotions in more recent days, what kinds of emotions are you feeling now?" The top category of responses is restoration: "feeling better," "all right," and "back to normal." The total share of the sample reporting positive feelings today is 42%.

While some respondents seem to be on the road to recovery, for others there is clearly a long way to go.

"A little bit better because we are getting a little bit of help, but it is still very difficult because we lost everything."

"A little better. But it's one thing after another. My children's father died. Seeing them grieving and all is very hard. So far I have been able to focus on my mom because she needed help for her healthcare."

"Adjusting to the way I have to live now. Other than that I am all right. I am adjusting day by day."

"Better; upbeat now. We've got power, we've got water, and we've got the leaks stopped in the roof. That's all temporary, of course."

"Thankful the Lord spared me."

"Very thankful that I have a house to come home to and my husband has his job. Some people weren't that fortunate."

Emotions in Recent Days
Positive Responses (net 42%)

Feeling better now/All right/Back to normal	24%
Relieved/Relief	8
Happy	4
Blessed (God was with me)	3
Hopeful/Hope	2
Thankful	2
Grateful	1
Calm/Stable	1
Lucky/Fortunate	1

(Table adds to more than 42% due to multiple responses.)

By contrast, the percentage naming one or more acutely negative feelings is only 31%. No single emotion dominates this category, but stress and depression lead the list.

Emotions in Recent Days
Acutely Negative Responses (net 31%)

Stressed/Stressed out	5%
Depressed	4
Lost/Don't know where to turn	3
Angry/Anger	2
Anxious/Anxiety	2
Devastated	2
Feelings of loss (loved one/home)	2
Overwhelmed	2
Upset	2
Bad	1
Crying	1
Disbelief	1
Disgusted	1
Fear	1
Helplessness	1
Scared/Afraid/Terrified	1
Shock/Shocked	1
Unbelievable	1

(Table adds to more than 31% due to multiple responses.)

Another 26% of respondents report feeling less severe negative emotions today, with the chief one being sadness.

"Sad for people who died and friends from New Orleans who died or lost everything."

"Sad, seeing all the trash. Depressing."

"Sadness for the people I have no idea where they are and the people I worked with."

Emotions in Recent Days
Negative Responses (net 26%)

Sad	8%
Emotional/All kinds of emotions	4
Frustrated	4
Confused	3
Uncertainty	3
Worried	2
Aggravated	1
Concerned	1
Nervous	1
Homesick	1
Hurt	1

(Table adds to more than 26% due to multiple responses.)

Separately, Gallup asked respondents to describe the extent to which they are currently experiencing specific post-traumatic stress disorder symptoms, including having trouble sleeping, feelings of anxiety, and feelings of depression. About two in five respondents report having a significant level of difficulty with each of these issues (saying it happens a great deal or quite a lot) and nearly two-thirds are experiencing at least some difficulty.

Victims Turn to Faith and Family to Soothe Their Pain

Respondents primarily credit family (37%) and faith (27%) as the twin pillars of support that have seen them through this emotionally

As a result of Hurricane Katrina, to what extent are you currently experiencing—[ITEM]—a great deal, quite a bit, some, very little, or none?

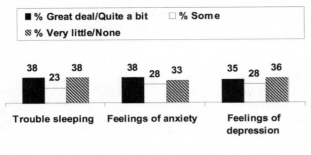

■ % Great deal/Quite a bit   □ % Some
▧ % Very little/None

| 38 | 23 | 38 | 38 | 28 | 33 | 35 | 28 | 36 |

Trouble sleeping   Feelings of anxiety   Feelings of depression

Sept. 30-Oct. 9, 2005

difficult period. Community members reaching out to help and friends are mentioned by 8% each. Just 4% cite FEMA, although this could be a reflection of the fact that FEMA's role in the relief effort is not specifically to provide emotional comfort.

What, if anything, has helped you to get through this difficult emotional time?

	2005 Sep 30-Oct 9 %
Family	37
Faith/Spirituality/Belief in Jesus/God/Prayer/Worship	27
Community/Neighbors/Citizens reaching out to help	8
Friends	8
FEMA	4
Getting back to work/Having a job/coworkers	4
Talking with others/Peace of mind/Local support	4
Keeping busy/Getting back into the daily structure	3
Various organizations	2
Services/Help provided by church/church members	2
Other	21
Nothing	3
No opinion	1
TOTAL	**124%**

(table adds to more than 100% due to multiple responses)

Survey Methods

This poll was conducted in cooperation with the American Red Cross. Results are based on telephone interviews with a sample of 1,510 adults, aged 18 and older, drawn randomly from the American Red Cross database of applicants seeking assistance due to the effects of Hurricane Katrina. Interviews were conducted Sept. 30-Oct. 9, 2005. Results based on the total sample have a margin of error of ±3 percentage points.

The vast majority of applicants provided a working contact telephone number to the Red Cross. Gallup did reverse phone lookups to obtain telephone numbers for the portion of the selected sample that did not provide a contact number. Where necessary, Gallup interviewers tracked down updated telephone numbers when respondents had moved from their previous locations. Interviews were conducted on both landline and cellular telephones. Full details on the poll methodology can be found at poll.gallup.com.

In addition to sampling error, question wording and practical difficulties in conducting surveys can introduce error or bias into the findings of public opinion polls.

October 18, 2005
POLITICAL MOOD SOURS
Bush approval at 39%; Congress approval 29%; satisfaction 31%

by David W. Moore, Gallup Poll Senior Editor

In the wake of Hurricane Katrina, higher gas prices, continued fighting in Iraq, and controversy over the Harriet Miers nomination to the Supreme Court, a new CNN/*USA Today*/Gallup survey finds the public in the most dour mood ever measured during the Bush presidency. The public's approval of the way President George W. Bush is handling his job is at 39%, a record low, though just a point lower than two ratings—in mid-September and mid-August of this year. The public's approval of Congress is at 29%, the first time it's dropped below the 30% level since 1994. And overall satisfaction with the way things are going is at 31%, the lowest level since January 1996.

Since mid-August, Bush's approval has fluctuated between a low of 40% and a high of 46%. Bush began the year with a 52% approval rating. It reached a high of 57% just after his state of the union speech, but then averaged between 47% and 48% from April through July. In August and September, it averaged 44%, and now for the first time in his presidency it has dropped to below 40%.

Bush's Overall Job Approval Rating
Selected Trend: January 2005 – October 2005

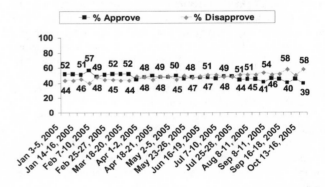

If the public is less than content about the president's performance, the public is downright sour about the performance of Congress. Just 29% of Americans approve of the way Congress is handling its job, the first time the approval rating has been close to this negative in eight years. In April 1997, only 30% of Americans approved of Congress' performance. The last time Gallup measured less than 30% approval was in December 1994.

These low numbers for the president and the Congress are similar to the low rating the public gives overall for the direction of the country. Just 31% of Americans say they are satisfied with the way things are going in the country, while 68% are dissatisfied. Since January 2004, a majority of Americans have expressed dissatisfaction, though the most recent dissatisfaction numbers represent a nine-point jump in just the last two weeks.

Harriet Miers Nomination

Bush's nomination of Harriet Miers has not been wildly welcomed by any major segment of the public. Among political activists, the nomination has split the Republican Party, with many conservatives disappointed that Bush did not nominate a person with more

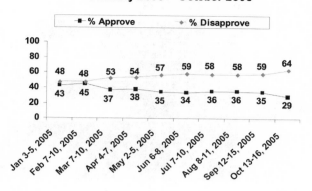

Congressional Job Approval
January 2005 – October 2005

U.S. Satisfaction
Selected Trend: January 2005 – October 2005

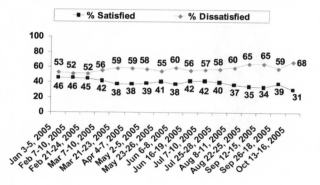

of a conservative judicial record. Among the general public, reaction to Miers is much less positive than it was to John Roberts, though the lower ratings are not found solely among conservatives and Republicans.

The public is about evenly split between having a favorable or unfavorable opinion of Miers (31% to 26%), with 43% of Americans expressing no opinion.

Next, we'd like to get your overall opinion of some people in the news. As I read each name, please say if you have a favorable or unfavorable opinion of these people—or if you have never heard of them.

U.S. Supreme Court nominee, Harriet Miers	Favor- able	Unfavor- able	Never heard of	No opinion
2005 Oct 13-16	31%	26	17	26

However, when asked whether the Senate should confirm her appointment to the Supreme Court, Americans say yes by a margin of 44% to 36%.

As you may know, Harriet Miers is the person nominated to serve on the Supreme Court. Would you like to see the Senate vote in favor of Miers serving on the Supreme Court, or not?

BASED ON 485 NATIONAL ADULTS IN FORM A

	Yes, vote in favor %	No, would not %	No opinion %
2005 Oct 13-16	44%	36	20

Trends for Comparison

John Roberts: As you may know, John Roberts is a federal judge who has been nominated to serve as chief justice on the Supreme Court. Would you like to see the Senate vote in favor of Roberts serving as chief justice on the Supreme Court, or not?

	Yes, vote in favor %	No, would not %	No opinion %
2005 Sep 16-18 ^	60	26	14
2005 Sep 8-11	58	27	15
2005 Aug 28-30 ^	52	26	22
2005 Aug 5-7 †	51	28	21
2005 Jul 22-24 †	59	22	19

^ WORDING: As you may know, John Roberts is a federal judge who has been nominated to serve on the Supreme Court. Would you like to see the Senate vote in favor of Roberts serving on the Supreme Court, or not?
† WORDING: As you may know, John Roberts is the person nominated to serve on the Supreme Court. Would you like to see the Senate vote in favor of Roberts serving on the Supreme Court, or not?

Similarly, when asked if Bush should withdraw the Miers nomination or continue to support it, Americans back Miers by a 46% to 36% margin.

Would you like to see President Bush—[ROTATED: withdraw his nomination of Harriet Miers to the Supreme Court, (or) continue to support his nomination of Harriet Miers to the Supreme Court]?

BASED ON 527 NATIONAL ADULTS IN FORM B

	Withdraw nomination	Continue to support	No opinion
2005 Oct 13-16	36%	46	18

The public was much more positive about Roberts' nomination, with 59% supporting it soon after Bush's announcement, and a majority giving support throughout the hearing process.

An analysis of support by party and ideology, however, shows that Miers' lower support is found among all the major partisan groups, and not just among conservatives and Republicans.

For example, 61% of conservatives support Miers' nomination, compared with 74% of conservatives who supported Roberts—a difference of 13 percentage points. But moderates show a 17-point greater level of support for Roberts (55% vs. 38%) and liberals show a 12-point advantage for Roberts (40% vs. 28%).

As you may know, Harriet Miers is the person nominated to serve on the Supreme Court. Would you like to see the Senate vote in favor of Miers serving on the Supreme Court, or not?

BASED ON 485 NATIONAL ADULTS IN FORM A

	Yes, vote in favor %	No, would not %	No opinion %
Miers			
Conservatives	61	21	18
Moderates	38	42	20
Liberals	28	49	23
Roberts			
Conservatives	74	12	14

	Yes, vote in favor %	No, would not %	No opinion %
Moderates	55	24	21
Liberals	40	36	24

Difference, in pct. pts.

Conservatives	-13	+9	+4
Moderates	-17	+18	-1
Liberals	-12	+13	-1

Survey Methods

Results are based on telephone interviews with 1,012 national adults, aged 18 and older, conducted Oct. 13-16, 2005. For results based on the total sample of national adults, one can say with 95% confidence that the maximum margin of sampling error is ±3 percentage points.

For results based on the 485 national adults in the Form A half-sample and 527 national adults in the Form B half-sample, the maximum margins of sampling error are ±5 percentage points.

In addition to sampling error, question wording and practical difficulties in conducting surveys can introduce error or bias into the findings of public opinion polls.

October 18, 2005
ARE AMERICANS FINANCIALLY PREPARED FOR DISASTER?
Only 4 in 10 have emergency cash on hand

by Dennis Jacobe, Chief Economist, The Gallup Organization

The aftermath of Hurricane Katrina exposed that many local, state, and federal agencies are not adequately prepared for such a significant natural disaster. A new Experian/Gallup Personal Credit Index poll* shows that, when it comes to being financially prepared for a disaster, the same may be true of many individual Americans. Although most Americans have basic emergency supplies readily available, only half have any emergency funds set aside.

Emergency Supplies

About 9 in 10 Americans say they have food, flashlights, and batteries available in case of an emergency. About three in four have bottled water, a portable radio, and a first-aid kit. Roughly half report having gasoline and 4 in 10 say they have an emergency meeting place designated for their families.

Emergency Funds

While two in three Americans say they have their credit card numbers, bank account numbers, and other financial information together in one place, only 51% say they have an "emergency fund" in case a disaster causes all their income to suddenly stop. Only about 4 in 10 Americans say they actually have cash on hand in case of an emergency. And only about 10% say they have $1,000 in cash available in case of an emergency.

Here is a list of items that people might have in case of an emergency. For each one, please tell me if you have this, or not. How about?

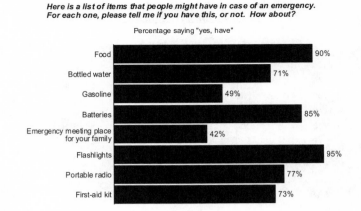

Percentage saying "yes, have"

Food	90%
Bottled water	71%
Gasoline	49%
Batteries	85%
Emergency meeting place for your family	42%
Flashlights	95%
Portable radio	77%
First-aid kit	73%

Do you have an emergency fund in case a disaster causes all of your income to suddenly stop, or not?

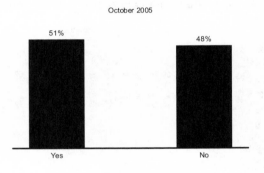

October 2005

Yes	No
51%	48%

Sources of Emergency Money

Three in four consumers say they would use their savings account as a money source in case of an emergency. Fifty-six percent say they would use credit cards and 50% would borrow from a relative. Thirty-nine percent say they would use their 401k retirement account and 37% say they would use their home equity account.

Here are some possible sources of money that some people might use in case of an emergency. For each one, please tell me if you would use that as a source for money in case of an emergency, or not. How about?

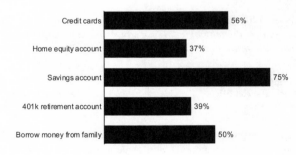

Credit cards	56%
Home equity account	37%
Savings account	75%
401k retirement account	39%
Borrow money from family	50%

Do Americans Feel Prepared?

Only 15% of Americans say they feel "very prepared" for a Katrina-like disaster. Another 43% say they feel "somewhat prepared," while 18% say they are "not too prepared" and 23% say they are "not prepared at all."

Bottom Line

One lesson every American should take from the Katrina experience is that every individual U.S. household needs to be prepared

Overall, how prepared do you think you and your family are in case of a natural disaster, like the one that was caused by Hurricane Katrina? Are you 1) very prepared, 2) somewhat prepared, 3) not too prepared, or 4) not prepared at all?

October 2005

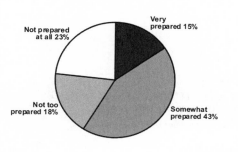

in case of a major natural disaster or terrorist event. Having adequate storm supplies and a preplanned family meeting place are important—but just as importantly, Americans need to be financially prepared. Financial records should not only be in one place, but easily portable in case of emergency. Families should also have some cash on hand.

During Katrina, power outages shut down ATMs, bank branches, and similar sources of cash—and while banks are required to have disaster plans in place, this does not mean that their systems will not be interrupted temporarily. Just as important a consideration is that a major disaster can shut down entire businesses, meaning that many employees could see their incomes come to a sudden stop.

Many Americans may feel that their chances of being directly affected by a major natural or terrorist-related disaster is small—therefore preparing for such an eventuality, though a good idea, is not a necessity. But one need only look at the plight of so many Katrina survivors to realize that unexpected disasters can affect the lives of millions, and that complete dependence on any government agency—local, state, or federal—in case of such an emergency can be disastrous.

Results for the survey are based on telephone interviews with 1,001 adults, aged 18 and older, conducted Sept. 20-26, 2005. For results based on the sample, one can say with 95% confidence that the maximum margin of sampling error is ±3 percentage points.

October 18, 2005
IRAQ WAR: AMERICANS' DOUBTS RISING
A third don't know what U.S. is fighting for

by Darren K. Carlson, Government and Politics Editor

The daily news from Iraq is rarely good. Bombing and body count reports eclipse even the brief shining moments, such as Iraqis' opportunity to vote on their new constitution last weekend. The bad news blitz may be collectively wearing on Americans. A recent CNN/*USA Today*/Gallup poll shows Americans are divided on whether the United States can win the war and are increasingly confused about what the United States is fighting for. They see mounting U.S. fatalities as a sign that the United States should leave Iraq, but they also think Iraq will descend into chaos if troops leave.

Can the United States Win?

The September poll found most Americans have doubts about whether the United States will win the war in Iraq. Fifty-four percent do not believe the United States will win, while 43% think it will. However, most Americans believe the United States *can* win—63% do, while 34% do not.

Which comes closer to your view about the war in Iraq – you think the U.S. will definitely win the war in Iraq, you think the U.S. will probably win the war in Iraq, you think the U.S. can win the war in Iraq, but you don't think it will win, (or) you do not think the U.S. can win the war in Iraq?

Sept. 16-18, 2005

Iraq War's Purpose

The poll also asked respondents if they had a clear idea of what the war is all about—what the United States is fighting for. Two-thirds say they do, while a third say they do not. The percentage who believe they understand the war's purpose has declined since March 2003, shortly after the war began. At that time, 8 in 10 said they felt they knew what the nation was fighting for. That percentage dropped to 70% in the fall of 2004.

Do you feel that you have a clear idea of what the war in Iraq is all about -- that is, what we are fighting for?

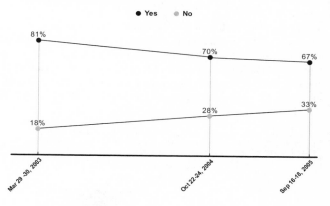

Gallup has asked this same question during other military conflicts. Typically, a majority of Americans say they know what the war in question is about. The most recent reading on Iraq is among the lowest Gallup has found historically. Two other measures were lower—in May 1967, just 49% of Americans said they understood what the Vietnam War was about, and in 1944, 59% had a clear idea of what World War II was about (down from 73% in 1942).

The highest reading Gallup obtained on this question was 89% in November 2001, in regard to the war on terrorism. During the first U.S.-Iraq conflict, the percentage of Americans who understood the conflict ranged from 69% in November 1990 to 81% in July 1991, which was a retrospective reading several months after the United States prevailed.

Withdraw or Stay the Course?

With U.S. military deaths in Iraq on track to surpass 2,000, the poll gauged what the public thinks the watermark means for the United States. A slim majority (55%) say the loss is tragic and is a sign that the United States should intensify efforts to withdraw troops, while 41% say it is tragic, but does not mean the United States should change its policy toward Iraq.

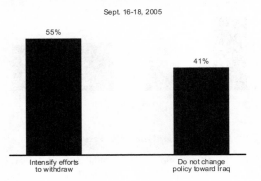

As you may know, the number of U.S. military deaths in Iraq will soon surpass 2,000. Which comes closer to your view about what this number of deaths means for the U.S. -- it is a tragic loss of life, and it is a sign that the U.S. should intensify its efforts to withdraw troops from Iraq, or it is a tragic loss of life, but it does not mean the U.S. should change its policy toward Iraq?

Sept. 16-18, 2005

Gallup asked a similarly worded question in August 2004, when the number of U.S. military deaths was poised to pass the 1,000 mark. The results at that time were different—a majority said the loss of life should not motivate a policy change for the United States, while slightly more than a third (37%) said it should cause the United States to step up its efforts to withdraw.

Maintaining Order in Iraq

Despite growing sentiment that the United States should withdraw some or all of its troops from Iraq, Americans remain doubtful that Iraq can remain stable without a U.S. military presence. Sixty-eight percent of Americans believe chaos or civil war would break out in Iraq if the United States withdrew its troops, while just about one-quarter (27%) say the Iraqi government would be able to maintain order in the country.

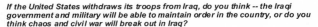

If the United States withdraws its troops from Iraq, do you think -- the Iraqi government and military will be able to maintain order in the country, or do you think chaos and civil war will break out in Iraq?

Sept. 16-18, 2005

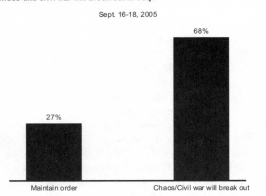

Results are based on telephone interviews with 818 national adults, aged 18 and older, conducted Sept. 16-18, 2005. For results based on the total sample of national adults, one can say with 95%

confidence that the margin of sampling error is ±4 percentage points. In addition to sampling error, question wording and practical difficulties in conducting surveys can introduce error or bias into the findings of public opinion polls.

October 18, 2005
HURRICANE VICTIMS' VIEWS VARY ON GOVERNMENT'S RESPONSE
FEMA named as most helpful agency

by Jeffrey M. Jones, Gallup Poll Managing Editor and Joseph Carroll, Assistant Editor

After major natural disasters, victims often look to the government—federal, state, or local—for aid and assistance. A recent CNN/*USA Today*/Gallup poll* of those affected by Hurricane Katrina finds generally mediocre ratings of the federal and state governments' responses to the disaster, and more positive ratings of the local government's response. Despite criticism about the Federal Emergency Management Agency's (FEMA) response, nearly half of those surveyed cite it as the agency that was most helpful to them. Louisiana and New Orleans residents are more critical of the government's response than are Alabama residents and Mississippi residents.

The poll, conducted in cooperation with the Red Cross, interviewed a random sample of 1,510 adults who applied for disaster relief from the Red Cross because of Hurricane Katrina. The vast majority of aid applicants were from Louisiana, with significant numbers also from Alabama and Mississippi.

Federal Government

Overall, slightly more than one in three of these hurricane survivors say the federal government did an excellent (10%) or good (26%) job in dealing with the hurricane and its aftermath. A similar percentage, 32%, say it did a poor job, while 30% rate its job as only fair.

Louisiana residents are the most negative toward the federal government—just 31% say it did an excellent or good job—compared with 42% of Mississippi residents and 56% of Alabama residents. Those who previously resided in New Orleans are even more negative in their evaluations—just 24% rate the federal government's response in positive terms, while nearly half, 47%, say it did a poor job.

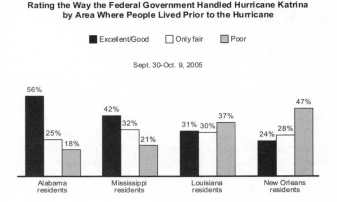

Rating the Way the Federal Government Handled Hurricane Katrina by Area Where People Lived Prior to the Hurricane

■ Excellent/Good   □ Only fair   ▨ Poor

Sept. 30-Oct. 9, 2005

State Government

State governments get only slightly better marks from these hurricane victims than the federal government does. Thirty-nine percent of respondents say their state government did an excellent (11%) or good (28%) job of dealing with Katrina and the aftereffects, 29% say fair and 30% poor.

Both Mississippians (58%) and Alabamans (67%) give positive evaluations to their state governments and more positive evaluations to their states than the federal government. Louisiana residents, however, rate the state government response no more positively than they rate the federal response, with 30% describing their state's response as excellent or good and 37% as poor (31% say only fair). Again, residents of New Orleans are even more negative, with 21% rating the state response as excellent or good and 49% as poor.

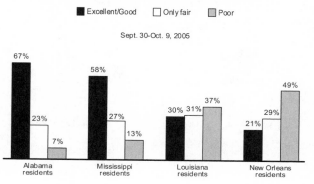

Rating the Way the State Government Handled Hurricane Katrina by Area Where People Lived Prior to the Hurricane

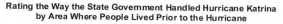

Sept. 30-Oct. 9, 2005

Local Government

A majority of hurricane survivors in the poll say their mayors and other local officials did an excellent (19%) or good (32%) job in responding to the hurricane. That includes 47% of Louisiana residents, 56% of Mississippi residents, and 72% of Alabama residents. New Orleans residents are again more negative than positive in rating their local officials' responses—33% say they did an excellent or good job, and 38% say poor.

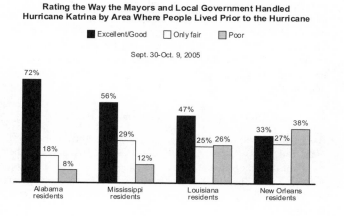

Rating the Way the Mayors and Local Government Handled Hurricane Katrina by Area Where People Lived Prior to the Hurricane

Sept. 30-Oct. 9, 2005

FEMA

Another set of survey questions asked respondents to say, on an open-ended basis, which government agencies were most helpful to them, and which they were most dissatisfied with. FEMA was the most frequently mentioned organization on both counts.

Nearly half of respondents, 49%, say FEMA was most helpful to them, somewhat surprising given the sharp criticism of FEMA's response to Hurricane Katrina. Six percent of respondents say food stamps, which are provided by federal and state governments, were most helpful. Two percent say the National Guard or military. About one in three respondents could not identify a government entity that helped them most.

In your experience, which government agencies have been most helpful to you, personally, since Hurricane Katrina?

	Sept. 30-Oct. 9, 2005
FEMA	49%
Food stamps (federal or state government)	6%
National Guard/Military	2%
State government agencies	1%
Department of Health and Human Services	1%
Local government agencies	1%
Unemployment/Department of Labor	*
Federal government (non-specific)	*
City offices	*
Sheriff's department	*
Housing Authority	*
Other	9%
None	31%
All	1%
No opinion	3%

Percentages add to more than 100% due to multiple responses.
*Less than 0.5%

Louisiana residents (57%) were about twice as likely as Mississippi (29%) or Alabama (26%) residents to cite FEMA as most helpful to them. An even higher percentage of New Orleans residents, 69%, say FEMA was most helpful.

Most respondents, more than 6 in 10 in total, could not name a government organization that they were most dissatisfied with. FEMA was most often mentioned, by 26% of the sample. Two percent mentioned state government agencies.

In your experience, which government agencies have you been least satisfied with in their response to any problems that you, personally, have had since Hurricane Katrina?

	Sept. 30-Oct. 9, 2005
FEMA	26%
State government agencies	2%
Federal government (non-specific)	1%
Housing Authority	1%
Unemployment/Department of Labor	1%
Local government agencies	1%
City offices	1%
Food stamps (federal or state government)	*
Department of Health and Human Services	*
National Guard/Military	*
Sheriff's department	*
Assisted living	*
Other	5%
None	57%
All	1%
No opinion	6%

Percentages add to more than 100% due to multiple responses.
*Less than 0.5%

Bottom Line

Hurricane Katrina victims are critical about the way the federal government handled the aftermath of the storm, with only a third rating it positively. State and local governments are rated more positively. Typically, Americans tend to be more positive in their evaluations of state, and especially local, governments than the federal government in general.

Louisiana residents and those who lived in New Orleans prior to Katrina are more negative in their assessments of all three levels of governments than those affected by the hurricane in other areas. The Red Cross list of applicants clearly shows that Louisiana residents were much more likely to seek assistance than Alabama or Mississippi residents, and the poll shows Louisiana residents were much more likely to be displaced following the hurricane than residents of neighboring states. As such, their need may be greater, and swift government response—certainly difficult in a disaster of this magnitude—is more important to their well-being.

This poll was conducted in cooperation with the American Red Cross.

Results are based on telephone interviews with a sample of 1,510 adults, aged 18 and older, drawn randomly from the American Red Cross database of applicants seeking assistance due to the effects of Hurricane Katrina. Interviews were conducted Sept. 30- Oct. 9, 2005.

The vast majority of applicants provided a working contact telephone number to the Red Cross. Gallup did reverse phone lookups to obtain telephone numbers for the portion of the selected sample that did not provide a contact number. Where necessary, Gallup interviewers tracked down updated telephone numbers when respondents had moved from their previous location. Interviews were conducted on both landline and cellular telephones. Full details on the poll methodology can be found at www.galluppoll.com.

In addition to sampling error, question wording and practical difficulties in conducting surveys can introduce error or bias into the findings of public opinion polls.

October 20, 2005
PUBLIC GROWS MORE PESSIMISTIC ABOUT U.S. CRIME
But Americans no more fearful for their personal safety

by Lydia Saad, Gallup Poll Senior Editor

Despite recently released government statistics showing crime is down in the United States—or at worst, holding steady at record low levels—Gallup's annual Crime Poll finds an increase in public pessimism about the nation's crime problem compared with a year ago. These perceptions seem to be focused on conventional crime, as Americans' fear of being the victim of terrorism shows no change since 2004. At the same time, the Oct. 13-16 survey gives little indication that Americans are more concerned about their personal safety.

Close to half of Americans (49%) now describe the nation's crime problem as either "extremely" or "very" serious. This is up slightly from 42% last year. Fifty percent rate the problem as either "moderately" or "not too" serious while less than 1% say it is "not at all serious."

The percentage perceiving more crime in the country than there was a year ago has increased more sharply, from 53% in October 2004 to 67% today.

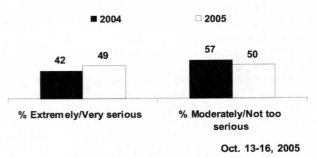

Perceptions of U.S. Crime Problem

■ 2004   □ 2005

% Extremely/Very serious: 42, 49
% Moderately/Not too serious: 57, 50

Oct. 13-16, 2005

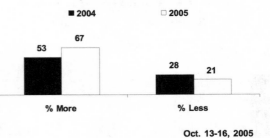

Is there more crime in the U.S. than there was a year ago, or less?

■ 2004   □ 2005

% More: 53, 67
% Less: 28, 21

Oct. 13-16, 2005

Perpetually Pessimistic, But to Varying Degrees

Since instituting this measure in 1989, Gallup has almost always found more Americans believing that U.S. crime is on the rise, even though federal statistics have shown property crimes declining since the 1970s, and violent crimes declining since about 1995.

Just a few years ago, the public did start to take notice of the striking decline in crime. Between 1996 and 1997, the percentage of Americans perceiving that crime was increasing fell from 71% to 64%. By 2001 it reached the low point in Gallup records of 41%—the only year that Gallup has found optimists outnumbering pessimists.

The next year, in 2002, Gallup recorded a sharp spike in negative perceptions about the national crime rate (rising to 62%), although this is most likely explained by the widely publicized Washington, D.C.-area sniper shootings that were going on at the time. Since then, it is less clear why the relatively higher levels of concern recorded in 2002 would be maintained, or why pessimism about national crime would increase again this year after declining somewhat in 2004.

Ratings of Local Area Crime Also Worse

As is typical with many perceptions (including education, government, and drugs), Americans have more positive perceptions of their local areas than of the nation as a whole when rating crime. Only 12% say that crime in the area where they live is extremely or very serious, but this was 8% last year—a small but statistically significant change.

Similar to perceptions about the crime trend nationally, more Americans than last year also believe that crime is up locally. Close to half (47%) now say there is more crime in their areas than there was a year ago, up from 37% who perceived this in 2004.

Crime in the U.S. vs. a Year Ago

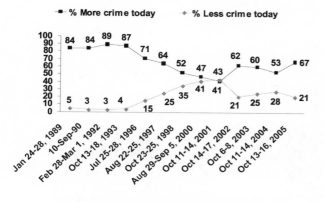

Rating of Crime Problem in Your Area

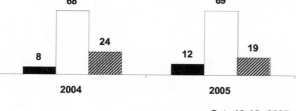

Oct. 13-16, 2005

Crime in Your Area vs. a Year Ago?

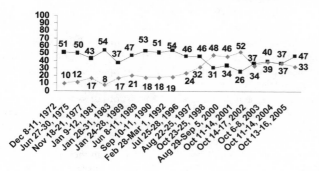

Mixed Indications of Trend in Personal Fear

Gallup's Crime Poll includes two measures of Americans' personal fears about being victimized by crime. A long-term trend question (first asked in 1965) asks respondents whether there is anywhere within a mile of their homes where they would be afraid to walk alone at night. The other is a more recent trend (started in 2000), asking Americans the degree to which they fear being the victim of several specific types of crime.

The long-term trend finds a slight increase since last year in the percentage of Americans feeling unsafe near their homes: 38% today, vs. 32% in 2004.

However, over the same period, Gallup's inventory of concerns about specific types of crime shows no change. Only minor, and not

statistically significant shifts, are seen in the percentage of Americans worried about each type of crime.

Percentage Worry Frequently/Occasionally
About Being a Victim of Each Crime

	2004	2005
	%	%
Having your car stolen or broken into	41	42
Your home being burglarized when you are not there	41	45
Being the victim of terrorism	39	38
Having a school-aged child physically harmed while attending school	30	29
Getting mugged	27	28
Your home being burglarized when you are there	24	24
Being attacked while driving your car	23	22
Being sexually assaulted	20	19
Being a victim of a hate crime	16	17
Getting murdered	16	15
Being assaulted/killed by a co-worker/ employee where you work	5	6

Crime Down, So Why Not Fear?

The two primary sources of federal statistics on crime are the FBI and the U.S. Justice Department. In late September the Justice Department, which bases its conclusions on a nationally representative survey of 42,000 households, reported that no significant changes in crime were observed between 2003 and 2004. The report said, "Violent and property crime rates in 2004 remained at the lowest levels since the Bureau of Justice Statistics (BJS) first conducted its annual National Criminal Victimization Survey in 1973."

The FBI, which relies on the actual number of crimes reported to law enforcement agencies nationwide, has a slightly different conclusion, saying that violent crime declined 2.2% last year, and property crime declined 2.1%.

Given this encouraging data, and without any high-profile national crime incidents to point to, it is unclear why Americans would show greater concern today about crime than they did a year ago. Not only have Americans' levels of fear about being the victim of specific types of conventional crime not changed, but their fears of terrorism have also held steady. As noted, 38% now say they worry frequently or occasionally about this, compared with 39% in 2004.

Also, a separate Gallup measure of public concern about terrorism found 47% in July—identical to the figure from last October—saying they were "very" or "somewhat" worried about themselves or a family member becoming a victim of terrorism. That is slightly higher than the 41% recorded in August 2003, but still lower than the 59% recorded shortly after the 9/11 terrorist attacks in 2001.

Partisanship can often be a factor in Americans' ratings of seemingly non-partisan aspects of the country such as the economy. And with President Bush's approval rating down to 39% in this poll, one has to question whether the more negative ratings of crime could be due to expanding criticism of the president. (Last year at this time, 48% approved of the job Bush was doing). However, partisanship does not appear to be the cause.

There is little difference between 2004 and today in perceptions of crime among Democrats or those who disapprove of the job Bush is doing as president. A high proportion of these groups were pessimistic in 2004 about the national crime rate, and they continue to be negative today. A much greater increase in pessimism about crime comes from Republicans and those who approve of the job Bush is doing as president.

Perceiving More Crime in the U.S. Than Year Ago

	2004 %	2005 %
Republicans	39	60
Independents	54	65
Democrats	67	74
Approve of Bush	46	60
Disapprove	62	71

Survey Methods

These results are based on telephone interviews with a randomly selected national sample of 1,012 adults, aged 18 and older, conducted Oct. 13-16, 2005. For results based on this sample, one can say with 95% confidence that the maximum error attributable to sampling and other random effects is ±3 percentage points. In addition to sampling error, question wording and practical difficulties in conducting surveys can introduce error or bias into the findings of public opinion polls.

October 21, 2005
BUSH FINISHES 19TH QUARTER IN OFFICE ON LOW NOTE
Quarterly average only in 18th percentile

by Jeffrey M. Jones, Gallup Poll Managing Editor

George W. Bush has now completed 19 quarters in office, and finds himself at the low point of his presidency with a quarterly average that puts him in the bottom 20% of all presidential quarters for which Gallup has job approval measures.

The latest CNN/*USA Today*/Gallup poll shows Bush with a 39% job approval rating. Bush's most recent quarterly average—for the period from July 20 to Oct. 19—is 43.9%. The president's 19th-quarter average represents a significant decline from his 18th-quarter average of 47.4%, which was, in turn, a significant decline from a 50.7% average in his 17th quarter in office.

The decline in Bush's job approval rating becomes starkly clear when put in the context of quarterly averages for all other presidents since Harry Truman. Bush's 19th-quarter average of 43.9% ranks in just the 18th percentile, meaning that just 18% of all quarterly averages for all other presidents in Gallup's historical database have been lower. By way of contrast, Bush's post-Sept. 11 averages in late 2001 and 2002 ranked at or near the top of the quarterly percentile rankings, scoring in the 94th to 99th percentiles.

George W. Bush Quarterly Approval Averages

Quarter	Dates	Average (%)	Percentile compared to other presidents since Truman
1	Jan 20-Apr 19, 2001	58.4	57
2	Apr 20-Jul 19, 2001	55.8	49
3	Jul 20-Oct 19, 2001	68.3	84

George W. Bush Quarterly Approval Averages

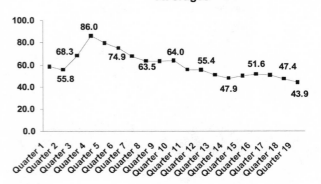

Quarter	Dates	Average (%)	Percentile compared to other presidents since Truman
4	Oct 20, 2001-Jan 19, 2002	86.0	99
5	Jan 20-Apr 19, 2002	79.5	98
6	Apr 20-Jul 19, 2002	74.9	94
7	Jul 20-Oct 19, 2002	67.7	82
8	Oct 20, 2002-Jan 19, 2003	63.5	74
9	Jan 20-Apr 19, 2003	63.3	73
10	Apr 20-Jul 19, 2003	64.0	76
11	Jul 20-Oct 19, 2003	55.7	49
12	Oct 20, 2003-Jan 19, 2004	55.4	48
13	Jan 20-Apr 19, 2004	50.9	38
14	Apr 20-Jul 19, 2004	47.9	30
15	Jul 20-Oct 19, 2004	50.1	36
16	Oct 20, 2004-Jan 19, 2005	51.6	39
17	Jan 20-Apr 19, 2005	50.7	37
18	Apr 20-Jul 19, 2005	47.4	28
19	Jul 20-Oct 19, 2005	43.9	18

The sharpest quarter-to-quarter decline in Bush's quarterly approval ratings came between his 10th and 11th quarters, at a time when approval of the Iraq war dropped precipitously. The only times at which Bush's ratings went up by at least a point since his fourth quarter were the two quarters in the midst of last year's presidential election—from July 20, 2004, to Jan. 19, 2005, when his quarterly average rose from the 30th percentile to the 39th percentile.

There are limited data available to compare Bush's standing with other presidents' standings at the same point in their presidencies. Only Truman, Dwight Eisenhower, Lyndon Johnson, Richard Nixon, Ronald Reagan, and Bill Clinton served second terms, and two of these—Truman and Johnson—initially became president on the death of their predecessors.

Bush compares unfavorably with three two-term presidents who served a full eight years. Eisenhower, Reagan, and Clinton all averaged close to a 60% job approval rating in their 19th quarters in office.

Nixon, who in July-October 1973 was mired in the Watergate scandal, averaged a 31.8% approval rating during his 19th quarter in office. During that time, former White House counsel John Dean alleged that Nixon was aware of plans to cover up the Watergate burglary. Later, the White House's secret taping system was revealed, and the Nixon administration refused to turn over the tapes to the special prosecutor and the Senate committee investigating the matter.

19th-Quarter Averages of Recent Presidents

President	Dates of 19th quarter	19th-quarter average (%)	Number of polls
Eisenhower	Jul 20-Oct 19, 1957	59.5	4
Nixon	Jul 20-Oct 19, 1973	31.8	6
Reagan	Jul 20-Oct 19, 1985	61.3	4
Clinton	Jul 20-Oct 19, 1997	58.8	6
Bush	Jul 20-Oct 19, 2005	43.9	11

Because Truman and Johnson served less than two full terms, their 19th-quarter averages were not their 3rd quarters after being re-elected, as it was for the other aforementioned presidents. Truman had a 45.0% average during his 19th quarter in office (October 1949-January 1950) and Johnson had a 41.8% average in his (April-July 1968). During his 19th term, Johnson was beset by the problems in Vietnam.

Survey Methods

The averages are based on telephone interviews with randomly selected national samples of approximately 1,000 adults each, aged 18 and older, conducted July 20-Oct. 19, 2005.

October 25, 2005

CAN A MORE INTEGRATED NEW ORLEANS RISE FROM THE RUBBLE?
Blacks more optimistic than whites

by Bryant Ott, Senior Staff Writer

On his most recent trip to the hurricane-ravaged Gulf Coast, President George W. Bush reaffirmed his confidence that New Orleans—one of the nation's largest cities and most vital seaports—would rise again. "Out of this rubble is going to come something good," the president said. "Out of this devastation will come a new city."

In a Sept. 5-6 Gallup Poll*, nearly two-thirds of Americans said they think New Orleans should be rebuilt as a major city. But in what ways will New Orleans be *new*? While it is among the nation's largest cities, more than two-thirds of New Orleans residents are black, and the city is among the most impoverished in the nation. Census figures reveal that people have been leaving New Orleans proper in droves since the 1960s, taking jobs and personal wealth with them. Whites flocked to suburbs and surrounding areas, more or less segregating the city by race and income.

Many people, from government officials and philanthropic groups to former New Orleans city planning director Kristina Ford, see the destruction as an opportunity to create a more integrated Crescent City. Gallup recently asked Americans nationwide** how successful they think government planners would be in rebuilding the Big Easy in such a way that neighborhoods would not be as segregated by race and class as they were before Katrina. Americans are dubious about the prospects for this; only 36% believe such an effort would be very (6%) or somewhat (30%) successful.

However, black Americans are more optimistic than white Americans on this question. Almost half of blacks (46%) say that government planners would succeed in making the city more integrated, while only a third (32%) of whites say they would be successful.

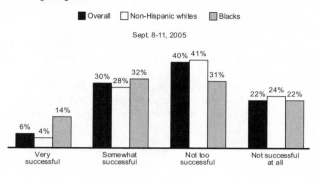

As you may know, government planners want to rebuild New Orleans in such a way that neighborhoods would not be as segregated by race and class as they were before the hurricane. How successful do you think they will be in achieving this goal?

If You Rebuild It, Will They Come?

Gallup, in conjunction with the American Red Cross, recently asked displaced victims of Hurricane Katrina who applied for disaster relief whether they would return to the community in which they lived before Hurricane Katrina hit. Four in 10 relief applicants who lived in the city of New Orleans prior to Hurricane Katrina say they will definitely (16%) or probably (23%) not return.

How many Americans share that reluctance to go back? That is, if a natural disaster destroyed their homes and left their communities in ruins, how many say they would return and try to rebuild and how many would move somewhere else and start over?

Two-thirds of Americans say they would go back and try to rebuild, while 32% would move to another area and start their new lives there. Again, there are differences by race. While majorities of blacks and whites would go back and rebuild, whites are more likely than blacks to say they'd go back. Sixty-seven percent of whites say they would try to rebuild their communities, compared with 54% of blacks.

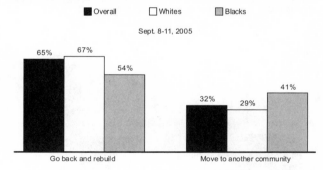

Suppose your home was destroyed due to a natural disaster and the community in which you lived was ruined. Would you want to go back to your community and try and rebuild or want to move to another community and start a new life there?

Results are based on telephone interviews with 609 national adults, aged 18 and older, conducted Sept. 5-6, 2005. For results based on the total sample of national adults, one can say with 95% confidence that the margin of sampling error is ±4 percentage points.

**Results are based on telephone interviews with 262 blacks, aged 18 and older, conducted Sept. 8-11, 2005, some of which were drawn from Gallup's Sept. 8-11 national sample and some of which were drawn from a special black oversample. The combined sample of blacks is weighted to be representative of U.S. blacks. For results based on the total sample, one can say with 95% confidence that the margin of sampling error is ±7 percentage points.

Results for the sample of 848 non-Hispanic whites, aged 18 and older, are based on telephone interviews conducted Sept. 8-11, 2005, drawn from the national sample poll. For results based on the total sample, one can say with 95% confidence that the margin of sampling error is ±4 percentage points.

In addition to sampling error, question wording and practical difficulties in conducting surveys can introduce error or bias into the findings of public opinion polls.

The poll did not dial into some of the areas of Louisiana and Mississippi that were declared federal disaster areas following Hurricane Katrina. This amounts to about 0.75% of the U.S. population.

October 25, 2005

AMERICANS DISSATISFIED WITH GOVERNMENT'S EFFORTS ON POVERTY

Most also say too little being spent

by Raksha Arora, Business and Economy Editor

In wealthy nations like the United States, it may be easy for some to forget that abject poverty exists. But it does, and it's not going anywhere. According to the latest figures from the U.S. Census Bureau, there were 37 million Americans living in poverty in 2004, up from 35.9 million in 2003.

In mid-September*, weeks after Hurricane Katrina's winds and waters clearly exposed the poverty in New Orleans, Gallup asked Americans whether they are satisfied or dissatisfied with the work the government is doing on the issue of poverty. Three in four Americans say they are dissatisfied, about the same as when the question was last posed in early September 2001. In both instances, the government's rating on poverty was among the worst of more than 15 items tested.

Next, we are going to name some major areas the federal government handles. For each one, please say whether you are satisfied or dissatisfied with the work the government is doing. How about -- poverty?

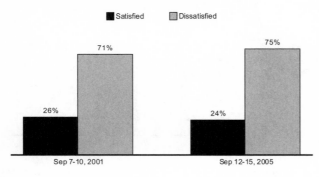

At a time when all questions regarding government performance are highly polarized between Republican and Democratic adherents, perceptions of the struggle against poverty are no different. Ninety percent of Democrats are dissatisfied with the government's efforts to curb poverty, but even among Republicans, 55% say they are dissatisfied.

Money for Poverty

A separate survey, conducted in early September**, clearly shows a majority (67%) believes the federal government is spending too little

to address the issue of poverty in this country. Twenty-two percent of Americans say the amount of spending is about right, and only 9% say too much is being spent.

A racial gap is evident, even though both most blacks and whites agree that the government is spending too little. Eighty-five percent of blacks say this, as do 64% of whites.

Do you think the federal government is spending -- too much, about the right amount, or too little -- money to address the issue of poverty in this country?

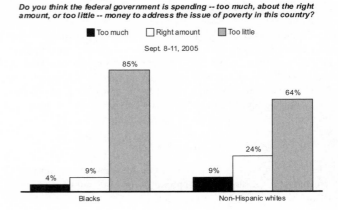

Again, the political divide is apparent. Eighty-seven percent of Democrats say the government is spending too little, while 41% of Republicans say too little is being spent (Republicans are equally as likely to say spending is about right). No more than one in seven identifying with any political party say the government is spending too much.

Bottom Line

With personal saving rates currently in negative territory, and low-skill jobs particularly vulnerable thanks to the rise of cheap labor overseas, the need for a reliable safety net could be particularly strong over the next few years in order to keep more Americans from sinking below the poverty line. But between tax cuts and the war in Iraq, that net is looking a little frayed. So with Americans calling for the federal government to step up spending to combat poverty—will the government change its priorities?

*These results are based on telephone interviews with a randomly selected national sample of 921 adults, aged 18 and older, conducted Sept. 12-15, 2005. For results based on this sample, one can say with 95% confidence that the maximum error attributable to sampling and other random effects is ±4 percentage points. In addition to sampling error, question wording and practical difficulties in conducting surveys can introduce error or bias into the findings of public opinion polls.

**Results are based on telephone interviews with 262 blacks, aged 18 and older, conducted Sept. 8-11, 2005, some of which were drawn from Gallup's Sept. 8-11 national sample and some of which were drawn from a special black oversample. The combined sample of blacks is weighted to be representative of U.S. blacks. For results based on the total sample, one can say with 95% confidence that the margin of sampling error is ±7 percentage points.

Results for the sample of 848 non-Hispanic whites, aged 18 and older, are based on telephone interviews conducted Sept. 8-11, 2005, drawn from the national sample poll. For results based on the total sample, one can say with 95% confidence that the margin of sampling error is ±4 percentage points.

In addition to sampling error, question wording and practical difficulties in conducting surveys can introduce error or bias into the findings of public opinion polls.

The poll did not dial into some of the areas of Louisiana and Mississippi that were declared federal disaster areas following Hurricane Katrina. This amounts to about 0.75% of the U.S. population.

October 25, 2005

KATRINA HURT BLACKS AND POOR VICTIMS MOST

Differences larger by race than income

by David W. Moore, Gallup Poll Senior Editor

Shortly after Hurricane Katrina hit New Orleans and the surrounding areas, critics charged that a lack of concern for poor and black people who lived in the devastated areas was behind the slow response to the disaster, the assumption being that low-income people and black people were disproportionately likely to be victims. Even among victims, blacks and poor people were seen as more likely to suffer hardships than whites and high-income people.

Results from a CNN/*USA Today*/Gallup survey* allow a comparison of racial and income effects among actual hurricane victims. The poll was conducted six weeks after the storm hit the Gulf Coast. Interviews were conducted Sept. 30-Oct. 9 among people who had applied for Red Cross assistance because of damage they had suffered from Katrina. The Red Cross database included more than 463,000 names, and the poll interviewed a random sample of 1,510 by telephone, some by landline and others by cell phone.

A comparison of the experiences reported by these people shows that blacks and poor people were indeed more likely than whites and high-income people, respectively, to suffer from the hurricane. It also shows that there were larger racial differences than income differences.

On 7 of the 10 hurricane-related hardships asked about in the poll, black victims were significantly more likely than white victims to say they experienced them. Blacks were significantly more likely than whites to have:

- worried about elderly family members living in the path of the hurricane (81% of blacks vs. 64% of whites)
- feared for their lives (63% vs. 39%)
- been separated from family members for at least a day (55% vs. 45%)
- gone without food for at least a day (53% vs. 24%)
- had a vehicle damaged (47% vs. 31%)
- gone without drinking water for at least a day (45% vs. 21%)
- spent at least one night in an emergency shelter (34% vs. 13%)

Similarly, low-income victims were more likely to suffer hardships than high-income victims. Compared with people earning more than $50,000 a year, the lowest income group of people (those earning less than $20,000 a year) were much more likely to have:

- worried about elderly family members living in the path of a hurricane (79% of low-income victims vs. 67% of high-income victims)
- feared for their lives (65% vs. 35%)
- been separated at least a day from their families (58% vs. 47%)
- gone without food for at least a day (52% vs. 21%)
- gone without drinking water for at least a day (44% vs. 17%)
- spent at least one night in an emergency shelter (33% vs. 13%)

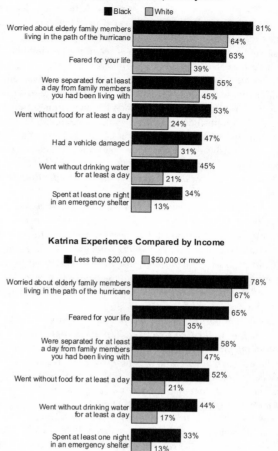

Katrina Experiences Compared by Race

■ Black ▨ White

Worried about elderly family members living in the path of the hurricane	81% / 64%
Feared for your life	63% / 39%
Were separated for at least a day from family members you had been living with	55% / 45%
Went without food for at least a day	53% / 24%
Had a vehicle damaged	47% / 31%
Went without drinking water for at least a day	45% / 21%
Spent at least one night in an emergency shelter	34% / 13%

Katrina Experiences Compared by Income

■ Less than $20,000 ▨ $50,000 or more

Worried about elderly family members living in the path of the hurricane	78% / 67%
Feared for your life	65% / 35%
Were separated for at least a day from family members you had been living with	58% / 47%
Went without food for at least a day	52% / 21%
Went without drinking water for at least a day	44% / 17%
Spent at least one night in an emergency shelter	33% / 13%

Because there is a high correlation between income and race, the differences between blacks and whites could be attributable to the different income levels of each group. But, taking the race of those in each income group into account, the data suggest that the differences between racial groups were, on average, much larger than the differences between high- and low-income groups.

These findings are illustrated by a comparison of high- and low-income blacks, with high- and low-income whites, on the question of whether they went without food for at least a day.

Went Without Food for at Least a Day, Compared by Race and Income

	High-income whites	High-income blacks	Low-income whites	Low-income blacks
% who went without food for at least a day	21	40	29	57

Among high-income victims (people with at least $30,000 in annual household income), there is a 19-point difference between the percentage of blacks who went without food (40%) and the percentage of whites (21%). Among low-income victims, the race gap is 28 points (57% of blacks vs. 29% of whites). The *weighted average*** of the two race differences (19 points and 28 points) is 24.2.

By contrast, the differences between income groups are not as large. Among whites, there is only an eight-point difference between low-income victims who went without food (29%) and high-income victims (21%). Among blacks, the income difference is larger—17 points (57% of high-income blacks vs. 40% of low-income blacks). But this income difference is still smaller than the two race differences noted earlier. The *weighted average* of the two income differences (8 points and 17 points) is 13.1.

The poll shows that both income and race played a significant role in the likelihood that hurricane victims suffered hardships. Separately, among whites and blacks, low-income victims suffered more hardship than high-income victims. Similarly, among low-income victims and high-income victims, blacks suffered more than whites. This analysis also suggests that race was a bigger factor in explaining hardship than income.

*This poll was conducted in cooperation with the American Red Cross.

**A simple average would just add the two differences and divide by two. In this case, the average was adjusted to take into account the number of cases for which each difference was calculated.

Results are based on telephone interviews with a sample of 1,510 adults, aged 18 and older, drawn randomly from the American Red Cross database of applicants seeking assistance due to the effects of Hurricane Katrina. Interviews were conducted Sept. 30-Oct. 9, 2005.

The vast majority of applicants provided a working contact telephone number to the Red Cross. Gallup did reverse phone lookups to obtain telephone numbers for the portion of the selected sample that did not provide a contact number. Where necessary, Gallup interviewers tracked down updated telephone numbers when respondents had moved from their previous location. Interviews were conducted on both landline and cellular telephones. Full details on the poll methodology can be found at www.galluppoll.com.

In addition to sampling error, question wording and practical difficulties in conducting surveys can introduce error or bias into the findings of public opinion polls.

October 26, 2005

MIDTERM ELECTIONS LOOK DICEY FOR GOP
Republicans trail by narrow margin on generic ballot, but other indicators look grim

by Lydia Saad, Gallup Poll Senior Editor

The latest CNN/*USA Today*/Gallup poll presents a fairly grim picture for the Republican Party one year out from the 2006 midterm elections. Several indicators reveal broad public dissatisfaction with the Republican-led Congress—dissatisfaction levels not seen since 1994. Additionally, given President Bush's low approval scores and that voters are more likely to say they'll vote for congressional candidates who oppose Bush than vote for those who support him, Bush could be the Republicans' liability-in-chief for retaining control of Congress.

Democrats Lead on Generic Ballot

The Oct. 21-23 survey finds Republicans trailing Democrats by seven points on the generic ballot. Half of registered voters now say they will vote for the Democratic congressional candidate on the ballot in their districts next fall; 43% say they will vote for the Republican.

That in itself is not a large deficit for Republicans on this measure. In the past two midterm elections (1998 and 2002), Republicans were down by nine points and five points, respectively, on the generic ballot among registered voters in Gallup's final pre-election surveys. By virtue of Republicans' higher turnout rates, the Republicans still went on to win a slim majority of seats in Congress.

The generic ballot result from late August was more worrisome for Republicans. At that time, Gallup found the Democrats leading by 12 points, 53% vs. 41% (a result mirrored in polls conducted by other organizations around the same time).

That 12-point Democratic advantage was a wider lead for the Democrats than anything Gallup has seen for most of the past decade that Republicans have been in power. The norm is for Republicans to be trailing by about five points among all registered voters on this measure, which converts to a slight lead among likely voters (that is, the smaller subset of voters who are most likely to go to the polls on Election Day).

This tendency is illustrated by the following table showing the projected percentage voting Republican, according to Gallup surveys, and by the actual results for the past three midterm elections.

Two-Party Vote: % Voting Republican for Congress in Recent Midterm Elections

	Registered Voters %	Likely Voters %	Actual Two-Party Vote %
2002	47.4	53.1	53.1
1998	46.5	50.0	50.5
1994	50.0	53.5	53.5

Given the precision with which the generic ballot (based on likely voters) typically matches the actual two-party vote for Congress, this is therefore an indicator that bears close monitoring over the next year. (Gallup will not institute its "likely voter" model until closer to the election, so until that time, it is necessary to interpret registered voter numbers in the context of their historical relationship to "likely voter" numbers.)

Mostly Dismal Ratings of Congress

Besides the generic ballot, there are some stronger indications that the Republican majority in Congress may be in trouble. Chiefly, Americans' overall approval rating of Congress is, according to Gallup's Oct. 13-16 poll, just 29%. That compares with 50% approval for Congress in October 2002 and 44% in October 1998. The last time congressional approval fell below 30% was in 1994—the year the previously entrenched Democratic majority was ousted by a Republican tidal wave.

Also, the percentage of registered voters who believe that most members of Congress deserve to be re-elected has fallen below 50% for the first time since 1994. Today, just 46% believe most members of Congress deserve another term, while 44% disagree. While not as low as the 38% found just before the 1994 elections, the 46% today is substantially lower than the 57%-58% recorded before the past two midterm elections.

One bright spot for Republicans is that the percentage of voters saying their own member of Congress deserves re-election is hold-

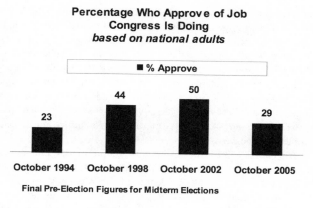

Percentage Who Approve of Job Congress Is Doing
based on national adults

■ % Approve

| October 1994 | October 1998 | October 2002 | October 2005 |
| 23 | 44 | 50 | 29 |

Final Pre-Election Figures for Midterm Elections

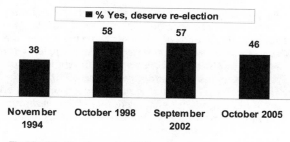

Percentage Saying Most Members of Congress Deserve Re-Election
based on registered voters

■ % Yes, deserve re-election

| November 1994 | October 1998 | September 2002 | October 2005 |
| 38 | 58 | 57 | 46 |

Final Pre-Election Figures for Midterm Elections

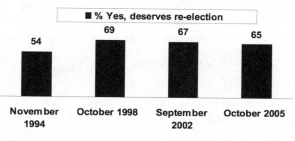

Percentage Saying Own Member of Congress Deserves Re-Election
based on registered voters

■ % Yes, deserves re-election

| November 1994 | October 1998 | September 2002 | October 2005 |
| 54 | 69 | 67 | 65 |

Final Pre-Election Figures for Midterm Elections

ing on at the two-thirds level, similar to where it was in 1998 and 2002, and higher than what was seen in 1994.

Bush Not a Draw With Voters

The impact Bush will have on the congressional elections is unclear, but in principle, his low approval ratings cannot help the Republican Party. If his ratings continue to dip into the low 40s, as they have for the past two months, he could be a greater liability to Republican candidates than was Bill Clinton in 1994.

This finding is underscored by a separate question asking voters what impact a candidate's relationship with Bush will have on their vote for that candidate. By a 55% to 39% margin, a majority of voters say they would be more likely to vote for a congressional can-

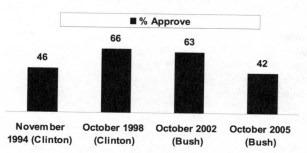

Percentage Who Approve of the Job the President Is Doing
based on national adults

■ % Approve

| November 1994 (Clinton) | October 1998 (Clinton) | October 2002 (Bush) | October 2005 (Bush) |
| 46 | 66 | 63 | 42 |

Final Pre-Election Figures for Midterm Elections

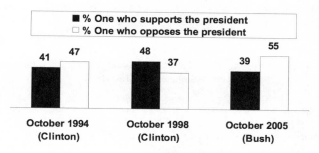

Which Candidate More Likely to Support?
based on registered voters

■ % One who supports the president
□ % One who opposes the president

| October 1994 (Clinton) | October 1998 (Clinton) | October 2005 (Bush) |
| 41 47 | 48 37 | 39 55 |

didate who opposes Bush than for a candidate who supports him. Only 6% say it would make no difference.

This is notably more negative than what Gallup found in 1994 and 1998 in reaction to Clinton. In neither case did a majority of voters say they would be more likely to vote for a candidate who opposed Clinton.

A follow-up question, asking voters how strongly they feel about a candidate's support for Bush, reveals an even more dramatic difference in Bush's potential impact on the election. Close to half of all voters today (47%) feel very strongly about voting for a candidate who opposes Bush. Even in 1994, when Clinton's approval rating was similar to Bush's current rating, a much lower percentage (36%) expressed this level of animosity toward Clinton.

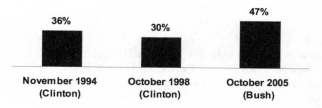

Percentage Who Feel Strongly About Voting for a Candidate Who Opposes the President
based on registered voters

| November 1994 (Clinton) | October 1998 (Clinton) | October 2005 (Bush) |
| 36% | 30% | 47% |

Results for this question are highly partisan, but Democrats are more unified in their support of candidates who oppose Bush than Republicans are in their support of candidates who support him (85% vs. 70%).

Intensity of Feeling About Impact of Bush on Vote for Congress
% preferring a candidate who ...

2005 Oct 21-23	Repub-lican %	Inde-pendent %	Democrat %
Supports Bush (feel strongly)	70	19	1
Supports Bush (don't feel strongly)	15	11	2
Opposes Bush (don't feel strongly)	4	10	9
Opposes Bush (feel strongly)	7	51	85
No opinion	4	9	3
	100%	100%	100%

In 1994, Republicans and Democrats were less strongly partisan in their responses with respect to Clinton. Then, two-thirds (68%) of Republicans felt strongly about picking a candidate who opposed Clinton. This contrasts with the 85% of Democrats today who feel strongly about choosing a candidate who opposes Bush.

Similarly, in 1994, 57% of Democrats felt strongly about backing a candidate who supported Clinton. This contrasts with 70% of Republicans today who feel strongly about voting for a candidate who supports Bush.

Intensity of Feeling About Impact of Clinton on Vote for Congress
% preferring a candidate who ...

1994 Nov 2-6	Repub-lican %	Inde-pendent %	Democrat %
Supports Clinton (feel strongly)	4	20	57
Supports Clinton (don't feel strongly)	5	15	18
Opposes Clinton (don't feel strongly)	14	13	6
Opposes Clinton (feel strongly)	68	31	10
No opinion	9	21	9
	100%	100%	100%

Survey Methods

These results are based on telephone interviews with a randomly selected national sample of 1,008 adults, aged 18 and older, conducted Oct. 21-23, 2005. For results based on this sample, one can say with 95% confidence that the maximum error attributable to sampling and other random effects is ±3 percentage points. In addition to sampling error, question wording and practical difficulties in conducting surveys can introduce error or bias into the findings of public opinion polls.

October 27, 2005

FOUR IN TEN AMERICANS BELIEVE BUSH ADMINISTRATION OFFICIALS ACTED ILLEGALLY

Majority still rates Bush administration's ethical standards in positive terms

by Jeffrey M. Jones, Gallup Poll Managing Editor

The federal grand jury hearing evidence concerning whether officials from President George W. Bush's administration broke the law by allegedly revealing a CIA agent's identity to the press is expected to vote by the end of October on whether to indict those officials. A new CNN/*USA Today*/Gallup poll finds that about 4 in 10 Americans think Bush administration officials did something illegal in this matter, while an equal percentage believe they did something unethical but not illegal. The public still gives a positive review to the Bush administration's ethical standards more generally, but the percent who rate these in strongly negative terms has increased. Since this summer, public opinion about White House advisor Karl Rove and Vice President Dick Cheney—two possible targets for indictments—has become more negative.

The Oct. 21-23 CNN/*USA Today*/Gallup poll asked the public for their views of whether Bush administration officials violated the law by allegedly revealing the identity of a CIA employee (Valerie Plame) to the media. Thirty-nine percent of Americans say some Bush administration officials did something illegal, 39% say some officials did something unethical but no one did anything illegal, while 10% said no one did anything wrong (an additional 12% have no opinion).

As you may know, several members of the Bush administration have been accused of leaking to reporters the identity of a woman working for the CIA. Which of the following statements best describes your view of top Bush administration officials in these matters–some Bush administration officials did something illegal, no Bush administration officials did anything illegal, but some officials did something unethical, or no Bush administration official did anything seriously wrong?

Oct. 21-23, 2005

Views of the matter are strongly related to one's political party affiliation. A majority of Democrats, 55%, believe Bush administration officials did something illegal. That view is shared by 45% of independents, but by only 19% of Republicans. A plurality of Republicans, 44%, say that Bush officials did something unethical, but not illegal.

More generally, the poll found that a slim majority of Americans still rate the Bush administration's ethical standards in positive terms, as either "excellent" (11%) or "good" (40%). Nineteen percent say the administration's ethical standards are "not good," and 29% say the standards are "poor." In July, about as many Americans gave the Bush administration positive ratings (55%) as do now, but significantly fewer rated the administration's ethical standards as poor (19%) back then.

Gallup has asked this question about Bush's administration and those of the previous three presidents. Americans tend to give positive ratings to the ethics of presidential administrations, although Gallup has only asked this question sporadically, and in most cases not following some of the larger presidential scandals such as Iran-

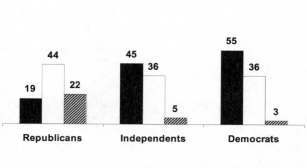

View of Bush Administration Officials
by party affiliation

■ % Illegal □ % Unethical ▨ % Nothing wrong

Republicans: 19, 44, 22
Independents: 45, 36, 5
Democrats: 55, 36, 3

Oct. 21-23, 2005

Contra and Monica Lewinsky. Thus, it is not possible to compare the effects of the current scandal to those of other recent scandals.

Overall, how would you rate the ethical standards of top Bush administration officials—excellent, good, not good, or poor?

	Excellent %	Good %	Not good %	Poor %	No opinion %
George W. Bush					
2005 Oct 21-23^	11	40	19	29	1
2005 Jul 22-24 ^	8	47	24	18	3
2002 Jul 26-28	15	59	15	8	3
Bill Clinton					
1994 Mar 7-8	4	53	20	21	2
1994 Jan 15-17	6	37	39	16	2
George H.W. Bush					
1989 May 12-16 †	5	54	20	7	13
Ronald Reagan					
1984 Oct 22-23 † ‡	7	60	17	12	4
1984 Sep 7-11 † ‡	6	58	19	15	3
1983 Jul 28-Aug 1 †	5	59	22	9	4

^ Asked of half sample
† ABC/*Washington Post* Trend
‡ Based on registered voters

A recent CNN/*USA Today*/Gallup poll assessed the public's overall views of some of the people who may have been involved in the Plame leak.

One of the central figures in the investigation is presidential adviser Rove, who was identified as a source for a *Time* magazine reporter. According to an Oct. 13-16 poll, Americans are more negative than positive toward Rove: 39% view him unfavorably, 22% favorably, while 39% have no opinion.

Opinions about Rove have become slightly more negative since July, the first time Gallup asked about him. At that time, 34% viewed Rove unfavorably, 25% favorably, and 41% did not have an opinion.

The other central figure in the investigation is I. Lewis "Scooter" Libby, the chief of staff for Vice President Cheney. Libby has been identified as the source for a *New York Times* reporter. There is speculation that Libby may have heard the information from Cheney.

Gallup has yet to ask the public about Libby; however, the Oct. 13-16 poll found Cheney's favorable ratings the worst they have been—47% view him unfavorably and 43% favorably. In June, 48% had a favorable opinion of the vice president and 44% had an unfavorable view. It is unclear if the recent change is due to his possible involvement in the CIA leak, or if it is just a reflection of more negative views toward the Bush administration more generally.

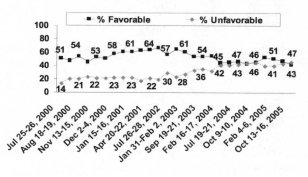

Opinion of Vice President Dick Cheney

■ % Favorable ◆ % Unfavorable

Favorable: 51, 54, 53, 58, 61, 64, 57, 61, 54, 45, 47, 46, 51, 47
Unfavorable: 14, 21, 22, 23, 23, 22, 30, 28, 36, 42, 43, 46, 41, 43

Jul 25-26, 2000 · Aug 18-19, 2000 · Nov 13-15, 2000 · Dec 2-4, 2000 · Jan 15-16, 2001 · Apr 20-22, 2001 · Jul 26-28, 2002 · Jan 31-Feb 2, 2003 · Sep 19-21, 2003 · Feb 16-17, 2004 · Jul 19-21, 2004 · Oct 9-10, 2004 · Feb 4-6, 2005 · Oct 13-16, 2005

Survey Methods

These results are based on telephone interviews with randomly selected national samples of 1,008 adults, aged 18 and older, conducted Oct. 21-23, 2005, and 1,012 adults, aged 18 and older, conducted Oct. 13-16, 2005. For results based on these samples, one can say with 95% confidence that the maximum error attributable to sampling and other random effects is ±3 percentage points. In addition to sampling error, question wording and practical difficulties in conducting surveys can introduce error or bias into the findings of public opinion polls.

October 28, 2005
PUBLIC MORE PLEASED THAN DISAPPOINTED BY MIERS' WITHDRAWAL
More concern about her qualifications and closeness to Bush than her ideology

by Frank Newport, Gallup Poll Editor in Chief

By a small margin, the American public is more pleased than disappointed with Harriet Miers' withdrawal as President Bush's nominee to fill the U.S. Supreme Court vacancy being created by the impending retirement of Sandra Day O'Connor.

The results of a special CNN/*USA Today*/Gallup poll conducted Thursday night suggest that Americans who are pleased with Miers' withdrawal are mostly concerned about Miers' qualifications and her closeness to Bush, rather than her ideology.

The poll contains some good news for Bush; most Americans consider Miers' withdrawal to be only a minor setback for the president, or no setback at all. Going forward, about 4 in 10 Americans want Bush's new nominee to be conservative, but only 3 in 10 think it is very important that he nominate another woman to replace O'Connor.

Most of the results of the special one-night poll are consistent with previous CNN/*USA Today*/Gallup polling. In Gallup's Oct. 21-23 poll, a plurality of Americans thought the Senate should reject the Miers nomination, and also showed significant disappointment over Bush's choice.

Initial Reaction

The Thursday night instant-reaction poll found that by a 42% to 35% margin, Americans are more pleased than disappointed by Miers' withdrawal.

As you may know, President Bush withdrew his nomination of Harriet Miers to the U.S. Supreme Court today.

First, would you say you are pleased or disappointed that Harriet Miers' nomination was withdrawn?

	Pleased	Disappointed	No opinion
2005 Oct 27	42%	35	23

This sentiment is roughly in line with results from this past weekend's poll in which Americans were asked about Bush's nomination of Miers. That poll found that 40% of Americans were pleased with Bush's choice, while 50% were disappointed.

Although the Thursday night poll's sample size is relatively small, it is informative to look at the responses by the self-reported ideology, partisanship, and gender of those interviewed.

Initial Reaction to Miers' Withdrawal

	Pleased	Disappointed
TOTAL SAMPLE	**42%**	**35%**
Conservatives	34	44
Moderates	45	33
Liberals	55*	25*
Republicans	31	53
Independents	39	33
Democrats	55	25
Men	47	32
Women	38	37

*Small sample size

The pattern of these responses follows typical lines. Conservatives and Republicans are most likely to be disappointed. This suggests rank-and-file conservatives may have been less negative about the nomination than highly visible conservative pundits and columnists.

Still, only 44% of conservatives describe themselves as disappointed with the withdrawal, while 34% are pleased (more than one in five conservatives didn't have an opinion in response to this question).

Men are more pleased than disappointed; women split almost precisely even in their reactions.

The Thursday night poll asked respondents who say they are pleased by the Miers withdrawal to indicate which of four possible explanations is the most important reason for their pleasure.

If you had to choose among the following, which would you say is the most important reason why you are pleased that Harriet Miers' nomination was withdrawn—[ROTATED: her views are too conservative, her views are not conservative enough, she does not have

strong enough qualifications to serve on the Supreme Court, (or) she is too close to George W. Bush personally]?*

BASED ON 241 ADULTS WHO SAY THEY ARE PLEASED THAT MIERS' NOMINATION WAS WITHDRAWN

	Views too conser-vative	Views not conser-vative enough	Does not have strong qualifi-cations	Too close to Bush person-ally	No opinion
2005 Oct 27	8%	4	49	35	4

Few of those who are pleased by the withdrawal say it was either because Miers was too conservative or because she was not conservative enough.

Instead, nearly half say they are pleased because Miers does not have strong enough qualifications, and a third feel she is too close to the president.

Impact on Bush

The long-term effect of the failed nomination on Bush is impossible to predict at this point. By all indications, Bush will name a new nominee in very short order, and the focus on that person will no doubt take attention away from the Miers situation in the days and weeks ahead.

For their part, Americans are highly likely to say that the Miers affair will be a minor setback or no setback at all for the Bush administration.

Do you consider the withdrawal of Harriet Miers to be a major setback for the Bush administration, a minor setback, or not a setback at all?

	Major setback	Minor setback	Not a setback at all	No opinion
2005 Oct 27	16%	42	34	8

Only 16% say it is a major setback, 42% say it is a minor setback, and 34% say it is not a setback at all.

Conservatives and Republicans are predictably less likely than other groups surveyed to say that it is a major setback.

Looking Ahead

Gallup polling has consistently shown that Americans have not been convinced that it is strongly necessary for Bush to nominate a woman to replace O'Connor.

The Thursday night poll confirms these findings.

Now that George W. Bush has withdrawn his nomination of Harriet Miers, how important is it to you that he nominates another woman to replace Sandra Day O'Connor on the Supreme Court—very important, somewhat important, not too important, or not at all important?

	Very important	Some-what important	Not too important	Not at all important	No opinion
2005 Oct 27	30%	29	14	25	2

Only 3 in 10 Americans interviewed say that it is very important that the new nominee be a woman, while another 29% say it is somewhat important. Roughly 4 in 10 say it is not too important or not at all important.

Are women more concerned than men that Bush's new nominee be a woman? The answer to that question is "yes," by a small margin. Thirty-six percent of women say it is very important that the new nominee be a woman, compared with 24% of men.

How Important Is It That Bush Nominate Another Woman to Replace Sandra Day O'Connor on the Supreme Court?

	Very important	Somewhat important	Not important/ Not at all important
TOTAL SAMPLE	30%	29%	39%
Men	24	28	47
Women	36	30	32

Republicans and conservatives—Bush's base—are less likely to think it is important that the new nominee be a woman than are others.

Should the new nominee be conservative? Americans give a mixed response to this question.

Do you think George W. Bush should nominate someone to the Supreme Court who is — [ROTATED: very conservative, somewhat conservative, moderate, somewhat liberal, (or) very liberal]?

	Very conser- vative	Some- what conser- vative	Mod- erate	Some- what liberal	Very liberal	No opinion
2005 Oct 27	14%	23	34	16	8	5

A little more than a third would like the new nominee to be conservative (with more of these saying "somewhat conservative" than "very conservative"). About one in four say the new nominee should be liberal, and a third say that the nominee should be moderate.

Not surprisingly, about two-thirds of both conservatives and Republicans say that the new nominee should be conservative.

Survey Methods

Results are based on telephone interviews with 516 national adults, aged 18 and older, conducted Oct. 27, 2005. For results based on the total sample of national adults, one can say with 95% confidence that the margin of sampling error is ±5 percentage points.

In addition to sampling error, question wording and practical difficulties in conducting surveys can introduce error or bias into the findings of public opinion polls.

Polls conducted entirely in one day, such as this one, are subject to additional error or bias not found in polls conducted over several days.

October 31, 2005
PUBLIC REACTION TO LIBBY INDICTMENTS IS LOW KEY
Majority denies that case demonstrates Bush administration has low ethics

by Lydia Saad, Gallup Poll Senior Editor

According to a CNN/*USA Today*/Gallup poll conducted this past weekend, less than half of the American public believes former senior White House aide I. Lewis Libby Jr. did anything illegal in the matter for which he was indicted; a majority says the controversy involving him is an isolated incident rather than symptomatic of low ethics at the White House; and there is little shift in the already low opinion ratings of the players closely associated with this controversy, including ratings of presidential adviser Karl Rove and Vice President Dick Cheney. President George W. Bush's job approval rating has also not changed compared with polling conducted a week ago.

Given the potential for a scandal of this magnitude to undermine support for the administration, it is worth noting that Republicans tend to stand by the administration when answering questions concerning the controversy over Libby's role in leaking a CIA operative's name to the press two years ago (while Democrats, predictably, do not).

Clearly, most Americans believe Libby did something wrong in connection with the case concerning the alleged outing of CIA operative Valerie Plame. While Libby was not charged with any crimes specific to the leak per se, he was indicted on five felony counts concerning the truthfulness of statements he made to FBI agents and of his testimony before the grand jury hearing the case. Albeit a plurality, fewer than half (45%) believe Libby's actions in the case were illegal, while 31% say they were unethical but not illegal. Only 8% say he did nothing wrong.

These results vary considerably by party, as only 28% of Republicans, but 56% of Democrats, consider Libby's actions illegal.

As you may know, a special prosecutor has investigated the leak of the name of a CIA employee by White House officials. On Friday, a grand jury indicted Lewis Libby on charges of perjury and obstruction of justice. From what you have heard or read about Libby's involvement in this matter, which of the following statements best describes your view of his actions—[ROTATED: he did something illegal, he did something unethical but nothing illegal, or he did not do anything seriously wrong]?

	Illegal %	Unethical %	Nothing wrong %	OTHER (vol.) %	No opinion %
National adults	45	31	8	1	15
Republicans	28	40	13	*	19
Independents	52	27	5	1	15
Democrats	56	26	5	1	12

*Less than 0.5%
(vol.) = Volunteered response

Despite much speculation that Libby's indictment will deepen public skepticism of Bush and spell the political unraveling of his administration, the initial reaction of Americans appears to downplay the matter's significance. Only 38% of Americans say the charges are a sign that "the Bush administration in general has low ethical standards." The majority, 56%, say the charges are "based on an isolated incident."

A majority of independents agree with most Republicans that the controversy stands alone, while most Democrats contend the charges are symptomatic that the Bush administration itself is corrupt.

Do you think these charges are a sign that the Bush administration in general has low ethical standards, or do you think these charges are based on an isolated incident?

	Sign of low ethical standards %	Isolated incident %	No opinion %
National adults	38	56	6
Republicans	10	83	7
Independents	38	54	8
Democrats	65	31	4

(An ABC News/*Washington Post* poll released this past weekend contained a question suggesting that the scandal does cast a broader shadow over the administration. However, the ABC News/*Washington Post* question sets a lower threshold, asking whether the Libby case indicates "broader problems with ethical wrongdoing in the Bush administration." With this wording, ABC News and the *Washington Post* found 55% saying the case does indicate broader problems, while 41% say it is an isolated incident.)

Bush Approval Is Steady

A key indicator of the Libby case's political impact is President Bush's overall job approval rating. According to the Oct. 28-30 poll, Bush's job approval remains exactly where it was in a poll conducted Oct. 24-26, just before Libby's indictment on Friday, and is statistically similar to two other polls conducted in the weeks before that. Forty-one percent of Americans now approve of the way Bush is handling his job as president, identical to the 41% who approved in a survey just before the indictments, and the same as his average rating spanning four Gallup Polls conducted this month.

Bush Job Approval

	Approve %	Disapprove %	No opinion %
2005 Oct 28-30	41	56	3
2005 Oct 24-26	41	56	3
2005 Oct 21-23	42	55	3
2005 Oct 13-16	39	58	3
Average for the month	**41**	**56**	**3**

At 41%, Bush's average approval rating for October is down compared with where it stood in September and August (44%), but Gallup's detailed October polling makes it clear that Bush's current job approval situation has not yet changed as a result of the Libby indictments. Bush's job approval ratings are at the low point of his administration, continuing a pattern of sagging approval ratings for him that has been evident since the start of the year. However, the events of the past week apparently have not pushed his ratings down further.

Bush Job Approval—Monthly Averages for 2005

	Approve %	Disapprove %
October	41	56
September	44	53
August	44	53
July	47	49
June	46	51
May	48	47
April	49	48
March	50	46
February	52	45
January	52	45

The weekend poll also does not support the hypothesis that the Plame controversy per se has hurt perceptions of Bush on other dimensions. Bush's ratings as being an effective manager of government, being honest and trustworthy, and being a strong leader have dropped since the summer. But trend data show the last two measures are statistically no different from September, suggesting again that Bush's image has been damaged in recent months, but not necessarily damaged further by the indictments.

Since July, those saying Bush can manage government effectively and that he is a strong and decisive leader each declined by 10 points. Over the same period, perceptions that he is honest and trustworthy dropped by only 5 points.

The result is that today, a slim majority of Americans say Bush is a strong and decisive leader (52% vs. 47%). Americans are evenly divided over whether Bush is honest and trustworthy (49% say this applies, while 48% say it does not). A majority now disagrees that he can manage the government effectively (56% vs. 43%).

Additionally, as would perhaps be expected for a president with only a 41% job approval rating and a 56% disapproval rating, the majority of Americans, 55%, say that the Bush presidency has been a failure so far, while 42% say it has been a success. (As can be seen, these numbers are essentially a reflection of the president's job approval rating.) Americans aren't optimistic that things are going to change for the better; 55% say the remaining three years will be a failure, while 41% say they will be a success for Bush.

Libby, Rove, and Cheney

Public reaction to Cheney's former chief of staff Libby is decidedly negative. Only 10% of Americans view Libby favorably (he resigned Friday shortly after the indictments were announced). Close to half (43%) hold an unfavorable view, but a roughly equal number, 47%, have no opinion of him. This is the first time Gallup has asked the public about this previously behind-the-scenes White House figure.

Although Rove has been, and remains, under investigation for his role in the Plame affair, Gallup finds only modest change in public attitudes toward him since these were first measured in July. His favorable rating has held steady at 24%, while his unfavorable rating has inched up slightly from 34% in July to 39% in mid-October and 40% today.

Last week it was reported that Cheney himself may have been Libby's source for Plame's identity, raising questions about his role in coordinating the leak of her name. Thus far it does not appear that

Cheney's image has been hurt further by the revelation. The weekend poll finds little change in favorable ratings of Cheney compared with mid-October. About 4 in 10 have a favorable view of him, while half hold an unfavorable view. These ratings are slightly more negative, however, than those recorded in June. At that time, 48% had a favorable view of Cheney and 44% unfavorable.

Where Is It Headed?

The weekend poll asked Americans how well they understand the Libby case. About two-thirds say they understand it very (22%) or somewhat (46%) well, while about one-third (31%) say they don't understand it very well or don't understand it at all.

Those who present themselves as knowledgeable about the case—saying they understand it "very well"—tend to be much more critical than others about the seriousness of the charges and the broader implications for the Bush administration. Whether this is an indication that public opinion will grow more critical as the facts become better known, or whether it merely reflects the somewhat higher proportion of Democrats among those highly familiar with the case, is not clear.

Seriousness of Charges According to Knowledge of Case

	Understand case very well %	Understand case somewhat well %	Do not understand case well %
Illegal	61	49	29
Unethical	21	38	27
Nothing wrong	15	7	4
No opinion/OTHER (vol.)	3	6	40
	100%	100%	100%

(vol.) = Volunteered response

Survey Methods

These results are based on telephone interviews with a randomly selected national sample of 800 adults, aged 18 and older, conducted Oct. 28-30, 2005. For results based on this sample, one can say with 95% confidence that the maximum error attributable to sampling and other random effects is ±4 percentage points. In addition to sampling error, question wording and practical difficulties in conducting surveys can introduce error or bias into the findings of public opinion polls.

A woman

	Essential %	Good idea, not essential %	Doesn't matter %	Bad idea %	No opinion %
2005 Oct 28-30	14	33	50	2	1
2005 Sep 26-28 ^	14	29	55	1	1

^ Asked of a half sample

A key factor to Bush's most vocal supporters is that the nominee be conservative, and there is little doubt that Alito is regarded that way. Only 21% of Americans say that it is essential that the nominee be conservative, however, while 24% say it is a good idea but not essential. Twenty percent say that nominating a conservative is a bad idea, while 32% say it doesn't matter.

A conservative

	Essential	Good idea, not essential	Doesn't matter	Bad idea	No opinion
2005 Oct 28-30	21%	24	32	20	3

One of the key issues dividing Republicans and Democrats is a potential nominee's position on abortion. Many prominent Christian conservatives have expressed a desire to reverse Roe v. Wade, the Supreme Court ruling that says a woman has a constitutional right to an abortion at least within the first three months of conception. And Americans have consistently indicated that they do not want to see Roe reversed.

In the current poll, only 16% of Americans say it is essential that a nominee be a person who would overturn Roe, and another 16% think it would be a good idea, but not essential. Forty-two percent say it would be a bad idea to have a justice who would overturn Roe, and 20% say it doesn't matter.

Someone who would vote to overturn the Roe v. Wade decision on abortion

	Essential %	Good idea, not essential %	Doesn't matter %	Bad idea %	No opinion %
2005 Oct 28-30	16	16	20	42	6
Republicans	19	22	23	31	5
Independents	13	15	20	45	7
Democrats	17	10	17	52	4
Conservatives	26	21	21	26	6
Moderates	12	15	21	46	6
Liberals	11	8	14	65	2

The results show that even Republicans are not especially intense on this issue, with 19% saying it's essential, compared with 17% of Democrats. But Democrats are much more likely than Republicans to say it is a bad idea—52% vs. 31%, respectively.

November 1, 2005
ALITO'S EXPERIENCE A PLUS WITH PUBLIC

Americans less concerned about ideology or gender of nominee

by David W. Moore, Gallup Poll Senior Editor

With the nomination of Judge Samuel Alito to replace Sandra Day O'Connor on the Supreme Court, President George W. Bush has found a candidate who apparently pleases most prominent conservatives. A description of Alito's record suggests that the American public will find the candidate generally acceptable on some qualifications, although the issue of abortion could be a source of contention.

The latest CNN/*USA Today*/Gallup survey, conducted Oct. 28-30, finds that 50% of Americans say it is essential that the nominee has experience as a judge, and another 36% say such experience is a "good idea," even if not essential. On this mark, Alito clearly qualifies. He has been a judge on the U.S. Court of Appeals for the 3rd Circuit since 1990.

Next, as you may know, President Bush will soon announce another nominee to the Supreme Court to fill the seat of retiring Justice Sandra Day O'Connor.

10. Which of the following best describes your view about whether the next Supreme Court justice is [RANDOM ORDER]—do you think it is—[RANDOM ORDER: essential that the next justice is (a woman/someone who has experience judge/a conservative/someone who would vote to overturn the Roe v. Wade decision), is it a good idea, but not essential, does it not matter to you, (or do you think it is) a bad idea]?

Someone who has experience as a judge

	Essential	Good idea, not essential	Doesn't matter	Bad idea	No opinion
2005 Oct 28-30	50%	36	11	2	1

Alito would replace O'Connor, the first woman ever appointed to the Supreme Court. However, Americans appear divided on the importance of replacing her with another woman. Fourteen percent say it is essential that the nominee be a woman, while 33% say it is a good idea to nominate a woman, but not essential. And 50% of Americans say it doesn't matter to them.

Conservatives are more likely than moderates or liberals to say it is essential to have a justice overturn Roe v. Wade, 26% vs. 12% and 11%, respectively. Still, 47% of conservatives say it either doesn't matter (21%) or it's a bad idea (26%). Sixty-five percent of liberals say it is a bad idea.

The last time Gallup asked the public's views of overturning Roe v. Wade was in July. The public opposed reversing the decision by greater than a two-to-one margin.

The 1973 Roe versus Wade decision established a woman's constitutional right to an abortion, at least in the first three months of pregnancy. Would you like to see the Supreme Court COMPLETELY OVERTURN its Roe versus Wade decision, or not?

	Yes, overturn %	No, not overturn %	No opinion %
2005 Jul 7-10 ^	29	68	3
2002 Mar 22-24	36	60	4
1992 Aug 13-14	34	60	6
1989 Oct 5-8	33	61	6
1989 Jul 6-7	31	58	11

^ Asked of a half sample

Would you like to see the Supreme Court overturn its 1973 Roe versus Wade decision concerning abortion, or not?

ASKED OF A HALF SAMPLE

	Yes, overturn	No, not overturn	No opinion
2005 Jul 7-10	28%	63	9

The purpose of asking two different versions was to see if the wording made a difference in the responses. The results show that with either wording, there is little support for overturning Roe v. Wade.

While it is difficult to predict how a judge will rule on a case, Alito's record suggests the nominee is at least more strongly anti-abortion than the justice he would replace. In 1991, he was the lone dissenter in a 3rd Circuit court decision that struck down a law requiring wives to tell their husbands before having an abortion. The Supreme Court upheld the 3rd Circuit court's decision by a 6-3 vote, including that of Justice O'Connor.

Despite its support for Roe v. Wade, the public itself is ambivalent about abortion. While a majority supports a woman's right to an abortion in the first three months, the public has also indicated majority support for requiring parental notification before a minor can have an abortion, and for prohibiting late-term abortions except if a woman's health is at risk.

Survey Methods

Results are based on telephone interviews with 800 national adults, aged 18 and older, conducted Oct. 28-30, 2005. For results based on the total sample of national adults, one can say with 95% confidence that the maximum margin of sampling error is ±4 percentage points.

In addition to sampling error, question wording and practical difficulties in conducting surveys can introduce error or bias into the findings of public opinion polls.

November 1, 2005
KATRINA VICTIMS FEAR WHAT FUTURE HOLDS
Next few months most worrisome

by Darren K. Carlson, Government and Politics Editor

In the aftermath of Hurricane Katrina, victims struggled just to get through each day. Only after basic needs like food, clothing, and shelter were met could victims even begin to consider the future. Now that they are able to look ahead, a significant number fear what that future holds. Results from a CNN/*USA Today*/Gallup poll of Katrina victims*, conducted six weeks after the hurricane hit, illustrate just how worried they are about what will happen to them in the months and years ahead.

The poll interviewed a random sample of 1,510 adults who applied for hurricane disaster relief from the American Red Cross. When respondents were asked how much they worry about what will happen to them in the next few months, more than a third say they are "very" worried.

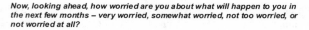

Now, looking ahead, how worried are you about what will happen to you in the next few months – very worried, somewhat worried, not too worried, or not worried at all?

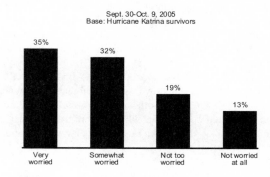

Sept. 30-Oct. 9, 2005
Base: Hurricane Katrina survivors

Black hurricane survivors are significantly more likely than white survivors to worry about their immediate futures. Specifically, 42% of black survivors say they are very worried, while 24% of white respondents report being this worried.

As one might expect, those who experienced the most severe damage from Katrina are more worried about the future than those who experienced less damage. Among those who say their homes were destroyed, 67% are very worried what will happen to them in the next few months. And 49% of those who had their homes damaged to the point where they can't live in them also say they are very worried. That compares with just 22% of those whose homes were not damaged or only suffered minor damage but are still livable.

Geographically speaking, half (53%) of survivors who previously resided in the city of New Orleans are very worried. This is significantly higher than the percentage among survivors who reside in the suburbs surrounding New Orleans, in different parts of Louisiana, or in Alabama or Mississippi.

Victims Less Worried About Long-Term

The survey also asked survivors to share their concerns about what will happen to them in the next five years. Fewer people express worry about the long-term than about the short-term, but one in four still report being very worried (24%) about what will happen to them within the next five years.

Now, looking ahead, how worried are you about what will happen to you in the next five years -- very worried, somewhat worried, not too worried, or not worried at all?

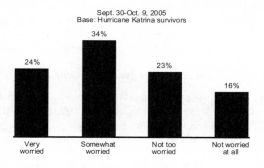

Sept. 30-Oct. 9, 2005
Base: Hurricane Katrina survivors

Very worried 24%
Somewhat worried 34%
Not too worried 23%
Not worried at all 16%

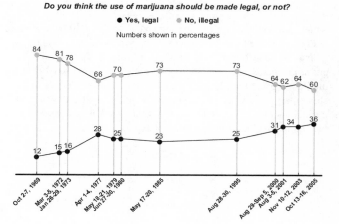

Do you think the use of marijuana should be made legal, or not?

● Yes, legal ● No, illegal

Numbers shown in percentages

Again, respondents' level of worry about the long-term future varies by race and extent of personal loss. While 15% of white respondents say they are very worried what's going to happen in the next five years, the percentage is twice as high among black survivors (30%). One-third of those whose homes were destroyed (36%) say they are very worried. That percentage falls to 25% among those whose homes were damaged to the point that they can't live in them, and 20% among those whose houses were not damaged or suffered only minimal damage.

Results are based on telephone interviews with a sample of 1,510 adults, aged 18 and older, drawn randomly from the American Red Cross database of applicants seeking assistance due to the effects of Hurricane Katrina. Interviews were conducted Sept. 30-Oct. 9, 2005.

The vast majority of applicants provided a working contact telephone number to the Red Cross. Gallup did reverse phone lookups to obtain telephone numbers for the portion of the selected sample that did not provide a contact number. Where necessary, Gallup interviewers tracked down updated telephone numbers when respondents had moved from their previous location. Interviews were conducted on both landline and cellular telephones. Full details on the poll methodology can be found at www.galluppoll.com

In addition to sampling error, question wording and practical difficulties in conducting surveys can introduce error or bias into the findings of public opinion polls.

November 1, 2005
WHO SUPPORTS MARIJUANA LEGALIZATION?
Support rising; varies most by age and gender

by Joseph Carroll, Gallup Poll Assistant Editor

Since the late 1960s, Gallup has periodically asked Americans whether the use of marijuana should be made legal in the United States. Although a majority of Americans have consistently opposed the idea of legalizing marijuana, public support has slowly increased over the years. In 1969, just 12% of Americans supported making marijuana legal, but by 1977, roughly one in four endorsed it. Support edged up to 31% in 2000, and now, about a third of Americans say marijuana should be legal.

Certain groups of Americans are more inclined than others to support the legalization of marijuana. In order to better understand which groups of Americans are more inclined to support legaliza-

tion, Gallup combined the results of three surveys, conducted in August 2001, November 2003, and October 2005*.

Gender, Age Shapes Support for Legalization

Support for marijuana legalization varies greatest by gender and age. Overall, younger Americans (aged 18 to 29) are essentially divided, with 47% saying marijuana should be legal and 50% saying it should not be. Support for legalization is much lower among adults aged 30 to 64 (35%) and those aged 65 and older (22%). Men (39%) are somewhat more likely than women (30%) to support the legalization of marijuana in the country.

When looking at the combined results by age and gender, the data show 44% of men aged 18 to 49 support the legalization of marijuana. This sentiment is lower among older men (33% for men aged 50 and older) and women of any age (34% for women aged 18 to 49 and 27% of women aged 50 and older).

Legalization of Marijuana by Gender and Age

■ Yes, legal ▨ No, illegal

2001-2005 aggregate

Men, aged 18 to 49: 44% / 52%
Men, aged 50 and older: 33% / 63%
Women, aged 18 to 49: 34% / 65%
Women, aged 50 and older: 27% / 70%

Gallup found similar patterns in 1973, a few years after it first started asking the question. That year, men were also slightly more likely than women, by 18% to 13%, to support legalization. A third of 18- to 29-year-olds (34%) agreed with legalizing marijuana, while no more than 11% of adults aged 30 and older agreed. And, about one in four men aged 18 to 49 (24%) supported legalization, compared with 7% of men aged 50 and older, 18% of women aged 18 to 49, and 6% of women aged 50 and older.

The data make it clear that despite the gender and age differences that still persist, all subgroups are more likely to support legalized marijuana today than three decades ago.

Westerners Divided in Views of Legalization

Americans residing in the western parts of the country are more likely than those living elsewhere to support the legalization of marijuana. These differences perhaps result from the fact that six Western states have, in various ways, already legalized marijuana for medicinal use. Overall, the data show that Westerners are divided about marijuana, with 47% saying it should be legal and 49% saying it should not be. No more than a third of adults living in other parts of the country feel marijuana should be legal.

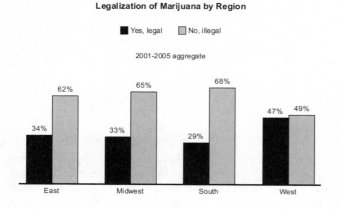

Legalization of Marijuana by Region

■ Yes, legal   ▨ No, illegal

2001-2005 aggregate

In 1973, Gallup found that residents in the East and West were more likely to support marijuana legalization than those in the Midwest and South. Roughly one in five Easterners (20%) and Westerners (22%) supported this idea, compared with 13% of Midwesterners and 10% of Southerners.

Church Attendance Related to Support

Only about one in six Americans who attend church or religious services weekly (17%) support the legalization of marijuana. Support is higher among those who attend less frequently—30% among those who attend almost weekly or monthly and 49% among those who rarely or never go.

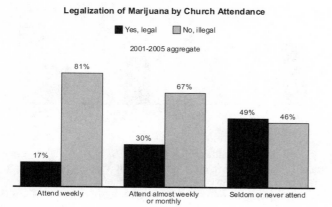

Legalization of Marijuana by Church Attendance

■ Yes, legal   ▨ No, illegal

2001-2005 aggregate

College-Educated Adults Give Slightly Higher Support for Legalization

Americans with some college education—from those who have attended at least one college course to those who have postgraduate degrees—are somewhat more likely than those without a college

degree to say marijuana should be legal in the country. Thirty-seven percent of adults with a college education support legalization, compared with 31% of those with no college education.

The differences between these two groups were much more pronounced in 1973. At that time, 29% of college-educated adults supported legalization, compared with just 11% of those with no college.

Politics and Marijuana Legalization

Support for legalizing marijuana is much lower among Republicans than it is among Democrats or independents. One in five Republicans (21%) say marijuana should be made legal in this country, while 37% of Democrats and 44% of independents share this view.

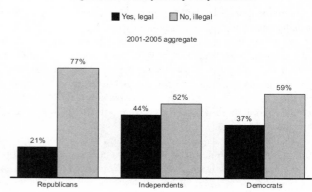

Legalization of Marijuana by Party Affiliation

■ Yes, legal   ▨ No, illegal

2001-2005 aggregate

When Gallup asked this question in 1973, independents (25%) were at least twice as likely as Democrats or Republicans to support this idea. However, at the time, there were only slight differences in support between Democrats (13%) and Republicans (9%).

The data also show differences by respondents' self-described political ideology. Twenty-two percent of conservatives feel marijuana should be made legal, compared with 36% of moderates and a majority of liberals (54%).

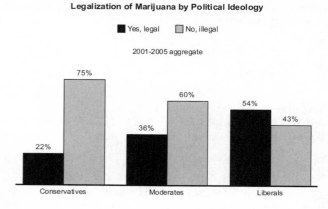

Legalization of Marijuana by Political Ideology

■ Yes, legal   ▨ No, illegal

2001-2005 aggregate

*Results are based on telephone interviews with 2,034 national adults, aged 18 and older, conducted Aug. 3-5, 2001, Nov. 10-12, 2003, and Oct. 21-23, 2005. For results based on the total sample of national adults, one can say with 95% confidence that the maximum margin of sampling error is ±2 percentage points.

In addition to sampling error, question wording and practical difficulties in conducting surveys can introduce error or bias into the findings of public opinion polls.*

November 3, 2005
AMERICANS' MAJOR FINANCIAL WORRIES: ENERGY, HEALTHCARE, INCOME
Is a spending decline on the horizon?

by Frank Newport, Gallup Poll Editor in Chief

Gallup's late October economic update shows little change in Americans' expressed worry about their families' financial situations. The three biggest money problems bedeviling the public at this point are energy costs, healthcare costs, and simply not having enough money. Americans' estimates of how much they are going to spend on clothing and dining out are lower now than they have been at previous points this year, suggesting at least the possibility of a pullback in discretionary spending in the face of higher gas prices.

Worried About Your Family's Finances?

About 4 in 10 Americans say they are worried about their families' personal financial situations.

Worried About Family's Finances?

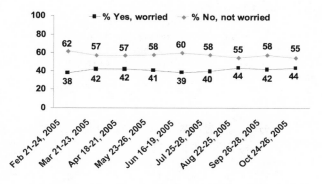

Expressed personal concern about family finances has remained remarkably stable so far this year. The average from February to October this year is 41%, with no one month's reading more than three percentage points above or below that average.

Over the last three months, the percentage expressing concern has averaged 43%, which is slightly higher than the year's average, but it is too soon to tell whether that represents any sort of trend toward more concern.

Those who say they are worried about their family finances are asked whether they are very worried or somewhat worried.

At this time, would you say you are worried about your family's finances, or not?

Are you very worried, or just somewhat worried?

COMBINED RESPONSES

	Very worried %	Somewhat worried %	Not worried %	No opinion %
2005 Oct 24-26	19	25	55	1
2005 Sep 26-28	18	24	58	*
2005 Aug 22-25	17	27	55	1
2005 Jul 25-28	15	25	58	2
2005 Jun 16-19	14	25	60	1
2005 May 23-26	15	26	58	1
2005 Apr 18-21	18	24	57	1
2005 Mar 21-23	18	24	57	1
2005 Feb 21-24	17	21	62	*

*Less than 0.5%

We do not detect any increase in the percentage of Americans saying they are "very worried" this year. The percentage "very worried" was slightly lower in May through July (averaging 15%), but over the past three months it is at a point very similar to where it was in February through April (averaging 18%).

This absence of any significant increase in expressed concern about family finances contrasts with changes in real economic conditions over the past nine months, including in particular the rapid increase in gas prices in August that lasted into September.

Family Financial Problems

Each month, Gallup asks Americans in an open-ended format to detail their families' most pressing financial problems.

What is the most important financial problem facing your family today? [OPEN-ENDED]

Recent Trend:

	Oct 24-27, 2005 %	Sep 26-28, 2005 %	Aug 22-25, 2005 %	Jul 25-28, 2005 %	Jun 16-19, 2005 %	May 23-26, 2005 %
Energy costs/Oil and gas prices	17	17	20	8	7	5
Healthcare costs	12	11	10	13	17	18
Lack of money/ Low wages	11	10	11	11	12	12
Too much debt/ Not enough money to pay debts	7	8	6	7	6	8
Unemployment/ Loss of job	6	6	7	8	7	8
High cost of living/ Inflation	6	7	6	6	8	5
College expenses	6	7	6	7	7	8
Cost of owning/ renting a home	5	5	3	4	6	6
Retirement savings	4	3	5	6	6	9
Taxes	4	4	3	4	3	3
State of the economy	2	1	*	1	1	—
Transportation/ Commuting costs	1	1	1	1	2	—
Social Security	1	1	2	1	2	2
Stock market/Investments	1	*	1	1	1	—
Interest rates	1	1	1	1	1	1
Lack of savings	1	1	1	1	2	—
Controlling spending	*	*	1	1	1	—
Other	3	4	4	4	6	4
None	16	18	16	17	16	16
No opinion	3	4	5	5	3	4

Percentages add to more than 100% due to multiple responses.
Contact Gallup for full trend.
*Less than 0.5%

The big change in the responses to this question throughout this year has been the uptick in expressed worry about energy costs, which occurred in August and continued through October. Energy costs have been the top problem for the last three months.

Other concerns have remained relatively stable. Sizable percentages of Americans continue to worry about healthcare costs (12%) and simply not having enough money (11%). These are the second- and third-most frequently occurring responses, followed by a variety of problems in the 5% to 7% range, including too much debt, unemployment, inflation, college expenses, and the cost of owning or renting a home.

The graph presents the trend of family financial worry and the trend in the top-of-mind mention of energy costs as the top family concern.

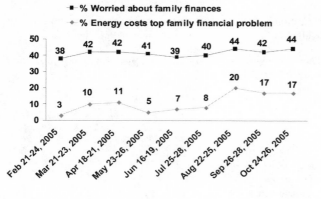

Comparing Worry About Family's Finances With Energy Costs as the Top Family Financial Problem

- ■ % Worried about family finances
- ◆ % Energy costs top family financial problem

There is little evidence that the increase in concern about gas prices caused a concomitant jump in worry about one's personal family financial situation.

Estimated Spending

Gallup also asks Americans to estimate how much they and their families are going to spend "this month" in each of four categories: groceries, clothing, eating dinner at a restaurant, and entertainment/vacation travel/recreational activities.

There is some fluctuation in these estimates by month, but the differences between many months are not statistically significant. Nevertheless, there has been a slight drop off in estimated spending in two discretionary categories for the last month or two, suggesting the possibility that the toll being taken by higher energy costs may be reflected in slightly lower spending in other areas of the family budget.

Groceries

The average American family estimates spending $362 on groceries in October, little changed from the average estimates on grocery spending found in each month going back to February this year.

Although the actual dollar amount varies from survey to survey, there has been no systematic trend showing that planned spending on groceries is steadily getting larger, or smaller.

The lowest estimate of the year so far came in August ($345), while the highest was in June ($383).

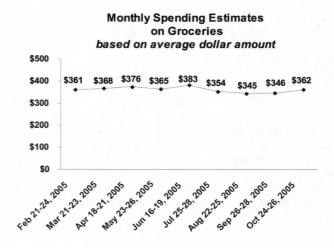

Monthly Spending Estimates on Groceries
based on average dollar amount

Clothing

Spending on clothing might be considered somewhat more discretionary than other family expenditures and perhaps as a result Gallup surveys have measured more variation in these estimates from month to month this year.

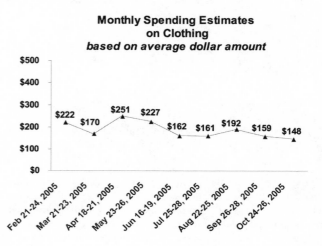

Monthly Spending Estimates on Clothing
based on average dollar amount

Americans indicated in October that they would be spending $148 on average on clothing in the month. That is the lowest such estimate this year. The previous low points were three measures in and around $160 found in September, July, and June. The highest estimates for clothing spending came earlier this year, including an estimate of $251 in April.

Does this indicate a slowdown in spending on this key retail category going forward? It's difficult to know at this point, but these data suggest that some consideration be given to this hypothesis.

Eating Dinner Out at a Restaurant

Estimates of monthly expenditures at restaurants have ranged from $109 to $133 this year.

The last two months have marked the lowest estimates measured so far this year: $109 in September and $110 in late October. The differences in these estimates by month are not great, and one should be appropriately hesitant to read too much into the slightly lower estimates.

Nevertheless, as was the case for the clothing estimates, the fact that the estimates have gone down suggests at least the possibility of

**Monthly Spending Estimates
on Dining Out**
based on average dollar amount

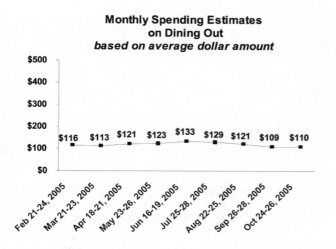

some increased financial concern on the part of consumers, perhaps in the face of rising energy costs.

Entertainment, Vacation Travel, Recreational Activities

**Monthly Spending Estimates
on Recreation or Entertainment**
based on average dollar amount

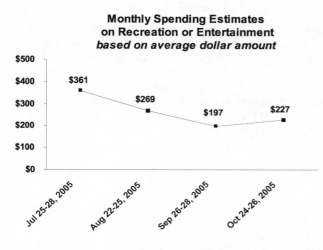

Gallup started measuring in this category in July, so there is only a four-month trend at this point.

The data show a significant drop in September ($197), with a slight recovery in October ($227)—compared with the two summer months of July ($361) and August ($269). This is entirely predictable given the assumption that recreational and vacation spending should be higher in the summer months.

Survey Methods

These results are based on telephone interviews with a randomly selected national sample of 840 U.S. adults, aged 18 and older, conducted Oct. 24-26, 2005. For results based on this sample, one can say with 95% confidence that the maximum error attributable to sampling and other random effects is ±4 percentage points. In addition to sampling error, question wording and practical difficulties in conducting surveys can introduce error or bias into the findings of public opinion polls.

November 7, 2005
GOP IMAGE TAKING A HIT
Democrats now have perceptual edge on most major issues

by Jeffrey M. Jones, Gallup Poll Managing Editor

Recent polling by CNN, *USA Today*, and Gallup shows a continued decline in the public's views of the Republican Party. The decline is evident in Americans' overall views of the party, as well as in its perceived ability to handle various issues compared with the Democratic Party's ability. The plurality of Americans believe the country would be better off if the Democrats controlled Congress. However, views of the Democratic Party have not necessarily improved; the party's current favorable rating is the same as it was earlier this year.

Opinions of the Parties

The Oct. 13-16 CNN/*USA Today*/Gallup poll found further deterioration in the public's views of the Republican Party, building on declines evident since February. Forty percent of Americans give the GOP a favorable rating and 50% an unfavorable one, compared with a 45%-45% split in September. Since Gallup began asking this question in 1992, the only other time the Republican Party had a majority viewing it unfavorably was in late 1998 and early 1999, during the Bill Clinton impeachment proceedings.

The recent trend on the public's overall opinion of the Republican Party shows just how much the party's image has suffered. Earlier this year, 56% of Americans viewed the party favorably, similar to the sentiment from last fall. But by the end of February, the party's favorable ratings began to decrease, dropping into the 50% range. In late July they fell further—below 50%—and today's ratings are even lower.

Opinion of the Republican Party

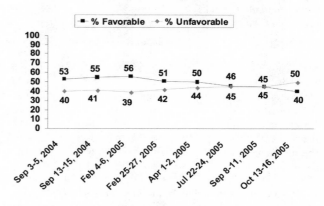

Currently, 52% of Americans have a favorable view and 36% an unfavorable view of the Democratic Party. While this does show some improvement from September (47%), the party's ratings are no more positive than they were earlier this year. In general, the Democratic Party's favorable rating has hovered around 50% this year.

The decline in positive ratings of the GOP has given the Democrats an edge on two key measures related to next year's elections. By a 45% to 32% margin, Americans say the country would be better off if the Democrats rather than Republicans controlled Congress (23% say it does not make any difference). Also, Gallup's latest reading of the generic congressional ballot shows a 50% to 43% edge for the Democratic candidates among registered voters. That suggests

Opinion of the Democratic Party

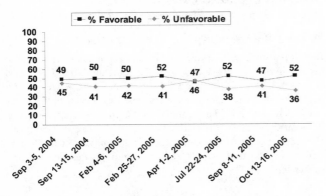

-■- % Favorable   ◆ % Unfavorable

Date	Favorable	Unfavorable
Sep 3-5, 2004	49	45
Sep 13-15, 2004	50	41
Feb 4-6, 2005	50	42
Feb 25-27, 2005	52	41
Apr 1-2, 2005	47	46
Jul 22-24, 2005	52	38
Sep 8-11, 2005	47	41
Oct 13-16, 2005	52	36

the Democrats would do well if the elections were held today, though a lot can change in the next year.

Despite the Democratic advantages on those two measures, the congressional parties get similar marks for how they are currently handling their jobs. Thirty-eight percent approve of the Republicans in Congress, while 41% approve of the Democrats. Both measures are higher than Congress' overall approval rating, which was 29% in the Oct. 13-16 poll.

Democrats Hold Edge on Issues

An Oct. 21-23 CNN/*USA Today*/Gallup poll asked the public whether the Democrats or the Republicans in Congress would better handle each of eight prominent issues. Democrats had the edge on seven of the eight, with terrorism being the only one that tilted in the Republican direction. Democrats hold advantages of 20 or more percentage points on healthcare, Social Security, and gas prices.

Do you think the Republicans in Congress or the Democrats in Congress would do a better job of dealing with each of the following issues and problems? How about—[RANDOM ORDER]?

2005 Oct 21-23	Republicans %	Democrats %	Advantage (pct pts)
Healthcare	30	59	D +29
Social Security	33	56	D +23
Gas prices	31	51	D +20
The economy	38	50	D +12
Corruption in government	33	44	D +11
Taxes	41	49	D +8
The situation in Iraq	40	46	D +6
Terrorism	49	38	R +11

What could be troubling for the Republicans is that Democrats now hold an edge on Iraq and taxes, two issues that had previously favored the Republicans.

The parties score about the same when they are rated on their governing approaches more generally. Just fewer than 6 in 10 Americans say the Democrats and, separately, the Republicans represent their values "very" or "moderately" well. Fifty-nine percent say the Democratic Party represents their attitudes about the role of government at least moderately well, and 57% say this about the Republican Party. Fifty-three percent of Americans say each party shares their attitudes about the role of religion in politics.

How well does the Republican/Democratic Party do each of the following—very well, moderately well, not too well, or not well at all?

Represent your values

	Very well	Moder- ately well	Not too well	Not well at all	No opinion
Republican	24%	33	19	22	2
Democratic	22%	36	22	18	2

Represent your attitude about the role of government

	Very well	Moder- ately well	Not too well	Not well at all	No opinion
Republican	21%	36	21	20	2
Democratic	18%	41	22	17	2

Share your attitudes about the role of religion in politics

	Very well	Moder- ately well	Not too well	Not well at all	No opinion
Republican	22%	31	22	23	2
Democratic	20%	33	21	22	4

Survey Methods

These results are based on telephone interviews with randomly selected national samples of 1,008 adults, aged 18 and older, conducted Oct. 21-23, 2005, and 1,012 adults, aged 18 and older, conducted Oct. 13-16, 2005. For results based on these samples, one can say with 95% confidence that the maximum error attributable to sampling and other random effects is ±3 percentage points. In addition to sampling error, question wording and practical difficulties in conducting surveys can introduce error or bias into the findings of public opinion polls.

November 8, 2005
LITTLE CHANGE IN CRIME RATE FROM LAST YEAR
Almost one in three households victimized by crime in past year

by David W. Moore, Gallup Poll Senior Editor

Gallup's annual update on crime shows that 32% of all U.S. households experienced some type of crime during the past year, including 18% with one incident and 14% with two or more incidents. The poll also shows that 39% of all crime incidents in the past year were not reported to the police.

Gallup added the category of Internet crime in 2003, which has increased the overall rate of crime victimization. Without Internet crime included, the household crime rate is 27%, compared with 25% last year and 26% the year before.

The rate of individual (as opposed to household) victimization is 21% for all crimes, and 16% for crimes not including Internet crimes. Individual crime victimization including Internet crime has been the same for 2003 through 2005. With Internet crime excluded from the computation, the individual crime rate was 18% in 2003, 17% in 2004, and 16% this year. The differences are within the polls' margins of error, suggesting no real change in the individual crime rate.

The two most frequently mentioned crimes in all the polls were having money or property stolen (11% to 16%) and having one's home, car, or property vandalized (11% to 15%). Those two crimes remain at the top of the list this year.

Please tell me which, if any, of these incidents have happened to you or your household within the last 12 months?

CRIME INCIDENT	2000 %	2001 %	2002 %	2003 %	2004 %	2005 %
Money or property stolen from you or another member of your household	14	11	12	14	14	16
A home, car, or property owned by you or other household member vandalized	12	11	15	15	15	15
Your house or apartment broken into	4	3	5	5	3	4
You or other household member mugged or physically assaulted	3	3	3	2	3	4
A car owned by you or other household member stolen	4	3	4	3	4	2
Money or property taken from you or other household member by force, with gun, knife, weapon or physical attack, or by threat of force	2	1	1	2	1	2
You or other household member sexually assaulted	1	na	2	1	*	1
You or another household member was victim of computer/Internet crime	na	na	na	6	8	8
Net percentage of households experiencing any crime	na	na	na	30	30	32
Net percentage of households experiencing any crime (excluding Internet crime)	24	22	25	26	25	27
Net percentage of households experiencing violent crime	3	4	4	5	4	5
Percentage of individuals victimized by crime in past year	na	na	na	21	21	21
Percentage of individuals victimized by crime in past year (not including Internet crime)	15	15	15	18	17	16
Percentage of individuals victimized by violent crime in past year	2	2	2	2	2	3
Percentage of all crime not reported to police	na	na	na	35	44	39

CRIME INCIDENT	2000 %	2001 %	2002 %	2003 %	2004 %	2005 %
Percentage of all crime not reported to police (excluding Internet crime)	29	33	29	32	38	33

*Less than 0.5%
na Not Available

Four percent of respondents this year say their house or apartment was broken into, 4% that someone in the household was mugged, 2% that a car owned by someone in the household was stolen, and 2% that someone in the household was robbed. One percent say that someone in the household was sexually assaulted.

In addition, 8% of Americans report being a victim of a computer or Internet crime, the same as last year.

A net total of 5% of all American households experienced one or more *violent* crimes this past year, compared with 4% the previous year and 5% the year before that.

For the first four years of the annual polls, the percentage of crimes not reported to the police varied between 29% and 33% (excluding Internet crimes). Last year, the percentage of unreported crime incidents jumped to 38%, up from 32% the previous year and 29% in 2002. However, this year, the percentage of unreported crimes (excluding Internet crimes) dropped back to 33%.

If Internet crimes are included in the calculation, roughly the same pattern prevails—44% of crimes were not reported last year, compared with 39% this year.

Crime Highest Among the Young and People in Urban Areas

While there are some variations over the past five years, the highest rates of victimization continue to be among young people and nonwhites. Urban residents have also consistently reported higher crime rates than suburban and rural residents, though the margin has varied over the years. (For purposes of comparison with previous years, Internet crime is excluded.)

CRIME INCIDENTS COMPARED BY SELECTED DEMOGRAPHICS
(Percentage Experiencing Any Crime During Past Year— Excluding Internet Crime)

	2000 %	2001 %	2002 %	2003 %	2004 %	2005 %
All Households	24	22	25	26	25	27
Age						
18-29	39	30	43	41	40	41
30-49	25	27	25	26	28	28
50-64	19	17	20	25	23	21
65+	8	8	12	10	8	17
Race						
Nonwhite	31	32	36	33	29	34
White	23	21	22	24	24	24
Community						
Urban	32	28	35	29	30	29
Suburban	23	20	20	27	23	26
Rural	16	21	23	20	25	24
Income						
<$20,000	18	21	27	25	35	34
$20,000-<$30,000	34	27	29	31	31	18

	2000 %	2001 %	2002 %	2003 %	2004 %	2005 %
$30,000-<$50,000	19	26	26	28	26	23
$50,000-<$75,000	28	19	21	26	22	33
$75,000+	19	22	28	20	21	23

Major Findings

- Forty-one percent of respondents in the youngest age group (18 to 29) report that their household experienced some crime in the past year, compared with 28% in the 30- to 49-year-old group, 21% in the 50 to 64 group, and 17% among people 65 or older. That pattern has been found in each of the past six years.
- White households consistently experience lower rates of crime than nonwhite households. The gap has varied over the past six years, from a low of 5 points last year (29% vs. 24%) to a high of 14 points in 2002 (36% vs. 22%). This year, the gap is 10 points (34% vs. 24%), slightly above the average gap for the half-dozen years.
- Urban households also consistently experience a higher rate of crime than suburban and rural households, but the margin has varied. This year, 29% of urban households report crime, compared with 26% of suburban households, and 24% of rural households. The differences between suburban and rural households have varied, with no clear pattern.
- This year, there is no clear correlation between income and victimization. Thirty-four percent of the lowest-income households report crime, while 33% of households with incomes in the $50,000 to $75,000 range also report some crime. Twenty-three percent of households with more than $75,000 a year report crime, the same percentage as households with $30,000 to $50,000 a year.

Survey Methods

The results reported here are based on telephone interviews with a randomly selected sample of 1,012 national adults, aged 18 and older, conducted Oct. 13-16, 2005. For results based on the total sample of national adults, one can say with 95% confidence that the maximum margin of sampling error is ±3 percentage points. In addition to sampling error, question wording and practical difficulties in conducting surveys can introduce error or bias into the findings of public opinion polls.

November 8, 2005
AMERICANS TENTATIVE ABOUT TEACHER TENURE
Half are at least somewhat familiar with the practice

by Linda Lyons, Education and Youth Editor

Among the ballot issues Californians will vote on in Tuesday's special election is whether to extend the probationary period before public school teachers become tenured from two to five years. If Proposition 74—also known as the "Put the Kids First" initiative—passes, California would become the third state to require a five-year trial period. A majority of states require three-year periods. Under California's initiative, it would also be easier for schools to fire

tenured public school teachers after two consecutive "unsatisfactory" performance reviews.

A recent Gallup Poll* asked about the issue of teacher tenure. Only half of Americans are at least somewhat familiar with the practice of granting tenure—or permanent status—to public school teachers.

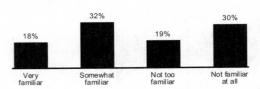

How familiar are you with the practice of granting tenure to public school teachers?

Respondents who currently have children enrolled in public schools are no more likely to be familiar with the policy of teacher tenure than are those with no children in grades kindergarten through 12. But acquaintance with the policy does vary by level of respondent education. Just 32% of Americans with a high school education or less are very or somewhat familiar with the practice, compared with 79% of those with a postgraduate education, 61% of college graduates, and 56% of Americans who have had at least some college.

Tenure-track positions are often coveted by professors at colleges and universities, which may be why familiarity is skewed toward Americans with higher education. Fred Glass, director of communications for the California Federation of Teachers, isn't surprised that many Americans are unfamiliar with the concept of tenure. "They've had far fewer opportunities to get to know and talk to educators," he says.

Tenure Pros and Cons

Gallup asked Americans whether they favor the practice of tenure for public school teachers. The majority, 58%, do not have an opinion. Among those who do, opinion is fairly evenly divided—19% of Americans say they favor tenure and 22% oppose it.

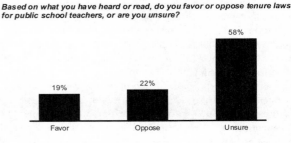

Based on what you have heard or read, do you favor or oppose tenure laws for public school teachers, or are you unsure?

Among the roughly 20% of Americans who are "very familiar" with the practice of tenure, 44% are in favor, 40% are opposed, and 16% have no opinion.

Those in favor, including teacher unions and state school board associations, have long held that tenure is necessary to protect teachers from dismissals based on unpopular opinions, arbitrary administrations, or simply the ebb and flow of cultural tides. "I'm in favor of job security for all types of work, including teaching," says Todd, a 45-year-old respondent from Maine who is "somewhat familiar" with tenure and likes what he sees. "Teachers put in a lot of time and they deserve to know their job will always be there."

Others feel granting tenure too often encourages teachers to become complacent about the quality of their work—or worse, keeps bad teachers in the classroom far too long. "I can understand why teachers want tenure," says Betty, a 73-year-old respondent from Michigan. "We have a lot of good teachers, but some bad ones, too—teachers who just put in their time. They know they can't be fired so they don't really care about the kids. It should be much easier to get rid of the bad apples and just keep the good ones."

Bottom Line

Tenure is a complex issue, even apart from the fact that specific tenure policies vary from state to state, so it's not surprising many Americans say they are not really familiar with it. It also affects only a small segment of the population. Many may be unclear as to just what rights tenured teachers have, or whether they can *ever* be fired.

Glass points out that tenured teachers can be fired—at least in his state. "Tenure is not a job for life," he says. "In California, it is simply the right to a hearing *before* being fired, during which reasons for termination must be presented. According to our attorney, 99% of cases in which a teacher *should* be fired but is not, it's because the administration has not documented the grievance properly—it's not the fault of tenure or the teacher's union."

Whether Proposition 74 passes—or is defeated, as Glass and his union hopes—Elizabeth, a 41-year-old respondent from Missouri, sums up a middle position that would probably sit well with many Americans. "Experience is important," she says, "and tenure is one way to reward experience. However, there has to be a system of due process, checks, and balances so that teachers *can* be fired—just not too easily."

Results are based on telephone interviews with 1,001 national adults, aged 18 and older, conducted Aug. 8-11, 2005. For results based on the total sample of national adults, one can say with 95% confidence that the margin of sampling error is ±3 percentage points.

November 8, 2005
GOVERNMENT REGULATION: PUBLIC BACK TO BUSINESS AS USUAL
Plurality thinks amount of involvement is "about right"

by Raksha Arora, Business and Economy Editor

Three years after a glut of business scandals, Americans have essentially returned to their pre-Enron comfort zone in regard to government regulation of business and industry. In a recent Gallup survey*, a plurality of Americans (40%) say they think there is about the right amount of regulation, a third say there is "too much," and roughly a quarter say there is "too little." Americans were less content only a few years ago.

In September 2001, Americans were more than twice as likely to say there was too much regulation as to say too little. However, all that was about to change. The Justice Department began its criminal investigation of the Enron's bankruptcy in January 2002 and a spate of corporate scandals followed at Adelphia, Tyco, Global Crossing, and WorldCom, among others. The percentage of Americans saying there was too little government regulation of business and industry reached a high point in June of that year.

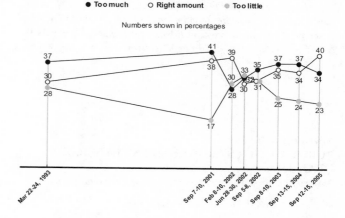

In general, do you think there is too much, too little, or about the right amount of government regulation of business and industry?

● Too much   ○ Right amount   ● Too little

Numbers shown in percentages

After the Sarbanes-Oxley Act that tightened accounting reporting requirements was signed into law in late 2002, the surge in support for more government regulation began to subside.

Demographic Differences

Interestingly, men favor less involvement than women do when it comes to regulation of business—41% of male respondents say there is too much regulation of business, compared with 28% of female respondents.

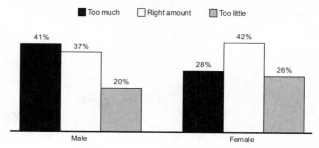

In general, do you think there is too much, too little, or about the right amount of government regulation of business and industry?

■ Too much   □ Right amount   ▨ Too little

The Republican Party is often characterized as anti-regulation and pro-business. Republicans are more likely than Democrats or political independents to say there is too much government regulation of business and industry. Forty-two percent of Republicans say

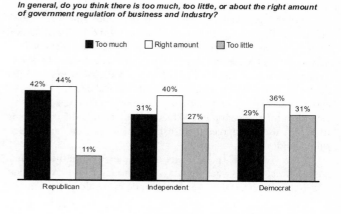

In general, do you think there is too much, too little, or about the right amount of government regulation of business and industry?

■ Too much   □ Right amount   ▨ Too little

there is too much regulation, compared with 31% of independents and 29% of Democrats.

Results are based on telephone interviews with 921 national adults, aged 18 and older, conducted Sept. 12-15, 2005. For results based on the total sample of national adults, one can say with 95% confidence that the margin of sampling error is ±4 percentage points.

November 8, 2005
PUBLIC DUBIOUS ABOUT BUSH'S LEADERSHIP QUALITIES
Majority disagrees with president on issues that matter most

by Joseph Carroll, Gallup Poll Assistant Editor

President George W. Bush's job approval ratings have hovered around the 40% mark for the last month. It appears much of the public is at odds with the president on a more personal level, too: Americans are divided as to whether Bush has the personality and leadership qualities a president should have, and a majority disagree with the president on issues that matter most to them.

A recent CNN/*USA Today*/Gallup poll*, conducted just prior to Supreme Court nominee Harriet Miers' withdrawal and former White House staffer Lewis "Scooter" Libby's indictment, finds the percentage of Americans who agree that Bush has the personality and leadership qualities a president should possess has dipped below the 50% mark for the first time in his presidency.

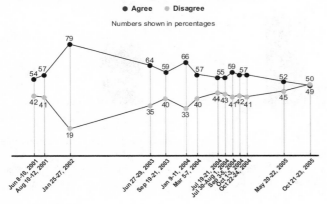

Please tell me whether you agree or disagree that George W. Bush has the personality and leadership qualities a president should have.

● Agree ● Disagree

Numbers shown in percentages

Gallup has asked this question many times since Bush took office in 2001. Early in his administration, a June 2001 Gallup Poll found a majority of Americans (54%) agreeing that Bush had the personality and leadership qualities that a president should possess. This percentage surged to 79% in January 2002, a few months after the Sept. 11 terrorist attacks. By June 2003, it had decreased to 64%, and then dropped again to 59% that September. Throughout Bush's campaign for re-election in 2004, a majority of Americans (ranging from 55% to 59%) agreed that Bush had the personality and leadership qualities to be president.

Views of Bush's personality and leadership qualities turned somewhat sour this year. In May, a slim majority of Americans (52%) said Bush has these qualities, while 45% said he does not.

Majority Disagrees With Bush on Important Issues

The Oct. 21-23 poll also finds only about 4 in 10 Americans say they agree with Bush on the issues that matter most to them.

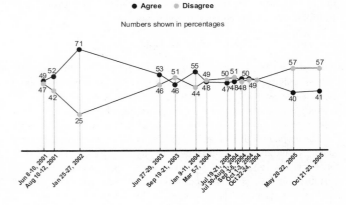

Please tell me whether you agree or disagree with George W. Bush on the issues that matter most to you.

● Agree ● Disagree

Numbers shown in percentages

Shortly after Bush took office, Americans were divided as to whether they agreed (49%) or disagreed (47%) with him on the issues that mattered most to them. By August 2001, Americans became slightly more positive on this question, with a slight majority (52%) saying they agreed with Bush.

In January 2002, as Bush's job ratings soared following the 9/11 attacks, the percentage saying they agreed with Bush on important issues jumped to 71%. But that accord began to fade after the United States military action began in Iraq in 2003. By September, the percentage had dropped to 46%.

A majority of Americans, 55%, again said in January 2004 that they agreed with Bush on important issues. But throughout the 2004 election campaign, Americans were more divided on this question.

Partisanship Shapes Perceptions of Leadership Qualities, Agreement on Issues

Both of these measures differ starkly between Republicans and Democrats.

- Nine in 10 Republicans (91%) say they agree that Bush has the personality and leadership qualities a president should have. Forty-one percent of independents and just 13% of Democrats share this view.

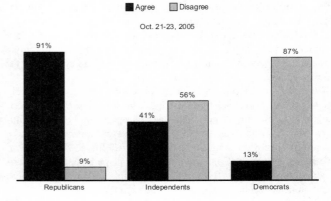

Agreement That Bush Has the Personality and Leadership Qualities to Be President

■ Agree ■ Disagree

Oct. 21-23, 2005

- More than 8 in 10 Republicans (84%) say they agree with Bush on the issues that matter most to them. Among independents, 34% agree with this statement, and among Democrats, just 5% agree.

Agreement With Bush on the Issues That Matter Most to You

■ Agree ☐ Disagree

Oct. 21-23, 2005

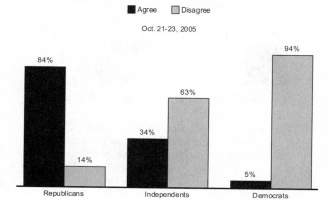

Gallup has consistently found vast partisan differences on both of the measures since Bush first took office. The single exception is the January 2002 poll, four months after the Sept. 11 attacks, in which partisan differences were not nearly as dramatic. In that poll, a majority of Republicans (98%), independents (76%), and Democrats (61%) agreed Bush had the personality and leadership qualities to be president. Ninety-seven percent of Republicans in that same poll said they agreed with Bush on the issues that matter most, while 65% of independents and 47% of Democrats concurred.

Results are based on telephone interviews with 1,008 national adults, aged 18 and older, conducted Oct. 21-23, 2005. For results based on the total sample of national adults, one can say with 95% confidence that the maximum margin of sampling error is ±3 percentage points. In addition to sampling error, question wording and practical difficulties in conducting surveys can introduce error or bias into the findings of public opinion polls.

November 8, 2005
INDEPENDENTS, MODERATE REPUBLICANS LEAD DECLINE IN BUSH RATINGS
Any further losses depend on Republican support

by Jeffrey M. Jones, Gallup Poll Managing Editor

About a year ago, George W. Bush was celebrating his re-election with a 51% majority of the popular vote. Much has changed in the meantime, and Bush's job approval rating is hovering in the low 40% range amid continued difficulties in Iraq, concerns about the economy, a White House scandal after the CIA leak, and a failed Supreme Court nomination.

Bush has been able to maintain the loyalties of most Republicans since he took office, although he gave conservative Republicans some possible reasons to be displeased with the nomination of Harriet Miers to the Supreme Court rather than a more credentialed jurist, record budget deficits, and increased government spending.

The near-universal rally in support that Bush enjoyed after the 9/11 terrorist attacks faded fairly quickly among Democrats.

Combined Gallup Poll data from post-election 2004 and late September and October 2005 allow for a more detailed comparison than is usually possible of where Bush's job approval rating has changed, spanning the political spectrum from liberal Democrats to conservative Republicans.

In the past year, conservative Republicans have become less likely to approve of Bush, but the decline has been more pronounced among moderate and liberal Republicans and independents.

Bush Approval Ratings, by Party and Ideology

	Nov-Dec 2004 %	Sep-Oct 2005 %	Change
Overall Approval Average	52	42	-10
Liberal Democrat	9	7	-2
Moderate Democrat	14	12	-2
Conservative Democrat	25	17	-8
Pure Independent	42	28	-14
Moderate/Liberal Republican	83	69	-14
Conservative Republican	94	87	-7

All six groups show at least some decline in approval of Bush. Liberal and moderate Democrats have shown the least change, but that is mainly because their support of Bush was so low to begin with.

There have been double-digit decreases in Bush approval ratings among pure independents (those who are independent and do not "lean" toward either party) and moderate and liberal Republicans. Pure independents' support has fallen from 42% to 28%, while moderate and liberal Republicans' support has dropped from 83% to 69%.

Conservative Republicans remain overwhelmingly likely to approve of Bush, but his support among this group has fallen below 90% in the past 11 months.

Implications

Any further significant losses in Bush approval will depend on whether he loses additional Republican support. If Bush lost *all* remaining support from Democrats (while maintaining his current levels of independent and Republican support), he would still have a 36% job approval rating, only slightly lower than his current 41% reading. If he also lost all support among pure independents as well, his rating would still be 34%. [These estimates also assume no change in the proportion of Republicans, Democrats, and independents in the adult population. If Bush were to lose additional popular support, it would not be unexpected for those party proportions to shift in a more Democratic direction.]

Falling below 40% approval, as Bush did in the Oct. 13-16 CNN/*USA Today*/Gallup poll, is not uncommon for presidents—all presidents since Lyndon Johnson have done so. But only four presidents since 1945—Harry Truman, Richard Nixon, Jimmy Carter, and the elder George Bush—have dropped below 30%. If the sitting president were to sink to those depths, he would be doing so because his own partisans were no longer supporting him.

Data are based on combined samples of 4,036 adults, taken from four polls conducted in November to December 2004, and 4,667 adults, taken from five polls conducted Sept. 26-Oct 30, 2005. Party and ideology groups are defined as follows:

Liberal Democrats: Self-identify as Democrat or independent who leans to the Democratic Party, and self-identifies as having a liberal ideology. N=748 in 2005, 679 in 2004.

Moderate Democrats: Self-identify as Democrat or independent who leans to the Democratic Party, and self-identifies as having a moderate ideology. N=1,099 in 2005, 808 in 2004.

Conservative Democrats: Self-identify as Democrat or independent who leans to the Democratic Party, and self-identifies as having a conservative ideology. N=391 in 2005, 317 in 2004.

Pure independent: Self-identify as independent and does not lean to either party. N=331 in 2005, 212 in 2004.

Liberal/Moderate Republicans: Self-identify as Republican or independent who leans to the Republican Party, and self-identifies as having a liberal or moderate ideology. Liberal and moderates are combined given the relatively low proportion of liberal Republicans. N=761 in 2005, 641 in 2004.

Conservative Republicans: Self-identify as Republican or independent who leans to the Republican Party, and self-identifies as having a conservative ideology. N=1,270 in 2005, 1,337 in 2004.

November 9, 2005

IRAQ ATTITUDES SHOW LITTLE CHANGE IMMEDIATELY AFTER LIBBY INDICTMENTS
Perceptions of the war are sour, but little different from recent months

by Lydia Saad, Gallup Poll Senior Editor

Political criticism of the Bush administration's Iraq policy intensified in recent weeks with the Oct. 28 indictment of White House aide I. Lewis Libby Jr. The larger controversy swirling around Libby, who resigned following his indictments, involves his role in an alleged White House plot to retaliate against former Ambassador Joseph C. Wilson for asserting that the Bush administration had exaggerated the nuclear threat Iraq posed.

Despite this renewed focus on the White House's tactics in leading the country to war, Gallup finds little change in the percentage of Americans saying the Bush administration deliberately misled the public about whether Iraq has weapons of mass destruction. This is according to a CNN/*USA Today*/Gallup poll conducted immediately after the announcement of the Libby indictments. As was true in late July, a slim majority of Americans (53%) surveyed Oct. 28-30 said Bush had misled Americans; 45% disagreed.

There has also been no noteworthy change in the percentage of Americans saying it was a mistake to send U.S. troops to Iraq to begin with. The latest CNN/*USA Today*/Gallup poll, conducted Oct. 28-30, finds 54% saying it was a mistake to send troops to Iraq. This is up from 49% saying the same a week earlier (as Iraqi voters were approving a new constitution), but is similar to the 53% to 59% recorded in August and September.

It is clear that the public is much more critical today of the Iraq war than it was at the outset. However, a broad view of Gallup trends suggests that most of this shift occurred within the first year of the war. Mounting U.S. casualties and renewed questions about Bush's motives for the war have triggered only a slight increase in public

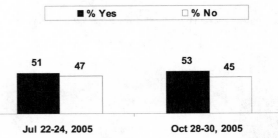

Do you think the Bush administration deliberately misled the American public about whether Iraq has weapons of mass destruction, or not?

■ % Yes   □ % No

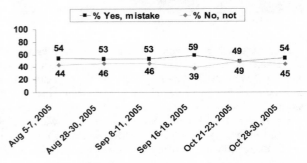

In view of the developments since we first sent our troops to Iraq, do you think the United States made a mistake in sending troops to Iraq, or not?

-■- % Yes, mistake   ◆ % No, not

opposition to the war—perhaps because these negatives are offset by positive factors surrounding Saddam Hussein's capture and democratic developments in Iraq, such as elections and the drafting of a constitution.

In the war's earliest stages, in the spring of 2003, only 31% of Americans believed Bush had deliberately misled the public about Iraq's weapons capacities, only 29% thought the war was going badly for the United States, and only 23% thought that sending U.S. troops to Iraq was a mistake. By the following year, in July 2004, these figures had risen to roughly 50% or more. Since then, the percentages saying Bush misled the public and that it was a mistake to send troops have each risen slightly, while the percentage saying things are going badly for the United States has remained about the same.

Summary of Iraq Views — Selected Trends

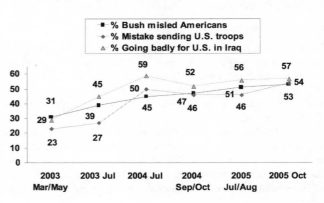

-■- % Bush misled Americans
◆ % Mistake sending U.S. troops
△ % Going badly for U.S. in Iraq

No Mere Exaggeration

Along with this rise in negative views about the United States' involvement in Iraq, there has been increased skepticism about the degree to which the Bush administration exaggerated the threat Iraq posed. At three different points, Gallup has asked respondents who think Bush misled Americans about the war to specify whether Bush merely exaggerated some specific details or greatly overstated the threat Iraq posed. And at each point, the majority of this group perceived that Bush had greatly overstated the threat.

Among the public as a whole, that figure is now 41%, up from 21% in May 2003 and 24% in July 2003.

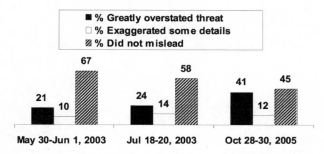

Perceptions of Bush Administration's Description of Iraqi Threat

■ % Greatly overstated threat
□ % Exaggerated some details
▨ % Did not mislead

These perceptions are highly related to partisan politics: only 14% of Republicans believe Bush greatly overstated the threat, compared with 66% of Democrats. Similarly, 8 in 10 Republicans say Bush did not deliberately mislead the public at all on this issue, compared with only 14% of Democrats.

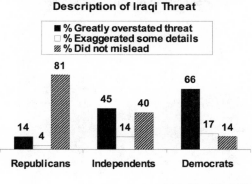

Perceptions of Bush Administration's Description of Iraqi Threat

■ % Greatly overstated threat
□ % Exaggerated some details
▨ % Did not mislead

Oct. 28–30, 2005

Survey Methods

These results are based on telephone interviews with a randomly selected national sample of 800 adults, aged 18 and older, conducted Oct. 28-30, 2005. For results based on this sample, one can say with 95% confidence that the maximum error attributable to sampling and other random effects is ±4 percentage points. In addition to sampling error, question wording and practical difficulties in conducting surveys can introduce error or bias into the findings of public opinion polls.

November 10, 2005
CONFIDENCE IN LOCAL POLICE DROPS TO 10-YEAR LOW
Percentage respecting police at a new low

by Jeffrey M. Jones, Gallup Poll Managing Editor

After several years of stable readings, Gallup's latest update on confidence in the police to protect people from violent crime has fallen this year, to a level not seen since 1995. The decline in confidence has generally occurred across demographic subgroups, as members of most key groups are less confident in the police this year than last. Gallup also finds a new low in the percentage of Americans who say they have a "great deal" of respect for the police in their area. Meanwhile, there has been no change in Americans' beliefs about police brutality occurring in their local areas.

Gallup's annual Crime Poll, conducted Oct. 13-16, finds 53% of Americans with "a great deal" or "quite a lot" of confidence in the police to protect them from violent crime. Last year, 61% expressed the same level of confidence. Confidence in this regard has been near or above 60% since 1998.

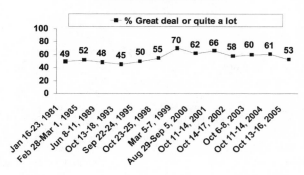

Confidence in the Police

The decline in confidence is probably a recent phenomenon. When Gallup asked its "confidence in institutions" question sequence in May 2005, there was little change in expressed confidence in the police compared with May 2004. One possible reason for the decline is that the poll was conducted shortly after media reports showed video of an Oct. 8 arrest during which New Orleans police allegedly beat a man outside a club in that city. Another possibility is that ratings of police are being dragged down by the same forces that are causing declines in ratings of the president, Congress, and overall satisfaction with the way things are going in the country.

The decline is evident among most demographic groups. There are some exceptions to that general pattern, as non-whites, older Americans (aged 65 and older), urban residents, political moderates, and independents have shown little change since 2004. Those whose households were victimized by crime in the last 12 months also show no change in confidence; however, their expressed level of confidence in 2004 was among the lowest of all subgroups.

A comparison of the current data with data from 1999 (the high point in measured confidence) shows that confidence in the police among non-whites, moderates, and independents decreased prior to this year, and no additional deterioration has occurred in the last 12 months.

Interestingly, older Americans are about as confident in the police now (72%) as they were during the high point of 1999 (76%).

Confidence in Police, Selected Years
by Demographic Subgroup

	1999 %	2004 %	2005 %
Overall	*70*	*61*	*53*
Men	68	58	50
Women	71	64	56
White	73	66	57
Non-white	57	44	40
Black	54	32	32
18- to 29-year-olds	66	51	43
30- to 49-year-olds	68	61	56
50- to 64-year-olds	71	60	46
65 years old and older	76	74	72
East	69	65	57
Midwest	71	62	52
South	67	58	52
West	73	62	54
Urban	N/A	55	54
Suburban	N/A	66	54
Rural	N/A	59	50
High school grad or less	68	59	52
Some college	67	60	49
College grad	77	64	59
Post-grad	78	68	59
Less than $30,000	66	52	50
$30,000 to $74,999	71	63	52
$75,000 or more	79	67	57
Liberal	64	57	40
Moderate	72	61	57
Conservative	71	66	58
Democrat	68	58	52
Independent	65	48	49
Republican	79	78	60
Married	N/A	68	58
Not married	N/A	53	48
Children under age 18	N/A	58	54
No children under age 18	N/A	63	54
Employed	N/A	60	49
Not employed	N/A	64	60
Attend church weekly	N/A	66	61
Attend church nearly weekly/monthly	N/A	68	57
Seldom/never attend	N/A	55	48
Gun in household	N/A	63	52
No gun	N/A	61	54
Crime victim, last 12 months	N/A	48	46
Not crime victim	N/A	67	56

Gallup also measures a new low in the public's respect for the police in their local area, a question that Gallup has asked periodically since 1965. Fifty-six percent of Americans now say they have a great deal of respect for the police in their area. The last time Gallup asked this question, in 2000, 60% said they respected the police in their area a great deal. During the 1960s, greater than 7 in 10 Americans had a great deal of respect for their local police.

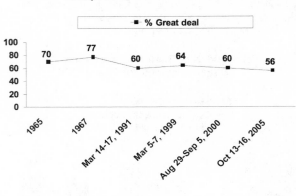

Respect for Police in Your Area

One measure that does not show any change is the public's perception of the existence of police brutality in their area. Thirty-one percent of Americans believe there is police brutality in their area, while 65% say there is not. That compares with a Gallup finding in 2000, when 32% said they believed police brutality existed in their area. The two most recent measurements represent a decline from the 1990s, but are much higher than Gallup measured in the 1960s, when fewer than 1 in 10 Americans thought police brutality was occurring in their local areas.

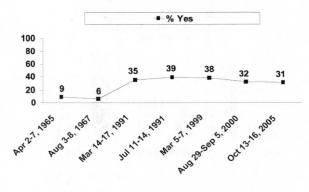

Police Brutality in Your Area?

Survey Methods

These results are based on telephone interviews with a randomly selected national sample of 1,012 adults, aged 18 and older, conducted Oct. 13-16, 2005. For results based on this sample, one can say with 95% confidence that the maximum error attributable to sampling and other random effects is ±3 percentage points. In addition to sampling error, question wording and practical difficulties in conducting surveys can introduce error or bias into the findings of public opinion polls.

November 11, 2005

AMERICANS SUPPORT CONGRESSIONAL INVESTIGATION INTO OIL PROFITS
Image of oil and gas industry remains very negative

by Frank Newport, Gallup Poll Editor in Chief

The nation's major oil and gas companies aren't regarded very highly by the American public. Americans strongly support the idea that Congress should investigate oil company profits, and as a result, most presumably welcomed Wednesday's televised Senate hearings at which oil company executives were grilled about their companies' huge third-quarter profits.

More generally, Gallup polling shows a sizable majority of Americans view the oil and gas industry negatively, that Americans blame the oil companies more than the Bush administration or Congress for the increase in gasoline prices, and that Americans believe the gas companies took unfair advantage of the late summer hurricanes to charge higher gas prices. Perhaps most troubling for oil company management, a majority of Americans—including half of Republicans—say the federal government should regulate the price of gasoline.

Investigation and Regulation of Oil Companies

The five oil company executives who testified at the Senate hearing were asked repeatedly about their companies' extraordinary profits and their own personal compensation at a time in which many Americans were having to stretch their pocketbooks to pay in the neighborhood of $3 a gallon for gas. An overwhelming 8 in 10 Americans want Congress to investigate oil company profits.

Do you think Congress should hold an investigation into the profits that oil companies have made in the past few months, or do you think an investigation is not necessary?

	Yes, should	*No, not necessary*	*No opinion*
2005 Oct 28-30	82%	17	1

There are often partisan differences on issues relating to regulating and investigating big business, but in this case, strong majorities of Republicans, independents, and Democrats say that Congress should investigate. This is not surprising. Even strong oil industry supporters such as Sen. Larry Craig, R-Idaho, said at the hearings that "it's not terribly fun" defending the oil companies to his constituents who repeatedly ask him about oil company profits at town hall meetings.

The oil company executives appeared to have escaped Wednesday's hearings relatively unscathed, but what presumably strikes fear in their hearts would be the idea of increased government regulation of their products and services. At this point, that proposal would pass if put to a vote of the American people.

Do you think the federal government should— or should not—regulate the price of gasoline?

	Yes, should	*No, should not*	*No opinion*
2005 Oct 28-30	53%	43	4

By a 10-point margin, Americans say the federal government should regulate the price of gasoline.

Interestingly, there is not a great deal of partisan differentiation on this issue either: 50% of Republicans and independents favor federal regulation of gas prices, compared with 59% of Democrats.

Oil as the Major Economic Problem Facing the U.S.

Americans' negative views of the oil and gas companies—and their desire to see the government do something about them—are certainly related to the fact that gas prices continue to be seen as the top economic problem facing the country today. One in four Americans named energy prices as the most important economic problem in September and October Gallup Poll surveys. (This was down from the high point of 34% who mentioned fuel prices in August.)

What is the most important economic problem facing the country today? [OPEN-ENDED]

Recent Trend:

	Oct 24-27, 2005 %	Sep 26-28, 2005 %	Aug 22-25, 2005 %	Jul 25-28, 2005 %	Jun 16-19, 2005 %	May 23-26, 2005 %
Fuel/oil prices	24	25	34	14	15	10
Unemployment/Jobs/ Wages	15	14	15	19	19	18
War in Iraq	10	11	10	11	9	11
Healthcare/Health insurance costs	6	6	6	7	12	11
Dealing with natural disasters	6	11	—	—	—	—
Inflation/Rising prices	5	4	4	4	5	5
Outsourcing of jobs	5	4	5	7	5	8
Federal budget deficit	4	6	5	5	6	4
Lack of money	4	3	2	4	5	4
Poorly run government/ Politics	3	2	1	1	2	1
Illegal immigrants	2	2	2	2	3	4
Poverty/Hunger/ Homelessness	2	2	3	2	2	2
Taxes	2	3	2	2	4	3
Social Security	2	1	3	4	6	6
Foreign aid/Focus on other countries	2	1	*	1	1	1
Education reform	2	2	2	1	4	2
Gap between rich and poor	1	1	1	1	1	1
Senior care/Medicare	1	1	1	1	1	1
Credit cards/Overspending	1	1	1	2	2	2
Trade deficit	1	1	1	3	2	3
Security/Threat of terrorism	1	*	2	3	1	—
George W. Bush/ His policies	1	1	1	1	1	1
Economy (non-specific)	1	1	2	1	2	1
Companies closing/ No growth	1	*	1	2	1	—
Interest rates	1	1	*	1	*	*
Welfare	*	1	1	1	1	1
International relations	*	*	1	*	*	*
Retirement	*	—	*	1	1	1
College tuition expenses	*	*	*	1	*	*
Stock market	*	—	—	*	*	*

	Oct 24-27, 2005 %	Sep 26-28, 2005 %	Aug 22-25, 2005 %	Jul 25-28, 2005 %	Jun 16-19, 2005 %	May 23-26, 2005 %
Other	4	5	5	6	9	7
None	1	*	1	1	1	2
No opinion	6	7	6	8	9	9

Percentages add to more than 100% due to multiple responses.
Contact Gallup for full trend.
*Less than 0.5%

Energy Industry Image

Some may ask whether the recent run-up in gas prices and the heat the oil companies are taking in Congress will hurt the image of the oil and gas industry. There's not much chance of that, given that its image is so negative to begin with.

Gallup's August rating of the images of various business and industry sectors showed that only 20% of Americans rated the oil and gas industry positively, while 62% rated it negatively. This net -42-point rating is by far the most negative of any of the 25 industry sectors tested, well below the second-most negative, the legal field, at -20 points. By contrast, Americans have a net positive image of +50 points for the restaurant industry, which is at the top of the list.

On another subject, for each of the following business sectors in the United States, please say whether your overall view of it is very positive, somewhat positive, neutral, somewhat negative or very negative. How about—[RANDOM ORDER]?

BASED ON 497 NATIONAL ADULTS IN FORM A

2005 Aug 8-11 (sorted by "net positive")	Total positive %	Neutral %	Total negative %	Net positive %
Restaurant industry	58	31	8	**+50**
Computer industry	57	30	10	**+47**
Farming and agriculture	58	27	13	**+45**
Grocery industry	58	27	15	**+43**
Retail industry	52	31	15	**+37**
Travel industry	48	35	13	**+35**
Accounting	42	40	14	**+28**
Internet industry	46	27	22	**+24**
Banking	46	31	22	**+24**
Real estate industry	46	29	23	**+23**
Education	52	18	29	**+23**
Publishing industry	42	35	20	**+22**
Automobile industry	42	29	26	**+16**
Telephone industry	40	31	27	**+13**
Airline industry	38	32	27	**+11**
Electric and gas utilities	36	24	38	**-2**
Television and radio industry	35	25	38	**-3**
Sports industry	33	26	38	**-5**
Advertising and public relations industry	30	32	35	**-5**
Movie industry	33	25	39	**-6**
The federal government	33	20	45	**-12**
Pharmaceutical industry	29	22	47	**-18**
Healthcare industry	32	16	50	**-18**
The legal field	27	24	47	**-20**
Oil and gas industry	20	17	62	**-42**

This negative image of the oil and gas industry is not something that has just developed as a result of the most recent increase in gas prices. The positive ratings for the industry have ranged only between the current 20% and 35% (2003) over the last five years, but in all instances, the negatives have far outweighed the positives.

This year, however, does mark the high point for "very" negative ratings of the oil and gas industry. Thirty-five percent of Americans give this rating, well above the previous high point of 23% very negative measured last year.

Oil and gas industry

	Very positive %	Somewhat positive %	Neutral %	Somewhat negative %	Very negative %	No opinion %
2005 Aug 8-11	9	11	17	27	35	1
2004 Aug 9-11	6	15	18	35	23	3
2003 Aug 4-6	9	26	22	29	14	*
2002 Aug 5-8	6	19	28	28	16	3
2001 Aug 16-19	7	17	21	33	21	1

*Less than 0.5%

Blame

Given these data, it is not surprising to find that Americans were quick to blame oil companies for the rapid run-up in gasoline prices at the end of August. A late August Gallup Poll found that 54% of Americans blamed oil companies a great deal for the recent increases in gasoline prices, compared with 38% who blamed the Bush administration this much, 27% who blamed the Republicans in Congress, and 12% who blamed the Democrats in Congress.

How much do you blame each of the following for the recent increase in gasoline prices—a great deal, a moderate amount, not much, or not at all? How about—[RANDOM ORDER]?

2005 Aug 28-30 (sorted by "great deal")	Great deal %	Great deal/ Moderate amount %	Not much/ Not at all %
Oil companies in the U.S.	54	84	15
The Bush administration	38	63	36
The Republicans in Congress	27	57	40
The Democrats in Congress	12	46	50

Americans also were overwhelmingly more likely to agree (in a Sept. 5-6 Gallup survey) that gas companies were taking advantage of the [hurricane] situation and charging unfair prices (79%), rather than to agree that the gas companies were charging fair prices given the conditions the hurricane caused (only 18% chose this option).

Survey Methods

These results are based on telephone interviews with a randomly selected national sample of 800 adults, aged 18 and older, conducted Oct. 28-30, 2005. For results based on this sample, one can say with 95% confidence that the maximum error attributable to sampling and other random effects is ±4 percentage points. In addition to sampling error, question wording and practical difficulties in conducting surveys can introduce error or bias into the findings of public opinion polls.

November 14, 2005
AMERICANS GENERALLY FAVOR ALITO APPOINTMENT
Closer to Roberts than to Miers in popularity

by Lydia Saad, Gallup Poll Senior Editor

The American public generally supports President George W. Bush's third nominee to replace Supreme Court Justice Sandra Day O'Connor. By a 2-to-1 margin, 50% to 25%, Americans say the Senate should vote to confirm Judge Samuel Alito. Another 25% of Americans have no opinion about his confirmation—not atypical for public attitudes about Supreme Court nominees.

This 50% support for Alito contrasts with the more restrained support received by the previous nominee, White House counsel Harriet Miers, before she withdrew her name amid growing controversy over her candidacy. In Gallup's initial reading on Miers, only 44% of Americans said she should be confirmed, while 36% disagreed.

Public support for Alito is only slightly less favorable than that for Judge John Roberts when Bush initially named him to succeed the retiring Justice O'Connor.

Initial Public Reaction to George W. Bush's Supreme Court Nominees: Should the Senate Vote in Favor?

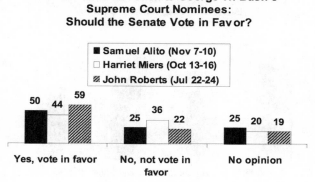

Reaction to Alito differs by party, although not overwhelmingly so. While the vast majority of Republicans (73%) favor Alito's confirmation, fewer than half of Democrats (40%) oppose it. In fact, by a 40% to 35% margin, only a slight plurality of Democrats oppose Alito's confirmation.

Initial Public Reaction to Alito Nomination: Should the Senate Vote in Favor?
by party ID

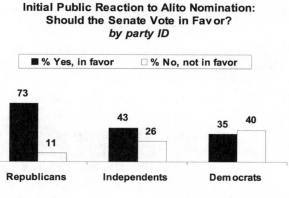

Nov. 7-10, 2005

The results are similar according to self-described ideology, although perhaps a bit starker. Those identifying themselves as politically conservative favor Alito's confirmation by a margin of 75%

to 6%. Those identifying themselves as liberals oppose it by a margin of 49% to 28%.

Alito v. Miers and Roberts

There has been about a 40-point gap between Republicans and Democrats in their initial support levels for each of the three Supreme Court nominees Bush has put forth this year—Alito, Miers, and Roberts. In each case, a majority of Republicans have favored the confirmation, but to varying degrees.

At the same time, differences in the overall level of public support for each nominee reflect important distinctions in the support levels among Democrats, with a plurality of Democrats supporting Roberts, Democrats closely divided on Alito, and generally opposing Miers.

In Miers' case, 73% of Republicans thought she should be confirmed while 16% disagreed. Democrats reacted quite differently, with 27% favoring her confirmation and 53% opposing it.

Initial Public Reaction to Miers Nomination: Should the Senate Vote in Favor?
by party ID

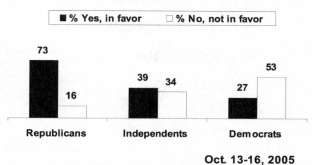

Oct. 13-16, 2005

In Roberts' case, the vast majority of Republicans (82%) wanted to see him confirmed; only 5% disagreed. This higher level of support (as compared with Miers) is also seen with Democrats, among whom the plurality (42%) favored his confirmation.

Initial Public Reaction to Roberts Nomination: Should the Senate Vote in Favor?
by party ID

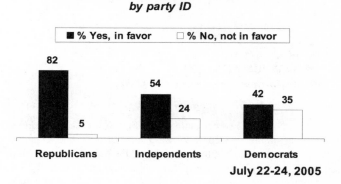

July 22-24, 2005

Historical Comparisons

Support for Alito's nomination puts him more in the company of Roberts, Ruth Bader Ginsburg (nominated by Bill Clinton in 1993), and Clarence Thomas (nominated by George H.W. Bush in 1991)—

all of whom were ultimately confirmed by the U.S. Senate—than it does in the category of unsuccessful nominees such as Miers and Robert Bork (nominated by Ronald Reagan in 1987).

Alito's 50% support from the general public compares with 31% for Bork, 44% for Miers, 52% for Thomas, 53% for Ginsburg, and 59% for Roberts.

When factoring in the percentage who did not want to see each of these nominees confirmed, the "net support" for Alito—as was true for Ginsburg, Roberts, and Thomas—is strongly positive, although Alito is at the bottom of the pack. By contrast, the "net support" for Miers and Bork (whose nomination was rejected by the U.S. Senate) was only in the single digits.

Net Support for Supreme Court Nominees
% confirm minus *% do not confirm*

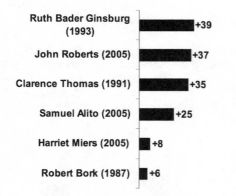

Survey Methods

These results are based on telephone interviews with a randomly selected national sample of 1,011 adults, aged 18 and older, conducted Nov. 7-10, 2005. For results based on this sample, one can say with 95% confidence that the maximum error attributable to sampling and other random effects is ±3 percentage points. In addition to sampling error, question wording and practical difficulties in conducting surveys can introduce error or bias into the findings of public opinion polls.

November 15, 2005
BUSH APPROVAL AT 37%
Lowest approval rating measured by Gallup

by David W. Moore, Gallup Poll Senior Editor

A new CNN/*USA Today*/Gallup survey finds just 37% of Americans approving of the job George W. Bush is doing as president, the lowest percentage measured by Gallup during the Bush presidency. Sixty percent say they disapprove. This rating is marginally worse than the previous low rating, measured by Gallup in an Oct. 13-16 poll, when 39% of Americans approved and 58% disapproved of Bush's job performance.

Bush began the year with a majority of Americans, 52%, indicating approval, which surged to 57% following his State of the Union speech and the elections in Iraq, but then fell below the 50%

Bush's Overall Job Approval Rating
Selected Trend: January 2005 – November 2005

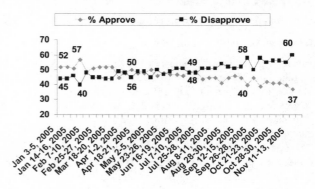

mark several times in the next three months. His average approval rating for the first quarter of the year was 51%, for the second quarter 48%, and for the third quarter 45%. His average for October and November has been 40%, including the 39% rating in mid-October and the current 37% rating.

Bush's Job Approval Ratings
2005 Quarterly Average

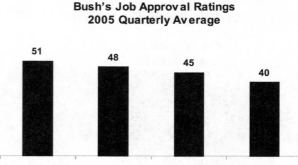

The low approval rating should not be interpreted as meaning that many people "hate" the president, however. Despite some blog commentaries, the poll finds that only 6% of Americans say they actually hate Bush. Another 27% say they dislike him "a lot," and 17% say they dislike him "a little"—a total of 50% who dislike him with some degree of intensity. Almost the same number, 48%, say they like the president, including 27% who say they like him a lot, and 21% who like him a little.

How would you describe your overall opinion of George W. Bush? Would you say you—[ROTATED: like Bush a lot, like him a little, dislike him a little, (or) dislike Bush a lot]?

Would you say you hate Bush, or would you say you dislike Bush but do not hate him?

COMBINED RESPONSES (Q.7-8)

	Like a lot %	Like a little %	Dislike a little %	Dislike a lot %	Hate Bush %	No opinion %
2005 Nov 11-13	27	21	17	27	6	2
2003 May 30-Jun 1	40	28	16	13	2	1

Bush's approval rating in other areas is as bad or worse than his overall approval rating, except for the issue of terrorism. On this

Bush Issues Approval on Selected Issues

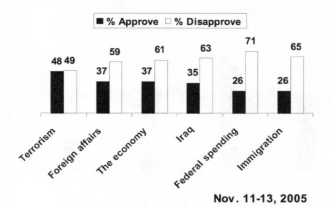

Nov. 11-13, 2005

Bush Qualities and Characteristics

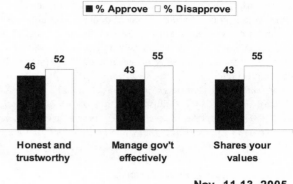

Nov. 11-13, 2005

issue, the public is about evenly divided, with 48% approving of the way Bush has been handling this issue, and 49% disapproving.

But on foreign affairs, the economy, the situation in Iraq, federal spending, and immigration, solid majorities of Americans disapprove of Bush's performance, with only a quarter to just over a third of Americans indicating their approval.

The lower rating on terrorism is especially significant, because Bush's 2004 electoral victory is widely attributed to the president's image as a strong leader opposing terrorism. About two weeks before the election, 57% of Americans approved of the way Bush was handling the issue, nine points higher than the current reading.

As for Bush's image as a strong president, again the poll finds a divided public: 49% say he is, while another 49% say he is a weak president.

Would you describe George W. Bush as a—[ROTATED: strong president (or a) weak president]?

	Strong president	*Weak president*	*No opinion*
2005 Nov 11-13	49%	49	2

Bush's integrity is also not immune to public criticism. With renewed questions being raised about the reasons for going to war in Iraq, Americans say the president is not honest and trustworthy by a 52% to 46% margin, the worst Gallup has measured for Bush. The previous low reading was found in a mid-September poll, when 50% said Bush was not honest and trustworthy, while 47% said he was.

George W. Bush as Honest and Trustworthy

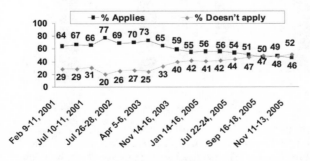

Majorities of Americans also say that Bush cannot manage the government effectively, and that he does not share their values. These low ratings are not new. In an October poll, Gallup got essentially

the same rating on Bush's ability to manage government, and in an August poll, Gallup got a similar rating on Bush's values.

The decline in Bush's integrity ratings can be seen in a separate question, when Americans were asked if they could trust Bush more or less than they could trust previous presidents. In June 2003, when Bush had a 61% job approval rating, Americans said they could trust him more than previous presidents, by 41% to 32%—with 25% indicating no difference. But the current poll shows a majority, 53%, saying they trust Bush less, 30% saying more, and 16% saying about the same.

Comparing George W. Bush with Previous Presidents

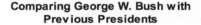

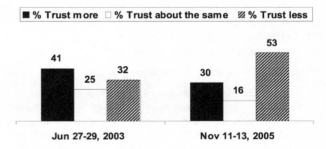

When Bush is compared explicitly with former President Bill Clinton, 48% say they would trust Bush less than Clinton, while 36% would trust Bush more—and the rest choose neither over the other.

Comparing George W. Bush With Previous Presidents and With Bill Clinton

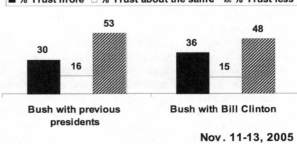

Nov. 11-13, 2005

Polarization on Bush remains substantial. The poll finds only 7% of Democrats who say they approve of Bush's performance, compared with 80% of Republicans—a 73-point difference. For 2005, the average polarization has been 72 points. In the period from when Bush first took office until the terrorist attacks on 9/11, the average polarization was 59 points, which declined to 18.5 points from then until the end of the year—as all partisan groups rallied around the president.

Approval among Democrats waned more quickly than among Republicans, and in 2002, the average polarization averaged 42 points. In 2003, it jumped to an average of 59 points. In election year 2004, it averaged 75 points over the whole period—but 72 points in the first six months and 78 points in the last six months.

Survey Methods

Results are based on telephone interviews with 1,006 national adults, aged 18 and older, conducted Nov. 11-13, 2005. For results based on the total sample of national adults, one can say with 95% confidence that the maximum margin of sampling error is ±3 percentage points.

For results based on the 491 national adults in the Form A half-sample and 515 national adults in the Form B half-sample, the maximum margins of sampling error are ±5 percentage points. In addition to sampling error, question wording and practical difficulties in conducting surveys can introduce error or bias into the findings of public opinion polls.

November 15, 2005
WAR THROUGH PARTISAN LENSES
Divide over Iraq war not necessarily typical

by Jeffrey M. Jones, Gallup Poll Managing Editor

Since August, a majority of Americans have fairly consistently said the United States made a mistake in sending troops to Iraq. By now, it is well established that Democrats and Republicans have starkly different views of the war in Iraq—the vast majority of Republicans support the war, and Democrats are overwhelmingly opposed.

Historically, Gallup has asked the same "mistake" question about other U.S. military engagements, starting with the Korean War. This history allows for an analysis of whether past wars divided the public along party lines as the Iraq war does, or if people viewed these other wars similarly regardless of their party affiliation.

Gallup Poll data from late September through October underscore just how divided Americans are politically about the Iraq war*. Eighty-one percent of Democrats say the United States made a mistake in sending troops there, while 78% of Republicans say it did not. Independents, as is typical, fall in between—but a majority of independents, 58%, believe the United States made a mistake.

The current popular perception is that Republicans are more inclined to support the use of military force than are Democrats, and thus should be more likely to support U.S. involvement in war. That general tendency could be complicated, however, if a Democratic president is the one who is arguing in favor of military action.

The Vietnam and Korean Wars present good tests of the link between party affiliation and support for wars historically. Both war efforts were primarily led by Democratic presidents—Harry Truman

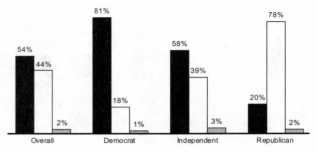

Views of War With Iraq by Party Affiliation

■ Mistake □ Not a mistake ▨ No opinion

Based on aggregated Gallup Poll data collected Sept. 26-Oct. 30, 2005

Overall: 54%, 44%, 2%
Democrat: 81%, 18%, 1%
Independent: 58%, 39%, 3%
Republican: 20%, 78%, 2%

and Lyndon Johnson—and both efforts were, as the Iraq war is now, not wholly embraced by the general public.

Vietnam War

Gallup began asking the "mistake" question about the Vietnam War in 1965. Similar to the current war in Iraq, initial opinion was favorable toward U.S. involvement in the war effort, but by 1968 more Americans were saying the United States made a mistake sending troops to Vietnam than were saying it did not. Once opinion reached that tipping point, it never recovered.

However, the Vietnam War was different from the Iraq war in that opinions were not strongly related to party affiliation. Aggregated Gallup data from August 1968 to September 1969 showed an average of 53% of Americans saying the United States made a mistake in sending troops to Vietnam, similar to the recent 54% average for the Iraq war. But a majority of Democrats, independents, and Republicans said the war was a mistake. In fact, there is little differentiation in the results by party—51% of Democrats, 55% of independents, and 56% of Republicans thought the United States made a mistake in going to Vietnam during that period. (The lack of partisan differences is evident in each of the four individual polls included in the aggregate, even though the presidency changed hands from Democrat Johnson to Republican Richard Nixon during that time.)

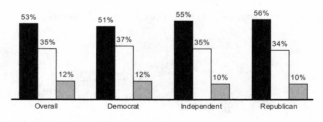

Views of Vietnam War by Party Affiliation

■ Mistake □ Not a mistake ▨ No opinion

Based on aggregated Gallup Poll data collected Aug. 7, 1968- Sept. 22, 1969

Overall: 53%, 35%, 12%
Democrat: 51%, 37%, 12%
Independent: 55%, 35%, 10%
Republican: 56%, 34%, 10%

Korean War

Gallup first asked about U.S. involvement in the Korean War in August 1950. Again, more Americans were supporting U.S. efforts at that time than not. The trend line on the mistake question during the Korean War, however, is very different from that for the Vietnam War. During the Korean War, support vacillated, with support outpacing opposition at certain times and the reverse being true at others.

Because of that, it is harder to combine data over time to get a read on support for the war by party. However, this analysis will look at two time points—February 1951 and February to March 1952, when opposition to the war was higher than support, and similar to what it is now for the Iraq war.

The data from February 1951 show a partisan division—with 55% of Republicans calling U.S. involvement in Korea a mistake, compared with 43% of Democrats***. Fifty-one percent of independents thought the United States made a mistake at that time.

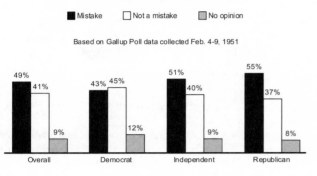

Views of Korean War by Party Affiliation

■ Mistake □ Not a mistake ▨ No opinion

Based on Gallup Poll data collected Feb. 4-9, 1951

Over a year later****, a partisan gap was evident, and was somewhat larger, as 61% of Republicans and 44% of Democrats thought the United States made a mistake in sending troops to Korea.

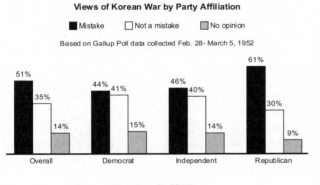

Views of Korean War by Party Affiliation

■ Mistake □ Not a mistake ▨ No opinion

Based on Gallup Poll data collected Feb. 28- March 5, 1952

Persian Gulf War

Unlike the three wars discussed, the 1991 Persian Gulf War with Iraq was won swiftly by the United States. As such, opposition to that war was never that high. But an analysis of Gallup data from early January (before the actual war began) showed a majority of both Republicans and Democrats supported the war, but Republicans were significantly more likely to do so.

Bottom Line

Historical Gallup Poll data show the current pattern of war support is not necessarily typical, compared with other lengthy wars involving U.S. troops. While there was a partisan divide during the Korean War, it was not nearly as pronounced as the division for the current war in Iraq. Democrats were more likely to support that war, while Republicans are more likely to support the current war. Also, Americans' views of the United States' role in the Vietnam War were not related to their political leanings in any meaningful way.

One possible explanation for the change is that the parties tend to be more homogeneous today than in the past. In the 1950s and 1960s,

conservative Democrats dominated the South. So the party was made up of conservative Southerners and moderates and liberals from other parts of the country. Since that time, the Republican Party has made significant inroads into the South in both party identification and in winning elections. Additionally, the Republican Party of the 1950s and 1960s was not as monolithically conservative as it is now.

*Results are based on 2,626 interviews with nationally representative samples of adults, age 18 and older, conducted in polls Sept. 26-28, Oct. 21-23, and Oct. 28-30, 2005. For results based on this combined sample, the maximum margin of sampling error is ±2 percentage points. This includes samples of 888 Republicans, 872 independents, and 848 Democrats. All have maximum margins of sampling error of ±4 percentage points.

**Results are based on 6,089 interviews with nationally representative samples of adults, age 18 and older, conducted in polls Aug. 7-12, 1968, Sept. 26-Oct. 1, 1968, Jan. 23-28, 1969, and Sept. 17-22, 1969. For results based on this combined sample, the maximum margin of sampling error is ±1 percentage point. This includes samples of 1,767 Republicans, 1,808 independents, and 2,373 Democrats. The Republican and independent samples have maximum margins of sampling error of ±3 percentage points; the Democratic sample has a maximum margin of sampling error of ±2 percentage points.

***Results are based on 1,403 interviews with a nationally representative sample of adults, age 18 and older, conducted Feb. 4-9, 1951. For results based on this sample, the maximum margin of sampling error is ±3 percentage points. This includes samples of 479 Republicans, 338 independents, and 563 Democrats. The Republican and Democratic samples have maximum margins of sampling error of ±5 percentage points; the independent sample has a maximum margin of sampling error of ±6 percentage points.

****Results are based on 1,922 interviews with a nationally representative sample of adults, age 18 and older, conducted Feb. 28-March 5, 1952. For results based on this sample, the maximum margin of sampling error is ±3 percentage points. This includes samples of 575 Republicans, 456 independents, and 737 Democrats. The Republican and independent samples have maximum margins of sampling error of ±5 percentage points; the Democratic sample has a maximum margin of sampling error of ±4 percentage points.

November 16, 2005
PUBLIC CONTINUES TO EXPRESS PESSIMISM ABOUT WAR IN IRAQ
Americans divided over whether U.S. can win war

by Jeffrey M. Jones, Gallup Poll Managing Editor

Gallup's latest update on Iraq shows no fundamental changes in recent weeks in attitudes about war support—more Americans say the United States made a mistake in sending troops to Iraq than say it did not. Though fairly closely divided, more Americans express pessimism than optimism that the United States will win the war in Iraq. Amid increased Senate discussion about setting concrete policies and objectives regarding the war, a majority of Americans say they favor withdrawing U.S. troops either immediately or within a year.

Basic Support for the War

Since August, an average of 54% of Americans have said the war with Iraq was a mistake, with an average of 45% saying it was not. The new CNN/*USA Today*/Gallup poll, conducted Nov. 11-13, shows no basic change in that sentiment; in fact, the poll's numbers exactly match the recent average.

In view of the developments since we first sent our troops to Iraq, do you think the United States made a mistake in sending troops to Iraq, or not?

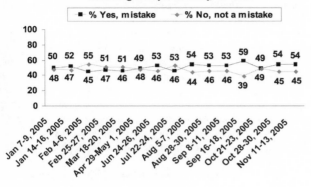

Americans are slightly more critical of the war when they are asked whether it was "worth going to war in Iraq." Thirty-eight percent of Americans say it was worth going; 60% say it was not. The latest measure is down slightly from recent readings, the last of which was a 45%-53% split in mid-September.

All in all, do you think it was worth going to war in Iraq, or not?

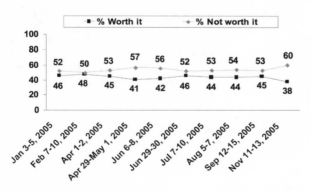

The current reading is the most negative evaluation of the war on this measure since the war began in March 2003.

Assessing Current Progress

Americans' assessments of the United States' prospects in the war are mixed. In fact, the public is largely divided as to whether the United States will win the war. Forty-six percent believe the United States will "definitely" or "probably win the war," while 50% believe the country will not win, including 17% who believe the United States is capable of winning the war, and 33% who believe it is not capable of winning.

These assessments are fairly stable when compared to the last reading, from mid-September. The percentage of Americans who

Which comes closer to your view about the war in Iraq: you think the U.S. will definitely win the war in Iraq, you think the U.S. will probably win the war in Iraq, you think the U.S. can win the war in Iraq, but you don't think it will win, (or) you do not think the U.S. can win the war in Iraq?

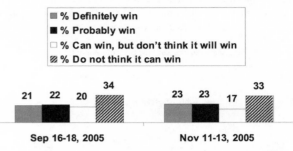

believe the U.S. *can* win the war (regardless of whether it will win) is the same now as then—63%.

The public's most critical attitudes toward the war concern the way George W. Bush is handling it. Just 35% of Americans approve of how Bush is handling the situation in Iraq, while 63% disapprove. This is just slightly higher than Bush's worst rating on Iraq, a 32% approval rating in September.

The public has grown increasingly negative in its review of Bush's handling of Iraq this year. Since February, the drop in Bush approval ratings has been more pronounced than the drops in basic war support evident on the "mistake" and "worth it" questions.

George W. Bush's Handling of the Situation in Iraq

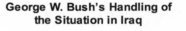
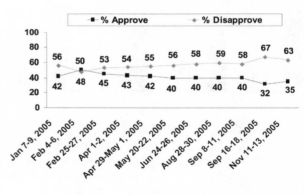

What Now?

On Tuesday, the U.S. Senate voted on proposals on Iraq, approving a Republican proposal and defeating a Democratic one. Both proposals called for the president to regularly update Congress and the American public on the progress of the war and the administration's strategy for completing the mission in Iraq. The Democratic proposal also asked the president to estimate dates for U.S. troop withdrawal.

The poll presented Americans with four options for dealing with the war in Iraq. Nineteen percent say the United States should immediately withdraw troops from Iraq, and another 33% say the United States should withdraw its troops by next November. Thirty-eight percent say the United States should withdraw, but should take as many years as needed to turn control of the country over to the Iraqis. Just 7% say the United States should send more troops to Iraq.

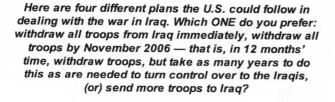

Here are four different plans the U.S. could follow in dealing with the war in Iraq. Which ONE do you prefer: withdraw all troops from Iraq immediately, withdraw all troops by November 2006 — that is, in 12 months' time, withdraw troops, but take as many years to do this as are needed to turn control over to the Iraqis, (or) send more troops to Iraq?

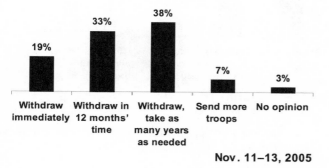

Nov. 11–13, 2005

Most Republicans, 58%, prefer that the United States withdraw troops but take as many years as needed to do so. A majority of independents and Democrats favor immediate withdrawal or withdrawal of troops by next November.

U.S. Troops in Iraq, by Party Affiliation

	Overall %	Democrat %	Independent %	Republican %
Immediate withdrawal	19	28	20	7
Withdraw by November 2006	33	39	36	25
Withdraw, take as many years as needed	38	25	34	58
Send more troops	7	5	8	8
No opinion	3	3	2	2

Gallup asked a similar question about the Vietnam War in July and August 1970, when a majority of Americans thought the United States made a mistake in sending troops to Vietnam. As is the case now, more Americans favored withdrawal in the short term than favored a longer-term withdrawal or increased troop deployments.

Forty-eight percent of Americans thought the United States should withdraw its troops immediately (23%) or within 12 months (25%). That compares with 33% who wanted to withdraw troops, but to take as many years as necessary in order to turn the war over to the South Vietnamese, and 10% who wanted to "send more troops to Vietnam and step up the fighting."

Survey Methods

These results are based on telephone interviews with a randomly selected national sample of 1,006 adults, aged 18 and older, conducted Nov. 11-13, 2005. For results based on this sample, one can say with 95% confidence that the maximum error attributable to sampling and other random effects is ±3 percentage points. In addition to sampling error, question wording and practical difficulties in conducting surveys can introduce error or bias into the findings of public opinion polls.

November 17, 2005

BUSH THE REPUBLICANS' LIABILITY-IN-CHIEF?

Majority would vote against candidates he endorses

by Lydia Saad, Gallup Poll Senior Editor

When pressed repeatedly by radio host Don Imus during an interview last week, Republican Congressman J.D. Hayworth admitted he would rather not have President George W. Bush campaign for him in his district in Arizona next year. "Would you like him to come to Arizona and cut campaign commercials for you and run them on all those TV stations in Phoenix, in Tucson, in Flagstaff, in Prescott, and everywhere?" asked Imus. "In a word, no. Not at this time," replied Hayworth.

Hayworth has since tried to soften the blow by saying he will do all he can to help the president with his current troubles, but his initial response merely bows to the reality that Bush seems to be more of a liability than an asset to Republican candidates.

The latest CNN/*USA Today*/Gallup poll, conducted Nov. 11-13, finds a majority of voters saying they would be less likely to vote for a candidate for political office in their area if Bush supported that person. Only one-third would be more likely to vote for such a candidate.

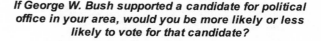

If George W. Bush supported a candidate for political office in your area, would you be more likely or less likely to vote for that candidate?

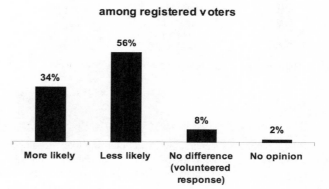

When asked specifically about their preferences for congressional candidates participating in next year's elections, only 9% of voters—including just 21% of Republicans—say they would be most likely to support a Republican candidate who agrees with Bush "on almost every major issue." That would seem to be a clear warning signal to candidates against associating themselves too closely with Bush.

Another 33% of voters say they would prefer a Republican who agrees as well as disagrees with Bush. Most Republican voters (69%) fall into this group.

However, the majority of all voters say they are most likely to support a Democratic candidate—one who either partially or mostly disagrees with Bush.

While Republican voters say they are most likely to vote for Republican candidates, a majority of independents (57%), as well as nearly all Democrats (96%), are inclined to vote Democratic. These groups are largely divided between those preferring a Democrat who disagrees with Bush on most issues and those who agree on only some issues. Just 35% of independents and 3% of Democrats say they are likely to vote Republican.

Which Type of Congressional Candidate Are You Most Likely to Support?
among registered voters

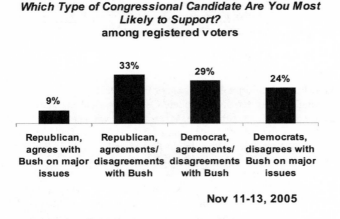

Nov 11-13, 2005

Candidate Preferences by Party Affiliation

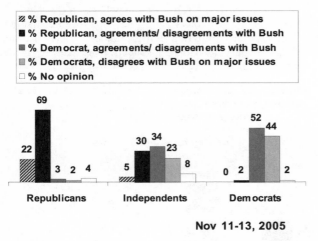

⊠ % Republican, agrees with Bush on major issues
■ % Republican, agreements/ disagreements with Bush
■ % Democrat, agreements/ disagreements with Bush
▨ % Democrats, disagrees with Bush on major issues
☐ % No opinion

Nov 11-13, 2005

Democrats Have the Edge

According to this assessment, 53% of all voters are likely to support the Democratic candidate in their congressional district, while 42% are likely to support the Republican. This is generally consistent with Gallup's latest "generic ballot" measure of voting intentions for Congress. According to an Oct. 21-23 Gallup poll, 50% of registered voters plan to vote for the Democratic candidate in their district, while 43% plan to vote Republican.

These results also mirror the 12-point lead Democrats have on a different question asking Americans whether the country would be better off if the Republicans or the Democrats controlled Congress. Close to half of Americans (46%) say the country would be better off with the Democrats in charge, while 34% choose the Republicans. Twelve percent say the country would be better if neither of the two major parties was in charge, and another 8% indicate that it makes no difference to them.

A Pox on Both Houses

Although Republicans are running behind in voter preferences, the terrain is not entirely smooth for the Democrats. A majority of Americans (53%) disapprove of the job the Democrats in Congress are doing, similar to the extent of disapproval directed at congressional Republicans (58%).

One difference between the two parties on this measure is the trend, which could be troubling for Republicans if it continues. In

Do you think the country would be better off if the Republicans controlled Congress, or if the Democrats controlled Congress?

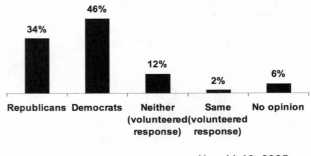

Nov 11-13, 2005

the past six months the Republicans' disapproval score has increased 8 points (from 50% to 58%), while ratings of the Democrats have been fairly steady.

Congressional Job Approval Ratings

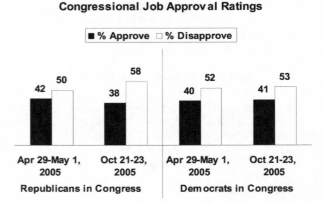

Of potential concern to the Democrats is the fact that independents are just as critical as Republicans of the job the Democrats in Congress are doing: 62% of independents disapprove of the Democrats, compared with 69% of Republicans.

This suggests that independents' tendency to support Democratic candidates for Congress is more a vote against the Republicans than it is for the Democrats—and that could make for a shakier base of support from this important group.

Job Performance of Parties in Congress by Party Affiliation

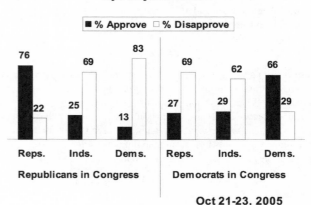

Oct 21-23, 2005

These results are based on telephone interviews with a randomly selected national sample of 1,006 adults, aged 18 and older, conducted Nov. 11-13, 2005. For results based on this sample, one can say with 95% confidence that the maximum error attributable to sampling and other random effects is ±3 percentage points. In addition to sampling error, question wording and practical difficulties in conducting surveys can introduce error or bias into the findings of public opinion polls.

November 18, 2005

BIRD FLU CONCERNS RISE AS MOST URGENT HEALTH PROBLEM

Cost of healthcare continues to rank as top problem

by Joseph Carroll, Gallup Poll Assistant Editor

Every year, Gallup asks Americans, without prompting, to name the most urgent health problem facing the country at the present time. While the cost of healthcare and health insurance remains the most urgent health problem in the latest survey, the percentage of Americans mentioning cancer and the flu or bird flu has increased. At the same time, mentions of access to healthcare and healthcare costs have declined.

The survey also shows that half of Americans say they are concerned about contracting a deadly virus, such as the bird flu, that spreads to the United States from a foreign country; fewer Americans are concerned about contracting an infectious disease that is brought into the United States by terrorists.

Most Urgent Health Problem

The poll, conducted Nov. 7-10, finds that one in four Americans mention the cost of healthcare or insurance as the most urgent health problem facing the country today. Access to healthcare (17%), cancer (15%), and the flu or bird flu (10%) follow health costs in the list of urgent problems. Fewer than 1 in 10 Americans say the top health problem in the country is obesity, AIDS, or heart disease.

Over the past year, there have been significant changes relating to four of these health problems.

Access to healthcare. There has been a 12-percentage point drop in the percentage of Americans mentioning access to healthcare as the nation's top health problem. Mentions of healthcare access are now at roughly the same level as in 2002, but healthcare access is still mentioned more frequently than in any year prior to that.

Health costs. The percentage of Americans who cite healthcare or insurance costs is down slightly from 29% last year to 25% this year. Since 2000, mentions of healthcare costs have been in the mid- to upper-20% range. (There was an exception to this in 2001, when Americans were much more likely to name bioterrorism as a top concern, following the anthrax scares that occurred after the 9/11 terrorist attacks.)

Flu. The poll finds an eight-point increase since last year (2% to 10%) in the percentage of respondents mentioning the flu or bird flu as the

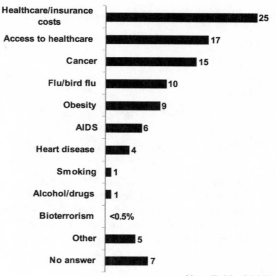

Most Urgent Health Problem 2005

Healthcare/insurance costs	25
Access to healthcare	17
Cancer	15
Flu/bird flu	10
Obesity	9
AIDS	6
Heart disease	4
Smoking	1
Alcohol/drugs	1
Bioterrorism	<0.5%
Other	5
No answer	7

Nov 7-10, 2005

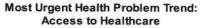

Most Urgent Health Problem Trend: Access to Healthcare

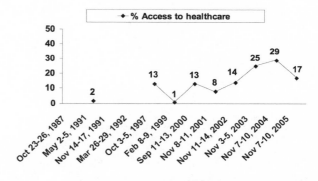

♦ % Access to healthcare

Most Urgent Health Problem Trend: Healthcare Costs or Health Insurance Costs

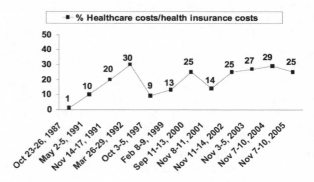

■ % Healthcare costs/health insurance costs

top health problem. This is almost certainly because of recent news accounts of the spread of the avian flu. Mentions of the flu are at the highest level Gallup has ever recorded in response to this question.

Cancer. Possibly related to the recent death of ABC News anchor Peter Jennings from lung cancer after years of smoking, Gallup

Most Urgent Health Problem Trend: Flu or Bird Flu

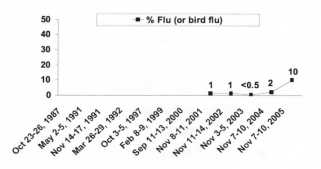

shows an increase—from 9% last year to 15% this year—in the percentage of Americans who say cancer is the most urgent health problem. The current results are at roughly the same level Gallup measured from 1987 through 1991, in 1997, and more recently in 2003. Cancer mentions were highest in the late 1990s and early 2000s, ranging from 19% to 23% over that period.

Most Urgent Health Problem Trend: Cancer

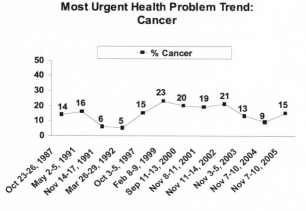

The results on this most urgent health problem question have changed substantially since the question was first asked in 1987. At that time, more than two in three Americans (68%) cited AIDS as the most urgent health problem. AIDS remained the top health problem until 2000, when healthcare costs and access became the top concerns. Since that time, access or costs have rated at the top of the list of health problems, with the exception of Gallup's 2001 survey.

Half of Americans Worried About Contracting Bird Flu

A separate poll question asked Americans how worried they are about contracting a deadly virus such as bird flu or a deadly infectious disease such as smallpox that is brought into the country by terrorists.

The results show that half of Americans say they are very (14%) or somewhat (36%) worried about contracting a "deadly virus, such as bird flu or something similar, that spreads to the United States from a foreign country." The other half of the public is not too (29%) or not at all (21%) concerned.

Americans are less concerned about a deadly infectious disease spread by terrorists. Roughly 4 in 10 Americans say they are very (11%) or somewhat (32%) worried about contracting "a deadly infectious disease, such as smallpox or something similar, that is brought into the United States by terrorists." The majority of Americans are not too (34%) or not at all (23%) worried.

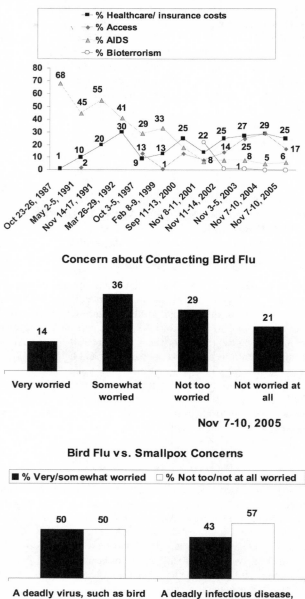

Survey Methods

Results are based on telephone interviews with 1,011 national adults, aged 18 and older, conducted Nov. 7-10, 2005. For results based on the total sample of national adults, one can say with 95% confidence that the maximum margin of sampling error is ±3 percentage points.

In addition to sampling error, question wording and practical difficulties in conducting surveys can introduce error or bias into the findings of public opinion polls.

November 21, 2005
CHENEY'S JOB APPROVAL AT 36%
Vice president's ratings similar to Bush's,
but less polarized

by David W. Moore, Gallup Poll Senior Editor

The latest CNN/*USA Today*/Gallup survey finds a 36% job approval rating for Vice President Dick Cheney, just a point lower than the job rating for President George W. Bush. While some observers have speculated that the vice president is losing popularity because of the indictment of his closest aide, Lewis "Scooter" Libby, the poll suggests that Cheney's ratings and Bush's ratings are closely tied to each other. Cheney's low rating in the most recent poll may be partially a result of the publicity surrounding Libby's indictment, but if that's the case, the Libby situation has most probably affected Bush as well.

Gallup has measured Cheney's job approval six times since Bush first assumed the presidency, and on five of the six occasions, the ratings of the two men were very similar.

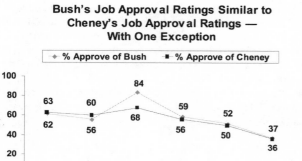

Bush's Job Approval Ratings Similar to Cheney's Job Approval Ratings — With One Exception

The one exception occurred in January 2002, just four months after the 9/11 terrorist attacks, when the country rallied around the president. That rally effect apparently did not extend as completely to the vice president, though his rating was higher at that time than at any other period Gallup has measured.

For each of the six times, Republicans gave a higher rating to Bush than to Cheney. The smallest gap was just 2 points (Bush's 89% to Cheney's 87% in May 2001), while the largest gap of 12 points shows up in the latest poll (80% for Bush vs. 68% for Cheney).

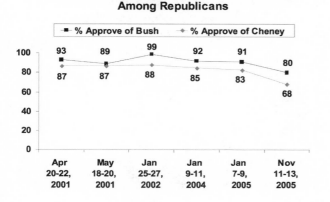

Bush's Ratings Higher Than Cheney's Ratings Among Republicans

On the other hand, on five of the six measures, Cheney received higher ratings from the Democrats than did Bush. The only exception was the January 2002 reading, which was apparently still influenced by the 9/11 rally effect.

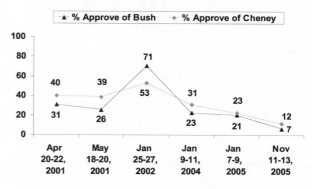

Cheney's Ratings Higher Than Bush's Ratings Among Democrats — With One Exception

These results suggest that Bush tends to polarize the country more than Cheney. The difference in the president's ratings between Republicans and Democrats is now at 73 points, with 80% of Republicans approving of the president's job performance, compared with only 7% of Democrats. By comparison, Cheney's polarization score is 56 points—68% of Republicans approve of Cheney's performance, compared with 12% of Democrats.

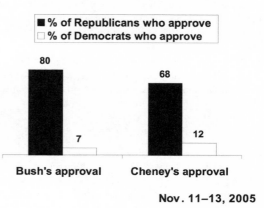

Polarization in Bush's Ratings Greater Than Polarization in Cheney's Ratings

Except for the January 2002 reading, when the polarization scores of both officials were much lower than normal, Bush's polarization score has been higher than Cheney's—by margins of 10 points to 17 points. The exception found Cheney with a polarization score of 35 points compared with Bush's 28 points.

Cheney's Advice Seen as Harmful

The poll also shows that a majority of Americans, 52%, rate Cheney's advice to the president as "bad," which "has created problems for the administration." Another 34% say his advice has been good and "has helped the administration."

Which comes closer to your view about the advice Vice President Dick Cheney has given to President George W. Bush over the past

Polarization in Bush's Ratings Greater Than
Polarization in Cheney's Ratings —
With One Exception

Polarization in Bush's Ratings Greater Than Polarization in Cheney's Ratings — With One Exception
(Republican ratings minus Democratic ratings, in percentage points)

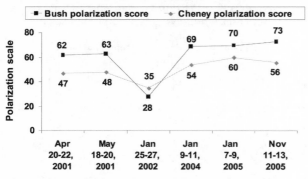

five years—[ROTATED: Cheney has generally given good advice that has helped the administration, (or) Cheney has generally given bad advice that has created problems for the administration]?

	Good advice	Bad advice	BOTH (vol.)	No opinion
2005 Nov 11-13	34%	52	2	12
2004 Aug 23-25 ^†	41%	39	3	17

^ Asked of a half sample
† WORDING: "… the past four years …"
(vol.) = Volunteered response

In August 2004, when Bush's job approval rating was 49% (and presumably, Cheney's rating was similar), the public was more evenly divided, with 41% saying the vice president's advice was good and 39% saying bad.

The pattern of responses to this question suggest that it closely mirrors job approval ratings, entailing mostly a general feeling about the overall performance of the Bush/Cheney administration rather than a specific critique of Cheney's advice to Bush.

Survey Methods

Results are based on telephone interviews with 1,006 national adults, aged 18 and older, conducted Nov. 11-13, 2005. For results based on the total sample of national adults, one can say with 95% confidence that the maximum margin of sampling error is ±3 percentage points.

In addition to sampling error, question wording and practical difficulties in conducting surveys can introduce error or bias into the findings of public opinion polls.

November 22, 2005
CHRISTMAS SPENDING INTENTIONS UP SLIGHTLY COMPARED TO LAST YEAR
Americans plan to spend an average of $763 on Christmas gifts

by Frank Newport, Gallup Poll Editor in Chief

Much of the discussion in recent months about the nation's economy has focused on the critical holiday spending season. Roughly a quarter of annual retail sales in the United States are accounted for in the Christmas time period. Analysts, this year in particular, have been speculating about the long-term impact of Hurricane Katrina and the late summer/early fall run up in gas prices on spending this year, and hoping that the season does not turn out to be a disappointment.

There are many factors that help determine retail holiday spending levels—including consumers' desires for new or exciting products, the degree to which retailers discount their products and run sales, the weather, and the scope of retail advertising. One critical piece of the puzzle is the mental state of consumers. Positive, upbeat, economically content consumers are presumed to be more likely to spend money than are depressed, worried, and concerned consumers.

Gallup has for years tracked consumers' holiday spending intentions by asking a simple question at about this time of year: "Roughly how much money do you think you personally will spend on Christmas gifts this year?" The answers to the question this year suggest that 2005 holiday sales will not lag far behind previous years', and that this holiday season may even see a higher than usual increase in spending for this period.

Spending Plans at Slightly Higher Level Than Mid-November 2004

The Gallup survey, conducted Nov. 7-10, finds that 30% of adults nationwide say they will spend $1,000 or more on gifts, while 26% plan to spend between $500 and $1,000, and 32% plan to spend less than $500. The average is $763.

The most relevant comparison for spending intentions comes from past data collected in mid-November each year. Not surprisingly, Christmas spending expectations were much higher at this time in 1999, when Americans were in the middle of the economic expansion and dot-com boom. At that point, Americans said they planned to spend, on average, $857 on gifts. Over the next three years, average Christmas spending intentions steadily declined, to $817 in 2000, $794 in 2001, and $690 in 2002. In 2003, the average moved up a little to $734, and stayed roughly the same—at $730—last year. This year, the average of $763 is modestly higher than last year and the highest measured since November 2000.

Christmas Spending Expectations
based on mean dollar amount

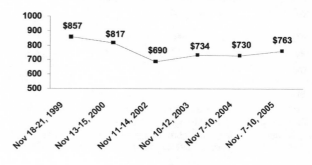

Americans' spending intentions generally change as the holiday season progresses; estimates obtained in December are higher than those measured in November. Last year, for example, Americans' spending estimates rose from $730 in mid-November to $862 in mid-December. Gallup will continue to measure these spending projections in the weeks ahead to see if the same pattern occurs this year.

Christmas Spending Expectations
October-December 2002 and
November-December 2003
based on mean dollar amount

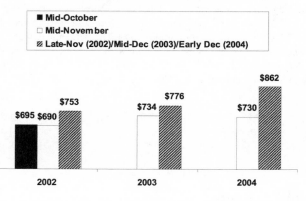

Fourteen percent of Americans say they will spend more than last year, while 26% say they will spend less, and 59% say they will spend about the same amount. These seemingly more negative attitudes are not unusual. For some reason, Americans have been saying that they are going to spend less for holiday gifts in the current year compared to the previous years for as long as Gallup has been asking the question.

In fact, this year's results on this question show essentially no change from those obtained last year at this time. The net-spending intentions figure this year (percentage who says they will spend more minus the percentage who says they will spend less) is -12. In 2004, the net-spending intentions figure was -10 points, and in 2003 it was -9 points.

Planning to Spend More, Less, or the Same?
polls conducted in November

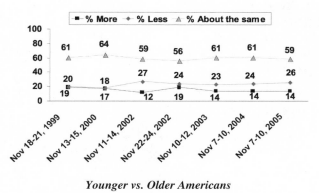

Younger vs. Older Americans

The results show a significant change in spending plans among younger Americans (those aged 18 to 29) and older Americans (those aged 65 and older). Younger adults will be spending significantly more than last year, while older Americans will be spending significantly less.

The sample sizes involved in these age groups are relatively small, which means that the margin of error for any year's estimate of spending in these groups is relatively high. Still, this year's changes among younger and older age groups are substantial:

- The current results show a significant increase in the amount of money that 18- to 29-year-olds plan to spend on Christmas gifts this year. On average, younger Americans plan to spend $713 on gifts, up from $548 last November.
- As has been the case in previous years, Americans aged 30 to 49 plan to spend more money on gifts than people in any other age group. Their average predicted expenditure for this year is $872, up from $817 in 2004. The most likely explanation for this finding is the higher incidence of children in the households of those within this age group. There has also been a modest increase in projected spending among this group compared to last year.
- Spending plans among those aged 50 to 64 show a gain compared to last year, from an average of $743 last year to $825 in the latest survey.
- Older Americans have significantly lowered their estimate of holiday spending compared to last year. Those aged 65 and older now plan to spend an average of $512 on gifts, down substantially from $726 last November. There has been quite a bit of year-to-year change in reported spending plans among those in this age group, so it is difficult to say if the current change represents a trend or simply a one-year aberration.

Average Amount of Money Spent on
Christmas Presents by Age
(Based on mean value including none)

	Mid-November 2004	Mid-November 2005	Change
18- to 29-year-olds	$548	$713	+$165
30- to 49-year-olds	$817	$872	+$55
50- to 64-year-olds	$743	$825	+$82
65 years and older	$726	$512	-$214

High Income vs. Low
Income Households

It is not surprising to find—as has always been the case in Gallup's tracking of this spending intention question—that higher income households plan to spend much more on gifts than lower income households. The following table gives stark evidence for the value of high-end retailers who appeal to upscale households; the average spending is nearly three times that of low-income households.

There has been an increase in projected spending across all three income groups used in this analysis compared to last year.

- Spending intentions increased by $59 over the past year among adults earning $75,000 a year or more, from an average of $1,107 in 2004 to $1,166 this year.
- People earning between $30,000 and $75,000 a year plan to spend an average of $769 on gifts this year, up $37 from last year.
- Americans living in households with annual incomes of less than $30,000 plan to spend an average of $371 on Christmas gifts this year, up only $10 from last year.

Average Amount of Money Spent on Christmas Presents by Income
(Based on mean value including none)

	Mid-November 2004	Mid-November 2005	Change
$75,000 a year or more	$1,107	$1,166	+$59
$30,000-$74,999	$732	$769	+$37
Less than $30,000 a year	$361	$371	+$10

The Gender Divide

Historically, men have reported higher levels of spending on Christmas gifts than have women. This pattern continues today, as men, on average, plan to spend $851 on Christmas gifts, while women plan to spend $682. Since last year's survey, the amount that men plan to spend has increased, while there has been no change in the projected spending of women.

Average Amount of Money Spent on Christmas Presents by Gender
(Based on mean value including none)

	Mid-November 2004	Mid-November 2005	Change
Men	$784	$851	+$67
Women	$682	$682	0

Survey Methods

These results are based on telephone interviews with a randomly selected national sample of 1,011 adults, aged 18 and older, conducted Nov. 7-10, 2005. For results based on this sample, one can say with 95% confidence that the maximum error attributable to sampling and other random effects is ±3 percentage points. In addition to sampling error, question wording and practical difficulties in conducting surveys can introduce error or bias into the findings of public opinion polls.

November 22, 2005

HAS KATRINA'S EFFECT ON ECONOMIC PERCEPTIONS BLOWN OVER?

by Raksha Arora, Business and Economy Editor

Now that pump prices aren't pinching them quite so hard and jobless claims are continuing to fall, economic concerns seem to be weighing a little lighter on Americans' minds than they have in recent months. In a recent Gallup Poll*, 28% of Americans mention some aspect of the economy as the most important problem

facing the nation. This is down somewhat from the 36% who mentioned economic concerns in October, and from 32% in September and August. Though specific mentions of energy prices and jobs continue to figure prominently among economic concerns, fewer Americans now mention the "economy in general" as the top problem.

Macro Optimism

In looking at opinion with respect to economic prospects, it is clear that Americans are prepared for a macroeconomic scenario dominated by higher inflation and rising interest rates. Seventy-nine percent of Americans expect interest rates to rise in the next six months, and 70% expect inflation to do the same. The percentage expecting interest rates to rise was essentially the same in November as it was in October, but slightly fewer Americans expect inflation to rise than thought so in September and October.

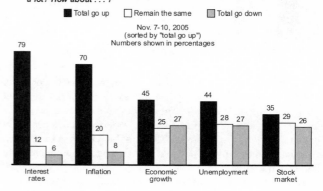

Over the next six months, do you think that each of the following will -- go up a lot, go up a little, remain the same, go down a little, or go down a lot? How about . . . ?

Despite expectations of higher interest rates and inflation, Americans' optimism about economic growth and the stock market appears to have rebounded somewhat from a gloomy October. Last month, 29% of Americans were bullish about the future of the stock market over the next six months; 35% now expect the market to go up. Forty-five percent of Americans currently expect economic growth to increase in the short term, compared with only 36% who said this last month.

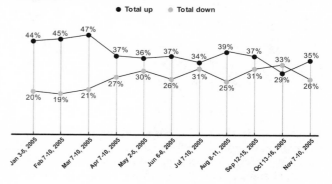

Over the next six months, do you think that each of the following will -- go up a little, remain the same, go down a little, or go down a lot? How about the Stock Market?

Over the next six months, do you think that each of the following will -- go up a little, remain the same, go down a little, or go down a lot? How about Economic Growth?

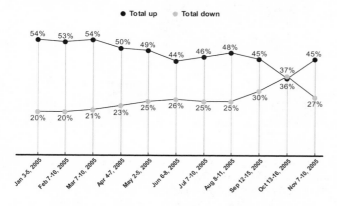

In September and October, a majority of Americans (52%) expected unemployment to rise in the next six months—likely related to higher unemployment that occurred in the aftermath of Hurricanes Katrina and Rita. This percentage moderated to 44% this month.

Over the next six months, do you think that each of the following will -- go up a little, remain the same, go down a little, or go down a lot? How about Unemployment?

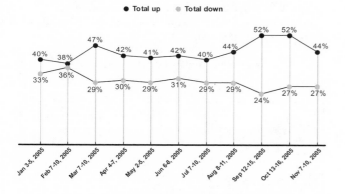

Results are based on telephone interviews with 1,011 national adults, aged 18 and older, conducted Nov. 7-10, 2005. For results based on the total sample of national adults, one can say with 95% confidence that the margin of sampling error is ±3 percentage points.

November 22, 2005
AMERICANS DEAL WITH CRIME BY STEERING CLEAR
One in 10 carry gun or knife

by Darren K. Carlson, Government and Politics Editor

Imagine you are walking alone at night after dinner in a neighborhood that is known as much for its crime as its great restaurants. You hear footsteps behind you. Your stomach churns. The hairs on the back of your neck stand up. You pick up your pace and desperately wish you had made dinner plans somewhere else. That tactic—avoiding certain neighborhoods or places—is the approach more Americans say they take than any other to deal with their concerns about crime.

According to Gallup's annual survey on crime*, one in six Americans report being the victim of a non-Internet-related crime in the last year. Theft and vandalism topped the list of crimes Americans say they experienced, and 3% say they were the victims of violent crimes. The survey delved into actions that people take because of their concerns about crime. Nearly half of Americans, 47%, say they simply avoid going to areas or neighborhoods they might otherwise want to go to as a means of staying safe. Fewer Americans say they keep a dog for protection, installed a burglar alarm, bought a gun, or carry Mace, a gun, or a knife for personal defense.

Next, I'm going to read some things people do because of their concern over crime. Please tell me which, if any, of these things you, yourself, do or have done. First, . . . Next, . . .

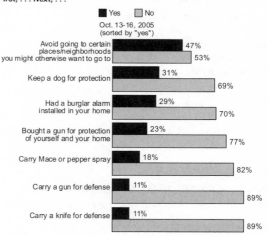

Avoidance Approach

Women are more likely than men to say they avoid going to certain places or neighborhoods they might otherwise want to go to. More than half of women (53%) avoid certain areas, compared with 40% of men.

Not surprisingly, more than half (57%) of those who say there is more crime in their areas now than a year ago say they avoid certain places or neighborhoods. Just 37% of those who don't observe more crime in their areas employ this tactic.

Safe at Home?

Roughly 3 in 10 Americans say they have taken steps to protect their homes from crime. Thirty-one percent say they keep a dog for protection. And, 29% of Americans say they had burglar alarms installed in their homes.

Keeping a dog for protection is more popular among younger Americans than older Americans; 34% of 18- to 49-year-olds say they do so, compared with 26% of those aged 50 and older.

People with annual household incomes of $75,000 or more are more likely to say they have installed burglar alarms in their homes; 39% of those in this income category say they have one, compared with 25% of those with annual household incomes under $75,000. Upper-income Americans are not only likely to have more to protect and secure in their homes, they're also more likely to be able to afford home security systems.

Armed and Secure?

Roughly a quarter of Americans (23%) say they have bought a gun to protect themselves or their homes. Significantly fewer—11%—report actually carrying a gun for defense. Men are more likely than women to say they have bought a gun for this purpose, 31% vs. 15% respectively, and to carry a gun for defense—14% vs. 7%.

Eighteen percent of Americans say they carry Mace or pepper spray. Women are far more likely than men to carry these; 26% of women report carrying them, compared with 9% of men. Eleven percent of Americans say their concerns about crime prompt them to carry a knife. More men than women say they carry knives for defense.

These results are based on telephone interviews with a randomly selected national sample of 1,012 adults, aged 18 and older, conducted Oct. 13-16, 2005. For results based on this sample, one can say with 95% confidence that the maximum error attributable to sampling and other random effects is ±3 percentage points. In addition to sampling error, question wording and practical difficulties in conducting surveys can introduce error or bias into the findings of public opinion polls.

November 22, 2005
GUN OWNERSHIP AND USE IN AMERICA
Women more likely than men to use guns for protection

by Joseph Carroll, Gallup Poll Assistant Editor

How many Americans personally own guns, and what do they use them for? A recent Gallup Poll* shows that 3 in 10 Americans personally own a gun; most gun owners say they use their guns to protect themselves against crime, for hunting, and for target shooting. Gun ownership varies by different groups in the country, with men more likely to be gun owners than women, Southerners and Midwesterners more likely than Easterners or Westerners, Republicans more so than Democrats, and older rather than younger Americans.

Gun Ownership

The poll, conducted Oct. 13-16, finds that 4 in 10 Americans report they have a gun in their homes, including 30% who say they personally own a gun and 12% who say another member of their household owns it. These results show essentially no change since this question was last asked in 2000. At that time, 27% of Americans said they personally owned a gun and 14% said another household member owned one.

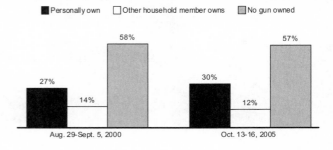

Do you have a gun in your home? Do you personally own a gun, or do the gun or guns in your household belong to another household member?

Certain groups of Americans—men, older Americans, Midwesterners, Southerners, Republicans, and whites—are more likely than other groups to say they personally own a gun.

- Nearly half of men (47%) report personal ownership, compared with just 13% of women.
- Americans aged 18 to 29 are slightly less likely than those who are older to be gun owners. Only one in five 18- to 29-year-olds (21%) say they own a gun, while 32% of 30- to 49-year-olds and 31% of those aged 50 and older report ownership.
- Roughly one in three Americans who live in the Midwest (34%) and the South (36%) say they personally own a gun. Ownership is lower among those residing in the East (22%) and the West (23%).
- Forty-one percent of Republicans say they own a gun, compared with 27% of independents and 23% of Democrats.
- One in three whites (33%) own a gun, while only about one in six nonwhites (18%) do.

Gun Ownership by Demographic Subgroups
Results are based on U.S. adults
Oct. 13-16, 2005

	Respondent personally owns	Other household member owns	Total (personally own gun/other member owns gun)
Overall	30%	12%	42%
Gender			
Men	47%	5%	52%
Women	13%	18%	31%
Region			
East	22%	9%	31%
Midwest	34%	13%	47%
South	36%	11%	47%
West	23%	15%	38%
Party Affiliation			
Republicans	41%	16%	57%
Independents	27%	10%	37%
Democrats	23%	10%	33%
Age			
18- to 29-year-olds	21%	13%	34%
30- to 49-year-olds	32%	12%	44%
50 years and older	31%	11%	42%
Race			
Whites	33%	13%	46%
Nonwhites	18%	9%	27%

Gun Use

The poll also shows that most gun owners use their guns for each of these three purposes: crime protection (67%), target shooting (66%), and hunting (58%).

These results represent essentially no change since the question was last asked in 2000. Because there is so little difference in results among the two polls, Gallup combined the data from its 2000 and 2005 surveys to provide a more detailed look at the reasons why different groups use guns.

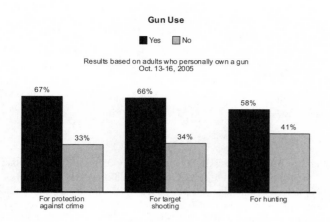

Gun Use

■ Yes ▨ No

Results based on adults who personally own a gun
Oct. 13-16, 2005

- 67% / 33% — For protection against crime
- 66% / 34% — For target shooting
- 58% / 41% — For hunting

Male gun owners are more likely than female owners to say they use a gun for hunting (63% to 45%, respectively) or for target shooting (68% to 59%), while female owners are slightly more likely than male gun owners to use a gun for protection (74% to 63%, respectively).

Gun owners aged 18 to 49, are more likely than those aged 50 and older to say they use a gun for hunting (65% to 52%) or for target practice (74% to 58%). There are essentially no differences between younger and older gun owners who use their guns for crime protection (67% among 18- to 49-year-olds and 64% of those aged 50 and older).

Republican and Democratic gun owners are almost equally likely to say they use a gun for protection against crime, 64% to 69%, respectively. However, Republicans are more likely than Democrats to say they use a gun for target shooting (71% to 53%) or for hunting (64% to 53%).

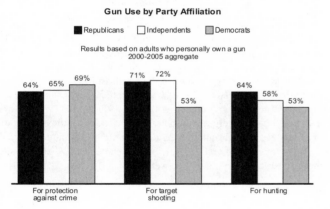

Gun Use by Party Affiliation

■ Republicans ☐ Independents ▨ Democrats

Results based on adults who personally own a gun
2000-2005 aggregate

- 64% / 65% / 69% — For protection against crime
- 71% / 72% / 53% — For target shooting
- 64% / 58% / 53% — For hunting

Results are based on telephone interviews with 1,012 national adults, aged 18 and older, conducted Oct. 13-16, 2005. For results based on the total sample of national adults, one can say with 95% confidence that the margin of sampling error is ±3 percentage points.

For results based on the sample of 305 adults who personally own a gun, the maximum margin of sampling error is ±6 percentage points.

For results based on the sample of 579 adults who personally own a gun, conducted Aug. 29-Sept. 5, 2000, and Oct. 13-16, 2005, the maximum margin of sampling error is ±4 percentage points.

In addition to sampling error, question wording and practical difficulties in conducting surveys can introduce error or bias into the findings of public opinion polls.

November 23, 2005
GIVING THANKS FOR A STEADY SCALE
Americans still overweight, but no increase in average weight

by Lydia Saad, Gallup Poll Senior Editor

As Americans sit down to Thanksgiving dinner with all of the trimmings, one thing for which they can be thankful is that the American public doesn't seem to have grown any heavier over the past year. In fact, for each of the past five years, the average weight reported by Americans in Gallup's annual Health survey has been between 171 and 174 pounds. This year's figure of 173 is identical to what was recorded in 2004.

That is small solace to the majority of the nation's adults who are either overweight or obese. According to respondents' self-reports of their current height and weight in Gallup's Nov. 7-10 survey, 21% of Americans are obese, 36% are overweight, 32% are normal, and 7% are underweight. These classifications conform to the standard body mass index (BMI) categories used by the National Institutes of Health for evaluating weight. A person's BMI score is based on a ratio of their weight and height (see Related Items).

The average weight of American men is 193 pounds; the average weight of American women is 154. Americans weighed a bit less in 1990, when Gallup first measured this. At that time, the average man weighed 180 and the average woman weighed 142. By 1999, these figures had jumped by 8 to 10 pounds, and they are now just slightly higher.

Average Body Weight (In Pounds)

	National adults	Women	Men
2005	173	154	193
2004	173	156	191
1999	170	150	190
1990	161	142	180

Americans Resist "Overweight" Label

Americans largely fail to acknowledge their weight problem, particularly when it comes to obesity. Whereas 21% of Americans today report height and weight measurements that put them in the government's obese category (and this is based on Gallup's self-reported data; federal statistics put the figure at 30%), only 5% of Americans describe themselves as "very overweight."

With another 37% calling themselves "overweight," this amounts to only 42% of Americans who consider themselves overweight to any degree. This contrasts with 57% who are overweight according to their Gallup BMI index (and with 65% who are overweight according to government data).

A Veritable Stew of Risk Factors

Stress and good health don't mix, so it is of potential concern that the vast majority of overweight Americans say they worry about their weight.

Close to half of all Americans say they worry all or some of the time about their weight. This jumps to 69% among those who describe themselves as overweight.

All of that worrying might be beneficial if it resulted in successful weight reduction. But the data on this are not encouraging. Since 1990, the percentage of Americans worrying about their weight has increased from 34% to 49%. At the same time, Americans' average weight has risen by 12 pounds (from 161 to 173).

How would you describe your own personal weight situation right now?

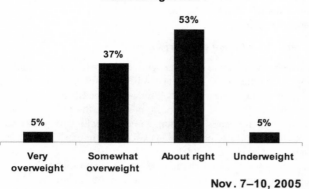

5%	37%	53%	5%
Very overweight	Somewhat overweight	About right	Underweight

Nov. 7–10, 2005

How Often Do You Worry About Your Weight?

■ % All/Some of the time　□ % Not too often　▨ % Never

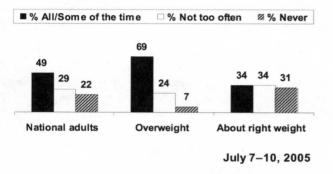

National adults	Overweight	About right weight
49　29　22	69　24　7	34　34　31

July 7–10, 2005

Trend in Worry About Weight
among national adults

■ % All/Some of the time　□ % Not too often　▨ % Never

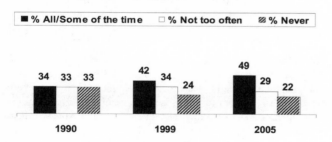

1990	1999	2005
34　33　33	42　34　24	49　29　22

The Catch-22 of being overweight is that one needs to exercise to lose weight, but it can be hard to exercise when overweight. Gallup's Health survey includes questions on people's activity level that are summarized in an exercise index. Overall, 29% of Americans score as high activity, 19% as medium activity, 24% as low activity, and 27% as sedentary.

However, there are some differences by weight. The majority of overweight Americans (60%) fall into the low activity or sedentary categories, while the majority of those who are about the right weight (55%) score as high or moderate activity.

Exercise Index

	National adults %	Overweight %	About right weight %
High activity	29	23	35
Moderate activity	19	17	20
Low activity	24	26	23
Sedentary	27	34	21
Total high/moderate	48	40	55
Total low/sedentary	51	60	44

Dieting Picks Up

Perhaps Americans are more worried about their weight today than in the past because they have experienced more dieting failures. Gallup has periodically asked Americans to estimate how many different times they have seriously tried to lose weight. The average number was only 4.0 in 1990. This increased to 4.6 in 1999, and is now 7.3.

Number of Times Have Seriously Dieted

▨ % Never　■ % 1-2 times　□ % 3-10 times　▥ % 11+ times

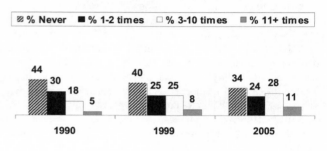

1990	1999	2005
44　30　18　5	40　25　25　8	34　24　28　11

A Gender Imbalance

While men and women are about equally likely to consider themselves overweight, men are substantially more likely than women to be classified as obese or overweight according to their BMI: 70% of men fall into these categories, compared with 44% of women.

In spite of this, it is women who are most likely to be worried about their weight. Nearly 6 in 10 women (57%) worry about it all or some of the time, compared with only 39% of men. Women are also much more likely to be on a dieting treadmill: they report an average of 9.6 serious attempts at losing weight, compared with 5.0 attempts for men. At present, 30% of women versus 23% of men say they are seriously trying to lose weight.

	% overweight (self-reported)	% overweight (BMI)	% worry all/some of the time about weight	% trying to lose weight now	Mean number of serious attempts to lose weight
Men	41	70	39	23	5.0
Women	44	44	57	30	9.6

Survey Methods

These results are based on telephone interviews with a randomly selected national sample of 1,011 adults, aged 18 and older, conducted Nov. 7-10, 2005. For results based on this sample, one can say with 95% confidence that the maximum error attributable to sampling and other random effects is ±3 percentage points. In addition to sampling error, question wording and practical difficulties in conducting surveys can introduce error or bias into the findings of public opinion polls.

November 28, 2005

HUSSEIN TRIAL TO RESUME UNDER TIGHT SECURITY

American public supports death penalty if Saddam convicted

by Mark Gillespie, Senior TV Broadcast Producer

The trial of former Iraqi President Saddam Hussein and his seven co-defendants, charged with crimes against humanity, is scheduled to resume Dec. 5 in Baghdad under tight security.

A new CNN/*USA Today*/Gallup poll, conducted Nov. 11-13, shows that nearly three out of four Americans (72%) would favor the death penalty for Hussein, should he be found guilty, while 25% would oppose such a sentence. This is similar to the results from a June poll, in which 71% of Americans favored the death penalty for Hussein, while 24% opposed it. By way of comparison, 64% of Americans in Gallup's Oct. 13-16 poll favored the death penalty for American defendants convicted of murder.

The charges against Hussein stem from mass executions carried out in 1982 in the Iraqi town of Dujail. More than 140 people were sentenced to death and still more imprisoned and tortured following an assassination attempt on Hussein. The trial could be the first of several for Hussein.

As with many aspects of the situation in Iraq, there is a degree of polarization among Americans on the issue. However, this aspect appears to have only minimal disagreement: 86% of those who approve of President Bush's handling of the Iraq situation favor the death penalty for Hussein, as do 63% of those who disapprove of Bush's approach. From a slightly different perspective, 63% of Democrats and Democratic-leaning independents favor Hussein's execution if he is found guilty, compared with 81% of Republicans and Republican-leaning independents.

Would a Conviction Hurt Iraqi Insurgents?

Each passing day brings more news reports of insurgent attacks on U.S. and coalition forces in Iraq, and Bush has said that setting a schedule for troop withdrawal would only embolden the insurgents.

Would a conviction and the resulting execution of Hussein undermine the insurgency? A majority of Americans do not think so. Three out of four (75%) say Hussein's execution would not weaken the insurgents, while just 22% say the insurgency would be weakened.

Here, there are partisan differences as well, but even a majority of Republicans and Republican-leaning independents (56%) say executing Hussein would not weaken the insurgency. This rises to 86% among Democrats and Democratic-leaning independents.

Survey Methods

These results are based on telephone interviews with a randomly selected national sample of 1,006 adults, aged 18 and older, conducted Nov. 11-13, 2005. For results based on this sample, one can say with 95% confidence that the maximum error attributable to sampling and other random effects is ±3 percentage points. For results based on the 491 national adults in the Form A half-sample and the 515 national adults in the Form B half-sample, the maximum margins of sampling error are ±5 percentage points. In addition to sampling error, question wording and practical difficulties in conducting surveys can introduce error or bias into the findings of public opinion polls.

November 29, 2005

PUBLIC BELIEVES U.S. GOVERNMENT HAS TORTURED PRISONERS

Majority unwilling to sanction torture of suspected terrorists

by Darren K. Carlson, Government and Politics Editor

"We do not torture," President George W. Bush said earlier this month as he defended the United States' anti-terrorism interrogation practices. Last week, CIA Chief Porter Goss echoed Bush's declaration, denying his agency tortures prisoners. But most Americans think otherwise. Further, most would be unwilling to sanction torture, even if it could potentially yield information about future terrorist attacks against the United States.

Has It Happened?

A CNN/*USA Today*/Gallup poll*, conducted Nov. 11-13, finds nearly three-quarters of Americans (74%) think that U.S. troops or government officials have tortured prisoners in Iraq and other countries.

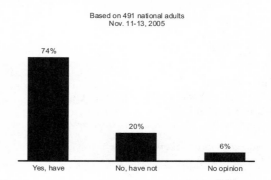

Just your best guess, do you think U.S. troops or government officials have -- or have not – tortured prisoners in Iraq or other countries?

Based on 491 national adults
Nov. 11-13, 2005

Yes, have: 74% No, have not: 20% No opinion: 6%

Majorities of both Democrats and Republicans believe U.S. troops and government officials have tortured prisoners in Iraq and elsewhere. However, Democrats are more likely than Republicans to believe torture has taken place, 80% vs. 65%, respectively.

Majority Not Willing to Allow Torture

In October, responding to revelations of prisoner mistreatment in Iraq's Abu Ghraib prison and allegations of mistreatment at the U.S. detention center at Guantanamo Bay, the Senate passed a ban on the torture of prisoners in U.S. custody. Because some interrogation techniques would be restricted under the ban, the Bush administration is arguing for an exemption for CIA-held prisoners if preventing a terrorist attack is at risk.

The Nov. 11-13 survey asked Americans whether they would be willing to have the government torture suspected terrorists if they may know details about future terrorist attacks against the United States. Slightly more than one in three, 38%, say they would be willing to have U.S. officials torture suspected terrorists, while the majority (56%) say they would not be willing.

Again, there is a schism along party lines. Just 27% of Democrats say they would be willing to have the government torture suspected terrorists if there's reason to believe they have information about future attacks, compared with slightly more than half of Republicans (51%).

Would you be willing – or not willing – to have the U.S. government torture suspected terrorists if they may know details about future terrorist attacks against the U.S.?

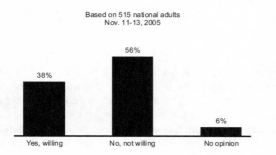

Based on 515 national adults
Nov. 11-13, 2005

38% Yes, willing

56% No, not willing

6% No opinion

These results are based on telephone interviews with randomly selected national samples of 491 and 515 adults, aged 18 and older, conducted Nov. 11-13, 2005. For results based on this sample, one can say with 95% confidence that the maximum error attributable to sampling and other random effects is ±5 percentage points. In addition to sampling error, question wording and practical difficulties in conducting surveys can introduce error or bias into the findings of public opinion polls.

November 29, 2005

WHAT'S THE PROGNOSIS FOR ANNUAL MEDICAL CHECKUPS?

Most Americans say it's important to have annual exams

by Lydia Saad, Senior Gallup Poll Editor

It used to be that visiting your doctor for an annual medical exam was the responsible thing to do. Good doctors were expected to pepper their patients with postcards reminding them it was checkup time, and good patients were expected to comply.

Evidence-based healthcare has changed all that. Studies show that the traditional top-to-bottom annual physical for healthy adults is largely a waste of time and healthcare dollars; it is too "low yield." So now the American Medical Association and other professional groups do not recommend the practice. Instead, they say medical care should be individualized according to a patient's age, health, and specific risk factors.

Traditions die hard, as is evident in a recent Gallup Poll* that shows 92% of Americans think it is important for people to have a routine medical checkup each year. When the question was phrased slightly differently, 95% say it is important for people their own age to have such a checkup. Young adults are as likely as seniors to believe this.

Not only do most people espouse this ideal; they live it. Nearly 8 in 10 Americans (78%) report that they personally had a routine exam in the past year.

There is a slight difference on this by gender: 83% of women versus 73% of men say they have had a routine checkup. This gender gap is primarily evident among adults under 50; 79% of women, but only 66% of men have had one. Men and women aged 50 and older are about equally likely to have had one.

These questions were asked as part of Gallup's annual health survey, which also includes a number of questions about respon-

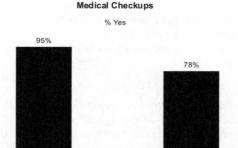

Medical Checkups

% Yes

95% Important for people your age to have routine annual checkup

78% Personally had a routine checkup in past year

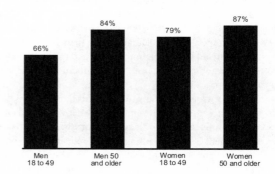

Had a Routine Checkup in Past Year, by Age and Gender

66% Men 18 to 49

84% Men 50 and older

79% Women 18 to 49

87% Women 50 and older

dents' own health and lifestyles. Speaking directly to the AMA's doubts about the value of annual physicals for healthy adults, people who describe their personal health as "excellent" or "good" are no less likely than those whose say their health is either "fair" or "poor" to have had a routine exam in the past year.

Percentage Had a Routine Medical Checkup in Past Year

Excellent/Good	Only fair/Poor
77%	82%

Although smokers have specific risk factors because of their habit, Gallup finds no significant difference in the percentage of smokers and nonsmokers who have had a routine checkup in the last year.

Percentage Had a Routine Medical Checkup in Past Year

Smoker	Nonsmoker
74%	80%

Also, those who are describe themselves as overweight are no more likely than those who say their weight is about right to have had a routine medical exam.

Percentage Had a Routine Medical Checkup in Past Year

Overweight	Weight About Right
79%	76%

While there is some relationship between household income and the likelihood of having had a routine exam, the likelihood varies a great deal by health insurance coverage. More than four in five insured Americans have had a routine medical checkup, compared with less than half of those without any insurance.

Percentage Had a Routine Medical Checkup in Past Year

Private insurance	Medicaid/Medicare	No insurance
81%	88%	44%

Bottom Line

The AMA and other professional groups may be exhibiting poor bedside manners in recommending against annual checkups. With so much emphasis on diseases and health risks in medical news, maybe patients have a legitimate need for annual reassurance that they are still OK.

That's the feeling of some doctors who argue the annual physical serves a vital function in nurturing the doctor-patient relationship—what Dr. Patrick G. O'Malley of Walter Reed Army Medical Center called the "less tangible benefits" of annual exams in a June WebMD *Medical News* article.

O'Malley is hardly alone. In a recent study reported in the *Archives of Internal Medicine*, 94% of primary doctors surveyed believed that annual physical exams improve the doctor-patient relationship and give doctors a unique opportunity to counsel patients on preventative healthcare.

But the healthcare train seems to be speeding in a different direction, albeit one that may provide a suitable compromise. The new approach to annual exams is called the "periodic health exam" or "PHE." The PHE is supposed to be regular (though not necessarily annual) and relies on a detailed family health history to tailor care to a patient's needs. The U.S. Surgeon General recently designated Thanksgiving 2005 as the second annual "National Family History Day"—hoping that people will take advantage of the assembly of relatives to chronicle their families' health history. Although PHEs appear to be the wave of the near future, it also appears there could be some resistance from patients and doctors who remain attached to the old system.

*Results are based on telephone interviews with 1,011 national adults, aged 18 and older, conducted Nov. 7-10, 2005. For results based on the total sample of national adults, one can say with 95% confidence that the margin of sampling error is ±3 percentage points.

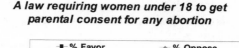

A recent *Newsweek* poll found even higher support—78%—when the question focused on parental notification, asking respondents whether they would favor or oppose an abortion restriction law "requiring that parents of teenagers must be notified."

Broad-Based Appeal

Gallup finds a high level of support for parental consent laws by gender as well as among different age groups. Women are only slightly less likely than men to favor parental consent (65% of women vs. 74% of men). There are no significant differences by age, as roughly 7 in 10 young adults, middle-aged adults, and seniors favor the laws.

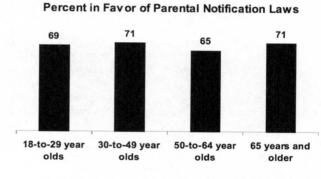

Percent in Favor of Parental Notification Laws

Nov 11-13, 2005

November 30, 2005

AMERICANS FAVOR PARENTAL INVOLVEMENT IN TEEN ABORTION DECISIONS

Think laws should require parental consent

by Lydia Saad, Gallup Poll Senior Editor

(The fate of a New Hampshire law requiring parents of minor girls to be notified before their daughters can have an abortion now rests with the Supreme Court. Opening arguments in Ayotte v. Planned Parenthood of Northern New England *begin Wednesday.)*

Most U.S. adults think parents should not just be notified, but should have to give their permission, before a minor daughter has an abortion. For more than a decade, Gallup has found roughly 7 in 10 Americans favoring laws that require women under 18 to receive parental consent for any abortion. The latest poll, conducted Nov. 11-13, finds 69% in favor and 28% opposed to such laws.

Support for such laws does vary according to partisan affiliation and political outlook; it is highest among Republicans and conservatives, and lowest among Democrats and liberals. Still, 59% of Democrats and a slim majority of liberals (51%) favor parental consent.

The popularity of parental involvement laws is evident in the fact that almost all states have them. According to Planned Parenthood, 44 states have laws requiring either parental notification or parental consent for minors seeking an abortion; but because of court challenges, such as the one that halted implementation of New Hampshire's law, only 35 are in effect.

The sticking point for New Hampshire's law, a point the *Ayotte* case will clarify, is whether parental consent laws must offer the same "health of the mother" exceptions that are required for laws that restrict abortions. The Supreme Court established this requirement in its 2000 decision nullifying a Nebraska ban on so-called partial-birth abortions; since then, lower courts have used this decision to strike down parental consent laws that fail to make the same exception.

Politics and Abortion
Percent in Favor of Parental Consent Laws

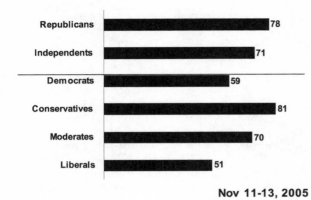

Republicans	78
Independents	71
Democrats	59
Conservatives	81
Moderates	70
Liberals	51

Nov 11-13, 2005

Gallup consistently finds that Americans are sympathetic to "health of the mother" exceptions to abortion restrictions. In January 2003, 77% of Americans said abortion should be legal when the woman's physical health is endangered. Whether this belief influences Americans' reactions to the New Hampshire case as it becomes better known will be interesting to see.

The Broader Strategy to Limit Abortion

The significance of *Ayotte* extends well beyond parental consent. Court watchers say it could set important precedents for how future challenges to state abortion laws are handled by the lower courts, and that could be critical to the strategy of abortion opponents.

Rather than tackling a complete ban on abortion or a sweeping overthrow of *Roe v. Wade*—which the public opposes—abortion opponents have, in recent years, taken an incremental approach to reducing the number of legal abortions. Gallup and other survey organizations document public support for many of the resulting abortion restrictions now being debated in the legislatures and courts. These include parental consent laws, "informed consent" for women, spousal notification for husbands, and bans on partial-birth abortions.

More generally, a majority of Americans (55%) favor a restrictive approach to abortion laws—saying abortion should be either legal "only in a few circumstances" or illegal in all circumstances, according to the latest poll. Just under half (42%) think it should be broadly legal—either in all or most circumstances.

Circumstances Under Which Abortion Should be Legal

Legal under any	Legal under most	Legal in only a few	Illegal in all
26	16	39	16

Nov 11-13, 2005

Attitudes about parental consent laws are clearly related to views about the legality of abortion. Opponents of abortion widely favor such laws. This includes more than four in five adults who believe abortion should be legal in only a few or no circumstances. However, rather than being solidly opposed to parental consent, abortion rights advocates are somewhat closely divided on the issue. Nearly half of those who think all abortions should be legal favor parental consent laws; just 52% oppose them. The majority (58%) of those who think abortions should be legal in most circumstances say they favor such laws.

Support for Parental Consent According to Position on Abortion

	Position on Abortion			
	Legal under any circum-stances	Legal under most circum-stances	Legal only in a few circum-stances	Illegal in all circum-stances
Parental Consent:	%	%	%	%
Favor	46	58	85	80
Oppose	52	39	13	19

Survey Methods

These results are based on telephone interviews with a randomly selected national sample of 1,006 adults, aged 18 and older, conducted Nov. 11-13, 2005. For results based on this sample, one can say with 95% confidence that the maximum error attributable to sampling and other random effects is ±3 percentage points. In addition to sampling error, question wording and practical difficulties in conducting surveys can introduce error or bias into the findings of public opinion polls.

December 1, 2005
AMERICANS SKEPTICAL BUSH HAS "VICTORY" PLAN

Few believe president's conditions for victory likely to be met soon, but reject fixed timetable

by David W. Moore, Gallup Poll Senior Editor

Wednesday morning, President George W. Bush outlined what he called his plan for victory in Iraq, but by late Wednesday evening, only a third of Americans had been exposed to the speech. Ten percent say they watched or listened to it live, and another 24% say they learned about it from news reports. Sixty-six percent had not heard of it.

That picture emerged from the results of a CNN/*USA Today*/Gallup poll conducted entirely on Wednesday evening, which found that 54% of Americans believe Bush is doing a poor job handling the situation in Iraq, while just 44% believe he is doing a good job.

How would you rate the job George W. Bush has done handling the situation in Iraq—as very good, good, poor, or very poor?

	Very good	Good	Poor	Very poor	No opinion
National adults	15%	29	25	29	2
(Combined good, poor)		44%		54	2

The poll also shows that a majority of Americans, 55%, believe Bush does not have a plan that will achieve victory in Iraq, while 41% believe he does. Among people who saw or listened to Bush give the speech, two-thirds say he has a plan and a third say he does not. But among people who learned of the speech in the news, only 42% say he has a plan, while 56% disagree—similar to the 37%-to-57% ratio among Americans who did not see or hear about the speech.

Do you think George W. Bush does—or does not—have a plan that will achieve victory for the United States in Iraq?

	Yes, does %	No, does not %	No opinion %	Sample size
National adults	41	55	4	606
Saw or listened to speech	67	33	0	69
Saw, heard, or read news coverage	42	56	2	145
Did neither	37	57	6	390

These results suggest the speech has had little immediate effect. Those who did not watch or listen to the speech but heard about it in the news hold similar views to people who had no exposure to the speech at all, while the speech watchers were already highly predisposed to agree with Bush given their partisan orientation. This group includes 45% who identify themselves as Republicans, more than twice the percentage who identify themselves as Democrats (20%). The other 35% are political independents.

In his speech, Bush vowed that the United States will not leave Iraq on the basis of a predetermined timetable, although U.S. troops will be withdrawn from Iraq as "conditions on the ground" permit. He specified at least three conditions that could signal victory in Iraq—establishing a stable democratic government there, making sure Iraqis can provide security without U.S. help, and ensuring that Iraq will not be used as base of operations for terrorists.

The poll suggests that Americans are inclined to agree with the president about not establishing a fixed timetable. On the other hand, most Americans do not believe that all three conditions are likely to be achieved within the next few years.

A clear majority of Americans, 59%, say that U.S. troops should be withdrawn from Iraq "only when certain goals are met," while 35% opt for setting a specific date and sticking to that timetable "regardless of conditions in Iraq at the time." This view would appear to coincide with Bush's position that "conditions on the ground" determine when troops should be withdrawn.

If you had to choose, which do you think is the better approach for deciding when the U.S. should withdraw its troops from Iraq—[ROTATED: to withdraw U.S. troops only when certain goals are met, (or) to withdraw U.S. troops by a specific date and stick to that timetable, regardless of conditions in Iraq at that time]?

	Withdraw only when certain goals are met %	Withdraw by specific and stick to date timetable %	No opinion %	Sample size
National adults	59	35	6	606
Saw or listened to speech	78	18	4	69
Saw, heard, or read news coverage	68	31	1	145
Did neither	53	40	7	390

These results suggest that people who heard about Bush's speech are more likely to agree with him than are people who had no exposure to his speech. Whatever the differences among the groups, majorities of each group reject the fixed timetable approach.

But the poll also suggests that most people believe Bush's three conditions of victory are not likely to be achieved soon.

- The public is about evenly divided as to whether a stable democratic regime can be established in Iraq in the next few years—47% say it is likely, 49% say unlikely.
- By a larger margin, 54% to 44%, Americans say it is unlikely that the Iraqi military and police will be able to ensure safety and security in Iraq without U.S. help.
- And by nearly a 2-to-1 margin, 63% to 33%, Americans think it unlikely that in the next few years, Iraq will be able to prevent terrorists from using that country as a base of operations for attacks against the United States.

Just your best guess, do you think each of the following is likely—or unlikely—to happen in Iraq in the next few years? How about— [RANDOM ORDER]?

	Likely %	Unlikely %	No opinion %
Iraq will have a democratic government that will not be overthrown by terrorists or supporters of Saddam Hussein	47	49	4
Iraqi military and police will be able to ensure safety and security in Iraq without assistance from the United States	44	54	2
Iraq will be able to prevent terrorists from using the country as a base of operations for planning attacks against the United States	33	63	4

Only 18% of Americans believe that all three conditions are likely to be met within the next few years, while another 35% believe that none of the conditions is likely to be met in that time frame. The rest say that at least one, but not all, of the conditions can be met.

At one point in his speech, Bush predicted that with a victory in Iraq, the United States will be safer from terrorism in the long run. Americans are divided on that point, with 48% agreeing and 50% disagreeing—43% saying the United States will actually be less safe, and another 7% volunteering that there would be no difference one way or the other.

In the long run, do you think the United States will be more safe—or less safe—from terrorism as a result of the war in Iraq?

	More safe	Less safe	NO CHANGE (vol.)	No opinion
National adults	48%	43	7	2

(vol.) = Volunteered response

Among the highly partisan group that watched or listened to the speech, most people say the country will be safer in the long run, by 72% to 25%. But among people who heard about Bush's speech in the news, and people who were not exposed to the speech, opinion is about evenly divided.

Survey Methods

Results are based on telephone interviews with 606 national adults, aged 18 and older, conducted Nov. 30, 2005. For results based on the total sample of national adults, one can say with 95% confidence that the maximum margin of sampling error is ±4 percentage points.

In addition to sampling error, question wording and practical difficulties in conducting surveys can introduce error or bias into the findings of public opinion polls.

Polls conducted entirely in one day, such as this one, are subject to additional error or bias not found in polls conducted over several days.

December 2, 2005
ANOTHER LOOK AT EVANGELICALS IN AMERICA TODAY
About 3 in 10 white, non-Catholic Christians describe themselves as "evangelical"

by Frank Newport, Gallup Poll Editor in Chief and Joseph Carroll, Assistant Editor

A great deal of attention has been placed on the special group of individuals within the American religious framework referred to as evangelicals. The term has been used for decades, but in more recent years has come to define a group of people who have become increasingly visible and active in American society. Evangelicals are not the only religious group in the United States that embraces certain more fundamental or orthodox beliefs, but it is one of the few such religious groups whose members are determined to have an impact on the society in which they live.

One does not have to look far to find evidence of this impact. The Family Research Council has scheduled another "Justice Sunday" event for this weekend, with the intent of mobilizing evangelicals to take action to change the types of judges in important positions. The role of evangelicals in electing President George W. Bush in the past two elections has been heavily documented, and evangelicals have been a major part of the news coverage in recent years of such issues as federal court nominees, evolution being taught in schools, and abortion debates.

Who Are the Evangelicals?

The term "evangelical" itself is vague, and has been defined and operationalized in a number of different ways in the past.

About 8 in 10 Americans at least nominally adhere to a Christian faith of one sort or another. The term evangelicals refers to a subset of this enormous group—a segment of Christians who by various definitions take their religion very seriously and also believe that the religious calling means that one should take action within the environment in which one lives. The most obvious such aspect of the environment is politics, and thus there has been an explosion of interest in the effect of the evangelical wing of the Republican Party on the political realm in recent years.

But, there is a great deal of confusion about exactly who evangelical Christians are. At various times, people have assumed that evangelicals are individuals who are adherents to certain denominations within the Christian faith, or that evangelicals are those who take their religion very seriously, adhere to more conservative or fundamental religious doctrine, have had specific religious experiences, or have specific beliefs about the correct relationship between religion and society.

Obviously, the aforementioned criteria produce quite different estimates of the percentage of the American population that is "evangelical." Some organizations have used a very strict criterion requiring respondents in surveys to answer affirmatively to a number of doctrinal and other questions before being considered to be evangelicals. Gallup has at times used a procedure consisting of three questions asking respondents if they have had a born-again experience committing themselves to Jesus Christ, if they have tried to encourage someone to believe in Jesus Christ, and if they believe the Bible is the actual word of God. Twenty-two percent of Americans agree with all three questions, according to a Gallup Poll conducted in May 2005.

Gallup also uses another, more straightforward approach. Americans are simply asked: "Would you describe yourself as a 'born again' or evangelical?" The percentage of Americans who say "yes" to this question has varied since Gallup first began using it in 1991, between a high point of 47% reached earlier this year, and a low of 35% in 1996.

The average agreement in four surveys conducted since December 2004 has been 43%.

Would you describe yourself as a "born again" or evangelical?

	Yes %	No %	No opin- ion %		Yes %	No %	No opin- ion %
2005 Nov 17-20	40	54	6	1998 Jun 22-23	44	48	8
				1997 Aug 12-13	45	47	8
2005 Sep 8-11	47	50	3	1997 Mar 24-26	43	51	6
2005 Apr 18-21	42	53	5	1996 Nov 21-24	41	52	7
2004 Dec 5-8	39	55	6	1996 Sep 3-5	42	52	6
2004 Jun 3-6	42	54	4	1996 Jul 26-28	36	59	5
2003 Nov 10-12	43	53	4	1996 Jun 27-30	35	58	7
2003 May 30-Jun 1	41	53	6	1995 Dec 15-18	43	52	5
2003 Feb 17-19	41	54	5	1995 Aug 28-30	39	54	7
2002 Dec 9-10	46	48	6	1995 May 11-14	39	53	8
2002 Mar 18-20	46	50	4	1994 Jun 25-28	39	53	8
2001 Dec 14-16	42	49	9	1994 Mar 28-30	45	48	7
2001 Feb 19-21	45	49	6	1993 Oct 28-30	43	51	6
2000 Aug 24-27	44	50	6	1993 Sep 13-15	44	51	5
2000 Mar 17-19	46	47	7	1993 Mar	46	50	4
1999 Dec 9-12	46	48	6	1992 Apr 9-12	42	52	6
1999 Apr 30-May 2	45	47	8	1991 Nov 21-24	41	54	5

^ November 1991-March 1997 wording: "Would you describe yourself as a 'born again' or evangelical Christian?"

But does this mean that the group of Americans who say "yes" to this question should be the group used as the popular representation of evangelicals? There are reasons to answer that question "no." Those who say "evangelical or born again" describes them include Catholics, blacks, and those who are not Christians. It seems reasonable to impose a more restrictive definition in order to isolate—for practical purposes—those who should be considered evangelicals.

The data shown in the table, compiled from December 2004 to November 2005, show that 19% of Catholics say "yes" when asked if they are evangelical or born again. While that is considerably lower than the 43% of all Americans who agree that they are born again, it is not an insignificant number.

The Catholic religion, it goes without saying, is very different from most Protestant or non-Catholic Christian denominations. There are major differences between the Catholic and Protestant approach to Christianity, differences in the structure of the church, and different historical traditions. There can certainly be debate on this issue, but many considerations of the impact of evangelicals in American society today focus mainly on Protestants. Given this fact, and the reality that Catholics at least nominally operate within a framework of much more prescribed dogma than is the case for Protestants, it seems defensible to exclude Catholics from a working definition of evangelicals.

What About Race?

Black Americans are among the most religious groups in America. They are also, for the most part, Protestant Christians. Therefore, it is not surprising to find that 70% of blacks in the combined aggregate sample of surveys say they are evangelical or born again.

But for most practical, analytic purposes, including blacks in the mix of those defined as evangelical makes little sense. Data show that blacks are overwhelmingly Democratic in political orientation regardless of their religion. At least 9 in 10 blacks vote for the Democratic candidate for president each election. So, the inclusion of blacks in a group of "evangelicals" being defined for analytic reasons obscures analysis to the degree that the purpose of defining the group is to measure their influence on political life in particular.

Thus, while it may be reasonable to look at black evangelicals in some situations and for some purposes, for the current purposes evangelicals will be defined as only whites.

Finally, there is a small percent of those who say they have no religion, or identify with non-Christian religions, that say they're evangelical or born again. Although this raises interesting questions in and of itself, it is reasonable to exclude these non-Christians from a practical definition of evangelicals.

Thus, when all is said and done, there is a group of about 28% of the adult population in America today who are white, non-Catholic Christians and who describe themselves as evangelical or born again.

Who are these people? One way is to look at the composition of evangelicals as defined thusly against the composition of the entire U.S. population:

	White, non-Catholic Christians who are evangelicals or born again %	All national adults %
Gender		
Men	44	48
Women	56	52
Region		
East	13	23
Midwest	25	23
South	45	32
West	16	22
Education		
High school or less	46	38
Some college	33	32
College graduate	12	14
Postgraduate	9	15
Income		
Less than $20,000 a year	14	14
$20,000 to $29,999 a year	13	12
$30,000 to $49,999 a year	31	26
$50,000 to $74,999 a year	16	17
$75,000 or more a year	25	30
Age		
18- to 29-year-olds	11	18
30- to 49-year-olds	38	40
50- to 64-year-olds	26	23
65 years and older	24	19
Party Affiliation		
Republicans	54	35
Independents	25	32
Democrats	22	33

	White, non-Catholic Christians who are evangelicals or born again %	All national adults %
Ideology		
Conservative	58	39
Moderate	31	40
Liberal	11	20

Several conclusions arise from consideration of these data:

- Evangelical Christians, as defined, are slightly more likely to be female and aged 50 and older than the overall national adult population.
- Evangelical Christians are somewhat less likely to be college graduates than the total population, but have an income structure that generally mirrors the national population.
- Evangelical Christians are overrepresented in the South, and are underrepresented in the East and, to a lesser degree, in the West compared with the basic U.S. population distribution.
- Evangelical Christians skew strongly Republican in terms of their political orientation. More than half (54%) identify themselves as Republicans, compared with 35% of the total population. On the other hand, 22% identify as Democrats, compared with 33% of the total population.
- Along these same lines, almost 6 in 10 evangelical Christians are conservatives, compared with just about 4 in 10 national adults, and they are less likely to identify themselves as moderates or liberals.

Bottom Line

There is no hard-and-fast definition of who "evangelicals" are in America today. For practical purposes, one approach is to define evangelicals as white, non-Catholic Christians who agree that the label "evangelical or born again" describes them. Recent survey data suggest that about 3 in 10 American adults meet these criteria. Compared with the overall national population, this group of evangelicals tends to be slightly more female and older, a little less well educated, more likely to live in the South, and much more likely to be Republican and conservative.

Survey Methods

Results are based on telephone interviews with 5,019 national adults, aged 18 and older, conducted across four surveys from December 2004 through November 2005. For results based on the total sample of national adults, one can say with 95% confidence that the maximum margin of sampling error is ±2 percentage points. In addition to sampling error, question wording and practical difficulties in conducting surveys can introduce error or bias into the findings of public opinion polls.

December 5, 2005
NURSES REMAIN ATOP HONESTY AND ETHICS LIST
Hold substantial lead over other professions

by Jeffrey M. Jones, Gallup Poll Managing Editor

Gallup's annual poll on the honesty and ethics of people in different professions finds that nurses continue to be rated most positively, by a substantial margin. Telemarketers and car salesmen rank at the bottom of this year's list. Most of the professions' ratings show little change from their last readings. However, there has been a slight increase in the ratings of bankers' honesty and ethics, and slight decreases for pharmacists and congressmen.

The Nov. 17-20 Gallup Poll asked Americans to rate the honesty and ethical standards of members of professions on a five-point scale that ranges from "very high" to "very low." Of the 21 professions tested this year, 6 have majority "high ethical" ratings—nurses (82%), pharmacists (67%), medical doctors (65%), high school teachers (64%), policemen (61%), and clergy (54%). Only one has a majority giving it low ethical ratings—telemarketers. Car salesmen come close, with 49% rating this profession as low on honesty and ethics.

Honesty and Ethical Ratings of People in Different Professions, 2005 Gallup Poll

(sorted by Very high/High)	%Very high/High	% Average	% Low/ Very low
Nurses	82	15	3
Druggists/Pharmacists	67	28	4
Medical doctors	65	31	4
High school teachers	64	27	7
Policemen	61	31	8
Clergy	54	35	8
Funeral directors	44	42	8
Bankers	41	48	10
Accountants	39	51	7
Journalists	28	44	27
Real estate agents	20	58	20
Building contractors	20	58	19
Lawyers	18	46	35
Labor union leaders	16	43	35
Senators	16	48	35
Business executives	16	52	30
Stockbrokers	16	56	23
Congressmen	14	44	41
Advertising practitioners	11	50	35
Car salesmen	8	41	49
Telemarketers	7	31	60

Gallup first asked the honesty and ethics question in 1976. Since that time, 57 different professions have been rated at one time or another. The following table shows the most positively and most negatively rated professions each year the question was asked.

Year	Most positive	Most negative
1976	Medical doctors (56% very high/high)	Political officeholders (10% low/very low)
1977	Clergy (61%)	Car salesmen (8%)
1981	Clergy (63%)	Car salesmen (6%)
1983	Clergy (64%)	Car salesmen (6%)

Year	Most positive	Most negative
1985	Clergy (67%)	Car salesmen (5%)
1988	Pharmacists (66%)	Car salesmen (6%)
1990	Pharmacists (62%)	Car salesmen (6%)
1991	Pharmacists (60%)	Car salesmen (8%)
1992	Pharmacists (66%)	Car salesmen (5%)
1993	Pharmacists (65%)	Car salesmen (6%)
1994	Pharmacists (62%)	Car salesmen (6%)
1995	Pharmacists (66%)	Car salesmen (5%)
1996	Pharmacists (64%)	Car salesmen (8%)
1997	Pharmacists (69%)	Car salesmen (8%)
1998	Pharmacists (64%)	Car salesmen (5%)
1999	Nurses (73%)	Car salesmen (8%)
2000	Nurses (79%)	Car salesmen (7%)
2001	Firefighters (90%)	Car salesmen (8%)
2002	Nurses (79%)	Telemarketers (5%)
2003	Nurses (83%)	Car salesmen (7%)
2004	Nurses (79%)	Car salesmen (9%)
2005	Nurses (82%)	Telemarketers (7%)

Nurses have averaged 80% high honesty ratings since Gallup first asked about the profession in 1999. That is significantly higher than any other profession that has been asked multiple times ("firefighters" was asked just once, following the publicity given that profession after the Sept. 11 terrorist attacks). The next highest averages belong to military officers (69%), veterinarians (66%), pharmacists (65%), and high school teachers (64%). Car salesmen (7%) and telemarketers (7%) have the lowest historical average ratings.

Other trends from this year's results:

- This is the first time bankers have exceeded 40% very high/high ratings. They have received ratings as low as 26%.
- Pharmacists' ratings dropped slightly this year, to 67% from 72% from last year. The current reading is more in line with the profession's average since Gallup first asked about it in 1981.
- Medical doctors and policemen have been rated more positively this decade than in previous decades. Doctors have a 65% average from 2000 to 2005, compared with a 54% average from 1976 to 1999. Policemen averaged 46% from 1981 to 1999, and have averaged 60% since then.
- Clergy ratings have not yet recovered since the Catholic priest sex abuse scandal became an issue. After a 64% rating in 2001, ratings of the clergy's honesty and ethics fell to 52% in 2002 and are at 54% today.
- Accountants' ratings, on the other hand, have almost fully recovered from the business scandals of 2002. Accountants' ratings went from 41% in 2001 to 32% during the Enron-era scandals and are at 39% today.
- Business executives had shown some improvement in recent years, but their ratings have fallen back this year. After dropping from 25% in 2001 to 16% in 2002, they inched up to 20% last year. However, this year, they returned to the 16% level.
- Funeral directors, last asked in 2002, improved from 39% then to 44% now.

Survey Methods

These results are based on telephone interviews with a randomly selected national sample of 1,002 adults, aged 18 and older, conducted Nov. 17-20, 2005. For results based on this sample, one can say with 95% confidence that the maximum error attributable to sampling and other random effects is ±3 percentage points. In addition to sampling error, question wording and practical difficulties in conducting surveys can introduce error or bias into the findings of public opinion polls.

December 6, 2005
REGULAR EXERCISE: WHO'S GETTING IT?
More than half fall into "low" or "sedentary" categories

by Joseph Carroll, Gallup Poll Assistant Editor

Every year, Gallup asks Americans to estimate the amount of time they spend exercising at different levels of intensity. The results show that nearly half of Americans work out regularly and vigorously, while slightly more than half do not. Which Americans are most likely to work out? The answers yield a few surprises.

Overall Results

Gallup's annual health survey asks Americans how many days each week they take part in "vigorous sports or physical activities for at least 20 minutes that cause large increases in breathing or heart rate" or in "moderate sports or recreational activities that cause slight increases in breathing or heart rate, such as walking, gardening, or other similar activities."

The results of these two questions are combined into four different categories in Gallup's exercise index:

- *High*: Adults who engage in vigorous activities three to seven days a week
- *Medium*: Adults who take part in vigorous physical activities one or two days a week
- *Low*: Adults who are rarely involved in vigorous activities but do partake in moderate activities three to seven days a week
- *Sedentary*: Adults who rarely take part in any vigorous or moderate activities

To better understand which groups of Americans are most likely to work out frequently and vigorously, Gallup combined the results of its last three surveys, conducted from November 2003 through November 2005. Overall, 29% of Americans fall into the "high" exercise category, while an additional 19% fall into the "medium" category. More than half of Americans fall into the "low" (23%) or "sedentary" (28%) exercise categories.

Men, Younger Americans More Inclined to Exercise Regularly

The data show that men are much more likely than women to say they exercise or engage in vigorous sports or activities on a regular basis. Fifty-six percent of men belong in the high (33%) or medium (23%) exercise categories, compared with only 42% of women (26% high, 16% medium). Nearly 6 in 10 women fall into the low (26%) or sedentary (32%) exercise groups.

The likelihood to exercise frequently and vigorously is most common among younger Americans and decreases substantially with age. Two in three adults aged 18 to 29 fall into the high or medium exercise categories. This compares with 52% of 30- to 49-year-olds, 41% of 50- to 64-year-olds, and 32% of adults aged 65 and older.

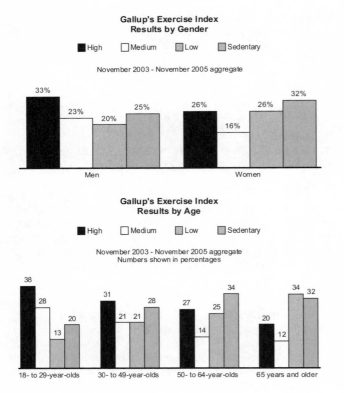

**Gallup's Exercise Index
Results by Gender**

■ High ☐ Medium ▨ Low ▨ Sedentary

November 2003 - November 2005 aggregate

**Gallup's Exercise Index
Results by Age**

■ High ☐ Medium ▨ Low ▨ Sedentary

November 2003 - November 2005 aggregate
Numbers shown in percentages

Interestingly, men are consistently more likely than women to say they exercise frequently and vigorously, regardless of the respondent's age, with men aged 18 to 29 the most likely group to work out.

Good Health Means More Exercise?

Healthier Americans are more likely to say they participate in frequent, vigorous exercise than those who are not as healthy. A majority of Americans who describe their physical health as excellent or good fall into the high (32%) or medium (21%) exercise categories, while only 3 in 10 adults who describe their health as only fair or poor do so (17% high, 13% medium). Nearly 7 in 10 adults who say their health is only fair or poor are in the low (23%) or sedentary (46%) groupings.

The direction of this relationship is not clear. Americans who are in poor health may not have the opportunity or ability to exercise as much as those in good health. It may also be, of course, that the exercise itself causes the differences in health situations.

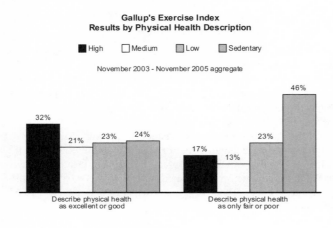

**Gallup's Exercise Index
Results by Physical Health Description**

■ High ☐ Medium ▨ Low ▨ Sedentary

November 2003 - November 2005 aggregate

Weight Affects Exercise Habits

Americans who describe themselves as overweight are much less likely to exercise frequently and vigorously than those who describe their weight as about right or underweight. Roughly 4 in 10 overweight adults fall into the high (22%) or medium (18%) exercise categories, while a majority of adults who are underweight or "about right" are in the high (34%) or medium (20%) range. Nearly 6 in 10 overweight adults fall into the low or sedentary groups.

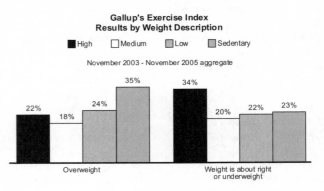

**Gallup's Exercise Index
Results by Weight Description**

■ High ☐ Medium ▨ Low ▨ Sedentary

November 2003 - November 2005 aggregate

Exercise Habits of Smokers

Gallup finds only modest variations in the exercise habits of smokers and nonsmokers. Forty-six percent of smokers—and 49% of nonsmokers—fall into the high or medium exercise groups.

**Gallup's Exercise Index
Results by Smoking Habits**

November 2003 - November 2005 aggregate

	Smokers	Nonsmokers
High	26%	30%
Medium	20%	19%
Low	22%	23%
Sedentary	32%	27%
High + Medium	46%	49%
Low + Sedentary	54%	50%

More You Earn, More You Exercise?

Americans residing in higher income households are more likely than those living in lower income households to exercise frequently. Among adults earning less than $30,000 per year, only about 4 in 10

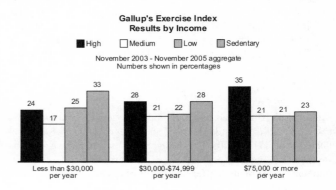

**Gallup's Exercise Index
Results by Income**

■ High ☐ Medium ▨ Low ▨ Sedentary

November 2003 - November 2005 aggregate
Numbers shown in percentages

belong in the high (24%) or medium (17%) exercise categories, while nearly half of adults earning between $30,000 and $75,000 exercise at the high or medium levels. Fifty-six percent of those earning $75,000 or more per year exercise at this level.

Results are based on telephone interviews with 3,027 national adults, aged 18 and older, conducted Nov. 3-5, 2003, Nov. 7-10, 2004, and Nov. 7-10, 2005. For results based on the total sample of national adults, one can say with 95% confidence that the margin of sampling error is ±2 percentage points. In addition to sampling error, question wording and practical difficulties in conducting surveys can introduce error or bias into the findings of public opinion polls.

December 6, 2005
AMERICANS APPROVE OF IMMIGRATION—IN PRINCIPLE
Quarter approve of how Bush has handled it

by Darren K. Carlson, Government and Politics Editor

President Bush traveled to Texas and Arizona last week to push new strategies for dealing with an issue that has divided the public and even his own party: immigration. His recent proposal on immigration reform hinges on hardened border security, a commitment to returning illegal immigrants to the interior of Mexico, and a controversial temporary worker program that allows illegal immigrants to get temporary legal status for a fixed period. Bush needs to gain political traction on this issue; a Nov. 11-13 Gallup Poll* shows that just 26% of Americans approve of the way he is handling immigration, while 65% disapprove.

Is Immigration Good or Bad for the U.S.?

For Americans, the problem doesn't appear to be the notion of immigration *per se*—a majority still views it as a good thing. Gallup's annual survey on minority relations, conducted last June**, found a majority of Americans (61%) saying they consider immigration a good thing for this country today. Slightly more than a third (34%) said it is a bad thing for the country. A majority of Americans have viewed immigration as a good thing since Gallup began asking this version of the question in 2001.

On the whole, do you think immigration is a good thing or a bad thing for this country today?

● Good thing   ● Bad thing

Nevertheless, when asked in the same survey about the level of immigration into the United States, Americans were more likely to favor decreasing it than increasing it. A plurality—46%—said they would like to see immigration decreased, 34% want to see it kept at its present level, and just 16% would like to see it increased.

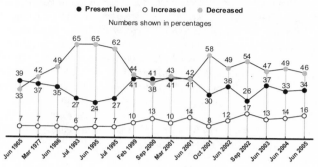

In your view, should immigration be kept at its present level, increased, or decreased?

● Present level   ○ Increased   ● Decreased

Numbers shown in percentages

Economic Interests Pervade Immigration Issue

The apparent contradiction may reflect Americans' ambivalence about the specific economic and social effects of immigration. The public is divided on whether immigrants mostly help or mostly hurt the economy. Forty-two percent believe immigrants help the economy by providing low-cost labor, while 49% think immigrants hurt it by driving down wages. There are differences of opinion by race and ethnicity. A majority of Hispanic Americans say immigrants mostly help the economy, while majorities of non-Hispanic white Americans and black Americans say immigrants mostly hurt the economy.

Americans are also divided on whether immigrants become productive citizens in the long run and pay their fair share of taxes, or cost the taxpayers too much by using government services such as public education and medical services. Forty-nine percent say immigrants pay their fair share, while 44% say they cost taxpayers too much. Non-Hispanic whites and blacks are fairly divided on this question, but two-thirds of Hispanics say immigrants pay their fair share.

Citizenship

The June survey also asked respondents whether they think it should be made easier for illegal immigrants to become citizens. Only 28% of Americans believe it should be made easier, while 70% disagree. Hispanic respondents are much more likely than non-Hispanic whites or blacks to think the United States should make it easier for illegal

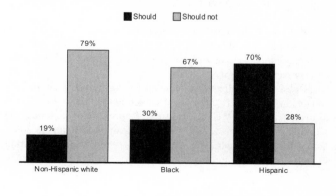

Do you think the United States should or should not make it easier for illegal immigrants to become citizens of the United States?

■ Should   ■ Should not

immigrants to become citizens. Seven in 10 Hispanic Americans think that it should be easier, compared with 30% of blacks and just 19% of non-Hispanic whites.

These results are based on telephone interviews with a randomly selected national sample of 1,006 adults, aged 18 and older, conducted Nov. 11-13, 2005. For results based on this sample, one can say with 95% confidence that the maximum error attributable to sampling and other random effects is ±3 percentage points. In addition to sampling error, question wording and practical difficulties in conducting surveys can introduce error or bias into the findings of public opinion polls.

**Results are based on telephone interviews with 2,264 national adults, aged 18 and older, conducted June 6-25, 2005, including oversamples of blacks and Hispanics that are weighted to reflect their proportions in the general population. For results based on the total sample of national adults, one can say with 95% confidence that the maximum margin of sampling error is ±5 percentage points.*

December 6, 2005

DELAY TRAILS "DEMOCRAT" IN OWN DISTRICT BY 13 POINTS

Majority of district voters believe charges against DeLay likely to be true

by David W. Moore, Gallup Poll Senior Editor

A CNN/*USA Today*/Gallup survey of registered voters in Texas' 22nd Congressional District finds incumbent Congressman Tom DeLay trailing a "generic" Democrat by 13 percentage points, with 49% of voters supporting the unnamed "Democratic Party's candidate for Congress," and 36% supporting DeLay. Another 12% of voters are unsure who they will vote for, and 3% choose another candidate.

If Tom DeLay runs for re-election in 2006, in general, are you more likely to vote for the Republican candidate Tom DeLay or for the Democratic Party's candidate for Congress?

	DeLay	Democratic candidate	OTHER (vol.)	No opinion
	%	%	%	%
Registered Voters				
2005 Dec 1-4	36	49	3	12
All Residents				
2005 Dec 1-4	34	47	4	15

(vol.) = Volunteered response

Among all adult residents, the unnamed Democrat's margin over DeLay is identical, though the percentages are two points lower for each candidate, 47% to 34%, with 15% unsure and 4% opting for another candidate.

DeLay was indicted on conspiracy and money laundering charges in September, and was subsequently forced to step down as Majority Leader of the U.S. House of Representatives, though he remained in office as a representative from his district. In 2003, DeLay helped engineer a mid-decade redistricting in Texas, in order to facilitate the election of more Republicans to the U.S. House in the 2004 election, an effort that was ultimately successful.

One of the victims of the new redistricting was Nick Lampson, a congressman from what had been the 9th Congressional District, before it was renumbered and re-configured, so that it contained more Republican voters than his old district. Lampson lost to a Republican in 2004, but in May 2005, he announced that he would run against DeLay in Texas' 22nd District next year.

The poll shows that only about 4 in 10 district voters have an opinion about Lampson, though it is more favorable (28%) than unfavorable (11%). Among all residents, the percentages are similar. These results suggest that while Lampson is not particularly well-known, he does not start out with a major negative image to overcome. (The poll does not include Lampson's name in the ballot question, because there could be other Democrats who run for the seat. Once a specific name is mentioned, the polling results are likely to change based on the actual candidate's own characteristics. Still, the unnamed Democratic ballot provides insight into DeLay's current electoral vulnerability.)

Opinion of Former Texas Congressman, Nick Lampson

	Favorable	Unfavorable	Never heard of	No opinion
Registered Voters	%	%	%	%
2005 Dec 1-4	28	11	37	24
All Residents				
2005 Dec 1-4	25	10	40	25

DeLay's favorability rating reflects the low level of his electoral support. By a margin of 52% to 37%, voters in the district say they have an unfavorable, rather than a favorable, view of the congressman. Among all adult residents in the district, the margin is identical.

Opinion of Texas Congressman, Tom DeLay

	Favorable	Unfavorable	Never heard of	No opinion
Registered Voters	%	%	%	%
2005 Dec 1-4	37	52	1	10
All Residents				
2005 Dec 1-4	35	50	3	12

A clear majority of residents and voters in the district are inclined to believe that the felony charges against DeLay are true—55% express that point of view, including 15% who say the charges are "definitely" true and 40% who say they are "probably" true.

As you may know, Tom DeLay has been indicted on charges that he broke campaign finance laws. Based on what you have heard or read, do you think the charges against DeLay are—[ROTATED: definitely true, probably true, probably not true, (or) definitely not true]?

	Definitely true	Probably true	Probably not true	Definitely not true	No opinion
Registered Voters	%	%	%	%	%
2005 Dec 1-4	15	40	26	8	11
All Residents					
2005 Dec 1-4	15	40	24	7	14

Only 34% of voters, or 31% of all residents, believe the charges are probably or definitely not true.

Oddly enough, given these negative views of DeLay, people in the district are evenly divided as to whether or not Travis County District Attorney Ronnie Earle is bringing the charges against the congressman primarily for political reasons. Forty-six percent say "it is mostly an effort to fairly enforce the law," while 45% say "it is mostly an attempt to hurt Tom DeLay politically."

Which best describes your view about the actions taken by the District Attorney in this case—[ROTATED: it is mostly an effort to fairly enforce the law, (or) it is mostly an attempt to hurt Tom DeLay politically]?

	Fairly enforce the law	Hurt DeLay politically	No opinion
Registered Voters	%	%	%
2005 Dec 1-4	46	45	9
All Residents			
2005 Dec 1-4	45	43	12

The public's skepticism about the reasons for bringing the charges is reflected in the evenly divided opinion that voters and residents express about Earle: 21% of voters have a favorable view of him, 22% unfavorable. Among all residents, the percentages are equal at 19%.

Opinion of Travis County District Attorney, Ronnie Earle

	Favorable	Unfavorable	Never heard of	No opinion
Registered Voters	%	%	%	%
2005 Dec 1-4	21	22	40	17
All Residents				
2005 Dec 1-4	19	19	44	18

Partisan Division

The poll shows that Republicans outnumber Democrats in the district by a 14-point margin, 39% to 25%, with 33% independents. When independents indicate the party they "lean" to, the 14-point difference between the two major parties reduces to nine points, with 50% saying they are Republicans (including "leaning" Republicans) and 41% saying they are Democrats (including "leaning" Democrats).

A comparison of voting intentions by party shows that two-thirds of Republican voters are inclined to choose DeLay, while 18% would vote for the Democrat, and 16% are undecided or would vote for another candidate. But by a two-to-one margin, independents prefer the Democratic candidate, 55% to 26%, and Democrats almost unanimously choose their own party's candidate, 91% to 3%.

2006 Vote for Congress in Texas' 22nd Congressional District

	DeLay	Democratic candidate	OTHER (vol.)	No opinion
	%	%	%	%
All registered voters	36	49	3	12
Republicans (39%)	66	18	3	13
Independents (33%)	26	55	4	15
Democrats (26%)	3	91	*	6

*Less than 0.5%
(vol.) = Volunteered response

Survey Methods

Results are based on telephone interviews with 803 adults in the 22nd Congressional district in Texas, aged 18 and older, conducted Dec. 1-4, 2005. For results based on the total sample of adults in the 22nd Congressional district in Texas, one can say with 95% confidence that the maximum margin of sampling error is ±4 percentage points.

Listed sample was provided by Survey Sampling International, with sampling done on a geographic basis (down to the census tract/block group level) that corresponded to the geographical definitions of Tom DeLay's district. These definitions were updated to reflect changes made to the geographical boundaries of DeLay's district prior to the 2004 election.

Ninety-two percent of the original sample lived in geographies that were entirely within Tom DeLay's district. The remaining 8% were flagged in the sample and were screened on self-reports of whether the respondent lived in the district. Of these, only those who were certain they lived in DeLay's district were interviewed.

Data were weighted on gender, age, education, race, and Hispanic ethnicity to match census figures for Tom DeLay's district.

Interviews were conducted in both English and Spanish (17 out of the 803 interviews were conducted in Spanish).

For results based on the sample of 713 registered voters, the maximum margin of sampling error is ±4 percentage points.

In addition to sampling error, question wording and practical difficulties in conducting surveys can introduce error or bias into the findings of public opinion polls.

December 7, 2005
U.S. HEALTHCARE RATINGS SLIP
Percentage favoring government healthcare system increases

by David W. Moore, Gallup Poll Senior Editor
and Jeffrey M. Jones, Managing Editor

The latest annual Gallup Poll on health finds a modest drop in the percentage of Americans giving a high rating to the quality and coverage of healthcare in this country, as well as a significant increase in the percentage of Americans favoring a government healthcare system. Overall, Americans continue to rate healthcare quality much higher than healthcare coverage, and to rate their own healthcare more positively than what the general public receives.

Healthcare in the United States

The poll, conducted Nov. 7-10, finds Americans somewhat more positive than negative about the overall quality of healthcare in the country. By a margin of 53% to 47%, Americans say U.S. healthcare quality is excellent or good, rather than fair or poor. Those figures are down from a 59% to 40% rating last year and a 60% to 40% rating in 2003. The current figures are in line with what Gallup measured in 2001 and 2002.

Increasingly negative perceptions of national healthcare quality this year compared to last are most evident among Republicans, women, and those with household incomes of $50,000 or greater.

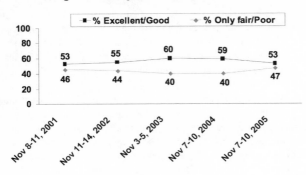

Rating the Quality of Healthcare in the Country

	% Excellent/Good	% Only fair/Poor
Nov 8-11, 2001	53	46
Nov 11-14, 2002	55	44
Nov 3-5, 2003	60	40
Nov 7-10, 2004	59	40
Nov 7-10, 2005	53	47

Quality of Healthcare in the United States: Percentage Saying Excellent or Good

	2004 %	2005 %	Difference
Overall	59	53	-6
Gender			
Male	63	60	-3
Female	57	46	-11
Age			
18-29	46	42	-4
30-49	67	53	-14
50-64	62	57	-5
65+	55	60	+5
Income			
<$30,000	45	48	+3
$30,000-<$50,000	54	50	-4
$50,000-<$75,000	72	50	-22
$75,000+	75	62	-13
Party			
Republican	74	63	-11
Independent	59	53	-6
Democrat	45	44	-1

Perceptions of healthcare coverage in the United States, which have been more negative than positive since Gallup first asked the question in 2001, have fallen to their lowest point in the last five years. Just 21% give an excellent or good rating to U.S. healthcare coverage, while 78% rate it as only fair (43%) or poor (35%). In the previous four years, excellent/good ratings ranged between 28% and 30%.

As with ratings of healthcare quality, women, Republicans, and those residing in higher-income households show the greatest declines in their ratings of national healthcare coverage compared

Rating Healthcare Coverage in the Country

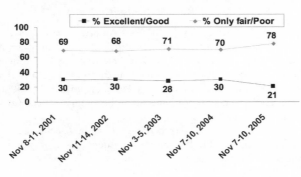

	% Excellent/Good	% Only fair/Poor
Nov 8-11, 2001	30	69
Nov 11-14, 2002	30	68
Nov 3-5, 2003	28	71
Nov 7-10, 2004	30	70
Nov 7-10, 2005	21	78

with last year. Those in the middle age categories—between ages 30 and 64—also show significant declines.

Healthcare Coverage in the United States: Percentage Saying Excellent or Good

	2004 %	2005 %	Difference
Overall	30	21	-9
Gender			
Male	32	26	-6
Female	28	17	-11
Age			
18-29	17	18	+1
30-49	31	17	-14
50-64	34	23	-11
65+	33	30	-3
Income			
<$30,000	21	16	-5
$30,000-<$50,000	27	17	-10
$50,000-<$75,000	42	29	-13
$75,000+	34	22	-12
Party			
Republican	47	32	-15
Independent	24	21	-3
Democrat	15	11	-4

Perhaps as a result of the increasingly negative perceptions of healthcare quality and coverage in the United States, the percentage of Americans favoring a government-run healthcare system has reached a five-year high at 41%. The plurality still favors maintaining the current system (49%); however, the percentage that does so is roughly 10 points lower than what it has been in previous surveys.

Replace the Current Healthcare System or Maintain Current System?

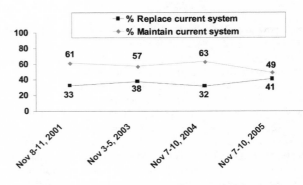

	% Replace current system	% Maintain current system
Nov 8-11, 2001	33	61
Nov 3-5, 2003	38	57
Nov 7-10, 2004	32	63
Nov 7-10, 2005	41	49

Other measures in the poll show stable results compared with previous years. Just 20% of Americans say they are satisfied with the total cost of healthcare in this country, while 79% are dissatisfied. Also, 70% of Americans say the healthcare system has major problems (52%) or go even further and say it is in a state of crisis (18%). The percentage of Americans giving either of these responses has been around 70% each time the question has been asked, aside from an unusually low 49% reading shortly after the Sept. 11 terrorist attacks.

Personal Healthcare

Respondents continue to be more positive when evaluating their own healthcare than the larger U.S. healthcare system. Seventy-eight percent rate the quality of healthcare they receive as excellent or good, and 63% rate their coverage in those terms.

Comparison of Healthcare Ratings, National vs. Personal

	Quality U.S. %	Coverage Personal %	U.S. %	Personal %
Excellent	16	29	2	20
Good	37	49	19	43
Only fair	33	17	43	21
Poor	14	3	35	11
Total Exc/Good	**53**	**78**	**21**	**63**
Total Fair/Poor	**47**	**20**	**78**	**32**

An analysis of individuals' responses to the national and personal healthcare questions shows that 44% rate their own healthcare quality higher than they rate national healthcare quality. Forty-seven percent give the same ratings to both, and 9% rate national healthcare quality better than their own healthcare.

Quality of Healthcare in the Country Compared With Quality of Healthcare Personally

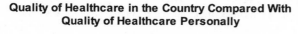

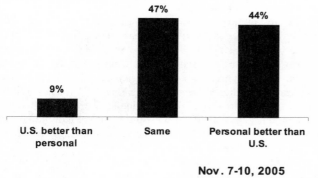

Nov. 7-10, 2005

Many more, 64%, rate their healthcare coverage more positively than they rate coverage in the United States more generally. Thirty percent give the same ratings to both, and 6% rate U.S. healthcare coverage as better than what they personally receive.

Healthcare Coverage in the Country Compared With Healthcare Coverage Personally

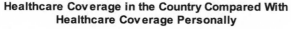

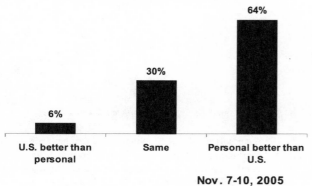

Nov. 7-10, 2005

Ratings of personal healthcare coverage overall show a modest decline, from a 69% excellent/good rating last year to 63% this year.

The percentage rating their coverage as excellent has dropped from 28% in 2004 to 20% this year.

Rating Your Healthcare Coverage

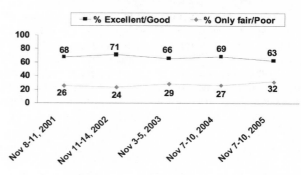

Apparently, the change is not due to increased insurance costs. The percentage of people with private insurance who say they are paying more for health premiums has not changed since last year, nor has the percentage of Americans who are satisfied with the total cost they pay for healthcare.

Costs of Health Insurance

Amount paying for insurance gone up in past year (among those who pay all or part of premiums on private health insurance)
2005	74%
2004	76%
2003	74%

Satisfied with total cost paid for healthcare (among all Americans)
2005	57%
2004	58%
2003	57%
2002	58%
2001	64%

Americans are about as likely to give excellent or good ratings to the quality of the healthcare they receive as they have been in the past. Seventy-eight percent rate their healthcare quality as excellent or good, compared with 80% in 2004, a change that is within the poll's margin of error.

Rating the Quality of Your Healthcare

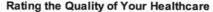

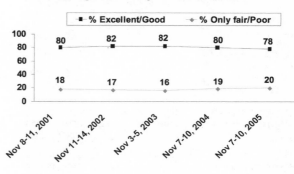

However, there has been a decline in the percentage of Americans rating their healthcare quality as excellent, from 38% last year to 29% this year. Last year's rating was slightly higher than what

Gallup had measured in previous years, so the change may just reflect a return to more typical levels.

Survey Methods

These results are based on telephone interviews with a randomly selected national sample of 1,011 adults, aged 18 and older, conducted Nov. 7-10, 2005. For results based on this sample, one can say with 95% confidence that the maximum error attributable to sampling and other random effects is ±3 percentage points. In addition to sampling error, question wording and practical difficulties in conducting surveys can introduce error or bias into the findings of public opinion polls.

December 8, 2005
SUPPORT FOR DEATH PENALTY STEADY AT 64%
Slightly lower than in recent past

by Lydia Saad, Gallup Poll Senior Editor

A criminal justice milestone was reached on Dec. 2, when Kenneth Lee Boyd became the 1,000th person executed in the United States since the Supreme Court reinstated the death penalty in 1976. Boyd was put to death by lethal injection in North Carolina for killing his wife and father-in-law.

Americans' broad support for the death penalty has not wavered in the past few years. Gallup's annual Crime survey, conducted Oct. 11-13, 2005, finds 64% of Americans in favor of the death penalty for persons convicted of murder; this is exactly the same percentage as found in 2003 and 2004.

However, according to the long-term trend, support for the death penalty is clearly lower today than in the recent past. From 2000 to 2002, the percentage in favor averaged 67%, and in the 1980s and 1990s, it averaged 75%. The highest individual measure of public support for the death penalty in Gallup's trend was 80%, recorded 11 years ago in September 1994. The low point was 42% in 1966.

Are you in favor of the death penalty for a person convicted of murder?

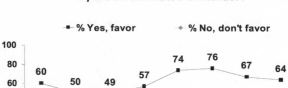

A separate question gauging death penalty support is asked each May as part of Gallup's annual Values survey. Respondents are offered a choice between the death penalty and life imprisonment without parole as the better penalty for murder. According to the May 2005 survey, 56% of Americans prefer the death penalty and 39%

prefer life imprisonment. This is a change from May 2004, when only 50% said they preferred the death penalty and 46% opted for life imprisonment. The current 56% is also higher than was recorded in 2001, when 52% preferred the death penalty.

These shifts run counter to the recent stability in the percentage saying they favor the death penalty for murder, and the slight decline in support for the death penalty seen since 2001.

Comparison of Trends in Death Penalty Support

	Favor death penalty for murder %	Prefer death penalty to life imprisonment %
2005	64	56
2004	64	50
2001	68	52

Historical Trends

Gallup's long-term trend on support for the death penalty suggests that shifting policy debates over the death penalty have shaped public opinion at times. In particular, it appears that the Supreme Court challenges to the death penalty in the 1970s may have sparked increased public support for the punishment.

For most of modern U.S. history, the death penalty was considered constitutional, and it was legal in most states. Then, in the 1972 landmark case of *Furman v. Georgia*, the Supreme Court determined the Georgia death penalty statute violated the Eighth Amendment's protection against cruel and unusual punishment because it gave juries complete latitude in sentencing. This decision voided 40 death penalty statutes nationwide. However, in the 1976 landmark *Gregg* decision, the court upheld the constitutionality of modified death penalty statutes in Florida, Georgia, and Texas, ushering in a new era of capital punishment.

After hovering around 50% in the early 1970s, the percentage of Americans in favor of the death penalty increased to 57% in November 1972 (after the *Furman* decision), and was 66% in April 1976 (three months before the *Gregg* decision was announced).

1970s Trend in Support for Death Penalty

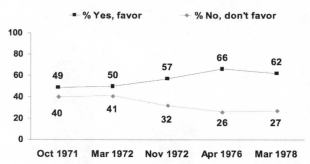

By 1985, support for the death penalty had reached 72% and it remained at approximately this level or higher through 1999.

More recently, the focus of death penalty legislation and litigation has been on limiting its application. In 2002, the Supreme Court ruled that the death penalty cannot be used with severely mentally retarded people, and in 2005, it ruled against executing juveniles. In January 2000, then-Gov. George Ryan of Illinois, a death penalty supporter, issued a moratorium in his state because of the high number of cases in which those on death row were ultimately proved not to be guilty of the crimes for which they were convicted.

Between February 1999 and February 2000, Gallup saw a five-point decline in the percentage of Americans favoring the death penalty (from 71% to 66%). And except for one measure in October 2002, the percentage favoring the death penalty has since remained below 70%.

Variations in Support

Today, 38 states have death penalty laws on the books, while 12 do not. An aggregate of Gallup Polls from 2002 through today show only a slight difference in public opinion about the death penalty in these two groups of states.

In those states allowing the death penalty, 68% of adults favor capital punishment, while 28% oppose it. In states where the death penalty is not allowed, 58% of adults are in favor, while 37% are opposed.

Support for Death Penalty According to State Law 2003-2005

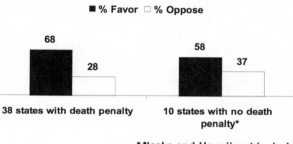

■ % Favor □ % Oppose

68 28   58 37

38 states with death penalty   10 states with no death penalty*

*Alaska and Hawaii not included

Greater variation in death penalty attitudes is seen by party affiliation. According to the latest poll, more than three-quarters of Republicans (77%) and nearly two-thirds of independents (63%) favor capital punishment, compared with 56% of Democrats. Similarly, 74% of self-described "conservatives" and 64% of "moderates," versus 51% of "liberals", favor it.

Men are a bit more likely than women to be in favor: 70% vs. 59%. Consistent with previous Gallup polling, there are strong differences by race, with most whites in favor of the death penalty and most nonwhites opposed to it, and no significant differences by age. While previous Gallup Polls have found churchgoers to be slightly more opposed to the death penalty than non-churchgoers, the current poll finds no difference between the two groups.

Survey Methods

These results are based on telephone interviews with a randomly selected national sample of 1,012 adults, aged 18 and older, conducted Oct. 13-16, 2005. For results based on this sample, one can say with 95% confidence that the maximum error attributable to sampling and other random effects is ±3 percentage points. In addition to sampling error, question wording and practical difficulties in conducting surveys can introduce error or bias into the findings of public opinion polls.

December 9, 2005

HALF OF AMERICANS CURRENTLY TAKING PRESCRIPTION MEDICATION
Nearly 9 in 10 seniors say they take prescriptions

by Joseph Carroll, Gallup Poll Assistant Editor

Gallup's annual survey about health and healthcare in the United States finds that about half of Americans report that they are currently taking prescription medication. Americans are much more likely to take medication for a long-term rather than short-term medical condition, and to take it for a physical rather than psychological or emotional condition. Americans also spend an average of $46 per month for their medications. (This average monthly spending is higher, at $89 per month, among those currently taking prescription medications.)

Prescription Drug Use

The poll, conducted Nov. 7-10, finds that 52% of Americans say they are currently taking prescription medication, while 48% say they are not. These results show a slight increase in reported prescription drug use from when Gallup first asked the question in 2003.

Prescription Drug Use

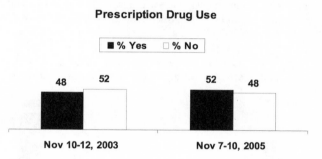

■ % Yes □ % No

48 52   52 48

Nov 10-12, 2003   Nov 7-10, 2005

Perhaps not surprisingly, senior citizens are more likely than any other group in the country to take prescription drugs. Only about one in four adults aged 18 to 29 (27%) currently take prescription medication. This percentage increases to 40% among 30- to 49-year-olds, 61% among 50- to 64-year-olds, and to an overwhelming 88% among adults aged 65 and older.

Prescription Drug Use
by age

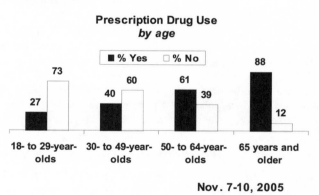

■ % Yes □ % No

27 73   40 60   61 39   88 12

18- to 29-year-olds   30- to 49-year-olds   50- to 64-year-olds   65 years and older

Nov. 7-10, 2005

By a 60% to 44% margin, women are more likely than men to say they are currently taking prescription medication. And, this difference is found more so among younger women. Forty-six percent of women in the 18 to 49 age group say they currently take prescription medication, compared with only 26% of men in this age group. At least 7 in 10 men and women aged 50 and older take prescriptions.

Prescription Drug Use
by gender and age

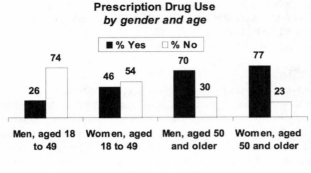

Nov. 7-10, 2005

**Take Prescription Medication for a
Physical Condition or Emotional Condition?**

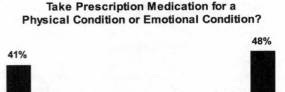

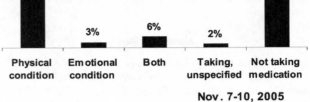

Nov. 7-10, 2005

For What Conditions Are Americans Taking Prescriptions?

The poll also finds that Americans take prescription medication to combat long-term conditions and for physical ailments.

One in three Americans (34%) say they take prescription drugs to treat a long-term illness or condition only, while 7% use them for a short-term condition only, and 9% use them for both. (Among those Americans currently taking prescription medication, 66% use it for a long-term condition, 13% for a short-term condition, and 18% for both.)

**Take Prescription Medication for a
Long-Term Condition or Short-Term Condition?**

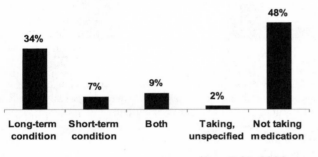

Nov. 7-10, 2005

Few Americans report that they are taking prescription medication for a psychological or emotional condition. The poll finds that 41% are taking prescriptions for a physical condition only, while 3% are taking them for an emotional condition only, and 6% are taking them for both. (Among prescription drug users, 78% take these drugs for a physical condition, 5% for an emotional condition, and 13% for both.)

Prescription Drug Costs

Americans report that they spend an average of $46 per month on prescription drugs. This average includes the one-half of Americans who do not currently take prescriptions, or do not spend money on them. Among those who currently take prescription drugs, the average monthly spending is $89 per month. Americans' spending on drugs breaks down as follows: 50% do not take prescriptions or spend nothing on them, 12% spend between $1 and $25 per month, 14% spend between $26 and $50 per month, 10% spend between $51 and $100 per month, and 12% spend more than that.

Prescription Drug Costs
among all Americans
Nov. 7-10, 2005

	%
Not taking prescription medication or costs nothing a month	50
Taking prescription medication, costs $1-$25 a month	12
Taking prescription medication, costs $26-$50 a month	14
Taking prescription medication, costs $51-$100 a month	10
Taking prescription medication, costs $101-$200 a month	7
Taking prescription medication, costs more than $200 a month	5
No opinion	2
Mean	*$46*

Seniors spend significantly more on prescription medication than do younger Americans. Americans aged 18 to 29 only spend an average of $13 per month on prescriptions, in large part because relatively few people in this age group are taking any prescription medication. This is slightly higher among 30- to 49-year-olds, who spend an average of $31 per month. Results are even higher among adults aged 50 to 64 who spend $58 per month, and among adults aged 65 and older, who spend $93 per month.

Prescription Medication Costs
by age
Nov. 7-10, 2005

	18- to 29-year-olds %	30- to 49-year-olds %	50- to 64-year-olds %	65 years and older %
Not taking any/costs nothing	78	63	42	14
Costs $1-$25 a month	7	13	12	14
Costs $26-$50 a month	10	9	15	23
Costs $51-$100 a month	1	7	14	15
Costs $101-$200 a month	3	4	9	15
Costs more than $200 a month	1	3	8	11
Mean	*$13*	*$31*	*$58*	*$93*

Survey Methods

Results are based on telephone interviews with 1,011 national adults, aged 18 and older, conducted November 7-10, 2005. For results based on the total sample of national adults, one can say with 95% confidence that the maximum error attributed to sampling and other random effects is ±3 percentage points.

For results based on the sample of 580 adults currently taking prescription medication, the maximum margin of sampling error is ±4 percentage points.

In addition to sampling error, question wording and practical difficulties in conducting surveys can introduce error or bias into the findings of public opinion polls.

December 12, 2005
AMERICANS' OPTIMISM ABOUT ECONOMY PERKS UP

But optimism about economy no better now than in January

by Frank Newport, Gallup Poll Editor in Chief

Gallup's first December reading on consumer views of the U.S. economy shows that the American public has become significantly more optimistic about the direction of the economy compared to recent months. Ratings of current economic conditions are, however, up only slightly from August lows, and there has been little change in the public's views about the job market. All in all, the public's confidence in the economy—although up in the short-term—has still not returned to the levels measured at the beginning of this year.

Economic Optimism

Gallup's Dec. 5-8 poll finds that 39% of Americans say the economy is getting better, while 50% say it is getting worse. This represents a net optimism score of -11—the least negative since March of this year, with the single exception of a May 23-26 poll where the net optimism was also -11.

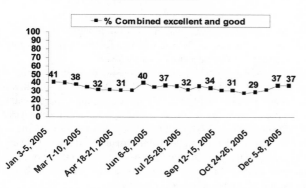

Current Economic Conditions Selected Trend: January 2005 – December 2005

9. Right now, do you think that economic conditions in the country as a whole are getting better or getting worse?

	Getting better %	Getting worse %	SAME (vol.) %	No opinion %
2005				
2005 Dec 5-8	39	50	8	3
2005 Nov 17-20	36	58	5	1
2005 Nov 7-10	30	61	7	2
2005 Oct 24-26	25	66	7	2
2005 Oct 13-16	24	68	6	2
2005 Sep 26-28	24	66	7	3
2005 Sep 12-15	25	66	7	2
2005 Aug 22-25	28	63	7	2
2005 Aug 8-11	36	52	9	3
2005 Jul 25-28	35	53	9	3
2005 Jul 7-10	35	54	8	3
2005 Jun 16-19	35	57	6	2
2005 Jun 6-8	35	55	8	2
2005 May 23-26	41	52	5	2
2005 May 2-5	32	61	6	1
2005 Apr 18-21	31	61	5	3
2005 Apr 4-7	35	56	6	3
2005 Mar 21-23	33	59	6	2
2005 Mar 7-10	41	50	6	3
2005 Feb 21-24	43	48	7	2
2005 Feb 7-10	47	44	7	2
2005 Jan 3-5	48	42	7	3

(vol.) = Volunteered response

In particular, the trend on this optimism measure is notably up from the depths to which it had descended at the end of August through the end of October of this year.

Looking at 2005 as a whole, however, suggests a generally mixed pattern. The year began on a robust note, with two surveys reflecting a net positive optimism score. Optimism then fell through April, rose slightly into the summer, and then fell sharply as the price of gas rose in late August.

Still, although Americans are more optimistic now than they have been at most points this year, the net negative rating of -11% is worse than what was measured for a good deal of 2004, for parts of 2003, and for the early months of 2002. In other words, the trend may be in the right direction, but it still has a good way to go to offer evidence of dramatically improved consumer optimism.

Rating the Current Economy

Perceptions of the current American economy typically are not as volatile as views of the future direction of the economy. In the recent survey, 37% of Americans rate current economic conditions as "excellent" or "good," identical to Gallup's late November rating, up slightly from earlier this fall, but little different from other points this year in the early summer and at the beginning of the year.

8. How would you rate economic conditions in this country today— as excellent, good, only fair, or poor?

	Excellent %	Good %	Only fair %	Poor %	No opinion %
2005					
2005 Dec 5-8	6	31	43	20	*
2005 Nov 17-20	5	32	39	24	*

*Less than 0.5%

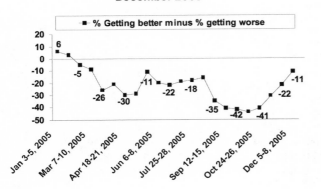

Economic Outlook
Selected Trend: January 2005 – December 2005

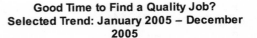

Good Time to Find a Quality Job?
Selected Trend: January 2005 – December 2005

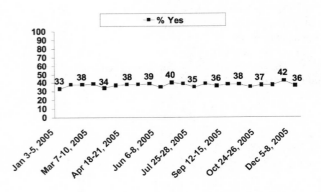

	Excellent %	Good %	Only fair %	Poor %	No opinion %
2005 Nov 7-10	3	29	47	21	*
2005 Oct 24-26	3	26	45	25	1
2005 Oct 13-16	3	25	46	26	*
2005 Sep 26-28	3	28	41	27	1
2005 Sep 12-15	3	28	44	25	*
2005 Aug 22-25	4	30	42	24	*
2005 Aug 8-11	4	32	46	18	*
2005 Jul 25-28	4	28	44	23	1
2005 Jul 7-10	3	33	45	18	1
2005 Jun 16-19	4	33	40	23	*
2005 Jun 6-8	4	31	45	20	*
2005 May 23-26	3	37	41	19	*
2005 May 2-5	1	30	44	25	*
2005 Apr 18-21	2	29	44	24	1
2005 Apr 4-7	3	29	49	18	1
2005 Mar 21-23	2	30	43	24	1
2005 Mar 7-10	3	32	48	16	1
2005 Feb 21-24	5	33	42	20	*
2005 Feb 7-10	3	37	44	16	*
2005 Jan 3-5	3	38	42	17	*

*Less than 0.5%

The data on the current conditions do not present a dramatically improved picture, although a 37% top-two category rating is roughly in line with what has been measured fairly consistently over the last several years. Indeed, one must look back as far as early 2001 to find a period of time when over 40% of the public routinely rated the economy as excellent or good.

The low point on this measure came in the period of time from late summer 2002 to late 2003, when combined excellent and good ratings were often below 30%, including an 18% reading in February 2003.

The Job Situation

There has been very little substantial change this year in the percentage of Americans who say that now is a good time to find a "quality job."

12. *Thinking about the job situation in America today, would you say that it is now a good time or a bad time to find a quality job?*

	Good time %	Bad time %	No opinion %
2005 Dec 5-8	36	60	4
2005 Nov 17-20	42	56	2
2005 Nov 7-10	37	59	4
2005 Oct 24-26	37	58	5
2005 Oct 13-16	35	62	3
2005 Sep 26-28	38	56	6
2005 Sep 12-15	38	59	3
2005 Aug 22-25	36	58	6
2005 Aug 8-11	39	58	3
2005 Jul 25-28	35	61	4
2005 Jul 7-10	39	58	3
2005 Jun 16-19	40	56	4
2005 Jun 6-8	35	62	3
2005 May 23-26	39	58	3
2005 May 2-5	38	59	3
2005 Apr 18-21	38	58	4
2005 Apr 4-7	37	59	4
2005 Mar 21-23	34	61	5
2005 Mar 7-10	39	57	4
2005 Feb 21-24	38	57	5
2005 Feb 7-10	38	59	3
2005 Jan 3-5	33	62	5

There have been minor variations from month to month on this measure, but the current 36% is within a few percentage points of most readings on this measure taken all year.

The low point on this quality job measure came in the spring and summer of 2003 when as few as 16% of Americans said it was a good time to find a quality job. More broadly, the average readings on this measure this year are generally higher than the averages for 2004, 2003, 2002, or 2001. Gallup did not routinely use this measure prior to 2001, but University of Connecticut and Rutgers University polling conducted in 1999 and 2000 found that upwards of 70% of employed adults said it was a good time to find a quality job in this time period of the booming dot.com economy.

The Economy as Number One Problem

Twenty-six percent of Americans mention some aspect of the economy when asked "What do you think is the most important problem facing this country today?" This is slightly less than the percentage mentioning the economy in recent months, including the 36% who mentioned the economy in October. Still, the current level of mentions of the economy is little different from earlier in the summer, and therefore does not appear to represent a dramatic change in the positioning of the economy in the public's mind when asked to think about the nation's problems.

The Bottom Line

Compared to several months ago, there are some signs of an improvement in the way in which Americans view the economy. This is particularly evident when the public is asked about the direction of the economy. Still, Americans' ratings of the current economy are no better than they were at the beginning of this year, and optimism levels are well below the level where they were at a number of different points over the last several years. The key will be what happens in the months ahead; whether there will be a continuing upward trend in positivity about the economy, or whether economic perceptions drop back down again.

Survey Methods

Results are based on telephone interviews with 1,013 national adults, aged 18 and older, conducted December 5-8, 2005. For results based on the total sample of national adults, one can say with 95% confidence that the maximum margin of sampling error is ±3 percentage points. In addition to sampling error, question wording and practical difficulties in conducting surveys can introduce error or bias into the findings of public opinion polls.

December 13, 2005
BUSH RATINGS IMPROVE, OVERALL JOB APPROVAL AT 42%
Public still negative toward Bush on most issues

by David W. Moore, Gallup Poll Senior Editor

Forty-two percent of Americans now approve of President George W. Bush's job performance, four points higher than the rating Gallup measured three weeks ago, in the Nov. 17-20 poll, and a point lower than the rating Gallup measured at the end of last week in the Dec. 5-8 poll. Compared with the November poll, Bush's ratings are also up slightly on the economy, Iraq, terrorism, and foreign affairs.

The increase in Bush's overall job approval is reinforced by comparing the average of two polls in November with two polls in

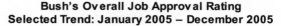

Bush's Overall Job Approval Rating
Selected Trend: January 2005 – December 2005

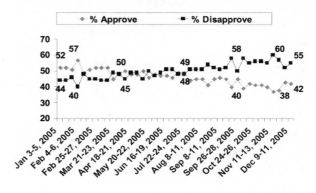

December—37.8% vs. 42.9%, respectively. That average five-point difference is well outside the margin of error of the combined polls, showing that the increase, while small, is statistically significant.

The improved ratings come in the wake of a more active effort by Bush to defend his administration's Iraq policy. On Nov. 30, the president launched a series of four speeches, which were intended to highlight the importance of the upcoming Iraqi parliamentary elections. Since then, he has delivered two additional addresses, all making the case for a continued U.S. military presence in Iraq until "victory" is achieved.

The poll suggests that Bush's increase in ratings comes primarily among independents, who typically are more susceptible than strong partisans to being influenced by new information. Republicans and Democrats apparently are little swayed in their positive and negative views, respectively, of the president.

In the two December polls, 35.3% of independents approved of Bush's job performance, up from 27.1% in the two November polls—an eight-point increase. By contrast, Republican approval increased by two points from November to December, and Democratic approval increased by just under two points.

On the economy, Bush's rating is up three percentage points since the Nov. 11-13 poll (37% to 40%); on Iraq up four points (35% to 39%); on terrorism up four points (48% to 52%); and on foreign affairs up five points (37% to 42%).

Other polls have also shown an increase in Bush's standing among the public, with some commentators suggesting the improvement is related not to Iraq but to the economy. The poll results here suggest perhaps an even broader interpretation—that Bush's improvement may be related to his making a more aggressive defense of his administration, regardless of the specific issue. With slight to modest increases across the various issues noted above, it would appear that many Americans (mostly independents) have more positive views of the president overall, not just on the way he is handling the war in Iraq.

The year-long trends on each of the issues show that despite the current upward movement, there has been little long-term change in the public's position on Bush and the various issues. Bush's most positive ratings still come on his handling of terrorism, with a slight majority now approving of his performance on this issue, up from an essential tie in November, and about the same level it has been since August.

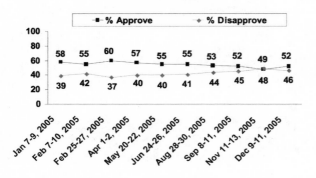

**Bush's Approval Ratings on Terrorism
Selected Trend: January 2005 –
December 2005**

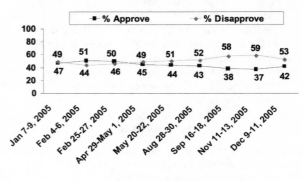

**Bush's Approval Ratings on Foreign Affairs
Selected Trend: January 2005 –
December 2005**

On Iraq, a clear majority continues to disapprove of Bush's performance, 59% to 39%, although not by the same margin as in mid-September. Still, the current rating is consistent with ratings taken this summer.

**Bush's Approval Ratings on Iraq
Selected Trend: January 2005 –
December 2005**

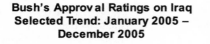

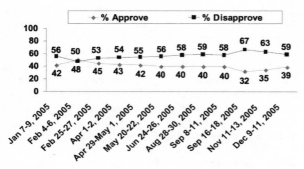

Bush's rating on the economy has fluctuated over the past year, but since the spring it has been more negative than positive. The current 58% disapproval to 40% approval is similar to ratings that go back to April.

**Bush's Approval Ratings on the Economy
Selected Trend: January 2005 –
December 2005**

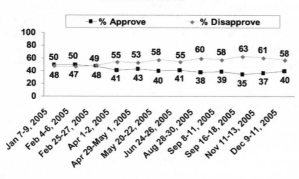

On foreign affairs, the same pattern prevails—more people disapprove of Bush's performance than approve, but the ratio is not as bad now as it was in November and September. However, the current rating is still worse than Bush's ratings from January through April.

Polarized Public

The poll also shows that the public is highly polarized in its evaluation of the president. One type of polarization is measured by calculating the difference between the views of Republicans and Democrats. While 81% of Republicans currently approve of Bush's job performance, just 10% of Democrats approve. This type of polarization has been noted in previous articles on the Gallup Web site.

Another type of polarization is reflected in the intensity of opinion people express on the issue. While people who approve of the president divide about equally between those who "strongly" approve and those who "moderately" approve, the people who "strongly" disapprove outnumber those who "moderately" disapprove by more than 3 to 1.

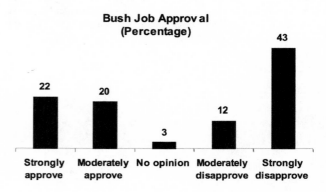

These results show that about twice as many people strongly disapprove of Bush's performance (43%) as strongly approve (22%).

Survey Methods

Results are based on telephone interviews with 1,003 national adults, aged 18 and older, conducted Dec. 9-11, 2005. For results based on the total sample of national adults, one can say with 95% confidence that the maximum margin of sampling error is ±3 percentage points. In addition to sampling error, question wording and practical difficulties in conducting surveys can introduce error or bias into the findings of public opinion polls.

December 13, 2005

AMERICANS HAVE LITTLE DOUBT GOD EXISTS

Belief strong, but not monolithic

by Albert L. Winseman, Religion and Social Trends Editor

For more than 60 years, Gallup has regularly asked Americans whether they believe in God, a universal spirit, or a higher power. Over the years, about 9 in 10 Americans have said they believe. But how strong are their convictions?

A recent Gallup Poll* looked a little more closely at Americans' certainty. Seventy-eight percent of Americans say they are "convinced" that God exists; another 12% think God probably exists, but have "a little doubt"; and 4% think God probably exists, but have "a lot of doubt." Only 4% think God "does not exist, but are not sure," and 1% are "convinced" that God does not exist.

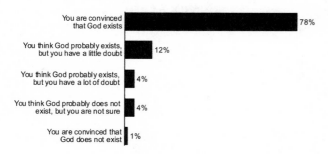

Which comes closest to describing you?

- You are convinced that God exists — 78%
- You think God probably exists, but you have a little doubt — 12%
- You think God probably exists, but you have a lot of doubt — 4%
- You think God probably does not exist, but you are not sure — 4%
- You are convinced that God does not exist — 1%

While the sample size of the doubters and disbelievers is insufficient to safely delve into any demographic differences, we can learn something about those who are "convinced" God exists.

Women are somewhat more likely to say they're convinced than are men—82% to 73%. This is no surprise, as women tend to score higher on most measures of religiosity Gallup has undertaken. Residents of the South are the most likely to express certainty about the existence of God (88%); least likely are Easterners (70%) and Westerners (71%). Those who live in the Midwest fall somewhere in between at 77%. Again, no surprise here: Gallup data demonstrate that Southerners tend to exhibit higher degrees of religiosity than do residents of other U.S. regions. Those who identify themselves as conservatives (87%) are more likely than moderates (76%) or liberals (61%) to say they are convinced.

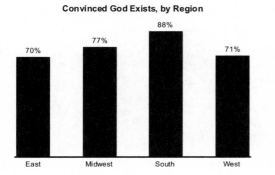

Convinced God Exists, by Region

- East — 70%
- Midwest — 77%
- South — 88%
- West — 71%

Naturally, weekly church attendees are particularly likely to be convinced; 94% are certain God exists. Even more interesting is that a solid majority—61%—of those who seldom or never attend church are nevertheless convinced that God exists. In the chicken-and-egg question about whether church attendance is more likely to drive religiosity or vice-versa, these data suggest that, for many Americans, belief in God is a personal conviction, and attending worship is an expression, rather than the cause, of that belief.

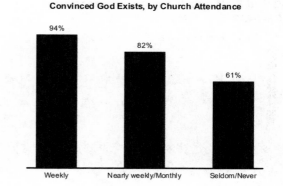

Convinced God Exists, by Church Attendance

- Weekly — 94%
- Nearly weekly/Monthly — 82%
- Seldom/Never — 61%

These initial responses show that even though belief in God is strong in America, it is not by any means a monolithic faith. Instead, it is streaked with some nuances and varying degrees of certainty. As we ask the question again in the future, the results should lead to more important insights about the status of religion in America.

*Results are based on telephone interviews with 1,002 national adults, aged 18 and older, conducted Nov. 17-20, 2005. For results based on the total sample of national adults, one can say with 95% confidence that the margin of sampling error is ±3 percentage points.

December 14, 2005

BASIC ATTITUDES TOWARD IRAQ WAR SLIGHTLY MORE POSITIVE

Americans divided over whether U.S. made mistake in going to war

by Jeffrey M. Jones, Gallup Poll Managing Editor

Over the last few weeks, President George W. Bush has mounted a campaign to change public perceptions on the Iraq war with a series of speeches. A new CNN/*USA Today*/Gallup poll suggests the strategy could be having some effect. The poll shows fewer Americans now say the United States made a mistake in going to war in Iraq than have so in recent weeks, though the public is still divided on this issue. Although ratings for Bush's handling of Iraq remain quite negative, the percentage of Americans approving of his job on Iraq has increased slightly.

Additionally, a majority of Americans do not believe Bush has a plan that will achieve victory in Iraq. Other measures show essentially no change, including attitudes about who is winning the war, whether the United States can win the war, and what the United States should do about its troops.

Late October and mid-November Gallup Polls showed Americans, by a 54% to 45% margin, saying the United States made a mistake in sending troops to Iraq. The new Dec. 9-11 CNN/*USA Today*/Gallup poll shows a more evenly divided public, with slightly more saying the war was not a mistake (50%) than saying it was (48%). The last time supporters outnumbered opponents on this measure was in late July.

In view of the developments since we first sent our troops to Iraq, do you think the United States made a mistake in sending troops to Iraq, or not?

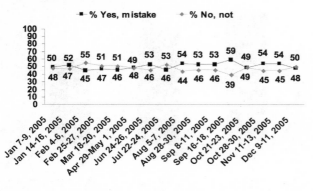

The more positive views on the war are apparent among Democrats and independents. Republicans have always been overwhelmingly supportive, and that support has not changed in recent weeks. Democrats still remain largely opposed to the war, but independents are now evenly divided after being mainly opposed in October and November.

Views of the Iraq War, by Party

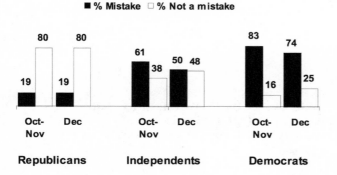

Americans' views of Bush's handling of the situation in Iraq have also noticeably improved. In mid-September, just 32% approved of how Bush has handled this issue, the lowest of his presidency. In mid-November, that percentage improved slightly to 35%, and is at 39% in the latest poll. Even so, the current percentage remains one of the lowest approval ratings for Bush on Iraq, and is now only back to where it was this summer.

In contrast to the improvement on the "mistake" and Bush approval measures, most other measures about the war are stable.

About half of all Americans, 49%, say neither side is winning the war in Iraq. Thirty-six percent say the United States and its allies are winning, 13% say the insurgents in Iraq are. These views have essentially not changed since June. No more than 44% of Americans have said the United States and its allies are winning since the question was first asked in October 2004.

A more forward-looking question on victory in Iraq also shows little change from recent months. The question asks Americans to assess whether the United States can win the war in Iraq, and whether

George W. Bush's Handling of the Situation in Iraq

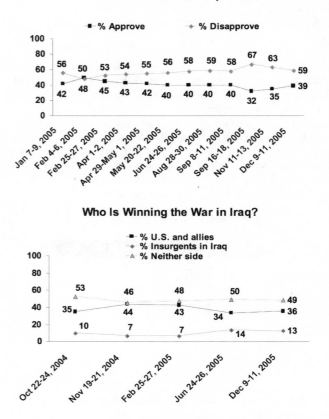

Who Is Winning the War in Iraq?

it will do so. Currently, 65% say the United States can win, but only 46% believe it will. Those percentages break down to 25% who say the United States will definitely win and 21% who say it probably will win, and 19% who think the United States can win the war but will not. Another 30% think the United States cannot win.

Which comes closer to your view about the war in Iraq—[ROTATED: you think the U.S. will definitely win the war in Iraq, you think the U.S. will probably win the war in Iraq, you think the U.S. can win the war in Iraq, but you don't think it will win, (or) you do not think the U.S. can win the war in Iraq]?

	Definitely win %	Probably win %	Can win, but don't think it will win %	Do not think it can win %	No opinion %	Net: Can win war %	Net: Will win war %
2005 Dec 9-11^	25	21	19	30	5	*65*	*46*
2005 Nov 11-13	23	23	17	33	4	*63*	*46*
2005 Sep 16-18	21	22	20	34	3	*63*	*43*

^Asked of a half sample

Americans' pessimism about the United States' prospects for victory could stem from a lack of confidence in the commander in chief. The majority of Americans do not believe Bush has a plan that will achieve victory in Iraq—38% say he has such a plan; 58% say he does not.

Popular sentiment is still firmly behind reducing the U.S. military presence in Iraq—64% of Americans say the United States should withdraw troops from Iraq, including 38% who say it should withdraw some troops and 26% who say all troops. Just 9% of Americans say the United States should send more troops, while an additional 25% say it should keep the same number of troops in Iraq that it has now.

A majority of Americans have favored a reduction in U.S. troop levels since June.

Which comes closest to your view about what the U.S. should now do about the number of U.S. troops in Iraq—[ROTATED: the U.S. should send more troops to Iraq, the U.S. should keep the number of troops as it is now, the U.S. should withdraw some troops from Iraq, (or) the U.S. should withdraw all of its troops from Iraq]?

	Send more troops %	Keep same number %	With- draw some %	With- draw all %	No opinion %	Net: With- draw %
2005 Dec 9-11	9	25	38	26	2	64
2005 Sep 16-18	8	26	33	30	3	63
2005 Aug 28-30	19	26	27	26	2	53
2005 Aug 5-7	13	28	23	33	3	56
2005 Jun 6-8	10	26	31	28	5	59
2005 Feb 4-6	10	38	32	17	3	49
2005 Jan 14-16	24	26	21	25	4	46
2004 Sep 24-26	21	35	21	18	5	39
2004 Jun 3-6	18	30	23	27	2	50
2004 May 7-9	25	24	18	29	4	47
2004 Apr 16-18	33	25	16	21	5	37
2004 Apr 5-8	20	29	18	28	5	46
2004 Jan 2-5	11	40	29	16	4	45
2003 Dec 15-16	14	40	27	15	4	42
2003 Dec 5-7	22	33	25	17	3	42
2003 Nov 3-5 ^	17	32	29	19	3	48
2003 Oct 24-26 ^	14	27	39	18	2	57
2003 Aug 25-26 ^	15	36	32	14	3	46

^WORDING: "Which comes closest to your view about what the U.S. should now do about the number of U.S. troops in Iraq—[ROTATED: the U.S. should send more troops to Iraq, the U.S. should keep the number of troops as it is now, the U.S. should begin to withdraw some troops from Iraq, (or) the U.S. should withdraw all of its troops from Iraq]?"

Survey Methods

These results are based on telephone interviews with a randomly selected national sample of 1,003 adults, aged 18 and older, conducted Dec. 9-11, 2005. For results based on this sample, one can say with 95% confidence that the maximum error attributable to sampling and other random effects is ±3 percentage points. In addition to sampling error, question wording and practical difficulties in conducting surveys can introduce error or bias into the findings of public opinion polls.

December 15, 2005
"HAPPY HOLIDAYS" RINGS HOLLOW FOR MOST AMERICANS
One-third bothered by the generic greeting

by Lydia Saad, Gallup Poll Senior Editor

Most Americans think the trend toward saying "Happy Holidays" or "Season's Greetings" at Christmastime is a change for the worse. But is it therefore a bad marketing decision for retailers to greet customers this way? Gallup finds some evidence of a consumer backlash, as 32% of Americans say it bothers them when stores use "Happy Holidays" or "Season's Greetings" in their displays at this time of year instead of "Merry Christmas."

The poll, conducted Dec. 5-8, also finds that Americans expect to spend an average of $840 on Christmas gifts this year. This amount is statistically unchanged from what Americans expected to spend last year at this time.

Retail Details

Sixty-two percent of Americans say that the now nearly ubiquitous use of "Happy Holidays" or "Season's Greetings," rather than "Merry Christmas," in many stores and public institutions is a change for the worse. Only 24% consider it a change for the better.

While the generic greetings bother a third of the public, there is almost unanimous public tolerance for the phrase, "Merry Christmas." Only 3% of national adults say it bothers them when stores specifically refer to the Christian holiday in their displays, rather than "Happy Holidays" or "Season's Greetings."

Consumer Reaction to Retailer Approaches

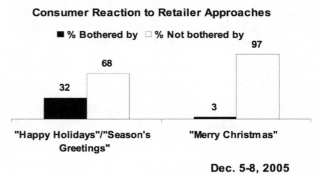

■ % Bothered by □ % Not bothered by

Dec. 5-8, 2005

Perhaps surprising, and counter to the inclusive rationale for saying "Happy Holidays," is the finding that only 5% of those who do not identify with any religion and just 8% of all non-Christians say they are bothered when confronted with "Merry Christmas" wishes while shopping.

Christian Right Is Most Bothered by Generic Greetings

Fierce debate over seasonal greetings is a regular occurrence on cable television these days, as dueling pundits argue about whether "Happy Holidays" is simply a more inclusive approach to dealing with a multicultural public, or a deliberate slap against Christians.

Despite the arguments, the use of the generic holiday expressions does *not* bother most Americans in general, including most major political and religious groups examined in this survey. But substantial minorities are bothered—enough, perhaps, to cause concern among some retailers.

Those generic greetings are most likely to irk Republicans (48%), conservatives (44%), and weekly churchgoers (42%). The greetings generate much less annoyance among Democrats (17%), liberals (21%), and those who seldom or never attend church (25%).

There is no significant difference between men and women in their reactions to holiday greetings. However, young adults (18- to 29-year-olds) are notably less bothered by the trend toward generic phrases than are adults aged 30 and older.

Reaction to "Happy Holidays"/ "Season's Greetings," by Age

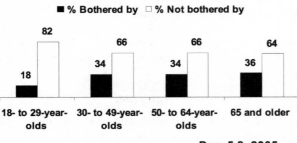

Dec. 5-8, 2005

Christmas Has Broad Appeal

One reason for the broad acceptance of "Merry Christmas" is that the vast majority of Americans are Christians. Gallup's 2004 polling (an aggregate of all religion questions asked last year) puts the total percentage affiliating with some form of Christianity at 84%. However, according to a December 2003 Gallup Poll, an even higher percentage of Americans—95%—celebrate Christmas; only 5% do not. Clearly large numbers of secular and non-Christian Americans take part in the holiday for cultural, if not religious, reasons.

Still, with Christmas, Hanukkah, and Kwanzaa all being celebrated around the same time, perhaps it was inevitable that the traditional salutation—"Merry Christmas"—would yield to a more generic greeting like "Happy Holidays." Not only is this shift evident with some major U.S. retailers, but a Gallup Poll last year found that 4 in 10 Americans themselves tended to say "Happy Holidays" when greeting someone they just met.

At this time of the year, which greeting would you be more likely to give to someone you just met: "Happy Holidays" (or) "Merry Christmas?"

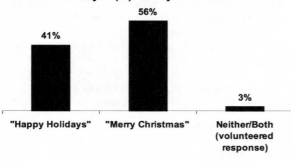

Dec. 5-8, 2004

Spending Intentions Are Flat

It is not clear whether consumers put off by advertisements for "holiday trees," "holiday cards," and by being wished "Happy Holidays" when paying for "holiday ornaments" will alter their Christmas shopping as a result. They could become selective about where they shop, they could do less shopping than in the past, or they could make no changes.

Gallup can only broadly address consumer Christmas spending, with a question asking Americans to estimate the amount they will spend on Christmas gifts in the current year. For each of the past three years, Gallup has measured this once in early November and again in early December. Because spending intentions change as Christmas draws near (the December estimate is always higher), November and December comparisons must be made separately.

This year, the November and December trends are seemingly contradictory. The November 2005 estimate of Americans' average spending on Christmas gifts was slightly higher than in November 2004: $763 vs. $730. The December estimate is down slightly from a year ago: $840 vs. $862. However, it is important to note that neither shift is statistically significant, and that the more likely finding is that consumers' year-to-year spending intentions are flat.

Trends in Estimated Spending Averages on Christmas Gifts

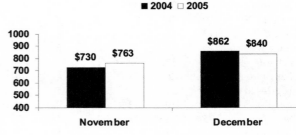

Survey Methods

These results are based on telephone interviews with a randomly selected national sample of 1,013 adults, aged 18 and older, conducted Dec. 5-8, 2005. For results based on this sample, one can say with 95% confidence that the maximum error attributable to sampling and other random effects is ±3 percentage points. In addition to sampling error, question wording and practical difficulties in conducting surveys can introduce error or bias into the findings of public opinion polls.

December 16, 2005
AMERICANS SKEPTICAL THAT DEMOCRACY WILL PREVAIL IN IRAQ
Poll also updates public's preferences for 2008 presidential nominees

by David W. Moore, Gallup Poll Senior Editor

On the eve of the Iraqi parliamentary elections, a CNN/*USA Today*/ Gallup poll shows skepticism among the American public about the likelihood of establishing a stable democracy in Iraq. The poll, conducted Dec. 9-11, was completed just days before the Iraqi election began. Americans seem to recognize the importance of those elections, as well as the importance of a vote last October on a new constitution for the country: Sixty-three percent say that Iraq has made "real progress" toward establishing a democratic government in the past two years, while just 34% say the country has not.

Now thinking about the past two years, do you think Iraq has made real progress toward establishing a democratic government, or don't you think Iraq has made any progress in this area?

	Yes, has made real progress	No, not made real progress	No opinion
2005 Dec 9-11	63%	34	3

Despite the perception of progress, 55% of Americans think the United States ultimately will not be able to establish a stable democratic government in Iraq, while 41% think it will.

Do you think the United States will—or will not—be able to establish a stable democratic government in Iraq?

	Yes, will %	No, will not %	No opinion %
2005 Dec 9-11	41	55	4
2005 Oct 21-23	40	56	4
2005 Jul 22-24	37	58	5
2004 Nov 19-21	46	49	5
2004 Apr 16-18	37	57	6

The public's skepticism expressed in this latest poll is similar to that measured last October and July, and in April 2004.

The current poll suggests that the more attention people have paid to the upcoming elections in Iraq, the more optimistic they are about the long-term success of establishing a democratic form of government. Overall, 15% say they have been following the news about the election "very" closely, 43% "somewhat" closely, and 42% not closely—including 28% who say "not too closely" and 14% who say "not closely at all."

How closely have you been following the news about the upcoming election in Iraq—very closely, somewhat closely, not too closely, or not closely at all?

	Very closely	Somewhat closely	Not too closely	Not closely at all	No opinion
2005 Dec 9-11	15	43	28	14	*

*Less than 0.5%

Americans who have been following the news "very" closely are most optimistic, with 54% expecting eventual success in forming a stable democratic government in Iraq, compared with 47% of people following the news "somewhat" closely, and just 31% who aren't paying much attention to the event.

Do you think the United States will—or will not—be able to establish a stable democratic government in Iraq?

	Yes, will %	No, will not %	No opinion %
All	41	55	4

How closely follow news about the Iraq election?

Very closely	54	45	1
Somewhat closely	47	48	5
Not closely	31	65	4

It is not clear if people are more optimistic because they are paying attention to the election and are receiving positive news, or if they are paying more attention to the news because they tend to be more upbeat about the ultimate success of U.S. efforts in Iraq.

If a democratic form of government is established, most Americans think it will make daily life better for the average Iraqi (68% say it will, 29% say it won't) and speed up the withdrawal of U.S. troops from Iraq (61% yes, 36% no). But, most Americans also think that the insurgent attacks will continue (67% say the attacks won't end, 29% say they will).

Suppose a democratic government is formed in Iraq in the next few months. Do you think that government will—or will not—be able to do each of the following? How about—[RANDOM ORDER]?

2005 Dec 9-11 (sorted by "yes, will")	Yes, will %	No, will not %	No opinion %
Make daily life better for the average Iraqi	68	29	3
Speed up the withdrawal of U.S. troops from Iraq	61	36	3
Make it harder for terrorists to establish a base of operations in Iraq	54	44	2
Help the U.S. achieve its goals in other countries in the region	45	51	4
End insurgent attacks against U.S. and Iraqi forces	29	67	4

Americans are more closely divided as to whether a democratic government in Iraq will make it harder for terrorists to operate out of Iraq (54% say yes, 44% no), and whether establishing this kind of government will help the United States achieve its goals in other countries in the region (45% say yes, 51% no).

Election 2008

The Dec. 9-11 poll also updates the preferences of Republicans and Democrats for their respective party's presidential nominee in 2008. Topping the GOP list is former New York Mayor Rudy Giuliani, with 30% of support, followed by Arizona Sen. John McCain (22%) and Secretary of State Condoleezza Rice (18% among registered voters, 17% among all Republicans).

Next, I'm going to read a list of people who may be running in the Republican primary for president in the next election. After I read all the names, please tell me which of those candidates you would be most likely to support for the Republican nomination for President in the year 2008, or if you would support someone else. [NAMES ROTATED: Virginia Senator, George Allen; Mississippi Governor, Haley Barbour; Tennessee Senator, Bill Frist; Former New York City Mayor, Rudy Giuliani; Arizona Senator, John McCain; Secretary of State, Condoleezza Rice; Massachusetts Governor, Mitt Romney]

BASED ON 405 REPUBLICANS AND REPUBLICAN LEANERS WHO ARE REGISTERED TO VOTE BASED ON 435 REPUBLICANS AND REPUBLICAN LEANERS

2005 Dec 9-11	Republican Registered voters %	All Republicans %
Rudy Giuliani	30	30
John McCain	22	22

2005 Dec 9-11	Republican Registered voters %	All Republicans %
Condoleezza Rice	18	17
George Allen	7	7
Bill Frist	3	2
Haley Barbour	2	3
Mitt Romney	2	3
Other	3	3
None	3	3
All/any	*	*
No opinion	10	10

*Less than 0.5%

Virginia Sen. George Allen receives 7% of support, while all other potential candidates receive less than 5% of support.

Massachusetts Gov. Mitt Romney just announced he would not seek re-election in 2006, opening the way for him to undertake a serious bid for his party's presidential nomination in 2008. Currently just 2% of registered Republicans would vote for him, though much can change in the next two years.

On the Democratic side, New York Sen. Hillary Rodham Clinton is the run-away leader, with 43% of support among registered voters, followed by former Sen. John Edwards (14%) and Sen. John Kerry (14%)—the Democratic vice presidential and presidential nominees in 2004, respectively.

Next, I'm going to read a list of people who may be running in the Democratic primary for president in the next election. After I read all the names, please tell me which of those candidates you would be most likely to support for the Democratic nomination for President in the year 2008, or if you would support someone else. [ROTATED: Indiana Senator, Evan Bayh; Delaware Senator, Joe Biden; New York Senator, Hillary Rodham Clinton; Former North Carolina Senator, John Edwards; Massachusetts Senator, John Kerry; New Mexico Governor, Bill Richardson; Iowa Governor, Tom Vilsack; Virginia Governor, Mark Warner]

BASED ON 446 DEMOCRATS AND DEMOCRATIC LEANERS WHO ARE REGISTERED TO VOTE BASED ON 491 DEMOCRATS AND DEMOCRATIC LEANERS

2005 Dec 9-11	Democratic Registered voters %	All Democrats %
Hillary Rodham Clinton	43	42
John Edwards	14	15
John Kerry	14	15
Joe Biden	8	7
Mark Warner	3	3
Bill Richardson	3	3
Evan Bayh	1	1
Tom Vilsack	1	1
Other	1	1
None	4	4
All/any	1	1
No opinion	7	7

Delaware Sen. Joe Biden, who ran for president unsuccessfully in 1988 and has indicated he will run again in 2008, receives 8% of support among registered voters, while other potential candidates receive less than 5% of support.

Survey Methods

Results are based on telephone interviews with 1,003 national adults, aged 18 and older, conducted Dec. 9-11, 2005. For results based on the total sample of national adults, one can say with 95% confidence that the maximum margin of sampling error is ±3 percentage points.

For results based on the 503 national adults in the Form A half-sample and 500 national adults in the Form B half-sample, the maximum margins of sampling error are ±5 percentage points.

For results based on the sample of 435 Republicans or Republican leaners, the maximum margin of sampling error is ±5 percentage points.

For results based on the sample of 405 Republicans or Republican leaners who are registered to vote, the maximum margin of sampling error is ±5 percentage points.

For results based on the sample of 491 Democrats or Democratic leaners, the maximum margin of sampling error is ±5 percentage points.

For results based on the sample of 446 Democrats or Democratic leaners who are registered to vote, the maximum margin of sampling error is ±5 percentage points.

In addition to sampling error, question wording and practical difficulties in conducting surveys can introduce error or bias into the findings of public opinion polls.

December 19, 2005
IRAQ AND TERRORISM ARE TOP PRIORITIES FOR PRESIDENT AND CONGRESS
Immigration issues given low priority

by Frank Newport, Gallup Poll Editor in Chief

Government activity in Washington, D.C., will begin to slow down as Christmas approaches and members of Congress retreat to their home districts and states for the holiday period. But January will bring a new year and new challenges for the nation's leaders. A recent CNN/*USA Today*/Gallup poll asked Americans to rate the importance they would place on a series of eight distinct issues as priorities for the president and Congress to deal with in the new year.

The results show that Americans ascribe the highest priority to two foreign policy issues—terrorism and the situation in Iraq—both given "extremely important" ratings by more than half of Americans. Between 41% and 48% of Americans say that healthcare costs, the economy, Social Security, and gas and home heating costs are extremely important for Congress and the president to deal with. Americans give the lowest importance to immigration issues—including the issue of controlling illegal immigration.

A Closer Look at the Issues

The basic question used on the survey is as follows: "How important is it to you that the president and Congress deal with each of the following issues in the next year—is it—extremely important, very important, moderately important, or not that important?"

It is clear that very few Americans rate the issues as "not that important," and large numbers rate the issues in one of the top two importance categories—extremely or very important. (The full responses for the eight issues are presented at the end of this article.)

This analysis focuses on the percentage of Americans who rate each issue as extremely important, under the assumption that it is this "top box" rating that identifies issues of real significance to the public.

The average extremely important rating across all eight items is 44.4%. Four of the items have extremely important ratings above this average, one is right at the average, and three have below-average importance. (It is important to remember that these items are being compared to the specific list included in this survey; had other issues been included, the relative priority for issues would have changed.)

How Important a Priority for the President and Congress in the New Year
% extremely important

	The economy %	Terrorism %	Healthcare costs %	The situation in Iraq %	Gas and home heating prices %	Immigration %	Controlling illegal immigration %	Social Security %
2005 Dec 9-11	47	58	48	59	41	27	31	44
Dec 2005 data normalized to 100 as average	106	131	108	133	92	61	70	99
2005 Apr 1-2	41	47	46	-	44	-	-	37
2005 Feb 4-6	44	54	49	53	-	-	-	41
2004 Dec 17-19	40	49	42	51	-	27	-	40
2003 Jan 3-5	49	59	45	46	-	-	-	41
2002 May 28-29 ^	38	53	-	-	-	-	-	41
2002 Jan 11-14	44	62	-	-	-	30	-	-
2001 Oct 5-6	54	70	-	-	-	-	-	-
2001 Jan 10-14	34		-	-	-	17	-	-
Avg. before Dec 2005	*43*	*56*	*46*	*50*	*44*	*25*	*-*	*40*
Change Avg. to Dec 05	*4*	*2*	*2*	*9*	*-3*	*2*	*-*	*4*

^Asked of a half sample

Key findings:
• The two issues with the highest perceived importance relate to foreign policy: the situation in Iraq and terrorism.

• Healthcare costs and the economy are slightly above the average in perceived importance.
• Americans ascribe average importance to Social Security.
• Gas and home heating prices are slightly below average importance.
• Both "immigration" and "controlling illegal immigration" come in significantly below average in terms of perceived importance.

Time Changes Perceived Importance

How have these priorities changed over time?

Perhaps the most important answer to this question is the finding that all items except for gas and home heating prices have risen in importance over time, even if slightly. In other words, each issue with the exception of gas and home heating prices is now more likely to be rated as extremely important than was the case across the previous times the issue had been measured in this fashion since 2001.

The two issues with the largest relative jump in importance in this survey (compared to the average importance rating in previous surveys) are the situation in Iraq and terrorism. This is of some interest. The current 59% extremely important rating for the situation in Iraq is the highest measure in the four times this item has been asked in this fashion. It is higher than in January 2003, just before the invasion, and is higher than the one time it was measured in 2004 and both times it was measured earlier this year.

Terrorism is perceived to be slightly more important now than its average across time. Note that 70% and 62% of Americans rated terrorism as extremely important in October 2001 and January 2002—just months after the Sept. 11, 2001 terrorist attacks. But the perceived importance of terrorism fluctuated from that point forward. Still, the current 58% extremely important rating given to terrorism is higher than the three previous measures stretching back to December 2004, and, as noted, is slightly higher than the average across all times the issue has been measured in this format.

Partisan Differences

The recent partisan wrangling in Congress over a number of issues such as budget cuts and the Patriot Act has highlighted differences in the ways Democrats and Republicans view the world today.

The table below displays the percentages of Republicans (including independents who lean Republican) and Democrats (including independents who lean Democratic) who rate each item as extremely important:

The data show that these issues are almost across the board of more importance to Democrats than Republicans. Republicans average an extremely important rating of 37% for the eight issues, while Democrats average a 51% extremely important rating. Democrats are in particular most likely to rate healthcare costs, gas and home heating prices, Social Security, the economy, and the situation in Iraq

How Important a Priority for the President and Congress in the New Year
% extremely important, by party
Dec. 9-11, 2005

Party	The economy %	Terrorism %	Healthcare costs %	The situation in Iraq %	Gas and home heating prices %	Immigration %	Controlling illegal immigration %	Social Security %	Avg. rating %
Reps w/leaners	36	60	32	50	28	28	31	33	37
Dems w/leaners	56	58	62	67	52	24	33	53	51
Difference: Dems minus Reps	*20*	*-2*	*30*	*17*	*24*	*-4*	*2*	*20*	

higher than do Republicans. The two partisan groups are roughly equal in the importance attached to terrorism and the two questions about immigration.

Age Differences

There are also differences in ascribed importance by age groups:

Key differences:
- The economy is of less importance to Americans aged 65 and older, many of whom are out of the workforce.
- Terrorism is also of less importance to Americans aged 65 and older.
- Healthcare costs are of most importance to those between ages 30 and 64; they are less important to those who are younger and older.
- The situation in Iraq is of less importance to Americans aged 65 and older.
- Gas and home heating prices are of slightly lower importance to those who are younger than age 50.
- Immigration and controlling illegal immigration are of slightly lower importance to younger Americans than older ones.
- Interestingly, Social Security is of most importance to those in the 30 to 64 age bracket; it is of less importance to those who are younger and older.

Regional Differences

- Illegal immigration is of most importance to those living in the South (a region that includes border states Texas and Florida).
- Gas and home heating costs are of most importance to those living in the East.
- Terrorism and the economy are of more importance to those living in the South and East.
- The situation in Iraq is of most importance to those on the two coasts, which is most likely an artifact of the fact that these areas have the highest percentage of Democrats.

- Social Security is of less importance to residents of the Midwest than in any other region.

Survey Methods

Results are based on telephone interviews with 1,003 national adults, aged 18 and older, conducted Dec. 9-11, 2005. For results based on the total sample of national adults, one can say with 95% confidence that the maximum margin of sampling error is ±3 percentage points. In addition to sampling error, question wording and practical difficulties in conducting surveys can introduce error or bias into the findings of public opinion polls.

December 20, 2005
NEGATIVE ATTITUDES ON IRAQ PROVE HARD TO CHANGE
Half still believe U.S. can't achieve victory in Iraq

by Lydia Saad, Gallup Poll Senior Editor

President George W. Bush's speech to the nation Sunday night squarely addressed several of the areas where there is the greatest divergence between the administration and the public on Iraq, including whether the United States is winning or losing the war, and whether Bush has a plan that can achieve victory.

A recent CNN/*USA Today*/Gallup poll suggests that despite hitting these same points in four previous speeches around the country since Thanksgiving, Bush has not succeeded in moving public opinion on Iraq in any significant way. The Dec. 16-18 survey was conducted after the Dec. 15 Iraqi election—widely hailed for its high turnout—but before Bush's Sunday night address to the nation in which he forcefully made the case for staying the course in Iraq.

How Important a Priority for the President and Congress in the New Year
% extremely important, by age
Dec. 9-11, 2005

Age	The economy %	Terrorism %	Health-care costs %	The situation in Iraq %	Gas and home heating prices %	Immi-gration %	Controlling illegal immi-gration %	Social Security %
18 to 29	50	60	41	66	35	23	27	39
30 to 49	50	60	50	64	43	25	27	47
50 to 64	47	59	54	58	45	29	35	47
65+	40	51	43	44	37	32	39	37

How Important a Priority for the President and Congress in the New Year
% extremely important, by region
Dec. 9-11, 2005

Region	The economy %	Terrorism %	Health-care costs %	The situation in Iraq %	Gas and home heating prices %	Immi-gration %	Controlling illegal immi-gration %	Social Security %
East	51	61	53	64	51	30	25	46
Midwest	42	54	46	50	39	26	28	38
South	53	62	49	56	40	30	40	46
West	39	55	45	69	33	19	28	45

The poll underscores the deep divisions that exist among the American public over the merits of the war in Iraq and the outlook for U.S. victory there—divisions Bush acknowledged in his speech to the nation on Sunday night.

Just slightly more than half of American adults, 52%, say that sending U.S. troops to Iraq was a mistake while 46% disagree. About half of Americans (49%) also tend to believe the United States will eventually win the war in Iraq, while 47% doubt this. These results are generally consistent with public opinion on Iraq throughout the fall.

Which comes closer to your view about the war in Iraq: you think the U.S. will definitely win the war in Iraq, you think the U.S. will probably win the war in Iraq, you think the U.S. can win the war in Iraq, but you don't think it will win, (or) you do not think the U.S. can win the war in Iraq?

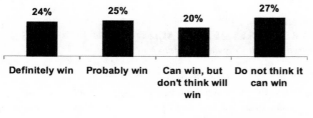

Dec. 16-18, 2005

The need for Bush to clearly articulate a plan for achieving victory in Iraq—as he did Sunday night—is evident as the weekend poll shows only 42% of Americans believe he has such a plan. Despite the administration's efforts, the majority of Americans have said in three polls conducted since Nov. 30 that Bush does not have a plan.

Does Bush Have a Plan That Will Achieve Victory in Iraq?

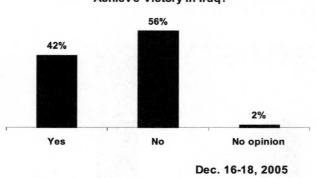

Dec. 16-18, 2005

Bush's latest job approval rating on Iraq (37% approve, 61% disapprove) is even more negative than his overall job rating. As of the weekend poll, 41% approved and 56% disapproved of the overall job Bush is doing as president. Both ratings are very similar to where they stood earlier this month, although Bush's overall job approval rating is slightly higher than the 38% average rating he received in three pre-Thanksgiving Gallup Polls in November.

In his Sunday night speech Bush defined the U.S. goal in Iraq as "a democratic Iraq that can defend itself, that will never again be a safe haven for terrorists, and that will serve as a model of freedom for the Middle East." He insisted that the United States is already winning the war on each dimension, and outlined a three-point plan for ultimate victory.

In contrast to Bush's optimism, the pre-speech poll finds only 40% of Americans convinced that the United States and its allies are currently winning the war. Half the public says neither side is winning while an additional 9% say the insurgents are winning.

Who do you think is currently winning the war in Iraq?

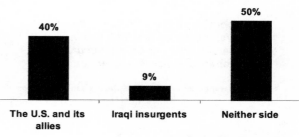

Dec. 16-18, 2005

Little Confidence in Iraqi Security Forces

A key to Bush's exit strategy in Iraq is training Iraqi forces to maintain law and order, but Americans are widely pessimistic about the chances of this happening in the next few years.

Only 37% of Americans foresee the Iraqi military and police forces being able to ensure safety and security in Iraq without U.S. assistance; 62% say this is unlikely.

Similarly, only 35% consider it likely that Iraq will be able to prevent terrorists from using the country as a base of operations for planning future attacks against the United States.

Americans Most Optimistic About Democracy Taking Hold in Iraq

Public opinion is closer to Bush's position when it comes to the perceived likelihood that Iraq will be able to establish a stable democratic government within the next few years—one that will not be overthrown by terrorists or supporters of Saddam Hussein. But even on this point, the public is closely divided. A 50% plurality of Americans believe Iraqi democracy will succeed; 47% say it is unlikely.

Exactly half of Americans also consider the recent election in Iraq to be either a "key step" (12%) or a "major step" (38%) toward ensuring the United States will achieve its goals in Iraq. Nearly as many view the election as only a "minor step" forward (29%) or as not helpful to the United States in achieving its goals (19%).

Importance of Recent Iraq Election for U.S. Achieving Victory in Iraq

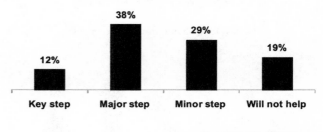

Dec. 16-18, 2005

Americans Dubious Iraq Is Part of War on Terror

The poll suggests Bush has a hard sell when it comes to convincing Americans that the Iraq war is part of the war on terrorism sparked by the events of Sept. 11, 2001. Only 43% of Americans associate Iraq with the war on terrorism while 55% consider it to be an entirely separate military action. Despite the president's emphasis on the connection between terrorism and the Iraq war in his recent speeches, the percentage linking the two is now significantly lower than it was a year ago (50% in October 2004), and well below where it stood in August 2003 (57%).

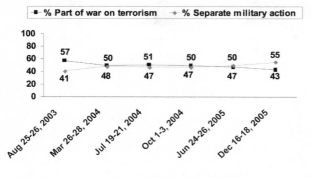

Do you consider the war in Iraq to be part of the war on terrorism which began on September 11, 2001, or do you consider it to be an entirely separate military action?

Outlook for Troops

In his Sunday address, Bush reiterated his opposition to setting a specific timetable for removing U.S. troops from Iraq, but he held out the hope that troops could start coming home as democracy takes hold, and as Iraqi security forces gain competency. In his words, "Our forces in Iraq are on the road to victory—and that is the road that will take them home."

Very few Americans (17%) predict there will be a significant withdrawal of U.S. troops from Iraq within one year, but a majority (53%) believes this will happen in one to three years. Only 29% foresee a significant number of troops in Iraq continuing after three years.

This contrasts with Americans' desire to see troops withdrawn much sooner. More than half (59%) say the United States should only maintain a significant number of troops for another year at most. Of this, 21% say the limit should be three months, 14% say three to six months, and 24% say six months to a year. More than a third

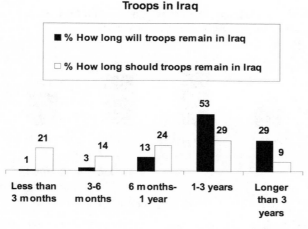

Troops in Iraq

Dec. 16-18, 2005

favor maintaining a significant U.S. military presence in Iraq for longer than a year, including 29% who would stay for one to three years, and 9% who would stay longer than three years.

Survey Methods

These results are based on telephone interviews with a randomly selected national sample of 1,003 adults, aged 18 and older, conducted Dec. 16-18, 2005. For results based on this sample, one can say with 95% confidence that the maximum error attributable to sampling and other random effects is ±3 percentage points. In addition to sampling error, question wording and practical difficulties in conducting surveys can introduce error or bias into the findings of public opinion polls.

December 20, 2005
PUBLIC STILL BEHIND ALITO
Democrats slightly more negative

by Joseph Carroll, Gallup Poll Assistant Editor

With less than a month to go before Judge Samuel Alito's Supreme Court confirmation hearings begin, pro- and anti-Alito camps are stepping up their rhetoric. A new CNN/*USA Today*/Gallup poll* finds Americans continue to generally support Alito's confirmation to the high court, but this support is becoming slightly more polarized along party lines.

The poll, conducted Dec. 9-11, finds that 49% of Americans say they would like to see the Senate vote in favor of Alito serving on the Supreme Court, while 29% say they would not, and 22% have no opinion. Gallup first asked about Alito's confirmation in November, and opinion has not changed substantially since. In early November, 50% were in favor of the Senate confirming Alito, 25% were opposed, and 25% had no opinion.

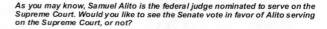

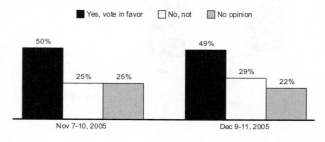

Public Support for Alito vs. Miers and Roberts

Public support for Alito's confirmation to the court is slightly higher than it was for Harriet Miers, who withdrew her nomination after mounting criticism over her qualifications to serve on the Supreme Court. Alito's current level of support is about the same as John Roberts' about a month after he was nominated, though Roberts' support reached as high as 60% prior to his confirmation.

Forty-four percent of Americans supported Miers' confirmation just after Bush nominated her, while 36% were opposed. Shortly before Miers withdrew her nomination, Gallup found Americans evenly divided: 42% were in favor and 43% were opposed to her serving on the Supreme Court.

Across five polls conducted from the time Bush first nominated Roberts to the time when his Senate confirmation hearings first began, Gallup found that 56% of Americans, on average, supported Roberts' confirmation, while 26% opposed it and 18% offered no opinion. Support for Roberts began at 59% right after he was nominated, but dropped to 51% in early August and stayed at 52% in late August. In September, as Bush nominated Roberts to the chief justice position and his confirmation hearings began, support for Roberts serving on the court grew to 58% and then 60%.

Public Support for Samuel Alito, Harriet Miers, and John Roberts

Gallup Polls, July 2005 - December 2005

	Yes, vote in favor	No, not	No opinion
Samuel Alito			
Average	50%	27%	23%
Dec 9-11, 2005	49%	29%	22%
Nov 7-10, 2005	50%	25%	25%
Harriet Miers			
Average	43%	40%	18%
Oct 21-23, 2005	42%	43%	15%
Oct 13-16, 2005	44%	36%	20%
John Roberts			
Average	56%	26%	18%
Sep 16-18, 2005	60%	26%	14%
Sep 8-11, 2005	58%	27%	15%
Aug 28-30, 2005	52%	26%	22%
Aug 5-7, 2005	51%	28%	21%
Jul 22-24, 2005	59%	22%	19%

Republicans More Likely Than Democrats to Support Alito Confirmation

Republicans and Democrats vary significantly in their overall level of support for Alito. More than 7 in 10 Republicans (73%) say the Senate should vote to confirm him, while just 12% say it should not. Democrats are much more likely to oppose (45%) than to support (29%) Alito's confirmation.

Public Support for Samuel Alito's Confirmation to the Supreme Court by Party Affiliation

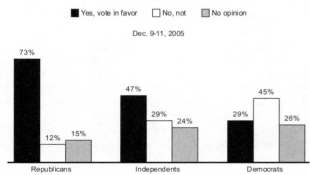

Dec. 9-11, 2005

Since Gallup first asked this question about Alito in November, Democrats have grown slightly more negative about Alito's confirmation. In early November, 35% of Democrats said the Senate should confirm Alito, while 40% opposed it. Support for Alito among Republicans shows no change since November.

There were similar partisan gaps in Americans' support of both Roberts and Miers.

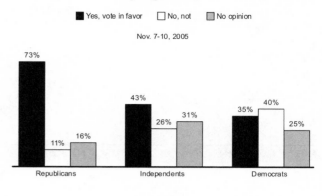

Public Support for Samuel Alito's Confirmation to the Supreme Court by Party Affiliation

Nov. 7-10, 2005

Bottom Line

Do the poll numbers reflect a nominee's chances to get confirmed to the Supreme Court? Gallup has polled the American public about its overall level of support for five recent Supreme Court nominees. The current 49% support level for Alito aligns him more closely with three individuals who were eventually confirmed—Clarence Thomas in 1991 (an average of 52% support), Ruth Bader Ginsburg (53%), and Roberts (56%). Alito's support is higher than it was for two nominees who were not confirmed: Robert Bork averaged just 35% support in 1987 and Miers averaged 43% earlier this year.

Results are based on telephone interviews with 1,003 national adults, aged 18 and older, conducted Dec. 9-11, 2005. For results based on the total sample of national adults, one can say with 95% confidence that the margin of sampling error is ±3 percentage points. In addition to sampling error, question wording and practical difficulties in conducting surveys can introduce error or bias into the findings of public opinion polls.

December 20, 2005

RELIGION "VERY IMPORTANT" TO MOST AMERICANS
Fewer have faith in its influence

by Albert L. Winseman, Religion and Social Trends Editor

Since the 1950s, Gallup has been asking Americans about the importance of religion in their lives—and about their perception of religion's influence on society as a whole. Answers to these questions provide some interesting insight into the contrast between Americans' personal experience and their perceptions of broader social conditions.

In 1952, the first year Americans were asked about the importance of religion in their lives, a record-high 75% said that religion was "very important" in their lives. When the question was asked again in 1978 (after a 70% reading in 1965), the "very important" percentage had dropped to 52%—which has proven to be the lowest Gallup has measured. The question has been asked regularly since the 1980s, with the percentage saying religion is very important remaining above the majority level. In the 1980s, the percentage saying religion is very important to them hovered in the mid-50s, and edged only slightly higher in 1990s and 2000s, remaining in the upper 50s and 60% range. In 2005, 57% of Americans, on average, said religion is very important in their lives.

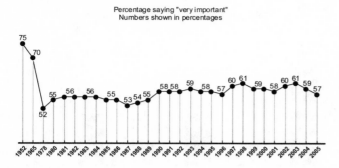

How important would you say religion is in your own life -- very important, fairly important, or not very important?

Percentage saying "very important"
Numbers shown in percentages

While religion plays an important role in Americans' lives, they are less sure about religion's influence on American life in general. Over the last 50 years, Gallup has also asked Americans to assess whether religion is increasing or losing its influence on American life. Overall, Americans have typically been more likely to feel religion is losing its influence than that its influence is increasing. However, responses to this question have moved around a lot, coinciding in some cases with major news events. Following the Sept. 11 terrorist attacks, for example, the proportion who felt the influence of religion was rising spiked 32 percentage points.

Since 2004, however, the public has been evenly split on the question. In 2005, on average, 49% said religion is gaining influence, while the 46% said it is losing influence.

These data show that Americans have been fairly consistent when it comes to religion's importance in their personal lives: a solid majority find their religious faith to be "very important" to them. But their opinions of religion's broader influence on society appears to hinge on events, underscoring a central paradox of contemporary American life: Americans view themselves as essentially spiritual and/or religious, but are acutely aware that they are living in a secular society—albeit a society that appears to be more secular at some times than at others.

December 20, 2005
AMERICANS' VACATION HABITS
About one in five traveled abroad in past year

by Jeffrey M. Jones, Gallup Poll Managing Editor

In the recent annual Lifestyle poll*, Gallup asked Americans about their vacation travel. The results show that most Americans took vacations away from home in the past year, but slightly fewer did so in 2005 than in 2001. Travel outside the United States is far less common. Vacations and foreign travel are much more common among wealthier Americans.

The Dec. 5-8 Lifestyle poll finds 64% of Americans saying they have taken a vacation away from home in the past year. That is down from 70% who said this in 2001. Nineteen percent of Americans say they have traveled outside the United States in the past year, the same percentage who said this in 2001.

One's economic resources and one's likelihood to take a vacation away from home are strongly related. Ninety percent of Americans whose annual household incomes are $75,000 or more took a vacation away from home in the past year. The percentage decreases steadily by income category and only 29% of those whose household incomes are less than $20,000 vacationed away from home last year.

Taken Vacation Away From Home in Last Year, by Household Income

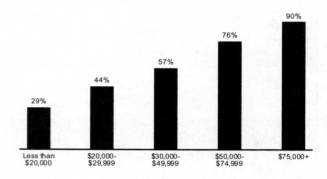

Generally speaking, those who are married (72%) are more likely to have taken a vacation away from home than those who are not married (52%), and those who have children under age 18 (71%) are more likely to vacation than those who do not have young children (60%). But the data suggest these relationships are somewhat complex and life situation interacts with household income when it comes to vacationing.

At the lowest level of household income ($30,000 or less), those who are married or who have children under age 18 are less likely than those who are not married or do not have young children to take a vacation. However, in the middle ($30,000 to $74,999) and upper ($75,000 or more) household income categories, the relationship reverses and those who are married or who have young children are more likely to vacation away from home.

The data also show that younger and older Americans are less likely to vacation than are those in the middle age categories. Fifty-seven percent of Americans between the ages of 18 and 29 and 47% of those aged 65 and older have taken a vacation away from home in the past year. That compares with 73% of Americans aged 30 to 49 and 67% of those aged 50 to 64.

These age differences are apparent in the lower and middle income categories, but at the highest income category ($75,000 and up), there are essentially no age differences.

Travel Abroad

Traveling outside the United States is not something many Americans have taken the opportunity to do in the past year. Only about one in five Americans have done so.

As with vacationing away from home, income and the likelihood of traveling outside the United States are strongly related. Slightly more than one in three Americans at the highest income level ($75,000 or more) have traveled abroad in the last 12 months. That percentage drops sharply at the next income category ($50,000 to $74,999) and levels off from there. Only 7% of Americans whose household incomes are less than $20,000 have traveled outside the United States in the past year.

Traveled Outside United States in Last Year, by Household Income

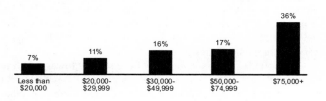

While Americans under age 30 are less likely than middle-aged Americans to vacation away from home, they are no less likely, and possibly more so, to have traveled outside the United States in the past year.

Twenty-five percent of Americans aged 18 to 29 have traveled abroad in the past year, compared with 22% of those aged 30 to 49, 16% of those aged 50 to 64, and 12% of those 65 and older.

Also, those living in the eastern (24%) or western (24%) regions of the United States are more likely to travel abroad than those living in the South (13%) or Midwest (17%). This may be because it is easier and likely more affordable for those living on the coasts to fly to other countries.

Results are based on interviews with 1,013 national adults, aged 18 and older, conducted Dec. 5-8, 2005. For results based on this sample of national adults, one can say with 95% confidence that the maximum margin of sampling error is ±3 percentage points.

December 21, 2005
AMERICANS PROTECTIVE OF CIVIL RIGHTS
Two-to-one majority opposes violation of civil rights in fight against terrorism

by David W. Moore, Gallup Poll Senior Editor

With President George W. Bush criticizing congressional Democrats and Republicans who have thus far blocked renewal of the Patriot Act, most Americans express reservations in principle about violating their civil rights in order to fight terrorism, though relatively few think the Patriot Act "goes too far."

A recent CNN/*USA Today*/Gallup poll finds 65% of Americans saying that while the government should make efforts to fight terrorism, it should not take steps that violate basic civil liberties. On the other hand, 31% would allow the government to take counter-terrorism steps to prevent terrorism, "even if that means your basic civil liberties would be violated."

Which comes closer to your view—[ROTATED: the government should take all steps necessary to prevent additional acts of terrorism in the U.S. even if it means your basic civil liberties would be violated, (or) the government should take steps to prevent additional acts of terrorism but not if those steps would violate your basic civil liberties]?

BASED ON 522 NATIONAL ADULTS IN FORM B

	Take steps, even if civil liberties violated %	Take steps but not violate civil liberties %	No opinion %
2005 Dec 16-18 ^	31	65	4
2003 Nov 10-12 ^	31	64	5
2003 Aug 25-26 ^	29	67	4
2003 Apr 22-23	33	64	3
2002 Sep 2-4 ^	33	62	5
2002 Jun 21-23	40	56	4
2002 Jan 25-27	47	49	4

^ Asked of a half sample

Americans were more permissive in their responses in a Jan. 2002 poll, only four months after the 9/11 terrorist attacks, when they were evenly divided about allowing the government to fight terrorism by violating basic civil rights—47% in favor, 49% opposed. But almost one year after 9/11, 62% of Americans were against, and just 33% in favor, of allowing civil rights violations in the war against terrorism—a pattern of division that has persisted since then.

When asked specifically about the Patriot Act—a broad anti-terrorism law which was initially enacted shortly after 9/11 and expires at the end of this month, unless renewed by Congress—34% of Americans say the law goes too far in restricting people's civil liberties, 41% say it is about right, and 18% say it doesn't go far enough. These views are little changed from a similar measure last June.

As you may know, shortly after the terrorist attacks on September 11, 2001, a law called the Patriot Act was passed. That law deals with the ways the federal government can obtain private information on people living in the U.S. who are suspected of having ties with terrorists. Based on what you have read or heard, do you think the Patriot Act—[ROTATED: goes too far, is about right, or does not go far enough]—in restricting people's civil liberties in order to investigate suspected terrorism?

BASED ON 481 NATIONAL ADULTS IN FORM A

	Goes too far	About right	Not far enough	No opinion
2005 Dec 16-18 ^	34%	44	18	4
2005 Jun 24-26	30%	41	21	8

^ Asked of a half sample

Partisan Differences

Given that President Bush and most congressional Republicans support the Patriot Act, while most Democrats (and only a few Republicans) oppose it, public opinion about this matter is likely to be highly related to party affiliation. The poll confirms that hypothesis:

Only 13% of Republicans say the law goes too far, compared with 40% of independents and 48% of Democrats. On the other hand, 65% of Republicans say the law is about right, compared with 37% of independents and 31% of Democrats.

Views of Patriot Act
by Party Affiliation

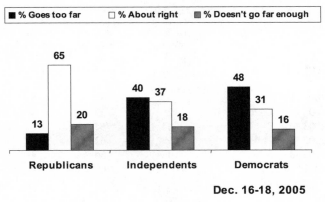

Dec. 16-18, 2005

The poll finds a similar pattern on whether the government should be able to violate basic civil liberties while fighting terrorism. A slight majority of Republicans, 51%, opposes such violations, compared with 73% of independents and 70% of Democrats.

Permissible to Violate Civil Liberties
While Fighting Terrorism?
by Party Affiliation

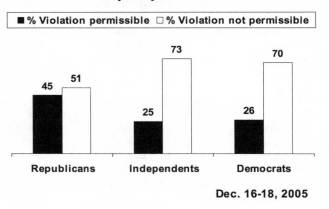

Dec. 16-18, 2005

Survey Methods

Results are based on telephone interviews with 1,003 national adults, aged 18 and older, conducted Dec. 16-18, 2005. For results based on the total sample of national adults, one can say with 95% confidence that the maximum margin of sampling error is ±3 percentage points.

For results based on the 481 national adults in the Form A half-sample and 522 national adults in the Form B half-sample, the maximum margins of sampling error are ±5 percentage points.

In addition to sampling error, question wording and practical difficulties in conducting surveys can introduce error or bias into the findings of public opinion polls.

December 22, 2005
CHRISTMAS A GOOD TIME FOR MOST AMERICANS
Fifteen percent say it is the best time of year for them

by Jeffrey M. Jones, Gallup Poll Managing Editor

As Americans prepare to celebrate Christmas, a new CNN/*USA Today/*Gallup poll finds most are apparently looking forward to it. Half say it is a "great time" or the "best time of the year." Slightly less than half of Americans say it is a "strongly religious" holiday for them. Most people say they usually feel some stress in getting ready for the holiday, but only about one in three say they feel a great deal or fair amount of stress.

The poll also shows Americans have shifted toward putting "Christmas" back in the holiday season, both in the way they greet others at this time of year and in the way they feel stores and other public institutions should acknowledge the season.

Celebrating Christmas

The Dec. 16-18 poll finds that 96% of all U.S. adults celebrate Christmas, a percentage that has been consistent over the past decade. This includes a high level of participation—84%—among non-Christians.

Most Americans feel positively toward Christmas. Half say it is a great time, including 15% who say it is the best time of the year for them. An additional 35% say it is a good time. Eight percent say it is neither good nor bad, and 3% say it is a bad time.

Younger adults are significantly more likely than older adults to describe Christmas in positive terms. Sixty-one percent of 18- to 29-year-olds say it is the best time of year or a great time. That percentage is 54% among those aged 30 to 49, 45% among those aged 50 to 64, and just 38% of those 65 and older.

Which of the following best describes the way you feel about Christmas — it is the best time of the year for you, it is a great time, it is a good time, it is neither a good nor a bad time, or it is a bad time for you?

Dec. 16–18, 2005

Also, parents of young children are more likely to express more positive attitudes toward the holiday—62% of parents of children under 18 say it is the best time or a great time of the year, compared with 43% of those who do not have young children.

Many Americans celebrate the holiday in ways that go beyond exchanging gifts and holiday greetings. The poll asked Americans how much time and effort they spend on Christmas-related activities—such as decorating the house, having parties, or baking cookies—compared with other people they know. Twelve percent believe they spend a lot more time and effort on these activities than most people they know, 30% say they spend a little more time and effort. Thirty-two percent say they spend a little less time, and 22% say a lot less time.

There are differences in the effort and time people put into Christmas activities by marital status. Fifty percent of those who are married believe they spend more time on Christmas activities than people they know. Only 31% of unmarried people say this.

There is a similar difference between those with young children and those without. Fifty-two percent of parents with children under 18 believe they spend more time "decking the halls" than most people, while only 37% of those who don't have young children say this.

A Dec. 9-11 CNN/*USA Today*/Gallup poll asked Americans specifically about sending Christmas cards. Eighty-one percent of Americans say they plan to give or send Christmas cards this year. According to the poll, the average American will send or give 31 Christmas cards this year. The average card-giver will send or give 37.

The Religious Aspect

Given that Christmas is the Christian celebration of the birth of Jesus Christ, and given that the United States is a predominantly Christian nation, religion plays an important part in the holiday for many Americans. According to the Dec. 16-18 poll, 47% of Americans say Christmas is a strongly religious holiday for them, up from 38% in 1989. Thirty percent say it is somewhat religious, and 19% say it is not too religious.

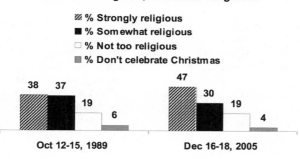

Thinking of the way you personally celebrate Christmas, is it a strongly religious holiday, somewhat religious, or not too religious?

▨ % Strongly religious
■ % Somewhat religious
☐ % Not too religious
▨ % Don't celebrate Christmas

Oct 12-15, 1989 — 38, 37, 19, 6
Dec 16-18, 2005 — 47, 30, 19, 4

Fifty-four percent of Christians say it is a strongly religious holiday, 33% say it is somewhat religious, and 11% say not too religious.

Weekly churchgoers are far more likely to say Christmas is a strongly religious holiday for them—80% of those who attend church weekly say so, compared with 49% of those who attend religious services nearly weekly or monthly and 24% of those who seldom or never attend.

Holiday Stress

Even though Christmas is largely a happy occasion for most Americans, the days and weeks leading up to it can be stressful with the shopping in crowded stores, decorations to put up, and holiday parties to attend. Most Americans admit to feeling at least a little stress or pressure around the holidays, but only about one in three say they feel a great deal (14%) or fair amount (23%) of stress. An additional 23% say they feel some stress, while 23% do not feel much and 13% do not feel any stress.

A similar question was asked in a 1989 Gallup Poll. Apparently, Christmas has not become any more stressful. At that time, 15% felt a great deal of pressure and 20% felt a fair amount from all the things they had to do to get ready for Christmas.

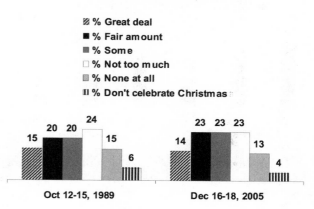

How much stress or pressure do you usually feel from all the things you have to do to get ready for Christmas?

▨ % Great deal
■ % Fair amount
■ % Some
☐ % Not too much
▨ % None at all
▥ % Don't celebrate Christmas

Oct 12-15, 1989 — 15, 20, 20, 24, 15, 6
Dec 16-18, 2005 — 14, 23, 23, 23, 13, 4

Happy Holiday Backlash?

There has been a major shift in Americans' attitudes toward holiday greetings in the last year—69% say they would greet someone they just met with the phrase "Merry Christmas," while 29% would opt to say "Happy Holidays." Last year, Americans still preferred the "Merry Christmas" greeting, but by a smaller 56% to 41% margin.

That change is also evident in Americans' attitudes about how stores and other public institutions acknowledge the holidays. An average of 62% of Americans in two polls (Dec. 5-8 and Dec. 16-18) say that public institutions' and stores' use of "Happy Holidays" or "Season's Greetings," rather than "Merry Christmas," is "a change for the worse," while just 26% say it is a "change for the better."

Last year, the public was evenly divided, with 44% saying the change was for the better and 43% for the worse.

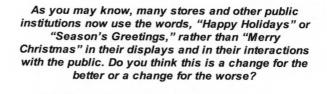

As you may know, many stores and other public institutions now use the words, "Happy Holidays" or "Season's Greetings," rather than "Merry Christmas" in their displays and in their interactions with the public. Do you think this is a change for the better or a change for the worse?

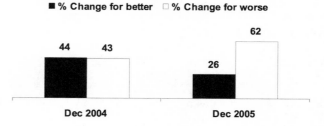

■ % Change for better   ☐ % Change for worse

Dec 2004 — 44, 43
Dec 2005 — 26, 62

This year, conservative talk-show hosts such as Bill O'Reilly have taken up the crusade against stores' use of the more universal greetings rather than the traditional "Merry Christmas." But it is not just conservatives who have changed their views from last year. In

2004, self-described liberals said the use of the universal greetings was a change for the better by a 68% to 18% margin. This year, liberals are evenly divided, with 43% saying it is for the worse, and 42% for the better.

Stores' Use of "Happy Holidays" or "Season's Greetings" Instead of "Merry Christmas"

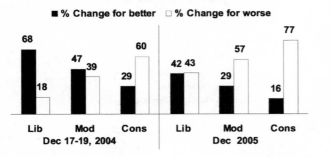

■ % Change for better □ % Change for worse

A more negative assessment of public institutions' use of the universal greetings this year compared to last is evident among most subgroups.

View of Use of Happy Holidays Instead of Merry Christmas, Selected Subgroups

| | 2004 | | 2005* | |
	Change for the better %	Change for the worse %	Change for the better %	Change for the worse %
All Americans	44	43	26	62
Democrat	56	32	37	48
Independent	45	39	30	57
Republican	30	59	13	80
Liberal	68	18	42	43
Moderate	47	39	29	57
Conservative	29	60	16	77
Weekly church	31	59	17	75
Monthly church	44	44	24	65
Seldom/Never	52	32	33	51
18 to 29	60	23	48	43
30 to 49	47	40	26	62
50 to 64	39	51	20	67
65+	30	57	15	69
High school or less	44	44	26	62
Some college	43	43	24	64
College grad	41	46	23	63
Postgrad	46	40	34	53
Christian	39	48	21	68
Non-Christian	61	23	47	35

*Based on combined data from Dec. 5-8 and Dec. 16-18 polls

The same patterns are evident in terms of which holiday greeting Americans would give to someone they just met—with many more saying they would say "Merry Christmas" this year than last.

Preferred Holiday Greeting to Give, Selected Subgroups

| | 2004 | | 2005 | |
	Merry Christmas %	Happy Holidays %	Merry Christmas %	Happy Holiday %
Democrat	44	54	60	38
Independent	54	43	64	34
Republican	71	25	83	15
Liberal	36	60	53	45
Moderate	57	40	65	33
Conservative	65	32	81	17
Weekly church	66	31	81	17
Monthly church	59	41	72	26
Seldom/Never	49	47	58	39
18 to 29	55	44	51	46
30 to 49	50	46	65	34
50 to 64	58	38	73	24
65+	65	32	84	12
High school or less	62	36	69	29
Some college	53	42	75	22
College grad	54	44	66	33
Postgrad	51	45	58	40
Christian	62	35	74	24
Non-Christian	31	63	45	53

Survey Methods

These results are based on telephone interviews with a randomly selected national sample of 1,003 adults, aged 18 and older, conducted Dec. 16-19, 2005. For results based on this sample, one can say with 95% confidence that the maximum error attributable to sampling and other random effects is ±3 percentage points. In addition to sampling error, question wording and practical difficulties in conducting surveys can introduce error or bias into the findings of public opinion polls.

December 23, 2005
AMERICANS INVENTORY THEIR GADGETS
Age, gender, household income related to ownership

by Joseph Carroll, Gallup Poll Assistant Editor

The Christmas season seems to be the time of year when Americans shop for nifty gadgets for their friends and family. This year, the gadget receiving the most buzz is the Xbox 360 gaming system, which has sold out in stores around the country and is being auctioned off on eBay and Craigslist for as much as $1,000 each.

Gallup recently asked Americans if they personally have each of 17 different technological gadgets. VCRs, DVD players, cell phones, cable television, and desktop computers are the most widely owned electronics, while wireless e-mail devices, satellite radio, and

GPS navigation systems are the least common. Younger Americans rather than older Americans, men rather than women, and those in high-income households rather than lower-income households are much more inclined to have many of the items listed in the survey.

Overall Results

The poll, conducted Dec. 5-8, finds that more than 8 in 10 Americans own a VCR or a DVD player. A large number of Americans— at least two in three—report that they have cell phones (78%), cable television (68%), and desktop computers (65%). Half say they have a digital camera.

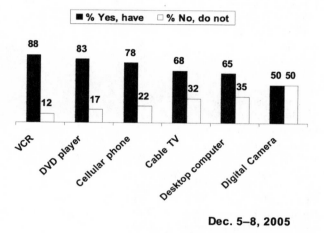

Most Popular Gadgets
(owned by at least half of Americans)

Dec. 5–8, 2005

Slightly less than half of Americans, 48%, have high-speed Internet. And, further down the list of electronic devices, Gallup finds that roughly a third of Americans say they currently have satellite television, a laptop computer, a portable DVD player, or a video game system, such as an Xbox or Playstation 2.

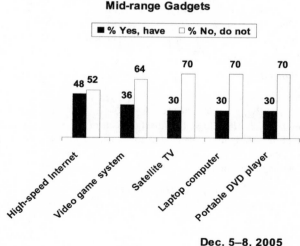

Mid-range Gadgets

Dec. 5–8, 2005

Six of the gadgets inventoried have more niched uses and are owned by fewer than one in four Americans: digital video recorders (22%), high-definition televisions (22%), iPods or MP3 music play-

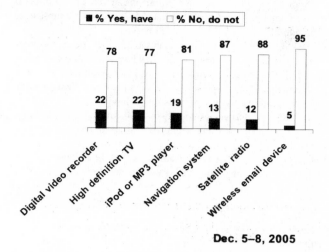

Least Popular Gadgets

Dec. 5–8, 2005

ers (19%), GPS or other navigation systems (13%), satellite radio (12%), or wireless e-mail devices (5%).

Younger vs. Older Americans

The generational gap in having high-tech devices is huge in some cases. Senior citizens are much less likely than those who are younger to have 10 out of the 17 items.

The largest differences between younger and older Americans involve video game systems and DVD players. A majority of Americans under age 50 say they have a video game system. This compares with just 18% of 50- to 64-year-olds and only 6% of those aged 65 and older. This difference may be due to the presence of children in the home, as two in three adults with children under age 18 have a gaming system and only 22% of adults with no children have one. The vast majority of adults under age 65 say they have a DVD player, but less than half of those 65 and older (48%) report having one at the present time.

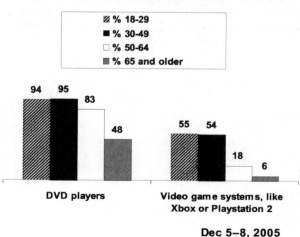

Gadgets Owned by Age Groups
(percentage who say they have each item)

Dec 5–8, 2005

The poll also finds significant age differences, albeit not nearly as dramatic, regarding the following items:

- Cell phones. More than 8 in 10 Americans between the ages of 18 and 49 say they have a cellular phone. This percentage is lower among 50- to 64-year-olds, at 75%, and among those aged 65 and older, just 54% own a cell phone.
- Desktop computers. Americans in the 30 to 49 age category are the most likely age group to say they have a desktop computer, with 80% saying they have one; two in three adults in the 18 to 29 and the 50 to 64 age categories say they have a desktop computer. Only one in three seniors report having one.
- High-speed Internet. A majority of adults under age 50 say they have high-speed Internet, while 46% of 50- to 64-year-olds and just 18% of adults aged 65 and older have this.
- Digital cameras. Again, those in the 30 to 49 age category are the most likely age group to say they have a digital camera, with 66% reporting this. Fifty-four percent of 18- to 29-year-olds and 47% of 50- to 64-year-olds have a digital camera. Just about one in five seniors have a digital camera.
- Laptop computers. More than 3 in 10 adults under age 65 say they have a laptop computer, while only 8% of seniors do.
- iPod or MP3 music player. Thirty-one percent of adults aged 18 to 29 have an iPod or MP3 music player. This compares with 26% of 30- to 49-year-olds, 11% of 50- to 64-year-olds, and only 2% of adults aged 65 and older.

Gadgets by Age Groups
(based on percentage who say "yes, have")
Dec. 5-8, 2005

	18- to 29-year-olds %	30- to 49-year-olds %	50- to 64-year-olds %	65 years and older %
A cellular phone	86	89	75	54
A desktop computer	65	80	68	33
High-speed Internet, such as DSL or cable	56	61	46	18
A digital camera	54	66	47	22
A laptop computer	37	39	31	8
An iPod or MP3 music player	31	26	11	2

The poll also shows slight age variations in having a portable DVD player, a digital video recorder, or a GPS or other navigation system, with seniors less likely than those under age 65 to have these devices.

Gadgets by Age Groups
(based on percentage who say "yes, have")
Dec. 5-8, 2005

	18- to 29-year-olds %	30- to 49-year-olds %	50- to 64-year-olds %	65 years and older %
A portable DVD player	31	38	28	17
A digital video recorder or Tivo	25	26	20	12
GPS or other navigation system	14	17	13	5

There are essentially no age differences for owning a VCR, cable or satellite television, high-definition television, satellite radio, or wireless e-mail devices.

Men vs. Women

Men are more likely than women to have 9 of the 17 items in the list, and women are no more likely than men to have any of these items.

Gadgets by Gender
(based on percentage who say "yes, have")
Dec. 5-8, 2005

	Men %	Women %	Difference (men – women)
A digital camera	57	44	+13
A laptop computer	36	25	+11
A GPS or other navigation system	19	8	+11
A desktop computer	70	61	+9
A video game system, such as XBox or Playstation 2	41	32	+9
A cellular phone	82	74	+8
High-speed Internet, such as DSL or cable	51	45	+6
Satellite TV	33	27	+6
A digital video recorder or Tivo	25	19	+6
A high-definition TV	25	20	+5
A wireless e-mail device, such as Blackberry or Treo	7	3	+4
A VCR	90	87	+3
A DVD player	84	81	+3
Cable TV	69	67	2
A portable DVD player	31	30	1
Satellite radio	12	11	1
An iPod or MP3 music player	18	19	-1

As the table illustrates, men are more likely than women to have the following gadgets: digital cameras (57% to 44%, respectively), laptop computers (36% to 25%), GPS or other navigation systems (19% to 8%), desktop computers (70% to 61%), video game systems (41% to 32%), and cellular phones (82% to 74%). Men are slightly more likely to have high-speed Internet, satellite television, digital video recorders, or high-definition television.

Men and women are just as likely to have wireless e-mail devices, VCRs, DVD players, cable television, portable DVD players, satellite radio, or MP3 players.

Higher-Income Households vs. Lower-Income Households

With the exception of video game systems and satellite television, Americans living in households earning $75,000 or more per year are more likely than those in households earning less than that to have all of these items in the table below. (The data show only modest variations by household income in having a video game system and satellite television.)

Gadgets by Household Income
(based on percentage who say "yes, have")
Dec. 5-8, 2005

	Less than $30,000 per year %	$30,000- $74,999 %	$75,000 or more per year %
A VCR	77	92	94
Cable TV	64	63	76

	Less than $30,000 per year %	$30,000-$74,999 %	$75,000 or more per year %
A DVD player	63	86	97
A cellular phone	49	85	96
A desktop computer	40	70	96
A video game system, such as Xbox or Playstation 2	32	40	38
Satellite TV	26	35	31
High-speed Internet, such as DSL or cable	23	49	74
A digital camera	21	53	80
A portable DVD player	21	30	43
A digital video recorder or Tivo	17	17	36
A high-definition TV	13	19	37
A laptop computer	12	30	54
An iPod or MP3 music player	10	16	34
Satellite radio	9	10	19
A GPS or other navigation system	6	12	25
A wireless e-mail device, such as Blackberry or Treo	2	4	12

The most significant difference is found in having a digital camera. Eighty percent of those earning $75,000 or more say they have a digital camera, compared with 53% of those earning between $30,000 and $75,000 and just 21% of those earning less than that.

The survey also finds large income differences in having high-speed Internet (74% among those earning $75,000 or more to 49% among those earning between $30,000 and $75,000 to 23% among those earning less than $30,000), a desktop computer (87% to 70% to 40%), a cell phone (96% to 85% to 49%), and a laptop computer (54% to 30% to 12%).

Survey Methods

Results are based on telephone interviews with 1,013 national adults, aged 18 and older, conducted Dec. 5-8, 2005. For results based on the total sample of national adults, one can say with 95% confidence that the maximum margin of sampling error is ±3 percentage points. In addition to sampling error, question wording and practical difficulties in conducting surveys can introduce error or bias into the findings of public opinion polls.

December 27, 2005
RESTAURANT DINING STILL THE EXCEPTION
Families eat dinner at home on most nights

by Lydia Saad, Gallup Poll Senior Editor

Anyone who has tried to find a parking spot at popular restaurants such as Olive Garden or P.F. Chang's on a typical weeknight, or who has waited at the door for an hour just to be seated, might wonder who still eats dinner at home.

Eating out is big business in the United States. According to the National Restaurant Association, with more than 12.2 million employees, the restaurant industry is the nation's second-biggest employer (behind government). Seventy billion "meal and snack occasions" were served at 900,000 locations across the United States in 2005. That works out to 233 restaurant stops for every man, woman, and child in this country of nearly 300 million residents.

While the numbers involved are huge, it may be that they overstate the importance of dining out to the average American—at least when focusing on the culturally celebrated dinner hour. Gallup's latest Lifestyle poll*, conducted Dec. 5-8, indicates that Americans eat dinner out only about once a week on average. Excluding those who generally never eat out (about a third of the public), the average number rises to twice a week.

Number of Times Ate Dinner Out at Restaurant Last Week

Zero	35%
1-2	49%
3+	15%
Mean	1.3
Mean excluding zero	2.0

A similar conclusion can be reached from a different question that asks adults with children under age 18 to estimate the number of nights a week their families eat dinner together at home. The average response is five nights per week, very close to what Gallup has recorded on this measure since 1997.

Number of Nights Per Week Family Dines Together at Home
(Based on adults with children under 18)

	2005	2003	2001	1997
Zero	2%	4%	4%	2%
1-2	10%	13%	10%	8%
3-4	21%	82%	87%	89%
5+	67%	64%	69%	72%
Mean	5.1	4.8	5.1	5.4

Dining out is naturally more common as one goes up the income ladder. But even among those in the highest income bracket reviewed ($75,000 or more in household income) fewer than one in five say they ate dinner out more than twice in the past week. The main difference in dining patterns between upper- and lower-income Americans is in the percentage eating out once or twice, versus not at all.

Restaurant Dining, by Annual Household Income

	Less than $30,000	$30,000-$49,999	$50,000-$74,999	$75,000 or more
# of times ate out in past week				
0 times	49	37	31	23
1-2 times	40	50	54	58
3+ times	11	13	16	18
	100%	100%	100%	100%

A similar pattern is seen by age. Young people are more frequent restaurant diners, but only a quarter eat dinner out three or more times a week (compared with 10% of those 65 and older). A much starker difference is seen in the percentage not eating out at all: only 19% among young adults compared with nearly half of seniors (19% vs. 46%). Middle-aged adults fall between these extremes.

Restaurant Dining, by Age

	18-29	30-49	50-64	65+
# of times ate out in past week				
0 times	19	32	41	46
1-2 times	55	55	45	44
3+ times	26	13	14	10
	100%	100%	100%	100%

Eating Up the Food Budget?

The financial impact on Americans of eating out may be greater than the reported frequency of restaurant dining indicates. Gallup asks Americans each month to estimate the total amount they will spend that month on various household activities, including buying groceries and eating dinner out at a restaurant. The average monthly dollar estimate for eating dinner out is $121, or a third of the total amount Americans say they typically spend on groceries for the entire month ($364).

Bottom Line

Tallying restaurant receipts for breakfast, lunch, and snacks, it is easy to see how, according to studies by Mintel International Group, Americans are estimated to spend nearly half of their household food budget on dining out. It's a significant factor in the nation's economy, and has major implications for Americans' waistlines, if not financial situations. However, given the still modest frequency of eating dinner away from home, it appears that the cultural impact of dining out may still be limited.

These latest results are based on telephone interviews with a randomly selected national sample of 1,013 adults, aged 18 and older, conducted Dec. 5-8, 2005. For results based on this sample, one can say with 95% confidence that the maximum error attributable to sampling and other random effects is ±3 percentage points. In addition to sampling error, question wording and practical difficulties in conducting surveys can introduce error or bias into the findings of public opinion polls.

December 28, 2005
BUSH, HILLARY MOST ADMIRED, AGAIN
Oprah Winfrey close second to Clinton

by Jeffrey M. Jones, Gallup Poll Managing Editor

President George W. Bush is the clear choice as the most admired man in Gallup's annual poll on this topic, while New York Sen. Hillary Rodham Clinton edges out talk-show host Oprah Winfrey and Secretary of State Condoleezza Rice as the most admired woman. This marks the fifth straight year that Bush has been most admired man, and the fourth straight year that Clinton has been most admired woman. Clinton has topped the list 10 times since 1993. Billy Graham finished among the top 10 most admired men for a record 49th time.

Gallup's Dec. 19-22 poll asked Americans to name, without prompting, the man and woman, living anywhere in the world, whom they admire most. Nineteen percent of Americans named Bush as the most admired man. Former president Bill Clinton, with 5%, and for-

mer president Jimmy Carter, Pope Benedict XVI, and Microsoft Chairman Bill Gates (each of whom garners 3%) round out the top five. The remainder of the top 10 includes the Rev. Billy Graham, former South African President Nelson Mandela, former U.S. Secretary of State Colin Powell, the Dalai Lama, Arizona Sen. John McCain, and rock singer Bono. British Prime Minister Tony Blair, Mormon Church President Gordon B. Hinckley, and former president George H.W. Bush also received mention from at least 1% of Americans.

Most Admired Man, 2005

	Name	% Mentioning	Number of Times in Top 10
1	George W. Bush	19	6
2	Bill Clinton	5	14
3	Jimmy Carter	3	24
4	Pope Benedict XVI	3	1
5	Bill Gates	3	7
6	(The Rev.) Billy Graham	2	49
7	Nelson Mandela	2	14
8	Colin Powell	2	14
9	The Dalai Lama	1	2
10	John McCain	1	2
	Bono	1	1

Graham's appearance marks the 49th time he has appeared on the top 10 list. Gallup began asking the "most admired" question in 1946. Graham first appeared in the top 10 in 1955 and has been in the top 10 every year since then except 1962 (the question was not asked in 1976). Ronald Reagan has the next most top 10 appearances among men, with 31.

Most Appearances, Top 10 List of Most Admired Men

Man	Number of Appearances
Billy Graham	**49**
Ronald Reagan	31
Pope John Paul II	27
Jimmy Carter	**24**
Dwight Eisenhower	21
Richard Nixon	21
Harry Truman	20
Edward Kennedy	**18**
Winston Churchill	17
George H.W. Bush	**16**
Douglas MacArthur	15
Bill Clinton	**14**
Nelson Mandela	**14**
Colin Powell	**14**
Henry Kissinger	**12**
Pope Paul VI	12
Adlai Stevenson	11
Albert Schweitzer	11
Jesse Jackson	**11**
Herbert Hoover	10
Pope Pius XII	10

Note: A bolded name indicates that the person is still living.

Bush owes his standing this year to the fact that he is easily the consensus choice among Republicans—44% of Republicans mention him. Bush is also the top choice among independents, but trails Clinton among Democrats.

Top 5 Most Admired Men, by Party Affiliation

Democrats		Independents		Republicans	
Bill Clinton	13%	George W. Bush	11%	George W. Bush	44%
George W. Bush	7%	Bill Clinton	3%	Billy Graham	5%
Jimmy Carter	6%	Pope Benedict XVI	3%	Gordon B. Hinckley	3%
Pope Benedict XVI	4%	Jimmy Carter	3%	Colin Powell	3%
Nelson Mandela	3%	Bill Gates	3%	Pope Benedict XVI	2%
				Bill Gates	2%

The president of the United States has been the most admired man every year since 1981. The last non-president to head the list was Pope John Paul II in 1980. The sitting president has been the most admired man 48 out of the 59 times the question has been asked.

Most Admired Woman

Hillary Rodham Clinton again leads the list of most admired women. Thirteen percent of Americans mention her, compared with 12% for Winfrey and 10% for Rice. Last year, Clinton was mentioned by 13%, Winfrey by 11%, and Rice by 7%.

The remainder of the top 10 for women this year includes first lady Laura Bush, former British Prime Minister Margaret Thatcher, actress Angelina Jolie, writer Maya Angelou, businesswoman and television personality Martha Stewart, North Carolina Sen. Elizabeth Dole, Supreme Court Justice Sandra Day O'Connor, and television journalist Barbara Walters. Former first lady Nancy Reagan and California Sen. Barbara Boxer were also mentioned by at least 1% of Americans.

Most Admired Woman, 2005

	Name	% Mentioning	Number of Times in Top 10
1	Hillary Rodham Clinton	13	14
2	Oprah Winfrey	12	18
3	Condoleezza Rice	10	5
4	Laura Bush	4	5
5	Margaret Thatcher	3	27
6	Angelina Jolie	1	1
7	Maya Angelou	1	9
8	Martha Stewart	1	2
9	Elizabeth Dole	1	11
10	Sandra Day O'Connor	1	9
	Barbara Walters	1	11

This marks the 27th consecutive year that Thatcher has been in the top 10, the 18th consecutive year for Winfrey, and the 14th for Clinton. Former first lady Barbara Bush failed to make the top 10 for the first time since 1987. Queen Elizabeth II of England has the most top 10 appearances among women. She did not finish in the top 10 this year after doing so in 2003 and 2004.

Most Appearances, Top 10 List of Most Admired Women

Woman	Number of Appearances
Queen Elizabeth II	**40**
Jacqueline Kennedy Onassis	28
Margaret Thatcher	**27**
Mamie Eisenhower	21
Margaret Chase Smith	20
Nancy Reagan	**19**
Oprah Winfrey	**18**
Mother Teresa	18
Clare Boothe Luce	18
Helen Keller	17
Mme Chiang Kai-Shek	17
Betty Ford	**17**
Barbara Bush	**17**
Patricia Nixon	15
Hillary Rodham Clinton	**14**
Eleanor Roosevelt	14
Elizabeth Dole	**11**
Barbara Walters	**11**
Lady Bird Johnson	**11**
Indira Gandhi	11
Princess Diana	10

Note: A bolded name indicates that the person is still living.

Each partisan group has a different woman atop its most admired list. Among Democrats, Clinton is the clear leader. Among independents, Winfrey is the top choice, and among Republicans, Rice is most frequently mentioned.

Top 5 Most Admired Women, by Party Affiliation

Democrat		Independent		Republican	
Hillary Clinton	24%	Oprah Winfrey	14%	Condoleezza Rice	21%
Oprah Winfrey	13%	Hillary Clinton	8%	Oprah Winfrey	9%
Condoleezza Rice	4%	Condoleezza Rice	7%	Laura Bush	9%
Maya Angelou	2%	Margaret Thatcher	3%	Hillary Clinton	6%
Angelina Jolie	2%	Laura Bush	2%	Margaret Thatcher	5%
Margaret Thatcher	2%				

There are interesting gender differences on the most admired woman question. Winfrey is the top choice among women, at 17%, followed by Clinton, at 12%. Only 7% of men mention Winfrey, compared with 13% for both Clinton and Rice.

While sitting presidents usually win the most admired title among men, sitting first ladies are most admired woman less than one-third of the time—only 18 times in the 56 times the question has been asked. However, former first ladies, such as Eleanor Roosevelt, Jacqueline Kennedy, and now Hillary Rodham Clinton, have frequently won the honor, 24 times in all. That means former first ladies have been most admired woman more often than sitting first ladies have been.

Survey Methods

These results are based on telephone interviews with a randomly selected national sample of 1,004 adults, aged 18 and older, conducted Dec. 19-22, 2005. For results based on this sample, one can say with 95% confidence that the maximum error attributable to sampling and other random effects is ±3 percentage points. In addition to sampling error, question wording and practical difficulties in conducting surveys can introduce error or bias into the findings of public opinion polls.

Index

character ratings of, 31, 32–33, 194, 277–78, 346, 351–52, 402, 416–17, 425–26

Cheney, Dick, compared with, 433–34

children and, 72

church and, 182–83

civil unions and, 3–4

Clinton, Bill, compared with, 425

confidence in, 31, 32, 38–39, 172–73, 227, 252, 352–53

Congress and, 32, 156, 397, 429–31

corporations and, 156

cost of living and, 155

democracy and, 72, 73

DNA evidence and, 72

economy and, 3–4, 15, 16, 19, 27, 31–32, 33–34, 52, 59–60, 65–67, 68–69, 72, 88, 112–13, 130, 131, 155, 156–57, 172–73, 194, 303–4, 325, 346, 351, 425, 461–62

education and, 3–4, 15, 16, 19, 27, 29, 31–32, 37, 39, 48, 65–67, 156, 157

election of 2006 (midterm) and, 397, 429

energy and, 3–4, 27, 102, 103, 155, 156–57

environment and, 3–4, 15, 16, 19, 27, 29, 37, 39, 156

ethics and, 276–77, 398–99, 402

expectations for, 28–31

federal budget and, 3–4, 15, 16, 19, 27, 31–32, 39, 68, 155, 425

first term of, 27, 28–29, 37

foreign affairs and, 3–4, 15, 16, 19, 27, 32, 33, 34, 59–60, 69, 88, 156, 194, 325, 351, 425, 461–62

foreign aid and, 156

foreign trade and, 155

gasoline and, 130, 155, 168–69, 325, 346, 422

geographic region and, 156–57

government and, 156, 374–75, 425

as greatest president, 74–75

healthcare and, 3–4, 15, 16, 19, 27, 29, 31–32, 37, 39, 52, 65–67, 130, 156, 157, 325

homelessness and, 3–4

homosexuality and, 188

honesty of, 32–33, 276, 277, 280, 300, 352, 402, 425

Hurricane Katrina and, 331, 337, 341–44, 345–47, 351–53, 393

ideology and, 309–10, 417

image of, 48–49, 49–50, 76, 206, 280–81, 309–10, 424–25

immigration and, 3–4, 15, 16, 19, 72, 156, 156–57, 425, 451

inauguration of, 24–25, 28, 30–31

inflation and, 155

intelligent design and, 354

Iraq and, 149, 150

Iraq war and, 3–4, 11–12, 15, 16, 19, 23, 27, 31–32, 41, 52, 59–60, 65–67, 72–73, 88, 90, 111–12, 131, 155, 156–57, 194, 214–16, 236, 241, 242, 243, 278–80, 297–98, 315, 317–18, 325, 326–28, 346, 351, 353–54, 359, 418–19, 425, 428, 445–46, 461–62, 463–65, 470–72

issues most important for, 3–4, 37–38, 65–67, 130, 468–70

judicial system and, 72, 130, 156

lawsuits and, 3–4, 65–67

leadership of, 32–33, 194, 277–78, 346, 351–52, 402, 416–17

marriage and, 3–4, 65–67, 72, 188

Medicare and, 27, 29, 37, 39, 156

military and, 32, 37, 39, 209

morality and, 27, 29, 37, 39, 130, 156

national security and, 27, 29, 39

natural disasters and, 352–53

oil and, 155

partisanship and, 27, 29, 37, 39

Plame, Valerie, and, 276–77, 398–99, 401–2

plans of, 31–32, 31–33, 41, 131, 236, 240, 242, 464, 471

policies of, 27, 52–53

political affiliation and, 28, 29–31, 31–32, 51–53, 69, 141–42, 157, 172–73, 214, 279, 310, 320, 331, 346, 397–98, 398–99, 402, 416–17, 419, 426, 433, 461, 462, 482–83

poverty and, 3–4, 156

power and, 374–75

presidency and, 27, 29, 37, 39

as problem, most important, 45, 113, 152, 198, 366, 421

prosperity and, 27, 29, 37

public opinion and, 377–78

race and, 3–4, 263–64, 341–44, 346

scandals and, 32

Schiavo, Terri, and, 105, 109, 110, 112, 122, 131

second term of, 28–31

September 11, 2001, terrorist attacks and, 26, 27

Sheehan, Cindy, and, 326–28

Social Security and, 3–4, 15, 16, 19, 27, 29, 31–32, 34, 35, 36–37, 39, 52, 55–59, 59–60, 62–65, 65–67, 68, 72, 73, 77–78, 87–89, 119–20, 130–31, 155, 156–57, 164–66, 194, 239–40

State of the Union address of, 50–53, 72–73

stem cell research and, 72, 194–95, 306

strength of, 425

Supreme Court and, 238–39, 246–47, 328, 363, 370–71, 384–85, 399–401, 423, 472–73

taxes and, 3–4, 6, 7, 15, 16, 19, 27, 29, 37, 37–39, 65–67, 155

terrorism and, 3–4, 15, 16, 18, 19–20, 27, 31–32, 39, 65–67, 72, 88, 130, 194, 227, 252, 297–98, 325, 327, 346, 352–53, 424–25, 446, 461–62

torture and, 441

trust in, 425

tsunami disaster and, 15

unemployment and, 3–4, 155

United States, image of, and, 27, 29, 37, 39

values of, 277, 300, 425

weapons of mass destruction and, 149, 150, 279–80, 418

welfare and, 156

Bush, Jeb, 310

Bush, Laura, 483

business. *See also* corporations
    confidence in, 201
    gender and, 415
    honesty of, 448
    image of, 310–13, 422
    political affiliation and, 415–16
    as problem, most important, 366, 421
    regulation of, 415–16, 421

California, 414

cameras, 478–81

campaign finance, 11, 20, 22, 40

Canada, 60–61, 79, 128

cancer, 99, 302, 431–32

Canseco, Jose, 115

careers, 153–55. *See also* occupations

Congress. *See also* Senate
abortion and, 3–4
age and, 145, 330
approval ratings of, 98, 144–45, 169–70, 212–13, 214, 330,
384, 385, 396–97, 412, 430
Bush, George W., and, 32, 156, 397, 429–31
civil unions and, 3–4
confidence in, 172–73, 201, 202
economy and, 3–4, 65–67, 130, 172–73, 412
education and, 3–4, 65–67, 144
election of 2006 (midterm) and, 396–98, 411–12, 429–31,
452–53
energy and, 3–4
environment and, 3–4
ethics and, 169–70
federal budget and, 3–4
foreign affairs and, 3–4
gasoline and, 130, 325, 412, 422
gender and, 145
government and, 412
healthcare and, 3–4, 65–67, 130, 412
homelessness and, 3–4
honesty of, 448
Hurricane Katrina and, 337, 343, 353
ideology and, 144–45
immigration and, 3–4
income and, 144
Iraq war and, 3–4, 65–67, 412
issues most important for, 3–4, 37–38, 65–67, 130, 468–70
judicial system and, 130
lawsuits and, 3–4, 65–67
lobbying and, 170
marriage and, 3–4, 65–67
military and, 209
morality and, 130
national security and, 334
political affiliation and, 98, 144, 169–70, 172–73, 202, 214,
330, 360, 396–98, 411–12, 429–31, 453
poverty and, 3–4
as problem, most important, 99, 174, 213, 348
race and, 3–4, 145
Schiavo, Terri, and, 105, 109, 110, 112, 122, 123, 145
Social Security and, 3–4, 34, 35, 36, 63, 65–67, 130, 240, 412
stem cell research and, 306
taxes and, 3–4, 6, 7, 37–38, 65–67, 412
terrorism and, 3–4, 65–67, 130, 334, 412
trust in, 359, 378
unemployment and, 3–4
conservatives:
abortion and, 245–46, 260, 405–6, 443, 444
affirmative action and, 288, 314–15
approval ratings and, 144–45, 417
blogs and, 98
Bush, George W., and, 309–10, 417
Christmas and, 477–78
Clinton, Hillary, and, 309
Congress and, 144–45
creationism v. evolution and, 191
death penalty and, 186, 457
drugs and, 408

economy and, 108
election of 2008 (presidential) and, 310
employment and, 287–88
euthanasia and, 179, 180
ghosts and, 253
Gonzales, Alberto, and, 246
guns and, 141
homelessness and, 134
hunger and, 134
Iraq war and, 244
law enforcement and, 420
McCain, John, and, 308–9
media and, 357–58
national pride and, 62
news and, 357–58
opportunities and, 287–88
poverty and, 134
religion and, 133, 151, 234, 448
Schiavo, Terri, and, 105
stem cell research and, 306–7
suicide and, 179, 180
Supreme Court and, 228–29, 244–46, 259, 370, 385–86, 400,
405–6
Constitution, 142–43, 188, 318–19
corporations. *See also* business
Bush, George W., and, 156
as problem, most important, 99, 174, 213, 347
satisfaction with, 20, 21, 22
taxes and, 38, 137
cost:
of energy, 222–23
of gasoline, 45, 93–95, 125, 195–97, 222–23, 285, 321–22, 325,
346, 420–21
of health insurance, 455
cost of living:
Bush, George W., and, 155
as problem, most important, 45, 93–95, 99, 113, 153, 174, 213,
304, 347, 366, 409
Craig, Larry, 420
creationism, 190–92, 354–56, 379–80
credit cards:
concern for, 159
as problem, most important, 45, 113, 152, 198, 366, 421
crime:
age and, 413–14, 438
assessment of, 390–92
Clinton, Bill, and, 73
community and, 413–14
concern for, 136, 162–64, 170–72, 391
gender and, 170–72, 437
government and, 356–57
guns and, 437, 438–39
income and, 171–72, 413–14, 438
policies concerning, satisfaction with, 11, 20, 22, 40, 356–57
political affiliation and, 356–57, 391–92
as problem, most important, 99, 174, 213
protection from, 437–38
race and, 413–14
rates of, 412–14, 437
State of the Union address and, 73

crystal meth, 162–64
Cuba, 71, 78–79, 128

Dalai Lama, 482
dating, 372–74
days, 224–25
dead, communication with, 221–22
Dean, Howard, 67, 206
Dean, John, 392
death, 117, 136
death penalty:
    accuracy of, 186
    age and, 186
    assessment of, 185–86
    church and, 186
    education and, 186
    gender and, 185, 186
    ideology and, 186
    income and, 186
    morality and, 177, 184–87, 192–93
    political affiliation and, 186, 192–93
    Protestantism and, 151
    race and, 186
    religion and, 131–32, 150
    support for, 184–87, 456–57
debt:
    age and, 209
    outlook for, 208–9
    as problem, most important, 45, 93–95, 113, 153, 223, 366, 409
    taxes and, 138, 139
defense. *See* military
DeLay, Tom, 170, 452–53
democracy:
    Bush, George W., and, 72, 73
    foreign affairs and, 73
    in Iraq, 40, 41, 278–79, 327, 445–46, 466–67, 471
    as problem, most important, 73
    State of the Union address and, 72, 73
Democratic National Committee (DNC), 67
Democratic Party:
    abortion and, 3–4, 175, 192–93, 245–46, 405, 443, 444
    admiration by, 483
    adultery and, 192–93
    Afghanistan and, 128, 129
    age and, 265
    agriculture and, 356–57
    American people and, 360
    Angelou, Maya, and, 483
    approval ratings and, 141–42, 144, 168, 169, 214, 320, 330, 346, 391–92, 397–98, 417, 426, 433, 461, 462
    approval ratings of, 412, 430
    Arctic National Wildlife Reserve (ANWR) and, 104–5
    Benedict XVI and, 483
    Bush, George H. W., and, 52
    Bush, George W., and, 28, 29–31, 31–32, 51–53, 141–42, 157, 172–73, 214, 279, 310, 320, 331, 346, 391–92, 397–98, 398–99, 402, 416–17, 419, 426, 433, 461, 462, 482–83
    business and, 415–16
    Canada and, 128

Carter, Jimmy, and, 483
Catholicism and, 133
Cheney, Dick, and, 433
China and, 128
Christmas and, 478
church and, 182–84, 268
civil liberties and, 475–76
civil unions and, 3–4
Clinton, Bill, and, 51, 52, 398, 483
Clinton, Hillary, and, 80–81, 82, 206, 289–90, 300–301, 309, 483
cloning and, 192–93
Congress and, 98, 144, 169–70, 172–73, 202, 214, 330, 360, 396–98, 411–12, 429–31, 453
crime and, 356–57, 391–92
Cuba and, 128
death penalty and, 186, 192–93, 457
DeLay, Tom, and, 453
divorce and, 192–93
drugs and, 408
economy and, 1, 3–4, 66, 108, 153, 356–57, 362, 469–70
education and, 3–4, 66, 356–57
Egypt and, 128
election of 2004 (presidential) and, 43, 68
election of 2006 (midterm) and, 396–98, 429–31, 452–53
election of 2008 (presidential) and, 67, 68, 80, 206, 289–90, 299–300, 467–68
election strategy of, 67–68
employment and, 290–92, 356–57
energy and, 3–4, 102–3, 104–5, 161, 356–57, 469–70
environment and, 3–4, 148, 356–57
ethics and, 169–70
euthanasia and, 179, 180
federal budget and, 3–4
filibuster debate and, 189–90
finances and, 94–95, 356–57
foreign affairs and, 1–2, 3–4, 356–57, 362
France and, 128
fur clothing and, 192–93
gambling and, 192–93
gasoline and, 104–5, 168, 169, 325, 421, 422, 469–70
Germany and, 128–29
Giuliani, Rudy, and, 289–90
Gonzales, Alberto, and, 246
government and, 356–57, 360, 374, 375
Great Britain and, 128
Greenspan, Alan, and, 173
Guantanamo Naval Base detention facility and, 226
guns and, 141, 438, 439
healthcare and, 3–4, 66, 356–57, 454, 469–70
homeland security and, 356–57
homelessness and, 3–4
homosexuality and, 142, 192–93
housing and, 356–57
Hurricane Katrina and, 331, 337, 343, 346
Hussein, Saddam, and, 441
identification with, 42–43, 114, 264–65, 281, 362
image of, 281, 360–62, 411–12
immigration and, 3–4, 469–70
India and, 128

Indonesia and, 128
intelligence system and, 149–50
Iran and, 128, 129
Iraq and, 40–41, 128, 129
Iraq war and, 3–4, 23–24, 40–41, 46, 66, 89, 145, 216, 225, 226, 244, 279, 326–27, 419, 426–27, 429, 464, 469–70
Israel and, 128
issues most important to, 469–70
Japan and, 128
Jolie, Angelina, and, 483
Jordan and, 128
judicial system and, 202, 360
Kerry, John, and, 289–90
labor unions and, 202, 313, 314, 323
law enforcement and, 295, 420
lawsuits and, 3–4, 66
Libby, I. Lewis ìScooter,î and, 401–2
Mandela, Nelson, and, 483
marriage and, 3–4, 66, 142
math and science aptitudes and, 96
McCain, John, and, 289–90, 309
media and, 360
Mexico and, 128
military and, 210, 218, 230, 356–57
morality and, 92–93, 178, 192–93
national parks and, 356–57
national pride and, 61
national security and, 295
natural disasters and, 356–57
news and, 360, 369
North Korea and, 128, 129
nuclear energy plants and, 161
nuclear weapons and, 292
oil and, 104–5, 469–70
open space and, 356–57
Pakistan and, 128
Palestinian Authority and, 128
Patriot Act and, 266, 475–76
patriotism and, 267
peace and, 1–2
Plame, Valerie, and, 277, 398–99, 401–2
Poland and, 128
polygamy and, 192–93
poverty and, 3–4, 356–57, 394
power and, 2, 374, 375
presidency and, 48, 74, 75, 202, 367–68
privacy and, 295
prosperity and, 1, 362
public officials and, 360
public opinion and, 378
race and, 3–4, 264–65, 268
religion and, 151, 234, 412, 447
Rice, Condoleezza, and, 116, 483
Roberts, John, and, 283–84
Rove, Karl, and, 277
Russia and, 128
Saudi Arabia and, 128
Schiavo, Terri, and, 105, 109, 110, 122
school prayer and, 318–19
September 11, 2001, terrorist attacks and, 334

sex and, 192–93, 192–93, 192–93
Sheehan, Cindy, and, 326–27
smoking and, 269
Social Security and, 3–4, 5, 6, 64, 66, 87–88, 119, 120, 130, 165, 239, 240, 469–70
State of the Union address and, 51–53
stem cell research and, 192–93, 195
suicide and, 179, 180, 192–93
Supreme Court and, 202, 228, 244–47, 259, 260, 283–84, 328, 329, 344–45, 370, 371, 400, 405, 423, 473
Syria and, 128
taxes and, 3–4, 6, 7, 39, 66
terrorism and, 3–4, 66, 272–73, 295, 469–70
Thatcher, Margaret, and, 483
torture and, 441
transportation and, 356–57
trust and, 360
tsunami relief and, 9–10
Ukraine and, 128
unemployment and, 3–4
United Nations and, 83–84
United States, satisfaction with, and, 214
values of, 412
voter turnout for, 42, 43
war and, 426–27
Winfrey, Oprah, and, 483
World War II and, 292
Diana, Princess, 8, 483
Diaz-Munoz, Javier, 268
diet, 296, 306, 440
dining out, 86–87, 222, 367, 410–11, 481–82
discretionary income, 86–87
disease, 99, 302, 431–32. *See also* health
divorce, 125, 131–32, 150–51, 177, 192–93
DNA evidence, 72
Dole, Elizabeth, 483
domestic problems, 368
donations, 8–10
draft, military, 230
drinking. *See* alcohol
driving age, 106–7
drugs. *See also* pharmaceutical industry
age and, 407
in baseball, 114–15
church and, 408
cocaine, 162–63
community and, 163, 164
concern for, 136, 162–64, 170–72
crystal meth, 162–64
education and, 408
gender and, 170–72, 407
geographic region and, 163, 408
ideology and, 408
income and, 171–72
marijuana, 407–8
Medicare and, 371–72
political affiliation and, 408
prescription drugs, 371–72, 457–59
as problem, most important, 99, 174, 213, 431
religion and, 408

Earle, Ronnie, 453
Easter, 114
economy:
    age and, 66, 108, 470
    approval ratings and, 15, 16, 19, 27, 33–34, 59–60, 68–69, 88,
        112–13, 131, 194, 325, 346, 351, 425, 461–62
    assessment of, 17, 69, 73, 112–13, 152, 153, 174, 197, 199,
        219–21, 255–56, 281, 285–87, 303–4, 347–49, 365–66,
        459–61
    Bush, George H. W., and, 33
    Bush, George W., and, 3–4, 15, 16, 19, 27, 31–32, 33–34,
        52, 59–60, 65–67, 68–69, 72, 88, 112–13, 130, 131,
        155,156–57, 172–73, 194, 303–4, 325, 346, 351, 425,
        461–62
    Clinton, Bill, and, 33
    community and, 108
    concern for, 136, 170–72
    Congress and, 3–4, 65–67, 130, 172–73, 412
    education and, 108
    employment and, 108
    gasoline and, 321–22
    gender and, 67, 108, 170–72
    geographic region and, 108, 156–57, 470
    government and, 356–57
    Hurricane Katrina and, 347–49, 365
    ideology and, 108
    immigration and, 248, 249, 451
    income and, 108, 171–72
    as issue, most important, 3–4, 38, 65–67, 130, 468–70
    outlook for, 1, 17, 52, 69, 73, 108–9, 112–13, 152, 153, 174,
        197, 220, 256, 281, 285, 286, 303–4, 321–22, 347, 365,
        436–37, 459–61
    plans for, 31–32
    political affiliation and, 1, 3–4, 66, 108, 153, 356–57, 362, 412,
        469–70
    as problem, most important, 17–18, 98, 99, 113, 148, 152, 174,
        198, 213, 220–21, 286, 304, 332, 347–48, 366, 409, 421,
        460–61
    problems with, most important, 45–46, 113, 152, 174, 197–98,
        213, 321–22, 365–66, 421–22
    race and, 108, 286–87
    Reagan, Ronald, and, 33
    satisfaction with, 11, 20, 22, 40, 356–57
    school and, 285–86
    State of the Union address and, 72
    unemployment and, 108
education. *See also* schools
    affirmative action and, 338
    age and, 66, 156
    approval ratings and, 15, 16, 19, 27, 144
    Bush, George W., and, 3–4, 15, 16, 19, 27, 29, 31–32, 37, 39,
        48, 65–67, 156, 157
    Christmas and, 478
    Congress and, 3–4, 65–67, 144
    creationism v. evolution and, 191, 355, 379
    death penalty and, 186
    drugs and, 408
    economy and, 108
    emphasis in, 333
    employment and, 340

    gender and, 67
    geographic region and, 157, 332
    goals of, 47–48
    government and, 356–57
    homosexuality and, 142
    image of, 311, 422
    income and, 340–41
    Iraq war and, 244
    as issue, most important, 3–4, 38, 65–67
    labor unions and, 323
    law enforcement and, 420
    marriage and, 142
    plans for, 31–32
    political affiliation and, 3–4, 66, 356–57
    as problem, most important, 18, 45, 99, 113, 152, 174, 198,
        213, 332, 348, 366, 421
    public opinion and, 378
    race and, 338–39
    reading and, 203
    religion and, 132, 234, 447
    satisfaction with, 20, 22, 40, 332–33, 356–57
Edwards, John, 80, 300, 468
Egypt, 79, 128
Eisenhower, Dwight D.:
    admiration of, 482
    approval ratings of, 24–25, 26, 27, 118–19, 141, 263, 320,
        392–93
    as greatest president, 74–75
    inauguration of, 24–25
Eisenhower, Mamie, 483
elderly, as most important problem, 99, 113, 152, 174, 198, 213,
    366, 421
election of 2004 (presidential), 8, 42, 43, 68, 175, 182
election of 2006 (midterm), 396–98, 411–12, 429–31, 452–53
election of 2008 (presidential):
    Allen, George, and, 300, 310, 468
    Barbour, Haley, and, 468
    Bayh, Evan, and, 300, 468
    Biden, Joe, and, 300, 468
    Brownback, Sam, and, 300, 310
    Bush, Jeb, and, 310
    Clark, Wesley, and, 300
    Clinton, Hillary, and, 80, 204–7, 288–90, 299–301, 468
    Democratic Party and, 67, 68, 80, 206, 299–300
    Edwards, John, and, 80, 300, 468
    Frist, Bill, and, 300, 310, 468
    Giuliani, Rudy, and, 288–90, 299–300, 310, 467–68
    Hagel, Chuck, and, 300, 310
    ideology and, 310
    Kerry, John, and, 80, 288–90, 300, 468
    McCain, John, and, 207, 288–90, 299–300, 308–10, 467–68
    Pataki, George, and, 300, 310
    political affiliation and, 289–90
    projections for, 288–90, 300, 467–68
    Republican Party and, 299–300, 310
    Rice, Condoleezza, and, 299–300, 310, 467–68
    Richardson, Bill, and, 300, 468
    Romney, Mitt, and, 300, 310, 468
    Vilsack, Tom, and, 468
    Warner, Mark, and, 300, 468

Christmas and, 436
church and, 114
Clinton, Hillary, and, 80–81, 82
concern and, 170–72
Congress and, 145
crime and, 170–72, 437
dating and, 372–73
death penalty and, 185, 186, 457
domestic problems and, 368
driving age and, 106
drugs and, 170–72, 407
economy and, 67, 108, 170–72
education and, 67
electronics and, 480
employment and, 135, 153–55, 287–88, 307–8, 336, 340
energy and, 161, 170–71
entrepreneurship and, 135
environment and, 148, 170–72
euthanasia and, 179, 180
exercise and, 449–50
finances and, 95
gasoline and, 196
Gonzales, Alberto, and, 246
guns and, 140, 438, 439
healthcare and, 46, 67, 170–71, 442, 454
health insurance and, 14
height and, 335–36, 375–77
homelessness and, 170–72
homosexuality and, 142
hunger and, 170–72
immigration and, 170–71
Iraq war and, 67, 243–44
labor unions and, 323
law enforcement and, 420
lawsuits and, 67
marriage and, 67, 142
math and science aptitudes and, 95–96
Medicaid and, 14
Medicare and, 14
military and, 217–18
money and, 162
national pride and, 62
national security and, 368
news and, 369
nuclear energy plants and, 161
nuclear weapons and, 292
occupations and, 340–41
opportunities and, 287–88
patriotism and, 267
poverty and, 170–72
prescription drugs and, 457–58
presidency and, 75–76, 367–68
race relations and, 170–71
reading and, 203
religion and, 132, 234, 447, 463
Rice, Condoleezza, and, 116
sex offender registries and, 212
Social Security and, 67, 170–72
spending and, 86–87, 436

sports and, 53–54
Stewart, Martha, and, 100–101
suicide and, 179, 180
Supreme Court and, 244–46, 259, 363, 370–71, 400–401, 405
taxes and, 67
terrorism and, 67, 170–72
tsunami relief and, 8–9
unemployment and, 170–71
violence and, 170–72
weight and, 296, 305–6, 440
World War II and, 292
geographic region:
Bush, George W., and, 156–57
church and, 114
drugs and, 163, 408
economy and, 108, 156–57, 470
education and, 157, 332
employment and, 198–99, 290–92
energy and, 156–57, 470
euthanasia and, 179
foreign affairs and, 157
gasoline and, 168, 196, 470
guns and, 140, 438
healthcare and, 157, 470
homosexuality and, 142
immigration and, 156–57, 470
Iraq war and, 156–57, 470
issues most important by, 470
labor unions and, 323
law enforcement and, 420
marriage and, 142
neighborhood and, 254
oil and, 470
religion and, 132, 133, 234, 447, 463
satisfaction by, 11
sex offender registries and, 212
Social Security and, 156–57, 470
sports and, 54–55
suicide and, 179
terrorism and, 470
vacation and, 475
Germany, 71–72, 79, 128–29
ghosts, 221–22, 252–54
Ginsburg, Ruth Bader, 283, 329, 423–24
Giuliani, Rudy, 288–90, 299–300, 310, 467–68
Glass, Fred, 414, 415
global warming, 148–49
God, 463
Goldman, Ronald, 91–92
golf, 53–55
Gonzales, Alberto, 211, 246
Gore, Al, 183
Goss, Porter, 441
government:
Bush, George W., and, 156, 374–75, 425
business regulated by, 415–16, 421
civil liberties and, 374
confidence in, 337, 358–59
Congress and, 412

food and, 349–50

gasoline and, 420–21

Hurricane Katrina and, 331, 336, 337, 341–44, 346, 352–53, 388–90

image of, 311, 312, 422

of Iraq, 11–12, 13, 234–35, 278–79, 327, 388, 445–46, 466–67, 471

natural disasters and, 337, 352–53, 356–57

political affiliation and, 356–57, 360, 374, 375, 412

poverty and, 356–57, 394–95

power of, 374–75

as problem, most important, 18, 45, 99, 113, 152, 174, 198, 213, 220, 348, 366, 421

race and, 341–44, 394

religion and, 412

role of, 356–57, 374, 375

satisfaction with, 20, 22, 356–57

spending on, 352, 353–54

terrorism and, 337, 352–53

trust in, 378

Graduated Driver Licensing (GDL) laws, 106

Graham, Billy, 230–32, 482, 483

Great Britain, 60–61, 79, 128

Greenspan, Alan, 172–73, 322

Griffin, Michael, 298, 299

groceries. *See* food

Guantanamo Naval Base detention facility, 225–26

guns:

age and, 140, 438, 439

on airplanes, 140

arming occupations with, 140

crime and, 437, 438–39

gender and, 140, 438, 439

geographic region and, 140, 438

ideology and, 141

in judicial system, 140

law enforcement and, 420

ownership of, 140–41, 438

policies concerning, satisfaction with, 20, 22, 39

political affiliation and, 141, 438, 439

as problem, most important, 99, 175, 213

race and, 438

recreation and, 438–39

in schools, 140

use of, 438–39

Hagel, Chuck, 300, 310, 315

happiness, 2–3

haunted houses, 221–22, 252–53

Hayworth, J. D., 429

health. *See also* disease; healthcare

alcohol and, 271–72

exercise and, 450

healthcare and, 442

prescription drugs and, 371–72, 457–59

as problem, most important, 175, 213

problems with, most important, 431–32

smoking and, 302

weight and, 296, 306

healthcare. *See also* health; health insurance

age and, 66, 156, 442, 454, 470

approval ratings and, 15, 16, 19, 27, 325

assessment of, 453–56

Bush, George W., and, 3–4, 15, 16, 19, 27, 29, 31–32, 37, 39, 52, 65–67, 130, 156, 157, 325

Clinton, Bill, and, 73

concern for, 135–36, 159, 170–71

confidence in, 201

Congress and, 3–4, 65–67, 130, 412

gender and, 46, 67, 170–71, 442, 454

geographic region and, 157, 470

government and, 356–57

health and, 442

health insurance and, 442–43

honesty of, 448–49

image of, 311, 422

income and, 454

as issue, most important, 3–4, 38, 65–67, 130, 468–70

medical checkups, 442–43

plans for, 31–32

political affiliation and, 3–4, 66, 356–57, 412, 454, 469–70

prescription drugs and, 371–72, 457–58

as problem, most important, 18, 45–46, 93–95, 98, 99, 113, 148, 152, 174, 198, 213, 220, 223, 348, 365–66, 409, 410, 421, 431, 432

race and, 136

satisfaction with, 11, 20, 22, 39, 40, 356–57, 453–56

smoking and, 442

State of the Union address and, 73

weight and, 442

health insurance, 13–15, 45, 152, 431, 442–43, 455. *See also* healthcare

health maintenance organizations (HMOs), 201

heart disease, 431

height, 335–36, 375–77

high school, 216–17

Hinckley, Gordon B., 483

Hispanics:

approval ratings and, 263–64

Bush, George W., and, 263–64

church and, 267–68

clothing and, 274

dating and, 372–74

economy and, 286–87, 286–87

employment and, 286–87

energy and, 286

food and, 274

gasoline and, 286

homelessness and, 286

hunger and, 286

immigration and, 248–49, 451–52

neighborhood and, 254–55

oil and, 286

opportunities and, 287

political affiliation and, 264–65, 268

poverty and, 133, 286

race relations and, 257–59, 274–75

religion and, 133, 267–68

on Supreme Court, 259
unemployment and, 286
hockey, ice, 53–55
homeland security, 356–57. *See also* national security
homelessness:
    Bush, George W., and, 3–4
    church and, 134
    concern for, 133–34, 136, 170–72
    Congress and, 3–4
    gender and, 170–72
    ideology and, 134
    income and, 171–72
    as issue, most important, 3–4, 38
    policies concerning, satisfaction with, 20, 22, 40
    political affiliation and, 3–4
    as problem, most important, 18, 45, 99, 113, 152, 174, 198, 213, 286, 348, 366, 421
    race and, 133, 286
    religion and, 134
homosexuality:
    acceptance of, satisfaction with, 11, 20, 21, 22, 40
    age and, 142
    attitudes toward, 187–89
    Bush, George W., and, 188
    church and, 142
    civil unions and, 143
    Constitution and, 142–43, 188
    education and, 142
    employment and, 187–88
    gender and, 142
    geographic region and, 142
    marriage and, 3–4, 38, 65–67, 72, 142–43, 188
    morality and, 177, 187, 192–93
    political affiliation and, 142, 192–93
    as problem, most important, 99, 174, 213
    religion and, 131–32, 150–51
    sex and, 188
honesty:
    of Bush, George W., 32–33, 276, 277, 280, 300, 352, 402, 425
    of Clinton, Bill, 300
    of Clinton, Hillary, 300
    of occupations, 448–49
    as problem, most important, 174, 213, 348
Hoover, Herbert, 482
households, 86–87, 222, 307–8, 366–67, 410–11. *See also* families; housing
housing. *See also* households
    concern for, 159
    cost of as most important problem, 93–95, 113, 153, 223, 366, 409
    government and, 356–57
    Hurricane Katrina and, 381
    political affiliation and, 356–57
    satisfaction with, 356–57
Howe, Neil, 47
human rights, 73. *See also* civil liberties
hunger:
    church and, 134
    concern for, 133–34, 136, 170–72

gender and, 170–72
ideology and, 134
income, 171–72
as problem, most important, 18, 45, 99, 113, 152, 174, 198, 213, 286, 348, 366, 421
race and, 133, 286
religion and, 134
hunting, 438–39
Hurricane Katrina:
    Alabama and, 388–90
    approval ratings and, 351
    assessment of, 330–32, 336–37, 341–44, 345–47
    attentiveness to, 336
    Bush, George W., and, 331, 337, 341–44, 345–47, 351–53, 393
    community and, 383–84
    Congress and, 353
    economy and, 347–49, 365
    emotions and, 382–84
    employment and, 381
    evacuation for, 331, 381
    families and, 380–81, 383–84
    federal budget and, 352, 354
    Federal Emergency Management Agency (FEMA) and, 336, 337, 341–44, 383–84, 389
    gasoline and, 331–32, 422
    government and, 331, 336, 337, 341–44, 352–53, 388–90
    housing and, 381
    income and, 337, 395–96
    investigation of, 353
    Iraq war and, 352, 353–54
    Louisiana and, 341–44, 388–90
    media and, 337
    Mississippi and, 388–90
    New Orleans and, 331, 337, 341–44, 388–90, 393–94
    paying for problems of, 352, 353–54
    as problem, most important, 348, 354, 365–66
    race and, 341–44, 395–96, 406, 407
    religion and, 383–84
    taxes and, 352, 354
    victims of, 337, 380–84, 388, 395–96, 406–7
Hussein, Saddam, 26, 441

identity theft, 162–63
ideology. See also *particular ideologies*; political affiliation
    abortion and, 245–46, 260, 405–6, 443, 444
    affirmative action and, 288, 314–15
    approval ratings and, 144–45, 417
    blogs and, 98
    Bush, George W., and, 309–10, 417
    Christmas and, 477–78
    of Clinton, Hillary, and, 207
    Clinton, Hillary, and, 309
    Congress and, 144–45
    creationism v. evolution and, 191
    death penalty and, 186, 457
    drugs and, 408
    economy and, 108
    election of 2008 (presidential) and, 310

employment and, 287–88
euthanasia and, 179, 180
ghosts and, 253
of Ginsburg, Ruth Bader, 329
Gonzales, Alberto, and, 246
guns and, 141
homelessness and, 134
hunger and, 134
Iraq war and, 244
of John Paul II, 85, 131
law enforcement and, 420
McCain, John, and, 308–9
of media, 357–58
national pride and, 62
of news, 357–58
opportunities and, 287–88
papacy and, 124–25
poverty and, 134
religion and, 124–25, 133, 151, 234, 448
of Roberts, John, 329
Schiavo, Terri, and, 105
stem cell research and, 306–7
suicide and, 179, 180
of Supreme Court, 238–39, 246, 259, 363, 401, 405
Supreme Court and, 228–29, 244–46, 259, 363–64, 370,
    385–86, 400, 405–6
of Thomas, Clarence, 329
image:
    of accounting, 311
    of advertising, 311
    of Afghanistan, 79, 128, 129
    of agriculture, 311, 312
    of airplanes, 311
    of Albright, Madeleine, 116
    of automobile industry, 311
    of banks, 311
    of Brown, Michael, 343
    of Bush, George H. W., 48–49
    of Bush, George W., 48–49, 49–50, 76, 206, 280–81, 309–10,
        424–25
    of business, 310–13, 422
    of Canada, 79, 128
    of Cheney, Dick, 399, 402–3
    of China, 79, 128
    of Clinton, Bill, 49, 76, 206
    of Clinton, Hillary, 79–82, 204–7, 288–89, 300–301, 309
    of computers, 311
    of Cuba, 79, 128
    of Dean, Howard, 206
    of DeLay, Tom, 170, 452
    of Democratic Party, 281, 360–62, 411–12
    of Earle, Ronnie, 453
    of education, 311
    of Egypt, 79, 128
    of food, 311, 422
    of France, 70–72, 79, 128
    of Frist, Bill, 206
    of gasoline, 311–12
    of Germany, 71–72, 79, 128–29
    of Giuliani, Rudy, 288–89

of Gonzales, Alberto, 246
of government, 311, 312
of Graham, Billy, 231–32
of Great Britain, 79, 128
of healthcare, 311
of India, 79, 128
of Indonesia, 79, 128
of Internet, 311
of Iran, 79, 128, 129
of Iraq, 79, 112, 128, 129
of Israel, 69–70, 79, 128
of Japan, 79, 128
of John Paul II, 85
of Jordan, 79, 128
of Kerry, John, 288–89
of Lampson, Nick, 452
of lawyers, 311
of Libby, I. Lewis ìScooter,î 402
of McCain, John, 288–89, 308–9
of Mexico, 79, 128
of Miers, Harriet, 385
of movies, 311, 312
of Nagin, Ray, 343
of National Aeronautics and Space Administration (NASA),
    250, 298–99
of National Rifle Association, 139–41
of North Korea, 79, 128, 129
of oil, 311–12
of Pakistan, 79, 128
of Palestinian Authority, 69–70, 79, 128
of pharmaceutical industry, 311
of Poland, 79, 128
political affiliation and, 360–62, 411–12
of Powell, Colin, 116
of publishing, 311
of radio, 311
of real estate, 311
of Rehnquist, William, 329
of Reid, Harry, 206
of Republican Party, 360–62, 411–12
of restaurants, 311
of retail industry, 311
of Rice, Condoleezza, 116
of Roberts, John, 283–84, 344–45
of Rove, Karl, 402
of Russia, 79, 128
of Saudi Arabia, 79, 128
of sports, 311, 312
of Stewart, Martha, 100–101
of Syria, 79, 128
of telephone industry, 311
of television, 311
of travel industry, 311
of Ukraine, 79, 128
of United Nations, 83, 84
of United States, 27, 29, 37, 39, 76–77
of utilities, 311
immigration:
    age and, 156, 470
    approval ratings and, 15, 16, 19, 425, 451

leadership:
    of Bush, George W., 32–33, 194, 277–78, 346, 351–52, 402, 416–17
    of Clinton, Hillary, 300
    of John Paul II, 85
    as problem, most important, 18, 174, 213, 348
    public opinion and, 377–79
Lewinsky, Monica, 49
Libby, I. Lewis ìScooter,î 399, 401–3, 418
liberals:
    abortion and, 245–46, 260, 405–6, 443, 444
    affirmative action and, 288, 314–15
    approval ratings and, 144–45, 417
    blogs and, 98
    Bush, George W., and, 309–10, 417
    Christmas and, 478
    Clinton, Hillary, and, 309
    Congress and, 144–45
    creationism v. evolution and, 191
    death penalty and, 186, 457
    drugs and, 408
    economy and, 108
    election of 2008 (presidential) and, 310
    employment and, 287–88
    euthanasia and, 179, 180
    ghosts and, 253
    Gonzales, Alberto, and, 246
    guns and, 141
    homelessness and, 134
    hunger and, 134
    Iraq war and, 244
    law enforcement and, 420
    McCain, John, and, 308–9
    media and, 357–58
    national pride and, 62
    news and, 357–58
    opportunities and, 287–88
    poverty and, 134
    religion and, 133, 151, 234, 448
    Schiavo, Terri, and, 105
    stem cell research and, 306–7
    suicide and, 179, 180
    Supreme Court and, 228–29, 244–46, 259, 370, 385–86, 400, 405–6
Libya, 71, 78–79
life, 1, 2, 20–22, 333–34. See also evolution
Lincoln, Abraham, 74–75
liquor, 260–62. See also alcohol
living wills, 123, 208
lobbying, 170, 260
long-term medical conditions, 14–15
Louisiana, 341–44, 388–90
Luce, Clare Boothe, 483
Lunsford, Jessica, 211
Lyne, Susan, 100

MacArthur, Douglas, 482
Mandela, Nelson, 482, 483
Mann, Horace, 47
marijuana, 407–8

marriage:
    age and, 66, 142
    Bush, George W., and, 3–4, 65–67, 72, 188
    children outside of, 177, 178
    Christmas and, 477
    church and, 142
    Clinton, Hillary, and, 81–82
    Congress and, 3–4, 65–67
    Constitution and, 142–43, 188
    education and, 142
    gender and, 67, 142
    geographic region and, 142
    homosexuality and, 3–4, 38, 65–67, 72, 142–43, 188
    as issue, most important, 3–4, 38, 65–67
    law enforcement and, 420
    political affiliation and, 3–4, 66, 142
    religion and, 125, 150–51
    State of the Union address and, 72
    vacation and, 474
Mars, 250–51, 299
mass transit, 273. See also transportation
math, 95–96
McCain, John, 207, 288–90, 299–300, 308–10, 467–68, 482
McGwire, Mark, 114–15
mealtime, 481
media. See also journalists; news
    confidence in, 201, 202, 357
    global warming and, 148–49
    Hurricane Katrina and, 337, 343
    ideology of, 357–58
    political affiliation and, 360
    as problem, most important, 100, 175, 213
    Schiavo, Terri, and, 110, 122
    trust in, 359–60, 378
Medicaid, 13–15, 443
medical checkups, 442–43
Medicare:
    age and, 13
    Bush, George W., and, 27, 29, 37, 39, 156
    coverage by, 13–15
    gender and, 14
    healthcare and, 443
    income and, 14, 372
    long-term medical conditions and, 14–15
    physical disability and, 14–15
    prescription drug program under, 371–72
    as problem, most important, 18, 45, 99, 113, 152, 174, 198, 213, 366, 421
    race and, 14
    satisfaction with, 20, 22, 40
    understanding of, 371–72
Megan's Law, 211–12
Mehlman, Ken, 263, 265
men:
    abortion and, 175, 245–46, 443
    admiration of, 482–83
    affirmative action and, 287, 288
    alcohol and, 262, 271–72
    approval ratings and, 145
    business and, 415

stem cell research and, 306–7
suicide and, 179, 180
Supreme Court and, 228–29, 244–46, 259, 370, 385–86, 400, 405–6
money:
  age and, 162
  concern for, 159
  for emergencies, 386–87
  gender and, 162
  preferences regarding, 162
  as problem, most important, 45, 93–95, 99, 113, 152, 153, 174, 198, 213, 223, 304, 347, 365–66, 409, 410, 421
months, 224
Moon, 299
morality. *See also* ethics
  abortion and, 177, 192–93
  adultery and, 177, 192–93
  age and, 92
  alcohol and, 270
  animal testing and, 177, 192–93
  assessment of, 177–78, 192–93
  Bush, George W., and, 27, 29, 37, 39, 130, 156
  Catholicism and, 131–32, 150–51
  children and, 92, 192–93
  church and, 132
  cloning and, 177, 192–93
  Congress, 130
  death penalty and, 177, 184–87, 192–93
  divorce and, 177, 192–93
  fur clothing and, 177, 192–93
  gambling and, 177, 192–93
  homosexuality and, 177, 187, 192–93
  as issue, most important, 130
  political affiliation and, 92–93, 178, 192–93
  polygamy and, 177, 192–93
  as problem, most important, 18, 99, 174, 213, 220, 348
  religion and, 150–51
  satisfaction with, 11, 20, 22, 92–93
  sex and, 177, 192–93
  stem cell research and, 177, 192–93, 195
  suicide and, 177, 192–93
morning, 225
mortality, 117, 136
movies:
  age and, 60
  attendance at, 60–61
  gadgets for, 478–81
  image of, 311, 312, 422
  income and, 60
  reading and, 203, 204

Nagin, Ray, 342–43, 380
National Aeronautics and Space Administration (NASA), 250–51, 298–99
National Gay and Lesbian Task Force, 142
national parks, 356–57
national pride, 61–62. *See also* patriotism
National Restaurant Association, 481
National Rifle Association, 139–41

national security:
  Bush, George W., and, 27, 29, 39
  Congress and, 334
  foreign affairs and, 73
  gender and, 368
  homeland security, 356–57
  in Iraq, 40, 41, 445–46, 471
  political affiliation and, 295
  privacy and, 293, 294–95
  as problem, most important, 99, 174, 213, 348, 366, 421
  racial profiling and, 294
  satisfaction with, 11, 20, 22, 39
  taxes and, 136–37
  terrorism and, 334
natural disasters, 337, 343, 352–53, 356–57, 386–87, 421. *See also* Hurricane Katrina; tsunami disaster
navigation systems, 478–81
neighborhood, 254–55. *See also* community
New Orleans, 330–32, 337, 341–44, 346, 352–53, 388–90, 393–94
news. *See also* journalists; media
  age and, 369
  attentiveness to, 368–69
  confidence in, 201, 202, 357
  gender and, 369
  Hurricane Katrina and, 337
  ideology of, 357–58
  political affiliation and, 360, 369
  registered voters and, 369
  sources for, 97
newspapers, 201, 202
nighttime, 225
Nixon, Patricia, 483
Nixon, Richard:
  admiration of, 482
  approval ratings of, 24, 25, 26, 27, 118–19, 141, 263, 320, 392–93, 417
  as greatest president, 74–75
  inauguration of, 24, 25
nonwhites. *See also* Asians; blacks; Hispanics
  alcohol and, 262
  Catholicism and, 133
  crime and, 413–14
  death penalty and, 186, 457
  economy and, 108
  employment and, 135
  entrepreneurship and, 135
  gasoline and, 196
  guns and, 438
  homelessness and, 133
  hunger and, 133
  Iraq war and, 145, 243–44
  Jackson, Michael, and, 91, 218
  law enforcement and, 420
  national pride and, 62
  patriotism and, 267
  poverty and, 133
  Rice, Condoleezza, and, 116
  Simpson, O. J., and, 218
  Social Security and, 46

sports and, 54
time of day and, 225
unemployment and, 46
North Korea, 71, 78–79, 128, 129
nuclear energy plants, 161
nuclear weapons, 73, 292–93. *See also* weapons of mass destruction

occupations:
  advice on, 153–55
  arming with guns, 140
  ethics of, 448–49
  gender and, 340–41
  homosexuality and, 187–88
  honesty of, 448–49
  income and, 340–41
  in military, 229–30
  survey of, 339–40
O'Connor, Sandra Day, 244, 483
oil:
  age and, 470
  from Arctic National Wildlife Reserve (ANWR), 103–5
  Bush, George W., and, 155
  geographic region and, 470
  image of, 311–12, 422
  as issue, most important, 468–70
  political affiliation and, 104–5, 469–70
  as problem, most important, 113, 152, 174, 198, 213, 220, 286, 304, 321, 347, 365–66, 409, 410, 421
  race and, 286
O'Malley, Patrick G., 443
open space, 356–57
opportunities, 11, 20, 22, 287–88, 314
O'Reilly, Bill, 477–78
organized labor. *See* labor unions
outlook:
  for debt, 208–9
  for economy, 1, 17, 52, 69, 73, 108–9, 112–13, 152, 153, 174, 197, 220, 256, 281, 285, 286, 303–4, 321–22, 347, 365, 436–37, 459–61
  for employment, 69
  for energy, 102
  for environment, 147
  for finances, 180–81, 208–9
  for foreign affairs, 1–2
  for income, 181, 208–9
  for inflation, 348, 436
  for interest rates, 436
  for labor unions, 313
  for peace, 1–2
  for prosperity, 1
  for race relations, 257–58
  for savings, 181, 208–9
  for spending, 181, 208–9, 348
  for stock market, 436–37
  for unemployment, 348, 436–37
outsourcing, 45, 113, 152, 198, 365–66, 421

Pakistan, 79, 128
Palestinian Authority, 69–70, 71, 78–79, 107–8, 128

Palmeiro, Rafael, 115
papacy, 85–86, 123–25. *See also individual popes*
paranormal, 221–22
parents:
  abortion and, 443–44
  Christmas and, 476, 477
  driving age and, 106–7
  law enforcement and, 420
  presidency, wishes for children on, 75–76
  sex offender registries and, 212
  vacation and, 474
partisanship, 27, 29, 30, 37, 39. *See also* political affiliation; unification
party identification, 42–43, 114, 264–65, 281, 362
Pataki, George, 300, 310
Patriot Act, 265–66, 294, 375, 475–76
patriotism, 266–67. *See also* national pride
Paul VI, 482
peace:
  in Iraq, 11, 13, 40, 41, 327–28, 388
  in Middle East, 70, 107–8
  outlook for, 1–2
periodic health exams, 443
Persian Gulf War, 8, 427
personal lives. *See* life
pharmaceutical industry, 311, 371–72, 422, 448, 449, 457–59
physical disability, 14–15
Pius XII, 482
Plame, Valerie, 276–77, 398–99, 401–3
Poland, 79, 128
police. *See* law enforcement
police brutality, 420
political affiliation. *See also* ideology; independents; *particular parties*
  abortion and, 3–4, 175, 192–93, 245–46, 405, 443, 444
  admiration by, 483
  adultery and, 192–93
  Afghanistan, 128, 129
  age and, 265
  agriculture and, 356–57
  American people and, 360
  Angelou, Maya, and, 483
  animal testing and, 192–93
  approval ratings and, 69, 120, 141–42, 144, 168, 169, 214, 320, 330, 346, 391–92, 397–98, 412, 417, 426, 430, 433, 461, 462
  Arctic National Wildlife Reserve (ANWR) and, 104–5
  Benedict XVI and, 483
  blogs and, 98
  Bush, George H. W. and, 52
  Bush, George W., and, 28, 29–31, 31–32, 51–53, 69, 141–42, 157, 172–73, 214, 279, 310, 320, 331, 346, 397–98, 398–99, 402, 416–17, 419, 426, 433, 461, 462, 482–83
  Bush, Laura, and, 483
  business and, 415–16
  Canada and, 128
  Carter, Jimmy, and, 483
  Cheney, Dick, and, 433
  children and, 192–93
  China and, 128

health insurance as, 45, 152, 431

homelessness as, 18, 45, 99, 113, 152, 174, 198, 213, 286, 348, 366, 421

homosexuality as, 99, 174, 213

honesty as, 174, 213, 348

housing costs as, 93–95, 113, 153, 223, 366, 409

hunger as, 18, 45, 99, 113, 152, 174, 198, 213, 286, 348, 366, 421

Hurricane Katrina as, 348, 354, 365–66

immigration as, 45, 99, 113, 152, 174, 198, 213, 348, 366, 421

income as, 45, 93–95, 99, 113, 152, 174, 198, 213, 304, 321, 347, 365–66, 409, 421

inflation as, 45, 93–95, 99, 113, 152, 153, 198, 213, 223, 304, 347, 366, 409, 421

interest rates as, 45, 93–95, 113, 152, 153, 198, 223, 366, 409, 421

Iraq war as, 18, 45–46, 72, 89, 98, 99, 113, 152, 174, 198, 213, 220, 317, 321, 332, 348, 354, 365–66, 421

judicial system as, 99, 174, 213, 348

leadership as, 18, 174, 213, 348

media as, 100, 175, 213

Medicare as, 18, 45, 99, 113, 152, 174, 198, 213, 366, 421

military as, 348

money as, 45, 93–95, 99, 113, 152, 153, 174, 198, 213, 223, 304, 347, 365–66, 409, 410, 421

morality as, 18, 99, 174, 213, 220, 348

national security as, 99, 174, 213, 348, 366, 421

natural disasters as, 421

oil as, 113, 152, 174, 198, 213, 220, 286, 304, 321, 347, 365–66, 409, 410, 421

outsourcing as, 45, 113, 152, 198, 365–66, 421

population as, 99, 175, 213

poverty as, 18, 45, 99, 113, 152, 174, 198, 213, 286, 347, 348, 366, 421

power as, 99, 175, 213

race relations as, 99, 174, 213, 348

racism as, 99, 174, 213, 348

recession as, 99

religion as, 18, 99, 174, 213, 348

respect as, 99, 174, 213, 348

retirement as, 45, 93–95, 113, 152, 153, 198, 223, 366, 409, 421

savings as, 366, 409

smoking as, 431

Social Security as, 18, 35, 45–46, 72, 73, 93–95, 98, 99, 100, 113, 148, 152, 153, 174, 198, 213, 214, 220, 223, 348, 366, 409, 421

spending as, 366, 409, 421

State of the Union address and, 72–73

stock market as, 45, 113, 152, 198, 366, 409, 421

taxes as, 45, 93–95, 99, 113, 152, 153, 174, 198, 213, 223, 304, 347, 366, 409, 421

terrorism as, 18, 98, 99, 174, 213, 220, 251–52, 332, 348, 366, 421, 431, 432

transportation as, 366, 409

unemployment as, 18, 45–46, 93–95, 99, 113, 152, 153, 174, 198, 213, 220, 223, 286, 304, 321, 347, 365–66, 409, 421

unification as, 99, 174, 213, 348

of United States, 17–18, 35, 45–46, 72–73, 89, 98, 99–100, 113, 148, 152, 174–75, 197–98, 213–14, 220–21, 251–52, 286, 304, 317, 321–22, 332, 347–48, 354, 365–66, 421–22, 460–61

Vietnam War as, 317

violence as, 99, 174, 213

war as, 148

weight as, 431

welfare as, 45, 99, 113, 152, 174, 198, 213, 348, 366, 421

prosperity, 1, 27, 29, 37, 362

Protestantism. *See also* Christianity

abortion and, 151

Catholicism compared with, 150, 151

church and, 233

death penalty and, 151, 186

divorce and, 151

euthanasia and, 179

Graham, Billy, and, 231

homosexuality and, 151

ideology and, 151

marriage and, 151

morality and, 150, 151

political affiliation and, 151, 183–84

preferences for, 114

race and, 268

religion and, 233

school prayer and, 318–19

sex and, 151

stem cell research and, 151

suicide and, 151, 179

Supreme Court and, 283

public officials, 359–60, 378

public opinion, 377–79

publishing, 311, 422

race. See also *particular races and ethnicities*; race relations; racism

abortion and, 245–46

affirmative action and, 314–15, 338

alcohol and, 262

approval ratings and, 145, 263–64, 342

Bush, George W., and, 3–4, 263–64, 341–44, 346

church and, 233, 267–68

clothing and, 274

college admissions and, 338–39

Congress and, 3–4, 145

crime and, 413–14

dating and, 372–74

death penalty and, 186, 457

economy and, 108, 286–87

education and, 338–39

employment and, 135, 286–87, 314

energy and, 286

entrepreneurship and, 135

finances and, 93, 94, 274

food and, 274

gasoline and, 196, 286

Gonzales, Alberto, and, 246

government and, 341–44, 394

guns and, 438

healthcare and, 136

health insurance and, 14

Canada and, 128
Cheney, Dick, and, 433
China and, 128
Christmas and, 478
church and, 182–84, 268
civil liberties and, 475–76
civil unions and, 3–4
Clinton, Bill, and, 51, 52, 398
Clinton, Hillary, and, 80–81, 82, 289–90, 300–301, 309, 483
cloning and, 192–93
Congress and, 98, 144, 169–70, 172–73, 202, 214, 330, 360, 396–98, 411–12, 429–31, 453
crime and, 356–57, 391–92
Cuba and, 128
death penalty and, 186, 192–93, 457
DeLay, Tom, and, 453
divorce and, 192–93
drugs and, 408
economy and, 1, 3–4, 66, 108, 153, 356–57, 362, 469–70
education and, 3–4, 66, 356–57
Egypt and, 128
election of 2004 (presidential) and, 43
election of 2006 (midterm) and, 396–98, 429–31, 452–53
election of 2008 (presidential) and, 289–90, 299–300, 310, 467–68
employment and, 290–92, 356–57
energy and, 3–4, 102–3, 104–5, 161, 356–57, 469–70
environment and, 3–4, 148, 356–57
ethics and, 169–70
euthanasia and, 179, 180
federal budget and, 3–4
filibuster debate and, 189–90
finances and, 94–95, 356–57
foreign affairs and, 1–2, 3–4, 356–57, 362
France and, 128
fur clothing and, 192–93
gambling and, 192–93
gasoline and, 104–5, 168, 169, 325, 421, 422, 469–70
Gates, Bill, and, 483
Germany and, 128–29
Giuliani, Rudy, and, 289–90
Gonzales, Alberto, and, 246
government and, 356–57, 360, 374, 375
Graham, Billy, and, 483
Great Britain and, 128
Greenspan, Alan, and, 173
Guantanamo Naval Base detention facility and, 226
guns and, 141, 438, 439
healthcare and, 3–4, 66, 356–57, 454, 469–70
Hinckley, Gordon B., and, 483
homeland security and, 356–57
homelessness and, 3–4
homosexuality and, 142, 192–93
housing and, 356–57
Hurricane Katrina and, 331, 337, 343, 346
Hussein, Saddam, and, 441
identification with, 42–43, 114, 264–65, 281, 362
image of, 360–62, 411–12
immigration and, 3–4, 469–70

India and, 128
Indonesia and, 128
intelligence system and, 149–50
Iran and, 128, 129
Iraq and, 40–41, 128, 129
Iraq war and, 3–4, 23–24, 40–41, 46, 66, 89, 145, 216, 225, 226, 244, 279, 326–27, 419, 426–27, 429, 464, 469–70
Israel and, 128
issues most important to, 469–70
Japan and, 128
Jordan and, 128
judicial system and, 202, 360
Kerry, John, and, 289–90
labor unions and, 202, 313, 314, 323
law enforcement and, 295, 420
lawsuits and, 3–4, 66
Libby, I. Lewis ìScooter,î and, 401–2
marriage and, 3–4, 66, 142
math and science aptitudes and, 96
McCain, John, and, 289–90, 309
media and, 360
Mexico and, 128
military and, 210, 218, 230, 356–57
morality and, 92–93, 178, 192–93
national parks and, 356–57
national pride and, 61
national security and, 295
natural disasters and, 356–57
news and, 360, 369
North Korea and, 128, 129
nuclear energy plants and, 161
nuclear weapons and, 292
oil and, 104–5, 469–70
open space and, 356–57
Pakistan and, 128
Palestinian Authority and, 128
Patriot Act and, 266, 475–76
patriotism and, 267
peace and, 1–2
Plame, Valerie, and, 277, 398–99, 401–2
Poland and, 128
polygamy and, 192–93
poverty and, 3–4, 356–57, 394
Powell, Colin, and, 483
power and, 2, 374, 375
presidency and, 48, 74, 202, 367–68
privacy and, 295
prosperity and, 1, 362
public officials and, 360
public opinion and, 378
race and, 3–4, 264–65, 268, 342
religion and, 133, 151, 234, 412, 447
Rice, Condoleezza, and, 116, 483
Roberts, John, and, 283–84
Rove, Karl, and, 277
Russia and, 128
Saudi Arabia and, 128
Schiavo, Terri, and, 105, 109, 110, 122
school prayer and, 318–19
September 11, 2001, terrorist attacks and, 334

sex and, 192–93, 192–93, 192–93
Sheehan, Cindy, and, 326–27
smoking and, 269
Social Security and, 3–4, 5, 6, 64, 66, 87–88, 119, 120, 130, 165, 239, 240, 469–70
State of the Union address and, 51–53
stem cell research and, 192–93, 195
suicide and, 179, 180, 192–93
Supreme Court and, 202, 228, 244–47, 259, 260, 283–84, 328, 329, 344–45, 370, 371, 400, 405, 423, 473
Syria and, 128
taxes and, 3–4, 6, 7, 39, 66
terrorism and, 3–4, 66, 272–73, 295, 469–70
Thatcher, Margaret, and, 483
torture and, 441
transportation and, 356–57
trust and, 360
tsunami relief and, 9–10
Ukraine and, 128
unemployment and, 3–4
United Nations and, 83–84
United States, satisfaction with, and, 214
values of, 412
voter turnout for, 42, 43
war and, 426–27
Winfrey, Oprah, and, 483
World War II and, 292
respect, 99, 174, 213, 336, 348
restaurants, 311, 349–50, 422, 481–82
retail industry, 311, 422
retirement:
    age for, 159, 160, 181–82
    concern for, 159
    income and, 159–60, 182
    plans for, 159–61
    as problem, most important, 45, 93–95, 113, 152, 153, 198, 223, 366, 409, 421
    Social Security and, 160
Rice, Condoleezza, 71, 115–16, 299–300, 310, 467–68, 483
Richardson, Bill, 300, 468
Ridge, John, 253–54
Roberts, John, 283–85, 328–30, 344–45, 370, 371, 385–86, 423–24, 472–73
Roe v. Wade, 245–46, 260, 284, 405–6
Roman Catholicism. *See* Catholicism
Romney, Mitt, 300, 310, 468
Roosevelt, Eleanor, 483
Roosevelt, Franklin D., 74–75, 135
Roosevelt, Theodore, 74–75
Rove, Karl, 276, 277, 399, 402
Rumsfeld, Donald, 234
rural areas:
    crime and, 413–14
    drugs and, 163, 164
    economy and, 108
    euthanasia and, 179
    guns and, 141
    law enforcement and, 420
    sex offender registries and, 212
    suicide and, 179

Russia, 71, 78–79, 128
Ryan, George, 456–57

sales, 222
satisfaction:
    with abortion policies, 20, 21, 22, 40
    with agriculture, 356–57
    with blacks, position of, 20, 22, 39
    with campaign finance, 11, 20, 22, 40
    with community, 11
    with corporations, 20, 21, 22
    with crime policies, 11, 20, 22, 40, 356–57
    with economy, 11, 20, 22, 40, 356–57
    with education, 20, 22, 40, 332–33, 356–57
    with employment, 356–57
    with energy, 11, 20, 22, 40, 356–57
    with environment, 20, 22, 40, 356–57
    with finances, nation's, 356–57
    with foreign affairs, 11, 20, 22, 39, 356–57
    by geographic region, 11
    with government, 20, 22, 356–57
    with gun policies, 20, 22, 39
    with healthcare, 11, 20, 22, 39, 40, 356–57, 453–56
    with homeland security, 356–57
    with homelessness policies, 20, 22, 40
    with homosexuality, acceptance of, 11, 20, 21, 22, 40
    with housing, 356–57
    with immigration, 20, 21, 22, 40
    income and, 2
    with life, 1, 2, 20–22
    with Medicare, 20, 22, 40
    with military, 11, 20, 22, 39, 210–11, 356–57
    with morality, 11, 20, 22, 92–93
    with national parks, 356–57
    with national security, 11, 20, 22, 39
    with natural disasters, handling of, 356–57
    with open space, 356–57
    with opportunities, 11, 20, 22
    with poverty policies, 20, 22, 40, 356–57
    with race relations, 20, 22, 40
    with religion, 11, 20, 21, 22, 46
    with Social Security, 20, 22, 40
    with states, 11
    with taxes, 11, 20, 21–22, 39–40
    with transportation, 356–57
    with United States, state of, 10–11, 39–40, 69, 98, 99, 112–13, 173–74, 213, 214, 281, 320–21, 384, 385
    with war on terrorism, 226–27, 334–35
    with women, position of, 20, 22, 39
Saudi Arabia, 71, 78–79, 128
savings, 162, 181, 208–9, 366, 386–87, 409
Sawyer, Diane, 9
scandals, 32
Scanlan, Suzanne, 253
Schiavo, Michael, 105, 109–10, 117–18, 122
Schiavo, Terri, 105–6, 109–10, 112, 116–18, 121–23, 131, 145, 208
Schindler, Bob and Mary, 109, 116–17, 117–18
schools. *See also* education
    confidence in, 201
    creationism v. evolution in, 190–92, 379

economy and, 285–86
educational emphasis in, 333
guns in, 140
high school, 216–17
prayer in, 318–19
safety at, concern for, 350–51
spending and, 285–86
teachers in, 414–15
Schweitzer, Albert, 482
science, 95–96
seasons, 223
Selig, Bud, 115
Senate. *See also* Congress
filibuster in, 189–90, 203–4, 239
honesty of, 448
Supreme Court and, 246–47, 283, 329, 344, 385, 423, 472–73
September 11, 2001, terrorist attacks, 8, 26, 27, 333–35, 336
sex, 150–51, 177, 188, 192–93
sex offender registries, 211–12
Sharon, Ariel, 69, 79, 107
Sheehan, Cindy, 315, 326–28
Shurlan, Danica, 252–53
Simpson, Nicole Brown, 91–92
Simpson, O. J., 91–92, 157–58, 218–19
smallpox, 432
Smith, Margaret Chase, 483
smoking, 269–70, 301–3, 431, 442, 450
sniper shootings, 8
Social Security:
age and, 5, 36, 64, 66, 77–78, 156, 165–66, 239–40, 470
approval ratings and, 15, 16, 19, 27, 59–60, 62, 63–64, 68, 87–89, 119, 120, 130–31, 164–66, 194, 239
assessment of, 34–35, 62–65
Bush, George W., and, 3–4, 15, 16, 19, 27, 29, 31–32, 34, 35, 36–37, 39, 52, 55–59, 59–60, 62–65, 65–67, 68, 72, 73, 77–78, 87–89, 119–20, 130–31, 155, 156–57, 164–66, 194, 239–40
concern for, 127–28, 136, 170–72
Congress and, 3–4, 34, 35, 36, 63, 65–67, 130, 240, 412
federal budget and, 5–6
gender and, 67, 170–72
geographic region and, 156–57, 470
income and, 5, 6, 127, 171–72
as issue, most important, 3–4, 35, 36, 38, 65–67, 130, 468–70
plans for, 31–32, 131, 240
political affiliation and, 3–4, 5, 6, 64, 66, 87–88, 119, 120, 130, 165, 239, 412, 469–70
privatization of, 4–6, 34–37, 55–59, 63–64, 68, 77–78, 88, 119–20, 130, 131, 164–66, 239–40
as problem, most important, 18, 35, 45–46, 72, 73, 93–95, 98, 99, 100, 113, 148, 152, 153, 174, 198, 213, 214, 220, 223, 348, 366, 409, 421
race and, 46
reform of, 35, 64–65, 87–88, 130, 164–66
reliance on, 35
retirement and, 160
satisfaction with, 20, 22, 40
State of the Union address and, 72, 73
understanding of, 119–20
Sosa, Sammy, 115

Souter, David, 176
space program, 250–51, 298–99
spending:
age and, 209, 435
on Christmas, 87, 434–36, 466, 477
on clothing, 86–87, 222, 367, 410
on dining, 86–87, 222, 367, 410–11, 482
of discretionary income, 86–87
on entertainment, 86–87, 222, 367, 411
estimates for, 86–87, 222, 366–67, 410–11
on food, 86–87, 222, 367, 410, 482
gender and, 86–87, 436
on government, 352, 353–54
income and, 86, 435–36
on Iraq war, 352
on military, 209–10
outlook for, 181, 208–9, 348
on poverty, 394
preferences for, 162
on prescription drugs, 458
as problem, most important, 366, 409, 421
on recreation, 86–87, 367, 411
school and, 285–86
sports, 53–55, 311, 312, 375–77, 422
standard of living, 73, 159
State of the Union address, 50–53, 72–73
states, 11, 42–43
stem cell research:
attentiveness to, 195
Bush, George W., and, 72, 194–95
funding for, 306–7
morality and, 177, 192–93, 195
policies concerning, 194–95
political affiliation and, 192–93, 195
religion and, 125, 131–32, 150, 151
State of the Union address and, 72
Stevenson, Adlai, 482
Stewart, Martha, 100–101, 483
stock market:
outlook for, 436–37
as problem, most important, 45, 113, 152, 198, 366, 409, 421
Strauss, William, 47
stress, 382–84, 477
suburban areas:
crime and, 413–14
drugs and, 163, 164
economy and, 108
euthanasia and, 179
guns and, 141
law enforcement and, 420
sex offender registries and, 212
suicide and, 179
suicide:
age and, 179
Catholicism and, 131–32, 150
church and, 179, 180
community and, 179
doctor-assisted, 117, 122–23, 131–32, 150, 151, 177, 178–80, 192–93
gender and, 179, 180

trust. *See also* confidence
    in American people, 359, 378
    in Bush, George W., 425
    in Clinton, Bill, 425
    in Congress, 359, 378
    in government, 378
    in judicial system, 359, 378
    in media, 359–60, 378
    political affiliation and, 360
    in presidency, 359, 378
    in public officials, 359–60, 378
tsunami disaster, 8–10, 15

Ukraine, 79, 128
understanding, 119–20, 148, 371–72, 403. *See also* familiarity
unemployment. *See also* employment
    Bush, George W., and, 3–4, 155
    concern for, 136, 170–71
    Congress and, 3–4
    economy and, 108
    gender and, 170–71
    as issue, most important, 3–4, 38
    outlook for, 348, 436–37
    political affiliation and, 3–4
    as problem, most important, 18, 45–46, 93–95, 99, 113, 152, 153, 174, 198, 213, 220, 223, 286, 304, 321, 347, 365–66, 409, 421
    race and, 46, 286
unification, 99, 174, 213, 300–301, 348. *See also* partisanship
United Nations, 82–84
United States:
    Bush, George W., and image of, 27, 29, 37, 39
    as enemy, own, 71, 78–79
    foreign affairs, role in, 76, 77
    image of, 27, 29, 37, 39, 76–77
    national pride in, 61–62
    partisanship in, 27, 29, 30, 37, 39
    patriotism in, 266–67
    power of, 1, 2
    problems with, most important, 17–18, 35, 45–46, 72–73, 89, 98, 99–100, 113, 148, 152, 174–75, 197–98, 213–14, 220–21, 251–52, 286, 304, 317, 321–22, 332, 347–48, 354, 365–66, 421–22, 460–61
    satisfaction with state of, 10–11, 39–40, 69, 98, 99, 112–13, 173–74, 213, 214, 281, 320–21, 384, 385
    September 11, 2001, terrorist attacks and, 333–35
    tsunami relief by, 8, 9–10
    unification of, 99, 174, 213, 300–301, 348
    world, position in, 76
urban areas:
    crime and, 413–14
    drugs and, 163, 164
    economy and, 108
    euthanasia and, 179
    guns and, 141
    law enforcement and, 420
    sex offender registries and, 212

suicide and, 179
U.S. Department of Health and Human Services, 371–72
U.S. Department of Justice, 391
utilities, 311, 422

vacation, 195–97, 474–75. *See also* recreation
values, 277, 300, 412, 425
vegetative state, 116–18, 121–22, 180. *See also* Schiavo, Terri
video games, 478–81
Vietnam War, 315–18, 426
Vilsack, Tom, 468
violence, 99, 136, 162–63, 170–72, 174, 213
voters, 42, 43, 369

wages. *See* income
Walters, Barbara, 483
war, 148, 426–27. See also *particular wars*
Warner, Mark, 300, 468
war on terrorism:
    assessment of, 18, 19, 252, 334–35
    Iraq war and, 236, 471–72
    prisoners of, 225–26
    satisfaction with, 226–27, 334–35
Washington, George, 74–75
weapons of mass destruction, 73, 149, 150, 279–80, 418. *See also* nuclear weapons
Web logs, 97–98
weight, 295–96, 304–6, 431, 439–40, 442, 450
welfare:
    Bush, George W., and, 156
    as problem, most important, 45, 99, 113, 152, 174, 198, 213, 348, 366, 421
West, Kayne, 346
whites. *See also* Hispanics
    abortion and, 245–46
    affirmative action and, 314–15
    alcohol and, 262
    approval ratings and, 263–64
    Bush, George W., and, 263–64, 341–44
    church and, 233
    clothing and, 274
    college admissions and, 338–39
    crime and, 413–14
    dating and, 372–74
    death penalty and, 186, 457
    economy and, 108, 286–87, 286–87
    education and, 338–39
    employment and, 135, 286–87, 314
    energy and, 286
    entrepreneurship and, 135
    finances and, 93, 94, 274
    food and, 274
    gasoline and, 196, 286
    Gonzales, Alberto, and, 246
    government and, 341–44, 394
    guns and, 438
    healthcare and, 136
    health insurance and, 14

homelessness and, 133, 286
hunger and, 133, 286
Hurricane Katrina and, 341–44, 395–96, 406, 407
immigration and, 248–49, 451–52
Iraq war and, 145, 243–44
Jackson, Michael, and, 91, 157, 158, 218
law enforcement and, 420
Medicaid and, 14
Medicare and, 14
morality and, 136
national pride and, 62
neighborhood and, 254–55
oil and, 286
opportunities and, 287, 314
patriotism and, 267
political affiliation and, 183–84, 264–65
poverty and, 133, 286, 394
race relations and, 257–59, 274–76
religion and, 133, 233, 447
Rice, Condoleezza, and, 116
school safety, concern for by, 351
Simpson, O. J., and, 157, 158, 218
Social Security and, 46
sports and, 54
Supreme Court and, 244–46, 345
time of day and, 225
unemployment and, 46, 286
Whittemore, James, 117
wills, 123, 207–8
Wilson, Joseph C., 418
wine, 260–62
Winfrey, Oprah, 483
witches, 221–22
women:
    abortion and, 175, 245–46, 443
    admiration of, 483
    affirmative action and, 287, 288
    alcohol and, 262, 271–72
    approval ratings and, 145
    business and, 415
    career advice and, 153–55
    caretaker role and, 307–8
    child abuse and, 163–64
    Christmas and, 436
    church and, 114
    Clinton, Hillary, and, 80–81, 82
    concern and, 170–72
    Congress and, 145
    crime and, 170–72, 437
    death penalty and, 185, 186, 457
    driving age and, 106
    drugs and, 170–72, 407
    economy and, 67, 108, 170–72
    education and, 67
    electronics and, 480
    employment and, 135, 153–55, 287–88, 307–8, 336, 340
    energy and, 161, 170–71
    entrepreneurship and, 135

environment and, 148, 170–72
    euthanasia and, 179, 180
    exercise and, 449–50
    finances and, 95
    gasoline and, 196
    Gonzales, Alberto, and, 246
    guns and, 140, 438, 439
    healthcare and, 46, 67, 170–71, 454
    health insurance and, 14
    height and, 335–36
    homelessness and, 170–72
    homosexuality and, 142
    hunger and, 170–72
    immigration and, 170–71
    Iraq war and, 67, 243–44
    labor unions and, 323
    law enforcement and, 420
    lawsuits and, 67
    marriage and, 67, 142
    math and science aptitudes and, 95–96
    Medicaid and, 14
    Medicare and, 14
    in military, 217–18
    money and, 162
    national pride and, 62
    news and, 369
    nuclear energy plants and, 161
    nuclear weapons and, 292
    occupations and, 287–88, 340–41
    patriotism and, 267
    position of, satisfaction with, 20, 22, 39
    poverty and, 170–72
    prescription drugs and, 457–58
    presidency and, 75–76, 367–68
    race relations and, 170–71
    reading and, 203
    religion and, 132, 234, 447, 463
    Rice, Condoleezza, and, 116
    sex offender registries and, 212
    Social Security and, 67, 170–72
    spending and, 86–87, 436
    sports and, 54
    Stewart, Martha, and, 100–101
    suicide and, 179, 180
    on Supreme Court, 259, 363, 370–71, 400–401, 405
    Supreme Court and, 244–46, 400–401
    taxes and, 67
    terrorism and, 67, 170–72
    tsunami relief by, 8–9
    unemployment and, 170–71
    violence and, 170–72
    weight and, 296, 305–6, 440
    World War II and, 292
World War II, 292–93
worry. See concern
wrestling, 53–55

youth. See children; teenagers